WILEY

GAAP 2015

Interpretation and Application of
GENERALLY ACCEPTED
ACCOUNTING PRINCIPLES

WILEY

GAAP 2015

Interpretation and Application of
GENERALLY ACCEPTED
ACCOUNTING PRINCIPLES

Joanne M. Flood

WILEY

This edition first published 2015

Registered office
John Wiley & Sons Ltd, The Atrium, Southern Gate, Chichester, West Sussex, PO19 8SQ, United Kingdom

For details of our global editorial offices, for customer services and for information about how to apply for permission to reuse the copyright material in this book please see our website at www.wiley.com.

ISBN 978-1-118-94519-3 (paperback)
ISBN 978-1-118-84506-3 (ebk)
ISBN 978-1-118-94515-5 (ebk)
ISBN 978-1-118-94505-6 (obk)

Set in 10/12pt Times LT Std by Laserwords Private Limited, Chennai, India
Printed in the United States of America by Bind Rite

CONTENTS

PREFACE

Sign Up for Free Monthly GAAP Newsletter

2014 brought one of the most significant Accounting Standards Updates in years—Revenue Recognition. The leases project continues to move forward, and FASB continues to make progress on its private company reporting initiative. Wiley's new free monthly newsletter will help you stay ahead in the face of growing challenges. Cutting through the complexity, the newsletter will give you, clearly and concisely, the latest information on critical technical developments and practical insights on the most recent standards setting activities of the FASB, AICPA, and others. Register today at www.wiley.com/go/GAAP2014, using password floodgaap2014.

Wiley GAAP 2015: Interpretation and Application provides analytical explanations, copious illustrations, and nearly 300 examples of all current generally accepted accounting principles. The book integrates principles promulgated by the FASB in its *Accounting Standards Codification.*™

This edition of *Wiley GAAP* is organized to align fully with the structure of the FASB Codification. Each chapter now begins with a list of the Subtopics included within the Topic, major scope and scope exceptions, technical alerts of FASB Updates, and an overview of the Topic. The remainder of each chapter contains a detailed discussion of the concepts and practical examples and illustrations. This organization facilitates the primary objective of the book—to assist financial statement preparers and practitioners in resolving the myriad practical problems faced in applying GAAP.

Meaningful, realistic examples abound, guiding users in the application of GAAP to complex fact situations that must be dealt with in the real world practice of accounting. In addition to this emphasis, a major strength of the book is that it explains the theory of GAAP in sufficient detail to serve as a valuable adjunct to accounting textbooks. Much more than merely a reiteration of currently promulgated GAAP, it provides the user with the underlying conceptual bases for the rules. It facilitates the process of reasoning by analogy that is so necessary in dealing with the complicated, fast-changing world of commercial arrangements and transaction structures. It is based on the author's belief that proper application of GAAP demands an understanding of the logical underpinnings of all its technical requirements.

As a bonus, a comprehensive disclosure checklist, following the main text, offers practical guidance to preparing financial statements in accordance with GAAP. For easy reference and research, the checklist follows the order of the codification.

The following FASB Accounting Standards Updates were issued since the Wiley GAAP 2013. Their requirements are incorporated in this edition of Wiley GAAP, as and where appropriate. Information on ASU 2014-09 is included in the chapter on ASC 605.

Number	Title	Issue Date
ASU 2014-09	Revenue from Contracts with Customers (Topic 606)	5/28/2014
ASU 2014-08	Presentation of Financial Statements (Topic 205) and Property, Plant, and Equipment (Topic 360): Reporting Discontinued Operations and Disclosures of Disposals of Components of an Entity	4/11/2014
ASU 2014-07	Consolidation (Topic 810): Applying Variable Interest Entities Guidance to Common Control Leasing Arrangements (a consensus of the Private Company Council)	3/20/2014
ASU 2014-06	Technical Corrections and Improvements Related to Glossary Terms	3/14/14
ASU 2014-05	Service Concession Arrangements (Topic 853) (a consensus of the FASB Emerging Issues Task Force)	01/23/14
ASU 2014-04	Receivables—Troubled Debt Restructurings by Creditors (Subtopic 310-40): Reclassification of Residential Real Estate Collateralized Consumer Mortgage Loans upon Foreclosure (a consensus of the FASB Emerging Issues Task Force)	01/17/14
ASU 2014-03	Derivatives and Hedging (Topic 815): Accounting for Certain Receive-Variable, Pay-Fixed Interest Rate Swaps—Simplified Hedge Accounting Approach (a consensus of the Private Company Council)	01/16/14
ASU 2014-02	Intangibles—Goodwill and Other (Topic 350): Accounting for Goodwill (a consensus of the Private Company Council)	01/16/14
ASU 2014-01	Investments—Equity Method and Joint Ventures (Topic 323): Accounting for Investments in Qualified Affordable Housing Projects (a consensus of the FASB Emerging Issues Task Force)	01/15/14
ASU 2013-12	Definition of a Public Business Entity—An Addition to the Master Glossary	12/23/13
ASU 2013-11	Income Taxes (Topic 740): Presentation of an Unrecognized Tax Benefit When a Net Operating Loss Carryforward, a Similar Tax Loss, or a Tax Credit Carryforward Exists (a consensus of the FASB Emerging Issues Task Force)	07/18/13

ASU 2013-10	Derivatives and Hedging (Topic 815): Inclusion of the Fed Funds Effective Swap Rate (or Overnight Index Swap Rate) as a Benchmark Interest Rate for Hedge Accounting Purposes (a consensus of the FASB Emerging Issues Task Force)	07/17/13
ASU 2013-09	Fair Value Measurement (Topic 820): Deferral of the Effective Date of Certain Disclosures for Nonpublic Employee Benefit Plans in Update No. 2011-04	07/08/13
ASU 2013-08	Financial Services—Investment Companies (Topic 946): Amendments to the Scope, Measurement, and Disclosure Requirements	06/07/13

Significant accounting changes are on the horizon. In the next year, the FASB is expected to make strides on the following major projects and others:

- Consolidation
- Going Concern
- Insurance Contracts
- Financial Instruments—Classification and Measurement

Readers are encouraged to check the FASB website for status updates to the above and other FASB projects.

In response to the 2011 report of the Blue Ribbon Panel on Standard Setting for Private Companies, the AICPA and the FASB began separate initiatives. In July 2013, the AICPA released its Financial Reporting Framework for Small- and Medium-sized Entities. The AICPA has positioned the Framework as an alternative to U.S. GAAP and one that will provide consistent, reliable information for small- and medium-sized entities that are not required to prepare financial statements in accordance with U.S. GAAP. The FASB created the Private Company Council to address the Blue Ribbon Panel's report. The FASB issued a framework for the FASB and the PCC to use in determining whether alternatives to existing and proposed U.S. GAAP are warranted for private companies. In 2014, FASB issued three ASUs that are consensuses of the PCC. Those are listed on the table above.

The author's wish is that this book will serve preparers, practitioners, faculty, and students, as a reliable reference tool to facilitate their understanding of, and ability to apply, the complexities of the authoritative literature.

Joanne M. Flood
June 2014

ABOUT THE AUTHOR

Joanne M. Flood, CPA, is an author and independent consultant on accounting and auditing technical topics and e-learning. She has experience as an auditor in both an international firm and a local firm and worked as a senior manager in the AICPA's Professional Development group. She received her MBA Summa Cum Laude in Accounting from Adelphi University and her Bachelor's degree in English from Molloy College.

While in public accounting, Joanne worked on major clients in retail, manufacturing, and finance and on small business clients in construction, manufacturing, and professional services. At the AICPA, Joanne developed and wrote e-learning, text, and instructor-led training courses on US and International Standards. She also produced training materials in a wide variety of media, including print, video, and audio, and pioneered the AICPA's e-learning product line. Joanne resides on Long Island, New York with her daughter, Elizabeth. Joanne is the author of the following Wiley publications:

Financial Disclosure Checklist
Wiley GAAP 2014: Interpretation and Application of Generally Accepted Accounting Principles
Wiley Practitioner's Guide to GAAS 2014: Covering all SASs, SSAEs, SSARSs, and Interpretations
Wiley GAAP: Financial Statement Disclosures Manual (Wiley Regulatory Reporting)
Wiley Revenue Recognition

And the following AICPA online and live CPE programs:

Audit Staff Essentials, Level 1 – New Hire
Audit Staff Essentials, Level 2 – Experienced Staff
Audit Staff Essentials, Level 3 – Audit Senior/In-Charge

CODIFICATION TAXONOMY

Topic # and title		Subtopic # and title	
I.	**General Principles and Objectives**		
105	Generally Accepted Accounting Principles	105-10	Overall
II.	**Overall Financial Reporting, Presentation, and Display Matters**		
A.	**Overall Presentation of Financial Statements**		
205	Presentation of Financial Statements	205-10	Overall
		205-20	Discontinued Operations
		205-30	Liquidation Basis of Accounting
210	Balance Sheet	210-10	Overall
		210-20	Offsetting
215	Statement of Shareholders' Equity	215-10	Overall
220	Comprehensive Income	220-10	Overall
225	Income Statement	225-10	Overall
		225-20	Extraordinary and Unusual Items
		225-30	Business Interruption Insurance
230	Statement of Cash Flows	230-10	Overall
235	Notes to Financial Statements	235-10	Overall
B.	**Various Financial Reporting, Presentation, and Display Matters**		
250	Accounting Changes and Error Corrections	250-10	Overall
255	Changing Prices	255-10	Overall
260	Earnings Per Share	260-10	Overall
270	Interim Reporting	270-10	Overall
272	Limited Liability Entities	272-10	Overall
274	Personal Financial Statements	274-10	Overall
275	Risks and Uncertainties	275-10	Overall
280	Segment Reporting	280-10	Overall
III.	**Transaction-Related Topics**		
A.	**Financial Statement Accounts**		
305	Cash and Cash Equivalents	305-10	Overall
310	Receivables	310-10	Overall
		310-20	Nonrefundable Fees and Other Costs
		310-30	Loans and Debt Securities Acquired with Deteriorated Credit Quality
		310-40	Troubled Debt Restructurings by Creditors
320	Investments—Debt and Equity Securities	320-10	Overall
323	Investments—Equity Method and Joint Ventures	323-10	Overall
		323-30	Partnerships, Joint Ventures, and Limited Liability Entities
325	Investments—Other	325-10	Overall
		325-20	Cost Method Investments
		325-30	Investments in Insurance Contracts
		325-40	Beneficial Interests in Securitized Financial Assets

Topic # and title		*Subtopic # and title*	
330	Inventory	330-10	Overall
340	Other Assets and Deferred Costs	340-10	Overall
		340-20	Capitalized Advertising Costs
		340-30	Insurance Contracts that Do Not Transfer Insurance Risk
350	Intangibles—Goodwill and Other	350-10	Overall
		350-20	Goodwill
		350-30	General Intangibles Other Than Goodwill
		350-40	Internal-Use Software
		350-50	Web Site Development Costs
360	Property, Plant, and Equipment	360-10	Overall
		360-20	Real Estate Sales
405	Liabilities	405-10	Overall
		405-20	Extinguishment of Liabilities
		405-30	Insurance-Related Assessments
		405-40	Obligations Resulting from Joint and Several Liabilities
410	Asset Retirement and Environmental Obligations	410-10	Overall
		410-20	Asset Retirement Obligations
		410-30	Environmental Obligations
420	Exit or Disposal Cost Obligations	420-10	Overall
430	Deferred Revenue	430-10	Overall
440	Commitments	440-10	Overall
450	Contingencies	450-10	Overall
		450-20	Loss Contingencies
		450-30	Gain Contingencies
460	Guarantees	460-10	Overall
470	Debt	470-10	Overall
		470-20	Debt with Conversion and Other Options
		470-30	Participating Mortgage Loans
		470-40	Product Financing Arrangements
		470-50	Modifications and Extinguishments
		470-60	Troubled Debt Restructurings by Debtors
480	Distinguishing Liabilities from Equity	480-10	Overall
505	Equity	505-10	Overall
		505-20	Stock Dividends and Stock Splits
		505-30	Treasury Stock
		505-50	Equity-Based Payments to Non-Employees
		505-60	Spin-offs and Reverse Spin-offs
605	Revenue Recognition	605-10	Overall
		605-15	Products
		605-20	Services
		605-25	Multiple-Element Arrangements
		605-28	Milestone Method
		605-30	Rights to Use
		605-35	Construction-Type and Production-Type Contracts
		605-40	Gains and Losses

Topic # and title		*Subtopic # and title*	
		605-45	Principal–Agent Considerations
		605-50	Customer Payments and Incentives
606	Revenue from Contracts with Customers	606-10	Overall[1]
610	Other Income	610-10	Overall[1]
705	Cost of Sales and Services	705-10	Overall
		705-20	Accounting for Consideration Received from a Vendor[1]
710	Compensation—General	710-10	Overall
712	Compensation—Nonretirement Postemployment Benefits	712-10	Overall
715	Compensation—Retirement Benefits	715-10	Overall
		715-20	Defined Benefit Plans—General
		715-30	Defined Benefit Plans—Pensions
		715-60	Defined Benefit Plans—Other Postretirement
		715-70	Defined Contribution Plans
		715-80	Multiemployer Plans
718	Compensation—Stock Compensation	718-10	Overall
		718-20	Awards Classified as Equity
		718-30	Awards Classified as Liabilities
		718-40	Employee Stock Ownership Plans
		718-50	Employee Share Purchase Plans
720	Other Expenses	720-10	Overall
		720-15	Start-Up Costs
		720-20	Insurance Costs
		720-25	Contributions Made
		720-30	Real and Personal Property Taxes
		720-35	Advertising Costs
		720-40	Electronic Equipment Waste Obligations
		720-45	Business and Technology Reengineering
		720-50	Fees Paid to the Federal Government by Pharmaceutical Manufacturers and Health Insurers
730	Research and Development	730-10	Overall
		730-20	Research and Development Arrangements
740	Income Taxes	740-10	Overall
		740-20	Intraperiod Tax Allocation
		740-30	Other Considerations or Special Areas
B.	**Broad Transactional Categories**		
805	Business Combinations	805-10	Overall
		805-20	Identifiable Assets and Liabilities, and Any Noncontrolling Interest
		805-30	Goodwill or Gain from Bargain Purchase, Including Consideration Transferred
		805-40	Reverse Acquisitions
		805-50	Related Issues
		805-740	Income Taxes

Topic # and title		*Subtopic # and title*	
808	Collaborative Arrangements	808-10	Overall
810	Consolidation	810-10	Overall
		810-20	Control of Partnerships and Similar Entities
		810-30	Research and Development Arrangements
815	Derivatives and Hedging	815-10	Overall
		815-15	Embedded Derivatives
		815-20	Hedging—General
		815-25	Fair Value Hedges
		815-30	Cash Flow Hedges
		815-35	Net Investment Hedges
		815-40	Contracts in Entity's Own Equity
		815-45	Weather Derivatives
820	Fair Value Measurements	820-10	Overall
825	Financial Instruments	825-10	Overall
		825-20	Registration Payment Arrangements
830	Foreign Currency Matters	830-10	Overall
		830-20	Foreign Currency Transactions
		830-30	Translation of Financial Statements
		830-230	Statement of Cash Flows
		830-740	Income Taxes
835	Interest	835-10	Overall
		835-20	Capitalization of Interest
		835-30	Imputation of Interest
840	Leases	840-10	Overall
		840-20	Operating Leases
		840-30	Capital Leases
		840-40	Sale-Leaseback Transactions
845	Nonmonetary Transactions	845-10	Overall
850	Related-Party Disclosures	850-10	Overall
852	Reorganizations	852-10	Overall
		852-20	Quasi-Reorganizations
		852-740	Income Taxes
853	Service Concession Arrangements	853-10	Overall
855	Subsequent Events	855-10	Overall
860	Transfers and Servicing	860-10	Overall
		860-20	Sales of Financial Assets
		860-30	Secured Borrowings and Collateral
		860-40	Transfers to Qualifying Special-Purpose Entities
		860-50	Servicing Assets and Liabilities

IV. Industry/Unique Topics

905	Agriculture	905-10	Overall
908	Airlines	908-10	Overall
910	Contractors—Construction	910-10	Overall
		910-20	Contract Costs
912	Contractors—Federal Government	912-10	Overall
		912-20	Contract Costs
915	Development Stage Entities	915-10	Overall
920	Entertainment—Broadcasters	920-10	Overall
922	Entertainment—Cable Television	922-10	Overall
924	Entertainment—Casinos	924-10	Overall

Topic # and title		*Subtopic # and title*	
926	Entertainment—Films	926-10	Overall
		926-20	Other Assets—Film Costs
928	Entertainment—Music	928-10	Overall
930	Extractive Activities—Mining	930-10	Overall
932	Extractive Activities—Oil and Gas	932-10	Overall
940	Financial Services—Brokers and Dealers	940-10	Overall
		940-20	Broker Dealer Activities
942	Financial Services—Depository and Lending	942-10	Overall
944	Financial Services—Insurance	944-10	Overall
		944-20	Insurance Activities
		944-30	Acquisition Costs
		944-40	Claim Costs and Liabilities for Future Policy Benefits
		944-50	Policyholder Dividends
		944-60	Premium Deficiency and Loss Recognition
		944-80	Separate Accounts
946	Financial Services—Investment Companies	946-10	Overall
		946-20	Investment Company Activities
948	Financial Services—Mortgage Banking	948-10	Overall
950	Financial Services—Title Plant		
952	Franchisors	952-10	Overall
954	Health Care Entities	954-10	Overall
958	Not-for-Profit Entities	958-10	Overall
		958-20	Financially Interrelated Entities
		958-30	Split-Interest Arrangements
960	Plan Accounting—Defined Benefit Pension Plans	960-10	Overall
		960-20	Accumulated Plan Benefits
		960-30	Net Assets Available for Plan Benefits
		960-40	Terminating Plans
962	Plan Accounting—Defined Contribution Pension Plans	962-10	Overall
		962-40	Terminating Plans
965	Plan Accounting—Health and Welfare Benefit Plans	965-10	Overall
		965-20	Net Assets Available for Plan Benefits
		965-30	Plan Benefits Obligations
		965-40	Terminating Plans
970	Real Estate—General	970-10	Overall
972	Real Estate—Common Interest Realty Associations	972-10	Overall
974	Real Estate—Real Estate Investment Trusts	974-10	Overall
976	Real Estate—Retail Land	976-10	Overall
978	Real Estate—Time-Sharing Activities	978-10	Overall

Topic # and title		*Subtopic # and title*	
980	Regulated Operations	980-10	Overall
		980-20	Discontinuation of Rate-Regulated Accounting
985	Software	985-10	Overall
		985-20	Costs of Software to Be Sold, Leased, or Marketed
995	US Steamship Entities		

V. Glossary

---

[1] ASU 2014-09 added the Codification section. For more information on ASU 2014-09, see the Preface.

1 ASC 105 GENERALLY ACCEPTED ACCOUNTING PRINCIPLES

PERSPECTIVES AND ISSUES

What Is GAAP?

The FASB Accounting Standards Codification™ (ASC) is the

> *...source of authoritative generally accepted accounting principles (GAAP) recognized by the FASB to be applied by nongovernmental entities. Rules and interpretive releases of the Securities and Exchange Commission (SEC) under authority of federal securities laws are also sources of authoritative GAAP for SEC registrants. In addition to the SEC's rules and interpretive releases, the SEC staff issues Staff Accounting Bulletins that represent practices followed by the*

staff in administering SEC disclosure requirements, and it utilizes SEC Staff Announcements and Observer comments made at Emerging Issues Task Force meetings to publicly announce its views on certain accounting issues for SEC registrants. ASC 105-10-05-1

In the absence of authoritative guidance, the FASB Codification (the Codification) offers the following approach.

If the guidance for a transaction or event is not specified within a source of authoritative GAAP for that entity, an entity shall first consider accounting principles for similar transactions or events within a source of authoritative GAAP for that entity and then consider nonauthoritative guidance from other sources. An entity shall not follow the accounting treatment specified in accounting guidance for similar transactions or events in cases in which those accounting principles either prohibit the application of the accounting treatment to the particular transaction or event or indicate that the accounting treatment should not be applied by analogy. ASC 105-10-05-2

Nonauthoritative Sources. The Codification lists some possible nonauthoriative sources:

- Practices that are widely recognized and prevalent either generally or in the industry
- FASB Concepts Statements
- American Institute of Certified Public Accountants (AICPA) Issues Papers
- International Financial Reporting Standards of the International Accounting Standards Board
- Pronouncements of professional associations or regulatory agencies
- Technical Information Service Inquiries and Replies included in AICPA Technical Practice Aids
- Accounting textbooks, handbooks, and articles.
  (ASC 105-10-05-3)

GAAP establishes

- The measurement of economic activity,
- The time when such measurements are to be made and recorded,
- The disclosures surrounding this activity, and
- The preparation and presentation of summarized economic information in the form of financial statements.

GAAP develops when questions arise about how to best accomplish those items. In response to those questions, GAAP is either prescribed in official pronouncements of authoritative bodies empowered to create it, or it originates over time through the development of customary practices that evolve when authoritative bodies fail to respond. Thus, GAAP is a reaction to and a product of the economic environment in which it develops. As such, the development of accounting and financial reporting standards has lagged the development and creation of increasingly intricate economic structures and transactions. There are two broad categories of accounting principles—recognition and disclosure.

Recognition Principles. Recognition principles determine the timing and measurement of items that enter the accounting cycle and impact the financial statements. These are quantitative standards that require economic information to be reflected numerically.

Disclosure Principles. Disclosure principles deal with factors that are not always quantifiable. Disclosures involve qualitative information that is an essential ingredient of a full set of financial statements. Their absence would make the financial statements misleading by omitting information relevant to the decision-making needs of the reader. Disclosure principles complement recognition principles by expanding on some quantitative data and explaining assumptions underlying the numerical information and providing additional information on accounting policies, contingencies, uncertainties, etc., which are essential to fully understand the performance and financial condition of the reporting enterprise.

DEFINITIONS OF TERMS

Source: ASC 105-10-20 Glossary

Nongovernmental Entity. An entity that is not required to issue financial reports in accordance with guidance promulgated by the Governmental Accounting Standards Board or the Federal Accounting Standards Advisory Board.

Nonpublic Entity. Any entity that does not meet any of the following conditions:

a. Its debt or equity securities trade in a public market either on a stock exchange (domestic or foreign) or in an over-the-counter market, including securities quoted only locally or regionally.
b. It is a conduit bond obligor for *conduit debt securities* that are traded in a public market (a domestic or foreign stock exchange or an over-the-counter market, including local or regional markets).
c. It files with a regulatory agency in preparation for the sale of any class of debt or equity securities in a public market.
d. It is required to file or furnish financial statements with the Securities and Exchange Commission.
e. It is controlled by an entity covered by criteria (a) through (d).

CONCEPTS, RULES, AND EXAMPLES

History of GAAP

From time to time, the bodies given responsibility for the promulgation of GAAP have changed, and indeed more than a single such body has often shared this responsibility. In response to the stock market crash of 1929, the AICPA appointed the Committee on Accounting Procedure. This was superseded in 1959 by the Accounting Principles Board (APB) created by the AICPA. Because of operational problems, in 1972 the profession replaced the APB with a three-part organization consisting of the Financial Accounting Foundation (FAF), Financial Accounting Standards Board (FASB), and the Financial Accounting Standards Advisory Council (FASAC). Since 1973 the FASB has been the organization designated to establish standards of financial reporting.

FASB is recognized as authoritative by the SEC, reaffirmed through the Sarbanes-Oxley Act of 2002, and by the AICPA through Rule 203 of the AICPA Code of Professional Conduct. FASB is an independent body relying on the FAF for selection of its members and approval of its budgets. FASB is supported by the sale of its publications and by fees assessed on all public companies based on their market capitalizations as mandated by the Sarbanes-Oxley Act.

From its inception through the mid-2009 implementation of the Accounting Standards Codification, FASB issued several types of pronouncements and used the following GAAP hierarchy (FAS 162, *The Hierarchy of Generally Accepted Accounting Principles*).

Pre Codification GAAP Hierarchy

Standard Setting Body	Type of Pronouncement	GAAP Level
AICPA	AICPA Accounting Research Bulletins (Not superseded by FASB actions)	A
APB	APB Opinions (Not superseded by FASB actions)	A
FASB	Statement of Financial Accounting Standard	A
FASB	Interpretation	A
FASB	Staff Positions	A
FASB	Technical Bulletins	B
AICPA - AcSEC	Statement of Position (if cleared by the FASB)	B
AICPA - AcSEC	Industry Audit and Accounting Guides (if cleared by the FASB)	B
EITF Task Force	Consensus Position	C
EITF Task Force	Topics discussed in Appendix D of EITF Abstracts (EITF D-Topics)	C
AICPA - AcSEC	Practice Bulletins	C
FASB	Implementation Guides (Q&As) published by the FASB Staff	D
AICPA	Accounting Interpretations	D
AICPA - AcSEC	Statement of Position not cleared by the FASB	D
	Practices widely recognized and prevalent either generally or in the industry	D

Other sources. Not all GAAP has resulted from the issuance of pronouncements by authoritative bodies. For example, depreciation methods such as straight-line and declining balance have both long been acceptable. There are, however, no definitive pronouncements that can be found to state this. Furthermore, there are many disclosure principles that evolved into general accounting practice because they were originally required by the SEC in documents submitted to them. Even much of the content of statements of financial position and income statements has evolved over the years in the absence of adopted standards.

GAAP Codification

FASB completed its project to codify GAAP and, on July 1, 2009, the Codification became the single official source of authoritative, nongovernmental US generally accepted accounting principles. It superseded all nongrandfathered (see ASC105-10-70-2 for a list of grandfathered guidance), non-SEC accounting guidance, that is, extant FASB, AICPA, EITF, and related literature. After that date, only one level of authoritative GAAP existed, excluding the guidance issued by the Securities and Exchange Commission (SEC). All other literature is nonauthoritative. In effect, therefore, all former Category A-D GAAP was compressed to two levels.

The Codification did not change GAAP, but rather introduced a new structure—one that is organized into an easily accessible, user-friendly online research system. The Codification reorganizes the large number of discrete US GAAP pronouncements into roughly 90 accounting Topics, and displays all Topics using a consistent structure.

SEC Guidance in the Codification. To increase the utility of the Codification for public companies, relevant portions of authoritative content issued by the SEC and selected SEC staff interpretations and administrative guidance are included for reference in the Codification. The sources include:

- Regulation S-X,
- Financial Reporting Releases (FRR)/Accounting Series Releases (ASR),
- Interpretive Releases (IR), and
- SEC staff guidance in:
  - Staff Accounting Bulletins (SAB),
  - EITF Topic D and SEC Staff Observer comments.

The Codification does not, however, incorporate the entire population of SEC rules, regulations, interpretive releases, and staff guidance, such as content related to matters outside of the basic financial statements, including Management's Discussion and Analysis (MD&A), or to auditing or independence matters.

Standards-setting Process

The FASB has long adhered to rigorous "due process" when creating new guidance. The goal is to involve constituents who would be affected by the newly issued guidance so that the standards created will result in information that reports economic activity as objectively as possible without attempting to influence behavior in any particular direction. Ultimately, however, the guidance is the judgment of the FASB, based on research, public input, and deliberation. The FASB's due process procedures are described below.

The FASB receives requests for new standards from all parts of its diverse constituency, including auditors, industry groups, the EITF, and the SEC. Requests for action include both suggestions for new topics and suggestions for reconsideration of existing pronouncements. In consultation with the FASB Members and others, and subject to FAF oversight, the FASB Chairman decides whether or not to add a project to the technical agenda. The FASB begins by appointing an advisory group, which may be a task force or advisory committee of outside experts. Care is taken to ensure that various points of view are represented in the advisory group. The group meets with and advises the Board and staff on the definition and scope of the project and the nature and extent of any additional research that may be needed. The FASB and its staff then debate the significant issues in the project and arrive at tentative conclusions. As it does so, the FASB and its staff study existing literature on the subject and conduct or commission any additional research as needed. The advisory group meetings and the Board meetings are open to public observation, and a public record is maintained. Many of these proceedings are also available by live or archived audio Webcast as well as via telephone. The basis of discussion for the meetings may be a Discussion Paper or an Exposure Draft.

Any individual or organization may request to speak at the public hearing, which is conducted by the FASB and the staff assigned to the project. Public observers are welcome. After each individual speaks, the FASB and staff ask questions. Questions are based on written material submitted by the speakers prior to the hearing as well as on the speaker's oral comments. In addition to the hearing, the staff analyzes all the written comments submitted. The FASB members study this analysis and read the comment letters to help them reach conclusions. The hearing transcript and written comments become part of the public record.

After the comment letters and oral presentations responding to the discussion document are considered, formal deliberations begin. (If the accounting problem is not as complex and no discussion document was issued, the due process begins at this point.) The FASB deliberates at meetings that are open to public observation, although observers do not participate in the discussions. The agenda for each meeting is announced in advance. Prior to each Board meeting, the staff presents a written analysis and recommendations of the issues to be discussed. During the meeting, the staff presents orally a summary of the written materials and the Board discusses each issue presented. The Board meets as many times as is necessary to resolve the issues.

When the Board has reached tentative conclusions on all the issues in the project, the staff prepares an Exposure Draft. The Exposure Draft sets forth the Board's conclusions about the proposed standards of financial accounting and reporting, the proposed effective date and method of transition, background information, and an explanation of the basis for the Board's conclusions. The Board reviews, and if necessary, revises, the Exposure Draft. A majority of the Board members must vote to approve an Exposure Draft for issuance for public comment. If the votes are not obtained, the FASB holds additional meetings and redrafts the Exposure Draft.

Any individual or organization can provide comments about the conclusions in the Exposure Draft during the exposure period, which is generally sixty days or more. The Board may also decide to have a public hearing to hear constituents' views. At the conclusion of the comment period, all comment letters and oral presentations are analyzed by the staff, and the Board members read the letters and the staff analysis. Then, the Board re-deliberates the issues, with the goal of issuing a final Accounting Standards Update (ASU).

All Board meetings are open to the public. During these meetings, the Board considers the comments received and may revise their earlier conclusions. If substantial modifications are made, the Board will issue a revised Exposure Draft for additional public comment. If so, the Board also may decide that another public hearing is necessary. When the Board is satisfied that all reasonable alternatives have been adequately considered, the staff drafts the proposed provisions. The Board deliberates the provisions and, if approved, the Board issues an Accounting Standards Update describing amendments to the Accounting Standards Codification. Once issued, the provisions become GAAP after the stated effective date.

Emerging Issues Task Force. The Emerging Issues Task Force (EITF) was formed in 1984 by the FASB to assist the Board in identifying current or emerging issues and implementation problems before divergent practices become entrenched. The guidance provided has often been restricted to narrow issues that were of immediate interest and importance. Task Force members are drawn primarily from public accounting firms but also include individuals who would be aware of issues and practices that should be considered by the group.

For each EITF agenda item, an issues paper is developed by members, their firms, or the FASB staff. These issues may be in especially narrow areas having little broad-based interest. Occasionally, FASB may include a narrow issue in the scope of a broader project and reaffirm or supersede the work of the Task Force. After discussion by the Task Force, a consensus may be reached on the issue, in which case the consensus is referred to the FASB for ratification. If the EITF consensus is approved by the FASB, it amends the FASB Codification through an ASU.

Accounting Standards Updates. Accounting Standards Updates (ASUs) are composed of:

- A summary of the key provisions of the project that led to the changes,
- The specific changes to the Codification, and
- The *Basis for Conclusions*.

The title of the combined set of new guidance and instructions is *Accounting Standards Update YY-XX,* where YY is the last two digits of the year and XX is the sequential number for each update. All authoritative GAAP issued by the FASB is issued in this format.

The FASB organizes the content of ASUs using the same Section headings as those used in the Codification. The ASU instructions display marked changes to the pertinent sections of the Codification. ASUs are not deemed authoritative in their own right; instead, they serve only to update the Codification and provide the historical basis for conclusions.

The content from updates that is not yet fully effective for all reporting entities appears in the Codification as boxed text and is labeled as *pending content.* The pending content text box includes the earliest transition date and a link to the related transition guidance, also found in the Codification.

For reference purposes, the Codification permits backward tracing to the actual literature from which the Codification was derived. Accounting Standards Updates add to or amend the Codification only, and no stand-alone FASB Statements or other guidance are promulgated. (ASC 105-10-05-5)

Maintenance Updates. As with any publishing practice, irregularities occur. To make necessary corrections, the FASB staff issues Maintenance Updates. These are not addressed by the Board and contain nonsubstantive editorial changes and link-related changes.

American Institute of Certified Public Accountants. Although it currently plays a greatly reduced standards-setting role, the American Institute of Certified Public Accountants (AICPA) has authorized the Financial Reporting Executive Committee (FinREC) to determine the AICPA's policies on financial reporting standards and to speak for the AICPA on accounting matters. FinREC, formerly the Accounting Standards Executive Committee (AcSEC), is the senior technical committee at the AICPA. It is composed of sixteen volunteer members, representative of industry, analysts, and both national and regional public accounting firms. All FinREC members are CPAs and members of the AICPA.

Researching GAAP Problems

The research procedures presented here are intended to serve as a general model for approaching research on accounting issues or questions you may have. These procedures should be refined and adapted to each individual fact situation.

Codification Structure. The FASB has compiled the Codification into a Web site, located through fasb.org. The site is intended to be easily searchable for research purposes. This section provides an overview of the site's contents and search functionality.

Areas. On all pages of the site, all categories of the Codification are listed down the vertical menu bar on the left side of the page, revealing the following Areas, and the numbering series for each one:

- General Principles (100) (Establishes the Codification as the source of GAAP.)
- Presentation—(200) (Topics in this area relate only to presentation matters; they do not address recognition, measurement, and derecognition matters. Examples of these topics are income statement, balance sheet, and earnings per share.)
- Assets (300).
- Liabilities (400).
- Equity (500).
- Revenue (600).
- Expenses (700). (Clusters all types of expense-related GAAP into five broad categories, which are cost of goods sold, research and development, compensation, income taxes, and other expenses.)

- Broad Transactions (800). (Contains the major transactional topics, such as business combinations, derivatives, and foreign currency matters.)
- Industry (900). (Itemizes GAAP for specific industries, such as entertainment, real estate, and software.)
- Master Glossary.

Topics. The Codification content is arranged by Area and then further divided by Topics, Subtopics, Sections, and Subsections. FASB has developed a classification system specifically for the Codification. The following is the structure of the classifications system: XXX-YY-ZZ-PP, where

- XXX = topic,
- YY = subtopic,
- ZZ = section, and
- PP = paragraph.

An "S" preceding the section number denotes SEC guidance. At the most granular level of detail, the Codification has a two-digit numerical code for a standard set of categories.

Below are the Codification Topics by Area. The entire numbering system is noted in the Codification Taxonomy section that precedes Chapter 1.

Codification Topics

General Principles
105 Generally Accepted Accounting Principles

Presentation
205 Presentation of Financial Statements
210 Balance Sheet
215 Statement of Shareholder Equity
220 Comprehensive Income
225 Income Statement
230 Statement of Cash Flows
235 Notes to Financial Statements
250 Accounting Changes and Error Corrections
255 Changing Prices
260 Earnings per Share
270 Interim Reporting
272 Limited Liability Entities
274 Personal Financial Statements
275 Risks and Uncertainties
280 Segment Reporting

Assets
305 Cash and Cash Equivalents
310 Receivables
320 Investments—Debt and Equity Securities
323 Investments—Equity Method and Joint Ventures
325 Investments—Other
330 Inventory
340 Other Assets and Deferred Costs
350 Intangibles—Goodwill and Other
360 Property, Plant, and Equipment

Liabilities
405 Liabilities
410 Asset Retirement and Environmental Obligations
420 Exit or Disposal Cost Obligations
430 Deferred Revenue
440 Commitments
450 Contingencies
460 Guarantees
470 Debt
480 Distinguishing Liabilities from Equity

Equity
505 Equity

Revenue
605 Revenue Recognition

Expenses
705 Cost of Sales and Services
710 Compensation—General
712 Compensation—Nonretirement Postemployment Benefits
715 Compensation—Retirement Benefits
718 Compensation—Stock Compensation
720 Other Expenses
730 Research and Development
740 Income Taxes

Broad Transactions
805 Business Combinations
808 Collaborative Arrangements
810 Consolidation
815 Derivatives and Hedging
820 Fair Value Measurement
825 Financial Instruments
830 Foreign Currency Matters
835 Interest
840 Leases
845 Nonmonetary Transactions
850 Related Party Disclosures
852 Reorganizations
853 Service Concession Arrangements
855 Subsequent Events
860 Transfers and Servicing

Industry
905 Agriculture
908 Airlines
910 Contractors—Construction
912 Contractors—Federal Government
915 Development Stage Entities
920 Entertainment—Broadcasters
922 Entertainment—Cable Television
924 Entertainment—Casinos
926 Entertainment—Films
928 Entertainment—Music
930 Extractive Activities—Mining
932 Extractive Activities—Oil and Gas
940 Financial Services—Broker and Dealers
942 Financial Services—Depository and Lending
944 Financial Services—Insurance
946 Financial Services—Investment Companies
948 Financial Services—Mortgage Banking
950 Financial Services—Title Plant
952 Franchisors
954 Health Care Entities
958 Not-for-Profit Entities
960 Plan Accounting—Defined Benefit Pension Plans
962 Plan Accounting—Defined Contribution Pension Plans
965 Plan Accounting—Health and Welfare Benefit Plans
970 Real Estate—General
972 Real Estate—Common Interest Realty Associations
974 Real Estate—Real Estate Investment Trusts
976 Real Estate—Retail Land
978 Real Estate—Time-Sharing Activities
980 Regulated Operations
985 Software
995 U.S. Steamship Entities

Subtopics. Subtopics represent subsets of a topic and are typically identified by type or by scope. For example, operating leases and capital leases are two separate subtopics of the leases topic. Each topic contains an *overall subtopic* (designated "-10") that generally represents the pervasive guidance for the topic, which includes guidance that applies to all other subtopics. Each additional subtopic represents incremental or unique guidance not contained in the overall subtopic.

Sections		
Title	**Number**	**Description**
Status	00	Includes references to the Accounting Standards Updates that affect the subtopic.
Overview and background	05	Provides overview and background material.
Objectives	10	States the high-level objectives of the Topic.
Scope and scope exceptions	15	Outlines the transactions, events and other occurrences to which the subtopic guidance does or does not apply.
Glossary	20	Contains definitions for terms found within the subtopic guidance.
Recognition	25	Defines the criteria, timing, and location for recording an item in the financial statements.
Initial measurement	30	Provides guidance on the criteria and amounts used to measure a transaction at the initial date of recognition.
Subsequent measurement	35	Provides guidance on the measurement of an item after the recognition date.
Derecognition	40	Relates almost exclusively to assets, liabilities, and equity. Provides criteria, the method to determine the amount of basis, and the timing to be used when derecognizing a particular item for purposes of determining gain or loss.
Other presentation matters	45	Provides guidance on presenting items in the financial statements.
Disclosure	50	Provides guidance regarding disclosure in the notes to or on the face of the financial statements.
Implementation guidance and illustrations	55	Contains illustrations of the guidance provided in the preceding sections.
Relationships	60	Contains links to guidance that may be helpful to the reader of the subtopic.
Transition and Open Effective Date Information	65	Contains references to paragraphs within the subtopic that have open transition guidance.
Grandfathered Guidance	70	Contains descriptions, references, and transition periods for content grandfathered after July 1, 2009, by an Accounting Standards Update.[1]
XBRL Elements	75	Contains the related XBRL elements for the subtopic
SEC Materials	S99	Contains selected SEC content for use by public companies.

[1] Certain accounting standards allowed for the continued application of superseded accounting standards for transactions that have an ongoing effect in an entity's financial statements. That superseded guidance has not been included in the Codification, is considered grandfathered, and continues to remain authoritative for those transactions after the effective date of the Codification. (ASC 105-10-70-2)

Sections. Sections represent the nature of the content in a subtopic—for example, recognition, measurement, and disclosure. The sectional organization for all subtopics is the same. In a manner similar to that used for topics, sections correlate closely with sections of individual International Accounting Standards. Sections are further broken down into *subsections, paragraphs,* and *subparagraphs*, depending on the specific content of each section.

Finding Information. By drilling down through the various topics and subtopics in the sidebar of the online Codification, a researcher can eventually locate the relevant GAAP information. However, there are other ways to access GAAP information through the Codification site that may prove to be easier.

- *Cross-referencing.* If the researchers know the reference number of an original GAAP source document, such as an EITF consensus or a FASB Staff Position, then they can enter this information through the Cross-Reference tab, which is located at the top center of the Codification home page.
- *Codification search.* If the researchers are searching for specific words or phrases, then the best search tool is the Codification search bar, which is located in the upper right corner of any page on the site. To use it for a precision search, enter quotes around the search text; for a less precise search that returns individual words within the search text, do not use quotes.

Codification Terminology. With issuance of the Codification, the FASB standardized on the term "entity" to replace terms such as company, organization, enterprise, firm, preparer, etc. So, too, the Codification uses "shall" throughout to replace "should," "shall," "is required to," "must," etc. The FASB believes these terms all represent the same concept—the requirement to apply a standard. "Would" and "should" are used to indicate hypothetical situations. To reduce ambiguity, the Codification also eliminated qualifying terminology, such as *usually*, *ordinarily*, *generally*, and similar terms.

Research Procedures

Step 1: Identify the problem. Most often it is found that incorrect answers (e.g., regarding the proper way to report revenue-producing activities) flow from improper definition of the actual question to be resolved. The process to be employed is to

- Gain an understanding of the problem or question.
- Challenge the tentative definition of the problem and revise, as necessary.
- Problems and research questions can arise from new authoritative pronouncements, changes in a firm's economic operating environment, or new transactions, as well as from the realization that the problem had not been properly defined in the past.
- If proposed transactions and potential economic circumstances are anticipated, more deliberate attention can be directed at finding the correct solution, and certain proposed transactions having deleterious reporting consequences might be avoided altogether or structured more favorably.
- If little is known about the subject area, it may be useful to consult general reference sources to become more familiar with the topic, that is, the basic what, why, how, when, who, and where. Web-based research vastly expands the ability to gather useful information.
- Ensure that the issue you are researching is a GAAP issue or is an auditing issue so that your search is directed to the appropriate literature.

Step 2: Analyze the problem.

- Identify critical factors, issues, and questions that relate to the research problem.
- What are the options? Brainstorm possible alternative accounting treatments.
- What are the goals of the transaction? Are these goals compatible with full and transparent disclosure and recognition?
- What is the economic substance of the transaction, irrespective of the manner in which it appears to be structured?
- What limitations or factors can impact the accounting treatment?

Step 3: Refine the problem statement.

- Clearly articulate the critical issues in a way that will facilitate research and analysis.

Step 4: Identify plausible alternatives.

- Plausible alternative solutions are based upon prior knowledge or theory.
- Additional alternatives may be identified as Steps 5–7 are completed.
- The purpose of identifying and discussing different alternatives is to be able to respond to key accounting issues that arise out of a specific situation.
- The alternatives are the potential methods of accounting for the situation from which only one will ultimately be chosen.
- Exploring alternatives is important because many times there is no single cut-and-dried financial reporting solution to the situation.
- Ambiguity often surrounds many transactions and related accounting issues and, accordingly, the accountant and business advisor must explore the alternatives and use professional judgment in deciding on the proper course of action.

Step 5: Develop a research strategy.

- Determine which literature to search.
- Generate keywords or phrases that will form the basis of an electronic search.
- Consider trying a broad search to
  - Assist in developing an understanding of the area,
  - Identify appropriate search terms, and
  - Identify related issues and terminology.
- Consider trying very precise searches to identify whether there is authoritative literature directly on point.

Step 6: Search authoritative literature (described in additional detail below).

This step involves implementation of the research strategy through searching, identifying, and locating applicable information.

- Research published GAAP.
- Research using *Wiley GAAP*.
- Research other literature.
- Research practice.
- Use theory.
- Find analogous events and/or concepts that are reasonably similar.

Step 7: Evaluation.

- Analyze and evaluate all of the information obtained.
- This evaluation should lead to the development of a solution or recommendation. Again, it is important to remember that Steps 3–7 describe activities that will interact with each other and lead to a more refined process in total, and a more complete solution. These steps may involve several iterations.

Search Authoritative Literature (Step 6)—Further Explanation

The following sections discuss in more detail how to search authoritative literature as outlined in Step 6.

Researching *Wiley GAAP*. This publication can assist in researching GAAP for the purpose of identifying technical answers to specific inquiries. You can begin your search in one of two ways: by using the contents page at the front of this book to determine the chapter in which the answer to your question is likely to be discussed, or by using the index at the back of this publication to identify specific pages of the publication that discuss the subject matter relating to your question. The path chosen depends in part on how specific the question is; an initial reading of the chapter or relevant section thereof will provide a broader perspective on the subject. However, if one's interest is more specific, it might be better to search the index, because securitizations are a very specialized type of transaction involving receivables and are addressed in only a few pages of the text.

Each chapter in this publication is organized in the following manner:

- A chapter table of contents on the first page of the chapter.
- Perspective and Issues, providing an overview of the chapter contents (noting any current controversy or proposed GAAP changes affecting the chapter's topics) and a list of major topics and subtopics in the FASB Accounting Standards Codification relevant to the chapter's topics.
- Definition of Terms, defining any specialized terms unique to the chapter's subject matter.
- Concepts, Rules, and Examples, setting forth the detailed guidance and examples.

After reading the relevant portions of this publication, the list of major topics and subtopics in the Codification can be used to find the sections in the Codification that are related to the topic, so that these can be appropriately understood and cited in documenting your research findings and conclusions. Readers familiar with the professional literature can use the Codification Taxonomy that precedes this chapter to quickly locate the pages in this publication relevant to each specific pronouncement.

Researching nonpromulgated GAAP. Researching nonpromulgated GAAP consists of reviewing pronouncements in areas similar to those being researched, reading accounting literature mentioned in ASC 105-10-05-3 and earlier in this chapter as "other sources," and carefully reading the relevant portions of the FASB Conceptual Framework (summarized later in this chapter). Concepts and intentions espoused by accounting experts offer essential clues to a logical formulation of alternatives and conclusions regarding problems that have not yet been addressed by the standard-setting bodies.

Both the AICPA and FASB publish a myriad of nonauthoritative literature. FASB publishes the documents it uses in its due process: Discussion Papers, Invitations to Comment, Exposure Drafts, and Preliminary Views as well as minutes from its meetings. It also publishes research reports, newsletters, and implementation guidance. The AICPA publishes Technical Practice Aids, Issues Papers, Technical Questions and Answers, Audit and Accounting Guides, as well as comment letters on proposals of other standard-setting bodies, and the monthly periodical, *Journal of Accountancy*. Technical Practice Aids are answers published by the AICPA to questions about accounting and auditing standards. AICPA Issues Papers are research documents about accounting and reporting problems that the AICPA believes should be resolved by FASB. They provide information about alternative accounting treatments used in practice.

The Securities and Exchange Commission issues Staff Accounting Bulletins and makes rulings on individual cases that come before it. These rulings create and impose accounting standards on those whose financial statements are to be submitted to the Commission. The SEC, through acts passed by Congress, has been given broad powers to prescribe accounting practices and methods for all statements filed with it.

Governmental agencies such as the Government Accountability Office, the Federal Accounting Standards Advisory Board, and the Cost Accounting Standards Board have certain publications that may assist in researching written standards. Also, industry organizations and associations may be other helpful sources.

Certain publications are helpful in identifying practices used by entities that may not be promulgated as standards. The AICPA publishes an annual survey of the accounting and disclosure policies of many public companies in *U. S. GAAP Financial Statements – Best Practices in Presentation and Disclosure* (formerly, *Accounting Trends and Techniques*) and offers an online version which contains a library of financial statements that can be accessed through a computerized search. EDGAR (Electronic Data Gathering, Analysis, and Retrieval) publishes the SEC filings of public companies, which includes the companies' financial statements. Through selection of keywords and/or topics, these services can provide information on how other entities resolved similar problems.

Internet-based research sources. There has been and continues to be an information revolution affecting the exponential growth in the volume of materials, authoritative and nonauthoritative, that are available on the Internet. A listing of just a small cross-section of these sources follows:

Accounting Web sites

AICPA Online	www.aicpa.org	Includes the Financial Reporting Center for your accounting and assurance information and resources; CPE information; Professional Ethics and Peer Review releases and information; information on relevant congressional/executive actions; online publications, such as the *Journal of Accountancy*; also has links to other organizations; includes links to standard-setting bodies and their authoritative standards for nonissuers including auditing standards, attestation standards, and quality control standards
American Accounting Association	www.aaahq.org	Accounting news; publications; faculty information; searchable; links to other sites
FASB	www.fasb.org	Information on FASB; ASUs, Project Status reports, Webcasts
FASB Codification	asc.fasb.org/home	Database using the accounting Codification; includes cross-referencing and tutorials

GASB	www.gasb.org	Information on GASB; new GASB documents; summaries/status of all GASB statements; proposed Statements; Technical Bulletins; Interpretations
International Accounting Standards Board (IASB)	www.ifrs.org	Information on the IASB; lists of Pronouncements, Exposure Drafts, project summaries, and conceptual framework
NASBA	www.nasba.org	National State Boards of Accountancy; includes listings of registered CPE sponsors and links to state boards of accountancy as well as joint AICPA/NASBA CPE standards
PCAOB	www.pcaobus.org	Sections on rulemaking, standards (including the interim auditing, attestation, quality control, ethics, and independence standards), enforcement, inspections and oversight activities
SEC	www.sec.gov	SEC digest and statements; EDGAR searchable database; information on current SEC rulemaking; links to other sites

The Concept of Materiality

Materiality has great significance in understanding, researching, and implementing GAAP. Disputes over financial statement presentations often turn on the materiality of items that were, or were not, recognized, measured, and presented in certain ways.

Materiality is defined by the FASB in Statement of Financial Concepts 2 (CON 2), *Qualitative Characteristics of Accounting Information,* as:

> *The magnitude of an omission or misstatement of accounting information that, in the light of surrounding circumstances, makes it probable that the judgment of a reasonable person relying on the information would have been changed or influenced by the omission or misstatement...*

This is in conformity with the U.S. Supreme Court. The Supreme Court has held that a fact is material if there is:

> *a substantial likelihood that the...fact would have been viewed by the reasonable investor as having significantly altered the "total mix" of information made available.*

However, due to its inherent subjectivity, the FASB definition does not provide specific or quantitative guidance in distinguishing material information from immaterial information. The individual accountant must exercise professional judgment in evaluating information and concluding on its materiality. Materiality as a criterion has both quantitative and qualitative aspects, and items should not be deemed *immaterial* unless all potentially applicable quantitative and qualitative aspects are given full consideration and found not relevant.

Quantitatively, materiality has been defined in relatively few pronouncements, which is a testament to the great difficulty of setting precise measures for materiality. For example, in ASC 280-10-50, which addresses segment disclosures, a material segment or customer is defined in ASC 280-10-50-12 as representing 10% or more of the reporting entity's revenues (although, even given this rule, qualitative considerations may cause smaller segments to be deemed reportable). The Securities and Exchange Commission has, in several of its pronouncements, defined materiality as 1% of total assets for receivables from officers and stockholders, 5% of total assets for separate balance sheet disclosure of items, and 10% of total revenue for disclosure of oil and gas producing activities.

Although materiality judgments have traditionally been primarily based on quantitative assessments, the nature of a transaction or event can affect a determination of whether that transaction or event is material. For example, a transaction that, if recorded, changes a profit to a loss or changes compliance with ratios in a debt covenant to noncompliance would be material even if it involved an otherwise immaterial amount. Also, a transaction that might be judged immaterial if it occurred as part of routine operations may be material if its occurrence helps meet certain objectives. For example, a transaction that allows management to achieve a target or obtain a bonus that otherwise would not become due would be considered material, regardless of the actual amount involved. So, too, offers to buy or sell assets for more or less than book value, litigation proceedings against the company pursuant to price-fixing or antitrust allegations, and active negotiations regarding their settlement can have a material impact on the enterprise's future profitability and, thus, are all examples of items that would not be capable of being evaluated for materiality based solely upon numerical calculations.

Another factor in judging materiality is the degree of precision that may be attained when making an estimate. For example, accounts payable can usually be estimated more accurately than a possible loss from the incurrence of an asset retirement obligation. An error amount that would be material in estimating accounts payable might be acceptable in estimating the retirement obligation.

The SEC in Staff Accounting Bulletin (SAB) Topics 1.M (SAB 99) and 1.N (SAB 108), provides useful discussions of this issue. Although not strictly applicable to nonpublic preparers of financial statements, this guidance is worthy of consideration by all accountants and auditors. Among other things, Topic 1.M notes that deliberate application of nonacceptable accounting methods cannot be justified merely because the impact on the financial statements is deemed to be immaterial. Topic 1.N also usefully reminds preparers and others that materiality has both quantitative and qualitative dimensions, and both must be given full consideration. Topic 1.N has added to the literature of materiality with its discussion of considerations applicable to prior period restatements.

The Conceptual Framework

FASB has issued eight pronouncements (five of which remain extant) called Statements of Financial Accounting Concepts (CON). The conceptual framework is designed to prescribe the nature, function, and limits of financial accounting and reporting and to be used as a guideline that will lead to consistent standards. These conceptual statements do **not** establish accounting standards or disclosure practices for particular items and are not enforceable under the AICPA Code of Professional Conduct. Since GAAP may be inconsistent with the principles set forth in the conceptual framework, the FASB expects to reexamine existing accounting standards. Until that time, a CON does not require a change in existing GAAP. CON do not amend, modify, or interpret existing GAAP, nor do they justify departing from GAAP based upon interpretations derived from them.

FASB's conceptual framework is intended to serve as the foundation upon which the Board can construct standards that are both sound and internally consistent. The fact that the framework was intended to guide FASB in establishing standards is embodied in the preface to CON 8, which states

> *The Board itself is likely to be the most direct beneficiary of the guidance provided by Concepts Statements. They will guide the Board in developing accounting and reporting standards by providing the Board with a common foundation and basic reasoning on which to consider merits of alternatives.*

The conceptual framework is also intended for use by the business community to help understand and apply standards and to assist in their development. This goal is also mentioned in the preface to CON 8:

> *However, knowledge of the objectives and concepts the Board will use in developing new guidance also should enable those who are affected by or interested in generally accepted accounting standards (GAAP) to understand better the purposes, content, and characteristics of information provided by financial accounting and reporting. That knowledge is expected to enhance the usefulness of, and confidence in, financial accounting and reporting. The objectives and fundamental concepts also may provide some guidance in analyzing new or emerging problems of financial accounting and reporting in the absence of applicable authoritative pronouncements.*

The FASB Special Report, *The Framework of Financial Accounting Concepts and Standards* (1998), states that the conceptual framework should help solve complex financial accounting or reporting problems by

- Providing a set of common premises as a basis for discussion;
- Providing precise terminology;
- Helping to ask the right questions;
- Limiting areas of judgment and discretion and excluding from consideration potential solutions that are in conflict with it; and
- Imposing intellectual discipline on what traditionally has been a subjective and ad hoc reasoning process.

Components of the conceptual framework. The components of the conceptual framework for financial accounting and reporting include objectives, qualitative characteristics, elements, recognition, measurement, and disclosure concepts.

Elements of financial statements are the components from which financial statements are created. They include assets, liabilities, equity, investments by owners, distributions to owners, comprehensive income, revenues, expenses, gains, and losses. In order to be included in financial statements, an element must meet criteria for recognition and possess a characteristic that can be reliably measured.

Reporting or display considerations are concerned with what information should be provided, who should provide it, and where it should be displayed. How the financial statements (financial position, earnings, and cash flow) are presented is the focal point of this part of the conceptual framework project.

Of the five extant Concepts Statements, the fourth, *Objectives of Financial Reporting by Nonbusiness Organizations*, is not covered here due to its specialized nature. Because the topics in CON 8 are foundational, this discussion begins with CON 8.

CON 8 is a result of a joint FASB/IASB project to improve and converge their frameworks. Chapter 1 of CON 8 replaced CON 1, and Chapter 2 of CON 8 is being reserved for a chapter on the Reporting Entity, a replacement of CON 3. The current status of the project can be found on FASB.org.

CON 8—Chapter 1: The Objective of General Purpose Financial Reporting

Chapter 1 identifies the objective of financial reporting and indicates that this objective applies to all financial reporting. It is not limited to financial statements. The objective is to provide information that is useful in making decisions about providing resources to the entity. Users of financial information are identified as existing and potential investors, lenders, and other creditors. Chapter 1 is directed at general-purpose external financial reporting by a business enterprise as it relates to the ability of that enterprise to generate favorable cash flows.

Investors and creditors need financial reports that provide understandable information that will aid in predicting the future cash flows of an entity. The expectation of cash flows affects an entity's ability to meet the obligations of loans and other forms of credit and to pay interest and dividends, which in turn affects the market price of that entity's stocks and bonds.

To assess cash flows, financial reporting should provide information relative to an enterprise's economic resources, the claims against the entity, and the effects of transactions, events, and circumstances that change resources and claims to resources. A description of these informational needs follows:

- *Economic resources, claims against the entity, and owners' equity.* This information provides the users of financial reporting with a measure of future cash flows and an indication of the entity's strengths, weaknesses, liquidity, and solvency.
- *Economic performance and earnings.* Past performance provides an indication of an entity's future performance. Furthermore, earnings based upon accrual accounting provide a better indicator of economic performance and future cash flows than do current cash receipts and disbursements. Accrual basis earnings are a better indicator because a charge for recovery of capital (depreciation/amortization) is made in determining these earnings. The relationship between earnings and economic performance results from matching the costs and benefits (revenues) of economic activity during a given period by means of accrual accounting. Over the life of an enterprise, economic performance can be determined by net cash flows or by total earnings since the two measures would be equal.
- *Liquidity, solvency, and funds flows.* Information about cash and other funds flows from borrowings, repayments of borrowings, expenditures, capital transactions, economic resources, obligations, owners' equity, and earnings may aid the user of financial reporting information in assessing a firm's liquidity or solvency.
- *Management stewardship and performance.* The assessment of a firm's management with respect to the efficient and profitable use of the firm's resources is usually made on the basis of economic performance as reported by periodic earnings. Because earnings are affected by factors other than current management performance, earnings may not be a reliable indicator of management performance.
- *Management explanations and interpretations.* Management is responsible for the efficient use of a firm's resources. Thus, it acquires knowledge about the enterprise and its performance that is unknown to the external user. Explanations by management concerning the financial impact of transactions, events, circumstances, uncertainties, estimates, judgments, and any effects of the separation of the results of operations into periodic measures of performance enhance the usefulness of financial information.

CON 8—Chapter 3: Qualitative Characteristics of Useful Financial Information

The purpose of financial reporting is to provide decision makers with useful information. Individuals or standard-setting bodies should make accounting choices based upon the usefulness of that information to the decision-making process. CON 8—Chapter 3 identifies the qualities or characteristics that make information useful in the decision-making process. It also establishes a terminology to provide a greater understanding of the characteristics.

Usefulness for decision. This is the most important characteristic of information. Information must be useful to be beneficial to the user. To be useful, accounting information must both be *relevant* and *faithfully represent* what it claims to represent. Both of these fundamental qualitative characteristics are affected by the completeness of the information.

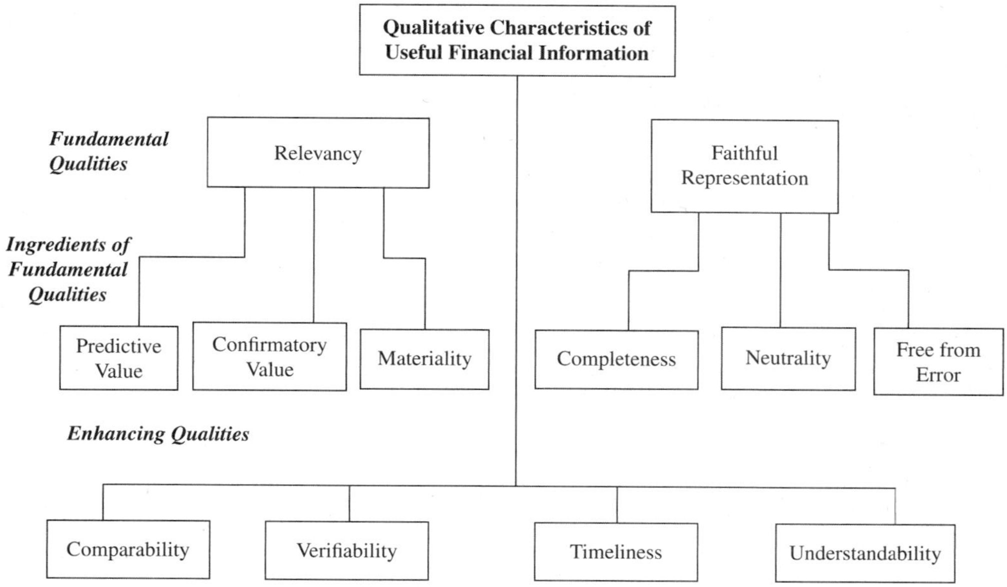

Relevance. Information is relevant to a decision if it makes a difference to the decision maker in his/her ability to predict events or to confirm or correct expectations. Relevant information will reduce the decision maker's assessment of the uncertainty of the outcome of a decision even though it may not change the decision itself. Information is relevant if it provides knowledge concerning.

- Past events (confirmatory value). Disclosure information is relevant because it provides information about past events.
- Future events (predictive value) and if it is timely. The predictive value of accounting information does not imply that such information is a prediction. The predictive value refers to the utility that a piece of information has as an input into a predictive model.

An item of information is material and should be reported if it is significant enough to have an effect on the decision maker. Materiality is entity specific. It is dependent upon the relative size of an item and nature of the item. Because materiality is evaluated in the context of an individual entity's financial report, the FASB could not offer quantitative standards of materiality.

Faithful representation. Financial statements are an abstraction of the activities of a business enterprise. They simplify the activities of the actual entity. To be faithfully representative, financial statements must portray the important financial relationships of the entity itself. Information is faithfully representative if it is

- Complete,
- Neutral, and
- Free from errors.

A complete representation contains all the information that would enable users to understand the information. In addition to quantitative information, a particular item may need to include a description and explanation.

Neutrality. Neutrality means that accounting information should serve to communicate without attempting to influence behavior in a particular direction. This does not mean that accounting should not influence behavior or that it should affect everyone in the same way. It means that information should not favor certain interest groups.

Free from error does not mean perfectly accurate. However, it does mean that a description is

- Accurately described,
- The explanation of the phenomenon are explained, and
- No errors have been made in selecting and reporting the process.

Information that is relevant and faithfully represented can be enhanced by

- Comparability,
- Verifiability,
- Timeliness, and
- Understandability.

Comparability. To be useful, accounting information should be comparable. The characteristic of comparability allows the users of accounting information to assess the similarities and differences either among different entities for the same time period or for the same entity over different time periods. Comparisons are usually made on the basis of quantifiable measurements of a common characteristic. Therefore, to be comparable, the measurements used must be reliable with respect to the common characteristic. Noncomparability can result from the use of different inputs, procedures, or systems of classification.

Related to comparability, consistency is an interperiod comparison that requires the use of the same accounting principles from one period to another. Although a change of an accounting principle to a more preferred method results in inconsistency, the change is acceptable if the effect of the change is disclosed. Consistency, however, does not insure comparability. If the measurements used are not representationally faithful, comparability will not be achieved.

Verifiability means that several independent measures will obtain the same accounting measure. An accounting measure that can be repeated with the same result (consensus) is desirable because it serves to detect and reduce measurer bias. Cash is highly verifiable. Inventories and depreciable assets tend to be less verifiable because alternative valuation methods exist. The direct verification of an accounting measure would serve to minimize measurer bias and measurement bias. The verification of the procedures used to obtain the measure would minimize measurer bias only. Finally, verifiability does not guarantee representational faithfulness or relevance.

Timeliness. Although timeliness alone will not make information useful, information must be timely to be useful.

Understandability. Financial reports must be understandable for users who have a "reasonable knowledge of business and economic activities and who review and analyze the information diligently" (Con 8, QC 32).

Trade-offs. Although it is desirable that accounting information contain the characteristics that have been identified above, not all of these characteristics are compatible. Often, one characteristic may be obtained only by sacrificing another. The trade-offs that must be made are determined on the basis of the relative importance of the characteristics. This relative importance, in turn, is dependent upon the nature of the users and their particular needs.

Cost constraint. The qualitative characteristics of useful accounting information are subject to a constraint: the relative cost-benefit of that information. Associated with the benefits to the user of accounting information is the cost of using that information and of providing it to the user. Information should be provided only if its benefits exceed its cost. Unfortunately, it is difficult to value the benefit of accounting information. It is also difficult to determine whether the burden of the cost of disclosure and the benefits of such disclosure are distributed fairly.

CON 5: Recognition and Measurement in Financial Statements of Business Enterprises

CON 5 indicates that financial statements are the principal means of communicating useful financial information. A full set of such statements contains

- Financial position at end of the period
- Earnings for the period
- Comprehensive income for the period
- Cash flows during the period
- Investments by and distributions to owners during the period.

Financial statements result from simplifying, condensing, and aggregating transactions. Therefore, no one financial statement provides sufficient information by itself and no one item or part of each statement can summarize the information.

A statement of financial position provides information about an entity's assets, liabilities, and equity. Earnings are a measure of entity performance during a period. Earnings are similar to net income but exclude accounting adjustments from earlier periods such as cumulative effect changes in accounting principles. Comprehensive income comprises all recognized changes in equity other than those arising from investments by and distributions to owners. A statement of cash flows reflects receipts and payments of cash by major sources and uses including operating, financing, and investing activities. The investments by and distributions to owners reflect the capital transactions of an entity during a period.

Income is determined by the concept of financial capital maintenance which means that only if the money amount of net assets increases during a period (excluding capital transactions) is there a profit. For recognition in financial statements, subject to both cost-benefit and materiality constraints, an item must meet the following criteria:

1. Definition—Meet the definition of an element in financial statements
2. Measurability—Have a relevant attribute measurable with sufficient reliability
3. Relevance
4. Reliability.

Items reported in the financial statements are based on historical cost, replacement cost, market value, net realizable value, and present value of cash flows. Price level changes are not recognized in these statements and conservatism guides the application of recognition criteria.

CON 6: Elements of Financial Statements

CON 3 was replaced by CON 6. CON 6 carried forward essentially all of the concepts in CON 3 and added the elements unique to the financial statements of not-for-profit organizations. CON 6 defines ten interrelated elements that are used in the financial statements of business enterprises.

1. *Assets*—Probable future economic benefits obtained or controlled by a particular entity as a result of past transactions or events.
2. *Liabilities*—Probable future sacrifices of economic benefits arising from present obligations of a particular entity to transfer assets or provide services to other entities in the future as a result of past transactions or events.
3. *Equity* (*Net Assets*)—The residual interest in the assets that remains after deducting its liabilities. In a business enterprise, equity is the ownership interest.
4. *Revenues*—Inflows or other enhancements of assets of an entity or settlement of its liabilities (or a combination of both) from delivering or producing goods, rendering services, or other activities that constitute the entity's ongoing major and central operations.
5. *Expenses*—Outflows or other using up of assets or incurrences of liabilities (or a combination of both) from delivering or producing goods, rendering services, or carrying out other activities that constitute the entity's ongoing major and central operations.
6. *Gains*—Increases in equity (net assets) from peripheral or incidental transactions of an entity and from all other transactions and other events and circumstances affecting the entity except those that result from revenues or investments by owners.
7. *Losses*—Decreases in equity (net assets) from peripheral or incidental transactions of an entity and from all other transactions and other events and circumstances affecting the entity except those that result from expenses or distributions to owners.
8. *Comprehensive Income*—The change in equity of a business enterprise during a period from transactions and other events and circumstances from sources other than investments by owners or distributions to owners.
9. *Investments by Owners*—Increases in equity of a particular business enterprise resulting from transfers to it for the purpose of increasing ownership interests.
10. *Distributions to Owners*—Decreases in the equity of a particular business enterprise resulting from transferring assets, rendering services, or incurring liabilities to owners.

Definitions of Terms. CON 6 also defines several significant financial accounting and reporting terms that are used in the Concepts Statements (and FASB pronouncements issued after the Concepts Statements).

An *event* is a happening of consequence to an entity. It can be an internal event (the use of raw materials) or an external event with another entity (the purchase of labor) or with the environment in which the business operates (a technological advance by a competitor).

A *transaction* is a particular kind of event. It is an external event that involves transferring something of value to another entity.

Circumstances are a condition, or set of conditions, that create situations that might otherwise have not occurred and might not have been anticipated.

Accrual is the accounting process of recognizing the effects of future cash receipts and payments in the current period. Accrual accounting attempts to record the financial effects on an entity of transactions and of other events and circumstances that have consequences for the entity in the periods in which those transactions, events, and circumstances occur rather than in the periods in which cash is received or paid by the entity.

Deferral is the accounting process of recognizing a liability resulting from a current cash receipt or an asset resulting from a current cash payment.

Realization is the process of converting noncash assets into cash.

Recognition is the process of formally incorporating a transaction or other event into the financial statements.

Matching is the simultaneous recognition of the revenues and expenses that result directly and jointly from the same transaction or other event.

Allocation is the process of assigning expenses to periods when the transactions or events that cause the using up of the benefits cannot be identified or when the cause can be identified but the actual amount of benefit used up cannot be reliably measured.

Elements of not-for-profit financial statements. CON 6 also discusses the elements used in the financial statements of not-for-profit organizations. Of the ten elements, seven are used by not-for-profit organizations. The three elements omitted are investments by owners, distributions to owners, and comprehensive income. The net assets (equity) of not-for-profit organizations is divided into three classes—unrestricted, temporarily restricted, and permanently restricted—based on the existence or absence of donor-imposed restrictions.

CON 7: Using Cash Flow Information and Present Value in Accounting Measurements

CON 7 provides a framework for using estimates of future cash flows as the basis for accounting measurements either at initial recognition or when assets are subsequently remeasured at fair value and for using the interest method of amortization. It provides the principles that govern measurement using present value, especially when the amount of future cash flows, their timing, or both are uncertain. However, it does not address recognition questions, such as which transactions and events should be valued using present value measures.

Fair value is the objective for most measurements at initial recognition and for fresh-start measurements in subsequent periods. At initial recognition, the cash paid or received (historical cost or proceeds) is usually assumed to be fair value, absent evidence to the contrary. For fresh-start measurements, a price that is observed in the marketplace for an essentially similar asset or liability is fair value. If purchase prices and market prices are available, there is no need to use alternative measurement techniques to approximate fair value. However, if alternative measurement techniques must be used for initial recognition and for fresh-start measurements, those techniques should attempt to capture the elements that when taken together would comprise a market price if one existed. The objective is to estimate the price likely to exist in the marketplace if there were a marketplace—fair value.

CON 7 states that the only objective of using present value in accounting measurements is fair value. It is necessary to capture, to the extent possible, the economic differences in the marketplace between sets of estimated future cash flows. A present value measurement that fully captures those differences must include the following elements:

1. An estimate of the future cash flow, or in more complex cases, series of future cash flows at different times
2. Expectations about possible variations in the amount or timing of those cash flows
3. The time value of money, represented by the risk-free rate of interest
4. The risk premium—the price for bearing the uncertainty inherent in the asset or liability
5. Other factors, including illiquidity and market imperfections.

How CON 7 measures differ from previously utilized present value techniques. Previously employed present value techniques typically used a single set of estimated cash flows and a single discount (interest) rate. In applying those techniques, adjustments for factors 2 through 5 described in the previous section are incorporated in the selection of the discount rate. In the CON 7 approach, only the third factor listed (the time value of money) is included in the discount rate; the other factors cause adjustments in arriving at risk-adjusted expected cash flows. CON 7 introduces the probability-weighted, expected cash flow approach, which focuses on the range of possible estimated cash flows and estimates of their respective probabilities of occurrence.

Previous techniques used to compute present value used estimates of the cash flows most likely to occur. CON 7 refines and enhances the precision of this model by weighting different cash flow scenarios (regarding the amounts and timing of cash flows) by their estimated probabilities of occurrence and factoring these scenarios into the ultimate determination of fair value. The difference is that values are assigned to the cash flows other than the most likely one. To illustrate, a cash flow might be $100, $200, or $300, with probabilities of 10%, 50%, and 40%, respectively. The most likely cash flow is the one with 50% probability, or $200. The expected cash flow is $230 [=($100 × .1) + ($200 × .5) + ($300 × .4)].

The CON 7 method, unlike previous present value techniques, can also accommodate uncertainty in the timing of cash flows. For example, a cash flow of $10,000 may be received in one year, two years, or three years, with probabilities of 15%, 60%, and 25%, respectively. Traditional present value techniques would compute the present value using the most likely timing of the payment—two years. The example below shows the computation of present value using the CON 7 method. Again, the expected present value of $9,030 differs from the traditional notion of a best estimate of $9,070 (the 60% probability) in this example.

Present value of $10,000 in 1 year discounted at 5%	$9,523	
Multiplied by 15% probability		$1,428
Present value of $10,000 in 2 years discounted at 5%	$9,070	
Multiplied by 60% probability		5,442
Present value of $10,000 in 3 years discounted at 5%	$8,638	
Multiplied by 25% probability		2,160
Probability weighted expected present value		$9,030

Measuring liabilities. The measurement of liabilities involves different problems from the measurement of assets; however, the underlying objective is the same. When using present value techniques to estimate the fair value of a liability, the objective is to estimate the value of the assets required currently to (1) settle the liability with the holder or (2) transfer the liability to an entity of comparable credit standing. To estimate the fair value of an entity's notes or bonds payable, accountants look to the price at which other entities are willing to hold the entity's liabilities as assets. For example, the proceeds of a loan are the price that a lender paid to hold the borrower's promise of future cash flows as an asset.

The most relevant measurement of an entity's liabilities should always reflect the credit standing of the entity. An entity with a good credit standing will receive more cash for its promise to pay than an entity with a poor credit standing. For example, if two entities both promise to pay $750 in three years with no stated interest payable in the interim, Entity A, with a good credit standing, might receive about $630 (a 6% interest rate). Entity B, with a poor credit standing, might receive about $533 (a 12% interest rate). Each entity initially records its respective liability at fair value, which is the amount of proceeds received—an amount that incorporates that entity's credit standing.

Present value techniques can also be used to value a guarantee of a liability. Assume that Entity B in the above example owes Entity C. If Entity A were to assume the debt, it would want to be compensated $630—the amount that it could get in the marketplace for its promise to pay $750 in three years. The difference between what Entity A would want to take the place of Entity B ($630) and the amount that Entity B receives ($533) is the value of the guarantee ($97).

Interest method of allocation. CON 7 describes the factors that suggest that an interest method of allocation should be used. It states that the interest method of allocation is more relevant than other methods of cost allocation when it is applied to assets and liabilities that exhibit one or more of the following characteristics:

1. The transaction is, in substance, a borrowing and lending transaction.
2. Period-to-period allocation of similar assets or liabilities employs an interest method.
3. A particular set of estimated future cash flows is closely associated with the asset or liability.
4. The measurement at initial recognition was based on present value.

Accounting for changes in expected cash flows. If the timing or amount of estimated cash flows changes and the asset or liability is not remeasured at a fresh-start measure, the interest method of allocation should be altered by a catch-up approach. That approach adjusts the carrying amount to the present value of the revised estimated future cash flows, discounted at the original effective interest rate.

Application of present value tables and formulas. *Present value of a single future amount.* To take the present value of a single amount that will be paid in the future, apply the following formula, in which *PV* is the present value of $1 paid in the future, *r* is the interest rate per period, and *n* is the number of periods between the current date and the future date when the amount will be realized.

$$PV = \frac{1}{(1+r)^n}$$

In many cases the results of this formula are summarized in a present value factor table.

(*n*) Periods	2%	3%	4%	5%	6%	7%	8%	9%	10%
1	0.9804	0.9709	0.9615	0.9524	0.9434	0.9346	0.9259	0.9174	0.9091
2	0.9612	0.9426	0.9246	0.9070	0.8900	0.8734	0.8573	0.8417	0.8265
3	0.9423	0.9151	0.8890	0.8638	0.8396	0.8163	0.7938	0.7722	0.7513
4	0.9239	0.8885	0.8548	0.8227	0.7921	0.7629	0.7350	0.7084	0.6830
5	0.9057	0.8626	0.8219	0.7835	0.7473	0.7130	0.6806	0.6499	0.6209

Example of a present value calculation

Suppose one wishes to determine how much would need to be invested today to have $10,000 in 5 years if the sum invested would earn 8%. Looking across the row with $n = 5$ and finding the present value factor for the $r = 8\%$ column, the factor of 0.6806 would be identified. Multiplying $10,000 by 0.6806 results in $6,806, the amount that would need to be invested today to have $10,000 at the end of 5 years. Alternatively, using a calculator and applying the present value of a single sum formula, one could multiply $10,000 by $1/(1+.08)^5$, which would also give the same answer—$6,806.

Present value of a series of equal payments (an annuity). Many times in business situations a series of equal payments paid at equal time intervals is required. Examples of these include payments of semiannual bond interest and principal or lease payments. The present value of each of these payments could be added up to find the present value of this annuity, or alternatively a much simpler approach is available. The formula for calculating the present value of an annuity of $1 payments over *n* periodic payments, at a periodic interest rate of *r* is

$$\text{PV Annuity} = \frac{\left(1 - \frac{1}{(1+r)^n}\right)}{r}$$

The results of this formula are summarized in an annuity present value factor table.

(*n*) Periods	2%	3%	4%	5%	6%	7%	8%	9%	10%
1	0.9804	0.9709	0.9615	0.9524	0.9434	0.9346	0.9259	0.9174	0.9091
2	1.9416	1.9135	1.8861	1.8594	1.8334	1.8080	1.7833	1.7591	1.7355
3	2.8839	2.8286	2.7751	2.7233	2.6730	2.6243	2.5771	2.5313	2.4869
4	3.8077	3.7171	3.6299	3.5460	3.4651	3.3872	3.3121	3.2397	3.1699
5	4.7135	4.5797	4.4518	4.3295	4.2124	4.1002	3.9927	3.8897	3.7908

Example of an annuity present value calculation

Suppose four annual payments of $1,000 will be needed to satisfy an agreement with a supplier. What would be the amount of the liability today if the interest rate the supplier is charging is 6% per year? Using the table to get the present value factor, the $n = 4$ periods row, and the 6% column, gives you a factor of 3.4651. Multiply this by $1,000 and you get a liability of $3,465.10 that should be recorded. Using the formula would also give you the same answer with $r = 6\%$ and $n = 4$.

Caution must be exercised when payments are not to be made on an annual basis. If payments are on a semiannual basis $n = 8$, but r is now 3%. This is because r is the periodic interest rate, and the semiannual rate would not be 6%, but half of the 6% annual rate. Note that this is somewhat simplified, since due to the effect of compound interest 3% semiannually is slightly more than a 6% annual rate.

Example of the relevance of present values. A measurement based on the present value of estimated future cash flows provides more relevant information than a measurement based on the undiscounted sum of those cash flows. For example, consider the following four future cash flows, all of which have an undiscounted value of $100,000:

1. Asset A has a fixed contractual cash flow of $100,000 due tomorrow. The cash flow is certain of receipt.
2. Asset B has a fixed contractual cash flow of $100,000 due in twenty years. The cash flow is certain of receipt.
3. Asset C has a fixed contractual cash flow of $100,000 due in twenty years. The amount that ultimately will be received is uncertain. There is an 80% probability that the entire $100,000 will be received. There is a 20% probability that $80,000 will be received.
4. Asset D has an *expected* cash flow of $100,000 due in twenty years. The amount that ultimately will be received is uncertain. There is a 25% probability that $120,000 will be received. There is a 50% probability that $100,000 will be received. There is a 25% probability that $80,000 will be received.

Assuming a 5% risk-free rate of return, the present values of the assets are

1. Asset A has a present value of $99,986. The time value of money assigned to the one-day period is $14 [$100,000 × .05/365 days]
2. Asset B has a present value of $37,689 [$100,000/$(1 + .05)^{20}$]
3. Asset C has a present value of $36,181 [(100,000 × .8 + 80,000 × .2)/$(1 + .05)^{20}$]
4. Asset D has a present value of $37,689 [($120,000 × .25 + 100,000 × .5 + 80,000 × .25)/$(1 + .05)^{20}$]

Although each of these assets has the same undiscounted cash flows, few would argue that they are economically the same or that a rational investor would pay the same price for each. Investors require compensation for the time value of money. They also require a risk premium. That is, given a choice between Asset B with expected cash flows that are certain and Asset D with cash flows of the same expected amount that are uncertain, investors will place a higher value on Asset B, even though they have the same expected present value. CON 7 says that the risk premium should be subtracted from the expected cash flows before applying the discount rate. Thus, if the risk premium for Asset D was $500, the risk-adjusted present values would be $37,500 {[($120,000 × .25 + 100,000 × .5 + 80,000 × .25) – 500]/ $(1 + .05)^{20}$}.

Practical matters. Like any accounting measurement, the application of an expected cash flow approach is subject to a cost-benefit constraint. The cost of obtaining additional information must be weighed against the additional reliability that information will bring to the measurement. As a practical matter, an entity that uses present value measurements often has little or no information about some or all of the assumptions that investors would use in assessing the fair value of an asset or a liability. Instead, the entity must use the information that is available to it without undue cost and effort when it develops cash flow estimates. The entity's own assumptions about future cash flows can be used to estimate fair value using present value techniques, as long as there are no contrary data indicating that investors would use different assumptions. However, if contrary data exist, the entity must adjust its assumptions to incorporate that market information.

2 ASC 205 PRESENTATION OF FINANCIAL STATEMENTS

PERSPECTIVE AND ISSUES

Subtopics

ASC 205, *Presentation of Financial Statements*, is divided into two subtopics:

- ASC 205-10, *Overall*, which emphasizes the value of comparative financial statements, and
- ASC 205-20, *Discontinued Operations*, which provides guidance
  - On reporting the results of operations when a component of an entity has been disposed of or is classified as held for sale and
  - On the allocation of interest and overhead of discontinued operations
- ASC 205-30, *Liquidation Basis of Accounting,* which is expanded upon in the technical alert below.

Scope Exceptions

ASC 205-30 does not apply to:

- Companies registered under the Investment Company Act of 1945 because legally they are not permitted to change the way they measure their net assets and
- Limited-life entities that are following liquidation plans established at their inception.

Technical Alert

In April 2014, the FASB issued ASU 2014-08. *Reporting Discontinued Operations and Disclosures of Disposals of Components of an Entity.* The ASU changes the criteria for determining which disposals can be presented as discontinued operations. The ASU also modifies related disclosure requirements.

Scope. Please note that this ASU applies to all entities and will significantly change current practice for assessing discontinued operations. It will also affect an entity's income and EPS from continuing operations.

Guidance. The ASU defines a discontinued operation as a disposal of a component or group of components that is disposed of or classified as held for sale and "represents a strategic shift that has (or will have) a major effect on an entity's operations and financial results." The Update goes on to state that a strategic shift could include:

- A major geographical area of operations,
- A major line of business,
- A major equity method investment, or
- Other major parts of an entity.

The disposal of a component or group of components must be reported in discontinued operations when any of the follow occurs:

1. The component of an entity or group of components of an entity meets all these criteria:
    a. Management commits to a plan to sell the entity.
    b. The entity to be sold is available for immediate sale.
    c. The entity has taken action to complete the plan, including a program to find a buyer or other actions.
    d. The sale or transfer of the entity to be sold is expected to be recognized as a completed sale within one year, unless events beyond the entity's control occur.
    e. The entity to be sold is being actively marketed at a price that is reasonable in relation to its current fair value.
    f. Action required to complete the plan to sell make it unlikely that the plan will be withdrawn or changed in any significant way.
2. The component or group of component is disposed of by sale.
3. The component or group of components is disposed of by other than sale.

Although "major" in major strategic shift is not defined, the Update does state a major strategic shift could have occurred when there has been a disposal of

- A major geographical area,
- A major line of business, or
- Other major parts of an entity.

The Update also provides several detailed examples. However, there will be a degree of judgment involved in making the determination.

The ASU removes the provisions that disallowed presentation as a discontinued operation if

1. There are operations and cash flows of the component that have not been eliminated from the reporting entity's ongoing operations, or
2. There is a significant continuing involvement with a component after its disposal.

Removal of these provisions should reduce complexity.

Disclosures. The Update details several new disclosures including:

- Presenting in the statement of cash flows or in a note:
  - Total operating and investing cash flows or discontinued operations or
  - Depreciation, amortization, capital expenditures, and significant operating and investing noncash items related to discontinued operations.
- Information about any significant continuing involvement after the disposal date. These may involve supply and distribution agreements, guarantees, repurchase option, and an equity method investment. The disclosure should include the nature of the activities that gave rise to the continuing involvement and how long the involvement is expected to continue.
- Cash inflows or outflow after the disposal transaction
- Revenues or expenses after the disposal that before the disposal were eliminated in consolidation
- If an entity retains an equity method investment after the disposal, the entity must present information that enables users to compare the financial performance of the entity from period to period if the entity held the same investment in all periods presented.

Effective Date. For public entities and not-for-profits that have issued, or is a conduit bond obligor for, securities that are traded, listed, or quoted on an exchange or an over-the-counter market, the provisions are prospectively to all disposals that occur within annual periods beginning on or after December 24, 2014 and interim periods within those years and all businesses or nonprofit activities that on acquisition are classified as held for sale.

All other entities should apply the guidance prospectively within annual periods beginning on or after December 12, 2014 and in interim periods beginning on or after December 15, 2015.

Early adoption is permitted for new disposals that have not been reported on financial statements previously issued or available for issuance.

DEFINITIONS OF TERMS

Source: ASC 205-10-20 *Glossary*

Asset Group. An asset group is the unit of accounting for a long-lived asset or assets to be held and used, which represents the lowest level for which identifiable cash flows are largely independent of the cash flows of other groups of assets and liabilities.

Component of an Entity. A component of an entity comprises operations and cash flows that can be clearly distinguished, operationally and for financial reporting purposes, from the rest of the entity. A component of an entity may be a reportable segment or an operating segment, a reporting unit, a subsidiary, or an asset group.

Comprehensive Income. The change in equity (net assets) of a business entity during a period from transactions and other events and circumstances from nonowner sources. It includes all changes in equity during a period except those resulting from investments by owners and distributions to owners. Comprehensive income comprises both of the following:

1. All components of net income
2. All components of other comprehensive income.

Net Income. A measure of financial performance resulting from the aggregation of revenues, expenses, gains, and losses that are not items of other comprehensive income. A variety of other terms such as net earnings or earnings may be used to describe net income.

Operating Segment. A component of a public entity. See Section 280-10-50 for additional guidance on the definition of an operating segment.

Other Comprehensive Income. Revenues, expenses, gains, and losses that under generally accepted accounting principles (GAAP) are included in comprehensive income but excluded from net income.

Reporting Unit. The level of reporting at which goodwill is tested for impairment. A reporting unit is an operating segment or one level below an operating segment (also known as a component).

(Additional terms from Source: ASC 205-20-20 Glossary)

Continuation of Activities. Continuation of activities means the continuation of any revenue-producing or cost-generating activity through active involvement with the disposed component.

Continuing Cash Flows. Continuing cash flows are cash inflows or outflows that are generated by the ongoing entity and are associated with activities involving a disposed component.

Disposal Group. A disposal group for a long-lived asset or assets to be disposed of by sale or otherwise represents assets to be disposed of together as a group in a single transaction and liabilities directly associated with those assets that will be transferred in the transaction.

Migration. Migration means the ongoing entity expects to continue to generate revenues and (or) incur expenses from the sale of similar products or services to specific customers of the disposed component.

Settlement of a Pension or Postretirement Benefit Obligation. A transaction that is an irrevocable action, relieves the employer (or the plan) of primary responsibility for a pension or postretirement benefit obligation, and eliminates significant risks related to the obligation and the assets used to effect the settlement.

(Additional terms from Source: ASC 205-30-20 Glossary)

Fair Value. The price that would be received to sell an asset or paid to transfer a liability in an orderly transaction between market participants at the measurement date.

Liquidation. The process by which an entity converts its assets to cash or other assets and settles its obligations with creditors in anticipation of the entity ceasing all activities. Upon cessation of the entity's activities, any remaining cash or other assets are distributed to the entity's investors or other claimants (albeit sometimes indirectly). Liquidation may be compulsory or voluntary. Dissolution of an entity as a result of that entity being acquired by another entity or merged into another entity in its entirety and with the expectation of continuing its business does not qualify as liquidation.

Statement of Changes in Net Assets in Liquidation. A statement that presents the changes during the period in net assets available for distribution to investors and other claimants during liquidation.

Statement of Net Assets in Liquidation. A statement that presents a liquidating entity's net assets available for distribution to investors and other claimants as of the end of the reporting period.

CONCEPTS, RULES, AND EXAMPLES

ASC 205-10, *Overall*

Comparative Statements. To increase the usefulness of financial statements, many entities include financial statements for one or more prior years in their annual reports. Some also include five- or ten-year summaries of condensed financial information. These comparative financial statements allow investment analysts and other interested readers to perform comparative analysis of pertinent information. ASC 205-10-45-1 states the presentation of comparative financial statements in annual reports enhances the usefulness of such reports and brings out more clearly the nature and trends of current changes affecting the enterprise. That presentation emphasizes the fact that the statements for a series of periods are far more significant than those for a single period and that the accounts for one period are but an installment of what is essentially a continuous history.

A full set of financial statements consists of:

1. Financial position at the end of the period
2. Earnings, which may be shown in a separate statement or within one continuous statement of comprehensive income
3. Comprehensive income for the period in one statement or two consecutive statements
4. Cash flows during the period
5. Investments by and distributions to the owners during the period.

Changes affecting comparability. ASC 205 emphasizes the principle of comparability. Any exceptions to comparability must be disclosed as described in ASC 205. If because of reclassification or other reasons, the manner of or basis of corresponding items have changed, that change must be explained. To the extent they remain significant, notes to financial statements should be repeated in comparative statements or at least referred to.

ASC 205-20, *Discontinued Operations*

(Important: See the Technical Alert section at the beginning of this chapter for information on an ASU that changes practice in this area. During this transitional period, the information below follows extant guidance and does not take into account the new guidance in the ASU.)

Determining when a Component of an Entity should be Classified as a Discontinued Operation. If a component of an entity is either classified as held-for-sale or has been disposed of during the period, the results of its operations are reported in discontinued operations, if *both* of the following conditions are met:

Condition 1. The operations and cash flows of the component have been or will be removed from the ongoing operations of the entity as a result of the disposal transaction, *and*

Condition 2. The entity will have no significant continuing involvement in the operations of the component after the disposal transaction. (ASC 205-20-45-1)

ASC 205-20-55-3 offers a four-step process to assess these two conditions, which is flowcharted in ASC 205-20-55-25 and in Exhibit 2-1:

Condition 1. ASC 205-20-55-4 provides guidance on evaluating whether operations and cash flows of a disposed component are eliminated from ongoing operations. This determination depends on

1. Whether continuing cash flows have been or are expected to be recognized and, if so,
2. Whether those continuing cash flows are direct or indirect.

If continuing cash flows are recognized, the determination as to whether those continuing cash flows are direct or indirect is based on their nature and significance. If any continuing cash flows are determined to be direct, the cash flows have not been eliminated and the operations of the component are not to be presented as a discontinued operation.

Exhibit 2-1

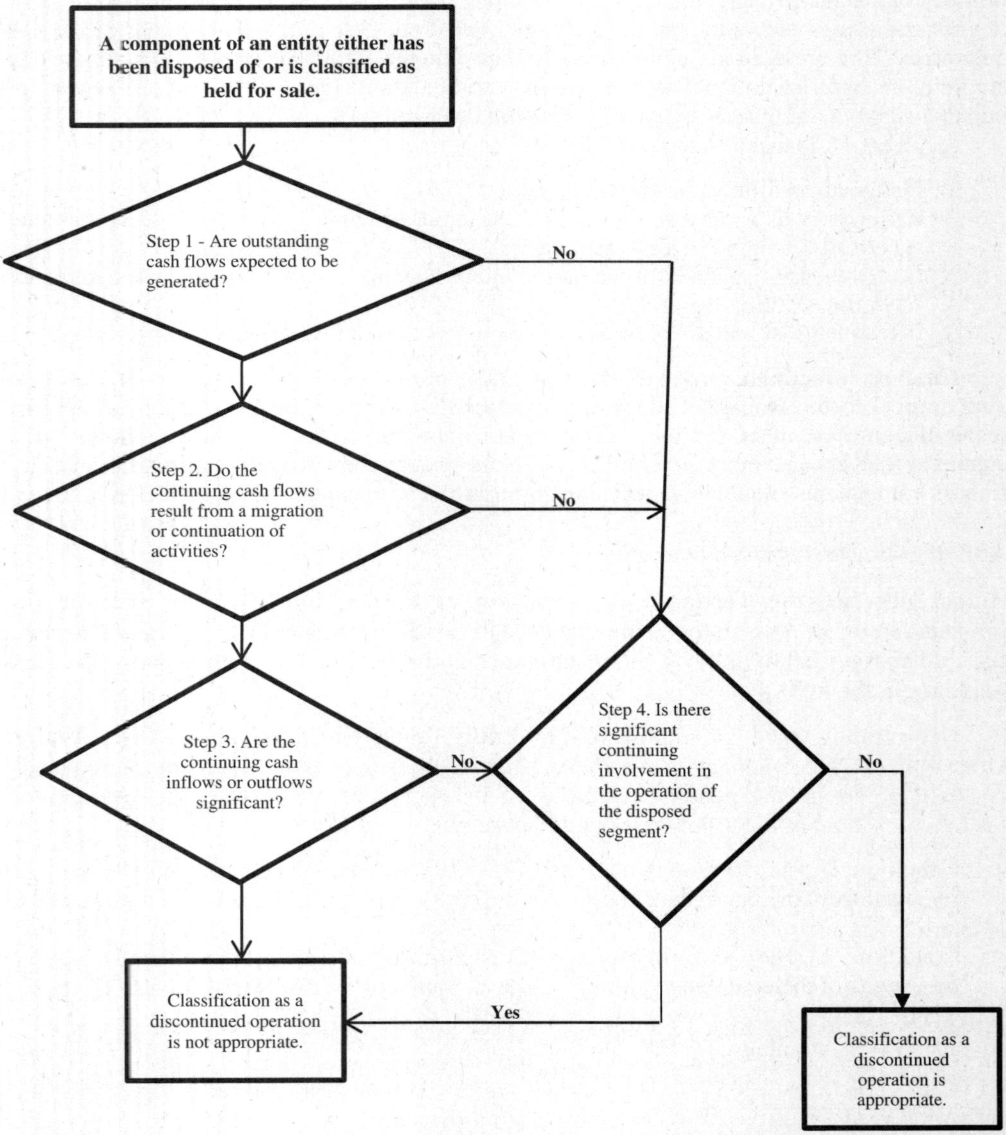

Condition 2. ASC 205-20-55 concluded that continuing involvement in the operations of the disposed component would provide the ongoing entity with the ability to influence the operating and/or financial policies of the disposed component. The retention of risk or the ability to obtain benefits associated with the ongoing operations for the disposed component might indicate that the ongoing entity has the ability to influence the operating and (or) financial policies of the disposed component, resulting in a finding of continuing involvement. The determination as to whether the continuing involvement is significant would be based on quantitative and qualitative assessments from the perspective of the disposed component. The assessment is to consider all types of continuing involvement, individually and in the aggregate.

The assessment period. The assessment of these conditions in light of certain fact situations has been the source of some confusion in practice. ASC 205-20-55 attempts to provide clarification and examples of appropriate application. Management's assessment must be based on all facts and circumstances including management's intent and ability to

1. Eliminate the disposed component's cash flows from its ongoing operations and
2. Not have significant continuing involvement in the operations of the disposed component.

The assessment is to take into consideration significant events or circumstances that occur during the period from the date of the statement of financial position to the date of issuance of the financial statements.

The assessment period commences on the date that the component initially meets the criteria to be classified as held-for-sale[1] or is disposed of. The assessment period ends one year from the date that the component is actually disposed of. During the year between disposal and the end of the assessment period, management must consider whether any significant events or circumstances had occurred that potentially would change its current assessment. If such an event or circumstance occurs, management must perform a reassessment to determine if it still expects to meet the two conditions necessary for discontinued operations reporting.

If the result of the reassessment is that management no longer expects to meet the two conditions by the end of the assessment period, the disposed component's operations are not to be presented as discontinued operations. If the reassessment indicates the opposite, that management expects to meet both conditions by the end of the assessment period, the component's operations are to be presented as discontinued operations. Each change in assessment that occurs during the assessment period will require reclassification of the operations for all periods presented in comparative financial statements.

If events or circumstances occur that are beyond the control of the reporting entity that extend the period required to meet the two conditions, the assessment period may extend beyond one year from the date of disposal provided that management (1) responds to the situation by taking the necessary actions, and (2) expects to successfully meet the two conditions.

The following discussion will analyze each of the conditions separately from the standpoint of management of the "ongoing entity," defined as the remaining operations of a reporting entity after it has disposed of a component or classified a component as held-for-sale.

Elimination of the component's operations and cash flows. Management of the ongoing entity is to assess whether any continuing cash flows have been generated or are expected to be generated. Continuing cash flows are cash inflows and/or outflows generated by the ongoing entity that are associated with activities involving the component that was disposed of

---

[1] ASC 360-10-45-9 has requirements for when a component should be classified as held-for-sale. See chapter on ASC 360.

or classified as held-for-sale. Cash inflows and/or outflows are assessed for this purpose in the same manner as under ASC 360-10-35-29 in assessing the recoverability of assets to be held and used.

Direct vs. indirect cash flows. If continuing cash flows have occurred or are expected to occur, their nature and significance must be evaluated to determine whether they are considered direct or indirect.

Cash flows are direct if they result from the ongoing entity's substantive continuation of the component's revenue-producing and/or cost-generating activities subsequent to the disposal transaction.

Significant cash *inflows* of the ongoing entity are direct if they result from a

1. Migration of revenues from the disposed component after the disposal transaction or
2. Continuation of revenue-producing activities by the ongoing entity through its active involvement with the disposed component after the disposal transaction.

Significant cash *outflows* of the ongoing entity are direct if they result from a

1. Migration of costs from the disposed component after the disposal transaction or
2. Continuation of cost-generating activities by the ongoing entity through its active involvement with the disposed component after the disposal transaction.

Cash flows considered indirect include but are not limited to

1. Interest income earned from seller financing associated with the disposal
2. Contingent consideration associated with a business combination
3. Dividends earned on investments
4. Royalties received based on passive interests in the operations of the disposed component.

The evaluation of whether the cash flows are direct or indirect is to be made by management by considering its expectations based on the best information available. If all of the significant continuing cash flows are direct, the first condition in ASC 360 is not met and the operations of the component are to be presented as part of continuing operations in the financial statements of the ongoing entity. If, however, all of the significant continuing cash flows are indirect, those cash flows are considered to have been eliminated from the ongoing entity and the component will have met the first of the two conditions for classification as a discontinued operation in the income statement of the ongoing entity.

Migration of revenues and costs. Migration in this context refers to the expectation of management that the ongoing entity will continue to sell products or services similar to those of the disposed component to the specific customers of the disposed component and that, in so doing, will continue to generate related revenues and/or incur related expenses. ASC 205-20-55 indicates that there is a rebuttable presumption that revenues and/or costs have migrated to the ongoing entity if, after the disposal transaction, the ongoing entity continues to sell a similar product or service. This presumption can be overcome by an analysis of specific facts and circumstances such as differences between the products or services or the markets in which they are provided.

Continuation of revenue-producing and cost-generating activities. Continuation of activities occurs when the ongoing entity remains actively involved with the disposed component after the disposal occurs. This can be evidenced, for example, by the continuation of predisposal purchases or sales of products or services between the ongoing entity and the disposed component or a related party.

Determining significance of continuing cash flows. ASC 205-20-55 prescribes a with-and-without approach to determining whether continuing cash flows are considered significant.

The determination of significance is to be made separately for gross cash inflows and gross cash outflows. Naturally, if gross cash inflows are determined to be significant, it is not necessary to determine the significance of gross cash outflows since it will already have been determined that the operations of the disposed-of component do not qualify for classification as discontinued operations in the financial statements of the ongoing entity.

Management makes the determination of the significance of cash inflows by comparing its estimate of the ongoing entity's cash inflows expected to result from the migration of the disposed component's sales after the disposal with a hypothetical estimate of what the cash inflows of the disposed component would have been had the disposal transaction not occurred. For the purpose of this estimate, the hypothetical cash inflows of the disposed component are to include cash inflows arising from external, third-party transactions and intercompany transactions as if they had been transactions between unrelated parties.

Significance of continuing involvement. The ASC Master Glossary defines continuing involvement as the ability of the ongoing entity to influence the operating and/or financial policies of the disposed component. This determination is to be based on both quantitative and qualitative assessments made from the standpoint of the disposed component. The ongoing entity's retention of risk or ability to obtain benefits from the ongoing operations associated with the disposed component is not, by itself, conclusive of the ability to influence. Management is to evaluate individually and in the aggregate, ownership interests, contractual arrangements, and other arrangements. Ownership interests include common stock, in-substance common stock as defined in the ASC Master Glossary, or a call option to acquire an interest in the disposed component. Ownership interests consisting of only common stock accounted for under the cost method or only of in-substance common stock do not constitute significant continuing involvement.

In evaluating contractual or other arrangements, the following factors are to be considered:

1. Significance of the contract or arrangement in the context of the disposed component's overall operations.
2. The extent of involvement of the ongoing entity in the disposed component's operations.
3. The rights that the contract or arrangement conveys to each of the parties.
4. The pricing terms included in the contract or arrangement.

The following circumstances are not considered to constitute continuing cash flows or continuing involvement:

1. *Resolution of transaction-related contingencies*—Subsequent resolution of contingencies related to the disposal transaction, such as adjustments to the purchase price and enforcement of any indemnification provisions in the disposal agreement.
2. *Resolution of operating contingencies*—Subsequent resolution of contingencies related to the operations of the disposed component that existed prior to the disposal, such as environmental and product warranty obligations that were retained by the seller (the ongoing entity).
3. *Settlement of employee benefit plan obligations*—Settlement of pension and other postemployment benefit-related obligations that are directly related to the disposal transaction.

In a period in which a component of an entity is either classified on the statement of financial position as held-for-sale or has been disposed of, the entity's income statement *for current and prior periods* is to report the component's results of operations (including gains or losses related to transfer of assets from the held-and-used to the held-for-sale category) as discontinued operations, net of applicable income taxes or benefit. Future losses may not be anticipated and accrued and are not to be recognized until the period in which they are incurred.

The gain or loss on disposal is permitted to be disclosed either on the face of the statement of income or in the notes to the financial statements.

In subsequent periods, certain adjustments may arise that affect amounts previously reported in discontinued operations. Examples of such adjustments include

- Resolution of contingencies associated with the terms of the disposal such as purchase price adjustments and indemnification issues with the purchaser
- Resolution of contingencies associated with the operation of the component prior to its disposal such as environmental or product warranty obligations retained by the seller
- Settlement of employee benefit plan obligations directly associated with the disposal transaction (generally settlements and curtailments of plan liabilities as contemplated by ASC 715).

When adjustments of this nature occur, they are classified separately in discontinued operations of the current period, and the notes to the financial statements are to disclose the nature and amount of these adjustments.

Assets and liabilities of a disposal group classified as held-for-sale are presented separately in their respective sections of the statement of financial position. Offsetting of these amounts is not permitted.

Cases - determination of whether to report discontinued operations

Software Solutions Plus develops and sells software for several markets. It has a children's educational line, a children's game line, a business office line, and a desktop publishing line. The product line is the lowest level at which the operations and cash flows can be clearly distinguished by management. Thus, each product line is an operating segment and a component of the entity.

Case 1 – Cash Flows Eliminated and No Continuing Involvement. Software Solutions Plus decides to exit the game business and commits to a plan to sell the children's game line. The assets and liabilities of the product line are classified as held-for-sale at that date. Software Solutions Plus will have no continuing involvement with the children's game software after the sale is closed. In addition, Software Solutions Plus has decided that it will not develop any new computer games for the children's market. In this case, the conditions are met to report the children's game line as a discontinued operation.

Case 2 – Continuing Direct Cash Flows. Instead of exiting the children's game business entirely as in Case 1, Software Solutions Plus decides to keep its game programmers on its staff and have them develop new children's games. However, instead of selling the games to the home market via distributors as it had been doing, each existing and newly developed game will be marketed and sold to other software game companies. Software Solutions Plus will not provide technical support for any particular game software after it is sold. In this case, although Software Solutions Plus will not have any continuing involvement with the games after they are sold, it will continue to have revenues and expenses related to the children's game product line. Thus, the first of the two conditions required for discontinued operations treatments is not met. The change in the manner of marketing the line cannot be reported in discontinued operations.

Case 3 – Discontinued Product Not a Component of the Entity. Software Solutions Plus decides to discontinue developing and selling its graphics drawing program product, which is part of the desktop publishing product line. In this case, because the graphics drawing program product is not a component of the entity on its own, but instead is part of the component desktop publishing product line, the sale of the graphics drawing program cannot be reported in discontinued operations.

Case 4 – Cash Flows and Significant Involvement Continue. Software Solutions Plus commits to a plan to sell the desktop publishing line to another software company. The assets and liabilities of the product line are classified as held-for-sale at that date. As part of the sales agreement, Software Solutions Plus will receive a sizable royalty for each program sold and will provide technical support to the buyer's programming staff and to customers for the next three years. In this case, because Software Solutions Plus will continue to receive cash flows from the product line and will continue to have significant involvement with the product line after the product line is sold, the sale of the desktop publishing product line cannot be reported in discontinued operations. In the third year after the sale, Software Solutions Plus should reassess whether the conditions necessary to report the activity in discontinued operations have been met.

Presentation. In the period in which a component of an entity is either classified as held-for-sale or has been disposed of, the results of operations of that component and any gain or loss recognized on disposal is reported as a separate component of income, before extraordinary items and the cumulative effect of accounting changes (if any). The income statements of any prior periods being presented should be restated to also reflect the results of operations of the component as discontinued operations. All amounts should be reported less applicable income taxes (benefits), as shown in the example below.

Example of income statement presentation for discontinued operations

	20X2	*20X1*
Income from continuing operations before income taxes	$ 598	$ 583
Income taxes	239	233
Income from continuing operations	359	350
Discontinued operations (Note ___)		
Loss from operations of discontinued component	1,165	1,045
Loss on disposal of discontinued component	167	
Income tax benefit	(532)	(418)
Loss on discontinued operations	800	627
Net income	$ (441)	$ (282)

This example shows the loss on disposal on the face of the income statement. Alternatively, the amount can be shown in the notes to the financial statements, as long as the disclosure identifies the caption in the income statement in which the loss is included.

The assets and liabilities of a disposal group must be presented separately on the face of the balance sheet or by reference in the notes.

Allocation of Overhead and Interest to Discontinued Operation. General corporate overhead may not be allocated to discontinued operations (ASC 205-20-45-9). Interest expense, however, is to be allocated to discontinued operations if, as a result of a disposal transaction, the buyer assumes debt of the seller/reporting entity or, as a result of the disposal transaction, the reporting entity is required to repay debt Allocation to discontinued operations of other consolidated interest is permitted but not required (ASC 205-20-45-6 through 8). If the corporation decides to allocate other consolidated interest, ASC 205-20-55 provides guidance regarding the maximum amount and methods of allocation.

Computing the gain or loss on disposal. To compute the loss (or gain) on disposal, the entity must first compute the fair value of the component; less the cost to sell it. Costs to sell are the incremental direct costs to transact the sale. In other words, costs to sell result directly from the decision to sell the component, are essential to the sales transaction, and would not have been incurred by the entity absent the decision to sell the component. Examples of costs to sell are broker commissions, legal fees, title transfer fees, and closing costs. In the limited situations in which the sale will occur more than one year after the component is classified as held-for-sale, the costs to sell should be discounted to present value.

Next, the entity must compute the carrying value of the component. The carrying amounts of assets (other than long-lived assets) and liabilities are first adjusted in accordance with GAAP, and any adjustments are excluded from the gain or loss from disposal. For example, if trade accounts receivable are being sold as part of a component, the adequacy of the valuation allowance would be assessed as of the date the component is classified as held-for-sale, and any adjustment needed to bring the allowance to the proper balance would be included in bad debt expense. Similarly, if the sale of the component includes assumption of bonds payable, the accumulated amortization of any premium or discount on those bonds would be brought up to date, and this adjustment would be included in interest expense.

The gain or loss on disposal is computed by comparing the total carrying amount to the fair value net of costs to sell. A loss is recognized in the period in which the component is classified as held-for-sale if the total carrying amount exceeds the fair value less costs to sell. On the other hand, if the fair value less costs to sell exceeds the carrying amount (that is, there is a gain on disposal), the gain is not recognized until the actual sale occurs. Fair value, as defined in ASC 820, is essentially the price the seller would receive on the open market for a product.

Under ASC 360, losses from operations of the component subsequent to the date the component is classified as held-for-sale are to be recognized in the period in which they are incurred. That is, expected future losses are not accrued prior to being incurred, since doing so would result in the creation of a liability (reserve) which fails to meet the definition in CON 6.

Example of computing the gain or loss on disposal

Today's Telecommunications has decided to close its pager division, which is a component of the reporting entity. It has committed to a plan to sell the assets and liabilities of the division and has properly reclassified the division as held-for-sale at that date. The following conditions apply:

- The division has incurred $1,750 losses from operations from the beginning of the year to the date it was reclassified as held-for-sale.
- The fair value of the assets and liabilities of the division is $10,775.
- Brokers' commissions and other costs to sell are estimated to be $1,650.
- The carrying value of the assets and liabilities of the division is $12,525 before the GAAP adjustments (depreciation, amortization, adjustment of valuation accounts, and similar periodic adjustments) are made.
- The GAAP adjustments reduce the carrying value of the assets and liabilities by $125.
- Losses from operations of the division from the date it is classified as held-for-sale to the end of the fiscal year are $580. (This loss does not include the GAAP adjustments noted above.)
- Anticipated future losses from operations of the division from the end of this fiscal year to the expected sales date are $1,999.
- The tax rate is 40%.

The income statement presentation of discontinued operations would be

Discontinued operations (Note ___)	
Loss from operations of discontinued division, net of tax of $982	$1,473
Loss on disposal of discontinued division, net of tax of $1,310	1,965
Loss on discontinued operations	$3,438

The loss from operations of the discontinued pager division is the sum of the $1,750 loss incurred prior to the date the assets and liabilities were classified as held-for-sale, plus the $125 GAAP adjustments that were recorded, plus the $580 loss incurred from the date the division was classified as held-for-sale to the end of the fiscal year. The sum ($2,455) less the tax effects of $982 ($2,455 × 40%) is the loss from operations of $1,473.

The loss on disposal is the difference between the carrying value of the division and its fair value less costs to sell. The carrying value of the division is $12,400 ($12,525 less the GAAP adjustments of $125). The fair value of the division less costs to sell is $9,125 ($10,775 fair value less costs to sell of $1,650). The difference of $3,275 less the tax effects of $1,310 ($3,275 × 40%) is the loss on disposal of $1,965. The anticipated future losses from operations of the division will be reported in discontinued operations in the future period in which they occur. They are not included in the loss on disposal in the current fiscal year.

Future periods. Subsequent to the fiscal year in which the assets and liabilities of a component are classified as held-for-sale, the discontinued operations section of an income statement includes:

1. Results of operations of the discontinued component
2. Certain adjustments that are directly related to the disposal of a component of an entity, such as:
   a. Resolution of contingencies associated with the terms of the disposal transaction, such as purchase price adjustments and indemnification issues with the purchaser
   b. Resolution of contingencies associated with the operations of the component prior to its disposal, such as environmental or product warranty obligations retained by the seller
   c. Settlement of employee benefit plan obligations directly associated with the disposal transaction that occur no later than one year after the disposal transaction.

When adjustments of this nature occur, they should be classified separately in discontinued operations of the current period and the notes to the financial statements should disclose the nature and amount of these adjustments (ASC 205-20-50-5).

Example of discontinued operations in a future period

Continuing the previous example, the sale of Today's Telecommunications' pager division, which is a component of the entity, closed in the year subsequent to the fiscal year in which the assets and liabilities were classified as held-for-sale.

- The actual sales price less costs to sell was $9,725.
- The net carrying value of the assets and liabilities on the date of sale was $12,225.
- The loss from operations from the end of the fiscal year to the date of sale was $2,045.
- The tax rate is 40%.

The income statement presentation of discontinued operations would be:

Discontinued operations (Note ___)	
Loss from operations of discontinued division, net of tax of $818	1,227
Gain on disposal of discontinued division, net of tax of $310	465
Loss on discontinued operations	762

The loss from operations of the discontinued pager division is the $2,045 less the tax effects of $818 ($2,045 × 40%).

The loss on disposal is the difference between the carrying value of the division and its sales price less the loss recognized in the prior period. The carrying value of the division was $12,225; the sales price less costs to sell was $9,725, for an actual loss of $2,500. The loss recognized in the prior period was $3,275, so an adjustment of $775 ($2,500 less $3,275) is necessary. The tax effects on the adjustment are $310 ($775 × 40%), so the net adjustment is a gain of $465 ($775 – $310).

Example of discontinued operations reporting

The Hewitt Candy Company sells its entire candy cane production line, recognizing a gain of $155,000 on the transaction prior to applicable taxes of $54,000. During the year in which the sale was completed, Hewitt lost $23,000 on its operation of the candy cane line, while it also lost $72,000 during the preceding year. Applicable tax reductions during these years were $8,000 and $25,000, respectively. It reports these results in the following portion of its income statement:

	20X0	*20X1*
Discontinued operations:		
Loss from operations of discontinued candy cane division (net of applicable taxes of $25,000 and $8,000)	$(47,000)	$(15,000)
Gain on disposal of candy cane division (net of applicable taxes of $54,000)	–	101,000

A clause in the sale agreement stipulates that Hewitt must reimburse the buyer for any maintenance problems found in the equipment. In the following year, the two parties negotiate a payment by Hewitt of $39,000 to address claims made under this clause. The applicable tax reduction associated with this payment is $14,000. It reports these results in the following portion of its income statement:

	20X0	*20X1*	*20X2*
Discontinued operations:			
Loss from operations of discontinued candy cane division (net of applicable taxes of $25,000 and $8,000)	$(47,000)	$(15,000)	–
Gain on disposal of candy cane division (net of applicable taxes of $54,000)	–	101,000	–
Adjustment to gain on disposal of candy cane division (net of applicable taxes of $14,000)	–	–	$(25,000)

ASC 205-30, *Liquidation Basis of Accounting*

In April 2013, the FASB issued ASU 2013-07, *Presentation of Financial Statements (Topic 205: Liquidation Basis of Accounting)*. ASU No. 2013-07 is effective for interim and annual reporting periods beginning after December 15, 2013. Early adoption is permitted. It applies to public, private, and not-for-profit entities. The ASU requires financial statements to be prepared using the liquidation basis of accounting when liquidation is imminent.

Per ASC 205-30-25-2, liquidation is considered imminent when either of the following occurs:

- A plan for liquidation is approved by the person or persons with the authority to make such a plan effective, and the likelihood is remote that any of the following will occur:
  - The execution of the plan will be blocked by other parties
  - The entity will return from liquidation

- A plan for liquidation is being imposed by other forces, such as involuntary bankruptcy, and the likelihood is remote that the entity will return from liquidation.

The guidance also addresses the recognition and measurement of assets and liabilities using the liquidation basis of accounting as well as the financial statement presentation and disclosure requirements.

Measurement. An entity using the liquidation basis of accounting may have items that it now intends to sell or use to settle liabilities, but that were previously recognized, e.g., trademarks. Those items may be recognized in the aggregate and should be recognized for the amount expected to be realized (ASC 205-30-30-1). Liabilities should be recognized in accordance with relevant guidance in other Topics. However, the entity should not anticipate being legally released from its debt (ASC 205-30-30-2). Estimated costs to dispose of assets or other items to be sold in liquidation should be accrued, but discount provisions should not be applied (ASC 205-30-30-3). Those costs should be presented in the aggregate, but separate from the related assets or items. If and when it has a reasonable basis for estimation, the entity should accrue costs and income expected to be incurred or earned through the end of the liquidation. (ASC 205-25-4 through 7)

The entity must remeasure its assets, liabilities, and disposal cost and income accruals at each measurement date.

Financial statements. The entity must at least prepare:

- A statement of net assets in liquidation and
- A statement of changes in net assets in liquidation.

(ASC 205-30-45-1)

The liquidation basis of accounting should be applied prospectively from the day the liquidation becomes imminent. The initial statement of changes in net assets in liquidation should present changes that occurred only during the period since liquidation became imminent. (ASC 205-30-45-2)

Disclosures. The disclosures should include all the disclosures required by other Topics and at a minimum:

- That the financial statements are prepared using the liquidation basis of accounting and the facts and circumstances surrounding the adoption of the liquidation basis of accounting and the entity's determination that liquidation is imminent.
- A description of the entity's plan for liquidation, including a description of: the manner by which it expects to dispose of its assets and other items it expects to sell that it had not previously recognized as assets; how it expects to settle its liabilities; and the date by which the entity expects to complete its liquidation.
- The methods and significant assumptions used to measure assets and liabilities, including any subsequent changes to those methods and assumptions.
- The type and amount of costs and income accrued and the period over which those costs are expected to be paid or income earned.

(ASC 205-30-50-2)

3 ASC 210 BALANCE SHEET

PERSPECTIVE AND ISSUES

Subtopics

ASC 210, Balance Sheets, is divided into two Subtopics:

- ASC 210-10, Overall, which focuses on the presentation of the balance sheet, particularly the operating cycle and current assets and liabilities, and
- ASC 210-20, Offsetting, which offers guidance on offsetting amounts for certain contracts and repurchase agreements accounted for as collateralize borrowings and reverse repurchase agreements accounted for as collateralize borrowings.

Scope and Scope Exceptions

The guidance in ASC 210-20 does not apply to:

> "The derecognition or nonrecognition of assets and liabilities. Derecognition by sale of an asset or extinguishment of a liability results in removal of a recognized asset or liability and generally results in the recognition of gain or loss. Although conceptually different, offsetting that results in a net amount of zero and derecognition with no gain or loss are indistinguishable in their effects on the statement of financial position. Likewise, not recognizing assets and liabilities of the same amount in financial statements achieves similar reported results." ASC 205-10-15-2

Generally, right of setoff involves only two parties. Exceptions are limited to the guidance in these subtopics and paragraphs:

1. ASC 840-30, paragraphs 32 through 52 (leveraged leases)
2. ASC 715-30 (accounting for pension plan assets and liabilities)

3. ASC 715-60 (accounting for plan assets and liabilities)
4. ASC 740-10 (net tax asset or liability amounts reported)
5. ASC 815, paragraphs 815-10-45-1 through 45-7 (derivative instruments with the right to reclaim cash collateral or the obligation to return cash collateral)
6. ASC 940-320 (trade date accounting for trading portfolio positions) and 910-405 (advances received on construction contracts)
7. ASC 942-305, paragraph 45-1 (reciprocal balances with other banks).

Overview

Statements of financial positions (also commonly known as balance sheets, and also referred to as statements of financial condition) present information about assets, liabilities, and owners' equity and their relationships to each other. They reflect an entity's resources (assets) and its financing structure (liabilities and equity) in conformity with generally accepted accounting principles. The statement of financial position reports the aggregate effect of transactions at a point in time, whereas the statements of income, retained earnings, comprehensive income, and cash flows all report the effect of transactions occurring during a specified period of time such as a month, quarter, or year.

It is common for the statement of financial position to be divided into classifications based on the length of the entity's operating cycle. Assets are classified as current if they are reasonably expected to be converted into cash, sold, or consumed either within one year or within one operating cycle, whichever is longer. Liabilities are classified as current if they are expected to be liquidated through the use of current assets or incurring other current liabilities. The excess or deficiency of current assets over or under current liabilities, which is referred to as net working capital, identifies, if positive, the relatively liquid portion of the entity's capital that is potentially available to serve as a buffer for meeting unexpected obligations arising within the ordinary operating cycle of the business.

Practice Alerts

Financial statement classification is a frequent topic of SEC comment letters. While SEC rules only apply to public entities, preparers of financial statements can benefit from the findings of SEC reviewers. The classification of current and noncurrent assets and liabilities, including debt, have been a source of SEC staff comments. Preparers should look to the guidance in ASC 210-10-45 and the discussion in this chapter when preparing classified balance sheets to determine whether an item should be classified as current or noncurrent.

DEFINITIONS OF TERMS

Source: ASC 210-10-20

Cash Equivalents. Cash equivalents are short-term, highly liquid investments that have both of the following characteristics:

a. Readily convertible to known amounts of cash.
b. So near their maturity that they present insignificant risk of changes in value because of changes in interest rates.

Generally, only investments with original maturities of three months or less qualify under that definition. Original maturity means original maturity to the entity holding the investment. For example, both a three-month U.S. Treasury bill and a three-year U.S. Treasury note purchased three months from maturity qualify as cash equivalents. However, a Treasury note purchased three years ago does not become a cash equivalent when its remaining maturity is three months. Examples of items commonly considered to be cash equivalents are Treasury bills, commercial paper, money market funds, and federal funds sold (for an entity with banking operations).

Current Assets. Current assets is used to designate cash and other assets or resources commonly identified as those that are reasonably expected to be realized in cash or sold or consumed during the normal operating cycle of the business.

Current Liabilities. Current liabilities is used principally to designate obligations whose liquidation is reasonably expected to require the use of existing resources properly classifiable as current assets, or the creation of other current liabilities.

Operating Cycle. The average time intervening between the acquisition of materials or services and the final cash realization constitutes an operating cycle.

Short-Term Obligations. Short-term obligations are those that are scheduled to mature within one year after the date of an entity's balance sheet or, for those entities that use the operating cycle concept of working capital, within an entity's operating cycle that is longer than one year.

Working Capital. Working capital (also called net working capital) is represented by the excess of current assets over current liabilities and identifies the relatively liquid portion of total entity capital that constitutes a margin or buffer for meeting obligations within the ordinary operating cycle of the entity.

Source: ASC 210-20

Cash. Consistent with common usage, cash includes not only currency on hand but demand deposits with banks or other financial institutions. Cash also includes other kinds of accounts that have the general characteristics of demand deposits in that the customer may deposit additional funds at any time and also effectively may withdraw funds at any time without prior notice or penalty. All charges and credits to those accounts are cash receipts or payments to both the entity owning the account and the bank holding it. For example, a bank's granting of a loan by crediting the proceeds to a customer's demand deposit account is a cash payment by the bank and a cash receipt of the customer when the entry is made.

Daylight Overdraft. Daylight overdraft or other intraday credit refers to the accommodation in the banking arrangements that allows transactions to be completed even if there is insufficient cash on deposit during the day provided there is sufficient cash to cover the net cash requirement at the end of the day. That accommodation may be through a credit facility, including a credit facility for which a fee is charged, or from a deposit of collateral.

Repurchase Agreement Accounted for as a Collateralized Borrowing. A repurchase agreement (repo) refers to a transaction in which a seller-borrower of securities sells those securities to a buyer-lender with an agreement to repurchase them at a stated price plus interest at a specified date or in specified circumstances. A repurchase agreement accounted for as a collateralized borrowing is a repo that does not qualify for sale accounting under Topic 860. The payable under a repurchase agreement accounted for as a collateralized borrowing refers to the amount of the seller-borrower's obligation recognized for the future repurchase of the securities from the buyer-lender. In certain industries, the terminology is reversed; that is, entities in those industries refer to this type of agreement as a reverse repo.

Reverse Repurchase Agreement Accounted for as a Collateralized Borrowing. A reverse repurchase agreement accounted for as a collateralized borrowing (also known as a reverse repo) refers to a transaction that is accounted for as a collateralized lending in which a buyer-lender buys securities with an agreement to resell them to the seller-borrower at a stated price plus interest at a specified date or in specified circumstances. The receivable under a reverse repurchase agreement accounted for as a collateralized borrowing refers to the amount due from the seller-borrower for the repurchase of the securities from the buyer-lender. In certain industries, the terminology is reversed; that is, entities in those industries refer to this type of agreement as a repo.

Right of Setoff. A right of setoff is a debtor's legal right, by contract or otherwise, to discharge all or a portion of the debt owed to another party by applying against the debt an amount that the other party owes to the debtor.

Securities Custodian. The securities custodian for a securities transfer system may be the bank or financial institution that executes securities transfers over the securities transfer system, and book entry securities exist only in electronic form on the records of the transfer system operator for each entity that has a security account with the transfer system operator.

CONCEPTS, RULES, AND EXAMPLES

Form of the Statement of Financial Position

The format of a statement of financial position is not specified by any authoritative pronouncement. Instead, formats and titles have developed as a matter of tradition and, in some cases, through industry practice.

Two basic formats are used.

1. The balanced format, in which the sum of the amounts for liabilities and equity are added together on the face of the statement to illustrate that assets equal liabilities plus equity
2. The less frequently presented equity format, which shows totals for assets, liabilities, and equity, but no sums illustrating that assets less liabilities equal equity.

Those two formats can take one of two forms.

1. The account form, presenting assets on the left-hand side of the page and liabilities and equity on the right-hand side
2. The report form, which is a top-to-bottom or running presentation.

The three elements customarily displayed in the heading of a statement of financial position are:

1. The legal name of the entity whose financial position is being presented
2. The title of the statement (e.g., statement of financial position or balance sheet)
3. The date of the statement (or statements, if multiple dates are presented for comparative purposes).

Entity's name. The entity's legal name appears in the heading exactly as specified in the document that created it (e.g., the certificate of incorporation, partnership agreement, LLC operating agreement, etc.). The legal form of the entity is often evident from its name when the name includes such designations as "incorporated," "LLP," or "LLC." Otherwise, the legal form is either captioned as part of the heading or disclosed in the notes to the financial statements. A few examples are as follows:

ABC Company
(a general partnership)
ABC Company
(a sole proprietorship)
ABC Company
(a division of DEF, Inc.)

The use of the titles "statement of financial position," "balance sheet," or "statement of financial condition" infers that the statement is presented using generally accepted accounting principles. If, instead, some financial reporting framework, such as income tax basis or cash basis is used, the financial statement title must be revised to reflect this variation. The use of a title such as "Statements of Assets and Liabilities—Income Tax Basis" is necessary to differentiate the financial statement being presented from a GAAP statement of financial position.

Date. The last day of the fiscal period is used as the statement date. Usually, this is a month-end date unless the entity uses a fiscal reporting period always ending on a particular day of the week such as Friday or Sunday. In these cases, the statement of financial position would be dated accordingly (i.e., December 26, October 1, etc.).

Consistency of Format. Statements of financial position generally are uniform in appearance from one period to the next with consistently followed form, terminology, captions, and patterns of combining insignificant items. If changes in the manner of presentation are made when comparative statements are presented, the prior year's information must be restated to conform to the current year's presentation.

ASC 205-10, *Overall*

Assets, liabilities, and shareholders' equity are separated in the statement of financial position so that important relationships can be shown and attention can be focused on significant subtotals.

Current Assets. Current assets are cash and other assets that are reasonably expected to be realized in cash or sold or consumed during the normal operating cycle of the business (ASC 210-10-05-4). When the normal operating cycle is less than one year, a one-year period is used to distinguish current assets from noncurrent assets. When the operating cycle exceeds one year, the operating cycle will serve as the proper period for purposes of current asset classification. When the operating cycle is very long, the usefulness of the concept of current assets diminishes. The following items are classified as current assets:

1. *Cash and cash equivalents* include cash on hand consisting of coins, currency, undeposited checks; money orders and drafts; demand deposits in banks; and certain short-term, highly liquid investments. Any type of instrument accepted by a bank for deposit would be considered to be cash. Cash must be available for withdrawal on demand. Cash that is restricted as to withdrawal, such as certificates of deposit, would not be included with cash because of the time restrictions. Cash must be available for current use in order to be classified as a current asset. Cash that is restricted in use would not be included in cash unless its restrictions will expire within the operating cycle. Cash restricted for a noncurrent use, such as cash designated for the purchase of property or equipment, would not be included in current assets. Cash equivalents include short-term, highly liquid investments that

    a. are readily convertible to known amounts of cash and
    b. are so near their maturity (maturities of three months or less from the date of purchase by the entity) that they present negligible risk of changes in value because of changes in interest rates.

    US Treasury bills, commercial paper, and money market funds are all examples of cash equivalents. Only instruments with original maturity dates of three months or less qualify as cash equivalents (ASC 205-10-45-1).

2. *Short-term investments* are readily marketable debt and equity securities. To be classified as current assets, management must be willing and able to sell the security to meet current cash needs, or the investment must mature within one year (or the operating cycle, if longer). These securities are accounted for under ASC 320. Securities classified as trading securities must be reported as current assets. Securities classified as held-to-maturity or available-for-sale are reported as either current or noncurrent depending upon management's intended holding period, the security's maturity date (if any), or both. It is not necessary to show the ASC 320 classification on the face of the statement of financial position. Short-term investments can be combined into a single line if the classification details appear in the notes to the financial statements. The statement of financial position presentation might be as follows:

Marketable securities	$xxx

3. *Receivables* include accounts and notes receivable, receivables from affiliated entities, and officer and employee receivables. The term "accounts receivable" is generally understood to represent amounts due from customers arising from transactions in the ordinary course of business (sometimes referred to as "trade receivables"). Valuation allowances, if any, are to be clearly stated. Estimates of needed allowances for uncollectibility may be based on historical correlations of bad debt experience as a percentage of sales or based on a direct credit quality analysis of the receivables. Valuation allowances to reflect the time value of money (discounts) are reported with the related receivable. If material, the different components that comprise receivables are to be separately stated. Receivables pledged as collateral are to be disclosed in the notes to the financial statements. The receivables section of a statement of financial position might be presented as follows:

Receivables:	
Accounts	$xxx
Notes	xxx
	xxx
Less allowance for uncollectible accounts	(xxx)
	xxx
Affiliated companies	xxx
Officers and employees	xxx
	$xxx

4. *Inventories* are goods on hand and available-for-sale. The basis of valuation and the method of pricing are to be disclosed. One form of presentation is as follows:

Inventories—at the lower of cost or market (specific identification)	$xxx

In the case of a manufacturing concern, raw materials, work in process, and finished goods must be stated separately on the statement of financial position or disclosed in the notes to the financial statements. Customarily, the components of manufacturing inventories are stated in order of their readiness for sale and ultimate conversion to cash—that is, finished goods are ready for sale, work in process is closer to being finished than raw materials and, of course, raw materials have not yet been placed into production. The disclosures must also include the basis upon which the amounts are stated and where practical the method of determining cost. A sample form of presentation is as follows:

Inventories:	
Finished goods	$xxx
Work in process	xxx
Raw materials	xxx
	$xxx

5. *Prepaid expenses* are amounts paid in advance to secure the use of assets or the receipt of services at a future date. Prepaid expenses will not be converted to cash, but they are classified as current assets because, if not prepaid, they would have required the use of current assets during the coming year or operating cycle, if longer (ASC 205-10-45-2). Prepaid rent and prepaid insurance are the most common examples of prepaid expenses.

Noncurrent Assets. ASC 205-10-45-4 excludes the following from current assets:

a. Cash and claims to cash that are

- restricted as to withdrawal or use for other than current operations,
- designated for expenditure in the acquisition or construction of noncurrent assets, or
- segregated for the liquidation of long-term debts.

Even though not actually set aside in special accounts, funds that are clearly to be used in the near future for the liquidation of long-term debts, payments to sinking funds, or for similar purposes shall also, under this concept, be excluded from current assets. However, if such funds are considered to offset maturing debt that has properly been set up as a current liability, they may be included within the current asset classification.

b. Receivables arising from unusual transactions (such as the sale of capital assets, or loans or advances to affiliates, officers, or employees) that are not expected to be collected within 12 months.
c. Investments that are intended to be held for an extended period of time (longer than one operating cycle). The following are the three major types of long-term investments:

1. *Debt and equity securities* - stocks, bonds, and long-term notes receivable. Securities that are classified as available-for-sale or held-to-maturity investments under ASC 320 would be classified as long-term if management intended to hold them for more than one year. Under ASC 320, the categories of these securities (held-to-maturity versus available-for-sale) need not be reported on the face of the statement of financial position if they are reported in the notes to the financial statements. The securities section of the statement of financial position could be presented as follows:

Long-term investments:		
Investments in A company common stock		$xxx
Notes receivable	$ xxx	
Less discount on notes receivable	(xxx)	xxx
Investment in B company bonds		xxx
		$xxx

2. *Tangible assets* not currently used in operations (e.g., land purchased as an investment and held for sale).

3. *Investments held in special funds* (e.g., sinking funds, pension funds, amounts held for plant expansion, and cash surrender values of life insurance policies).

d. Property, plant, and equipment. These are disclosed with related accumulated depreciation/depletion as follows:

Property, plant, and equipment	$xxx
Less accumulated depreciation	(xxx)
Or	$xxx
Property, plant, and equipment (net of $xxx accumulated depreciation)	$xxx

Accumulated depreciation may be shown in total or by major classes of depreciable assets. In addition to showing this amount on the statement of financial position, the notes to the financial statements must disclose the amounts of major classes of depreciable assets, by nature or function, at the date of the statement of financial position. Assets under capital leases are separately disclosed. A general description of the method or methods used in computing depreciation with respect to major classes of depreciable assets (ASC 360-10-50) must be included in the notes to financial statements.

e. Intangible assets include legal and/or contractual rights that are expected to provide future economic benefits and purchased goodwill. Patents, copyrights, logos, and trademarks are examples of rights that are recognized as intangible assets. Intangible assets with finite useful lives are amortized to expense over those lives. Generally, the amortization of an intangible asset is credited directly to the recorded amount of the asset although it is acceptable to use an accumulated amortization valuation allowance. Intangible assets with indefinite economic useful lives are tested for impairment at least annually.

f. Other assets. An all-inclusive heading that incorporates assets that do not fit neatly into any of the other asset categories (e.g., long-term prepaid expenses, deposits made to purchase equipment, deferred income tax assets (net of any required valuation allowance), bond issue costs, noncurrent receivables, and restricted cash).

Liabilities

Liabilities are displayed on the statement of financial position in the order of expected payment.

Current liabilities. Obligations are classified as current if their liquidation is reasonably expected to require the use of existing resources properly classifiable as current assets or to create other current obligations (ASC 210-45-5). Current liabilities also includes obligations that are due on demand or that are callable at any time by the lender are classified as current regardless of the intent of the entity or lender. ASC 470-10-45 includes more guidance on those and on short-term debt expected to be refinanced (ASC 205-10-45-7). The following items are classified as current liabilities:

1. *Accounts payable.* Accounts payable is normally comprised of amounts due to suppliers (vendors) for the purchase of goods and services used in the ordinary course of running a business.
2. *Trade notes payable* are also obligations that arise from the purchase of goods and services. They differ from accounts payable because the supplier or vendor finances the purchase on terms longer than the customary period for trade payables. The

supplier or vendor generally charges interest for this privilege. If interest is not charged, it is imputed in accordance with ASC 835.

A valuation allowance is used to reduce the carrying amount of the note for the resulting discount as follows:

Notes payable, net of imputed interest of $xx		$ xxx
Or		
Notes payable	$ xxx	
Less discounts	(xxx)	$ xxx

3. *Accrued expenses* represent estimates of expenses incurred on or before the date of the statement of financial position that have not yet been paid and that are not payable until a succeeding period within the next year. Examples of accrued expenses include salaries, vacation pay, interest, and retirement plan contributions.
4. *Dividends payable* are obligations to distribute cash or other assets to shareholders that arise from the declaration of dividends by the entity's board of directors.
5. *Advances and deposits* are collections of cash or other assets received in advance to ensure the future delivery of goods or services. Advances and deposits are classified as current liabilities if the goods and services are to be delivered within the next year (or the operating cycle, if longer). Advances and deposits include such items as advance rentals and customer deposits. Certain advances and deposits are sometimes captioned as deferred or unearned revenues.
6. *Agency collections and withholdings* are liabilities that arise because the entity acts as an agent for another party. Employee tax withholdings, sales taxes, and wage garnishments are examples of agency collections.
7. *Current portion of long-term debt* is the portion of a long-term obligation that will be settled during the next year (or operating cycle, if longer) by using current assets. Generally, this amount includes only the payments due within the next year under the terms of the underlying agreement. However, if the entity has violated a covenant in a long-term debt agreement and, as a result, the investor is legally entitled to demand payment, the entire debt amount is classified as current unless the lender formally (in writing) waives the right to demand repayment of the debt for a period in excess of one year (or one operating cycle, if longer). In two cases, obligations to be paid in the next year are not classified as current liabilities. Debt expected to be refinanced through another long-term issue and debt that will be retired through the use of noncurrent assets, such as a bond sinking fund, are treated as noncurrent liabilities because the liquidation does not require the use of current assets or the creation of other current liabilities.

Noncurrent liabilities. Obligations that are not expected to be liquidated within one year (or the current operating cycle, if longer) are classified as noncurrent. The following items would be classified as noncurrent:

1. *Notes and bonds payable* are obligations that will be paid in more than one year (or one operating cycle, if longer).
2. *Capital lease obligations* are contractual obligations that arise from obtaining the use of property or equipment via a capital lease contract.
3. *Written put options on the option writer's (issuer's) equity shares and forward contracts to purchase an issuer's equity shares that require physical or net cash settlement* are classified as liabilities on the issuer's statement of financial position. The obligation is classified as noncurrent unless the date at which the contract will be settled is within the next year (or operating cycle, if longer).

4. *Certain financial instruments that embody an unconditional obligation to issue a variable number of equity shares and financial instruments other than outstanding shares that embody a conditional obligation to issue a variable number of equity shares* are classified as a liability in the issuer's statement of financial position. The obligation is classified as noncurrent unless the date at which the financial instrument will be settled is within the next year (or operating cycle, if longer).
5. *Contingent obligations* are recorded when it is probable that an obligation will occur as the result of a past event. In most cases, a future event will eventually confirm the amount payable, the payee, or the date payable. The classification of a contingent liability as current or noncurrent depends on when the confirming event will occur and how soon afterwards payment must be made.
6. *Mandatorily redeemable shares* are recorded as liabilities per ASC 480. A mandatory redemption clause requires common or preferred stock to be redeemed (retired) at a specific date(s) or upon occurrence of an event which is uncertain as to timing although ultimately certain to occur. The obligation is classified as noncurrent unless the date at which the shares must be redeemed is within the next year (or operating cycle, if longer).
7. *Other noncurrent liabilities* include defined benefit pension obligations, postemployment obligations, and postretirement obligations. Deferred income taxes are liabilities to pay income taxes in the future that result from differences between the carrying amounts of assets and liabilities for income tax and financial reporting purposes.

Presentation

The classification and presentation of information in a statement of financial position may be highly aggregated, highly detailed, or anywhere in between. In general, highly aggregated statements of financial position are used in annual reports and other presentations provided to the public. Highly detailed statements of financial position are used internally by management. The following highly aggregated statement of financial position includes only a few line items. The additional details required by GAAP are found in the notes to the financial statements.

Example: Statement of financial position – highly aggregated

ABC Corporation
Statement of Financial Position
December 31, 20X1

Assets	
Current assets	xxx
Long-term investments	xxx
Property, plant, and equipment, net	xxx
Deferred income tax assets	xxx
Goodwill	xxx
Intangible and other assets	xxx
Total assets	xxx
Liabilities and Shareholders' Equity	
Current liabilities	xxx
Deferred income tax liabilities	xxx
Long-term debt	xxx
Total liabilities	xxx

Capital stock	xxx
Additional paid-in capital	xxx
Retained earnings	xxx
Accumulated other comprehensive income	xxx
Total shareholders' equity	xxx
Total liabilities and shareholders' equity	xxx

The following more comprehensive statement of financial position includes more line items (for details about specific assets and liabilities) than are found in most statements of financial position.

Example: Statement of financial position – highly detailed

ABC Corporation
Statement of Financial Position
December 31, 20X1

Assets			
Current assets:			
Cash and bank deposits:			
Restricted to current bond maturity	$xxx		
Unrestricted	xxx	$xxx	
Short-term investments:			
Marketable equity securities (trading)		xxx	
Marketable debt securities (available-for-sale)		xxx	
Refundable income taxes		xxx	
Receivables from affiliates		xxx	
Accounts receivable	xxx		
Less allowance for uncollectible accounts	(xxx)	xxx	
Notes receivable due in 20X2	xxx		
Less discounts on notes receivable	(xxx)	xxx	
Installment notes receivable due in 20X2		xxx	
Interest receivable		xxx	
Creditors' accounts with debit balances		xxx	
Advances to employees		xxx	
Inventories (carried at the lower of cost or market using FIFO):			
Finished goods	xxx		
Work in process	xxx		
Raw materials	xxx	xxx	
Deferred income taxes (net of valuation allowance of $xxx)			
Prepaid expenses:			
Prepaid rent	xxx		
Prepaid insurance	xxx	xxx	
Total current assets			$xxx
Long-term investments:			
Investments in equity securities (available-for-sale)		xxx	
Investments in bonds (held-to-maturity)		xxx	
Investments in equity securities (at cost, plus equity in undistributed net earnings since acquisition)		xxx	
Investments in unused land and facilities		xxx	
Cash surrender value of officers' life insurance policies		xxx	
Sinking fund for bond retirement		xxx	
Plant expansion fund		xxx	
Total long-term investments			$xxx

Property, plant, and equipment:			
Land		$xxx	
Buildings (including capitalized interest of $xxx)		xxx	
Machinery and equipment		xxx	
Furniture and fixtures		xxx	
Assets under capital leases		xxx	
Leasehold improvements		xxx	
Less accumulated depreciation and amortization		(xxx)	
Total property, plant, and equipment			xxx
Intangible assets net of amortization:			
Goodwill of acquired businesses		$xxx	
Patents		xxx	
Trademarks		xxx	
Total intangible assets, net			xxx
Other assets:			
Installment notes due after 20X2		$xxx	
Unamortized bond issue costs		xxx	
Deferred income taxes (net of valuation allowance of $xxx)			xxx
Total other noncurrent assets			xxx
Total assets			$xxx
Liabilities and Shareholders' Equity			
Current liabilities:			
Current maturities of long-term debt		$xxx	
Current maturities of capital lease obligations		xxx	
Commercial paper and other short-term notes payable		xxx	
Accounts payable		xxx	
Accrued salaries, wages, and commissions		xxx	
Payroll taxes withheld and accrued		xxx	
Employee 401(k) contributions withheld		xxx	
Accrued rent		xxx	
Income taxes payable		xxx	
Sales taxes payable		xxx	
Dividends payable		xxx	
Rent revenue collected in advance		xxx	
Other advances from customers		xxx	
Deferred income taxes		xxx	
Short-term portion of accrued warranty costs		xxx	
Other accrued liabilities		xxx	
Total current liabilities			$xxx
Noncurrent liabilities:			
Notes payable due after 20X2	$xxx		
Plus unamortized note premium	xxx	$xxx	
Long-term bonds:			
10% debentures due 20Y0	xxx		
9 1/2% collateralized obligations maturing serially to 20X3	xxx		
8% convertible subordinated debentures due 20Y3	xxx		
Less unamortized discounts net of premiums	(xxx)	xxx	
Accrued pension cost		xxx	
Capital lease obligations		xxx	
Asset retirement obligations (net of accumulated accretion of $xxx)		xxx	
Deferred income taxes		xxx	
Long-term portion of accrued warranty costs		xxx	
Total noncurrent liabilities			xxx
Total liabilities			$xxx

Shareholders' equity			
Capital stock:			
$12.50 convertible preferred stock, $100 stated value, 200,000 shares authorized, 175,000 outstanding	$xxx		
12% cumulative preferred stock, $100 stated value, callable at $115, 100,000 shares authorized and outstanding	xxx		
Common stock, $10 stated value, 500,000 shares authorized, 450,000 issued, 15,000 held in treasury	xxx		
Common stock subscribed 10,000 shares	xxx		
Less: Subscriptions receivable	(xxx)	$xxx	
Additional paid-in capital:			
From 12% cumulative preferred	xxx		
From common stock	xxx		
From treasury stock transactions	xxx		
From stock dividends	xxx		
From expiration of share options	xxx		
Warrants outstanding	xxx	xxx	
Retained earnings		xxx	
Accumulated other comprehensive income		(xxx)	
Less: Treasury stock at cost		(xxx)	
Total shareholders' equity			$xxx
Total liabilities and shareholders' equity			$xxx

ASC 210-20, *Offsetting*

In general, assets and liabilities are not permitted to be offset against each other unless certain specified criteria are met. ASC 210-20-45-1 permits offsetting only when *all* of the following conditions are met that constitute a right of setoff:

1. Each of the two parties owes the other determinable amounts (although they may be in different currencies and bear different rates of interest).
2. The reporting party has the right to set off the amount it owes against the amount owed to it by the other party.
3. The reporting party intends to set off the two amounts.
4. The right of setoff is legally enforceable.

Furthermore, when maturities differ, only the party with the nearest maturity can offset, because the party with the later maturity must settle in the manner determined by the party with the earlier maturity (ASC 210-20-45-3).

Bankruptcy. In particular cases, state laws or bankruptcy laws may impose restrictions or prohibitions against the right of setoff (ASC 210-20-45-8).

Taxes Payable. The offsetting of cash or other assets against a tax liability or other amounts due to governmental bodies is acceptable only under the following, limited circumstances:

- When it is clear that a purchase of securities is in substance an advance payment of taxes payable in the near future and
- The securities are acceptable for the payment of taxes.

Primarily this occurs as an accommodation to governmental bodies that issue tax anticipation notes in order to accelerate the receipt of cash from future taxes (ASC 210-20-45-6 and 7).

Repurchase Agreements. ASC 210-20-45-11 permits the offset of amounts recognized as payables in repurchase agreements accounted for as collateralized borrowings against amounts recognized as receivables in reverse repurchase agreements accounted for as collateralized borrowings with the same counterparty. If certain conditions are met, an entity may, but is not required to, offset the amounts recognized. The additional conditions are

1. The repurchase agreements and the reverse repurchase agreements must have the same explicit settlement date.
2. The repurchase agreements and the reverse repurchase agreements must be executed in accordance with a master netting agreement.
3. The securities underlying the repurchase agreements and the reverse repurchase agreements exist in "book entry" form and can be transferred only by means of entries in the records of the transfer system operator or the security custodian.
4. The repurchase agreements and the reverse repurchase agreements will be settled on a securities transfer system that transfers ownership of "book entry" securities, and banking arrangements are in place so that the entity must only keep cash on deposit sufficient to cover the net payable.
5. Cash settlements for securities transferred are made under established bank arrangements that provide that an entity to have case on deposit for net amounts due at close of business. The entity uses the same account for cash inflows and outflow related to the settlement. (Also see ASC 210-20-45-14 through 17 for additional details.)
6. The same account at the clearing bank is used for the cash inflows of the settlement of the reverse repurchase agreements and the cash outflows in the settlement of the repurchase agreements.

Disclosures. For additional information on disclosures, please see the Appendix to this volume.

Scope. The following requirements apply to derivatives accounted for in accordance with Topic 815, *Derivatives and Hedging,* including:

- Bifurcated embedded derivatives,
- Repurchase agreements accounted for as collateralized borrowings and reverse repurchase agreements
- Securities borrowing and securities lending transactions that are either offset in accordance with Section 210-20-45 or Section 815-10-45 or subject to an enforceable master netting arrangement or similar agreement.

(ASC 210-20-50-1)

Derivatives that fall within one of the scope exceptions in ASC 815 are outside the scope of the offsetting disclosure requirements.

Requirements. Entities must disclose offsetting and related arrangements within the scope outlined above. The requirements apply to financial and derivative instruments that are either offset on the statement of financial position or subject to an enforceable netting arrangement or similar agreement. The disclosures must include:

- Both net and gross information for those assets and liabilities.
- Amounts subject to an enforceable netting arrangement not included in the statement of financial position, instruments that management makes an election not to offset, and the amounts related to financial collateral.
  (ASC 210-20-50-3).

Unless another format is more appropriate, the disclosure must be presented in tabular format, separately by assets and liabilities (ASC 210-20-50-4). In addition to the quantitative information, management must present a description of the rights of setoff for recognized assets and liabilities subject to an enforceable master netting or similar arrangement (ASC 210-20-50-5).

Other Sources

See ASC Location – Wiley *GAAP* Chapter…	***For information on…***
ASC 310-10-45-8	The presentation of unearned discounts (other than cash or quantity discounts and the like), finance charges, and interest.
ASC 605-35-45-2	The presentation of provisions for losses on contracts.
ASC 852-10-45-4	The presentation of liabilities subject to compromise and those not subject to compromise during reorganization proceedings.
ASC 926-20-45-1	The presentation of film costs in a classified balance sheet.

4 ASC 215 STATEMENT OF SHAREHOLDER EQUITY

PERSPECTIVE AND ISSUES

ASC 215, *Statement of Shareholder Equity*, contains one subtopic:

ASC 215-10, *Overall*

That subtopic merely provides a referral to ASC 505, *Equity*.

5 ASC 220 COMPREHENSIVE INCOME

PERSPECTIVE AND ISSUES

Subtopic

ASC 220, *Comprehensive Income,* consists of one topic:

- ASC 220-10, *Overall,* which provides guidance on the reporting, presentation, and disclosure of comprehensive income.

Scope Exceptions

Per ASC 220-10-15-4, the ASC 220 does *not* apply to the following entities:

1. Those that do not have any items of comprehensive income
2. Those not-for-profit entities that are required to follow the guidance in ASC 958-205.

Overview

In financial reporting, performance is primarily measured by net income and its components, which are provided in the income statement. A second performance measure—comprehensive income—is a more inclusive notion of performance than net income. It includes all recognized changes in equity that occur during a period except those resulting from investments by owners and distributions to owners.

Because comprehensive income includes the effects on an entity of economic events largely outside of management's control, some have said that net income is a measure of management's performance and comprehensive income is a measure of entity performance.

DEFINITIONS OF TERMS

Source: ASC 220-10-20

Available-for-Sale Securities. Investments not classified as either trading securities or as held-to-maturity securities.

Comprehensive Income. The change in equity (net assets) of a business entity during a period from transactions and other events and circumstances from nonowner sources. It includes all changes in equity during a period except those resulting from investments by owners and distributions to owners. Comprehensive income comprises both of the following:

a. All components of net income
b. All components of other comprehensive income.

Net Income. A measure of financial performance resulting from the aggregation of revenues, expenses, gains, and losses that are not items of other comprehensive income. A variety of other terms such as net earnings or earnings may be used to describe net income.

Noncontrolling Interest. The portion of equity (net assets) in a subsidiary not attributable, directly or indirectly, to a parent. A noncontrolling interest is sometimes called a minority interest.

Nonpublic Entity. Any entity that does not meet any of the following conditions:

a. Its debt or equity securities trade in a public market either on a stock exchange (domestic or foreign) or in an over-the-counter market, including securities quoted only locally or regionally.
b. It is a conduit bond obligor for *conduit debt securities* that are traded in a public market (a domestic or foreign stock exchange or an over-the-counter market, including local or regional markets).
c. It files with a regulatory agency in preparation for the sale of any class of debt or equity securities in a public market.
d. It is required to file or furnish financial statements with the Securities and Exchange Commission.
e. It is controlled by an entity covered by criteria (a) through (d).

Other Comprehensive Income. Revenues, expenses, gains, and losses that under generally accepted accounting principles (GAAP) are included in comprehensive income but excluded from net income.

Parent. An entity that has a controlling financial interest in one or more subsidiaries. (Also, an entity that is the primary beneficiary of a variable interest entity.)

Reclassification Adjustments. Adjustments made to avoid double counting in comprehensive income items that are displayed as part of net income for a period that also had been displayed as part of other comprehensive income in that period or earlier periods.

Subsidiary. An entity, including an unincorporated entity such as a partnership or trust, in which another entity, known as its parent, holds a controlling financial interest. (Also, a variable interest entity that is consolidated by a primary beneficiary.)

CONCEPTS, RULES, AND EXAMPLES

Limitations of the Income Statement

Economists have generally adopted a wealth maintenance concept of income. Under this concept, income is the maximum amount that can be consumed during a period and still leave the enterprise with the same amount of wealth at the end of the period as existed at the beginning. Wealth is determined with reference to the current market values (fair values) of the net productive assets at the beginning and end of the period. Therefore, the economists' definition of income would fully incorporate market value changes (both increases and decreases in wealth) in the determination of periodic income.

Accountants, on the other hand, have generally defined income by reference to specific events that give rise to recognizable elements of revenue and expense during a reporting period. The events that produce reportable items of revenue and expense are a subset of economic events that determine economic income. Many changes in the market values of wealth components are deliberately excluded from the measurement of accounting income, but are included in the measurement of economic income.

Accountants have moved closer to an economic measure of income by introducing the measure comprehensive income into the financial statements. Because of the realization and recognition of accounting principles discussed earlier, comprehensive income remains a subset of economic income.

Other Comprehensive Income

Comprehensive income is the change in equity that results from revenue, expenses, gains, and losses during a period, as well as any other recognized changes in equity that occur for reasons other than investments by owners and distributions to owners.

Items of Comprehensive Income. ASC 220-10-45-10A lists the following as items currently within other comprehensive income:

- Foreign currency translation adjustments (see paragraph 830-30-45-12)
- Gains and losses on foreign currency transactions that are designated as, and are effective as, economic hedges of a net investment in a foreign entity, commencing as of the designation date (see paragraph 830-20-35-3(a))
- Gains and losses on intra-entity foreign currency transactions that are of a long-term-investment nature (that is, settlement is not planned or anticipated in the foreseeable future), when the entities to the transaction are consolidated, combined, or accounted for by the equity method in the reporting entity's financial statements (see paragraph 830-20-35-3(b))
- Gains and losses (effective portion) on derivative instruments that are designated as, and qualify as, cash flow hedges (see paragraph 815-20-35-1(c))
- Unrealized holding gains and losses on available-for-sale securities (see paragraph 320-10-45-1)
- Unrealized holding gains and losses that result from a debt security being transferred into the available-for-sale category from the held-to-maturity category (see paragraph 320-10-35-10(c))
- Amounts recognized in other comprehensive income for debt securities classified as available-for-sale and held-to-maturity related to an other-than-temporary impairment recognized in accordance with Section 320-10-35 if a portion of the impairment was not recognized in earnings

- Subsequent decreases (if not an other-than-temporary impairment) or increases in the fair value of available-for-sale securities previously written down as impaired (see paragraph 320-10-35-18)
- Gains or losses associated with pension or other postretirement benefits (that are not recognized immediately as a component of net periodic benefit cost) (see paragraph 715-20-50-1(j))
- Prior service costs or credits associated with pension or other postretirement benefits (see paragraph 715-20-50-1(j))
- Transition assets or obligations associated with pension or other postretirement benefits (that are not recognized immediately as a component of net periodic benefit cost) (see paragraph 715-20-50-1(j)).

Other comprehensive income is recognized and measured in accordance with the accounting pronouncement that deems it part of other comprehensive income. The Codification notes that additional classifications or additional items within current classifications may result from future accounting standards.

Format of Statement of Income and Comprehensive Income

ASC 220 requires that the components of other comprehensive income along with totals for net income, other comprehensive income, and comprehensive income must appear in a statement of the same prominence as other financial statements. (An entity that has no items of other comprehensive income in any period presented is required to report only net income.) Presenting those required amounts in a combined statement of income and comprehensive income is one of two permissible methods. The other is two separate, but consecutive statements.

Not-for-profit entities and entities with no OCI items are outside the scope of this requirement. For interim reporting, entities must present a total for comprehensive income but are *not* required to present the individual components of other comprehensive income (OCI). Entities that present two statements in their annual financial reports have the option of using a single-statement approach in their condensed interim financial statements. Using one statement avoids the presentation of a separate statement of comprehensive income that contains only one line item for total comprehensive income.

Reclassification adjustments. Some items impact other comprehensive income in one period and then affect net income in the same or a later period. For example, an unrealized holding gain on an available-for-sale security is included in other comprehensive income in the period in which the market fluctuation occurs. Later, perhaps years later, the security is sold, and the realized gains are included in net income. An adjustment to the unrealized holding gain component of other comprehensive income is necessary to avoid double counting the gain—once in net income in the current year and once in other comprehensive income in the earlier period. Adjustments of that type are called reclassification adjustments. The process of including in net income an item previously reported in other comprehensive income is often referred to as "recycling."

Usually, a sale triggers the need for a reclassification adjustment. The sale of an available-for-sale security in the current period triggers the need for an adjustment for the gains (losses) that had been included in other comprehensive income in a prior period. Likewise, the sale of an investment in a foreign entity triggers an adjustment for foreign currency items that had been included in other comprehensive income previously (i.e., accumulated translation gains or losses). Amounts accumulated in other comprehensive income from cash flow hedges are reclassified into earnings in the same period(s) in which the hedged forecasted transactions (such as a forecasted sale) affect earnings. If it becomes probable that the forecasted transaction will not occur, the net gain or loss in accumulated other comprehensive income must be immediately reclassified. An adjustment is also necessary upon the complete (or substantially complete) liquidation of an investment in a foreign entity. Only minimum pension liabilities will not require reclassification adjustments (because they will not be reported in net income in any future period).

Reclassification adjustments can be presented by component of other comprehensive income, either:

- In a single note *or*
- Parenthetically on the face of their annual financial statement.

(ASC 220-10045-11)

Public companies also have to include this information in their interim reports. All required information must be in a single location. New disclosures for items reclassified out of AOCI include:

- The effect of significant amounts reclassified from each component of AOCI based on its source
- The income statement line items affected by the reclassification.

If a component is only partially reclassified to net income, entities must cross reference to the related footnote for additional information.

The tax effects of each component of other comprehensive income must be presented in the statement in which those components are presented or in the notes of the financial statements. The items of other comprehensive income can be reported either:

- Net of related tax effects in the statement or
- Gross with the tax effects related to all components reported on a single, separate line.

If gross reporting is used, the notes to the financial statements must disclose the tax effects related to each component (if there is more than one component). The following examples illustrate the two presentations.

Example of single statement of income and comprehensive income with "net of tax" presentation

Hypothetical Corporation
Statement of Comprehensive Income
For the Year Ended December 31, 20X1
($000 omitted)

Revenues	$395,400
Expenses	(251,220)
Other gains and losses	1,500
Income from operations before tax	145,680
Income tax expense	(62,430)
Net income	83,250
Earnings per share	
Basic and diluted 0.73	

Other comprehensive income		
Foreign currency translation adjustment, net of $5,100 tax		11,900
Unrealized gain on securities:		
Unrealized holding gains arising during period, net of $7,500 tax	17,500	
Less: Reclassification adjustment, net of $1,500 tax, for gain included currently in net income	(3,500)	14,000
Cash flow hedges		
Net derivative losses arising during the period, net of $4,800 tax	(11,200)	
Less: Reclassification adjustment for losses included currently in net income, net of $7,762 tax	18,113	6,913
Defined benefit pension plans:		(4,550)
Prior service cost arising during period	(3,900)	
Net loss arising during period	(2,900)	
Less: Amortization of prior service cost included with net period pension cost	300	
Less: Tax effects	1,950	(4,550)
Other comprehensive income		28,263
Comprehensive income		$111,513

Example of single statement of income and comprehensive income with "gross of tax" presentation

Hypothetical Corporation
Statement of Comprehensive Income
For the Year Ended December 31, 20X1
($000 omitted)

Sales		$395,400
Expenses		(251,220)
Other gains and losses		1,500
Income from operations before tax		145,680
Income tax expense		(62,430)
Net earnings		83,250
Earnings per share		
Basic and diluted 0.73		
Other comprehensive income		
Foreign currency translation adjustment		17,000
Unrealized gains on securities:		
Unrealized holding gains arising during period	25,000	
Less: Reclassification adjustment for gain included currently in net income	(5,000)	20,000
Cash flow hedges		
Net derivative losses arising during the period	(16,000)	
Less: Reclassification adjustment for losses included currently in net income	25,875	9,875
Defined benefit plans adjustment		
Prior service cost arising during period	(3,900)	
Net loss arising during period	(2,900)	
Less: Amortization of prior service cost included with net period pension cost	300	(6,500)
Other comprehensive income, before tax		40,375
Income tax expense related to items of other comprehensive income		(12,112)
Other comprehensive income, net of tax		28,263
Comprehensive income		$111,513

If the "gross" approach illustrated above is utilized, it is also necessary to present in the notes to the financial statements details regarding the allocation of the tax effects to the several items included in other comprehensive income. An example of that note disclosure follows.

Example Note X: Income Taxes

The tax effects of items included in other comprehensive income for the year ended December 31, 20X1, are as follows:

	Before-tax amount	*Tax expense (benefit)*	*Net-of-tax amount*
Foreign currency translation adjustments	$17,000	$ 5,100	$11,900
Unrealized gains on securities:			
Unrealized holding gains arising during period	25,000	7,500	17,500
Less: Reclassification adjustment for gains realized in net income	(5,000)	(1,500)	(3,500)
Net unrealized holding gains	20,000	6,000	14,000
Cash flow hedges:			
Net derivative losses arising during the period	(16,000)	4,800	(11,200)
Plus: Reclassification adjustment for losses realized in net income	25,875	(6,913)	18,113
Net effects of cash flow hedges	9,875	(2,113)	6,913
Defined benefit plans	(6,500)	(1,950)	(4,550)
Other comprehensive income	$40,375	$12,112	$28,263

Reporting Comprehensive Income in Two Separate but Consecutive Statements of Income and Comprehensive Income

Entities are not required to present information about comprehensive income in a continuous statement of income and comprehensive income. Instead, they can present the components of other comprehensive income, the totals of other comprehensive income, and a total for comprehensive income in a statement which must immediately follow a statement of net income.

Example of two separate but consecutive statements of income and comprehensive income—net of tax presentation

Hypothetical Corporation
Statement of Income
For the Year Ended December 31, 20X1
($000 omitted)

Revenues, (includes $12,000 accumulated other comprehensive income reclassifications for net gains in cash flow hedges)	$395,400
Expenses, (includes ($10,000) accumulated other comprehensive income reclassifications for net loss in cash flow hedges)	(251,220)
Other gains and losses	1,500
Income from operations before tax	145,680
Income tax expense	(62,430)
Net income	83,250
Earnings per share	
Basic and diluted 0.73	

Hypothetical Corporation
Statement of Comprehensive Income
For the Year Ended December 31, 20X1
($000 omitted)

Net income		83,250
Other comprehensive income		
Foreign currency translation adjustment, net of $5,100 tax		11,900
Unrealized gain on securities:		
Unrealized holding gains arising during period, net of $7,500 tax	17,500	
Less: Reclassification adjustment, net of $1,500 tax, for gain included currently in net income	(3,500)	14,000
Cash flow hedges		
Net derivative losses arising during the period, net of $4,800 tax	(11,200)	
Less: Reclassification adjustment for losses included currently in net income, net of $7,762 tax	18,113	6,913
Defined benefit pension plans: tax		
Prior service cost arising during period	(3,900)	
Net loss arising during period	(2,900)	
Less: Amortization of prior service cost included with net period pension cost	300	
Less: Tax effects	1,950	(4,550)
Other comprehensive income		28,263
Comprehensive income		$111,513

6 ASC 225 INCOME STATEMENT

PERSPECTIVE AND ISSUES

Subtopics

ASC, *Income Statement,* contains three subtopics:

- ASC 220-10, *Overall,* which provides general income statement guidance and on the structure of the Topic.
- ASC 220-20, *Extraordinary Items,* which addresses the classification, presentation, and disclosure of extraordinary events and transactions and the presentation and disclosure of unusual and infrequently occurring items that do not meet the extraordinary criteria.
- ASC 220-30, *Business Interruption Insurance,* which provides presentation and disclosure requirements for business interruption insurance.

The three subtopics provide discrete information and are not interrelated.

Scope and Scope Exceptions

The guidance in ASC 225 applies to all entities. ASC 225-20-15-2 specifically mandates that "The net effect of discontinuing the application of regulatory operations accounting addressed in Section 980-20-40 shall be recognized as an extraordinary item and thus shall be subject to the scope of this Subtopic regardless of whether the criteria discussed in paragraph 225-20-45-2 are met."

Overview

The primary focus of financial reporting is to provide information about an entity's performance that is useful to present and potential investors, creditors, and others when they are making financial decisions. In financial reporting, performance is primarily measured by net income and its components, which are provided in the income statement.

In contrast to the statement of financial position, which provides information about an entity at a point in time, an income statement provides information about a period of time. It reflects information about the transactions and other events occurring within the period. Most of the weaknesses of an income statement are a result of its periodic nature. Entities are continually creating and selling goods and services, and at any single point in time some of those processes will be incomplete.

DEFINITIONS OF TERMS

Source: ASC 220-20-20

Extraordinary Items. Extraordinary items are events and transactions that are distinguished by their unusual nature and by the infrequency of their occurrence. Thus, both of the following criteria should be met to classify an event or transaction as an extraordinary item:

a. Unusual nature. The underlying event or transaction should possess a high degree of abnormality and be of a type clearly unrelated to, or only incidentally related to, the ordinary and typical activities of the entity, taking into account the environment in which the entity operates (see paragraph 225-20-60-3).
b. Infrequency of occurrence. The underlying event or transaction should be of a type that would not reasonably be expected to recur in the foreseeable future, taking into account the environment in which the entity operates (see paragraph 225-20-60-3).

Infrequency of Occurrence. See Extraordinary Items.
Unusual Nature. See Extraordinary Items

Source ASC 220-30-20

Business Interruption Insurance. Insurance that provides coverage if business operations are suspended due to the loss of use of property and equipment resulting from a covered cause of loss. Business interruption insurance coverage generally provides for reimbursement of certain costs and losses incurred during the reasonable period required to rebuild, repair, or replace the damaged property.

Gross Margin. The excess of sales over cost of goods sold. Gross margin does not consider all operating expenses.

CONCEPTS, RULES, AND EXAMPLES

Recognition and Measurement

Revenues. Revenues represent actual or expected cash inflows that result from an entity's central operations. Revenues are generally recognized at the culmination of the earnings process—when the entity has substantially completed all it must do to be entitled to future cash inflows (or to retain cash already transferred). Most often, an exchange transaction indicates that revenues have been earned. Merchandise is delivered or services are rendered to a customer, resulting in the receipt of cash or the right to receive cash in the future. Revenues are generally measured by the values of the assets exchanged (or liabilities incurred).

Revenues are commonly distinguished from gains for three reasons. See the table below.

Revenues	*Gains*
Result from an entity's central operations	Result from incidental or peripheral activities of the entity
Are usually earned	Result from nonreciprocal transactions (such as winning a lawsuit or receiving a gift) or other economic events for which there is no earnings process
Are reported gross	Are reported net

Exchange transactions. The existence of an exchange transaction generally is critical to the accounting recognition of revenue. However, an exchange transaction is viewed in a broader sense than the legal concept of a sale. Whenever an exchange of rights and privileges takes place, an exchange transaction is deemed to have occurred. For example, interest revenue and interest expense are earned or incurred ratably over a period without a discrete transaction taking place. Accruals are recorded periodically in order to reflect the interest realized by the passage of time. In a like manner, the percentage-of-completion method recognizes revenue based upon the measure of progress on a long-term construction project. The earnings process is considered to occur simultaneously with the measure of progress (e.g., the incurrence of costs).

Timing. The timing of revenue recognition also varies based on the realizability of the future cash flows. For example, the production of certain commodities takes place in an environment in which the ultimate realization of revenue is so assured that revenue can be recognized upon the completion of the production process. At the opposite extreme is the situation in which an exchange transaction has taken place, but significant uncertainty exists as to the ultimate collectibility of the amount. For example, in certain sales of real estate, where the down payment percentage is extremely small and the security for the buyer's notes is minimal, revenue is often not recognized until the time collections are actually received.

Expenses. Expenses represent actual or expected cash outflows that result from an entity's central operations. Expenses are generally recognized when an asset either is consumed in an entity's central operations or is no longer expected to provide the level of future benefits expected when that asset was recognized.

Expenses are commonly distinguished from losses for three reasons:

Expenses	*Losses*
Result from an entity's central operations	Result from incidental or peripheral activities of the entity
Often incurred during the earnings process	Often result from nonreciprocal transactions (such as thefts or fines) or other economic events unrelated to an earnings process
Reported gross	Reported net

Although many cash outflows are recognized directly as expenses, this accounting is often done for expediency since most expenses are first assets, if only for a brief moment. Measuring the consumption of assets is done by one of three pervasive measurement principles:

- Associating cause and effect,
- Systematic and rational allocation, or
- Immediate recognition.

Matching principle. The general approach for recognizing expenses is first to attempt to match costs with the related revenues. Next, a method of systematic and rational allocation should be attempted. If both of those measurement principles are inappropriate, the cost should be immediately expensed.

Some costs, such as materials and direct labor consumed in the manufacturing process, are relatively easy to identify with the related revenue elements. The matching principle requires that all expenses incurred in the generation of revenue should be recognized in the same accounting period as the related revenues are recognized. Thus, those cost elements are included in inventory and expensed as cost of sales when a product is sold and revenue from the sale is recognized. That process is associating cause and effect.

Systematic and rational allocation. Other costs are more closely associated with specific accounting periods. In the absence of a cause and effect relationship, the asset's cost should be allocated to the accounting periods benefited in a systematic and rational manner. This form of expense recognition involves assumptions about the expected length of benefit and the relationship between benefit and cost of each period. Depreciation of plant, property, and equipment, amortization of intangibles, and allocation of rent and insurance are examples of costs that are recognized by the use of a systematic and rational method.

Expense as incurred. All other costs are normally expensed in the period in which they are incurred. This includes costs for which no clear-cut future benefits can be identified, costs that were recorded as assets in prior periods but for which no remaining future benefits can be identified, and costs for which no rational allocation scheme can be devised.

Distributions to owners. Expenses do not include distributions to owners. Expenses of a corporation are easily identified and separated from distributions to stockholders. In both the sole proprietorship and partnership form of entity, the identification process can be more difficult. Items such as interest or salaries paid to partners or owners may be thought of as distributions of profits rather than expenses. However, many entities adopt the philosophy that financial reporting should be the same regardless of legal form (economic substance takes precedence over legal form). Under the corporate form of business, interest on stockholder loans and salaries paid to stockholders are clearly classified as expenses and not as distributions. Accordingly, these items may be treated as expenses for both partnerships and sole proprietorships. However, full disclosure and consistency of financial reporting treatment would be required. Circumstances may involve treating certain payments, such as guaranteed salaries, as expenses while classifying other "salaries" as profit distributions.

Gains and losses. Gains are increases in equity resulting from transactions and economic events other than those that generate revenues or are investments from owners. Losses are decreases in equity resulting from transactions and economic events other than those that generate expenses or are distributions to owners. Gains and losses result from an entity's peripheral transactions (e.g., sale of used equipment), from economic events outside of the control of management (e.g., holding gains on securities), or from nonreciprocal transactions (e.g., lawsuit settlements, fines, and thefts).

Gains and losses are often described in financial statements by their sources, for example, realized gains (losses) on sale of securities or earthquake loss. They are usually measured at net amounts. For example, gains (losses) from sales of assets are measured by subtracting the unexpired cost of the asset from the proceeds, and holding gains (losses) are measured by subtracting the value at the beginning of the period from the value at the end of the period.

Gains often result from transactions and other events that involve no earnings process. In terms of recognition, it is more significant that the gain be realized or realizable than earned. Losses are recognized when it becomes evident that future economic benefits of a previously recognized asset have been reduced or eliminated, or that a liability has been incurred without associated economic benefits.

Format of Statements of Income and Comprehensive Income

The basic order of presentation of information in an income statement (or statement of income and comprehensive income) is defined by accounting standards, as shown by the diagram below. Other than in the section "income from continuing operations," the display of revenues, expenses, gains, losses, and other comprehensive income is predetermined by the Codification guidance. Only within income from continuing operations does tradition and industry practice determine the presentation.

Statement of Income	*Report net of tax?*	*Reference*
Income from continuing operations	No	ASC 225
Sales or service revenues		
Costs of goods sold		
Operating expenses		
Remaining excess of fair value over cost of acquired net assets in a business combination		ASC 805
Gains and losses		
Other revenues and expenses		
Items that are unusual or infrequent, but not both		
Income tax expense related to continuing operations		
Results from discontinued operations	Yes	ASC 360,
Income (loss) from operations of a discontinued component		ASC 250
Gain (loss) from disposal of a discontinued component		
Extraordinary items	Yes	ASC 225,
Items that are both unusual and infrequent		ASC 980-20,
Investor's share of an equity method investee's extraordinary item		ASC 225-20
Net income		
Earnings per share information		ASC 260
Other comprehensive income	Optional	ASC 220, 320, 715, 815, 830
Foreign currency translation adjustments		
Unrealized gains (losses) on securities		
Adjustments related to pension liabilities or assets		
Gains/losses on cash-flow hedging items		
Gains/losses on hedges of forecasted foreign-currency-denominated transactions		
Reclassification adjustment (may be shown gross or net of tax, details may be disclosed in note)		
Income tax related to other comprehensive income (if components are not shown net of tax)		
Comprehensive income		
Earnings per share information		ASC 260

The three items that are shown in the heading of an income statement are

1. The name of the entity whose results of operations is being presented
2. The title of the statement
3. The period of time covered by the statement.

Entity name. The entity's legal name should be used and supplemental information could be added to disclose the entity's legal form as a corporation, partnership, sole proprietorship, or other form if that information is not apparent from the entity's name.

Statement Titles. The use of the titles "Income Statement," "Statement of Income and Comprehensive Income," "Statement of Operations," or "Statement of Earnings" denotes preparation in accordance with GAAP. If another comprehensive basis of accounting were used, such as the cash or income tax basis, the title of the statement would be modified accordingly. "Statement of Revenue and Expenses—Income Tax Basis" or "Statement of Revenue and Expenses—Modified Cash Basis" are examples of such titles.

Statement date. The date of an income statement must clearly identify the time period involved, such as "Year Ending March 31, 2013." That dating informs the reader of the length of the period covered by the statement and both the starting and ending dates. Dating such as "The Period Ending March 31, 2013" or "Through March 31, 2013" is not useful because of the lack of precision in those titles. Income statements are rarely presented for periods in excess of one year but are frequently seen for shorter periods such as a month or a quarter. Entities whose operations form a natural cycle may have a reporting period end on a specific day (e.g., the last Friday of the month). These entities should head the income statement "For the 52 Weeks Ended March 29, 2013" (each week containing seven days, beginning on a Saturday and ending on a Friday). Although that fiscal period includes only 364 days (except for leap years), it is still considered an annual reporting period.

Consistency of form. Income statements generally should be uniform in appearance from one period to the next. The form, terminology, captions, and pattern of combining insignificant items should be consistent. If comparative statements are presented, the prior year's information should be restated to conform to the current year's presentation if changes in presentation are made.

Aggregation. Aggregation of items should not serve to conceal significant information, such as netting revenues against expenses or combining dissimilar types of resources, expenses, gains, or losses. The category "other or miscellaneous expense" should contain, at maximum, an immaterial total amount of aggregated insignificant items. Once this total approaches a material amount of total expenses, some other aggregations with explanatory titles should be selected.

Income from Continuing Operations

The section "income from continuing operations" includes all revenues, expenses, gains, and losses that are not required to be reported in other sections of an income statement.

There are two generally accepted formats for the presentation of income from continuing operations: the single-step and the multiple-step formats.

In the single-step format, items are classified into two groups: revenues and expenses. The operating revenues and other revenues are itemized and summed to determine total revenues. The cost of goods sold, operating expenses, and other expenses are itemized and summed to determine total expenses. The total expenses (including income taxes) are deducted from the total revenues to arrive at income from continuing operations.

Example of a single-step format for income from continuing operations

Revenues:		
Sales (net of discounts and returns and allowances)	$xxx	
Gain on sale of equipment	xxx	
Interest income	xxx	
Dividend income	xxx	$xxx
Expenses:		
Cost of goods sold	$xxx	
Selling expenses	xxx	
General and administrative expenses	xxx	
Interest expense	xxx	xxx
Income from continuing operations		xxx

Multiple-step format. Some believe that a multiple-step format enhances the usefulness of information about an entity's performance by reporting the interrelationships of revenues and expenses, using subtotals to report significant amounts. In a multiple-step format, operating revenues and expenses are separated from nonoperating revenues and expenses to provide more information concerning the firm's primary activities. This format breaks the revenue and expense items into various intermediate income components so that important relationships can be shown and attention can be focused on significant subtotals. Some examples of common intermediate income components are as follows:

1. Gross profit (margin)—The difference between net sales and cost of goods sold.
2. Operating income—Gross profit less operating expenses.
3. Income before income taxes—Operating income plus any other revenue items and less any other expense items.

Example of a multiple-step format for income from continuing operations

Sales:			
Sales			$xxx
Less: Sales discounts		$xxx	
Sales returns and allowances		xxx	(xxx)
Net sales			$xxx
Cost of goods sold			xxx
Gross profit			$xxx
Operating expenses:			
Selling expenses			
Sales salaries	$xxx		
Commissions	xxx		
Advertising expense	xxx		
Delivery expense	xxx		
Selling supplies expense	xxx		
Depreciation of store furniture and equipment	xxx	$xxx	
General and administrative expenses			
Officers' salaries	$xxx		
Office salaries	xxx		
Bad debts expense	xxx		
Office supplies expense	xxx		
Depreciation of office furniture and fixtures	xxx		
Depreciation of building	xxx		
Insurance expense	xxx		
Utilities expense	xxx	xxx	
Total operating expense			(xxx)

Operating income		$xxx
Other revenues:		
Dividend income	$xxx	
Gain on business acquisition ("bargain purchase")	xxx	
Interest income	xxx	xxx
Other expenses:		
Interest expense		(xxx)
Income from continuing operations		$xxx

Income from Continuing Operations. The following items of revenue, expense, gains, and losses are included within income from continuing operations:

1. *Sales or service revenues* are charges to customers for the goods and/or services provided during the period. This section should include information about discounts, allowances, and returns in order to determine net sales or net revenues.
2. *Cost of goods sold* is the cost of the inventory items sold during the period. In the case of a merchandising firm, net purchases (purchases less discounts, returns, and allowances plus freight-in) are added to beginning inventory to obtain the cost of goods available-for-sale. From the cost of goods available-for-sale amount, the ending inventory is deducted to obtain the cost of goods sold.
3. *Operating expenses* are primary recurring costs associated with central operations (other than cost of goods sold) that are incurred in order to generate sales. Operating expenses are normally reported in the following two categories:

   a. Selling expenses
   b. General and administrative expenses.

   Selling expenses are those expenses directly related to the company's efforts to generate sales (e.g., sales salaries, commissions, advertising, delivery expenses, depreciation of store furniture and equipment, and store supplies). General and administrative expenses are expenses related to the general administration of the company's operations (e.g., officers and office salaries, office supplies, depreciation of office furniture and fixtures, telephone, postage, accounting and legal services, and business licenses and fees).
4. *Gains and losses* result from the peripheral transactions of the entity. If immaterial, they are usually combined and shown with the normal, recurring revenues and expenses. If they are individually material, they should be disclosed on a separate line. Examples are write-downs of inventories and receivables, effects of a strike, gains and losses on the disposal of equipment, and gains and losses from exchange or translation of foreign currencies. Holding gains on available-for-sale securities are included in other comprehensive income rather than income from continuing operations.
5. *Other revenues and expenses* are revenues and expenses not related to the central operations of the company (e.g., interest revenues and expenses, and dividend revenues).
6. *Unusual or infrequent* items should be reported as a separate component of income from continuing operations.
7. *Goodwill impairment losses* are presented as a separate line item in the income from continuing operations section of the income statement.
8. *Exit or disposal activity costs* are included in income from continuing operations before income taxes.
9. *Income tax expense* related to continuing operations is that portion of the total income tax expense applicable to continuing operations.

Net income. The section ends in a subtotal that varies depending upon the existence of discontinued operations[1] and extraordinary items. Net income reflects all items of profit and loss recognized during the period, except for error corrections. The effects of changes in accounting principles (under ASC 250) are dealt with by *retrospective application* to all prior periods being presented. For example, the subtotal is usually titled "income from continuing operations" only when there is a section for discontinued operations in one of the years presented. If there is only a section for extraordinary items, the subtotal is usually titled "income before extraordinary items." The titles are adjusted accordingly if more than one of these additional sections are necessary. If there are no discontinued operations or extraordinary items, the subtotal is titled "net income."

The requirement that net income be presented as one amount does not apply to those entities that have statements different in format from commercial enterprises:

- Investment companies
- Insurance entities
- Certain not-for-profit entities (NFPs).
  (ASC 225-10-45-1)

Example of the format for presentation of discontinued operations and an extraordinary item

Discontinued operations and an extraordinary item

Income (loss) from continuing operations		$ xxx
Discontinued operations		
Income (loss) from operations of Division Z, less applicable income taxes of $xxx	$xxx	
Income (loss) on disposal of Division Z, less applicable income taxes of $xxx	xxx	xxx
Income (loss) before extraordinary item		$ xxx
Extraordinary item, less applicable income taxes of $xxx (Note _)		xxx
Net income		$ xxx
Per share of common stock*		
Income (loss) from continuing operations		$x.xx
Net income		$x.xx

Example of format for presentation of discontinued operation only

Discontinued operations only

Income (loss) from continuing operations		$ xxx
Discontinued operations		
Income (loss) from operations of Division Z, less applicable income taxes of $xxx	$xxx	
Income (loss) on disposal of Division Z, less applicable income taxes of $xxx	xxx	xxx
Net income		$ xxx
Per share of common stock*		
Income (loss) from continuing operations		$x.xx
Net income		$x.xx

* *Assume that per share amounts of discontinued operations and extraordinary items are shown in the notes.*

[1] Also see the chapter on ASC 205 for information on ASU 2014-08, an update related to discontinued operations.

ASC 225-20, *Extraordinary and Unusual Items*

Extraordinary items. An event or transaction should be presumed to be an ordinary and usual activity and not to be described as extraordinary unless the event or transaction is both of an unusual nature and infrequent in its occurrence. (ASC 225-20-45-2)

An extraordinary item, if material, should appear separately in the income statement. Generally, extraordinary items should be evaluated individually. However if the effects of related transactions relate to a single event. the effects should be aggregated to determine materiality. (ASC 225-20-45-3)

Unusual nature. To meet this criterion, the underlying event or transaction should

- Possess a high degree of abnormality and
- Be clearly unrelated to, or only incidentally related to, the ordinary and typical activities of the reporting entity, taking into account the environment in which it operates.

In determining whether an event or transaction is of an unusual nature, the following special characteristics of the reporting entity are considered:

1. Type and scope of operations
2. Lines of business
3. Operating policies
4. Industry (or industries) in which the reporting entity operates
5. Geographic locations of its operations
6. Nature and extent of government regulation.

An event that is of an unusual nature for one reporting entity can be an ordinary and usual activity of another because of the above characteristics. Whether an event or transaction is beyond the control of management is irrelevant in the determination of whether it is of an unusual nature.

Infrequency of occurrence. To satisfy this requirement, the underlying event or transaction should be of a type that would not reasonably be expected to recur in the foreseeable future, again taking into account the environment in which the reporting entity operates.

Items specifically included or excluded from extraordinary items. Accounting pronouncements have specifically required the following items to be presented as extraordinary, irrespective of whether they meet the criteria stated above:

1. The investor's share of an investee's extraordinary item when the investor uses the equity method of accounting for the investee (ASC 323-10-45).
2. The net effect of adjustments relating to the discontinuation of the application of ASC 980 by a public utility or other reporting entity with regulated operations. (ASC 225-20-45-8)
3. The remaining excess of the fair value of acquired net assets over their cost pursuant to ASC 805.
4. Estimated losses recognized due to obligations under the Coal Industry Retiree Health Benefit Act of 1992 (ASC 930-715-25).

The following items are, by definition, *not* extraordinary items:

1. Write-down or write-off of receivables, inventories, equipment leased to others, or intangible assets.
2. Foreign currency gains and losses.
3. Gains and losses on the disposal of a segment of a business.

4. Gains and losses from sale or abandonment of property, plant, or equipment used in operations.
5. Effects of a strike.
6. Adjustments of accruals on long-term contracts.
   (ASC 225-20-45-4)

Presentation. Extraordinary items should be segregated from the results of ordinary operations and shown net of taxes in a separate section of the income statement, following "discontinued operations." If more than one extraordinary item occurs during a period, they should be reported separately with details about the nature and amount included in the notes to the financial statements. (ASC 225-20-45-9) EPS should be presented on the face of the income statement or in related notes. (ASC 225-20-45-12)

Example of the format for presentation of extraordinary item

Income (loss) before extraordinary item	$ xxx
Extraordinary item, less applicable income taxes of $xxx (Note _)	xxx
Net income	$ xxx
Per share of common stock*	
Income (loss) before extraordinary item	$x.xx
Net income	$x.xx

* *These examples assume that per share amounts of discontinued operations and extraordinary items are shown in the notes.*

Unusual or Infrequent Items

Items that are unusual or infrequent, but not both, should be reported as a separate component of income from continuing operations. The EPS effect of these items should not be separated on the face of the income statement. (ASC 225-20-45-16)

Pro Forma Earnings

Companies have increasingly made reference in press releases and published materials to an alternative measure of performance, referred to as "pro forma earnings." This practice has generated confusion because there is no standard definition for "pro forma earnings." Different reporting entities can, and have, defined pro forma earnings on a wide range of ad hoc bases, and sometimes a given entity fails even to consistently define this amount from period to period.

Often, even when GAAP-basis earnings are stated in the same announcement as the pro forma measure, it is the latter that receives most of the attention. In a number of instances, pro forma earnings have been based on very aggressive exclusions of operating costs and, sometimes, the inclusion of onetime gains. Such practices ultimately came to be widely recognized as being misleading and inappropriate, and popular sentiment turned against employment of such devices.

For reporting entities, part of the allure of pro forma earnings is that they can be defined to exclude some or all of a range of "unusual" items. Not surprisingly, most of the excluded items have been charges, such as those for worker layoffs, restructurings, assets impairments, and inventory obsolescence. Even if truly not expected to recur annually, many of these charges are quite normal and may be anticipated to recur at irregular intervals in the life of a given business. Furthermore, many such charges can be viewed as "catch-ups" for underrecognition of expenses in earlier periods, and since those charges would have been fully reflected in current earnings, the subsequent period's catch-up should, logically, also be included in the current period measure of operating results.

A further practice, which is improper but has not been uncommon, has been for reporting entities to opportunistically charge off an exaggerated loss in the current period, perhaps in connection with such randomly occurring events as discontinued operations. The loss is then excluded from pro forma earnings. The excess reserves then become available to be drawn down in future periods, as the provided-for expenses fail to materialize in the amounts reserved. The draw-downs of the excess reserves increase net income in future periods, but those draw-downs will not be excluded from pro forma earnings the way the original loss had been. The result will be to boost both GAAP-basis net income and pro forma earnings in future years.

The SEC adopted Regulation G to curtail the use of pro forma earnings statements. Regulation G states that a public company, or a person acting on its behalf, is not to make public a non-GAAP financial measure that, taken together with the information accompanying that measure, either contains an untrue statement of a material fact or omits a material fact that would be necessary to make the presentation of the non-GAAP financial measure not misleading. Further, Regulation G requires a public company that discloses or releases a non-GAAP financial measure to include in that disclosure or release a presentation of the most directly comparable GAAP financial measure and a reconciliation of the disclosed non-GAAP measure to that directly comparable GAAP financial measure.

The regulations also prohibit certain non-GAAP measures from inclusion in SEC filings. Public companies must not:

1. Exclude from non-GAAP liquidity measures charges or liabilities that required, or will require, cash settlement, or would have required cash settlement absent an ability to settle in another manner. However, earnings before interest and taxes (EBIT) and earnings before interest, taxes, depreciation, and amortization (EBITDA) are permissible.
2. Create a non-GAAP performance measure that eliminates items identified as nonrecurring, infrequent, or unusual if the nature of the excluded item is such that it is (a) reasonably likely to recur within two years or (b) similar to a charge or gain that occurred within the prior two years.
3. Present non-GAAP financial measures on the face of the registrant's financial statements prepared in accordance with GAAP or in the accompanying notes.
4. Present non-GAAP financial measures on the face of any pro forma financial information required to be disclosed by Article 11 of Regulation S-X (e.g., business combinations or disposals).
5. Use titles or descriptions of non-GAAP financial measures that are the same as, or confusingly similar to, titles or descriptions used for GAAP measures.

The SEC's action has curbed the abuse of pro forma earnings measures, but it does little to standardize the measures in use.

ASC 225-30, *Business Interruption Insurance*

ASC 225-30 provides guidance on presentation and disclosure of business interruption insurance. This type of insurance may cover gross margin lost because of the suspension of normal operations, fixed charges, expenses related to gross margin, and expenses incurred to reduce the loss from business interruption, etc.

Entities may choose how to record proceeds from business interruption insurance as long as it does not conflict with other standards. Disclosure requirements can be found in the Appendix.

7 ASC 230 STATEMENT OF CASH FLOWS

PERSPECTIVE AND ISSUES

Subtopic

ASC 230, *Statement of Cash Flows,* contains one subtopic:

- ASC 230-10 *Overall*, that establishes standards for cash flow reporting in general purpose financial statements.

Scope and Scope Exceptions

A statement of cash flows is a required part of a complete set of financial statements for business enterprises and not-for-profit organizations. The following are not required to present a statement of cash flows:

- Defined pension plans that present financial information under Topic 960,
- Other employee plans that present information similar to ASC 960,
- Certain investment companies, and
- "A common trust fund, variable annuity account, or similar fund maintained by a bank, insurance entity, or other entity in its capacity as a trustee, administrator, or guardian for the collective investment and reinvestment of moneys."

(ASC 230-10-15-4)

Overview

The primary purpose of the statement of cash flows is to provide information about cash receipts and cash payments of an entity during a period. A secondary purpose is to provide information about the entity's investing and financing activities during the period.

Specifically, the statement of cash flows helps investors and creditors assess

1. Ability to generate future positive cash flows
2. Ability to meet obligations and pay dividends
3. Reasons for differences between net income and net cash receipts and payments
4. The cash and noncash aspects of investing and financing transactions on an entity's financial position.

The ultimate objective of investment and credit decisions is the maximization of net cash inflows, so information for assessing the amounts, timing, and uncertainty of prospective cash flows is needed.

Cash flows involving trading securities must be classified based on the nature of, and purpose for which, the financial assets or liabilities are acquired or incurred.

DEFINITIONS OF TERMS

Definitions are from ASC 230-10-20 Glossary, except for "direct method" and "indirect method."

Cash. Consistent with common usage, cash includes not only currency on hand but demand deposits with banks or other financial institutions. Cash also includes other kinds of accounts that have the general characteristics of demand deposits, in that the customer may deposit additional funds at any time and also effectively may withdraw funds at any time without prior notice or penalty. All charges and credits to those accounts are cash receipts or payments to both the entity owning the account and the bank holding it. For example, a bank's granting of a loan by crediting the proceeds to a customer's demand deposit account is a cash payment by the bank and a cash receipt of the customer when the entry is made.

Cash equivalents. Short-term, highly liquid investments that have both of the following characteristics

a. Readily convertible to known amounts of cash and
b. So near their maturity that they present insignificant risk of changes in value because of changes in interest rates. Generally, only investments with original maturities of three months or less qualify under that definition.

Original maturity means original maturity to the entity holding the investment. For example, both a three-month US Treasury bill and a three-year US Treasury note purchased three months from maturity qualify as cash equivalents. However, a Treasury note purchased three years ago does not become a cash equivalent when its remaining maturity is three months. Examples of items commonly considered to be cash equivalents are Treasury bills, commercial paper, money market funds, and federal funds sold (for an entity with banking operations).

Direct method. A method that derives the net cash provided by operating activities from the components of operating cash receipts and payments as opposed to adjusting net income for items not affecting cash.

Fair Value. The price that would be received to sell an asset or paid to transfer a liability in an orderly transaction between market participants at the measurement date.

Financial Asset. Cash, evidence of an ownership interest in an entity, or a contract that conveys to one entity a right to do either of the following:

a. Receive cash or another financial instrument from a second entity
b. Exchange other financial instruments on potentially favorable terms with the second entity.

Financing activities. Financing activities include obtaining resources from owners and providing them with a return on, and a return of, their investment; receiving restricted resources that by donor stipulation must be used for long-term purposes; borrowing money and repaying amounts borrowed, or otherwise settling the obligation; and obtaining and paying for other resources obtained from creditors on long-term credit.

Indirect (reconciliation) method. A method that derives the net cash provided by operating activities by adjusting net income for revenue and expense items not resulting from cash transactions.

Investing activities. Investing activities include making and collecting loans and acquiring and disposing of debt or equity instruments and property, plant, and equipment and other productive assets, that is, assets held for or used in the production of goods or services by the entity (other than materials that are part of the entity's inventory). Investing activities exclude acquiring and disposing of certain loans or other debt or equity instruments that are acquired specifically for resale, as discussed in paragraphs ASC 230-10-45-12 and 230-10-45-21.

Operating activities. Operating activities include all transactions and other events that are not defined as investing or financing activities (see paragraphs 230-10-45-12 through 45-15). Operating activities generally involve producing and delivering goods and providing services. Cash flows from operating activities are generally the cash effects of transactions and other events that enter into the determination of net income.

CONCEPTS, RULES, AND EXAMPLES

Cash Focus

The statement of cash flows includes only inflows and outflows of cash and cash equivalents. Cash equivalents include any short-term highly liquid investments (see definition for criteria) used as a temporary investment of idle cash. The effects of investing and financing activities that do not result in receipts or payments of cash are to be reported in a separate schedule immediately following the statement or in the notes to the financial statements. The reasoning for not including noncash items in the statement of cash flows and placing them in a separate schedule is that it preserves the statement's primary focus on cash flows from operating, investing, and financing activities. Thus, if a transaction is part cash and part noncash, only the cash portion is reported in the body of the statement of cash flows.

Classification of Cash Receipts and Disbursements

ASC 230-10-45-10 through 17 discusses classification of cash receipts and disbursements. The statement of cash flows requires classification of cash receipts and cash disbursements into three categories:

- Investing activities
- Financing activities
- Operating activities.

See the Definitions of Terms section above for more information on these categories. The following are examples of the classification of cash inflows and outflows within the statement of cash flows:

	Operating	*Investing*	*Financing*
Cash Inflows	• Receipts from sale of goods or services	• Principal collections from loans and sales of other entities' debt instruments held in available-for-sale or held-to-maturity portfolios	• Proceeds from issuing stock (or other ownership interests)
	• Sale of loans, debt, or equity instruments carried in a trading portfolio	• Sale of equity instruments, held in available-for-sale or held-to-maturity portfolios, of other enterprises and from returns of investment in those instruments	• Proceeds from issuing debt (short-term or long-term)
	• Returns on loans (interest) • Returns on equity securities (dividends) • Not-for-profits' cash receipts from nearly immediate sale of donated financial assets unless donor-restricted for long-term purposes • All other cash receipts that are not from investing or financing activities	• Sale of property, plant, and equipment • Not-for-profits cash proceeds from sales of donated financial assets that are not classified as operation or financing activities	• Not-for-profits' donor-restricted cash gifts that are limited to long-term purposes • Not-for-profits' cash receipts from nearly immediate sale of donor-restricted for long-term purposes financial assets[2] • Income tax benefits received due to increases in the fair value of equity instruments issued in share-based payment arrangements • Proceeds received from derivative instruments that include financing elements at inception
Cash Outflows	• Payments for inventory • All other cash payments that are not from investing or financing activities	• Loans made and acquisitions of other entities' debt instruments held in available-for-sale or held-to-maturity portfolios	• Payment of dividends or other distributions to owners, including repurchase of entity's stock • Distributions to counterparties of derivative instruments that include financing elements at inception • Payments for debt issue costs

Operating	*Investing*	*Financing*
• Payments to employees and other suppliers for goods and services	• Purchase of equity instruments, held in available-for-sale or held-to-maturity portfolios, of other enterprises	
• Payments of income taxes including cash that would have been paid for income taxes if the reporting entity had not received an income tax benefit due to increases in the fair value of equity instruments issued in share-based payment arrangements	• Purchase of property, plant, and equipment and other productive assets	• Repayment of debt principal, including capital lease obligations
• Payments of interest		
• Purchase of loans, debt, or equity instruments carried in trading portfolio		
• Payments of asset retirement obligations		
• All other cash payments that are not from investing or financing activities		

Other Classification Items. ASC 230-10-45-18 through 21A provides additional guidance on specific acquisitions and sales of certain securities and loans:

- Topics 255 and 940 offer guidance on securities and other assets held in trading accounts carried by banks, brokers, and dealers in securities.
- Cash receipts and payments from purchases and sales of securities and other assets classified as trading securities (Topic 320) are classified as cash flows based on the nature and purpose for which the securities were acquired.
- When a cash receipt or payment has aspects of more than one cash flow category, it should be in the category that is likely to be the predominant source of cash flows.

Disclosure of the following noncash investing and financing activities may be appended to the statement or reported in the accompanying notes:

- Acquiring an asset through a capital lease or by incurring long-term debt
- Conversion of debt to equity
- Exchange of noncash assets or liabilities for other noncash assets or liabilities
- Issuance of ownership shares to acquire assets
- Obtaining an investment asset or a building by receiving a contribution.

The following example reveals the classification of cash receipts and disbursements into the investing and financing activities of a statement of cash flows (though without detail of the required operating activities section):

Liquid Corporation
Statement of Cash Flows
For the Year Ended December 31, 20X1

Net cash flows from operating activities		$ xxx
Cash flows from investing activities:		
Purchase of property, plant, and equipment	$(xxx)	
Sale of equipment	xx	
Collection of notes receivable	xx	
Net cash used in investing activities		(xx)
Cash flows from financing activities:		
Sale of common stock	xxx	
Repayment of long-term debt	(xx)	
Reduction of notes payable	(xx)	
Net cash provided by financing activities		xx
Effect of exchange rate changes on cash		xx
Net increase (decrease) in cash		$ xxx
Cash and cash equivalents at beginning of year		xxx
Cash and cash equivalents at end of year		$ xxx
Schedule of noncash financing and investing activities:		
Conversion of bonds into common stock		$ xxx
Property acquired under capital leases		xxx
		$ xxx

Operating Activities Presentation

Direct vs. indirect. The operating activities section of the statement of cash flows can be presented under the direct method or the indirect method. However, the FASB has long expressed a preference for the direct method of presenting net cash from operating activities. Conversely, the indirect method has always been vastly preferred by preparers.

The *direct method* shows the items that affected cash flow. Cash received and cash paid are presented, as opposed to converting accrual-basis income to cash flow information. At a minimum, entities using the direct method are required to report the following classes of operating cash receipts and payments:

1. Cash collected from customers
2. Interest and dividends received
3. Other operating cash receipts
4. Cash paid to employees and other suppliers
5. Interest paid
6. Income taxes paid including separate identification of the cash that would have been paid if the reporting entity had not received an income tax benefit resulting from increases in the fair value of its shares associated with share-based compensation arrangements.
7. Other operating cash payments.

The direct method allows the user to clarify the relationship between the company's net income and its cash flows. For example, payments of expenses are shown as cash disbursements and are deducted from cash receipts. In this way, the user is able to recognize the cash receipts and cash payments for the period. The information needed to prepare the operating activities section using the direct method can often be obtained by converting information already appearing in the statement of financial position and income statement. Formulas for conversion of various income statement amounts for the direct method of presentation from the accrual basis to the cash basis are summarized next.

Accrual basis		Additions		Deductions		Cash basis
Net sales	+	Beginning A/R	–	Ending A/R A/R written off	=	Cash received from customers
Cost of goods sold	+	Ending inventory Beginning A/P	–	Manufacturing depreciation and amortization Beginning inventory Ending A/P	=	Cash paid to suppliers
Operating expenses	+	Ending prepaid expenses Beginning accrued expenses	–	Sales and administrative depreciation and amortization Beginning prepaid expenses Ending accrued expenses payable Bad debts expense	=	Cash paid for operating expenses

When the direct method is used, a separate schedule reconciling net income to net cash flows from operating activities must also be provided. That schedule reports the same information as the operating activities section prepared using the indirect method. Therefore, a firm must prepare and present both the direct and indirect methods when using the direct method for reporting cash from operating activities.

The *indirect method* is the most widely used presentation of cash from operating activities, because it is easier to prepare. It focuses on the differences between net income and cash flows. The indirect format begins with net income, which is obtained directly from the income statement. Revenue and expense items not affecting cash are added or deducted to arrive at net cash provided by operating activities. For example, depreciation and amortization would be added back because they reduce net income without affecting cash.

The statement of cash flows prepared using the indirect method emphasizes changes in the components of most current asset and current liability accounts. Changes in inventory, accounts receivable, and other current accounts are used to determine the cash flow from operating activities. Calculate the change in accounts receivable using the balances net of the allowance account in order to ensure that write-offs of uncollectible accounts are treated properly. Other adjustments under the indirect method include changes in the account balances of deferred income taxes and the income (loss) from investments reported using the equity method. However, short-term borrowing used to purchase equipment is classified as a financing activity.

The following diagram shows the adjustments to net income necessary for converting accrual-based net income to cash-basis net income when using the indirect method. The diagram is simply an expanded statement of financial position equation.

	*Current assets**	+	*Noncurrent assets*	=	*Current liabilities*	+	*Long-term liabilities*	+	*Income*	*Accrual income adjustment to convert to cash flow*
1.	Increase			=					Increase	Decrease
2.	Decrease			=					Decrease	Increase
3.				=	Increase				Decrease	Increase
4.				=	Decrease				Increase	Decrease

* *Other than cash and cash equivalents.*

For example, using Row 1, a credit sale would increase accounts receivable and accrual-basis income but would not affect cash. Therefore, its effect must be removed from the accrual income in order to convert to cash income. The last column indicates that the increase in a current asset balance must be deducted from income to obtain cash flow. Using Row 2, a decrease in a current asset, such as prepaid rent, indicates that net income was decreased by rent expense, without a cash outflow in the current period. Thus, the decrease in prepaid rent would be added back to convert to cash income.

Similarly, using Row 3, an increase in a current liability must be added to income to obtain cash flows (e.g., accrued wages are on the income statement as an expense, but they do not require cash; the increase in wages payable must be added back to remove this non-cash expense from accrual-basis income). Using Row 4, a decrease in a current liability, such as accounts payable, indicates that cash was used but the expense was incurred in an earlier period. Thus, the decrease in accounts payable would be subtracted to include this disbursement in cash income.

If the indirect method is chosen, then the amount of interest and income tax paid must be included in the related disclosures.

The major drawback to the indirect method involves the user's difficulty in comprehending the information presented. This method does not show the sources or uses of cash. Only adjustments to accrual-basis net income are shown. In some cases, the adjustments can be confusing. For instance, the sale of equipment resulting in an accrual-basis loss would require that the loss be added to net income to arrive at net cash from operating activities. (The loss was deducted in the computation of net income, but because the sale will be shown as an investing activity, the loss must be added back to net income.)

The direct method portrays the amounts of cash both provided by and used in the reporting entity's operations, instead of presenting net income and reconciling items. The direct method reports only the items that affect cash flow (inflows/outflows of cash) and ignores items that do not affect cash flow (depreciation, gains, etc.). The general formats of both the direct method and the indirect method are shown below.

Direct method

Cash flows from operating activities:		
Cash received from sale of goods	$xxx	
Cash interest received	xxx	
Cash dividends received	xxx	
Cash provided by operating activities		$xxx
Cash paid to suppliers	(xxx)	
Cash paid for operating expenses	(xxx)	
Cash interest paid	(xxx)	
Cash paid for taxes	(xxx)	
Cash disbursed for operating activities		(xxx)
Net cash flows from operating activities		$xxx

Indirect method

Cash flows from operating activities:	
Net income	$ xx
Add/deduct items not affecting cash:	
Decrease (increase) in accounts receivable	(xx)
Depreciation expense	xx
Increase (decrease) in accounts payable	xx
Decrease (increase) in inventories	xx
Loss on sale of equipment	xx
Net cash flows from operating activities	$xxx

Other Requirements

Gross vs. net basis. The emphasis in the statement of cash flows is on gross cash receipts and payments. For instance, reporting the net change in bonds payable would obscure the financing activities of the entity by not disclosing separately cash inflows from issuing bonds and cash outflows from retiring bonds. In a few circumstances, netting of cash flows is allowed. Items having quick turnovers, large amounts, and short maturities may be presented as net cash flows if the cash receipts and payments pertain to

(1) investments (other than cash equivalents),
(2) loans receivable, and
(3) debts (original maturity of three months or less).

Extraordinary items and discontinued operations. ASC 230 permits, but does not require, separate disclosure of cash flows related to extraordinary items and to discontinued operations. If an entity chooses to disclose this information, disclosure must be consistent for all periods affected.

Cash flow per share. This information may *not* be displayed in the financial statements of a reporting entity.

Entities Exempt from Providing a Statement of Cash Flows

Per ASC 962-205-45-9, a statement of cash flows is not required for a defined benefit pension plan that presents the financial information under the guidelines of ASC 960. Other employee benefit plans are exempted, provided that the financial information presented is similar to the requirements of ASC 960. Investment enterprises or a common trust fund held for the collective investment and reinvestment of moneys are not required to provide a statement of cash flows if the following conditions are met:

1. Substantially all of the entity's investments are highly liquid.
2. The entity's investments are carried at market value.
3. The entity has little or no debt, based on average debt outstanding during the period, in relation to average total assets.
4. The entity provides a statement of changes in net assets.

Net Reporting by Financial Institutions

Per ASC 230-10-45, banks, savings institutions, and credit unions are allowed to report net cash receipts and payments for the following:

1. Deposits placed with other financial institutions
2. Withdrawals of those deposits
3. Time deposits accepted
4. Repayments of time deposits
5. Loans made to customers
6. Principal collections of loans made to customers.

Not-for-Profit Organizations

ASC 958-230 requires not-for-profit organizations to include a statement of cash flows in a complete set of financial statements. The statement of cash flows is prepared as it is for business enterprises with the following differences:

1. The indirect method of reporting cash flows from operations (or reconciliation of net income to net cash flows from operations required when the direct method is used) is prepared beginning with the change in net assets.
2. Investing activities also include receiving contributions that are restricted by the donor to the purchase or improvement of long-lived assets or for long-term investment such as permanent or term endowment.
3. Noncash activities include gifts of long-lived assets and gifts of securities held for long-term investment.

Reporting Hedging Transactions

Per ASC 230-10-45, the cash flows resulting from derivative instruments that are accounted for as fair value hedges or cash flow hedges may be classified as the same type of cash flows as the hedged items provided that the accounting policy is disclosed. However, if the derivative instrument used to hedge includes at inception an other-than-insignificant financing element, all cash inflows and outflows associated with the derivative instrument are reported by the borrower as cash flows from financing activities. (ASC 230-10-45-27) A derivative that at inception includes off-market terms, or requires up-front cash payment, or both, often contains a financing element. A derivative instrument is viewed as including a financing element if its contractual terms have been structured to ensure that net payments will be made by one party in the earlier periods of the derivative's term and subsequently returned by the counterparty in the later periods (other than elements that are inherent in at-the-money derivative instruments with no prepayments). If for any reason hedge accounting is discontinued, then any cash flows subsequent to the date of discontinuance are classified consistent with the nature of the instrument.

Reporting Foreign Currency Cash Flows

If an entity has foreign currency transactions or foreign operations, it should look to ASC 830 for guidance.

Preparation of the Statement

Under a cash and cash equivalents basis, the changes in the cash account and any cash equivalent account is the "bottom line" figure of the statement of cash flows. Using the 20X1 and 20X2 statements of financial position shown below, an increase of $25,000 can be computed. This is the difference between the totals for cash and treasury bills between 20X1 and 20X2 ($41,000 – $16,000).

When preparing the statement of cash flows using the direct method, gross cash inflows from revenues and gross cash outflows to suppliers and for expenses are presented in the operating activities section.

In preparing the reconciliation of net income to net cash flow from operating activities (indirect method), changes in all accounts (other than cash and cash equivalents) that are related to operations are additions to or deductions from net income to arrive at net cash provided by operating activities.

A T-account analysis may be helpful when preparing the statement of cash flows. A T-account is set up for each account, and beginning (20X1) and ending (20X2) balances are taken from the appropriate statement of financial position. Additionally, a T-account for cash and cash equivalents from operating activities and a master or summary T-account of cash and cash equivalents should be used.

Example of preparing a statement of cash flows

The financial statements below will be used to prepare the statement of cash flows.

Johnson Company
Statements of Financial Position
December 31, 20X2 and 20X1

	20X2	20X1
Assets		
Current assets:		
Cash	$ 37,000	$ 10,000
Treasury bills	4,000	6,000
Accounts receivable—net	9,000	11,000
Inventory	14,000	9,000
Prepaid expenses	10,000	13,000
Total current assets	$ 74,000	$ 49,000
Noncurrent assets:		
Investment in available-for-sale securities	7,500	15,000
Add (less) adjustment for changes in fair value	1,000	(3,000)
Investment in XYZ (35%)	16,000	14,000
Patent	5,000	6,000
Leased asset	5,000	–
Property, plant, and equipment	39,000	37,000
Less accumulated depreciation	(7,000)	(3,000)
Total assets	$140,500	$115,000
Liabilities		
Current liabilities:		
Accounts payable	$ 2,000	$ 12,000
Notes payable—current	9,000	–
Interest payable	3,000	2,000
Dividends payable	5,000	2,000
Income taxes payable	2,180	1,000
Lease obligation	700	–
Total current liabilities	21,880	17,000
Noncurrent liabilities:		
Deferred tax liability	9,360*	4,920*
Bonds payable	10,000	25,000
Lease obligation	4,300	–
Total liabilities	$ 45,540	$ 46,920
Stockholders' equity		
Common stock, $10 par value	$ 33,000	$ 26,000
Additional paid-in capital	16,000	3,000
Retained earnings	45,320	41,000
Accumulated other comprehensive income		
Net unrealized loss on available-for-sale securities	640	(1,920)
Total stockholders' equity	$ 94,960	$ 68,080
Total liabilities and stockholders' equity	$140,500	$115,000

* *Net of deferred tax asset ($540) and ($1,080) respectively.*

Johnson Company
Statement of Earnings and Comprehensive Income
For the Year Ended December 31, 20X2

Sales		$100,000
Other income		8,500
		$108,500
Cost of goods sold, excluding depreciation		60,000
Selling, general, and administrative expenses		12,000
Depreciation		8,000
Amortization of patents		1,000
Interest expense		2,000
		$ 83,000
Income before taxes		$ 25,500
Income taxes:		
Current	$6,180	
Deferred	3,000	9,180
Net income		$ 16,320
Other comprehensive income, net of tax		
Unrealized gains on securities:		
Unrealized holding gains (less applicable income taxes of $900)		1,600
Add reclassification adjustment (less applicable income taxes of $540)		960
Total other comprehensive income		$ 2,560
Comprehensive income		$ 18,880

Additional information (all relating to 20X2)

1. Equipment costing $6,000 with a book value of $2,000 was sold for $5,000.
2. The company received a $3,000 dividend from its investment in XYZ, accounted for under the equity method and recorded income from the investment of $5,000 that is included in other income.
3. The company issued 200 shares of common stock for $5,000.
4. The company signed a note payable for $9,000.
5. Equipment was purchased for $8,000.
6. The company converted $15,000 bonds payable into 500 shares of common stock. The book value method was used to record the transaction.
7. A dividend of $12,000 was declared.
8. Equipment was leased on December 31, 20X2. The principal portion of the first payment due December 31, 20X3, is $700.
9. The company sold half of their available-for-sale investments during the year for $8,000. The fair value of the remaining available-for-sale investments was $8,500 on December 31, 20X2.
10. The income tax rate is 36%.

Summary of
Cash and Cash Equivalents

Inflows	Outflows	
(d) 5,000		
	8,000 (g)	
(h) 5,000	9,000 (i)	
(n) 9,000		
(s) 8,000		
(t) 15,000		
42,000	17,000	
	25,000	Net increase in cash
42,000	42,000	

Cash and Cash
Equivalents—Operating

(a) 16,320	
(b) 8,000	
(c) 1,000	3,000 (d)
(e) 3,000	5,000 (f)
(f) 3,000	
(j) 2,000	5,000 (k)
(l) 3,000	10,000 (m)
(o) 1,000	
(p) 1,180	500 (s)
38,500	23,500
	15,000 (t)
38,500	38,500

Accounts Receivable (net)

11,000	
	2,000 (j)
9,000	

Inventory

9,000	
(k) 5,000	
14,000	

Prepaid Expenses

13,000	
	3,000 (l)
10,000	

Investment in AFS Securities

15,000	
	7,500 (s)
7,500	

Adjustment for Changes in FV of AFS Securities

	3,000
(s) 1,500	
(s) 2,500	
1,000	

Investment in XYZ

14,000	
(f) 5,000	3,000 (f)
16,000	

Patent

6,000	
	1,000 (c)
5,000	

Leased Equipment

(r) 5,000	
5,000	

Property, Plant, & Equipment

37,000	
	6,000 (d)
(g) 8,000	
39,000	

Accumulated Depreciation

	3,000
	8,000 (b)
(d) 4,000	
	7,000

Accounts Payable

	12,000
(m) 10,000	
	2,000

Notes Payable

	9,000 (n)
	9,000

Interest Payable

	2,000
(o) 1,000	2,000 (o)
	3,000

Dividends Payable

	2,000
(i) 9,000	12,000 (i)
	5,000

Income Taxes Payable

	1,000
(p) 5,000	6,180 (p)
	2,180

Deferred Tax Liability (Net)

	4,920
	3,000 (e)
	540 (s)
	900 (s)
	9,360

Bonds Payable

	25,000
(q) 15,000	
	10,000

Lease Obligation

	5,000 (r)
	5,000

Common Stock

	26,000
	2,000 (h)
	5,000 (q)
	33,000

Addl. Paid-in Capital

	3,000
	3,000 (h)
	10,000 (q)
	16,000

Retained Earnings

	41,000
	16,320 (a)
(i) 12,000	
	45,320

Unrealized Gain (Loss) on AFS Securities

1,920	
	960 (s)
	1,600 (s)
	640

Explanation of entries

a. Cash and Cash Equivalents—Operating Activities is debited for $16,320 (net income) and the credit is to Retained Earnings.

b. Depreciation is not a cash flow; however, depreciation expense was deducted to arrive at net income. Therefore, Accumulated Depreciation is credited and Cash and Cash Equivalents—Operating Activities is debited.

c. Amortization of patents is another expense not requiring cash; therefore, Cash and Cash Equivalents—Operating Activities is debited and Patent is credited.

d. The sale of equipment (additional information, item 1) resulted in a $3,000 gain. The gain is computed by comparing the book value of $2,000 with the sales price of $5,000. Cash proceeds of $5,000 are an inflow of cash. Since the gain was included in net income, it must be deducted from net income to determine cash provided by operating activities. This is necessary to avoid counting the $3,000 gain both in cash provided by operating activities and in investing activities. The following entry would have been made on the date of sale:

Cash	5,000	
Accumulated depreciation ($6,000 – $2,000)	4,000	
Property, plant, and equipment		6,000
Gain on sale of equipment ($5,000 – $2,000)		3,000

Adjust the T-accounts as follows: debit Summary of Cash and Cash Equivalents for $5,000, debit Accumulated Depreciation for $4,000, credit Property, Plant, and Equipment for $6,000, and credit Cash and Cash Equivalents—Operating Activities for $3,000.

e. The deferred income tax liability account shows an increase of $4,440. The $3,000 increase that pertains to amounts reported in the income statement must be added to income from operations. Although the $3,000 was deducted as part of income tax expense in determining net income, it did not require an outflow of cash. Therefore, debit Cash and Cash Equivalents—Operating Activities and credit Deferred Taxes. The other two amounts in the deferred tax liability account are covered below, under paragraph "p."

f. Item 2 under the additional information indicates that the investment in XYZ is accounted for under the equity method. The investment in XYZ had a net increase of $2,000, which is the result of the equity in the earnings of XYZ of $5,000 and the receipt of a $3,000 dividend. Dividends received (an inflow of cash) would reduce the investment in XYZ, while the equity in the income of XYZ would increase the investment without affecting cash. The journal entries would have been

Cash (dividend received)	3,000	
Investment in XYZ		3,000
Investment in XYZ	5,000	
Equity in earnings of XYZ		5,000

The dividend received ($3,000) is an inflow of cash, and the equity earnings are not. Debit Investment in XYZ for $5,000, credit Cash and Cash Equivalents—Operating Activities for $5,000, debit Cash and Cash Equivalents—Operating Activities for $3,000, and credit Investment in XYZ for $3,000.

g. The Property, Plant, and Equipment account increased because of the purchase of $8,000 (additional information, item 5). The purchase of assets is an outflow of cash. Debit Property, Plant, and Equipment for $8,000 and credit Summary of Cash and Cash Equivalents.

h. The company sold 200 shares of common stock during the year (additional information, item 3). The entry for the sale of stock was:

Cash	5,000	
Common stock (200 shares × $10)		2,000
Additional paid-in capital		3,000

This transaction resulted in an inflow of cash. Debit Summary of Cash and Cash Equivalents $5,000, credit Common Stock $2,000, and credit Additional Paid-in Capital $3,000.

i. Dividends of $12,000 were declared (additional information, item 7). Only $9,000 was actually paid in cash, resulting in an ending balance of $5,000 in the Dividends Payable account. Therefore, the following entries were made during the year:

Retained earnings	12,000	
Dividends payable		12,000
Dividends payable	9,000	
Cash		9,000

These transactions result in an outflow of cash. Debit Retained Earnings $12,000 and credit Dividends Payable $12,000. Additionally, debit Dividends Payable $9,000 and credit Summary of Cash and Cash Equivalents $9,000 to indicate the cash dividends paid during the year.

j. Accounts Receivable (net) decreased by $2,000. This is added as an adjustment to net income in the computation of cash provided by operating activities. The decrease of $2,000 means that an additional $2,000 cash was collected on account above and beyond the sales reported in the income statement. Debit Cash and Cash Equivalents—Operating Activities and credit Accounts Receivable for $2,000.

k. Inventories increased by $5,000. This is subtracted as an adjustment to net income in the computation of cash provided by operating activities. Although $5,000 additional cash was spent to increase inventories, this expenditure is not reflected in accrual-basis cost of goods sold. Debit Inventory and credit Cash and Cash Equivalents—Operating Activities for $5,000.

l. Prepaid Expenses decreased by $3,000. This is added back to net income in the computation of cash provided by operating activities. The decrease means that no cash was spent when incurring the related expense. The cash was spent when the prepaid assets were purchased, not when they were expensed on the income statement. Debit Cash and Cash Equivalents—Operating Activities and credit Prepaid Expenses for $3,000.

m. Accounts Payable decreased by $10,000. This is subtracted as an adjustment to net income. The decrease of $10,000 means that an additional $10,000 of purchases were paid for in cash; therefore, income was not affected but cash was decreased. Debit Accounts Payable and credit Cash and Cash Equivalents—Operating Activities for $10,000.

n. Notes Payable increased by $9,000 (as listed under additional information, item 4). This is an inflow of cash and would be included in the financing activities. Debit Summary of Cash and Cash Equivalents and credit Notes Payable for $9,000.

o. Interest Payable increased by $1,000, but interest expense reported on the income statement was $2,000. Therefore, although $2,000 was expensed, only $1,000 cash was paid ($2,000 expense – $1,000 increase in interest payable). Debit Cash and Cash Equivalents—Operating Activities for $1,000 for the noncash portion, debit Interest Payable for $1,000 for the cash portion, and credit Interest Payable for $2,000 for the expense.

p. The following entry was made to record the incurrence of the tax liability:

Income tax expense	9,180	
Income taxes payable		6,180
Deferred tax liability		3,000

Therefore, $9,180 was deducted in arriving at net income. The $3,000 credit to Deferred Income Taxes was accounted for in entry e. above. The $6,180 credit to Taxes Payable does not, however, indicate that $6,180 cash was paid for taxes. Since Taxes Payable increased $1,180, only $5,000 must have been paid and $1,180 remains unpaid. Debit Cash and Cash Equivalents—Operating Activities for $1,180, debit Income Taxes Payable for $5,000, and credit Income Taxes Payable for $6,180.

q. Item 6 under the additional information indicates that $15,000 of bonds payable were converted to common stock. This is a *noncash* financing activity and should be reported in a separate schedule. The following entry was made to record the transaction:

Bonds payable	15,000	
Common stock (500 shares × $10 par)		5,000
Additional paid-in capital		10,000

Adjust the T-accounts with a debit to Bonds Payable, $15,000; a credit to Common Stock, $5,000; and a credit to Additional Paid-in Capital, $10,000.

r. Item 8. under the additional information indicates that leased equipment was acquired on the last day of 2012. This is also a noncash financing activity and should be reported in a separate schedule. The following entry was made to record the lease transaction:

Leased asset	5,000	
Lease obligation		5,000

s. The company sold half of its available-for-sale investments during the year for $8,000 (additional information, item 9). The entry for the sale of the investments was

Cash	8,000	
Investment in available-for-sale securities		7,500
Gain on sale of investments		500

This transaction resulted in an inflow of cash. Debit Summary of Cash and Cash Equivalents $8,000, credit Investment in Available-for-Sale Securities $7,500, and credit Cash and Cash Equivalents—Operating Activities $500. The following additional journal entries were made:

Adjustment for changes in FV	1,500	
Other comprehensive income ($1,500 × 64%)		960
Deferred tax liability ($1,500 × 36%)		540

To adjust the allowance account for the sale, one-half of the amounts provided at the end of 2012 must be taken off the books when the related securities are sold.

Adjustment for changes in FV	2,500	
Unrealized gain on available-for-sale securities ($2,500 × 64%)		1,600
Deferred tax liability ($2,500 × 36%)		900

The change in fair value of the remaining securities at year-end (as listed under additional information, item 9) must be adjusted. The book value of the securities before the adjustment above is $6,000 ($7,500 – $1,500). The fair value of the securities is $8,500. An adjustment of $2,500 is necessary.

t. The cash and cash equivalents from operations ($15,000) is transferred to the Summary of Cash and Cash Equivalents.

All of the changes in the noncash accounts have been accounted for and the balance in the Summary of Cash and Cash Equivalents account of $25,000 is the amount of the year-to-year increase in cash and cash equivalents. The formal statement may now be prepared using the T-account, Summary of Cash and Cash Equivalents. The alphabetic characters in the statement below refer to the entries in that T-account. The following statement of cash flows is prepared under the direct method. The calculations for gross receipts and gross payments needed for the direct method are shown below the statement.

Johnson Company
Statement of Cash Flows
For the Year Ended December 31, 20X2

Cash flow from operating activities			
Cash received from customers	$102,000		
Dividends received	3,000		
Cash provided by operating activities			$105,000
Cash paid to suppliers	$ 75,000		
Cash paid for expenses	9,000		
Interest paid	1,000		
Income taxes paid	5,000		
Cash paid for operating activities			(90,000)
Net cash flow provided by operating activities		(t)	$ 15,000
Cash flow from investing activities			
Sale of equipment	5,000	(d)	
Sale of investments	8,000	(s)	
Purchase of property, plant, and equipment	(8,000)	(g)	
Net cash provided by investing activities			5,000
Cash flow from financing activities			
Sale of common stock	$ 5,000	(h)	
Increase in notes payable	9,000	(n)	
Dividends paid	(9,000)	(i)	
Net cash provided by financing activities			5,000
Net increase in cash and cash equivalents			$ 25,000
Cash and cash equivalents at beginning of year			16,000
Cash and cash equivalents at end of year			$ 41,000

Calculation of amounts for operating activities section

Cash received from customers = Net sales + Beginning A/R – Ending A/R
$100,000 + $11,000 – $9,000 = $102,000

Cash paid to suppliers = Cost of goods sold + Beginning A/P – Ending A/P + Ending inventory – Beginning inventory
$60,000 + $12,000 – $2,000 + $14,000 – $9,000 = $75,000

Cash paid for operating expenses = Operating expenses + Ending prepaid expenses – Beginning prepaid expenses – Depreciation expense (and other noncash operating expenses)
$12,000 + $8,000 + $1,000 + $10,000 – $13,000 – $8,000 – $1,000 = $9,000

Interest paid = Interest expense + Beginning interest payable – Ending interest payable
$2,000 + $2,000 – $3,000 = $1,000

Taxes paid = Income taxes + Beginning income taxes payable – Ending income taxes payable – Change in deferred income taxes—operating portion
$9,180 + $1,000 – $2,180 – $3,000 = $5,000

When a statement of cash flows is prepared using the direct method of reporting operating cash flows, the reconciliation of net income to operating cash flows must also be provided. The T-account, Cash and Cash Equivalents—Operating Activities is used to prepare the reconciliation. The alphabetic characters in the reconciliation below refer to the entries in the T-account.

Reconciliation of net income to net cash provided by operating activities			
Net income		(a)	$16,320
Add (deduct) items not using (providing) cash:			
Depreciation	8,000	(b)	
Amortization	1,000	(c)	
Gain on sale of equipment	(3,000)	(d)	
Increase in deferred taxes	3,000	(e)	
Equity in XYZ	(2,000)	(f)	
Decrease in accounts receivable	2,000	(j)	
Increase in inventory	(5,000)	(k)	
Decrease in prepaid expenses	3,000	(l)	
Decrease in accounts payable	(10,000)	(m)	
Increase in interest payable	1,000	(o)	
Increase in income taxes payable	1,180	(p)	
Gain on sale of AFS securities	(500)	(s)	(1,320)
Net cash flow provided by operating activities		(t)	$15,000
Schedule of noncash transactions			
Conversion of bonds into common stock		(q)	$15,000
Acquisition of leased equipment		(r)	$ 5,000

Statement of Cash Flows for Consolidated Entities

A consolidated statement of cash flows must be presented when a complete set of consolidated financial statements is issued. The consolidated statement of cash flows would be the last statement to be prepared, as the information to prepare it will come from the other consolidated statements (consolidated statement of financial position, income statement, and statement of retained earnings). The preparation of a consolidated statement of cash flows involves the same analysis and procedures as the statement for an individual entity with a few additional items. When the indirect method is used, the additional noncash transactions relating to the business combination, such as the differential amortization, must also be reversed, and all transfers to affiliates must be eliminated, as they do not represent cash inflows or outflows of the consolidated entity.

All unrealized intercompany profits should have been eliminated in preparation of the other statements. Any income or loss allocated to noncontrolling parties would need to be added back, as it would have been eliminated in computing consolidated net income but does not represent a true cash outflow or inflow. Finally, only dividend payments that are not intercompany should be recorded as cash outflows in the financing activities section.

In preparing the operating activities section of the statement by the indirect method following a purchase business combination, the changes in assets and liabilities related to operations since acquisition should be derived by comparing the consolidated statement of financial position as of the date of acquisition with the year-end consolidated statement of financial position. These changes will be combined with those for the acquiring company up to the date of acquisition as adjustments to net income. The effects due to the acquisition of these assets and liabilities are reported under investing activities.

Disclosures

Cash Equivalents Policy. The policy for determining which items are treated as cash equivalents must be disclosed. Any change to that policy is considered a change in accounting principle requiring restating financial statements for earlier years presented in comparative statements.

Interest and Income Taxes Paid. Entities using the indirect method must disclose the amounts of interest paid (net of amounts capitalized) and income taxes paid during the period.

Noncash Investing and Financing Activities. If an entity engages in investing and financing activities during a period that affect recognized assets or liabilities but that do not result in cash receipts or cash payments in the period, information about those activities must be disclosed. Those disclosures may be either narrative or summarized in a schedule, and they must clearly relate the cash and noncash aspects of transactions involving similar items.

Some transactions are part cash and part noncash; only the cash portion is reported in the statement of cash flows. If there are only a few such noncash transactions, it may be convenient to include them on the same page as the statement of cash flows. Otherwise, the transactions may be reported elsewhere in the financial statements, clearly referenced to the statement of cash flows.

Other Sources (ASC 230-10-60)

See ASC Location – Wiley *GAAP* Chapter	***For information on…***
ASC 320	Classification and reporting in the statement of cash flows of cash flows from available-for-sale, held-to-maturity, and trading securities.
ASC 325-30-45	Classification in the statement of cash flows of cash receipts and cash payments related to life settlement contracts.
ASC 830	Reporting and implementation guidance for presenting a statement of cash flows of an entity with foreign currency transactions or foreign currency operations.
ASC 915	The required presentation of and the additional information required in the statement of cash flows of a development stage entity.

8 ASC 235 NOTES TO FINANCIAL STATEMENTS

PERSPECTIVE AND ISSUES

Subtopic

ASC 235, *Notes to Financial Statements*, contains one Subtopic:

- ASC 235-10, *Overall*, which addresses "the content and usefulness of the accounting policies judged by management to be most appropriate to fairly present the entity's financial statement."

The topic does not address specific disclosures. Those are addressed in the related topics. The topic does, however, list accounting policy disclosures commonly required:

- Basis of consolidation
- Depreciation methods
- Amortization of intangibles
- Inventory pricing
- Accounting for recognition of profit on long-term construction-type contracts
- Recognition of revenue from franchising and leasing operations.
  (ASC 235-10-50-4)

Technical Alert

Disclosures have drawn the attention of both the FASB and the SEC. As the disclosure requirements have accumulated over the years, there has been a growing concern about information overload and whether more is necessarily better.

The FASB has a project to develop a framework to increase the effectiveness of disclosures. The framework will address the process for establishing disclosure and for determining which disclosures to make. More information can be found on the FASB's website.

The SEC is reviewing specific sections of regulations S-K and S-X, with a goal of updating requirements and eliminating duplicate disclosures. The Commission also wants to continue to provide material information and reduce cost burdens on companies. There are several suggestions for decreasing disclosure overload. Here are some excerpts from an April 2014 speech by Keith Higgins, SEC Division of Corporation Finance Director. The full speech is available on sec.gov.

- ***Reduce Repetition***—Think twice before repeating something. There are plenty of examples of companies including—verbatim—disclosure from their significant accounting policies footnote in their MD&A discussions of critical accounting estimates. Setting aside the fundamental question of whether our MD&A guidance on critical accounting estimates requires a recitation of the accounting principle itself, if there were ever a place in a report that cried out for a cross reference—and there are likely plenty of them—this is near the top of the list. The purpose of the discussion of critical accounting estimates is to educate the reader about the aspects of the particular accounting policy that are the most uncertain and subject to possible revision, not to repeat how the accounting policy works, which is described elsewhere. Before you repeat anything in a filing, please step back and ask yourself—do I need to say it again?
- ***Focus Your Disclosure***—I wonder if Abe Lincoln—who wrote the Gettysburg Address in 272 words—ever dreamed we would have annual reports with risk factor disclosure exceeding 30 or 40 pages. Some have suggested, only partly in jest, that we implement a page limit for risk factors or require companies to list their top ten risk factors. We can all probably agree that risk factors could be written better—less generic and more tailored—and they should explain how the risks would affect the company if they came to pass. There is no question that many companies have come to view these discussions as an insurance policy. After taking into account the safe harbor in the Private Securities Litigation Reform Act of 1995, and courts' lack of uniformity about the interpretation of "meaningful cautionary statements," the result is that companies have little incentive to limit the number of risk factors. I recognize this is a problem. But, are there effective ways to incentivize companies—and their lawyers—to write better risk factors that would allow investors to zero in on the material risks?

  Turning to a different example, the transparency of our review and comment process has had a generally salutary effect, which has been far reaching. One effect that may not be as salutary is the tendency for companies to simply follow what others have done when making disclosure decisions or to include disclosures because a client alert says that it is a "hot button" issue for the staff. However, the first question should be "does this issue apply to the company?" And when the answer is no, it should be the last question as well.
- ***Eliminate Outdated Information***—Disclosure should evolve over time. In a survey of 122 public companies, 74% said that once they include disclosure in a public filing in response to an SEC comment, it is rarely, if ever, removed.[1] Companies and their representatives should regularly evaluate their disclosures to determine whether they are material to investors. If they are not material, and they are not required, you can take them out. Yes, as unsettling as I am sure this can be for some, it is perfectly all right to remove disclosure when it is immaterial or outdated even if it was included in a prior filing in response to a staff comment. A response to a staff comment is not carved in stone and enshrined for time immemorial in each filing going forward—unless, of course, it remains material. And if it does, keep it in.

---

[1] See KPMG LLP and Financial Executives Research Foundation, Inc., Disclosure overload and complexity: hidden in plain sight, Available at: http://www.kpmg.com/US/en/IssuesAndInsights/ArticlesPublications/Documents/disclosure-overload-complexity.pdf.

For those interested in the SEC's disclosure project, a staff report to Congress was issued in December 2013 and is also available on the SEC site at http://www.sec.gov/news/studies/2013/reg-sk-disclosure-requirements-review.pdf. This report was mandated by the Jumpstart Our Business Startups (JOBS) Act. It provides the staff's preliminary conclusions and recommendations about disclosure reform.

DEFINITIONS OF TERMS

There is no glossary in ASC 235.

CONCEPTS, RULES, AND EXAMPLES

Accounting Policies

The reporting entity's management is responsible for adopting and adhering to the highest quality accounting policies possible. ASC 235 requires management, in discharging this responsibility, to adopt accounting principles and methods of applying them that are "the most appropriate in the circumstances to present fairly financial position, results of operations, and cash flows in accordance with generally accepted accounting principles."

There are many different methods of valuing assets, recognizing revenues, and assigning costs. Financial statement users must be aware of the accounting policies used by an entity so that sound economic decisions can be made. Per ASC 235, financial statement disclosures should identify and describe

- All significant accounting policies followed by the entity and
- Methods of applying those principles that materially affect the determination of financial position, changes in cash flows, or results of operations.

This requirement applies even in reporting situations where one or more of the basic financial statements have been omitted. However, it does not apply to unaudited interim statements where the accounting policies have not changed since the issuance of the last annual statements. (ASC 275-10-50-2)

The accounting policies disclosure should encompass those accounting principles and methods that involve the following:

1. Selection from acceptable alternatives
2. Principles and methods peculiar to the industry
3. Unique applications of GAAP.

In theory, if only one method of accounting for a type of transaction is acceptable under GAAP, it is not necessary to explicitly cite it in the accounting policies note, although many entities do routinely identify all accounting policies affecting the major financial statement captions.

In the accounting policy disclosure, it is not necessary to repeat details that are provided in other disclosures. Many preparers simply cross-reference accounting policy disclosures to relevant details provided in other notes to the financial statements.

The "summary of significant accounting policies" is customarily, but not necessarily, the first note disclosure included in the financial statements. A more all-encompassing title such as "Nature of business and summary of significant accounting policies" is frequently used.

Commonly disclosed accounting policies. A listing of accounting policies commonly disclosed by reporting entities follows (the listing is not intended to be all-inclusive):

- Advertising costs
- Advertising, direct response arrangements
- Cash equivalents
- Changes in accounting policies
- Combined financial statements, principles of combination
- Concentrations of credit risk, major customers and/or suppliers
- Consolidated financial statements, principles of consolidation
- Consolidated financial statements, variable interest entities
- Deferred income taxes
- Deferred income taxes, undistributed earnings of subsidiaries and/or joint ventures
- Derivatives and hedging activities
- Fair value elections, methods, assumptions, inputs used
- Financial instruments
- Fiscal year, 52–53 week year
- Fiscal year, difference between fiscal year used for financial reporting and for income tax purposes
- Foreign currency translation
- Foreign sales corporations
- Goodwill
- Guarantees
- Impairment of long-lived assets, goodwill, other intangibles, investments, etc.
- Income taxes, deposit to retain fiscal year
- Income taxes, nonaccrual by flow-through entity
- Income taxes, liability for unrecognized income tax positions
- Intangibles, amortizable and/or nonamortizable
- Interest capitalization
- Internal-use software
- Inventories
- Investments, cost method
- Investments, debt and marketable equity securities including reclassifications between portfolios
- Investments, equity method
- Long-term contracts
- Nature of operations
- Not-for-profits; restrictions that are satisfied in the year they originate
- Operating cycle
- Out-of-pocket costs (typically for service businesses)
- Pension and other postretirement or postemployment plans
- Property and equipment, depreciation and amortization
- Property and equipment, changes from held-and-used to held-for-sale
- Rebates
- Receivables, past due, interest and late charges, determination of allowance for bad debts
- Reclassifications

- Revenue recognition, lessor leasing activities
- Revenue recognition, long-term contract accounting
- Revenue recognition, methods for each significant product or service
- Revenue recognition, multiple-element arrangements
- Revenue recognition, product returns
- Revenue recognition, real estate (time-sharing) sales (e.g., installment cost recovery, full accrual)
- Revenue recognition, software sold or otherwise marketed
- Share-based payment arrangements
- Shipping and handling costs
- Start-up costs
- Syndication costs
- Use of estimates
- Warranties.

Timing of adoption decisions. Upon formation of a business or nonprofit organization, management makes decisions regarding the adoption of accounting policies, based on the types of activities in which the entity engages and the industry and environment in which it operates. Certain ASC Topics permit choices to be made from among alternative, acceptable accounting treatments. The principles selected from among the available alternatives and the methods of applying those principles constitute the reporting entity's accounting policies.

Management initially adopts accounting principles at two distinct times:

1. Upon formation of the reporting entity
2. Upon the occurrence of a new type of event or transaction that had either not happened in the past or had previously been judged to be immaterial.

Once the initial adoption decisions are made, the users of the financial statements expect a reporting entity's financial statements to be prepared consistently over time. This facilitates comparisons across periods and among different reporting entities.

Disclosure Techniques

The following five disclosure techniques are used in varying degrees in contemporary financial statements:

1. Parenthetical explanations
2. Notes to the financial statements
3. Cross-references
4. Valuation allowances (sometimes referred to as "contra" amounts)
5. Supporting schedules.

Parenthetical explanations. Information is sometimes disclosed by means of parenthetical explanations appended to the appropriate statement of financial position caption. For example

Common stock ($10 par value, 200,000 shares authorized, 150,000 issued)	$1,500,000

Parenthetical explanations have an advantage over both notes to the financial statements and supporting schedules. Parenthetical explanations place the disclosure prominently in the body of the statement instead of in a note or schedule where it is more likely to be overlooked.

Notes to financial statements. If the information cannot be disclosed in a relatively short and concise parenthetical explanation, a note disclosure is used. For example

Inventories (see note 1)	$2,550,000

The notes to the financial statements would contain the following:

> **Note 1:** Inventories are stated at the lower of cost or market. Cost is determined using the first-in, first-out (FIFO) method.

Cross-references. Cross-referencing is used when there is a direct relationship between two accounts on the statement of financial position. For example, among the current assets, the following might be shown if $1,500,000 of accounts receivable were pledged as collateral for a $1,200,000 bank loan:

Accounts receivable pledged as collateral on bank loan payable	$1,500,000

Included in the current liabilities would be the following:

Bank loan payable—collateralized by accounts receivable	$1,200,000

Valuation allowances. Valuation allowances are used to reduce or increase the carrying amounts of certain assets and liabilities. Accumulated depreciation reduces the carrying value of property, plant, and equipment, and a bond premium (discount) increases (decreases) the face value of a bond payable as shown in the following illustrations:

Equipment	$18,000,000	
Less accumulated depreciation	(1,625,000)	$16,375,000
Bonds payable	$20,000,000	
Less discount on bonds payable	(1,300,000)	$18,700,000
Bonds payable	$20,000,000	
Add premium on bonds payable	1,300,000	$21,300,000

9 ASC 250 ACCOUNTING CHANGES AND ERROR CORRECTIONS

PERSPECTIVE AND ISSUES

Subtopics

ASC 250, *Accounting Changes and Error Corrections,* contains one subtopic: ASC 250-10, *Overall*, which:

- Provides guidance on accounting for and reporting on accounting changes and error corrections
- Requires, unless impractical, retrospective application of a change in accounting principle
- Provides guidance on when retrospective application is impractical and how to report on the impracticability.

ASC 250-10 also:

- Specifies the method of treating error correction in comparative statements
- Specifies the disclosures required upon restatement of previously issued statements of income
- Recommends methods of presentation of historical, statistical-type financial summaries affect by error corrections.
  (ASC 250-10-5-5)

Scope

ASC 250 applies to all entities' financial statements and summaries of information that reflect an accounting period affected by accounting change or error.

Overview

Under US GAAP, management is granted the flexibility of choosing between or among certain alternative methods of accounting for the same economic transactions. Examples of the availability of such choices are provided throughout this publication, in such diverse areas as alternative cost-flow assumptions used to account for inventory and cost of sales, different methods of depreciating long-lived assets, and varying methods of identifying operating segments. The professional literature (in the areas of accounting principles, auditing standards, quality control standards, and professional ethics) is emphatic that, in choosing among the various alternatives, management is to select principles and apply them in a manner that results in financial statements that faithfully represent economic substance over form and that are fully transparent to the user.

Changes in accounting can be necessitated over time due to changes in the assumptions and estimates underlying the application of accounting principles and methods of applying them, changes in the principles defined as acceptable by a standards-setting authority, or other types of changes.

Changes in the accounting for given transactions can have a profound influence on investing and operational decisions. Financial statement analysts and management decision makers both generally presume the consistency and comparability of financial statements across periods and among entities within industry groupings. Any type of accounting change potentially can create inconsistency. The challenge is to present the effects of the change in a manner that is most readily comprehended by users of financial statements, who may impose various adjustments of their own in their efforts to make the information comparable for analysis purposes.

When contemplating a potential change in accounting principle, a primary focus of management should be to consider its effect on financial statement comparability. This should not, however, dissuade preparers from adopting preferable accounting standards, where otherwise warranted.

ASC 250 contains the underlying presumption that in preparing financial statements an accounting principle, once adopted, should not be changed in accounting for events and transactions of a similar type. This consistent use of accounting principles is intended to enhance the utility of financial statements. The presumption that a reporting entity should not change an accounting principle may be overcome only if management justifies the use of an alternative acceptable accounting principle on the basis that it is actually preferable.

ASC 250 does not provide a definition of preferability or criteria by which to make such assessments, so this remains a matter of professional judgment. What is preferable for one industry or company is not necessarily considered preferable for another.

DEFINITIONS OF TERMS

Source: ASC 250-10-20

Accounting Change. A change in an accounting principle, an accounting estimate, or the reporting entity. The correction of an error in previously issued financial statements is not an accounting change.

Change in Accounting Estimate. A change that has the effect of adjusting the carrying amount of an existing asset or liability or altering the subsequent accounting for existing or future assets or liabilities. A change in accounting estimate is a necessary consequence of the assessment, in conjunction with the periodic presentation of financial statements, of the present status and expected future benefits and obligations associated with assets and liabilities. Changes in accounting estimates result from new information. Examples of items for which estimates are necessary are uncollectible receivables, inventory obsolescence, service lives and salvage values of depreciable assets, and warranty obligations.

Change in Accounting Estimate Effected by a Change in Accounting Principle. A change in accounting estimate that is inseparable from the effect of a related change in accounting principle. An example of a change in estimate effected by a change in principle is a change in the method of depreciation, amortization, or depletion for long-lived, nonfinancial assets.

Change in Accounting Principle. A change from one generally accepted accounting principle to another generally accepted accounting principle when there are two or more generally accepted accounting principles that apply or when the accounting principle formerly used is no longer generally accepted. A change in the method of applying an accounting principle also is considered a change in accounting principle.

Change in the Reporting Entity. A change that results in financial statements that, in effect, are those of a different reporting entity. A change in the reporting entity is limited mainly to the following:

a. Presenting consolidated or combined financial statements in place of financial statements of individual entities
b. Changing specific subsidiaries that make up the group of entities for which consolidated financial statements are presented
c. Changing the entities included in combined financial statements.

Neither a business combination accounted for by the acquisition method nor the consolidation of a variable interest entity (VIE) pursuant to Topic 810 is a change in reporting entity.

Direct Effects of a Change in Accounting Principle. Those recognized changes in assets or liabilities necessary to effect a change in accounting principle. An example of a direct effect is an adjustment to an inventory balance to effect a change in inventory valuation method. Related changes, such as an effect on deferred income tax assets or liabilities or an impairment adjustment resulting from applying the lower-of-cost-or-market test to the adjusted inventory balance, also are examples of direct effects of a change in accounting principle.

Error in Previously Issued Financial Statements. An error in recognition, measurement, presentation, or disclosure in financial statements resulting from mathematical mistakes, mistakes in the application of generally accepted accounting principles (GAAP), or oversight or misuse of facts that existed at the time the financial statements were prepared. A change from an accounting principle that is not generally accepted to one that is generally accepted is a correction of an error.

Indirect Effects of a Change in Accounting Principle. Any changes to current or future cash flows of an entity that result from making a change in accounting principle that is applied retrospectively. An example of an indirect effect is a change in a nondiscretionary profit sharing or royalty payment that is based on a reported amount such as revenue or net income.

Restatement. The process of revising previously issued financial statements to reflect the correction of an error in those financial statements.

Retrospective Application. The application of a different accounting principle to one or more previously issued financial statements, or to the statement of financial position at the beginning of the current period, as if that principle had always been used, or a change to financial statements of prior accounting periods to present the financial statements of a new reporting entity as if it had existed in those prior years.

CONCEPTS, RULES, AND EXAMPLES

Accounting Changes

There are legitimate reasons why a reporting entity would change its accounting:

1. Changing to an existing alternative accounting principle that management deems to be preferable to the one it is currently following
2. Adopting a newly issued accounting principle
3. Refining an estimate made in the past as a result of further experience and better information
4. Correcting an error made in previously issued financial statements. Although technically not an "accounting change" as defined in GAAP literature, this involves restating previously issued financial statements and is also governed by ASC 250.

To facilitate accurate analysis, it is important for management of the reporting entity to adequately inform the financial statement users when one or more of these changes are made, and to provide sufficient information to enable the reader to distinguish the effects of the change from other factors affecting results of operations.

Each of the types of accounting changes and the proper treatment prescribed for them is summarized in the following chart and discussed in detail in the following sections.

Summary of Accounting Changes and Error Corrections

Type and description of change or correction	*Treatment in financial statements, historical summaries, financial highlights, and other similar presentations of businesses and not-for-profit organizations*		
	Retrospective application to all periods presented[1]	*Affects period of change and, if applicable, future periods*	*Restatement of all prior period financial statements presented*
Accounting Changes Change in accounting principle *New principle required to be preferable*	✓		
Change in accounting estimate		✓	
Change in accounting estimate effected by a change in accounting principle *New principle required to be preferable*		✓	
Change in reporting entity[2]	✓		
Restatements[3] Correction of errors in previously issued financial statements			✓

Change in Accounting Principle

Management is permitted to change from one generally accepted accounting principle to another only when

1. It voluntarily decides to do so and can justify the use of the alternative accounting principle as being preferable to the principle currently being followed, or
2 It is required to make the change as a result of a newly issued accounting pronouncement. (ASC 250-10-45-2)

Per ASC 250-45-1, the following are not considered a change in accounting principle:

- Initial adoption of an accounting principle.

---

[1] *ASC 250 provides an exception to the requirement for retroactive restatement when it is impracticable to make the restatement. This exception is only permitted to be used under specified conditions.*

[2] *This is generally limited to (a) presentation of consolidated or combined financial statements instead of financial statements of individual entities, (b) a change in the specific subsidiaries making up a group of entities for which consolidated financial statements are presented, and (c) changing the entities included in combined financial statements.* ***Neither a business combination under ASC 805 nor consolidation of a variable interest entity under ASC 810 is considered a change in reporting entity.***

[3] *The word "restatement" is only to be used to describe and/or present corrections of prior period errors.*

- Adoption or modification of an accounting principle for transactions or events substantially different from previous transactions.
  (ASC 250-45-1)

If a change in accounting principle is being made voluntarily, the financial statements of the period of change must include disclosure of the nature of and reason for the change and an explanation of why management believes the newly adopted accounting principle is preferable. This preferability assessment is required to be made from the perspective of financial reporting, and not solely from an income tax perspective. Thus, favorable income tax consequences alone do not justify making a change in financial reporting practices.

According to ASC 250, the term *accounting principle* includes not only the accounting principles and practices used by the reporting entity, but also its methods of applying them. A change in the components used to cost a firm's inventory is considered a change in accounting principle and, therefore, is only permitted when the new inventory costing method is preferable to the former method.

Preferability. As stated, management is only permitted to voluntarily change the reporting entity's accounting principles when the newly employed principle is preferable to the principle it is replacing. The independent auditors are then charged with concurring with management's assessment. If the auditors do not believe management has provided reasonable justification for the change, AU-C §708.07 requires the auditors to express either a qualified or adverse opinion, depending on the materiality of the effects of the unacceptable accounting principle on the financial statements.

When management of a public company voluntarily changes the registrant's accounting principles, a letter from the registrant's independent public accountants is required to be filed with the Securities and Exchange Commission (SEC). This "preferability letter" is to be included as an exhibit in 10-Q and 10-K filings (Regulation S-K Item 601, Exhibit 18) and must indicate whether the change in principle or practice (or method of applying that principle or practice) is to an acceptable alternative that, in the auditors' judgment, is preferable under the circumstances. (ASC 250-10-S99-4)

Retrospective application. ASC 250-10-45-5 provides that changes in accounting principle be reflected in financial statements by retrospective application to all prior periods presented unless it is impracticable to do so. ASC 250-45-3 points out that Accounting Standards Updates include specific provisions regarding transitioning to the new principles that are to be followed by adopting entities. The default method is retrospective restatement, whereas previously the default procedure was to recognize a cumulative effect adjustment in current results of operations. If FASB believes this to be the most beneficial method of transition, updates may still provide for adoption using cumulative effect adjustments.

Retrospective application is accomplished by the following steps:

At the beginning of the first period presented in the financial statements,

Step 1 Adjust the carrying amounts of assets and liabilities for the cumulative effect of changing to the new accounting principle on periods prior to those presented in the financial statements.

Step 2 Offset the effect of the adjustment in Step 1 (if any) by adjusting the opening balance of retained earnings (or other components of equity or net assets, as applicable to the reporting entity).

For each individual prior period that is presented in the financial statements,

Step 3 Adjust the financial statements for the effects of applying the new accounting principle to that specific period.

(ASC 250-10-45-5)

Example of retrospective application of a new accounting principle

In 20X1, upon the incorporation of Newburger Company, its management elected to recognize advertising costs as incurred. Newburger has been consistently following that policy in its financial statements. In 20Y3, Newburger's management reviewed its accounting policies and concluded that application of its current policy was resulting in substantial costs associated with the production of television advertising being recognized in financial reporting periods that preceded the periods in which the related revenues were earned. Consequently, management decided to change Newburger's policy to elect to expense advertising costs the first time the advertising takes place as permitted by ASC 720-35, *Advertising Costs*. Additional assumptions follow:

- As has been its policy in the past, Newburger plans to issue comparative financial statements presenting two years, 20Y3 and 20Y2.
- Newburger does not engage in direct-response advertising activities.
- A combined federal and state income tax rate of 40% was in effect for all relevant periods.
- Prior to the change in accounting principle, there were no temporary differences or loss carryforwards and, thus, there were no deferred income tax assets or liabilities.
- Advertising costs are deductible for income tax purposes when incurred and, therefore, upon adoption of the new accounting policy, Newburger will have a temporary difference between the book and income tax bases of its asset, deferred advertising costs. These advertising costs that are being recognized in the financial statements in the year after they are deducted on Newburger's income tax return represent a future taxable temporary difference that will give rise to a deferred income tax liability.
- The financial statements originally issued as of and for the years ended December 31, 20Y2 and 20Y1, prior to the adoption of the new accounting principle are presented below with advertising-related captions shown separately for illustrative purposes.

Newburger Company
Statements of Income and Retained Earnings
Prior to Change in Accounting Principle
Years Ended December 31, 20Y2 and 20Y1

	20Y2	*20Y1*
Sales	$ 2,300,000	$ 2,000,000
Cost of sales	(850,000)	(750,000)
Gross profit	1,450,000	1,250,000
Advertising expense	65,000	55,000
Other selling, general, and administrative expenses	385,000	445,000
	450,000	500,000
Income from operations	1,000,000	750,000
Other income (expense)	11,000	10,000
Income before income taxes	1,011,000	760,000
Income taxes	(404,000)	(304,000)
Net income	607,000	456,000
Retained earnings, beginning of year	13,756,000	14,500,000
Dividends	(1,400,000)	(1,200,000)
Retained earnings, end of year	$12,963,000	$13,756,000

Newburger Company
Statements of Financial Position
Prior to Change in Accounting Principle
December 31, 20Y2 and 20Y1

	20Y2	*20Y1*
Assets		
Current assets		
Cash and cash equivalents	$ 2,200,000	$ 2,400,000
Deferred advertising cost	–	–
Prepaid expenses	125,000	120,000
Other current assets	22,000	20,000
Total current assets	2,347,000	2,540,000
Property and equipment	10,729,000	11,311,000
Total assets	$13,076,000	$13,851,000
Liabilities and Stockholders' Equity		
Deferred income taxes	$ –	$ –
Other current liabilities	35,000	12,000
Total current liabilities	35,000	12,000
Noncurrent liabilities	65,000	70,000
Total liabilities	100,000	82,000
Stockholders' equity		
Common stock	13,000	13,000
Retained earnings	12,963,00	13,756,000
Total stockholders' equity	12,976,000	13,769,000
Total liabilities and stockholders' equity	$13,076,000	$13,851,000

Newburger Company
Statements of Cash Flows
Prior to Change in Accounting Principle
Years Ended December 31, 20Y2 and 20Y1

	20Y2	*20Y1*
Operating activities		
Net income	$ 607,000	$ 456,000
Depreciation	715,000	715,000
Deferred income taxes	–	–
Gain on sale of property and equipment	–	–
Changes in		
Deferred advertising costs	–	–
Prepaid expenses	(5,000)	1,000
Other current assets	(2,000)	1,500
Other current liabilities	23,000	900
Net cash provided by operating activities	1,338,000	1,174,400
Investing activities		
Property and equipment		
Acquisition	(133,000)	(120,000)
Proceeds from sale	–	–
Net cash used for investing activities	(133,000)	(120,000)
Financing activities		
Dividends paid to stockholders	(1,400,000)	(1,200,000)
Long-term debt		
Borrowed	–	–
Repaid	(5,000)	(5,000)

	20Y2	*20Y1*
Net cash used for financing activities	(1,405,000)	(1,205,000)
Decrease in cash and cash equivalents	(200,000)	(150,600)
Cash and cash equivalents, beginning of year	2,400,000	2,550,600
Cash and cash equivalents, end of year	$2,200,000	$2,400,000

Step 1 Adjust the carrying amounts of assets and liabilities at the beginning of the first period presented in the financial statements (January 1, 20Y2, in this example). For the cumulative effect of changing to the new accounting principle on periods prior to those presented in the financial statements.

In this example, the preparer refers to the previously issued 2011 financial statements presented above. Assume the following data regarding advertising costs at December 31, 20Y1/January 1, 20Y2:

Costs incurred during 20Y1 for advertising that will not take place for the first time until 20Y2	$25,000
Deferred income tax liability that would have been recognized at December 31, 20Y1, computed at 40% of the temporary difference	(10,000)
Net adjustment to beginning assets and liabilities	$15,000

Step 2 Offset the effect of the adjustment in Step 1 by adjusting the opening balance of retained earnings (or other components of equity or net assets, as applicable to the reporting entity).

The $15,000 net effect of the adjustment in Step 1 is presented in the statement of income and retained earnings as an adjustment to the January 1, 20Y2 retained earnings as previously reported at December 31, 20Y1.

Step 3 Adjust the financial statements of each individual prior period presented for the effects of applying the new accounting principle to that specific period.

In this case, the following adjustments are necessary to adjust the 20Y2 financial statements for the period-specific effects of the change in accounting principle:

Cost incurred in	*Year the advertising was first run*	
20Y1	20Y2	$ 25,000
20Y2	20Y3	(45,000)
Pretax, period-specific adjustment to advertising costs at 12/31/Y1		(20,000)
× 40% income tax effect		8,000
Effect on 20Y2 net income		$(12,000)

Adjustments to the 20Y2 financial statements for the period-specific effects of retrospective application of the new accounting principle are:

Adjustments to 20Y2 financial statements

	Deferred advertising costs	*Deferred income tax liability*	*Advertising expense*	*Income tax expense*
Balance at 12/31/Y2 prior to adjustment	$ –	$ –	$65,000	$404,000
Adjustment to opening balances from retrospective application to 20Y2	25,000	10,000	–	–
Advertising costs incurred in 2010, first run in 20Y2	(25,000)	–	25,000	–
Advertising costs incurred in 2011, first run in 20Y3	45,000	–	(45,000) (20,000)	–
Income tax effect of net adjustment to 20Y2 advertising expense (40%)	–	8,000	–	8,000
Adjusted amounts for 20Y12 financial statements	$45,000	$18,000	$45,000	$412,000

The adjusted comparative financial statements, reflecting the retrospective application of the new accounting principle, follow.

Newburger Company
Statements of Income and Retained Earnings
Reflecting Retrospective Application of Change in Accounting Principle
Years Ended December 31, 20Y3 and 20Y2

	20Y3	*20Y2 as adjusted*
Sales	$ 2,700,000	$ 2,300,000
Cost of sales	995,000	850,000
Gross profit	1,705,000	1,450,000
Advertising expense	66,000	45,000
Other selling, general, and administrative expenses	423,000	385,000
	489,000	430,000
Income from operations	1,216,000	1,020,000
Other income (expense)	9,000	11,000
Income before income taxes	1,225,000	1,031,000
Income taxes	490,400	412,000
Net income	734,600	619,000
Retained earnings, beginning of year, as originally reported		13,756,000
Adjustment for retrospective application of new accounting principle (Note X)		15,000
Retained earnings, beginning of year, as adjusted	12,990,000	13,771,000
Dividends	1,600,000	1,400,000
Retained earnings, end of year	$12,124,600	$12,990,000

Newburger Company
Statements of Financial Position
Reflecting Retrospective Application of Change in Accounting Principle
Years Ended December 31, 20Y3 and 20Y2

	20Y3	*20Y2 as adjusted*
Assets		
Current assets		
Cash and cash equivalents	$ 2,382,000	$ 2,200,000
Deferred advertising costs	16,000	45,000
Prepaid expenses	123,000	125,000
Other current assets	21,000	22,000
Total current assets	2,542,000	2,392,000
Property and equipment	9,800,000	10,729,000
Total assets	$12,342,000	$13,121,000
Liabilities and stockholders' equity		
Deferred income taxes	$ 6,000	$ 18,000
Other current liabilities	36,000	35,000
Total current liabilities	42,400	53,000
Noncurrent liabilities	162,000	65,000
Total liabilities	204,400	118,000
Stockholders' equity		
Common stock	13,000	13,000
Retained earnings	12,124,600	12,990,000
Total stockholders' equity	12,137,600	13,003,000
Total liabilities and stockholders' equity	$12,342,000	$13,121,000

Newburger Company
Statements of Cash Flows
Reflecting Retrospective Application of Change in Accounting Principle
Years Ended December 31, 20Y13 and 20Y2

	20Y3	*20Y2 as adjusted*
Operating activities		
Net income	$ 734,600	$ 619,000
Depreciation	725,000	715,000
Deferred income taxes	(11,600)	8,000
Gain on sale of property and equipment	(1,200,000)	–
Changes in		
Deferred advertising costs	29,000	(20,000)
Prepaid expenses	2,000	(5,000)
Other current assets	1,000	(2,000)
Other current liabilities	1,000	23,000
Net cash provided by operating activities	$ 281,000	$1,338,000
Investing activities		
Property and equipment		
Acquisition	(1,096,000)	(133,000)
Proceeds from sale	2,500,000	–
Net cash provided by (used for) investing activities	1,404,000	(133,000)

	20Y3	20Y2 as adjusted
Financing activities		
Dividends paid to stockholders	(1,600,000)	(1,400,000)
Long-term debt		
Borrowed	105,000	–
Repaid	(8,000)	(5,000)
Net cash used for financing activities	(1,503,000)	(1,405,000)
Increase (decrease) in cash and cash equivalents	182,000	(200,000)
Cash and cash equivalents, beginning of year	2,200,000	2,400,000
Cash and cash equivalents, end of year	$2,382,000	$2,200,000

It is important to note that, in presenting the previously issued financial statements for 20Y2, the caption "as adjusted" is included in the column heading. Prior to ASC 250, many preparers used the caption "as restated." ASC 250 explicitly defines a restatement as a revision to previously issued financial statements to correct an error. Therefore, to avoid misleading the financial statement reader, use of the terms restatement or restated are to be limited to prior period adjustments to correct errors, as discussed later in this chapter.

Indirect effects. The example above only reflects the direct effects of the change in accounting principle, net of the effect of income taxes. Changing accounting principles sometimes results in indirect effects from legal or contractual obligations of the reporting entity, such as profit sharing or royalty arrangements that contain monetary formulas based on amounts in the financial statements. In the preceding example, if Newburger Company had an incentive compensation plan that required it to contribute 15% of its pretax income to a pool to be distributed to its employees, the adoption of the new accounting policy would potentially require Newburger to provide additional contributions to the pool computed as:

	Pretax effect of retroactive application	*Contractual rate*	*Indirect effect*
Prior to 20Y2	$25,000	15%	$3,750
20Y2	(20,000)	15%	(3,000)
			$ 750

Contracts and agreements are often silent regarding how such a change might affect amounts that were computed (and distributed) in prior years. Management of Newburger Company might have discretion over whether to make the additional contributions. Further, it would probably consider it undesirable to reduce the 20Y2 incentive compensation pool because of an accounting change of this nature, and it might thus decide for valid business reasons not to reduce the pool under these circumstances.

ASC 250 specifies that irrespective of whether the indirect effects arise from an explicit requirement in the agreement or are discretionary, if incurred they are to be recognized in the period in which the reporting entity makes the accounting change, which is 2013 in the example above.

Impracticability exception. All prior periods presented in the financial statements are required to be adjusted for the retroactive application of the newly adopted accounting principle, unless it is impracticable to do so (ASC 250-10-45-9). FASB recognizes that there are certain circumstances when there is a change in accounting principle when it will not be feasible to compute (1) the retroactive adjustment to the prior periods affected or (2) the period-specific adjustments relative to periods presented in the financial statements presented.

For management to assert that it is impracticable to retrospectively apply the new accounting principle, one or more of the following conditions must be present:

1. Management has made a reasonable effort to determine the retrospective adjustment and is unable to do so.
2. If it were to apply the new accounting principle retrospectively, management would be required to make assumptions regarding its intent in a prior period that would not be able to be independently substantiated.
3. If it were to apply the new accounting principle retrospectively, management would be required to make significant estimates of amounts for which it is impossible to develop objective information that would have been available at the time the original financial statements for the prior period (or periods) were issued to provide evidence of circumstances that existed at that time regarding the amounts to be measured, recognized, and/or disclosed by retrospective application.

Inability to determine period-specific effects. If management is able to determine the adjustment to beginning retained earnings for the cumulative effect of applying the new accounting principle to periods prior to those presented in the financial statements, but is unable to determine the period-specific effects of the change on all of the prior periods presented in the financial statements, ASC 250-10-45-6 requires the following steps to adopt the new accounting principle:

1. Adjust the carrying amounts of the assets and liabilities for the cumulative effect of applying the new accounting principle at the beginning of the earliest period presented for which it is practicable to make the computation.
2. Any offsetting adjustment required by applying Step 1 is made to beginning retained earnings (or other applicable components of equity or net assets) of that period.

Inability to determine effects on any prior periods. If it is impracticable to determine the cumulative effect of adoption of the new accounting principle on any prior periods, ASC 250-10-45-7 requires that the new principle be applied prospectively as of the earliest date that it is practicable to do so. The most common example of this occurs when management of a reporting entity decides to change its inventory costing assumption from first-in, first-out (FIFO) to last-in, first-out (LIFO), as illustrated in the following example:

Example of change from FIFO to LIFO

During 20X3 Warady Inc. decided to change the method used for pricing its inventories from FIFO to LIFO. The inventory values are as listed below using both FIFO and LIFO methods. Sales for the year were $15,000,000 and the company's total purchases were $11,000,000. Other expenses were $1,200,000 for the year. The company had 1,000,000 shares of common stock outstanding throughout the year.

Inventory values

	FIFO	*LIFO*	*Difference*
12/31/X2 Base year	$ 2,000,000	$2,000,000	$ –
12/31X3	4,000,000	1,800,000	2,200,000
Variation	$ 2,000,000	$ (200,000)	$ 2,200,000

The computations for 20X3 would be as follows:

	FIFO	*LIFO*	*Difference*
Sales	$15,000,000	$15,000,000	$ –
Cost of goods sold			
Beginning inventory	2,000,000	2,000,000	–
Purchases	11,000,000	11,000,000	–
Goods available for sale	13,000,000	13,000,000	–
Ending inventory	4,000,000	1,800,000	2,200,000
	9,000,000	11,200,000	(2,200,000)
Gross profit	6,000,000	3,800,000	2,200,000
Other expenses	1,200,000	1,200,000	–
Net income	$ 4,800,000	$ 2,600,000	$2,200,000

The following is an example of the required disclosure in this circumstance:

Example Note A: Change in method of accounting for inventories

During 20X3, management changed the company's method of accounting for all of its inventories from first-in, first-out (FIFO) to last-in, first-out (LIFO). The change was made because management believes that the LIFO method provides a better matching of costs and revenues. In addition, with the adoption of LIFO, the company's inventory pricing method is consistent with the method predominant in the industry. The change and its effect on net income ($000 omitted except for per share amounts) and earnings per share for 20X3 are as follows:

	Net income	*Earnings per share*
Net income before the change	$4,800	$4.80
Reduction of net income due to the change	2,200	2.20
Net income as adjusted	$2,600	$2.60

Management has not retrospectively applied this change to prior years' financial statements because beginning inventory on January 1, 20X3, using LIFO is the same as the amount reported on a FIFO basis at December 31, 20X2. As a result of this change, the current period's financial statements are not comparable with those of any prior periods. The FIFO cost of inventories exceeds the carrying amount valued using LIFO by $2,200,000 at December 31, 20X3.

Disclosure of Prospective Changes in GAAP

Disclosing the impact of newly established GAAP that has not yet become effective. The accounting principles used in the reporting entity's financial statements may comply with GAAP as of the reporting date, but those principles may become unacceptable at a specified future date due to the issuance of a new accounting standard that is not yet effective. If the new GAAP, when adopted, is expected to materially affect the future financial statements, it is necessary to inform the users of the current financial statements about the future change. The objective of such a disclosure is to ensure that the financial statements are not misleading and that the users are provided adequate information to assess the significance of adopting the new GAAP on the reporting entity's future financial statements.

In some cases, the effect of the future change will be so pervasive as to necessitate the presentation of pro forma financial data to supplement the historical financial statements. The pro forma data would present the effects of the future adoption as if it had occurred at the date of the statement of financial position. The pro forma data may be presented in a column next to the historical data, in the notes to the financial statements, or separately accompanying the basic historical financial statements. Disclosure may also be needed of other future effects that may be triggered by the adoption of the new GAAP, such as adverse effects on the reporting entity's compliance with its debt covenants.

The best source of guidance in determining the form and content of these disclosures is ASC 250-10-S99. While this guidance is applicable to public companies, it also can be interpreted to apply to nonpublic companies as "practices that are widely recognized and prevalent." Under this requirement management is to disclose:

1. A brief description of the new standard.
2. The date the reporting entity is required to adopt the new standard.
3. If the new standard permits early adoption and the reporting entity plans to do so, the date that the planned adoption will occur.
4. The method of adoption that management expects to use. If this determination has not yet been made, then a description of the alternative methods of adoption that are permitted by the new standard.
5. The impact that the new standard will have on reported financial position and results of operations. If management has quantified the impact, then it is to disclose the estimated amount. If management has not yet determined the impact or if the impact is not expected to be material, this is to be disclosed.

The SEC staff also encourages the following additional disclosures:

1. The potential impact of adoption on such matters as loan covenant compliance, planned or intended changes in business practices, changes in availability of or cost of capital, and the like.
2. Newly issued standards that are not expected to materially affect the reporting entity should nevertheless be disclosed with an accompanying statement that adoption is not expected to have a material effect on the reporting entity.
3. When the newly issued standard only affects disclosure and the future disclosures are expected to be significantly different from the current disclosures, it is desirable to provide the reader with details.

Proposed GAAP. There is no requirement under GAAP or under SEC rules to disclose the potential effects of standards that have been proposed but not yet issued. If management wishes to voluntarily disclose information that it believes will provide the financial statement users with useful, meaningful information, the SEC provides guidance (§501.11 of the Codification of Financial Reporting Policies) on how to present this information, either in narrative form or as pro forma information, in a manner that "is reasonable, balanced and not misleading." In its guidance, the SEC notes that it may be reasonable to cover only those proposals where, based on the standard setter's published agenda, adoption appears imminent. When management chooses to make these disclosures, the disclosures should:

1. Provide a brief description of the proposed standard.
2. Explain the purpose of the disclosures, the basis of presentation, and any significant assumptions made in preparing them.
3. Discuss, in a balanced manner:

    a. The positive and negative effects of applying the proposed standard,
    b. The effects the proposed standard would have had on prior results of operations,
    c. The potential effects of the proposed standard on future periods,
    d. The effects that can be quantified, and
    e. The effects, if any, that cannot be quantified.

4. Address the entire proposed standard, not just certain aspects of it.
5. Limit any disclosures that quantify the effects of the proposed standard to covering only the most recent fiscal year.

6. Warn the readers that the final standard, when and if issued, could differ from the proposal that was used as a basis for these disclosures and that, as a result, the actual application of any final standard could result in effects different than those disclosed.
7. If necessary for a fair and balanced presentation, provide information regarding more than one proposed standard. There is a risk to the reporting entity that the disclosure may appear to be incomplete or misleading if it discusses the effects of one significant proposed standard but not another.

Reclassifications

Occasionally, a company will choose to change the way it applies an accounting principle, resulting in a change in the way that a particular financial statement caption is displayed or in the individual general ledger accounts that comprise a caption. These reclassifications may occur for a variety of reasons, including:

1. In management's judgment, the revised methodology more accurately reflects the economics of a type or class of transaction.
2. An amount that was immaterial in previous periods and combined with another number has become material and warrants presentation as a separately captioned line item.
3. Due to changes in the business or the manner in which the financial statements are used to make decisions, management deems a different form of presentation to be more useful or informative.

To maintain comparability of financial statements when such changes are made, the financial statements of all periods presented must be reclassified to conform to the new presentation.

Such reclassifications, which usually affect only the statement of income, do not affect reported net income or retained earnings for any period since they result in simply recasting amounts that were previously reported. Normally a reclassification will result in an increase in one or more reported numbers with a corresponding decrease in one or more other numbers. In addition, these changes reflect changes in the application of accounting principles either for which there are multiple alternative treatments, or for which GAAP is silent and thus management has discretion in presentation.

Reclassifications are not explicitly dealt with in GAAP but nevertheless do commonly occur in practice. The following examples are adapted from actual notes that appeared in the summary of significant accounting policies of publicly held companies:

Example 1

Effective January 1, 20X3, the company removed the impact of intellectual property income, gains and losses on sales and other-than-temporary declines in market value of certain investments, realized gains and losses on certain real estate activity, and foreign currency transaction gains and losses from the caption "Selling, General and Administrative Expenses" in the Consolidated Statement of Income. Custom development income was also removed from the "Research, Development, and Engineering" caption on the Consolidated Statement of Income. Intellectual property and custom development income are now presented in a separate caption in the Consolidated Statement of Income. The other items listed above are now included as part of "Other Income and Expense." Results of prior periods have been reclassified to conform to the current year presentation.

Example 2

Effective January 1, 20X3, management has elected to reclassify certain expenses in its consolidated statements of income. Costs of the order entry function and certain accounting and information technology services have been reclassified from cost of sales to selling, general, and administrative expense. Costs related to order fulfillment have been reclassified from selling, general, and administrative expense to cost of sales. These reclassifications resulted in a decrease to cost of sales and an increase to selling, general, and administrative expense of $31.8 million, and $36.2 million for the years ended December 31, 20X2 and 20X1, respectively.

Change in Accounting Estimate

The preparation of financial statements requires frequent use of estimates for such items as asset service lives, salvage values, lease residuals, asset impairments, collectability of accounts receivable, warranty costs, pension costs, and the like. Future conditions and events that affect these estimates cannot be estimated with certainty. Therefore, changes in estimates will be inevitable as new information and more experience is obtained. ASC 250-10-45-17 requires that changes in estimates be recognized currently and prospectively. The effect of the change in accounting estimate is accounted for in "(a) the period of change if the change affects that period only or (b) the period of change and future periods if the change affects both." The reporting entity is precluded from retrospective application, restatement of prior periods, or presentation of pro forma amounts as a result of a change in accounting estimate.

Example of a change in accounting estimate

On January 1, 20X1, a machine purchased for $10,000 was originally estimated to have a ten-year useful life and a salvage value of $1,000. On January 1, 20X5 (five years later), the asset is expected to last another ten years and have a salvage value of $800. As a result, both the current period (the year ending December 31, 20X1) and subsequent periods are affected by the change. Annual depreciation expense over the estimated remaining useful life is computed as follows:

Original cost	$10,000
Less estimated salvage (residual) value	(1,000)
Depreciable amount	9,000
Accumulated depreciation, based on original assumptions (10-year life)	
20X1	900
20X2	900
20X3	900
20X4	900
20X5	900
	4,500
Carrying value at 1/1/20X6	5,500
Revised estimate of salvage value	(800)
Depreciable amount	4,700
Remaining useful life at 1/1/20X6	10 years
	$ 470 depreciation per year
Effect on 20X6 net income	$470 – $900 = $430 increase

Example Note A: Change in accounting estimate

During 20X6, management assessed its estimates of the useful lives and residual values of the Company's machinery and equipment. Management revised its original estimates and currently estimates that its production equipment acquired in 20X1 and originally estimated to have a 10-year useful life and a residual value of $1,000 will have a 15-year useful life and a residual value of $800. The effects of reflecting this change in accounting estimate on the 2018 financial statements are as follows:

Increase in	
Income from continuing operations and net income	$430.00
Earnings per share (for public companies)*	$ 0.02

* *Assuming 25,000 shares were outstanding for all of 2018*

Example of a change in accounting estimate

The industry in which ABC Company operates suffers a significant downturn, resulting in a decline in the financial condition of its customers and a noticeable worsening of the days required to collect its accounts receivable. ABC had formerly provided an amount equal to 2% of its credit sales as an increment to the bad debt allowance, resulting in a current balance in the allowance of $105,000. However, the new economic conditions mandate an immediate change to a 4% allowance. Accordingly, ABC provides an additional $105,000 in the current period to increase the previously recorded allowance to meet the new 4% estimate, and also begins providing 4% in the bad debt allowance on all new credit sales. Both of these adjustments are reflected in current period expense, even though the increased allowance on existing receivables pertains to sales made (in part) in a prior reporting period, because the change in estimate was made in the current period based on new circumstances that arose in that period—specifically, the declining credit standing of its customers.

Accounting for long-term construction contracts under the percentage-of-completion method necessarily involves ongoing revisions to estimates of total contract revenue, total contract cost, and extent of progress toward project completion. These revisions represent changes in accounting estimate and, in accordance with ASC 605-35, the change in estimate is accounted for using the cumulative catch-up method. This is applied by

1. Computing the percentage of completion, earned revenues, cost of earned revenues, and gross profit on a contract-to-date basis at the date of the statement of financial position using the reporting entity's consistently applied accounting policy for the contract and reflecting the revised estimates.
2. Reflecting in the current period's earned revenue and cost of earned revenue the difference between the newly computed contract-to-date results computed in item 1 and those amounts recognized in previous periods.

This approach results in the effect of the change in accounting estimate being reflected in the current period statement of income, and prospectively accounting for the contract using the revised assumptions.

Note that an impairment of a long-lived asset, as described by ASC 360-10-35, is not a change in accounting estimate. Rather, it is an event that is to be treated as an operating expense of the period in which it is recognized, in effect as additional depreciation. (See further discussion in chapter in this volume on ASC 360.)

Change in Accounting Estimate Effected by a Change in Accounting Principle

To change certain accounting estimates, management must adopt a new accounting principle or change the method it uses to apply an accounting principle. In contemplating such a change, management would not be able to separately determine the effects of changing the accounting principle from the effects of changing its estimate. The change in estimate is accomplished by changing the method.

Under ASC 250-10-45-18, a change in accounting estimate that is effected by a change in accounting principle is accounted for in the same manner as a change in accounting estimate, that is, prospectively in the current and future periods affected. However, because management is changing the company's accounting principle or method of applying it, the new accounting principle, as previously discussed, must be preferable to the accounting principle being superseded.

Management may decide, for example, to change its depreciation method for certain types of assets from straight-line to an accelerated method, such as double-declining balance to recognize the fact that those assets are more productive in their earlier years of service because they require less downtime and do not require repairs as frequently. Such a change is permitted by ASC 250-10-45-19 only if management justifies it based on the fact that using the new method is preferable to the old one, in this case because it more accurately matches the costs of production to periods in which the units are produced.

A distinction is made in ASC 250-10-45-20, however, for entities that elect to apply a depreciation method that results in accelerated depreciation until the point during the useful life of the depreciable asset when it is useful to change to straight-line depreciation in order to fully depreciate the asset over the remaining term. At this point, the remaining carrying value (net book value) is depreciated using the straight-line method over its remaining useful life. ASC 250 provides that, if this method is consistently followed by the reporting entity, the changeover to straight-line depreciation is not considered to be an accounting change.

Change in Reporting Entity

An accounting change resulting in financial statements that are, in effect, of a different reporting entity than previously reported on, is retrospectively applied to the financial statements of all prior periods presented in order to show financial information for the new reporting entity for all periods (ASC 250-10-45-21). The change is also retrospectively applied to previously issued interim financial information.

The following qualify as changes in reporting entity:

1. Consolidated or combined financial statements in place of individual entities' statements
2. A change in the members of the group of subsidiaries that comprise the consolidated financial statements
3. A change in the companies included in combined financial statements.

Specifically *excluded* from qualifying as a change in reporting entity are:

1. A business combination accounted for by the purchase method and
2. Consolidation of a variable interest entity under ASC 810.

Error Corrections

Errors are sometimes discovered after financial statements have been issued. Errors result from mathematical mistakes, mistakes in the application of GAAP, or the oversight or misuse of facts known or available to the accountant at the time the financial statements were prepared. Errors can occur in recognition, measurement, presentation, or disclosure. A change from an unacceptable (or incorrect) accounting principle to a correct principle is also considered a correction of an error and not a change in accounting principle. Such a change should not be confused with the preferability determination discussed earlier that involves two or more acceptable principles. An error correction pertains to the recognition that a previously used method was not an acceptable method at the time it was employed.

The essential distinction between a change in estimate and the correction of an error depends upon the availability of information. An estimate requires revision because by its nature it is based upon incomplete information. Later data will either confirm or contradict the estimate and any contradiction will require revision of the estimate. An error results from the misuse of existing information available at the time which is discovered at a later date. However, this discovery is not as a result of additional information or subsequent developments.

ASC 250 specifies that, when correcting an error in prior period financial statements, the term "restatement" is to be used. That term is exclusively reserved for this purpose so as to effectively communicate to users of the financial statements the reason for a particular change in previously issued financial statements.

Restatement consists of the following steps:

Step 1 Adjust the carrying amounts of assets and liabilities at the beginning of the first period presented in the financial statements for the cumulative effect of correcting the error on periods prior to those presented in the financial statements.

Step 2 Offset the effect of the adjustment in Step 1 (if any) by adjusting the opening balance of retained earnings (or other components of equity or net assets, as applicable to the reporting entity) for that period.

Step 3 Adjust the financial statements of each individual prior period presented for the effects of correcting the error on that specific period (referred to as the period-specific effects of the error).

Example of a prior period adjustment

Assume that Truesdell Company had overstated its depreciation expense by $50,000 in 20X0 and $40,000 in 20X2, both due to mathematical mistakes. The errors affected both the financial statements and the income tax returns in 20X1 and 20X2 and are discovered in 20X3.

Truesdell's statements of financial position and statements of income and retained earnings as of and for the year ended December 31, 20X2, prior to the restatement were as follows:

Truesdell Company
Statement of Income and Retained Earnings
Prior to Restatement
Year Ended December 31, 20X2

	20X2
Sales	$2,000,000
Cost of sales	
Depreciation	750,000
Other	390,000
	1,140,000
Gross profit	860,000
Selling, general, and administrative expenses	450,000
Income from operations	410,000
Other income (expense)	10,000
Income before income taxes	420,000
Income taxes	168,000
Net income	252,000
Retained earnings, beginning of year	6,463,000
Dividends	(1,200,000)
Retained earnings, end of year	$5,515,000

Truesdell Company
Statement of Financial Position
Prior to Restatement
December 31, 20X2

	20X12
Assets	
Current assets	$2,540,000
Property and equipment	
Cost	3,500,000
Accumulated depreciation and amortization	(430,000)
	3,070,000
Total assets	$5,610,000
Liabilities and stockholders' equity	
Income taxes payable	$ –
Other current liabilities	12,000
Total current liabilities	12,000
Noncurrent liabilities	70,000
Total liabilities	82,000
Stockholders' equity	
Common stock	13,000
Retained earnings	5,515,000
Total stockholders' equity	5,528,000
Total liabilities and stockholders' equity	$5,610,000

The following steps are followed to restate Truesdell's prior period financial statements:

Step 1 Adjust the carrying amounts of assets and liabilities at the beginning of the first period presented in the financial statements for the cumulative effect of correcting the error on periods prior to those presented in the financial statements.

The first period presented in the financial statements is 2012. At the beginning of that year, $50,000 of the mistakes had been made and reflected on both the income tax return and financial statements. Assuming a flat 40% income tax rate and ignoring the effects of penalties and interest that would be assessed on the amended income tax returns, the following adjustment would be made to assets and liabilities at January 1, 20X2:

Decrease in accumulated depreciation	$50,000
Increase in income taxes payable	(20,000)
	$30,000

Step 2 Offset the effect of the adjustment in Step 1 by adjusting the opening balance of retained earnings (or other components of equity or net assets, as applicable to the reporting entity) for that period.

Retained earnings at the beginning of 20X2 will increase by $30,000 as the offsetting entry resulting from Step 1.

Step 3 Adjust the financial statements of each individual prior period presented for the effects of correcting the error on that specific period (referred to as the period-specific effects of the error).

The 20X2 prior period financial statements will be corrected for the period-specific effects of the restatement as follows:

Decrease in depreciation expense and accumulated depreciation	$40,000
Increase in income tax expense and income taxes payable	(16,000)
Increase 2012 net income	$24,000

The restated financial statements are presented below.

Truesdell Company
Statements of Income and Retained Earnings
As Restated
Years Ended December 31, 20X3 and 20X2

	20X3	*20X2 restated*
Sales	$2,100,000	$2,000,000
Cost of sales		
Depreciation	740,000	710,000
Other	410,000	390,000
	1,150,000	1,100,000
Gross profit	950,000	900,000
Selling, general, and administrative expenses	460,000	450,000
Income from operations	490,000	450,000
Other income (expense)	(5,000)	10,000
Income before income taxes	485,000	460,000
Income taxes	200,000	184,000
Net income	285,000	276,000
Retained earnings, beginning of year, as originally reported	5,569,000	6,463,000
Restatement to reflect correction of depreciation (Note X)	–	30,000
Retained earnings, beginning of year, as restated	5,569,000	6,493,000
Dividends	(800,000)	(1,200,000)
Retained earnings, end of year	$5,054,000	$5,569,000

Truesdell Company
Statements of Financial Position
As Restated
December 31, 20X3 and 20X2

	20X3	*20X2 restated*
Assets		
Current assets	$2,840,000	$2,540,000
Property and equipment		
Cost	3,750,000	3,500,000
Accumulated depreciation and amortization	(1,050,000)	(340,000)
	2,700,000	3,160,000
Total assets	$5,540,000	$5,700,000
Liabilities and stockholders' equity		
Income taxes payable	$50,000	$ 36,000
Other current liabilities	110,000	12,000
Total current liabilities	160,000	48,000
Noncurrent liabilities	313,000	70,000
Total liabilities	473,000	118,000
Stockholders' equity		
Common stock	13,000	13,000
Retained earnings	5,054,000	5,569,000
Total stockholders' equity	5,067,000	5,582,000
Total liabilities and stockholders' equity	$5,540,000	$5,700,000

When restating previously issued financial statements, management is to disclose

1. The fact that the financial statements have been restated
2. The nature of the error
3. The effect of the restatement on each line item in the financial statements
4. The cumulative effect of the restatement on retained earnings (or other applicable components of equity or net assets)
    a. At the beginning of the earliest period presented in comparative financial statements, or
    b. At the beginning of the period in single-period financial statements
5. The effect on net income, both gross and net of income taxes
    a. For each prior period presented in comparative financial statements or
    b. For the period immediately preceding the period presented in single-period financial statements
6. For public companies (or others electing to report earnings per share data), the effect of the restatement on affected per-share amounts for each prior period presented.

These disclosures need not be repeated in subsequent periods.

The correction of an error in the financial statements of a prior period discovered subsequent to their issuance is reported as a prior period adjustment in the financial statements of the subsequent period.

Evaluating Uncorrected Misstatements

Misstatements, particularly if detected after the financial statements have been produced and distributed, may under certain circumstances be left uncorrected. This decision is directly impacted by judgments about materiality, an important concept discussed in Chapter 1. The financial statement preparer is expected to exercise professional judgment in determining the level of materiality to apply in order to cost-effectively prepare full, complete, and accurate financial statements in a timely manner. However, there have been instances where the materiality concept has been used to rationalize the noncorrection of errors that should have been dealt with, and indeed even to excuse errors known when first committed. The fact that the concept of materiality has sometimes been abused led to the promulgation of further guidance relative to error corrections.

Although independent auditors are charged with obtaining sufficient evidence to enable them to provide the financial statement user with reasonable assurance that management's financial statements are free of material misstatement, the financial statements are primarily the responsibility of the preparers. Certain auditing literature is therefore germane to the preparers' consideration of matters such as error corrections and application of materiality guidelines. These matters are further explored in the following paragraphs.

Types of misstatements. Preparers of financial statements need to have control procedures to reduce the risk of accounting errors being committed and not detected. From the auditors' perspective, it is required that the examination be conducted in a manner that will provide reasonable assurance of detecting material misstatements, including those resulting from errors. Known misstatements arise from:

1. Incorrect selection or application of accounting principles
2. Errors in gathering, processing, summarizing, interpreting, or overlooking relevant data
3. An intent to mislead the financial statement user to influence their decisions
4. To conceal theft.

Likely misstatements arise from

1. Differences in judgment between management and the auditor regarding accounting estimates where the amount presented in the financial statements is outside the range of what the auditor believes is reasonable
2. Amounts that the auditor has projected based on the results of performing statistical or nonstatistical sampling procedures on a population.

Management, in assessing the impact of uncorrected misstatements, is required to assess materiality both quantitatively and qualitatively from the standpoint of whether a financial statement user would be misled if a misstatement were not corrected or if, in the case of informative disclosure errors, full disclosure was not made. Qualitative considerations include (but are not limited to) whether the misstatement

1. Arose from estimates or from items capable of precise measurement and, if the misstatement arose from an estimate, the degree of precision inherent in the estimation process
2. Masks a change in earnings or other trends
3. Hides a failure to meet analysts' consensus expectations for the reporting entity
4. Changes a loss to income or vice versa
5. Concerns a segment or other portion of the reporting entity's business that has been identified as playing a significant role in operations or profitability

6. Affects compliance with loan covenants or other contractual commitments
7. Increases management's compensation by affecting a performance measure used as a basis for computing it
8. Involves concealment of an unlawful transaction.

Misstatements from prior years. Management may have decided to not correct misstatements that occurred in one or more prior years because, in their judgment at the time, the financial statements were not materially misstated. Two methods of making that materiality assessment—sometimes referred to as the "rollover" and the "iron curtain" methods—have been widely used in practice. These are described and illustrated in the following paragraphs.

The *rollover method* quantifies a misstatement as its originating or reversing effect on the *current period's* statement of income, irrespective of the potential effect on the statement of financial position of one or more prior periods' accumulated uncorrected misstatements.

The *iron curtain method,* on the other hand, quantifies a misstatement based on the *accumulated uncorrected amount* included in the current, end-of-period statement of financial position, irrespective of the year (or years) in which the misstatement originated.

Each of these methods, when considered separately, has strengths and weaknesses, as follows:

Method	*Focuses on*	*Strength*	*Weakness*
Rollover	Current period income statement	Focuses on whether the income statement of the current period is materially misstated, assuming that the statement of financial position is not materially misstated	Material misstatement of the statement of financial position can accumulate over multiple periods
Iron curtain	End of period statement of financial position	Focuses on ensuring that the statement of financial position is not materially misstated, irrespective of the year or years in which a misstatement originated	Does not consider whether the effect of correcting a statement of financial position misstatement that arose in one or more periods is material to the current period income statement

Guidance for SEC registrants. The SEC staff issued, Staff Accounting Bulletin (SAB) 108, *Considering the Effects of Prior Year Misstatements in Current Year Financial Statements,* to address how registrants (i.e., publicly held corporation) are to evaluate misstatements. SAB 108 prescribes that if a misstatement is material to *either* the income statement or the statement of financial position, it is to be corrected in a manner set forth in the bulletin and illustrated in the example and diagram below.

Example

Lenny Payne, the CFO of Flamingo Industries, is preparing the company's 20X3 financial statements. The company has consistently overstated its accrued liabilities by following a policy of accruing the entire audit fee it will pay its independent auditors for auditing the financial statements for the reporting year, even though approximately 80% of the work is performed in, and is thus an expense of, the following year.

Due to regular increases in audit fees, the overstatement of liabilities at 12/31/20X5 has accumulated as follows:

Year ended 12/31	*Amount of misstatement originating during year*	*End-of-year accumulated misstatement*
20X1	$15	$15
20X2	5	20
20X3	5	25
20X4	5	30
20X5	10	40

Lenny has consistently used the rollover approach to assess materiality and, in all previous years, had judged the amount of the misstatement that originated during that year to be immaterial. The guidance in SAB 108 is illustrated in the following decision diagram:

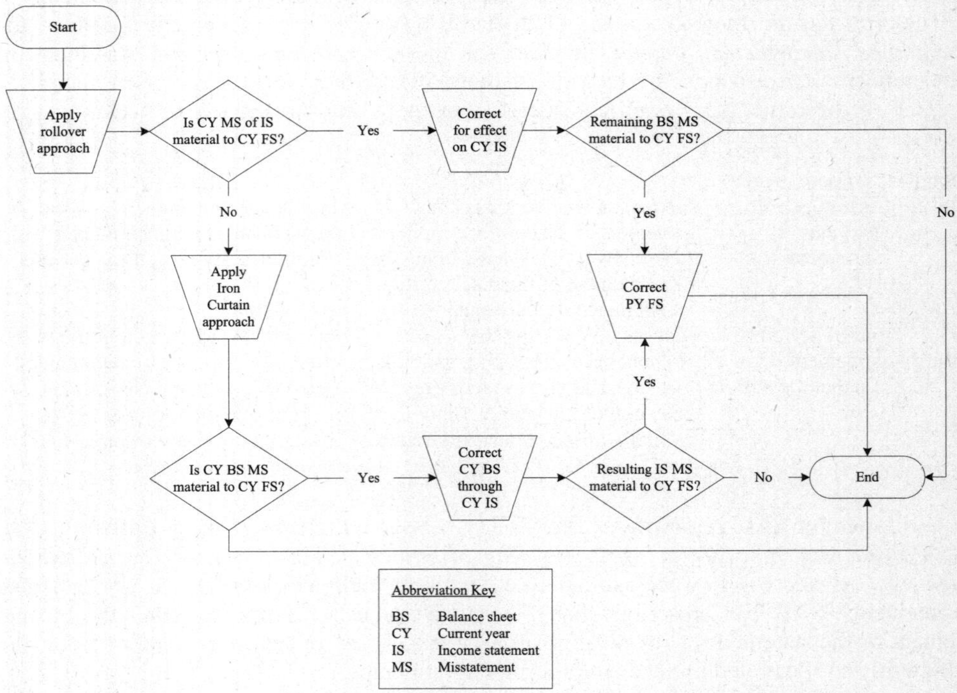

Following the decision tree, Lenny analyzes the misstatement as follows:

1. Applying the *rollover* approach, as he had done consistently in the past, Lenny computes the misstatement as the $10 that originated in 20X5. In his judgment, this amount is immaterial to the 20X5 income statement.
2. Applying the *iron curtain* approach, Lenny evaluates whether the accumulated misstatement of $40 materially misstates the statement of financial position at 12/31/20X5. Lenny believes that, considering both quantitative and qualitative factors, the misstatement has grown to the point where it does result in a materially misstated statement of financial position.

According to SAB 108 and as shown on the diagram, Lenny would record an adjustment to correct the statement of financial position as follows:

	Debit	Credit
Accrued professional fees	40,000	
Professional fees (general and administrative expenses)		40,000

To correct statement of financial position by reversing misstated accrual for audit fees not yet incurred.

Upon review of the effect of the correcting entry, Lenny believes that recording the entry will result in a material misstatement to the 20X5 income statement. Consequently, to avoid this result, the prior years' financial statements of Flamingo Industries would, under normal circumstances, be required to be restated as previously discussed in the section of this chapter titled "Error Corrections." This would be the case even if the adjustment to the prior year financial statements was, and continues to be, immaterial to those financial statements. The SEC would not, however, require Flamingo Industries to amend previously filed reports; instead, registrants are permitted to make the correction in the next filing submitted to the SEC that includes the prior year financial statements.

If the cumulative effect adjustment occurs in an interim period other than the first interim period, the SEC waived the requirement that previously filed interim reports for that fiscal year be amended. Instead, comparative information presented for interim periods of the first year subsequent to initial application are to be adjusted to reflect the cumulative effect adjustment as of the beginning of the fiscal year of initial application. The adjusted results are also required to be included in the disclosures of selected quarterly information that are required by Regulation S-K, Item 302.

Entities that do not meet the criteria to use the cumulative effect adjustment are required to follow the provisions of ASC 250 that require restatement of all prior periods presented in the filing.

Interim Reporting Considerations

If a change in accounting principle is made in an interim period, the change is made using the same methodology for retrospective application discussed and illustrated earlier in this chapter. Management is precluded from using the impracticability exception to avoid retrospective application to prechange interim periods of the same fiscal year in which the change is made. Thus, if it is impracticable to apply the change to those prechange interim periods, the change can only be made as of the beginning of the following fiscal year. FASB believes this situation will rarely occur in practice.

ASC 270 requires that interim financial reports disclose any changes in accounting principles or the methods of applying them from those that were employed in:

1. The prior fiscal year;
2. The comparable interim period of the prior fiscal year; and
3. The preceding interim periods of the current fiscal year.

The disclosures required by ASC 250 for changes in accounting principle are to be made, in full, in the financial statements of the interim period in which the change is made.

Public companies. When a public company adopts a new standard in an interim period, the ASC 270 disclosures cited above are to be supplemented, as applicable, with all disclosures required by the newly adopted standard to be included in annual financial statements. If the change is made in a period other than the first quarter, prior filings are not required to be amended; however, adjustment of each prior quarter's results is to be included in the filing for the quarter in which the new principle is being adopted. If the newly adopted standard requires retrospective application to all prior periods, the prior interim quarters are also to be presented on an adjusted basis.

In addition, a special disclosure rule applies to a public company that

1. Changes accounting principles in the fourth quarter of a fiscal year;
2. Regularly reports interim financial information; and
3. Does not separately disclose in its annual report (or in a separate report) the minimum summarized information required by ASC 270 for the fourth quarter of the fiscal year.

When all three of these conditions are present, management is required to disclose in a note to the annual financial statements the effects of the change on interim period results.

Going concern considerations. Financial statements prepared in accordance with GAAP presume that the reporting entity is expected to remain in operation for the foreseeable future. This "going concern" assumption is important, since in its absence many accounting conventions and practices (e.g., depreciation of long-lived assets over expected economic lives) would not be sensible, as the ability to realize the economic benefits of such assets would be in doubt.

US auditing standards have long required auditors to affirmatively evaluate whether there was substantial doubt about the ability of the reporting entity to continue as a going concern for a reasonable period following the date of the financial statements, but not for longer than one year from that date. When substantial doubt was found to exist, this was cited in the auditors' report, and the financial statements were required to include, as footnote disclosure, information about the reasons for such doubts, as well as about management's plans to cope with the circumstances. (When such informative disclosures were not provided by management, the auditors were generally required to qualify their opinions due to lack of adequate disclosure, notwithstanding inclusion of "going concern" language in the auditors' report itself.)

Other Sources

See ASC Location – Wiley *GAAP* Chapter…	***For information on…***
ASC 260-10-55-15 through 55-16	The effect of restatements expressed in per-share terms
ASC 323-10-45-1 through 45-2.	The classification of an investor's share of error corrections reported in the financial statements of the investee

10 ASC 255 CHANGING PRICES

PERSPECTIVE AND ISSUES

Subtopic

ASC 255, *Changing Prices,* contains one subtopic:

- ASC 255-10, *Overall,* that provides guidance on reporting the effects of changing prices or inflation

Scope

The topic applies to business entities that prepare US GAAP financial statements and "foreign entities that prepare financial statements in the currency for which the operations and that operate in countries with hyperinflationary economies."

The ASC disclosures are **encouraged**, but not required.

DEFINITIONS OF TERMS

Consumer Price Index for All Urban Consumers. An index of price level changes affecting consumers generally often used to measure changes in the general purchasing power of the monetary unit itself.

Current Cost-Constant Purchasing Power Accounting. A method of accounting based on measures of current cost or lower recoverable amount in units of currency, each of which has the same general purchasing power. For operations in which the dollar is the functional currency, the general purchasing power of the dollar is used and the Consumer Price Index for All Urban Consumers is the required measure of purchasing power. For operations in which the functional currency is other than the dollar, the general purchasing power of either the dollar or the functional currency is used (see paragraphs 255-10-50-45 through 50-47).

Fair Value. The price that would be received to sell an asset or paid to transfer a liability in an orderly transaction between market participants at the measurement date.

Historical Cost. The generally accepted method of accounting used in the primary financial statements that is based on measures of historical prices without restatement into units, each of which has the same general purchasing power.

Historical Cost-Constant Purchasing Power Accounting. A method of accounting based on measures of historical prices in units of a currency, each of which has the same general purchasing power.

Income from Continuing Operations. Income after applicable income taxes but excluding the results of discontinued operations, extraordinary items, the cumulative effect of accounting changes, translation adjustments, purchasing power gains and losses on monetary items, and increases and decreases in the current cost or lower recoverable amount of nonmonetary assets and liabilities.

Income-Producing Real Estate. Properties that meet all of the following criteria:

a. Cash flows can be directly associated with a long-term leasing agreement with unaffiliated parties.
b. The property is being operated. (It is not in a construction phase.)
c. Future cash flows from the property are reasonably estimable.
d. Ancillary services are not a significant part of the lease agreement.

Hotels, which have occupancy rates and related cash flows that may fluctuate to a relatively large extent, do not meet the criteria for income-producing real estate.

Mineral Resource Assets. Assets that are directly associated with and derive value from all minerals that are extracted from the earth. Such minerals include oil and gas, ores containing ferrous and nonferrous metals, coal, shale, geothermal steam, sulphur, salt, stone, phosphate, sand, and gravel. Mineral resource assets include mineral interests in properties, completed and uncompleted wells, and related equipment and facilities and other facilities required for purposes of extraction. This definition does not cover support equipment because that equipment is included in the property, plant, and equipment for which current cost measurements are required.

Monetary Assets. Money or a claim to receive a sum of money the amount of which is fixed or determinable without reference to future prices of specific goods or services.

Monetary Liability. An obligation to pay a sum of money the amount of which is fixed or determinable without reference to future prices of specific goods and services.

Motion Picture Films. All types of film, including feature films, television specials, television series, or similar products (including animated films and television programming) that are sold, licensed, or exhibited, whether produced on film, video tape, digital, or other video recording format.

Parity Adjustment. The effect of the difference between local and U.S. inflation for the year on net assets (that is, shareholders' equity) measured in nominal dollars. If only the differential rates of U.S. and local inflation are reflected in the exchange rates (parity), the parity adjustment, and the translation adjustment net to zero. Therefore, the sum of the parity adjustment and the translation adjustment represents the effect of exchange rate changes in excess of (or less than) that needed to maintain purchasing power parity between the functional currency and the dollar.

Probable Reserves. Probable reserves are reserves for which quantity and grade and/or quality are computed from information similar to that used for proven reserves, but the sites for inspection, sampling, and measurement are farther apart or are otherwise less adequately spaced. The degree of assurance, although lower than that for proven (measured) reserves, is high enough to assume continuity between points of observation.

Proven Reserves. Proven reserves are reserves for which both of the following conditions are met:

a. Quantity is computed from dimensions revealed in outcrops, trenches, workings, or drill holes; grade and/or quality are computed from the results of detailed sampling.

b. The sites for inspection, sampling, and measurement are spaced so closely and the geologic character is so well defined that size, shape, depth, and mineral content of reserves are well established.

Purchasing Power Gain or Loss. The net gain or loss determined by restating in units of constant purchasing power the opening and closing balances of, and transactions in, monetary assets and liabilities.

Recoverable Amount. Current worth of the net amount of cash expected to be recoverable from the use or sale of an asset.

Restate-Translate. An approach to converting current cost-nominal functional currency data of a foreign operation into units of constant purchasing power expressed in dollars. Using this approach, the current cost-nominal functional currency data are restated into units of constant purchasing power using a general price index for the foreign currency. After restatement into units of constant functional currency purchasing power, the current cost data are translated into dollars. This approach often necessitates a parity adjustment.

Translate-Restate. An approach to converting current cost-nominal functional currency data of a foreign operation into units of constant purchasing power expressed in dollars. Using this approach, the current cost-nominal functional currency data are first translated into dollars and then restated into units of constant purchasing power using the Consumer Price Index for All Urban Consumers.

Translation Adjustments. Translation adjustments result from the process of translating financial statements from the entity's functional currency into the reporting currency.

Value in Use. The amount determined by discounting the future cash flows (including the ultimate proceeds of disposal) expected to be derived from the use of an asset at an appropriate rate that allows for the risk of the activities concerned.

CONCEPTS, RULES, AND EXAMPLES

Elective Disclosures

Business entities are encouraged, but not required, to present supplementary information on the effects of changing prices. ASC 255-10-50-3 contains a list of items that should be disclosed in a five-year summary of financial data:

- Net sales and other operating revenues
- Income from continuing operations on a current cost basis
- Purchasing power gain or loss on net monetary items
- Increase or decrease in the current cost or lower recoverable amount of inventory and property, plant, and equipment, net of inflation
- The aggregate foreign currency translation adjustment on a current cost basis, if applicable
- Net assets at year-end on a current cost basis
- Income per common share from continuing operations on a current cost basis
- Cash dividends declared per common share
- Market price per common share at year-end.

In addition to the disclosures above, if income from continuing operations on a current cost-constant purchasing power basis would differ significantly from income from continuing operations in the primary financial statements, an entity should provide the following information (ASC 255-10-50-11 through 16):

- Components of income from continuing operations for the current year on a current cost basis, applying the same constant purchasing power option used for presentation of the five-year summary.
- Separate amounts for the current cost or lower recoverable amount at the end of the current year of inventory and property, plant, and equipment.
- Increase or decrease in current cost or lower recoverable amount before and after adjusting for the effects of inflation of inventory a property, plant, and equipment for the current year.
- Any differences between (1) the depreciation methods, estimates of useful lives, and salvage values of assets used for calculations of current cost-constant purchasing power and (2) the methods and estimates used for calculations of depreciation in the primary financial statements.

ASC 255 includes other elective disclosures related to entities with mineral resource assets. Entities that have elected to make ASC 255 disclosures should refer to the Codification for additional guidance.

Other Sources

See ASC 912-255-50-1 for guidance on supplementary information provided by federal government contractors on the effects of changing prices when calculating the purchasing power gain or loss on net monetary items.

11 ASC 260 EARNINGS PER SHARE

PERSPECTIVE AND ISSUES

Subtopic

ASC 260, *Earnings per Share,* consist of one subtopic:

- ASC 260-10, *Overall,* that provides the guidance for computation, presentation, and disclosure for earnings per share (EPS) for entities with publicly held common stock or potential common stock.

The subtopic also includes master limited partnership subsections that clarify the application to master limited partnership of the Other Presentation Matters subsection.

Scope and Scope Exceptions

ASC 260 applies to all entities whose common stock or potential common stock is traded in a public market or who have made a filing or are in the process of making a filing to trade their stock publicly. If an entity that is not required to report under ASC 260 chooses to provide EPS information, the entity must comply with the ASC 260 guidance.

The guidance does not apply to investment companies who comply with ASC 946 or in statements of wholly owned subsidiaries.

Overview

Earnings per share (EPS) is an indicator widely used by investors to gauge the profitability of a corporation. Its purpose is to indicate how effective an enterprise has been in using the resources provided by its common stockholders. In its simplest form, EPS is net income (loss) divided by the weighted average number of shares of outstanding common stock. The EPS computation becomes more complex with the existence of securities that are not common stock but have the potential of causing additional shares of common stock to be issued to dilute EPS upon conversion or exercise (e.g., convertible preferred stock, convertible debt, options, and warrants). Diluted EPS considers the potential dilution that could occur from other financial instruments that would increase the total number of outstanding shares of common stock. Omission of an EPS number that takes into account the potential dilutive effects of such securities would be misleading. In addition, a lack of standardization in the way in which these securities are included in such an EPS computation would make comparisons among corporations extremely difficult.

Publicly traded corporations with a complex capital structure are obligated to report basic EPS and diluted EPS. The dual presentation is required on the face of the corporation's income statement even if both of these computations result in the same EPS amount. In addition, a reconciliation of the numerator and the denominator of the basic EPS computation to the numerator and denominator of the diluted EPS computation is required.

DEFINITIONS OF TERMS

Source: ASC 260-10-20, *Glossary*

Antidilution. An increase in earnings per share amounts or a decrease in loss per share amounts.

Basic Earnings Per Share. The amount of earnings for the period available to each share of common stock outstanding during the reporting period.

Call Option. A contract that allows the holder to buy a specified quantity of stock from the writer of the contract at a fixed price for a given period. See Option and Purchased Call Option.

Common Stock. A stock that is subordinate to all other stock of the issuer. Also called common shares.

Consolidated Financial Statements. The financial statements of a consolidated group of entities that include a parent and all its subsidiaries presented as those of a single economic entity.

Consolidated Group. A parent and all its subsidiaries.

Contingent Issuance. A possible issuance of shares of common stock that is dependent on the satisfaction of certain conditions.

Contingent Stock Agreement. An agreement to issue common stock (usually in connection with a business combination) that is dependent on the satisfaction of certain conditions. See Contingently Issuable Shares.

Contingently Convertible Instruments. Contingently convertible instruments are instruments that have embedded conversion features that are contingently convertible or exercisable based on either of the following:

a. A market price trigger
b. Multiple contingencies if one of the contingencies is a market price trigger and the instrument can be converted or share settled based on meeting the specified market condition.

A market price trigger is a market condition that is based at least in part on the issuer's own share price. Examples of contingently convertible instruments include contingently convertible debt, contingently convertible preferred stock, and the instrument described by paragraph 260-10-45-43, all with embedded market price triggers.

Contingently Issuable Shares. Shares issuable for little or no cash consideration upon the satisfaction of certain conditions pursuant to a contingent stock agreement. Also called contingently issuable stock. See Contingent Stock Agreement.

Conversion Rate. The ratio of the number of common shares issuable upon conversion to a unit of a convertible security. For example, $100 face value of debt convertible into 5 shares of common stock would have a conversion ratio of 5:1. Also called conversion ratio.

Convertible Security. A security that is convertible into another security based on a conversion rate. For example, convertible preferred stock that is convertible into common stock on a two-for-one basis (two shares of common for each share of preferred).

Diluted Earnings Per Share. The amount of earnings for the period available to each share of common stock outstanding during the reporting period and to each share that would have been outstanding assuming the issuance of common shares for all dilutive potential common shares outstanding during the reporting period.

Dilution. A reduction in EPS resulting from the assumption that convertible securities were converted, that options or warrants were exercised, or that other shares were issued upon the satisfaction of certain conditions.

Earnings Per Share. The amount of earnings attributable to each share of common stock. For convenience, the term is used to refer to either earnings or loss per share.

Employee Stock Ownership Plan. An employee stock ownership plan is an employee benefit plan that is described by the Employee Retirement Income Security Act of 1974 and the Internal Revenue Code of 1986 as a stock bonus plan, or combination stock bonus and money purchase pension plan, designed to invest primarily in employer stock. Also called an employee share ownership plan.

Exercise Price. The amount that must be paid for a share of common stock upon exercise of an option or warrant.

If-Converted Method. A method of computing EPS data that assumes conversion of convertible securities at the beginning of the reporting period (or at time of issuance, if later).

Income Available to Common Stockholders. Income (or loss) from continuing operations or net income (or net loss) adjusted for preferred stock dividends.

Noncontrolling Interest. The portion of equity (net assets) in a subsidiary not attributable, directly or indirectly, to a parent. A noncontrolling interest is sometimes called a minority interest.

Option. Unless otherwise stated, a call option that gives the holder the right to purchase shares of common stock from the reporting entity in accordance with an agreement upon payment of a specified amount. Options include, but are not limited to, options granted to employees and stock purchase agreements entered into with employees. Options are considered securities. See Call Option.

Participating Security. A security that may participate in undistributed earnings with common stock, whether that participation is conditioned upon the occurrence of a specified event or not. The form of such participation does not have to be a dividend—that is, any form of participation in undistributed earnings would constitute participation by that security, regardless of whether the payment to the security holder was referred to as a dividend.

Potential Common Stock. A security or other contract that may entitle its holder to obtain common stock during the reporting period or after the end of the reporting period.

Preferred Stock. A security that has preferential rights compared to common stock.

Purchased Call Option. A contract that allows the reporting entity to buy a specified quantity of its own stock from the writer of the contract at a fixed price for a given period. See Call Option.

Put Option. A contract that allows the holder to sell a specified quantity of stock to the writer of the contract at a fixed price during a given period.

Reverse Treasury Stock Method. A method of recognizing the dilutive effect on EPS of satisfying a put obligation. It assumes that the proceeds used to buy back common stock (pursuant to the terms of a put option) will be raised from issuing shares at the average market price during the period. See Put Option.

Rights Issue. An offer to existing shareholders to purchase additional shares of common stock in accordance with an agreement for a specified amount (which is generally substantially less than the fair value of the shares) for a given period.

Security. The evidence of debt or ownership or a related right. It includes options and warrants as well as debt and stock.

Stock Dividend. An issuance by a corporation of its own common shares to its common shareholders without consideration and under conditions indicating that such action is prompted mainly by a desire to give the recipient shareholders some ostensibly separate evidence of a part of their respective interests in accumulated corporate earnings without distribution of cash or other property that the board of directors deems necessary or desirable to retain in the business. A stock dividend takes nothing from the property of the corporation and adds nothing to the interests of the stockholders; that is, the corporation's property is not diminished and the interests of the stockholders are not increased. The proportional interest of each shareholder remains the same.

Subsidiary. An entity, including an unincorporated entity such as a partnership or trust, in which another entity, known as its parent, holds a controlling financial interest. (Also, a variable interest entity that is consolidated by a primary beneficiary.)

Treasury Stock Method. A method of recognizing the use of proceeds that could be obtained upon exercise of options and warrants in computing diluted EPS. It assumes that any proceeds would be used to purchase common stock at the average market price during the period.

Warrant. A security that gives the holder the right to purchase shares of common stock in accordance with the terms of the instrument, usually upon payment of a specified amount.

Weighted-Average Number of Common Shares Outstanding. The number of shares determined by relating the portion of time within a reporting period that common shares have been outstanding to the total time in that period. In computing diluted EPS, equivalent common shares are considered for all dilutive potential common shares.

CONCEPTS, RULES, AND EXAMPLES

Simple Capital Structure

Simple capital structures are those with only common stock outstanding, having no potential common shares (options, warrants, etc.). Simple capital structures only have basic EPS. All other entities are considered to have a complex capital structure. Entities with a complex capital structure will have potential common stock in the form of potentially dilutive securities, options, warrants, or other rights that upon conversion or exercise would dilute earnings per common share. Dilutive securities have the potential upon their issuance to reduce EPS.

Computational guidelines. The basic EPS calculation is income available to common stockholders (the numerator) divided by the weighted-average number of common shares outstanding (the denominator) during the period (ASC 260-10-45-10). The objective of the basic EPS calculation is to measure the performance of the entity over the reporting period. Complexities arise because net income does not necessarily represent the earnings available to the common stockholder, and a simple weighted-average of common shares outstanding does not necessarily reflect the true nature of the situation.

Numerator. The net income available to common stockholders used as the numerator in any of the EPS computations must be reduced by any preferential claims against it by other securities (ASC 260-10-45-11). The justification for this reduction is that the preferential claims of the other securities must be satisfied before any income is available to the common stockholder. These other securities are usually in the form of preferred stock, and the deduction from income is the amount of the dividend declared (whether or not paid) during the year on the preferred stock. If the preferred stock is cumulative,[1] the dividend is deducted from income (added to the loss) whether or not declared. Dividends in arrears do not affect the calculation of EPS in the current period; such dividends have been included in prior periods' EPS computations. However, the amount in arrears is required to be disclosed, as well as the effects on the EPS calculation of the rights given to holders of preferential securities.

If an entity is presenting consolidated financial statements with less than wholly owned subsidiaries, then it should exclude from net income the income attributable to the noncontrolling interest in subsidiaries (ASC 45-11A).

Denominator. The computation of the weighted-average of common stock shares outstanding is complicated by the effect that various transactions have on the computation of common shares outstanding. While it is impossible to analyze all the possibilities, ASC 260

---

[1] Cumulative preferred stock requires that if the entity fails to pay a dividend in any year, it must make it up in a later year before paying any dividends to holders of common stock.

provides discussion of some of the more common transactions affecting the number of common shares outstanding. By analogy, the theoretical model set forth in these relatively simple examples can be applied to situations that are not explicitly discussed.

Treasury stock. If a company reacquires its stock (treasury stock), the number of shares reacquired is excluded from EPS calculations as of the date of reacquisition. The same theory holds for the issuance of common stock during the period. The number of shares newly issued is included in the computation only for the period after their issuance date. The logic for this treatment is that the proceeds from issuance of the shares were not available to the company to generate earnings until the shares were issued. This same logic applies to the reacquired shares, because the cash paid to reacquire those shares was no longer available to generate earnings after the reacquisition date.

Stock dividend or stock split. When an entity issues a dividend in the form of its own stock or splits its stock, it does not receive any consideration, but it does increase the number of shares outstanding. ASC 260 states that the increase in shares as a result of a stock split or dividend, or decrease in shares as a result of a reverse split, is to be given retroactive recognition as an appropriate equivalent charge for all periods presented. Thus, even if a stock dividend or split occurs at the end of the period, it is considered outstanding for the entirety of each period presented. The reasoning is that a stock dividend or split has no effect on the ownership percentage of the common stockholder. As such, to show a dilution in the EPS reported would erroneously give the impression of a decline in profitability when in fact it was merely an increase in the shares outstanding due to the stock dividend or split. ASC 260 carries this principle one step further by requiring the retroactive adjustment of outstanding shares for stock dividends or splits occurring after the end of the period, but before the release of the financial statements. The rationale for this adjustment is that the primary interest of the financial statement user is considered to be the company's current capitalization. If this situation occurs, disclosure of both the end-of-year outstanding shares and those used to compute EPS is required.

When shares are issued in connection with a business combination that occurs during the period, they are treated as issued and outstanding as of the date of the acquisition.

Weighted-Average Computation

Transaction	*Effect on weighted-average computation*
• Common stock outstanding at the beginning of the period	• Included in number of shares outstanding
• Issuance of common stock	• Increase number of shares outstanding by the number of shares issued times the portion of the year outstanding
• Conversion into common stock	• Increase number of shares outstanding by the number of shares converted times the portion of the year outstanding
• Reacquisition of common stock	• Decrease number of shares outstanding by number of shares reacquired times portion of the year since reacquisition
• Stock dividend or split	• Increase number of shares outstanding by number of shares issued for the dividend or resulting from the split retroactively as of the beginning of the earliest period presented

• Reverse split	• Decrease number of shares outstanding by decrease in shares retroactively as of the beginning of the earliest period presented
• Business combination	• Increase number of shares outstanding by number of shares issued times portion of year since acquisition

The table does not provide for all of the possible complexities arising in the EPS computation; however, most of the others occur under a complex capital structure. The complications arising under a complex capital structure are discussed and illustrated in detail later in this chapter and in the final Section, "Comprehensive Example." The illustration below applies some of the foregoing concepts to a simple capital structure.

Example of EPS computation—simple capital structure

Assume the following information:

	Numerator information			Denominator information	
a.	Income from continuing operations before extraordinary items	$130,000	a.	Common shares outstanding 1/1/X1	100,000
b.	Extraordinary loss (net of income tax)	(30,000)	b.	Shares issued for cash 4/1/ X1	20,000
c.	Net income	100,000	c.	Shares issued in 10% stock dividend declared in July 20 X1	12,000
d.	6% cumulative preferred stock, $100 par, 1,000 shares issued and outstanding	100,000	d.	Shares of treasury stock reacquired 10/1/X1	10,000

When calculating the numerator, the claims related to the preferred stock are deducted to arrive at the income available to the common stockholders. In this example, the preferred stock is cumulative. Thus, regardless of whether or not the board of directors declares a preferred dividend, holders of the preferred stock have a claim of $6,000 (= 1,000 shares × $100 par × 6%) against 20X1 earnings. Therefore, $6,000 must be deducted from the numerator to arrive at the income available to common stockholders. Note that any cumulative preferred dividends in arrears are ignored in computing this period's EPS since they would have been incorporated into previous periods' EPS calculations. Also note that this $6,000 would have been deducted for *non*cumulative preferred stock only if a dividend of this amount had been declared during the period.

The EPS calculations follow:

Earnings per common share

On income from continuing operations before extraordinary item $\frac{\$130,000 - \$6,000}{\text{Common shares outstanding}}$

On net income $\frac{\$100,000 - \$6,000}{\text{Common shares outstanding}}$

The computation of the denominator is based upon the weighted-average number of common shares outstanding. A simple weighted-average is not considered appropriate because of the various complexities. Table 1 illustrates one way of computing the weighted-average number of shares outstanding.

Table 1

Item	*Actual number of shares*	*Retroactive effects of July stock dividend*	*Subtotal number of shares deemed outstanding*	*Fraction of the year deemed outstanding*	*Shares times fraction of the year deemed outstanding*
Number of shares as of beginning of the year 1/1/X1	100,000	10,000 [10%(100,000)]	110,000	12/12	110,000
Shares issued 4/1/X1	20,000	2,000 [10%(20,000)]	22,000	9/12	16,500
Treasury shares reacquired 10/1/X1	(10,000)	–	(10,000)	3/12	(2,500)
Weighted-average number of common shares outstanding					124,000

The stock dividend declared in July is treated as being retroactive to the beginning of the year. Thus, for the period 1/1 through 4/1, 110,000 shares are considered to be outstanding. When shares are issued, they are included in the weighted-average beginning with the date of issuance. The shares issued as a result of the stock dividend applicable to the 20,000 newly issued shares are also assumed to have been outstanding for the same period as the 20,000 shares. Thus, we can see that of the 12,000-share stock dividend, 10,000 shares relate to the beginning balance and 2,000 shares to the new issuance (10% of 100,000 and 20,000, respectively). The reacquisition of the treasury stock requires that these shares be excluded from the calculation for the remainder of the period after their reacquisition date. This amount is subtracted from the calculation because the shares were reacquired from shares outstanding prior to their reacquisition.

To complete the example, we divide the previously computed numerator by the weighted-average number of common shares outstanding to arrive at EPS.

Earnings per common share:

On income from continuing operations before extraordinary item $\frac{\$130{,}000 - \$6{,}000}{124{,}000 \text{ common shares}} = \$1.00$

On net income $\frac{\$100{,}000 - \$6{,}000}{124{,}000 \text{ common shares}} = \$0.76$

The numbers computed above are required to be presented on the face of the income statement. Reporting a $.24 extraordinary loss per share ($30,000 extraordinary item ÷ 124,000 common shares) is required either on the face of the income statement or in the notes to the financial statements.

Preferred stock dividends payable in common shares. All dividends represent distributions of accumulated earnings, and accordingly are not reported as expenses on the income statement under GAAP. However, as illustrated above, for purposes of computing EPS, preferred dividends must be deducted in order to ascertain how much income is available for common stockholders. In some cases, preferred dividends are not payable in cash, but rather in common shares (based on market value as of the date of declaration, typically). In certain cases, the dividends may be payable in common shares or cash at the issuer's option.

ASC 260 defines income available to common stockholders as "income (or loss) from continuing operations or net income (or net loss) adjusted for preferred stock dividends." This adjustment in computing income available to common stockholders is consistent with the treatment of common stock issued for goods or services. (ASC 260-10-45-12)

Example of preferred stock dividends payable in common shares

Delta Corporation has three classes of preferred stock outstanding, as noted in the following table:

Stock type	*Preferred stock description*	*Total $ issued*
Series A	7% preferred stock, $100 par value, 3,000 shares outstanding, payable in common stock priced at market value on declaration date	$300,000
Series B	5% preferred stock, $100 par value, 2,000 shares outstanding, payable in common stock at fixed price of $2.00/share	200,000
Series C	8% preferred stock, $100 par value, 1,000 shares outstanding, payable in cash or in common stock at market price on declaration date, at Delta's option	100,000

On the dividend declaration date, the price of a share of common stock is $2.50. Delta's Board of Directors approves the payment of the Series C dividend as 50% cash, 50% common stock. The following table shows the types and amounts of dividends due for all types of preferred stock:

Stock type	*Total dividend due*	*Applicable common stock price*	*Number of common shares issued*	*Cash issued*
Series A	$21,000	$2.50	8,400	
Series B	10,000	2.00	5,000	
Series C	8,000	2.50	1,600	$4,000
	$39,000		15,000	$4,000

Delta has net income of $110,000, from which the total dividend due, regardless of the form of payment, must be subtracted. The calculation follows:

$$\frac{\$110{,}000 \text{ net income} - \$39{,}000 \text{ dividend}}{\text{Common shares outstanding}}$$

Delta's fiscal year is the calendar year. Delta had 200,000 shares of common stock outstanding on January 1, issued an additional 30,000 common shares on May 1, and declared the previously described preferred stock dividends on 12/31. Based on this information, the weighted-average number of shares outstanding follows:

Description	*Number of shares*	*Fraction of the year deemed outstanding*	*Weighted-average shares outstanding*
Number of shares as of 1/1	200,000	12/12	200,000
Common stock issuance on 5/1	30,000	8/12	20,000
Common stock issued on 12/31 as part of preferred stock dividend	15,000	12/12	15,000
Weighted-average number of common shares outstanding			235,000

Delta divides the 235,000 common shares outstanding into the adjusted net income to arrive at the following EPS calculation:

$$\frac{\$110{,}000 - \$39{,}000}{235{,}000 \text{ common shares}} = \$0.30$$

Effect of preferred stock dividends payable in common shares on computation of EPS. At the option of the issuer, preferred stock dividends are sometimes payable in either cash or common stock. According to ASC 260-10-45, the form of payment is not a determinant in accounting for the effect of the preferred dividend on net income available to common stockholders. Therefore, for the purposes of the numerator in EPS computations, net income or loss is adjusted to compute the portion available to common stockholders.

Complex Capital Structure

The computation of EPS under a complex capital structure involves all of the complexities discussed under the simple structure and many more. A complex capital structure is one that includes securities that grant rights with the potential to be exercised and reduce EPS (dilutive securities). The denominator is increased to include the number of additional shares that would have been outstanding had the dilutive shares been issued. The numerator is also adjusted for any change in income or loss that would have resulted from the conversion. Any antidilutive securities (those that increase EPS) are not included in the computation of EPS.

Note that a complex capital structure requires dual presentation of basic EPS and DEPS. The common stock outstanding and all other dilutive securities are used to compute DEPS.

Diluted earnings per share. DEPS represents the earnings attributable to each share of common stock after giving effect to all potentially dilutive securities which were outstanding during the period. The computation of DEPS requires that the following steps be performed:

1. Identify all potentially dilutive securities.
2. Compute dilution, the effects that the other dilutive securities have on net income and common shares outstanding.

Identification of potentially dilutive securities. Dilutive securities are those that have the potential of being exercised and reducing the EPS figure. Some examples of dilutive securities identified by ASC 260 are convertible debt, convertible preferred stock, options, warrants, participating securities, two-class common stocks, and contingent shares.

Convertible securities. A convertible security is one type of potentially dilutive security. A security of this type has an inherent dual nature. Convertibles are comprised of two distinct elements:

- The right to receive dividends or interest, and
- The right to potentially participate in earnings by becoming a common stockholder.

This security is included in the DEPS computation due to the latter right.

Options and warrants. Options, warrants, and their equivalents generally derive their value from the right to obtain common stock at specified prices over an extended period of time.

Participating securities and two-class common stocks. The capital structure of some entities includes securities that may participate in dividends with common stocks according to a predetermined formula, or a class of common stock with different dividend rates from those of another class of common stock but without prior or senior rights. ASC 260-10-55 nullified the option of using the if-converted method for those securities that are convertible into common stock, if the effect is dilutive. For these securities, participating securities, and two-class common stocks the two-class method of computing EPS, as described below, is used.

Financial instruments with characteristics of both liabilities and equity. ASC 480 specifies that certain freestanding financial instruments (as distinguished from compound financial instruments) that may resemble equity are nevertheless required to be classified as liabilities on the issuer's statement of financial position. Such instruments include mandatorily redeemable financial instruments (including mandatorily redeemable common or preferred stock) and certain forward contracts that require physical settlement by repurchase of a fixed number of the issuer's equity shares. Issuers of these instruments are required to

1. Exclude any shares of common stock that are required to be redeemed or repurchased from the denominator of the EPS and DEPS computations, and
2. Apply the two-class method described below to deduct from income available to common stockholders (the numerator of EPS and DEPS computations) any amounts that are attributable to shares that are to be redeemed or repurchased, including contractual dividends and participation rights in undistributed earnings.

The deduction described in (2) is limited to amounts not recognized in the issuer's financial statements as interest expense. More information can be found in the chapter on ASC 480.

Contingent issuances of common stock. Another consideration is contingent issuances of common stock (e.g., stock subscriptions). If shares are to be issued in the future with no restrictions on issuance other than the passage of time, they are to be considered issued and treated as outstanding in the computation of DEPS. Other issuances that are dependent upon certain conditions being met are to be evaluated in a different manner. ASC 260 uses as examples the maintenance of current earnings levels and the attainment of specified earnings increases. If the contingency is to merely maintain the earnings levels currently being attained, then the shares are considered outstanding for the entire period and considered in the computation of DEPS if the effect is dilutive. If the requirement is to increase earnings over a period of time, the DEPS computation includes those shares that would be issued based on the assumption that the current amount of earnings will remain unchanged if the effect is dilutive. Previously reported DEPS are not restated to give recognition to shares issued as a result of the earnings level attainment. If a contingent issuance is based upon the lapsing of time *and* the market price of the stock (which generally affects the number of shares issued), both conditions must be met to include the contingently issuable shares in the DEPS computation. FASB prohibits restatement of DEPS data should fluctuations in the market price occur in future periods. (ASC 260-10-45-48 through 45-55)

Example of the impact of contingent stock issuances on EPS

Arturo Corporation offers its management team the following set of stock-based incentives that apply to the current year of operations:

- A stock grant of 25,000 common shares if the company attains full-year net income of at least $1 million.
- An additional stock grant of 1,000 common shares for every additional $100,000 of net income recorded above $1 million.
- A stock grant of 50,000 common shares if the company is granted ISO 9001 certification, to be issued immediately upon completion of the certification.

Arturo has 500,000 shares of common stock outstanding throughout the calendar year, which is its fiscal year. It obtains the ISO 9001 certification on April 1. Arturo's full-year net income is $1,300,000. It records the following basic EPS:

$$\frac{\$1{,}300{,}000 \text{ net income}}{537{,}500 \text{ common shares}} = \$2.42$$

The denominator incurs 3/4 of the 50,000 stock grant (e.g., 37,500 shares) associated with completion of the ISO 9001 certification, since the grant occurs after 1/4 of the fiscal year had been completed. The stock grant that is contingent on full-year earnings is not included in the basic EPS calculation, since the grant cannot occur until the last day of the year, and therefore has a negligible impact on the calculation.

For the DEPS calculation, the contingent stock grant of 25,000 shares associated with the $1 million net income goal is included in the full-year weighted-average, as well as the 3,000 shares associated with the incremental increase in net profits above $1 million and the 50,000 shares associated with the ISO 9001 project completion. The calculation of shares to include in the DEPS denominator follows:

Common stock outstanding	$500,000
Stock grant associated with ISO 9001 project completion	50,000
Stock grant associated with attainment of $1 million net income goal	25,000
Stock grant associated with attainment of incremental $300,000 net income goal	3,000
Total DEPS shares	$578,000

By including these shares in the denominator of the DEPS calculation, Arturo arrives at the following diluted EPS:

$$\frac{\$1{,}300{,}000 \text{ net income}}{578{,}000 \text{ common shares}} = \$2.25$$

Computation of DEPS. The second step in the process is the actual computation of DEPS. There are basically two methods used to incorporate the effects of other dilutive securities on EPS (excluding participating and two-class common securities for which the two-class method described above is used).

1. The treasury stock method, and
2. The if-converted method

The treasury stock method. The treasury stock method, used for the exercise of most warrants or options, requires that DEPS be computed as if

- The options or warrants were exercised at the beginning of the period (or actual date of issuance, if later), and
- That the funds obtained from the exercise were used to purchase (reacquire) the company's common stock at the average market price for the period.

The incremental shares (the difference between the number of shares assumed issued and the number of shares assumed purchased) shall be included in the denominator of the diluted EPS computation. (ASC 260-10-45-23)

An example of the requirements under ASC 260 follows. If a corporation has warrants outstanding for 1,000 shares of common stock exercisable at $10 per share, and the average market price of the common stock is $16 per share, the following would occur: The company would receive $10,000 (1,000 × $10) and issue 1,000 shares from the exercise of the warrants which would enable it to repurchase 625 shares ($10,000 ÷ $16) in the open market. The net increase in the denominator (which effects a dilution in EPS) is 375 shares (1,000 issued less 625 repurchased). If the exercise price is greater than the average market price, the exercise is not assumed since the result would be antidilutive. In that case, DEPS of prior periods presented in comparative form are not restated to reflect the change in market price.

Treasury Stock Method

Denominator must be increased by net dilution, as follows:

Net dilution	= Shares issued – Shares assumed to be repurchased
where	
Shares issued	= Proceeds received ÷ Exercise price per share
Shares assumed to be repurchased	= Proceeds received ÷ Average market price per share

The if-converted method. The if-converted method is used for those convertible securities that are currently sharing in the earnings of the company through the receipt of interest or dividends as preferential securities, but that have the potential for sharing in the earnings as common stock (e.g., convertible bonds or convertible preferred stock). The if-converted method logically recognizes that the convertible security can only share in the earnings of the company as one or the other, not both. Thus, the dividends or interest less income tax effects applicable to the convertible security as a preferential security are not recognized in income available to common stockholders used to compute DEPS, and the weighted-average number of shares is adjusted to reflect the assumed conversion as of the beginning of the year (or actual date of issuance, if later). (ASC 260-10-45-40)

If-Converted Method

Numerator

Income available to common stockholders recomputed to reflect assumed and/or actual conversion

- Add back interest expense less income tax effects
- Convertible preferred dividends are no longer subtracted
- Add back other expenses attributable to convertible issues

Denominator

Weighted-average number of shares of common stock outstanding adjusted to reflect the assumed and/or actual conversion of convertible securities at the beginning of the period or actual date of issuance, if later

Exceptions. Generally, the if-converted method is used for convertible securities, while the treasury stock method is used for options and warrants. There are some situations specified by ASC 260 for which this does not hold true.

1. If options or warrants permit or require that debt or other securities of the issuer be tendered for all or a portion of the exercise price, the if-converted method is used.
2. If options or warrants require that the proceeds from the exercise are to be used to retire existing debt, the if-converted method is used.
3. If convertible securities require cash payment upon conversion, and are, therefore, considered equivalent to warrants, the treasury stock method is used.

Dual presentation of EPS. DEPS is a pro forma presentation which reflects the dilution of EPS that would have occurred if all contingent issuances of common stock that would individually reduce EPS had taken place at the beginning of the period (or the date actually issued, if later). The presentation of the concept of dual EPS provides the reader with factually supportable EPS that range from no dilution to the maximum potential dilution. DEPS assumes that all issuances that have the legal right to become common stock exercise that right (unless the exercise would be antidilutive), and therefore anticipates and measures all potential dilution. The underlying basis for the computation is that of conservatism. The DEPS considers all other potentially dilutive securities, but only uses those securities that are dilutive. Thus, in most cases, the DEPS is less than the basic EPS. DEPS can never be greater than the basic EPS, but it could potentially be the same if all of the convertible securities were antidilutive.

Examples of EPS Computation—Complex Capital Structure

Each of the following independent examples is presented to illustrate the foregoing principles. The procedural guidelines are detailed to enable the reader to understand the computation without referring back to the preceding explanatory text.

Example of the treasury stock method

Assume that net income is $50,000 and the weighted-average number of common shares outstanding has been computed as 10,000. Additional information regarding the capital structure is:

1. 4% nonconvertible, cumulative preferred stock, par value of $100 per share, 1,000 shares issued and outstanding the entire year.
2. Options and warrants to purchase 1,000 shares of common stock at $8 per share were outstanding all year.
3. The average market price of common stock during the year was $10.

The first step in applying this method is the determination of basic EPS. This calculation appears as follows:

$$\frac{\text{Net income} - \text{Preferred dividends}}{\text{Weighted-average number of common shares outstanding}} = \frac{\$50{,}000 - \$4{,}000}{10{,}000 \text{ shares}} = \$4.60$$

The second step is the calculation of DEPS, which is based upon outstanding common stock and other dilutive securities. The options and warrants are the only potentially dilutive securities in the example. However, remember that only dilutive options (Market price > Exercise price) are included in the computation. The treasury stock method is used to compute the number of shares to be added to the denominator as illustrated below.

Proceeds from assumed exercise of options and warrants (1,000 shares × $8 per share)	$8,000
Number of shares issued	1,000
Number of shares assumed to be reacquired ($8,000 ÷ $10 average market price per share)	800
Number of shares assumed issued and not reacquired	200*

* *An alternative approach that can be used to calculate this number for DEPS is demonstrated below.*

$$\frac{\text{Average market price} - \text{Exercise price}}{\text{Average market price}} \times \text{Number of shares under options/warrants} = \text{Shares not reacquired}$$

$$\frac{\$10 - \$8}{\$10} \times 1{,}000 \text{ shares} = 200 \text{ shares}$$

DEPS can now be calculated as follows, including the effects of applying the treasury stock method:

$$\frac{\text{Net income} - \text{Preferred dividends}}{\text{Weighted-average number of common shares outstanding + Number of shares assumed issued and not reacquired with proceeds from options and warrants}} = \frac{\$50{,}000 - \$4{,}000}{10{,}200 \text{ shares}} = \$4.51$$

Note the dilutive effect of the options and warrants shown in Table 2, as EPS of $4.60 is reduced to DEPS of $4.51.

Table 2
Computations of Basic EPS and Diluted EPS

	EPS on outstanding common stock (Basic EPS)			*DEPS*		
Item	*Numerator*		*Denominator*	*Numerator*		*Denominator*
Net income	$50,000			$50,000		
Preferred dividends	(4,000)			(4,000)		
Common shares outstanding			10,000 shs			10,000 shs
Options and warrants						200
Totals	$46,000	÷	10,000 shs	$46,000	÷	10,200 shs
EPS		$4.60			$4.51	

Example of the if-converted method

Assume net income of $50,000 and weighted-average common shares outstanding of 10,000. Additional information regarding capital structure is:

1. 7% convertible debt, 200 bonds each convertible into forty common shares. The bonds were outstanding the entire year. The income tax rate is 40%. The bonds were issued at par ($1,000 per bond). No bonds were converted during the year.
2. 4% convertible, cumulative preferred stock, par value of $100 per share, 1,000 shares issued and outstanding. Each preferred share is convertible into two common shares. The preferred stock was issued at par value and was outstanding the entire year. No shares were converted during the year.

The first step is to compute basic EPS. As in the previous example, this is $4.60. The next step is the computation of DEPS, assuming conversion of the convertible debt in order to determine whether their conversion would be dilutive. The convertible bonds are assumed to have been converted to common stock at the beginning of the year, since no bonds were actually converted during the year. The effects of this assumption are twofold. One, if the bonds are converted, interest expense would be reduced by $14,000 (= 7% × 200 bonds × $1,000 par value per bond); and two, there will be an additional 8,000 shares of common stock outstanding during the year (= 200 bonds × 40 common shares per bond). The effect of avoiding $14,000 of interest expense will increase net income, but it will also increase income tax expense due to the lost income tax deduction. Consequently, the net after-tax effect of avoiding interest expense of $14,000 is $8,400 [= (1 – .40) × $14,000]. DEPS is computed as follows:

$$\frac{\text{Net income} - \text{Preferred dividends} + \text{Interest expense (net of tax)}}{\text{Weighted-average number of common shares outstanding} + \text{Shares issued upon conversion of bonds}} = \frac{\$50{,}000 - \$4{,}000 + \$8{,}400}{10{,}000 + 8{,}000 \text{ shares}} = \$3.02$$

The convertible debt is dilutive because EPS of $4.60 is reduced to DEPS of $3.02.

To determine the dilutive effect of the preferred stock, the preferred stock is assumed to have been converted to common stock at the beginning of the year, since no shares of preferred stock were actually converted during the year. The effects of this assumption are twofold. One, if the preferred stock is converted, there will be no preferred dividends of $4,000 for the year; and two, there will be an additional 2,000 shares of common stock outstanding during the year (the conversion rate is 2 for 1 on 1,000 shares of outstanding preferred stock). DEPS considering the preferred stock is computed, as follows, reflecting these two assumptions:

$$\frac{\text{Net income} + \text{Interest expense (net of tax)}}{\text{Weighted-average number of common shares outstanding} + \text{Shares issued upon conversion of bonds and conversion of preferred stock}} = \frac{\$50{,}000 + \$8{,}400}{10{,}000 + 8{,}000 + 2{,}000 \text{ shares}} = \$2.92$$

The convertible preferred stock is also dilutive because DEPS of $3.02 is reduced to DEPS of $2.92.

Together, the effect of the convertible bonds and preferred stock reduces EPS of $4.60 to DEPS of $2.92. In this example, the convertible bonds must be considered first, prior to the inclusion of the convertible preferred stock in the computation. For a complete explanation of the sequencing process of including multiple dilutive securities in the computations of DEPS, see the comprehensive example at the end of the chapter. Table 3 summarizes the computations made for this example.

Table 3
Computations of Basic EPS and Diluted EPS

	EPS on outstanding common stock (Basic EPS)			*DEPS*		
Item	*Numerator*		*Denominator*	*Numerator*		*Denominator*
Net income	$50,000			$50,000		
Preferred dividend	(4,000)					
Common shares outstanding			10,000 shs			10,000 shs
Conversion of preferred						2,000
Conversion of bonds				8,400		8,000
Totals	$46,000	÷	10,000 shs	$58,400	÷	20,000 shs
EPS		$4.60			$2.92	

In the preceding example, all of the potentially dilutive securities were outstanding the entire year and no conversions or exercises were made during the year. If a potentially dilutive security was not outstanding the entire year, then the numerator and denominator effects would have to be *time-weighted.* For instance, suppose the convertible bonds in the above example were issued during the current year on July 1. If all other facts remain unchanged, DEPS would be computed as follows:

$$\frac{\text{Net income + Interest expense (net of tax)}}{\text{Weighted-average number of common shares outstanding + Shares issued upon conversion of preferred stock and conversion bonds}} = \frac{\$50{,}000 + \tfrac{1}{2}(8{,}400)}{10{,}000 + 2{,}000 + \tfrac{1}{2}(8{,}000)} = \$3.39$$

Since the DEPS of $3.39 is still less than the EPS of $4.60, the convertible debt is dilutive whether or not it is outstanding the entire year.

If actual conversions or exercises take place during a period, the common shares issued upon conversion will be outstanding from their date of issuance and therefore, will be included in the computation of the weighted-average number of common shares outstanding. These shares are then weighted from their respective dates of issuance. Assume that all the bonds in the above example are converted on July 1 into 8,000 common shares; the following effects should be noted:

1. For basic EPS, the weighted-average of common shares outstanding will be increased by (8,000 shares) (6 months outstanding/12 months in the period) or 4,000. Income will increase $4,200 net of income tax, because the bonds were only outstanding for the first half of the year.
2. For DEPS, the if-converted method is applied to the period January 1 to June 30 because it was during this period that the bonds were potentially dilutive. The interest expense, net of income tax, of $4,200 is added to the net income in the numerator, and 4,000 shares are added to the denominator.
3. Interestingly, the net effect of items 1 and 2 is the same for the period, whether these dilutive bonds were outstanding the entire period or converted during the period.

Participating Securities and the Two-Class Method

Reporting entities that issue securities that are entitled to participate in dividends with common shares will report lower EPS under the guidance in ASC 260-10-55. This issue addresses the computation of EPS by entities that have issued securities, other than common stock, that entitle the holder to participate in dividends when, and if, dividends are declared on common stock. In addition, ASC 260-10-55 provides further guidance on calculating EPS using a two-class method and requires companies to retroactively restate EPS amounts presented. (ASC 260-10-45-59)

Participation rights are defined based solely on whether the holder is entitled to receive any dividends if the entity declares them during the period. The codification also requires the use of the two-class method for computing basic EPS when participating convertible securities exist. The use of the two-class method was also expanded by ASC 260-10-55 to encompass other forms of participating securities, including options, warrants, forwards, and other contracts to issue an entity's common shares (including unvested share-based compensation awards).

Presentation and disclosure. Presentation of participating securities' basic and diluted EPS is not required, but is permitted for other than common stock. What is required by ASC 260-10-55 is adjustment to the earnings that are used to compute EPS for the common stock.

Participating security defined. ASC 260-10-55 formally defines participating securities as any "security that may participate in undistributed earnings with common stock, whether that participation is conditioned upon the occurrence of a specified event or not… regardless of the whether the payment to the security holder was referred to as a dividend."

Additional guidance clarifies that instruments granted in share-based payment transactions can be participating securities prior to the requisite service having been rendered. However, the right to receive dividends or dividend equivalents that the holder will forfeit if the award does not vest does not qualify as a participation right, as the award does not meet the definition of a participation security. Also not considered to be participation rights are dividends, or their equivalents, that can be transferred to the holder of a share-based payment award as a reduction in the exercise price of the award.

Allocating earnings and losses. In addition to the amount of dividends declared in the current period, net dividends must be reduced by the contractual amount of dividends or other participation payments that are paid or accumulated for the current period. The allocation of undistributed earnings for a period should be done for a participating security based on the contractual participation rights of the security to share in the current earnings assuming all earnings for the period are distributed. The allocation process is not based on a fair-value analysis, but is based on the term of the securities. For losses, an entity would allocate to the participating securities a portion of the net losses of the entity in accordance with the contractual provisions that may require the security to have an obligation to share in the issuing entity's losses. This occurs when the participating security holder has an obligation to share in the losses of the issuing entity if the holder is obligated to fund the issuing authority's losses or if losses incurred by the issuing entity reduce the security's principal or mandatory redemption amount.

Two-class method. This is an earnings allocation formula for computing EPS. It determines EPS for each class of common stock and participating securities according to dividends declared/accumulated and participation rights in undistributed earnings. The codification requires that the two-class method be applied for participating convertible securities when computing basic EPS. This changes earlier guidance, which permitted reporting entities to make an accounting policy election to use the if-converted method, rather than the two-class method, in the basic EPS calculation, as long as the if-converted method was not less dilutive.

ASC 260-10-55 states that use of the two-class method is dependent upon having no unsatisfied *contingencies* or objectively determinable contingent events. Thus, if preferred shares are entitled to participate in dividends with common shareholders only if management declares the distribution to be "extraordinary," this would not invoke the use of the two-class computation of EPS. However, if classification of dividends as extraordinary is predetermined by a formula, then undistributed earnings would be allocated to common stock and the participating security based on the assumption that all of the earnings for the period are distributed, with application of the defined sharing formula used for the determination of the allocation to the participating security.

If the participating security participates with common stock in earnings for a period in which a specified event occurs, regardless of whether a dividend is actually paid during the period (e.g., achievement of a target market price or achievement of threshold earnings), then undistributed earnings would be allocated to common stock and the participating security based on the assumption that all of the earnings for the period are distributed. Undistributed earnings would be allocated to the participating security if the contingent condition would have been satisfied at the reporting date, even if no actual distribution were made.

Example—Participating convertible preferred stock

Assume that Struthers Corp. had 20,000 shares of common stock and 5,000 shares of preferred stock outstanding during 20X1, and reported net income of $65,000 for 20X1. Each share of preferred stock is convertible into two shares of common stock. The preferred stock is entitled to a noncumulative annual dividend of $5 per share. After the common has been paid a dividend of $1 per share, the preferred stock then participates in any additional dividends on a 2:3 per share ratio with the common. For 20X1, the common shareholders have been paid $26,000 (or $1.30 per share), and the preferred shareholders have been paid $26,000 (or $5.20 per share). Basic EPS under the two-class method for 20X1 would be computed as follows:

Net income		65,000
Less dividends paid:		
Common	$26,000	
Preferred stock	26,000	52,000
Undistributed 20X1 earnings		$13,000

Allocation of undistributed earnings

To preferred

0.2(5,000) ÷ [0.2(5,000) + 0.3(20,000)] × $13,000 = $1,857

$1,857 ÷ 5,000 shares = $0.37 per share

To common

0.3(20,000) ÷ [0.2(5,000) + 0.3(20,000)] × $13,000 = $11,143

$11,143 ÷ 20,000 shares = $0.56 per share

Basic EPS amounts for 20X1

	Preferred	*Common*
Distributed earnings	$5.20	$1.30
Undistributed earnings	0.37	0.56
Total	$5.57	$1.86

Example—Participating convertible debt instrument

Assume that Wincomp, Inc. had 20,000 shares of common stock outstanding during 20X1 and reported net income of $85,000 for the year. On January 1, 20X1, Wincomp issues 1,000 30-year,

3% convertible bonds with an aggregate par value of $1,000,000. Each bond is convertible into 8 shares of common stock. After the common has been paid a dividend of $1 per share, the bondholders then participate in any additional dividends on a 2:3 per share ratio with common shareholders. The bondholders receive common stock dividends based on the number of shares of common stock into which the bonds are convertible. The bondholders do not have any voting rights prior to conversion into common stock. For 20X1, the Wincomp common shareholders have been paid $20,000 (or $1.00 per share). Basic EPS under the two-class method for 20X1 would be computed as follows:

Net income		$85,000
Less dividends paid:		
Common	$20,000	20,000
Undistributed 20X1 earnings		$65,000

Allocation of undistributed earnings

To convertible bonds

0.2(8,000) ÷ [0.2(8,000) + 0.3(20,000)] × $65,000 = $13,684

$13,684 ÷ 8,000 shares = $1.71 per share

To common

0.3(20,000) ÷ [0.2(8,000) + 0.3(20,000)] × $65,000 = $51,316

$51,316 ÷ 20,000 shares = $2.57 per share

Basic EPS amounts for 20X1

	Convertible bonds	*Common*
Distributed earnings	$ –	$1.00
Undistributed earnings	1.71	2.57
Total	$1.71	$3.57

Example—Participating warrants

Assume that SmithCo. had 15,000 shares of common stock and 1,000 warrants to purchase shares of common stock outstanding during 20X1. SmithCo. reported net income of $75,000 for the year. Each warrant entitles the holder to purchase one share of common stock at $10 per share. In addition, the warrant holders receive dividends on the underlying common stock to the extent they are declared. For 20X1, common shareholders have been paid $30,000 ($2.00 per share), and the warrant holders have been paid $2,000 (also $2.00 per share). Basic EPS under the two-class method for 20X1 would be computed as follows:

Net income		$75,000
Less dividends paid:		
Common stock	$30,000	
Warrants	2,000	32,000
Undistributed 20X1 earnings		$43,000

Allocation of undistributed earnings

To warrants

0.5(1,000) ÷ [0.5(1,000) + 0.5(15,000)] × $43,000 = $2,687.50

$2,687.50 ÷ 1,000 shares = $2.69 per share

To common

0.5(15,000) ÷ [0.5(1,000) + 0.5(15,000)] × $43,000 = $40,312.50

$40,312.50 ÷ 15,000 shares = $2.69 per share

Basic EPS amounts for 20X1

	Common	*Warrants*
Distributed earnings	$2.00	$2.00
Undistributed earnings	2.69	2.69
Total	$4.69	$4.69

Effect of Contracts That May Be Settled in Stock or Cash on the Computation of DEPS

There is an issue regarding how the option to settle contracts (e.g., written puts on the reporting entity's shares) in stock or cash influences the computation of EPS. FASB staff concluded that in calculating EPS, adjustments should be made to the numerator for contracts that are classified, in accordance with ASC 815-40-15, as equity instruments, but for which the company has a stated policy or for which past experience provides a reasonable basis to believe that such contracts will be paid partially or wholly in cash (in which case there will be no potential common shares included in the denominator). Thus, a contract that is reported as an equity instrument for accounting purposes may require an adjustment to the numerator for any changes in income or loss that would result if the contract had been reported as an asset or liability for accounting purposes during the period.

For purposes of computing diluted EPS, the adjustments to the numerator described above are only permitted for instruments for which the effect on net income (the numerator) is different depending on whether the instrument is accounted for as an equity instrument or as an asset or liability (e.g., those that are within the scope of ASC 480 or ASC 815-40-15). The provisions of ASC 260 require that for contracts that provide the company with a choice of settlement methods, the company will assume that the contract will be settled in shares. That presumption may be overcome if past experience or a stated policy provides a reasonable basis to believe that it is probable that the contract will be paid partially or wholly in cash.

ASC 260-10-55-36 also states that, for contracts in which the holder controls the means of settlement, past experience or a stated policy is not determinative. In those situations, the more dilutive of cash or share settlement should be used.

Adjustment to the numerator in year-to-date diluted EPS calculations may be required in certain circumstances. ASC 260-10-55-34 cites the example of contracts in which the holder controls the method of settlement and that would have a more dilutive effect if settled in shares, where the numerator adjustment is equal to the earnings effect of the change in the fair value of the asset/liability recorded during the year-to-date period. In that situation, the number of incremental shares included in the denominator is to be determined by calculating the number of shares that would be required to settle the contract using the average share price during the year-to-date period.

ASC 260-10-55 also notes that antidilutive contracts, such as purchased put options and purchased call options, should be excluded from diluted EPS.

ASC 480 requires entities that issue mandatorily redeemable financial instruments or that enter into forward purchase contracts that require physical settlement by repurchase of a fixed number of shares in exchange for cash to exclude the common shares that are to be redeemed or repurchased in calculating EPS and DEPS. Amounts attributable to shares that are to be redeemed or repurchased that have not been recognized as interest costs (e.g., amounts associated with participation rights) are deducted in computing the income available to common shareholders (the numerator of the EPS calculations) consistently under the "two-class" method. Therefore, ASC 480's requirements for calculating EPS partially nullify ASC 260-10-55 for those financial instruments. For other financial instruments, including those that are liabilities under ASC 480, the guidance in ASC 260-10-55 remains applicable.

Inclusions/Exclusions from Computation of DEPS

Certain types of instruments and contracts having characteristics of both liabilities and equity require special treatment using the two-class method described previously; if under ASC 480, they are required to be classified as liabilities on the statement of financial position of the issuer. Examples of these instruments include mandatorily redeemable common or preferred stock; and forward purchase contracts or written put options on the issuer's equity shares that require physical settlement or net cash settlement.

The computations of DEPS also does not include contracts such as purchased put options and purchased call options (options held by the entity on its own stock). The inclusion of such contracts would be antidilutive.

Sometimes entities issue contracts that may be settled in common stock or in cash at the election of either the issuing entity or the holder. The determination of whether the contract is reflected in the computation of DEPS is based on the facts available each period. It is presumed that the contract will be settled in common stock and the resulting common shares will be included in DEPS if the effect is dilutive. This presumption may be overcome if past experience or a stated policy provides a reasonable basis to believe that the contract will be paid partially or wholly in cash. If during the reporting period the exercise price exceeds the average market price for that period, the potential dilutive effect of the contract on EPS is computed using the reverse treasury stock method. Under this method:

1. Issuance of sufficient common shares is assumed to have occurred at the beginning of the period (at the average market price during the period) to raise enough proceeds to satisfy the contract.
2. The proceeds from issuance of the shares are assumed to have been used to satisfy the contract (i.e., to buy back shares).
3. The denominator of the DEPS calculation includes the incremental number of shares (the difference between the number of shares assumed issued and the number of shares assumed received from satisfying the contract).

The Effect of Contingently Convertible Instruments on DEPS

In recent years contingently convertible securities have become more common. ASC 260-10-45 addresses the impact of the existence of such instruments on the computation of EPS. Contingently convertible instruments are those that have embedded conversion features that are contingently convertible or exercisable based either on a market price trigger or on multiple contingencies, if one of the contingencies is a market price trigger and the instrument can be converted or share settled based on meeting the specified market condition. A market price trigger is a condition that is based at least in part on the reporting entity's share price. Examples include contingently convertible debt and contingently convertible preferred stock. A typical trigger occurs when the market price exceeds a defined conversion price by a specified percentage (e.g., when the market price first equals or exceeds 20% more than the conversion price of $33 per share). Others have floating market price triggers for which conversion is dependent upon the market price of the reporting entity's stock exceeding the conversion price by a specified percentage(s) at specified times during the term of the debt. Yet other contingently convertible instruments require that the market price of the issuer's stock exceed a specified level for a specified period (for example, 20% above the conversion price for a 30-day period). In addition, these instruments may have additional features such as parity features, issuer call options, and investor put options.

ASC 260-10-45-44 holds that contingently convertible instruments are to be included in diluted EPS, if dilutive, regardless of whether the market price trigger has been met. The reasoning is that there is no substantive economic difference between contingently convertible instruments and conventional convertible instruments with a market price conversion premium. ASC 260-10-45-44 is to be applied to instruments that have multiple contingencies, if one of these is a market price trigger and the instrument is convertible or settleable in shares based on a market condition being met—that is, the conversion is not dependent on a substantive non-market-based contingency.

Example—Contingently convertible debt with a market price trigger

The holder of the Frye Corp. 4% interest-bearing bonds, amounting to $100,000 face value, may convert the debt into shares of Frye common stock when the share price exceeds the market price trigger; otherwise, the holder is only entitled to the par value of the debt. The conversion ratio is 20 shares per bond, or a total of 2,000 shares of stock. The implicit conversion price, therefore, is $50 per share.

At the time of issuance of the bonds, Frye common stock has a market price of $40. Frye's effective tax rate is 35%. Frye has 20,000 shares of its common shares outstanding. The bonds become convertible when the average share price for the year exceeds $65 (130% of conversion price).

The contingently convertible bonds are issued on January 1, 20X1. Income available to common shareholders for the year ended December 31, 20X1, is $80,000, and the average share price for the year is $55. The issuer of the contingently convertible debt would apply ASC 260-10-45, which requires the reporting entity to include the dilutive effect of the convertible debt in diluted EPS even though the market price trigger of $65 has not been met.

Basic EPS is ($80,000 ÷ 20,000 shares =) $4.00 per share. Applying the if-converted method to the debt instrument dilutes EPS to $3.77. (To compute DEPS, net income is increased by the after-tax effect of interest, and this is then divided by the total of outstanding plus potential common shares.)

Consolidated DEPS

When computing consolidated DEPS entities with subsidiaries that have issued common stock or potential common shares to parties other than the parent company (minority interests) follow these general guidelines.

1. Securities issued by a subsidiary that enable their holders to obtain the subsidiary's common stock are included in computing the subsidiary's EPS. Per-share earnings of the subsidiary are included in the consolidated EPS calculations based on the consolidated group's holding of the subsidiary's securities.
2. For the purpose of computing consolidated DEPS, securities of a subsidiary that are convertible into its parent company's common stock, along with subsidiary's options or warrants to purchase common stock of the parent company, are all considered among the potential common shares of the parent company.

Partially Paid Shares

If an entity has common shares issued in a partially paid form and the shares are entitled to dividends in proportion to the amount paid, the common-share equivalent of those partially paid shares is included in the computation of basic EPS to the extent that they were entitled to participate in dividends. Partially paid stock subscriptions that do not share in dividends until paid in full are considered the equivalent of warrants and are included in the calculation of DEPS using the treasury stock method.

Example of impact of partially paid shares on EPS

Orion Corporation has 200,000 shares of common stock outstanding. In addition, under a stock subscription plan, investors have paid $30,000 towards the purchase of 4,000 common shares at the fixed price of $15 per share. Investors purchasing shares under the plan are entitled to dividends in proportion to the amount paid. Thus, there are 2,000 shares in the stock subscription plan for the purpose of calculating basic EPS, calculated as follows:

$$\frac{\text{4,000 common shares}}{\text{(4,000 common shares} \times \text{\$15/share) / \$30,000 paid}} = \text{2,000 shares}$$

Orion records net income of $50,000 for the fiscal year. Its calculation of basic EPS follows:

$$\frac{\text{\$50,000 net income}}{\text{2,000 existing common shares + 2,000 stock subscription shares}} = \text{\$0.25}$$

Once the stock subscription plan is completed, with all shares paid for and issued under that earlier plan, Orion creates another plan, which is one that does not allow participants to share in dividends until all payments are completed. Again, participants have thus far paid $30,000 to acquire 4,000 common shares at a fixed price of $15 each. Orion has 204,000 shares of common stock outstanding, and its net income for the current fiscal year is $80,000. The average market price of Orion's stock during the period is $20. Orion calculates the number of additional common shares with the following calculation, which is the same approach used to calculate the number of shares associated with warrants:

Proceeds from assumed purchase of shares in subscription plan (4,000 shares × $15/share)	$60,000
Number of shares to be issued	4,000
Number of shares assumed to be reacquired ($60,000 / $20 average market price)	3,000
Number of shares assumed issued and not reacquired	1,000

Orion's DEPS calculation follows:

$$\frac{\text{80,000 net income}}{\text{204,000 existing common shares + 1,000 shares from stock purchase plan}} = \text{\$0.39}$$

Note that Orion's basic EPS is not affected by the shares to be issued under this plan, since no right to dividends exists until the subscription has been fully paid.

Effect of Certain Derivatives on EPS Computations

ASC 260 did not contemplate certain complex situations having EPS computation implications. In ASC 815-40-15, the accounting for derivative financial instruments that are indexed to, and potentially to be settled in, the reporting entity's own shares has been addressed. It establishes a model for categorization of a range of such instruments and deals with the EPS effects of each of these. This approach assumes that when the entity can elect to settle these instruments by payment of cash or issuance of shares, the latter will be chosen; if the holder (counterparty) has that choice, payment of cash must be presumed. (Certain exceptions exist when the settlement alternatives are not economically equivalent; in those instances, accounting is to be based on the economic substance of the transactions.) Statement of financial position classification of such instruments is based on consideration of a number of factors, and classification may change from period to period if there are certain changes in circumstances.

For EPS computation purposes, for those contracts that provide the company with a choice of either cash settlement or settlement in shares, ASC 815-40-15 states that settlement in shares should be assumed, although this can be overcome based on past experience or stated policy. If the counterparty controls the choice, however, the more dilutive assumption must be made, irrespective of past experience or policy.

ASC 260 requires the use of the "reverse treasury stock method" to account for the dilutive impact of written put options and similar derivative contracts, if they are "in the money" during the reporting period. Using this method, an incremental number of shares is determined to be the excess of the number of shares that would have to be sold for cash, at the average market price during the period, to satisfy the put obligation over the number of shares obtained via the put exercise. ASC 815-40-15 states that, for contracts giving the reporting entity a choice of settlement methods (stock or cash), it should assume share settlement, although this can be overcome if past behavior makes it reasonable to presume cash settlement. If the holder controls the settlement method, however, the more dilutive method of settlement must be presumed.

Effect on EPS of Redemption or Induced Conversion of Preferred Stock

Companies may redeem shares of their outstanding preferred stock for noncash consideration such as by exchanges for other securities. Sometimes the company induces conversion by offering additional securities or other consideration to the holders. Such offers are sometimes referred to as "sweeteners." The accounting for "sweeteners" offered to convertible debt holders was addressed by ASC 470-20-05, and is explained in the chapter on ASC 470. ASC 260-10-S99 deals with the anomalous situation of "sweeteners" offered to induce conversion of convertible preferred shares.

The position of the SEC staff is that any excess of the fair value of consideration given over the book value of the preferred stock represents a return to the preferred stockholder and, consequently, is to be accounted for similar to dividends paid to the preferred stockholders for purposes of computing EPS. This means that the excess should be deducted from earnings to compute earnings available for common stockholders in the calculation of EPS.

If the converse is true, with consideration given being less than carrying value, including when there is an excess of the carrying amount of the preferred stock over the fair value of the consideration transferred, this should be added to net income to derive earnings available for common stockholders in the calculation of EPS.

This SEC staff position applies to redemptions of convertible preferred stock, whether or not the embedded conversion feature is "in the money" or not at the time of redemption.

If the redemption or induced conversion is effected by offering other securities, rather than cash, fair values would be the referent to determine whether an excess was involved. If the conversion includes the reacquisition of a previously recognized beneficial conversion feature, then reduce the fair value of the consideration by the intrinsic value of the conversion option on the commitment date.

Furthermore, per ASC 260-10-S99, in computing the carrying amount of preferred stock that has been redeemed or been subject to an induced conversion, the carrying amount of the preferred stock is to be reduced by the related issuance costs irrespective of how those costs were classified in the stockholders' equity section of the statement of financial position upon initial issuance.

Since ASC 480-10-25-4 defines mandatorily redeemable preferred stock as a liability, not as equity, the guidance in ASC 260-10-S99 would not apply. Rather, any excess or shortfall offered in an induced conversion situation involving mandatorily redeemable preferred stock would be reported as gain or loss on debt extinguishment, not as a dividend.

In a related matter, ASC 260-10-S99 discusses the accounting required when a reporting entity effects a redemption or induced conversion of only a portion of the outstanding securities of a class of preferred stock. Reflecting an SEC staff position, any excess consideration should be attributed to those shares that are redeemed or converted. Thus, for the purpose of determining whether the "if-converted" method is dilutive for the period, the shares redeemed or converted should be considered separately from those shares that are not redeemed or converted. It would be inappropriate to aggregate securities with differing effective dividend yields when determining whether the "if-converted" method is dilutive, which would be the result if a single, aggregate computation was made for the entire series of preferred stock.

Example of partial conversion

Hephaestus Construction has 1,000 shares of convertible preferred stock outstanding at the beginning of the reporting period. Hephaestus issued the preferred stock at its fair value, which matched its $15/share par value. The shares have a stated dividend of 7 percent ($1.05), and each convertible preferred share converts into one share of Hephaestus common stock. During the reporting period, Hephaestus redeemed 250 shares for $18/share.

Hephaestus should determine whether the conversion is dilutive for the remaining 750 shares by applying the "if-converted" method for the entire period, comparing the $1.05 stated dividend to the effect of assuming their conversion into 750 shares of Hephaestus common stock.

Hephaestus should use the same calculation for the converted 250 shares, weighted from the beginning of the period to their redemption date. In this case, Hephaestus should apply the "if-converted" method using the $1.05 stated dividend and redemption premium of $3/share, in comparison to the effect of assuming their conversion into 250 shares of Hephaestus common stock.

EPS Impact of Tax Effect of Dividends Paid on Unallocated ESOP Shares

Under the provisions of ASC 718-40, dividends paid on unallocated shares are not charged to retained earnings. Since the employer controls the use of dividends on unallocated shares, these dividends are not considered dividends for financial reporting purposes. Consequently, the dividends do not affect the DEPS computation.

Earnings Per Share Implications of ASC 718

ASC 718 mandates that share-based employee compensation arrangements must, with very few exceptions, be recognized as expenses over the relevant employee service period. ASC 260-10-45-28A requires that employee equity share options, nonvested shares, and similar equity instruments granted to employees be treated as potential common shares in computing diluted EPS. DEPS is to be based on the actual number of options or shares granted and not yet forfeited, unless doing so would be antidilutive. If vesting in or the ability to exercise (or retain) an award is contingent on a performance or market condition (e.g., as the level of future earnings), the shares or share options shall be treated as contingently issuable shares. If equity share options or other equity instruments are outstanding for only part of a reporting period, the shares issuable are to be weighted to reflect the portion of the period during which the equity instruments are outstanding.

ASC 260 provides guidance on applying the treasury stock method for equity instruments granted in share-based payment transactions in determining DEPS.

Presentation

The reason for the differentiation between simple and complex capital structures is that ASC 260 requires different financial statement presentation for each. ASC 260 mandates that EPS be shown on the face of the income statement for each of the following items (when applicable):

1. Income from continuing operations
2. Net income.

An entity that reports a discontinued operation, an extraordinary item, or the cumulative effect of a change in accounting principle presents basic and diluted EPS amounts for these line items either on the face of the income statement or in the notes to the financial statements. These requirements must be fulfilled regardless of whether the capital structure is simple or complex. The difference in the two structures is that a simple capital structure requires presentation of only a single EPS number for each item, while a complex structure requires the dual presentation of basic EPS and DEPS for each item.

EPS data is to be presented for all periods for which an income statement or summary of earnings is presented. If DEPS is reported for at least one period, it is to be reported for all periods presented, regardless of whether or not DEPS differs from basic EPS. (ASC 260-10-45-7) However, if basic and diluted EPS are the same amounts for all periods presented, dual presentation may be accomplished in one line on the face of the income statement.

Rights issue. A rights issue whose exercise price at issuance is below the fair value of the stock contains a bonus element. If a rights issue contains a bonus element (somewhat similar to a stock dividend) and is offered to all existing stockholders, basic and diluted EPS are adjusted retroactively for the bonus element for all periods presented. However, if the ability to exercise the rights issue is contingent on some event other than the passage of time, this retroactive adjustment does not apply until the contingency is resolved.

Restated EPS. When a restatement of the results of operations of a prior period is required to be included in the income statement, EPS for the prior period(s) is also restated. The effect of the restatement, expressed in per-share terms, is disclosed in the period of restatement. Restated EPS data is computed as if the restated income (loss) had been reported in the prior period(s).

Year-to-date diluted EPS. ASC 260-10-45 addresses the matter of how to compute year-to-date diluted EPS (1) when a company has a year-to-date loss from continuing operations including one or more quarters with income from continuing operations, and (2) when in-the-money options or warrants were not included in one or more quarterly diluted EPS computations because there was a loss from continuing operations in those quarters.

ASC 260 directs that in applying the treasury stock method in year-to-date computations, the number of incremental shares to be included in the denominator is to be determined by computing a year-to-date weighted-average of the number of incremental shares included in each quarterly diluted EPS computation.

However, ASC 260 includes a prohibition against antidilution, which states that the computation of diluted EPS is not to assume conversion, exercise, or contingent issuance of securities that would have an antidilutive effect on EPS. There may be a conflict between these provisions when a period longer than three months has an overall loss but includes quarters with income. For periods with year-to-date income (as in quarterly filings on Form 10-Q), in computing year-to-date diluted EPS, SEC staff believes that year-to-date income (or loss) from continuing operations should be the basis for determining whether or not dilutive potential common shares not included in one or more quarterly computations of diluted EPS should be included in the year-to-date computation.

According to ASC 260-10-45, (1) when there is a year-to-date loss, potential common shares should never be included in the computation of diluted EPS, because to do so would be antidilutive, and (2) when there is year-to-date income, if in-the-money options or warrants were excluded from one or more quarterly diluted EPS computations because the effect was antidilutive (there was a loss from continuing operations in those periods), then those options or warrants should be included in the diluted EPS denominator (on a weighted-average basis) in the year-to-date computation as long as the effect is not antidilutive. Similarly, contingent shares that were excluded from a quarterly computation solely because there was a loss from continuing operations should be included in the year-to-date computation unless the effect is antidilutive.

Other Disclosure Requirements

The additional items required to be disclosed for all periods for which an income statement is presented can be found in the disclosure checklist in the appendix to this volume.

COMPREHENSIVE EXAMPLE

The examples within the text used a simplified approach for determining whether or not options, warrants, convertible preferred stock, or convertible bonds have a dilutive effect on DEPS. If the DEPS number computed was lower than basic EPS, the security was considered dilutive. This approach is adequate when the company has only *one* potentially dilutive security. If the firm has *more than one* potentially dilutive security, a more complex ranking procedure must be employed (ASC 260).

For example, assume the following facts concerning the capital structure of a company:

1. Income from continuing operations and net income are both $50,000. Income from continuing operations is not displayed on the firm's income statement.
2. The weighted-average number of common shares outstanding is 10,000 shares.
3. The income tax rate is a flat 40%.
4. Options to purchase 1,000 shares of common stock at $8 per share were outstanding all year.
5. Options to purchase 2,000 shares of common stock at $13 per share were outstanding all year.
6. The average market price of common stock during the year was $10.
7. 200 7% convertible bonds, each convertible into 40 common shares, were outstanding the entire year. The bonds were issued at par value ($1,000 per bond) and no bonds were converted during the year.
8. 4% convertible, cumulative preferred stock, par value of $100 per share, 1,000 shares issued and outstanding the entire year. Each preferred share is convertible into one common share. The preferred stock was issued at par value and no shares were converted during the year.

Note that reference is made below to some of the tables included in the body of the chapter because the facts above represent a combination of the facts used for the examples in the chapter.

To determine both basic EPS and DEPS, the following procedures must be performed:

1. Calculate basic EPS as if the capital structure were simple.
2. Identify other potentially dilutive securities.
3. Calculate the per-share effects of assuming issuance or conversion of each potentially dilutive security on an individual basis.
4. Rank the per-share effects from smallest to largest.
5. Recalculate EPS (Step 1 above) adding the potentially dilutive securities one at a time in order, beginning with the security with the *smallest* per-share effect.
6. Continue adding potentially dilutive securities to each successive calculation until all have been added or until the addition of a security increases EPS (antidilution) from its previous level.

Applying these procedures to the facts above

1. Basic EPS

$$\frac{\text{Net income} - \text{Preferred dividends}}{\text{Weighted-average number of common shares outstanding}} = \frac{\$50{,}000 - \$4{,}000}{10{,}000 \text{ shares}} = \$4.60$$

2. Identification of other potentially dilutive securities

   a. Options (two types)
   b. 7% convertible bonds
   c. 4% convertible cumulative preferred stock.

Diluted EPS (DEPS)

3. Per-share effects of conversion or issuance of other potentially dilutive securities calculated individually

   a. Options—Only the options to purchase 1,000 shares at $8.00 per share are potentially dilutive. The options to purchase 2,000 shares of common stock are antidilutive because the exercise price is greater than the average market price. Thus, they are not included in the computation.
   Proceeds if options exercised:

   $$1{,}000 \text{ shares} \times \$8 \text{ per share} = \underline{\underline{\$8{,}000}}$$

   Shares that could be acquired:

   $$\$8{,}000 \div \$10 = \underline{\underline{800}}$$

   $$\text{Dilutive shares: } 1{,}000 - 800 = \underline{\underline{200}}$$

   $$\frac{\text{Increase/decrease in net income}}{\text{Increase in weighted-average number of common shares outstanding}} = \frac{\$0}{200 \text{ shares}} = \$0$$

   b. 7% convertible bonds (see Table 3)

   $$\frac{\text{Increase/decrease in net income}}{\text{Increase in weighted-average number of common shares outstanding}} = \frac{\$8{,}400}{8{,}000 \text{ shares}} = \$1.05$$

   c. 4% convertible cumulative preferred stock—The outstanding common shares increase by 1,000 when all shares are converted. This results in total dividends of $4,000 not being paid.

   $$\frac{\text{Increase/decrease in net income}}{\text{Increase in weighted-average number of common shares outstanding}} = \frac{\$4{,}000}{1{,}000 \text{ shares}} = \$4.00$$

4. Rank the per-share effects from smallest to largest

a.	Options	$ 0
b.	7% convertible bonds	1.05
c.	4% convertible cumulative preferred stock	4.00

5. Recalculate the EPS in rank order starting from the security with the smallest per-share dilution and adding one potentially dilutive security at a time

a. DEPS—options added

$$\frac{\text{Net income} - \text{Preferred dividends}}{\text{Weighted-average number of common shares outstanding} + \text{Shares not acquired with proceeds of options}} = \frac{\$50{,}000 - \$4{,}000}{10{,}000 + 200 \text{ shares}} = \$4.51$$

b. DEPS—options and 7% convertible bonds added

$$\frac{\text{Net income} - \text{Preferred dividends} + \text{Interest expense (net of tax)}}{\text{Weighted-average number of common shares outstanding} + \text{Shares not acquired with proceeds of options} + \text{Shares issued upon conversion of bonds}} = \frac{\$50{,}000 - \$4{,}000 + \$8{,}400}{10{,}000 + 200 + 8{,}000 \text{ shares}} = \$2.99$$

c. DEPS—options, 7% convertible bonds and 4% convertible cumulative preferred stock added

$$\frac{\text{Net income} + \text{Interest expense (net of tax)}}{\text{Weighted-average number of common shares outstanding} + \text{Shares not acquired with proceeds of options} + \text{Shares issued upon conversion of bonds and preferred stock}} = \frac{\$50{,}000 + \$8{,}400}{10{,}000 + 200 + 8{,}000 + 1{,}000 \text{ shares}} = \$3.04$$

DEPS = $2.99

Since the addition of the 4% convertible cumulative preferred stock raises DEPS from $2.99 to $3.04, the preferred stock is antidilutive and is therefore excluded from the computation of DEPS.

A dual presentation of basic EPS and DEPS is required. The dual presentation on the face of the income statement would appear as follows:

Net income	$50,000
Earnings per common share* (Note X)	$ 4.60
Earnings per common share, assuming dilution* (Note X)	$ 2.99

* *The captions "Basic EPS" and "Diluted EPS" may be substituted, respectively.*

Note X: Earnings per Share (Illustrative Disclosure Based on Facts from the Example)

The following adjustments were made to the numerators and denominators of the basic and diluted EPS computations:

	Year Ended December 31, 20X1		
	Income (numerator)	*Weighted-average number of outstanding shares (denominator)*	*Amount per share*
Net income	$50,000		
Less: Preferred stock dividends	(4,000)		
Basic EPS			
Income available to common stockholders	46,000	10,000	$4.60
Effects of Dilutive Securities			
Options to purchase common stock		200	
7% convertible bonds	8,400	8,000	
Diluted EPS			
Income available to common stockholders adjusted for the effects of assumed exercise of options and conversion of bonds	$54,400	18,200	$2.99

There were 1,000 shares of $100 par value, 4% convertible, cumulative preferred stock issued and outstanding during the year ended December 31, 20X1, that were not included in the above computation because their conversion would not have resulted in a dilution of EPS.

Example of the presentation and computation of earnings per share

Assume that 100,000 shares were outstanding throughout the year.

ABC Company
Income Statement
For the Year Ended December 31, 20X1

Sales		$2,000,000
Cost of goods sold		750,000
Gross profit		$1,250,000
Selling and administrative expenses		500,000
Income from operations		$ 750,000
Other revenues and expense		
Interest income	$40,000	
Interest expense	(30,000)	10,000
Income before unusual or infrequent items and income taxes		$ 760,000
Unusual or infrequent items:		
Loss from permanent impairment of value of manufacturing facilities		(10,000)
Income from continuing operations before income taxes		$ 750,000
Income taxes		300,000
Income from continuing operations		$ 450,000
Discontinued operations:		
Loss from operations of Division X, including loss on disposal of $100,000 and income tax benefit of $20,000		$ 30,000
Income before extraordinary item		$ 420,000
Extraordinary item—loss from earthquake less applicable income tax benefit of $38,000		(72,000)
Net income		$ 348,000
Basic EPS computation		
Income from continuing operations ($450,000/100,000)		$ 4.50
Extraordinary items* ($72,000/100,000)		(0.72)
Discontinued operations* ($30,000/100,000)		(0.30)
Net income available for common stockholders		$ 3.48

* *May instead be shown in the notes to the financial statements.*

Other Sources

See ASC Location – Wiley *GAAP* Chapter	*For information on…*
ASC 710-10-45	The effects of employer shares held by a rabbi trust in computing basic and diluted EPS.
ASC 718-10-45	The effects of employee equity share options, nonvested shares, and similar equity instruments in computing diluted EPS.
ASC 718-40-45 and 718-40-50	The effects of issues resulting from the existence of employee stock ownership plans in computing basic and diluted EPS and the related disclosure requirements.

12 ASC 270 INTERIM REPORTING

PERSPECTIVE AND ISSUES

Subtopic

ASC 270, *Interim Reporting,* contains one subtopic:

- ASC 270-10, *Overall,* that provides guidance on
  - Accounting and disclosure issues for reporting on periods less than one year and
  - Minimum disclosure requirements for interim reporting for publicly traded companies.

Overview

The term "interim reporting" refers to financial reporting for periods of less than a year. GAAP does not mandate interim reporting. However, in the United States the Securities and Exchange Commission (SEC) requires public companies to file quarterly summarized interim financial data on its Form 10-Q. The level of detail of the information required in those interim reports is substantially less than is specified under GAAP for annual financial statements.

Objective. The objective of interim reporting is to provide current information regarding enterprise performance to existing and prospective investors, lenders, and other financial statement users. This enables users to act upon relevant information in making informed decisions in a timely manner. SEC filings on Form 10-Q are due in no more than 45 days after period end. The demand for timely information means that interim data will often be more heavily impacted by estimates and assumptions.

Integral Approach. Historically, there have been two competing views of interim reporting. Under the *integral* view, the interim period is considered an integral part of the annual accounting period. It thus follows that annual operating expenses are to be estimated and allocated to the interim periods based on forecasted annual activity levels such as sales volume. The results of subsequent interim periods are adjusted to reflect the effect of estimation errors in earlier interim periods of the same fiscal year. ASC 270-10-45-1 prefers the integral view.

Discrete Approach. Under the *discrete* view, each interim period is considered a discrete accounting period. Thus, estimations and allocations are made using the same methods used for annual reporting. It follows that the same expense recognition rules apply as under annual reporting, and no special interim accruals or deferrals would be necessary or permissible. Annual operating expenses are recognized in the interim period incurred, irrespective of the number of interim periods benefited (i.e., no special deferral rules would apply to interim periods).

Integral/Discrete Pros and Cons. Proponents of the integral view argue that unique interim expense recognition procedures are necessary to avoid fluctuations in period-to-period results that might be misleading to financial statement users. Applying the integral view results in interim earnings which are indicative of annual earnings and, thus, arguably more useful for predictive purposes. Proponents of the discrete view argue that the smoothing of interim results for purposes of forecasting annual earnings has undesirable effects. For example, a turning point during the year in an earnings trend could be obscured if smoothing techniques implied by the integral view were to be employed.

The debate between integral and discrete views of interim reporting can result in very different interim measures of results of operations. This can occur, for example, because certain annual expenses may be concentrated in one interim period, yet benefit the entire year's operations. Examples include advertising expenses and major repairs and maintenance of equipment. Also, in the United States (and many other jurisdictions) progressive (graduated) income tax rates are applied to total annual income and various income tax credits may arise, all of which are computed on annual pretax earnings, often adding complexity to the determination of quarterly income tax expense.

Other Issues. Interim reporting is problematic for reasons other than the choice of an underlying measurement philosophy. As reporting periods are shortened, the effects of errors in estimation and allocation are magnified, and randomly occurring events which might not be material in the context of a full fiscal year could create major distortions in short interim period summaries of reporting entity performance. The effects of seasonal fluctuations and temporary market conditions further limit the reliability, comparability, and predictive value of interim reports.

DEFINITIONS OF TERMS

Source: ASC 270-10-20

Acquiree. The business or businesses that the acquirer obtains control of in a business combination. This term also includes a nonprofit activity or business that a not-for-profit acquirer obtains control of in an acquisition by a not-for-profit entity.

Acquirer. The entity that obtains control of the acquiree. However, in a business combination in which a variable interest entity (VIE) is acquired, the primary beneficiary of that entity always is the acquirer.

Acquisition by a Not-for-Profit Entity. A transaction or other event in which a not-for-profit acquirer obtains control of one or more nonprofit activities or businesses and initially recognizes their assets and liabilities in the acquirer's financial statements. When applicable guidance in Topic 805 is applied by a not-for-profit entity, the term business combination has the same meaning as this term has for a not-for-profit entity. Likewise, a reference to business combinations in guidance that links to Topic 805 has the same meaning as a reference to acquisitions by not-for-profit entities.

Business. An integrated set of activities and assets that is capable of being conducted and managed for the purpose of providing a return in the form of dividends, lower costs, or other economic benefits directly to investors or other owners, members, or participants. Additional guidance on what a business consists of is presented in paragraphs 805-10-55-4 through 55-9.

Business Combination. A transaction or other event in which an acquirer obtains control of one or more businesses. Transactions sometimes referred to as true mergers or mergers of equals also are business combinations. See also Acquisition by a Not-for-Profit Entity.

Financing Receivable. A financing arrangement that has both of the following characteristics:

a. It represents a contractual right to receive money in either of the following ways:
    1. On demand
    2. On fixed or determinable dates.
b. It is recognized as an asset in the entity's statement of financial position.

See paragraphs 310-10-55-13 through 55-15 for more information on the definition of financing receivable, including a list of items that are excluded from the definition (for example, debt securities).

Legal Entity. Any legal structure used to conduct activities or to hold assets. Some examples of such structures are corporations, partnerships, limited liability companies, grantor trusts, and other trusts.

Not-for-Profit Entity. An entity that possesses the following characteristics, in varying degrees, that distinguish it from a business entity:

a. Contributions of significant amounts of resources from resource providers who do not expect commensurate or proportionate pecuniary return
b. Operating purposes other than to provide goods or services at a profit
c. Absence of ownership interests like those of business entities.

Entities that clearly fall outside this definition include the following:

a. All investor-owned entities
b. Entities that provide dividends, lower costs, or other economic benefits directly and proportionately to their owners, members, or participants, such as mutual insurance entities, credit unions, farm and rural electric cooperatives, and employee benefit plans.

Publicly Traded Company. A publicly traded company includes any company whose securities trade in a public market on either of the following:

a. A stock exchange (domestic or foreign)
b. In the over-the-counter market (including securities quoted only locally or regionally), or any company that is a conduit bond obligor for conduit debt securities that are traded in a public market (a domestic or foreign stock exchange or an over-the-counter market, including local or regional markets).

Additionally, when a company is required to file or furnish financial statements with the SEC or makes a filing with a regulatory agency in preparation for sale of its securities in a public market it is considered a publicly traded company for this purpose.

Conduit debt securities refer to certain limited-obligation revenue bonds, certificates of participation, or similar debt instruments issued by a state or local governmental entity for the express purpose of providing financing for a specific third party (the conduit bond obligor) that is not a part of the state or local government's financial reporting entity. Although conduit debt securities bear the name of the governmental entity that issues them, the governmental entity often has no obligation for such debt beyond the resources provided by a lease or loan agreement with the third party on whose behalf the securities are issued. Further, the conduit bond obligor is responsible for any future financial reporting requirements.

Variable Interest Entity. A legal entity subject to consolidation according to the provisions of the Variable Interest Entities Subsections of Subtopic 810-10.

CONCEPTS, RULES, AND EXAMPLES

Differentiation between Public and Nonpublic Companies

The explanations and interpretations in this chapter have been divided into two sections. Part I discusses issues applicable to *both* public and nonpublic reporting entities (including, where applicable, not-for-profit organizations). Part II discusses issues applicable *only* to publicly traded companies.

The usefulness of interim reports rests on the relationship to annual reports. Therefore, ASC 270-10-45-1 states that "each interim period should be viewed primarily as an integral part of an annual period," and the accounting should be based on the principles and practices used in the entity's annual reporting. The exception to this is if the entity has adopted a change in accounting in the interim period. Certain principles and practices may also have to be modified so that the interim reporting better relates to the annual results. The modifications are detailed in ASC 270-10-45-4 through 45-11 and are detailed in the sections below.

PART I—REQUIREMENTS APPLICABLE TO ALL REPORTING ENTITIES

Revenues

Revenues are recognized as earned during an interim period using the same principles followed in annual reports (ASC 270-10-45-3). This rule applies to both product sales and service revenues. For example, product sales cutoff procedures are applied at the end of each interim period in the same manner that they are applied at year-end, and revenue from long-term construction contracts is recognized at interim dates using the same method used at year-end.

Product Costs and Direct Costs

Product costs and costs directly associated with service revenues are treated in interim reports in the same manner as in annual reports. ASC 270-10-45 provides for four integral view exceptions:

1. The gross profit method may be used to estimate cost of goods sold and ending inventory for interim periods.
2. When inventory consists of LIFO layers, and a portion of the base period layer is liquidated at an interim date, and it is expected that this inventory will be replaced by year-end, the anticipated cost of replacing the liquidated inventory is included in cost of sales of the interim period.
3. An inventory market decline reasonably expected to reverse by year-end (i.e., a decline deemed to be temporary in nature) need not be recognized in the interim period. ASC 330-10-55 states that there must be substantial evidence available to support the contention that the market value will recover before the inventory is sold, which generally limits this interim exception to seasonal price fluctuations. If an inventory loss from a market decline that is recognized in one period is followed by a market price recovery, the reversal is recognized as a gain in the subsequent interim period. Recognition of this gain in the later interim period is limited to the extent of loss previously recognized. This is in marked contrast to lower of cost or market write-downs in annual financial statements, which are not permitted to be restored in a later period.
4. Entities using standard cost accounting systems ordinarily report purchase price, wage rate, and usage or efficiency variances in the same manner as year-end. Planned purchase price and volume variances are deferred if expected to be absorbed by year-end.

The first exception above eliminates the need for a physical inventory count at the interim date. The other three exceptions attempt to synchronize the quarterly financial statements with the annual report. For example, consider the LIFO liquidation exception. Without this exception, interim cost of goods sold could include low earlier year or base-period costs, while annual cost of goods sold would include only current year costs.

Several questions arise when using LIFO for interim reporting.

1. What is the best approach to estimate interim LIFO cost of sales?
2. As noted above, when an interim liquidation occurs that is expected to be replaced by year-end, cost of sales includes the expected cost of replacement. How is this adjustment treated on the interim statement of financial position?
3. How is an interim liquidation that is not expected to be replaced by year-end recorded?

These problems are not addressed in ASC 270. The only literature related to these problems is a 1984 American Institute of Certified Public Accounts (AICPA) Task Force LIFO Issues Paper.[1]

---

[1] *AICPA Accounting Standards Executive Committee Task Force on LIFO Inventory Problems, "Identification and Discussion of Certain Financial Accounting and Reporting Issues Concerning LIFO Inventories." American Institute of Certified Public Accountants, November 30, 1984. The paper can be found at* tinyurl.com/8j3f8t7.

The Issues Paper describes two acceptable approaches to measuring interim LIFO cost of sales. The first approach makes specific quarterly computations of the effect of using LIFO based on year-to-date amounts. This is accomplished by reviewing quarterly price level changes and inventory levels. The second approach projects the expected annual effect of using LIFO and then allocates the results of that projection to the individual quarters. The allocation can be made equally to each quarter or can be made in relation to certain operating criteria per quarter.

The Issues Paper also describes two acceptable approaches to treating the interim liquidation replacement on the statement of financial position. The first approach is to record the adjustment for the effect on pretax income of the replacement as a deferred credit in the current liabilities section. The second approach is to record the adjustment as a credit to an inventory valuation allowance.

When an interim LIFO liquidation occurs that is not expected to be reinstated by year-end, the effect of the liquidation is recognized in the period in which it occurs to the extent that it can be reasonably determined. A reporting entity using dollar-value LIFO may allocate the expected effect of the liquidation to the quarters affected.

Example of interim reporting of product costs

Dakota Corporation encounters the following product cost situations as part of its quarterly reporting:

- It takes physical inventory counts at the end of the second quarter and end of the fiscal year. Its typical gross profit is 30% of sales. The actual gross profit applicable to the first six months of the year is 32%. The actual full-year gross profit is 29%.
- It carries one type of its inventory at LIFO and the remaining inventory at first-in, first-out (FIFO).
- It suffers a clearly temporary decline of $10,000 in the market value of a specific part of its FIFO inventory in the first quarter, which it recovers in the second quarter.
- It liquidates earlier-period, lower-cost LIFO inventories during the second quarter. The liquidation results in second quarter cost of goods sold being $90,000 less (and, of course, second quarter gross profit being $90,000 more) than it would have been absent the LIFO liquidation. Dakota expects to, and does, restore these inventory levels by year-end.
- It suffers a decline of $65,000 in the market value of its FIFO inventory during the third quarter. The inventory value increases by $75,000 in the fourth quarter.

Dakota computes interim cost of goods sold to reflect the effect of these situations as follows:

	Quarter 1	*Quarter 2*	*First 6 months*	*Quarter 3*	*Quarter 4*	*Full year*
Sales	$10,000,000	$8,500,000	$18,500,000	$7,200,000	$11,800,000	$37,500,000
Complement of normal gross profit percentage	70%			70%		
Cost of goods sold using gross profit method	7,000,000			5,040,000		
Complement of year-to-date gross profit percentage based on actual count			68%			71%
Cost of goods sold based on actual count			12,580,000			26,625,000
Sales	$10,000,000	$8,500,000	$18,500,000	$7,200,000	$11,800,000	$37,500,000
Adjustment for effect of temporary LIFO liquidation[3]			90,000			
Decline in inventory value[4]				65,000		
Adjusted cost of goods sold	$7,000,000	$5,670,000[1]	$12,670,000	$5,105,000	$8,850,000[2]	$26,625,000

1 *Calculated as: Adjusted cost of goods sold for first six months based on actual inventory count – Cost of goods sold recognized during the first quarter using the gross profit method.*

2 *Calculated as Full year cost of goods sold of $26,625,000 – $12,670,000 Cost of goods sold for first half of year – $5,105,000 Cost of goods sold recognized during the third quarter.*

3 *Full recognition of replacement of earlier period LIFO layer in the period that the temporary liquidation was incurred.*

4 *No recognition is given to the first quarter temporary decline in value or the subsequent increase because, at the time it occurred, it was expected to be temporary. Full recognition is given to the third quarter market value decline assuming that it was not expected to be temporary. This is followed by recognition of the market value increase, but only to offset the amount of the initial decline.*

To illustrate that the fourth quarter is appropriately adjusted for the effects of applying the interim costing rules to the other quarters, the fourth quarter cost of goods sold is proved as follows:

	Fourth quarter
Fourth quarter sales × actual annual gross profit complement (100% – 29% = 71%)	$8,378,000
Adjustment for the difference between the 68% complement based on the second quarter physical inventory count and the 71% annual complement multiplied by sales for the first six months	555,000
Adjustment for the difference between the 70% complement used under the gross profit method in the third quarter and the actual 71% annual complement multiplied by sales for the third quarter	72,000
Fourth quarter recovery of the third quarter FIFO market decline	(65,000)
Effect of replacing the second quarter temporary decline in LIFO inventory levels	(90,000)
	$8,850,000

Other Costs and Expenses

The integral view is evident in how current US GAAP treats costs incurred in interim periods. Most costs and expenses are recognized in interim periods as incurred. However, a cost that clearly benefits more than one interim period (e.g., annual repairs or property taxes) is allocated among the periods benefited (ASC 270-10-45-8). The allocation is based on

- Estimates of time expired,
- Benefit received, or
- Activity related to the specific periods.

Allocation procedures are to be consistent with those used at year-end reporting dates. However, if a cost incurred during an interim period cannot be readily associated with other interim periods, it is not arbitrarily assigned to those periods. The following parameters (ASC 270-45-10-9) are used in interim periods to account for certain types of expenses incurred in those periods:

1. Costs that benefit two or more interim periods (e.g., annual major repairs) are assigned to interim periods through the use of deferrals or accruals.
2. Quantity discounts given to customers based on annual sales volume are allocated to interim periods on the basis of sales to customers during the interim period relative to estimated annual sales.
3. Property taxes (and like costs) are deferred or accrued at a year-end date to reflect a full year's charge to operations. Charges to interim periods follow similar procedures.
4. Advertising costs are permitted to be deferred to subsequent interim periods within the same fiscal year if the costs clearly benefit those later periods. Prior to actually receiving advertising services, advertising costs may be accrued and allocated to interim periods on the basis of sales if the sales arrangement implicitly includes the advertising program. See Chapter 3 for a discussion of the specialized accounting for direct-response advertising prescribed by ASC 340-20. Those rules apply to both interim and annual reporting periods.

Costs and expenses subject to year-end determination, such as discretionary bonuses and profit-sharing contributions, are assigned to interim periods in a reasonable and consistent manner to the extent they can be reasonably estimated (ASC 270-10-45-10).

Application of interim expense reporting principles is illustrated in the following examples.

Example of interim reporting of other expenses

Dakota Corporation encounters the following expense scenarios as part of its quarterly reporting (for illustrative purposes, all amounts are considered to be material):

- Its largest customer, Floor-Mart, placed firm orders for the year that will result in sales of \$1,500,000 in the first quarter, \$2,000,000 in the second quarter, \$750,000 in the third quarter, and \$1,650,000 in the fourth quarter. Dakota gives Floor-Mart a 5% rebate if Floor-Mart buys at least \$5 million of goods each year. Floor-Mart exceeded the \$5 million goal in the preceding year and is expected to do so again in the current year.
- It incurs \$24,000 of trade show fees in the first quarter for a trade show that will occur in the third quarter.
- It pays \$64,000 in advance in the second quarter for a series of advertisements that will run during the third and fourth quarters.

- It receives a $32,000 property tax bill in the second quarter that applies to the following twelve-month period (July 1 to June 30).
- It incurs annual air filter replacement costs of $6,000 in the first quarter.
- Its management team is entitled to a year-end cash bonus of $120,000 if it meets an annual sales target of $40 million, prior to any sales rebates, with the bonus dropping by $10,000 for every million dollars of sales not achieved.

Dakota used the following calculations to record these scenarios:

	Quarter 1	Quarter 2	Quarter 3	Quarter 4	Full year
Sales	$10,000,000	$8,500,000	$7,200,000	$11,800,000	$37,500,000
Deduction from sales	(75,000)[1]	(100,000)	(37,500)	(82,500)	(295,000)
Marketing expense			24,000[2]		24,000
Advertising expense			32,000[3]	32,000	64,000
Property tax expense			8,000[4]	8,000	16,000
Maintenance expense	1,500[5]	1,500	1,500	1,500	6,000
Bonus expense	30,000[6]	25,500	21,600	17,900	95,000

1 *The sales rebate is based on 5% of actual sales to the customer in the quarter when the sale is made. The actual payment back to the customer does not occur until the end of the year when the $5 million goal is definitively reached.*

2 *The $24,000 trade show payment is initially recorded as a prepaid expense and then charged to marketing expense when the trade show occurs in the third quarter.*

3 *The $64,000 advertising payment is initially recorded as a prepaid expense and then charged to advertising expense when the advertisements run.*

4 *The $32,000 property tax payment is initially recorded as a prepaid expense and then charged to property tax expense on a straight-line basis over the next four quarters.*

5 *The $6,000 air filter replacement payment is initially recorded as a prepaid expense and then charged to maintenance expense over the one-year life of the air filters.*

6 *The management bonus is recognized in proportion to the amount of revenue recognized in each quarter. Once it becomes apparent that the full sales target will not be reached, the bonus accrual is adjusted downward. In this case, the downward adjustment is assumed to be in the fourth quarter, since past history and seasonality factors made achievement of the full goal unlikely until fourth quarter results were known.*

Income Taxes

At each interim date, the reporting entity is required to make its best estimate of the effective income tax rate expected to apply to the full fiscal year. This estimate reflects expected federal, state, local, and foreign income tax rates, income tax credits, and the effects of applying income tax planning techniques. However, changes in income tax legislation are reflected in interim periods only after the enactment date of the legislation. This process is necessary to avoid distortions that would result if early interim periods reflected the entire effect of lower income tax brackets, while later periods suffered from having all income taxed at higher bracket rates. Since income taxes apply to annual income, not to interim periods on stand-alone bases, an integral approach is clearly warranted.

Fair Value of Financial Instruments

ASC 825-10-50 requires disclosures about the fair value of financial instruments in interim reporting periods, as well as in annual financial statements. Specifically, an entity should disclose the fair value of all financial instruments for which it is practicable to create such an estimate, alongside their carrying values. The format of this presentation should clarify whether these items are assets or liabilities. The entity should also disclose the methods and significant assumptions that it used to estimate the fair value of the financial instruments, as well as note any changes in these methods and assumptions from the preceding period. In interim periods, nonpublic entities are not required to disclose the level in which a fair value measurement would be categorized within the fair value hierarchy for assets and liabilities not recognized at fair value but for which disclosure of fair value is required.

Discontinued Operations and Extraordinary Items

Extraordinary items and the effects of the disposal of a component of the entity (ASC 270-10-45-11A) are reported separately in the interim period in which they occur. The same treatment is given to other unusual or infrequently occurring events. No attempt is made to allocate the effects of these items over the entire fiscal year in which they occur.

Materiality is evaluated by relating the item to the expected annual results of operations. Thus, an item to be reported in an early interim period may be judged material but later, when estimated results for the full fiscal year are known with greater precision, be judged immaterial; the opposite pattern may also occur, with a presumed immaterial item being later found material to full-year results of operations. Either of such eventualities is inherent in the interim reporting process and would not be deemed an error requiring restatement.

Example of discontinued operations and extraordinary items

Dakota Corporation's Helena, Montana, facility suffers a direct hit from a tornado during the second quarter. Dakota's management believes the loss warrants treatment as an extraordinary item since the state of Montana does not typically experience tornadoes. Dakota's insurance does not cover tornados, and the loss resulting from cleanup costs and writing down the net book value of the damaged portion of the building is $620,000, or $403,000 net of applicable income taxes computed at a flat 35% rate. As required by ASC 360-10-35, Dakota's management estimates the expected future cash flows from the use and ultimate disposition of the property and determines that the building does not require any further write-down for impairment.

In the third quarter, before the tornado repairs are completed, this unfortunate facility is subjected to a flood; however, the unreimbursed damage is only $68,000, or $44,200 net of applicable income taxes. The flood damage is considered material in the third quarter, but subsequently, during the fourth quarter, is determined to be immaterial for annual reporting purposes.

Finally, in the fourth quarter, management declares the facility too damaged to repair, and reclassifies it as held-for-sale. The facility meets the criteria of ASC 360-10-35 to be classified as a component of the entity since its operations and cash flows are clearly distinguishable from the rest of Dakota Corporation. Activities conducted at the facility generated income from operations of $82,000 in the first quarter, followed by losses of $102,000, $129,000, and $104,000 in the succeeding quarters, prior to 35% income taxes. Upon classification of the facility as held for sale, the carrying value is written down to its fair value less cost to sell resulting in a further loss of $117,000, which is net of $63,000 in applicable income taxes.

Dakota includes these circumstances in its quarterly and annual financial statement in the following manner:

	Quarter 1	*Quarter 2*	*Quarter 3*	*Quarter 4*	*Full year*
Income from continuing operations	$814,000	$629,000	$483,000	$505,000	$2,483,650[1]
Discontinued operations:					
Loss from operations of discontinued component, net of applicable income taxes of $36,400				(67,600)[2]	
Loss from operations of discontinued component, net of applicable income taxes of $88,550					(164,450)[3]
Income from continuing operations	$814,000	$629,000	$483,000	$505,000	$2,483,650[1]

	Quarter 1	*Quarter 2*	*Quarter 3*	*Quarter 4*	*Full year*
Loss from reclassification of Montana facility as held for sale and adjusting the carrying value to fair value less costs to sell, net of applicable income taxes of $63,000				(117,000)	(117,000)
Loss from discontinued operations				(184,600)	(281,450)
Extraordinary items:					
Tornado loss (less applicable income taxes of $217,000)		(403,000)			(403,000)
Flood loss (less applicable income taxes of $23,800)			(44,200)		0[1]
Net income	$814,000	$226,000	$438,800	$320,400	$1,799,200

[1] *The full-year income from continuing operations does not match the total of quarterly income from continuing operations, because the third-quarter classification of flood damage is not considered extraordinary for annual reporting purposes, and so is added back into annual income from continuing operations. Annual income is also reduced by operating losses in the discontinued facility for the full year, which were retained in income from continuing operations for the first three quarters. Full-year income from continuing operations is computed as follows:*

Sum of operating income for four quarters	*$2,431,000*
– Extraordinary loss shifted back to operating income	*(44,200)*
+ After-tax effect of first three quarters of losses on discontinued operations	*96,850*
= Full-year income from continuing operations	*$2,483,650*

[2] *The facility is classified as discontinued in the fourth quarter; there is no requirement to restate prior interim statements to show the loss from operations of the facility in earlier quarters.*

[3] *The full-year financial statement reflects the full-year loss from discontinued operations.*

Note that classification as an extraordinary item is based on facts and circumstances, given the requirement under GAAP that the event be both infrequent in occurrence and unusual in nature. If the plant were located in Kansas, for example, and tornado damage did not qualify under both criteria given its location, then this would not have been presented as an extraordinary item.

Contingencies

In general, contingencies and uncertainties that exist at an interim date are accrued or disclosed in the same manner required for annual financial statements. For example, contingent liabilities that are probable and subject to reasonable estimation are to be accrued. The materiality of the contingency is evaluated in relation to the expected annual results. Disclosures regarding material contingencies and uncertainties are to be repeated in all interim and annual financial statements until they have been settled, adjudicated, transferred, or judged to be immaterial.

The following adjustments or settlements are accorded special treatment in interim reports if they relate to prior interim periods of the current fiscal year:

1. Litigation or similar claims
2. Income taxes (except for the effects of retroactive tax legislation enacted during an interim period)
3. Renegotiation proceedings associated with government contracts
4. Utility revenue under rate-making processes.

If the item is material, directly related to prior interim periods of the current fiscal year in full or in part, and becomes reasonably estimable in the current interim period, it is reported as follows:

1. The portion directly related to the current interim period is included in that period.
2. Prior interim periods are restated to reflect the portions directly related to those periods.
3. The portion directly related to prior years is recognized in the restated first interim period of the current year.

Example of interim reporting of contingencies

Dakota Corporation is sued over its alleged violation of a patent in one of its products. Dakota settles the litigation in the fourth quarter. Under the settlement terms, Dakota must retroactively pay a 3% royalty on all sales of the product to which the patent applies. Sales of the product are $150,000 in the first quarter, $82,000 in the second quarter, $109,000 in the third quarter, and $57,000 in the fourth quarter. In addition, the cumulative total of all sales of the product in prior years is $1,280,000. Dakota restates its quarterly financial results to include the following royalty expense:

	Quarter 1	*Quarter 2*	*Quarter 3*	*Quarter 4*	*Full year*
Sales related to lawsuit	$150,000	$82,000	$109,000	$57,000	$398,000
Royalty expense	4,500	2,460	3,270	1,710	11,940
Royalty expense related to prior years' sales	38,400				38,400

Seasonality

The operations of many businesses are subject to recurring material seasonal variations. Such businesses are required to disclose the seasonality of their activities to avoid the possibility of misleading interim reports. ASC 270-10-45-11 also recommends that such businesses present results of operations for twelve-month periods ending at the interim date of the current and preceding year.

Accounting Changes

Change in accounting principle. The discussion commencing at ASC 270-10-45-12 requires disclosure in interim financial statements of any changes in accounting principles or the methods of applying them from those that were followed in:

1. The prior fiscal year,
2. The comparable interim period of the prior fiscal year, and
3. The preceding interim periods of the current fiscal year.

The information to be included in these disclosures is the same as is required to be included in annual financial statements and is to be provided in the interim period in which the change occurs, subsequent interim periods of that same fiscal year, and the annual financial statements that include the interim period of change.

ASC 250 requires changes in accounting principle to be adopted through retrospective application to all prior periods presented. This accounting treatment is the same in both interim and annual financial statements. The impracticability exception provided by ASC 250 is only applicable to annual financial statements and may not be invoked for prechange interim periods occurring in the same fiscal year as the change is made.

ASC 270-10-45-15 recommends making a change in accounting principle in the first interim report of a fiscal year wherever possible.

Change in accounting estimate. ASC 250 requires that changes in accounting estimate be accounted for currently and prospectively. Retroactive restatement and presentation of pro forma amounts are not permitted. This accounting is the same whether the change occurs at the end of a year or during an interim reporting period.

Change in reporting entity. When an accounting change results in the financial statements presenting a different reporting entity than was presented in the past, all prior periods presented in the new financial statements, including all previously issued interim financial information, are to be retroactively restated to present the financial statements of the new reporting entity. In restating the previously issued information, however, interest previously capitalized under ASC 835 with respect to equity-method investees that have not yet commenced their planned principal operations, is not to be changed.

Restatements. The term "restatement" may only be used to describe a correction of an error from a prior period. Under ASC 250, when a restatement is made, the financial statements of each individual prior period presented (whether interim or annual) are to be adjusted to reflect correction of the effects of the error that relate to that period. Full disclosure of the restatement is to be provided in the financial statements of the:

1. Interim period in which the restatement is first made,
2. Subsequent interim periods during the same fiscal year that includes the interim period in which the restatement is first made, and
3. Annual period that includes the interim period in which the restatement is first made.

PART II—REQUIREMENTS APPLICABLE TO PUBLIC REPORTING ENTITES

Quarterly Reporting to the SEC

Summarized interim financial data. The SEC does not require registrants to file complete sets of quarterly financial statements. Rather, on a quarterly basis, condensed (summarized) unaudited interim financial statements are required to be filed with the SEC on its Form 10-Q (Regulation S-X, Rule 10-01—ASC 270-10-S99-1). The minimum captions and disclosures required to be included in these financial statements are summarized in the Disclosure Checklist in the Appendix. Although such financial statements are informational tools used by investors, creditors, and analysts, they are not presented in sufficient detail to constitute a fair presentation of the reporting entity's financial position and results of operations in accordance with US GAAP.

Changes in accounting principle. In the interim period in which a new accounting principle is adopted, the SEC expects registrants to include in the quarterly condensed financial statements a complete set of the disclosures required to be included in annual financial statements. In addition, these complete disclosures are to be repeated in the interim condensed financial statements of each of the quarters immediately succeeding the quarter of adoption until an annual Form 10-K is filed that reflects the registrant's adoption of the new accounting principle.

Fourth quarter adjustments. When, as is typical, the fourth quarter results are not reported separately, the annual financial statements of publicly traded companies are required to disclose the effects on the fourth quarter of accounting changes made during the quarter; disposals of components of the reporting entity; extraordinary, unusual, or infrequently occurring items; and the aggregate effect of year-end adjustments having a material effect on the quarter's results.

Earnings per share. The same procedures used at year-end are used for earnings per share computations and disclosures in interim reports. Note that annual earnings per share generally will not equal the sum of the interim earnings per share amounts, due to such factors as stock issuances during the year and market price changes. No reconciliation requirements exist for such disparities.

Accelerated reporting requirements. To provide stakeholders with relevant, actionable information on a more timely basis, the SEC requires certain events that occur between regular quarterly reporting deadlines to be reported on its Form 8-K in accordance with an accelerated timetable. Events subject to accelerated reporting requirements are set forth below.

Form 8-K item number	*Event requiring disclosure*
Section 1 – Registrant's Business and Operations	
1.01	Entry into or amendment of a "material definitive agreement" that provides for rights or obligations material to and enforceable by or against the registrant
1.02	Termination of material definitive agreement
1.03	Bankruptcy or receivership
1.04	Mine safety – reporting of shutdowns and patterns of violations
Section 2 – Financial Information	
2.01	Completion of acquisition or disposition of significant amounts of assets by registrant or any of its majority-owned subsidiaries (other than in the ordinary course of business)
2.02	Results of operations and financial condition—disclosure of material nonpublic information regarding a completed fiscal year or quarter included in a public announcement or release including an update of an earlier announcement or release
2.03	Creation of a direct financial obligation or an obligation under an off-balance-sheet arrangement
2.04	Triggering events that accelerate or increase a direct financial obligation or an obligation under an off-balance-sheet arrangement
2.05	Costs associated with exit or disposal activities
2.06	Material impairments
Section 3 – Securities and Trading Markets	
3.01	Notice of delisting or failure to satisfy a continued listing rule or standard; transfer of listing
3.02	Unregistered sales of equity securities
3.03	Material modification to rights of security holders, including working capital restrictions and other limitations on the payment of dividends
Section 4 – Matters Related to Accountants and Financial Statements	
4.01	Changes in registrant's certifying accountant
4.02	Nonreliance on previously issued financial statements or a related audit report or completed interim review
Section 5 – Corporate Governance and Management	
5.01	Changes in control of the registrant
5.02	Departure of directors or principal officers; election of directors; appointment of certain officers; compensatory arrangements of certain officers
5.03	Amendments to articles of incorporation or bylaws; change in fiscal year
5.04	Temporary suspension of trading under registrants's employee benefit plans
5.05	Amendments to the registrant's code of ethics, or waivers of a provision of the code of ethics
5.06	Change in shell company status
5.07	Submission of matters to a vote of security holders
5.08	Shareholder director nominations

Form 8-K item number	*Event requiring disclosure*
Section 6 – Asset-Backed Securities	
6.01	Asset-backed securities' informational and computational material
6.02	Change of servicer or trustee
6.03	Change in credit enhancement or other external support for asset-backed securities
6.04	Failure to make a required distribution
6.05	Securities act updating disclosure
Section 7 – Regulation FD	
7.01	Regulation FD disclosure—
Section 8 – Other Events	
8.01	Other events that the registrant deems important to security holders that is not otherwise called for by the Form 8-K.
Section 9 – Financial Statements and Exhibits	
9.01	Financial statements, pro forma information, and exhibits relative to business combinations described in item number 2.01 including certain shell-company transactions; or acquisitions of one or more real estate properties.

Other Sources

See ASC Location – Wiley *GAAP* Chapter	***For information on…***
820-10-50	For additional disclosure guidance on fair value measurements and disclosures for the reporting entity

13 ASC 272 LIMITED LIABILITY ENTITIES

PERSPECTIVE AND ISSUES

Subtopic

ASC 272, *Limited Liability Entities,* contains one subtopic:

- ASC 272-10, *Overall,* that contains guidance for limited liability entities organized in the United States that prepare financial statements under US GAAP.

DEFINITIONS OF TERMS

ASC 272 does not contain a glossary. However, it does define a limited liability company as having the following characteristics:

- It is an unincorporated association of two or more persons
- Its members have limited personal liability for the obligations or debts of the entity
- It is classified as a partnership for federal income tax purposes.

Further, ASC 272 states that for a limited liability company to be classified as a partnership for federal tax purposes, it must lack at least two of the following characteristics:

- Limited liability
- Free transferability of interests
- Centralized management
- Continuity of life.
  (ASC 272-10-5-6)

CONCEPTS, RULES, AND EXAMPLES

Reporting by Limited Liability Companies and Partnerships

Accounting theory and practice have overwhelmingly developed within the context of businesses organized as traditional corporations. Accordingly, there is little official guidance to entities organized as partnerships or other forms of business, which is generally not a serious concern given that most transactions entered into by such entities do not differ generically from those conducted by corporations. The primary differences relate to equity transactions and to the display of the equity section of the statement of financial position.

ASC 272 addresses certain issues pertaining to accounting and reporting by limited liability companies and partnerships. This Topic establishes that, when an entity restructures itself as a limited liability company or a limited liability partnership, the basis of all assets and liabilities from its predecessor entity are carried forward. Also, as suggested by ASC 740, *Income Taxes,* if the new entity is not a taxable one, any deferred tax assets or liabilities existing previously are to be written off at the time the change in tax status becomes effective; with the elimination of any debit or credit balance being effected by a charge or credit to current period tax expense.

Presentation. With regard to financial statement display issues, the Codification establishes that the headings of each statement identify the entity as being a limited liability company or a limited liability partnership, similar to the common practice of identifying partnership entities. The apparent logic is that this alerts the user to certain anomalies, such as (most commonly) an absence of income tax expense and a related liability, and the use of somewhat distinctive captions in the equity section of the statement of financial position. In the case of limited liability companies and partnerships, the term "members' equity" has been prescribed, and the changes in members' equity are to be communicated either in a separate financial statement, in a combined statement of operations and changes in members' equity, or in the notes to the financial statements.

Members' equity. A limited liability company (LLC) presents its equity using the caption "members' equity." In accordance with ASC 272-10-45-3, the equity attributable to each class of member is to be separately stated on the face of the statement of financial position or disclosed in the notes to the financial statements.

A deficit, if one exists, should be reported in the members' equity account(s), even if there is limited liability for the members. This is consistent with the "going concern" assumption that underlies GAAP. It is not required to disaggregate members' equity into separate components (undistributed earnings, unallocated capital, etc.) on the face of the statement of financial position or in the notes, although this is of course permissible. (ASC 272-10-45-4).

Amounts due from members for capital contributions, if any remain unpaid at the date of the statement of financial position, should be shown as deductions from members' equity. This is entirely consistent with practice for unpaid stock subscriptions receivable. (ASC 272-10-45-5).

Comparative Statements. GAAP presumes that comparative financial statements are more useful than those for a single period, and accordingly that comparative statements should normally be presented. However, for such financial statements to be meaningful, the information for the earlier period must be truly comparable to that of the more recent period. (ASC 272-10-45-6). If the formation of the limited liability company or the limited liability partnership results in a new reporting entity being created, the guidance of ASC 250 dealing with changes in accounting entities should be consulted. (ASC 272-10-45-7).

Disclosures. ASC 272 sets forth certain disclosures to be made in the financial statements of limited liability companies. There should be a description of any limitations on members' equity and of the different *classes* of members' interests and the respective rights, preferences, and privileges of each class and amounts thereof. If the entity will cease to exist at a stipulated date, this must be disclosed. As suggested above, any change in tax status, and the impact of eliminating any tax liability or benefit from the entity's statement of financial position, must be adequately explained in the notes to the financial statements in the period the change in status occurs.

Other Sources

See ASC Location – Wiley *GAAP* Chapter	***For information on…***
ASC 740-10-25-6	Recognizing the financial statement effects of a tax position
ASC 740-10-25-32	Recognizing a deferred tax liability or asset for temporary differences at the date that a nontaxable entity becomes a taxable entity
ASC 740-10-50-9	Adjustments of a deferred tax liability or asset for enacted changes in tax laws or rates or a change in the tax status of the entity
ASC 805-50	Common control transactions in business combinations

14 ASC 274 PERSONAL FINANCIAL STATEMENTS

PERSPECTIVE AND ISSUES

Subtopic

ASC 274, *Personal Financial Statements,* consists of one subtopic:

- ASC 274-10, *Overall,* that addresses the preparation and presentation of financial statements of individuals or groups of related individuals (i.e., families).

Overview

Personal financial statements are generally prepared to organize and plan an individual's financial affairs on a more formal basis. Specific purposes that might require the preparation of personal financial statements include the obtaining of credit, income tax planning, retirement planning, gift and estate planning, or the public disclosure of financial affairs. Third-party recipients of personal financial statements use them in deciding whether to grant credit, in evaluating the financial condition of individuals, in assessing the financial affairs of public officials and candidates for public office, and for other purposes. Estimated current values of assets and liabilities are almost always specified for use in the preparation of personal financial statements as this information is more relevant to users than historical cost.

DEFINITIONS OF TERMS

Source: ASC 274-10-20

Estimated current value of an asset. The amount for which an item could be exchanged between a buyer and a seller, each of whom is well informed and willing, and neither of whom is compelled to buy or sell.

Net worth. The difference between total assets and total liabilities, after deducting estimated income taxes on the differences between the estimated current values of assets and the estimated current amounts of liabilities and their income tax bases.

CONCEPTS, RULES, AND EXAMPLES

Personal financial statements can be prepared for an individual, jointly for a husband and wife, or collectively for a family.

Personal financial statements consist of:

1. *Statement of financial condition*—The only required financial statement, the statement of financial condition presents the estimated current values of assets and the estimated current amounts of liabilities. A liability is recognized for estimated income taxes on the difference between the asset and liability amounts set forth in the statement of financial condition and their respective income tax bases. Naturally, the residual amount after deducting the liabilities (including the estimated income tax liability) from the assets is presented as net worth at that date.
2. *Statement of changes in net worth*—An optional statement that presents the primary sources of increases and decreases in net worth over a period of time.
3. *Comparative financial statements*—The inclusion of a comparison of the current period's financial statements with one or more previous period's financial statements is optional.

(Source: 274-10-45-4)

Basis of presentation. The accrual basis, rather than the cash basis, of accounting is used in preparing personal financial statements. The presentation of personal financial statements does not require the classification of assets and liabilities as current and noncurrent. Instead, assets and liabilities are presented in order of liquidity and maturity.

Measurement. In personal financial statements, assets are presented at their estimated current values. This is defined by ASC 274 as the amount at which the item could be exchanged between a buyer and a seller, assuming both parties are well informed, and neither party is compelled to buy or sell. Disposal costs, if material, are deducted to arrive at current values. It is important to note that this definition has not been amended to conform to the definition of fair value as set forth in ASC 820. The definition of estimated current value in ASC 274 more closely resembles the definition of fair value less cost to sell that is used in FAS ASC 360, *Property, Plant, and Equipment*. Futhermore, ASC 274 specifically provides for adjustment of the current value of securities for the effects of transferability restrictions or the effects of the investor holding a large block of securities (blockage factor). Adjustments for blockage factors are specifically prohibited by ASC 820.

A specialist may need to be consulted in the determination of the current value of certain types of assets (e.g., works of art, jewelry, restricted securities, investments in closely held businesses, and real estate). If property is held in joint tenancy, as community property, or through a similar joint ownership arrangement, the financial statement preparer may require the advice of an attorney to determine, under applicable state law, the portion of the property interest that should be included in the individual's assets.

Liabilities are presented at the lesser of the discounted amount of cash to be paid or the current cash settlement amount. The discount rate should be the rate implicit in the transaction that gave rise to the liability. As a practical matter, the preparer may decide to use the individual's incremental borrowing rate at the inception of the transaction to discount the remaining cash flows.

The use of information about recent transactions involving similar types of assets and liabilities, in similar circumstances, constitutes a satisfactory means of determining the estimated current value of an asset and the estimated current amount of a liability. If recent transactional information cannot be obtained, it is permissible to use other methods (e.g., capitalization of past or prospective earnings, the use of liquidation values, the adjustment of historical cost based on changes in a specific price index, the use of appraisals, and the use of the discounted amounts of projected cash receipts and payments). The methods used should be followed consistently from period to period unless the facts and circumstances dictate a change to different methods.

Income taxes payable are to include unpaid income taxes for completed tax years and the estimated amount for the elapsed portion of the current tax year. Additionally, personal financial statements are required to include estimated income tax on the difference between the current value (amount) of assets (liabilities) and their respective income tax bases as if they had been realized or liquidated.

The table below summarizes the methods of determining "estimated current values" for assets and "estimated current amounts" for liabilities.

Assets and liabilities	*Discounted cash flow*	*Quoted market price*	*Appraised value*	*Other*
• Receivables	x			
• Marketable debt and equity securities		x		If traded on valuation day: closing price. If not traded: valuation must fall in range (between bid and ask price); adjustments may be required for factors such as the holding of a large block of equity securities in an enterprise (blockage factor) or for restrictions on transfer of the securities
• Options—securities		x		If a quoted market price for the option is not available, compute based on the value of the asset subject to option considering factors such as the exercise price and length of option period
• Options—other assets*				Difference between the exercise price and the current value of the contracted asset, discounted at the interest rate that would be available to the individual to borrow with the asset under option as collateral
• Investment in life insurance				Cash surrender value less outstanding loans
• Investment in closely held business	x		x	Liquidation value, multiple of earnings, reproduction value, adjustment of book value or cost
• Real estate (including leaseholds)	x		x	By reference to sales of comparable property, appraisals used for the purpose of borrowing, by reference to assessed values used for property tax purposes, and to the relationship of assessed value to current value of properties in the geographic area

Assets and liabilities	Discounted cash flow	Quoted market price	Appraised value	Other
• Intangible assets	x			Net proceeds from current sale or discounted cash flows from asset; otherwise, may use cost of purchasing a similar asset, if available
• Future interests (nonforfeitable rights)**	x			
• Payables and other liabilities	x			Discharge amount if lower than discounted amount
• Noncancelable commitments***	x			
• Income taxes payable				Unpaid income tax for completed tax years and estimated income tax for elapsed portion of current tax year to date of financial statements
• Estimated income tax on difference between current values of assets and current amounts of liabilities and their respective tax bases				Computed as if current value of assets and liabilities had been respectively realized or liquidated considering applicable tax laws and regulations, recapture provisions and carryovers.
• Uncertain obligations*				Not covered by SOP 82-1; follow recognition, measurement, and disclosure guidance in ASC 450

* *Adapted from: "Personal Financial Statements: Valuation Challenges and Solutions," Michael D. Kinsman, CPA, PhD, and Bruce Samuelson,CPA, DBA,* Journal of Accountancy, *September 1987, pp. 138–148.*

** *Rights have all of the following attributes: (1) are for fixed or determinable amounts; (2) are not contingent on holder's life expectancy or occurrence of a particular event (e.g., disability/death), and (3) do not require future performance of service by holder.*

*** *Commitments have all of the following attributes: (1) are for fixed or determinable amounts; (2) are not contingent on others' life expectancies or occurrence of a particular event (e.g., disability/death); and (3) do not require future performance of service by others.*

Business interests that comprise a large portion of a person's total assets should be presented separately from other investments. An investment in a separate entity that is marketable as a going concern (e.g., a closely held corporation) should be presented as one amount. If the investment is a limited business activity, not conducted in a separate legal entity, separate asset and liability amounts should be shown (e.g., investment in real estate and related mortgage; only the person's beneficial interest in the investment is included in his/her personal financial statements).

The preparer must decide whether to value the net investment him/herself or to engage a qualified specialist. The possible valuation methods available are discounted cash flow, appraised value, liquidation value, multiple of earnings, reproduction value, adjustment of book value (e.g., equity method), or cost. In some cases, it is appropriate to use a combination of approaches to reasonably estimate the current value.

Disclosures. The following disclosures are typically made in either the body of the financial statements or in the accompanying notes. (This list is not all-inclusive.)

1. A clear identification of the individuals covered by the financial statements
2. That assets are presented at their estimated current values and liabilities are presented at their estimated current amounts
3. The methods used in determining the estimated current values of major assets and the estimated current amounts of major liabilities or major categories of assets and liabilities, and
4. Changes in methods used in 3 from one period to the next
5. If assets held jointly by the person and by others included in the statements, the nature of the joint ownership
6. If the person's investment portfolio is material in relation to his or her other assets and is concentrated in one or a few companies or industries, the names of the companies or industries and the estimated current values of the securities
7. If the person has a material investment in a closely held business:
   a. The name of the company
   b. The person's percentage of ownership
   c. The nature of the business
   d. Summarized financial information about assets, liabilities, and results of operations for the most recent year based on the businesses' own financial statements as well as the basis of presentation (e.g., GAAP, cash basis, income tax basis, etc.), and any significant loss contingencies
8. Description of intangible assets and their estimated useful lives
9. The face amount of life insurance the individual owns
10. Certain nonforfeitable rights, such as pensions based on life expectancy
11. The methods and assumptions used to calculate estimated income taxes on the differences between the estimated current values of assets and the estimated current amounts of liabilities and their tax bases as well as a statement that the provision will probably differ from the amounts eventually paid as the timing and method of disposal as well as changes in the tax laws and regulations will affect the actual taxes to be paid
12. Unused operating loss and capital loss carryforwards and any other unused deductions or credits and, if applicable, the tax year in which they expire (under the current income tax code, there will frequently be unused alternative minimum tax credit carryforwards)
13. The differences between the estimated current values of major assets and the estimated current amounts of major liabilities or categories of assets and liabilities and their tax bases
14. Maturities, interest rates, collateral, and other pertinent details relating to receivables and debt
15. Certain noncancellable commitments such as operating leases.

(Source: ASC 274-10-50-2)

EXAMPLE: HYPOTHETICAL SET OF PERSONAL FINANCIAL STATEMENTS

Marcus and Kelly Imrich
Statements of Financial Condition
December 31, 2013 and 2012

	20X2	*20X1*
Assets		
Cash	$ 381,437	$ 207,621
Certificate of deposit	20,000	10.000
Securities		
Marketable (Note 2)	128,787	260,485
Tax-exempt bonds (Note 3)	1,890,222	986,278
Loans receivable (Note 4)	262,877	362,877
Partnership and joint venture interests (Note 5)	935,000	938,000
Real estate interests (Note 6)	890,000	2,500,000
David Corporation (Note 7)	2,750,687	2,600,277
Cash surrender value of life insurance (Note 8)	388,000	265,000
Personal residences (Note 9)	2,387,229	2,380,229
Deferred losses from partnerships	68,570	60,830
Vested interest in David Corporation benefit plan	545,960	530,960
Personal jewelry and furnishings (Note 10)	513,000	6,700
Total assets	$11,161,769	$11,109,257
Liabilities		
Mortgage payable (Note 11)	$ 254,000	$ 267,000
Security deposits—rentals	–	5,700
Income taxes payable—current year balance	9,800	10,680
Total liabilities	263,800	283,380
Estimated income taxes on difference between estimated current values of assets and estimated current amounts of liabilities and their tax bases (Note 12)	555,400	731,000
Net Worth	10,342,569	10,094,877
Total liabilities and net worth	$11,161,769	$11,109,257

Marcus and Kelly Imrich
Statement of Changes in Net Worth
For the Years Ended December 31, 2013 and 2012

	20X2	*20X1*
Realized increases in net worth		
Salary and bonus	$ 200,000	$ 175,000
Dividends and interest income	184,260	85,000
Distribution from limited partnerships	280,000	260,000
Gain on sales of marketable securities	58,240	142,800
	722,500	662,800
Realized decreases in net worth		
Income taxes	180,000	140,000
Interest expense	25,000	26,000
Real estate taxes	21,000	18,000
Personal expenditures	242,536	400,000
	468,536	584,000
Net realized increase in net worth	253,964	78,800

	20X2	*20X1*
Unrealized increases in net worth		
Marketable securities (net of realized gains on securities sold)	37,460	30,270
Benefit plan—David Corporation	15,000	14,000
Personal jewelry and furnishings	20,000	18,000
	72,460	62,270
Unrealized decreases in net worth		
Estimated income taxes on the difference between the estimated current values of assets and the estimated current amounts of liabilities and their tax bases	78,732	64,118
Net unrealized decrease in net worth	(6,272)	(1,848)
Net increase in net worth	247,692	76,952
Net worth at the beginning of year	10,094,877	10,017,925
Net worth at the end of year	$10,342,569	$10,094,877

Marcus and Kelly Imrich
Notes to Financial Statements

Note 1: The accompanying financial statements include the assets and liabilities of Marcus and Kelly Imrich. Assets are stated at their estimated current values, and liabilities at their estimated current amounts.

Note 2: The estimated current values of marketable securities are either (1) their quoted closing prices or (2) for securities not traded on the financial statement date, amounts that fall within the range of quoted bid and asked prices.

Marketable securities consist of the following:

	December 31, 20X2		*December 31, 20X1*	
Stocks	*Number of shares*	*Estimated current values*	*Number of shares*	*Estimated current values*
Susan Schultz, Inc.			1,000	$122,000
Ripley Robotics Corp.	500	$ 51,927	1,000	120,485
L.A.W. Corporation	300	20,700	100	5,000
Jay & Kelly Corp.	300	20,700	200	5,000
J.A.Z. Corporation	200	35,460	200	8,000
		$128,787		$260,485

Note 3: The interest income from state and municipal bonds is generally not subject to federal income taxes but is, except in certain cases, subject to state income tax and federal alternative minimum tax.

Note 4: The loan receivable from Carol Parker, Inc. matures January 2020 and bears interest at the prime rate.

Note 5: Partnership and joint venture interests consist of the following:

	Percent owned	*Cost*	*Estimated current value 12/31/20X2*	*Estimated current value 12/31/20X1*
East Third Partnership	50.0%	$ 50,000	100,000	100,000
631 Lucinda Joint Venture	20.0	10,000	35,000	38,000
27 Wright Partnership	22.5	10,000	40,000	50,000
Eannarino Partnership	10.0	40,000	60,000	50,000
Sweeney Joint Venture	30.0	100,000	600,000	600,000
Kelly Parker Group	20.0	20,000	100,000	100,000
707 Lucinda Joint Venture	50.0	(11,000)	–	–
			$935,000	$938,000

Note 6: Mr. and Mrs. Imrich own a one-half interest in an apartment building in DeKalb, Illinois. The estimated current value was determined by Mr. and Mrs. Imrich. Their income tax basis in the apartment building was $1,000,000 for both 20X2 and 20X1.

Note 7: Kelly Imrich owns 75% of the common stock of the David Corporation. A condensed statement of assets, liabilities, and stockholders' equity (income tax basis) of David Corporation as of December 31, 20X2 and 20X1 is summarized below.

	20X2	*20X1*
Current assets	$2,975,000	$3,147,000
Investments	200,000	200,000
Property and equipment (net)	145,000	165,000
Loans receivable	110,000	120,000
Total assets	$3,430,000	$3,632,000
Current liabilities	$2,030,000	$2,157,000
Other liabilities	450,000	400,000
Total liabilities	2,480,000	2,557,000
Stockholders' equity	950,000	1,075,000
Total liabilities and stockholders' equity	$3,430,000	$3,632,000

Note 8: At December 31, 20X2 and 20X1, Marcus Imrich owned a $1,000,000 whole life insurance policy. Mrs. Imrich is the sole beneficiary under the policy.

Note 9: The estimated current values of the personal residences are their purchase prices plus their cost of improvements. Both residences were purchased in 20X0.

Note 10: The estimated current values of personal effects and jewelry are the appraised values of those assets, determined by an independent appraiser for insurance purposes.

Note 11: The mortgage (collateralized by the residence) is payable in monthly installments of $2,479, including interest at an annual rate of 6% through 20X5.

Note 12: The estimated current amounts of liabilities at December 31, 2013, and December 31, 2012, equaled their income tax bases. Estimated income taxes have been provided on the excess of the estimated current values of assets over their tax bases as if the estimated current values of the assets had been realized on the dates of the statements of financial condition, using applicable income tax laws and regulations. The provision will probably differ from the amounts of income taxes that eventually will be paid because those amounts are determined by the timing and the method of disposal or realization and the income tax laws and regulations in effect at the time of disposal or realization.

The excess of estimated current values of major assets over their income tax bases are:

	December 31	
	20X2	*20X1*
Investment in David Corporation	$1,400,000	$1,350,000
Vested interest in benefit plan	350,000	300,000
Investment in marketable securities	100,000	120,300
	$1,850,000	$1,770,300

15 ASC 275 RISKS AND UNCERTAINTIES

PERSPECTIVE AND ISSUES

Subtopic

ASU 275, *Risks and Uncertainties,* contains one subtopic:

- ASU 275-10, *Overall,* that provides guidance on disclosures of risks and uncertainties inherent in entity's operations.

This topic recognizes that all businesses face risk and uncertainty. The objective of ASC 275 is to provide guidelines that will enable the preparer to screen the many risks and uncertainties faced by entities and focus on those most useful to the readers of the particular entity's report, those that will enable the readers to assess the future cash flows and result of operations. Thus, the topic focuses on screening criteria for risks and uncertainties and the resulting required disclosures.

Scope and Scope Exceptions

The guidance applies to all GAAP financial statements, interim and annual, but not to condensed or summarized financial statements. The guidance does not apply to risks and uncertainties associated with:

- "Management or key personnel
- Proposed changes in accounting principles
- Deficiencies in the internal control structure
- The possible effects of acts of God, war, or sudden catastrophes."
  ASC 275-10-15-4

The Codification points out that there is overlap between this topic and the requirements of the SEC and other Codification topics. The guidance in ASC 275 does not alter any of those requirements.

DEFINITIONS OF TERMS

Source: ASC 275, *Risks and Uncertainties*

Fair Value. The price that would be received to sell an asset or paid to transfer a liability in an orderly transaction between market participants at the measurement date.

Near Term. A period of time not to exceed one year from the date of the financial statements.

Severe Impact. (Used in reference to current vulnerability due to certain concentrations.) A significant financially disruptive effect on the normal functioning of an entity. Severe impact is a higher threshold than material. Matters that are important enough to influence a user's decisions are deemed to be material, yet they may not be so significant as to disrupt the normal functioning of the entity. Some events are material to an investor because they might affect the price of an entity's capital stock or its debt securities, but they would not necessarily have a severe impact on (disrupt) the entity itself. The concept of severe impact, however, includes matters that are less than catastrophic. Matters that are catastrophic include, for example, those that would result in bankruptcy.

CONCEPTS, RULES, AND EXAMPLES

ASC 275-10-50, *Risks and Uncertainties*, requires disclosure in financial statements about risks and uncertainties existing as of the date of those statements that could significantly affect the amounts reported in the near term. The four areas of disclosure required by ASC 275-10-50 are risks and uncertainties relating to

- The nature of the entity's operations,
- Use of estimates in the preparation of financial statements,
- Certain significant estimates, and
- Vulnerability due to certain concentrations.

These areas are not mutually exclusive and may overlap with other requirements. The disclosures may be grouped together or placed in other parts of the financial statements or made as part of the disclosures required by other topics.

Nature of Operations

ASC 275-10-50 requires that entities disclose the major products or services that they sell or provide, the principal markets that they serve, and the location of those markets.

If an entity operates in more than one industry, it must disclose all industries it is operating within as well as the relative importance of each industry. The basis for determining the relative importance of each industry (assets, revenue, or earnings) is also to be disclosed. Not-for-profit entities should disclose the nature of their principal services and the revenue sources for those services. Quantification is not required in disclosures about the nature of operations. Comparisons of relative importance an entity operating in more than one business can be conveyed by the use of words such as predominantly, equally, or major. (ASC 275-10-50-2)

Use of Estimates in the Preparation of Financial Statements

Financial statements must include an explanation that the preparation of financial statements in accordance with GAAP requires the use of estimates by management. The purpose of this disclosure is to clearly alert users to the pervasiveness of estimates. (ASC 275-10-50-4)

Certain Significant Estimates

ASC 275-10-50 requires disclosures regarding estimates used in valuing assets, liabilities, or gain or loss contingencies if both of the following conditions are met:

1. It is at least reasonably possible that the estimate of the effect on the financial statements of a condition, situation, or set of circumstances that existed at the date of the financial statements will change in the near term due to one or more future confirming events.
2. The effect of the change would be material to the financial statements.

For the purposes of determining materiality, it is not the amount of an estimate that determines whether an item is material and must be disclosed, but rather the effect of using a different estimate that determines materiality.

The disclosure is to indicate the nature of the uncertainty and that it is reasonably possible that the estimate will change in the near term. ASC 275-10-50 is separate from and does not change ASC 450, *Contingencies*. If an estimate is covered under ASC 450 as a loss contingency, the disclosure also is to include an estimate of the possible range of loss, or state that an estimate cannot be made. Disclosure of any factors that would make an estimate sensitive to change is encouraged but not required.

Examples of items that may be based on estimates that are particularly sensitive to change in the near term (ASC 275-10-50-15)

1. Inventory subject to rapid technological obsolescence
2. Specialized equipment subject to technological obsolescence
3. Valuation allowances for deferred income tax assets based on future taxable income
4. Capitalized motion picture film production costs
5. Capitalized computer software costs
6. Deferred policy acquisition costs of insurance entities
7. Valuation allowances for commercial and real estate loans
8. Environmental remediation-related obligations
9. Litigation-related obligations
10. Contingent liabilities for guarantees of other entities' obligations
11. Amounts reported for long-term obligations, such as amounts reported for pensions and postemployment benefits
12. Net proceeds recoverable, the provisions for expected loss to be incurred, or both, on disposition of a business or assets
13. Amounts reported for long-term contracts.

Current Vulnerability Due to Concentrations

Vulnerability from concentrations occurs when entities fail to diversify in order to mitigate risk. Financial statements must disclose such concentrations if management knows prior to issuance of the financial statements that all of the following conditions exist (ASC 275-10-50-16):

1. The concentration exists at the date of the financial statements.
2. The concentration makes the entity vulnerable to the risk of a near-term severe impact.
3. It is at least reasonably possible that the events that could cause the severe impact will occur in the near term.

Examples of concentrations that require disclosure (ASC 275-10-50)

1. Concentrations in the volume of business transacted with a particular customer, supplier, lender, grantor, or contributor
2. Concentrations in revenue from particular products, services, or fundraising events
3. Concentrations in the available sources of supply of materials, labor, services, or of licenses or other rights used in the entity's operations
4. Concentrations in the market or geographic area in which an entity conducts its operations.

The potential for severe impact can occur as the result of the total or partial loss of a business relationship, price or demand changes, loss of patent protection, changes in the availability of a resource or right, or the disruption of operations in a market or geographic area. For purposes of ASC 275-10-50, it is always considered reasonably possible in the near term that any customer, grantor, or contributor will be lost and that operations located outside an entity's home country will be disrupted.

For concentrations of labor subject to collective bargaining agreements and concentrations of operations outside an entity's home country, the following additional disclosures are required (ASC 275-10-50-20):

1. For labor subject to collective bargaining agreements, disclosure is to include both the percentage of the labor force covered by collective bargaining agreements and the percentage of the labor force covered by collective bargaining agreements that will expire within one year.
2. For operations located outside the entity's home country, disclosure is to include the carrying amounts of net assets and the geographic areas in which they are located.

Example Disclosure – Geographic Concentration

The Group's operations are conducted in Hong Kong and the PRC. Accordingly, the Group's business, financial condition, and results of operations may be influenced by the political, economic, and legal environment in the PRC, and by the general state of the PRC economy.

The Group's operations in the PRC are subject to special considerations and significant risks not typically associated with companies in North America and Western Europe. These include risks associated with, among others, the political, economic, and legal environment and foreign currency exchange. The Group's results may be adversely affected by changes in the political and social conditions in the PRC, and by changes in governmental policies with respect to laws and regulations, anti-inflationary measures, currency conversion, remittances abroad, and rates and methods of taxation, among other things.

Other Sources

See ASC Location – Wiley *GAAP* Chapter	*For guidance on…*
ASC 270-10-50-6	Disclosure of contingencies in summarized interim financial information of publicly traded entities
See ASC Location – Wiley *GAAP* Chapter	***For an illustration of…***
ASC 205-20-55-80	The kinds of disclosures required for risks and uncertainties related to discontinued operations.
ASC 330-10-55-8	The kinds of disclosures required for risks and uncertainties related to inventory.
ASC 360-10-55-50 through 55-54	The kinds of disclosures required for risks and uncertainties related to specialized manufacturing equipment.
ASC 410-30-55-7	The kinds of disclosures required for risks and uncertainties related to environmental remediation liabilities.
ASC 450-20-55-36	The kinds of disclosures required for risks and uncertainties related to loss contingencies.
ASC 460-10-55-25	The kinds of disclosures required for risks and uncertainties related to guarantees of debt.
ASC 605-35-55-2	The kinds of disclosures for risks and uncertainties related to long-term construction contracts.
ASC 740-10-55-218	The kinds of disclosures required for risks and uncertainties related to income taxes.
958-605-55-69	The kinds of disclosures required for risks and uncertainties related to contributions.
ASC 985-20-55-23	The kinds of disclosures for risks and uncertainties related to capitalized software costs.

16 ASC 280 SEGMENT REPORTING

PERSPECTIVE AND ISSUES

Subtopic

ASC 280, *Segment Reporting,* has one subtopic:

- ASC 280-10, *Overall,* that provides guidance to public business entities on how to report certain information about
  - Operating segments in complete sets of financial statements and in
  - Condensed financial statements of interim periods issued to shareholders.

ASC 280 also requires public entities to disclose certain information about:

- Their products and services,
- The geographic areas in which they operate, and
- Their major customers.

Overview

Benefits. With many companies organized as conglomerates, the presentation of basic consolidated financial statements on an aggregated basis does not provide users with sufficient information for decision-making purposes. The objective of segment reporting, as set forth in ASC 280-10-1 is to

> . . . *Provide information about the different types of business activities in which an enterprise engages and the different economic environments in which it operates to help users of financial statements:*

a. *Better understand the enterprise's performance*
b. *Better assess its prospects for future net cash flows*
c. *Make more informed judgments about the enterprise as a whole.*

The primary benefit of segment reporting is the release of "hidden data" from consolidated financial information. Different segments may possess different levels of profitability, risk, and growth. Assessing future cash flows and their associated risks can be aided by segment data. For example, knowledge of the level of reporting entity operations in a growing or declining product line can help in the prediction of cash flow, while knowledge of the scope of reporting entity operations in an unstable geographic area can help in the assessment of risk. In general, information about the nature and relative size of an enterprise's various business operations is considered useful by decision makers.

ASC 280 governs the way publicly held businesses are required to report disaggregated information in interim and annual financial reports to stockholders. The statement defines operating segments as distinct revenue-producing components of the reporting entity about which separate financial information is produced internally, and whose operating results are regularly reviewed by the reporting entity.

Management Approach. The disclosure approach adopted by ASC 280-10-05-03 and 04 is the "management approach," meaning it is based on the way management organizes segments internally to make operating decisions and assess performance. The management approach, in general, provides that external financial reporting will closely conform to internal reporting, thus giving financial statement users the ability to view the reporting entity's segments in the same manner as internal decision makers.

Financial information can be segmented in several ways: by types of products or services, by geography, by legal entity, or by type of customer. ASC 280 provides a methodology to identify the operating segments that are separately reportable (referred to as "reportable segments") and requires that each reportable segment disclose, among other items, its profit or loss, certain specific revenues and expenses, and its assets. Management is required to reconcile segment information with its consolidated general-purpose financial statements.

In addition, ASC 280 requires that all public companies report information on a company-wide basis about revenues for each product and service, about countries in which revenues are earned and assets are held, and about its major customers, even if this information is not used by management in making operating decisions.

The Codification does not limit segment reporting to purely financial information. It also requires a description of the company's rationale or methods employed in determining the composition of the segments. This description includes the products or services produced by each segment, differences in measurement practices between segments and the consolidated entity, and differences in the segments' measurement practices between periods.

Practice Alert

Segment reporting is a frequent topic of SEC comment letters. While SEC rules only apply to public entities, preparers of financial statements can benefit from the findings of SEC reviewers. For segment reporting, these are some of the topics found in SEC comment letters:

- How operating segments were identified
- The basis of aggregation of operating segments
- Confirmation that prior periods were revised so that information is consistent
- Lack of quantitative disclosure about products and services
- Lack of disclosure about geographic information.

DEFINITIONS OF TERMS

Source: ASC 280-10-20, unless otherwise noted

Chief operating decision maker (CODM). The person(s) at the reporting entity level whose general function (not specific title) is to allocate resources to, and assess the performance of, the segments. Within a reporting entity, this authority does not necessarily need to be vested in a single individual; rather, the responsibilities can be fulfilled by a group of individuals. (ASC 280-10-50-5)

Operating segment. A component of a reporting entity that earns revenues and incurs expenses, about which separate financial information is available that is evaluated regularly by the CODM in deciding how to allocate resources and in assessing performance has all of the following characteristics:

a. It engages in business activities from which it may earn revenues and incur expenses (including revenue and expenses relating to transactions with other components of the same entity).
b. Its operating results are regularly reviewed by the public entity's chief operating decision maker to make disclosures about resources to be allocated to the segment and assess its performance.
c. Its discrete financial information is available.

Source: ASC 280-10-50-1

Public entity. A business entity or a not-for-profit entity that meets any of the following conditions:

1. It has issued debt or equity securities or is a conduit bond obligor for conduit debt securities that are traded in a public market (a domestic or foreign stock exchange or an over-the counter market, including local or regional markets).
2. It is required to file financial statements with the SEC.
3. It provides financial statements for the purpose of issuing any class of securities in a public market.

Segment manager. The person(s) accountable to the reporting entity's CODM (defined earlier) for one or more operating segment's activities, financial results, budgets, forecasts, and operating plans. The reporting entity's CODM can also serve as segment manager for one or more operating segments. (ASC 280-10-50-7 and 8)

CONCEPTS, RULES, AND EXAMPLES

Applicability of ASC 280

ASC 280 applies to issuers (i.e., public companies). The statement does not mandatorily apply to not-for-profit organizations or to nonissuers (i.e., nonpublic companies)—which are, nevertheless, encouraged to voluntarily provide the segment disclosures prescribed by ASC 280. It also does not apply to "parent entities, subsidiaries, joint ventures, or investees accounted for by the equity method if those entities' separate company statements also are consolidated or combined in a complete set of financial statements and both the separate company statements and the consolidated or combined statements are included in the same financial report." However, ASC 280 does not apply to those entities if they are public entities, whose financial statements are issued separately. (ASC 280-15-3)

Operating Segments

Operating segments frequently have a segment manager function that communicates on an ongoing basis with the reporting entity's CODM. The segment manager is not necessarily a single individual but rather the segment management responsibility can vest functionally in a committee or group of designated individuals. Additionally, an operating segment may not be revenue generating from its inception, as it may be in a start-up phase.

Not all activities that occur within the reporting entity are allocable to its operating segments. Activities that are non-revenue-producing or that are incidental to the reporting entity, such as corporate headquarters or certain service or support departments, are not to be attributable to operating segments. ASC 280 specifies that the reporting entity's pension and other postretirement benefit plans are not considered to be operating segments. (ASC 280-10-50-4)

Reportable Segments

An operating segment is considered to be a reportable segment if it is significant to the enterprise as a whole because it satisfies one of the three quantitative 10% tests described below. (ASC 280-10-50-12)

Revenue test. Segment revenue (unaffiliated and intersegment) is at least 10% of the combined revenue (unaffiliated and intersegment) of all operating segments.

Profit and loss test. The absolute amount of segment profit or loss is at least 10% of the greater, in absolute amount, of:

1. Combined profits of all operating segments reporting a profit
2. Combined losses of all operating segments reporting a loss.

ASC 280-10-55 clarifies that, if the CODM uses different measures of profit or loss to evaluate the performance of different segments (e.g., net income versus operating income), the reporting entity is to use a single, consistent measure for the purposes of this profit and loss test. This does not, however, affect the requirement that the reporting entity disclose the measure of profit or loss used by the CODM for the purposes of decision making regarding the segment's performance and resources to be allocated to the segment.

Assets test. Segment assets are at least 10% of the combined assets of all operating segments. Segment assets include those assets used exclusively by the segment and the allocated portion of assets shared by two or more segments. Assets held for general corporate purposes are not assigned to segments.

Comparability. Interperiod comparability must be considered in conjunction with the results of the 10% tests. If a segment fails to meet the tests in the current reporting period but has satisfied the tests in the past and is expected to in the future, it is considered as being reportable in the current year for the sake of comparability. Similarly, if a segment which rarely passes the tests does so in the current year as the result of an unusual event, that segment may be excluded to preserve comparability.

75% Test. After the 10% tests are completed, a 75% test must be performed. The combined external revenue of all reportable segments must be at least 75% of the combined unaffiliated revenue of all operating segments. If the 75% test is not satisfied, additional segments must be designated as reportable until the test is satisfied. The purpose of this test is to ensure that reportable segments account for a substantial portion of the entity's operations.

Example of segment testing

The following example illustrates the three 10% tests and the 75% test.

Operating segment	*External revenue*	*Intersegment revenue*	*Total revenue*	*Segment profit*	*Segment (loss)*	*Assets*
A	$ 90	$ 12	$ 102	$11	$ –	$ 70
B	120	–	120	10	–	50
C	110	20	130	–	(40)	90
D	200	–	200	–	–	140
E	140	300	440	–	(100)	230
F	380	–	380	60	–	260
G	144	–	144	8	–	30
Total	$1,184	$332	$1,516	$89	$(140)	$870

NOTE: Because the $140 total segment losses exceed the $89 total segment profits, the $140 is used for the 10% test.

Summary of Test Results

x = Passed test – Reportable segment

Operating segment	*Total revenues (10% of $1,516 = $152)*	*Segment profit/loss (10% of $140 = $14)*	*Assets (10% of $870 = $87)*	*75% of unaffiliated revenues test*
A				
B				
C		x	x	$110
D	x		x	200
E	x	x	x	140
F	x	x	x	380
G				
				830
			75% of $1,184	888
			Revenue shortfall	$ (58)

Note that the aggregate revenues of the reportable segments that passed the 10% tests are $58 short of providing the required coverage of 75% of external revenues. Consequently, an additional operating segment (A, B, or G) will need to be added to the reportable segments in order to obtain sufficient coverage.

Aggregating Segments. Certain other factors must be considered when identifying reportable segments. Management may consider aggregating two or more operating segments if:

1. They have similar economic characteristics,
2. Aggregation is consistent with the objective and basic principles of ASC 280, and
3. The segments are similar in all of the following areas:

    a. The nature of the products and services
    b. The nature of the production processes
    c. The type of customer for their products and services
    d. The methods used to distribute their products or provide their services
    e. The nature of the regulatory environment.

This aggregation can occur prior to performing the 10% tests if management desires.

Management may *optionally* combine information on operating segments that do not meet any of the 10% tests to produce a reportable segment, but only if the segments being combined have similar economic characteristics and also share a majority of the five aggregation criteria listed above (ASC 280-10-50).

Note that information about operating segments that do not meet any of the 10% thresholds may still be disclosed separately. (ASC 280-10-50-15) By utilizing the aggregation criteria and quantitative thresholds (10% tests) for determining reportable segments, ASC 280 uses what should be considered a modified management approach.

The number of reportable segments should not be so great as to decrease the usefulness of segment reporting. As a rule of thumb, FASB suggests that if the number of reportable segments exceeds ten, segment information may become too detailed. In this situation, the most closely related operating segments should be combined into broader reportable segments, again, however, subject to the objectives inherent in ASC 280's requirements. (ASC 280-10-50-18)

Refer to the "Alternative Statement of Financial Position Segmentation" section and the accompanying diagram that follows. It provides an example of the different components of a reporting entity used for various accounting and reporting purposes.

Measurement Issues

Transfer pricing. Since segment revenue as defined by ASC 280 includes intersegment sales, transfer pricing becomes an issue. Rather than establishing a basis for setting transfer prices, FASB requires companies to use the same transfer prices for segment reporting purposes as are used internally. Since most segments are organizational profit centers, internal transfer prices would generally reflect market prices, but even if this is not the case, these same transfer prices must be used for segment disclosures.

Common costs. Another issue in determining profit or loss is the allocation of common costs. Common costs are expenses incurred by the reporting entity for the benefit of more than one operating segment. Again, segment reporting is required to conform to internal management reporting. Accordingly, these costs are only allocated to a segment for external reporting purposes if they are included in the measure of the segment's profit or loss that is used internally by the CODM.

General corporate cxpense. Difficulties can arise in distinguishing common costs from general corporate expenses. General corporate expenses are not direct expenses from the point of view of any operating segment; they are incurred for the benefit of the corporation as a whole and cannot be reasonably attributed to any operating segment. Common costs, on the other hand, benefit two or more segments and can be allocated to those segments in a manner determined by management to support internal decision making by the reporting entity.

Corporate assets. Similarly, only those assets that are included internally in the measure of the segment's assets used to make operating decisions are reported as assets of the segment in external financial reports. If management allocates amounts to segment profit or assets internally and those amounts are used by the CODM, then those amounts are to be allocated on a reasonable basis and disclosed.

Segment Disclosures

ASC 280 requires disclosures regarding the reporting entity's reportable segments that include

1. **General information**—Explain how management identified the reporting entity's reportable segments, including whether operating segments have been aggregated.

Alternative Balance Sheet Segmentation

The Parent Holding Company *Owns subsidiaries, land and headquarters building that they all use*						
Subsidiary 1 *Division a* *Business i*	Subsidiary 2 *Business iv*	Subsidiary 3 *Business v* *2 Product Lines*	Subsidiary 4 *2 Similar Businesses* Business vi	Subsidiary 5 2 Similar Businesses *Business viii*	Subsidiary 6 *Business ix*	Subsidiary 7 *2 Nonsimilar Businesses* Business x
Asset Group (a)	Asset Group (d) with Primary Asset	Asset Group (e) and Disposal Group (f)	Asset Group (g)	Asset Group (i)	Asset Group (j)	Asset Group (k) Reporting Unit (6)
Reporting Unit (1)	Reporting Unit (2)	Reporting Unit (3)	Reporting Unit (4)	Reporting Unit (5)		Business xi
Division b Business ii: Asset Group (b) Business iii: Asset Group (c)			Business vii Asset Group (h)			Asset Group (l) Reporting Unit (7)
Operating Segment A		Operating Segment B	Operating Segment C	Operating Segment D		Operating Segment E
Reportable Segment I			Reportable Segment II	Reportable Segment III		Reportable Segment IV

Additionally, describe the types of products and services from which each reportable segment derives its revenues. (ASC 280-10-50-21)

2. **Certain information about reported segment profit and loss, segment assets and the basis of measurement**—This will include:
   a. Revenues from external customers
   b. Revenues from transactions with other operating segments of the same public entity
   c. Interest revenue
   d. Interest expense
   e. Depreciation, depletion, and amortization expense
   f. Unusual items as described in paragraph 225-20-45-16
   g. Equity in the net income of investees accounted for by the equity method
   h. Income tax expense or benefit
   i. Extraordinary items
   j. Significant noncash items other than depreciation, depletion, and amortization expense.

   (ASC 280-10-50-22)
3. Disclose the basis of measurement for these items. (ASC 280-10-50-29)
4. **Reconciliations**—Management must reconcile the segment amounts disclosed to the corresponding consolidated reporting entity amounts. (ASC 280-10-50-30)
5. **Interim period information**—Although the interim period disclosure requirements are not as extensive as those that apply to the annual financial statements, certain segment disclosures are required in interim financial statements. Public entities must disclose revenues from external customers, intersegment revenues, measure of segment profit or loss, total assets where there have been a material change from the last annual report, description of differences from the last annual report in the segmentation basis or basis of profit and loss measurement, reconciliation. (ASC 280-10-50-32)

See the comprehensive illustration of the disclosures required for segment reporting provided later in this chapter. Additionally, ASC 280 provides an illustrative example.

Entity-Wide Disclosures

In addition to segment data, ASC 280-10-50-38 through 42 mandates that certain entity-wide disclosures be made. The entity-wide disclosures are required for all reporting entities subject to ASC 280, even those that have only a single reportable segment.

Products and services. Revenue from external customers for each product and service or each group of similar products and services is to be reported by the reporting entity unless impracticable. If deemed to be impracticable, disclose that fact. If the company's reportable segments have been organized around products and services, then this disclosure will generally not be required.

Geographic areas. A reporting entity separately discloses revenues from external customers and long-lived assets attributable to its domestic operations and foreign operations. If the reportable segments have been organized around geographic areas, then these disclosures will generally not be required because they would be duplicative.

Domestic operations are those operations located in the reporting entity's home country that generate either unaffiliated or intersegment revenues. Foreign operations are similar operations located outside of the home country of the reporting entity. For the purposes of these disclosures, US reporting entities' operations in Puerto Rico are not considered to be foreign operations, although management is not precluded from voluntary disclosure regarding Puerto Rican operations (ASC 280-10-55).

If the reporting entity functions in two or more foreign geographic areas, to the extent revenues or assets of an individual foreign geographic area are material, then separately disclose these amounts. In addition, disclosure is required of the basis for attributing revenue to different geographic areas. A geographic area is defined as an individual country. If providing this information is impracticable, disclose that fact.

Major customers. If the reporting entity earns 10% or more of its revenue on sales to a single external customer, disclose that fact and the amount of revenue from each such customer. Also, disclose the segment making these sales. This disclosure provides information on concentrations of risk.

For the purpose of this disclosure, a group of customers under common control, such as subsidiaries of a common parent, is regarded as a single customer. Similarly the various agencies of a government are considered to be a single customer. An insuring entity (such as Blue Cross) is not considered to be the customer unless that entity (rather than the patient) controls the decision as to the doctor, type of service, etc.

Restatement of Previously Reported Segment Information

ASC 280-10-50-34 requires segment reporting on a comparative basis when the associated financial statements are comparative. Therefore, restate the information to preserve comparability whenever the reporting entity has changed the structure of its internal organization in a manner that causes a change to its reportable segments. Management must explicitly disclose that it has restated the segment information of earlier periods.

Comprehensive Illustration

The following illustration is provided for a hypothetical company, Resources Unlimited. The illustration provides segment disclosures by legal entity.

NOTE: ASC 280 provides illustrative segment disclosures by product line.

Description of the types of products and services from which each reportable segment derives its revenues. Resources Unlimited has four reportable segments: Wholesale Corporation, Retail Corporation, Library Corporation, and Software Corporation. Wholesale Corporation buys and resells used elementary and college textbooks. Retail Corporation operates 200 college book stores and a related e-commerce Web site selling both new and used college textbooks, trade books, sports apparel, and other sundries. Library Corporation sells library books primarily to elementary school libraries. Software Corporation develops and sells library systems application software.

Measurement of segment profit or loss and segment assets. The accounting policies of the segments are the same as those described in the summary of significant accounting policies except the first-in, first-out (FIFO) method of inventory valuation is used for segment reporting. In addition, Resources Unlimited allocates interest expense to each segment based on the segment's average borrowings from the corporate office. However, the related debt is not allocated to the segments and remains on the corporate statement of financial position. Resources Unlimited evaluates performance based on profit or loss before income taxes not including nonrecurring gains and losses.

Resources Unlimited accounts for intersegment sales and transfers as if the sales or transfers were transacted with third parties (i.e., at current market prices).

Factors management used to identify reportable segments. Resources Unlimited's business is conducted through four separate legal entities that are wholly owned subsidiaries. At the company's inception, each entity was founded and managed by a different Resources Unlimited stockholder/family member. Each corporation is still managed separately, as each business has a distinct customer base and requires different strategic and marketing efforts.

Information about profit and loss and assets. The amounts in the illustration are assumed to be the amounts in reports used by the CODM. Resources Unlimited allocates interest expense to the segments; however, it does not allocate income taxes and unusual items to them.

($000 omitted)

	Wholesale Corporation	*Retail Corporation*	*Library Corporation*	*Software Corporation*	*Totals*
Revenues from external customers	$197,500	$263,000	$182,300	$102,200	$745,000
Intersegment revenues	23,000	–	–	–	23,000
Interest revenue	250	150	–	–	400
Interest expense	1,570	2,150	1,390	2,700	7,810
Depreciation and amortization*	8,600	13,100	7,180	6,070	34,950
Segment profit	12,100	13,500	9,900	5,100	40,600
Segment assets	121,200	153,350	100,600	85,000	460,150
Expenditures for segment assets	7,200	12,700	5,600	6,700	32,200

* *Depreciation and amortization are required to be disclosed for each operating segment even if the CODM evaluates segment performance using predepreciation measures such as earnings before income taxes, depreciation, and amortization (EBITDA) (ASC 280-10-55).*

Reconciliations. An illustration of reconciliations for revenues, profit and loss, assets, and other significant items is shown below. In general, this illustration assumes that there are no unreported operating segments, but there is a corporate headquarters, thus most reconciling items relate to corporate revenues and expenses.

As discussed previously, the company recognizes and measures inventory based on FIFO valuation for segment reporting. The consolidated financial statements are assumed not to include discontinued operations or the cumulative effect of a change in accounting principle.

	($000 omitted)
Revenue	
Total revenues for reportable segments	$768,000
Elimination of intersegment revenue	(23,000)
Total consolidated revenue	$745,000
Profit and loss	
Total profit for reportable segments	$40,600
Elimination of intersegment profits	(6,100)
Unallocated amounts relating to corporate operations:	
Interest revenue	500
Interest expense	(800)
Depreciation and amortization	(1,900)
Unrealized gain on trading securities	1,865
Income before income taxes and extraordinary items	$34,165
Assets	
Total assets for reportable segments	$460,150
Corporate short-term investments, land and building	25,100
Adjustment for LIFO reserve in consolidation	(9,200)
	$476,050

Other significant items

	Segment totals	*Adjustments*	*Consolidated totals*
Expenditures for segment assets	$32,200	800	$33,000

The reconciling adjustment is the amount of expenditures incurred for additions to the corporate headquarters building, which is not included in the segment information.

Products and services

Used textbooks	$296,125
New textbooks	72,150
Trade books	45,700
Sports apparel	41,325
Sundries	5,200
Library books	182,300
Library software	102,200
Total consolidated revenue	$745,000

Geographic information

	*Revenues**	*Long-lived assets*
United States	$687,400	$253,200
Foreign countries	57,600	18,800
Total	$745,000	$272,000

* *Revenues are attributed to countries as follows: For Wholesale Corporation and Library Corporation, the country in which the customer takes delivery. For Retail Corporation, the country in which the retail store is located or, for internet sales, the country to which the merchandise is delivered. For Software Corporation, the country where the host server on which the software is installed is located.*

Major customers. No single customer represents 10% or more of the consolidated revenues. Consequently, management believes that the Companies' sales are appropriately diversified.

Other Sources

See ASC Location – Wiley *GAAP* Chapter	*For information on...*
ASC 350	Information to be disclosed about goodwill in each reportable segment and significant changes in the allocation of goodwill by reportable segments
ASC 350	Segment disclosures related to each impairment loss recognized related to an intangible asset
ASC 420-10-50-1	Segment information to be disclosed in the period in which an exit or disposal activity is initiated
ASC 908-280	Segmentation in the airline industry
ASC 924-280	Segment guidance in the casino industry

17 ASC 305 CASH AND CASH EQUIVALENTS

PERSPECTIVE AND ISSUES

Subtopic

ASC 305, *Cash and Cash Equivalents,* contains one subtopic:

- ASC 305-10, *Overall,* that provides implementation guidance on cash on deposit at a financial institution.

Scope

ASC 305 applies to all entities and has no scope exceptions.

Overview

Assets displayed on the statement of financial position are the resources available to the reporting entity to support its current and future operations. To provide information about liquidity, the assets are often divided into current and noncurrent assets. Current assets consist of cash and other assets that are reasonably expected to be realized in cash or sold or consumed during the normal operating cycle of the business. When the normal operating cycle is less than one year, a one-year period is used to distinguish current assets from noncurrent assets. If the operating cycle exceeds one year, the operating cycle is the proper period to use for current asset identification. When information about current assets is accompanied by information about current liabilities, readers of the financial statements can assess the amount of net working capital (current assets less current liabilities) possessed by the reporting entity and its *current ratio* (current assets divided by current liabilities). Each of those measures provides useful information about the liquidity of the reporting entity.

Cash is the most liquid of assets, and cash items are generally classified as a current asset.

Practice Alert

The classification of investments as cash equivalents is a frequent topic of SEC comment letters. While SEC rules only apply to public entities, preparers of financial statements can benefit from the findings of SEC reviewers. Preparers should bear in mind that an investment does not meet the ASC 230-10-20 definition of a cash equivalent unless the security is purchased very near its stated maturity date. Unless the investments are purchased three months or less before their maturity date, investments with stated maturities greater than three months cannot be classified as cash equivalents. For further information, see the Definitions of Terms section below and discussion of cash classification later in this chapter.

DEFINITIONS OF TERMS

Source: ASC 305-10-20

Cash. Consistent with common usage, cash includes not only currency on hand but demand deposits with banks or other financial institutions. Cash also includes other kinds of accounts that have the general characteristics of demand deposits in that the customer may deposit additional funds at any time and also effectively may withdraw funds at any time without prior notice or penalty. All charges and credits to those accounts are cash receipts or payments to both the entity owning the account and the bank holding it. For example, a bank's granting of a loan by crediting the proceeds to a customer's demand deposit account is a cash payment by the bank and a cash receipt of the customer when the entry is made.

Cash Equivalents. Cash equivalents are short-term, highly liquid investments that have both of the following characteristics:

a. Readily convertible to known amounts of cash
b. So near their maturity that they present insignificant risk of changes in value because of changes in interest rates.

Generally, only investments with original maturities of three months or less qualify under that definition. Original maturity means original maturity to the entity holding the investment. For example, both a three-month U.S. Treasury bill and a three-year U.S. Treasury note purchased three months from maturity qualify as cash equivalents. However, a Treasury note purchased three years ago does not become a cash equivalent when its remaining maturity is three months. Examples of items commonly considered to be cash equivalents are Treasury bills, commercial paper, money market funds, and federal funds sold (for an entity with banking operations).

CONCEPTS, RULES, AND EXAMPLES

Cash

To be included as cash in the statement of financial position, funds must be represented by coins, currency, undeposited checks, money orders, drafts, and demand deposits that are immediately available without restriction. Recognition and measurement of cash is generally straightforward. However, it is necessary to inform readers of the financial statements about any limitations on the ability to use cash in current operations.

Cash whose use is restricted would not be included with cash unless the restrictions on it expire within the year (or the operating cycle, if longer). Thus, cash contractually required to be held in a sinking fund is classified as a current asset if it will be used to retire the current portion of long-term debt. However, if material, it would be reported on a separate line rather than within cash. Cash in a demand deposit account that is being held for the retirement of long-term debts that do not mature currently is excluded from current assets and shown as a noncurrent investment. Cash in transit to the reporting entity (e.g., checks already mailed by the customer) cannot be included in cash because it is not under the control of the reporting entity.

Compensating balances. An entity will often be required to maintain a minimum amount of cash on deposit, generally in connection with having a borrowing arrangement with a financial institution (compensating balance). The purpose of this balance may be to substitute for service fees foregone by the bank (or fees at a rate less than market) or simply to increase the yield on a loan to the lender. Since most organizations must maintain a certain working balance in their cash accounts simply to handle routine transactions and to cushion against unforeseen variations in the demand for cash, borrowers often will not find compensating balance arrangements objectionable. Nevertheless, the compensating balance is not available for unrestricted use and penalties will result if it is used. If material, the portion of the reporting entity's cash account that is a compensating balance must be segregated and shown as a separate caption on the statement of financial position, and this should be included in noncurrent assets if related borrowings are noncurrent liabilities. If the borrowings are current liabilities or if the compensating balance reduces fees that would have been incurred in the next year, it is acceptable to show the compensating balance as a separately captioned current asset.

Example of compensating balance disclosure

The Arkansas Billboard Company (ABC) has obtained a short-term, $10 million line of credit with Premier Bank. The loan agreement with Premier includes a requirement that ABC maintain a compensating balance of 5% of the maximum amount of the line of credit (5% × $10 million = $500,000). ABC also has a loan with First National Bank involving a single balloon payment of $200,000 due in two years, and requiring a compensating balance of 10% (10% × $200,000 = $20,000). At year-end, ABC has cash balances of $782,000 at Premier and $28,000 at First National. ABC's reporting of cash on its statement of financial position is as follows:

Current assets:	
Cash	290,000
Restricted cash compensating balances	500,000
Noncurrent assets:	
Restricted cash compensating balances	20,000

Cash not immediately available. Cash in savings accounts subject to a statutory notification requirement and cash in certificates of deposit maturing during the current operating cycle or within one year may be included as current assets but, if material, is to be separately captioned in the statement of financial position to avoid the misleading implication that these funds are available immediately upon demand. Typically, such items will be included in the short-term investments caption, but these could be labeled as time deposits or restricted cash deposits.

Overdrafts. A reporting entity may issue checks with a dollar value exceeding the balance in its checking account. If the excess amount of these checks over the checking account balance has not yet cleared the bank, the overage is called a *book overdraft*, since the overdraft only exists in the reporting entity's accounting records. For reporting purposes, although the bank is yet unaware of this situation, the overdraft is reported as a liability, since the checks have already been released and are thus no longer under the control of the reporting entity. If the checks have cleared the bank, and the bank has advanced the reporting entity the funds (sometimes marketed as "automatic overdraft protection"), then this borrowing is also reported as a liability.

Petty cash. Petty cash and other imprest cash accounts are usually combined in financial statements with other cash accounts.

18 ASC 310 RECEIVABLES

PERSPECTIVE AND ISSUES

Subtopics

ASC 310, *Receivables,* consists of four subtopics:

- ASC 310-10, *Overall,* which provides general guidance for receivables and has two subsections:
  - *General*, which provides guidance on receivables in general and standby commitments to purchase loans, factoring arrangements, and rebates,
  - *Acquisition, Development, and Construction Arrangements,* which provides guidance on whether a lender should account for the arrangement as a loan or as an investment in real estate or in a joint venture.
- ASC 310-20, *Nonrefundable Fees and Other Costs,* provides guidance on nonrefundable fees, origination costs, and acquisition costs associated with lending activities and loan purchases.
- ASC 310-30, *Loans and Debt Securities Acquired with Deteriorated Credit Quality*, which provides guidance regarding loans acquired with evidence of deterioration of credit quality since origination acquired by completion of a transfer for which it is probable, at acquisition, that the investor will be unable to collect all contractually required payments receivable.
- ASC 310-40, *Troubled Debt Restructurings by Creditors,* which provides guidance focused on the creditor's records. Guidance for the debtor's accounting in a trouble debt restructuring (TDR) is found in ASC 470-60.

Scope and Scope Exceptions

ASC 310-10, *Overall.* ASC 310-10-15-3 lists two exceptions to the guidance in the General Subsections of ASC 310-10: mortgage banking activities and contracts accounted for as derivative instruments under ASC 815-10. ASC 310-10-15-5 states that the Acquisition, Development, and Construction Subsections guidance applies only to those acquisition, development, and construction arrangements in which the lender participates in expected residual profit.

ASC 310-20, *Nonrefundable Fees and Other Costs.* ASC 310-20-15-3 specifically excludes from ASC 310-20 guidance:

a. Loan origination or commitment fees that are refundable; however, the guidance does apply when such fees subsequently become nonrefundable.
b. Costs that are incurred by the lender in transactions with independent third parties if the lender bills those costs directly to the borrower.
c. Nonrefundable fees and costs associated with originating or acquiring loans that are carried at fair value if the changes in fair value are included in earnings of a business entity or change in net assets of a not-for-profit entity (NFP). The exclusion provided in this paragraph and the preceding paragraph applies to nonrefundable fees and costs associated with originating loans that are reported at fair value and premiums or discounts associated with acquiring loans that are reported at fair value. Loans that are reported at cost or the lower of cost or fair value, loans or debt securities reported at fair value with changes in fair value reported in other comprehensive income (includes financial assets subject to prepayment as defined in paragraph 860-20-35-2, and debt securities classified as available-for-sale under Topic 320), and loans that

have a market interest rate, or adjust to a market interest rate, are not considered to be loans carried at fair value.

d. Fees and costs related to a commitment to originate, sell, or purchase loans that is accounted for as a derivative instrument under Subtopic 815-10.
e. Fees and costs related to a standby commitment to purchase loans if the settlement date of that commitment is not within a reasonable period or the entity does not have the intent and ability to accept delivery without selling assets. For guidance on fees and costs related to such a commitment, see paragraph 310-10-30-7.

ASC 310-30, ***Loans and Debt Securities Acquired with Deteriorated Credit Quality.*** ASC 310-30-15-2 excludes the following transactions from ASC 310-30 guidance:

a. Loans that are measured at fair value if all changes in fair value are included in earnings or, for an NFP, loans that are measured at fair value if all changes in fair value are included in the statement of activities and included in the performance indicator if a performance indicator is presented. Examples include those loans classified as trading securities under Topic 320 and Subtopic 948-310.
b. Mortgage loans classified as held for sale under paragraph 948-310-35-1.
c. Leases as defined in Topic 840. Only contracts that are classified by the purchaser as leases under that Topic meet this exclusion. The distinction between purchasing a lease and purchasing a stream of cash flows must be drawn to determine applicability of this Section.
d. Loans acquired in a business combination accounted for at historical cost, including business combinations of two or more NFPs, the acquisition of a for-profit business entity by an NFP, and combinations of two or more mutual entities.
e. Loans held by liquidating banks (financial reporting by liquidating banks is discussed in Topic 942).
f. Revolving credit agreements, such as credit cards and home equity loans, if at the acquisition date the borrower has revolving privileges.
g. Loans that are a transferor's interests (see Subtopic 325-40).

ASC 310-30-15-4 further excludes the following transactions and activities:

a. Loans that are derivative instruments subject to the requirements of Topic 815. If a loan would otherwise be in the scope of this paragraph of this Section and has within it an embedded derivative that is subject to that Topic, the host instrument (as described in that Topic) remains within the scope of this paragraph of this Section if it satisfies the conditions in this paragraph.
b. Loans for which it is possible, but not probable, that the investor will be unable to collect all amounts due according to the contractual terms of the loan.
c. Situations in which credit is still being offered, and the entire relationship is excluded if, at the acquisition date, the borrower has revolving privileges. This scope exclusion is appropriate because lenders generally will not continue to make credit available to borrowers from whom it is probable that the lender will not collect all contractually required payments receivable.

ASC 310-40, ***Troubled Debt Restructuring by Creditors.*** ASC 310-40 applies to all troubled debt restructurings by creditors. Accounting by debtors is found in ASC 470-60. Interestingly the two Subtopics use different applicability tests and so, creditors and debtors applying the same facts and circumstances may not reach the same conclusion as to whether a troubled debt restructuring (TDR) has occurred.

ASC 310-40-15-9 states that TDRs may include, but are not limited to, one or a combination of:

- Transfer from the debtor to the creditor of receivables from third parties, real estate, or other assets to satisfy fully or partially a debt
- Issuance or other granting of an equity interest to the creditor by the debtor to satisfy fully or partially a debt unless the equity interest is granted pursuant to existing terms for converting the debt into an equity interest
- Modifications of terms of a debt, such as
  - Reduction of the stated interest rate
  - Extension of the maturity date at a stated interest rate lower than the current market rate
  - Reduction of accrued interest.

ASC 310-40-15-11 *excludes* the following for consideration under the TDR guidance:

- Changes in lease agreements
- Changes in employment-related agreements
- Unless they involve an agreement between debtor and creditor to restructure,
  - Debtors' failures to pay trade accounts according to their terms or
  - Creditors' delays in taking legal action to collect overdue amounts of interest and principal
- Modifications of loans within a pool accounted for as impaired loans
- Changes in expected cash flows of a pool of loans accounted for as impaired loans resulting from the modification of one or more loans within the pool.

Overview

Receivables come from credit sales, loans, or other transactions and may be in the form of loans, notes, or other type of financial instruments. Trade receivables and other customary trade term receivables that are due in no longer than one year are measured at

- outstanding face value (principal),
- adjusted for any write-offs and the allowance for doubtful accounts,
- provided that management has the intent and ability to hold those receivables for the foreseeable future or until maturity or payoff.

Loans receivable that management will hold until maturity or payoff are valued at outstanding principal adjusted for

- any write-offs,
- the allowance for loan losses,
- any deferred fees or costs on originated loans, and
- any unamortized premiums of discounts on purchased loans.

If a receivable is due on terms exceeding one year, the proper valuation is the present value of future payments to be received. These future payments are computed by using an interest (discount) rate commensurate with the risks involved, as of the date of the receivable's creation. In many situations where an explicit interest rate is provided, the rate commensurate with the risks involved is the rate stated in the agreement between the payee and the obligor. However, if the receivable is noninterest-bearing or if the rate stated in the agreement is not indicative of the market rate for a debtor of similar creditworthiness under similar terms, interest must be imputed at the market rate. The resulting discount is amortized as additional interest income over the life of the agreement, per ASC 835.

Receivables that are pledged or assigned to a lender as collateral for a lending agreement remain under the control of the reporting entity and, therefore, remain on its statement of financial position to inform readers of the financial statements about the pledge or assignment.

As an alternative to borrowing against the value of the receivables, customer obligations are sometimes sold to generate cash before their due dates. If the transferor has no continuing involvement with the transferred assets or with the transferee, it is clear that a sale has taken place, and a gain or loss on sale is measured and recognized. However, in many cases, the transferor of the receivables has continuing involvement with the transferred assets because it sells the receivables with recourse for uncollectible amounts, retains an interest in the receivables, or agrees to service the receivables after the sale. The greater the control that the transferor retains over the receivables, the more likely that the transfer will be accounted for as a secured borrowing rather than a sale.

Technical Alert

In response to the increased rate of default on loans collateralized by residential real estate and a lack of clarity around when a creditor should be considered to have received physical possession of residential real property collateralizing a mortgage loan, FASB issued ASU 2014-04, *Receivables—Troubled Debt Restructurings by Creditors* (Subtopic 310-40): Reclassification of Residential Real Estate Collateralized Consumer Mortgage Loans upon Foreclosure (a consensus of the FASB Emerging Issues Task Force). The ASU clarifies that the receivable should be derecognized and the real property recognized when either:

1. The creditor obtains legal title to the property upon completion of foreclosure or
2. The borrower conveys all interest in the property to the creditor to satisfy the loan through completion of a deed in lieu of foreclosure or a similar legal agreement.

The ASU is effective for public business entities for annual periods, and interim periods within those annual periods, beginning after December 15, 2014. For other entities, it is effective for annual periods beginning after December 15, 2014, and interim periods within annual periods beginning after December 15, 2015. Early adoption is permitted. The amendments should be applied using either a modified retrospective transition method or a prospective transition method.

DEFINITIONS OF TERMS

Accretable yield. The excess of a loan's cash flows expected to be collected over the investor's initial investment in the loan.

Acquisition, development, and construction arrangements. Acquisition, development, or construction arrangements, in which a lender, usually a financial institution, participates in expected residual profit from the sale or refinancing of property.

Blended-rate loans. Blended-rate loans involve lending new funds at market interest rates combined with existing loans at rates currently lower than market rates. (Those funds are not advanced under a line of credit.)

Carrying Amount. For a receivable, the face amount increased or decreased by applicable accrued interest and applicable unamortized premium, discount, finance charges, or issue costs and also an allowance for uncollectible amounts and other valuation accounts. For a payable, the face amount increased or decreased by applicable accrued interest and applicable unamortized premium, discount, finance charges, or issue costs.

Cash flows expected at acquisition. The investor's estimate, at acquisition, of the amount and timing of undiscounted principal, interest, and other cash flows expected to be collected. This would be the investor's best estimate of cash flows, including the effect of prepayments if considered, that is used in determining the acquisition price, and, in a business combination, the investor's estimate of fair value for purposes of acquisition price assignment in accordance with Subtopic 805-20. One acceptable method of making this estimate is described in paragraphs 820-10-55-3F through 55-3G and 820-10-55-4 through 55-20, which provide guidance on present value techniques.

Class of financing receivable. A group of financing receivables determined on the basis of all of the following:

a. Initial measurement attribute (for example, amortized cost or purchased credit impaired)
b. Risk characteristics of the financing receivable
c. An entity's method for monitoring and assessing credit risk.

See paragraphs 310-10-55-16 through 55-18 and 310-10-55-22.

Collateral-dependent loan. A loan for which the repayment is expected to be provided solely by the underlying collateral.

Commitment Fees. Fees charged for entering into an agreement that obligates the entity to make or acquire a loan or to satisfy an obligation of the other party under a specified condition. Commitment fees include fees for letters of credit and obligations to purchase a loan or group of loans and pass-through certificates.

Common risk characteristics. Loans with similar credit risk (for example, evidenced by similar Fair Isaac Company [FICO] scores, an automated rating process for credit reports) or risk ratings, and one or more predominant risk characteristics, such as financial asset type, collateral type, size, interest rate, date of origination, term, and geographic location.

Completion of a transfer. A completion of a transfer occurs for a transaction with any of the following characteristics:

a. It satisfies the conditions in paragraph 860-10-40-5 to be accounted for as a sale.
b. It is in a business combination.
c. It is to a newly created subsidiary if the transferee has written the loan down to its fair value with the intent of transferring the stock of the subsidiary as a dividend to the shareholders of the parent entity.
d. It is a contribution receivable or a transfer that satisfies a prior promise to give.
e. Contractually Required Payments Receivable. The total undiscounted amount of all uncollected contractual principal and contractual interest payments both past due and scheduled for the future, adjusted for the timing of prepayments, if considered, less any reduction by the investor. For an acquired asset-backed security with required contractual payments of principal and interest, the contractually required payments receivable is represented by the contractual terms of the security. However, when contractual payments of principal and interest are not specified by the security, it is necessary to consider the contractual terms of the underlying loans or assets.

Contractually Required Payments Receivable. The total undiscounted amount of all uncollected contractual principal and contractual interest payments both past due and scheduled for the future, adjusted for the timing of prepayments, if considered, less any reduction by the investor. For an acquired asset-backed security with required contractual payments of principal and interest, the contractually required payments receivable is represented by the contractual terms of the security. However, when contractual payments of principal and interest are not specified by the security, it is necessary to consider the contractual terms of the underlying loans or assets.

Control. The possession, direct or indirect, of the power to direct or cause the direction of the management and policies of an entity through ownership, by contract, or otherwise.

Credit card fees. The periodic uniform fees that entitle cardholders to use credit cards. The amount of such fees generally is not dependent upon the level of credit available or frequency of usage. Typically the use of credit cards facilitates the cardholder's payment for the purchase of goods and services on a periodic, as-billed basis (usually monthly), involves the extension of credit, and, if payment is not made when billed, involves imposition of interest or finance charges. Credit card fees include fees received in similar arrangements, such as charge card and cash card fees.

Credit quality indicator. A statistic about the credit quality of financing receivables.

Current assets. Current assets is used to designate cash and other assets or resources commonly identified as those that are reasonably expected to be realized in cash or sold or consumed during the normal operating cycle of the business.

Debt. A receivable or payable (collectively referred to as debt) represents a contractual right to receive money or a contractual obligation to pay money on demand or on fixed or determinable dates that is already included as an asset or liability in the creditor's or debtor's balance sheet at the time of the restructuring.

Debt security. Any security representing a creditor relationship with an entity. The term debt security also includes all of the following:

a. Preferred stock that by its terms either must be redeemed by the issuing entity or is redeemable at the option of the investor
b. A collateralized mortgage obligation (or other instrument) that is issued in equity form but is required to be accounted for as a nonequity instrument regardless of how that instrument is classified (that is, whether equity or debt) in the issuer's statement of financial position
c. U.S. Treasury securities
d. U.S. government agency securities
e. Municipal securities
f. Corporate bonds
g. Convertible debt
h. Commercial paper
i. All securitized debt instruments, such as collateralized mortgage obligations and real estate mortgage investment conduits
j. Interest-only and principal-only strips.

The term debt security *excludes* all of the following:

a. Option contracts
b. Financial futures contracts
c. Forward contracts
d. Lease contracts
e. Receivables that do not meet the definition of security and, so, are not debt securities (unless they have been securitized, in which case they would meet the definition of a security), for example:

    1. Trade accounts receivable arising from sales on credit by industrial or commercial entities

2. Loans receivable arising from consumer, commercial, and real estate lending activities of financial institutions.

Direct loan origination costs. Direct loan origination costs represent costs associated with originating a loan. Direct loan origination costs of a completed loan shall include only the following:

a. Incremental direct costs of loan origination incurred in transactions with independent third parties for that loan
b. Certain costs directly related to specified activities performed by the lender for that loan. Those activities include all of the following:

    1. Evaluating the prospective borrower's financial condition
    2. Evaluating and recording guarantees, collateral, and other security arrangements
    3. Negotiating loan terms
    4. Preparing and processing loan documents
    5. Closing the transaction.

The costs directly related to those activities shall include only that portion of the employees' total compensation and payroll-related fringe benefits directly related to time spent performing those activities for that loan and other costs related to those activities that would not have been incurred but for that loan. See Section 310-20-55 for examples of items.

Effective interest rate. The rate of return implicit in the loan, that is, the contractual interest rate adjusted for any net deferred loan fees or costs, premium, or discount existing at the origination or acquisition of the loan.

Expected residual profit. The amount of profit, whether called interest or another name, such as equity kicker, above a reasonable amount of interest and fees expected to be earned by a lender.

Fair value. The price that would be received to sell an asset or paid to transfer a liability in an orderly transaction between market participants at the measurement date.

Financing receivable. A financing arrangement that has both of the following characteristics:

a. It represents a contractual right to receive money in either of the following ways:

    1. On demand
    2. On fixed or determinable dates.

b. It is recognized as an asset in the entity's statement of financial position.

See paragraphs 310-10-55-13 through 55-15 for more information on the definition of financing receivable, including a list of items that are excluded from the definition (for example, debt securities).

Idle time. Idle time represents the time that a lender's employees are not actively involved in performing origination activities for specific loans. Idle time can be caused by many factors, including lack of work, delays in work flow, and equipment failure. Idle time can be measured through the establishment of standard costs, time studies, ratios of productive and nonproductive time, and other methods.

Incremental direct costs. Costs to originate a loan that have both of the following characteristics:

a. Result directly from and are essential to the lending transaction
b. Would not have been incurred by the lender had that lending transaction not occurred.

Initial investment. The amount paid to the seller plus any fees paid or less any fees received.

Lending activities. Lending, committing to lend, refinancing or restructuring loans, arranging standby letters of credit, syndicating loans, and leasing activities are lending activities.

Loan. A contractual right to receive money on demand or on fixed or determinable dates that is recognized as an asset in the creditor's statement of financial position. Examples include but are not limited to accounts receivable (with terms exceeding one year) and notes receivable.

Loan Origination Fees. Origination fees consist of all of the following:

a. Fees that are being charged to the borrower as prepaid interest or to reduce the loan's nominal interest rate, such as interest buy-downs (explicit yield adjustments)
b. Fees to reimburse the lender for origination activities
c. Other fees charged to the borrower that relate directly to making the loan (for example, fees that are paid to the lender as compensation for granting a complex loan or agreeing to lend quickly)
d. Fees that are not conditional on a loan being granted by the lender that receives the fee but are, in substance, implicit yield adjustments because a loan is granted at rates or terms that would not have otherwise been considered absent the fee (for example, certain syndication fees addressed in paragraph 310-20-25-19)
e. Fees charged to the borrower in connection with the process of originating, refinancing, or restructuring a loan. This term includes, but is not limited to, points, management, arrangement, placement, application, underwriting, and other fees pursuant to a lending or leasing transaction and also includes syndication and participation fees to the extent they are associated with the portion of the loan retained by the lender.

Loan participation. A transaction in which a single lender makes a large loan to a borrower and subsequently transfers undivided interests in the loan to groups of banks or other entities.

Loan syndication. A transaction in which several lenders share in lending to a single borrower. Each lender loans a specific amount to the borrower and has the right to repayment from the borrower. It is common for groups of lenders to jointly fund those loans when the amount borrowed is greater than any one lender is willing to lend.

Net investment in an original loan. The net investment in an original loan includes the unpaid loan principal, any remaining unamortized net fees or costs, any remaining unamortized purchase premium or discount, and any accrued interest receivable.

Nonaccretable difference. A loan's contractually required payments receivable in excess of the amount of its cash flows expected to be collected.

Portfolio segment. The level at which an entity develops and documents a systematic methodology to determine its allowance for credit losses. See paragraphs 310-10-55-21 through 55-22.

Probable. The future event or events are likely to occur.

Recorded investment. The amount of the investment in a loan, which is not net of a valuation allowance, but which does reflect any direct write-down of the investment.

Recorded investment in the receivable. The recorded investment in the receivable is the face amount increased or decreased by applicable accrued interest and unamortized premium, discount, finance charges, or acquisition costs and may also reflect a previous direct write-down of the investment.

Recourse. The right of a transferee of receivables to receive payment from the transferor of those receivables for any of the following:

a. Failure of debtors to pay when due
b. The effects of prepayments
c. Adjustments resulting from defects in the eligibility of the transferred receivables.

Related Parties. Related parties include:

a. Affiliates of the entity
b. Entities for which investments in their equity securities would be required, absent the election of the fair value option under the Fair Value Option Subsection of Section 825-10-15, to be accounted for by the equity method by the investing entity
c. Trusts for the benefit of employees, such as pension and profit-sharing trusts that are managed by or under the trusteeship of management
d. Principal owners of the entity and members of their immediate families
e. Management of the entity and members of their immediate families
f. Other parties with which the entity may deal if one party controls or can significantly influence the management or operating policies of the other to an extent that one of the transacting parties might be prevented from fully pursuing its own separate interests
g. Other parties that can significantly influence the management or operating policies of the transacting parties or that have an ownership interest in one of the transacting parties and can significantly influence the other to an extent that one or more of the transacting parties might be prevented from fully pursuing its own separate interests.

Revolving Privileges. A feature in a loan that provides the borrower with the option to make multiple borrowings up to a specified maximum amount, to repay portions of previous borrowings, and to then reborrow under the same loan.

Standby Letter of Credit. A letter of credit (or similar arrangement however named or designated) that represents an obligation to the beneficiary on the part of the issuer for any of the following:

a. To repay money borrowed by or advanced to or for the account of the account party
b. To make payment on account of any evidence of indebtedness undertaken by the account party
c. To make payment on account of any default by the account party in the performance of an obligation.

A standby letter of credit would *not* include the following:

a. Commercial letters of credit and similar instruments where the issuing bank expects the beneficiary to draw upon the issuer and which do not guarantee payment of a money obligation
b. A guarantee or similar obligation issued by a foreign branch in accordance with and subject to the limitations of Regulation M of the Federal Reserve Board.

Time of Restructuring. Troubled debt restructurings may occur before, at, or after the stated maturity of debt, and time may elapse between the agreement, court order, and so forth, and the transfer of assets or equity interest, the effective date of new terms, or the occurrence of another event that constitutes consummation of the restructuring. The date of consummation is the time of the restructuring.

Troubled Debt Restructuring. A restructuring of a debt constitutes a troubled debt restructuring if the creditor for economic or legal reasons related to the debtor's financial difficulties grants a concession to the debtor that it would not otherwise consider.

CONCEPTS, RULES, AND EXAMPLES

Receivables

Types of receivables. Financing receivables include

- loans,
- trade accounts receivable,
- credit cards, and
- receivables relating to a lessor's right to payments from a lease other than an operating lease that should be recognized as assets.

Accounts receivable, open accounts, or trade accounts are agreements by customers to pay for services received or merchandise obtained. Notes receivable are formalized obligations evidenced by written promissory notes. Notes receivable generally arise from cash advances but could result from sales of merchandise or the provision of services.

The nature of amounts due from trade customers is often different from that of balances receivable from related parties, such as employees or shareholders. Thus, generally accepted accounting principles (GAAP) require that the different classes of receivables be separately identified either on the face of the statement of financial position itself, or in the notes thereto.

The FASB has given entities the option of using fair value as the measurement basis in the financial statements. Entities can record most financial instruments, including receivables, at fair value.

Receivables due within one year (or one operating cycle, if longer) generally are presented at outstanding face value (principal amount), adjusted for any write-offs already taken and valuation allowances, provided that management has the intent and ability to hold those receivables for the foreseeable future or until maturity or payoff. Valuation allowances adjust the carrying amount of receivables downward because not all of those receivables will ultimately be realized as cash. For example, valuation allowances are reported for amounts estimated to be uncollectible and also for the estimated returns, allowances, and other discounts to be taken by customers prior to or at the time of payment. If it is known that sales are recorded for merchandise that is shipped "on approval" and available data suggests that a sizable proportion of such sales are returned by the customers, then the estimated future returns must be accrued. Similarly, material amounts of anticipated discounts and allowances are to be recorded in the period of sale.

Example of different classes of receivables

Snowy Winters & Sons is a purveyor of fine books about the Alaskan heartland. Its total ending receivable balance is $420,000. The receivable balance is affected by the following items:

- The allowance for uncollectible accounts receivable is $17,000, reflecting a historical rate of bad debts equal to 4% of receivables.
- It ships books on a subscription basis, resulting in a 15% return rate. Winters has recorded an allowance for returns of $63,000.
- It offers an early payment discount of 1%, which is generally taken. Winters maintains a 1% early payments allowance of $4,200 to reflect this arrangement.
- One large customer, Anchorage Book Company (ABC), is delinquent in its payments, so the collections department has converted ABC's outstanding balance of $58,000 into a short-term note receivable, payable over ten months at a 12% interest rate.
- The Winters legal staff has won a lawsuit from which the company can expect to receive a total of $12,000, payable over two years.

- Early Winters, the family patriarch, borrowed $15,000 from the company to purchase an antique dogsled.

Snowy Winters' controller reports this information on the Winters statement of financial position in the following manner:

Accounts receivable, trade	335,000	
Less: Allowances for doubtful accounts	(17,000)	
Returns allowance	(63,000)	
Early payment for discount allowance	(4,200)	250,800
Receivables due from officers		15,000
Notes receivable due in current year		58,000
Noncurrent receivables		
Claims receivable (litigation settlement to be collected over two years)		12,000

Valuation Allowance for Uncollectible Amounts

The recording of a valuation allowance for anticipated uncollectible amounts is almost always necessary. The *direct write-off method*, in which a receivable is charged off only when it is clear that it cannot be collected, is unsatisfactory since it overstates assets and also results in a mismatching of revenues and expenses. (Note that the direct write-off method may be required for tax purposes, but if so, this results in temporary differences for which interperiod tax allocation will generally be required.) Proper matching, which remains a valid financial reporting objective, can only be achieved if bad debts are recorded in the same fiscal period as the revenues to which they are related. Since the amount of uncollectible accounts is not known with certainty, however, an estimate must generally be made.

There are two popular estimation techniques, both acceptable under GAAP:

- The *percentage-of-sales method*, is principally oriented towards achieving the best possible matching of revenues and expenses.
- The *aging the accounts* method is more inclined toward the presentation of the correct net realizable value of the trade receivables in the statement of financial position.

Percentage of sales method. For the percentage-of-sales method, historical data are analyzed to ascertain the relationship between bad debts and credit sales. The derived percentage is then applied to the current period's sales revenues to arrive at the appropriate debit to bad debts expense for the year. The offsetting credit is made to allowance for uncollectible accounts (often still referred to as the *reserve for bad debts*). When specific customer accounts are subsequently identified as uncollectible, they are written off against this allowance.

Example of percentage-of-sales method

Total credit sales for year:	$7,500,000	
Bad debt ratio from prior years or other data source:	1.75%	of credit sales
Computed year-end adjustment for bad debts expense:	$ 131,250	($7,500,000 × .0175)

The entry required is

Bad debts expense	131,250	
Allowance for uncollectible receivables		131,250

Care must be taken to ensure that the bad debt ratio computed will be representative of uncollectibility of the current period's credit sales. A ratio based on historical experience may require an adjustment to reflect the current economic climate. For example, if a large percentage of customers are concentrated in a geographic area that is experiencing an economic downturn, the rate of default may increase over that previously suffered. Changes in credit terms and in customer mix may also affect the relationship between sales and bad debts, and should be given consideration in determining the bad debt percentage to be applied to current period credit sales. In practice, these relationships evolve slowly over time and may not always be observed over the short term.

Aging the accounts method. When aging the accounts, an analysis is prepared of the customer receivables at the date of the statement of financial position. Each customer's balance is categorized by the number of days or months the underlying invoices have remained outstanding. Based on the reporting entity's past experience or on other available statistics, such as industry trends, historical bad debts percentages are applied to each of these aggregate amounts, with larger percentages being applied to the older accounts. The end result of this process is a computed total dollar amount that implies the proper ending balance in the allowance for uncollectible receivables at the date of the statement of financial position. The computed amount is compared to the balance in the valuation account, and an adjustment is made for the differences.

Example of the aging method

	Age of accounts			
	Under 30 days	*30–90 days*	*Over 90 days*	*Total*
Gross receivables	$1,100,000	$425,000	$360,000	
Bad debt percentage	0.5%	2.5%	15%	
Provision required	$ 5,500	$ 10,625	$ 54,000	$70,125

The credit balance required in the allowance account is $70,125. Assuming that a debit balance of $58,250 already exists in the allowance account (from charge-offs during the year that exceeded the credit balance in the allowance account at the previous year-end), the necessary entry is

Bad debts expense	128,375	
Allowance for uncollectible receivables		128,375

Change in estimate. Both of the estimation techniques should produce approximately the same result over the course of a number of years. Nonetheless, these adjustments are based upon estimates and will never precisely predict ultimate results. When facts subsequently become available to indicate that the amount provided as an allowance for uncollectible accounts was incorrect, an adjustment classified as a change in estimate is made, unless this was the consequence of a failure to consider facts available at the time the estimate was made, in which case a correction of an accounting error will have to be recognized.

Imputed interest. If a receivable is due on terms exceeding one year, the proper valuation is the present value of future payments to be received, determined by using an interest rate commensurate with the risks involved at the date of the receivable's creation. In many situations the interest rate commensurate with the risks involved is the rate stated in the agreement between the payee and the debtor. However, if the receivable is noninterest-bearing or if the rate stated in the agreement is not indicative of the market rate for a debtor of similar creditworthiness under similar terms, interest is imputed at the market rate. A valuation allowance is used to adjust the face amount of the receivable to the present value at the market rate. The balance in the valuation allowance is amortized as additional interest income so that interest income is recognized using a constant rate of interest over the life of the agreement. Initial recording of such a valuation allowance also results in the recognition of an expense, typically (for customer receivables) reported as selling expense or as a contra revenue item (sales discounts). Accounting Standards Codification (ASC) 835-30 specifies when and how interest is to be imputed when the receivable is noninterest-bearing or the stated rate on the receivable is not reasonable. It applies to transactions conducted at arm's length between unrelated parties, as well as to transactions in which captive finance companies offer favorable financing to increase sales of related companies.

Detailed information and examples can be found in the chapter on ASC 835.

Lending and financing activities, including trade receivables. Receivables generally arise from extending credit to others.

If the reporting entity has the intent and ability to hold trade receivables or loans for the foreseeable future or until maturity or payoff, those receivables are reported in the statement of financial position at their outstanding principal (face) amounts less any write-offs and allowance for uncollectible receivables or at fair value. Loans originated by the reporting entity are reported net of deferred fees or costs of originating them, and purchased loans are reported net of any unamortized premium or discount. If a decision has been made to sell loans, those loans are transferred to a held-for-sale category on the statement of financial position and reported at the lower of cost or fair value. Any amount by which cost exceeds fair value is accounted for as a valuation allowance.

When a trade receivable or loan is deemed uncollectible, the balance is written off against the allowance for uncollectible receivables. Recoveries of loans and trade receivables that were previously written off are recorded when received—either by a credit directly to earnings or by a credit to the allowance for uncollectible receivables. A credit loss on a financial instrument with off-statement-of-financial-position risk is recorded as a liability rather than being included in a valuation allowance netted against a recognized financial instrument. When settled, the credit loss is deducted from the liability.

ASC 310-10 requires disclosures about

- the nature of the credit risk in an entity's financing receivables,
- how any risk is incorporated into the allowance for credit losses, and
- the reasons for any changes in the allowance.

This information is required to be disaggregated primarily at the level at which an entity calculates its allowance for credit losses. The specific disclosures are noted in the Appendix at the end of this book. Not many entities will need to disclose this information, since ASC 310-10 exempts short-trade trade receivables or receivables measured at fair value or lower of cost or fair value from the disclosure.

ASC 310-25 also includes standards for recognizing fees related to receivables. Delinquency fees are recognized when chargeable, provided that collectibility is reasonably assured. Prepayment fees are not recognized until prepayments have occurred. Rebates of finance charges due because payments are made earlier than required are to be recognized when the receivables are prepaid and are accounted for as adjustments to interest income.

Example of delinquency fees, prepayment fees, and rebates

The DitchWay Company sells a ditch-digging machine called the DitchMade that contractors use to lay utility lines and pipes. DitchWay invoices customers a standard monthly fee for two years, using a book of 24 preprinted invoices, after which they receive title to their DitchMade machines. The DitchMade machine is patent-protected and unique, so contractors must purchase from DitchWay. If a contractor makes a late payment, DitchWay bills them a $150 late fee. Since DitchWay can withhold title to the equipment if all fees are not received, the collection of these fees is reasonably assured. Its entry to record a late fee follows:

Accounts receivable	150	
Income—delinquency fees		150

One contractor enters bankruptcy proceedings. It has accumulated $450 of unpaid delinquency fees by the time it enters bankruptcy. DitchWay uses the following entry to eliminate the fees from its accounts receivable:

Bad debt reserve	450	
Accounts receivable		450

DitchWay's sale agreement recognizes that its billing schedule is essentially a series of loan payments with an implied interest rate of 12%. About 20% of all contractors obtain better financing elsewhere and prepay their invoices in order to reduce the interest payment. DitchWay charges a flat $500 prepayment fee when a prepayment occurs. Though the proportion of early payments is predictable, DitchWay cannot recognize prepayment fees until each prepayment actually occurs. One contractor makes a prepayment, so DitchWay records the following entry:

Accounts receivable	500	
Income—prepayment fees		500

The DitchWay sales agreement also states that, when a contractor prepays an invoice, it should pay the full amount of the invoice, even if paid early, and DitchWay will rebate the unearned portion of the interest expense associated with the early payment. In one case, a contractor prepays a single $2,500 invoice for which the original sales entry was as follows:

Accounts receivable	2,500	
Interest income		450
Revenue		2,050

The amount of interest to be rebated back to the contractor is $225, which DitchWay records with the following entry:

Interest income—rebated	225	
Cash		225

The use of the contra account, interest income—rebated, provides the reporting entity with greater control and information for management purposes. However, the debit could be made directly to interest income if these enhancements are not useful.

Pledging, Assigning, and Factoring Receivables

An organization can alter the timing of cash flows resulting from sales to its customers by using its accounts receivable as collateral for borrowings or by selling the receivables outright. A wide variety of arrangements can be structured by the borrower and lender, but the most common are pledging, assignment, and factoring.

Pledging. Accounts receivable pledging is an agreement in which accounts receivable are used as collateral for loans. The customers whose accounts have been pledged are not aware of this event, and their payments are still remitted to the original entity to which the debt was owed. The pledged accounts merely serve as security to the lender, giving comfort that sufficient assets exist to generate cash flows adequate in amount and timing to repay the debt. However, the debt is paid by the borrower whether or not the pledged receivables are collected and whether or not the pattern of their collection matches the payments due on the debt.

Disclosures. The only accounting issue relating to pledging is that of adequate disclosure. The accounts receivable, which remain assets of the borrowing entity, continue to be shown as current assets in its financial statements but must be identified as having been pledged.

This identification can be accomplished either parenthetically or by note disclosures. Similarly, the related debt should be identified as having been collateralized by the receivables.

Example of disclosure for pledged receivables

Current assets:	
Accounts receivable ($3,500,000 of which has been pledged as collateral for bank loans), net of allowance for doubtful accounts of $600,000	8,450,000
Current liabilities:	
Bank loans payable (collateralized by pledged accounts receivable)	2,700,000

A more common practice is to include the disclosure in the notes to the financial statements. Since the borrower has not surrendered control of the pledged receivables, it continues to carry the pledged receivables as its assets (ASC 860).

Assignment. Accounts receivable assignment is a more formalized transfer of the receivables to the lending institution. The lender investigates the specific receivables that are being proposed for assignment and will approve those that it deems worthy as collateral. Usually customers are not aware that their accounts have been assigned and they continue to forward their payments to the original obligee (the borrowing entity). In some cases, the assignment agreement requires that collection proceeds be immediately delivered to the lender. The borrower is, however, the primary obligor of the debt and is required to make timely payment on the debt whether or not the receivables are collected as anticipated. The borrowing is with recourse, and the general credit of the borrower is pledged to the payment of the debt.

Since the lender knows that not all the receivables will be collected on a timely basis by the borrower, only a fraction of the face value of the receivables will be advanced as a loan to the borrower. Typically, this amount ranges from 70 to 90%, depending upon the credit history and collection experience of the borrower.

Assigned accounts receivable remain the assets of the borrower and continue to be presented in its financial statements, with appropriate disclosure of the assignment similar to that illustrated for pledging. Prepaid finance charges would be recorded as a prepaid expense and amortized to expense over the period to which the charges apply.

In the typical case involving the assignment of receivables, the borrower retains control of the receivables, and it is clear that the transaction is a secured borrowing rather than a sale. If it is unclear whether the borrower has retained control of the receivables, a determination must be made as to whether to account for the transfer as a sale or as a secured borrowing. Making that determination is discussed in the chapter on ASC 860, *Transfers of Financial Assets under ASC 860.*

Factoring. Accounts receivable factoring traditionally involves the outright sale of receivables to a finance company known as a factor. These arrangements involve (1) notification to the customer to remit future payments to the factor and (2) the transfer of receivables to the factor without recourse to the transferor. The factor assumes the risk of an inability to collect. Thus, once a factoring arrangement is completed, the transferor has no further involvement with the accounts, except for a return of merchandise.

In its simplest form, the receivables are sold and the difference between the cash received and the carrying value is recognized as a gain or loss.

Example 1: Example of accounting for the factoring of receivables without recourse

Thirsty Corp. enters into an agreement with Rich Company to sell a group of its receivables without recourse for $180,055. A total face value of $200,000 accounts receivable (against which a 5% allowance had been recorded) is involved. The entries required are as follows:

Cash	180,055	
Allowance for bad debts (200,000 × .05)	10,000	
Loss on sale of receivables	19,945	
Bad debts expense		10,000
Accounts receivable		200,000

The classic variety of factoring provides two financial services to the business: it permits the reporting entity to obtain cash earlier than waiting for customers to pay, and it transfers the risk of bad debts to the factor. The factor is compensated for each of these services. Interest is charged based on the anticipated length of time between the date the factoring arrangement is consummated and the expected collection date of the receivables sold. A fee is charged based upon the factor's anticipated bad debt losses.

Example 2: Example of accounting for the factoring of receivables without recourse

Thirsty Corp. enters into an agreement with Rich Company to sell a group of its receivables without recourse. The receivables have a total face value of $200,000 (against which a 5% allowance had been recorded). The factor will charge 20% interest computed on the weighted-average time to maturity of the receivables of thirty-six days plus a 3% fee.

The entries required are as follows:

Cash	180,055	
Allowance for bad debts (200,000 × .05)	10,000	
Interest expense (or prepaid) (200,000 × .20 × 36/365)	3,945	
Factoring fee (200,000 × .03)	6,000	
Loss on sale of receivables	10,000	
Bad debts expense		10,000
Accounts receivable		200,000

The interest expense, factor's fee and loss can be combined into a $19,945 loss on the sale of receivables.

Some companies factor receivables as a means of transferring bad debt risk, but leave the cash on deposit with the factor until the weighted-average due date of the receivables, thereby avoiding interest charges. This arrangement is still referred to as factoring, since the customer receivables have been sold. However, the borrowing entity does not receive cash but instead records a new receivable, usually captioned "Due from Factor." This receivable, in contrast to the original customer receivables, is essentially without risk and is presented in the statement of financial position without a deduction for estimated uncollectible receivables.

Merchandise returns are normally the responsibility of the transferor, who must then make the appropriate settlement with the factor. To protect against the possibility that merchandise returns will diminish the total of receivables to be collected, a factor will frequently advance only a portion of the face amount of the factored receivables (less any interest and factoring fee deductions). The factor will retain a certain fraction of the total proceeds relating to the portion of sales that are anticipated to be returned by customers. This sum is known as the factor's *holdback*. When merchandise is returned to the transferor, an entry is made offsetting the receivable from the factor. At the end of the return privilege period, any remaining holdback will become due and payable to the transferor.

Example 3: Example of accounting for the factoring of receivables without recourse

1. Thirsty Corp. enters into an agreement with Rich Company to sell a group of its receivables without recourse. The receivables have a total face value of $200,000 (against which a 5% allowance had been recorded). The factor will charge 20% interest computed on the weighted-average time to maturity of the receivables of thirty-six days plus a 3% fee. A 5% holdback will also be retained.
2. Thirsty's customers return for credit $4,800 of merchandise.
3. The customer return privilege period expires and the remaining holdback is paid to the transferor.

The entries required are as follows:

1. Cash	180,055	
Allowance for bad debts (200,000 × .05)	10,000	
Interest expense (or prepaid) (200,000 × .20 × 36/365)	3,945	
Factoring fee (200,000 × .03)	6,000	
Factor's holdback receivable	9,500	
[$10,000/($10,000 + $190,000) × $190,000]		
Loss on sale of receivables	500	
Bad debts expense		10,000
Accounts receivable		200,000

The interest expense, factor's fee and loss can be combined into a $10,445 charge to loss on the sale of receivables.

2. Sales returns and allowances	4,800	
Factor's holdback receivable		4,800
3. Cash	5,200	
Factor's holdback receivable		4,700
Loss on sale of receivables		500

The factor's holdback receivable recorded by the seller is required by ASC 860 to be an allocation of the carrying value of the receivables ($190,000) between the assets sold (the receivables) and the assets retained (the holdback) based on their relative fair values at the date of the factoring agreement. The factor holds back 5% of the face value ($200,000) for a total of $10,000. Upon settlement the loss or gain recorded at the origination of the factoring arrangement needs to be adjusted because the factor pays the remaining holdback of $5,200 ($10,000 holdback – $4,800 returns) in settlement of an asset with a carrying value of $4,700 ($9,500 – $4,800).

Factoring results in a transfer of title to the factored receivables. Where there is a no recourse provision or other continuing involvement with the receivables, the removal of the receivables from the borrower's statement of financial position is clearly warranted.

Another variation is known as factoring with recourse. Accounting for factoring with recourse requires a determination of whether the transfer is a sale or a secured borrowing. That determination is made by applying ASC 860. See the chapter on ASC 860 for more information.

Loan Impairment

ASC 310-10-35 applies:

- To all creditors,
- To all troubled debt restructurings involving a modification of terms, and
- To all loans *except*:
  - Groups of similar small balance loans that are collectively evaluated
  - Loans measured at fair value or lower of cost or fair value

- Leases
- ASC 320 debt securities.
  (ASC 310-10-35-13)

If it is probable that a creditor will not collect all amounts (principal and interest) owed to the degree specified in the loan agreement, a loan is considered impaired. (ASC 310-10-35-16) A delay does not impair the loan if the creditor collects all amounts due (including accrued interest during the delay at the contractual rate).

Measurement. An impaired loan can be measured on a loan-by-loan basis in any of the following ways:

1. Present value of expected future cash flows using the loan's original effective interest rate (the contractual interest rate adjusted for premium or discount and net deferred loan costs or fees at acquisition or origination)
2. Loan's observable market price
3. Fair value of the collateral if the loan is collateral dependent (repayment expected to be provided by the collateral). If foreclosure is probable, this measurement must be used.

(ASC 310-10-35-22)

Other measurement considerations include:

1. Costs to sell, on a discounted basis, if they will reduce cash flows to satisfy the loan
2. Creation of or adjustment to a valuation allowance account with the offset to bad-debt expense if the recorded investment is greater than the impaired loan measurement
3. If the contractual interest rate varies based on changes in an independent factor, the creditor can choose between (ASC 310-10-35-28):
   a. Calculating the effective interest on the factor as it changes over the loan's life, or
   b. Calculating the effective interest as fixed at the rate in effect at the date of impairment.

   The choice must be consistently applied. Projections of factor changes should not be made.
4. Cash flow estimates should be the creditors' best estimate based on reasonable and supportable assumptions.
5. Significant changes occurring in measurement values require recalculation and adjustment of the valuation allowance. Net carrying amount of the loan should not exceed the recorded investment.

After impairment, creditors use existing methods to record, measure, and display interest income. If the existing policy results in a recorded investment less than fair value, no additional impairment is recognized.

Under ASC 310-10-35-16, the creditor would account for the examples above as follows.

Example 1

Land	80,000	
Bad debt expense	20,000	
Note receivable		90,000
Interest receivable		10,000

Example 2

Future cash flows (after restructuring) at the agreement's original effective interest rate:

		5% 5 yrs PV Factor
Principal	$ 56,806	($72,500 × .78353)
Interest	12,555	($ 2,900 × 4.32948)
Total present value	$ 69,361	
Amount prior to restructure ($90,000 principal + $10,000 accrued interest)	(100,000)	
Creditor's loss	$(30,639)	

Beginning of Year 1

Bad debt expense	30,639	
Interest receivable		10,000
Valuation allowance		20,639

End of Year 1

Cash	2,900	
Valuation allowance	568	
Bad debt expense (or interest income)		3,468 (69,361 × .05)

End of Year 2

Cash	2,900	
Valuation allowance	596	
Bad debt expense (or interest income)		3,496 [(69,361 + 568) = 69,929 × .05]

End of Year 3

Cash	2,900	
Valuation allowance	626	
Bad debt expense (or interest income)		3,526 [(69,929 + 596) = 70,525 × .05]

End of Year 4

Cash	2,900	
Valuation allowance	658	
Bad debt expense (or interest income)		3,558 [(70,525 + 626) = 71,151 × .05]

End of Year 5

Cash	2,900	
Valuation allowance	691	
Bad debt expense (or interest income)		3,591 [(71,151 + 658) = 71,809 × .05]
Cash	72,500	
Valuation allowance	17,500	
Note receivable		90,000

Example 3

Future cash flows (after restructuring) at the agreement's original effective interest rate:

		5% 5 yrs PV Factor
Principal	$ 74,435	($95,000 × .78353)
Interest	16,452	($ 3,800 × 4.32948)
Total present value	$ 90,887	
Amount prior to restructure ($90,000 principal + $10,000 accrued interest)	(100,000)	
Creditor's loss	$(9,113)	

Beginning of Year 1		
Bad debt expense	9,113	
Note receivable—new	95,000	
Note receivable—old		90,000
Interest receivable		10,000
Valuation allowance		4,113
End of Year 1		
Cash	3,800	
Valuation allowance	744	
Bad debt expense (or interest income)		4,544 (90,887 × .05)
End of Year 2		
Cash	3,800	
Valuation allowance	781	
Bad debt expense (or interest income)		4,581 [(90,887 + 744) = 91,631 × .05]
End of Year 3		
Cash	3,800	
Valuation allowance	821	
Bad debt expense (or interest income)		4,621 [(91,631 + 781) = 92,412 × .05]
End of Year 4		
Cash	3,800	
Valuation allowance	862	
Bad debt expense (or interest income)		4,662 [(92,412 + 821) = 93,233 × .05]
End of Year 5		
Cash	3,800	
Valuation allowance	905	
Bad debt expense (or interest income)		4,705 [(93,233 + 862) = 94,095 × .05]
Cash	95,000	
Note receivable		95,000

ASC 310-20, *Nonrefundable Fees and Other Costs*

Loan origination fees. These fees should be deferred and recognized over the life of the loan as an adjustment of interest income. If there are any related direct loan origination costs, the origination fees and origination costs should be netted, and only the net amount should be deferred and amortized via the interest method. Origination costs include those incremental costs such as credit checks and security arrangements, among others, pertaining to a specific loan.

The only exception to the foregoing rule would be in the instance of certain loans that also qualify as debt instruments under ASC 320. For those carried in the "trading securities" portfolio, related loan origination fees should be charged to expense when incurred; the requirement that these be carried at fair value would make adding these costs to the asset carrying amounts a useless exercise.

Example of a loan origination fee

Debtor Corp. wishes to take out a loan with Klein Bank for the purchase of new machinery. The fair value of the machinery is $614,457. The loan is for ten years, designed to give Klein an implicit return of 10% on the loan. The annual payment is calculated as follows:

$$\text{Annual payment} = \frac{\$614{,}457}{PV_{10,\ 10\%}} = \frac{614{,}457}{6.14457} = \$100{,}000$$

Unearned interest on the loan would be $385,543 [(10 × $100,000) – $614,457].

Klein also is to receive a "nonrefundable origination fee" of $50,000. Klein incurred $20,000 of direct origination costs (for credit checks, etc.). Thus, Klein has *net* nonrefundable origination fees of $30,000. The new net investment in the loan is calculated below.

Gross investment in loan (10 × $100,000)	$1,000,000
Less: Unamortized net nonrefundable origination fees	(30,000)
	970,000
Less: Unearned interest income (from above)	385,543
Net investment in loan	$ 584,457

The new net investment in the loan can be used to find the new implicit interest rate.

$$\frac{100{,}000}{(1+i)^1} + \frac{100{,}000}{(1+i)^2} + \ldots + \frac{100{,}000}{(1+i)^{10}} = \$584{,}457$$

where i = implicit rate

Thus, the implicit interest rate is 11.002%. The amortization table for the first three years is set up as follows:

(a) Loan payments	*(b)* Reduction in unearned interest	*(c)* Interest revenue (PV × implicit rate of 11.002%)	*(d)* Reduction in net orig. fees (c-b)	*(e)* Reduction in PV of net invest (a-c)	*(f)* PV of net loan investment
					$584,457
$100,000	$61,446*	$64,302	$2,856	$35,689	548,759
100,000	57,590**	60,374	2,784	39,626	509,133
100,000	53,349***	56,015	2,666	43,985	465,148

* *($614,457 × 10%) = $61,446*

** *[$614,457 – ($100,000 – $61,446)] × 10% = $57,590*

*** *[$575,900 – ($100,000 – $57,590)] × 10% = $53,349*

Commitment fees and costs. Often fees are received in advance in exchange for a commitment to originate or purchase a loan. These fees should be deferred and recognized upon exercise of the commitment as an adjustment of interest income over the life of the loan, as in Example 1 for origination costs and fees. If a commitment expires unexercised, the fees should be recognized as income upon expiration.

As with loan origination fees and costs, if both commitment fees are received and commitment costs are incurred relating to a commitment to originate or purchase a loan, the net amount of fees or costs should be deferred and recognized over the life of the loan.

If there is a remote possibility of exercise, the commitment fees may be recognized on a straight-line basis over the commitment period as "service fee income." If there is a subsequent exercise, the unamortized fees at the date of exercise should be recognized over the life of the loan as an adjustment of interest income, as in the previous example.

In certain cases, commitment fees are determined retroactively as a percentage of available lines of credit. If the commitment fee percentage is nominal in relation to the stated rate on the related borrowing, with the borrowing earning the market rate of interest, the fees shall be recognized in income as of the determination date.

Example of a commitment fee

Glass Corp. has a $2 million, 10% line of credit outstanding with Ritter Bank. Ritter charges its annual commitment fee as 0.1% of any available balance as of the end of the prior period. Ritter will report $2,000 ($2 million × 0.1%) as service fee income in its current income statement.

Fees and costs in refinancing or restructurings. (Assume this is not a troubled debt restructuring.) When the terms of a refinanced/restructured loan are as favorable to the lender as the terms for loans to customers with similar risks who are not in a restructuring, the refinanced loan is treated as a new loan, and all prior fees of the old loan are recognized in interest income when the new loan is made. This condition is met if:

1. The new loan's effective yield at least equals the effective yield for similar loans and
2. Modifications of the original debt are more than minor.
   (ASC 310-20-35-9)

When the above situation is not satisfied, the fees or costs from the old loan become part of the net investment in the new loan.

Example of a refinanced loan – favorable terms – origination fees

Jeffrey Bank refinanced a loan receivable to $1,000,000, at 10% interest, with annual interest receipts for ten years. Jeffrey's "normal" loan in its portfolio to debtors with similar risks is for $500,000 at 9% interest for five years. Jeffrey had loan origination fees from the original loan of $20,000. These fees are recognized in income *immediately* because the terms of the restructuring are as favorable to Jeffrey as a loan to another debtor with similar risks.

Example of a refinanced loan – unfavorable terms – origination fees

Assume the same facts as in Example 3 except that the refinanced terms are $500,000 principal, 7% interest for three years. Since the terms of the restructuring are not as favorable to Jeffrey as a loan to another debtor with similar risks, the $20,000 origination fees become part of the new investment in the loan and recognized in interest income over the life of the new loan, as in Example 1.

Purchase of a loan or group of loans. Fees paid or fees received when purchasing a loan or group of loans should normally be considered part of the initial investment; to be recognized in income over the lives of the loans. However, if the loans qualify as debt securities under ASC 320 and are held in the lender's "trading securities" portfolio, these fees should be reported in income when paid or received, and not added to the cost of the loans.

Special arrangements. Often lenders provide demand loans (loans with no scheduled payment terms). In this case, any net fees or costs should be recognized on a straight-line basis over a period determined by mutual agreement of the parties, usually over the estimated length of the loan.

Under a revolving line of credit, any net fees or costs are recognized in income on a straight-line basis over the period that the line of credit is active. If the line of credit is terminated due to the borrower's full payment, any unamortized net fees or costs are recognized in income.

Example of a line of credit – origination fee

Green Bank received $50,000 as a nonrefundable origination fee on a $2 million demand loan. Green's loan dictates that any fees are to be amortized over a period of ten years. Therefore, $5,000 (= $50,000 × 1/10) of origination fees will be recognized as an addition to interest income each year for the next ten years.

Financial statement presentation. The unamortized balance of origination, commitment, and other fees/costs that are recognized as an adjustment of interest income are reported on the statement of financial position as part of the loan balance to which they relate. Except for any special cases as noted in the above paragraphs, the amount of net fees/costs recognized each period as an adjustment will be reported in the income statement as part of interest income.

ASC 310-30, *Certain Loans or Debt Securities Acquired in Transfers*

Overview. ASC 310-30 requires the preparer to differentiate between securities investments acquired directly from the issuer and those obtained on the secondary market. It imposes accounting requirements for debt instruments acquired in transfers when the purchase price reflects a change in the debtor's credit standing since the original issuance of the instrument. This standard is applicable to all acquirers of loans or debt securities (bonds, securitized loans, etc.), not merely financial institutions, although fewer commercial or industrial entities would tend to be making such purchases.

Debt instruments (whole loans or loan participations, as well as securities) will generally trade in the secondary market at prices that vary from the amount at which they were issued originally. The prices may be higher or lower than the face amount, depending on the confluence of several factors. Because interest rates change almost continually, it is rare that market rates will correspond to the nominal rate on any given loan or debt security, even if the loan or instrument originally carried a market yield. Furthermore, many instruments are issued at premiums or discounts at inception, for various reasons. In the secondary market, prices will be adjusted continually to reflect current market conditions as they pertain to the loan's (or security's) coupon rate and the credit standing of the issuer/borrower, within the context of market rates of interest and other factors. If current rates are higher than the instrument's coupon (i.e., contractual) rate, it will trade at a discount from par value, while if the current rates are below the coupon rate, it will sell for a premium, if other variables are held constant.

Furthermore, the borrower's creditworthiness may well have changed since the loan was originated or the debt instrument was issued. This also impacts the price at which the loan or security will trade, with a decline in credit standing resulting in a drop in value, and an improvement in credit standing causing a rise in the value of the entity's debt. Creditworthiness pertains to the risk of default, and a number of well-regarded private sector companies closely monitor the outstanding debt of publicly held and private corporations and various governmental agencies and political subdivisions. Examples of rating agencies or measures are Moody's, Standard & Poor's, and Fitch's for publicly held companies and the Fair Isaac credit score for private companies.

Loans or debt securities may trade in the secondary market at their original issuance prices as the coincidental result of offsetting changes in the above-noted variables. Thus, market yields may have declined—which, taken alone, would cause a rise in the price of fixed coupon debt instruments—but concurrently the issuer's creditworthiness may have been reassessed downward by rating agencies—which, absent other events, would cause the price of the debt to decline. In tandem, the credit downgrade may have essentially negated the price response to lower market interest rates. In applying ASC 310-30, it is necessary to refer not simply to the price at which the loan or security has been transferred, in relation to its "par" or original issuance price, but also to examine whether there is information to suggest that there has been a change in the issuer's credit quality since inception of the obligation. Only in the latter circumstance will the provisions of this standard be applied.

ASC 310-30 in greater detail. The purpose of ASC 310-30 is to prescribe the accounting for debt instruments (comprising most loans and debt securities, with certain exceptions) which are acquired via a transfer (i.e., in the secondary market) and which have been affected by changes in credit quality. The standard requires that the accretable yield be determined. This derived from the relationship between the future cash flows expected to be collected and the price paid for the acquired instrument. The accretable yield is distinguished from the nonaccretable difference, which is generally the excess of the total of contractual future cash flows over the expected cash flows.

Neither the accretable yield nor the nonaccretable difference can be displayed in the financial statements. For example, consider a loan that contractually is obligated to pay a total of $85,000 in future interest and principal, but which can be purchased for $50,00 and is expected to provide future cash flows of only $73,500. The $23,500 ($73,500 – 50,000) spread between the purchase price and the undiscounted expected future cash flows is the accretable yield. The further $11,500 ($85,000 – 73,500) spread between expected and contractual cash flows, however, is the nonaccretable difference, which cannot be given accounting recognition under ASC 310-30. That is, the loan (which is an investment in the hands of the transferee) cannot be recorded or displayed at the higher $85,000 amount, with a contra account or valuation allowance pertaining to the pretransfer estimated uncollectible amount being reported. Instead, the purchase cost, $50,000, must be the initial representation of this acquired asset, which is later increased by virtue of the accretion of yield (and reduced by collections).

While ASC 310-30 applies to loans and debt securities, there are important exceptions. Derivative instruments are excluded entirely from the scope of the standard, although debt instruments that contain embedded derivatives are not excluded. Also, debt securities that are accounted for at fair value with changes taken into income currently (i.e., those held in trading portfolios) are exempted, since these are not accreted to face value or to an expected level of future cash flows. Similarly, since changes in the fair values of trading and available-for-sale securities held by not-for-profit organizations both are reflected currently in the changes in net assets (the parallel performance measure for not-for-profit entities, roughly corresponding to net income), these are also exempted. Mortgage loans classified by mortgage bankers as held-for-sale (and presented at fair value) are also exempted from the provisions of ASC 310-30.

Upon acquisition, the effective yield is to be computed based on the expected pattern (i.e., timings and amounts) of future cash flows, so that interest can be accreted on the level-yield basis (a constant rate on a changing base). Over the holding term of the investment, expected cash flows may be altered: They may decline due to perceived impairment or may increase due to upgrading of creditworthiness. The accounting for such changes will vary, with decreases in expectations triggering immediate impairment loss recognition, while increases will generally be reported prospectively over the holding period of the instrument. The precise accounting for changes in expected future cash flows also depends, per ASC 310-30, on whether the instrument is accounted for as a loan (under ASC 310-30) or as a debt security (under ASC 320). These matters are addressed in the following sections.

Under ASC 310-30, reductions in expected future cash flows will trigger the recognition of a loss in the current reporting period.

Accounting for investments in loans acquired by transfer. Loans acquired by transfer (i.e., in the secondary market) are recorded initially at acquisition cost. If the acquisition price differs from the par or face amount (i.e., there is a premium or a discount), the effective yield has to be computed and used to accrete the discount (or, if a premium, amortize it) over the expected term of the instrument.

However, if there is evidence of a decline in creditworthiness since the instrument's inception, such that it is deemed probable at the date of transfer that the full amount of contractual cash flows will not be received, the provisions of ASC 310-30 must be applied. In this context, *probable* is used in the same way as it is under ASC 450, and only if that rather high-threshold criterion is satisfied will this standard be invoked. In such cases, the transferee must estimate cash flows to be received, and accrete the initial carrying amount to that amount, rather than to the gross amount of future contractual cash flows. An uncertainty regarding future cash flows that suggests only a possible shortfall versus contractual amounts owed would not qualify under the standard for the accounting set forth in this discussion. (In such a situation, there would be disclosure of reasonably possible contingent losses, and if at a later date the loss is deemed to have become probable, a loss accrual would be recognized per ASC 450.)

The estimation of the amounts of expected future cash flows, and the timing of those cash flows, is obviously a matter of some complexity and inevitable subjectivity. For example, if payments from a credit-impaired obligor are expected to be made, say, fifteen days late on average, this will impact the computed effective yield on the loan and is to be given explicit consideration in ascertaining the effective yield, subject to the usual materiality threshold concerns. The calculation of accretable yield is made at the acquisition date, but as described in the following example, it may later have to be adjusted as expectations regarding future cash flow amounts change. Subsequent reduced expectations of cash flows will result in the recognition of impairment, while expectations of enhanced or improved cash flows may result in reversal of previously recognized impairment (if any), or increased effective yield over the instrument's remaining holding period.

Basic example of loans acquired via transfer

Assume that Investor Co. acquires a loan with a remaining principal balance of $650,000 on January 1, 20X1. The contractual terms of the loan call for interest-only payments, at 9%, annually through December 31, 20X5, at which time the full principal balance is due. The debtor's credit rating has been reduced subsequent to the initiation of the borrowing, and the 20X0 interest payment was not made when due. Investor Co. pays $500,000 (flat) for the loan and any unpaid interest. The expectation is that the debtor will pay $40,000 at the end of 20X1, $60,000 at the end of years 20X2 and 20X1 (each year), $70,000 at the end of 20X4, and $600,000 at the end of 20X5. Total projected cash inflows, $830,000, are lower than the contractually due amount, $1,001,000 (including the arrearage for 2010), and the effective yield will be about 12.6% at transfer; the investment is recorded at cost, as follows:

Investment in loan receivable	500,000	
Cash		500,000

At the end of 20X1, immediately prior to receipt of the payment, the entry to record the accretion for the year, at the effective yield, is:

Investment in loan receivable	62,974	
Accretion (interest income)		62,974

The collection of the anticipated amount at December 31, 20X1, is recorded as follows:

Cash	40,000	
Investment in loan receivable		40,000

Entries for subsequent years' accretion and collections would follow in the same manner. This presumes, of course, that amounts expected to be received indeed are received, and that expectations about the future receipts do not depart from what had been anticipated when the loan was purchased.

The changes in carrying amount and recognition of income over the full five-year period are illustrated in the following chart.

	A	*B*	*C*	*D*	*E*
Year ending December 31	*Beginning carrying amount*	*Cash flows expected to be collected*	*Interest income*	*Reduction (increase) in carrying amount (B–C)*	*Ending carrying amount of loan (A–D)*
20X1	$500,000	$ 40,000	$ 62,974	$ (22,974)	$522,974
20X2	522,974	60,000	65,867	(5,867)	528,841
20X3	528,841	60,000	66,606	(6,606)	535,447
20X4	535,447	70,000	67,438	2,562	532,885
20X5	532,885	600,000	67,115	532,885	–
		$830,000	$330,000	$500,000	

In the foregoing chart total cash collected, $830,000, consisted of $330,000 in interest, accreted at the 12.6% computed yield, and $500,000 return of investment in the loan receivable.

Contrast this result with the examples that follow.

Example with decrease in expected cash flows

If, subsequent to acquisition and computation of effective yield, the expected cash flows associated with a loan are revised downward, ASC 310-30 directs that this be accounted for as an impairment, with the adjustment being such that the previously determined yield percentage is maintained in future periods by applying the constant return to a downwardly adjusted carrying value. While some might argue that a diminished expectation of cash flows would imply a new lower rate of return, ASC 310-30 instead opts for recognizing an immediate impairment, measured as the then-present value of the stream of cash flow shortfalls being projected. This results in a continuing rate of return equal to the original estimate, but with a step-down in the carrying value of the loan.

To illustrate, using the same basic facts above, assume now that immediately after the 20X3 payment is made, Investor Co. revises its expectation of cash flows to be received in 20X4 and 20X5. It now anticipates zero cash collection in 20X3, and only $500,000 at year-end 20X5. The present value of these shortfalls—a $70,000 shortage one year hence, followed by a $100,000 shortfall two years later—discounted at the 12.6% yield on the investment computed at the date of transfer, reveals an impairment of $141,039 as of the start of 20X4. The entry to record this, given that the investment is treated as a loan rather than as a debt security, is as follows:

Bad debt expense	141,039	
Allowance for uncollectible loan receivable		141,039

The reduced net carrying value of the loan receivable, which is $394,408 immediately following this adjustment, will continue to accrete at 12.6%, as the following table illustrates:

	A	B	C	D	E
Year ending December 31	*Beginning carrying amount of loan*	*Cash flows expected to be collected*	*Interest income*	*Reduction (increase) in carrying amount (B–C)*	*Ending carrying amount of loan (A–D)*
20X1	$500,000	$ 40,000	$ 62,974	$ (22,974)	$522,974
20X2	522,974	60,000	65,867	(5,867)	528,841
20X3	528,841	60,000	66,606	(6,606)	
20X4*				141,039	394,408
20X5	394,408	–	49,675	(49,675)	444,083
20X6	444,083	500,000	55,917	444,083	–
		$660,000	$301,039	$500,000	

* *Provision of allowance for estimated uncollectible future cash flows, computed at present value using the effective yield of the loan.*

It will be observed in the foregoing chart that total cash collected, $660,000, consisted of $301,039 in interest, accreted at the 12.6% computed yield, and the recovery of only $358,961 of the $500,000 investment in the loan receivable. In other words, SOP 03-3 treats the decrease in expected cash flows as a loss of principal, accounted for as a bad debt and a provision of a valuation allowance against the $500,000 loan receivable. Note that the decreased cash flow expectation was *not* accounted for as a lowered future return on the investment (which would have resulted in lower interest income recognition in years 20X4 and 20X5, in this example, coupled with a full recovery of the principal invested).

Example with decrease in expected cash flows followed by increase in expected cash flows (recovery of uncollectible loan receivable)

If Investor Co., above, first lowers its expectation regarding future cash flows and then partially reverses its estimate, so that some or all (but not more than all) of the allowance of the uncollectible loan receivable proves unneeded, this is accounted for under ASC 310-30 as a reversal of the valuation allowance account (i.e., as a change in an accounting estimate).

To illustrate, consider again the facts in the basic example, and now assume that in 20X3 Investor Co. has the expectation that no interest will be collected in 20X4 and that only $500,000 will be collected in 20X5. In 20X4, however, $20,000 is in fact collected, and Investor Co. then expects a full collection of the $600,000 in 20X5 (but no recovery of the $50,000 missed payment in 20X4)

The entry to record the reduced expectation of future cash flows at the end of 20X2 or beginning of 20X3 is as shown previously.

Bad debt expense	141,039	
Allowance for uncollectible loan receivable		141,039

In 20X4, the collection of the $20,000 (when no collection at all was anticipated) coupled with the renewed expectation of collecting $600,000 in 20X5 required that some of the previously provided valuation allowance be reversed. The amount of valuation allowance to be restored, per ASC 310-30, is that amount which will result in interest accretion thereafter at the previously determined 12.6% yield through the final collection of the loan. Assuming that the $20,000 collection in December 20X4 came as a surprise, the adjustment will be computed with reference to the final remaining collection, $600,000, expected in December 20X5, and to the $20,000 unexpected 20X6 collection.

The entry to partially restore the carrying value of the loan, net of the valuation allowance, is as follows:

Allowance for uncollectible loan receivable	108,802	
Bad debt expense		108,802

The computation of the foregoing amount may be somewhat confusing, unless one keeps in mind that the objective of ASC 310-30 is to provide for the reporting of interest income over the full carrying term of the loan receivable, at a constant rate on a changing balance, with that rate being the rate computed at the date of transfer. The only exception, which will be illustrated later in this section, is for situations where the total cash to be collected exceeds the estimate made at the date of transfer; in that case, a higher rate of return is reported in periods after the change in estimate, to avoid the alternative of reporting a gain at the date the new estimate is made. In this example, the anticipated "extra" 20X5 collection of $100,000 ($600,000 – $500,000) has a present value at the end of 20X14 of $88,802, so this previously provided valuation allowance is no longer needed. Furthermore, the $20,000 collection in 20X4 was unexpected, and had previously been fully included in the valuation allowance as being uncollectible, so this too must be reversed. Therefore, the total reversal of valuation allowance is the sum of these two amounts, or $108,802. Alternatively, this can be computed as the adjustment necessary to bring the net carrying value of the loan receivable to the amount of "principal" to be collected in December 20X5 (i.e., the present value, discounting at 12.6%, of the expected $600,000 collection).

The net carrying value of the loan receivable will continue to accrete at 12.6%, both after the recognition of the valuation allowance at the end of 20X3 and after the partial elimination of the valuation allowance in 20X4, as the following table illustrates:

	A	*B*	*C*	*D*	*E*
Year ending December 31	*Beginning carrying amount of loan*	*Cash flows expected to be collected*	*Interest income*	*Reduction (increase) in carrying amount (B–C)*	*Ending carrying amount of loan (A–D)*
20X1	$500,000	$ 40,000	$ 62,974	$ (22,974)	$522,974
20X2	522,974	60,000	65,867	(5,867)	528,841
20X3	528,841	60,000	66,606	(6,606)	
20X3*				141,039	394,408
20X4	394,408	20,000	49,675	(29,675)	
20X4**				(108,802)	532,885
20X5	532,885	600,000	67,115	532,885	–
		$780,000	$312,237	$500,000	

* *Provision of allowance for estimated uncollectible future cash flows, computed at present value using the effective yield on the loan.*

** *Restoration of a portion of the previously provided allowance, computed at present value using the effective yield on the loan, relative to expected 20X5 collection, plus the $20,000 unanticipated collection in 20X4 at full accreted amount.*

It will be observed in the foregoing chart that total cash collected, $780,000, consisted of $312,237 in interest, accreted at the 12.6% computed yield, and the recovery of only $467,763 of the $500,000 investment in the loan receivable. As in the immediately preceding example, ASC 310-30 treats the decrease in expected cash flows as a loss of principal, accounted for as a bad debt and a provision of a valuation allowance against the $500,000 loan receivable. In this case, $32,237 of "principal" (i.e., of the amount recognized at the time of transfer) was lost, which is the net of the $141,039 valuation allowance provision in 20X3 and the $108,802 recovery recognized in 20X4.

Note that in all of the preceding examples the carrying value of the loan receivable continues to earn the computed 12.6% yield throughout the holding period. This was true if the initially estimated future cash flows were all collected as planned, or if changes to the estimated amounts or timings later were made—as long as the total cash to be collected did not exceed the amount originally (i.e., upon transfer to Invest Co.) estimated. In the next example, the collections exceed what was anticipated when the loan was acquired, and this necessitates a different approach to accounting for the interest yield on the investment.

In all cases where an allowance for uncollectible loan amounts has been provided, if the loan is subsequently foreclosed, the lender must measure the long-lived asset received in full satisfaction of a receivable at fair value less cost to sell as prescribed by ASC 310-40. That standard prescribes that after a troubled debt restructuring, the creditor must account for assets received in satisfaction of a receivable the same as if the assets had been acquired for cash. Accordingly there will be a new cost basis for the long-lived asset received in full satisfaction of a receivable; the valuation allowance would not be carried over as a separate element of the cost basis for purposes of accounting for the long-lived asset under ASC 360 subsequent to foreclosure. This treatment has been confirmed by ASC 310-40.

Example with increase in expected cash flows

Assume again the basic facts of the investment in the loan receivable made by Investor Co. However, after fully collecting the anticipated amounts in 20X1 and 20X2, Investor revises its estimates of the amounts to be collected in 20X3, 20X4, and 20X5. Specifically, it now expects to receive $75,000 at the end of 20X3 and again at the end of 20X4, and to collect the full remaining balance, $650,000, at the end of 20X5. ASC 310-30 does not permit recognition of a gain or other income upon making this new estimate, but does instead require that the effective yield be recomputed and that future receipts be allocated between interest income and principal reduction consistent with the new accretable yield.

Note that no entry is required at the time of the new estimate of future cash flows because no gain or loss (or reversal of previously recognized loss) is being affected. As with changes in accounting estimates under ASC 250, this is handled strictly on a prospective basis.

Year ending December 31	*A* *Beginning carrying amount of loan*	*B* *Cash flows expected to be collected*	*C* *Interest income*	*D* *Reduction (increase) in carrying amount (B–C)*	*E* *Ending carrying amount of loan (A–D)*
20X1	$500,000	$ 40,000	$ 62,974	$ (22,974)	$522,974
20X2	522,974	60,000	65,867	(5,867)	528,841
20X3*					
20X4	528,841	75,000	88,086	(13,086)	541,927
20X5	541,927	75,000	90,265	(15,265)	557,192
20X6	557,192	650,000	92,808	557,192	–
		$900,000	$400,000	$500,000	

* *Based on new expectations regarding future cash flows, a new yield is computed in an amount that equates the present value of expected receipts in 20X3–X5 to the carrying value at the end of 20X2, $528,841. This yield is about 16.7%.*

In the foregoing example, $900,000 in cash is ultimately collected, allocated $400,000 to interest income and $500,000 to recovery of the amount recorded at the date of transfer, which was the sum paid for the loan receivable.

Accounting for investments in pools of loans acquired by transfer. Loans that are acquired as a pool present special accounting considerations. Each individual loan must meet the criteria of ASC 310-30 in order to apply the accounting set forth in this standard. Thus, if a group of loans are acquired together and in the aggregate have expected future cash flows in an amount lower than the aggregate contractual cash flows, this does not qualify each of the loans to be accounted for under ASC 310-30. Rather, each loan must be reviewed for impairment due to credit quality, and only those individual loans exhibiting the defined characteristic would be subject to the specified accounting.

After making a determination that each loan in a proposed pool has met the threshold conditions set forth under ASC 310-30 (i.e., that there has been evidence of credit quality deterioration subsequent to the origination, and that it is probable that, as of the transfer date, the transferee will not collect all the contractually required payments), a further determination must be made that the loans share common risk characteristics. Under provisions of ASC 310-30, loans with similar credit risk or risk ratings, and one or more predominant risk characteristics, such as financial asset type, collateral type, size, interest rate, date of origination, term, and geographic location, will be considered to have common risk characteristics.

Credit risk can be assessed by reference to publicly available ratings of publicly held companies or by automated ratings such as that produced by FICO (formerly Fair Isaac Corporation), called FICO scores.

The aggregate cost of the loans to be aggregated is to be apportioned to the loans in the pool in proportion to their respective fair values at date of acquisition. The aggregate accretable yield of the pool is allocated among the loans in this same manner.

Only loans acquired in a given fiscal *quarter* (not year!) are subject to aggregation for financial reporting purposes. Once a pool is established, its integrity must be maintained, and thus loans can only be removed from the pool upon sale, foreclosure, write-off, or settlement. New loans cannot be added to an existing pool. The excess of contractually required cash flows over the acquisition cost of the pool may not be used to offset or absorb changes to anticipated cash flows associated with other loans or pools of loans having other common risk characteristics.

Removal of a loan from a portfolio is effected at the loan's then-carrying value, and accordingly a gain or loss would be reflected in income of the period, measured as the difference between the carrying value and the fair value of the amount received in settlement (e.g., cash or collateral). Any difference between the carrying amount of the loan being removed from the pool and the fair value of the amount received will not impact the percentage yield being used to accrete value on the remainder of the pool.

Example of an investment in a pool of loans acquired by transfer

Garfield Corporation acquires the following seven loans for $600,000 during the same fiscal quarter:

Loan no.	*Fair value*	*Remaining term*	*Interest rate*	*FICO score*
1	$53,000	4 years	9%	450
2	260,000	4 years	6%	800
3	125,000	4 years	10%	600
4	78,000	4 years	8%	480
5	50,000	4 years	7%	730
6	92,000	4 years	10%	390
7	67,000	4 years	9%	340
	$725,000			

Garfield elects to split these loans into two groups—those having FICO scores below the minimum Fannie Mae acceptance score of 620, and those above it. Accordingly, loan numbers 2 and 5 are shifted into a separate Pool A, with the remaining loans in Pool B. The $600,000 acquisition cost is allocated to the two pools based on the relative fair values of the loans within the pools, as shown below.

Pool no.	*Aggregate fair value*	*Proportion of total fair value*	*Cost allocation*
A	$310,000	43%	$258,000
B	415,000	57%	342,000
	$725,000	100%	$600,000

Garfield expects $117,376 annual payments from the Pool B loans. It determines that the discount rate equating all cash flows expected to be collected with the $342,000 allocated purchase price is 14%. Using the 14% rate, Garfield constructs the following amortization table for Pool B:

Year	Expected cash receipts	Interest income (14%)	Reduction of carrying amount	Carrying amount
Inception				$342,000
1	$117,376	$ 47,880	$ 69,496	272,504
2	117,376	38,151	79,225	193,279
3	117,376	27,059	90,317	102,962
4	117,376	14,414	102,962	0
	$469,504	$127,504	$342,000	

At the beginning of Year 3, Garfield writes off the remaining balance of Loan 7. Prior to the final payment, Loan 7 has a carrying value of $31,204, as determined by apportioning the carrying amount of Pool B at the end of Year 2 amongst the five loans in the pool based on their relative fair values at the date of acquisition. This apportionment calculation is shown in the following table:

Loan no.	Fair value at inception	Relative values	Apportionment of year 2 carrying amount
1	$ 53,000	12.77%	$24,684
3	125,000	30.12%	58,217
4	78,000	18.80%	36,327
6	92,000	22.17%	42,847
7	67,000	16.14%	1,204
	$415,000	100.00%	$193,279

Garfield records the loan write-off with the following entry:

Loss on loan write-off	31,204	
Investment in loan receivable		31,204

The following amortization table reflects the removal of Loan 7 from Pool B, along with its proportionate share of the expected cash receipts in Years 3 and 4.

Year	Expected cash receipts	Interest income (14%)	Reduction of carrying amount	Carrying amount
Inception				$342,000
1	$117,376	$ 47,880	$ 69,496	272,504
2	117,376	38,151	79,225	193,279
Write-off			31,204	162,075
3	98,426	22,690	75,736	86,339
4	98,426	12,087	86,339	0
	$431,604	$120,808	$342,000	

If loans are accounted for in a pool and you subsequently modify one or more of these loans, do not remove the loans from the pool even if the modification would otherwise be considered a troubled debt restructuring. The entity must continue to evaluate whether the pool is impaired if the expected cash flows associated with the pool change.

Accounting for investments in debt securities acquired by transfer. If the debt instrument acquired in a transfer to be accounted for under ASC 310-30 meets the definition of a security, as set forth in ASC 320 (namely, that it constitutes a share, participation, or other interest that is represented by a registered or bearer instrument or by book entry, and is one of a class or series of participations, interests, or obligations), then ASC 310-30 prescribes a slightly different mode of accounting for changes in expected cash flows. To conform to ASC 320's requirements, an anticipated downward change in expected future cash flows must be examined to determine whether merely a temporary change in value has occurred, or whether an other than temporary decline has been signaled. While temporary impairment is not impossible, if in fact the transferee of debt securities—the issuer of which had suffered an adverse change in creditworthiness prior to the transfer—now anticipates further reduced cash flows from the security, there is a substantial likelihood that the impairment in value is other than temporary. Under ASC 320, other-than-temporary impairment must be recognized by writing down the carrying value of the investment and reflecting the charge in current earnings, whether the security is being held in the available-for-sale portfolio or is being held to maturity.

If, on the other hand, the estimated future cash flows from the debt security are increased from the amounts anticipated at transfer, then similar to what was illustrated above, the accretable yield is to be recomputed and periodic interest income thereafter appropriately adjusted. This is considered a change in accounting estimate under ASC 250.

To illustrate, consider the same facts as set forth above, except now assume that the loan was instead a debt security meeting the definition set forth in ASC 320. When acquired, it was treated as being available for sale, but for this example no changes in value are addressed other than that associated with the changed expectation of cash flows.

Example of reduction in cash flow expectations

The anticipated cash flows occurred in 20X1, 20X2, and 20X3, but at the beginning of 20X4 Investor Co. revises its expectations, and now believes that there will be a zero cash collection in 20X4, and only $500,000 at year-end 20X5. The present value of these shortfalls—a $70,000 shortage at year-end 20X4, followed by a $100,000 gap at year-end 20X5—discounted at the same 12.6% rate computed as the yield on the investment at transfer, reveals an impairment of $141,039 as of the start of 20X4. The entry to record this, given that the investment is treated as a debt security, rather than as a loan, is as follows:

Loss on impairment of investment	141,039	
Investment in available-for-sale debt securities		141,039

Apart from the bookkeeping (writing down the investment directly rather than crediting a contra asset account), the treatment is very similar to that previously presented. Most importantly, the reduced net carrying value of the debt security held as an available for sale security will continue to accrete at 12.6%, as the following table illustrates:

	A	*B*	*C*	*D*	*E*
Year ending December 31	*Beginning carrying amount of investment*	*Cash flows expected to be collected*	*Interest income*	*Reduction (increase) in carrying amount (B–C)*	*Ending carrying amount of investment (A–D)*
20X1	$500,000	$ 40,000	$ 62,974	$ (22,974)	$522,974
20X2	522,974	60,000	65,867	(5,867)	528,841
20X3	528,841	60,000	66,606	(6,606)	
20X3*				141,039	394,408
20X4	394,408	–	49,675	(49,675)	444,083
20X5	444,083	500,000	55,917	444,083	–
		$660,000	$301,039	$500,000	

* *Write-down of carrying value of investment in debt security, due to reduced expectation of future cash flows, which is judged to be an OTTI, computed at present value using the effective yield on the loan.*

The total cash collected, $660,000, is accounted for as interest income, in the total amount $301,039, and recovery of the "principal" of the investment, net of the impairment recorded in 20X3, amounting to $358,961.

Example with decrease in expected cash flows followed by increase in expected cash flows

Unlike in the earlier examples, where the investment was accounted for as a loan receivable, here the investment is in a debt security accounted for under ASC 320, which prohibits restoring an other-than-temporary decline in value. For this reason, the write-down was not reflected through a contra asset (allowance) account, and a later improvement in the outlook for future cash flows must instead be accounted for prospectively as a yield adjustment.

Assume, therefore, that Investor Co. first lowers its expectation regarding future cash flows and then partially reverses its estimate, so that some or all of the amount of future cash flow thought not to be forthcoming now again is expected to be received. Specifically, assume that in 20X3 Investor Co. has the expectation that no interest will be collected in 20X4 and that only $500,000 will be collected in 20X5. In 20X4, however, $20,000 is in fact collected, and Investor Co. then expects a full collection of the $600,000 in 20X5 (but no recovery of the $50,000 missed payment in 20X4).

The entry to record the reduced expectation of future cash flows at the end of 20X2 or beginning of 20X3 is as shown below.

Loss on impairment of investment	141,039	
Investment in available-for-sale debt securities		141,039

In 20X4, the collection of the $20,000 (when no collection at all was anticipated), coupled with the renewed expectation of collecting $600,000 in 20X5, requires that the yield through the end of the expected holding period (final payoff, in this case) be recomputed. Assuming that the $20,000 payment for 20X4 is received before the financial statements for 20X4 have been prepared, it would be appropriate to recompute accretable yield as of the beginning of that year, so that both 20X4 and 20X5 will report interest income consistent with the pattern of cash flows over that two-year period. The calculated yield on an investment equal to the carrying value at the beginning of 20X4 ($394,408), which is expected to generate cash inflows of $20,000 at the end of that year and $600,000 at the end of the next year, is 25.9%, and this is used to accrete yield over the remaining term.

Since this will be reported prospectively, no entry is made as of the beginning of the year (nor would the necessary information have been available), but the entry to record interest income and the accretion for uncollected interest would be as follows:

Cash	20,000	
Investment in available-for-sale debt securities	82,156	
Interest income		102,156

The accretion of value is akin to an amortization of discount, and represents interest earned but not received, based on the most recent estimates of future cash flows. It does not represent a recovery of the previously written down carrying value of the investment because of permanent impairment. The complete analysis can be seen in the chart that follows:

	A	*B*		*C*	*D*
Year ending December 31	*Beginning carrying amount of investment*	*Cash flows expected to be collected*	*Interest income*	*Reduction (increase) in carrying amount (B–C)*	*Ending carrying amount of investment (A–D)*
20X1	$500,000	$ 40,000	$ 62,974	$ (22,974)	$522,974
20X2	522,974	60,000	65,867	(5,867)	528,841
20X3	528,841	60,000	66,606	(6,606)	
20X3*				141,039	394,408
20X4**	394,408	20,000	102,156	(82,156)	476,564
20X5	476,564	600,000	123,436	476,564	–
		$780,000	$421,039	$500,000	

Column letters as printed above the chart: *A*, *B*, *C*, *D*, *E*.

* *Write-down of carrying value of investment in debt security, due to reduced expectation of future cash flows, which is judged to be an OTTI computed at present value using the effective yield on the loan.*

** *Interest is accreted at the new rate of 25.9% hereafter.*

It will be observed in the foregoing chart that total cash collected, $780,000, consisted of $421,039 in interest, accreted first at the 12.6% computed yield through the end of 20X3, and then at the 25.9% computed yield in light of higher expected cash flows for 20X4 and 20X5. The remainder of the cash flows, totaling $358,961, was attributable to the recovery of the investment, net of the write-down for impairment in 20X3.

In contrast to the example where the investment was accounted for as a loan receivable, here the yield is adjusted prospectively when a recovery in value is observed, and this causes relatively more of the future cash flows to be treated as interest income, and relatively less as recovery of the investment principal.

Note that if no reduction in future cash flows had been anticipated, but if an increase in cash flows was expected at some point during the holding period of the investment, the result, from an accounting standpoint, would be as shown immediately above. The accretable yield would have been computed and recognized prospectively over the remaining holding period of the security.

Troubled Debt Restructuring, ASC 310-40

Is it a TDR loan? A TDR loan is one that is restructured or modified for economic or legal reasons, where these conditions are present:

1. The creditor grants a concession that it otherwise would not consider and
2. The borrower is having financial difficulties.

(ASC 310-40-15-5)

Because of the framework in the guidance, creditors only have to evaluate modifications for debtors that are experiencing financial difficulties. "Concession" and "financial difficulties" have specific meaning under the guidance.

Financial difficulty. Lenders should consider the following factors when evaluating the first condition for a TDR – borrower's financial difficulty:

- Borrower is in payment default on any of its debt; or it is probable the debtor will be in payment default on any of its debt in the foreseeable future without the modification.
- The borrower has declared or is in the process of declaring bankruptcy.
- There is significant doubt about the borrower's business continuing as a going concern.
- Borrower has securities that have been delisted or are in the process or threat of being delisted from an exchange.
- Based on estimates and projections that encompass only the current business capabilities, The creditor forecasts that the debtor's entity-specific cash flows will be insufficient to service any of its debt in accordance with contractual terms for the foreseeable future.
- Without the modification, the borrower cannot obtain funds from sources other than the existing creditors at an effective interest rate equal to the current market interest rate for similar debt for a nontroubled debtor.

(ASC 310-40-15-20)

The assessment regarding whether it is probable the debtor will be in default in the significant future is a significant change. However, the guidance does not specify how a creditor should determine that it is probable that it will be unable to collect all amounts due according to the contractual terms of a loan. A creditor should apply its normal loan review procedures in making that judgment. An insignificant delay or insignificant shortfall in amount of payments does not require application of this guidance.

Granting a concession. A concession has been granted as a result of a restructuring when the creditor does not expect to collect all amounts due, including interest accrued at the original contract rate. The creditor should also consider changes to underlying collateral if the principal payment is dependent on the value of the collateral.

The first thing the creditor should consider in determining whether a TDR has occurred is whether it expects to collect all amounts due. If contractual amounts due have not changed or have increased, the Codification provides additional guidance.

Additional collateral and guarantees. When a creditor has restructured a debt in exchange for additional collateral or guarantees from the debtor and the nature and amount of that additional collateral or guarantees received as part of a restructuring do not serve as adequate compensation for other terms of the restructuring, the creditor needs to consider whether a concession has occurred. (ASC 310-40-15-14)

Access to market-rate funds. In a declining-rate environment, the loan may be restructured with a lower interest rate. The creditor needs to evaluate whether the debtor would be able to get the same terms and market rate from another lender. If so, a concession has not occurred. If not, the restructuring would be considered to be at a below-market rate and this may indicate that the creditor has granted a concession. (ASC 310-40-15-15)

Guidance specifically prohibits creditors from using the borrower's effective rate test in ASC 470-60 in evaluating whether a concession has been granted to a borrower. (ASC 310-40-15-8A) If it is determined that a TDR exists, the lender is required to:

- Make certain disclosures and
- Calculate the allowance for credit losses following the impairment guidance for impaired receivables in 310-10-35, discussed earlier in this chapter. (ASC 310-40-65-1)

All TDRs are considered impaired loans.

Temporary/permanent increases in interest rate. The borrower cannot assume that a temporary or permanent increase in the contractual interest rate as a result of a restructuring is not a concession. The new contractual interest rate could still be below market interest rates for new debt with similar risk characteristics. Borrowers have to perform the TDR evaluation based on consideration of any other changes as a result of the restructuring. (ASC 310-40-15-16)

Insignificant delay. A delay in payments is not considered a concession if the delay is insignificant. This is aligned with the impairment guidance in ASC 310-10.

ASC 310-40-15-17 provides that a delay may be insignificant depending on the following factors:

1. The amount of payment subject to delay is insignificant relative to the unpaid principal
2. The restructuring results in an insignificant shortfall in the contractual amount due
3. The delay in the timing is insignificant with respect to:
    a. The frequency of payments due
    b. The original contractual maturity
    c. The original expected duration.

The preparer should use judgment in evaluating the factors listed, and other factors may also be considered in evaluating whether an insignificant delay has occurred.

Substituted debtors in a troubled debt restructuring. ASC 310-40-40-1 addresses the situation of a sale of real estate collateral by a debtor in a troubled debt situation, with the acquirer assuming the obligation to the creditor (the reporting entity) such that the fair value of the obligation (the present value of payments, less than the net investment) was less than the creditor's carrying value of the loan receivable. In such circumstances, the creditor would be required to recognize a loss in the amount by which the net investment in the loan exceeds the fair value of the payments to be received. The fair value of the payments should be recorded as an asset by the creditor.

19 ASC 320 INVESTMENTS—DEBT AND EQUITY SECURITIES

PERSPECTIVE AND ISSUES

Subtopics

The Codification contains several Topics dealing with investments, including:

- ASC 320, *Investments—Debt and Equity Securities*
- ASC 323, *Investments—Equity Method and Joint Ventures*
- ASC 325, *Investments—Other*

ASC 320, *Investments–Debt and Equity Securities* contains one subtopic:

- ASC 320-10, *Overall,* that contains guidance for
  - Passive investments in all debt securities and
  - Those equity securities that have a readily determinable fair value.

Scope and Scope Exceptions

ASC 320 applies to all entities that do not belong to specialized industries for purposes of ASC 320. The entities to which it applies include

- Cooperatives,
- Mutual entities and
- Trusts that do not report substantially all their securities at fair value.

ASC 320 does not apply to "entities whose specialized accounting practices include accounting for substantially all investments in debt securities and equity securities at fair value, with changes in value recognized in earnings (income) or in the change in net assets," such as brokers and dealers in securities, defined benefit and other portretirement plans, and investment companies. (ASC 320-15-3)

ASC 320 does not apply to

- Derivative instruments
- Cost method investments accounted for under ASC 325-20, except with respect to the impairment guidance in ASC 320-10-35
- Equity method investments absent the election of the fair value option under ASC 825-10-25-1
- Investments in consolidated subsidiaries.
  (ASC 320-10-15-7)

In the case of an investment subject to ASC 320 with an embedded derivative, the host instrument is accounted for under ASC 320, and the embedded derivative is accounted for under ASC 815.

Overview

ASC 320 classifies these securities into one of three categories:

- Held-to-maturity,
- Trading, or
- Available-for-sale.

Because equity securities have no maturity date, the held-to-maturity category can only be applied to debt securities, which are then reported at amortized cost. The trading category can include both debt and equity securities, which are reported at fair value, via charges or credits included in current earnings. The available-for-sale category is used for those investments that do not fit in either of the other two classifications. Available-for-sale securities are also reported at fair value in the statement of financial position, however, changes in fair value are not reflected in current earnings.

Practice Alert

While SEC rules only apply to public entities, preparers of financial statements can benefit from the findings of SEC reviewers. Investments are a frequent topic of SEC comment letters. Determining when an investment is other-than-temporarily-impaired requires significant judgment. Neither the SEC nor the ASC offer definitive guidelines. The SEC commonly requests:

- Support for the preparer's conclusion that unrealized losses are temporary
- Information on how the preparer determined which period to report the impairment
- More transparent disclosures
- Basis for determining that unrealized losses are recoverable
- How entities separate their OTTI losses on debt securities between credit and noncredit components.

With the worldwide economy continuing to experience volatility, the SEC recently has focused on disclosures related to holdings of sovereign debt issued by Eurozone member countries experiencing financial difficulty. Entities need to determine whether those debt securities will recover their entire amortized cost basis. Equity and privately debt securities issued in those areas also need a careful evaluation.

DEFINITIONS OF TERMS

Source: ASC 320-10-20 *Glossary*.

Amortized cost basis. The amount at which an investment is acquired, adjusted for accretion, amortization, collection of cash, previous other-than-temporary impairments recognized in earnings (less any cumulative-effect adjustments), foreign exchange, and fair value hedge accounting adjustments.

Asset group. An asset group is the unit of accounting for a long-lived asset or assets to be held and used that represents the lowest level for which identifiable cash flows are largely independent of the cash flows of other groups of assets and liabilities.

Available-for-sale-securities. Investments not classified as either trading securities or as held-to-maturity securities.

Cash equivalents. Cash equivalents are short-term, highly liquid investments that have both of the following characteristics:

1. Readily convertible to known amounts of cash
2. So near their maturity that they present insignificant risk of changes in value because of changes in interest rates.

Generally, only investments with original maturities of three months or less qualify under that definition. Original maturity means original maturity to the entity holding the investment. For example, both a three-month U.S. Treasury bill and a three-year U.S. Treasury note purchased three months from maturity qualify as cash equivalents. However, a Treasury note purchased three years ago does not become a cash equivalent when its remaining maturity is three months. Examples of items commonly considered to be cash equivalents are Treasury bills, commercial paper, money market funds, and federal funds sold (for an entity with banking operations).

Component of an entity. A component of an entity comprises operations and cash flows that can be clearly distinguished, operationally and for financial reporting purposes, from the rest of the entity. A component of an entity may be a reportable segment or an operating segment, a reporting unit, a subsidiary, or an asset group.

Debt security. Any security representing a creditor relationship with an entity. The term debt security also includes all of the following:

1. Preferred stock that by its terms either must be redeemed by the issuing entity or is redeemable at the option of the investor
2. A collateralized mortgage obligation (or other instrument) that is issued in equity form but is required to be accounted for as a nonequity instrument regardless of how that instrument is classified (that is, whether equity or debt) in the issuer's statement of financial position
3. US Treasury securities
4. US government agency securities
5. Municipal securities
6. Corporate bonds
7. Convertible debt
8. Commercial paper
9. All securitized debt instruments, such as collateralized mortgage obligations and real estate mortgage investment conduits
10. Interest-only and principal-only strips.

The term debt security excludes all of the following:

1. Option contracts
2. Financial futures contracts
3. Forward contracts
4. Lease contracts
5. Receivables that do not meet the definition of security and so are not debt securities (unless they have been securitized, in which case they would meet the definition of a security), for example:
    a. Trade accounts receivable arising from sales on credit by industrial or commercial entities
    b. Loans receivable arising from consumer, commercial, and real estate lending activities of financial institutions.

Equity security. Any security representing an ownership interest in an entity (for example, common, preferred, or other capital stock) or the right to acquire (for example, warrants, rights, and call options) or dispose of (for example, put options) an ownership interest in an entity at fixed or determinable prices. The term equity security does not include any of the following:

1. Written equity options (because they represent obligations of the writer, not investments)
2. Cash-settled options on equity securities or options on equity-based indexes (because those instruments do not represent ownership interests in an entity)
3. Convertible debt or preferred stock that by its terms either must be redeemed by the issuing entity or is redeemable at the option of the investor.

Fair value. The price that would be received to sell an asset or paid to transfer a liability in an orderly transaction between market participants at the measurement date.

Holding gain or loss. The net change in fair value of a security. The holding gain or loss does not include dividend or interest income recognized but not yet received or write-downs for other-than-temporary impairment.

Operating segment. A component of a public entity. See Section 280-10-50 for additional guidance on the definition of an operating segment.

Readily determinable fair value. An equity security has a readily determinable fair value if it meets any of the following conditions:

1. The fair value of an equity security is readily determinable if sales prices or bid-and-asked quotations are currently available on a securities exchange registered with the US Securities and Exchange Commission (SEC) or in the over-the-counter market, provided that those prices or quotations for the over-the-counter market are publicly reported by the National Association of Securities Dealers Automated Quotations systems (NASDAQ) or by OTC Markets Group Inc. Restricted stock meets that definition if the restriction terminates within one year.
2. The fair value of an equity security traded only in a foreign market is readily determinable if that foreign market is of a breadth and scope comparable to one of the U.S. markets referred to above.
3. The fair value of an investment in a mutual fund is readily determinable if the fair value per share (unit) is determined and published and is the basis for current transactions.

Reporting unit. The level of reporting at which goodwill is tested for impairment. A reporting unit is an operating segment or one level below an operating segment (also known as a component).

Retrospective interest method. A method of interest income recognition under which income for the current period is measured as the difference between the amortized cost at the end of the period and the amortized cost at the beginning of the period, plus any cash received during the period.

Security. A share, participation, or other interest in property or an entity of the issuer or an obligation of the issuer that has all of the following characteristics:

1. It is either represented by an instrument issued in bearer or registered form or, if not represented by an instrument, is registered in books maintained to record transfers by or on behalf of the issuer.
2. It is of a type commonly dealt in on securities exchanges or markets or, when represented by an instrument, is commonly recognized in any area in which it is issued or dealt in as a medium for investment.
3. It is either one of a class or series or, by its terms, is divisible into a class or series of shares, participations, interests, or obligations.

Structured note. A debt instrument whose cash flows are linked to the movement in one or more indexes, interest rates, foreign exchange rates, commodities prices, prepayment rates, or other market variables. Structured notes are issued by US government-sponsored enterprises, multilateral development banks, municipalities, and private entities. The notes typically contain embedded (but not separable or detachable) forward components or option components such as caps, calls, and floors. Contractual cash flows for principal, interest, or both can vary in amount and timing throughout the life of the note based on nontraditional indexes or nontraditional uses of traditional interest rates or indexes.

Trading. An activity involving securities sold in the near term and held for only a short period of time. The term trading contemplates a holding period generally measured in hours and days rather than months or years. See paragraph 948-310-40-1 for clarification of the term trading for a mortgage banking entity.

Trading securities. Securities that are bought and held principally for the purpose of selling them in the near term and therefore held for only a short period of time. Trading generally reflects active and frequent buying and selling, and trading securities are generally used with the objective of generating profits on short-term differences in price.

CONCEPTS, RULES, AND EXAMPLES

Debt Securities and Equity Securities with Readily Determinable Fair Values

ASC 320, *Investments—Debt and Equity Securities*, governs the accounting

- for passive investments in all debt securities and
- for equity securities with readily determinable fair values.

Classification of investment securities. Classification is made and documented at the time of the initial acquisition of each investment. (ASC 320-10-25-1 and 2) The appropriateness of classification is reassessed at each reporting date. ASC 320 requires all debt securities and equity securities with readily determinable fair values to be placed into one of three categories.

Classification of Debt Securities and Equity Securities with Readily Determinable Fair Values

Category	Type	Characteristics	*Reported on statement of* financial position	*Reported* in income
1. Held-to-maturity	Debt	Positive intent and ability to hold until maturity	Amortized cost	Interest Realized gains and losses[1]
2. Trading	Debt or equity	Bought and held principally to sell short-term	Fair value	Interest and dividends Realized gains and losses Unrealized gains and losses
3. Available-for-sale	Debt or equity	Neither held-to-maturity nor trading securities	Fair value Unrealized gains and losses in accumulated other comprehensive income (component of equity)[2]	Interest and dividends Realized gains and losses

Presentation. If a classified statement of financial position is presented, the debt and equity securities owned by an entity are grouped into current and noncurrent portfolios. By definition all trading securities are classified as current assets. The determination of current or noncurrent status for individual held-to-maturity and individual available-for-sale securities is made on the basis of whether or not the securities are considered working capital available for current operations (ASC 210-10-45). Investments that are held for purposes of control of another entity or pursuant to an ongoing business relationship, for example, stock held in a supplier, would be excluded from current assets and would instead be listed as other assets or long-term investments.

Fair Value Readily Determinable. The fair value of an equity security is considered readily determinable if it meets the definition in ASC 320-10-20. See the Definition of Terms section in this chapter for the criteria.

---

1 A transaction gain or loss on a foreign-currency-denominated held-to-maturity security is accounted for according to ASC 830-20.

2 "If an available for sale security is designated as being held in a fair value hedge, all or a portion of the unrealized gain or loss should be recognized in earnings." (ASC 815-25-35-1)

Held-to-Maturity Debt Securities

If an entity has both the *positive intent* and the *ability* to hold debt securities to maturity, those maturities are measured and presented at amortized cost. Each investment in a debt security is evaluated separately. The held-to-maturity category does not include securities available for sale in response to a need for liquidity or changes in:

1. Market interest rates
2. Foreign currency risk
3. Funding sources and terms
4. Yield and availability of alternative investments
5. Prepayment risk.

(ASC 320-10-25-4)

For asset-liability management purposes, similar or identical securities may be classified differently depending upon intent and ability to hold. (ASC 320-10-25-4)

Under ASC 860-20-35, securities such as interest-only strips, which can be settled in a manner that could cause the recorded amounts to not be substantially recovered, cannot be classified as held-to-maturity. Dependent upon the circumstances, those securities are categorized as either trading or available-for-sale.

Transfers. In general, transfers to or from this category are not permitted. In those rare circumstances when there are transfers or sales of securities in this category, disclosure must be made of the following in the notes to the financial statements for each period for which the results of operations are presented:

1. Amortized cost
2. Realized or unrealized gain or loss
3. Circumstances leading to the decision to sell or transfer.

ASC 320-10-25-6 lists changes in circumstances that are not considered inconsistent with the transfer, including:

1. Material deterioration in creditworthiness of the issuer
2. Elimination or reduction of tax-exempt status of interest through a change in tax law
3. Major business disposition or combination
4. Statutory or regulatory changes that materially modify what a permissible investment is or the maximum level of the security to be held
5. Downsizing in response to a regulatory increase in the industry's capital requirements
6. A material increase in risk weights for regulatory risk-based capital purposes.

Other events may prompt a sale or transfer of a held-to-maturity security before maturity (ASC 320-10-25-9). These events should be:

- Isolated
- Nonrecurring
- Unusual for the reporting entity
- Not able to be reasonably anticipated.

Sales Within Three Months of Maturity date. The sale of a security within three months of its maturity meets the requirement to hold to maturity, since the interest rate risk is substantially diminished. Likewise, if a call is considered probable, a sale within three months of that date meets the requirement. The sale of a security after collection of at least 85% of the principal outstanding at acquisition (due to prepayments or to scheduled payments of principal and interest in equal installments) also qualifies, since the "tail" portion no longer represents an efficient investment due to the economic costs of accounting for the remnants. Scheduled payments are not required to be equal for variable-rate debt.

Example of held-to-maturity debt securities

The 12/31/X1 debt security portfolio categorized as held-to-maturity is as follows:

Security	*Maturity value*	*Amortized cost*	*Assumed fair value*
DEF 12% bond, due 12/31/X2	$ 10,000	$10,320	$10,200
PQR mortgage-backed debt, due 12/31/X4	$100,000	$92,000	$90,000
JKL 8% bond, due 12/31/X8	$ 10,000	$ 8,929	$ 9,100

The statement of financial position would report all the securities in this category at amortized cost and would classify them as follows:

Security	*Maturity date*	*Statement of financial position*	*Classification*
DEF	12/31/X2	$10,320	Current
PQR	12/31/X4	92,000	Noncurrent
JKL	12/31/X8	8,929	Noncurrent

Interest income, including premium and discount amortization, is included in income. Any realized gains or losses are also included in income.

Trading Securities

If an entity has debt and/or equity securities (with readily determinable fair value) that it intends to actively and frequently buy and sell for short-term profits, those securities are classified as trading securities. Unless classified as held-to-maturity securities, under ASC 948 mortgage-backed securities held for sale require classification as trading securities. The securities in this category are required to be carried at fair value on the statement of financial position as current assets. All applicable interest and dividends, realized gains and losses, and unrealized gains and losses on changes in fair value are included in income from continuing operations.

Example of accounting for trading securities

The year one current trading securities portfolio is as follows:

Security	*Cost*	*Fair value*	*Difference (fair value minus cost)*
ABC	$1,000	$ 900	$(100)
MNO calls	1,500	1,700	200
STU	2,000	1,400	(600)
XYZ 7% bond	2,500	2,600	100
	$7,000	$6,600	$(400)

A $400 adjustment is required in order to recognize the decline in fair value. The entry required is

Unrealized loss on trading securities	400	
Trading securities—MNO calls	200	
Trading securities—XYZ 7% bond	100	
Trading securities—ABC		100
Trading securities—STU		600

The unrealized loss would appear on the income statement as part of other expenses and losses. (ASC 320-10-35-1) Dividend income and interest income (including premium and discount amortization) is included in income. Any realized gains or losses from the sale of securities are also included in income.

An alternative to direct write-up and write-down of securities is the use of an asset valuation allowance account to adjust the portfolio totals. In the above example, the entry would be:

Unrealized loss on trading securities	400	
Valuation allowance (contra asset)		400

The valuation allowance of $400 would be deducted from historical cost to obtain a fair value of $6,600 for the trading securities on the statement of financial position.

All trading securities are classified as current assets and the statement of financial position would appear as follows:

Current assets:	
Trading securities at fair value (cost = $7,000)	$6,600

The year 2 current trading portfolio is as follows:

Security	New securities cost	Old securities X1 fair value	X2 fair value	Difference*
ABC		$ 900	$1,000	$100
DEF Puts	$1,500		1,500	0
STU		1,400	1,800	400
VWX	2,700		2,800	100
	$4,200	$2,300	$7,100	$600

* *Difference = X2 fair value – (Cost or X1 fair value)*

A $600 adjustment is required in order to recognize the increase in fair value. The entry required is

Trading securities—ABC	100	
Trading securities—STU	400	
Trading securities—VWX	100	
Unrealized gain on trading securities		600

The unrealized gain would appear on the income statement as part of other income.

Example of accounting for a realized gain on trading securities

1. The same information as given in the above example for year one
2. In year 2, the MNO calls are sold for $1,600 and the XYZ 7% bonds are sold for $2,700.

The entry required to record the sale is:

Cash	4,300	
Realized loss on sale of trading securities	100	
Realized gain on sale of trading securities		100
Trading securities—MNO calls (X1 fair value)		1,700
Trading securities—XYZ 7% bonds (X1 fair value)		2,600

Under the valuation allowance method, the current trading portfolio would appear as follows:

Security	Cost	X2 fair value
ABC	$1,000	$1,000
DEF Puts	1,500	1,500
STU	2,000	1,800
VWX	2,700	2,800
	$7,200	$7,100

The required entries to recognize the increase in fair value and the realized gain are:

Valuation allowance	300	
Unrealized gain on trading securities		300

To adjust the valuation allowance to reflect the unrealized loss of $100 at the end of year two on the remaining trading portfolio

Cash	4,300	
Trading securities—MNO calls (Cost)		1,500
Trading securities—XYZ 7% bonds (Cost)		2,500
Realized gain on sale of trading securities		300

The statement of financial position under both methods would appear as follows:

Current assets:

Trading securities at fair value (cost = $7,200) $7,100

Available-for-Sale Securities

Investments in debt securities and in equity securities with a readily determinable fair value that are *not* classified as either trading securities or held-to-maturity are classified as available-for-sale. The securities in this category are required to be carried at fair value on the statement of financial position. (ASC 320-10-35-1) The determination of current or noncurrent status for individual securities depends on whether the securities are considered working capital (ASC 210-10-45).

Other than the possibility of having some noncurrent securities on the statement of financial position, the major difference between trading securities and available-for-sale securities is the handling of unrealized gains and losses. Unlike trading securities, the *unrealized* gains and losses of available-for-sale securities are excluded from net income. Instead, they are reported in other comprehensive income. An exception to this is if all or part of the gain or loss is designated as a fair value hedge. In that case, the unrealized gain or loss is recognized in earnings. (ASC 320-10-35-1)

All applicable interest (including premium and discount amortization) and any realized gains or losses from the sale of securities are included in income from continuing operations.

Example of available-for-sale equity securities

Bonito Corporation purchases 2,500 shares of equity securities at $6 each, which it classifies as available-for-sale. At the end of one year, the quoted market price of the securities is $4, which rises to $9 at the end of the second year, when Bonito sells the securities. The company has an incremental tax rate of 25%. The calculation of annual gains and losses follows:

	Gain/(loss) before tax	Tax on gain/(loss)	Gain/(loss) net of tax
End of Year 1	(5,000)	(1,250)	(3,750)
End of Year 2	12,500	3,125	9,375
Net gain	7,500	1,875	5,625

Bonito reports these gains and losses in net income and other comprehensive income in the indicated years as follows:

	Year 1	*Year 2*
Net income:		
Gain on sale of securities		$7,500
Income tax expense		(1,875)
Net gain realized in net income		5,625
Other comprehensive income:		
Gain/(loss) on available-for-sale securities arising during period, net of tax	$(3,750)	9,375
Reclassification adjustment, net of tax		(5,625)
Other comprehensive income net gain/(loss)	(3,750)	3,750

Example of available-for-sale debt securities

Bonito Corporation purchases 10,000 bonds of Easter Corporation maturing in 6 years, at a price of $95.38, and classifies them as available-for-sale. The bonds have a par value of $100 and pay interest of 7% annually. At the price Bonito paid, the effective interest rate is 8%. The calculation of the bond discount follows:

Maturity value of bonds receivable		$1,000,000
Present value of $1,000,000 due in 6 years at 8% (multiplier = 0.63017)	630,170	
Present value of $70,000 interest payable annually for 6 years at 8% annually (multiplier = 4.6229)	323,600	
Purchase price of bonds		953,770
Discount on bonds payable		46,230

The complete table of interest income and discount amortization calculations for the remaining life of the bonds follows:

Year	*Beginning value*	*Interest received*	*Recognized interest income**	*Discount amortization*	*Ending value*
1	$953,800	$70,000	$76,304	6,304	960,104
2	960,104	70,000	76,808	6,808	966,912
3	966,912	70,000	77,353	7,353	974,265
4	974,265	70,000	77,941	7,941	982,206
5	982,206	70,000	78,576	8,576	990,782
6	990,782	70,000	79,218	9,218	1,000,000

* *(Beginning value) × (Effective interest rate of 8%)*

At the end of year 1, the quoted market price of the bonds is $98, and it is $94 at the end of year 2. The company has an incremental tax rate of 25%. The following table calculates the before-tax and after-tax holding gains and losses on the investment.

Year	*Ending carrying value*	*Ending fair value*	*Holding gain/(loss)*	*Income tax*	*Net of tax*
1	$960,104	$980,000	$19,896	4,974	14,922
2	966,912	940,000	(26,912)	(6,728)	(20,184)
Net			(7,016)	(1,754)	(5,262)

Bonito sells the bonds at the end of year 2, and reports these gains and losses in net income and other comprehensive income in the indicated years as follows:

	Year 1	*Year 2*
Net income:		
Interest income	76,304	76,808
Loss on sale of bonds		(7,016)
Income tax expense	(19,076)	(17,448)
Net gain/(loss) realized in net income	57,228	52,344
Other comprehensive income:		
Gain/(loss) on available-for-sale securities arising during period, net of tax	14,922	(20,184)
Reclassification adjustment, net of tax		5,262
Other comprehensive income net gain/(loss)	14,922	(14,922)

Deferred Income Tax Effects

The recognition of unrealized gains and losses for financial statement purposes is likely to have deferred income tax effects. See the discussion in the chapter on ASC 740, *Income Taxes*.

Transfers Between Categories

A major reason for the development of the guidance in ASC 320 was the concern that under the prior rules there had been too many instances where management had been able to deliberately affect reported net income by careful selection of portfolio securities to be sold in a given period. The practice, typically known as "gains trading," was widely blamed for misleading financial reporting, primarily by financial institutions (which generally hold significantly larger investment portfolios than do other business enterprises). In a gains trading situation, management seeking additional net income would sell securities from the nontrading portfolio having low carrying values based on their original acquisition cost versus current market values. Since these securities had not previously been reported at fair value, the gain would be reported in net income of the period of sale. In a variation on this process, securities held in a trading account, but suffering declining value, would be reclassified to a nontrading portfolio, thus averting a charge against net income to reflect the decline.

ASC 320 includes provisions intended to curtail the abuses described above. Transfers from one of the three portfolio classifications to any other are expected to be rare. ASC 320 provisions impose limitations on situations in which it would be permissible to transfer investments between portfolios. With respect to debt securities (discussed in detail earlier in this chapter), ASC 320 prohibits the use of the "held-to-maturity" classification once it has been "tainted" by sales of securities that had been classified in that portfolio. (ASC 320-10-35-8 and 9)

Securities purchased for the trading portfolio are so classified because it is management's intent to seek advantage in short-term price movements. The fact that management does not in fact dispose of those investments quickly would not necessarily mean that the original categorization was improper or that an expressed changed intent calls for an accounting entry. While transfers out of the trading category are not completely prohibited, they would have to be supported by facts and circumstances making the assertion of changed intent highly credible.

Measurement. Transfers among portfolios are accounted for at fair value as of the date of the transfer. Generally, investments in the trading category transferred to the available-for-sale category warrant no further recognition of gain or loss, as the carrying value of the investments already reflects any unrealized gains or losses experienced since their original acquisition. The only caveat is that, if the reporting entity's accounting records of its investments, as a practical matter, have not been updated for fair values since the date of the most recently issued statement of financial position, any changes occurring since that time need to be recognized at the date the transfer occurs. The fair value at the date of transfer becomes the new "cost" of the equity security in the available-for-sale portfolio.

In brief, fair value is used for transfers between categories. When the security is transferred, any unrealized holding gains and losses are accounted for in the following manner:

1. From trading—Already recognized and not to be reversed
2. Into trading—Recognize immediately in income
3. Available-for-sale debt security into held-to-maturity—Report the unrealized holding gain or loss at the transfer date as other comprehensive income and amortize the gain or loss over the investment's remaining life as an adjustment of yield in the same manner as a premium or discount. The transferred-in security will probably record a premium or discount since fair value is used. Thus, the two amortizations will tend to cancel each other on the income statement.
4. Held-to-maturity debt security into available-for-sale—Recognize in other comprehensive income per ASC 220. Few transfers are expected from the held-to-maturity category.

Example of a transfer between trading and available-for-sale portfolios

Neihaus Corporation's investment in Rabin Restaurants' common stock was assigned to the trading portfolio and at December 31, 20X1, was reflected at its fair value of $88,750. Assume that in April 20X2 management now determines that this investment will not be traded, but rather will continue to be held indefinitely. Under the criterion established by ASC 320, this investment now belongs in the available-for-sale portfolio. Assume also that the fair value at the date this decision is made is $92,000, and that no adjustments have been made to the accounting records since the one that recognized the fair value increase to $88,750. The entry to record the transfer from the trading portfolio to the available-for-sale portfolio is:

Investment in equity securities—available-for-sale	92,000	
Investment in equity securities—held-for-trading		88,750
Unrealized gain on holding equity securities		3,250

Unrealized gains and losses on trading securities are always recognized in income, and in this example the additional increase in fair value since the last fair value adjustment, $3,250, is recognized at the time of the transfer to the available-for-sale portfolio. Further gains after this date, however, will not be recognized in net income, but rather will be included in other comprehensive income.

For securities being transferred into the trading category, any unrealized gain or loss (that had previously been recorded in accumulated other comprehensive income, as illustrated above) is deemed to have been realized at the date of the transfer. Also, any fair value changes since the date of the most recent statement of financial position may need to be recognized at that time.

Example of a transfer between available-for-sale and trading portfolios

NOTE: Items affecting other comprehensive income or loss are required to be recorded net of income tax. For illustrative purposes, the income tax effects of such transactions have been ignored.

The investment in Mitzen preferred stock was held in the available-for-sale portfolio and had been adjusted at December 31, 20X1, from its original acquisition cost of $125,000 to an end-of-year fair value of $109,500 by reflecting in other comprehensive loss the $15,500 unrealized decline in fair value that management judged to be temporary.

At March 31, 20X2, the fair value of Mitzen remained at $109,500 and management now believed the unrealized loss to be an other-than-temporary impairment. As discussed in detail later in this chapter, this loss was recognized as a charge to net income at March 31, 2013, and reclassified ("recycled") from accumulated other comprehensive income into net income to prevent duplication in the financial statements (see summary table below).

At June 30, 20X2, the fair value of Mitzen had increased slightly from $109,500 to $112,000. Because Mitzen shares were classified as "available-for-sale," this increase is reflected in other comprehensive income and is computed as:

Fair value of $112,000 – Cost adjusted for OTTI $109,500 = $2,500.

On July 15, 20X2, management reverses course and decides to try to sell the investment in the short term. Thus, the shares no longer qualify to be classified as available-for-sale and are now considered securities held for trading purposes. The fair value of the shares held at the date of decision is $114,700.

The activity described above with respect to Mitzen is summarized as follows:

				Reflected in	
Date	*Description*	*Memo: Cost (adjusted cost)*	*Fair value (carrying amount)*	*Net income (loss)*	*OCI*
3/5/20X1	Original acquisition	$125,000	$125,000		
12/31/20X1	Unrealized loss		(15,500)		$(15,500)
			$109,500		(15,500)
3/31/20X2	OTTI	(15,500)	0	(15,500)	15,500
		109,500	109,500	(15,500)	0
6/30/20X2	Partial recovery		2,500		2,500
			112,000		2,500
7/15/20X2	Reclassification and further recovery		2,700	5,200	(2,500)
		$109,500	$114,700	$(10,300)	$0

Abbreviations

OCI	Other comprehensive income (loss)
OTTI	Other-than-temporary impairment
AOCI	Accumulated other comprehensive income (loss)
FV	Fair value
AFS	Available-for-sale

On July 15, 20X2, immediately preceding the reclassification of the investment from available-for-sale to trading, the accounting records reflect the following componentized balances (assuming these were the only transactions occurring during the period):

Statement of financial position	
Cost adjusted for OTTI of AFS equity securities (asset)	109,500
Change in FV of AFS equity securities (valuation account)	2,500
	$112,000
Accumulated other comprehensive loss (equity)	$ (15,500)
Statement of comprehensive income	
Loss on impairment of AFS equity securities (net income)	$ (15,500)
Reclassification of AOCI to net income (OCI)	15,500
Unrealized appreciation of AFS equity securities (OCI)	2,500
	$ 2,500

The entry to record the transfer from available-for-sale to trading and the "realization" of the increase in fair value from $112,000 to $114,700 at that date is as follows:

	Debit	Credit
July 15, 20X2		
Change in FV of AFS equity securities (valuation account)	2,700	
Unrealized appreciation of AFS equity securities (OCI)		2,700
To record appreciation in AFS portfolio at 7/15/20X2		
Equity securities held for trading purposes	114,700	
Cost adjusted for OTTI of AFS equity securities		109,500
Change in FV of AFS equity securities (valuation account)		5,200
Unrealized appreciation of AFS equity securities (OCI)	5,200	
Unrealized gain on equity securities held for trading (net income)		5,200
To reclassify equity securities from the AFS portfolio to the trading portfolio, to recognize the appreciation in fair value of those securities in current net income, and to reclassify the previously unrecognized appreciation on those securities from AOCI		

The recognized gain at the time of transfer, in this case, is the sum of the previously unrecognized gain that had been recorded in accumulated other comprehensive income (AOCI), the additional equity account ($2,500) plus the further gain not yet recognized in the investor's financial statements ($2,700). Note that the elimination of the additional equity representing the previously reported unrealized gain will be included in comprehensive income in the current period as a debit, since the additional equity account is being reversed at this time.

Other-than-Temporary Impairment (OTTI)

ASC 320-10-35-17 through 34E addresses the impairment of individual available-for-sale and held-to-maturity securities.

Scope. The guidance on impairment of individual available-for-sale and held to maturity securities applies to

1. Debt and equity securities within the scope of ASC 320 with the following clarifications:
   - All equity securities held by insurance entities are included in the scope of the guidance.
   - Entities are not to "look through" the form of their investment to the nature of the securities held by the investee entity. So, for example, if the reporting entity holds an investment in shares of a mutual fund whose investment strategy is to invest primarily in debt securities, management is to assess the mutual fund investment as an equity security, since the shares held by the reporting entity represent equity in the mutual fund, irrespective of the fact that the mutual fund's holdings are comprised primarily of debt.
   - If the application of ASC 815-15-25 (recognition of embedded derivatives) results in bifurcating an investment into a host instrument and an embedded derivative, the host instrument would be evaluated for impairment under this guidance if it falls within its scope.
2. The standard applies to debt and equity securities that are (a) within the scope of ASC 958-320 (not-for-profit entities' investments in debt and equity securities) and (b) that are held by an investor that reports a performance indicator.
3. Cost-method investments in equity securities.

ASC 320-10-35 establishes a multistep decision process to determine if an investment has been impaired, evaluate whether the impairment is other than temporary, and if OTTI is determined to have occurred, measure the impairment loss. It also establishes a discrete model for assessing impairment of cost-method investments that present unique challenges since reasonable estimation of their fair value is often not practical or cost effective.

Unit of accounting. The unit of accounting to be used for the purpose of performing these steps is the individual security level. This is defined as the level and method of aggregation used by the reporting entity to measure realized and unrealized gains and losses on its debt and equity securities. An example of an acceptable method of aggregation would be for the reporting entity to consider equity securities of an issuer that carry the same Committee on Uniform Security Information Procedures (CUSIP) number that were purchased in separate trade lots to be considered together on an average cost basis.

In considering whether the issuer (i.e., borrower or debtor) of a debt security can prepay or settle the security in a manner that would result in the investor not recovering substantially all of its cost, the investor is not permitted to combine separate contracts such as a debt security and a guarantee or other credit enhancement.

The model set forth for investments, other than those accounted for using the cost method follows.

Step 1—Determine whether the investment is impaired. An investment is impaired if its fair value is less than its cost. Cost as defined for this purpose includes adjustments made to the cost basis of an investment for accretion, amortization, previous OTTIs, and hedging.[3]

In assessing impairment of debt securities, the investor is not permitted to combine separate contracts such as guarantees or other credit enhancements.

The assessment of whether an investment is impaired is to be made for each interim and annual reporting period, subject to special provisions that apply to cost-method investments discussed separately below.

After comparing fair value to cost, if cost exceeds fair value, the investment is considered impaired, and the evaluator is to then proceed to Step 2 to evaluate whether the impairment is considered to be "other than temporary."

Step 2—Evaluate whether the impairment is other than temporary. If the fair value of the investment is less than its cost at the ending date of a reporting period (the date of the latest statement of financial position), management is tasked with evaluating whether the impairment is temporary, or whether it is "other-than-temporary." While the term "other-than-temporary" is not defined, FASB affirmatively states that it *does not mean permanent*. Thus a future recovery of all or a portion of the decline in fair value is not necessarily indicative that an assessment of OTTI made in prior periods was incorrect.

OTTI of available-for-sale (AFS) equity securities (ASC 320-10-35-32A). When the fair value of an equity security declines, management is to start with a working premise that the decline may necessitate a write-down of the security. With that mindset, management is to investigate the reasons for the decline by considering all available evidence to evaluate the AFS equity investment's realizable value. Many factors should be considered by management in performing the evaluation and, of course, the evaluation will depend on the individual facts and circumstances. The SEC's Stafff Accounting Bulletin Series, Topic 5.M provides a few examples of factors that, when considered individually or in the aggregate, indicate that a decline in fair value of an AFS equity security is other-than-temporary, and that an impairment write-down of the carrying value is required.

---

[3] *ASC 815-25-35 indicates that, with respect to a qualifying fair value hedge, the change in fair value of the hedged item that is attributable to the hedged risk is recorded as an adjustment to the carrying amount of the hedged item and is recognized currently in net income.*

1. The period of time and the extent to which the fair value has been less than cost.
2. The financial condition and near-term prospects of the issuer, including any specific events that might influence the operations of the issuer such as changes in technology that may impair the earnings potential of the investment or the discontinuance of a segment of the business that may affect the future earnings potential; *or*
3. The intent or ability of the holder to retain its investment in the issuer for a period of time sufficient to allow for any anticipated recovery in fair value.

Unless there is existing evidence supporting a realizable value greater than or equal to the carrying value of the investment, a write-down to fair value accounted for as a realized loss is to be recorded. The loss is to be recognized as a charge to net income in the period in which it occurs and the written-down value of the investment in investee becomes the new cost basis of the investment.

It is important to note that, if an investor has decided to sell an impaired AFS equity security, and the investor does not expect the fair value of the security to fully recover prior to the expected time of sale, the security is to be considered OTTI in the period in which the investor decides to sell the security. However, even if a decision to sell the security has not been made, the investor is to recognize OTTI when that impairment has been determined to have been incurred.

OTTI of debt securities. (ASC 320-10-35-33A through 33I) If the fair value of a debt security is less than its amortized cost basis at the date of the statement of financial position, management is to assess whether the impairment is an OTTI.

If management intends to sell the security, then an OTTI is considered to have been incurred.

If management does not intend to sell the security, management should consider all available evidence to assess whether, it is more likely than not, that it will be required to sell the security prior to recovery of its amortized cost basis (e.g., whether the entity's cash or working capital requirements, or contractual or regulatory obligations, will require sale of the security prior to the occurrence of a forecasted recovery). If it is more likely than not that a sale will be required prior to recovery of the security's amortized cost basis, OTTI is considered to have been incurred.

If, at the measurement date, management does not expect to recover the *entire* amortized cost basis, this precludes an assertion that it will recover the amortized cost basis irrespective of whether management's intent is to continue holding the security or to sell the security. Therefore, when this is the case, OTTI is considered to have been incurred.

Expected recovery is computed by comparing the present value of cash flows expected to be collected (PVCF) from the security to the security's amortized cost basis.

If PVCF is less than amortized cost basis, the entire amortized cost basis of the security will not be recovered; a credit loss has occurred, and an OTTI has been incurred.

Amortized cost basis (ACB) includes adjustments made to the original cost of the investment for such items as:

1. Accretion
2. Amortization
3. Cash collections
4. Previous OTTI recognized as charges to net income (less any cumulative-effect adjustments recognized in transitioning to the provisions of FSP 115-2)
5. Fair value hedge accounting adjustments.

In determining whether a credit loss has been incurred, management must use its best estimate of the present value of cash flows expected to be collected from the debt security.

The computation, in simple terms, is made by discounting the expected cash flows at the effective interest rate implicit in the security at the date of its acquisition. A methodology for estimation of that amount is described in ASC 310, which is codified in the ASC as follows:

- ASC 310-10-35-21 through 35-37
- ASC 310-30-30-2
- ASC 310-40-35-12.

Many factors influence the estimate of whether a credit loss has occurred and the period over which the debt security is expected to recover (ASC 320-10-35-33F). Examples of these factors include, but are not limited to:

1. The length of time and the extent to which the fair value of the security has been less than its amortized cost basis
2. Adverse conditions that relate specifically to the security, an industry, or a geographic locale such as:
   a. Changes in the financial condition of the issuer of the security or, in the case of asset-backed securities, changes in the financial condition of the underlying loan obligors
   b. Changes in technology
   c. Discontinuance of a segment of the business that may affect the future earnings potential of the issuer or underlying loan obligors of the security
   d. Changes in the quality of a credit enhancement
3. The historical and implied volatility of the fair value of the security
4. The payment structure of the debt security and the likelihood of the issuer being able to make payments that are scheduled to increase in the future; examples of nontraditional loan terms are described in ASC 310-10-50-25, ASC 825-10-55-1, and ASC 825-10-55-2
5. Failure of the security's issuer to make scheduled interest or principal payments
6. Changes in the rating of the security by a ratings agency
7. Recoveries or additional declines in fair value that occur subsequent to the date of the statement of financial position.

In developing the estimate of PVCF for the purpose of assessing whether OTTI has occurred (or recurred), management should consider all available information relevant to the collectability of sums due under the terms of the security, including information about past events, current conditions, and reasonable and supportable forecasts. That information generally is to include:

1. The remaining payment terms of the security,
2. Prepayment speeds,
3. The financial condition of the issuer(s),
4. Expected defaults, and
5. The value of the collateral.

(ASC 320-10-35-33G)

To accomplish this objective, management should consider, for example:

1. Industry analyst reports and forecasts,
2. Sector credit ratings, and

3. Other market data relevant to the collectability of the security.

(ASC 320-10-35-33H)

Management must also consider how other credit enhancements affect the expected performance of the security, including:

1. The current financial condition of the guarantor of the security (unless the guarantee is a separate contract under ASC 320-10-35-23), and/or
2. Whether any subordinated interests are capable of absorbing estimated losses on the loans underlying the security.

(ASC 320-10-35-33I)

The remaining payment terms of the security could differ significantly from the payment terms in prior periods, such as when securities are backed by nontraditional loans (e.g., reverse mortgages, interest-only debt, adjustable-rate products). As a result, management must consider whether currently performing loans that back a security will continue to perform when required payments increase in the future, including any required "balloon" payments. Management should also consider how the value of any collateral would affect the security's expected performance. If there has been a decline in the fair value of the collateral, management is to assess the effect of that decline on the ability of the entity to collect the balloon payment.

Recognition of an other-than-temporary impairment. If, as a result of Step 2, management judges the impairment to be other than temporary, the reporting entity recognizes an impairment loss as a charge to net income for the entire difference between the investment's cost and its fair value at the date of the statement of financial position. The impairment measurement must not to include any partial recoveries that might have occurred subsequent to the date of the statement of financial position but prior to issuance of the financial statements.

The reduced carrying amount of the investment becomes that investment's new cost basis. This new cost basis is not changed for any subsequent recoveries in fair value. Subsequent recoveries in the fair value of available-for-sale securities are included in other comprehensive income; subsequent decreases in fair value are evaluated as to whether they are other than temporary in nature. If considered temporary, the decrease is recorded in other comprehensive income. If considered other than temporary, the decrease is to be recognized as a component of net income for the period as previously described.

Determining OTTI of debt securities to be recognized in net income and in other comprehensive income (OCI). ASC 320 permits reporting entities to split OTTI of debt securities into two components and thus recognize only a portion of the OTTI as a charge to net income when incurred. The remaining portion is to be accounted for through other comprehensive income as described in the following paragraphs.

When an OTTI has been incurred with respect to a debt security, the amount of the OTTI recognized in net income is dependent upon whether management intends to sell the security or more likely than not will be required to sell the security prior to recovery of its ACB, less any recognized current period credit loss, as explained below.

As discussed previously, if management intends to sell the security or more likely than not will be required to sell the security prior to recovery of its amortized cost basis, less any current period credit loss, the OTTI to be recognized in net income equals the entire difference between the investment's amortized cost basis and its fair value at the date of the statement of financial position. Stated differently, in this situation, the entire amount of the OTTI is deemed to be a credit loss and is recognized as an immediate charge to net income in its entirety.

If, however,

1. Management does not intend to sell the security, *and*
2. It is more likely than not the entity will not be required to sell the security prior to recovery of its amortized cost basis less any current period credit lost, the OTTI is to be separated into two components as follows:

   Component 1: The amount representing the credit loss, *and*
   Component 2: The remaining amount, which is presumed to be related to all other factors (but that economically is inseparable from the factors that would cause a loss to be characterized as being from deteriorated credit quality).

Component 1 is to be recognized in its entirety in net income and Component 2 is to be recognized in OCI, net of applicable income taxes.

The previous ACB less Component 1 of the current year's OTTI that represents the current period credit loss is to become the new amortized cost basis of the investment prospectively. That new ACB is not to be adjusted for subsequent recoveries in fair value. The amortized cost basis is to be adjusted, however, for accretion and amortization, as described in the next section.

Example of other-than-temporary impairment of an available-for-sale security

In January 20X2 new information comes to the attention of Neihaus Corporation management regarding the viability of Mitzen Corp. Based on this information, it is determined that the decline in Mitzen preferred stock is probably not a temporary one, but rather is other than temporary (i.e., the asset impairment requires financial statement recognition). ASC 320 prescribes that such a decline be reflected in net income and the written-down value be treated as the new cost basis. The fair value has remained at the amount last reported, $109,500. Accordingly, the entry to recognize the fact of the investment's permanent impairment is as follows:

Loss on holding equity securities	15,500	
Unrealized loss on securities—available-for-sale (other comprehensive income)		15,500

Any subsequent recovery in this value would not be recognized in net income unless realized through a sale of the investment to an unrelated entity in an arm's-length transaction, as long as the investment continues to be categorized as "available-for-sale," as distinct from "held-for-trading." However, if there is an increase in value (not limited to just a recovery of the amount of the loss recognized above, of course) the increase will be added to the investment account and shown in a separate account in stockholders' equity, since the asset is to be marked to fair value on the statement of financial position.

It should be noted that the issue of other-than-temporary impairment does not arise in the context of investments held for trading purposes, since unrealized holding gains and losses are immediately recognized without limitation. In effect, the distinction between realized and unrealized gains or losses does not exist for trading securities.

Example of temporary impairment

In March 20X2 further information comes to management's attention, which now suggests that the decline in Mitzen preferred was indeed only a temporary decline; in fact, the value of Mitzen now rises to $112,000. Since the carrying value after the recognition of the impairment was $109,500, which is treated as the new cost basis for purposes of measuring further declines or recoveries, the increase to $112,000 will be accounted for as an increase to be reflected in the additional stockholders' equity account (AOCI), as follows:

Investment in equity securites—available-for-sale	2,500	
Unrealized gain on securities—available-for-sale (other comprehensive income)		2,500

Note that this increase in fair value is not recognized in current net income, since the investment is still considered to be available-for-sale, rather than a part of the trading portfolio. Even though the previous decline in Mitzen stock was realized in current net income, because judged at the time to be an OTTI, the recovery is not permitted to be recognized in net income. Rather, the change in fair value will be included in other comprehensive income and then displayed in AOCI.

Subsequent measurement after recognition of an OTTI. After recognition of an OTTI, the impaired security is to be accounted for as follows. Management is to account for the debt security subject to OTTI as if that security had been purchased on the measurement date of the OTTI at an amortized cost basis equal to the previous amortized cost basis less Component 1 of the OTTI (the portion recognized as a charge to net income as a current period credit loss).

Debt securities classified as available-for-sale (AFS). Subsequent increases and decreases in the fair value of AFS securities, if not caused by an additional OTTI, are to be included in OCI.

Debt securities classified as held-to-maturity. The OTTI recognized in OCI for held-to-maturity securities is to be prospectively accreted (sometimes referred to as "recycling") from other comprehensive income (OCI) to the amortized cost of the debt security over its remaining life based on the amount and timing of future estimated cash flows. That accretion is to increase the security's carrying value and is to continue until the security is sold, matures, or there is an additional OTTI charged to net income. If the security is sold, guidance on the effect of changes in circumstances that would not call into question management's intent to hold other debt securities to maturity in the future is discussed in a previous section of this chapter and is provided in the following authoritative literature:

- ASC 320-10-25-6, and 25-9
- ASC 320-10-25-14
- ASC 320-10-50-11.

Additional guidance with respect to subsequent period accounting. For debt securities for which OTTI has been recognized as a charge to net income, the difference between the new amortized cost bais and the cash flows expected to be collected is to be accreted following existing guidance on interest income. Management is to continue to estimate the PVCF expected to be collected over the remaining life of the debt security.

For debt securities accounted for under Emerging Issues Task Force (EITF) 99-20 (i.e., specified beneficial interests in securitized financial assets) management is to apply the provisions of ASC 325-40 to account for changes in the PVCF.

For all other debt securities, if subsequent evaluation indicates a significant increase in the PVCF or if actual cash flows are significantly greater than cash flows previously expected, those changes are to be accounted for as a prospective adjustment to the accretable yield of the security under ASC 310-30, even if the debt security would not otherwise be subject to the scope of that standard.

Income statement presentation. In periods in which management determines that a decline in the fair value of a security below its amortized cost basis is other than temporary, management is to present the total OTTI in the income statement with an offset for the amount of the total OTTI that is recognized in OCI, if any (Component 2).

Example of income statement presentation of OTTI

Total losses from other-than-temporary impairment	$(30,000)
Portion of loss recognized in other comprehensive income (before income taxes)	22,000
Net impairment losses recognized in net income	$ (8,000)

When reporting the components of accumulated other comprehensive income (AOCI), management must present separately the amounts recognized in AOCI related to held-to-maturity and available-for-sale debt securities for which a portion of an OTTI has been recognized as a charge to net income.

Subsequent accounting for debt securities after recognition of OTTI. After recognizing a loss from other-than-temporary impairment with respect to a debt security, the investor is to treat the security as if it had been purchased on the measurement date on which the impairment was recognized. If the security had been originally purchased at a premium, the impairment charge will either reduce or eliminate the premium or if the impairment is large enough cause the reporting entity to record a discount. If the security had been purchased at its face amount or a discount, the impairment charge will result in recording or increasing the discount.

After recording the adjustment for the impairment, the adjusted premium or discount is to be amortized prospectively over the remaining term of the debt security based on the amount and timing of future estimated cash flows.

Cost-Method Investments

By their nature, cost-method investments normally do not have readily determinable fair values. Consequently, ASC 320-10-35-25 provides a different model for determining whether a cost-method investment is other-than-temporarily impaired. The determination is made as follows:

1. If the investor has estimated the investment's fair value (e.g., for the purposes of the disclosures of the fair value of financial assets required by ASC 825-10-50), that estimate is to be used to determine if the investment is impaired for those reporting periods in which the investor estimates fair value. If the fair value is less than cost, the investor would proceed to Step 2 of the impairment protocol described previously.
2. For reporting periods in which the investor has not estimated the fair value of the investment, the investor is required to evaluate whether an event or change in circumstances has occurred during the period that may have a significant adverse effect on the fair value of the investment. Such events and circumstances are referred to as impairment indicators and include, but are not limited to:
    a. A significant deterioration in the earnings performance, credit rating, asset quality, or business prospects of the investee
    b. A significant adverse change in the economic, regulatory, or technological environment of the investee
    c. A significant adverse change in the general market condition of either the geographic area or the industry in which the investee operates
    d. A solicited or unsolicited bona fide offer to purchase, an offer by the investee to sell, or a completed auction process for the same or similar security for an amount less than the cost of the investment
    e. Existing factors that raise significant concerns regarding the ability of the investee to continue as a going concern, such as negative cash flows from operations,

working capital deficiencies, or noncompliance with debt covenants or statutory capital requirements.

(ASC 320-10-35-27)

If an impairment indicator is present, the investor is required to estimate the investment's fair value and compare the estimated fair value to the cost of the investment. If the fair value is less than cost, the investor is to proceed to Step 2, as previously described, to evaluate whether the impairment is other than temporary.

Additionally, if a cost-method investment had previously been evaluated under Step 2 as to whether impairment was other than temporary, and the investor had previously concluded that the investment was not other-than-temporarily impaired, the investor is required to continue to make this evaluation by estimating the investment's fair value in each subsequent interim and annual reporting period until either

(1) the investment's fair value recovers to an amount that equals or exceeds the cost of the investment, or
(2) the investor recognizes an other-than-temporary impairment loss.

(ASC 320-10-35-28)

Option Contracts

Call and put options can serve as valuable hedging instruments or as highly leveraged speculative investments. Options give one party, the *holder,* the right but not the obligation to either buy (call) or sell (put) a fixed quantity of an instrument at a defined price. The counterparty, known as the *writer* of the option, has no choice to make and must perform if called upon to do so by the holder.

For example, a call contract gives the holder the right to buy 100 shares of the underlying security at a specific exercise price, regardless of the market price. The seller (writer) of the call, on the other hand, must sell the security to the buyer at that specified exercise price, regardless of the market price. For example, assume a Dreamy July 35 call has a quoted market price of $6 (per share or $600 per contract). These facts indicate that a buyer that pays $600 to a seller for a call has the right to purchase 100 shares of Dreamy at any time until July (typically, the end of trading on the third Friday of the month quoted) for $35 per share. The buyer can exercise this right at any time until it expires. The writer of the call must stand ready to deliver 100 shares to the buyer for $35 per share until expiration. Typically, the holder expects the market price to rise and the writer expects the market price to stay the same or to fall.

A put is the opposite of a call. A put gives the holder of the put the right to sell the underlying security at the exercise price regardless of the market price. It gives the writer of the put the obligation to buy at the exercise price, if so demanded by the holder. Typically, the holder of a put option expects the market price to fall, and the writer expects the market price to stay the same or to rise.

There are many compound options used by traders and investors, all of which consist of combinations of one or more calls and puts, in some cases having differing expiration dates. Strips, straps, straddles, and spreads are combinations and/or variations of the basic call and the basic put. These and other compound instruments should be analyzed in terms of their constituent elements, and accounted for accordingly.

Example

Writer D owns 100 shares of Dreamy at a cost of $75 per share and sells 1 Dreamy July 35 call to Holder E at $6. The following positions result if the market price:

	Position	
	Writer (D)	*Holder (E)*
1. Stays at 35 and there is no exercise	+$600	–$600

D receives the $600 premium and E pays for the right to call the stock. If the market price doesn't move, the option expires; E is out $600 and D collects it.

2. Rises to 55 and there is an exercise and immediate sale	+$600 (0 + $600)	+$1,400 ($2,000 – $600)

If the price rises to $55 per share and the security is called, D sells the security to E at $35 ($0 profit on the shares) and is effectively $600 (the amount of the premium) better off. E, however, buys the security at $35 per share and immediately sells it for $55 per share. E gains $2,000 from the security sale less the $600 premium, and so is $1,400 better off.

3 Falls to 15 and there is no exercise	–$1,400 (– $2,000 + $600)	–$600 (0 – $600)

If the market price falls to $15 per share, D incurs an effective $2,000 decrease in value of the shares held, less the $600 premium received. E does not exercise the option and loses the premium paid.

The issue in accounting for options is whether cost or fair value—or some combination—is to be used in accounting for the option itself and for the associated underlying security. For instance, assume M buys 100 shares of XYZ at $15 per share and the security price immediately moves to $25 per share. At this point, M buys a November 25 put contract at $100 for the contract. M has effectively hedged and guaranteed a minimum profit of $900 [(100 shares × $10) – (100 shares × $1)] regardless of market price movement, since XYZ can be sold for $25 per share until the third Friday in November. If the price continues upward, the put will expire unexercised and M will continue to benefit point for point. If the price stays the same, M locks in a profit of $900. If the price falls, M has locked in a profit of $900. The question is whether, under this fact pattern, both the option and the security can be accounted for at historical cost or at fair value or at some combination of the two.

Change in Fair Value Measurements After Year-end, Disclosures, and Elections

Changes in fair value after the date of the statement of financial position. Under GAAP, events occurring after the date of the statement of financial position are generally not recognized as adjustments to the financial statements. However, disclosure may be necessary if, absent that information, the user of the financial statements would be misled. While not addressed explicitly by ASC 320, presumably material changes in fair value occurring subsequent to the date of the statement of financial position but prior to issuance of the financial statements should be disclosed by management.

Sometimes changes in fair value can be indicative of the underlying cause of the price fluctuations. Of most interest here would be declines in value of available-for-sale securities held at the date of the statement of financial position, which suggest that an "other-than-temporary" impairment has occurred. If the decline actually occurred after year-end as evidenced by a bankruptcy filing, then the event would be disclosed but not reflected in the year-end statement of financial position. However, in some instances, the subsequent decline would be seen as a "confirming event" which provided evidence that the classification or other treatment of an item on the date of the statement of financial position was incorrect. Thus, if a decline in the fair value of available-for-sale securities at the date of the statement of financial position had been accounted for as temporary (and hence reported in other comprehensive income) a further decline after the statement of financial position date might suggest that the decline as of the statement of financial position date had, in fact, been a permanent impairment. Note that any further value decline after year-end would not be recorded in the financial statements; the only question to be addressed is whether the decline that occurred prior to year-end should have been treated as a permanent impairment rather than as a temporary market fluctuation.

If it is clear that the impairment at year-end had, in fact, been other than temporary in nature, then the financial statements are to be adjusted to reflect this loss in net income. Absent sufficient basis to reach this conclusion, the appropriate course of action is to not adjust the statements, but merely to disclose the (material) change in fair value that occurred subsequent to year-end including, if appropriate, a statement to the effect that the later decline was deemed to be an OTTI and will be reflected in the net income of the next year's financial statements. It should also be made clear that the decline occurring prior to year-end was not considered to be an other-than-temporary impairment at that time.

The FASB staff noted that when an entity has decided to sell a security classified as available-for-sale having a fair value less than cost at year-end, and it does not reasonably expect a recovery in value before the sale is to occur, then a write-down for an other-than-temporary decline is prescribed. This would most obviously be necessary if the actual sales transaction, anticipated at year-end, occurs prior to the issuance of the financial statements.

Mutual funds invested in US government contracts. ASC 320-10-50 holds that investments in open-end mutual funds that invest in US government securities are to be reported at fair value per ASC 320. Investments in mutual funds that invest solely in US government debt securities are deemed to be equity investments (since it is the shares of the fund, and not the ultimate debt securities, that are owned), and therefore cannot be classified as held-to-maturity investments.

Forward contracts and options. ASC 815-10-35 addresses the accounting for certain forward contracts and purchased options to acquire securities covered by ASC 320. It applies only when the terms require physical settlement. It stipulates that forward contracts and purchased options (which are not classified as derivatives, having no intrinsic value at acquisition) are to be designated and accounted for as prescribed by ASC 320. These forwards and options would not be eligible for designation as hedging instruments.

Structured Notes. ASC 320-10-35 deals with the complex area of "structured notes," in particular with the matters of the recognition of interest income and of the statement of financial position classification of such instruments. According to this consensus, when recognizing interest income on structured note securities in an available-for-sale or held-to-maturity portfolio, the retrospective interest method is to be used if three conditions are satisfied. These conditions are:

1. Either the original investment amount or the maturity amount of the contractual principal is at risk
2. Return of investment on note is subject to volatility arising from either:
    a. No stated rate or stated rate that is not a constant percentage or in the same direction as changes in market-based interest rates or interest rate index, or
    b. Fixed or variable coupon rate lower than that for interest for traditional notes with similar maturity, and a portion of potential yield based on occurrence of future circumstances or events

3. Contractual maturity of bond is based on a specific index or on occurrence of specific events or situations outside the control of contractual parties.

This does not apply to structured note securities that, by their nature, subject the holder to reasonably possible loss of all, or substantially all, of the original invested amount (other than due to debtor failure to pay amount owed). In those instances, the investment is to be carried at fair value with changes in value recognized in current earnings.

The retrospective interest method requires that periodic income be measured by reference to the change in amortized cost from period beginning to period end, plus any cash received during the period. Amortized cost is determined with reference to the conditions applicable as of the respective date of the statement of financial position. Other-than-temporary declines in fair value would also have to be recognized in earnings, consistent with ASC 320 requirements for held-to-maturity investments.

20 ASC 323 INVESTMENTS—EQUITY METHOD AND JOINT VENTURES

PERSPECTIVE AND ISSUES

Topics Related to Investments

The Codification contains several Topics on the various forms of investments:

- ASC 320, *Investments – Debt and Equity Securities*
- ASC 323, *Investments – Equity Method and Joint Ventures*
- ASC 325, *Investments – Other.*

ASC 323 Subtopics

ASC 323, *Investments – Equity Method and Joint Ventures* contains three subtopics:

- ASC 323-10, *Overall*
- ASC 323-30, *Partnerships, Joint Ventures, and Limited Liability Entities*, which provides guidance on applying the equity method to partnerships, joint ventures, and limited liability entities
- ASC 323-740, *Income Taxes,* provides stand-alone guidance on a specific type of real estate investment, Qualified Affordable Housing Project Subsections.

Investments in stock of entities joint ventures and other noncontrolled entities are usually accounted for by one of three methods:

1. The cost method (ASC 325)
2. The fair value method (ASC 320) or
3. The equity method (this topic – ASC 323).

ASC 323-10, *Overall*

Overview. When an investor has significant influence over an investee, the investor is no longer considered to be a passive investor, and the equity method is an appropriate way to account for the investment. If an investor has the ability to influence significantly the operations and financial policies of an investee, it is appropriate for the investor to reflect that responsibility in the investor's financial statements. The advantages of the equity method are that it:

- Recognizes changes to the underlying economic resources
- More closely meets the objectives of accrual accounting than the cost method
- Best enables investors in corporate joint ventures to reflect their investment in those ventures.
(ASC 323-10-15-4)

Significant Influence. According to ASC 323-10-15-6, indications of significant influence are:

- Representation on the board of directors
- Participation in policy-making processes

- Material intra-entity transactions
- Interchange of managerial personnel
- Technological dependency
- Extent of ownership in relation to other investors.

Generally, significant influence is presumed to exist when the investor owns between 20 to 50% of the investee's voting shares. However, ASC 323, allows for consideration of circumstances where such influence is present with under 20% ownership, or conversely is absent with holdings of 20% or greater. Over 50% is a strong indicator of control, and full consolidation of the investee's financial statements is mandatory unless the investor lacks control.

Accounting Overview. To the extent that the cost of acquiring the investment exceeds the fair value of the investor's share of the investee's underlying net assets, the excess must be accounted for in a manner analogous to the accounting prescribed for goodwill. Therefore, ASC 350, *Intangibles—Goodwill and Other,* affects the application of the equity method of accounting because the portion of the purchase cost identified as representing goodwill is not subject to amortization unless the entity is eligible for applies the alternative available under ASU 2014-02. (See the chapter on ASC 350 for more information on this new guidance.)

The equity method involves increasing the original cost of the investment by the investor's pro rata share of the investee's periodic net income, and decreasing it for the investor's share of the investee's periodic net losses and for dividends paid.

Scope and Scope Exception—ASC 323-10, *Overall*

ASC 323 (ASC 323-10-15-2 through 5) applies to all entities and their investments in common stock or in-substance common stock, including common stock of joint ventures. The guidance in ASC 323 guidance does not apply to an investment:

- Accounted for in accordance with ASC 815-10, *Derivatives and Hedging—Overall*
- In common stock held by a nonbusiness entity, such as an estate, trust, or individual
- In common stock within the scope of ASC 810, *Consolidation*
- Held by an investment company within the scope of ASC 946, except as discussed in paragraph 946-323-45-2.

ASC 323-10 does not apply to an investment in a partnership or unincorporated joint venture (covered in ASC 323-30) and an investment in a limited liability company that maintains specific ownership accounts for each investor (discussed in ASC 272-10).

Scope—ASC 323-30, *Partnerships, Joint Ventures, and Limited Liability Entities*

ASC 323-30 follows the same scope and scope exceptions as ASC 323-10, providing guidance specifically on:

- Partnerships
- Unincorporated joint ventures
- Limited liability companies.

ASC 323-740, *Income Taxes*

Overview. ASC 323-740 provides guidance on a specific tax issue—investments in a Qualified Affordable Housing Project. Created under the Tax Reform Act of 1986, this federal program gives incentives for the utilization of private equity in the development of affordable housing for low-income Americans. The Revenue Reconciliation Act of 1993 retroactively extended and made permanent the affordable housing credit. C corporations eligible for the credits generally purchase an interest in a limited partnership that operates the qualified affordable housing projects. So, the guidance in ASC 323-740 applies to investments in limited partnerships that operate qualified affordable housing projects.

Scope and Scope Exception. ASC 323-740 follows the same scope and scope exceptions as ASC 323-10 and the guidance applies to investments in limited partnerships that operate qualified affordable housing projects.

Technical Alert

In January 2014, the FASB issued ASU 2014-01, *Accounting for Investments in Qualified Affordable Housing Projects*. The ASU is a consensus of the EITF and is effective for public companies for annual and interim periods beginning after December 15, 2014. For all other entities, the amendments are effective for periods beginning after December 15, 2014 and interim periods with annual reporting periods beginning after December 15, 2015. The guidance should be applied retrospectively.

The ASU introduces a "proportional amortization method" that can be elected to amortize the investment basis of investments that meet certain conditions. If elected, the method is required for all eligible investments in qualified affordable housing projects and must be applied consistently. It replaces the effective yield method. Under the proportional method, an investor amortizes the costs of its investment, in proportion to the tax credits and other tax benefits it receives, to income tax expense.

To elect the proportional method, all of the following conditions must be met:

1. It is probable that the tax credits allocable to the investor will be available.
2. The investor does not have the ability to exercise significant influence over the operating and financial policies of the limited liability entity.
3. Substantially all of the projected benefits are from tax credits and other tax benefits (for example, tax benefits generated from the operating losses of the investment).
4. The investor's projected yield based solely on the cash flows from the tax credits and other tax benefits is positive.
5. The investor is a limited liability investor in the limited liability entity for both legal and tax purposes, and the investor's liability is limited to its capital investment.

(Pending content: ASC 323-740-25-1)

It is expected that the new guidance will enable more investors to present amortization of investments in qualified affordable housing projects. Investors that do not qualify for the proportional amortization presentation under the new guidance will continue to account for their investments under the equity method or cost method, which results in losses recognized in pretax income and tax benefits recognized in income taxes ("gross" presentation of investment results).

DEFINITIONS OF TERMS

Source: ASC 323-10-20, 323-30-20, 323-740-20

Common stock. A stock that is subordinate to all other stock of the issuer. Also called common shares.

Corporate joint venture. A corporation owned and operated by a small group of entities (the joint venturers) as a separate and specific business or project for the mutual benefit of the members of the group. A government may also be a member of the group. The purpose of a corporate joint venture frequently is to share risks and rewards in developing a new market, product or technology; to combine complementary technological knowledge; or to pool resources in developing production or other facilities. A corporate joint venture also usually provides an arrangement under which each joint venturer may participate, directly or indirectly, in the overall management of the joint venture. Joint venturers thus have an interest or relationship other than as passive investors. An entity that is a subsidiary of one or the joint venturers is not a corporate joint venture. The ownership of a corporate joint venture seldom changes, and its stock is usually not traded publicly. A noncontrolling interest held by public ownership, however, does not preclude a corporation from being a corporate joint venture.

Current tax expense. The amount of income taxes paid or payable (or refundable) for a year as determined by applying the provisions of the enacted tax law to the taxable income or excess of deductions over revenues for that year.

Dividends. Dividends paid or payable in cash, other assets, or another class of stock and does not include stock dividends or stock splits.

Earnings or losses of an investee. Net income (or net loss) of an investee determined in accordance with US GAAP.

Event. A happening of consequence to an entity. The term encompasses both transactions and other events affecting an entity. [FAS 109, paragraph 289, sequence 1058.]

In-substance common stock. An investment in an entity that has risk and reward characteristics that are substantially similar to that entity's common stock.

Income tax expense (or benefit). The sum of current tax expense (or benefit) and deferred tax expense (or benefit).

Income Taxes. Domestic and foreign federal (national), state, and local (including franchise) taxes based on income.

Investee. An entity that issued an equity instrument that is held by an investor.

Investor. A business entity that holds an investment in voting stock of another entity.

Noncontrolling interest. The portion of equity (net assets) in a subsidiary not attributable, directly or indirectly, to a parent. A noncontrolling interest is sometimes called a minority interest.

Not-for-profit entity. An entity that possesses the following characteristics, in varying degrees, that distinguish it from a business entity:

1. Contributions of significant amounts of resources from resource providers who do not expect commensurate or proportionate pecuniary return
2. Operating purposes other than to provide goods or services at a profit
3. Absence of ownership interests like those of business entities.

Entities that clearly fall outside this definition include the following:

1. All investor-owned entities
2. Entities that provide dividends, lower costs, or other economic benefits directly and proportionately to their owners, members, or participants, such as mutual insurance entities, credit unions, farm and rural electric cooperatives, and employee benefit plans.

Parent. An entity that has a controlling financial interest in one or more subsidiaries. (Also, an entity that is the primary beneficiary of a variable interest entity.)

Public business entity. A public business entity is a business entity meeting any one of the criteria below. Neither a not-for-profit entity nor an employee benefit plan is a business entity.

1. It is required by the U.S. Securities and Exchange Commission (SEC) to file or furnish financial statements, or does file or furnish financial statements (including voluntary filers), with the SEC (including other entities whose financial statements or financial information are required to be or are included in a filing).
2. It is required by the Securities Exchange Act of 1934 (the Act), as amended, or rules or regulations promulgated under the Act, to file or furnish financial statements with a regulatory agency other than the SEC.
3. It is required to file or furnish financial statements with a foreign or domestic regulatory agency in preparation for the sale of or for purposes of issuing securities that are not subject to contractual restrictions on transfer.
4. It has issued, or is a conduit bond obligor for, securities that are traded, listed, or quoted on an exchange or an over-the-counter market.
5. It has one or more securities that are not subject to contractual restrictions on transfer, and it is required by law, contract, or regulation to prepare U.S. GAAP financial statements (including footnotes) and make them publicly available on a periodic basis (for example, interim or annual periods). An entity must meet both of these conditions to meet this criterion.

An entity may meet the definition of a public business entity solely because its financial statements or financial information is included in another entity's filing with the SEC. In that case, the entity is only a public business entity for purposes of financial statements that are filed or furnished with the SEC.

Significant influence. See ASC 323-10-15-6 through 15-11 and information in the Perspectives and Issues Section at the beginning of this chapter.

Standstill agreement. An agreement signed by the investee and investor under which the investor agrees to limit its shareholding in the investee.

Subsidiary. An entity, including an unincorporated entity such as a partnership or trust, in which another entity, known as its parent, holds a controlling financial interest. (Also, a variable interest entity that is consolidated by a primary beneficiary.)

CONCEPTS, RULES, AND EXAMPLES

The Equity Method of Accounting for Investments

Introduction and background. The equity method of accounting has been referred to as "one-line consolidation," because the net result of applying ASC 323 on reported net income and on net worth should be identical to what would have occurred had full consolidation been applied. However, rather than include its share of each component (e.g., sales, cost of sales, operating expenses, etc.) in its financial statements, the investor only includes its share of the investee's net income as a separate line item in its income. Note that there are exceptions to this one-line rule. The investor's share of investee extraordinary items and prior period adjustments retain their identities in the investor's income and retained earnings statements and are separately reported if material in relation to the investor's income. It should be noted that the final bottom-line impact on the investor's financial statements is identical whether the equity method or full consolidation is employed; only the amount of detail presented within the financial statements differs.

Significant influence. The equity method is not a substitute for consolidation. It is employed where the investor has significant influence over the operations of the investee but lacks control. In general, significant influence is inferred when the investor owns between 20% and 50% of the investee's voting common stock. Any ownership percentage over 50% presumably gives the investor actual voting control, making full consolidation of financial statements necessary. The 20% threshold stipulated in ASC 323 is presumptive, but not absolute. Circumstances may suggest that significant influence exists even though the investor's level of ownership is less than 20%, or that it is absent despite a level of ownership above 20%. In considering whether significant influence exists, ASC 323-10-15-10 identifies the following factors:

1. Opposition by the investee,
2. Agreements under which the investor surrenders shareholder rights,
3. Majority ownership by a small group of shareholders,
4. Inability to obtain desired information from the investee,
5. Inability to obtain representation on investee board of directors, etc.

Whether sufficient contrary evidence exists to negate the presumption of significant influence is a matter of judgment. Judgment requires a careful evaluation of all pertinent facts and circumstances, over an extended period of time in some cases.

As a practical matter, absence of control by the parent is the only remaining reason to not consolidate a majority-owned investee.

Recognition and initial measurement. Investment in the stock of an investee is recognized as an asset. The investor measures its initial equity method investment at cost.

Determination of cost. When the consideration is in the form of cash, the cost of the acquisition is measured as the amount of cash paid to acquire the investment, including transaction costs associated with the acquisition.[1]

In some transactions, noncash consideration is surrendered by the investor. This can take the form of

- Noncash assets,
- Liabilities incurred or assumed, or
- Equity interests issued.

The measurement of consideration in these transactions is based on either the cost to the acquirer or the fair value of the assets (or net assets) acquired, whichever is considered more reliably measurable. No gain or loss is recognized by the investor, unless the value of noncash assets surrendered as consideration differs from their carrying amounts in the investor's accounting records.

Contingent consideration arrangements. All business combinations are required to be accounted for using the acquisition method as prescribed in ASC 805. Contingent consideration should, in general, only be included in the initial measurement of an equity method investment if required to be so included by guidance contained in GAAP other than ASC 805.

If an equity method investment agreement involves a contingent consideration arrangement in which the fair value of the investor's share of the investee's net assets exceeds the

[1] *This treatment of transaction costs is unique to an asset acquisition or acquisition of an equity method investment. In a business combination accounted for under the acquisition method, transaction costs are expensed as incurred.*

investor's initial cost (referred to as the "differential"), a liability is to be recognized for the *lesser* of the:

1. Excess of the investor's share of the investee's net assets over the measurement of initial cost (including contingent consideration otherwise recognized), *or*
2. Maximum amount of contingent consideration not otherwise recognized.

Subsequently, upon the resolution of a contingent liability recorded under this provision (ASC 323-10-30-2B), when the consideration is issued or becomes issuable:

1. An excess of the fair value of the contingent consideration issued or issuable over the amount previously recognized as a liability is to be recognized as an additional cost of the investment.
2. An excess of the amount previously recognized as a liability over the contingent consideration issued or issuable is to be applied to reduce the cost of the investment.

Basis differences. ASC 323 requires that the investor account for any differential between its cost and its proportionate share of the fair value of the investee's net identifiable assets consistent with the accounting for a business combination under the acquisition method prescribed by ASC 805.

In almost all instances, the price paid by an investor to acquire shares of an investee will differ from the corresponding underlying book value (i.e., the investee's net assets per its GAAP-basis financial statements). The differential can be broken down into the following components from the authoritative literature on business combinations:

1. Tangible and intangible assets recognized in the accounting records of the investee at carrying values that are below their fair values.
2. Intangible assets not recognized in the accounting records of the investee because of the longstanding prohibition in GAAP against recognizing internally developed intangibles (with the notable exception of internal-use software). These might include in-process research and development assets, customer lists, and other amortizable or nonamortizable intangibles as discussed in detail in the chapters on ASC 730, *Research and Development* and ASC 350, *Intangibles—Goodwill and Other.*
3. Contingent consideration.
4. Goodwill.

This means that premiums or discounts versus underlying book values must be identified, analyzed, and dealt with. It also means that assets or liabilities *not* recognized by the investee must be identified and assigned, on a memo basis, the appropriate shares of the investor's purchase cost.

In the simplest example of applying this principle, if the investor identifies fixed assets with appreciated fair values, part of the price paid by the investor must be allocated (in a notional sense only—since the entire investment is presented as a single caption in the investor's financial statements, consistent with the "one-line consolidation" characteristic of equity method accounting) to the "step-up" in the values of those assets. Since those assets (other than land) are subject to depreciation, the investor must amortize a part of the investment cost to reduce the proportionate share of investee earnings that it would otherwise recognize in its entirety. This can require a costly and time-consuming effort on the part of the investor, particularly when a range of assets having varying depreciable lives is involved, as is almost always the case.

Under ASC 323, any premium paid by the investor that cannot be identified as being attributable to appreciated recognized tangible and intangible assets or unrecognized internally developed intangible assets of the investee (1 and 2 above) is analogous to goodwill.

Since the ultimate income statement effects of applying the equity method of accounting must generally be the same as full consolidation, an adjustment must be made to account for these differentials.

Subsequent accounting. In periods subsequent to the initial acquisition of the investment, the investor recognizes

- Increases to the carrying value of the investment for the investor's proportionate share of the investee's net income and
- Decreases in the carrying value of the investment for the investor's proportionate share of the investee's net losses, and by dividends received.

The basic procedure is illustrated below.

Example of the equity method—a simple case that ignores deferred income taxes

On January 2, 20X1, R Corporation (the investor) acquired 40% of E Company's (the investee) voting common stock from the former owner for $100,000. Unless demonstrated otherwise, it is assumed that R Corporation can exercise significant influence over E Company's operating and financing policies. On January 2, E's stockholders' equity consists of the following:

Common stock, $1.00 par value per share; 100,000 shares authorized, 50,000 shares issued and outstanding	$ 50,000
Additional paid-in capital	150,000
Retained earnings	50,000
Total stockholders' equity	$250,000

Note that, although improbable in practice, for this simple example, the cost of E Company common stock was exactly equal to 40% of the book value of E's net assets. Assume also that there is no difference between the book value and the fair value of E Company's assets and liabilities. Accordingly, the balance in the investment account in R's records represents exactly 40% of E's stockholders' equity (net assets). Assume further that E Company reported net income for 20X1 of $30,000 and paid cash dividends of $10,000. Its stockholders' equity at year-end would be as follows:

Common stock, $1.00 par value per share; 100,000 shares authorized, 50,000 shares issued and outstanding	$ 50,000
Additional paid-in capital	150,000
Retained earnings	70,000
Total stockholders' equity	$270,000

R Corporation would record its share of the increase in E Company's net assets during 20X1 as follows:

Investment in E Company	12,000	
Equity in E income		12,000
($30,000 × 40%)		
Cash	4,000	
Investment in E Company		4,000
($10,000 × 40%)		

When R's statement of financial position is prepared at December 31, 20X1, the balance reported as the carrying value of the equity method investment in E Company would be $108,000 (= $100,000 + $12,000 – $4,000). This amount continues to represent 40% of the book value of

E's net assets at the end of the year (40% × $270,000). Note also that the equity in E income is reported as a separate caption in R's income statement, typically as a component of income from continuing operations before income taxes.

Deferred income tax accounting. The equity method is not a recognized accounting method for federal income tax purposes under the US Internal Revenue Code (IRC). For income tax purposes, the investor's share of the investee's net income is not recognized until it is realized through either the investor's receipt of dividends from the investee or through the investor's sale of the investment. Thus, when the investor, under the equity method, recognizes its proportionate share of the net income of the investee as an increase to the carrying value of the investment, a future taxable temporary difference between the carrying value of the equity method investment for financial reporting purposes and the income tax basis of the investment will arise. The temporary difference will give rise to recognition of a deferred income tax liability.

In computing the deferred income tax effects of income recognized by applying the equity method, the investor must make an assumption regarding the means by which the undistributed earnings of the investee will be realized. The earnings can be realized either through later dividend receipts or by disposition of the investment at a gain. The former assumption would result in income taxes at the investor's marginal income tax rate on ordinary income (net of the 80% dividends received deduction permitted by the Internal Revenue Code for intercorporate investments of less than 80% but at least 20%; a lower deduction of 70% applies if ownership is below 20%). The latter option would be treated as a capital gain.

Example of the equity method—a simple case that includes deferred income taxes

Assume the same information as in the example above. In addition, assume that R Corporation has a combined (federal, state, and local) marginal income tax rate of 34% on ordinary income and that it anticipates realization of E Company earnings through future dividend receipts.

R Corporation's current income tax expense associated with its investment is computed based on its current dividends received less the dividends received deduction under IRC §243. Since R owns a 40% interest in E, the applicable percentage for the dividends received deduction is 80%. Note that the dividends received deduction constitutes a permanent difference under ASC 740 that never reverses. The provision for income taxes currently payable is computed as follows:

Dividends received	$4,000
Less—dividends received deduction (80%)	3,200
Taxable income from investment in E	800
× current combined federal and state tax rate	× 34%
Income taxes currently payable	$ 272

To compute deferred income taxes under the liability method used in ASC 740, at each reporting date we must determine the temporary difference between the carrying amount of the investment for financial reporting purposes and its income tax basis. In this case, this is done as follows:

Carrying value of equity method investment for financial reporting purposes	
Original cost	$100,000
Equity method earnings	12,000
Dividends	(4,000)
Income tax basis	
Original cost	100,000
Temporary difference	$ 8,000

Since R expects to realize this difference in the future through the receipt of dividends, it adjusts the difference for the permanent difference that arises from benefit of the dividends received deduction of 80% of $8,000 or $6,400 thus leaving $1,600 that would be subject to the effective rate that R expects to apply to reversal of the temporary difference, which, as provided in the assumptions above, is 34%. Applying the 34% expected future effective tax rate to the $1,600 taxable portion of the temporary difference would yield a deferred income tax expense (and related liability) of $544. The entry to record these items at December 31, 20X1, is as follows:

Income tax expense—Current	272	
Income tax expense—Deferred	544	
Income taxes currently payable		272
Deferred income tax liability		544

To record provision for income taxes for the year ended 12/31/20X1 attributable to equity method investment in E

The deferred income tax liability is originally computed with reference to the projected income tax effect of the "temporary difference reversal." It may be subsequently adjusted for a variety of reasons, including changed income tax rates and altered management expectations (see the chapter on ASC 740 for a complete discussion).

Notwithstanding ASC 740's requirement that deferred income taxes be adjusted for changed expectations at the date of each subsequent statement of financial position, the actual income tax effect of the temporary difference reversal may still differ from the deferred income tax liability provided. This difference may occur because the actual income tax effect is a function of the entity's other current items of income and expense in the year of reversal (while ASC 740 requires the use of a projected effective income tax rate, actual rates may differ). It may also result from a realization of the investee's earnings in a manner other than anticipated (assuming that income tax rates on "ordinary" income differ from those on capital gains).

Example of income tax effects resulting from the sale of an equity method investment

Assume that in 20X2, before any further earnings or dividends are reported by the investee, the investor sells the entire investment for $115,000. The income tax impact is:

Selling price	$115,000
Less income tax basis (original cost)	100,000
Gain	$ 15,000
Capital gain rate (marginal corporate rate)	× 34%
Income tax liability	$ 5,100

The entries to record the sale, the income tax thereon, and the reversal of the previously provided deferred income taxes on the undistributed 20X3 earnings of the investee are as follows:

1.	Cash	115,000	
	Investment in E Company		108,000
	Gain on sale of investment		7,000
2.	Income tax expense—Current	5,100	
	Deferred income tax liability	544	
	Income taxes payable—Current		5,100
	Income tax benefit—Deferred		544

Note that if the realization through a sale of the investment had been anticipated at the time the 20X1 statement of financial position was prepared, the deferred income tax liability would have been adjusted (possibly to reflect the entire $5,100 amount of the ultimate obligation), with the offset included in 20X1's ordinary income tax expense. The above example explicitly assumes that the sale of the investment was not anticipated prior to 20X2.

Differences in fiscal year. If the investor and investee have different fiscal years, ASC 323-10-35-6 permits the investor to use the most recent financial statements available as long as the lag in reporting is consistent from period to period. Analogizing from ASC 810, the lag period is not to exceed three months.

If the investee changes its fiscal year-end to reduce or eliminate the lag period, ASC 810-10-45 stipulates that the change be treated as a voluntary change in accounting principle under ASC 250 (discussed in detail in the chapter on ASC 250). Although ASC 250 requires such changes to be made by retrospective application to all periods presented, it provides an exception if it is not practical to do so.

Goodwill Impairment Testing. Under ASC 350-20-35-58 and 35-59 the goodwill component is subject not to amortization, unless the entity is eligible for and applies the alternative available under ASU 2014-02, but rather to impairment testing. (See the chapter on ASC 350 for more information on this new guidance.)

The impairment testing regime to be applied is not, however, that specified in ASC 350, which only pertains to testing by entities which actually record an asset explicitly as goodwill (i.e., the acquirer in a business combination accounted for under ASC 805). Equity method investors assess impairment of investments in investees by considering whether declines in the fair values of those investments, versus the carrying values of the underlying assets, may be other than temporary in nature as discussed previously in this chapter.

There is a requirement, applicable to the accounting for business combinations, and equity method investments, to identify intangible assets that require recognition separately from goodwill. Accordingly, in analyzing the purchase cost of an equity method investment, an investor needs to identify the portions of the premium paid that relate to identifiable intangibles per ASC 350, as well as to goodwill, with appropriate treatments regarding varying amortizable lives or, in some instances, amortization not being recognized due to the identifiable intangible assets having indefinite lives.

Although infrequently encountered in practice, the amount paid by the investor for its interest in the investee may imply that there had been a discount, analogous to a bargain purchase in the GAAP that relates to business combinations. In the rare instances where this occurs, this would be treated in the same manner as negative goodwill or gain from a bargain purchase. These are discussed in greater detail in the chapter on ASC 805.

In the following examples, the accounting for equity method investments involving both positive goodwill and negative goodwill are presented.

Example of a complex case that ignores deferred income taxes—equity method goodwill

Foxen Corporation (FC) acquired 40% of Besser, Inc.'s (BI) shares on January 2, 20X1, for $140,000. BI's assets and liabilities at that date had the following book values and fair values:

	Book values	*Fair values*
Cash	$ 10,000	$ 10,000
Accounts receivable (net)	40,000	40,000
Inventories (FIFO cost)	80,000	90,000
Land	50,000	40,000
Plant and equipment (net of accumulated depreciation)	140,000	220,000
Total assets	$320,000	$400,000
Liabilities	$ (70,000)	$ (70,000)
Net assets (stockholders' equity)	$250,000	$330,000

The first order of business is the calculation of the differential, as follows:

FC's cost for 40% of BI's common	$ 140,000
Book value of 40% of BI's net assets ($250,000 × 40%)	(100,000)
Total differential	$ 40,000

Next, the $40,000 differential is allocated to those individual assets and liabilities for which fair value differs from book value. In the example, the differential is allocated to inventories, land, and plant and equipment, as follows:

Item	*Book value*	*Fair value*	*Difference debit (credit)*	*40% of difference debit (credit)*
Inventories	$ 80,000	$ 90,000	$10,000	$ 4,000
Land	50,000	40,000	(10,000)	(4,000)
Plant and equipment	140,000	220,000	80,000	32,000
Differential allocated				$32,000

Assuming that there are no unrecognized identifiable intangibles included in the allocation, the difference between the allocated differential of $32,000 and the total differential of $40,000 is goodwill of $8,000. Goodwill, as shown by the following computation, represents the excess of the cost of the investment over the fair value of the net assets acquired.

FC's cost for 40% of BI's common	$ 140,000
40% of the fair value of BI's net assets ($330,000 × 40%)	$(132,000)
Excess of cost over fair value (goodwill)	$ 8,000

It is important to note that the allocation of this differential is not recorded formally by either FC or BI. Furthermore, FC, the investor, does not remove the differential from the investment account and recategorize it in its own respective asset categories, since the use of the equity method (one-line consolidation) does not involve the recording of individual assets and liabilities of the investee in the financial statements of the investor. FC leaves the differential of $40,000 in the investment account, as a part of the balance of $140,000 at January 2, 20X1. Accordingly, information pertaining to the allocation of the differential is maintained by the investor, but this information is outside the formal accounting system, presumably on a spreadsheet maintained for this purpose.

After the differential has been allocated, the amortization pattern is developed. To develop the pattern in this example, assume that BI's plant and equipment have ten years of useful life remaining and that BI depreciates its fixed assets on a straight-line basis. FC would prepare the following amortization schedule covering the years 20X1 through 20X3:

Item	*Differential debit (credit)*	*Remaining useful life*	*Amortization 20X1*	*20X2*	*20X3*
Inventories (FIFO)	$ 4,000	Sold in 20X1	$4,000	$ –	$ –
Land	(4,000)	Indefinite	–	–	–
Plant and equipment (net)	32,000	10 years	3,200	3,200	3,200
Goodwill	8,000	Not relevant			
Totals	$40,000		$7,200	$3,200	$3,200

Note that the entire differential allocated to inventories is amortized in 20X3 because the cost flow assumption used by BI is FIFO. If BI had been using LIFO instead of FIFO, no amortization would take place until BI sold some of the inventory included in the LIFO layer that existed at January 2, 20X1. Since this sale could be delayed for many years under LIFO, the differential allocated to LIFO inventories would not be amortized until BI sold more inventory than it manufactured/purchased. Note, also, that the differential (in this example, a negative valuation amount) allocated to BI's land is not amortized, because land is not a depreciable asset. The goodwill component of the differential is not amortized, but instead is evaluated along with the investment as a whole as to whether it is other-than-temporarily impaired.

The amortization of the differential is recorded formally in the accounting system of FC. Recording the amortization adjusts the equity in BI's income that FC records based upon BI's income statement. BI's income must be adjusted because it is based upon BI's book values, not upon the cost that FC incurred to acquire its interest in BI. FC makes the following entries in 20X1, assuming that BI reported net income of $30,000 and paid cash dividends of $10,000:

1.	Investment in BI	12,000	
	Equity in BI income		12,000
	$30,000 net income × 40% proportionate share		
2.	Equity in BI income (amortization of differential)	7,200	
	Investment in BI		7,200
3.	Cash	4,000	
	Investment in BI		4,000
	Record dividends received by investor $10,000 × 40%		

The balance in the investment account on FC's records at the end of 20X1, after giving effect to these entries is $140,800 [$140,000 + $12,000 – ($7,200 + $4,000)], and BI's stockholders' equity is $250,000 + net income of $30,000 – dividends of $10,000 = $270,000. The investment account balance as reflected by FC, the investee of $140,800 is not equal to $108,000 (40% of $270,000). However, this difference can easily be reconciled, as follows:

Balance in investment account at December 31, 20X1		$140,800
40% of BI's net assets at December 31, 20X1		108,000
Difference at December 31, 20X1		$ 32,800
Differential at January 2, 20X1	$40,000	
Differential amortized during 20X1	(7,200)	
Unamortized differential at December 31, 20X1		$ 32,800

With the passing years, the balance in the investment account approaches the amount representing 40% of the book value of BI's net assets, as the differential is amortized as a component of equity method income or loss. However, since a part of the differential was allocated to land, which is not depreciating, and to goodwill, which is not subject to amortization, the carrying value will most likely never exactly equal the equity in the investee's net assets. However, if the investee disposes of the land, the investor must also eliminate the associated portion of the differential. If the carrying value of the investment becomes impaired and the impairment is considered other than temporary, the goodwill portion of the differential may also be reduced or eliminated. Thus, under certain conditions the investor's carrying value may subsequently be adjusted to equal the underlying net asset value.

To illustrate how the sale of land would affect equity method procedures, assume that BI sold the land in the year 20X6 for $80,000. Since BI's cost for the land was $50,000, it would report a gain of $30,000, of which $12,000 (= $30,000 × 40%) would be recorded by FC, when it records its 40% share of BI's reported net income, ignoring income taxes. However, from FC's viewpoint, the gain on sale of land should have been $40,000 ($80,000 – $40,000) because the cost of the land from FC's perspective was $40,000 at January 2, 20X3 (since the allocated fair value of the land was below its book value). Therefore, in addition to the $12,000 share of the gain recorded above, FC should record an additional $4,000 gain [($40,000 – $30,000) × 40%] by debiting the investment account and crediting the equity in BI's income account. This $4,000 debit to the investment account will eliminate the $4,000 differential allocated to land on January 2, 20X2, since the original differential was a credit (the fair value of the land was $10,000 less than its book value).

Adjustments to the goodwill portion of the differential are somewhat more complex. ASC 323 requires that the difference between cost and underlying book value be accounted for as if the investee were a consolidated subsidiary. An investor is therefore required to determine the individual components that comprise the differential as illustrated above, and this may result in the identification of part of the differential as goodwill (referred to as "equity method goodwill"). Under GAAP, goodwill associated with a business combination is required to be evaluated annually for impairment. FASB decided, however, that equity method investments would continue to be tested for impairment in accordance with ASC 323 (i.e., the equity method investment as a whole, not the underlying net assets, are to be evaluated for impairment) and that equity method goodwill will not be treated as being separable from the related investment. Accordingly, goodwill is not to be tested for impairment in accordance with the current goodwill and intangible assets standard, ASC 350.

Example of adjustment of goodwill for other-than-temporary impairment of an equity method investment—that ignores income taxes

Building on the facts from the previous example, BI's reported net income in 20X2 and loss in 20X3 are $15,000 and ($12,000), respectively. No dividends are paid by BI after 20X1. FC's carrying value, before considering possible impairment in value, as of year-end 20X2 is computed as follows:

Carrying value of investment, December 31, 20X1	$140,800
FC's interest in BI's 20X2 net income ($15,000 × 40%)	6,000
Amortization of differential between fair value and carrying value	(3,200)
Carrying value, December 31, 20X2	143,600
FC's interest in BI's 20X3 net loss ($12,000 × 40%)	(4,800)
Amortization of differential between fair value and carrying value	(3,200)
Carrying value, December 31, 20X3, before considering additional charge for impairment	$135,600

If, at December 31, 20X3, FC determines that the fair value of its investment in BI has declined to $130,000, and this decline in value is judged to be other than temporary in nature, then FC must, per ASC 323, recognize a further loss amounting to $5,600 for the year. Notice that this fair value decline is assessed with reference to the fair (presumably, but not necessarily, market) value of the investment in BI. It would not be determined with specific reference to the value of BI's business operations, in the manner that the implied fair value of goodwill is assessed in connection with business combinations accounted for by the presentation of consolidated financial statements, although such a decline in value of the investment would likely be related to the value of BI's operations.

While the ASC is silent on this issue, it is reasonable that any recognized decline in value be assigned first to the implicit goodwill component of the investment account. In this example, since the decline, $5,600, is less than the $8,000 goodwill component of the differential, it will be fully absorbed, and future periods' amortization of the differential assigned to other assets will not be affected. On the other hand, if the value decline had exceeded $8,000, the excess would logically have been allocated to the underlying nonmonetary assets of the investee, such that the remaining differential previously identified with plant and equipment might have been reduced or eliminated, thereby altering future amortization on a prospective basis.

The impact of interperiod income tax allocation in the foregoing example is similar to that demonstrated earlier in the simplified example. Under GAAP goodwill rules, unless goodwill has been reduced for financial reporting purposes due to other-than-temporary impairment of the investment, there will be no book-tax difference and hence no deferred income tax issue to be addressed. The other components of the differential in the foregoing example are all temporary differences, with normal deferred income tax implications.

Example of a complex case that ignores deferred income taxes—computation of negative goodwill

The facts in this example are similar to those in the immediately preceding examples, but in this instance the price paid by the investor, Lucky Corp., is less than its proportionate share of the investee's net assets, at fair value. This is analogous to negative goodwill in a business combination, and the accounting for the negative differential between cost and fair value follows that mandated for bargain purchases either under the business combinations and goodwill standards, ASC 805 and ASC 350 or, if the stock is acquired after its effective date, under the bargain purchase provisions of ASC 805.

Assume that Lucky Corp. acquired 40% of Compliant Company's shares on January 2, 20X1, for a cash payment of $120,000. Compliant Company's assets and liabilities at that date had the following book and fair values:

	Book values	*Fair values*
Cash	$ 10,000	$ 10,000
Accounts receivable (net)	40,000	40,000
Inventories (FIFO cost)	80,000	90,000
Land	50,000	40,000
Plant and equipment (net of accumulated depreciation)	140,000	220,000
Total assets	$320,000	$400,000
Liabilities	$ (70,000)	$ (70,000)
Net assets (stockholders' equity)	$250,000	$330,000

The first step is to compute the differential, which is as follows:

Lucky's cost for 40% of Compliant's common stock	$120,000
Book value of 40% of Compliant's net assets ($250,000 × 40%)	(100,000)
Total differential	$ 20,000

Next, the $20,000 is allocated, on a preliminary basis, to those individual assets and liabilities for which fair value differs from book value. In the example, the differential is initially allocated to inventories, land, and plant and equipment, as follows:

Item	*Book value*	*Fair value*	*Difference debit (credit)*	*40% of difference debit (credit)*
Inventories	$ 80,000	$ 90,000	$ 10,000	$ 4,000
Land	50,000	40,000	(10,000)	(4,000)
Plant and equipment	140,000	220,000	80,000	32,000
Differential allocated				$32,000

The difference between the allocated differential of $32,000 and the actual differential of $20,000 is negative goodwill of $12,000. Negative goodwill, as shown by the following computation, represents the excess of the fair value of the net assets acquired over the cost of the investment.

Lucky's cost for 40% of Compliant's common stock	$ 120,000
40% of the fair value of Compliant's net assets ($330,000 × 40%)	(132,000)
Excess of fair value over cost (negative goodwill)	$ 12,000

Although the topic is not addressed explicitly by ASC 350, the investor's handling of negative goodwill should track how this would be dealt with by a parent company preparing consolidated financial statements following a "bargain purchase" business combination. It is important to note that the treatment of negative goodwill in this regard will depend on the date on which the investor obtained its interest.

Investor share of investee losses in excess of the carrying value of the investment. As demonstrated in the foregoing paragraphs, the carrying value of an investment which is accounted for by the equity method is increased by the investor's share of investee earnings and reduced by its share of investee losses and by dividends received from the investee. Sometimes the losses are so large that the carrying value is reduced to zero, and this raises the question of whether the investment account should be allowed to "go negative," or whether losses in excess of the investment account should be recognized in some other manner.

In general, an equity method investment would not be permitted to have a negative (i.e., credit) balance, since this would imply that it represented a liability. In the case of normal corporate investments, the investor would enjoy limited liability and would not be held liable to the investee's creditors should, for instance, the investee become insolvent. For this reason, excess losses of the investee would not be reflected in the financial statements of the investor. The practice is to discontinue application of the equity method when the investment account reaches a zero balance, with adequate disclosure being made of the fact that further investee losses are not being reflected in the investor's earnings. If the investee later returns to profitability, the investor ignores its share of earnings until the previously ignored losses have been fully offset; thereafter, normal application of the equity method is resumed.

There are, however, limited circumstances in which further investee losses would be reflected. Often the investor has guaranteed or otherwise committed to indemnify creditors or other investors in the investee entity for losses incurred, or to fund continuing operations of the investee. Having placed itself at risk in the case of the investee's insolvency, continued application of the equity method is deemed to be appropriate, since the net credit balance in the investment account (reportable as a liability entitled "losses in excess of investment made in investee") would indeed represent an obligation of the investor.

The other situation in which investee losses in excess of the investor's actual investment in common stock of the investee are to be reflected is somewhat more complicated. When the investor has investments consisting of both common stock holdings accounted for under ASC 323, and other investments in or loans to the investee, such as in its preference shares (including mandatorily redeemable preferred stock) or debt obligations of the investee, there will not only be further application of ASC 323, but also possible interaction between the provisions of ASC 323 and those of ASC 310 and/or ASC 320. In addition, there will be the question of the appropriate proportion of the investee's loss to be recognized by the investor—that is, should the investor's share of further investee losses be computed based only on its common stock ownership interest, or would some other measure of economic interest be more relevant?

ASC 323-10-35 addresses the accounting to be applied under the circumstances described in the preceding paragraph. A principal concern was that an anomaly could develop if, for example, the common shareholdings were being accounted for by application of the equity method (including a suspension of the method when the carrying value declined to zero due to investee losses) while investments in the same investee's debt or preferred shares were being carried at fair value per ASC 320 (assuming that the debt was not being carried at amortized cost due to classification as a held-to-maturity investment). A parallel concern invokes the accounting for loans under ASC 310-10-35 when investee debt is being held by the investor.

According to ASC 323-10-35, the adjusted basis of the other investments (preferred stock, debt, etc.) are to be adjusted for the equity method losses, after which the investor is to apply ASC 310-10-35 and ASC 320 to the other investments, as applicable. Those equity method losses are applied to the other investments in reverse order of seniority (that is, the respective priority in liquidation). This sequence is logical because it tracks the risk of investor loss: Common shareholders' interests are the first to be eliminated, followed by those of the preferred shareholders, and so on—with debt having the highest claim to investee assets in the event of liquidation. If the investee later becomes profitable, equity method income subsequently recorded (if, as described earlier, any unrecognized losses have first been exceeded) is applied to the adjusted basis of the other investments in reverse order of the application of the equity method losses (i.e., equity method income is applied to the more senior securities first).

In applying ASC 323, the cost basis of the other investments is taken to mean the original cost of those investments adjusted for the effects of

- Other than temporary write-downs,
- Unrealized holding gains and losses on ASC 320 securities classified as trading, and
- Amortization of any discount or premium on debt securities or loans.

The adjusted basis is defined as the cost basis, as adjusted for the ASC 310-10-35 valuation allowance account for an investee loan and for the cumulative equity method losses applied to the other investments.

The interaction of ASC 323 and ASC 310-10-35 and ASC 320 could mean, for example, that investee losses are recognized via a reduction in carrying value of preferred shares, which might then be immediately upwardly adjusted to recognize fair value as of the date of the statement of financial position in accordance with ASC 320. In a situation such as this, the equity method downward adjustment would be a loss recognized currently in net income, while the upward revaluation to fair value would typically be credited to other comprehensive income, and thus excluded from current period net income (unless defined as being held for trading purposes, which would be unusual).

ASC 323-10-35 addresses only the situation where the investor had the same percentage interests in common stock and all the other equity or debt securities of the investee. However, a further complication can arise when the investor's share in the common stock of the investee is not mirrored in its investment in the other debt or equity securities of the investee that it also holds. While this possibility is discussed in ASC 323, GAAP is not definitive regarding the mechanism by which the investor's share of further losses should be recognized in such situations. What is clear, however, is that merely applying the investor's percentage interest in the investee's common stock to the period's loss would not be appropriate in these cases.

In the absence of definitive guidance, two approaches are justifiable. The first is to eliminate the carrying value of first, the common stock and then, the other securities of the investee (including loans made to the investee), in reverse order of seniority, as set forth under ASC 323-10-35. The percentage of the investee's loss to be absorbed against each class of investment other than common stock would be governed by the proportion of that investment held by the investor—and emphatically not by its common stock ownership percentage. The logic is that, if the investor entity were to be harmed by the investee's further losses (once the common stock investment were reduced to zero carrying value), the harm would derive from being forced to take a reduced settlement in a liquidation of the investee, at which point the percentage ownership in separate classes of stock or in holdings of classes of debt would determine the amount of the investor's losses.

The second acceptable approach also takes into account the investor's varying percentage interests in the different equity and debt holdings. However, rather than being driven by the investee's reported loss for the period, the investor's loss recognition is determined by the period-to-period change in its claim on the net assets of the investee, as measured by book value. This approach implicitly assumes that fair values upon a hypothetical liquidation of the investee would equal book values—an assumption which is obviously unlikely to be borne out in any actual liquidation scenario. Nonetheless, given the enormous difficulty of applying this measurement technique to the continuously varying fair values of the investee's assets and liabilities, this was deemed to be a necessary compromise.

Thus, both methods of computing the excess investee losses to be recognized by an investor having more than just a common stock interest in the investee depend on the varying levels of those other investment vehicles. These two alternative, acceptable approaches are described and illustrated below.

Example of accounting for excess loss of investee when other investments are also held in same entity, when proportions of all investments are identical

Assume the following facts: Dardanelles Corporation owns 25% of the common stock of Bosporus Company. Dardanelles also owns 25% of Bosporus' preferred shares, and 25% of its commercial debt. Bosporus has $50,000 of debt and $100,000 of preferred stock outstanding.

As of 1/1/20X1 the carrying (i.e., book) value of Dardanelles' investment in Bosporus common stock was $12,000, after having applied the equity method of accounting in prior periods, per ASC 323. In 20X1, 20X2, and 20X3, Bosporus incurs net losses of $140,000, $50,000, and $30,000, respectively.

As of 1/1/20X1, the carrying (book) values of Dardanelles' investment in Bosporus' preferred stock and commercial debt were $25,000 and $12,500, respectively. Due to its continuing losses, the market or fair value of Dardanelles' outstanding preferred shares and its commercial debt decline over the years 20X1–20X3; Bosporus' portion of these values are as follows:

	Fair value of preferred shares, consistent with ASC 320	*Fair value of commercial debt, consistent with ASC 310-10-35*
1/1/20X1	N/A	N/A
12/31/20X1	$20,000	$12,000
12/31/20X2	9,500	8,000
12/31/20X3	2,000	7,000

The following table indicates the adjustments that would be made on the books of Dardanelles to record its share of Bosporus' losses in 20X1–20X3:

	Common stock	*Preferred stock*		*Commercial debt*	
	Book value	*Book value*	*Fair value*	*Book value*	*Fair value*
1/1/20X1	$ 12,000	$ 25,000	N/A	$ 12,500	N/A
20X1 loss (25% × 140,000 = 35,000)	(12,000)	(23,000)		–	
		2,000	$20,000	12,500	$12,000
Adjust pfd. stk. to FMV and debt to FV		18,000		(500)	
12/31/20X1 values	0	20,000		12,000	
20X1 loss (25% × 50,000 = 12,500)		(2,000)		(10,500)	
		18,000	9,500	1,500	8,000
Adjust pfd. stk. to FMV and debt to FV		(8,500)		–	
12/31/20X2 values	0	9,500		1,500	
20X2 loss (25% × 30,000 = 7,500)		–		(1,500)	
		9,500	2,000	0	7,000
Adjust pfd. stk. to FMV and debt to FV		(7,500)		–	
12/31/20X3 values	$ 0	$ 2,000		$ 0	

Actual journal entries and explanations for the foregoing are given as follows:

12/31/X1	Investee losses	35,000	
	Investment in Bosporus common stock		12,000
	Investment in Bosporus preferred stock		23,000

To record Dardanelles' share of Bosporus' loss for the year; the excess over the carrying value of the common stock is used to reduce the carrying value of the preferred shares

12/31/X1	Investment in Bosporus preferred stock	18,000	
	Unrealized gain on securities available for sale (other comprehensive income)		18,000

Since the fair value of the preferred shares is $20,000, per ASC 320 the carrying value must be upwardly revalued, and the adjustment is included in other comprehensive income for the year

12/31/X1	Loss from impairment of loan	500	
	Investment in Bosporus commercial debt		500

As required by ASC 310-10-35, the impairment of the loan to Bosporus must be recognized by a charge against current period net income

12/31/X2	Investee losses	12,500	
	Investment in Bosporus preferred stock		2,000
	Investment in Bosporus commercial debt		10,500

To record Dardanelles' share of Bosporus' loss for the year; the excess over the remaining carrying value of the preferred stock (without consideration of the ASC 320 adjustment) is used to reduce the carrying value of the commercial debt held

12/31/X2	Unrealized gain on securities available for sale (other comprehensive income)	8,500	
	Investment in Bosporus preferred stock		8,500

Since the fair market value of the preferred shares is not $9,500, the adjustment booked in the prior period must be partially reversed, this adjustment is included in other comprehensive income for the year

12/31/X3	Investee losses	1,500	
	Investment in Bosporus commercial debt		1,500

To record Dardanelles' share of Bosporus' loss for the year; the maximum to be recognized is the carrying value of the commercial debt since the carrying value of common and preferred stock investments have already been reduced to zero

	Unrealized gain on securities available for sale (other comprehensive income)	7,500	
	Investment in Bosporus preferred stock		7,500

Since the fair value of the preferred shares are now $2,000, the carrying value must be further reduced, with the adjustment included in other comprehensive income

It should be noted in the foregoing example that in year 20X3 there will be $6,000 of unrecognized investee losses, since as of the end of that year the carrying value of all the investor's investments in the investee will have been reduced to zero, except for the fair value of the preferred stock which is presented pursuant to ASC 320. Also note that the carrying value of the commercial debt is reduced for an impairment in 20X1 because the fair value is lower than the cost basis; in later years the fair value exceeds the cost basis, but under ASC 310-10-35 net upward adjustments would not be permitted.

Example of accounting for excess loss of investee when other investments are also held in same entity, when proportions of investments vary—first method: investee's reported loss used as basis for recognition

When the percentage interest in common stock of the investee is not mirrored by the level of ownership in its other securities, the process of recognizing the investor's share of investee losses becomes much more complex. Per ASC 323, there are two acceptable approaches, both of which are illustrated here. The first approach is to recognize the investor's share of investee losses by reducing the various investments held in the investee (common and preferred stock and commercial debt, in this example) by the relevant percentages applicable to each class of investment.

In the following, the same facts as in the preceding example are continued, except that the percentage of ownership in the equity and debt instruments is as follows:

	Percentage ownership by Dardanelles Corporation
Common stock	25%
Preferred stock	50%
Commercial debt	100%

Note that the fair values of the securities held (using the new assumed percentages of ownership of each class) are as follows:

	Fair value of preferred shares, consistent with ASC 320	*Fair value of commercial debt, consistent with ASC 310-10-35*
1/1/20X1	N/A	N/A
12/31/20X1	$40,000	$48,000
12/31/20X2	19,000	32,000
12/31/20X3	4,000	28,000

Given the foregoing, the period-by-period adjustments are summarized in the following table:

	Common stock	*Preferred stock*		*Commercial debt*	
	Book value	*Book value*	*Fair value*	*Book value*	*Fair value*
1/1/20X1	$ 12,000	$ 50,000	N/A	$50,000	N/A
20X1 loss = $140,000					
Eliminate @ 25% ratio	(12,000)				
Reduce preferred @ 50% ratio		(46,000)			
		4,000	$40,000		$48,000
Adjust pfd. stk. to FMV and debt to FV		36,000		(2,000)	
12/31/20X1 values	0	40,000		48,000	
20X2 loss = $50,000					
Eliminate preferred @50% ratio		(4,000)			
Reduce commercial debt @ 100% ratio				(42,000)	
		36,000	19,000	6,000	32,000
Adjust pfd. stk. to FMV and debt to FV		17,000		–	
12/31/20X2 values	0	19,000		6,000	
20X3 loss = $30,000					
Reduce commercial debt @ 100% ratio				(6,000)	
			4,000	0	7,000
Adjust pfd. stk. to FMV and debt to FV		(15,000)		–	
12/31/20X3 values	$ 0	$ 4,000		$ 0	

Journal entries and explanations for the adjustments that would be made consistent with the foregoing fact pattern are as follows:

12/31/X1	Investee losses	58,000	
	Investment in Bosporus common stock		12,000
	Investment in Bosporus preferred stock		46,000

To record Dardanelles' share of Bosporus' loss for the year; the excess over the carrying value of the common stock is used to reduce the carrying value of the preferred shares based on Dardanelles' 50% ownership interest in the preferred stock outstanding

Investment in Bosporus preferred stock	36,000	
Unrealized gain on securities available for sale (other comprehensive income)		36,000

Since the fair value of the preferred shares is $40,000, per ASC 320 the carrying value must be upwardly revalued and the adjustment is included in other comprehensive income for the year

Loss from impairment of loan	2,000	
Investment in Bosporus commercial debt		2,000

As required by ASC 310-10-35, the impairment of the loan to Bosporus must be recognized by a charge against current period net income

12/31/X2	Investee losses	46,000	
	Investment in Bosporus preferred stock		4,000
	Investment in Bosporus commercial debt		42,000
	To record Dardanelles' share of Bosporus' loss for the year; the excess over the remaining carrying value of the preferred stock (without consideration of the ASC 320 adjustment) is used to reduce the carrying value of the commercial debt held		
12/31/X2	Unrealized gain on securities available for sale (other comprehensive income)	17,000	
	Investment in Bosporus preferred stock		17,000
	Since the fair value of the preferred shares is not $19,000, the adjustment booked in the prior period must be partially reversed; this adjustment is included in other comprehensive income for the year		
12/31/X3	Investee losses	6,000	
	Investment in Bosporus commercial debt		6,000
	To record Dardanelles' share of Bosporus' loss for the year; the maximum to be recognized is the carrying value of the commercial debt since the carrying value of common and preferred stock investments have already been reduced to zero		
	Unrealized gain on securities available for sale (other comprehensive income)	15,000	
	Investment in Bosporus preferred stock		15,000
	Since the fair value of the preferred shares are now $4,000, the carrying value must be further reduced, with the adjustment included in other comprehensive income		

It should be noted in the foregoing example that the limitation on loss recognition each year is given by reference to the investor's percentage interests in the various classes of equity or debt held. The 20X1 loss is allocated between the common and preferred interests. A $12,000, 25% interest in the common stock equates to a total of $48,000 of common stock ($12,000 ÷ 25%). Therefore, if the full $140,000 loss were first allocated to reduce the book value of the common stock, $48,000 would have been applied to reduce that book value to zero. That would leave $92,000 of loss ($140,000 – $48,000) that remains to be allocated to the preferred interests. $92,000 × the 50% preferred interest of the investor is $48,000. Since the carrying value of the preferred stock investment is greater than this amount, the full loss is recognized by the investor proportional to its interest.

Similarly, the investee loss of $50,000 in 20X2 is first used to eliminate the remaining carrying value (before the ASC 320 adjustment) of the preferred stock investment, at a 50% ratio. The total of the preferred interests is computed by dividing the remaining carrying value of the preferred stock, $4,000, by the 50% interest that it represents. Therefore, the $8,000 of the $50,000 loss would be allocated to the preferred interests, thus leaving $42,000 to allocate to the commercial debt. Since Dardanelles owns all of this debt issue, the limitation on loss recognition would be the lesser of the remaining loss ($42,000) or the carrying value of the debt (before the ASC 310-10-35 adjustment) of $48,000.

Finally, note that in year 20X3 there will be $24,000 of unrecognized investee losses, since as of the end of that year the carrying value of all the investor's investments in the investee will have been reduced to zero (except for the fair value of the preferred stock which is presented pursuant to ASC 320).

Example of accounting for excess loss of investee when other investments are also held in same entity, when proportions of investments vary—second method: investee's reported change in net assets used as basis for recognition

The alternative, equally acceptable approach to investee loss recognition when various equity and debt interests are held in the investee, at varying percentage ownership levels, ignores the investee's reported loss for the period in favor of an indirect approach, making reference to the change in the investor's interest in the investee's reported net assets (net book value). In theory, the results will often be very similar if not identical, but investee capital transactions with other owners (e.g., issuing another series of preferred shares) could impact the loss recognition by the investor under some circumstances. Furthermore, since the investor's cost of its investments in the investee will normally vary from the investee's book value of those investments (e.g., if the investments were acquired in the secondary market), the losses computed by this method may differ from those computed by the first of the two alternative approaches.

To illustrate, again assume all the facts above, including the percentage interests in the immediately preceding example. Also, the condensed statements of financial position of Bosporus Corporation as of the relevant dates are given as follows:

	1/1/X1	*12/31/X1*	*12/31/X2*	*12/31/X3*
Total assets	$270,000	$135,000	$ 90,000	$ 50,000
Commercial debt	50,000	50,000	50,000	50,000
Other liabilities	20,000	25,000	30,000	20,000
Preferred stock	100,000	100,000	100,000	100,000
Common stock + retained earnings	100,000	(40,000)	(90,000)	$(120,000)
Total liabilities and equity	$270,000	$135,000	$ 90,000	$ 50,000

The investor's share of the investee's net assets at these respective dates and the changes to be recognized therein as the investor's share of investee losses for the years 20X1–20X3 are given below.

	1/1/X1	*12/31/X1*	*12/31/X2*	*12/31/X3*
		(At investee's book values)		
Investor's shares of:				
Commercial debt (100%)	$ 50,000	$ 50,000	$ 50,000	$ 30,000
Preferred stock (50%)	50,000	30,000	5,000	0
Common stock + retained earnings (25%)	25,000	0	0	0
Total share of investee's net assets	$125,000	$ 80,000	$ 55,000	$ 30,000
Change in share from prior year (investor's share of investee loss for year)		$(45,000)	$(25,000)	$(25,000)

In terms of how the actual investee losses should be recorded by the investor, the standard is not explicit, but there is no reason to depart from the approach illustrated above. Thus, the investment in Bosporus common stock would be eliminated first, then the investment in the preferred stock, and finally the investment in the debt securities. The provisions of ASC 310-10-35 and ASC 320 would have to be adhered to as well, again similar to the illustration above.

One part of the foregoing analysis that may need elaboration is the decision, in 20X3, to absorb all the excess investee losses against the investor's interest in the commercial debt. In many cases the commercial debt will be secured or for other reasons have preference over the other liabilities (which would tend to include accruals, trade payables, etc.). Therefore, in an actual liquidation situation the unsecured creditors would be eliminated before the commercial debtholders. However, the purpose of this computation—determining how much of the investee's losses should be reported by the investor—is not predicated on an actual liquidation but, rather, is based on a going concern assumption and conservatism. Since the investor in this example owns a major position in the common stock, half of the preferred stock, and all of the debt, presumably if the ongoing losses were indicative of imminent demise the investor would have already put the investee into liquidation or taken other dramatic steps. Since this has not occurred, the appropriate computational strategy, it is believed, is to allocate further losses against the investor's remaining interest, which is in the commercial debt. (If actual liquidation were being contemplated, it would be necessary to consider an even greater write-down of the carrying value of this investment.)

Note that the loss recognized each period differs from that under the previous approach, since the allocation is based on the book values of the various interests on the investee's statement of financial position, not the cost basis from the investor's perspective, as detailed below.

	Common stock Book value	Preferred stock Book value	Preferred stock Fair value	Commercial debt Book value	Commercial debt Fair value
1/1/20X1	$12,000	$50,000	N/A	$ 50,000	N/A
20X1 change in investor's share of investee's net book value = –45,000					
Eliminate carrying value of common	(12,000)				
Reduce carrying value of preferred		(33,000)			
		17,000	$40,000		$48,000
Adjust pfd. stk. to FMV and debt to FV		23,000		(2,000)	
12/31/20X1 values	0	40,000		48,000	
20X2 change in investor's share of investee's net book value = –25,000					
Reduce carrying value of commercial debt		(17,000)		(8,000)	
		23,000	19,000	40,000	32,000
Adjust pfd. stk. to FMV and debt to FV		(4,000)		(8,000)	
12/31/20X2 values	0	19,000		32,000	
20X3 change in investor's share of investee's net book value = –25,000					
Reduce carrying value of commercial debt				(25,000)	
			4,000	7,000	7,000
Adjust pfd. stk. to FMV and debt to FV		(15,000)		—	
12/31/20X3 values	$ 0	$ 4,000		$ 7,000	

Journal entries and explanations for the adjustments that would be made consistent with the foregoing fact pattern would be similar to those shown earlier in this section and therefore will not be repeated here.

Accounting for subsequent investments in an investee after suspension of equity method loss recognition. Recognition of investee losses by the investor is suspended when the investment account is reduced to zero, subject to the further reduction in the carrying value of any other investments (preferred stock, debt, etc.) in that investee, as circumstances warrant. In some cases, after the recognition of investee losses is suspended, the investor will make a further investment in the investee, and the question arises whether recognition of some or all of the previously unrecognized investee losses should immediately be given recognition, up to the amount of the additional investment.

ASC 323-10-S99 addresses the situation where the increased investment in the equity method investee triggered a need to consolidate (i.e., the 50% ownership threshold was exceeded), and cites the Securities and Exchange Commission (SEC)'s position against further loss recognition. ASC 323-10-35-29 deals with the situation where the increased investment did not cause control to be assumed, but rather where equity method accounting was specified both before and after the further investment is made (e.g., the investor owned 30% of the investee's common stock previously, and then increased the interest to 35%) has been dealt with.

ASC 323-10-35-29 holds that recognition of some or all of the previously unrecognized ("suspended") losses is conditioned on whether the new investment represents funding of prior investee losses. To the extent that it does, the previously unrecognized share of prior losses will be given recognition (i.e., reported in the investor's current period net income). Making this determination requires the use of judgment and is fact-specific, but some of the considerations would be as follows:

- Whether the additional investment is acquired from a third party or directly from the investee, since it is unlikely that funding of prior losses occurs unless funds are infused into the investee;
- The fair value of the consideration received in relation to the value of the consideration paid for the additional investment, with an indicated excess of consideration paid over that received being suggestive of a funding of prior losses;
- Whether the additional investment results in an increase in ownership percentage of the investee, with investments being made without a corresponding increase in ownership or other interests (or, alternatively, a pro rata equity investment made by all existing investors) being indicative of the funding of prior losses; and
- The seniority of the additional investment relative to existing equity of the investee, with investment in subordinate instruments being suggestive of the funding of prior losses.

When additional investments are made in an investee that has experienced losses, the corollary issue of whether the investor has committed to further investments may arise. If such is the case, then yet-unrecognized (suspended) investee losses may also need to be recognized in investor net income currently—in effect, as a loss contingency that is deemed probable of occurrence.

Example of subsequent investments in investee with losses in excess of original investment

R Corp. invested $500,000 in an investee, E Company, representing a 40% ownership interest. Investee losses caused R Corp. to completely eliminate the carrying value of this investment, and the recognition of R Corp.'s share of a further $200,000 of E Company losses ($200,000 × 40% = $80,000) was suspended. Later, R Corp. invested another $100,000 in E Company. Application of the criteria above led to the conclusion that one-half of its investment was in excess of the value of the consideration received, and thus the entry to record the further investment would be:

Investment in E Company stock	50,000	
Loss on equity method investment in E Company	50,000	
Cash		100,000

If it is determined, however, that R Corp. has "otherwise committed" to further investment in E Company, the investor might have to recognize losses up to the full amount of the suspended losses. The entry might therefore be:

Investment in E Company stock	20,000	
Loss on equity method investment in E Company	80,000	
Cash		100,000

Intercompany transactions between investor and investee. Transactions between the investor and the investee may require that the investor make certain adjustments when it records its share of the investee earnings. According to the realization concept, profits can be recognized by an entity only when realized through a sale to outside (unrelated) parties in arm's-length transactions (sales and purchases) between the investor and investee. Similar problems, however, can arise when sales of fixed assets between the parties occur. In all cases, there is no need for any adjustment when the transfers are made at book value (i.e., without either party recognizing a profit or loss in its separate accounting records).

In preparing consolidated financial statements, all intercompany (parent-subsidiary) transactions are eliminated. However, when the equity method is used to account for investments, only the profit component of intercompany (investor-investee) transactions is eliminated. This is because the equity method does not result in the combining of all income statement accounts (such as sales and cost of sales), and therefore will not cause the financial statements to contain redundancies. In contrast, consolidated statements would include redundancies if the gross amounts of all intercompany transactions were not eliminated.

Another distinction between the consolidation and equity method situations pertains to the percentage of intercompany profit to be eliminated. In the case of consolidated statements, the entire intercompany profit is eliminated, regardless of the percentage ownership of the subsidiary. However, only the investor's pro rata share of intercompany profit is to be eliminated in equity accounting, whether the transaction giving rise to the profit is "downstream" (a sale to the investee) or "upstream" (a sale to the investor). An exception is made when the transaction is not "arm's-length" or if the investee company was created by or for the benefit of the investor. In these cases, 100% profit elimination would be required, unless realized through a sale to a third party before year-end.

Example of accounting for intercompany transactions

Continue with the basic facts set forth in an earlier example and also assume that E Company sold inventory to R Corporation in 20X1 for $2,000 above E's cost. Of this inventory, 30% remains unsold by R at the end of 20X1. E's net income for 20X1, including the gross profit on the inventory sold to R, is $15,000; E's income tax rate is 34%. R should make the following journal entries for 20X1 (ignoring deferred income taxes):

1.	Investment in E Company	6,000	
	Equity in E income		6,000
	$15,000 × 40%		
2.	Equity in E income (amortization of differential)	3,200	
	Investment in E Company		3,200
3.	Equity in E income	158	
	Investment in E Company		158
	$2,000 × 30% × 66% × 40%		

The amount in the last entry needs further elaboration. Since 30% of the inventory remains unsold, only $600 of the intercompany profit remains unrealized at year-end. This profit, net of income taxes, is $396. R's share of this profit ($158) is included in the first ($6,000) entry recorded. Accordingly, the third entry is needed to adjust or correct the equity in the reported net income of the investee.

Eliminating entries for intercompany profits in fixed assets are similar to those in the examples above. However, intercompany profit is realized only as the assets are depreciated by the purchasing entity. In other words, if an investor buys or sells fixed assets from or to an investee at a price above book value, the gain would only be realized piecemeal over the asset's remaining depreciable life. Accordingly, in the year of sale the pro rata share (based on the investor's percentage ownership interest in the investee, regardless of whether the sale is upstream or downstream) of the unrealized portion of the intercompany profit would have to be eliminated. In each subsequent year during the asset's life, the pro rata share of the gain realized in the period would be added to income from the investee.

Example of eliminating intercompany profit on fixed assets

Assume that Investor Co., which owns 25% of Investee Co., sold to Investee a fixed asset, having a five-year remaining life, at a gain of $100,000. Investor Co. is in the 34% marginal income tax bracket. The sale occurred at the end of 20X1; Investee Co. will use straight-line depreciation to amortize the asset over the years 20X3 through 20X5.

The entries related to the foregoing are

20X1

1.	Gain on sale of fixed asset	25,000	
	Deferred gain		25,000
	To defer the unrealized portion of the gain		
2.	Deferred income tax benefit	8,500	
	Income tax expense		8,500
	Income tax effect of gain deferral		

Alternatively, the 20X1 events could have been reported by this single entry.

Equity in investee income	16,500	
Investment in Investee Co.		16,500

20X2 through 20X6 (each year)

1.	Deferred gain	5,000	
	Gain on sale of fixed assets		5,000
	To amortize deferred gain		
2.	Income tax expense	1,700	
	Deferred income tax benefit		1,700
	Income tax effect of gain realization		

The alternative treatment would be

Investment in Investee Co.	3,300	
Equity in investee income		3,300

In the above example, the income tax currently paid by Investor Co. (34% × $25,000 taxable gain on the transaction) is recorded as a deferred income tax benefit in 20X1 since current income taxes will not be due on the book gain recognized in the years 20X2 through 20X6. Under provisions of ASC 740, deferred income tax assets are recorded to reflect the income tax effects of all future deductible temporary differences. Unless Investor Co. could demonstrate that future taxable amounts arising from existing future taxable temporary differences exist (or, alternatively, that a net operating loss [NOL] carryback could have been elected), this deferred income tax asset will be offset by an equivalent valuation allowance in Investor Co.'s statement of financial position at year-end 20X1. Thus, the deferred income tax asset might not be recognizable, net of the valuation allowance, for financial reporting purposes unless other future taxable temporary differences not specified in the example generate future taxable income to offset the net deductible effect of the deferred gain.

NOTE: The deferred income tax impact of an item of income for book purposes in excess of tax is the same as a deduction for income tax purposes in excess of book.

Investee income items separately reportable by the investor. In the examples thus far, the investor has reported its share of investee income, and the adjustments to this income, as a single item described as equity in investee income. However, when the investee has extraordinary items and/or prior period adjustments that are material, the investor is to report its share of these items separately on its statements of income and retained earnings.

Example of accounting for separately reportable items

Assume that both an extraordinary item and a prior period adjustment reported in an investee's income and retained earnings statements are individually considered material from the investor's viewpoint.

Statement of income

Income before extraordinary item	$ 80,000
Extraordinary loss from earthquake (net of income taxes of $12,000)	(18,000)
Net income	$ 62,000

Statement of changes in retained earnings

Retained earnings at January 1, 20X1, as originally reported	250,000
Add restatement for prior period adjustment—correction of an error made in 20X0 (net of income taxes of $10,000)	20,000
Retained earnings at January 1, 20X1, restated	$270,000

If an investor owned 30% of the voting common stock of this investee, the investor would make the following journal entries in 20X1:

1.	Investment in investee company	24,000	
	Equity in investee income before extraordinary item		24,000
	$80,000 × 30%		
2.	Equity in investee extraordinary loss	5,400	
	Investment in investee company		5,400
	$18,000 × 30%		
3.	Investment in investee company	6,000	
	Equity in investee prior period adjustment		6,000
	$20,000 × 30%		

The equity in the investee's prior period adjustment should be reported on the investor's statement of changes in retained earnings which is often presented in a more all-encompassing format with the statement of changes in stockholders' equity, and the equity in the extraordinary loss is reported separately in the appropriate section on the investor's statement of income.

Obtaining significant influence subsequent to initial investment. An investor that holds an investment accounted for using the cost method may subsequently qualify to use the equity method of accounting. This can occur, for example, if the investor acquires additional voting shares or if the investor's voting percentage increases as a result of repurchase of voting stock by the investee.

Accounting for a partial sale or additional purchase of an equity method investment. This section covers the accounting issues that arise when the investor sells some or all of its equity in the investee, or acquires additional equity in the investee.

Example of accounting for a discontinuance of the equity method

Assume that an investor owns 10,000 shares (30%) of XYZ Company common stock, for which it paid $250,000 ten years ago. On July 1, 20X1, the investor sells 5,000 XYZ shares for $375,000. The balance in the investment in XYZ Company account at January 1, 20X1, was $600,000. Assume that the original differential between cost and book value has been fully amortized. To calculate the gain (loss) upon this sale of 5,000 shares, it is first necessary to adjust the investment account so that it is current as of the date of sale. Assuming that the investee had net income of $100,000 for the six months ended June 30, 20X1, the investor would record the following entries:

1.	Investment in XYZ Company	30,000	
	Equity in XYZ income		30,000
	$100,000 × 30%		
2.	Income tax expense	2,040	
	Deferred income tax liability		2,040
	$30,000 × 20% × 34%		

The gain upon sale can now be computed, as follows:

Proceeds upon sale of 5,000 shares	$375,000
Book value of the 5,000 shares ($630,000 × 50%)	315,000
Gain from sale of XYZ common	$ 60,000

Two entries will be needed to reflect the sale: one to record the proceeds, the reduction in the investment account, and the gain (or loss); and the other to record the related income tax effects. Remember that the investor must have computed the deferred tax effects of the undistributed earnings of the investee that it had recorded each year, on the basis that those earnings either would eventually be paid as dividends or would be realized as capital gains. When those dividends are ultimately received or when the investment is disposed of, the previously recorded deferred income tax liability must be reversed.

To illustrate, assume that the investor in this example provided deferred income taxes at an effective rate for dividends (considering the 80% exclusion) of 6.8%. The realized capital gain will be taxed at an assumed 34%. For income tax purposes, this gain is computed as $375,000 – $125,000 = $250,000, yielding an income tax effect of $85,000. For accounting purposes, the deferred income taxes already provided are 6.8% × ($315,000 – $125,000), or $12,920. Accordingly, an additional income tax expense of $72,080 is incurred upon the sale, due to the fact that an additional gain was realized for book purposes ($375,000 – $315,000 = $60,000; income tax at 34% = $20,400) and that the deferred income tax previously provided for at dividend income rates was lower than the real capital gains rate [$190,000 × (34% – 6.8%) = $51,680 extra income tax due]. The entries are as follows:

1.	Cash	375,000	
	Investment in XYZ Company		315,000
	Gain on sale of XYZ Company stock		60,000
2.	Deferred income tax liability	12,920	
	Income tax expense	72,080	
	Income taxes payable—current		85,000

The gains (losses) from sales of investee stock are reported on the investor's income statement in the "Other income and expense" section, assuming that a multistep income statement is presented.

In this example, the sale of investee stock reduced the percentage owned by the investor to 15%. In such a situation, the investor would discontinue use of the equity method. The balance in the investment account on the date the equity method is suspended ($315,000 in the example) will be accounted for on the basis of fair value, under ASC 320, presumably being reported in the available-for-sale investment portfolio. This accounting principle change does not require the computation of a cumulative effect or any retroactive disclosures in the investor's financial statements. In periods subsequent to this principles change, the investor records cash dividends received from the investment as dividend income and subjects the investment to the appropriate GAAP used to assess "other-than-temporary" impairment. Any dividends received in excess of the investor's share of postdisposal net income of the investee are credited to the investment, rather than to income.

The process of discontinuing the use of the equity method and adopting ASC 320, as necessitated by a reduction in ownership below the significant influence threshold level, does not require retroactive application. However, the opposite situation having the 20% ownership level equaled or exceeded again (or for the first time) is more complex. ASC 323 stipulates that this change in accounting principle (i.e., to the equity method) requires that the investment account, results of operations (all periods being presented, current and prior), and retained earnings of the investor company be retroactively adjusted.

Investor accounting for investee capital transactions. According to ASC 323, investee transactions of a capital nature that affect the investor's share of the investee's stockholders' equity are accounted for as if the investee were a consolidated subsidiary. These transactions principally include situations where the investee purchases treasury stock from, or sells unissued shares or reissues treasury shares it holds to, outside shareholders. (If the investor participates in these transactions on a pro rata basis, its percentage ownership will not change and no special accounting will be necessary.) Similar results are obtained when holders of outstanding options or convertible securities acquire investee common shares.

When the investee engages in one of the above capital transactions, the investor's ownership percentage is changed. This gives rise to a gain or loss, depending on whether the price paid (for treasury shares acquired) or received (for shares issued) is greater or lesser than the per share carrying value of the investor's interest in the investee. However, since no gain or loss can be recognized on capital transactions, these purchases or sales will affect additional paid-in capital and/or retained earnings directly, without being reflected in the investor's income statement. This method is consistent with the treatment that would be accorded to a consolidated subsidiary's capital transaction. An exception is that, under certain circumstances, the SEC will permit income recognition based on the concept that the investor is essentially selling part of its investment.

Example of accounting for an investee capital transaction

Assume R Corp. purchases, on 1/2/X1, 25% (2,000 shares) of E Corp.'s outstanding shares for $80,000. The cost is equal to both the book and fair values of R's interest in E's underlying net assets (i.e., there is no differential to be accounted for). One week later, E Corp. buys 1,000 shares of its stock from other shareholders for $50,000. Since the price paid ($50/share) exceeded R Corp.'s per share carrying value of its interest, $40, R Corp. has in fact suffered an economic loss by the transaction. Also, its percentage ownership of E Corp. has increased as the number of shares held by third parties has been reduced.

R Corp.'s new interest in E's net assets is

$$\frac{\text{2,000 shares held by R}}{\text{7,000 shares outstanding}} \times \text{E Corp. net assets}$$

$$.2857 \times (\$320{,}000 - \$50{,}000) = \$77{,}143$$

The interest held by R Corp. has thus been diminished by $80,000 – $77,143 = $2,857. Therefore, R Corp. should make the following entry:

Additional paid-in capital (or retained earnings)	2,857	
Investment in E Corp.		2,857

R Corp. charges the loss against additional paid-in capital if such amounts have accumulated from past transactions of a similar nature; otherwise the debit is to retained earnings. Had the transaction given rise to a gain it would have been credited to additional paid-in capital only (never to retained earnings) following the rule that transactions in one's own shares cannot produce net income.

Note that the amount of the charge to additional paid-in capital (or retained earnings) in the entry above can be verified as follows: R Corp.'s share of the posttransaction net equity (2/7) times the "excess" price paid ($50 – $40 = $10) times the number of shares purchased = 2/7 × $10 × 1,000 = $2,857.

Investor's proportionate share of other comprehensive income items. ASC 323-10-35-37 holds that an investor's proportionate share of an investee's equity adjustments for other comprehensive income items (e.g., fair value adjustments to available-for-sale investments) is to be offset against the carrying value of the investment in the investee entity at the time significant influence is lost. To the extent that the offset results in a carrying value of the investment that is less then zero, an investor will (1) reduce the carrying value of the investment to zero; and (2) record the remaining balance in income.

Exchanges of equity method investments. According to ASC 845, an exchange of an equity method investment for another such investment is to be accounted for at book value, without gain or loss recognition (other than what may be necessary to record impairment, of course).

Change in level of ownership or degree of influence. An equity method investor is to account for an issuance of shares by the investee as if the investor had sold a proportionate share of its investment. Any gain or loss to the investor that results from the investee's share issuance is to be recognized in net income.

Significant influence in the absence of ownership of voting common stock. ASC 323 was written to apply to investments in voting common stock of an investee, and authoritative guidance has been lacking regarding the accounting for investments in other investment vehicles, such as options and warrants, and complex licensing and/or management agreements, where significant influence might also be present. These nontraditional modes of investment, providing the investor with significant influence, have become more common over the years, and thus the need for guidance became acute. ASC 323-10-15-13 addresses the accounting for these alternative investments.

ASC 323-10-15-13 states that a reporting entity that has the ability to exercise significant influence over the operating and financial policies of an investee is to apply the equity method only when it has an investment(s) in common stock and/or an investment that is in-substance common stock. In-substance common stock is an investment in an entity that has risk and reward characteristics that are substantially similar to the investee's common stock. Whether or not significant influence is wielded is a fact question, and suggested criteria are not provided in the ASC.

Management is to consider certain characteristics when determining whether an investment in an entity is substantially similar to an investment in that entity's common stock. These are conjunctive constraints: thus, if the entity determines that any one of the following characteristics indicates that an investment in an entity is not substantially similar to an investment in that entity's common stock, the investment is not in-substance common stock.

1. *Subordination.* It must be determined whether the investment has subordination characteristics substantially similar to the investee's common stock. If there are substantive liquidation preferences, the instrument would not be deemed substantially similar to common stock. On the other hand, certain liquidation preferences are not substantive (e.g., when the stated liquidation preference that is not significant in relation to the purchase price of the investment), and would be discounted in this analysis.
2. *Risks and rewards of ownership.* A reporting entity must determine whether the investment has risks and rewards of ownership that are substantially similar to an investment in the investee's common stock. If an investment is not expected to participate in the earnings (and losses) and capital appreciation (and depreciation) in

a manner that is substantially similar to common stock, this condition would not be met. Participating and convertible preferred stocks would likely meet this criterion, however.

3. *Obligation to transfer value.* An investment is not substantially similar to common stock if the investee is expected to transfer substantive value to the investor and the common shareholders do not participate in a similar manner. For example, if the investment has a substantive redemption provision (for example, a mandatory redemption provision or a non-fair-value put option) that is not available to common shareholders, the investment is not substantially similar to common stock.

In some instances it may be difficult to assess whether the foregoing characteristics are present or absent. ASC 323-10-15-13 suggests that, in such circumstances, management of the reporting entity (the investor) is also to analyze whether the future changes in the fair value of the investment are expected to be highly correlated with the changes in the fair value of the investee's common stock. If the changes in the fair value of the investment are not expected to be highly correlated with the changes in the fair value of the common stock, then the investment is not in-substance common stock.

According to ASC 323-10-15-13, the determination of whether an investment vehicle is in-substance common stock must be made upon acquisition, if the entity has the ability to exercise significant influence. The assessment is to be revisited if one or more of these occur:

1. The contractual terms of the investment are changed resulting in a change to any of its characteristics described above.
2. There is a significant change in the capital structure of the investee, including the investee's receipt of additional subordinated financing.
3. The reporting entity obtains an additional interest in an investment in which the investor has an existing interest. As a result, the method of accounting for the cumulative interest is based on the characteristics of the investment at the date at which the entity obtains the additional interest (that is, the characteristics that the entity evaluated in order to make its investment decision), and will result in the reporting entity applying one method of accounting to the cumulative interest in an investment of the same issuance.

The mere fact that the investee is suffering losses is not a basis for reconsideration of whether the investment is in-substance common stock.

Upon implementation of ASC 323-10-15-13, for investments in which the entity has the ability to exercise significant influence over the operating and financial policies of the investee, the reporting entity is to make an initial determination about whether existing investments are in-substance common stock. The initial determination is to be based on circumstances that existed on the date of adoption, rather than on the date that the investment was made.

Equity Investments in Corporate Joint Ventures and Noncorporate Entities (ASC 323-30)

A wide variety of noncorporate entities and structures are used to:

- Operate businesses,
- Hold investments in real estate or in other entities, or
- Undertake discrete projects as joint ventures.

These include:

- Partnerships, for example, limited partnerships, general partnerships, limited liability partnerships, and
- Limited liability companies (LLC).

Practice questions persistently arise regarding whether directly or by analogy, authoritative GAAP literature that applies to corporate structures is also applicable to investors in noncorporate entities.

By analogy, investors with controlling interests in unincorporated, such as partnerships and other unincorporated joint ventures, generally should account for their investments using the equity method.

General partnerships. There is a rebuttable presumption that a general partner that has a majority voting interest is in control of the partnership. If voting rights are indeterminate under the provisions of the partnership agreement or applicable law, the general partner with a majority of the financial interests in the partnership's profits or losses would be presumed to have control. If this presumption is not overcome, the general partner with voting control or the majority financial interest would consolidate the partnership in its financial statements and the other noncontrolling general partners would use the equity method (ASC 323, ASC 970-323).

Limited Liability Companies. A limited liability company may maintain a specific ownership account for each investor—similar to a partnership capital account structure. In that case, the investment in the limited liability company is viewed as similar to an investment in a limited partnership for purposes of determining whether a noncontrolling investment in a limited liability company is accounted for using the cost method or the equity method.

Qualified Affordable Housing Project Investments (ASC 323-740)

(The Perspectives and Issues Section at the beginning of this chapter gives a brief summary of this Federal tax provision.) See the Technical Alert section as the beginning of this chapter for an important update on this guidance.

These investments are accounted for using:

- Effective yield method or
- The guidance in ASC 970-323, *Real Estate General—Investments-Equity Method and Joint Ventures*.

Effective Yield Method. The effective yield is the internal rate of return on the investment, based on the cost of the investment and the guaranteed tax credits allocated to the investor, excluding any expected residual value of the investment (ASC 323-740-35-2). Investors may use the effective yield method if the following conditions are met:

- The investor is a limited partner, for both legal and tax purposes, with liability limited to its capital investment.
- A creditworthy entity guarantees the availability of the tax credits allocable to the investor.
- Based solely on the cash flows from the guaranteed tax credits, the investor's projected yield is positive.

The decision to use the effective yield method is an accounting policy decision.

Recognition. The investor should recognize a liability for:

- Delayed equity contributions that are unconditional and legally binding.
- Equity contributions that are contingent upon a future event.

An investor should not recognize credits before their inclusion in the investor's tax return.

Subsequent Measurement. Investors recognize tax credits as they are allocated and amortize the initial cost of the investment to provide a constant effective yield over the period that tax credits are allocated to the investor. Investors include in earnings any cash received from operations of the limited partnership or sale of the property.

The tax credit allocated, net of the amortization of the investment in the limited partnership, is recognized in the income statement as a component of income taxes attributable to continuing operations (ASC 323-740-45-2).

Other Sources

Investments – Debt and Equity Securitites – Overall	
See ASC Location – Wiley *GAAP* Chapter…	***For information on…***
ASC 260-10-55-20	The computation of consolidated earnings per share (EPS) if equity method investees or corporate joint ventures have issued options, warrants, and convertible securities
ASC 958-810-15-4	The use of the equity method if a not-for-profit entity (NFP) has common stock investments that are 50% or less of the voting stock of for-profit entities
ASC 958-810-15-4	NFPs that choose to report investment portfolios at fair value instead of applying the equity method
ASC 974-323-25-1	The use of the equity method by a real estate investment trust with an investment in a service corporation
Equity Investments in Corporate Joint Ventures and Noncorporate Entities	
ASC 310-10-25	Accounting for an acquisition, development, and construction arrangement, see the Acquisition, Development, and Construction Arrangements Subsection
ASC 320-10-55-8 through 55-9	An investment in a limited partnership interest (or a venture capital entity) that meets the definition of an equity security but does not have a readily determinable fair value
ASC 970-323	An investment in real estate or real estate development projects in a form that otherwise would be within the scope of this Subtopic
ASC 808	Collaborative arrangements

21 ASC 325 INVESTMENTS—OTHER

PERSPECTIVE AND ISSUES

Topics

The Codification contains several Topics on the various forms of investments:

- ASC 320, *Investments – Debt and Equity Securities*
- ASC 323, *Investments – Equity Method and Joint Venures*
- ASC 325, *Investments – Other.*

Subtopics

ASC 325 contains four subtopics:

- ASC 325-10, *Overall,* which merely identifies the other three topics
- ASC 325-20, *Cost Method Investments,* which offers guidance on stocks of entities not accounted for under the fair value method (ASC 320) or the equity method (ASC 323)
- ASC 325-30, *Investments in Insurance Contracts,* which provides guidance on investments, life insurance contracts in general, and life settlement contracts
- ASC 325-40, *Beneficial Interests in Securitized Financial Assets,* which provides guidance on accounting for a transferor's interest in securitized transaction accounted for as sales and purchased beneficial interests.

Scope

ASC 325-40 "applies to a transferor's interests in securitization transactions that are accounted for as sales under Topic 860 and purchased beneficial interests in securitized financial assets." (ASC 325-40-15-2)

According to ASC 325-15-40-3, the guidance applies to beneficial interests that have *all* of the following characteristics:

1. "Are either debt securities under Subtopic 320-10 or required to be accounted for like debt securities under that Subtopic pursuant to paragraph 860-20-35-2."
2. Involve securitized financial assets that have contractual cash flows. The guidance does not apply to securitized financial assets that do not involve contractual cash flows.
3. Do not result in consolidation of the entity issuing the beneficial interest by the holder of the beneficial interests.
4. Are not within the scope of ASC 310-30.
5. Are not beneficial interests in securitized financial assets that have both of the following characteristics:
    a. Are of high credit quality (for example, guaranteed by the U.S. government, its agencies, or other creditworthy guarantors, and loans or securities sufficiently collateralized to ensure that the possibility of credit loss is remote)
    b. Cannot contractually be prepaid or otherwise settled in such a way that the holder would not recover substantially all of its recorded investment.

(ASC 325-40-15-3)

Note that a beneficial interest in securitized financial assets that is in equity form may meet the definition of a debt security. These beneficial interests would be in the scope of this topic and ASC 320 because ASC 320 requires them to be accounted for as debt securities:

- If the beneficial interests issued in the form of equity,
    - Represent solely a right to receive a stream of future cash flows to be collected under preset terms and conditions, or
    - According to the terms of the special-purpose entity, must be redeemed by the issuing entity or must be redeemable at the option of the investor.
    (ASC 325-40-15-5)

ASC 325-40 does not apply to hybrid beneficial interests measured at fair value pursuant to paragraphs 815-15-25-4 through 25-6 for which the transferor does not report interest income as a separate item in its income statements. (ASC 325-40-15-9)

Overview

ASC 325-30 provides guidance on investments in insurance contracts. A life settlement contract is an agreement executed between a third-party investor and the owner of a life insurance policy where (1) the investor does not have an insurable interest in the life of the insured, (2) the investor pays an amount in excess of this policy's cash surrender value to the policy owner, and (3) upon the death of the insured, the face value of the policy is paid to the investor. These investments may be facilitated by a broker or transacted directly between the investor and the policy owner.

ASC 325-40 provides guidance on another type of investment. When a reporting entity sells a portion of an asset that it owns, the portion retained becomes an asset separate from the portion sold and separate from the assets obtained in exchange. This is the situation when financial assets such as loans are securitized with certain interests being retained (e.g., a defined portion of the contractual cash flows). Management of the reporting entity must allocate the previous carrying amount of the assets sold based on the relative fair values of each component at the date of sale. In most cases, the initial carrying amount (i.e., the allocated cost) of the retained interest will be different from the fair value of the instrument. Furthermore, cash flows from those instruments may be delayed depending on the contractual provisions of the entire structure (for example, cash may be retained in a trust to fund a cash collateral account). The issue is addressed by ASC 325-40.

DEFINITIONS OF TERMS

Source: ASC 325-20-20

Publicly Traded Company. A publicly traded company includes any company whose securities trade in a public market on either of the following:

a. A stock exchange (domestic or foreign)
b. In the over-the-counter market (including securities quoted only locally or regionally), or any company that is a conduit bond obligor for conduit debt securities that are traded in a public market (a domestic or foreign stock exchange or an over-the-counter market, including local or regional markets).

Additionally, when a company is required to file or furnish financial statements with the SEC or makes a filing with a regulatory agency in preparation for sale of its securities in a public market it is considered a publicly traded company for this purpose.

Conduit debt securities refers to certain limited-obligation revenue bonds, certificates of participation, or similar debt instruments issued by a state or local governmental entity for the express purpose of providing financing for a specific third party (the conduit bond obligor) that is not a part of the state or local government's financial reporting entity. Although conduit debt securities bear the name of the governmental entity that issues them, the governmental entity often has no obligation for such debt beyond the resources provided by a lease or loan agreement with the third party on whose behalf the securities are issued. Further, the conduit bond obligor is responsible for any future financial reporting requirements.

Source: ASC 325-30-20

Cash surrender value. The amount of cash that may be realized by the owner of a life insurance contract or annuity contract upon discontinuance and surrender of the contract before its maturity. The cash surrender value may be different from the policy account balance due to outstanding loans (including accrued interest) and surrender charges. (Note: The use of this glossary term is not consistent among legal contracts. When determining the applicability of this term, the economic substance of the item shall be taken into consideration.)

Certificates. An insurance entity issues to each individual in a group contract a certificate of insurance for each person insured under the group contract. The certificate is merely a summary of the rights, duties, and benefits available under a group policy. If there is any conflict between the certificate and a group policy, the group policy is the controlling document. (Note: The use of this glossary term is not consistent among legal contracts. When determining the applicability of this term, the economic substance of the item shall be taken into consideration.)

Claims stabilization reserve. The claims stabilization reserve is established through deductions from the policy account balance through the cost of insurance charge and is sometimes held in a general account (that is, an account that is intermingled with the insurance entity's assets) as opposed to a legally segregated account (sometimes referred to as a separate account). The amounts are accumulated in this account until a death benefit is paid. The death benefit represents a combination of the policy account balance and the claims stabilization reserve based on the contractual terms. The cost of insurance is recalculated periodically based on actual experience of the insured class. Annually, the claims stabilization reserve is reviewed and an experience credit may be issued back to the policyholder if the experience has been favorable. The balance in the claims stabilization reserve will be reviewed annually and to the extent the balance is greater than the forecasted or expected amount, an experience refund would get credited to the entity's policy account balance. An entity's claims stabilization reserve will generally be realized through the collection of death benefits or an experience refund that gets credited to the policyholder's policy account balance or upon surrender of the group policy. A claims stabilization reserve is included in a policy as a mechanism for the policyholder and the insurance entity to share in the mortality risk, which in this case is the risk that the deaths will occur sooner than originally expected. Absent a claims stabilization reserve, the policyholder's net cost of insurance would typically be higher than in a policy without a claims stabilization reserve. The claims stabilization reserve is sometimes referred to as a mortality reserve or a mortality retention reserve. (Note: The use of this glossary term is not consistent among legal contracts. When determining the applicability of this term, the economic substance of the item shall be taken into consideration.)

Deferred acquisition costs tax. Section 848 of the Internal Revenue Code requires insurance entities to capitalize certain policy acquisition costs and defer deducting them in determining the insurer's tax liability. These costs are known as the deferred acquisition costs tax and are based on a percentage of the premium received as specified by the Internal Revenue Code. The initial deferred acquisition costs tax is deducted from a policyholder's policy account balance when the premium is paid. The deferred acquisition costs tax is credited back to the policyholder's policy account balance as the tax deduction is recognized in the insurer's tax return. (Note: The use of this glossary term is not consistent among legal contracts. When determining the applicability of this term, the economic substance of the item shall be taken into consideration.)

Insurance policy. The legal agreement between the policyholder and the insurance entity that states the terms of the arrangement. The term insurance policy includes all riders, attachments, side agreements, and other related documents that are either directly or indirectly part of the contractual arrangement. (Note: The use of this glossary term is not consistent among legal contracts. When determining the applicability of this term, the economic substance of the item shall be taken into consideration.)

Life settlement contract. A life settlement contract is a contract between the owner of a life insurance policy (the policy owner) and a third-party investor (investor), and has all of the following characteristics:

1. The investor does not have an insurable interest (an interest in the survival of the insured, which is required to support the issuance of an insurance policy).
2. The investor provides consideration to the policy owner of an amount in excess of the current cash surrender value of this life insurance policy.
3. The contract pays the face value of the life insurance policy to an investor when the insured dies.

Policy account balance. At any point in time, this is the amount held by the insurance entity on behalf of the policyholder. This balance may be held in a general account, a separate account (a legally segregated account), or a combination of both on the insurance entity's balance sheet. This account includes premiums received from the policyholder, plus any credited income, less any relevant charges (acquisition costs, cost of insurance, and so forth). (Note: The use of this glossary term is not consistent among legal contracts. When determining the applicability of this term, the economic substance of the item shall be taken into consideration.)

Probable. The future event or events are likely to occur.

Surrender charge. A contractual fee imposed by the insurance entity when a policyholder surrenders the insurance policy that typically decreases over the life of the policy. The surrender charge represents a recovery of costs incurred by the insurance entity in originating the policy. It may or may not be explicitly called a surrender charge and can be embedded in other agreements besides the insurance contract. (Note: The use of this glossary term is not consistent among legal contracts. When determining the applicability of this term, the economic substance of the item shall be taken into consideration.)

Source: ASC 323-40-20 Glossary

Beneficial interests. Rights to receive all or portions of specified cash inflows received by a trust or other entity, including, but not limited to, all of the following:

1. Senior and subordinated shares of interest, principal, or other cash inflows to be passed-through
2. Premiums due to guarantors
3. Commercial paper obligations
4. Residual interests, whether in the form of debt or equity.

Debt security. Any security representing a creditor relationship with an entity. The term debt security also includes all of the following:

1. Preferred stock that by its terms either must be redeemed by the issuing entity or is redeemable at the option of the investor
2. A collateralized mortgage obligation (or other instrument) that is issued in equity form but is required to be accounted for as a nonequity instrument regardless of how that instrument is classified (that is, whether equity or debt) in the issuer's statement of financial position
3. U.S. Treasury securities
4. U.S. government agency securities
5. Municipal securities
6. Corporate bonds
7. Convertible debt
8. Commercial paper
9. All securitized debt instruments, such as collateralized mortgage obligations and real estate mortgage investment conduits
10. Interest-only and principal-only strips.

The term debt security excludes all of the following:

1. Option contracts
2. Financial futures contracts
3. Forward contracts
4. Lease contracts

5. Receivables that do not meet the definition of security and, so, are not debt securities (unless they have been securitized, in which case they would meet the definition of a security), for example:
   a. Trade accounts receivable arising from sales on credit by industrial or commercial entities
   b. Loans receivable arising from consumer, commercial, and real estate lending activities of financial institutions.

CONCEPTS, RULES, AND EXAMPLES

Cost Method Investments

An entity may hold stock in entities other than subsidiaries. The entity should account for these investments by one of three methods—

- The cost method (addressed in this subtopic),
- The fair value method (Topic 320), or
- The equity method (Topic 323).

The cost method is generally followed for most investments

- In noncontrolled corporations,
- In some corporate joint ventures, and
- To a lesser extent in unconsolidated subsidiaries, particularly foreign.

For investments using the cost method, the investor recognizes, initially at cost, investments in stock of investees as assets on the statement of financial position.

Dividends. Dividends are the vehicle for an investor to recognize earnings from an investment under the cost method. From the date of the investment entities recognize dividends received from an investee in one of two ways:

- If the dividends are distributed from net accumulated earnings, the investor recognizes them as income.
- If the dividends are in excess of earnings, they are considered a return on investment and the investor records them as reductions in the cost of the investment.

Impairment. The value of the investment in stock accounted for under the cost method may lose its value because of a series of operating losses or other factors. If the impairment is considered other than temporary, investors should look to ASC 320-10-35-17 through 35-35. Those paragraphs discuss the methodology for determining impairment and evaluating whether the impairment is other than temporary and, therefore, must be recognized.

Changes in Accounting Method. The level of ownership in stock of an investee may change. An investor may lose the ability to influence policy or gain the ability to influence policy. These circumstances call for a change to or from the equity method of accounting. In those cases, preparers should look to ASC 323-10-35 for guidance.

Other Accounting Issues. ASC 325-20 provides guidance on Accounting for a Cost Method Investment in Affordable Housing Projects with Allocated Tax Credits. Disclosures required by ASC 325 may be found in the disclosure checklist included with this volume.

Other Sources. For guidance on the use of the cost method by real estate investment trusts with related service corporations, see Topic 974. (ASC 325-20-60)

ASC 325-30, *Investments in Insurance Contracts*

Investments in Life Settlement Contracts. For a life settlement contract, ASC 325-30 requires the investor to elect to account for these investments using either the "investment method" or the "fair value method." This irrevocable election is made in one of two ways:

1. On an instrument-by-instrument basis supported by documentation prepared concurrently with acquisition of the investment, or
2. Based on a preestablished, documented policy that automatically applies to all such investments.

The investment method. The investor recognizes the initial investment at the transaction price plus all initial direct external costs. Continuing costs (payments of policy premiums and direct external costs, if any) necessary to keep the policy in force are capitalized. Gain recognition is deferred until the death of the insured. At that time the investor recognizes in net income (or other applicable performance indicator) the difference between the carrying amount of the investment and the policy proceeds.

The investor is required to test the investment for impairment upon the availability of new or updated information that indicates that, upon the death of the insured, the expected proceeds from the insurance policy may not be sufficient for the investor to recover the carrying amount of the investment plus anticipated gross future premiums (undiscounted for the time value of money) and capitalizable external direct costs, if any. Indicators to be considered include, but are not limited to:

1. A change in the life expectancy of the insured
2. A change in the credit standing of the insurer.

As a result of performing an impairment test, if the undiscounted expected cash inflows (the expected proceeds from the policy) are less than the carrying amount of the investment plus the undiscounted anticipated gross future premiums and capitalizable external direct costs, an impairment loss is recognized. The loss is recorded by reducing the carrying value of the investment to its fair value. The fair value computation is to employ current interest rates. Note that a change in interest rates would not by itself require an impairment test.

The fair value method. The initial investment is recorded at the transaction price. Each subsequent reporting period, the investor remeasures the investment at fair value and recognizes changes in fair value in current period net income (or other relevant performance indicators for reporting entities that do not report net income). Cash outflows for policy premiums and inflows for policy proceeds are to be included in the same financial statement line item as the changes in fair value are reported.

Presentation in the statement of financial position. On the face of its statement of financial position, the investor is required to differentiate between investments remeasured at fair value and those accounted for using the investment method. This may be accomplished by either:

1. Presenting separate line items for each type of investment, or
2. Parenthetical disclosure.

Examples of presentation alternatives in the statement of financial position

1. Separate line items

Investments in life settlement contracts measured at	
Fair value	$xxx,xxx
Initial investment and accumulated costs	$xxx,xxx

2. Parenthetical disclosure

Investments in life settlement contracts	$xxx,xxx
(Portion stated at fair value $xxx,xxx)	

Income statement presentation. Investment income attributable to fair value remeasurements is presented on the face of the income statement separately from investment income attributable to contracts accounted for using the investment method. This may be accomplished by either:

1. Presenting separate line items for investment income attributable to each type of investment, or
2. Parenthetical disclosure.

Examples of income statement presentation alternatives

1. Separate line items

Investment income from life settlement contracts measured at	
Fair value	$xxx,xxx
Initial investment and accumulated costs	$xxx,xxx

2. Parenthetical disclosure

Investment income from life settlement contracts	$xxx,xxx
(Portion from contracts carried at fair value $xxx,xxx)	

Cash flow statement presentation. Cash inflows and outflows attributable to investments in life settlement contracts are to be classified based on the nature and purpose for which the contracts were acquired.

Disclosure of accounting policy. In addition to other applicable GAAP disclosures, the investor is to disclose the policy it follows to account for life settlement contracts, including the classification in the cash flow statement of cash inflows and outflows associated with these contracts.

Disclosures when using the investment method. For life settlement contracts accounted for under the investment method, the investor is required to disclose the following information based on the remaining life expectancy of the insured individuals:

1. By year, for each of the first five fiscal years ending after the date of the statement of financial position, in total for the years succeeding those first five years, and in the aggregate:
   a. The number of life settlement contracts in which it has invested
   b. The carrying value of those contracts
   c. The face value (death benefits) of the life insurance policies covered by those contracts.
2. By year, for each of the first five fiscal years ending after the date of the most recent statement of financial position presented, the life insurance premiums expected to be paid in order to keep the life insurance policies related to the life settlement contracts in force.
3. If management becomes aware of new or updated information that causes it to change its estimates of the expected timing of its receipt of the proceeds from the investments, it is to disclose the nature of the information and its related effect on the

timing of the expected receipt of the policy proceeds. This disclosure is to include significant effects of the change in estimate on the disclosure described in item 1.[1]

Disclosures when using the fair value method. For life settlement contracts accounted for under the fair value method, the investor is required to disclose the following information based on the remaining life expectancy of the insured individuals:

1. The method(s) and significant assumptions used to estimate the fair value of the contracts, including any mortality assumptions.
2. By year, for each of the first five fiscal years ending after the date of the statement of financial position, in total for the years succeeding those first five years, and in the aggregate
   a. The number of life settlement contracts in which it has invested
   b. The carrying value of those contracts
   c. The face value (death benefits) of the life insurance policies covered by those contracts.
3. The reasons for changes in its estimates of the expected timing of its receipt of the proceeds from the investments including significant effects of the change in estimates on the information disclosed in item 2.

ASC 325-40, *Beneficial Interests in Securitized Financial Assets*

This subtopic provides that the holder of the beneficial interest is to recognize the excess of all cash flows anticipated at the acquisition transaction date over the initial investment (ASC 325-40-30-2) as interest income using the effective yield method (ASC 325-40-35-1). The holder is required to update the estimate of cash flows over the life of the beneficial interest. If the estimated cash flows change (but there was still an excess over the carrying amount), the adjustment is accounted for prospectively as a change in estimate with the amount of the periodic accretion adjusted over the remaining life of the beneficial interest. If the fair value of the beneficial interest declines below its carrying amount, the reporting entity should determine if the decline is other than temporary and apply the impairment guidance in ASC 320-10-35-18. If it is not practicable for a holder/transferor to estimate the fair value of the beneficial interest at the securitization date, interest income is recognized using the cash basis rather than the effective yield method.

Impairment and interest income on purchased and retained beneficial interests in securitized financial assets. If, based on current information and events that the reporting entity anticipates a market participant would use in determining the current fair value of the beneficial interest, there is a change in estimated cash flows, the amount of accretable yield is recalculated. If the change in estimated cash flows is adverse, an other-than-temporary impairment would be considered to have occurred.

OTTI evaluations. The objective of the analysis as to whether an impairment is other-than-temporary is to determine whether it is probable that the holder will realize some portion of the unrealized loss on an impaired security. Under US GAAP, a holder may ultimately realize an unrealized loss on the impaired security because, for example

1. It is probable that the holder will not collect all of the contractual or estimated cash flows, considering both their amount and timing, or

---

[1] *This disclosure requirement does not impose an obligation on management to actively seek out new or updated information in order to update the assumptions used in determining the remaining life expectancy of the life settlement contracts.*

2. The holder of the security lacks the intent and ability to hold it until recovery of the loss.

It is inappropriate for management to automatically conclude that, because all of the scheduled payments to date have been received, a security has not incurred an OTTI. Conversely, it is also inappropriate for management to automatically conclude that every decline in fair value of a security represents OTTI. The longer and/or the more severe the decline in fair value, the more persuasive the evidence that would be needed to overcome the premise that it is probable that the holder will not collect all of the contractual or estimated cash flows from the security. (ASC 325-40-35-10A)

Further analysis and the exercise of judgment are required to assess whether a decline in fair value indicates that it is probable that the holder will not collect all of the contractual or estimated cash flows from the security.

In performing the assessment of OTTI and developing estimates of future cash flows, the holder should look to the guidance in ASC 320-10-35-33G through 35-33I and consider all information available that is relevant to collectibility, including information about past events, current conditions, and forecasts that are reasonable and supportable. ASC 320-10-35 provides that this information should generally include:

1. The remaining payment terms of the security,
2. Prepayment speeds,
3. The issuer's financial condition,
4. Expected defaults,
5. The value of the underlying collateral,
6. Industry analyst reports and forecasts, sector credit ratings, and other relevant market data,
7. The effect, if applicable, of any credit enhancements on the expected performance of the security, including consideration of the current financial condition of a guarantor of the security.

(ASC 320-10-35-33G through 35-33I)

NOTE: This applies only if the guarantee is not a separate contract. Per ASC 320-10-35-23, the holder is not to combine separate contracts (such as a debt security and a guarantee or other credit enhancement) for the purpose of the determination of impairment or the determination of whether the debt security can be contractually prepaid or otherwise settled in a manner that would preclude the holder from recovering substantially all of its cost.

Some or all of the securitized loans that comprise many beneficial interests may be structured with payment streams that are not level over the life of the loan. Thus, the remaining payments expected to be received from the security could differ significantly from those received in prior periods. These so-called "nontraditional" loans may have features such as:

1. Terms permitting principal payment deferral (interest-only)
2. Interest accruals exceeding the required payments (negative amortization or reverse mortgages)
3. A high loan-to-value ratio
4. Collateral applying to multiple loans that, when considered together, result in a high loan-to-value ratio
5. Option adjustable rate mortgages (Option ARMs) or similar products that may expose the borrower to future increases in required payments

6. An initial interest rate ("teaser rate") below the market rate of interest for the initial period of the term of the loan that will increase significantly at the end of that initial period
7. Interest-only loans
8. Loans requiring a "balloon" payment at maturity.

In achieving this objective, the holder considers information such as:

1. Reports and forecasts from industry analysts
2. Sector credit ratings
3. Other market data relevant to the collectibility of the security.

The existence of these or other features necessitates consideration by the holder of whether a security backed by loans that are currently performing will continue to perform when the contractual provisions of those loans require increasing payments on the part of the borrowers. In addition, the holder is to consider how the value of any collateral would affect the expected performance of the security. Naturally, if the fair value of the collateral has declined, the holder must assess the effect of the decline on the ability of the borrower to make the balloon payment since the decline in value may preclude the borrower from obtaining sufficient funds from a potential refinancing of the debt.

Timing of recognition of an OTTI. If management of the entity *both* holds an available-for-sale beneficial interest whose fair value is less than its amortized cost basis *and* does not expect the fair value to recover prior to an expected sale shortly after the date of the statement of financial position, a write-down for other-than-temporary impairment is recognized as a charge to net income in the period in which the decision to sell the beneficial interest is made. (ASC 325-40-35-13)

22 ASC 330 INVENTORY

PERSPECTIVE AND ISSUES

Subtopic

ASC 330, *Inventory,* consists of one subtopic:

- ASC 330-10, *Overall,* that provides guidance on the accounting and reporting practices on inventory.

ASC 330, *Inventory*, discusses the definition, valuation, and classification of inventory, as well as the measurement and classification of inventories during interim periods.

Scope

ASC 330 applies to all entities but is not necessarily applicable to:

- Not-for-profit entities
- Regulated utilities.
  (ASC 330-10-15-2 and 15-3)

Practice Alert

While SEC comments do not pertain to nonpublic entities, their comments can often provide valuable guidance. In the area of inventory, the SEC has commented on the selection and disclosure of valuation methods, how spoilage is estimated, cost capitalized in inventory, and disclosure of adjustments. Preparers should pay close attention to the accounting and disclosures in those areas.

Overview

The accounting for inventories is a major consideration for many entities because of its significance to both the income statement (cost of goods sold) and the statement of financial position (current assets).

The complexity of accounting for inventories arises from factors that include:

1. The high volume of activity (or turnover) and the associated challenges of keeping accurate, up-to-date records.
2. Choosing from among various cost flow alternatives that are permitted by GAAP.
3. Ensuring compliance with complex US income tax laws and regulations when electing to use the last-in, first-out (LIFO) method.
4. Monitoring and properly accounting for adjustments necessitated by applying the lower of cost or market method to the inventory.

There are two types of entities for which the accounting for inventories is relevant. The merchandising entity purchases inventory for resale to its customers. The manufacturer buys raw materials, and processes those raw materials using labor and equipment into finished goods that are then sold to its customers. While the production process is progressing, the costs of the raw materials, salaries and wages paid to the labor force (and related benefits), depreciation of the machinery, and an allocated portion of the manufacturer's overhead are accumulated by the accounting system as work in process (WIP). Finished goods inventory is the completed product which is on hand awaiting shipment or sale.

In the case of either type of entity, we are concerned with answering the same basic questions.

1. At what point in time should the items be included in inventory (ownership)?
2. What costs incurred should be included in the valuation of inventories?
3. What cost flow assumption should be used?
4. At what value should inventories be reported (determination of the lower of cost or market, or LCM)?

DEFINITIONS OF TERMS

Source: ASC 330-10-20

Direct Effects of a Change in Accounting Principle. Those recognized changes in assets or liabilities necessary to effect a change in accounting principle. An example of a direct effect is an adjustment to an inventory balance to effect a change in inventory valuation method. Related changes, such as an effect on deferred income tax assets or liabilities or an impairment adjustment resulting from applying the lower-of-cost-or-market test to the adjusted inventory balance, also are examples of direct effects of a change in accounting principle.

Inventory. The aggregate of those items of tangible personal property that have any of the following characteristics:

a. Held for sale in the ordinary course of business
b. In process of production for such sale
c. To be currently consumed in the production of goods or services to be available for sale.

The term inventory embraces goods awaiting sale (the merchandise of a trading concern and the finished goods of a manufacturer), goods in the course of production (work in process), and goods to be consumed directly or indirectly in production (raw materials and supplies). This definition of inventories excludes long-term assets subject to depreciation accounting, or goods which, when put into use, will be so classified. The fact that a depreciable asset is retired from regular use and held for sale does not indicate that the item should be classified as part of the inventory. Raw materials and supplies purchased for production may be used or consumed for the construction of long-term assets or other purposes not related to production, but the fact that inventory items representing a small portion of the total may not be absorbed ultimately in the production process does not require separate classification. By trade practice, operating materials and supplies of certain types of entities such as oil producers are usually treated as inventory.

Market. As used in the phrase lower of cost or market, the term market means current replacement cost (by purchase or by reproduction, as the case may be) provided that it meets both of the following conditions:

a. Market shall not exceed the net realizable value
b. Market shall not be less than net realizable value reduced by an allowance for an approximately normal profit margin.

Net Realizable Value. Estimated selling price in the ordinary course of business less reasonably predictable costs of completion, disposal, and transportation.

CONCEPTS, RULES, AND EXAMPLES

Ownership of Goods

Generally, in order to obtain an accurate measurement of inventory quantity, it is necessary to determine when title legally passes between buyer and seller. The exception to this general rule arises from situations when the buyer assumes the significant risks of ownership of the goods prior to taking title and/or physical possession of the goods. Substance over form in this case would dictate that the inventory is an asset of the buyer and not the seller, and that a purchase and sale of the goods be recognized by the parties irrespective of the party that holds legal title.

The most common error made in this area is to assume that an entity has title only to the goods it physically holds. This may be incorrect in two ways:

1. Goods held may not be owned, and
2. Goods that are not held may be owned.

Four issues affect the determination of ownership:

1. Goods in transit,
2. Consignment arrangements,
3. Product financing arrangements, and
4. Sales made with the buyer having the right of return.

Goods in transit. At year-end, any goods in transit from seller to buyer must be included in one of those parties' inventories based on the conditions of the sale. Such goods are included in the inventory of the firm financially responsible for transportation costs. This responsibility may be indicated by a variety of peculiar shipping acronyms such as FOB, which is used in overland shipping contracts, or FAS, CIF, C&F, and ex-ship, which are used in maritime contracts.

The term FOB is an abbreviation of "free on board." If goods are shipped FOB destination, transportation costs are paid by the seller and title does not pass until the carrier delivers the goods to the buyer. These goods are part of the seller's inventory while in transit. If goods are shipped FOB shipping point, transportation costs are paid by the buyer and title passes when the carrier takes possession of the goods. These goods are part of the buyer's inventory while in transit. The terms FOB destination and FOB shipping point often indicate a specific location at which title to the goods is transferred, such as FOB Cleveland. This means that the seller retains title and risk of loss until the goods are delivered to a common carrier in Cleveland who will act as an agent for the buyer. The rationale for these determinations originates in agency law, since transfer of title is conditioned upon whether the carrier with physical possession of the goods is acting as an agent of the seller or the buyer.

A seller who ships FAS (free alongside) must bear all expense and risk involved in delivering the goods to the dock next to (alongside) the vessel on which they are to be shipped. The buyer bears the costs of loading and shipment. Title passes when the carrier, as agent for the buyer, takes possession of the goods.

In a CIF (cost, insurance, and freight) contract, the buyer agrees to pay in a lump sum the cost of the goods, insurance costs, and freight charges. In a C&F (cost and freight) contract, the buyer promises to pay a lump sum that includes the cost of the goods and all freight charges. In either case, the seller must deliver the goods to the buyer's agent/carrier and pay the costs of loading. Both title and risk of loss pass to the buyer upon delivery of the goods to the carrier.

A seller who delivers goods ex-ship bears all expense and risk until the goods are unloaded, at which time both title and risk of loss pass to the buyer.

Examples of goods in transit

The Meridian Vacuum Company is located in Santa Fe, New Mexico, and obtains compressors from a supplier in Hong Kong. The standard delivery terms are free alongside (FAS) a container ship in Hong Kong harbor, so that Meridian takes legal title to the delivery once possession of the goods is taken by the carrier's dockside employees for the purpose of loading the goods on board the ship. When the supplier delivers goods with an invoiced value of $120,000 to the wharf, it e-mails an advance shipping notice (ASN) and invoice to Meridian via an electronic data interchange (EDI) transaction, itemizing the contents of the delivery. Meridian's computer system receives the EDI transmission, notes the FAS terms in the supplier file, and therefore automatically logs it into the company computer system with the following entry:

Inventory	120,000	
Accounts payable		120,000

The goods are assigned an "In Transit" location code in Meridian's perpetual inventory system. When the compressor eventually arrives at Meridian's receiving dock, the receiving staff records a change in inventory location code from "In Transit" to a code designating a physical location within the warehouse.

Meridian's secondary compressor supplier is located in Vancouver, British Columbia, and ships overland using free on board (FOB) Santa Fe terms, so the supplier retains title until the shipment arrives at Meridian's location. This supplier also issues an advance shipping notice by EDI to inform Meridian of the estimated arrival date, but in this case Meridian's computer system notes the FOB Santa Fe terms, and makes no entry to record the transaction until the goods arrive at Meridian's receiving dock.

Consignment arrangements. In consignment arrangements, the consignor ships goods to the consignee, who acts as the agent of the consignor in trying to sell the goods. In some consignments, the consignee receives a commission upon sale of the goods to its customer. In other arrangements, the consignee "purchases" the goods simultaneously with the sale of the goods to the customer. Goods on consignment are included in the inventory of the consignor and excluded from the inventory of the consignee.

Example of a consignment arrangement

The Portable Handset Company (PHC) ships a consignment of its cordless phones to a retail outlet of the Consignee Corporation. PHC's cost of the consigned goods is $3,700. PHC shifts the inventory cost into a separate inventory account to track the physical location of the goods. The entry follows:

Consignment out inventory	3,700	
Finished goods inventory		3,700

A third-party shipping company ships the cordless phone inventory from PHC to Consignee. Upon receipt of an invoice for this $550 shipping expense, PHC charges the cost to consignment inventory with the following entry:

Consignment out inventory	550	
Accounts payable		550

To record the cost of shipping goods from the factory to Consignee

Consignee sells half the consigned inventory during the month for $2,750 in credit card payments, and earns a 22% commission on these sales, totaling $605. According to the consignment arrangement, PHC must also reimburse Consignee for the 2% credit card processing fee, which is $55 ($2,750 × 2%). The results of this sale are summarized as follows:

Sales price to Consignee's customer earned on behalf of PHC	$2,750
Less: Amounts due to Consignee in accordance with arrangement	
22% sales commission	(605)
Reimbursement for credit card processing fee	(55)
	(660)
Due to PHC	$2,090

Upon receipt of the monthly sales report from Consignee, PHC records the following entries:

Accounts receivable	2,090	
Cost of goods sold	55	
Commission expense	605	
Sales		2,750

To record the sale made by Consignee acting as agent of PHC, the commission earned by Consignee and the credit card fee reimbursement earned by Consignee in connection with the sale

Costs of goods sold	2,125	
Consignment out inventory		2,125

To transfer the related inventory cost to cost of goods sold, including half the original inventory cost and half the cost of the shipment to consignee [($3,700 + $550 = $4,250) × ½ = $2,125]

Product financing arrangements. ASC 470-40 addresses the issues involved with product financing arrangements. A product financing arrangement is a transaction in which an entity (referred to as the "sponsor") simultaneously sells and agrees to repurchase inventory to and from a financing entity. The repurchase price is contractually fixed at an amount equal to the original sales price plus the financing entity's carrying and financing costs. The purpose of the transaction is to enable the sponsor enterprise to arrange financing of its original purchase of the inventory.

FASB ruled that the substance of this transaction is that of a borrowing transaction, not a sale. That is, the transaction is, in substance, no different from the sponsor directly obtaining third-party financing to purchase inventory. ASC 470-40 specifies that the proper accounting by the sponsor is to record a liability in the amount of the selling price when the funds are received from the financing entity in exchange for the initial transfer of the inventory. The sponsor proceeds to accrue carrying and financing costs in accordance with its normal accounting policies. These accruals are eliminated and the liability satisfied when the sponsor repurchases the inventory. The inventory is not removed from the statement of financial position of the sponsor and a sale is not recorded. Thus, although legal title has passed to the financing entity, for purposes of measuring and valuing inventory, the inventory is considered to be owned by the sponsor.

For more information, see the chapter on ASC 470.

Sales made with the buyer having the right of return. Another issue requiring special consideration exists when a buyer is granted a right of return, as defined by ASC 605-15. The seller must consider the propriety of recognizing revenue at the point of sale under such a situation. The sale is recorded only when six specified conditions are met including the condition that the future amount of returns can be reasonably estimated by the seller. If a reasonable estimate cannot be made, then the sale is not recorded until the earlier of the expiration date of the return privilege or the date when all six conditions are met. Similar to product financing costs, this situation results in the seller continuing to include the goods in its measurement and valuation of inventory even though legal title has passed to the buyer. For more information see chapter on ASC 605.

Accounting for Inventories

A major objective of accounting for inventories is the matching of appropriate costs to the period in which the related revenues are earned in order to properly compute gross profit, also referred to as gross margin. Inventories are recorded in the accounting records using either a periodic or perpetual system.

In a periodic inventory system, inventory quantities are determined by physical count. The quantity of each item counted is then priced using the cost flow assumption that the enterprise had adopted as its accounting policy for that type of inventory. Cost of goods sold is computed by adding beginning inventory and net purchases (or cost of goods manufactured) and subtracting ending inventory.

A perpetual inventory system keeps a running total of the quantity (and possibly the cost) of inventory on hand by maintaining subsidiary inventory records that reflect all sales and purchases as they occur. When inventory is purchased, inventory (rather than purchases) is debited. When inventory is sold, the cost of goods sold and corresponding reduction of inventory are recorded.

Using a periodic inventory system necessitates the taking of physical inventory counts to determine the quantity of inventory on hand at the end of a reporting period. To facilitate accurate annual financial statements, in practice physical counts are performed at least annually on the last day of the fiscal year.

If the enterprise maintains a perpetual inventory system, it must regularly and systematically verify the accuracy of its perpetual records by physically counting inventories and comparing the quantities on hand with the perpetual records. GAAP does not provide explicit requirements regarding the timing and frequency of physical counts necessary to verify the perpetual records; however there is a US income tax requirement (IRC§471[b][1]) that a taxpayer perform "... a physical count of inventories at each location on a regular and consistent basis...." The purpose of this requirement is to enable the taxpayer to support any tax deductions taken for inventory shrinkage if it elects not to take a complete physical inventory at all locations on the last day of the fiscal year. The IRS, in its Rev. Proc. 98-29, provided a "retail safe harbor method" that permits retailers to deduct estimated shrinkage where the retailer takes physical inventories at each location at least annually. (ASC 330-10-30-1)

Initial Measurement—Valuation of Inventories

The primary basis of accounting for inventories is cost. Cost is defined as the sum of the applicable expenditures and charges directly or indirectly incurred in bringing an article to its existing condition and location. This definition allows for a wide interpretation of the costs to be included in inventory.

Raw materials and merchandise inventory. For raw materials and merchandise inventory which are purchased outright, the identification of cost is relatively straightforward. The cost of these purchased inventories will include all expenditures incurred in bringing the goods to the point of sale and converting them to a salable condition. These costs include the purchase price, transportation costs (freight-in), insurance while in transit, and handling costs charged by the supplier.

Example of recording raw material costs

Aruba Bungee Cords, Inc. (ABC) purchases rubber bands, a raw material that it uses in manufacturing its signature product. The company typically receives delivery of all its raw materials and uses them in manufacturing its finished products during the winter, and then sells its stock of finished goods in the spring. The supplier invoice for a January delivery of rubber bands includes the following line items:

Rubber band (1,681 pounds at $3 per pound)	$5,043
Shipping and handling	125
Shipping insurance	48
Subtotal	5,216
Sales tax	193
Total	$5,409

Since ABC is using the rubber bands as raw materials in a product that it resells, it will not pay the sales tax. However, both the shipping and handling charge and the shipping insurance are required for ongoing product acquisition, and so are included in the following entry to record receipt of the goods:

Inventory raw materials	5,216	
Accounts payable		5,216

To record purchase of rubber bands and related costs

On February 1, ABC purchases a $5,000, two-month shipping insurance policy (paradoxically, this type of policy is sometimes referred to as "inland marine" coverage) that applies to all incoming supplier deliveries for the remainder of the winter production season, allowing it to refuse shipping insurance charges on individual deliveries. Since the policy insures all inbound raw materials deliveries (not just rubber bands), it is too time-consuming to charge the cost of this policy to individual raw material deliveries using specific identification, and accordingly, the controller can estimate a flat charge per delivery based on the number of expected deliveries during the two-month term of the insurance policy as follows:

$5,000 insurance premium ÷ 200 expected deliveries during the policy term = $25 per delivery and then charge each delivery with $25 as follows:

Inventory—raw materials	25	
Prepaid insurance		25

To allocate cost of inland marine coverage to inbound insured raw materials shipments

In this case, however, the controller determined that shipments are expected to occur evenly during the two-month policy period and therefore will simply make a monthly standard journal entry as follows:

Inventory—raw materials	2,500	
Prepaid insurance		2,500

To amortize premium on inland marine policy using the straight-line method

Note that the controller must be careful, under either scenario, to ensure that perpetual inventory records appropriately track unit costs of raw materials to include the cost of shipping insurance. Failure to do so would result in an understatement of the cost of raw materials inventory on hand at the end of any accounting period.

Purchases can be recorded at their gross amount or net of any allowable discount. If recorded gross, the discounts taken represent a reduction in the purchase cost for purposes of determining cost of goods sold. On the other hand, if they are recorded net, any lost discounts are treated as a financial expense, not as cost of goods sold. The net method is considered to be theoretically preferable, but the gross method is simpler and, thus, more commonly used. Either method is acceptable under GAAP, provided that it is consistently applied.

Inventory purchases and sales with the same counterparty. Some enterprises sell inventory to another party from whom they also acquire inventory in the same line of business. These transactions may be part of a single or separate arrangements and the inventory purchased or sold may be raw materials, work-in-process, or finished goods. These arrangements require careful analysis to determine if they are to be accounted for as a single exchange transaction under ASC 845, *Nonmonetary Transactions,* and whether they are to be recognized at fair value or at the carrying value of the inventory transferred.[1] More detailed information can be found in the chapter on ASC 845.

Inventory hedges. One notable exception to recording inventories at cost is provided by the hedge accounting requirements of ASC 815. If inventory has been designated as the hedged item in a fair value hedge, changes in the fair value of the hedged inventory are recognized on the statement of financial position as they occur, with the offsetting charge or credit recognized currently in net income. Hedging is discussed in detail in Chapter 10.

Manufacturing inventories. Inventory cost in a manufacturing enterprise includes both acquisition and production costs. This concept is commonly referred to as *full absorption* or *full costing*. As a result, the WIP and finished goods inventories include direct materials,

[1] *This guidance does not apply to arrangements accounted for as derivatives under ASC 815, or to exchanges of software or real estate.*

direct labor, and an appropriately allocated portion of indirect production costs referred to as indirect overhead.

Under full absorption costing, indirect overhead costs—costs that are incidental to and necessary for production—are allocated to goods produced and, to the extent those goods are uncompleted or unsold at the end of a period, are included in ending WIP or finished goods inventory, respectively. Indirect overhead costs include such costs as

- Depreciation and cost depletion
- Repairs
- Maintenance
- Factory rent and utilities
- Indirect labor
- Normal rework labor, scrap, and spoilage
- Production supervisory wages
- Indirect materials and supplies
- Quality control and inspection
- Small tools not capitalized.

Indirect overhead is comprised of two elements, variable and fixed overhead. ASC 330-10-30-3 clarifies that variable overhead is to be allocated to work-in-process and finished goods based on the actual usage of the production facilities. Fixed overhead, however, is to be allocated to work-in-process and finished goods based on the normal expected capacity of the enterprise's production facilities, with the overhead rate recomputed in instances when actual production exceeds the normal capacity. Initially, this may appear to be an inconsistent accounting method; however, the use of this convention ensures that the inventory is not recorded at an amount in excess of its actual cost, as illustrated in the following example:

Example of allocating fixed overhead to units produced

Brewed Refreshment Plant, Inc. (BRP), located in Washington, D.C., has historically produced between 3,200 and 3,800 barrels of beer annually with its average production approximating 3,500 barrels. This average takes into account its normal number of work shifts and the normal operation of its machinery adjusted for downtime for normal maintenance and recalibration. BRP's average capacity and overhead costs (partial list) are presented below.

(a) Normal expected annual productive capacity		3,500 barrels
Fixed overhead costs (partial list):		
Depreciation of machinery	$600	
Factory rent	800	
Plant superintendent	80	
(b) Total fixed overhead to allocate		$ 1,480
(c) Fixed overhead rate per barrel produced (b ÷ a)		$ 0.4229 per barrel

Scenario 1: The Washington Nationals major-league baseball team outperforms expectations; since BRP's beer is sold at the Nationals' stadium, BRP substantially increases production beyond the normal level expected.

Actual production level	4,500 barrels

If BRP were to apply fixed overhead using the rate based on its normal productive capacity, the calculation would be as follows:

4,500 barrels produced × $0.4229 per barrel = $1,903 of overhead applied

This would result in an over-allocation of $423, the difference between the $1,903 of overhead applied and the $1,480 of overhead actually incurred. This violates the lower of cost or market principle, since the inventory would be valued at an amount that exceeded its actual cost. Therefore, BRP applied ASC 330 and recomputed its fixed overhead rate as follows:

1,480 fixed overhead incurred ÷ Revised production level of 4,500 barrels = $0.3289 per barrel

Scenario 2: The Washington Nationals experience a cold, rainy summer and worse-than-expected attendance. If production lags expectations and BRP only produces 2,500 barrels of beer, the original overhead rate is not revised. The fixed overhead is allocated as follows:

2,500 barrels produced × $0.4229 per barrel = $1,057 of overhead applied

Per ASC 330, when production levels decline below the original expectation, the fixed overhead rate is not recomputed. The $423 difference between the $1,480 of actual fixed overhead incurred and the $1,057 of overhead applied is accounted for as an expense in the period incurred.

For the purpose of determining normal productive capacity, it is expected that capacity will vary from period to period based on enterprise-specific or industry-specific experience. Management is to formulate a judgment regarding a reasonable range of normal production levels expected to be achieved under normal operating conditions.

The enterprise may incur unusually large expenses resulting from idle facilities, excessive waste, spoilage, freight, or handling costs. ASC 330 clarifies that when this situation occurs, the abnormal portion of these expenses is to be treated as a cost of the period incurred and not to be allocated to inventory.

Generally, interest costs incurred during the production of inventory are not capitalized under ASC 835-20. A complete discussion regarding the capitalization of interest costs is provided in the chapter on ASC 835.

Example of variable and fixed overhead allocation

The InCase Manufacturing Company (IMC) uses injection molding to create two types of plastic CD cases—regular size and mini—on a seven-day, three-shift production schedule. During the current month, it records the following overhead expenses:

Depreciation of machinery	$232,000	Rent	$36,000
Indirect labor	208,000	Repairs	12,000
Indirect materials	58,000	Small tools	28,000
Maintenance	117,000	Scrap and spoilage	49,000
Production supervisory wages	229,000	Utilities	37,000
Quality control	82,000		

IMC's controller analyzed scrap and spoilage statistics and determined that abnormal losses of $32,000 were incurred due to a bad batch of plastic resin pellets. She adjusted scrap and spoilage expense by charging the cost of those pellets to cost of goods sold during the current period, resulting in a reduced scrap and spoilage expense of $17,000. Also, the rent cost includes a $6,000 lease termination penalty payable to the lessor of a vacant factory. Since this cost is considered an exit or disposal activity under ASC 420, it does not benefit production and is therefore charged directly to expense in the current period.

For allocation purposes, IMC's controller elects to group the adjusted overhead expenses into two cost pools. Pool #1 contains all expenses related to machinery operation, which includes depreciation, indirect labor, indirect materials, maintenance, rent, repairs, small tools, and utilities. Pool #2 contains all expenses related to production runs, which includes production supervisory wages, quality control, scrap, and spoilage. The following three journal entries record (1) the recognition of excess scrap and unused facilities in the current period, (2) the allocation of costs to the machinery cost pool, and (3) the allocation of costs to the production runs cost pool:

Cost of goods sold expense	38,000	
Scrap and spoilage expense		32,000
Rent expense		6,000

Overhead pool #1—Machinery operation	722,000	
Depreciation		232,000
Indirect labor		208,000
Indirect materials		58,000
Maintenance		117,000
Rent		30,000
Repairs		12,000
Small tools		28,000
Utilities		37,000
Overhead pool #2—Production runs	328,000	
Production supervisory wages		229,000
Quality control		82,000
Scrap and spoilage		17,000

Since the costs in overhead pool #1 are centered on machine usage, the controller elects to use the total operating hours used for the production of each product as the allocation basis for that pool. The accumulated production hours by machine for the past month are as follows:

Machinery type	*Regular CD production hours*	*Mini CD production hours*
50-ton press	0	710
55-ton press	310	290
70-ton press	480	230
85-ton press	690	0
Total hours	1,480	1,230
Percentage of total hours	55%	45%

Since the costs in overhead pool #2 are centered on production volume, the controller decides to use the total pounds of plastic resin pellets used for production during the month as the allocation basis for that cost pool. The total plastic resin usage, adjusted for spoilage, was 114,000 pounds of resin for the regular CD cases and 76,000 pounds for the mini CD cases, which is a percentage split of 60% for regular CD cases and 40% for mini CD cases.

With the calculation of allocation bases completed, the split of overhead costs between the two products follows:

	Total costs in pool	*55% regular CD allocation*	*45% mini CD allocation*
Overhead pool #1	722,000	397,100	324,900
	Total costs in pool	*60% regular CD allocation*	*40% mini CD allocation*
Overhead pool #2	328,000	196,800	131,200

Thus, the total overhead allocated to regular CD cases is $593,900 (397,100 + 196,800), while the total overhead allocated to mini CD cases is $456,100 (324,900 + 131,200). Of the case quantities produced, 85% of the regular CD cases and 70% of the mini CD cases were sold during the month, with the remainder being transferred into finished goods inventory. IMC's controller uses these percentages to apportion the cost of allocated overhead between the cost of goods sold and finished goods inventory, as shown in the following entry:

Cost of goods sold—regular CD cases	504,815	
Cost of goods sold—mini CD cases	319,270	
Finished goods inventory—regular CD cases	89,085	
Finished goods inventory—mini CD cases	136,830	
Overhead pool #1—Machinery operation		722,000
Overhead pool #2—Production runs		328,000

Determining inventory cost. The theoretical basis for valuing inventories and cost of goods sold requires assigning production and/or acquisition costs to the specific goods to which they relate. This method of inventory valuation is usually referred to as specific identification.

Specific identification is generally not practical inasmuch as the product will generally lose its separate identity as it passes through the production and sales process. Exceptions to this would arise in situations involving small inventory quantities with high unit value and low turnover rate, such as automobiles or heavy machinery. Because of the limited applicability of specific identification, it is necessary to make certain assumptions regarding the cost flows associated with inventory. Although these cost flow assumptions are used for accounting purposes, they may or may not reflect the actual physical flow of the inventory.

Cost flow assumptions. The most common cost flow assumptions used are specified in ASC 330-10-30-9:

1. first-in, first-out (FIFO),
2. last-in, first-out (LIFO), and
3. weighted-average.

Additionally, there are variations in the application of each of these assumptions which are commonly used in practice. ASC 330-10-30-9 points out that:

> "The major objective in selecting a method should be to choose the one which, under the circumstances, most clearly reflects periodic income."

In selecting which cost flow assumption to adopt as its accounting policy for a particular type of industry, management should consider a variety of factors. First, the industry norm should be examined, as this will facilitate intercompany comparison by financial statement users. The appropriateness of using a particular cost flow assumption will vary depending on the nature of the industry and the expected economic climate. The appropriate method in a period of rising prices differs from the method that is appropriate for a period of declining prices. Each of the foregoing assumptions and their relative advantages or disadvantages are discussed below. Examples are provided to enhance understanding of the application.

First-in, first-out (FIFO). The FIFO method of inventory valuation assumes that the first goods purchased are the first goods used or sold, regardless of the actual physical flow. This method is thought to most closely parallel the physical flow of the units in most industries. The strength of this cost flow assumption lies in the inventory amount reported on the statement of financial position. Because the earliest goods purchased are the first ones removed from the inventory account, the remaining balance is composed of items priced at more recent cost. This yields results similar to those obtained under current cost accounting on the statement of financial position. However, the FIFO method does not necessarily reflect the most accurate income figure as older, historical costs are being charged to cost of goods sold and matched against current revenues.

Example of the basic principles involved in the application of FIFO

	Units available	*Units sold*	*Actual unit cost*	*Actual total cost*
Beginning inventory	100	–	$2.10	$210
Sale	–	75	–	–
Purchase	150	–	2.80	420
Sale	–	100	–	–
Purchase	50	–	3.00	150
Total	300	175		$780

Given this data, the cost of goods sold and ending inventory balance are determined as follows:

	Units	Unit cost	Total cost
Cost of goods sold	100	$2.10	$210
	75	2.80	210
	175		420
Ending inventory	50	3.00	150
	75	2.80	210
	125		360
Totals	300		$780

Notice that the total of the units in cost of goods sold and ending inventory, as well as the sum of their total costs, is equal to the goods available for sale and their respective total costs.

The FIFO method provides the same results under either the periodic or perpetual inventory tracking system.

Last-in, first-out (LIFO). The LIFO method of inventory valuation assumes that the last goods purchased are the first goods used or sold. This allows the matching of current costs with current revenues and provides the best measure of gross profit. However, unless costs remain relatively unchanged over time, the LIFO method will usually misstate the ending inventory statement of financial position amount, because LIFO inventory usually includes costs of acquiring or manufacturing inventory that were incurred in earlier periods. LIFO does not usually follow the physical flow of merchandise or materials. However, the matching of physical flow with cost flow is not an objective of accounting for inventories.

LIFO accounting is actually an income tax concept. Consequently, the rules regarding the application of the LIFO method are not set forth in U.S. GAAP, but rather, are found in the US Internal Revenue Code (IRC) §472. U.S. Treasury regulations provide that any taxpayer that maintains inventories may select LIFO application for any or all inventoriable items. This election is made with the taxpayer's income tax return on Form 970 after the close of the first tax year that the taxpayer intends to use (or expand the use of) the LIFO method.

The quantity of ending inventory on hand at the beginning of the year of election is termed the "base layer." This inventory is valued at actual (full absorption) cost, and unit cost for each inventory item is determined by dividing total cost by the quantity on hand. At the end of the initial and subsequent years, increases in the quantity of inventory on hand are referred to as increments, or LIFO layers. These increments are valued individually by applying one of the following costing methods to the quantity of inventory representing a layer:

1. The actual cost of the goods most recently purchased or produced
2. The actual cost of the goods purchased or produced in order of acquisition
3. An average unit cost of all goods purchased or produced during the current year
4. A hybrid method that more clearly reflects income (for income tax purposes, this method must meet with the approval of the IRS Commissioner).

Thus, after using the LIFO method for five years, it is possible that an enterprise could have ending inventory consisting of the base layer and five additional layers (or increments) provided that the quantity of ending inventory increased every year.

Example of the single goods (unit) LIFO approach

Rose Co. is in its first year of operation and elects to use the periodic LIFO method of inventory valuation. The company sells only one product. Rose applies the LIFO method using the order of current year acquisition cost. The following data are given for years 1 through 3:

		Units			Purchase cost	
Year 1	Beginning inventory	Purchased	Sold	Ending inventory	Unit cost	Total cost
Purchase		200			$2.00	$400
Sale			100		–	–
Purchase		200			3.00	600
Sale			150		–	–
	–	400	250	150		

		Units			Purchase cost	
Year 2	Beginning inventory	Purchased	Sold	Ending inventory	Unit cost	Total cost
Purchase		300			$3.20	$960
Sale			200		–	–
Purchase		100			3.30	330
	150	400	200	350		
Year 3						
Purchase		100			$3.50	$350
Sale			200		–	–
Sale			100		–	–
	350	100	300	150		

In year 1 the following occurred:

1. The total goods available for sale were 400 units.
2. The total sales were 250 units.
3. Therefore, the ending inventory was 150 units.

The ending inventory is valued at the earliest current year acquisition cost of $2.00 per unit. Thus, ending inventory is valued at $300 (150 × $2.00).

Another way to look at this is to analyze both cost of goods sold and ending inventory.

Year 1	Units	Unit cost	Total cost
Cost of goods sold	200	$3.00	$600
	50	2.00	100
	250		$700
Ending inventory	150	2.00	$300

Note that the base-year cost is $2.00 and that the base-year level is 150 units. Therefore, if ending inventory in the subsequent period exceeds 150 units, a new layer (or increment) will be created.

Year 2	Units	Unit cost	Total cost	
Cost of goods sold	100	$3.30	$330	
	100	3.20	320	
	200		$650	
Ending inventory	150	2.00	$300	Base-year layer
	200	3.20	640	Year 2 increment
	350		$940	

If ending inventory exceeds 350 units in the next period, a third layer (increment) will be created.

Year 3	*Units*	*Unit cost*	*Total cost*	
Cost of goods sold	100	$3.50	$350	
	200	3.20	640	
	300		$990	
Ending inventory	150	2.00	$300	Base-year layer

Notice how the decrease (decrement) of 200 units in year 3 eliminated the entire year 2 increment. Thus, any year 4 increase in the quantity of inventory would result in a *new* increment, which would be valued at year 4 prices.

In situations where the ending inventory decreases from the level established at the close of the preceding year, the enterprise experiences a decrement or LIFO liquidation. Decrements reduce or eliminate previously established LIFO layers. Once any part of a LIFO layer has been eliminated, it cannot be reinstated after year-end. For example, if in its first year after the election of LIFO an enterprise establishes a LIFO layer (increment) of ten units, then in the next year inventory decreases by four units, leaving the first layer at six units, the enterprise is not permitted in any succeeding year to increase the number of units in the first year layer back up to the original ten units. The quantity in the first layer remains at a maximum of six units subject to further reduction if decrements occur in future years. Any unit increases in future years will create one or more new layers. The effect of LIFO liquidations in periods of rising prices is to transfer, from ending inventory into cost of goods sold, costs that are below the current cost being paid. Thus, the resultant effect of a LIFO liquidation is to increase income for both accounting and income tax purposes. Because of this, LIFO is most commonly used by companies in industries in which levels of inventories are consistently maintained or increased over time.

LIFO liquidations can be either voluntary or involuntary. A voluntary liquidation occurs when an enterprise deliberately lets its inventory levels drop. Voluntary liquidations may be desirable for a number of reasons. Management might consider the current price of purchasing the goods to be too high, a smaller quantity of inventory might be needed for efficient production due to conversion to a "just-in-time" production model, or inventory items may have become obsolete due to new technology or transitions in the enterprise's product lines.

Involuntary LIFO liquidations stem from reasons beyond the control of management, such as a strike, material shortages, shipping delays, etc. Whether voluntary or involuntary, all LIFO liquidations result in a corresponding increase in income in periods of rising prices.

To determine the effect of the liquidation, management must compute the difference between actual cost of sales and what cost of sales would have been had the inventory been reinstated. The Internal Revenue Service has ruled that this hypothetical reinstatement must be computed under the company's normal pricing procedures for valuing its LIFO increments. In the preceding example the effect of the year 3 LIFO liquidation would be computed as follows:

Hypothetical inventory reinstatement

200 units @ $3.50 – $3.20 = $60

Hypothetically, if there had been an increment instead of a decrement in year 3 and the year 2 inventory layer had remained intact, 200 more units (out of the 300 total units sold in year 3) would have been charged to cost of goods sold at the year 3 price of $3.50 instead of the year 2 price of $3.20. Therefore, the difference between $3.50 and the actual amount charged to cost of sales for these 200 units liquidated ($3.20) measures the effect of the liquidation.

The following is considered acceptable GAAP disclosure in the event of a LIFO liquidation:

> During 2013, inventory quantities were reduced below their levels at December 31, 2012. As a result of this reduction, LIFO inventory costs computed based on lower prior years' acquisition costs were charged to cost of goods sold. If this LIFO liquidation had not occurred and cost of sales had been computed based on the cost of 2013 purchases, cost of goods sold would have increased by approximately $xxx and net income decreased by approximately $xx or $x per share.

Applying the unit LIFO method requires a substantial amount of recordkeeping. The recordkeeping becomes more burdensome as the number of products increases. For this reason a "pooling" approach is often used to compute LIFO inventories.

Pooling is the process of grouping items that are naturally related and then treating this group as a single unit in determining LIFO cost. Because the ending inventory normally includes many items, decreases in one item can be offset by increases in others, whereas under the unit LIFO approach a decrease in any one item results in a liquidation of all or a portion of a LIFO layer.

Complexity in applying the pooling method arises from the income tax regulations. These regulations require that the opening and closing inventories of each type of good be compared. In order to be considered comparable for this purpose, inventory items must be similar as to character, quality, and price. This qualification has generally been interpreted to mean identical. The effect of this interpretation is to require a separate pool for each item under the unit LIFO method. To provide a simpler, more practical approach to applying LIFO and allow for increased use of LIFO pools, election of the dollar-value LIFO method is permitted.

Dollar-value LIFO. Dollar-value LIFO may be elected by any taxpayer. Under the dollar-value LIFO method of inventory valuation, the cost of inventories is computed by expressing base-year costs in terms of total dollars rather than specific prices of specific units. The dollar-value method also provides an expanded interpretation of the use of LIFO pools. Increments and decrements are treated the same as under the unit LIFO approach but are reflected only in terms of a *net* increment or liquidation for the entire pool.

Identifying pools. Three alternatives exist for determining pools under dollar-value LIFO: (1) the natural business unit method, (2) the multiple pooling method, and (3) pools for wholesalers, retailers, jobbers, and the like.

The natural business unit is defined by the existence of separate and distinct processing facilities and operations and the maintenance of separate income (loss) records. The concept of the natural business unit is generally dependent upon the type of product being produced, not the various stages of production for that product. Thus, the pool of a manufacturer can (and will) contain raw materials, WIP, and finished goods. The three examples below, adapted from the treasury regulations, illustrate the application of the natural business unit concept.

Example 1 – Identifying Pools

A corporation manufactures, in one division, automatic clothes washers and dryers of both commercial and domestic grade as well as electric ranges and dishwashers. The corporation manufactures, in another division, radios and television sets. The manufacturing facilities and processes used in manufacturing the radios and television sets are distinct from those used in manufacturing the automatic clothes washers, etc. Under these circumstances, an enterprise consisting of two business units and two pools would be appropriate: one consisting of all of the LIFO inventories involved with the manufacture of clothes washers and dryers, electric ranges and dishwashers and the other consisting of all the LIFO inventories involved with the production of radios and television sets.

Example 2 – Identifying Pools

A taxpayer produces plastics in one of its plants. Substantial amounts of the production are sold as plastics. The remainder of the production is shipped to a second plant of the taxpayer for the production of plastic toys which are sold to customers. The taxpayer operates its plastics plant and toy plant as separate divisions. Because of the different product lines and the separate divisions, the taxpayer has two natural business units.

Example 3 – Identifying Pools

A taxpayer is engaged in the manufacture of paper. At one stage of processing, uncoated paper is produced. Substantial amounts of uncoated paper are sold at this stage of processing. The remainder of the uncoated paper is transferred to the taxpayer's finishing mill where coated paper is produced and sold. This taxpayer has only one natural business unit, since coated and uncoated paper are within the same product line.

The treasury regulations require that a pool consist of all items entering into the entire inventory investment of a natural business unit, unless the taxpayer elects to use the multiple-pooling method.

The multiple-pooling method is the grouping of "substantially similar" items. In determining substantially similar items, consideration is given to the processing applied, the interchangeability, the similarity of use, and the customary practice of the industry. While the election of multiple pools will necessitate additional recordkeeping, it may result in a better estimation of gross profit and periodic net income.

According to Reg. §1.472-8(c), inventory items of wholesalers, retailers, jobbers, and distributors are to be assigned to pools by major lines, types, or classes of goods. The natural business unit method may be used with permission of the Commissioner.

All three methods of pooling allow for a change in the components of inventory over time. New items which properly fall within the pool may be added, and old items may disappear from the pool, but neither will necessarily cause a change in the total dollar value of the pool.

Computing dollar-value LIFO. The purpose of the dollar-value LIFO method of valuing inventory is to convert inventory priced at end-of-year prices to that same quantity of inventory priced at base-year (or applicable LIFO layer) prices. The dollar-value method achieves this result through the use of a conversion price index. The inventory computed at current year cost is divided by the appropriate index to arrive at its base-year cost. The main computational focus is on the determination of the conversion price index. There are four types of methods that can be used in the computation of the ending inventory amount of a dollar-value LIFO pool: (1) double-extension, (2) link-chain, (3) indexing, and (4) alternative LIFO for automobile dealers.

Double-extension method. This method was originally developed to compute the conversion price index. It involves extending the entire quantity of ending inventory for the current year at both base-year prices and end-of-year prices to arrive at a total dollar value for each, hence the title "double-extension." The dollar total computed at end-of-year prices is then divided by the dollar total computed at base-year prices to arrive at the index, usually referred to as the conversion price index. This index indicates the relationship between the base-year and current prices in terms of a percentage. Each layer (or increment) is valued at its own percentage. Although a representative sample is allowed (meaning that not all of the items need to be double-extended; this is discussed in more detail under indexing), the recordkeeping under this method is very burdensome. The base-year price must be maintained for each inventory item. Depending upon the number of different items included in the inventory of the enterprise, the necessary records may be too detailed to keep past the first year or two.

The following example illustrates the double-extension method of computing the LIFO value of inventory. The example presented is relatively simple and does not attempt to incorporate all of the complexities of LIFO inventory accounting.

Example of the dollar-value LIFO method

Isaacson, Inc. uses the dollar-value method of LIFO inventory valuation and computes its price index using the double-extension method. Isaacson has a single pool that contains two inventory items, A and B. Year 1 is the company's initial year of operations. The following information is given for years 1 through 4:

Year	Ending inventory current prices	Ending quantity (units) and current unit price A		B	
1	$100,000	5,000	$6.00	7,000	$10.00
2	120,300	6,000	6.30	7,500	11.00
3	122,220	5,800	6.40	7,400	11.50
4	133,900	6,200	6.50	7,800	12.00

In year 1 there is no computation of an index; the index is 100%. The LIFO cost is the same as the actual current year cost. This is the base year.

In year 2 the first step is to double-extend the quantity of ending inventory at base-year and current year costs.

Item	Quantity	Base-year cost/unit	Extended	Current year cost/unit	Extended
A	6,000	$ 6.00	$ 36,000	$ 6.30	$ 37,800
B	7,500	10.00	75,000	11.00	82,500
			$111,000		$ 120,300*

* *When using the double-extension method and extending **all** of the inventory items to arrive at the index, this number must equal the ending inventory at current prices. If a sampling method is used (as discussed under indexing), this number **divided by** your ending inventory at current prices is the percentage sampled.*

Now we can compute the conversion price index which is

$$\frac{\text{Ending inventory at current year prices}}{\text{Ending inventory at base-year prices}}$$

In this case $\frac{120,300}{111,000} = 108.4\%$ (rounded)

Next, compute the year 2 layer at base-year cost by taking the current year-ending inventory at base-year prices (if you only extend a sample of the inventory, this number is arrived at by dividing the ending inventory at current year prices by the conversion price index) of $111,000 and subtracting the base-year cost of $100,000. In year 2 we have an increment (layer) of $11,000 valued at base-year costs.

The year 2 layer of $11,000 at base-year cost must be converted so that the layer is valued at the prices in effect when it came into existence (i.e., at year 2 prices). This is done by multiplying the increment at base-year cost ($11,000) by the rounded conversion price index (1.084). The result is the year 2 layer at LIFO prices.

Base-year layer	$100,000
Year 2 layer ($11,000 × 1.084)	11,924
	$111,924

In year 3 the same basic procedure is followed.

Item	*Quantity*	*Base-year cost/unit*	*Extended*	*Current year cost/unit*	*Extended*
A	5,800	$ 6.00	$ 34,800	$ 6.40	$ 37,120
B	7,400	10.00	74,000	11.50	85,100
			$108,800		$122,220

There has been a decrease in the base-year cost of the ending inventory ($111,000 – $108,800 = $2,200) which is referred to as a decrement. A decrement results in the decrease (or elimination) of previously provided layers. In this situation, the computation of the index is not necessary as there is no LIFO layer that requires a valuation. If a sampling approach has been used, the index is needed to arrive at the ending inventory at base-year cost and thus determine if there has been an increment or decrement.

Now the ending inventory at base-year cost is $108,800. The base-year cost layer is still intact at $100,000, so the cumulative increment is $8,800. Since this is less than the $11,000 increment of year 2, no additional increment is established in year 3. The LIFO cost of the inventory is shown below.

Base-year layer	$100,000
Year 2 layer ($8,800 × 1.084)	9,539
	$109,539

The fourth year then follows the same steps.

Items	*Quantity*	*Base-year cost/unit*	*Extended*	*Current year cost/unit*	*Extended*
A	6,200	$ 6.00	$ 37,200	$ 6.50	$ 40,300
B	7,800	10.00	78,000	12.00	93,600
			$115,200		$133,900

The conversion price index is 116.2% (133,900/115,200).

A current year increment exists because the ending inventory at base-year prices in year 4 of $115,200 exceeds the year 3 number of $108,800. The current year increment of $6,400 must be valued at year 4 prices. Thus, the LIFO cost of the year 4 inventory is

Base-year layer	$100,000
Year 2 layer ($8,800 × 1.084)	9,539
Year 4 layer ($6,400 × 1.162)	7,437
	$116,976

It is important to point out that once a layer is reduced or eliminated it is never reinstated (as with the year 2 increment) after year-end.

Link-chain method. Since the double-extension method computations are arduous even if only a few items exist in the inventory, consider the complexity that arises when there is a constant change in the inventory mix or when there is a large number of inventory items. The link-chain method of applying dollar-value LIFO was developed to mitigate the effects of this complexity.

Consider the situation where the components of inventory are constantly changing. The regulations require that any new products added to the inventory be recorded at base-year prices. If these are not available, then the earliest cost available after the base year is used. If the item was not in existence in the base year, the taxpayer may reconstruct the base cost, using a reasonable method to determine what the cost would have been if the item had been in existence in the base year. Finally, as a last resort, the current year purchase price can be used. While this does not appear to be a problem on the surface, imagine a base period that is twenty-five to fifty years in the past. The difficulty involved with finding the base-year cost may require using a more current cost, thus eliminating some of the LIFO benefit. Imagine a situation faced by a company in a "high-tech" industry where inventory is continually being replaced by newer, more advanced products. The effect of this rapid change under the double-extension method (because the new products did not exist in the base period) is to use current prices as base-year costs. When inventory has such a rapid turnover, the overall LIFO advantage becomes diluted as current and base-year costs are often identical. This situation necessitated the development of the link-chain method.

The link-chain method was originally developed for (and limited to) those companies that wanted to use LIFO but, because of a substantial change in product lines over time, were unable to reconstruct or maintain the historical records necessary to make accurate use of the double extension method. It is important to note that the double-extension and link-chain methods are not elective alternatives for the same situation. For income tax purposes, the link-chain election requires that substantial changes in product lines be evident over the years, and may not be elected solely because of its ease of application. The double-extension and index methods must be demonstrably impractical in order to elect the link-chain method. However, an enterprise may use different computational techniques for financial reporting and income tax purposes. Therefore, the link-chain method could be used for financial reporting purposes even if a different application is used for income tax purposes. Obviously, the recordkeeping burdens imposed by using different LIFO methods for GAAP and income tax purposes (including the deferred income tax accounting that would be required for the temporary difference between the GAAP and income tax bases of the LIFO inventories) would make this a highly unlikely scenario.

The link-chain method is the process of developing a single cumulative index which is applied to the ending inventory amount priced using beginning-of-the-year costs. Thus, the index computed at the end of each year is "linked" to the index from all previous years. A separate cumulative index is used for each pool regardless of the variations in the components of these pools over the years. Technological change is accommodated by the method used to calculate each current year's index. The index is calculated by double-extending a representative sample of items in the pool at both beginning-of-year prices and end-of-year prices. This annual index is then applied to (multiplied by) the previous period's cumulative index to arrive at the new current year cumulative index.

An example of the link-chain method is shown below. The end-of-year costs and inventory quantities used are the same as those used in the double-extension example.

Example – Link-chain method

Assume the following inventory data for years 1–4 for Dickler Distributors, Inc. Year 1 is assumed to be the initial year of operation for the company. The LIFO method is elected on the first income tax return. Assume that A and B constitute a single pool.

	Ending inventory	Cost per unit		Extension	
Product	*quantity*	*Beg. of yr.*	*End of yr.*	*Beginning*	*End*
Year 1					
A	5,000	N/A	$ 6.00	N/A	$ 30,000
B	7,000	N/A	10.00	N/A	70,000
					$100,000
Year 2					
A	6,000	$ 6.00	6.30	$ 36,000	$ 37,800
B	7,500	10.00	11.00	75,000	82,500
				$111,000	$120,300

Year 3					
A	5,800	6.30	6.40	$ 36,540	$ 37,120
B	7,400	11.00	11.50	81,400	85,100
				$117,940	$122,220
Year 4					
A	6,200	6.40	6.50	$ 39,680	$ 40,300
B	7,800	11.50	12.00	89,700	93,600
				$129,380	$133,900

The initial year (base year) does not require the computation of an index under any LIFO method. The base-year index will always be 1.00.

Thus, the base-year inventory layer is $100,000 (the end-of-year inventory stated at base-year cost). The second year requires the first index computation. Notice that in year 2 our extended totals are:

Product	*Beginning-of-year prices*	*End-of-year prices*
A	$ 36,000	$ 37,800
B	75,000	82,500
	$111,000	$120,300

The year 2 index is 1.084 (120,300/111,000). This is the same as computed under the double-extension method because the beginning-of-the-year prices reflect the base-year price. This will not always be the case, as sometimes new items may be added to the pool, causing a change in the index. Thus, the cumulative index is the 1.084 current year index multiplied by the preceding year index of 1.00 to arrive at a link-chain index of 1.084.

This index is then used to restate the inventory to base-year cost by dividing the inventory at end-of-year prices by the cumulative index: $120,300/1.084 = $111,000. The determination of the LIFO increment or decrement is then basically the same as the double-extension method. In year 2 the increment (layer) at base-year cost is $11,000 ($111,000 – 100,000). This layer must be valued at the prices effective when the layer was created, or extended at the cumulative index for that year. This results in an ending inventory at LIFO cost of:

	Base-year cost	*Index*	*LIFO cost*
Base-year layer	$100,000	1.000	$100,000
Year 2 layer	11,000	1.084	11,924
	$111,000		$111,924

The index for year 3 is computed as follows:

	Beginning-of-year prices	*End-of-year prices*
A	$ 36,540	$ 37,120
B	81,400	85,100
	$117,940	$122,220

122,220/117,940 = 1.036

The next step is to determine the cumulative index which is the product of the preceding year's cumulative index and the current year index, or 1.123 (1.084 × 1.036). The new cumulative index is used to restate the inventory at end-of-year dollars to base-year cost. This is accomplished by dividing the end-of-year inventory by the new cumulative index. Thus, current inventory at base-year cost is $108,833 ($122,220 ÷ 1.123). In this instance we have experienced a decrement (a decrease from the prior year's $111,000). The determination of ending inventory is:

	Base-year cost	*Index*	*LIFO cost*
Base-year layer	$100,000	1.000	$100,000
Year 2 layer	8,833	1.084	9,575
Year 3 layer	–	1.123	–
	$108,833		$109,575

Finally, the same steps are performed for the year 4 computation. The current year index is 1.035 (133,900/129,380). The new cumulative index is 1.162 (1.035 × 1.123). The base-year cost of the current inventory is $115,232 (133,900/1.162). Thus, LIFO inventory at the end of year 4 is:

	Base-year cost	*Index*	*LIFO cost*
Base-year layer	$100,000	1.000	$100,000
Year 2 layer	8,833	1.084	9,575
Year 3 layer	–	1.123	–
Year 4 layer	6,399	1.162	7,435
	$115,232		$117,010

Notice how even though the numbers used were the same as those used in the double-extension example, the results were different (year 4 inventory under double-extension was $116,976)—however, not by a significant amount. It is much easier to keep track of beginning-of-the-year prices than base-year prices, but perhaps more importantly, it is easier to establish beginning-of-the-year prices for new items than to establish their base-year price. This latter reason is why the link-chain method is so much more desirable than the double-extension method. However, before electing or applying this method, a company must be able to establish a sufficient need as defined in the treasury regulations.

Indexing methods. Indexing methods can basically be broken down into two types: (1) an internal index and (2) an external index.

The internal index is merely a variation of the double-extension method. The regulations allow for the use of a statistically valid representative sample of the inventory to be double-extended. The index computed from the sample is then used to restate the inventory to base-year cost and to value the new layer.

The external index method, referred to in treasury regulations as the Inventory Price Index Computation (IPIC) Method, involves using indices published by the US Department of Labor's Bureau of Labor Statistics (BLS)[2] and applying them to specified categories of inventory included in the taxpayer's LIFO pools. Taxpayers wanting to change to the IPIC Method from another LIFO method must obtain IRS consent by filing Form 3115, *Application for Change in Accounting Method.*

Alternative LIFO method for automobile dealers. A simplified dollar-value method is available for use by retail automobile dealers for valuing inventory of new automobiles and light-duty trucks. The use of this method and its acceptance for income tax purposes is conditioned on the application of several LIFO submethods, definitions and special rules. The reader is referred to Rev. Proc. 92-79 for a further discussion of this method.

LIFO accounting literature. GAAP for the application of LIFO has been based upon income tax rules rather than on financial accounting pronouncements. LIFO is cited in GAAP as an acceptable inventory method, but specific rules regarding its implementation are not provided. The income tax regulations, as discussed below, do provide specific rules for the implementation of LIFO and require financial statement conformity. For this reason, income tax rules have essentially defined the financial accounting treatment of LIFO inventories.

In recognition of the lack of authoritative accounting guidelines in the implementation of LIFO, the American Institute of Certified Public Accountants (AICPA)'s Accounting Standards Division formed a task force on LIFO inventory problems to prepare an Issues Paper on this topic. "Identification and Discussion of Certain Financial Accounting and Reporting Issues Concerning LIFO Inventories," issued in 1984, identifies financial accounting issues resulting from the use of LIFO and includes advisory guidance on resolving them. Issues Papers,

---

2 *For more information see http://www.bls.gov.*

however, do not establish authoritative standards of financial accounting. The guidance provided by the task force is described below.[3]

1. **Specific goods versus dollar-value.** Either the specific goods approach or dollar-value approach to LIFO is acceptable for financial reporting. Disclosure of whether the specific goods or dollar-value approach is used is not required.
2. **Pricing current year purchases.** Three approaches to pricing LIFO inventory increments are available under income tax regulations—earliest acquisition price, latest acquisition price, and average acquisition price. The earliest acquisition price approach is the most compatible with financial reporting objectives, but all three are acceptable for financial reporting.
3. **Quantity to use to determine price.** The price used to determine the inventory increment should be based on the cost of the quantity or dollars of the increment rather than on the cost of the quantity or dollars equal to the ending inventory. Disclosure of which approach is used is not required.
4. **Disclosure of LIFO reserve or replacement cost.** The LIFO reserve or replacement cost and its basis for determination should be disclosed for financial reporting.
5. **Partial adoption of LIFO.** If a company changes to LIFO, it should do so for all of its inventories. Partial adoption should only be allowed if there exists a valid business reason for not fully adopting LIFO. A planned gradual adoption of LIFO over several time periods is considered acceptable if valid business reasons exist (lessening the income statement effect of adoption in any one year is not a valid business reason). Where partial adoption of LIFO has been justified, the extent to which LIFO has been adopted should be disclosed. This can be disclosed by indicating either the portion of the ending inventory priced on LIFO or the portion of cost of sales resulting from LIFO inventories.
6. **Methods of pooling.** An entity should have valid business reasons for establishing its LIFO pools. Additionally, the existence of a separate legal entity that has no economic substance is not reason enough to justify separate pools. Disclosure of details regarding an entity's pooling arrangements is not required.
7. **New items entering a pool.** New items should be added to a pool based on what the items would have cost had they been acquired in the base period (reconstructed cost) rather than based on their current cost. The reconstructed cost should be determined based on the most objective sources available, including published vendor price lists, vendor quotes, and general industry indexes. Where necessary, the use of a substitute base year in making the LIFO computation is acceptable. Disclosure of the way that new items are priced is not required.
8. **Dollar-value index.** The required index can be developed using two possible approaches, the unit cost method or the cost component method. The unit cost method measures changes in the index based on the weighted-average increase or decrease in the unit costs of raw materials, work in process, and finished goods inventory. The cost component method, on the other hand, measures changes in the index by the weighted-average increase or decrease in the component costs of material, labor, and overhead that make up ending inventory. Either of these methods is acceptable.
9. **LIFO liquidations.** The effects on income of LIFO inventory liquidations should be disclosed in the notes to the financial statements. A replacement reserve for the liquidation should not be provided. When an involuntary LIFO liquidation occurs, the effect on income of the liquidation should not be deferred.

---

[3] The issues paper can be found at tinyurl.com/8j3f8t7.

When a LIFO liquidation occurs, there are three possible ways to measure its effect on income:

a. The difference between actual cost of sales and what cost of sales would have been had the inventory been reinstated under the entity's normal pricing procedure
b. The difference between actual cost of sales and what cost of sales would have been had the inventory been reinstated at year-end replacement cost
c. The amount of the LIFO reserve at the beginning of the year which was credited to income (excluding the increase in the reserve due to current year price changes)

The first method is considered preferable. Disclosure of the effect of the liquidation should give effect only to pools with decrements (i.e., there should be no netting of pools with decrements against other pools with increments).

10. **Lower of cost or market.** The most reasonable approach to applying the lower of cost or market rules to LIFO inventory is to base the determination on groups of inventory rather than on an item-by-item approach. A pool constitutes a reasonable grouping for this purpose. An item-by-item approach is permitted by authoritative accounting literature, particularly for obsolete or discontinued items.

    For companies with more than one LIFO pool, it is permissible to aggregate the pools in applying the lower of cost or market test if the pools are similar. Where the pools are significantly dissimilar, aggregating the pools is not appropriate.

    Previous write-downs to market value of the cost of LIFO inventories should be reversed after a company disposes of the physical units of the inventory for which reserves were provided. The reserves at the end of the year should be based on a new computation of cost or market.

11. **LIFO conformity and supplemental disclosures.** A company may present supplemental non-LIFO disclosures within the historical cost framework. If nondiscretionary variable expenses (i.e., profit sharing based on earnings) would have been different based on the supplemental information, then the company should give effect to such changes. Additionally, the supplemental disclosure should reflect the same type of income tax effects as required by generally accepted accounting principles in the primary financial statements.

    A company may use different LIFO applications for financial reporting than it uses for income tax purposes. Any such differences should be accounted for as temporary differences with the exception of differences in the allocation of cost to inventory in a business combination. Any differences between LIFO applications used for financial reporting and those used for income tax purposes need not be disclosed beyond the requirements of ASC 740.

12. **Interim reporting and LIFO.** The Task Force's conclusions on interim reporting of LIFO inventory are discussed in the chapter on interim reporting.

13. **Different financial and income tax years.** A company with different fiscal year-ends for financial reporting and income tax reporting should make a separate LIFO calculation for financial purposes using its financial reporting year as a discrete period for that calculation.

14. **Business combinations accounted for by the purchase method.** Inventory acquired in a business combination accounted for by the purchase method will be recorded at fair value at the date of the combination. The acquired company may be able to carry over its prior basis for that inventory for income tax purposes, causing a difference between GAAP and income tax basis. An adjustment should be made to the fair value of the inventory only if it is reasonably estimated that it will be

liquidated in the future. The adjustment would be for the income tax effect of the difference between income tax and GAAP basis.

Inventory acquired in such a combination should be considered the LIFO base inventory if the inventory is treated by the company as a separate business unit or a separate LIFO pool. If instead the acquired inventory is combined into an existing pool, then the acquired inventory should be considered as part of the current year's purchases.

15. **Changes in LIFO applications.** A change in a LIFO application is a change in accounting principle. LIFO applications refer to the approach (i.e., dollar value or specific goods), computational technique, or the numbers or contents of the pools.

ASC 810-10-55 provides guidance for intercompany transfers. The focus of this section is the LIFO liquidation effect caused by transferring inventories, which in turn creates intercompany profits. This liquidation can occur when (1) two components of the same taxable entity transfer inventory, for example, when a LIFO method component transfers inventory to a non-LIFO component, or (2) when two separate taxable entities that consolidate transfer inventory, even though both use the LIFO method.

This LIFO liquidation creates profit that must be eliminated along with other intercompany profits.

LIFO income tax rules and restrictions. As discussed previously, most of the rules and regulations governing LIFO originate in the U.S. IRC and the related regulations, revenue rules, revenue procedures, and judicial decisions. Taxpayers electing to use the LIFO inventory method are subject to myriad rules and restrictions, such as:

1. The inventory is to be valued at cost regardless of market value (i.e., application of the lower of cost or market rule is not allowed).
2. Changes in the LIFO reserve can potentially cause the taxpayer to be subject to alternative minimum tax (AMT) or increase the amount of AMT.
3. Corporations that use the LIFO method whose stockholders subsequently elect to be taxed as an "S" Corporation are required to report as income their entire LIFO reserve resulting in a special tax under IRC §1363(d) that is payable in four annual installments. The "S" Corporation is, however, permitted to retain LIFO as its inventory accounting method after the election.
4. Once elected, the LIFO method must continue to be used consistently in future periods. A taxpayer is permitted, subject to certain restrictions, to revoke its LIFO election in accordance with Rev. Proc. 99-49. After revocation however, the taxpayer is precluded from reelecting LIFO for a period of five taxable years beginning with the year of the change. For GAAP purposes, a change to or from the LIFO method is accounted for as a change in accounting principle under ASC 250.

A unique rule regarding LIFO inventories is referred to as the LIFO Conformity Rule. A taxpayer may not use a different inventory method in reporting profit or loss of the entity for external financial reports. Thus, if LIFO is elected for income tax purposes, it must also be used for accounting purposes.

Treasury regulations permit certain exceptions to this general rule. Among the exceptions allowable under the regulations are the following:

1. The use of an inventory method other than LIFO in presenting information reported as a supplement to or explanation of the taxpayer's primary presentation of income in financial reports to outside parties. (Reg. §1.472-2[e][1][i])
2. The use of an inventory method other than LIFO to determine the value of the taxpayer's inventory for purposes of reporting the value of such inventory as an asset on the statement of financial position. (Reg. §1.472-2[e][1][ii])

3. The use of an inventory method other than LIFO for purposes of determining information reported in internal management reports. (Reg. §1.472-2[e][1][iii])
4. The use of an inventory method other than LIFO for financial reports covering a period of less than one year. (Reg. §1.472- 2[e][1][iv])
5. The use of lower of LIFO cost or market to value inventories for financial statements while using LIFO cost for income tax purposes. (Reg. §1.472-2[e][1][v])
6. For inventories acquired by a corporation in exchange for issuing stock to a stockholder that, immediately after the exchange, is considered to have control (a section 351 transaction), the use of the transferor's acquisition dates and costs for GAAP while using redetermined LIFO layers for tax purposes. (Reg. §1.472-2[e][1][vii])
7. The inclusion of certain costs (under full absorption) in inventory for income tax purposes, as required by regulations, while not including those same costs in inventory under GAAP (full absorption). (Reg. §1.472-2[e][8][i])
8. The use of different methods of establishing pools for GAAP purposes and income tax purposes. (Reg. §1.472-2[e][8][ii])
9. The use of different determinations of the time sales or purchases are accrued for GAAP purposes and tax purposes. (Reg. §1.472-2[e][8][xii])
10. In the case of a business combination, the use of different methods to allocate basis for GAAP purposes and income tax purposes. (Reg. §1.472-29[e][8][xiii])

Another important consideration in applying the LIFO conformity rule is the law concerning related corporations. In accordance with the Tax Reform Act of 1984, all members of the same group of financially related corporations are treated as a single taxpayer when applying the conformity rule. Previously, taxpayers were able to circumvent the conformity rule by having a subsidiary on LIFO, while the non-LIFO parent presented combined non-LIFO financial statements. This is a violation of the conformity requirement [Sec. 472(g)].

The LIFO conformity rule is viewed as a major obstacle to the adoption of International Financial Reporting Standards (IFRS) in the United States. Since IFRS does not permit the use of LIFO for valuing inventories, should a U.S. taxpayer convert from U.S. GAAP to IFRS in presenting its basic financial statements, that taxpayer would violate the LIFO conformity rule, which would result in an automatic revocation of the LIFO election. Thus, the adoption of IFRS would likely cause a heavy income tax burden for those taxpayers using LIFO to value their inventories.

Weighted-average and moving-average. Another method of inventory valuation involves averaging and is commonly referred to as the weighted-average method.

Under this method the cost of goods available for sale (beginning inventory plus net purchases) is divided by the number of units available for sale to obtain a weighted-average cost per unit. Ending inventory and cost of goods sold are then priced at this average cost.

Example of the weighted-average method

Assume the following data:

	Units available	*Units sold*	*Actual unit cost*	*Actual total cost*
Beginning inventory	100	–	$2.10	$210
Sale	–	75	–	–
Purchase	150	–	2.80	420
Sale	–	100	–	–
Purchase	50	–	3.00	150
Total	300	175		$780

The weighted-average cost per unit is $780/300, or $2.60. Ending inventory is 125 units (300 – 175) at $2.60, or $325; cost of goods sold is 175 units at $2.60, or $455.

When the weighted-average assumption is applied using a perpetual inventory system, the average cost is recomputed after each purchase. This process is referred to as a moving average. Cost of goods sold is recorded using the most recent average. This combination is called the moving-average method and is applied below to the same data used in the weighted-average example above.

	Units on hand	*Purchases in dollars*	*Cost of sales in dollars*	*Inventory total cost*	*Inventory moving-average unit cost*
Beginning inventory	100	$ –	$ –	$210.00	$2.10
Sale (75 units @ $2.10)	25	–	157.50	52.50	2.10
Purchase (150 units, $420)	175	420.00	–	472.50	2.70
Sale (100 units @ $2.70)	75	–	270.00	202.50	2.70
Purchase (50 units, $150)	125	150.00	–	352.50	2.82

Cost of goods sold is 75 units at $2.10 and 100 units at $2.70, or $427.50.

This method is permitted for financial reporting purposes but had historically been prohibited for income tax purposes (Rev. Ruling 71-234). The IRS has issued Revenue Procedure 2008-43, which grants limited use of this method for income tax reporting purposes. This relief is only available to taxpayers that were already using an average cost method for financial reporting purposes. In addition, an electing taxpayer is required to meet both of the following safe harbors:

1. The taxpayer must recompute the rolling average inventory price with every new purchase, or no less frequently than monthly.
2. The results under the rolling average method may not vary by more than 1% from the results using a FIFO or specific identification method. A shortcut method is permitted to be used to meet this safe harbor. If the taxpayer's annual turnover for its entire inventory exceeds four times, this safe harbor is considered to have been met.

Comparison of cost flow assumptions. Of the three cost flow assumptions, FIFO and LIFO produce the most extreme results, while results from using the weighted-average method generally fall somewhere in between. The selection of one of these methods involves a detailed analysis of the organization's objectives, industry practices, current and expected future economic conditions, and most importantly, the needs of the intended users of the financial statements.

The following table compares the relative effects of using FIFO and LIFO cost assumptions on the statement of financial position and statement of income under differing economic conditions:

Changes in price levels	*Relative effect on statement of financial position*		*Relative effect on statement of income*	
	FIFO	*LIFO*	*FIFO*	*LIFO*
Inflation (i.e., rising prices)	Higher inventory carrying value	Lower inventory carrying value	Lower cost of sales; higher gross profit and net income	Higher cost of sales; lower gross profit and net income
Deflation (i.e., falling prices)	Lower inventory carrying value	Higher inventory carrying value	Higher cost of sales; lower gross profit and net income	Lower cost of sales; higher gross profit and net income

In periods of rising prices, the LIFO method is generally thought to best fulfill the objective of providing the clearest measure of periodic net income. It does not, however, provide an accurate estimate of inventory cost in an inflationary environment. However, this shortcoming can usually be overcome by providing additional disclosures in the notes to the financial statements. In periods of rising prices, a prudent business should use the LIFO method because it will result in a decrease in the current income tax liability when compared to other alternatives. In a deflationary period, the opposite is true.

FIFO is a balance-sheet-oriented costing method. It gives the most accurate estimate of the current cost of inventory during periods of changing prices. In periods of rising prices, the FIFO method will result in higher income taxes than the other alternatives, while in a deflationary period FIFO provides for a lesser income tax burden. However, a major advantage of the FIFO method is that it is not subject to all of the complex regulations and requirements of the income tax code that govern the use of LIFO.

The average methods do not provide an estimate of current cost information on either the statement of financial position or income statement. The average methods are not permitted to be used for income tax purposes and therefore, their use for financial reporting purposes would necessitate the use of FIFO for income tax reporting purposes since LIFO requires financial statement conformity.

Although price trends and underlying objectives are important to consider in selecting a cost flow assumption, other considerations are the risk of experiencing unintended liquidations of LIFO layers, as well as the effects of the chosen method on cash flow, capital maintenance, collateral requirements, and restrictive covenants imposed by lenders, etc.

Lower of Cost or Market (LCM)

As stated in ASC 330-10-20:

> *...as used in the phrase lower of cost or market, the term market means current replacement cost, provided that it meets both the following conditions: a) market shall not exceed the net realizable value, and b) market shall not be less than net realizable value reduced by an allowance for an approximately normal profit margin.*

Inventory can lose value for a variety of reasons including damage, spoilage, obsolescence, changes in market prices, and the like. The application of LCM is a means of attempting to measure loss of value and recognize the effects in the period in which this occurs.

The term "market" means current replacement cost not to exceed a ceiling of net realizable value (selling price less reasonably estimable costs of completion and disposal) or be less than a floor of net realizable value adjusted for a normal profit margin.

LCM is not applied in conjunction with the LIFO method of inventory valuation for income tax purposes. However, it is important to note that LCM/LIFO is applied for financial reporting purposes. Such application gives rise to a temporary difference in the carrying value of inventory between financial statements and income tax returns. LCM/LIFO for financial reporting was discussed earlier in this chapter.

LCM may be applied to either the entire inventory or to each individual inventory item. The primary objective for selecting between the alternative methods of applying the LCM rule is to select the one that most clearly reflects periodic income. The rule is most commonly applied to the inventory on an item-by-item basis. The reason for this application is twofold.

1. It is required by income tax purposes unless it involves practical difficulties, and
2. It provides the most conservative valuation of inventories, because decreases in the value of one item are not offset by increases in the value of another.

Example of the lower of cost or market calculation

The application of these principles is illustrated in this example. Assume the following information for products A, B, C, D, and E:

Item	*Cost*	*Replacement cost*	*Est. selling price*	*Cost to complete*	*Normal profit percentage*	*Normal profit amount*
A	$2.00	$1.80	$ 2.50	$0.50	24%	$0.60
B	4.00	1.60	4.00	0.80	24%	0.96
C	6.00	6.60	10.00	1.00	18%	1.80
D	5.00	4.75	6.00	2.00	20%	1.20
E	1.00	1.05	1.20	0.25	12.5%	0.15

First, determine the market value and then compare this to historical cost. Market value is equal to the replacement cost, but cannot exceed the net realizable value (NRV) nor be below net realizable value less the normal profit percentage.

Market Determination

Item	*Cost*	*Replacement cost*	*NRV (ceiling)*	*NRV less profit (floor)*	*Market*	*LCM*
A	$2.00	$1.80	$2.00	$1.40	$1.80	$1.80
B	4.00	1.60	3.20	2.24	2.24	2.24
C	6.00	6.60	9.00	7.20	7.20	6.00
D	5.00	4.75	4.00	2.80	4.00	4.00
E	1.00	1.05	0.95	0.80	0.95	0.95

NRV (ceiling) equals selling price less costs of completion (e.g., item A: $2.50 – .50 = $2.00). NRV less profit (floor) is self-descriptive (e.g., item A: $2.50 – .50 –.60 = $1.40). Market is replacement cost unless lower than the floor or higher than the ceiling. Note that market must be designated before LCM is determined. Finally, LCM is the lower of cost or market value.

Replacement cost is a valid measure of the future utility of the inventory item, since increases or decreases in the enterprise's purchase price generally foreshadow related increases or decreases in the price at which it is able to sell the item. The ceiling and the floor provide safeguards against the recognition of either excessive profits or excessive losses in future periods in those instances where the selling price and replacement cost do not move in the same direction in a proportional manner. The ceiling avoids the recognition of additional losses in the future when the selling price is falling faster than replacement cost. Without the ceiling constraint, inventories would be carried at an amount in excess of their net realizable value. The floor avoids the recognition of abnormal profits in the future when replacement cost is falling faster than the selling price. Without the floor, inventories would be carried at a value less than their net realizable value minus a normal profit.

The loss from writing inventories down to LCM is generally reflected on the income statement in cost of goods sold. If material, the loss must be separately captioned in the income statement. While GAAP is not explicit as to presentation, it would appear that this adjustment could either be displayed as a separately identified charge within cost of goods sold, or as an administrative expense. The write-down is recorded as a debit to a loss account and a credit either to an inventory or a valuation allowance account.

Inventory estimation methods. There are instances in which an accountant must estimate the value of inventories without an actual physical count. Some of the estimation methods used to accomplish this are the retail method, the LIFO retail method, and the gross profit method. These methods are not cost flow assumptions like LIFO and FIFO; rather, they are computational methods that have been devised to assist in estimating inventory cost under the relevant cost flow assumption.

Retail method. The retail method is used by retailers to estimate the cost of their ending inventory. The retailer can either take a physical inventory at retail prices or estimate ending retail inventory and then use a computed cost-to-retail ratio to convert the ending inventory priced at retail to its estimated cost. This method eliminates the process of going back to original vendor invoices or other documents in order to determine the original cost for each inventoriable item. The retail method can be used under any of the three cost flow assumptions discussed earlier: FIFO, LIFO, or average cost. As with ordinary FIFO or average cost, the LCM rule is also applied when either one of these two cost assumptions is used in conjunction with the retail method.

The key to applying the retail method is determining the cost-to-retail ratio. The calculation of this ratio varies depending upon the cost flow assumption selected. The cost-to-retail ratio provides a measure of the relationship between the cost of goods available for sale and the retail price of these same goods. This ratio is used to convert the ending retail inventory back to cost. The computation of the cost-to-retail ratio for the FIFO and average cost methods is described below. The use of the LIFO cost flow assumption with this method is discussed in the succeeding section.

1. **FIFO cost**—The FIFO method assumes that the ending inventory is made up of the latest purchases. Therefore, beginning inventory is excluded from the computation of the cost-to-retail ratio, and the computation uses the cost of current year net purchases divided by their retail value adjusted for both net markups and net markdowns as will be further explained and illustrated.
2. **FIFO (LCM)**—The computation is basically the same as FIFO cost, except that markdowns are excluded from the computation of the cost-to-retail ratio.
3. **Average cost**—Average cost assumes that ending inventory consists of all goods available for sale. Therefore, the cost-to-retail ratio is computed by dividing the cost of goods available for sale (Beginning inventory + Net purchases) by the retail value of these goods adjusted for both net markups and net markdowns.
4. **Average cost (LCM)**—Is computed in the same manner as average cost, except that markdowns are excluded from the calculation of the cost-to-retail ratio.

Example of the cost-to-retail ratio

A simple example illustrates the computation of the cost-to-retail ratio under both the FIFO cost and average cost methods in a situation where no markups or markdowns exist.

	FIFO cost		*Average cost*	
	Cost	*Retail*	*Cost*	*Retail*
Beginning inventory	$100,000	$ 200,000	$100,000	$ 200,000
Net purchases	500,000 (a)	800,000 (b)	500,000	800,000
Total goods available for sale	$600,000	1,000,000	$600,000 (c)	1,000,000 (d)
Sales at retail		(800,000)		(800,000)
Ending inventory—retail		$ 200,000		$ 200,000
Cost-to-retail ratio	(a) 500,000 / (b) 800,000	= 62.5%	(a) 600,000 / (b)1,00,000	= 60%
Ending inventory—cost				
200,000 × 62.5%		$ 125,000		
200,000 × 60%				$ 120,000

Note that the only difference in the two examples is the numbers used to calculate the cost-to-retail ratio.

The lower of cost or market aspect of the retail method is a result of the treatment of net markups and net markdowns. Net markups (markups less markup cancellations) are net increases above the original retail price, which are generally caused by changes in supply and demand. Net markdowns (markdowns less markdown cancellations) are net decreases below the original retail price. An approximation of "lower of cost or market" pricing is achieved by including net markups but excluding net markdowns, from the cost-to-retail ratio.

To understand this approximation, assume a toy is purchased for $6, and the retail price is set at $10. It is later marked down to $8. A cost-to-retail ratio including markdowns would be $6 divided by $8 or 75%, and ending inventory would be valued at $8 times 75%, or $6 (original cost). The logic behind including markdowns in the cost-to-retail ratio is the assumption that these inventories would eventually be marked down and that markdowns are a normal part of business for this enterprise and/or these types of inventories. A cost-to-retail ratio excluding markdowns would be $6 divided by $10 or 60%, and ending inventory would be valued at $8 times 60%, or $4.80 (LCM). The logic behind excluding markdowns from the cost-to-retail ratio is that the enterprise did not expect to mark these inventory items down and that this is not a normal occurrence. The write-down to $4.80 reflects the loss in utility which is evidenced by the reduced retail price.

The application of the lower of cost or market rule is illustrated for both the FIFO and average cost methods in the example below. Remember, if the markups and markdowns below had been included in the previous example, both would have been included in the cost-to-retail ratio.

Example of the lower of cost or market rule – FIFO and average cost methods

	FIFO cost (LCM)			*Average cost (LCM)*		
	Cost	*Retail*		*Cost*	*Retail*	
Beginning inventory	$100,000	$ 200,000		$100,000	$ 200,000	
Net purchases	500,000 (a)	800,000 (b)		500,000	800,000	
Net markups	–	250,000 (b)		–	250,000	
Total goods available for sale	$600,000	1,250,000		$600,000 (c)	1,250,000 (d)	
Net markdowns		(50,000)			(50,000)	
Sales at retail		(800,000)			(800,000)	
Ending inventory—retail		$ 400,000			$ 400,000	
Cost-to-retail ratio	(a) 500,000 / (b) 1,050,000 =	47.6%		(c) 600,000 / (d) 1,250,000 =	48%	
Ending inventory—LCM						
400,000 × 47.6%		$ 190,400				
400,000 × 48%					$ 192,000	

Under the FIFO (LCM) method all of the markups are considered attributable to the current period purchases. While this is not necessarily accurate, it provides the most conservative estimate of the ending inventory.

There are a number of additional issues that affect the computation of the cost-to-retail ratio. Purchase discounts and freight-in affect only the cost column in this computation. The sales figure that is subtracted from the adjusted cost of goods available for sale in the retail column must be gross sales after adjustment for sales returns. Sales discounts are not included in the computation. If sales are recorded gross, then deduct the gross sales figure. If sales are recorded net, then both the recorded sales and sales discount must be deducted to give the same effect as deducting gross sales. Normal spoilage is generally allowed for in the enterprise's pricing policies, and for this reason it is deducted from the retail column after the calculation of the cost-to-retail ratio. Abnormal spoilage, on the other hand, is deducted from both the cost and retail columns before the cost-to-retail calculation as it could otherwise distort the ratio. It is then generally reported as a separate loss, either within cost of goods sold or administrative expenses. Abnormal spoilage generally arises from a major theft or casualty, while normal spoilage is usually due to shrinkage or breakage. These determinations and their treatments will vary depending upon the enterprise's policies.

When applying the retail method, separate computations are made for any departments that experience significantly higher or lower gross profit margins. Distortions arise in applying the retail method when a department sells goods with gross profit margins that vary in a proportion different from the gross profit margins of goods purchased during the period. In this case, the cost-to-retail percentage would not be representative of the mix of goods in ending inventory. Also, manipulations of income are possible by planning the timing of markups and markdowns.

The retail method is an acceptable method of estimating inventories under FIFO (LCM) for income tax purposes. Income tax regulations require valuation at lower of cost or market (except for LIFO) and regular and consistent physical counts of inventory at each location.

LIFO retail method. As with other LIFO methods, treasury regulations are the governing force behind the LIFO retail method. The regulations differentiate between a "variety" store, which is required to use an internally computed index, and a "department" store, which is permitted to use a price index published by the Bureau of Labor Statistics. The computation of an internal index was previously discussed in the dollar-value LIFO section. It involves applying the double-extension method to a representative sample of the ending inventory. Selection of an externally published index is to be in accordance with the Treasury regulations.

The steps used in computing the value of ending inventory under the LIFO retail method are listed below and then applied in an example for illustrative purposes.

1. Calculate (or select) the current year conversion price index. Recall that in the base year this index will be 1.00.
2. Calculate the value of the ending inventory at both cost and retail. Remember, as with other LIFO methods, income tax regulations do not permit the use of LCM, so both markups and markdowns are included in the computation of the cost-to-retail ratio. However, the beginning inventory is excluded from goods available for sale at cost and at retail.
3. Restate the ending inventory at retail to base-year retail. Divide the current ending inventory at retail by the current year index determined in Step 1.
4. Layers are then treated as they were for the dollar-value LIFO example presented earlier. If the ending inventory restated to base-year retail exceeds the previous year's amount at base-year retail, a new layer is established.
5. The computation of LIFO cost is the last step and requires multiplying each layer at base-year retail by the appropriate price index and multiplying this product by the cost-to-retail ratio in order to arrive at the LIFO cost for each layer.

Example of the LIFO retail method

The following example illustrates a two-year period to which the LIFO retail method is applied. The first period represents the first year of operations for the company and is its base year.

Year 1

Step 1—Because this is the base year, there is no need to compute an index, as it will always be 1.00.

Step 2—

	Cost	*Retail*
Beginning inventory	$ –	$ –
Purchases	582,400	988,600
Markups	–	164,400
Markdowns	–	(113,000)
Subtotal	582,400	1,040,000
Total goods available for sale	$582,400	1,040,000
Sales—at retail		840,000
Ending year 1 inventory—at retail		$ 200,000

Cost-to-retail ratio $\frac{(a)\ 582{,}400}{(b)\ 1{,}040{,}000}$ = 56%

Ending inventory at cost $200,000 × 56% $112,000

Step 3—Because this is the base year, the restatement to base-year cost is not necessary; however, the computation would be $200,000/1.00 = $200,000.

Steps 4 and 5—The determination of layers is again unnecessary in the base year; however, the computation would take the following format:

	Ending inventory at base-year retail	*Conversion price index*	*Cost-to-retail ratio*	*LIFO cost*
Base year ($200,000/1.00)	$200,000	1.00	0.56	$112,000

Year 2

Step 1—We make the assumption that the computation of an internal index yields a result of 1.12 (obtained by double-extending a representative sample).

Step 2—

	Cost	*Retail*
Beginning inventory	$112,000	$ 200,000
Purchases	716,300	1,168,500
Markups	–	87,500
Markdowns	–	(21,000)
Subtotal	$716,300	1,235,000
Total goods available for sale		1,435,000
Sales—at retail		1,171,800
Ending year 2 inventory—at retail		$ 263,200

Cost-to-retail ratio $\frac{716{,}300}{1{,}235{,}000}$ = 58%

Step 3—The restatement of ending inventory at current year retail to base-year retail is done using the index computed in Step 1. In this case it is $263,200/1.12 = $235,000.

Steps 4 and 5—There is a LIFO layer in year 2 because the $235,000 inventory at base-year retail exceeds the year 1 amount of $200,000.

The computation of the LIFO cost for each layer is shown below.

	Ending inventory at base-year retail	*Conversion price index*	*Cost-to-retail ratio*	*LIFO cost*
Base year ($200,000/1.00)	$200,000	1.00	0.56	$112,000
Year 2 layer	35,000	1.12	0.58	22,736
	$235,000			
Ending year 2 inventory at LIFO cost				$134,736

The treatment of subsequent increments and decrements is the same for this method as it is for the regular dollar-value method.

Gross profit method. The gross profit method is used to estimate ending inventory when a physical count is not taken. It can also be used to evaluate the reasonableness of a given inventory amount. Assume the following data:

Beginning inventory	$125,000
Net purchases	450,000
Sales	600,000
Estimated gross profit percentage	32%

Ending inventory is estimated as follows:

Beginning inventory	$125,000
Net purchases	450,000
Cost of goods available for sale	575,000
Cost of goods sold [$600,000 – (32% × $600,000)] or (68% × $600,000)	408,000
Estimated ending inventory	$167,000

The gross profit method is used for interim reporting estimates, for conducting analytical review procedures by independent accountants in audits and review engagements, and for estimating inventory lost in fires or other catastrophes. The method is not acceptable, however, for either income tax or annual financial reporting purposes.

Standard costs. Standard costs are predetermined unit costs used by manufacturing firms for planning and control purposes. Standard costs are often used to develop approximations of GAAP inventories for financial reporting purposes. The use of standard cost approximations in financial reporting is acceptable only if adjustments to the standards are made periodically to reflect current conditions and if their use approximates the results that would be obtained by directly applying one of the recognized cost flow assumptions.

Example of standard costing

The Bavarian Clock Company (BCC) uses standard costing to value its FIFO inventory. One of its products is the Men's Chronometer wristwatch, for which the following bill of materials has been constructed:

Part description	*Quantity*	*Cost*
Titanium watch casing	1	$212.25
Leather strap	1	80.60
Scratch resistant crystal bezel	1	120.15
Double timer shock-resistant movement	1	42.80
Multilingual instruction sheet	1	0.80
Ornamental box	1	2.75
Overhead charge	1	28.00
Total		$487.35

The industrial engineering department designed the following labor routing for assembly of the Men's Chronometer and determined the standard process times:

Labor routing description	*Quantity/ minutes*	*Labor type*	*Cost/ minute*	*Cost*
Quality review of raw materials received	3.5	Quality assurance	$0.42	$ 1.47
Attach strap to casing	7.5	Watch maker	0.79	5.93
Insert movement in casing	10.8	Watch maker	0.79	8.53
Attach bezel	3.2	Watch maker	0.79	2.53
Final quality review and testing	11.0	Quality assurance	0.42	4.62
Insert into packing case	1.5	Assembler	0.13	.20
Total	37.5			$23.28

Thus, the total standard cost of the Men's Chronometer is $510.63 ($487.35 material and overhead cost + $23.28 labor cost). At the beginning of December, there are 1,087 Men's Chronometers in finished goods inventory, which are recorded at standard cost, resulting in a beginning inventory valuation of $555,054.81 (= $510.63 × 1,087 units).

During December, BCC records actual material costs of $1,915,312.19, actual labor costs of $111,844.40, and actual overhead costs of $124,831.55 related to the Men's Chronometer, which are charged to the inventory account. During the month, BCC manufactures 4,105 Men's Chronometers and ships 4,385, leaving 807 units in finished goods inventory. At a standard cost of $510.63 per unit, this results in a month-end finished goods inventory balance of $412,078.41. The monthly charge to cost of goods sold is calculated as follows:

Beginning inventory at standard cost	$ 555,054.81
+ Actual material costs incurred	1,915,312.19
+ Actual labor costs incurred	111,844.40
+ Actual overhead costs incurred	124,831.55
– Ending inventory at standard cost	(412,078.41)
= Cost of goods sold	$2,294,964.54

At month-end, the purchasing manager conducts his quarterly review of the bill of materials and determines that the cost of the bezel has permanently increased by $4.82, bringing the total standard bezel cost to $124.97 and therefore the total standard cost of the Men's Chronometer to $515.45. This increases the value of the ending inventory by $3,889.74 ($4.82 standard cost increase × 807 units in finished goods inventory), to $415,968.15, while reducing the cost of goods sold to $2,291,074.80. The following entry records the month-end inventory valuation at standard cost:

Cost of goods sold	2,291,074.80	
Finished goods inventory		2,291,074.80

As a cross-check, BCC's controller divides the cost of goods sold by the total number of units shipped, and arrives at an actual unit cost of $522.48, as opposed to the standard costs of $515.45. The variance from the standard cost is $7.03 per unit, or a total of $30,826.55. Upon further investigation, she finds that overnight delivery charges of $1,825 were incurred for a shipment of watch casings, while there was a temporary increase in the cost of the leather strap of $2.83 for a 1,000-unit purchase, resulting in an additional charge of $2,830. She elects to separately track these excess material-related costs with the following entry:

Material price variance	4,655.00	
Cost of goods sold		4,655.00

In addition, the production staff incurred overtime charges of $16,280 during the month. Since overtime is not included in the labor routing standard costs, the controller separately tracks this information with the following entry:

Labor price variance	16,280.00	
Cost of goods sold		16,280.00

Finally, the controller determines that some costs comprising the overhead cost pool exceeded the budgeted overhead cost during the month, resulting in an excess charge of $9,891.55 to the Men's Chronometer cost of goods sold. She separates this expense from the cost of goods sold with the following entry:

Overhead price variance	9,891.55	
Cost of goods sold		9,891.55

Her variance analysis has identified all causes of the $30,826.55 cost overage, as noted in the following table:

Total cost of goods sold	$ 2,291,074.80
– Standard cost of goods sold	(2,260,248.25)
– Material price variance	(4,655.00)
– Labor price variance	(16,280.00)
– Overhead price variance	(9,891.55)
= Remaining unresolved variance	–

As explained previously, variances resulting from abnormal costs incurred are considered period costs and, thus, are not allocated to inventory.

Other inventory valuation methods.

Base stock. The base stock method assumes that a certain level of inventory investment is necessary for normal business activities and is, therefore, permanent. The base stock inventory is carried at historical cost. Decreases in the base stock are considered temporary and are charged to cost of goods sold at replacement cost. Increases are carried at current year costs. The base stock approach is seldom used in practice, since it is not allowed for income tax purposes, and the LIFO method yields similar results.

Direct costing. An alternative to full absorption costing is direct costing. Direct costing (also referred to as variable costing) requires classifying only direct materials, direct labor, and variable production overhead as inventory costs. Under this method, all fixed costs are accounted for as period costs. The exclusion of all overhead from inventory costs is not an acceptable accounting method for GAAP or under the US Treasury Regulations for income tax purposes.

Relative sales value. Relative sales (or net realizable) values are used to assign costs to inventory items purchased or manufactured in groups. This method is applicable to joint products, subdivided assets such as real estate lots, and basket purchases.

For example, products A and B have the same processes performed on them up to the split-off point. The total cost incurred to this point is $80,000. This cost can be assigned to products A and B using their relative sales value at the split-off point. If A could be sold for $60,000 and B for $40,000, the total sales value is $100,000. The cost would be assigned on the basis of each product's relative sales value. Thus, A would be assigned a cost of $48,000 (60,000/100,000 × 80,000) and B a cost of $32,000 (40,000/100,000 × 80,000).

Differences between GAAP and Income Tax Accounting for Inventories

Full absorption costing—income tax. The Tax Reform Act (TRA) of 1986 included provisions referred to as Uniform Capitalization (UNICAP) requiring certain additional indirect costs that are not capitalizable under GAAP be capitalized rather than expensed for income tax purposes.

1. Depreciation and amortization in excess of that reported in financial statements
2. Percentage depletion in excess of cost
3. Rework labor, scrap, and spoilage costs
4. Allocable general and administrative costs related to the production function.

For income tax purposes, these costs, as well as the indirect production costs listed above for inventory costing under GAAP, are allocated to the WIP and finished goods inventories. Examples of general and administrative costs that must be allocated include payroll department costs, wages of security guards, and the president's salary. The difference between the GAAP and income tax inventory carrying values is a temporary difference, which requires deferred income tax accounting (discussed in Chapter 24).

Uniform capitalization rules—income tax versus GAAP. TRA 1986 established the UNICAP rules for inventory costs for tax purposes. ASC 330-10-55 states that capitalizing a cost for income tax purposes does not, by itself, indicate that it is preferable or even appropriate to capitalize the cost for financial reporting purposes. Although a cost may be required to be capitalized for income tax purposes, management must analyze the individual facts and circumstances based on the nature of its operations and industry practice to determine whether to capitalize the cost for financial reporting purposes.

Inventory capitalization for retailers/wholesalers—income tax versus GAAP. Prior to TRA 1986, retailers and wholesalers recorded their inventory as the invoice price plus the cost of applicable sales tax and freight-in under both GAAP and income tax law. TRA 1986 applied UNICAP to certain retailers and wholesalers and introduced a requirement that additional costs be capitalized. Inventories of retailers/wholesalers whose average annual gross receipts for the preceding three years are $10 million or less are exempt from applying UNICAP.

The costs which must be capitalized have been divided into two categories. The first category is direct costs and includes the inventory invoice price plus transportation. Also included in direct costs is the cost of labor for purchasing, storing, and handling inventory items. The second category is indirect costs and consists of any costs that directly benefit or are incurred because of the performance of a resale activity. The following types of indirect costs must be capitalized under UNICAP:

1. Off-site storage or warehousing
2. Purchasing
3. Handling, processing, assembly, and repackaging
4. Allocable general and administrative costs related to the above three functions.

The indirect costs are allocated between inventory and cost of goods sold by using traditional methods (specific identification, standard costing methods, etc.) or one of three simplified methods. Temporary differences require deferred income tax accounting as discussed in the chapter on ASC 740, *Income Taxes.*

Other Inventory Topics

Purchase commitments. Purchase commitments generally are not recognized in the financial statements because they are executory in nature. However, disclosure in the notes to the financial statements is required for firm purchase commitments that are material in amount.

If at the date of a statement of financial position the contract price of these commitments exceeds the market value, the estimated loss is accrued and reported as a loss in the income statement. This results in recognition of the loss before the inventory is actually purchased.

Inventories valued at selling price. In exceptional cases, inventories may be reported at sales price less estimated disposal costs. Such treatment is justified when cost is difficult to determine, quoted market prices are available, marketability is assured, and units are interchangeable. Precious metals, certain agricultural products, and meat are examples of inventories valued in this manner. When inventory is valued above cost, revenue is recognized before the time of sale. Naturally full disclosure in the financial statements is required.

Stripping costs incurred during production in the mining industry. ASC 930-330 states that stripping costs incurred during a mine's production phase are to be accounted for as variable production costs and therefore allocated to inventory. The ASC is limited to stripping costs incurred during the period when inventory is being produced (i.e., extracted) and did not address the accounting for these costs when incurred during the preproduction phase of the mine.

Interim reporting. The principles used to determine ending inventory and cost of goods sold in annual reports are also used in interim reports, although four exceptions are allowed (under ASC 270). These are:

1. The gross profit method may be used to estimate cost of goods sold and ending inventory.
2. When LIFO layers are liquidated during the interim period but are expected to be replaced by year-end, cost of goods sold is adjusted to reflect current costs rather than older LIFO costs.
3. Temporary market declines need not be recognized if substantial evidence exists that market prices will recover. If LCM losses are recorded in one or more interim periods and are recovered by year-end, the recovery is recognized as a fourth-quarter gain
4. Planned standard cost variances expected to reverse by year-end are not recognized.

For a complete discussion of interim financial reporting see the chapter on ASC 270.

23 ASC 340 OTHER ASSETS AND DEFERRED COSTS

PERSPECTIVE AND ISSUES

Subtopics

ASC 340, *Other Assets and Deferred Costs,* contains three subtopics:

- ASC 340-10, *Overall,* which provides guidance on certain deferred costs and prepaid expenses.
- ASC 340-20, *Capitalized Advertising Costs,* which provides guidance on the initial measurement, amortization, realizability, and disclosure of direct response advertising costs reported as assets.
- ASC 340-30, *Insurance Contracts that Do Not Transfer Insurance Risk,* which provides guidance on how to apply the deposit method of accounting when it is required for insurance and reinsurance contracts that do not transfer risk.

The guidance in ASC 340-10 is limited to a discussion of the nature of prepaid expenses and guidance for preproduction costs related to long-term supply arrangements. The specific guidance for many other deferred costs is included in various other areas of the Codification.

Scope and Scope Exceptions

Per ASC 340-20-15-4:

"Direct-response advertising activities exclude advertising that, though related to the direct-response advertising, is directed to an audience that could not be shown to have responded specifically to the direct-response advertising. For example, a television commercial announcing that order forms (that are direct-response advertising) soon will be distributed directly to some people in the viewing area would not be a direct-response advertising activity because the television commercial is directed to a broad audience, not all of which could be shown to have responded specifically to the direct-response advertising."

ASC 340-30-15 provides guidance on which transactions are covered and which are not covered by subtopic ASC 340-30. The guidance in the Subtopic includes the following transactions

- Short-duration insurance and reinsurance contracts that do not transfer insurance risk as described in paragraph 720-20-25-1 and, for reinsurance contracts, as described in Section 944-20-15
- Multiple-year insurance and reinsurance contracts that do not transfer insurance risk or for which insurance risk transfer is not determinable.
  (ASC 340-30-15-3)

The guidance in ASC 340-30 does not apply to the following transactions and activities:

- Long-duration life and health insurance contracts that do not indemnify against mortality or morbidity risk shall be accounted for as investment contracts under Topic 944. Therefore, such contracts are not covered by this Subtopic.
  (ASC 340-30-15-4)

Overview

Prepaid expenses are amounts paid to secure the use of assets or the receipt of services at a future date or continuously over one or more future periods. Prepaid expenses will not be converted to cash, but they are classified as current assets because, if they are not prepaid, they would have required the use of current assets during the coming year (or operating cycle, if longer).

Manufacturers often incur preproduction costs related to products and services they will supply to their customers under long-term arrangements. The supplier may be contractually guaranteed reimbursement of design and development costs, implicitly guaranteed reimbursement of design and development costs through the pricing of the product or other means, or not guaranteed reimbursement of the design and development costs incurred under the long-term supply arrangement.

DEFINITION OF TERMS

Source: ASC 340-30-20

Assuming Entity. The party that receives a reinsurance premium in a reinsurance transaction. The assuming entity (or reinsurer) accepts an obligation to reimburse a ceding entity under the terms of the reinsurance contract.

Ceding Entity. The party that pays a reinsurance premium in a reinsurance transaction. The ceding entity receives the right to reimbursement from the assuming entity under the terms of the reinsurance contract.

Experience Adjustment. A provision in an insurance or reinsurance contract that modifies the premium, coverage, commission, or a combination of the three, in whole or in part, based on experience under the contract.

Insurance Risk. The risk arising from uncertainties about both underwriting risk and timing risk. Actual or imputed investment returns are not an element of insurance risk. Insurance risk is fortuitous; the possibility of adverse events occurring is outside the control of the insured.

Timing Risk. The risk arising from uncertainties about the timing of the receipt and payments of the net cash flows from premiums, commissions, claims, and claim settlement expenses paid under a contract.

Underwriting Risk. The risk arising from uncertainties about the ultimate amount of net cash flows from premiums, commissions, claims, and claim settlement expenses paid under a contract.

CONCEPTS, RULES, AND EXAMPLES

Prepaid Expenses

Types of prepaid expenses. Prepaid expenses are amounts paid to secure the use of assets or the receipt of services at a future date or continuously over one or more future periods. Prepaid expenses will not be converted to cash, but they are classified as current assets because, if they are not prepaid, they would have required the use of current assets during the coming year (or operating cycle, if longer). Examples of items that are often prepaid include dues, subscriptions, maintenance agreements, memberships, licenses, rents, and insurance.

The examples of prepaid expenses cited in the previous paragraph are unambiguous. This is, however, not always the case. In negotiating union labor contracts, the parties may agree that the union employees will be entitled to receive a lump-sum cash payment or series of payments in exchange for agreeing to little or no increase in the employees' base wage rate. These lump-sum arrangements ordinarily do not require the employee to refund any portion of the lump sum to the employer in the event that the employee terminates employment during the term of the labor agreement. Further, it is assumed by the parties that, upon termination of a union member, the employer will replace that individual with another union member at the same base wage rate to whom no lump sum would be due. Management believes that the lump-sum payment arrangement will reduce or eliminate raises during the contract term and that these lump-sum payments will benefit future periods. To record these lump sums as prepaid expenses, ASC 710-10-25 specifies that, based on a careful review of the facts and circumstances around the contract and negotiations, the payments must clearly benefit a future period in the form of a lower base wage rate than would otherwise have been in effect. Further, the amortization period is not permitted to extend beyond the term of the union contract. The presumption of replacing terminating union members with other union members at the same wage rate is essential to this conclusion and, thus, this accounting treatment is only applicable to union contracts and is not permitted to be applied by analogy to account for individual employment contracts or other compensation arrangements. The SEC observer noted that accounting for this transaction as a prepaid expense is only appropriate when there is no evidence of any kind that the lump-sum payment or payments are related to services rendered in the past.

Amortization. Prepaid expenses are amortized to expense on a ratable basis over the period during which the benefits or services are received. For example, if rent is prepaid for the quarter at the beginning of the quarter, two months of the rent will be included in the prepaid rent account. At the beginning of the second month, the equivalent of one month's rent (half the account balance) would be charged to rent expense. At the beginning of the third month, the remaining prepayment would be charged to rent expense.

Example of prepaid expenses

The PipeTrak Company starts using geographical information systems (GIS) software to track the locations of the country's pipeline infrastructure under a contract for the Department of Homeland Security. It pays maintenance fees on three types of GIS software, for which the following maintenance periods are covered:

Software name	*Maintenance start date*	*Maintenance duration*	*Maintenance fee*
Culture Data (CD)	February	Annual	$4,800
Map Layering (ML)	April	Semiannual	18,000
Land Grid (LG)	June	Quarterly	6,000

It initially records these fee payments as prepaid expenses. PipeTrak's controller then uses the following amortization table to determine the amount of prepaid expenses to charge to expense each month:

Software	*Feb*	*Mar*	*Apr*	*May*	*Jun*	*Jul*	*Aug*	*Sep*	*Oct*	*Nov*	*Dec*
CD	400	400	400	400	400	400	400	400	400	400	400
ML			3,000	3,000	3,000	3,000	3,000	3,000			
LG					2,000	2,000	2,000				
Totals	400	400	3,400	3,400	5,400	5,400	5,400	3,400	400	400	400

In June, PipeTrak records the following entry to charge a portion of its prepaid software maintenance to expense:

Software maintenance expense	5,400	
Prepaid expenses		5,400

Preproduction Costs Related to Long-Term Supply Arrangements

Manufacturers often incur costs referred to as preproduction costs, related to products that they will provide to their customers under long-term supply arrangements. ASC 340-10-25 states the following with respect to these costs:

1. Costs of design and development of products to be sold under long-term supply arrangements are expensed as incurred.
2. Costs of design and development of molds, dies, and other tools that the supplier will own and that will be used in producing the products under the long-term supply arrangement are capitalized as part of the molds, dies, and other tools (subject to an ASC 360 recoverability assessment when one or more impairment indicators is present). There is an exception, however, for molds, dies, and other tools involving new technology, which are expensed as incurred as research and development costs under ASC 730.
3. If the molds, dies, and other tools described in 2 above are *not to be owned* by the supplier, then their costs are expensed as incurred unless the supply arrangement provides the supplier the noncancelable right (as long as the supplier is performing under the terms of the supply arrangement) to use the molds, dies, and other tools during the term of the supply arrangement. (ASC 340-10-25-1)
4. If there is a legally enforceable contractual guarantee for reimbursement of design and development costs that would otherwise be expensed under these rules, the costs are recognized as an asset as incurred. Such a guarantee must contain reimbursement provisions that are objectively measurable and verifiable. The ASC provides examples illustrating this provision. (ASC 340-20-25-3)

Under these rules, preparers are encouraged (and SEC registrants are required) to disclose the following information (ASC 340-10-S99-3):

1. The accounting policy for preproduction design and development costs.
2. The aggregate amounts of:
   a. Assets recognized pursuant to agreements providing for contractual reimbursement of preproduction design and development costs.
   b. Assets recognized for molds, dies, and other tools that the supplier owns.
   c. Assets recognized for molds, dies, and other tools that the supplier does not own.

It is important to note that the above provisions do not apply to assets acquired in a business combination that are used in research and development activities. Instead, such assets are accounted for in accordance with ASC 805, which permits recognition of in-process research and development assets.

Capitalized Advertising Costs

The costs of advertising are expensed either as costs are incurred or the first time the advertising takes place (e.g., when the television advertisement is aired or printed copy is published), if later (720-35-25). However, if both of the following conditions are met, those costs can be capitalized:

1. The primary purpose is to elicit sales to customers who could be shown to have responded specifically to the advertising, and
2. The advertising results in probable future economic benefits.

The future benefits to be received are the future revenues arising as a direct result of the advertising. The company is required to provide entity-specific persuasive evidence that there is a linkage between the direct-response advertising and these future benefits. These costs are then amortized over the period in which the future benefits are expected to be received.

Advertising expenditures are sometimes made subsequent to the recognition of revenue (such as in "cooperative advertising" arrangements with customers). In order to achieve proper matching, these costs are to be estimated, accrued, and charged to expense when the related revenues are recognized. (ASC 340-20-25-2)

Insurance contracts that do not translate insurance risk

Deposit accounting. Insurance risk is comprised of timing risk and underwriting risk, and one or both of these may not be transferred to the insurer (assuming entity in the case of reinsurance) under certain circumstances. For example, many workers' compensation policies provide for *experience adjustments* which have the effect of keeping the underwriting risk with the insured, rather than transferring it to the insurer; in such instances, deposit accounting would be prescribed.

Under the provisions of ASC 340-30, for contracts that transfer only significant timing risk, or that transfer neither significant timing nor underwriting risk, a deposit asset (from the insured's or ceding entity's perspective, respectively, for insurance and reinsurance arrangements) or liability (from the insurer's or assuming entity's perspective, respectively, for insurance and reinsurance arrangements) should be recognized at inception. The deposit asset or liability should be remeasured at subsequent financial reporting dates by calculating the effective yield on the deposit to reflect actual payments to date and expected future payments. Yield is to be determined as set forth in ASC 310-20, using the estimated amounts and timings of cash flows. The deposit is to be adjusted to that which would have existed at the statement of financial position date had the new effective yield been applied since inception of the contract; thus, expense or income for a period will be determined by first calculating the necessary amount in the related statement of financial position account.

For contracts that transfer only significant underwriting risk, a deposit asset or liability is also established at inception. However, subsequent remeasurement of the deposit does not occur until such time as a loss is incurred that will be reimbursed under the contract; instead, the deposit is reported at its amortized amount. Once the loss occurs, the deposit should be remeasured by the present value of expected future cash flows arising from the contract, plus the remaining unexpired portion of the coverage. Changes in the deposit arising from the present value measure are to be reported in the insured's income statement as an offset against the loss to be reimbursed; in the insurer's income statement, the adjustment should be reported as an incurred loss. The reduction due to amortization of the deposit is reported as an adjustment to incurred losses by the insurer. The discount rate used to compute the present value is to be the rate on government obligations with similar cash flow characteristics, adjusted for differences in default risk, which is based on the insurer's credit rating. Rates are determined at the loss date(s) and not revised later, absent further losses.

For insurance contracts with indeterminate risk, the procedures set forth in ASC 944-605 (the open-year method) should be applied. (ASC 340-25-05-8) This involves the segregation, in the statement of financial position, of amounts that have not been adjusted due to lack of sufficient loss or other data. When sufficient information becomes available, the deposit asset or liability is adjusted, which is to be reported as an accounting change per ASC 250.

Other Sources

See ASC Location – Wiley *GAAP* Chapter…	***For information on…***
ASC 340-10-60	
ASC 310-20	Nonrefundable fees and costs associated with lending, committing to lend, or purchasing a group of loans and for accounting for fees and initial direct costs associated with leasing
ASC 350-40	Capitalization of internal and external costs incurred to develop internal-use computer software
ASC 410-30	Capitalization of costs incurred to treat asbestos and criteria for environmental contamination treatment costs
ASC 605-20	Deferral of costs directly related to the acquisition of a contract and costs incurred in anticipation of future construction and certain production-type contract sales
ASC 720-45	The cost of business process reengineering activities
ASC 912-45	The allocation of general and administrative costs to government contract inventories and cost-reimbursement contracts
ASC 915-810	The assessment of recoverability of capitalized or deferred costs in a development stage subsidiary
ASC 922-360	The capitalization and subsequent measurement of initial subscriber installation costs
ASC 928-340	Reporting of an advance royalty to an artist as an asset
ASC 940-340	Consideration of a membership as an asset by broker dealers and distribution fees by broker dealers
ASC 940-20	Accounting guidance for underwriting expenses by broker dealers

ASC 946-20	Accounting for offering costs by investment companies
ASC 950-350-30	Capitalization guidance for costs incurred to construct a title plant
ASC 985-20	Accounting for costs of computer software to be sold, leased, or otherwise marketed
ASC 340-20-60	
ASC 720-35	Additional information on advertising costs

24 ASC 350 INTANGIBLES— GOODWILL AND OTHER

PERSPECTIVE AND ISSUES

Subtopics

ASC 350, *Intangibles—Goodwill and Other,* consists of five subtopics:

- ASC 350-10, *Overall,* which provides guidance for accounting and reporting on intangible assets
- ASC 350-20, *Goodwill,* which provides guidance on accounting for goodwill subsequent to acquisition and for the cost of internally developed goodwill. The guidance in this section is presented in two subsections – a. General and b. Accounting Alternative.
- ASC 350-30, *General Intangibles Other Than Goodwill,* which provides guidance on accounting and reporting for intangible assets other than goodwill acquired individually or with a group of other assets
- ASC 350-40, *Internal-Use Software,* which provides guidance on accounting for software developed for internal use and determining whether that software *is* for internal use

- ASC 350-50, *Website Development Costs,* which provides guidance on accounting for costs associated with the development of a website, including costs incurred:
  - In the planning, application development, infrastructure development, and operating stages
  - To develop graphics and content.

Scope Exceptions

All of the subtopics above adopt the following scope limitations of ASC 350-10, the overall subtopic. The guidance does *not* apply to:

- Accounting at acquisition for goodwill acquired in a business combination (see ASC 805-30) or in an acquisition by a not-for-profit entity (see ASC 958-805).
- Accounting at acquisition for intangible assets other than goodwill acquired in a business combination or in an acquisition by a not-for-profit entity (see ASC 805-20 and ASC 958-805).

ASC 350-10-15-4 goes on to list locations that are *not* changed by the guidance in ASC 350:

- Research and development costs under Subtopic 730-10
- Extractive activities under Topic 932
- Entertainment and media, including records and music under Topic 928
- Financial services industry under Topic 950
- Entertainment and media, including broadcasters under Topic 920
- Regulatory operations under paragraphs 980-350-35-1 through 35-2
- Software under Topic 985
- Income taxes under Topic 740
- Transfers and servicing under Topic 860.

Issues

For manufacturing companies, the primary assets typically are tangible, such as buildings and equipment. For financial institutions, the major assets are financial instruments. For high-technology, knowledge-based companies, however, the primary assets are intangible, such as patents and copyrights, and for professional service firms the key assets may be "soft" resources, such as knowledge bases and client relationships. Overall, enterprises for which intangible assets constitute a large and growing component of total assets are a rapidly growing part of the economy, and there is pressure to improve the relevance of financial reporting in light of changing business and economic conditions.

Intangible assets are defined as both current and noncurrent assets that lack physical substance. Specifically excluded, however, are financial instruments and deferred income tax assets. The value of intangible assets is based on the rights or privileges to which they entitle the reporting entity. Most of the accounting issues associated with intangible assets involve their characteristics, valuation and amortization. Adequate consideration must be given to the economic substance of the transaction.

Note: For a summary and comparison of accounting and impairment rules for property, plant and equipment and intangibles, see the Perspectives and Issues section of the chapter on ASC 360.

Technical Alert

In January 2014, the FASB issued ASU No. 2014-02, "Intangibles—Goodwill and Other (Topic 350): Accounting for Goodwill." This ASU is a consensus of the Private Company Council and amends a long-standing policy of not allowing amortization of goodwill. Public companies, not-for-profit entities, and employee benefit plans within the scope of Topics 960 through 965 on plan accounting are outside the scope of these amendments. Companies within scope are now allowed to amortize goodwill on a straight-line basis over a period of no more than ten years. A period of less than ten years is allowed if a shorter life is more appropriate.

Entities electing this alternative are subject to its related subsequent measurement, derecognition, other presentation, and disclosure requirements. Once an entity elects the alternative, it applies to existing goodwill and any goodwill recognized in the future.

Entities electing this alternative must make an accounting policy decision to test goodwill for impairment at either the reporting-unit level or the entity level. Under this alternative impairment model, goodwill should be tested when a triggering event occurs, rather than once a year as required for other entities. A triggering event is one that indicates that the fair value of the reporting unit or the company may be below its carrying value. In addition, for companies electing the alternative, the ASU eliminates step two of the existing impairment model. Once impairment is indicated, no further testing is necessary.

Disclosures under the alternative are similar to existing GAAP. However, entities are not required to present changes in goodwill in tabular format.

The ASU is effective prospectively for new goodwill recognized in annual periods beginning after December 15, 2014 and interim periods within annual periods beginning after December 15, 2015. Goodwill existing at the beginning of the period of adoption should be amortized prospectively on a straight-line basis over not more than ten years. Early adoption is permitted.

DEFINITIONS OF TERMS

Source: ASC 350 Glossary sections

Acquiree. The business or businesses that the acquirer obtains control of in a business combination. This term also includes a nonprofit activity or business that a not-for-profit acquirer obtains control of in an acquisition by a not-for-profit entity.

Acquirer. The entity that obtains control of the acquire. However, in a business combination in which a variable interest entity (VIE) is acquired, the primary beneficiary of that entity always is the acquirer.

Acquisition by a non-for-profit entity. A transaction or other event in which a not-for-profit acquirer obtains control of one or more nonprofit activities or businesses and initially recognizes their assets and liabilities in the acquirer's financial statements. When applicable guidance in ASC 805 is applied by a not-for-profit entity, the term business combination has the same meaning as this term has for a not-for-profit entity. Likewise, a reference to business combinations in guidance that links to ASC 805 has the same meaning as a reference to acquisitions by not-for-profit entities.

Business. An integrated set of activities and assets that is capable of being conducted and managed for the purpose of providing a return in the form of dividends, lower costs, or other economic benefits directly to investors or other owners, members, or participants. Additional guidance on what a business consists of is presented in ASC 805-10-55-4 through 55-9.

Business combination. A transaction or other event in which an acquirer obtains control of one or more businesses. Transactions sometimes referred to as true mergers or mergers of equals also are business combinations. See also **Acquisition by a not-for-profit entity.**

Defensive intangible asset. An acquired intangible asset in a situation in which an entity does not intend to actively use the asset but intends to hold (lock up) the asset to prevent others from obtaining access to the asset.

Goodwill. An asset representing the future economic benefits arising from other assets acquired in a business combination or an acquisition by a not-for-profit entity that are not individually identified and separately recognized. For ease of reference, this term also includes the immediate charge recognized by not-for-profit entities in accordance with ASC 958-805-25-29.

Intangible asset class. A group of intangible assets that are similar, either by their nature or by their use in the operations of an entity.

Intangible assets. Assets (not including financial assets) that lack physical substance. (The term intangible assets is used to refer to intangible assets other than goodwill.)

Legal entity. Any legal structure used to conduct activities or to hold assets. Some examples of such structures are corporations, partnerships, limited liability companies, grantor trusts, and other trusts.

Mutual entity. An entity other than an investor-owned entity that provides dividends, lower costs, or other economic benefits directly and proportionately to its owners, members, or participants. Mutual insurance entities, credit unions, and farm and rural electric cooperatives are examples of mutual entities.

Nonprofit activity. An integrated set of activities and assets that is capable of being conducted and managed for the purpose of providing benefits, other than goods or services at a profit or profit equivalent, as a fulfillment of an entity's purpose or mission (for example, goods or services to beneficiaries, customers, or members). As with a not-for-profit entity, a nonprofit activity possesses characteristics that distinguish it from a business or a for-profit business entity.

Nonpublic entity. Any entity other than one with any of the following characteristics:

1. Whose debt or equity securities trade in a public market either on a stock exchange (domestic or foreign) or in the over-the-counter market, including securities quoted only locally or regionally
2. That is a conduit bond obligor for conduit debt securities that are traded in a public market (a domestic or foreign stock exchange or an over-the-counter market, including local or regional markets)
3. That makes a filing with a regulatory agency in preparation for the sale of any class of debt or equity securities in a public market
4. That is controlled by an entity covered by 1, 2, or 3.

Conduit debt securities refers to certain limited-obligation revenue bonds, certificates of participation, or similar debt instruments issued by a state or local governmental entity for the express purpose of providing financing for a specific third party (the conduit bond obligor) that is not a part of the state or local government's financial reporting entity. Although conduit debt securities bear the name of the governmental entity that issues them, the governmental entity often has no obligation for such debt beyond the resources provided by a lease or loan agreement with the third party on whose behalf the securities are issued. Further, the conduit bond obligor is responsible for any future financial reporting requirements.

Not-for-profit entity. An entity that possesses the following characteristics, in varying degrees, that distinguish it from a business entity:

1. Contributions of significant amounts of resources from resource providers who do not expect commensurate or proportionate pecuniary return
2. Operating purposes other than to provide goods or services at a profit
3. Absence of ownership interests like those of business entities.

Entities that clearly fall outside this definition include the following:

1. All investor-owned entities
2. Entities that provide dividends, lower costs, or other economic benefits directly and proportionately to their owners, members, or participants, such as mutual insurance entities, credit unions, farm and rural electric cooperatives, and employee benefit plans.

Operating segment. A component of a public entity that has all of the following characteristics:

1. It engages in business activities from which it may earn revenues and incur expenses,
2. Its operating results are regularly reviewed by the public entity's chief operating decision maker to make decisions about resources to be allocated to the segment and assess its performance.
3. Its discrete financial information is available.

Preliminary Project Stage. When a computer software project is in the preliminary project stage, entities will likely do the following:

1. Make strategic decisions to allocate resources between alternative projects at a given point in time. For example, should programmers develop a new payroll system or direct their efforts toward correcting existing problems in an operating payroll system?
2. Determine the performance requirements (that is, what it is that they need the software to do) and systems requirements for the computer software project it has proposed to undertake.
3. Invite vendors to perform demonstrations of how their software will fulfill an entity's needs.
4. Explore alternative means of achieving specified performance requirements. For example, should an entity make or buy the software? Should the software run on a mainframe or a client server system?
5. Determine that the technology needed to achieve performance requirements exists.
6. Select a vendor if an entity chooses to obtain software.

Private company. An entity other than a public business entity, a not-for-profit entity, or an employee benefit plan within the scope of Topics 960 through 965 on plan accounting.

Public business entity. A public business entity is a business entity meeting any one of the criteria below. Neither a not-for-profit entity nor an employee benefit plan is a business entity.

1. It is required by the U.S. Securities and Exchange Commission (SEC) to file or furnish financial statements, or does file or furnish financial statements (including voluntary filers), with the SEC (including other entities whose financial statements or financial information are required to be or are included in a filing).
2. It is required by the Securities Exchange Act of 1934 (the Act), as amended, or rules or regulations promulgated under the Act, to file or furnish financial statements with a regulatory agency other than the SEC.

3. It is required to file or furnish financial statements with a foreign or domestic regulatory agency in preparation for the sale of or for purposes of issuing securities that are not subject to contractual restrictions on transfer.
4. It has issued, or is a conduit bond obligor for, securities that are traded, listed, or quoted on an exchange or an over-the-counter market.
5. It has one or more securities that are not subject to contractual restrictions on transfer, and it is required by law, contract, or regulation to prepare U.S. GAAP financial statements (including footnotes) and make them publicly available on a periodic basis (for example, interim or annual periods). An entity must meet both of these conditions to meet this criterion.

An entity may meet the definition of a public business entity solely because its financial statements or financial information is included in another entity's filing with the SEC. In that case, the entity is only a public business entity for purposes of financial statements that are filed or furnished with the SEC.

Reporting Unit. The level of reporting at which goodwill is tested for impairment. A reporting unit is an operating segment or one level below an operating segment (also known as a component).

Residual Value. The estimated fair value of an intangible asset at the end of its useful life to an entity, less any disposal costs.

Useful Life. The period over which an asset is expected to contribute directly or indirectly to future cash flows.

Variable interest entity. A legal entity subject to consolidation according to the provisions of the Variable Interest Entities Subsections of Subtopic 810-10.

CONCEPTS, RULES, AND EXAMPLES

Goodwill (ASC 350-20)[1]

Goodwill is not considered an identifiable intangible asset, and accordingly, under ASC 350-20, it is accounted for differently from identifiable intangibles. The lack of identifiability is the critical element in the definition of goodwill. Accordingly, *identifiable* intangible assets that are reliably measurable are recognized and reported separately from goodwill.

Costs of internally developed goodwill are expensed as incurred (ASC 350-20-25-3) Accounting at acquisition for goodwill acquired during the acquisition of an entire entity is accounted for under the provisions of ASC 805-30. Accounting at acquisition for goodwill acquired at acquisition by a not-for-profit entity is accounted for under the provisions of 958-805.

Amortization and impairment testing. Goodwill is considered to have an indefinite life and, therefore, is not amortized. (See the Technical Alert section for an important update on the new alternative for private companies.) Goodwill is, however, subject to unique impairment testing techniques. Goodwill is impaired when its *implied* fair value is less than its carrying amount. The fair value of goodwill cannot be measured directly; it can only be "implied," that is, measured as a residual.

Reporting unit. The impairment test for goodwill is performed at the level of the reporting unit. A reporting unit, as detailed in ASC 350-20-35-33 through 46, is an operating segment or one level below an operating segment. In the chapter on ASC 280, the diagram entitled *"Alternative Balance Sheet Segmentation"* illustrates how different groupings in a

[1] See the Technical Alert section of this chapter for an important update to this guidance.

business can be characterized as reporting units. The diagram is accompanied by definitions of reporting units, operating segments, and other organizational groupings. The reporting entity may internally refer to reporting units by terms such as business units, operating units, or divisions.

Determination of reporting units is largely dependent on how the business is managed and its structure for reporting and management accountability. An entity may have only one reporting unit, which would, of course, result in the goodwill impairment test being performed at the entity level. This can occur when the entity has acquired a business that it has integrated with its existing business in such a manner that the acquired business is not separately distinguishable as a reporting unit.

On the date an asset is acquired or a liability is assumed, the asset or liability is assigned to a reporting unit if it meets both of the following conditions:

1. The asset will be used in or the liability is related to the operations of a reporting unit
2. The asset or liability will be considered in determining the fair value of the reporting unit.

The methodology used to determine reporting units must be reasonable and supportable and must be applied similarly to how aggregate goodwill is determined in a purchase business combination.

Net assets include assets and liabilities that are recognized as "corporate" items if they, in fact, relate to the operations of the reporting unit. Examples of corporate items are environmental liabilities associated with land owned by a reporting unit, and pension assets and liabilities attributable to employees of a reporting unit. Executory contracts (e.g., operating leases, contracts for purchase or sale, construction contracts) are considered part of net assets only if the amount reflected in the acquirer's financial statements is based on a fair value measurement subsequent to entering into the contract. To illustrate, if an acquiree had a preexisting operating lease on either favorable or unfavorable terms as compared to its fair value on the date of acquisition, the acquirer would recognize, in its purchase price allocations, an asset or liability for the fair value of the favorable or unfavorable terms, respectively. ASC 350 distinguishes between accounting for this fair value of an otherwise unrecognized executory contract and prepaid rent or rent payable, which generally have carrying values that approximate their fair values.

Implied fair value. The implied fair value of goodwill is the excess of the fair value of the reporting unit as a whole over the fair values that would be assigned to its assets and liabilities in a purchase business combination.

Timing of testing. The annual goodwill impairment test may be performed at any time during the fiscal year as long as it is done consistently at the same time each year. Each reporting unit is permitted to establish its own annual testing date. ASC 350-20-35-30 indicates that additional impairment tests are required between annual impairment tests if:

1. They are warranted by a change in events and circumstances, *and*
2. It is more likely than not that the fair value of the reporting unit is below its carrying amount.

ASC 350-20-35-30 references ASC 350-20-35-3C to provide examples of events or circumstances that require goodwill of a reporting unit to be tested for impairment between annual tests:

a. Macroeconomic conditions, such as a deterioration in general economic conditions, limitations on accessing capital, fluctuations in foreign exchange rates, or other developments in equity and credit markets

b. Industry and market considerations, such as a deterioration in the environment in which city an entity operates, an increased competitive environment, a decline in market-dependent multiples or metrics (consider in both absolute terms and relative to peers), a change in the market for entity's products or services, or a regulatory or political development
c. Cost factors, such as increases in raw materials, labor, or other costs that have a negative effect on earnings and cash flows
d. Overall financial performance, such as negative or declining cash flows or a decline in actual or planned revenue or earnings compared with actual and projected results of relevant prior periods
e. Other relevant entity-specific events, such as changes in management, key personnel, strategy, or customers; contemplation of bankruptcy; or litigation
f. Events affecting a reporting unit, such as a change in the composition or carrying amount of its net assets, a more-likely-than-not expectation of selling or disposing all, or a potion, of a reporting unit, or recognition of a goodwill impairment loss in the financial statements of a subsidiary that is a component of a reporting unit
g. If applicable, a sustained decrease in share price (consider in both absolute terms and relative to peers).

This list is not intended to be all-inclusive. Other indicators may come to the attention of management that would indicate that goodwill impairment testing should be performed between annual tests. Goodwill must also be tested for impairment if a portion of goodwill is allocated to a business to be disposed of.

If indicators exist requiring impairment testing of goodwill, impairment testing of nonamortizable intangibles, and/or recoverability evaluation of tangible long-lived assets or amortizable intangibles, the other assets are tested/evaluated first and any impairment loss is recognized prior to testing goodwill for impairment.

Performing the impairment test. To what had been a two-step process, the FASB has, in effect, introduced "Step 0." Step 0 gives entities the option of performing a qualitative assessment before calculating the fair value in Step 1. In the qualitative assessment, entities determine whether it is more likely than not that the fair value of the reporting unit is less than the carrying amount. The qualitative assessment is optional and entities may bypass it for any reporting unit in any period.

The factors listed previously that indicate impairment testing should be done between annual tests are the same as those that should be considered in the qualitative assessment. (See ASC 350-20-35-3C examples above.)

ASC 350-20-35-3F goes on to say that these examples are not all-inclusive, and offers other events and circumstances than an entity must consider:

> *An entity shall consider the extent to which each of the adverse events and circumstances identified could affect the comparison of a reporting unit's fair value with its carrying amount. An entity should place more weight on the events and circumstances that most affect a reporting unit's fair value or the carrying amount of its net assets. An entity also should consider positive and mitigating events and circumstances that may affect its determination of whether it is more likely than not that the fair value of a reporting unit is less than its carrying amount. If an entity has a recent fair value calculation for reporting unit, it also should include as a factor in its consideration the difference between the fair value and the carrying amount in reaching its conclusion about whether to perform the first step of the goodwill impairment test.*

ASC 350-20-35-3G advises that the events and circumstances should be considered in context and no one event necessarily requires the entity to perform Step 1.

If it is *not* more likely than not that the fair value of the reporting unit is less than the carrying amount, further testing is not performed. If it *is* more likely than not the fair value of the reporting unit is less than the carrying amount, the entity proceeds to Step 1.

Step 1. Compare the fair value of the reporting unit as a whole to its carrying value, including goodwill.

- If the reporting unit's carrying amount is greater than zero and its fair value exceeds its carrying value, goodwill is not impaired and no further computations are required.
- If the reporting unit has a zero or negative carrying amount, then the entity must proceed to the next step if it is more likely than not that a goodwill impairment exists. In making this evaluation, the entity should consider whether there are significant differences between the carrying amount and the estimated fair value of the assets and liabilities, and the existence of significant unrecognized intangible assets. (ASC 350-20-35-8)
- If the carrying value of the reporting unit exceeds its fair value, the second step of the impairment test is required.

Step 2. Determine whether and by how much goodwill is impaired as follows:

a. Estimate the implied fair value of goodwill.
b. Compare the implied fair value of goodwill to its carrying amount.
c. If the carrying amount of goodwill exceeds its implied fair value, it is impaired and is written down to the implied fair value.

Consistent with long-standing practice in GAAP, upon recognition of an impairment loss, the adjusted carrying amount of goodwill becomes its new cost basis, and future restoration of the written down amount is prohibited.

Determining the implied fair value of goodwill. The fair value of a reporting unit is defined in the ASC 350 Glossary as the price that would be received to sell the unit as a whole in an orderly transaction between market participants at the measurement date. The determination of the implied fair value of goodwill is based on the assumption that the fair value of a reporting unit as a whole differs from the fair value of its identifiable net assets. This is the general principle that gives rise to goodwill in the first place. The acquirer assigns additional value to the acquiree (as evidenced by a purchase price that exceeds the collective fair values of the assets and liabilities to be acquired) based on the acquirer's perceived ability to take advantage of synergies and other benefits that flow from its control over the acquiree.

Determining the fair value of a reporting unit. Quoted market prices in active markets are considered the best evidence of fair value and are to be used if available. However, market capitalization of a publicly traded business unit is computed based on a quoted market price per share that does not consider any advantages that might inure to an acquirer in a situation where control is obtained. For this reason, ASC 350-20-35-23 cautions that the market capitalization of a reporting unit with publicly traded stock may not be representative of its fair value. Presumably, estimating the fair value of a privately held business using earnings multiples derived from publicly traded companies in the same line of business might have the same limitation.

ASC 350 also prescribes that when a significant portion of a reporting unit is comprised of an acquired entity, the same techniques and assumptions used to determine the purchase price of the acquisition are to be used to measure the fair value of the reporting unit unless such techniques and assumptions are not consistent with the objective of measuring fair value.

If quoted market prices are not available, the estimate of fair value is to be based on the best information available, including prices for similar assets and liabilities or the results of applying available valuation techniques. Such techniques include expected present value methods, option pricing models, matrix pricing, option-adjusted spread models, and fundamental analysis. The weight given to evidence gathered in the valuation process must be proportional to the ability to objectively observe it. When an estimate is in the form of a range of either the amount or timing of estimated future cash flows, the likelihood of possible outcomes should be considered (i.e., probability weightings are assigned in order to estimate the most likely outcome).

The measurement techniques and assumptions used to estimate the fair values of the reporting unit's net assets should be consistent with those used to measure the fair value of the reporting unit as a whole. For example, estimates of the amounts and timing of cash flows used to value the significant assets of the reporting unit are to be consistent with those assumptions used to estimate such cash flows at the reporting unit level when a cash flow model is used to estimate the reporting unit's fair value as a whole.

For the purposes of determining the fair value of a reporting unit, the relevant facts and circumstances are to be carefully evaluated with respect to whether to assume that the reporting unit could be bought or sold in a taxable or nontaxable transaction. The factors to consider in making the evaluation are set forth in ASC 350-20-35.

1. The assumptions that marketplace participants would make in estimating fair value
2. The feasibility of the assumed structure considering
    a. The ability to sell the reporting unit in a nontaxable transaction, and
    b. Any limits on the entity's ability to treat a sale as a nontaxable transaction imposed by income tax laws or regulations, or corporate governance requirements.
3. Whether the assumed structure would yield the best economic after-tax return to the (hypothetical) seller for the reporting unit.

If a reporting unit is not wholly owned by the reporting entity, the fair value of that reporting unit and the implied fair value of goodwill are to be determined in the same manner as prescribed by ASC 805. If the reporting unit includes goodwill that is solely attributable to the parent, any impairment loss would be attributed entirely to the parent. If, however, the reporting unit's goodwill is attributable to both the parent and the noncontrolling interest, the impairment loss would need to be allocated to both the parent and the noncontrolling interest in a rational manner. The same logic applies to gain or loss on disposal of all or a portion of a reporting unit. When that reporting unit is disposed of, the gain or loss on disposal is to be attributed to both the parent and to the noncontrolling interest.

For the purpose of goodwill impairment testing, the carrying value of a reporting unit includes deferred income taxes irrespective of whether fair value of the reporting unit was determined assuming taxable or nontaxable treatment.

Measuring Fair Value

Implied Fair Value Computation. For the purpose of computing the implied fair value of reporting unit goodwill, assumptions must be made as to the income tax bases of the reporting unit's assets and liabilities in order to compute any relevant deferred income taxes. If the computation of the reporting unit's fair value in Step 1 of the goodwill impairment test assumed that the reporting unit was structured as a taxable transaction, then new income tax bases are used. Otherwise the existing income tax bases are used (ASC 350-20-35).

Recognition of impairment loss. If the carrying amount of the reporting unit's good will exceeds the implied fair value of that goodwill, an impairment loss in the amount equal to the excess is recognized. The recognized loss cannot exceed the carrying amount of goodwill. The new carrying amount of the goodwill is the adjusted amount after recognizing the loss. Once the loss is recognized, it cannot be reversed subsequently.

If the second step of the impairment test is not completed before the financial statements are issued and a loss is probable, the entity should recognized the loss and disclose the fact that it is an estimate. Upon completion of the test, the entity may make an adjustment to that estimated loss in the subsequent period.

Example of the goodwill impairment test

Spectral Corporation acquires FarSite Binocular Company for $5,300,000; of this amount, $3,700,000 is assigned to a variety of assets, with the remaining $1,600,000 assigned to goodwill, as noted in the following table:

Purchase price	$ 5,300,000
– Accounts receivable	(450,000)
– Inventory	(750,000)
– Production equipment	(1,000,000)
– Acquired formulas and processes	(1,500,000)
= Goodwill	$ 1,600,000

The asset allocation related to acquired formulas and processes is especially critical to the operation, since it refers to the use of a proprietary lens coating system that allows FarSite's binoculars to yield exceptional clarity in low-light conditions. This asset is being depreciated over ten years.

One year after the acquisition date, the FarSite division has recorded annual cash flow of $1,450,000; assuming the same cash flow for the next five years, the present value of the expected cash flows, discounted at the corporate cost of capital of 8%, is roughly $5,789,000. Also, an independent appraisal firm assigns a fair value of $3,600,000 to FarSite's identifiable assets. With this information, the impairment test follows:

FarSite division's fair value	$ 5,789,000
– Fair value of identifiable assets	(3,600,000)
= Implied fair value of goodwill	$ 2,189,000

Though the implied fair value of FarSite's goodwill has increased, Spectral's controller cannot record this increase.

A few months later, Spectral's management learns that a Czech optics company has created a competing optics coating process that is superior to and less expensive than FarSite's process. Since this will likely result in a reduction in FarSite's fair value below its carrying amount, Spectral conducts another impairment test. Management assumes that the forthcoming increase in competition will reduce the expected present value of its cash flows to $3,900,000. In addition, the appraisal firm now reduces its valuation of the acquired formulas and processes asset by $1,200,000. The revised impairment test follows:

FarSite division's fair value	$ 3,900,000
– Fair value of identifiable assets	(2,400,000)
= Implied fair value of goodwill	1,500,000
– Carrying amount of goodwill	1,600,000
= Impairment loss	$ (100,000)

Since the implied fair value of goodwill is $100,000 less than its current carrying amount, Spectral's controller uses the following entry to record reduction in value:

Impairment loss	100,000	
Goodwill		100,000

In addition, Spectral's controller writes down the value of the acquired formulas and processes by the amount recommended by the appraisal firm with the following entry:

Impairment loss	1,200,000	
Accumulated depreciation		1,200,000

A year later, FarSite's research staff discovers an enhancement to its optical coating process that will restore FarSite's competitive position against the Czech firm. However, Spectral's controller cannot increase the carrying cost of the acquired formulas and processes or goodwill to match their newly increased fair value and implied fair value, respectively.

Other goodwill considerations. Other provisions included in ASC 350 include the following:

- Equity method goodwill continues to be recognized under ASC 323 and is not subject to amortization. This goodwill is not tested for impairment under ASC 350, but rather, is tested under ASC 323. This test considers whether the fair value of the underlying investment has declined and whether that decline is "other than temporary."
- Goodwill of a reporting unit that is fully disposed of is included in the carrying amount of the net assets disposed of in computing the gain or loss on disposal.
- If a significant portion of a reporting unit is disposed of, the goodwill of that unit is required to be tested for impairment. In performing the impairment test, only the net assets to be retained after the disposal are included in the computation. If, as a result of the test, the carrying amount of goodwill exceeds its implied fair value, the excess carrying amount is allocated to the carrying amount of the net assets disposed of in computing the gain or loss on disposal and, consequently, is not considered an impairment loss.

Presentation. To provide financial statement users with transparent information about goodwill, ASC 350-20-45 requires separate line item treatment as follows:

- *Balance sheet (statement of financial position)*—the aggregate amount of goodwill included in assets is captioned separately from other assets and may not be combined with other intangibles.
- *Income statement*—the aggregate amount of goodwill impairment losses is captioned separately in the operating section unless associated with discontinued operation. If the goodwill impairment loss is associated with a discontinued operation, the loss should be presented net of tax within discontinued operations.

General Intangibles Other Than Goodwill (ASC 350-30)

Intangible assets, other than goodwill, fall into two categories:

- Those with finite useful lives, which are amortized and subject to impairment testing
- Those with indefinite lives, which are not amortized, but are subject to impairment testing.

Initial recognition of intangible assets. Intangibles acquired individually or with a group of other assets[2] are initially recognized and measured based on their fair values. Fair value, consistent with ASC 820 *Fair Value*, is determined based on the assumptions that market participants would use in pricing the asset. Even if the reporting entity does not intend to use an intangible asset in a manner that is its highest and best use, the intangible is nevertheless measured at its fair value.

Per 805-20-S99-3, the SEC does not allow an entity to assign a purchase price, rather than fair value, to intangible assets, and then allocate the remainder of the acquisition price to an "indistinguishable" intangible asset.

The aggregate amount assigned to a group of assets acquired in other than a business combination is to be allocated to the individual assets acquired based on their relative fair values. Goodwill is prohibited from being recognized in such an asset acquisition (ASC 350-30-25-2).

Although a reporting entity can purchase intangibles that were developed by others, U.S. GAAP continues to maintain a strict prohibition against capitalizing costs of internally developing, maintaining, or restoring intangibles, including goodwill (ASC 350-30-25-3). Exceptions to this general rule are software developed for internal use and Website development costs. Both are discussed later in this chapter.

Determining the useful of life of intangible assets. An income approach is commonly used to measure the fair value of an intangible asset. The period of expected cash flows used to measure fair value of the intangible, adjusted for applicable entity-specific factors, is to be considered by management in determining the useful life of the intangible for amortization purposes.

Under ASC 350-30-35-3, in estimating the useful life of an intangible asset, the reporting entity is to consider:

1. The entity's expected use of the asset
2. The expected useful life of another asset or asset group to which the useful life of the intangible asset may be related
3. Any provisions contained in applicable law, regulation, or contract that may limit the useful life
4. The entity's own historical experience in renewing or extending similar arrangements if such experience is consistent with the intended use of the intangible asset by the reporting entity, irrespective of whether those similar arrangements contained explicit renewal or extension provisions. In the absence of such historical experience, management is to consider the assumptions that market participants would use about the renewal or extension consistent with their highest and best use of the asset, and adjusted for relevant entity-specific factors.
5. The effects of obsolescence, demand, competition, and other economic factors such as
    a. Stability of the industry,
    b. Known technological advances,
    c. Legislative action that results in an uncertain or changing regulatory environment, and
    d. Expected changes in distribution channels.
6. The level of maintenance expenditures that would be required to obtain the expected future cash flows from the asset.

[2] *See discussion in the chapter on ASC 805, Business Combinations.*

If no legal, regulatory, contractual, competitive, economic, or other factors limit the useful life of an intangible asset to the reporting entity, the useful life of the asset is considered to be indefinite (which, of course, is not the same as unlimited or infinite). (ASC 350-30-35-4)

Defensive intangible assets. In connection with a business combination or asset acquisition, management of the acquirer may acquire intangible assets that it does not intend to actively use but, rather, wishes to hold in order to prevent other parties from employing them or obtaining access to them. As noted in ASC 350-30-25-5, these intangibles are often referred to as defensive assets, or as "locked-up assets."[3]

To qualify as a defensive intangible asset, the asset must be either

1. Acquired with the intent to not use it *or*
2. Used by the acquirer with the intent to discontinue its use after completion of a transition period.

(ASC 350-30-55-1)

Obviously, upon being characterized as a defensive intangible, the asset is precluded from being considered abandoned upon acquisition, regardless of the fact that it is not being used.

Subsequent to the asset being characterized as a defensive intangible, management may decide to actively employ the asset. If so, it would cease to be considered a defensive intangible. (ASC 350-30-55-1B)

At acquisition, defensive intangibles are subject to the same fair value valuation principles as any other acquired intangible asset, including that they be measured considering exit price to marketplace participants that would put them to their highest and best use. In making the measurement, defensive intangibles are accounted for as a separate unit of accounting and are not to be grouped with other intangibles.

It would be rare for defensive intangible assets to have an indefinite life, since lack of market exposure and competitive and other factors contribute to diminish the fair value of these assets over time (ASC 350-30-35-5B).

Defensive intangible assets are, in theory, to be assigned a useful life representing how (and for how long) the entity expects to consume the expected benefits related to them in the form of direct and indirect cash flows that would result from the prevention of others from realizing any value from them. In practice, however, such estimates would be difficult to make and highly subjective; consequently, ASC 350-30-35-5A substituted what it believed to be a more workable determination of useful life based on management's estimate of the period over which the defensive intangible asset diminishes in fair value.

Amortization of intangible assets. Identifiable intangible assets, such as franchise rights, customer lists, trademarks, patents and copyrights, and licenses are to be amortized over their expected useful economic life with required impairment reviews of their recoverability when necessitated by changes in facts and circumstances in the same manner as set forth in ASC 360 for tangible long-lived assets.

ASC 350-30-35-8 also requires consideration of the intangible's residual value (analogous to salvage value for a tangible asset) in determining the amount of the intangible to amortize. Residual value is defined as the value of the intangible to the entity at the end of its (entity-specific) useful life reduced by any estimated disposition costs. The residual value of an amortizable intangible is assumed to be zero unless the intangible will continue to have a useful life to another party after the end of its useful life to its current holder, and one or both of the following criteria are met:

[3] *Defensive assets exclude intangible assets used in research and development activities, since such assets are subject to different accounting rules under ASC 730-10-25-2c.*

1. The current holder has received a third-party commitment to purchase the intangible at the end of its useful life, *or*
2. A market for the intangible exists and is expected to continue to exist at the end of the asset's useful life as a means of determining the residual value of the intangible by reference to marketplace transactions.

The entity should evaluate the residual value each reporting period.

Amortization and impairment considerations. Many intangible assets are based on rights that are conveyed legally by contract, statute, or similar means. For example, governments grant franchises or similar rights to taxi companies, cable companies, and hydroelectric plants; and companies and other private-sector organizations grant franchises to automobile dealers, fast-food outlets, and professional sports teams. Other rights, such as airport landing rights, are granted by contract. Some of those franchises or similar rights are for finite terms, while others are perpetual. Many of those with finite terms are routinely renewed, absent violations of the terms of the agreement, and the costs incurred for renewal are minimal. Many such assets are also transferable, and the prices at which they trade reflect expectations of renewal at minimal cost. However, for others, renewal is not assured, and their renewal may entail substantial cost.

Trademarks, service marks, and trade names may be registered with the government for a period of twenty years and are renewable for additional twenty-year periods as long as the trademark, service mark, or trade name is used continuously. (Brand names, often used synonymously with trademarks, are typically not registered and thus the required attribute of control will be absent.) The U.S. government now grants copyrights for the life of the creator plus fifty years. Patents are granted by the government for a period of seventeen years but may be effectively renewed by adding minor modifications that are patented for additional seventeen-year periods. Such assets also are commonly transferable.

A broadcast license, while nominally subject to expiration in five years, might be indefinitely renewable at little additional cost to the broadcaster. If cash flows can be projected indefinitely, and assuming a market exists for the license, no amortization is to be recorded until such time as a finite life is predicted. However, impairment is required to be tested at least annually to ensure that the asset is carried at no more than its fair value. (ASC 350-30-55-12)

The foregoing examples all addressed identifiable intangibles, which are recognized in the financial statements when purchased separately or in connection with a business combination. There are other intangibles, which are deemed to not be identifiable because they cannot be reliably measured. Technological know-how and an assembled workforce are examples of such intangible assets. Intangibles that cannot be separately identified are considered integral components of goodwill.

Indefinite-Lived Intangible Assets. Identifiable intangible assets having indefinite useful economic lives supported by clearly identifiable cash flows are not subject to regular periodic amortization. Instead, the carrying amount of the intangible is tested for impairment annually, and again between annual tests if events or circumstances warrant such a test. An impairment loss is recognized if the carrying amount exceeds the fair value. Furthermore, amortization of the asset commences when evidence suggests that its useful economic life is no longer deemed indefinite.

Testing for Impairment of Indefinite-Lived Intangible Assets. The ASC gives entities the option to first assess qualitatively whether it is more likely than not (more than 50 percent) that the asset is impaired. The qualitative assessment test can be performed on some or all of the assets, or the entity can bypass the qualitative test and perform the quantitative test.

If it is not more likely than not that the asset is impaired, the entity does not have to calculate the fair value of the intangible asset and perform the quantitative impairment test.

If it is more likely than not that the asset is impaired, the entity must perform the quantitative impairment test and calculate the fair value of an indefinite-lived intangible asset.

If performing the qualitative assessment, the entity needs to identify and consider those events and circumstances that, individually or in the aggregate, most significantly affect an indefinite-lived intangible asset's fair value. Examples of events and circumstances that should be considered include those listed in ASC 350-30-35-18B:

a. Cost factors such as increases in raw materials, labor, or other costs that have a negative effect on future expected earnings and cash flows that could affect significant inputs used to determine the fair value of the indefinite-lived intangible asset
b. Financial performance such as negative or declining cash flows or a decline in actual or planned revenue or earnings compared with actual and projected results of relevant prior periods that could affect significant inputs used to determine the fair value of the indefinite-lived intangible asset
c. Legal, regulatory, contractual, political, business, or other factors, including asset-specific factors that could affect significant inputs used to determine the fair value of the indefinite-lived intangible asset
d. Other relevant entity-specific events such as changes in management, key personnel, strategy, or customers; contemplation of bankruptcy; or litigation that could affect significant inputs used to determine the fair value of the indefinite-lived intangible asset
e. Industry and market considerations such as a deterioration in the environment in which an entity operates, an increased competitive environment, a decline in market-dependent multiples or metrics (in both absolute terms and relative to peers), or a change in the market for an entity's products or services due to the effects of obsolescence, demand, competition, or other economic factors (such as the stability of the industry, known technological advances, legislative action that results in an uncertain or changing business environment, and expected changes in distribution channels) that could affect significant inputs used to determine the fair value of the indefinite-lived intangible asset
f. Macroeconomic conditions such as deterioration in general economic conditions, limitations on accessing capital, fluctuations in foreign exchange rates, or other developments in equity and credit markets that could affect significant inputs used to determine the fair value of the indefinite-lived intangible asset.

Any positive and mitigating events and circumstances should also be considered, as well as the difference between the fair value in a recent calculation of an indefinite-lived intangible asset and the then carrying amount, whether there have been changes to the carrying amount of the indefinite-lived intangible asset (ASC 350-30-35-18C).

Determining the unit of accounting. ASC 350-30-35 provides guidance about when it is appropriate to combine into a single "unit of accounting" for impairment testing purposes, separately recorded indefinite-life intangibles, whether acquired or internally developed.

The assets may be combined into a single unit of accounting for impairment testing if they are operated as a single asset and, as such, are inseparable from one another. The following indicators are to be used in evaluating the individual facts and circumstances to enable the exercise of judgment (ASC 350-30-35-21).

Indicators that indefinite-lived intangibles are to be combined as a single unit of accounting. (ASC 350-30-35-23):

1. The intangibles will be used together to construct or enhance a single asset.
2. If the intangibles had been part of the same acquisition, they would have been recorded as a single asset.
3. The intangibles, as a group, represent "the highest and best use of the assets" (e.g., they could probably realize a higher sales price if sold together than if they were sold separately). Indicators pointing to this situation are:
   a. The unlikelihood that a substantial portion of the assets would be sold separately, or
   b. The fact that, should a substantial portion of the intangibles be sold individually, there would be a significant reduction in the fair value of the remaining assets in the group.
4. The marketing or branding strategy of the entity treats the assets as being complementary (e.g., a trademark and its related trade name, formulas, recipes, and patented or unpatented technology can all be complementary to an entity's brand name).

Indicators that indefinite-lived intangibles are *not* to be combined as a single unit of accounting. (ASC 350-30-35-24):

1. Each separate intangible generates independent cash flows.
2. In a sale, it would be likely that the intangibles would be sold separately. If the entity had previously sold similar assets separately, this would constitute evidence that combining the assets would not be appropriate.
3. The entity is either considering or has already adopted a plan to dispose of one or more of the intangibles separately.
4. The intangibles are used exclusively by different asset groups (as defined in the ASC Master Glossary).
5. The intangibles have differing useful economic lives.

ASC 350-30-35-26 provides guidance regarding the "unit of accounting" determination.

1. Goodwill and finite-lived intangibles are not permitted to be combined in the "unit of accounting" since they are subject to different impairment rules.
2. If the intangibles collectively constitute a business, they may not be combined into a unit of accounting.
3. If the unit of accounting includes intangibles recorded in the separate financial statements of consolidated subsidiaries, it is possible that the sum of impairment losses recognized in the separate financial statements of the subsidiaries will not equal the consolidated impairment loss.

NOTE: Although counterintuitive, this situation can occur when:

1. *At the separate subsidiary level, an intangible asset is impaired since the cash flows from the other intangibles included in the unit of accounting that reside in other subsidiaries cannot be considered in determining impairment, and*
2. *At the consolidated level, when the intangibles are considered as a single unit of accounting, they are not impaired.*

---

4. Should a unit of accounting be included in a single reporting unit, that same unit of accounting and associated fair value is to be used in computing the implied fair value of goodwill for measuring any goodwill impairment loss.

Quantitative impairment test for indefinite-lived intangible asset. This test consists simply of comparing the fair value of the asset with its carrying amount.

Recognition of impairment loss for indefinite-lived intangible asset. If the carrying amount exceeds its fair value, the entity recognizes an impairment loss equal to that excess. After recognition of the loss, the adjusted carrying amount becomes the new basis for that intangible asset.

Presentation. To provide financial statement users with transparent information about intangible assets, ASC 350-30-45 requires:

- *Statement of Financial Position:* All intangible assets must be aggregated and presented as a separate line item in the statement of financial position. The entity may also choose to present individual intangible assets or classes of intangible assets as separate line items.
- *Income Statement:* As appropriate, the entity should present amortization expense and impairment losses in line items within continuing operations.

Software Developed for Internal Use (ASC 350-40)

ASC 350-40-05-02 and 03 provide guidance on accounting for the costs of software developed for internal use. Software must meet two criteria to be accounted for as internal-use software:

1. The software's specifications must be designed or modified to meet the reporting entity's internal needs, including costs to customize purchased software.
2. During the period in which the software is being developed, there can be no plan or intent to market the software externally, although development of the software can be jointly funded by several entities that each plan to use the software internally.

To justify capitalization of related costs, it is necessary for management to conclude that it is probable that the project will be completed and that the software will be used as intended. Absent that level of expectation, costs must be expensed currently as research and development costs. Entities that engage in both research and development of software for internal use and for sale to others must carefully identify costs with one or the other activity, since the former is (if all conditions are met) subject to capitalization, while the latter is expensed as research and development costs until technological feasibility is demonstrated, per ASC 985-20.

Costs subject to capitalization. Cost capitalization commences when an entity has completed the conceptual formulation, design, and testing of possible project alternatives, including the process of vendor selection for purchased software, if any. These early-phase costs (referred to as "preliminary project stage" in ASC 350-40) are analogous to research and development costs and must be expensed as incurred. These cannot be later restored as assets if the development proves to be successful.

Costs incurred subsequent to the preliminary project stage that meet the criteria under GAAP as long-lived assets are capitalized and amortized over the asset's expected economic life. Capitalization of costs begins when both of two conditions in ASC 350-40-25-12 are met.

- *First,* management having the relevant authority authorizes and commits to funding the project and believes that it is probable that it will be completed and that the resulting software will be used as intended.
- *Second,* the conceptual formulation, design, and testing of possible software project alternatives (i.e., the preliminary project stage) have all been completed.

Application development stage. Costs capitalized include those of the application development stage of the software development process. These include coding and testing activities and various implementation costs. ASC 350-40-30-1 limits these costs to:

1. External direct costs of materials and services consumed in developing or obtaining internal-use computer software;
2. Payroll and payroll-related costs for employees who are directly associated with and who devote time to the internal-use computer software project to the extent of the time spent directly on the project; and
3. Interest cost incurred while developing internal-use computer software, consistent with the provisions of ASC 835-20.

Costs expensed. General and administrative costs, overhead costs, and training costs are expensed as incurred (ASC 350-40-30-3). Even though these may be costs associated with the internal development or acquisition of software for internal use, under GAAP those costs relate to the period in which they are incurred. The issue of training costs is particularly important, since internal-use computer software purchased from third parties often includes, as part of the purchase price, training for the software (and often fees for routine maintenance as well). When the amount of training or maintenance fees is not specified in the contract, entities are required to allocate the cost among training, maintenance, and amounts representing the capitalizable cost of computer software. Training costs are recognized as expense as incurred. Maintenance fees are recognized as expense ratably over the maintenance period.

Examples of computer software developed for internal use. ASC 350-40-55-1 provides examples of when computer software is acquired or developed for internal use. The following is a list of examples illustrating when computer software is for internal use:

1. A manufacturing entity purchases robots and customizes the software that the robots use to function. The robots are used in a manufacturing process that results in finished goods.
2. An entity develops software that helps it improve its cash management, which may allow the entity to earn more revenue.
3. An entity purchases or develops software to process payroll, accounts payable, and accounts receivable.
4. An entity purchases software related to the installation of an online system used to keep membership data.
5. A travel agency purchases a software system to price vacation packages and obtain airfares.
6. A bank develops software that allows a customer to withdraw cash, inquire about balances, make loan payments, and execute wire transfers.
7. A mortgage loan servicing entity develops or purchases computer software to enhance the speed of services provided to customers.
8. A telecommunications entity develops software to run its switches that are necessary for various telephone services such as voice mail and call forwarding.
9. An entity is in the process of developing the accounts receivable system. The software specifications meet the entity's internal needs and the entity did not have a marketing plan before or during the development of the software. In addition, the entity has not sold any of its internal-use software in the past. Two years after completion of the project, the entity decided to market the product to recoup some or all of its costs.

10. A broker-dealer entity develops a software database and charges for financial information distributed through the database.
11. An entity develops software to be used to create components of music videos (for example, the software used to blend and change the faces of models in music videos). The entity then sells the final music videos, which do not contain the software, to another entity.
12. An entity purchases software to computerize a manual catalog and then sells the manual catalog to the public.
13. A law firm develops an intranet research tool that allows firm members to locate and search the firm's databases for information relevant to their cases. The system provides users with the ability to print cases, search for related topics, and annotate their personal copies of the database.
(ASC 350-40-55-1)

On the other hand, software that does not qualify as being for internal use includes software sold by a robot manufacturer to purchasers of its products; the cost of developing programs for microchips used in automobile electronic systems; software developed for both sale to customers and internal use; computer programs written for use in research and development efforts; and costs of developing software under contract with another entity. ASC 350-40-55-2 contains more examples.

Impairment. Impairment of capitalized internal-use software is recognized and measured in accordance with the provisions of ASC 360 in the same manner as tangible long-lived assets and other amortizable intangible assets. Per ASC 350-40-35-1, circumstances that might suggest that an impairment has occurred and that would trigger a recoverability evaluation include

1. A realization that the internal-use computer software is not expected to provide substantive service potential;
2. A significant change in the extent or manner in which the software is used;
3. A significant change has been made or is being anticipated to the software program; or
4. The costs of developing or modifying the internal-use computer software significantly exceed the amount originally expected. These conditions are analogous to those generically set forth by ASC 360, *Property, Plant, and Equipment*.

In some instances, ongoing software development projects will become troubled before being discontinued. ASC 350-40 indicates that management needs to assess the likelihood of successful completion of projects in progress. When it becomes no longer probable that the computer software being developed will be completed and placed in service, the asset is to be written down to the lower of the carrying amount or fair value, if any, less costs to sell. Importantly, it is a rebuttable presumption that any uncompleted software has a zero fair value.

ASC 350-40-35-3 provides indicators that the software is no longer expected to be completed and placed in service. These include

1. A lack of expenditures budgeted or incurred for the project;
2. Programming difficulties that cannot be resolved on a timely basis;
3. Significant cost overruns;
4. Information indicating that the costs of internally developed software will significantly exceed the cost of comparable third-party software or software products, suggesting that management intends to obtain the third-party software instead of completing the internal development effort;

5. The introduction of new technologies that increase the likelihood that management will elect to obtain third-party software instead of completing the internal project, and
6. A lack of profitability of the business segment or unit to which the software relates or actual or potential discontinuation of the segment.

Amortization. Paragraphs 4, 5, and 6 in ASC 350-40-35 provided guidance on amortization. As for other long-lived assets, the cost of computer software developed or obtained for internal use should be amortized in a systematic and rational manner over its estimated useful life. The intangible nature of the asset contributes to the difficulty of developing a meaningful estimate, however. Among the factors to be weighed are the effects of obsolescence, new technology, and competition. Management would especially need to consider if rapid changes are occurring in the development of software products, software operating systems, or computer hardware, and whether it intends to replace any technologically obsolete software or hardware.

Amortization commences for each module or component of a software project when the software is ready for its intended use, without regard to whether the software is to be placed in service in planned stages that might extend beyond a single reporting period. Computer software is deemed ready for its intended use after substantially all testing has been completed.

Internal-use software subsequently marketed. In some cases internal-use software is later sold or licensed to third parties, notwithstanding the original intention of management that the software was acquired or developed solely for internal use. In such cases, ASC 350-40 provides that any proceeds received are to be applied first as a reduction of the carrying amount of the software. No profit is recognized until the aggregate proceeds from sales exceed the carrying amount of the software. After the carrying value is fully recovered, any subsequent proceeds are recognized in revenue as earned.

Example of software developed for internal use

The Da Vinci Invention Company employs researchers based in countries around the world. The far-flung nature of its operations makes it extremely difficult for the payroll staff to collect timesheets, so the management team authorizes the design of an in-house, Web-based timekeeping system. The project team incurs the following costs:

Cost type	Charged to expense	Capitalized
Concept design	$ 2,500	
Evaluation of design alternatives	3,700	
Determination of required technology	8,100	
Final selection of alternatives	1,400	
Software design		$ 28,000
Software coding		42,000
Quality assurance testing		30,000
Data conversion costs	3,900	
Training	14,000	
Overhead allocation	6,900	
General and administrative costs	11,200	
Ongoing maintenance costs	6,000	
Totals	$57,700	$100,000

Thus, the total capitalized cost of this development project is $100,000. The estimated useful life of the timekeeping system is five years. As soon as all testing is completed, Da Vinci's controller begins amortizing using a monthly charge of $1,666.67. The calculation follows:

$100,000 capitalized cost ÷ 60 months = $1,666.67 amortization charge

Once operational, management elects to construct another module for the system that issues an e-mail reminder for employees to complete their timesheets. This represents significant added functionality, so the design cost can be capitalized. The following costs are incurred:

Labor type	Labor cost	Payroll taxes	Benefits	Total cost
Software developers	$11,000	$ 842	$1,870	$13,712
Quality assurance testers	7,000	536	1,190	8,726
Totals	$18,000	$1,378	$3,060	$22,438

The full $22,438 amount of these costs can be capitalized. By the time this additional work is completed, the original system has been in operation for one year, thereby reducing the amortization period for the new module to four years. The calculation of the monthly straight-line amortization follows:

$22,438 capitalized cost ÷ 48 months = $467.46 amortization charge

The Da Vinci management then authorizes the development of an additional module that allows employees to enter time data into the system from their cell phones using text messaging. Despite successfully passing through the concept design stage, the development team cannot resolve interface problems on a timely basis. Management elects to shut down the development project, requiring the charge of all $13,000 of programming and testing costs to expense in the current period.

After the system has been operating for two years, a Da Vinci customer sees the timekeeping system in action and begs management to sell it as a stand-alone product. The customer becomes a distributor, and lands three sales in the first year. From these sales Da Vinci receives revenues of $57,000, and incurs the following related expenses:

Expense type	Amount
Distributor commission (25%)	$14,250
Service costs	1,900
Installation costs	4,300
Total	$20,450

Thus, the net proceeds from the software sale is $36,550 ($57,000 revenue less $20,450 related costs). Rather than recording these transactions as revenue and expense, the $36,550 net proceeds are offset against the remaining unamortized balance of the software asset with the following entry:

Revenue	$57,000	
Fixed assets—software		$36,550
Commission expense		14,250
Service expense		1,900
Installation expense		4,300

At this point, the remaining unamortized balance of the timekeeping system is $40,278, which is calculated as follows:

Original capitalized amount	$100,000
+ Additional software module	22,438
– 24 months amortization on original capitalized amount	(40,000)
– 12 months amortization on additional software module	(5,610)
– Net proceeds from software sales	(36,550)
Total unamortized balance	$ 40,278

Immediately thereafter, Da Vinci's management receives a sales call from an application service provider who manages an Internet-based timekeeping system. The terms offered are so good that the company abandons its in-house system at once and switches to the ASP system. As a result of this change, the company writes off the remaining unamortized balance of its timekeeping system with the following entry:

Accumulated depreciation	45,610	
Loss on asset disposal	40,278	
Fixed assets—software		85,888

Website Development Costs (ASC 350-50)

The costs of developing a website, including the costs of developing services that are offered to visitors (e.g., chat rooms, search engines, blogs, social networking, e-mail, calendars, and so forth), are often quite significant. The SEC staff had expressed the opinion that a large portion of those costs should be accounted for in accordance with ASC 350-50, which sets forth certain conditions which must be met before costs may be capitalized.

Per ASC 350-50, costs incurred in the planning stage must be expensed as incurred. The cost of software used to operate a website must be accounted for consistent with ASC 350-40, unless a plan exists to market the software externally, in which case ASC 985-20, *Software-Costs of Software to Be Sold, Leased, or Marketed,* governs. Costs incurred to develop graphics (broadly defined as the "look and feel" of the web page) are included in software costs, and thus accounted for under ASC 350-40 or ASC 985-20, as noted in the foregoing. Costs of operating websites are accounted for in the same manner as other operating costs analogous to repairs and maintenance.

ASC 350-50-55 includes a detailed exhibit stipulating how a variety of specific costs are to be accounted for under its requirements.

25 ASC 360 PROPERTY, PLANT, AND EQUIPMENT

PERSPECTIVE AND ISSUES

Subtopic

ASC 360, *Property, Plant, and Equipment,* consists of two subtopics:

- ASC 360-10, *Overall,* which is further divided into two subsections:

  a. *General,* which provides guidance on accounting and reporting on property, plant, and equipment, including accumulated depreciation
  b. *Impairment or disposal of long-lived assets*, which contains guidance for

     1. Recognizing impairment of long-lived assets to be held and used and
     2. Long-lived assets to be disposed of by sale

- ASC 360-20, *Real Estate Sales,* which provides guidance on the sale of real estate other than retail land.

Scope and Scope Exceptions

ASC 360-10. The guidance in ASC the 360-10 general subsection applies to all entities. The guidance in the ASC 360-10 impairment or disposal subsections applies to

- Capital leases of lessees,
- Long-lived assets of lessors subject to operating leases,
- Proved oil and gas properties accounted for using the successful-efforts method of accounting, and long-term prepaid assets.

The subsection guidance does *not* apply to the following transactions and activities that are considered part of an asset or disposal group:

- If a long-lived asset (or assets) is part of a group that includes other assets and liabilities not covered by the Impairment or Disposal of Long-Lived Assets Subsections, the guidance in the Impairment or Disposal of Long-Lived Assets Subsections applies to the group. In those situations, the unit of accounting for the long-lived asset is its group. For a long-lived asset or assets to be held and used, that group is referred to as an asset group. For a long-lived asset or assets to be disposed of by sale or otherwise, that group is referred to as a disposal group. Examples of liabilities included in a disposal group are legal obligations that transfer with a long-lived asset, such as certain environmental obligations, and obligations that, for business reasons, a potential buyer would prefer to settle when assumed as part of a group, such as warranty obligations that relate to an acquired customer base.
- The guidance in the Impairment or Disposal of Long-Lived Assets Subsections does not change GAAP applicable to those other individual assets (such as accounts receivable and inventory) and liabilities (such as accounts payable, long-term debt, and asset retirement obligations) not covered by the Impairment or Disposal of Long-Lived Assets Subsections that are included in such groups.

The guidance in the Impairment or Disposal of Long-Lived Assets Subsections does not apply to the following transactions and activities:

1. Goodwill
2. Intangible assets not being amortized that are to be held and used
3. Servicing assets
4. Financial instruments, including investments in equity securities accounted for under the cost or equity method
5. Deferred policy acquisition costs
6. Deferred tax assets
7. Unproved oil and gas properties that are being accounted for using the successful-efforts method of accounting
8. Oil and gas properties that are accounted for using the full-cost method of accounting as prescribed by the Securities and Exchange Commission (SEC) (see Regulation S-X, Rule 4-10, Financial Accounting and Reporting for Oil and Gas Producing Activities Pursuant to the Federal Securities Laws and the Energy Policy and Conservation Act of 1975)
9. Certain other long-lived assets for which the accounting is prescribed elsewhere in the standards:
    a. For guidance on financial reporting in the record and music industry, see Topic 928.
    b. For guidance on financial reporting in the broadcasting industry, see Topic 920.
    c. For guidance on accounting for the costs of computer software to be sold, leased, or otherwise marketed, see Subtopic 985-20.
    d. For guidance on accounting for abandonments and disallowances of plant costs for regulated entities, see Subtopic 980-360.

The guidance in ASC 360-20 applies to all entities, and ASC 360-20-15-3 includes the following transactions in ASC 360-20 guidance.

1. All sales of real estate, including real estate with property improvements or integral equipment. The terms *property improvements* and *integral equipment* as they are used in this Subtopic refer to any physical structure or equipment attached to the real estate that cannot be removed and used separately without incurring significant cost. Examples include an office building, a manufacturing facility, a power plant, and a refinery.
2. Sales of property improvements or integral equipment subject to an existing lease of the underlying land should be accounted for in accordance with paragraphs 360-20-40-56 through 40-59.
3. The sale or transfer of an investment in the form of a financial asset that is in substance real estate.
4. The sale of timberlands or farms (that is, land with trees or crops attached to it).
5. Real estate time-sharing transactions (see Topic 978).
6. Loss of a controlling financial interest (as described in Subtopic 810-10) in a subsidiary that is in substance real estate because of a default by the subsidiary on its nonrecourse debt.

ASC 360-20 *excludes* the following transactions and activities:

- The sale of only property improvements or integral equipment without a concurrent (or contemplated) sale of the underlying land. However ASC 360-20 does apply to sales of property improvements or integral equipment with the concurrent lease (whether explicit or implicit in the transaction) of the underlying land to the buyer
- The sale of the stock or net assets of a subsidiary or a segment of a business if the assets of that subsidiary or that segment contain real estate. If such a transaction is, in substance, the sale of real estate, ASC 360-20 does apply.
- Exchanges of real estate for other real estate. See the accounting for nonmonetary transactions in ASC 845.
- The sale of debt and equity securities accounted for under ASC 320
- Retail land sales
- Natural assets such as those that have been extracted from the land (for example, oil, gas, coal, and gold). See ASC 932.

(ASC 360-20-15-10)

Overview

ASC 360-10, *Overall.* Property, plant, and equipment (sometimes referred to as "fixed assets," "tangible long-lived assets," or as "plant assets") are tangible property used in a productive capacity that will benefit the reporting entity for a period exceeding one year.

Among the accounting issues that can arise in accounting for fixed assets are

1. Determination of the amounts at which to initially record the assets, whether acquired through purchase or nonmonetary exchange or through construction by the reporting entity.
2. Whether management capitalizes discrete assets in groups or separately capitalizes the major individual components of individual assets (determination of the unit of account)
3. The proper accounting for postacquisition costs incurred with respect to the assets during their useful lives

4. The rate and pattern of allocation of amounts capitalized to the proper future periods, including, if applicable, periods during which the assets become impaired
5. Events that cause the assets to be reclassified to or from categories such as held and used, held for sale, or idle
6. Derecognition—the recording of sale, exchange, retirement, and/or disposal of the assets at or before the end of their productive lives.

Comparison of accounting and impairment rules. The following diagram summarizes and compares the rules affecting the accounting for tangible and intangible long-lived assets.

Summary and Comparison of Accounting and Impairment Rules

Attribute	PP&E. Website Dev., Internal-use software	Amortizable intangibles	Indefinite-lived intangibles	Goodwill[1]
Useful life?	Estimated useful life or, for leasehold improvements, the lesser of that life or the term of the lease		Indefinite	Indefinite for public; alternative for other entities of 10 year maximum
Consider residual or salvage value?	Yes	Yes—with either 3rd party commitment or ready market	No	
Capitalize interest if self-constructed?	Yes			
Recoverability evaluation or impairment test?	Recoverability evaluation		Optional qualitative and then quantitative impairment test	Optional Step 0 qualitative assessment and Special 2-step impairment test
Frequency	When events and circumstances warrant		At least annually; more often if events and circumstances warrant, unless entity has elected alternative, then triggering event.	
Change between amortizable and nonamortizable		Test for impairment, adjust if required		
Subsequent increases recognized?	No			
Level of aggregation for impairment purposes	Asset group or disposal group		Unit of accounting as specified by ASC 350-30-35	Reporting unit

ASC 360-20, *Real Estate Sales*. The substance of a sale of any asset is that the transaction unconditionally transfers the risks and rewards of ownership to the buyer. However, the economic substance of many real estate sales is that the risks and rewards of

1 See the chapter on ASC 350 for a technical update on the new alternative related to amortization and impairment testing for other than public entities.

ownership have *not* been clearly transferred. The turbulent and cyclical environments in the real estate and debt markets have led to the evolution of many complex methods of financing real estate transactions. For example, in some transactions the seller, rather than an independent third party, finances the buyer, while in others, the seller may be required to guarantee a minimum return to the buyer or continue to operate the property for a specified period of time. In many of these complex transactions, the seller still has some association with the property even after the property has been sold. The question that must be answered in these transactions is: At what point does the seller become disassociated enough from the property that profit may be recognized on the transaction?

Another question is under what circumstances is a transaction in substance the sale of real estate. To make that determination, ASC 360-20 suggests the preparer considers the nature of the entire component being sold, that is, not just the land, but the land plus the property improvements and integral equipment. Further, that determination shall not consider whether the operations in which the assets are involved are traditional or nontraditional real estate activities. For example, if a ski resort is sold and the lodge and ski lifts are considered to be affixed to the land (that is, they cannot be removed and used separately without incurring significant cost), then it would appear that the sale is in substance the sale of real estate and that the entire sale transaction would be subject to the provisions of this Subtopic. Transactions involving the sale of underlying land (or the sale of the property improvements or integral equipment subject to a lease of the underlying land) shall not be bifurcated into a real estate component (the sale of the underlying land) and a non-real-estate component (the sale of the lodge and lifts) for purposes of determining profit recognition on the transaction.

Accounting for retail land sales is governed by ASC 976. The purpose of ASC 360-20 is to present the guidelines that need to be considered when analyzing nonretail real estate transactions. ASC 840-40 dealing with sales-type real estate leases and sales-leaseback real estate transactions is covered in the chapter on ASC 840.

DEFINITIONS OF TERMS

Source: ASC 360-10-20 and 360-20-20 Glossaries, unless otherwise noted

Activities. The term activities is to be construed broadly. It encompasses physical construction of the asset. In addition, it includes all the steps required to prepare the asset for its intended use. For example, it includes administrative and technical activities during the preconstruction stage, such as the development of plans or the process of obtaining permits from governmental authorities. It also includes activities undertaken after construction has begun in order to overcome unforeseen obstacles, such as technical problems, labor disputes, or litigation.

Asset group. An asset group is the unit of accounting for a long-lived asset or assets to be held and used, which represents the lowest level for which identifiable cash flows are largely independent of the cash flows of other groups of assets and liabilities.

Buy-sell agreement. A contractual arrangement that gives both investors in a jointly owned entity the ability to offer to buy the other's interest. (EITF 07-6)

Component of an entity. A component of an entity comprises operations and cash flows that can be clearly distinguished, operationally and for financial reporting purposes, from the rest of the entity. A component of an entity may be a reportable segment or an operating segment, a reporting unit, a subsidiary, or an asset group.

Continuing investment. Payments that the buyer is contractually required to pay on its total debt for the purchase price of the property. (ASC 360-20-40-20)

Cost recovery method. Under the cost recovery method, no profit is recognized until cash payments by the buyer, including principal and interest on debt due to the seller and on existing debt assumed by the buyer, exceed the seller's cost of the property sold.

Deposit method. Under the deposit method, the seller does not recognize any profit, does not record notes receivable, continues to report in its financial statements the property and the related existing debt even if it has been assumed by the buyer, and discloses that those items are subject to a sales contract.

Disposal group. A disposal group for a long-lived asset or assets to be disposed of by sale or otherwise represents assets to be disposed of together as a group in a single transaction and liabilities directly associated with those assets that will be transferred in the transaction. A disposal group may include a discontinued operation along with other assets and liabilities that are not part of the discontinued operation.

Fair Value. The price that would be received to sell an asset or paid to transfer a liability in an orderly transaction between market participants at the measurement date.

Firm purchase commitment. A firm purchase commitment is an agreement with an unrelated party, binding on both parties and usually legally enforceable, that meets both of the following conditions:

1. It specifies all significant terms, including the price and timing of the transactions.
2. It includes a disincentive for nonperformance that is sufficiently large to make performance probable.

Full accrual method. A method that recognizes all profit from a real estate sale at the time of sale.

Impairment. Impairment is the condition that exists when the carrying amount of a long-lived asset (asset group) exceeds its fair value.

Initial investment. The sales value received by the seller at the time of sale. It includes a cash down payment, buyer's notes supported by an irrevocable letter of credit, payments by the buyer to third parties to reduce or eliminate the seller's indebtedness on the property, and any other amounts paid by the buyer that are part of the sales value. (ASC 360-20-40-10)

A method that recognizes revenue on the basis of payments made by the buyer on debt owed to the seller and payments by the buyer to the holder of primary debt. Each payment is apportioned between profit and cost recovery.

Installment method. The installment method apportions each cash receipt and principal payment by the buyer on debt assumed between cost recovered and profit. The apportionment is in the same ratio as total cost and total profit bear to the sales value.

Integral equipment. Integral equipment is any physical structure or equipment attached to the real estate that cannot be removed and used separately without incurring significant cost.

Nonpublic entity. Any entity that does not meet any of the following conditions:

1. Its debt or equity securities trade in a public market either on a stock exchange (domestic or foreign) or in an over-the-counter market, including securities quoted only locally or regionally.
2. It is a conduit bond obligor for *conduit debt securities* that are traded in a public market (a domestic or foreign stock exchange or an over-the-counter market, including local or regional markets).
3. It files with a regulatory agency in preparation for the sale of any class of debt or equity securities in a public market.

4. It is required to file or furnish financial statements with the Securities and Exchange Commission (SEC).
5. It is controlled by an entity covered by criteria 1 through 4.

Not-for-profit entity. An entity that possesses the following characteristics, in varying degrees, that distinguish it from a business entity:

1. Contributions of significant amounts of resources from resource providers who do not expect commensurate or proportionate pecuniary return
2. Operating purposes other than to provide goods or services at a profit
3. Absence of ownership interests like those of business entities.

Entities that clearly fall outside this definition include the following:

1. All investor-owned entities
2. Entities that provide dividends, lower costs, or other economic benefits directly and proportionately to their owners, members, or participants, such as mutual insurance entities, credit unions, farm and rural electric cooperatives, and employee benefit plans.

Operating segment. A component of a public entity. See ASC 280-10-50 for additional guidance on the definition of an operating segment.

Probable. The future event or events are likely to occur.

Public business entity. A public business entity is a business entity meeting any one of the criteria below. Neither a not-for-profit entity nor an employee benefit plan is a business entity.

1. It is required by the U.S. Securities and Exchange Commission (SEC) to file or furnish financial statements, or does file or furnish financial statements (including voluntary filers), with the SEC (including other entities whose financial statements or financial information are required to be or are included in a filing).
2. It is required by the Securities Exchange Act of 1934 (the Act), as amended, or rules or regulations promulgated under the Act, to file or furnish financial statements with a regulatory agency other than the SEC.
3. It is required to file or furnish financial statements with a foreign or domestic regulatory agency in preparation for the sale of or for purposes of issuing securities that are not subject to contractual restrictions on transfer.
4. It has issued, or is a conduit bond obligor for, securities that are traded, listed, or quoted on an exchange or an over-the-counter market.
5. It has one or more securities that are not subject to contractual restrictions on transfer, and it is required by law, contract, or regulation to prepare U.S. GAAP financial statements (including footnotes) and make them publicly available on a periodic basis (for example, interim or annual periods). An entity must meet both of these conditions to meet this criterion.

An entity may meet the definition of a public business entity solely because its financial statements or financial information is included in another entity's filing with the SEC. In that case, the entity is only a public business entity for purposes of financial statements that are filed or furnished with the SEC.

Reduced-profit method. A reduced profit is determined by discounting the receivable from the buyer to the present value of the lowest level of annual payments required by the sales contract over the maximum period, specified in ASC 360-20-40-19 through 360-20-40-20 and excluding requirements to pay lump sums.

Reporting unit. The level of reporting at which goodwill is tested for impairment. A reporting unit is an operating segment or one level below an operating segment (also known as a component).

CONCEPTS, RULES, AND EXAMPLES

Property, Plant, and Equipment

Cost considerations – initial acquisition. Determination of costs is critical to proper accounting for property, plant, and equipment. Upon acquisition, the reporting entity should capitalize all the costs necessary to deliver the asset to its intended location and prepare it for its productive use. This includes interest costs incurred during the period of time necessary to ready the asset for use (ASC 835-20-05-1). Examples of delivery and asset preparation costs relative to personal property include:

1. Sales, use, excise, and other taxes imposed on the purchase
2. Import duties
3. Finders' fees
4. Freight costs and related shipping insurance
5. Storage and handling costs
6. Installation and setup costs
7. Testing and breaking-in costs
8. Foundations and other costs related to providing proper support for the asset
9. Costs of reconditioning assets that are purchased used in order to prepare them for use.

When the asset consists of one or more buildings, capitalized costs include such items as:

1. Demolition of preexisting structures occupying the land, as well as costs related to excavating, grading, or filling the land to ready it for the new structure
2. Contract price paid to the general contractor and subcontractors
3. Architectural and engineering costs
4. Building permits
5. Costs of renovating a preexisting purchased building to convert it for use by the buyer.

Construction of tangible assets for internal use. All direct costs (labor, materials, payroll, and related benefit costs) of constructing an entity's own tangible fixed assets are capitalized. However, a degree of judgment is involved in allocating costs between indirect costs—a reasonable portion of which are allocable to construction costs—and general and administrative costs, which are treated as period costs.

The FASB has not addressed this issue. In ASC 605-35, the FASB (in the context of long-term construction contracts) indicates that, in order for costs to be capitalized (rather than be treated as period costs), they should be "… clearly related to production either directly or by an allocation based on their discernible future benefits." Later in that same section, illustrative examples of capitalizable costs are provided with a qualifier: "in *some circumstances*, support costs such as central preparation and processing of payrolls [are allocable as indirect costs]."

In ASC 350-40, (addressing the capitalization of costs of software self-developed for internal use), the FASB indicates that "general and administrative costs *and overhead costs* should not be capitalized as costs of internal-use software." The distinction between the two conflicting rules may be due to the former being applicable to tangible assets and the latter to intangible software costs, although both types of internally constructed assets are subject to interest capitalization during the production period.

Prudence suggests that management establish a carefully reasoned policy that is consistently followed and fully disclosed in the notes to the financial statements, to unambiguously inform the user about the methods used and amounts involved.

Interest cost. The recorded amount of an asset includes all of the costs necessary to get the asset set up and functioning properly for its intended use, including interest.

The principal purposes accomplished by the capitalization of interest costs are:

1. To obtain a more accurate measurement of the costs associated with the investment in the asset
2. To achieve a better matching of costs related to the acquisition, construction, and development of productive assets to the future periods that will benefit from the revenues that the assets generate.

All assets that require a time period to get ready for their intended use should include a capitalized amount of interest. However, accomplishing this level of capitalization would usually violate a reasonable cost/benefit test because of the added accounting and administrative costs that would be incurred. In many such situations, the effect of interest capitalization would be immaterial. Accordingly, interest cost is only capitalized as a part of the historical cost of the following qualifying assets when such interest is considered to be material. For more detailed information on capitalization of interest costs, see the chapter on ASC 835.

Acquisition of the residual value in leased assets. Upon acquisition, an interest in the residual value of a leased asset is recorded as an asset. The asset is recorded initially at:

- The amount of cash disbursed,
- The fair value of other consideration, and
- The present value of liabilities assumed.

To measure cost, use the fair value of the interest acquired if it is more evident than the fair value of assets or services surrendered or liabilities assumed.

Accounting for assets acquired in a group. It is important to differentiate the acquisition of assets in a group from those acquired in a business combination. To aid the practitioner in this endeavor, ASC 805 provides that, if the assets acquired and liabilities assumed constitute a "business," the transaction is a business combination; otherwise, it is accounted for as an asset acquisition.

The definition of a business is

> *... an integrated set of activities and assets that is capable of being conducted and managed for the purpose of providing a return in the form of dividends, lower costs, or other economic benefits directly to investors or other owners, members, or participants.*

Significantly, the definition does not

1. Require that outputs be present, although they frequently are present
2. Require that a business be self-sustaining. Rather it emphasizes that the activities and assets be *capable* of providing a return. Thus, an entity that is in its development stage and has not yet commenced its planned principal operations that otherwise meets the definition is considered to be a business.

When a reporting entity acquires assets and assumes liabilities that do not constitute a business, the transaction is accounted for as an asset acquisition. Assets acquired in an asset acquisition are initially recognized at their cost to the acquirer, including related transaction costs. The costs of assets acquired as a group are allocated to the individual assets acquired or liabilities assumed based on their relative fair values. Goodwill is not to be recognized in a transaction of this nature.

If assets are transferred between entities under common control, the entity receiving the net assets or equity interests initially recognizes the assets and liabilities transferred at their carrying amounts to the transferring entity at the transfer date. If there is a difference between the carrying amounts of the net assets transferred and their historical cost of the parent company because, for example, push-down accounting had not been applied, then the financial statements of the recipient entity are to reflect the transferred assets and liabilities at the historical cost of the parent of the entities under common control.

Unit of accounting. No specific guidance is provided in GAAP as to the unit of accounting to be used by management in capitalizing long-lived assets. Management might choose, with respect to assets it acquires or constructs, to aggregate individually identifiable assets and record them as if they were a single asset, and then depreciate them accordingly. Conversely, management might choose, with respect to longer-lived assets such as buildings or aircraft, to disaggregate the purchase price and separately record and depreciate the asset's major components over each component's own, individually determined estimated useful life. (Note that there may be significant tax advantages to separately accounting for components.)

Absent specific guidance regarding such practices, it is important that the financial statements provide sufficient information regarding the reporting entity's policies regarding capitalization of fixed assets and the criteria used by management to determine whether to record specified categories of assets in groups and/or by component. These policies are to be followed consistently, once adopted, with any future voluntary, postadoption changes in the policies subject to ASC 250, *Accounting Changes and Error Corrections*.

Other Asset Acquisition Concerns. For general guidance on assets acquired

- In a business combination, see ASC 805-20-25
- In a nonmonetary transaction, see ASC 845-10-30-1 through 30-10
- Under a capital lease, see ASC 840-30
- In a troubled debt restructuring, see ASC 310-40.

Cost considerations – postacquisition. Many different terms are used to describe costs that occur subsequent to initial acquisition including, but not limited to, the following:

Addition	Overhaul	Rehabilitation	Retrofitting
Alteration	Planned major maintenance	Renovation	Turnaround
Betterment	Rearrangement	Repair	
Improvement	Redevelopment	Replacement	
Maintenance	Refurbishment	Retooling	

Irrespective of the terminology used to describe a cost, the proper accounting treatment depends on a careful analysis of whether the cost is expected to provide future benefits to the reporting entity and, if so, the nature of those expected benefits.

Costs that increase the value of the asset. If the cost adds to the existing asset, in effect a new asset has been acquired that is subject to the same capitalization considerations applied in recognizing the original asset. As a practical expedient, most reporting entities establish a dollar threshold under which such costs are charged to expense, irrespective of their purpose (e.g., all costs under $1,500 are charged to expense). This is done under the assumption that the costs of capitalizing and depreciating the item exceed the benefits to users of the financial statements. In effect, these items are considered to be immaterial to the financial statements, both individually and in the aggregate.

Costs that increase the future service potential of the asset. If the cost increases the future service potential of the asset, it is accounted for in one of the following manners, depending on the individual facts and circumstances:

1. *Costs that do not extend the overall useful life of the asset.* If a portion of the original asset is being replaced, theoretically, the carrying value, if any, of the corresponding portion of the asset that is being replaced (cost less accumulated depreciation and less any impairment charges recognized in prior periods) should be removed from the accounting records and recorded as a loss in the period of the replacement. This accounting is seldom used in practice because, in general, accounting records for fixed assets are not maintained in the painstaking detail necessary to determine the carrying value of the individual components that comprise each asset. Instead, most companies will capitalize the replacement components under the rationale that the portion of the asset being replaced would have been depreciated sufficiently based on the useful life of the host asset so that at the time of replacement, little or no carrying value would remain to be removed.
2. *Costs that extend the overall useful life of the asset.* If, as a result of incurring a cost, the useful life of the host asset is extended without increasing its productivity or capacity, it has been suggested that the costs be recorded as a charge to accumulated depreciation, rather than capitalizing them as additions to fixed assets. Recording the transaction in this manner effectively recovers previously recognized depreciation and has the same effect on the net carrying value as capitalizing the addition. This treatment is seldom used in practice and has little theoretical appeal unless it is accompanied by a prospective change in the remaining estimated useful life of the host asset.

Planned major maintenance activities. ASC 908-360 contains guidance on accounting for the expenses related to airline maintenance activities. Line maintenance and other routine maintenance activities should be expenses as incurred. There are three acceptable methods for accounting for planned major maintenance activities:

1. Expense as incurred
2. Deferral
3. Built-in overhaul method

Additional guidance can be found in ASC 908-360-25-2 and in the AICPA's *Airlines – Audit and Accounting Guide.*

Reinstallations and rearrangements. If, as a result of reinstallation and rearrangement activities, the reporting entity expects to obtain benefits that extend into future years arising from improved production efficiency or reduced production costs, these costs can be capitalized and depreciated. If the activities are not expected to provide those future benefits, the costs are to be recognized as expense as incurred.

Relocation. The costs of moving a fixed asset to a new location at which it will operate in the same manner and with the same functionality as it did at its former location does not result in any future benefits, and therefore the costs of dismantlement, packaging/crating, shipping, and reinstallation are to be recognized as expenses as incurred.

Repairs and maintenance. If a cost does not extend an asset's useful life, increase its productivity, improve its operating efficiency, or add additional production capacity, the cost is to be recognized as an expense as incurred.

Depreciation and depletion. The costs of fixed assets are allocated to the periods of their expected useful life through depreciation or depletion. The method of depreciation chosen is that which results in a systematic and rational allocation of the cost of the asset (less its residual or salvage value) over the asset's expected useful life. The estimation of useful life takes a number of factors into consideration, including technological change, normal deterioration, and actual physical usage. The method used is to be selected based on either a function of time (e.g., technological change or normal deterioration) or as a function of actual physical usage. (ASC 360-10-35-8)

Depreciation methods based on time. Each of the examples below is based on the following facts.

Michele Corporation purchased a production machine and placed it in service on January 1, 20X1. The machine cost $100,000, has an estimated salvage value of $10,000, and an estimated useful life of five years.

1. Straight-line method—Depreciation expense is recognized evenly over the estimated useful life of the asset.

   Formula

   a. Compute the straight-line depreciation rate as

   $$\frac{1}{\text{Estimated useful life}}$$

   b. Multiply the depreciation rate by the cost less estimated salvage value.

Example of straight-line depreciation

a. Straight-line depreciation $= \frac{1}{5} = 20\%$ per year

b. 20% × ($100,000 – $10,000) = $18,000 annual depreciation

2. Accelerated methods—Depreciation expense is higher in the early years of the asset's useful life and lower in the later years. These methods are more appropriate than straight-line if the asset depreciates more quickly or has greater production capacity in the earlier years than it does as it ages. They are also sometimes used on the theory that maintenance and repair costs typically increase as assets age; therefore, in conjunction with accelerated depreciation total ownership costs (depreciation, maintenance, and repairs) will approximate straight-line.

   a. Declining balance—Annual depreciation is computed by multiplying the book value at the beginning of the fiscal year by a multiple of the straight-line rate of depreciation as computed above. (ASC 360-10-35-7)

      Formula

      Double-declining balance (ceases when the book value = the estimated salvage value)
      2 × Straight-line depreciation rate × Book value at the beginning of the year

The ASC specifically prohibits use of the IRS's Accelerated Cost Recovery System (ACRS) if a reasonable range of the asset's useful life is not reflected within the years specified by the ACRS. The ASC also states that the annuity method of depreciation is not acceptable. (ASC 360-10-35-9)

Example of double-declining balance depreciation

Year	*Net book value, beginning of year*	*Double-declining balance depreciation computed as 2 × SL rate × beginning NBV*	*Net book value, end of year*
1	$100,000	$40,000	$60,000
2	60,000	24,000	36,000
3	36,000	14,400	21,600
4	21,600	8,640	12,960
5	12,960	2,960	10,000 limited by salvage value
Total		$90,000	

b. Sum-of-the-years' digits (SYD) depreciation

Formula

(Cost – Estimated salvage value) × Applicable percentage

$$\text{Applicable percentage} = \frac{\text{Number of years of estimated life remaining at the beginning of the year}}{\text{SYD}}$$

$$\text{SYD} \quad \frac{n(n+1)}{2} \quad \text{where } n = \text{estimated useful life}$$

Example of sum-of-the-years' digits (SYD) depreciation

$$\text{SYD} = \frac{5(5+1)}{2} = 15$$

This formula yields the sum of each year of the estimated useful life
1 + 2 + 3 + 4 + 5 = 15

Year	*Remaining estimated useful life at beginning of year*	*SYD*	*Applicable percentage*	*Annual depreciation*
1	5	5/15	33.33%	$30,000
2	4	4/15	26.67	24,000
3	3	3/15	20.00	18,000
4	2	2/15	13.33	12,000
5	1	1/15	6.67	6,000
Totals	15		100.00%	$90,000

3. Present value methods—Depreciation expense is lower in the early years and higher in the later years. The rate of return on the investment remains constant over the life of the asset. Time value of money formulas are used.

   a. Sinking fund—Uses the future value of an annuity formula.
   b. Annuity fund—Uses the present value of an annuity formula.

Partial-year depreciation. When an asset is either acquired or disposed of during the year, the full-year depreciation calculation is prorated between the accounting periods involved.

Example of partial-year depreciation

Ginger Corporation, a calendar-year entity, acquired a machine on June 1, 2012 that cost $40,000 with an estimated useful life of four years and a $2,500 salvage value. The depreciation expense for each full year of the asset's life is calculated as:

	Straight-line	Double-declining balance		Sum-of-years' digits	
Year 1	37,500* ÷ 4 = 9,375	50% × 40,000 =	20,000	4/10 × 37,500* =	15,000
Year 2	9,375	50% × 20,000 =	10,000	3/10 × 37,500 =	11,250
Year 3	9,375	50% × 10,000 =	5,000	2/10 × 37,500 =	7,500
Year 4	9,375	50% × 5,000 =	2,500	1/10 × 37,500 =	3,750
	37,500		37,500		37,500

* *(40,000 – 2,500)*

Because the first full year of the asset's life does not coincide with the company's fiscal year, the amounts shown above must be prorated as follows:

	Straight-line		Double-declining balance		Sum-of-years' digits	
2012	7/12 × 9,375 =	5,469	7/12 × 20,000 =	11,677	7/12 × 15,000 =	8,750
2013		9,375	5/12 × 20,000 =	8,333	5/12 × 15,000 =	6,250
			7/12 × 10,000 =	5,833	7/12 × 11,250 =	6,563
				14,166		12,813
2014		9,375	5/12 × 10,000 =	4,167	5/12 × 11,250 =	4,687
			7/12 × 5,000 =	2,917	7/12 × 7,500	4,375
				7,084		9,062
2015		9,375	5/12 × 5,000 =	2,083	5/12 × 7,500 =	3,125
			7/12 × 2,500 =	1,458	7/12 × 3,750 =	2,188
				3,541		5,313
2016	5/12 × 9,375 =	3,096	5/12 × 2,500 =	1,042	5/12 × 3,750 =	1,562
		37,500		37,500		37,500

As an alternative to proration, an entity may follow any one of several simplified conventions.

1. Record a full year's depreciation in the year of acquisition and none in the year of disposal.
2. Record one-half year's depreciation in the year of acquisition and one-half year's depreciation in the year of disposal.

Depreciation method based on actual physical usage—units of production. Depreciation is based upon the number of units produced by the asset in a given year.

$$\text{Depreciation rate} = \frac{\text{Cost less salvage value}}{\text{Estimated number of units to be produced by the asset over its estimated useful life}}$$

$$\text{Units of production depreciation} = \text{Depreciation rate} \times \text{Number of units produced during the current year}$$

Other depreciation methods. In addition to the foregoing, a group (composite) method is sometimes used. This method averages the service lives of a number of assets using a weighted-average of the units and depreciates the group or composite as if it were a single unit. A group consists of similar assets, while a composite is made up of dissimilar assets.

$$\text{Depreciation rate} = \frac{\text{Sum of the straight-line depreciation of individual assets}}{\text{Total asset cost}}$$

Depreciation expense: Depreciation rate × Total group (composite) cost

Gains and losses are not recognized on the disposal of an asset but are netted into accumulated depreciation.

Depletion. Depletion is the annual charge for the use of natural resources. In order to compute depletion, it is first necessary to establish a depletion base, the amount of the depletable asset.

The depletion base includes the following elements:

1. *Acquisition costs*—The cost to obtain the property rights through purchase or lease, royalty payments to the property owner,
2. *Exploration costs*—Typically, these costs are expenses as incurred; however in certain circumstances in the oil and gas industry, they may be capitalized,
3. *Development costs*—Intangible development costs such as drilling costs, tunnels, shafts, and wells,
4. *Restoration costs*—The costs of restoring the property to its natural state after extraction of the natural resources has been completed.

The amount of the depletion base, less its estimated salvage value is charged to depletion expense each period using a depletion rate per unit extracted, or *unit depletion rate* that is computed using the following formula:

$$\frac{1}{\text{Total expected recoverable units}} \times \text{Depletion base} \times \text{Units extracted}$$

The unit depletion rate is revised frequently due to the uncertainties surrounding the recovery of natural resources. The revision is made prospectively; the remaining undepleted cost is allocated over the remaining expected recoverable units.

Example of depletion

The Cheyenne Oil Company drills a well in the Denver Basin oil field. It expects to incur the following acquisition, development, and restoration costs associated with the well:

Land acquisition	$172,000
Land preparation (road and drill pad)	38,000
Well drilling	301,000
Trunk line construction	29,000
Estimated site restoration cost	50,000
Total	$590,000

A considerable amount of extraction equipment is also positioned at the well, but since it can be moved among well sites and is therefore not a fixed part of this well, it is depreciated separately.

The entire $590,000 is capitalized. Cheyenne's geologists calculate that the well has proven reserves of 250,000 barrels of crude oil. In the first year of production, the well produces 45,000 barrels of oil. The depletion charge for the first year of operation follows:

$$\frac{1}{\text{250,000 barrels of proven reserves}} \times \$590{,}000 = \$2.36 \text{ per barrel extracted unit depletion rate}$$

$2.36 per barrel extracted × 45,000 barrels extracted = $106,200 first-year depletion charge

During the second year of the well's operation, Cheyenne's engineers revise the estimated remaining proven reserves upward by 20,000 barrels from 250,000 barrels to 270,000 barrels, based on improved oil recovery techniques. Also, due to new environmental laws, the estimated site restoration cost increases by $10,000, increasing the depletion base from $590,000 to $600,000.

Total production for the second year is 62,000 barrels of oil. The depletion charge for the first year is not retroactively adjusted; instead changes in cost and estimated total production are accounted for prospectively. The depletion calculation for the second year follows:

$$\frac{1}{\text{225,000 barrels of proven reserves remaining}} \times \$493{,}800 \times 62{,}000 \text{ barrels extracted in year 2}$$

= $136,069, which is the depletion charge of $2.19 per barrel extracted

These depletion expenses leave $357,731 of capitalized costs yet to be amortized over remaining proven reserves of 163,000 barrels, representing a future depletion charge of $2.19 per barrel, barring any further future changes in estimates.

Income tax methods. Income tax deductions for depreciation (referred to in income tax law as "cost recovery deductions"), including the Section 179 and bonus depreciation deductions discussed below, are not in accordance with generally accepted accounting principles because, in general, they are not based on estimated useful lives and do not allocate cost to future periods benefited on a systematic and rational basis. Therefore, differences between financial statement and income tax depreciation result in temporary differences between the carrying values of the long-lived assets for income tax and financial reporting purposes. These temporary differences are taken into account in the calculation of deferred income taxes, as discussed in the chapter on ASC 740.

Accelerated Cost Recovery System. Assets placed in service between 1981 and 1986 are depreciated under the Accelerated Cost Recovery System (ACRS). ACRS ignores salvage value. Thus, the asset's entire income tax basis is depreciable over the specified recovery period to be used for each class of asset. Property is placed into classes and the depreciation method and life for each class is specified. Election of optional depreciation methods was also permitted. Depreciation deductions are calculated by multiplying the asset's unadjusted basis by the specified depreciation percentage for the related time period. The depreciation percentage will depend upon the asset's class, recovery year, depreciation method, and convention used to compute depreciation in the year of acquisition.

Modified Accelerated Cost Recovery System. For assets placed in service after 1986, income tax depreciation is calculated using the Modified Accelerated Cost Recovery System (MACRS) under IRC §168, which also ignores salvage value and divides assets into classes. Depreciation deductions are calculated by multiplying the asset's unadjusted basis by the appropriate depreciation percentage. The percentages are based on the type of property, class life, depreciation method, and acquisition-year convention. Depreciation deductions are limited for certain assets such as listed property (primarily automobiles). Optional depreciation methods may also be elected.

Additional deductions available in year placed in service. The US Congress has frequently passed legislation providing businesses substantial income tax benefits in the form of accelerated first-year deductions for newly purchased depreciable property placed in service.

Two such provisions of note that are and have been available to businesses are (1) the "Election to Expense Certain Property under Section 179" ("§179 deduction"), and (2) the special allowance for "Bonus Depreciation: in IRC §168(k)," as recently amended by the American Recovery and Reinvestment Act of 2009.

The benefits of these deductions are taken prior to computing depreciation as described above and, of course, the amount of the deductions reduces the depreciable basis of the affected assets for income tax purposes.

Income tax depreciation will differ in amount from financial statement depreciation because of differences in treatment of salvage value, recovery methods, recovery periods, and the use of conventions for assets placed in service during the year.

The difference between income tax depreciation and financial statement depreciation is reported as a reconciling item (referred to as a "Schedule M-1 or Schedule M-3 adjustment") on a corporation's US federal income tax return.

Impairment and disposal. The GAAP rules for measuring and recording impairment of assets are not uniform for all assets or for all specialized industries. The table below distinguishes between those assets subject to the general impairment rules and those for which different, specialized rules apply.

Subject to General Impairment Rules (ASC 360-10-35)

Assets associated with discontinued operations
Cable television plant
Capitalized interest costs
Capitalized motion picture film costs
Development stage enterprises' assets
Financial institutions' depositor-relationship, borrower-relationship, and credit cardholder intangibles
Real estate
Software developed or obtained for internal use
Title plant costs of title insurance and title abstract companies, and title agents
Website development costs

Subject to Specialized Impairment Rules

Broadcasters' program rights (ASC 920-350-35)
Computer software to be sold, leased, or otherwise marketed (ASC 985-20-35)
Cost-method investments (ASC 325-20-35-2)
Deferred income tax assets (ASC 740-10-30-16 et seq.)
Equity method investments (ASC 323-10-35-31 et seq.)
Financial institutions' servicing assets (ASC 860-50)
Financial instruments—Available-for-sale and held-to-maturity securities (ASC 320-10-35)
Goodwill (ASC 350-20-35)
Loans receivable (these rules are not limited to lending institutions) (ASC 310-30)
Recording masters in the recorded music industry (ASC 928-340-25-2)

Split between General and Specialized Impairment Standards

Subject to general impairment standard	*Subject to specialized impairment standard*
Public utilities and certain other regulated enterprises	Abandoned plants and disallowed plant costs of regulated enterprises (ASC 980-360-35)
Intangibles that are amortized	Intangibles that are not amortized (ASC 350-30-35-15)
Lessee capital leases	Lessor direct financing, sales-type, and leveraged leases (ASC 840-30-35-25)
Lessor assets subject to operating leases	
Proved properties and wells of oil and gas producing companies with related facilities and equipment that are accounted for using the successful efforts method of accounting	Unproved properties of oil and gas producing companies (ASC 932-360-35-11)
All insurance assets except deferred insurance policy acquisition costs	Deferred insurance policy acquisition costs (ASC 944-30-35)

Impairment of long-lived assets to be held and used. Under US GAAP, impairment losses are only recognized when the carrying amount of the impaired asset (or asset group) is not *recoverable* (ASC 360-10-35-17). Recoverability is determined by comparing the carrying amount of the asset (or asset group) on the date it is being evaluated for recoverability to the sum of the *undiscounted* cash flows expected to result from its use and eventual disposition. It is important to note that under ASC 360-10-35, an asset's carrying value can exceed its fair value (thus technically it could be considered to be impaired), yet if the carrying value is recoverable from expected future cash flows from its use and disposition, as defined, no impairment loss is recognized.

When to test. ASC 360-10-35 uses "events and circumstances" criteria to determine when, if at all, an asset (or asset group) is evaluated for recoverability. Thus, there is no set interval or frequency for recoverability evaluation. ASC 360-10-35-21 provides a list of examples of events or changes in circumstances that indicate the carrying amount of an asset (asset group) *may* not be recoverable and thus is to be evaluated for recoverability. It is important to note that the list of events and circumstances below is not intended to be all-inclusive. Rather, it is intended to provide examples of situations that warrant evaluation of an asset or group of assets for recoverability to determine whether an impairment loss must be recognized.

1. A significant decrease in the market price of a long-lived asset (asset group)
2. A significant adverse change in the extent or manner in which a long-lived asset (asset group) is being used or in its physical condition
3. A significant adverse change in legal factors or in the business climate that could affect the value of a long-lived asset (asset group), including an adverse action or assessment by a regulator
4. An accumulation of costs significantly in excess of the amount originally expected for the acquisition or construction of a long-lived asset (asset group)
5. A current period operating or cash flow loss combined with a history of operating or cash flow losses or a projection or forecast that demonstrates continuing losses associated with the use of a long-lived asset (asset group)
6. A current expectation that, more likely than not, a long-lived asset (asset group) will be sold or otherwise disposed of significantly before the end of its previously estimated useful life.

Financial statement preparers are required to consider, for each interim and annual reporting period, the applicability of these indicators as well as other indicators not included in the list that might be applicable in the circumstances. Reliance should not be placed on "disclosure checklists" for this purpose as they are not designed to be used to determine the correct application of GAAP recognition and measurement requirements.

Measurement of the impairment loss. Under ASC 360-10-35-17, if the carrying amount of an asset or asset group (in use or under development) is evaluated and found not to be fully recoverable (the carrying amount exceeds the estimated gross, undiscounted cash flows from use and disposition), then an impairment loss must be recognized. The impairment loss is measured as the excess of the carrying amount over the asset's (or asset group's) fair value.

Fair value (as defined in the ASC Master Glossary) is the price that the reporting entity would receive to sell the asset on the measurement date in an orderly transaction between market participants in the principal (or most advantageous) market for the asset. To measure fair value, management must determine the asset's (or group of assets') highest and best use, which may not coincide with the manner in which the reporting entity is currently using it. Fair value measurements are discussed and illustrated in the chapter on ASC 820.

In conjunction with the recoverability evaluation, it may also be necessary to review the appropriateness of the method of depreciation (amortization) and depreciable (amortizable) lives of the asset or group of assets. If, as a result of that review the remaining useful life of the asset (group) is revised, the revised useful life is used to develop the cash flow estimates used to evaluate recoverability. Changes to the accounting method (e.g., from straight-line to accelerated depreciation), however, would be made prospectively after the application of ASC 360 (ASC 360-10-35-22).

Asset group impairment analysis. ASC 360 includes the concept of the *asset group*, defined as the lowest level for which identifiable cash flows are largely independent of the cash flows of other assets and liabilities (ASC 360-10-35-23).

An asset group could be

- The whole company
- An operating segment as defined in the ASC Master Glossary
- A reporting unit as defined in the ASC Master Glossary
- A business
- A part of a business (such as a division or department).

Refer to asset groups shown in the diagram entitled *"Alternative Balance Sheet Segmentation"* in the chapter on ASC 280.

- Asset group (a) is a single division of a subsidiary
- Asset groups (b) and (c) are each separate businesses that comprise another division of the same subsidiary
- Asset group (d) is an entire subsidiary consisting of a single business
- Asset group (e) is a product line that is part of a larger business and, after the disposal of disposal group (f), will constitute an entire operating segment
- Asset groups (g) and (h) are each separate businesses that comprise a subsidiary.

If a long-lived asset cannot be assigned to any asset group because it does not have identifiable cash flows largely independent of other long-lived assets individually or in asset groups (such as a corporate headquarters), then that asset is evaluated for recoverability by reference to all assets and liabilities of the entity (ASC 360-10-35-24).

The assets and liabilities in the group that are neither long-lived assets nor goodwill are separately identified. Since those assets and liabilities are not subject to the provisions of ASC 360, the GAAP applicable to their valuation is applied *before* applying ASC 360 to the group. For example, allowances for uncollectible accounts receivable and inventory obsolescence are recorded as necessary. (ASC 360-10-35-27)

Effect of goodwill on grouping. In assessing the composition of asset groups, management must be aware of the interrelationship between ASC 360, *Property, Plant, and Equipment,* and ASC 350, *Intangibles—Goodwill and Other.* Goodwill can only be assigned to an asset group that is being evaluated for recoverability if the asset group is either a reporting unit or includes a reporting unit.

Estimates of future cash flows. For the purposes of recoverability evaluation, future cash flows are defined as cash inflows less the associated cash outflows directly associated with, and that are expected to arise as a direct result of, the use and eventual disposition of the asset group excluding interest that is recognized as a period expense when incurred. (ASC 360-10-35-29)

The estimate of future cash flows:

- Is based on all available evidence
- Incorporates assumptions that marketplace participants would use in their estimates of fair value when that information is available without undue cost or effort; otherwise, the entity incorporates its own assumptions, including the "highest and best use" of the asset (or group)
- Is to be consistent with assumptions used by the entity for comparable periods such as internal budgets and projections, accruals related to incentive compensation plans, or information communicated to others
- Is made for the remaining estimated useful life of the asset (or the primary asset of an asset group) to the entity

NOTE: The primary asset is the long-lived asset being depreciated (or intangible asset being amortized) that is the most significant component asset from which the group derives its cash-flow generating capacity. The primary asset cannot be land or nonamortizing intangible assets. If the primary asset does not have the longest useful life of the long-lived assets in the group, cash flow estimates must assume that the entire group will be sold at the end of the primary asset's useful life. (ASC 360-10-35-31)

- Takes into account future expenditures necessary to complete an asset under development including interest capitalized under ASC 835-20
- Includes future outflows necessary to maintain the existing service potential of all or a component of the asset or group of assets
- Excludes cash flows for future capital expenditures that increase the service potential of a long-lived asset or group of assets
- Is required to take into account the likelihood of possible cash flow outcomes if alternative courses of action are being contemplated, or if ranges of cash flows are estimated to occur under different scenarios.

(ASC 360-10-35-30)

NOTE: ASC 360 indicates that, when uncertainties exist with respect to timing and amount of future cash flows, using an expected present value technique will be the appropriate way to estimate fair value.

Allocating impairment losses to a group. If an asset group is found to have sustained an impairment loss, the loss is only applied to reduce the carrying amounts of the long-lived asset or assets in the group. In general, the loss is allocated to the long-lived assets in the group based on their relative carrying values. However, the carrying value of any individual asset in the group that has a fair value that is separately identifiable without "undue cost or effort" is not to be reduced below that fair value. (ASC 360-10-35-28)

After recognition of impairment losses, the adjusted carrying amounts of the impaired long-lived assets constitute their new cost bases. Depreciation (amortization) is recognized prospectively over their remaining estimated useful lives. The adjustment to carrying values to reflect an impairment loss may never be restored.

Example of impairment

(Refer to the diagram under the section entitled, "Alternative Balance Sheet Segmentation." in the chapter on ASC 280)

The Parent Holding Company (PHC) owns and operates seven subsidiaries comprising eleven businesses, primarily engaged in the manufacturing and distribution of food and beverages. All of the businesses are headquartered in the same building that is owned by PHC. Additional facts are as follows:

- Due to general economic conditions and the failure, in 20X4, of several high-tech start-ups in the city in which PHC is headquartered, the local commercial real estate market is depressed. PHC's headquarters building has eight years remaining in its expected useful life and its carrying value is $4,500,000. PHC has substantial excess space in the building, which it does not expect to need in the foreseeable future. PHC management expects the real estate market to remain depressed for the next two years and when the market recovers, it will consider selling the building and either leasing or purchasing a smaller facility in the area.
- Subsidiary 2 operates a South American bottling plant that produces a line of carbonated beverages that is sold exclusively on that continent. A large increase in sugar prices during 2012 has resulted in lower margins and, due to partial price increases, a 30% decrease in units sold during the year. The plant operates in a building that Subsidiary 2 leases under an operating lease with five years remaining. The primary asset owned by Subsidiary 2 is what it refers to as its "bottling line" which consists of equipment that mixes ingredients, adds carbon dioxide, and fills and caps the bottles. The bottling line has a remaining useful life of four years. The other assets in the asset group have remaining useful lives of seven years. Subsidiary 2 has been profitable for the past three years (20X1–20X2) but is showing a small operating loss for 20X4. Additional information regarding Subsidiary 2 follows:

	Bottling line (primary asset)	*Asset B*	*Asset C*	*Totals*
Net book value	$87,000	$19,000	$17,000	$123,000
Remaining life	4 years	7 years	7 years	
Expected cash inflows, net of outflows				
20X5				4,000
20X6				6,000
20X7				7,000
20X8				8,000
From assumed disposition—end of 20X8				75,000
Total expected net operating cash flows				$100,000

- PHC is in the process of preparing its consolidated financial statements for the year ended December 31, 20X4. Thus far, normal depreciation of PHC and its subsidiaries' fixed assets has been recorded and impairment has not yet been considered.

Analysis.

Step 1—*Identify asset groups.* This has been diagrammed in the diagram in the chapter on ASC 280. Note that the headquarters building cannot be assigned to any specific asset group since it does not generate independent cash flows. Therefore, its potential impairment is assessed at the PHC level on a consolidated basis.

Step 2—*Consider the applicability of impairment indicators.* Assess each of PHC's asset groups (and on a consolidated basis), as to whether the example events and circumstances provided by ASC 360 or any other events and circumstances indicate that PHC's long-lived assets may be impaired. Based on the decline in the local real estate market, it would be presumed that the market price of the headquarters building has declined, and thus the building should be evaluated for recoverability. Analysis of the situation of Subsidiary 2 is more complex. Two of the factors in ASC 360 warrant consideration. First, it could be argued that the increase in sugar prices constitutes a significant adverse change in the business climate. This might be mitigated if management believed the price increase to be a short-term condition and assuming this belief was supportable by past experience. Second, the current period operating loss should be considered. Since there has not been a history of such losses, the relevance of this factor depends on management's forecast of future results. If Subsidiary 2 were forecast to continue to experience operating losses, this would indicate that the asset group needs to be evaluated for recoverability. For the purposes of this example, we will assume that continuing losses are forecast.

Step 3—*Evaluate recoverability.* Two recoverability evaluations are required, one for the headquarters building and the other for the asset group represented by Subsidiary 2. Since the headquarters building is not allocable to an asset group, its recoverability is evaluated using consolidated cash flows that include the cash flows of Subsidiary 2. Thus, the recoverability evaluation for Subsidiary 2 is performed first.

Subsidiary 2's recoverability evaluation is performed by reference to the four-year remaining useful life of the bottling line, its primary asset. The cash flows used to evaluate recoverability are required to assume that the asset group will be sold in its entirety at the end of four years.

Comparison of the $100,000 sum of the undiscounted expected cash flows from use and disposition to the carrying amount of $123,000 indicates that the carrying amount of the asset group is not expected to be fully recoverable. Therefore, the asset group is impaired.

The recoverability evaluation for the building is performed using an estimate of expected cash flows, weighted for the probabilities as to whether management will pursue the sale of the facility when the local economy recovers in two years, versus retaining it for the remaining eight years of its expected useful life. In addition, depending on different scenarios of future economic conditions and business performance by PHC's businesses, different levels of cash flows could result both from operations and from disposition. Acknowledging the inherent uncertainties associated with predicting future results and the subjectivity involved in the estimation process, management formulated its best judgment regarding the probabilities of the best, worst, and most-likely scenarios.

Estimate of Future Cash Flows

Course of action	*Use of the asset (consolidated basis)*	*Disposition of the asset*	*Total*	*Probability assessment*	*Probability-weighted possible cash flows*
Sale at the end of 2 years	$100,000	$3,500,000	$3,600,000	20%	$720,000
	130,000	4,600,000	4,730,000	60%	2,838,000
	150,000	4,600,000	4,750,000	20%	950,000
				100%	$4,508,000
Sale at the end of 8 years	$410,000	$4,000,000	$4,410,000	20%	$882,000
	550,000	4,700,000	5,250,000	60%	3,150,000
	620,000	4,800,000	5,420,000	20%	1,084,000
				100%	$5,116,000

Upon review of the analysis above, management determined that it is 70% probable that it will sell the building at the end of two years. Consequently, the expected cash flows from the use and disposition of the building are as follows:

Course of action	*Probability-weighted possible cash flows*	*Probability assessment for course of action*	*Undiscounted Expected cash flows*
Sale at the end of 2 years	$4,508,000	70%	$3,155,600
Sale at the end of 8 years	5,116,000	30%	1,534,800
		100%	$4,690,400

Comparison of the undiscounted expected cash flows or $4,690,400 per above to the $4,500,000 carrying value of the building at December 31, 20X4, indicates that the carrying value of the building is expected to be fully recoverable, and thus the building is not impaired.

As a result of the above analysis, management may decide upon one of the alternative courses of action. If so, the expected cash flows from that course of action would be used in the recoverability evaluation since it would no longer be necessary to probability-weight the outcomes.

Step 4—*Compute impairment, if any*. Market information regarding the asset group of Subsidiary 2 is not available "without undue cost and effort." Management elects to use the traditional present value of estimated cash flows method to estimate fair value because it believes that uncertainty regarding the timing and amounts of cash flows is minimal (but, if this were not the case, management would use an *expected present value* technique to make this estimate). This estimation method is referred to in ASC 820 as a *discount rate adjustment* technique. Using this technique requires:

- A single set of most-likely cash flows that includes assumptions regarding the likelihood of occurrence or nonoccurrence of events that potentially influence the estimated amounts
- A discount rate approximating a market rate of return based on observable rates of return for comparable assets traded in the same market as the asset or group of assets being measured

The 8% interest rate used for this illustration is assumed to be a rate commensurate with the risks involved (unlike the risk-free rate sometimes used in applying an expected present value technique). The computation is as follows:

Year	*Net cash flows*	*Present value at 8%*[2]	*Carrying value of asset group*	*Impairment adjustment required*
20X5	$ 4,000	$ 3,704		
20X6	6,000	5,144		
20X7	7,000	5,557		
20X8–Use	8,000	5,880		
20X8–Sale	75,000	55,127		
	$100,000	$75,412	$123,000	$47,588

Asset	*Carrying value*	*Pro rata allocation factor*	*Allocation of impairment loss*	*Tentative adjusted carrying amount*
Bottling line	$ 87,000	71%	$33,660	$53,340
Asset B	19,000	15%	7,351	11,649
Asset C	17,000	14%	6,577	10,423
Total	$123,000	100%	$47,588	$75,412

Note that the adjusted carrying amount is captioned "tentative." This is because Subsidiary 2 was able to obtain a quoted market price of $16,000 for Asset B. ASC 360 specifies that assets are not to be reduced to an amount below their fair value. To obtain the proper result, the impairment loss requires reallocation among the assets comprising the asset group.

Asset	*Tentative adjusted carrying amount*	*Pro rata reallocation factor*	*Reallocation of excess impairment loss*	*Adjusted carrying amount*
Bottling line	$53,340	84%	$(3,640)	$49,700
Asset C	10,423	16%	(711)	9,712
Subtotal	63,763	100%	(4,351)	
Asset B	11,649		4,351	16,000
Total	$75,412		$ --	$75,412

[2] *These present values can be calculated using standardized spreadsheet software; specialized software used to compute time value of money and amortization schedules; the table of factors in Chapter 1 for the present value of a single future amount; or the formula used to derive that table, which is also cited in Chapter 1.*

Step 5—*Record the impairment adjustment.* The entry to record impairment in the accounting records of Subsidiary 2 is as follows:

Impairment loss (operating section of income statement)	47,588	
Accumulated depreciation—Machinery and equipment		47,588

To adjust the carrying value of the bottling line and related assets to reflect an impairment loss for 2012.

Other impairment considerations. Besides the foregoing, other issues arise as a consequence of applying the impairment rules.

Going concern. The example above included an estimate of cash flows at the entity level to assess whether the building was impaired. If the estimate had indicated that the building was impaired, management must consider whether the cash flows estimated for at least the ensuing year will be sufficient for the entity to continue as a going concern. Disclosure in the financial statements of management's plans may be required under ASC 205-30, *Going Concern.*

Significant estimates. If, in the example above, the expected cash flows used to assess the recoverability of the building were closer to the building's $4,500,000 carrying value, consideration is given to the applicability of ASC 275, *Risks and Uncertainties.* The assumptions used in the cash flow estimates could be considered significant estimates for which it is reasonably possible changes could occur in the near term (the ensuing year) and, consequently, disclosure would be required.

Treatment of certain site restoration/environmental exit costs. ASC 360-10-55 discusses how, for the purpose of performing the recoverability evaluation under ASC 360, to treat the costs of future site restoration or closure (referred to as "environmental exit costs") that may be incurred if the asset is sold, abandoned, or ceases operations. To conform to ASC 360, references to an "asset" are also applicable to an "asset group."

ASC 410-20, *Asset Retirement and Environmental Obligations,* requires asset retirement obligations recognized as liabilities to be included as part of the capitalized cost of the related asset and, to avoid double-counting, the cash settlement of those liabilities to be excluded from the expected future cash flows used to evaluate recoverability under ASC 360. If the asset retirement costs have not yet been recognized under ASC 410-20 because the obligation is being incurred over more than one reporting period during the useful life of the asset, then the cash flows for those unrecognized costs are to be included in the expected future cash flows.

The cash flows for environmental exit costs that are not recorded as liabilities under ASC 410-30 may not occur until the end of the asset's life if the asset ceases to be used or may be delayed indefinitely as long as management retains ownership of the asset and chooses not to sell or abandon it. Consequently, management's intent regarding future actions with respect to the asset is to be taken into account in determining whether to include or exclude these cash flows from the computation of the expected future cash flows used to evaluate recoverability under ASC 360. If management is contemplating alternative courses of action to recover the carrying amount of the asset or if a range is estimated for the amount of possible future cash flows, the likelihood (probability) of these possible outcomes is to be considered in connection with the recoverability evaluation under ASC 360.

ASC 360-10-55 provides examples illustrating situations where cash flows for environmental exit costs not recognized as liabilities under ASC 410-30 are either included in or excluded from the undiscounted expected future cash flows used to evaluate a long-lived asset or group of assets for recoverability under ASC 360.

Deferred income taxes. Impairment losses are not deductible for US federal income tax purposes. Consequently, financial statement recognition of these losses will result in differences between the carrying amounts of the impaired assets for financial reporting purposes and income tax purposes. These differences are considered temporary differences and are accounted for under the provisions of ASC 740.

Long-lived assets to be disposed of by sale. An asset may be disposed of individually or as part of a disposal group (see Definition of Terms section in this chapter).

Long-lived assets (or disposal groups) are classified as held-for-sale in the period in which *all* of the following six criteria are met (ASC 360-10-45-9):

1. Management possessing the necessary authority commits to a plan to sell the asset (disposal group)
2. The asset (disposal group) is immediately available for sale on an "as is" basis (i.e., in its present condition subject only to usual and customary terms for the sale of such assets)
3. An active program to find a buyer and other actions required to execute the plan to sell the asset (disposal group) have commenced
4. An assessment of remaining actions required to complete the plan indicates that it is unlikely that significant changes will be made to the plan or that the plan will be withdrawn
5. Sale of the asset (disposal group) is probable, as that term is used in the context of ASC 450-20 (i.e., likely to occur), and transfer of the asset (disposal group) is expected to qualify for recognition as a completed sale within one year

NOTE: Certain exceptions to the one-year requirement are set forth in ASC 360-10-45-11 for events and circumstances beyond the entity's control that extend the period required to complete the sale.

6. The asset (disposal group) is being actively marketed for sale at a price that is reasonable in relation to its current fair value.

For a long-lived asset (disposal group) that has been newly acquired in a business combination to be classified as held for sale at that date, it must

- Meet criterion 5 above (subject to the same exceptions noted in 5), *and*
- Any other of the required criteria that are not met at the date of acquisition are judged to be probable of being met within a short period (approximately three months or less) of acquisition.

(ASC 360-10-45-12)

If the criteria are met after the date of the statement of financial position but prior to issuance of the entity's financial statements, the long-lived asset continues to be classified as held-and-used at the date of the statement of financial position (ASC 360-10-45-13). Appropriate subsequent events disclosures would be included in the financial statements in accordance with ASC 855, *Subsequent Events*.

Measurement. (ASC 360-10-35-43) Long-lived assets (disposal groups) classified as held-for-sale are measured at the lower of their carrying amount or fair value less cost to sell. A loss is recognized for any initial or subsequent write-down to fair value less cost to sell. A gain is recognized for any subsequent increase in fair value less cost to sell, but recognized gains may not exceed the cumulative losses previously recognized. Long-lived assets that are classified as held-for-sale are presented separately on the statement of financial position.

Long-lived assets (disposal groups) being held for sale are not to be depreciated (amortized) while being presented under the held-for-sale classification. Interest and other expenses related to the liabilities of a held-for-sale disposal group are accrued as incurred.

Cost to sell consists of costs that directly result from the sales transaction that would not have been incurred if no sale were transacted. Cost to sell includes brokerage commissions, legal fees, title transfer fees, and other closing costs that must be incurred prior to transfer of legal title to assets. Prior to measurement of fair value less cost to sell, the entity adjusts the carrying amounts of any assets included in the disposal group not covered by ASC 360 including any goodwill (e.g., establishes appropriate valuation allowances for receivables and inventory, recognizes other-than-temporary impairment of applicable investment securities, etc.).

The entity may not accrue, as part of cost to sell, expected future losses associated with operating the long-lived asset (disposal group) while it is classified as held-for-sale (ASC 360-10-35-38). Costs associated with the disposal, including costs of consolidating or closing facilities, are only recognized when the actual costs are incurred. If the exception to the one-year requirement applies (permitted when there are certain events and circumstances beyond the entity's control), and the sale is expected to occur in more than one year, the cost to sell is discounted to its present value.

Reclassification. If, at any time after meeting the criteria to be classified as held-for-sale, the asset (disposal group) no longer meets those criteria, the long-lived asset (disposal group) is to be reclassified from held-for-sale to held-and-used, measured at the *lower of:*

- Carrying value prior to classification as held-for-sale, adjusted for any depreciation (amortization) that would have been recognized had the asset (disposal group) continued to be classified as held-and-used, or
- Fair value at the date of the subsequent decision not to sell the asset (disposal group).

The adjustment required to the carrying amount of an asset (disposal group) being reclassified from held-for-sale to held-and-used is included in income from continuing operations in the period that the decision is made not to sell. FASB concluded that impairment losses from long-lived assets to be held and used, gains or losses recognized on long-lived assets to be sold, and other costs associated with exit or disposal activities (as defined in ASC 420) should be accounted for consistently. Therefore, if the entity reports a measure of operations (e.g., income from operations), these amounts are reported in operations unless they qualify as discontinued operations, as explained below. The income statement classification of these amounts is to be consistent with the accounting policy for classifying the depreciation of the underlying assets per the following examples:

Machinery and equipment used in production	Cost of goods sold
Office equipment	General and administrative
Trucks and delivery equipment	General and administrative or, if a separate category of expenses, selling expense
Combination factory/office building	Allocate between cost of goods sold, and general and administrative in the same manner as depreciation

If a component of an entity (as defined below) is reclassified as held-and-used, the results of that component that had previously been reported in discontinued operations are reclassified and included in income from continuing operations for all periods presented.

Upon removal of an individual asset or liability from a disposal group classified as held-for-sale, the remaining part of the group is to be evaluated as to whether it still meets all six of the criteria to be classified as held-for-sale. If all of the criteria are still met, then the remaining assets and liabilities will continue to be measured and accounted for as a group. If not all of the criteria are met, then the remaining long-lived assets are to be measured individually at the lower of their carrying amounts or fair value less cost to sell at that date. Any assets that will not be sold are reclassified as held-and-used as described above. (ASC 360-10-35-45)

Example of long-lived assets to be disposed of by sale

The Hewitt Candy Company chooses to stop sales of its candy cane product line, and accordingly shifts the $840,000 carrying cost (i.e., book value) of its candy cane twister equipment into a held-for-sale account. After several months of trying to close a sale of the equipment, Hewitt's controller determines that the fair value of the twister equipment is now $855,000. However, after projected sale costs that include commissions, legal fees, and title transfer fees are included, the net fair value is only $825,000. The controller accordingly writes down the equipment cost to $825,000 with the following entry:

Loss on decline of fair value of equipment held-for-sale	15,000	
Equipment held-for-sale		15,000

After another two months, the controller determines that the equipment's fair value, net of estimated disposition costs, has increased to $860,000. Although this represents a gain of $35,000 over the adjusted carrying cost of the equipment, he can only recognize a gain up to the amount of all previously recorded losses, which he does with the following entry:

Equipment held-for-sale	15,000	
Recovery of fair value of equipment held-for-sale		15,000

Six months after the twister equipment is classified as held-for-sale, Hewitt's management concludes that it will wait for better economic conditions to market and sell the equipment. Hewitt's controller reclassifies the equipment as held-and-used with the following entry:

Equipment held-and-used	840,000	
Equipment held-for-sale		840,000

Prior to its classification as held-for-sale, the equipment had been depreciated on a straight-line basis over a ten-year life span using an original equipment base cost of $1.2 million, so $60,000 would otherwise have been incurred while the equipment was classified as held-for-sale; this would have reduced the equipment's net carrying cost (i.e., book value) from $840,000 to $780,000. Since this is lower than the estimated fair value of $860,000 as of the date when the decision was made to halt sale activities, the controller records the following entry:

Depreciation—equipment	60,000	
Accumulated depreciation—equipment		60,000

After four more months, Hewitt receives an unsolicited cash offer of $875,000 for the twister equipment, which it accepts. During these additional four months, the equipment has been depreciated by a further $40,000. Hewitt's controller records the sale with the following entry:

Cash	875,000	
Accumulated depreciation—equipment	460,000	
Equipment held-and-used		1,200,000
Gain on equipment sale		135,000

Long-lived assets to be disposed of other than by sale. Long-lived assets may be abandoned, exchanged, or distributed to owners in a spin-off. Until the actual disposal occurs, the assets continue to be classified on the statement of financial position as "held and used." During the period prior to disposal, they are subject to conventional impairment rules applicable to assets held and used.

Abandoned assets are considered disposed of under ASC 360 when they cease to be used. Temporary idling of an asset, however, is not considered abandonment (ASC 360-10-35-49). At the time an asset is abandoned, ASC 360 prescribes that its carrying value be adjusted to its salvage value, if any, but not less than zero (i.e., a liability cannot be recorded upon abandonment). If an acquired asset meets the criteria to be considered a defensive intangible asset, it is prohibited from being considered abandoned upon its acquisition.

If the entity commits to a plan to abandon the asset before the end of its previously estimated useful life, the depreciable life is revised in accordance with the rules governing a change in estimate under ASC 250 and depreciation of the asset continues until the end of its shortened useful life (ASC 360-10-35-46).

Per ASC 360-10-40-4 if a long-lived asset is to be disposed of either by spinning it off to owners of the company or in an exchange transaction for a similar productive long-lived asset, the disposal is recognized when the actual exchange or spin-off occurs. If that asset (group) is evaluated for recoverability while held and used and before the disposal, the estimates of future cash flows are to assume that the disposal will not occur and that the asset will continue to be held and used for the remainder of its useful life. Two separate impairment losses might be recognized in this scenario.

1. An impairment loss for the asset while it is held and used
2. An additional impairment loss if, upon exchange or spin-off, which are recorded under ASC 845 at the asset's recorded amount, the recorded amount/carrying value exceeds fair value.

Discontinued operations. ASC 360 introduced the concept of a "component of an entity." A component of an entity is distinguishable from the rest of the reporting entity because it has its own operations and cash flows. It may be a reportable segment or operating segment (as defined by ASC 280), a reporting unit (as defined in the ASC Master Glossary, a subsidiary, or an asset group.

If a component of an entity is either classified as held-for-sale as a discontinued operation or has been disposed of during the period, the results of its operations are to be reported in discontinued operations. Discontinued operations are covered in depth in the chapter on ASC 205, *Presentation of Financial Statements.*

Long-lived assets temporarily idled. The only reference in ASC 360 to the temporary idling of long-lived assets is the provision that prohibits recognizing temporary idling as abandonment. At a minimum, however, if material assets are temporarily idled, the following considerations apply:

1. Idling constitutes a "significant adverse change in the extent or manner in which…" the asset (or asset group) is being used, which is an indicator requiring a recoverability evaluation under ASC 360.
2. The estimates of future cash flows used in performing the recoverability evaluation are to consider, on a probability-weighted basis, the range of outcomes under consideration by management regarding when the asset will be returned to service, sold, or abandoned.
3. Idle property and equipment is to be clearly and unambiguously captioned and segregated on the statement of financial position from both the "held-and-used" and

"held-for-sale" categories, since it does not qualify for either classification, with appropriate disclosure of the relevant circumstances.

4. As part of the ongoing review of the appropriateness of useful lives, the remaining useful life of the idle equipment is to be reassessed.
5. Evaluation by management of whether temporary suspension of depreciation or amortization of the asset is warranted until it is returned to service.

Real Estate Sales Other than Retail Land Sales

Scope. ASC 360-20-15 explicitly states that real estate sales transactions under ASC 360 include real estate with property enhancements or integral equipment. This defines property improvements and integral equipment as (ASC 360-20-15-3a) "any physical structure or equipment attached to real estate or other parts thereof that cannot be removed and used separately without incurring significant cost." Examples include an office building or manufacturing plant. (For guidance on retail land sales that are sales, on a volume basis, of lots that are subdivisions of large tracts of land, see ASC 976.)

Criteria for using full accrual method. Profit from real estate sales is recognized in full, provided the following (ASC 360-20-40-3):

1. The profit is determinable (i.e., the collectability of the sales price is reasonably assured or the amount that will not be collectible can be estimated).
2. The earnings process is virtually complete, that is, the seller is not obliged to perform significant activities after the sale to earn the profit.

When both of these conditions are satisfied, the method used to recognize profits on real estate sales is referred to as the full accrual method. If both of these conditions are not satisfied, recognition of all or part of the profit is postponed.

The Codification goes on to say (ASC 360-20-40-4) that for real estate sales, the collectibility of the sales price is reasonably assured when the buyer has demonstrated a commitment to pay. This commitment is supported by a substantial initial investment, along with continuing investments that give the buyer a sufficient stake in the property such that the risk of loss through default motivates the buyer to honor its obligations to the seller. Collectibility of the sales price is also assessed by examining the conditions surrounding the sale (e.g., credit history of the buyer; age, condition, and location of the property; and history of cash flows generated by the property).

The full accrual method is appropriate and profit is recognized in full at the point of sale for real estate transactions when all of the following criteria are met (ASC 360-20-40-5):

1. A sale is consummated.
2. The buyer's initial and continuing investments are adequate to demonstrate a commitment to pay for the property.
3. The seller's receivable is not subject to future subordination.
4. The seller has transferred to the buyer the usual risks and rewards of ownership in a transaction that is in substance a sale, and the seller does not have a substantial continuing involvement in the property.

On sales in which an independent third party provides all of the financing for the buyer, the seller is most concerned that criterion number 1 above is met. For such sales, the sale is usually consummated on the closing date. When the seller finances the buyer, the seller must analyze the economic substance of the agreement to ascertain that criteria 2, 3, and 4 are also met (i.e., whether the transaction clearly transfers the risks and rewards of ownership to the buyer).

Consummation of a sale. A sale is considered consummated when the following conditions are met (ASC 360-20-40-7):

1. The parties are bound by the terms of a contract.
2. All consideration has been exchanged.
3. Any permanent financing for which the seller is responsible has been arranged.
4. All conditions precedent to closing have been performed.

When a seller is constructing office buildings, condominiums, shopping centers, or similar structures, item 4 may be applied to individual units rather than the entire project. These four conditions are usually met on or after closing, not at the point the agreement to sell is signed or at a preclosing meeting. Closing refers to the final steps of the transaction (i.e., when consideration is paid, the mortgage is secured, and the deed is delivered or placed in escrow). If the consummation criteria have not been satisfied, the seller uses the deposit method of accounting until all of the criteria are met (i.e., the sale has been consummated).

Buyer's initial and continuing involvement. The initial and continuing investment requirements for the full accrual method apply unless the seller receives any of the following as the full sales value of the property (ASC 360-20-40-15):

a. Cash without any seller contingent liability on any debt on the property incurred or assumed by the buyer,
b. The buyer's assumption of the seller's existing nonrecourse debt on the property,
c. The buyer's assumption of all recourse debt on the property with the complete release of the seller from those obligations, or
d. Any combination of such cash and debt assumption.

In computing the buyer's initial investment, debt incurred by the buyer that is secured by the property is not considered part of the buyer's initial investment. This is true whether the debt was incurred directly from the seller or other parties or indirectly through assumption. Payments to the seller from the proceeds of such indebtedness are not included as part of the buyer's initial investment. (ASC 360-20-40-17)

If the transaction does not qualify for full accrual accounting and, consequently, is being accounted for using installment, cost recovery or reduced profit methods, payments made on debt the preceding paragraph are not considered to be buyer's cash payments. However, if the profit deferred under the applicable method exceeds the outstanding amount of seller financing and the outstanding amount of buyer's debt secured by the property for which the seller is contingently liable, the seller recognizes the excess in income.

Adequacy of the buyer's initial investment. Once the sale is consummated, the next step is to determine whether the buyer's initial investment adequately demonstrates a commitment to pay for the property and the reasonable likelihood that the seller will collect it. This determination is made by comparing the buyer's initial investment to the sales value of the property. ASC 360-20-55-1 and 55-2 specifically detail items that are includable as the initial investment and the minimum percentages that the initial investment must bear to the sales value of the property. To make the determination of whether the initial investment is adequate, the sales value of the property must also be computed.

Computation of sales value. The sales value of property in a real estate transaction is computed as follows:

Stated sales price
\+ Proceeds from the issuance of an exercised purchase option
\+ Other payments that are, in substance, additional sales proceeds (e.g., management fees,

points, prepaid interest, or fees required to be maintained in advance of the sale that will be applied against amounts due to the seller at a later point)
- A discount that reduces the buyer's note to its present value
- Net present value of services seller agrees to perform without compensation
- Excess of net present value of services seller performs over compensation that seller will receive

= Sales value of the property

Composition of the initial investment. Sales transactions are characterized by many different types of payments and commitments made between the seller, buyer, and third parties; however, the buyer's initial investment only includes the following (ASC 360-20-40-10):

1. Cash paid to the seller as a down payment
2. Buyer's notes given to the seller that are supported by irrevocable letters of credit from independent lending institutions
3. Payments by the buyer to third parties that reduce existing indebtedness the seller has on the property
4. Other amounts paid by the buyer that are part of the sales value
5. Other consideration received by the seller that can be converted to cash without recourse to the seller; for example, other notes of the buyer.

ASC 360-20-40-13 specifically states that the following items are not included as initial investment:

1. Payments by the buyer to third parties for improvements to the property
2. A permanent loan commitment by an independent third party to replace a loan made by the seller
3. Funds that have been or will be loaned, refunded, or directly or indirectly provided to the buyer by the seller or loans guaranteed or collateralized by the seller for the buyer.

ASC 360-20-40-15 deals with a range of possible forms of financing and the implications of each for profit recognition under ASC 360. The following guidelines are to be used by a seller of real estate in applying ASC 360:

1. In determining whether a transaction qualifies for accounting using the full accrual method of profit recognition, the initial and continuing investment requirements of ASC 360 must be considered unless the seller has unconditionally received all amounts due and is not at risk related to the financing.
2. In determining the buyer's initial investment, payments made on debt incurred by the buyer that is secured by the property (irrespective of whether the debt is incurred directly from the seller or other parties or indirectly by assumption) is not part of the initial investment. Also excluded from the initial investment are payments made to the seller out of the proceeds from debt described in the preceding sentence.
3. Under the installment method, cost recovery method, and reduced-profit recognition methods, payments described in 2. above are not considered to be cash payments from the buyer. If, however, the deferred profit under the method applied under ASC 360 exceeds the sum of (1) the outstanding amount of seller financing, and (2) the outstanding amount of the buyer's debt secured by the property for which the seller is contingently liable, the excess amount is recognized as income by the seller.

Size of initial investment. Once the initial investment is computed, its size must be compared to the sales value of the property. To qualify as an adequate initial investment, the initial investment must be equal to at least a major part of the difference between usual loan limits established by independent lending institutions and the sales value of the property. The minimum initial investment requirements for real estate sales (other than retail land sales) vary depending upon the type of property being sold (ASC 360-20-40-18). The following table from ASC 360-20-55-2 provides the limits for the various properties:

Type of property	Minimum initial investment expressed as a percentage of sales value
Land	
Held for commercial, industrial, or residential development to commence within two years after sale	20
Held for commercial, industrial, or residential development to commence more than two years after sale	25
Commercial and Industrial Property	
Office and industrial buildings, shopping centers, and so forth:	
Properties subject to lease on a long-term lease basis to parties with satisfactory credit rating; cash flow currently sufficient to service all indebtedness	10
Single-tenancy properties sold to a buyer with a satisfactory credit rating	15
All other	20
Other income-producing properties (hotels, motels, marinas, mobile home parks, and so forth):	
Cash flow currently sufficient to service all indebtedness	15
Start-up situations or current deficiencies in cash flow	25
Multifamily Residential Property	
Primary residence:	
Cash flow currently sufficient to service all indebtedness	10
Start-up situations or current deficiencies in cash flow	15
Secondary or recreational residence:	
Cash flow currently sufficient to service all indebtedness	15
Start-up situations or current deficiencies in cash flow	25
Single-Family Residential Property (including condominium or cooperative housing)	
Primary residence of the buyer	5[a]
Secondary or recreational residence	10[a]

[a] *If collectibility of the remaining portion of the sales price cannot be supported by reliable evidence of collection experience, the minimum initial investment [is to] be at least 60% of the difference between the sales value and the financing available from loans guaranteed by regulatory bodies such as the Federal Housing Authority (FHA) or the Veterans Administration (VA), or from independent, established lending institutions. This 60% test applies when independent first-mortgage financing is not utilized and the seller takes a receivable from the buyer for the difference between the sales value and the initial investment. If independent first mortgage financing is utilized, the adequacy of the initial investment on sales of single-family residential property [is] determined [as described in the next paragraph].*

Lenders' appraisals of specific properties often differ. Therefore, if the buyer has obtained a permanent loan or firm permanent loan commitment for maximum financing of the property from an independent lending institution, the minimum initial investment must be the greater of the following (ASC 360-20-55-1):

1. The minimum percentage of the sales value of the property specified in the above table or

2. The lesser of
   a. The amount of the sales value of the property in excess of 115% of the amount of a newly placed permanent loan or firm loan commitment from a primary lender that is an independent established lending institution
   b. 25% of the sales value.

To illustrate the determination of whether an initial investment adequately demonstrates a commitment to pay for property, consider the following example.

Example determining adequacy of initial investment

Marcus, Inc. exercised a $2,000 option for the purchase of an apartment building from Rubin, Inc. The terms of the sales contract required Marcus to pay $3,000 of delinquent property taxes, pay a $300,000 cash down payment, assume Rubin's recently issued first mortgage of $1,200,000, and give Rubin a second mortgage of $500,000 at a prevailing interest rate.

Step 1 — Compute the sales value of the property.

Payment of back taxes to reduce Rubin's liability to local municipality	$ 3,000
Proceeds from exercised option	2,000
Cash down payment	300,000
First mortgage assumed by Marcus	1,200,000
Second mortgage given to Rubin	500,000
Sales value of the apartment complex	$2,005,000

Step 2 — Compute the initial investment.

Cash down payment	$ 300,000
Payment of back taxes to reduce Rubin's liability to local municipality	3,000
Proceeds from exercised option	2,000
	$ 305,000

Step 3 — Compute the minimum initial investment required.

a. The minimum percentage of the sales value of the property as specified in the table is 200,500 (= $2,005,000 × 10%).

b. 1. The amount of the sales value of the property in excess of 115% of the recently placed permanent mortgage is $625,000 (sales value of $2,005,000 – $1,380,000 [= 115% of $1,200,000]).

   2. 25% of the sales value ($2,005,000) is $501,250.

The lesser of b.1 and b.2 is b.2, $501,250. The greater of a and b is b, $501,250. Therefore, to record this transaction under the full accrual method (assuming all other criteria are met), the minimum initial investment must be equal to or greater than $501,250. Since the actual initial investment is only $305,000, all or part of the recognition of profit from the transaction must be postponed.

If the sale has been consummated but the buyer's initial investment does not adequately demonstrate a commitment to pay, the transaction is accounted for using the installment method when the seller is reasonably assured of recovering the cost of the property if the buyer defaults. However, if the recovery of the cost of the property is not reasonably assured should the buyer default or if the cost has been recovered and the collection of additional amounts is uncertain, the cost recovery or deposit method is used.

Adequacy of the buyer's continuing investments. The collectibility of the buyer's receivable must be reasonably assured; therefore, for full profit recognition under the full accrual method, the buyer must be contractually required to pay each year on its total debt for the purchase price of the property an amount at least equal to the level annual payment that would be needed to pay that debt (both principal and interest) over a specified period. This period is no more than twenty years for land, and no more than the customary amortization term of a first mortgage loan by an independent lender for other types of real estate. For continuing investment purposes, the contractually required payments must be in a form that is acceptable for an initial investment. If the seller provides funds to the buyer, either directly or indirectly, these funds must be subtracted from the buyer's payments in determining whether the continuing investments are adequate. (ASC 360-20-40-19 and 50-20)

The indebtedness on the property does not have to be reduced proportionately. A lump-sum (balloon) payment will not affect the amortization of the receivable as long as the level annual payments still meet the minimum annual amortization requirement. For example, a land real estate sale may require the buyer to make level annual payments at the end of each of the first five years and then a balloon payment at the end of the sixth year. The continuing investment criterion is met provided the level annual payment required in each of the first five years is greater than or equal to the level annual payment that would be made if the receivable were amortized over the maximum twenty-year (land's specified term) period.

Release provisions. An agreement to sell real estate may provide that part or all of the property sold will be released from liens by payment of an amount sufficient to release the debt or by an assignment of the buyer's payments until release. To meet the criteria of an adequate initial investment, the investment must be sufficient both to pay the release on property released and to meet the initial investment requirements on property not released. If not, profit is recognized on each released portion as if it were a separate sale when a sale has been deemed to have taken place. (ASC 360-20-21 and 40-23)

Seller's receivable subject to future subordination. The seller's receivable should not be subject to future subordination. Future subordination by a primary lender would permit the lender to obtain a lien on the property, giving the seller only a secondary residual claim. This subordination criterion does not apply if either of the following occur (ASC 360-20-40-25):

1. A receivable is subordinate to a first mortgage on the property existing at the time of sale.
2. A future loan, including an existing permanent loan commitment, is provided for by the terms of the sale and the proceeds of the loan will be applied first to the payment of the seller's receivable.

If the seller's receivable is subject to future subordination, profit is recognized using the cost recovery method. The cost recovery method is justified because the collectibility of the sales price is not reasonably assured in circumstances when the receivable may be subordinated to amounts due to other creditors.

Seller's continuing involvement. Sometimes sellers continue to be involved with property for periods of time even though the property has been legally sold. The seller's involvement often takes the form of profit participation, management services, financing, guarantees of return, construction, etc. The seller does not have a substantial continuing involvement with property unless the risks and rewards of ownership have been clearly transferred to the buyer.

If the seller has some continuing involvement with the property and does not clearly transfer substantially all of the risks and rewards of ownership, profit is recognized by a method other than the full accrual method. The method chosen is determined by the nature and extent of the seller's continuing involvement. As a general rule, profit is only recognized at the time of sale if the amount of the seller's loss due to the continued involvement with the property is limited by the terms of the sales contract. In this event, the profit recognized at this time is reduced by the maximum possible loss from the continued involvement. (ASC 360-20-40-37)

Continuing investment not qualifying. If the sale has been consummated and the minimum initial investment criteria have been satisfied but the continuing investment by the buyer does not meet the stated criterion, the seller recognizes profit by the reduced profit method at the time of sale if payments by the buyer each year will at least cover both of the following (ASC 360-20-40-33):

1. The interest and principal amortization on the maximu first mortgage loan that could be obtained on the property
2. Interest, at an appropriate rate, on the excess of the aggregate actual debt on the property over such a maximum first mortgage loan.

If the payments by the buyer do not cover both of the above, the seller recognizes profit by either the installment or cost recovery method. (ASC 360-20-40-34)

Graduated payment mortgages. Graduated payment mortgages for which negative principal amortization is recognized do not meet the continuing investment tests in ASC 360, and thus full profit is not to be recognized immediately. (ASC 360-20-40-35) Mortgage insurance is not to be considered the equivalent of an irrevocable letter of credit in determining whether profit is to be recognized, and the purchase of such insurance is not in itself a demonstration of commitment by the buyer to honor its obligation to pay for the property. The sole exception to this rule is that an irrevocable financial instrument from an established independent insuring institution, such as FHA (Federal Housing Administration) and VA (Veteran's Affairs), profits may be recognized under the full accrual method. (ASC 360-20-40-12) The seller may consider these to be the equivalent of irrevocable letters of credit.

Profit-sharing, financing, and leasing arrangements. In real estate sales, it is often the case that economic substance takes precedence over legal form. Certain transactions, though possibly called sales, are in substance profit-sharing, financing, or leasing arrangements and are accounted for as such. These include situations in which (ASC 360-20-40-38):

1. The seller has an obligation to repurchase the property, or the terms of the transaction allow the buyer to compel the seller to repurchase the property or give the seller an option to do so.
2. The seller is a general partner in a limited partnership that acquires an interest in the property sold and holds a receivable from the buyer for a significant part (15% of the maximum first-lien financing) of the sales price.
3. The seller guarantees the return of the buyer's investment or a return on that investment for an extended period of time.
4. The seller is required to initiate or support operations, or continue to operate the property at its own risk for an extended period of time.

Seller's continuing involvement without risks and rewards. Sometimes sellers continue to be involved with property for periods of time even though the property has been legally sold. The seller's involvement often takes the form of profit participation, management services, financing, guarantees of return, construction, etc. The seller does not have a substantial continuing involvement with property unless the risks and rewards of ownership have been clearly transferred to the buyer.

If the seller has some continuing involvement with the property and does not clearly transfer substantially all of the risks and rewards of ownership, profit is recognized by a method other than the full accrual method. The method chosen is determined by the nature and extent of the seller's continuing involvement. As a general rule, profit is only recognized at the time of sale if the amount of the seller's loss due to the continued involvement with the property is limited by the terms of the sales contract. In this event, the profit recognized at this time is reduced by the maximum possible loss from the continued involvement. (ASC 360-20-40-37)

Antispeculation clauses. ASC 360-20-40-39 deals with antispeculation clauses sometimes found in land sale agreements, requiring the buyer to develop the land in a specific manner or within a specific period of time and giving the seller the right, but not the obligation, to reacquire the property when the condition is not met. This option does not preclude recognition of a sale if the probability of the buyer not complying is remote.

Options to purchase real estate property. Often a buyer will buy an option to purchase land from a seller with the hopeful intention of obtaining a zoning change, building permit, or some other contingency specified in the option agreement. Proceeds from the issue of an option by a property owner (seller) are accounted for by the deposit method. If the option is exercised, the seller includes the option proceeds in the computation of the sales value of the property. If the option is not exercised, the seller recognizes the option proceeds as income at the time the option expires. (ASC 360-20-40-45)

Partial sales of property. Per ASC 360-20-40-46, "a sale is a partial sale if the seller retains an equity interest in the property or has an equity interest in the buyer." Profit on a partial sale may be recognized on the date of sale if the following occur:

1. The buyer is independent of the seller.
2. Collection of the sales price is reasonably assured.
3. The seller will not be required to support the operations of the property on its related obligations to an extent greater than its proportionate interest.

Per ASC 360-20-46 and 47, if the buyer is not independent of the seller, the seller may not be able to recognize any profit that is measured at the date of sale (see the following Buy-sell agreements section).

If the seller is not reasonably assured of collecting the sales price, the cost recovery or installment method is used to recognize profit on the partial sale. (ASC 360-20-40-48)

A seller who separately sells individual units in condominium projects or time-sharing interests recognizes profit by the percentage-of-completion method on the sale of individual units or interests if all of the following criteria are met (ASC 360-20-40-50):

1. Construction is beyond a preliminary stage (i.e., engineering and design work, execution of construction contracts, site clearance and preparation, excavation, and completion of the building foundation have all been completed).
2. The buyer is unable to obtain a refund except for nondelivery of the units or interest.
3. Sufficient units have been sold to assure that the entire property will not revert to being rental property.
4. Sales prices are collectible.
5. Aggregate sales proceeds and costs can be reasonably estimated.

The deposit method is used to account for these sales up to the point all the criteria are met for recognition of a sale. (ASC 360-20-40-54)

Leases involving real estate. (ASC 360-20-40-60) ASC 840-40 dealing with sales-type real estate leases and sale-leaseback real estate transactions is covered in the chapter on ASC 840.

***Buy-sell agreements*.** A buy-sell clause is not a prohibited form of continuing involvement precluding partial sales treatment, but only if

1. The buyer can act independently from the seller, or if
2. The seller is not compelled to reacquire the other investor's interest in the jointly owned entity.

The decision is judgmental, requiring consideration of numerous factors.

Factors to consider in determining whether the buyer cannot act independently from the seller are

1. The presence of a predetermined buy-sell price,
2. The seller has a strategic necessity barring it from relinquishing its ownership rights to the buyer,
3. The seller has business arrangements with the jointly owned entity that economically require it to reacquire the real estate to avoid losing economic benefits or escaping negative consequences of the arrangements, or
4. Tax implications compelling the seller to acquire the buyer's interest in the entity.

Factors to consider in determining if the buyer can compel the seller to repurchase the property include

1. The buyer is financially unable to acquire the seller's interest,
2. The buy-sell clause contains a specified rate of return for either party,
3. The buyer has a strategic necessity requiring it to sell its interest to the seller,
4. The buyer is legally restricted from acquiring the seller's interest,
5. The buyer cannot realize its economic interest by sale to a third party, due to the integration of the real estate into the seller's business, or
6. Tax implications compelling the buyer to sell its interest to the seller.

Methods of Accounting for Real Estate Sales other than Retail Land Sales

Selection of method. The full accrual method of accounting for nonretail sales of real estate is appropriate when all four of the recognition criteria have been satisfied:

1. The sale is consummated,
2. The buyer has demonstrated a commitment to pay,
3. The seller's receivable is not subject to future subordination.
4. The seller has transferred the risks and rewards of ownership and does not have a substantial continuing involvement with the property.

If all of the criteria have not been met, the seller records the transaction by one of the following methods as indicated by ASC 360-20:

1. Deposit
2. Cost recovery
3. Installment
4. Reduced profit
5. Percentage-of-completion.

The installment method is used if the full accrual method cannot be used due to an inadequate initial investment by the buyer, provided that recovery of cost is reasonably assured if the buyer defaults.

The cost recovery method or the deposit methods are used if such cost recovery is not assured.

The reduced profit method is used when the buyer's initial investment is adequate but the continuing investment is not adequate, and payments by the buyer at least cover the sum of

1. The amortization (principal and interest) on the maximum first mortgage that could be obtained on the property and
2. The interest, at an appropriate rate, on the excess of aggregate debt over the maximum first mortgage.

Full accrual method. The full accrual method is simply the application of the revenue recognition principle. Profit under the full accrual method is computed by subtracting the cost basis of the property surrendered from the sales value given by the buyer. Also, the computation of profit on the sale includes all costs incurred that are directly related to the sale, such as accounting and legal fees.

If a loss is apparent (e.g., the carrying value of the property exceeds the sum of the deposit, fair value of unrecorded note receivable, and the debt assumed by the buyer), then immediate recognition of the loss is required.

A real estate sale is recognized in full when the profit is determinable and the earnings process is virtually complete. The profit is determinable when the first three recognition criteria listed above have been met. The earnings process is virtually complete when the fourth criterion has been met.

Installment method. Under the installment method (ASC 360-20-55-7), each cash receipt and principal payment by the buyer on debt assumed with recourse to the seller consists of part recovery of cost and part recovery of profit. The apportionment between cost recovery and profit is in the same ratio as total cost and total profit bear to the sales value of the property sold. Therefore, under the installment method, the seller recognizes profit on each payment that the buyer makes to the seller and on each payment the buyer makes to the holder of the primary debt. When a buyer assumes debt that is without recourse to the seller, the seller recognizes profit on each payment made to the seller and on the entire debt assumed by the buyer. The accounting treatment differs because the seller is subject to substantially different levels of risk under the alternative conditions. For debt that is without recourse, the seller recovers a portion, if not all, of the cost of the asset surrendered at the time the buyer assumes the debt.

Example of the installment method

Assume Tucker sells to Price a plot of undeveloped land for $2,000,000. Price will assume, with recourse, Tucker's existing first mortgage of $1,000,000 and also pay Tucker a $300,000 cash down payment. Price will pay the balance of $700,000 by giving Tucker a second mortgage payable in equal installments of principal and interest over a ten-year period. The cost of the land to Tucker was $1,200,000 and Price will commence development of the land immediately.

1. Computation of sales value:

Cash down payment	$ 300,000
First mortgage	1,000,000
Second mortgage	700,000
Sales value	$2,000,000

2. Computation of the initial investment:

Cash down payment	$ 300,000

3. Computation of the minimum required initial investment:

   a. $400,000 ($2,000,000 × 20%)

   b 1. $850,000 [$2,000,000 – (115% × 1,000,000)]

   2. $500,000 ($2,000,000 × 25%)

The minimum initial investment is $500,000 since b.2 is less than b.1 and b.2 is greater than a.

The initial investment criterion has not been satisfied because the actual initial investment is less than the minimum initial investment. Therefore, assuming the sale has been consummated and Tucker is reasonably assured of recovering the cost of the land from Price, the installment method is to be used. The gross profit to be recognized over the installment payment period by Tucker is computed as follows:

Sales value	$ 2,000,000
Cost of land	(1,200,000)
Gross profit	$ 800,000

The gross profit percentage to apply to each payment by Price to Tucker and the primary debt holder is 40% ($800,000/$2,000,000).

If Price also pays $50,000 of principal on the first mortgage and $70,000 of principal on the second mortgage in the year of sale, Tucker would recognize the following profit in the year of sale:

Profit recognized on the down payment ($300,000 × 40%)	$120,000
Profit recognized on the principal payments:	
First mortgage ($50,000 × 40%)	20,000
Second mortgage ($70,000 × 40%)	28,000
Total profit recognized in year of sale	$168,000

Note that Tucker recognizes profit only on the payment applicable to the first mortgage. This is because Tucker may be called upon to satisfy the liability on the first mortgage if Price defaults.

If Tucker's first mortgage was assumed without recourse, Tucker would recognize the following profit in the year of sale:

Profit recognized on the down payment ($300,000 × 40%)	$120,000
Profit recognized on Price's assumption of Tucker's first mortgage without recourse ($1,000,000 × 40%)	400,000
Profit recognized on the principal payment of the second mortgage ($70,000 × 40%)	28,000
Total profit recognized in year of sale	$548,000

The income statement (or related footnotes) for the period of sale includes the sales value received, the gross profit recognized, the gross profit deferred, and the costs of sale. In future periods when further payments are made to the buyer, the seller realizes gross profit on these payments. This amount is presented as a single line item in the revenue section of the income statement.

If, in the future, the transaction meets the requirements for the full accrual method of recognizing profit, the seller may change to that method and recognize the remaining deferred profit as income at that time.

Cost recovery method. When the cost recovery method (ASC 360-20-55-13) is used (e.g., when the seller's receivable is subject to subordination or the seller is not reasonably assured of recovering the cost of the property if the buyer defaults), no profit is recognized on the sales transaction until the seller has recovered the cost of the property sold. If the buyer assumes debt that is with recourse to the seller, profit is not recognized by the seller until the cash payments by the buyer, including both principal and interest on debt due the seller and on debt assumed by the buyer, exceed the seller's cost of the property sold. If the buyer assumes debt that is without recourse to the seller, profit may be recognized by the seller when the cash payments by the buyer, including both principal and interest on debt due the seller, exceed the difference between the seller's cost of the property and the nonrecourse debt assumed by the buyer.

For the cost recovery method, principal collections reduce the seller's related receivable, and interest collections on such receivable increase the deferred gross profit on the statement of financial position. (ASC 360-20-55-14)

Example of the cost recovery method

Assume that on January 1, 20X1, Simon, Inc. purchased undeveloped land with a sales value of $365,000 from Davis Co. The sales value is represented by a $15,000 cash down payment, Simon assuming Davis's $200,000 first mortgage (10%, payable in equal annual installments over the next twenty years), and Simon giving Davis a second mortgage of $150,000 (12%, payable in equal annual installments over the next ten years). The sale has been consummated, but the initial investment is below the minimum required amount and Davis is not reasonably assured of recovering the cost of the property if Simon defaults. The cost of the land to Davis was $300,000. The circumstances indicate the cost recovery method is appropriate. The transaction is recorded by Davis as follows:

1/1/X1	Notes receivable	150,000	
	First mortgage payable	200,000	
	Cash	15,000	
	Revenue from sale of land		365,000
	Revenue from sale of land	365,000	
	Land		300,000
	Deferred gross profit		65,000

Case 1 — The first mortgage was assumed with recourse to Davis. Immediately after the sale, the unrecovered cost of the land is computed as follows:

Land	$300,000
Less: Cash down payment	(15,000)
Unrecovered cost	$285,000

The note (second mortgage) is reported as follows:

Note receivable	$150,000	
Less: Deferred gross profit	(65,000)	$ 85,000

At the end of the year Simon pays $26,547.64 ($8,547.64 principal and $18,000.00 interest) on the second mortgage note and $23,491.94 ($3,491.94 principal and $20,000.00 interest) on the first mortgage. At 12/31/12 the unrecovered cost of the land is computed as follows:

Previous unrecovered cost		$285,000.00
Less: Note receivable payment	$26,547.64	
First mortgage payment	23,491.94	(50,039.58)
Unrecovered cost		$234,960.42

The receivable is reported on the 12/31/12 statement of financial position as follows:

Note receivable ($150,000 – 8,547.64)	$141,452.36	
Less: Deferred gross profit ($65,000 + 18,000)	83,000.00	$58,452.36

Case 2 — The first mortgage is assumed without recourse to Davis. The reporting of the note is the same as Case 1; however, the unrecovered cost of the property is different. Immediately after the sale, the unrecovered cost of the property is computed as follows:

Land	$ 300,000
Less: Cash down payment	(15,000)
Nonrecourse debt assumed by Simon	(200,000)
Unrecovered cost	$ 85,000

After Simon makes the payments at the end of the year, the unrecovered cost is computed as follows:

Previous unrecovered cost	$85,000.00
Less: Notes receivable payment	26,547.64
Unrecovered cost	$58,452.36

For the cost recovery method, the income statement for the year the real estate sale occurs includes the sales value received, the cost of the property given up, and the gross profit deferred. In future periods, after the cost of the property has been recovered, the income statement includes the gross profit earned as a separate revenue item.

If, after accounting for the sale by the cost recovery method, circumstances indicate that the criteria for the full accrual method are satisfied, the seller may change to the full accrual method and recognize any remaining deferred gross profit in full.

Deposit method. When the deposit method (ASC 360-20-55-17) is used (e.g., when the sale is, in substance, the sale of an option and not real estate), the seller does not recognize any profit, does not record a receivable, continues to report in its financial statements the property and the related existing debt even if the debt has been assumed by the buyer, and discloses that those items are subject to a sales contract. The seller also continues to recognize depreciation expense on the property for which the deposits have been received, unless the property has been classified as held for sale (per ASC 360-10). Cash received from the buyer (initial and continuing investments) is reported as a deposit on the contract. However, some amounts of cash may be received that are not subject to refund, such as interest on the unrecorded principal. These amounts are used to offset any carrying charges on the property (e.g., property taxes and interest on the existing debt). If the interest collected on the unrecorded receivable is refundable, the seller records this interest as a deposit before the sale is consummated and then includes it as a part of the initial investment once the sale is consummated. If deposits on retail land sales are eventually recognized as sales, the interest portion of the deposit is separately recognized as interest income. For contracts that are cancelled, the nonrefundable amounts are recognized as income and the refundable amounts returned to the depositor at the time of cancellation.

As stated, the seller's statement of financial position continues to present the debt assumed by the buyer (this includes nonrecourse debt) among its other liabilities. However, the seller reports any principal payments on the mortgage debt assumed as additional deposits, while correspondingly reducing the carrying amount of the mortgage debt.

Example of a deposit transaction

Elbrus Investments enters into two separate property acquisition transactions with the Buena Vista Land Company.

1. Elbrus pays a $50,000 deposit and promises to pay an additional $800,000 to buy land and a building in an area not yet properly zoned for the facility Elbrus intends to construct. Final acquisition of the property is contingent upon these zoning changes. Buena Vista does not record the receivable, and records the deposit with the following entry:

Cash	50,000	
Customer deposits		50,000

Part of the purchase agreement stipulates that Buena Vista will retain all interest earned on the deposit, and that 10% of the deposit is nonrefundable. Buena Vista earns 5% interest on Elbrus' deposit over a period of four months, resulting in $208 of interest income that is offset against the property tax expenses of the property with the following entry:

Cash	208	
Property tax expense		208

Immediately thereafter, the required zoning changes are turned down, and Elbrus cancels the sales contract. Buena Vista returns the refundable portion of the deposit to Elbrus and records the nonrefundable portion as income with the following entry:

Customer deposits	50,000	
Income from contract cancellation		10,000
Cash		40,000

2. Elbrus pays a $40,000 deposit on land owned and being improved by Buena Vista. Elbrus immediately begins paying $5,000/month under a four-year, 7% loan agreement totaling $212,000 of principal payments, and agrees to pay an additional $350,000 at closing, subject to the land being approved for residential construction. After two months, Buena Vista has earned $167 of refundable interest income on Elbrus' deposit and has been paid $7,689 of refundable principal and $2,311 of refundable interest on the debt. Buena Vista records these events with the following entry:

Cash	10,167	
Customer deposits		10,167

The land is approved for residential construction, triggering sale of the property. Buena Vista's basis in the property is $520,000. Buena Vista uses the following entry to describe completion of the sale:

Cash	350,000	
Note receivable	204,311	
Customer deposits	50,167	
Gain on asset sale		84,478
Land		520,000

Reduced profit method. The reduced profit method is appropriate when the sale has been consummated and the initial investment is adequate but the continuing investment does not clearly demonstrate the buyer's willing commitment to pay the remaining balance of the receivable. For example, a buyer may purchase land under an agreement in which the seller will finance the sale over a thirty-year period. ASC 976 specifically states twenty years as the maximum amortization period for the purchase of land; therefore, the agreement fails to meet the continuing investment criteria.

Under the reduced profit method (ASC 360-20-55-16), the seller recognizes a portion of the profit at the time of sale with the remaining portion recognized in future periods. The amount of reduced profit recognized at the time of sale is determined by discounting the receivable from the buyer to the present value of the lowest level of annual payments required by the sales contract over the maximum period of time specified for that type of real estate property (twenty years for land and the customary term of a first mortgage loan set by an independent lending institution for other types of real estate). The remaining profit is recognized in the periods that lump-sum or other payments are made.

Example of the reduced profit method

Assume Levinson, Inc. sells a parcel of land to Raemer Co. Levinson receives sales value of $2,000,000. The land cost $1,600,000. Raemer gave Levinson the following consideration:

Cash down payment	$ 500,000
First mortgage note payable to an independent lending institution (payable in equal installments of principal and 12% interest, $133,887 payable at the end of each of the next twenty years)	1,000,000
Second mortgage note payable to Levinson (payable in equal installments of principal and 10% interest, $53,039 payable at the end of each of the next thirty years)	500,000
Total sales value	$2,000,000

The amortization term of the second mortgage (seller's receivable) exceeds the twenty-year maximum permitted by ASC 976. It is assumed that the payments by the buyer will cover the interest and principal on the maximum first mortgage loan that could be obtained on the property and interest on the excess aggregate debt on the property over such a maximum first mortgage loan; consequently, the reduced profit method is appropriate. It is also assumed that the market interest rate on similar agreements is 14%.

The present value of $53,039 per year for twenty years at the market rate of 14% is $351,278 ($53,039 × 6.623).

The gross profit on the sale ($400,000) is reduced by the difference between the face amount of the seller's receivable ($500,000) and the reduced amount ($351,278) or $148,722. The profit recognized at the time of sale is the sales value less the cost of the land less the difference between the face amount of the receivable and the reduced amount. Therefore, the reduced profit recognized on the date of sale is computed as follows:

Sales value		$ 2,000,000
Less:	Cost of land	(1,600,000)
	Excess	(148,722)
Reduced profit		$ 251,278

Under the reduced profit method, the seller amortizes its receivable at the market rate, not the rate given on the second mortgage. The receivable's carrying balance is zero after the specified term expires (in this case, twenty years). The remaining profit of $148,722 is recognized in the years after the specified term expires as the buyer makes payments on the second mortgage (years twenty-one through thirty).

Other Guidance to Accounting for Real Estate Sales Transactions

Integral equipment. Sales of integral equipment are within the scope of ASC 360, and thus the determination of whether equipment is integral is an important one. A determination of whether equipment to be leased is integral is also necessary to enable lessors to determine the proper accounting for sales-type leases. This determination is to be made based on two factors.

1. The first is the significance of the cost to remove the equipment from its existing location (which would include any costs of repairing the damage done to that location by the act of removal). (ASC 360-20-15-4)
2. The second is the decrease in value of the equipment that results from its removal (which is, at a minimum, the cost to ship and reinstall the equipment at a new site). (ASC 360-20-15-5)

The nature of the equipment and whether others can use it is considered in determining whether there would be any further diminution in fair value. When the combined total of the cost to remove and any further diminution of fair value exceeds 10% of the fair value of the equipment (installed), the equipment is to be deemed integral equipment, and thus accounted for under the provisions of ASC 360. (ASC 360-20-15-7)

Collateralized loan valuation allowance. ASC 310-40-55 deals with the question of whether a valuation allowance previously established for a loan which is collateralized by a long-lived asset should be carried forward after the asset is foreclosed due to loan default. It holds that, when such a loan is foreclosed, any valuation allowance established for the foreclosed loan should not be carried over as a separate element of the cost basis for purposes of accounting for the long-lived assets under ASC 360. Rather, upon foreclosure the lender must measure the long-lived asset received in full satisfaction of a receivable at fair value less cost to sell as prescribed by ASC 310-40. Application of ASC 310-40 results in the identification of a new cost basis for the long-lived asset received in full satisfaction of a receivable.

Foreclosure – subsequent recovery of value. ASC 310-40-55 also addresses the limitation on gain recognition when an impaired asset obtained by means of foreclosure later recovers some value. ASC 360-10-35-40 states that "a loss shall be recognized for any initial or subsequent write-down to fair value less cost to sell. A gain shall be recognized for any subsequent increase in fair value less cost to sell, but not in excess of the cumulative loss previously recognized (for a write-down to fair value less cost to sell)." Thus gain recognition is limited to the cumulative extent that losses have been recognized while the assets were accounted for as long-lived assets under ASC 360. Put differently, ASC 360 does not allow the lender to "look back" to lending impairments measured and recognized under ASC 450 or ASC 310, for purposes of measuring the cumulative loss previously recognized. "Recovery" of losses not recognized is thus not permitted.

Homebuilder builds home on own lot. ASC 970-360-55 addresses the timing of income recognition when a homebuilder enters into a contract to build a home on its own lot, relinquishing title to both the lot and the home at closing. It states that profit recognition is not appropriate until the conditions specified in ASC 360 have been met. Deposit accounting is to be used for both the land and building activity until the conditions are met.

Homeowners's equity interest securitizes note. ASC 360-20-55-66 addresses the situation in which a homeowner's equity interest in property is pledged as security for a note and finds that this cannot be included as part of the buyer's initial investment in determining whether profit can be recognized under ASC 976.

Repossessed real estate. ASC 310-40-40-7 deals with the proper valuation for repossessed real estate which is recorded at the lower of the net receivable due to the seller at foreclosure or the fair value of the property.

Minority interests in REITs. ASC 974-810-30 addresses the proper treatment of minority interests in certain real estate investment trusts. It holds that the net equity of the operating partnership (after the contributions of the sponsor and the Real Estate Investment Trusts, or REIT) multiplied by the sponsor's ownership percentage in the operating partnership represents the amount to be initially reported as the minority interest in the REIT's consolidated financial statements. Also, if a minority interest balance is negative, the related change in the REIT's income statement would be the greater of the minority interest holder's share of current earnings or the amount of distributions to the minority interest holder during the year. Any excess is to be credited directly to equity until elimination of the minority interest deficit that existed at the formation of the REIT. Other REIT accounting matters are also addressed in the codification; for example, subsequent acquisitions by the REIT, for cash, of a sponsor's minority interest in an operating partnership are accounted for consistent with the accounting for formation of the REIT.

ADC loans. The matter of appropriate accounting for transfers of investments that are in substance real estate was addressed by ASC 360-20-15-3, which held that in such circumstances the accounting is to follow ASC 360. Thus transfers of acquisition, development, and construction loans (ADC loans), which are deemed in substance real estate under ASC 815-15-55-10, are subject to this rule, and transfers of marketable investments in a REIT which are accounted for under ASC 320 are to be accounted for per ASC 860.

Condominium unit sales. ASC 360-20-40 addresses the applicability of a buyer's continuing investment to an entity's recognition of revenue when selling condominium units. An entity can assess the collectibility of the sales price as per ASC 360 by requiring the buyer to either make additional payments during the construction term at least equal to the level annual payments that would be required to fund principal and interest on a customary mortgage for the remaining purchase price of the property, or increase the minimum initial investment by an equivalent aggregate amount. If these criteria cannot be met, then the seller should record the transaction under the deposit method.

Investments in real estate ventures. ASC 970-323, specifying the accounting for investments in real estate ventures, has been widely applied in practice—even to the extent that its guidance has been analogized to other equity investment situations. It requires that owners of real estate ventures should generally use the equity method of accounting to account for their investments. However, limited partners may have such a minor interest and have no influence or control, in which case the cost method would instead be appropriate.

According to ASC 970-323, if losses exceed the investment, the losses are to be recognized regardless of any increase in the estimated fair value of the venture's assets. Losses in excess of the amount of the investment are a liability. Losses which cannot be borne by certain investors require the remaining investors to use ASC 450 to determine their share of any additional loss. Limited partners are not required to record losses in excess of investment. As usual, if investors do not recognize losses in excess of investment, the equity method is resumed only after the investor's share of net income exceeds the cumulative net losses not recognized previously.

The codification also notes that venture agreements may designate different allocations for profits, losses, cash distributions and cash from liquidation. Accounting for equity in profits and losses therefore requires careful consideration of allocation formulas because the substance over form concept requires equity method accounting to follow the ultimate cash allocations.

Contributions of real estate to a venture as capital are recorded by the investor at cost, and cannot result in the recognition of a gain, since a capital contribution does not represent the culmination of the earnings process.

Real estate syndications. ASC 970-323 states that interest on loans and advances that are, in substance, capital contributions and so are accounted for as distributions and not interest.

In ASC 970-605, the related topic of appropriate accounting for real estate syndication income is addressed. This applies to all income recognition from real estate syndication activities. ASC 976 applies to profit and loss recognition on sales of real estate by syndicators to partnerships. ASC 970-605 requires that the same concepts be applied to the syndicators—even though they may have never owned the property.

Under the provisions of ASC 970-605, all fees charged by syndicators are includable in the determination of sales value, as required by ASC 976, except for syndication fees and fees for which future services must be performed. Syndication fees are recognized as income when the earning process is complete and collectibility is reasonably assured. If fees are unreasonable, they are to be adjusted, and the sales price of the real estate is to be appropriately adjusted as well. If a partnership interest is received by the syndicator, the value is included in the test of fee reasonableness. If it is part of the fee, the syndicators are to account for this interest as a retained interest from the partial sale of real estate in conformity with ASC 976. Fees for future services are recognized when the service is rendered.

Fees received from blind pool transactions are recognized ratably as the syndication partnership invests in property but only to the extent that the fees are nonrefundable. If syndicators are exposed to future losses from material involvement or from uncertainties regarding collectibility, income is deferred until the losses can be reasonably estimated. For purposes of determining the ASC 976 requirement concerning the buyer's initial and continuing investment for profit recognition, before cash received by syndicators can be allocated to initial and continuing investment, it is allocated to (1) unpaid syndication fees until such fees are paid in full, and (2) amounts previously allocated to fees for future services (to the extent such services have already been performed when the cash is collected). If syndicators receive or retain partnership interests that are subordinated, these are accounted for as participations in future profits without risk of loss.

26 ASC 405 LIABILITIES

PERSPECTIVE AND ISSUES

Subtopics

ASC 405, *Liabilities,* consists of four subtopics:

- ASC 405-10, *Overall,* which merely points to other areas of the codification which contain guidance on liabilities
- ASC 405-20, *Extinguishments of Liabilities,* which provides guidance on when an entity should consider a liability settled
- ASC 405-30, *Insurance-Related Assessments,* which provides guidance on items such as assessments for state guaranty funds and workers' compensation second-injury funds
- ASC 405-40, *Obligations Resulting from Joint and Several Liabilities,* which provides guidance on arrangements where the total amount of the obligation is fixed at the reporting date.

ASC 405 provides accounting and reporting guidance related to short-term liabilities and certain guidance that may apply broadly to any liability. The Codification has several topics on liabilities, including ASC 470, *Debt,* and ASC 480, *Distinguishing Liabilities from Equity.*

Scope and Scope Exceptions

ASC 405 guidance applies to all entities with the covered transactions.

ASC 405-30 does not apply to the following:

a. Amounts payable or paid as a result of reinsurance contracts or arrangements that are in substance reinsurance, including assumed reinsurance activities and certain involuntary pools that are covered by Topic 944.
b. Assessments of depository institutions related to bank insurance and similar funds.
c. The annual fee imposed on health insurers by the Patient Protection and Affordable Care Act as amended by the Health Care and Education Reconciliation Act (the Acts). The accounting for the Acts' fee is addressed in Subtopic 720-50.

ASC 405-40 applies to all entities and obligations such as debt arrangements, other contractual obligations, and settled litigation and judicial rulings. The guidance does not apply to obligations accounted for under the following topics:

- ASC 410, *Asset Retirement and Environmental Obligations*
- ASC 450, *Contingencies*
- ASC 460, *Guarantees*
- ASC 715, *Compensation – Retirement Benefits*
- ASC 740, *Income Taxes*.

Overview

The FASB has declared, as a long-term goal, that all financial liabilities are to be recognized in the statement of financial position at fair values, rather than at amounts based on their historical cost. The proper calculation of fair value, as presented in ASC 820, *Fair Value Measurements and Disclosures*, is described in detail in the chapter on ASC 820. Under ASC 825, *Financial Instruments*, an entity has the option to record certain of its current liabilities that meet the definition of "financial liabilities" at their respective fair values, with changes in fair value recognized each period in net income. Liabilities that require the entity to provide goods or services to settle the obligation, instead of cash settlement, are not financial liabilities and thus are not eligible for the fair value measurement election permitted by ASC 825. This option is addressed in detail in the chapter on ASC 825.

Although measurement of liabilities is generally straightforward, some liabilities are difficult to measure because of uncertainties. Uncertainties regarding subsequent events, whether an obligation exists, how much of an entity's assets will be needed to settle the obligation, and when the settlement will take place can impact whether, when, and for how much an obligation will be recognized in the financial statements.

Most entities continue to measure their current liabilities at their settlement value, which is the amount of cash (or its equivalent amount of other assets) that will be paid to the creditor to liquidate the obligation during the current operating cycle. Accounts payable, dividends payable, salaries payable, and other current obligations are measured at settlement value because they require the entity to pay a determinable amount of cash within a relatively short period of time. If a current liability is near its payment date, there will be only an insignificant risk of changes in fair value because of changes in market conditions or the entity's credit standing, and settlement value and fair value will be essentially the same.

Other current liabilities are measured at the proceeds received when the obligation arose. Liabilities that are measured in this manner generally require the entity to discharge the obligation by providing goods or services rather than by paying cash. Deposits payable, or rents paid in advance on the statement of financial position of a lessor are examples of current liabilities measured by reference to proceeds received.

DEFINITIONS OF TERMS

Source: ASC 405-30-20 and ASC 405-40-20

In-Force Policies. Policies effective before a specified date that have not yet expired or been cancelled.

Incurred Losses. Losses paid or unpaid for which the entity has become liable during a period.

Involuntary Pools. A residual market mechanism for insureds who cannot obtain insurance in the voluntary market.

Life, Annuity, and Health Insurance Entities. An entity that may issue annuity, endowment, and accident and health insurance contracts as well as life insurance contracts. Life and health insurance entities may be either stock or mutual entities.

Nonpublic Entity. Any entity that does not meet any of the following conditions:

a. Its debt or equity securities trade in a public market either on a stock exchange (domestic or foreign) or in an over-the-counter market, including securities quoted only locally or regionally.
b. It is a conduit bond obligor for *conduit debt securities* that are traded in a public market (a domestic or foreign stock exchange or an over-the-counter market, including local or regional markets).
c. It files with a regulatory agency in preparation for the sale of any class of debt or equity securities in a public market.
d. It is required to file or furnish financial statements with the Securities and Exchange Commission.
e. It is controlled by an entity covered by criteria (a) through (d).

Obligated to Write. A circumstance in which an entity has no discretion to cancel a policy because of legal obligation under state statute, contract terms, or regulatory practice and is required to offer or issue insurance policies for a period in the future.

Premium Tax Offsets. Offsets against premium taxes levied on insurance entities by states.

Premiums Written. The premiums on all policies an entity has issued in a period.

Property and Casualty Insurance Entity. An entity that issues insurance contracts providing protection against either of the following:

a. Damage to or loss of property caused by various perils, such as fire and theft.
b. Legal liability resulting from injuries to other persons or damage to their property.

Property and liability insurance entities may be either stock or mutual entities.

CONCEPTS, RULES, AND EXAMPLES

ASC 405-10, *Overall*

ASC 405-10 contains no guidance. Its purpose is to point to guidance in other areas of the Codification. ASC 410-10-02 points to the following Codification Topics which contain guidance on accounting and reporting on liabilities:

- *Asset Retirement and Environmental Obligations* – ASC 410
- *Exit or Disposal Cost Obligations* – ASC 420
- *Deferred Revenue* – ASC 430
- *Commitments* – ASC 440
- *Contingencies* – ASC 450
- *Guarantees* – ASC 460
- *Debt* – ASC 470
- *Distinguishing Liabilities from Equity* – Topic 480.

ASC 405-20, *Extinguishments of Liabilities*

A liability is extinguished when

- The debtor pays the creditor
- The debtor is legally given relief from the liability.

If the entity becomes a guarantor on the debt, the entity applies the guidance in ASC 460.

ASC 405-40, *Obligations Resulting from Joint and Several Liabilities*

ASC 405-40 requires an entity to measure obligations resulting from joint and several liability arrangements for which the total amount of the obligation within the scope of the guidance is fixed at the reporting date as the sum of:

1. The amount the reporting entity agreed to pay on the basis of its arrangement among its obligors and
2. Any additional amount the entity expects to pay on behalf of its co-obligors.

The corresponding entry depends on the particular facts and circumstances.

The guidance above is effective for fiscal years, and interim periods within those years, beginning after December 15, 2013 for public entities. For nonpublic entities, the amendments are effective for fiscal years ending after December 14, 2014, and interim periods and annual periods thereafter. The guidance should be applied retrospectively to all prior periods presented. Early adoption is permitted.

27 ASC 410 ASSET RETIREMENT AND ENVIRONMENTAL OBLIGATIONS

PERSPECTIVE AND ISSUES

Subtopics

ASC 410, *Asset Retirement and Environmental Obligations*, consists of three subtopics:

- ASC 410-10, *Overall,* which merely points out the differences between the other two Subtopics
- ASC 410-20, *Asset Retirement Obligations,* which provides guidance on asset retirement obligation and environmental remediation liabilities resulting from normal operations of long-lived assets.
- ASC 410-30, *Environmental Obligations,* which provides guidance on environmental remediation liabilities.

Scope and Scope Exceptions

ASC 410-20 applies to all entities. It does not apply to these transactions:

1. Obligations that arise solely from a plan to sell or otherwise dispose of a long-lived asset.
2. An environmental remediation liability that results from the improper operation of a long-lived asset.
3. Activities necessary to prepare an asset for an alternative use as they are not associated with the retirement of the asset.
4. Historical waste held by private households.

5. Obligations of a lessee in connection with leased property, whether imposed by a lease agreement or by a party other than the lessor, that meet the definition of either minimum lease payments or contingent rentals in paragraphs.
6. An obligation for asbestos removal resulting from the other-than-normal operation of an asset.
7. Costs associated with complying with funding or assurance provisions.
8. Obligations associated with maintenance, rather than retirement, of a long-lived asset.
9. The cost of a replacement part that is a component of a long-lived asset.

(ASC 410-20-15-3)

ASC 410-30 applies to all entities. It does not apply to these transactions:

1. Environmental contamination incurred in the normal operation of a long-lived asset.
2. Pollution control costs with respect to current operations or on accounting for costs of future site restoration or closure that are required upon the cessation of operations or sale of facilities, as such current and future costs and obligations represent a class of accounting issues different from environmental remediation liabilities.
3. Environmental remediation actions that are undertaken at the sole discretion of management and that are not induced by the threat, by governments or other parties, of litigation or of assertion of a claim or an assessment.
4. Recognizing liabilities of insurance entities for unpaid claims.
5. Natural resource damages and toxic torts.
6. Asset impairment issues.

(ASC 410-30-1503)

DEFINITIONS OF TERMS

Source: ASC 410

Accretion Expense. An amount recognized as an expense classified as an operating item in the statement of income resulting from the increase in the carrying amount of the liability associated with the asset retirement obligation.

Asset Retirement Cost. The amount capitalized that increases the carrying amount of the long-lived asset when a liability for an asset retirement obligation is recognized.

Asset Retirement Obligation. An obligation associated with the retirement of a tangible long-lived asset.

Closure. Related to the Resource Conservation and Recovery Act of 1976: the process in which the owner-operator of a hazardous waste management unit discontinues active operation of the unit by treating, removing from the site, or disposing of on site all hazardous wastes in accordance with an Environmental Protection Agency or state-approved plan. Included, for example, are the process of emptying, cleaning, and removing or filling underground storage tanks and the capping of a landfill. Closure entails specific financial guarantees and technical tasks that are included in a closure plan and must be implemented.

Conditional Asset Retirement Obligation. A legal obligation to perform an asset retirement activity in which the timing and (or) method of settlement are conditional on a future event that may or may not be within the control of the entity.

Discount Rate Adjustment Technique. A present value technique that uses a risk-adjusted discount rate and contractual, promised, or most likely cash flows.

Disposal. Related to the Comprehensive Environmental Response, Compensation, and Liability Act of 1980 and the Resource Conservation and Recovery Act of 1976: under the Resource Conservation and Recovery Act of 1976, the discharge, deposit, injection, dumping, spilling, leaking, or placing of any solid waste or hazardous waste into or on any land or water so that such solid waste or hazardous waste or any constituent thereof may enter the environment or be emitted into the air or discharged into any waters, including groundwaters. Similarly under the Comprehensive Environmental Response, Compensation, and Liability Act of 1980 with regard to hazardous substances.

Fair Value, The price that would be received to sell an asset or paid to transfer a liability in an orderly transaction between market participants at the measurement date.

Hazardous Waste. Related to Resource Conservation and Recovery Act of 1976: a waste, or combination of wastes, that because of its quantity, concentration, toxicity, corrosiveness, mutagenicity or inflammability, or physical, chemical, or infectious characteristics may cause, or significantly contribute to, an increase in mortality or an increase in serious irreversible, or incapacitating reversible illness or pose a substantial present or potential hazard to human health or the environment when improperly treated, stored, transported, or disposed of, or otherwise managed. Technically, those wastes that are regulated under the Resource Conservation and Recovery Act of 1976 40 CFR Part 261 are considered to be hazardous wastes.

Legal Obligation. An obligation that a party is required to settle as a result of an existing or enacted law, statute, ordinance, or written or oral contract or by legal construction of a contract under the doctrine of promissory estoppel.

Natural Resources. Under the Comprehensive Environmental Response, Compensation, and Liability Act of 1980, natural resources are defined as land, fish, wildlife, biota, air, water, groundwater, drinking water supplies, and other such resources belonging to, managed or held in trust by, or otherwise controlled by the United States, state or local governments, foreign governments, or Indian tribes.

Orphan Share. Equitable share of liability for response or remediation costs attributed to orphan-share potentially responsible parties, or the amount by which the equitable share of liability for response or remediation costs attributable to other parties exceeds the amount for which those parties have settled their liability.

Orphan Share Potentially Responsible Party. An identified potentially responsible party that cannot be located or that is insolvent. Some of these parties may be identified by the Environmental Protection Agency; others may be identified as the site is investigated or as the remediation is performed. However, no contributions will ever be made by these parties.

Participating Potentially Responsible Party. A party to a Superfund site that has acknowledged potential involvement with respect to the site. Active potentially responsible parties may participate in the various administrative, negotiation, monitoring, and remediation activities related to the site. Others may adopt a passive stance and simply monitor the activities and decisions of the more involved potentially responsible parties. This passive stance could result from a variety of factors such as the entity's lack of experience, limited internal resources, or relative involvement at a site. This category of potentially responsible parties (both active and passive) is also referred to as players.

Potentially Responsible Party. Any individual, legal entity, or government—including owners, operators, transporters, or generators—potentially responsible for, or contributing to, the environmental impacts at a Superfund site. The Environmental Protection Agency has the authority to require potentially responsible parties, through administrative and legal actions, to remediate such sites. At early stages of the remediation process, the list of potentially responsible parties may be limited to a handful of entities that either were significant contributors of waste to the site or were easy to identify, for example, because of their proximity to the site or because of labeled material found at the site. As further investigation of the site occurs and as remediation activities take place, additional potentially responsible parties may be identified. Once identified, the additional potentially responsible parties would be reclassified from this category to either the participating potentially responsible party or recalcitrant potentially responsible party category. The total number of parties in this category and their aggregate allocable share of the remediation liability varies by site and cannot be reliably determined before the specific identification of individual potentially responsible parties. For example, some ultimately may be dropped from the potentially responsible party list because no substantive evidence is found to link them to the site. For others, substantive evidence eventually may be found that points to their liability. The presentation of that evidence to the entity would result in a reclassification of the party from this category of potentially responsible parties (sometimes referred to as hiding in the weeds) to either the participating potentially responsible party or recalcitrant potentially responsible party category.

Promissory Estoppel. "The principle that a promise made without consideration may nonetheless be enforced to prevent injustice if the promisor should have reasonably expected the promisee to rely on the promise and if the promisee did actually rely on the promise to his or her detriment." (See Black's Law Dictionary, seventh edition.)

Recalcitrant Potentially Responsible Party. A party whose liability with respect to a Superfund site is substantiated by evidence, but that refuses to acknowledge potential involvement with respect to the site. Recalcitrant potentially responsible parties adopt a recalcitrant attitude toward the entire remediation effort even though evidence exists that points to their involvement at a site. Some may adopt this attitude out of ignorance of the law; others may do so in the hope that they will be considered a nuisance and therefore ignored. Typically, parties in this category must be sued in order to collect their allocable share of the remediation liability; however, it may be that it is not economical to bring such suits because the parties' assets are limited. This category of potentially responsible parties is also referred to as nonparticipating potentially responsible parties.

Release. Related to Superfund: any spilling, leaking, pumping, pouring, emitting, emptying, discharging, injecting, escaping, leaching, dumping, or disposing into the environment. Includes the abandonment or discarding of barrels, containers, and other closed receptacles containing any hazardous substance, pollutant, or contaminant. The law provides for several exclusions. Release also means the substantial threat of release.

Remedial Action. Related to Superfund: generally long-term actions taken to do any of the following:

1. Investigate, alleviate, or eliminate the effects of a release of a hazardous substance into the environment
2. Investigate, alleviate, or eliminate a threat of the release of an existing hazardous substance that could potentially harm human health or the environment
3. Restore natural resources.

Also refers to corrective action under the Resource Conservation and Recovery Act of 1976.

Remedial Investigation-Feasibility Study. Extensive technical studies conducted by the government or by the potentially responsible parties to investigate the scope of site impacts and determine the remedial alternatives that, consistent with the National Contingency Plan, may be implemented at a Superfund site. Government-funded remedial investigation-feasibility studies do not recommend a specific alternative for implementation. Remedial investigation-feasibility studies conducted by potentially responsible parties usually do recommend and technically support a remedial alternative. A remedial investigation-feasibility study may include a variety of on- and off-site activities, such as monitoring, sampling, and analysis.

Removal Action. Under the Comprehensive Environmental Response, Compensation, and Liability Act of 1980, generally short-term actions taken to respond promptly to an urgent need. The cleanup or removal of released hazardous substances from the environment; actions in response to the threat of release; actions that may be necessary to monitor, assess, and evaluate the release or threat; disposal of removed material; or other actions needed to prevent, minimize, or mitigate damage to public health or welfare or to the environment. Removal also includes, without being limited to, security fencing or other measures to limit access; provision of alternative water supplies; temporary evacuation and housing of threatened individuals not otherwise provided for; and any emergency assistance provided under the Disaster Relief Act.

Retirement. The other-than-temporary removal of a long-lived asset from service. That term encompasses sale, abandonment, recycling, or disposal in some other manner. However, it does not encompass the temporary idling of a long-lived asset. After an entity retires an asset, that asset is no longer under the control of that entity, no longer in existence, or no longer capable of being used in the manner for which the asset was originally acquired, constructed, or developed.

Unknown Potentially Responsible Party. A party that has liability with respect to a Superfund site, but that has not yet been identified as a potentially responsible party by the Environmental Protection Agency or by an analogous state agency.

Unproven Potentially Responsible Party. A party that has been identified as a potentially responsible party for a Superfund site by the U.S. Environmental Protection Agency or by an analogous state agency, but that does not acknowledge potential involvement with respect to the site because no evidence has been presented linking the party to the site. Also referred to as a hiding-in-the-weeds potentially responsible party.

CONCEPTS, RULES, AND EXAMPLES

ASC 410-20, *Asset Retirement Obligations*

ASC 410-20 provides standards for measuring the future cost to retire an asset and recognizing that cost in the financial statements as a liability, and correspondingly, as part of the depreciable cost of the asset. ASC 410-20 applies to *legal obligations* associated with the *retirement* of tangible long-lived assets that result from their acquisition, construction, development, and/or normal operation (ASC 410-20015-2a). Lessee capital lease assets and lessor assets that are leased under operating leases are also subject to these rules (ASC 410-20-15-2d).

For the purposes of applying ASC 410-20, a legal obligation is "an obligation that a party is required to settle as a result of an existing or enacted law, statute, ordinance, or written or oral contract or by legal construction of a contract under the doctrine of *promissory estoppel*." Promissory estoppel is a legal doctrine whereby a court of law will enforce a promise made by one party (the promisor) to another party (the promisee) even though no formal contract exists between the two parties or no consideration was exchanged. This situation can arise when a party (the promisee) relies on a promise to his or her detriment and the person making the promise (the promisor) should have reasonably expected the promisee to rely on the promise.

Asset retirement obligations requiring recognition. When an entity acquires, constructs, and operates assets, it often incurs obligations that are unavoidable. Much of the discussion in ASC 410-20 pertains to specialized industry applications such as offshore oil platforms, nuclear power plants, mining operations, landfills, and underground storage tanks. However, the criteria for recognizing asset retirement obligations are intended to apply to situations encountered more frequently in practice, such as in the following examples.

Examples of the scope of ASC 410-20

Example 1—Leased premises. In accordance with the terms of a lease, the lessee is obligated to remove its specialized machinery from the leased premises prior to vacating those premises, or to compensate the lessor accordingly. The lease imposes a legal obligation on the lessee to remove the asset at the end of the asset's useful life or upon vacating the premises, and therefore this situation would be covered by ASC 410-20.

Example 2—Owned premises. The same machinery described in example 1 is installed in a factory that the entity owns. At the end of the useful life of the machinery, the entity will either incur costs to dismantle and remove the asset or will leave it idle in place. If the entity chooses to do nothing and not remove the equipment, this would adversely affect the fair value of the premises should the entity choose to sell the premises on an "as is" basis. Conceptually, to apply the matching principle in a manner consistent with example 1, the cost of asset retirement should be recognized systematically and rationally over the productive life of the asset and not in the period of retirement. However, in this example, there is no *legal obligation* on the part of the owner of the factory and equipment to retire the asset and, thus, this would *not* be covered by ASC 410-20.

Example 3—Promissory estoppel. Assume the same facts as in example 2. In this example, however, the owner of the property sold to a third party an option to purchase the factory, exercisable at the end of five years. In offering the option to the third party, the owner verbally represented that the factory would be completely vacant at the end of the five-year option period and that all machinery, furniture and fixtures would be removed from the premises. The property owner would reasonably expect that the purchaser of the option relied to the purchaser's detriment (as evidenced by the financial sacrifice of consideration made in exchange for the option) on the representation that the factory would be vacant. This would trigger promissory estoppel and the owner's obligation would be covered by ASC 410-20.

Example of timing of recognition

Phyl Corporation owns and operates a chemical company. At its premises, it maintains underground tanks used to store various types of chemicals. The tanks were installed when Phyl Corporation purchased its facilities seven years prior. On February 1, 2012, the governor of the state signed a law requiring removal of such tanks when they are no longer being used. Since the law imposes a legal obligation on Phyl Corporation, upon enactment, recognition of an asset retirement obligation (ARO) would be required.

Example of ongoing additions to the obligation

Joyce Manufacturing Corporation (JMC) operates a factory. As part of its normal operations it stores production byproducts and uses cleaning solvents on site in a reservoir specifically designed for that purpose. The reservoir and surrounding land, all owned by JMC, are contaminated with these chemicals. On February 1, 2012, the governor of the state signed a law requiring cleanup and disposal of hazardous waste from an already existing production process upon retirement of the facility. Upon enactment of the law, immediate recognition would be required for the ARO associated with the contamination that had already occurred. In addition, liabilities will continue to be recognized over the remaining life of the facility as additional contamination occurs.

Accounting considerations. Several important accounting issues merit careful consideration.

Recognition and allocation. Upon initial recognition, the entity records an increase to the carrying amount of the related long-lived asset and an offsetting liability. The entity then depreciates the combined cost of the asset and the capitalized asset retirement obligation using a systematic and rational allocation method over the period during which the long-lived asset is expected to provide benefits, taking into consideration any expected salvage value. Conceptually, this accounting treatment is an application of the matching principle in that the total investment in the asset, including the cost of its eventual retirement, is charged to expense over the periods benefited. Depending on the pattern and timing of obligating events, an entity could, under these rules, capitalize an amount of asset retirement cost during a period and, in the same period, allocate an equal amount to depreciation expense. It is important to note that, for the purpose of capitalizing interest under ASC 835-20, these additions to the carrying amounts of long-lived assets are not considered expenditures.

Impairment. Retirement obligations added to the carrying amounts of long-lived assets must be included in those carrying amounts for the purpose of testing those assets for impairment. In estimating future cash flows under the impairment rules (ASC 360-10-35), the cash flows related to settling the liability for an asset retirement obligation are to be excluded from both the undiscounted cash flows used to assess the recoverability of the asset's carrying amount and the discounted cash flows used to measure the asset's fair value.

Measurement. Asset retirement obligations are initially measured at fair value. Fair value (as defined in ASC 820 and discussed in detail in the chapter on ASC 820) is the price that would be paid to transfer the liability in an orderly transaction between market participants at the measurement date. This measurement is not based on the amount that the reporting entity (the obligor) would be required to pay to settle the liability on the measurement date (which would be difficult, if not impossible, to estimate in the absence of a market for the transfer of such obligations). Rather, the measurement assumes that the reporting entity remains the obligor under the ARO and that the obligee has transferred its rights by selling them to a hypothetical market participant on the measurement date. In determining the price it would be willing to pay for the rights associated with the ARO, a third-party market participant would consider the risk of nonperformance of the reporting entity, since that entity will continue to be the obligor after the measurement date. Thus, the fair value measurement of the obligation, under ASC 820, takes into consideration the reporting entity's own risk of nonperformance that includes, but is not limited to, the effect of its own credit standing.

FASB conforms ASC 410-20 to its fair value guidance, but when it issued FAS 143 on AROs, acknowledged that

> *Rarely, if ever, would there be an observable rate of interest for a liability that has cash flows similar to an asset retirement obligation being measured. In addition, an asset retirement obligation usually will have uncertainties in both timing and amount. In that circumstance, employing a discount rate adjustment technique, where uncertainty is incorporated into the rate, will be difficult, if not impossible.*

This lack of observability means that management, in order to estimate the ARO, will be required to use an expected present value technique that uses its own assumptions regarding the necessary adjustment for market risk. These are referred to as "Level 3 inputs" by ASC 820.

Initially applying an expected present value method. ASC 820-10-55 provides two alternative methods for determining expected present value. To apply Method 1, management adjusts the expected cash flows for market risk by incorporating a cash risk premium in them and uses a risk-free interest rate to discount the risk-adjusted expected cash flows.

To apply Method 2, management does not adjust the expected cash flows, but instead adjusts the risk-free interest rate by incorporating a risk premium in it.

As discussed later in this section, Method 1 cannot be used to estimate the expected present value of an ARO due to computational difficulties that cannot be overcome. As a result, the following discussion, adapted from ASC 410-20, uses Method 2 to illustrate the estimation of expected present value.

Management begins by estimating a series of cash flows that reflect its marketplace estimates of the cost and timing of performing the required retirement activities. Marketplace amounts are those amounts that would be expended by the entity to hire a third party to perform the work. Explicit assumptions are to be developed and incorporated in the estimates about all of the following matters:

1. The costs that a third party would incur in performing the necessary tasks associated with retiring the asset.
2. Additional amounts that the third party would include in pricing the work, related to such factors as inflation, overhead, equipment charges, profit margins, anticipated technological advances, and offsetting cash inflows, if any.
3. The extent to which the amount of the third party's costs or their timing might differ under various future scenarios and the relative probabilities of those scenarios actually occurring.
4. The price that the third party would demand and could expect to receive for bearing the uncertainties and unforeseeable circumstances inherent in the obligation. This is referred to as a *market-risk premium.*

If data is available regarding assumptions that marketplace participants would make that contradicts management's own assumptions, management must adjust its assumptions accordingly. For example, if the costs of labor in the marketplace exceed those of the entity, the higher marketplace costs are to be used in the cash flow estimates. Even if the entity can and will retire the asset using internal resources, the obligation must be computed as if a third party will be retained to perform the work, including provisions for recovery of the contractor's overhead and profit.

The discount rate to be used in the present value calculations is the *credit-adjusted risk-free rate* that adjusts a risk-free rate of interest for the effects of the entity's own credit standing. The risk-free interest rate is the interest rate on monetary assets with maturity dates or durations that coincide with the period covered by the estimated cash flows associated with the ARO. When the measurement involves cash flows denominated in US dollars, the yield curve for US Treasury securities is used.

In adjusting the risk-free rate for the entity's credit standing, the entity takes into account the effects on the fair value estimate of all terms, collateral, and existing guarantees. In ASC 820, FASB indicated that it believed, when it issued ASC 410, that it would be more practical for management to reflect an estimate of its own credit standing as an adjustment to the risk-free rate rather than as an adjustment to the expected cash flows. In fact, based on the model FASB chose to account for subsequent upward and downward changes in the ARO, ASC 410 would not be operational unless the adjustment for credit standing was made to the risk-free interest rate.

As a practical matter, for companies whose debt is not rated by a bond-rating agency, the adjustment for credit standing may be difficult to establish. For such companies, the incremental borrowing rate used for lease testing may serve as an acceptable approximation of the credit-adjusted risk-free rate.

The ARO may be incurred in one or more of the entity's reporting periods. Each period's incremental liability incurred is recognized as a separate liability and is estimated using these principles based on market and interest rate assumptions existing in the period of recognition.

ASC 410-20 clarifies that an ARO is required to be recognized when incurred (or acquired), even if uncertainty exists regarding the timing and/or method of eventually settling the obligation. In effect, ASC 410-20 distinguishes between a contingency and an uncertainty. If the obligation to perform the retirement activities is unconditional, the fact that uncertainty exists regarding the timing and/or method of retirement does not relieve the reporting entity of the requirement to estimate and record the obligation if, in fact, it is reasonably estimable. The assumptions regarding the probabilities of the various outcomes used in the computation are to take into account that uncertainty. An ARO is considered reasonably estimable if:

1. It is evident that the obligation's fair value is included in an asset's acquisition price,
2. An active market exists for the transfer of the obligation, or
3. Sufficient information is available to enable the use of the CON 7 expected present value technique to estimate the obligation.

Sufficient information is considered to be available to reasonably estimate the obligation if either:

1. The settlement date and method of settlement have been specified by others (e.g., the end of a lease term or the end of a statutory period) or
2. Information is available to reasonably estimate:

   a. The settlement date or range of potential settlement dates
   b. The settlement method or potential settlement methods
   c. The probabilities of occurrence of the dates and methods in a. and b.

The information necessary to make these estimates can be based on the reporting entity's own historical experience, industry statistics or customary practices, management's own intent, or estimates of the asset's economic useful life.

The determination of fair value for an ARO may be difficult, especially if the volume and level of activity for the asset or liability have significantly decreased to the extent where there are few recent transactions or price quotations vary substantially. If so, it may be necessary to use multiple valuation techniques, and select a point within the derived range of values that is most representative of fair value.

Even if management concludes that sufficient information does not exist to record the obligation at inception, management is expected to continuously consider whether this remains true in future accounting periods, and to recognize the obligation in the first period when sufficient information becomes available to enable the fair value estimate.

Accounting in subsequent periods. After the initial period of ARO recognition, the liability will change as a result of either the passage of time or revisions to the original estimates of either the amounts of estimated cash flows or their timing. Such changes can arise due to the effects of inflation, changes in the probabilities used in the original estimate, changes in interest rates, changes in laws, regulations, statutes, and contracts.

ASC 410-20 does not require detailed cash flow estimates every reporting period, but rather allows the exercise of judgment as to when facts and circumstances indicate that the initial estimate requires updating.

If a change to the liability is deemed necessary, it is recognized by first adjusting its carrying amount for changes due to the passage of time (referred to as *accretion* and discussed in detail below) and then, if applicable, for changes due to revisions in either amounts or timing of estimated cash flows.

Changes due to the passage of time increase the carrying amount of the liability because there are fewer periods remaining from the initial measurement date until the settlement date; thus, the present value of the discounted future settlement amount increases. These changes are recorded as a period cost called *accretion expense* and classified separately in the operating section of the statement of income (or not-for-profit statement of activities). Accretion is computed using an interest method of allocation that results in periodic accretion expense that represents a level effective interest rate applied to the carrying amount of the liability at the beginning of each period. The effective interest rate used to calculate accretion is the credit-adjusted risk-free rate or rates (or incremental borrowing rate) applied when the liability or portion of the liability (as explained below) was initially measured and recognized. Accretion expense is not combined with interest expense, and is not considered interest cost for the purpose of applying the interest capitalization criteria of ASC 835-20.

Changes in the ARO that result from changes in the estimates of the timing or amounts of future cash flows are accounted for differently for increases and decreases. If the expected present value increases, the increase gives rise to a new obligation accounted for separately just as the ARO was originally measured but using current market value assumptions, and the current credit-adjusted risk-free rate. Thus, over time, a particular long-lived asset may have multiple layers of obligations associated with it that are based on different assumptions measured at different dates during the asset's useful life. The incremental obligation is recorded by increasing the recorded ARO and capitalizing the additional cost as a part of the carrying amount of the related long-lived asset. If multiple layers have been recorded and it is not practical to separately identify the period (or layer) to which subsequent revisions in estimated cash flows relate, management is permitted to use a *weighted-average credit-adjusted risk-free rate* to measure the change in the liability resulting from that revision.

If, however, the expected present value subsequently decreases, the difference between the remeasured amount and the carrying amount of the liability (after adjustment for inception-to-date accretion) is recorded as a gain in the current period. In this case, the previously recognized layers of liabilities are reduced pro rata so as not to affect the overall effective rate of accretion over the remaining life of the obligation.

For the purposes of measurement in subsequent periods, in the unlikely event that an entity originally determined its ARO based on available market prices rather than using the expected present value method, it would be required to determine the undiscounted cash flows embedded in that market price. This process is analogous to computing the rate of interest implicit in a lease.

If the increase in carrying amount of the affected long-lived asset resulting from the remeasurement of ARO in a subsequent period impacts only that period, then the increase is fully depreciated in that period. Otherwise, the increase is depreciated in the period of change and future periods as a change in estimate in accordance with ASC 250. Both depreciation and accretion are classified as operating expenses in the statement of income.

Other provisions. Other provisions of ASC 410 affect the calculation of the credit-adjusted rate as well as how it is to be applied by rate-regulated entities.

Funding and assurance provisions. Factors such as laws, regulations, public policy, the entity's creditworthiness, or the sheer magnitude of the future obligation may cause an entity to be required to provide third parties with assurance that the entity will be able to satisfy its ARO in the future. Such assurance is provided using such instruments as surety bonds, insurance policies, letters of credit, guarantees by other entities, establishment of trust funds, or by custodial arrangements segregating other assets dedicated to satisfying the ARO.

Although providing such means of assurance does not satisfy the underlying obligation, the credit-adjusted interest rate used in calculating the expected present value is adjusted for the effect on the entity's credit standing of employing one or more of these techniques.

Rate-regulated entities. Many rate-regulated entities (as defined in ASC 980 and discussed in the chapter on ASC 980) follow current specialized accounting that capitalizes costs not otherwise afforded that treatment under GAAP. These entities recover these additional costs in the rates that they charge their customers. These additional capitalized costs may or may not meet the definition of ARO under ASC 410. The differences in the amounts and timing of assets and liabilities between GAAP and regulatory accounting used for rate-making purposes give rise to temporary differences and the resultant deferred income tax accounting.

ASC 410 provides that, if the criteria in ASC 980 are met, the rate-regulated entity is to recognize a regulatory asset or liability for differences in the timing of recognition of the period costs associated with ARO for financial reporting and rate-making purposes. Accounting for the ARO arising from closed or abandoned long-lived assets of rate-regulated entities is covered by ASC 980-360.

Example—initial measurement and recognition

Gerald Corporation constructs and places into service on January 1, 20X1, specialized machinery on premises that it leases under a fifteen-year lease. The machinery cost $1,750,000 and has an estimated useful life of ten years. Gerald Corporation is contractually obligated, under the terms of the lease, to remove the machinery from the premises when it is no longer functional. Gerald is unable to obtain current market-related information regarding the costs of settling the liability at inception and, therefore, chooses to estimate the initial fair value of the ARO using an expected present value technique. The significant assumptions used by Gerald in applying this technique are as follows:

1. Labor costs are based on prevailing wage rates in that geographic area that a contractor would pay to hire qualified workers. Gerald assigns probability assessments to the range of cash flow estimates as follows:

Cash flow estimate	*Probability assessment*	*Expected cash flows for labor costs*
$40,000	25%	$10,000
60,000	50	30,000
75,000	25	18,750
	100%	$58,750

2. Based on its own experience, which Gerald believes is indicative of local market conditions, Gerald estimates that a contractor will apply a 75% rate to labor costs to charge for overhead and equipment usage and that, based on published industry statistics for the region, a contractor would add a markup of 8% to the combined labor, overhead, and equipment costs.
3. Since the eventual dismantlement and removal will be occurring ten years later, Gerald expects that a contractor would receive a market-risk premium of 5% of the expected cash flows adjusted for inflation. This premium is to compensate the contractor for assuming the risks and uncertainties of contracting now for a project ten years later.
4. The risk-free rate of interest as evidenced by the price of zero-coupon US Treasury instruments that mature in ten years is 4.5%. Gerald adjusts that rate by 2.5% to reflect the effect of its credit standing as evidenced by its incremental borrowing rate of 7%. Therefore, the credit-adjusted risk-free rate used to compute the expected present value is 7%.
5. Gerald assumes an average rate of inflation of 3.5% over the ten-year period.

The ARO is initially measured as follows as of January 1, 20X1:

	Expected cash flows as of January 1, 2012
Expected cash flows for labor costs	$ 58,750
Allocated overhead and equipment charges (75% × $58,750)	44,063
Contractor's markup [8% × ($58,750 + $44,063)]	8,225
Expected cash flows before inflation adjustment	111,038
Average annual compounded inflation rate of 3.5% for 10 years (1.035^{10})	× 1.4106
Expected cash flows adjusted for inflation	156,630
Market-risk premium (5% × $156,630)	7,832
Expected cash flows adjusted for market risk	164,462
Present value using credit-adjusted risk-free rate of 7% for 10 years, compounded annually	$ 83,604

On January 1, 20X1, Gerald would record the initial ARO as follows:

Machinery and equipment	83,604	
ARO liability		83,604

Example—accounting in subsequent periods

Assuming the same facts as above, during the ten-year life of the machinery, Gerald would record entries to recognize accretion and depreciation as follows (assuming no remeasurement of the ARO is required):

Year	*Liability balance as of January 1*	*Annual accretion*	*Liability balance as of December 31*
20X1	$ 83,604	$ 5,852	$ 89,456
20X2	89,456	6,262	95,718
20X3	95,718	6,700	102,418
20X4	102,418	7,169	109,587
20X5	109,587	7,671	117,258
20X6	117,258	8,208	125,466
20X7	125,466	8,783	134,249
20X8	134,249	9,397	143,646
20X9	143,646	10,055	153,701
20Y0	153,701	10,761	164,462

Entries to record annual accretion

The accretion for each year presented in the table is recorded as follows:

Accretion expense (presented on the income statement as part of operating expense)	xx,xxx	
Asset retirement obligation		xx,xxx

Depreciation computations

Acquisition cost of asset	$ 1,750,000
Capitalized ARO	83,604
Adjusted carrying amount of asset	$ 1,833,604
Estimated salvage value (assumed)	100,000
	$ 1,733,604
Estimated useful life	÷ 10 years
Annual depreciation expense	$ 173,360

Entry to record annual depreciation

Depreciation expense	173,360	
Accumulated depreciation		173,360

Settlement of ARO

On December 31, 20Y0, Gerald uses its internal workforce to dismantle and dispose of the machinery and incurred costs as follows:

Labor	$ 70,000
Internally allocated overhead and equipment charges (75% of labor)	52,500
Total costs incurred	122,500
ARO liability	164,462
Gain on settlement of ARO	$ 41,962

Note that, because Gerald chose to perform the retirement activities using its own workforce, the "market approach" mandated by ASC 410 and ASC 820 does not achieve an even matching of the total costs of acquisition and retirement to the periods benefited. The period of the retirement reflects a gain on settlement that would not have occurred had Gerald hired a contractor to perform the work instead of using its own employees.

Electronic equipment waste obligations. ASC 720-40 prescribes the proper treatment of electronic equipment waste obligations.

A commercial user of electronic equipment acquired on or prior to August 13, 2005, is required to capitalize an asset retirement cost, as outlined in ASC 410, by increasing the carrying amount of the related asset by the same amount as the liability associated with the waste disposal obligation. If the asset is subsequently replaced, the obligation is shifted to the producer of the replacement equipment, so the user must calculate that portion of the payment to the replacement equipment producer relating to the transfer of the ARO, and eliminate the associated liability from its statement of financial position, while recognizing a gain or loss based on the difference between the liability on the sale date and that portion of the payment related to the ARO. Meanwhile, the producer of the new asset recognizes revenue for the total amount of the sale, less the fair value of the ARO.

ASC 410-30, *Environmental Obligations*

Environmental remediation costs, the costs of cleaning up environmental contamination, are generally expensed as incurred as operating expenses (ASC 410-30-25-16). The exceptions to this general rule that result in capitalizing these costs are as follows:

1. If the costs result from legal obligations associated with the eventual retirement of an asset or group of assets they will be capitalized as an ARO, as discussed and illustrated in the previous section of this chapter on ASC 410-20.
2. If the costs do not qualify as ARO, but they meet one of the following criteria, they may be capitalized subject to reduction for impairment, if warranted:
    a. The costs extend the life, increase the capacity, or improve the safety or efficiency of property owned by the reporting entity.
    b. The costs mitigate or prevent future environmental contamination while also improving the property compared with its condition when originally constructed or acquired by the reporting entity.
    c. The costs are incurred in preparing for sale a property that is currently held for sale (the application of this criterion must be balanced with the limitation in ASC

360 regarding assets held for sale being carried at the lower of carrying value or, fair value less cost to sell).

(ASC 410-30-25-17)

SEC registrants are required to disclose any significant exposure for asbestos treatment in the management discussion and analysis (MD&A).

Environmental costs associated with the improper operation or use of an asset (e.g., penalties and fines) are specifically excluded from the accounting guidance with respect to ARO and, should they be incurred, under ASC 410-30, they would most likely not qualify to be capitalized under GAAP.

Environmental remediation liabilities. Obligations arising from pollution of the environment have become a major cost for businesses. ASC 410-30 sets forth a very detailed description of relevant laws, remediation provisions, and other pertinent information, which is useful to auditors as well as to reporting entities. In terms of accounting guidance, ASC 430-20 contains the principal rules with respect to accounting for environmental obligations (e.g., determining the threshold for accrual of a liability, etc.) and its sets "benchmarks" for liability recognition. The benchmarks for the accrual and evaluation of the estimated liability (i.e., the stages which are deemed to be important to ascertaining the existence and amount of the liability) are:

1. The identification and verification of an entity as a potentially responsible party (PRP), since ASC 410-30 stipulates that accrual is to be based on the premise that expected costs will be borne by only the "participating potentially responsible parties" and that the "recalcitrant, unproven and unidentified" PRP will not contribute to costs of remediation
2. The receipt of a "unilateral administrative order"
3. Participation, as a PRP, in the remedial investigation/feasibility study (RI/FS)
4. Completion of the feasibility study
5. Issuance of the Record of Decision (RoD)
6. The remedial design through operation and maintenance, including postremediation monitoring.

(ASC 410-30-25-15)

The amount of the liability that is to be accrued is affected by the entity's allocable share of liability for a specific site and by its share of the amounts related to the site that will not be paid by the other PRP or the government. The categories of costs to be included in the accrued liability include incremental direct costs of the remediation effort itself, as well as the costs of compensation and benefits for employees directly involved in the remediation effort. Costs are to be estimated based on existing laws and technologies and are not to be discounted to estimated present values unless timing of cash payments is fixed or reliably determinable.

Incremental direct costs will include such items as fees paid to outside law firms for work related to the remediation effort, costs relating to completing the RI/FS, fees to outside consulting and engineering firms for site investigations and development of remedial action plans and remedial actions, costs of contractors performing remedial actions, government oversight costs and past costs, the cost of machinery and equipment dedicated to the remedial actions that do not have an alternative use, assessments by a PRP group covering costs incurred by the group in dealing with a site, and the costs of operation and maintenance of the remedial action, including costs of postremediation monitoring required by remedial action plan.

ASC 410-30 states that potential recoveries cannot be offset against the estimated liability, and further notes that any recovery recognized as an asset is to be reflected at fair value, which implies that only the present value of future recoveries can be recorded. It also stipulates that environmental clean-up costs are not unusual in nature, and thus cannot be shown as extraordinary items in the income statement. Furthermore, it is presumed that the costs are operating in nature and thus cannot normally be included in the "other income and expense" category of the income statement, either. Disclosure of accounting policies regarding recognition of the liability and of any related asset (for recoveries from third parties) is also needed, where pertinent.

28 ASC 420 EXIT OR DISPOSAL COST OBLIGATIONS

PERSPECTIVE AND ISSUES

Subtopic

ASC 420, *Exit or Disposal Cost Activities,* consists of one subtopic:
ASC 420-10, *Overall,* which provides guidance on the definition, reporting, and disclosure of such costs.

Scope and Scope Exceptions

ASC 420 applies to all entities. It does not apply to:

- Costs associated with the retirement of a long-lived asset covered by ASC 410-20
- Impairment of an unrecognized asset while it is being used.
(ASC 420-10-15-5)

Overview

ASC 420-10-15-4 clarifies that an exit activity includes, but is not limited to:

- A restructuring
- The sale or termination of a line of business
- The closure of business activities in a particular location
- The relocation of business activities
- Changes in management structure
- A fundamental reorganization that affects the nature and focus of operation.

DEFINITIONS OF TERMS

Source: ASC 420-10-20

Acquiree. The business or businesses that the acquirer obtains control of in a business combination. This term also includes a nonprofit activity or business that a not-for-profit acquirer obtains control of in an acquisition by a not-for-profit entity.

Acquirer. The entity that obtains control of the acquiree. However, in a business combination in which a variable interest entity (VIE) is acquired, the primary beneficiary of that entity always is the acquirer.

Acquisition by a Not-for-Profit Entity. A transaction or other event in which a not-for-profit acquirer obtains control of one or more nonprofit activities or businesses and initially recognizes their assets and liabilities in the acquirer's financial statements. When applicable guidance in Topic 805 is applied by a not-for-profit entity, the term business combination has the same meaning as this term has for a not-for-profit entity. Likewise, a reference to business combinations in guidance that links to Topic 805 has the same meaning as a reference to acquisitions by not-for-profit entities.

Business. An integrated set of activities and assets that is capable of being conducted and managed for the purpose of providing a return in the form of dividends, lower costs, or other economic benefits directly to investors or other owners, members, or participants. Additional guidance on what a business consists of is presented in paragraphs 805-10-55-4 through 55-9.

Business Combination. A transaction or other event in which an acquirer obtains control of one or more businesses. Transactions sometimes referred to as true mergers or mergers of equals also are business combinations. See also Acquisition by a Not-for-Profit Entity.

Cease-Use Date. The date the entity ceases using the right conveyed by the contract, for example, the right to use a leased property or to receive future goods or services.

Communication Date. The date the plan of termination for one-time employee termination benefits meets all of the criteria in paragraph 420-10-25-4 and has been communicated to employees.

Legal Entity. Any legal structure used to conduct activities or to hold assets. Some examples of such structures are corporations, partnerships, limited liability companies, grantor trusts, and other trusts.

Legal Notification Period, The notification period that an entity is required to provide to employees in advance of a specified termination event as a result of an existing law, statute, or contract.

Not-for-Profit Entity. An entity that possesses the following characteristics, in varying degrees, that distinguish it from a business entity:

1. Contributions of significant amounts of resources from resource providers who do not expect commensurate or proportionate pecuniary return
2. Operating purposes other than to provide goods or services at a profit
3. Absence of ownership interests like those of business entities.

Entities that clearly fall outside this definition include the following:

1. All investor-owned entities
2. Entities that provide dividends, lower costs, or other economic benefits directly and proportionately to their owners, members, or participants, such as mutual insurance

entities, credit unions, farm and rural electric cooperatives, and employee benefit plans.

One-Time Employee Termination Benefits. Benefits provided to current employees that are involuntarily terminated under the terms of a one-time benefit arrangement.

Restructuring. A program that is planned and controlled by management, and materially changes either the scope of a business undertaken by an entity, or the manner in which that business is conducted, as defined by the International Accounting Standard No. 37 in 2002.

Variable Interest Entity. A legal entity subject to consolidation according to the provisions of the Variable Interest Entities Subsections of Subtopic 810-10.

CONCEPTS, RULES, AND EXAMPLES

Employee Termination Benefits

ASC 420, *Exit or Disposal Cost Obligations,* applies to termination benefits provided to current employees that are involuntarily terminated under the terms of a benefit arrangement that applies for a specified termination event or for a specified future period. Those benefits are referred to as onetime termination benefits. If an entity has a history of providing similar benefits to employees involuntarily terminated in earlier events, the benefits are presumed to be part of an ongoing benefit arrangement (rather than a onetime benefit arrangement) unless there is evidence to the contrary.

A onetime benefit arrangement first exists at the date the plan of termination meets *all* of the following criteria:

1. Management approves and commits to the termination plan.
2. The termination plan specifies the number of employees to be terminated, their job classifications or functions, and their locations, as well as the expected completion date.
3. The termination plan establishes the terms of the benefit arrangement in sufficient detail that employees are able to determine the type and amount of benefits that they will receive if they are involuntarily terminated.
4. Actions required to complete the plan indicate that significant changes to the plan are unlikely.

(ASC 460-10-25-4)

Communicating the plan to employees creates a liability at the communication date (ASC 420-10-25-5).

Measurement. Exit or disposal costs should be measured at fair value. Often, quoted market values are not available for those costs. A present value technique may be the best option. However, in some situations the use of estimates may not be materially different from present value techniques and those are acceptable if consistent with a fair value measurement objective. (ASC 420-10-30-1 through 3)

Timing. (ASC 420-10-6 through 8) The timing of recognition of the liability for onetime termination benefits depends on whether the employees are required to render service beyond a minimum retention period. The minimum retention period is the notification period that an entity is required to provide to employees in advance of a termination event as a result of law, statute, or contract, or in the absence of a legal notification period, the minimum retention period cannot exceed sixty days.

If employees are entitled to receive the termination benefits regardless of when they leave or if employees will not be retained to render service beyond the minimum retention period, the liability for the termination benefits is recognized and measured at its fair value at the communication date.

If employees are required to render service until they are terminated in order to receive the termination benefit and will be retained beyond the minimum retention period, the liability for the termination benefits is measured at its fair value at the communication date and recognized ratably over the service period.

Examples of the determination of the minimum retention period and recognition

Master Mobile Communications announces that it will close its Donnybrook plant and terminate all 120 employees there. The terms of the plan meet the criteria above. There are three major groups of employees: management, union workers, and nonunion workers. Management is required to stay and render service until the plant's closing, which is four months from now, and each of the twelve management employees will receive $10,000. The union workers' contract states that they must be notified ninety days in advance before they can be terminated. The union workers will be terminated in ninety days. The termination benefit for each of the fifty union employees is one week per every six months of employment. The nonunion workers can leave at any time within the next three months and still collect the termination benefit. Each of the fifty-eight nonunion employees will receive a termination benefit of $1,000 for each year of service. There is no state statute specifying a notification period.

Case 1: Management

Management is required to work until termination, so it is necessary to determine whether the service period is beyond the minimum retention period. There is no state statute specifying a notification period, but the Worker Adjustment and Retraining Act, which applies to entities with over 100 employees, requires a sixty-day notification period for this plant's closing. Thus, the minimum retention period is sixty days. Management must work beyond the minimum retention period, so the $120,000 liability (12 × $10,000) is recognized at $30,000 per month for the next four months. Present value techniques are not necessary to measure the liability because the discount period is so short that the face amount would not differ materially from the fair value.

Case 2: Union employees

The union employees' contract requires a ninety-day notification period, so the minimum retention period for these employees is ninety days. The union workers will be terminated at the end of the ninety-day period, so they will not be required to work beyond the minimum retention period. If the total of the termination benefits for the fifty union employees is $142,500, a liability of $142,500 is recognized at the communication date. Present value techniques are not necessary to measure the liability because the discount period is so short that the face amount would not differ materially from the fair value.

Case 3: Nonunion workers

Nonunion workers are not required to work until the termination date to collect the termination benefit. Therefore, it is not necessary to determine the minimum retention period for these employees. If the 58 nonunion employees have 230 years of service among them, a liability of $230,000 is recognized at the communication date. Present value techniques are not necessary to measure the liability because the discount period is so short that the face amount would not differ materially from the fair value.

Subsequent measurement. If subsequent to the communication date there are changes in either the timing or amount of the expected termination benefit cash flows, the cumulative effect of the change should be computed and reported in the same line item(s) in the income statement in which the costs were initially reported. If present value techniques were used to measure the initial liability, the same credit-adjusted risk-free rate should be used to remeasure the liability.

Changes in the liability due to the passage of time (accretion) are recognized as accretion expense in the income statement. If employees are not required to provide services or are required to provide services only during the minimum retention period, accretion expense is charged for the passage of time after the communication date. If employees are required to provide services beyond the minimum retention period, accretion expense is charged for the passage of time after the termination date. Accretion expense should not be titled interest expense or be considered interest costs subject to capitalization.

According to ASC 420-10-55, if newly offered benefits represent a revision to an ongoing arrangement that is not limited to a specified termination event or to a specified future period, the benefits represent an enhancement to an ongoing benefit arrangement.

If a plan of termination changes and employees that were expected to be terminated within the minimum retention period are retained to render service beyond that period, the liability amount should be recomputed as though it had been known at the initial communication date that those employees would be required to render services beyond the minimum retention period. The cumulative effect of the change is recognized as a change in the liability and reported in the same line item(s) in the income statement in which the costs were initially reported. The remainder of the liability is recognized ratably from the date of change to the termination date.

Plan includes voluntary and involuntary benefits. If a plan of termination includes both voluntary and involuntary termination benefits, a liability for the involuntary benefits is recognized as described above. A liability for the incremental voluntary benefits (the excess of the voluntary benefit amount over the involuntary benefit amount) is recognized in accordance with ASC 712-10-25-1 through 25-3. That is, if the benefits are special termination benefits offered only for a short period of time, the liability is recognized when the employees accept the offer and the amount can be reasonably estimated. If, instead, the voluntary termination benefits are contractual termination benefits (for example, required by a union contract or a pension contract) the liability is recognized when it is probable that employees will be entitled to benefits and the amount can be reasonably estimated.

Contract Termination Costs

In addition to employee termination costs, an entity may incur contract termination costs, relocation costs, plant consolidation costs, and other costs associated with the exit or disposal activity. ASC 420 sets forth the following standards for recognition.

A liability for the costs to terminate a contract before the end of its term is recognized and measured at its fair value when the entity actually terminates the contract in accordance with the contractual term (e.g., by written notice).

A liability for the costs that will continue to be incurred under a contract for its remaining term without economic benefit to the entity is recognized and measured at its fair value when the entity ceases using the right conveyed by the contract (the cease-use date). If the contract is an operating lease, the fair value of the liability should be determined based on the remaining lease rentals, reduced by estimated sublease rentals, even if the entity does not intend to find a sublease. However, remaining operating lease payments should not be reduced to an amount less than zero by the estimated sublease payments.

Other Associated Costs to Exit an Activity

Other associated costs are items such as employee relocation costs and costs associated with facility closings or consolidations. A liability for other costs associated with the exit or disposal activity should be recognized when the liability is incurred, which is generally when the goods or services associated with the activity are received. The liability should not be recognized before it is incurred even if the costs are incremental and a direct result of the exit or disposal plan. (ASC 420-10-25-14 and 15)

Reporting and Disclosure

The costs of exit or disposal activities must be included in income from continuing operations before income taxes and are specifically prohibited from being presented in any manner that implies they are similar to an extraordinary item. If the subtotal "income from operations" is presented, the costs must be included in that subtotal. If the costs are associated with exit or disposal activities that involve a discontinued operation, they are included in the results of discontinued operations. If an entity's responsibility to settle the liability associated with an exit or disposal activity is removed or discharged, the related costs are reversed through the same line item(s) in the income statement that were used when those costs were initially recognized. (ASC 420-10-45-3)

Disclosure requirements can be found in the Appendix.

29 ASC 430 DEFERRED REVENUE

The only guidance this Topic provides is a link to guidance on deferred revenue related to vendor sales incentives (refunds or rebated) that will be claimed by customers at ASC 605-50-25-4.

30 ASC 440 COMMITMENTS

PERSPECTIVE AND ISSUES

Subtopics

ASC 440, *Commitments,* contains only one subtopic:

- ASC 440-10, *Overall,* which provides general guidance on financial accounting and reporting for certain commitments.

The Subtopic has two Subsections:

1. *General*
2. *Unconditional Purchase Obligations.*

The *General* Subsection provides guidance for

- Unused letters of credit,
- Preferred stock dividends in arrears,
- Commitments such as those for plant acquisitions, and
- Obligations to reduce debts, maintain working capital, or restrict dividends.

The *Unconditional Purchase Obligation* subsection provides guidance for unconditional purchase obligations, such as throughput and take-or-pay contracts.

Scope and Scope Exceptions

ASC 440 applies to all transactions. However, for guidance on product financing arrangements, the preparer should look to ASC 470-40-15.

Overview

All significant contractual commitments must be disclosed in the notes to the financial statements. For example, lease contract provisions, pension obligations, requirements contracts, bond indenture covenants, commitments to purchase or construct new facilities, and employee share-based compensation plans are to be clearly disclosed in the notes.

DEFINITIONS OF TERMS

Source: ASC 440-20

Purchaser's Incremental Borrowing Rate. The rate that, at the inception of an unconditional purchase obligation, the purchaser would have incurred to borrow over a similar term the funds necessary to discharge the obligation.

Take-or-Pay Contract. An agreement between a purchaser and a seller that provides for the purchaser to pay specified amounts periodically in return for products or services. The purchaser must make specified minimum payments even if it does not take delivery of the contracted products or services.

Throughput Contract. An agreement between a shipper (processor) and the owner of a transportation facility (such as an oil or natural gas pipeline or a ship) or a manufacturing facility that provides for the shipper (processor) to pay specified amounts periodically in return for the transportation (processing) of a product. The shipper (processor) is obligated to provide specified minimum quantities to be transported (processed) in each period and is required to make cash payments even if it does not provide the contracted quantities.

Unconditional Purchase Obligation. An obligation to transfer funds in the future for fixed or minimum amounts or quantities of goods or services at fixed or minimum prices (for example, as in take-or-pay contracts or throughput contracts).

CONCEPTS, RULES, AND EXAMPLES

Through-Put and Take-or-Pay Contracts

Through-put and take-or-pay contracts are sometimes used to help a supplier pay for new facilities, machines, or other expenditures. They are negotiated as a way of arranging financing for the facilities that will produce the goods or provide the services desired by a purchaser. A through-put contract is an agreement between the owner of a transportation facility or manufacturing facility (such as a pipeline) and a purchaser (such as an oil processor) that requires the purchaser to pay specified amounts at future dates to the owner in return for the transportation or manufacture of a product. A take-or-pay contract is similar. It is an agreement between a purchaser and a supplier that requires the purchaser to pay specified amounts at future dates in return for products or services. In both types of contracts, the purchaser is required to make the specified payments even if it does not receive goods or services.

Some of these contracts are reported on the statement of financial position as an asset and a liability. Others are not reported. Other than standards relating to recognition of losses on unconditional purchase obligations (ASC 330-10-35), there are no standards that require the contracts to be recognized on the statement of financial position. However, ASC 440 requires certain disclosures to be made.

Example of a through-put contract

Aramarck Oil contracts with the Persian Pipeline Company to ship a minimum of three million barrels a month of unprocessed sour crude oil from the Ahwaz oil field in Iran to the pipeline terminus at Char Bahar, an amount which constitutes 1/3 of the capacity of the pipeline. The contract term is twelve years. Under the contract, Aramarck is obligated to pay Persian for 1/3 of the fixed operating costs of the pipeline, depreciation, interest on the $500 million of 5% debt used to finance the pipeline (to be paid off in equal annual payments over twelve years), and a 7% rate of return on equity to Persian. Estimated annual payments are $20 million. Aramarck's disclosure of the agreement follows:

> Aramarck has signed an agreement reserving pipeline capacity for twelve years. Under the terms of the agreement, Aramarck is obligated to make the following minimum payments, whether or not it ships through the pipeline:

20X1 through 20X5 ($20 million annually)	$100,000,000
Later years	140,000,000
Total	240,000,000
Less: Amount representing interest	(58,984,000)
Total at present value	$181,016,000

Disclosures required by ASC 440 can be found in the Appendix.

31 ASC 450 CONTINGENCIES

PERSPECTIVE AND ISSUES

Subtopics

ASC 450, *Contingencies,* contains guidance for reporting and disclosure of gain and loss contingencies and has three subtopics:

- ASC 450-10, *Overall,* which, along with ASC 450-20450-30, provides guidance on accounting and disclosures for contingencies.
- ASC 450-20, *Loss Contingencies,* which describes accounting for potential liabilities in circumstances involving uncertainties.
- ASC 450-30, *Gain Contingencies,* which describes accounting and disclosure requirements for gain contingencies.

Scope and Scope Exceptions

ASC 450 applies to all entities. Not all uncertainties are contingencies. ASC 450-10-55 points out several common estimates that do not fall under the contingency guidance:

- Depreciation
- Estimates used in accruals
- Changes in tax law.

ASC 450-10-15-2A has the following transaction exception:

"The guidance in the Contingencies Topic does not apply to the recognition and initial measurement of assets or liabilities arising from contingencies that are measured at fair value or assets arising from contingencies measured at an amount other than fair value on the acquisition date in a business combination or an acquisition by a not-for-profit entity under the requirements of Subtopic 805-20 or 958-805. Those Subtopics provide the recognition and initial measurement requirements for assets and liabilities arising from contingencies measured at fair value and for assets arising from contingencies measured at an amount other than fair value as part of a business combination or an acquisition by a not-for-profit entity."

ASC 450-20-15-2 excludes the following transactions because their guidance is elsewhere in the Codification:

- Stock issued to employees (ASC 718).
- Employment-related costs, including deferred compensation contracts (ASC 710, 712, and 715). However, certain postemployment benefits are included in the scope of this ASC 450-20 by reference in 712-10-25-4 through 25-5.
- Uncertainty in income taxes (ASC 740-10-25).
- Accounting and reporting by insurance entities (ASC 944).

Overview

ASC 450-20 requires a liability to be recognized

1. If it is *probable* that an obligation has been incurred because of a transaction or event that occurred on or before the date of the financial statements and
2. If the amount of the obligation can be *reasonably estimated.*

Thus, uncertainties about the existence of an obligation need not be resolved before the liability is recorded.

DEFINITIONS OF TERMS

Source: ASC 450-10-20, ASC 450-20-20, ASC 450-30-20

Acquiree. The business or businesses that the acquirer obtains control of in a business combination. This term also includes a nonprofit activity or business that a not-for-profit acquirer obtains control of in an acquisition by a not-for-profit entity.

Acquirer. The entity that obtains control of the acquiree. However, in a business combination in which a variable interest entity (VIE) is acquired, the primary beneficiary of that entity always is the acquirer.

Acquisition by a Not-for-Profit Entity. A transaction or other event in which a not-for-profit acquirer obtains control of one or more nonprofit activities or businesses and initially recognizes their assets and liabilities in the acquirer's financial statements. When applicable guidance in Topic 805 is applied by a not-for-profit entity, the term business combination has the same meaning as this term has for a not-for-profit entity. Likewise, a reference to business combinations in guidance that links to Topic 805 has the same meaning as a reference to acquisitions by not-for-profit entities.

Acquisition Date. The date on which the acquirer obtains control of the acquiree.

Business. An integrated set of activities and assets that is capable of being conducted and managed for the purpose of providing a return in the form of dividends, lower costs, or other economic benefits directly to investors or other owners, members, or participants. Additional guidance on what a business consists of is presented in paragraphs 805-10-55-4 through 55-9.

Business Combination. A transaction or other event in which an acquirer obtains control of one or more businesses. Transactions sometimes referred to as true mergers or mergers of equals also are business combinations. See also Acquisition by a Not-for-Profit Entity.

Contingency. An existing condition, situation, or set of circumstances involving uncertainty as to possible gain (gain contingency) or loss (loss contingency) to an entity that will ultimately be resolved when one or more future events occur or fail to occur.

Gain Contingency. An existing condition, situation, or set of circumstances involving uncertainty as to possible gain to an entity that will ultimately be resolved when one or more future events occur or fail to occur.

Legal Entity. Any legal structure used to conduct activities or to hold assets. Some examples of such structures are corporations, partnerships, limited liability companies, grantor trusts, and other trusts.

Loss Contingency. An existing condition, situation, or set of circumstances involving uncertainty as to possible loss to an entity that will ultimately be resolved when one or more future events occur or fail to occur. The term loss is used for convenience to include many charges against income that are commonly referred to as expenses and others that are commonly referred to as losses.

Not-for-Profit Entity. An entity that possesses the following characteristics, in varying degrees, that distinguish it from a business entity:

a. Contributions of significant amounts of resources from resource providers who do not expect commensurate or proportionate pecuniary return
b. Operating purposes other than to provide goods or services at a profit
c. Absence of ownership interests like those of business entities.

Entities that clearly fall outside this definition include the following:

a. All investor-owned entities
b. Entities that provide dividends, lower costs, or other economic benefits directly and proportionately to their owners, members, or participants, such as mutual insurance entities, credit unions, farm and rural electric cooperatives, and employee benefit plans.

Probable. The future event or events are likely to occur.

Reasonably Possible. The chance of the future event or events occurring is more than remote but less than likely.

Remote. The chance of the future event or events occurring is slight.

Variable Interest Entity. A legal entity subject to consolidation according to the provisions of the Variable Interest Entities Subsections of Subtopic 810-10.

CONCEPTS, RULES, AND EXAMPLES

ASC 450-10, *Overall*

ASC 450 defines a contingency as an existing condition, situation, or set of circumstances involving uncertainty as to possible gain or loss and that will result in the acquisition of an asset, the reduction of a liability, the loss or impairment of an asset, or the incurrence of a liability (ASC 450-10-05-5). The uncertainty will ultimately be resolved when one or more future events occur or fail to occur.

ASC 450-20, *Loss Contingencies*

Loss contingencies are recognized only if there is an impairment of an asset or the incurrence of a liability as of the date of the statement of financial position. ASC 450-20-25-2 states that a loss must be accrued if *both* of the following conditions are met:

1. It is probable that an asset has been impaired or a liability has been incurred at the date of the financial statements.
2. The amount of loss can be reasonably estimated.

For example, estimated settlement amounts for ongoing lawsuits are recognized prior to a court's decision if it is probable that the outcome will be unfavorable. Further, difficulty in measuring an obligation is not, by itself, a reason for not recording a liability if the amount can be estimated. For example, warranty obligations are commonly recognized as liabilities even though the number of claims and the amount of each claim are unknown at the time of the sale of the item covered by the warranty. Although future events will eventually resolve the uncertainties (the warranty claims will be paid and the lawsuit will be adjudicated or settled), the liabilities are required to be recognized before all of the uncertainties are resolved so that relevant information is provided on a timely basis.

Levels of probability. ASC defines the different levels of probability as to whether or not future events will confirm the existence of a loss as follows:

1. *Probable*—The future event or events are likely to occur.
2. *Reasonably possible*—The chance of the future event or events occurring is more than remote but less than likely.
3. *Remote*—The chance of the future event or events occurring is slight.

(ASC 450-20-25-2)

Professional judgment is required to classify the likelihood of the future events occurring. All relevant information that can be acquired concerning the uncertain set of circumstances needs to be obtained and used to determine the classification.

Estimating the loss. When estimating the fair value of the loss, it is not necessary that a single amount be identified. A range of amounts is sufficient to indicate that some amount of loss has been incurred and is required to be accrued (ASC 450-20-25-5). The amount accrued is the amount within the range that appears to be the best estimate. If there is no best estimate, the minimum amount in the range is accrued, since it is probable that the loss will be at least that amount (ASC 450-20). The maximum amount of loss is required to be disclosed (ASC 450-20-30-1). If future events indicate that the minimum loss originally accrued is inadequate, an additional loss is to be accrued in the period when this fact becomes known. This accrual is a change in estimate, not a prior period adjustment.

Probable. When a loss is probable and no estimate is possible, these facts are also to be disclosed in the current period. The accrual of the loss is to be made in the earliest period in which the amount of the loss can be estimated. Accrual of that loss in future periods is a change in estimate. It is not treated as a restatement (prior period adjustment).

Reasonably possible. If the occurrence of the loss is reasonably possible, the facts and circumstances of the possible loss and an estimate of the amount, if determinable, are to be disclosed. If the occurrence of the loss is remote, no accrual or disclosure is usually required.

Amount not estimable. When a public company cannot estimate the reasonably likely impact of a contingent liability, but a range of amounts are determinable, the SEC requires disclosure of those amounts. Disclosure of contingencies for public companies is also to include quantification of the related accruals and adjustments, costs of legal defense, and reasonably likely exposure to additional loss, as well as the assumptions that management has made about those amounts and the extent to which the resulting estimates of loss are sensitive to changes in those assumptions.

Events subsequent to balance sheet date. Events that give rise to loss contingencies that occur after the date of the statement of financial position (i.e., bankruptcy or expropriation) but before issuance of the financial statements may require disclosure so that statement users are not misled. Note disclosures or pro forma financial statements may be prepared as supplemental information to show the effect of the loss.

Unasserted claims or assessments. It is not necessary to disclose loss contingencies for an unasserted claim or assessment where there has been no manifestation of an awareness of possible claim or assessment by a potential claimant unless it is deemed probable that a claim will be asserted and a reasonable possibility of an unfavorable outcome exists. Under the provisions of ASC 450, general or unspecified business risks are not loss contingencies and therefore no accrual is necessary. Disclosure of these business risks may be required under ASC 275.

Estimate versus contingency. Distinguishing between an estimate and a contingency can be difficult because both involve an uncertainty that will be resolved by future events. However, an estimate exists because of uncertainty about the amount of a loss resulting from an event requiring an acknowledged accounting recognition. The event has occurred and the effect is known, but the amount itself is uncertain. For example, depreciation is an estimate, but not a contingency because the actual fact of physical depreciation is acknowledged, although the amount is obtained by an assumed accounting method.

In a contingency, the amount is also usually uncertain, although that is not an essential characteristic. Instead, the uncertainty lies in whether the event has occurred (or will) and what the effect, if any, on the enterprise would be. Collectibility of receivables is a contingency because it is uncertain whether a customer will not pay at a future date, although it is probable that some customers will not pay. Similar logic would hold for obligations related to product warranties. That is, it is uncertain whether a product will fail, but it is probable that some will fail within the warranty period.

Other contingencies are rarely recognized until specific events confirming their existence occur. Every business risks loss by fire, explosion, government expropriation or casualties in the ordinary course of business. To the extent those losses are not (or cannot be) insured, the risks are contingencies. Because those events are often random in their occurrence, uncertainty surrounds whether the future event confirming the loss will or will not take place. The passage of time usually resolves the uncertainty. Until the event confirming the loss occurs (or is probable of occurrence) and the amount of the loss can be reasonably estimated, the potential loss is not recognized in financial statements.

Litigation. The most difficult area of contingencies is litigation. Accountants must rely on attorneys' assessments concerning the likelihood of such events. Unless the attorney indicates that the risk of loss is remote or slight, or that the loss if it occurs would be immaterial to the company, disclosure in financial statements is necessary and an accrual may also be necessary. In practice, attorneys are loathe to state that the risk of loss is remote, as that term is defined by ASC 450, although the likelihood of obtaining a definitive response to lawyers' letters under AU-C Section 501 is improved if the auditors explicitly cite a materiality threshold. In cases where judgments have been entered against the reporting entity, or where the attorney gives a range of expected losses or other amounts and indicates that an unfavorable outcome is probable, accruals of loss contingencies for at least the minimum point of the range must be made. In most cases, however, an estimate of the contingency is unknown and the contingency is reflected only in footnotes.

Accruals for contingencies, including those arising in connection with litigation, are limited under GAAP to expected losses resulting from events occurring prior to the date of the statement of financial position (ASC 450-20-25-6). One unresolved issue is whether expected legal costs to be incurred in connection with a loss contingency that is being accrued should be accrued as well. Apparently, GAAP would permit such an accrual, but practice is varied. With respect to SEC registrants, the SEC staff expects consistency and the decision to do so to be disclosed in the financial statements and applied consistently (ASC 450-20-S99).

ASC 450-30, *Gain Contingencies*

The guidance in ASC 450-30 states simply that a "contingency that might result in a gain usually should not be reflected in the financial statements because to do so might be to recognize revenue before its realization. (ASC 450-30-25-2)" However, it also states that entities may consider disclosing a gain contingency as long as the disclosure is adequate and is not misleading.

Other Sources

The Contingencies Subtopics do not include all guidance related to contingencies. The following chart, based on information in the ASC Subtopics "60" sections, references other Codification sources of guidance.

See ASC Location – Wiley *GAAP* Chapter…	*For information on…*
From ASC 450-10, *Overall*	
ASC 270-10-50-6	Contingencies and other uncertainties that could be expected to affect the fairness of presentation of financial data at an interim date
ASC 340-30	Contingencies associated with insurance and reinsurance contracts that do not transfer insurance risk
ASC 605-15	Recognition of revenue when uncertainties exist about possible returns
ASC 605-40-25-4	Cases in which a nonmonetary asset is destroyed or damaged (that is, an involuntary conversion) and the amount of monetary assets to be received is uncertain
ASC 720-20	Accounting by an insured entity for the contingencies associated with a multiple-year retrospectively rated insurance contract accounted for as insurance
ASC 740-10-25	Accounting for uncertainty in income taxes
ASC 805-20-55-50 through 55-51	Recognition of contingent obligations for contractual termination benefits and curtailment losses under employee benefit plans that will be triggered by the consummation of the business combination
ASC 840-10-25-35	Contingent rentals
ASC 944-40	Contingencies that arise when an insurance entity or a reinsurance entity issues an insurance contract
ASC 944-20-15	Contingencies associated with a reinsurance contract between insurance entities (including retrocession)
ASC 944-20	Contingencies associated with multiple-year retrospectively rated contracts

ASC 985-605	Revenue recognition when uncertainties exist if licensing, selling, leasing, or otherwise marketing computer software
ASC 450-20, *Loss Contingencies*	
ASC 275	Disclosure of certain risks and uncertainties that stem from the nature of an entity's operations and from significant concentrations in certain aspects of an entity's operations, many of which are noninsured or underinsured risks
ASC 310-10-35	Contingencies related to the collectibility of receivables
ASC 310-10-35	Application of this Subtopic to the collectibility of a loan portfolio
ASC 330-10-35	Inventories that are impaired by damage, deterioration, obsolescence, changes in price levels, or other causes
ASC 330-10-35	Losses that are expected to arise from firm, uncancelable, and unhedged commitments for the future purchase of inventory
ASC 405-30	Assessments by state guaranty funds and workers' compensation second-injury funds and other assessments related to insurance activities, including insurance activities of an entity that self-insures
ASC 410-20	Contingencies associated with the retirement of a tangible long-lived asset that result from the acquisition, construction, or development and/or the normal operation of a long-lived asset
ASC 410-30	Contingencies related to environmental remediation liabilities that arise from the improper operation of a long-lived asset
The Product Warranties Subsections of Subtopic 460-10	Contingencies related to product warranties and product defects
ASC 460	Contingencies related to guarantees of indebtedness of others
ASC 460	Contingencies related to obligations of commercial banks under financial standby letters of credit
ASC 470-60-35	Contingent payments of a troubled debt restructuring
ASC 715-80-35-2 and 715-80-50-2	Contingencies related to withdrawal from a multiemployer plan

ASC 720-20-25-1	Contingencies related to an insurance contract or reinsurance contract that does not, despite its form, provide for indemnification of the insured or the ceding company by the insurer or reinsurer against loss or liability
ASC 840-10-25-12	Classification effects of a provision in a lease that requires lessee indemnifications for environmental contamination caused by the lessee during its use of the property
ASC 840-10-25-35	Contingent rent
ASC 860-10-40	Contingencies related to agreements to repurchase receivables (or to repurchase the related property) that have been sold or otherwise assigned
ASC 930-715	Contingencies resulting from the Coal Industry Retiree Health Benefit Act of 1992
ASC 944-40	Contingencies related to the risk of loss that is assumed by a property and casualty insurance entity or reinsurance entity when it issues an insurance policy covering risk of loss from catastrophes
ASC 946-320-35-17 to 35-19	Contingencies related to the collectibility of interest receivable, including purchased interest
ASC 954-450	Contingencies related to malpractice claims
ASC 450-30, *Gain Contingencies*	
ASC 210-20-45	The determination of whether a receivable resulting from the recognition of a gain contingency may be offset against an existing liability
ASC 225-30-45	The presentation of business interruption insurance recoveries in the income statement
ASC 225-30-50	Disclosure of information about business interruption insurance recoveries
ASC 720-20-25-3	Recognition of insurance recoveries by an entity insured through a purchased retroactive insurance contract (other than for core insurance operations of an insurance entity)
ASC 840-10-50-5	A lessor's accounting for contingent rental income

32 ASC 460 GUARANTEES

PERSPECTIVE AND ISSUES

Subtopic

ASC 460, *Guarantees,* consists of one subtopic:

- ASC 460-10, *Overall,* which provides requirements to be met by a guarantor for certain guarantees issued and outstanding.

ASC 460-10 has two Subsections:

- General, which discusses the guarantor's recognition and disclosure of a liability at the inception of a guarantee
- Product Warranties.

Additional sources of guidance are listed in the Other Sources section at the end of this chapter.

Scope and Scope Exceptions

ASC 460 applies to all entities. ASC 460 applies to guarantee contracts that contingently require the guarantor to make payments (either in cash, financial instruments, shares of its stock, other assets or in services) to the guaranteed party based on any of the following circumstances (ASC 460-10-15-4):

a. Changes in a specified interest rate, security price, commodity price, foreign exchange rate, index of prices or rates, or any other variable, including the occurrence or nonoccurrence of a specified event that is related to an asset or liability of the guaranteed party. For example, the provisions apply to the following, as cited by ASC 460:
    1. A financial standby letter of credit
    2. A market value guarantee on either securities (including the common stock of the guaranteed party) or a nonfinancial asset owned by the guaranteed party

3. A guarantee of the market price of the common stock of the guaranteed party
4. A guarantee of the collection of the scheduled contractual cash flows from individual financial assets held by a variable interest entity (VIE)
5. A guarantee granted to a business or its owners that the revenue received by the business will equal or exceed some stated amount.

(ASC 460-10-55-2, with reference to ASC 460-10-15-4(a)

One common example of this type of situation is where a hospital lures a doctor to open a practice in an underserved community with a guarantee of fee income for an initial period. ASC 460 explicitly states that these types of assurances are guarantees and must be given accounting recognition.

b. Another entity's failure to perform under an obligating agreement. For example, the provisions apply to a performance standby letter of credit, which obligates the guarantor to make a payment if the specified entity fails to perform its nonfinancial obligation.
c. The occurrence of a specified event or circumstance (an indemnification agreement), such as an adverse judgment in a lawsuit or the imposition of additional taxes due to either a change in the tax law or an adverse interpretation of the tax law, provided that the guarantor is an entity other than an insurance or reinsurance company.
d. The occurrence of specified events under conditions whereby payments are legally available to creditors of the guaranteed party and those creditors may enforce the guaranteed party's claims against the guarantor under the agreement (an indirect guarantee of the indebtedness of others).

Per ASC 460-10-15-7, ASC 460 does *not* apply to

1. A guarantee or an indemnification that is excluded from the scope of Topic 450, *Contingencies*, primarily employment-related guarantees.
2. A lessee's guarantee of the residual value of leased property if the lessee accounts for the lease as a capital lease
3. Contingent rents
4. A guarantee contract or an indemnification agreement that is issued by either an insurance or a reinsurance company
5. Vendor rebates (by the guarantor) based on either the sales revenues of or the number of units sold by the guaranteed party
6. Vendor rebates (by the guarantor) based on the volume of purchases by the buyer (because the underlying relates to an asset of the seller not the buyer who receives the rebate).
7. Guarantees that prevent the guarantor from recognizing either the sale of the asset underlying the guarantee or the profits from that sale
8. A registration payment arrangement within the scope of ASC 825-20-15, *Financial Instruments, Registration Payment Arrangements*
9. A guarantee or an indemnification of an entity's own future performance.
10. A guarantee accounted for as a credit derivative instrument at fair value under ASC 815-10-50-4J through 4L.

(ASC 460-10-15-7)

Initial measurements. ASC 460's requirement to recognize an initial liability does *not* apply to the following types of guarantees (i.e., these guarantees are subject only to ASC 460's disclosure requirements):

1. A guarantee that is accounted for as a derivative instrument at fair value under ASC 815.
2. A contract that guarantees the functionality of nonfinancial assets that are owned by the guaranteed party (product warranties)
3. Contingent consideration in a business combination or an acquisition of a business or nonprofit activity by a not-for-profit entity
4. A guarantee that requires the guarantor to issue its own equity shares
5. A guarantee by an original lessee that has become secondarily liable under a new lease that relieved the original lessee of the primary obligation under the original lease
6. A guarantee issued between parents and their subsidiaries or between corporations under common control
7. A parent's guarantee of a subsidiary's debt to a third party (irrespective of whether the parent is a corporation or an individual)
8. A subsidiary's guarantee of a parent's debt to a third party or the debt of another subsidiary of the parent.

(ASC 460-10-25-1)

Product warranties. Per ASC 460-10-15-9 the guidance in the Product Warranties Subsections applies only to product warranties, which include all of the following:

1. Product warranties issued by the guarantor, regardless of whether the guarantor is required to make payment in services or cash
2. Separately priced extended warranty or product maintenance contracts.
3. Warranty obligations that are incurred in connection with the sale of the product, that is, obligations that are not separately priced or sold but are included in the sale of the product.

Overview

There had been a longstanding requirement in GAAP for specific disclosures to be provided about direct and indirect guarantees of the indebtedness of others. ASC 460, *Guarantees*, explains that guarantees actually embody two separate obligations:

1. The contingent obligation to make future payments under the guarantee in the event of nonperformance by the party whose obligation is guaranteed, and
2. An obligation to be ready to perform, referred to as a standby obligation, during the period that the guarantee is in effect.

As a result of this bifurcation of the obligation, many guarantees are now required to be recognized as liabilities on the statement of financial position.

DEFINITIONS OF TERMS

Source: ASC 460-10-20

Acquiree. The business or businesses that the acquirer obtains control of in a business combination. This term also includes a nonprofit activity or business that a not-for-profit acquirer obtains control of in an acquisition by a not-for-profit entity.

Acquirer. The entity that obtains control of the acquiree. However, in a business combination in which a variable interest entity (VIE) is acquired, the primary beneficiary of that entity always is the acquirer.

Acquisition by a Not-for-Profit Entity. A transaction or other event in which a not-for-profit acquirer obtains control of one or more nonprofit activities or businesses and initially recognizes their assets and liabilities in the acquirer's financial statements. When applicable guidance in Topic 805 is applied by a not-for-profit entity, the term business combination has the same meaning as this term has for a not-for-profit entity. Likewise, a reference to business combinations in guidance that links to Topic 805 has the same meaning as a reference to acquisitions by not-for-profit entities.

Bargain Purchase Option. A provision allowing the lessee, at his option, to purchase the leased property for a price that is sufficiently lower than the expected fair value of the property at the date the option becomes exercisable that exercise of the option appears, at lease inception, to be reasonably assured.

Bargain Renewal Option. A provision allowing the lessee, at his option, to renew the lease for a rental sufficiently lower than the fair rental of the property at the date the option becomes exercisable that exercise of the option appears, at lease inception, to be reasonably assured. Fair rental of a property in this context shall mean the expected rental for equivalent property under similar terms and conditions.

Business. An integrated set of activities and assets that is capable of being conducted and managed for the purpose of providing a return in the form of dividends, lower costs, or other economic benefits directly to investors or other owners, members, or participants. Additional guidance on what a business consists of is presented in paragraphs 805-10-55-4 through 55-9

Business Combination. A transaction or other event in which an acquirer obtains control of one or more businesses. Transactions sometimes referred to as true mergers or mergers of equals also are business combinations. See also Acquisition by a Not-for-Profit Entity.

Commercial Letter of Credit. Document issued typically by a financial institution on behalf of its customer (the account party) authorizing a third party (the beneficiary), or in special cases the account party, to draw drafts on the institution up to a stipulated amount and with specified terms and conditions; it is a conditional commitment (except if prepaid by the account party) on the part of the institution to provide payment on drafts drawn in accordance with the terms of the document.

Contingency. An existing condition, situation, or set of circumstances involving uncertainty as to possible gain (gain contingency) or loss (loss contingency) to an entity that will ultimately be resolved when one or more future events occur or fail to occur.

Credit Derivative. A derivative instrument that has both of the following characteristics:

1. One or more of its underlyings are related to any of the following:
    a. The credit risk of a specified entity (or a group of entities)
    b. An index based on the credit risk of a group of entities.
2. It exposes the seller to potential loss from credit-risk-related events specified in the contract.

Examples of credit derivatives include, but are not limited to, credit default swaps, credit spread options, and credit index products.

Direct Guarantee of Indebtedness. An agreement in which a guarantor states that if the debtor fails to make payment to the creditor when due, the guarantor will pay the creditor. If the debtor defaults, the creditor has a direct claim on the guarantor.

Fair Value. The price that would be received to sell an asset or paid to transfer a liability in an orderly transaction between market participants at the measurement date.

Financial Standby Letter of Credit. An undertaking (typically by a financial institution) to guarantee payment of a specified financial obligation.

Gain Contingency. An existing condition, situation, or set of circumstances involving uncertainty as to possible gain to an entity that will ultimately be resolved when one or more future events occur or fail to occur.

Indirect Guarantee of Indebtedness. An agreement that obligates the guarantor to transfer funds to a debtor upon the occurrence of specified events, under conditions whereby:

1. After funds are transferred from the guarantor to the debtor, the funds become legally available to creditors through their claims against the debtor
2. Those creditors may enforce the debtor's claims against the guarantor under the agreement.

In contrast with a direct guarantee of indebtedness, if the debtor defaults, the creditor has a direct claim on the guarantor. Examples of indirect guarantees include agreements to advance funds if a debtor's net income, coverage of fixed charges, or working capital falls below a specified minimum.

Indirectly Related to the Leased Property. The provisions or conditions that in substance are guarantees of the lessor's debt or loans to the lessor by the lessee that are related to the leased property but are structured in such a manner that they do not represent a direct guarantee or loan. Examples include a party related to the lessee guaranteeing the lessor's debt on behalf of the lessee, or the lessee financing the lessor's purchase of the leased asset using collateral other than the leased property.

Lease Term. The fixed noncancelable lease term plus all of the following, except as noted in the following paragraph:

1. All periods, if any, covered by bargain renewal options.
2. All periods, if any, for which failure to renew the lease imposes a penalty on the lessee in such amount that a renewal appears, at lease inception, to be reasonably assured.
3. All periods, if any, covered by ordinary renewal options during which any of the following conditions exist:
    a. A guarantee by the lessee of the lessor's debt directly or indirectly related to the leased property is expected to be in effect.
    b. A loan from the lessee to the lessor directly or indirectly related to the leased property is expected to be outstanding.
4. All periods, if any, covered by ordinary renewal options preceding the date as of which a bargain purchase option is exercisable.
5. All periods, if any, representing renewals or extensions of the lease at the lessor's option.

The lease term shall not be assumed to extend beyond the date a bargain purchase option becomes exercisable.

Legal Entity. Any legal structure used to conduct activities or to hold assets. Some examples of such structures are corporations, partnerships, limited liability companies, grantor trusts, and other trusts.

Loss Contingency. An existing condition, situation, or set of circumstances involving uncertainty as to possible loss to an entity that will ultimately be resolved when one or more future events occur or fail to occur. The term loss is used for convenience to include many charges against income that are commonly referred to as expenses and others that are commonly referred to as losses.

Minimum Revenue Guarantee. A guarantee granted to a business or its owners that the revenue of the business (or a specific portion of the business) for a specified period of time will be at least a specified minimum amount.

Noncancelable Lease Term. That portion of the lease term that is cancelable only under any of the following conditions:

1. Upon the occurrence of some remote contingency
2. With the permission of the lessor
3. If the lessee enters into a new lease with the same lessor
4. If the lessee incurs a penalty in such amount that continuation of the lease appears, at inception, reasonably assured.

Not-for-Profit Entity. An entity that possesses the following characteristics, in varying degrees, that distinguish it from a business entity:

1. Contributions of significant amounts of resources from resource providers who do not expect commensurate or proportionate pecuniary return
2. Operating purposes other than to provide goods or services at a profit
3. Absence of ownership interests like those of business entities.

Entities that clearly fall outside this definition include the following:

1. All investor-owned entities
2. Entities that provide dividends, lower costs, or other economic benefits directly and proportionately to their owners, members, or participants, such as mutual insurance entities, credit unions, farm and rural electric cooperatives, and employee benefit plans.

Penalty. Any requirement that is imposed or can be imposed on the lessee by the lease agreement or by factors outside the lease agreement to do any of the following:

1. Disburse cash
2. Incur or assume a liability
3. Perform services
4. Surrender or transfer an asset or rights to an asset or otherwise forego an economic benefit, or suffer an economic detriment. Factors to consider in determining whether an economic detriment may be incurred include, but are not limited to, all of the following:
   a. The uniqueness of purpose or location of the property
   b. The availability of a comparable replacement property
   c. The relative importance or significance of the property to the continuation of the lessee's line of business or service to its customers
   d. The existence of leasehold improvements or other assets whose value would be impaired by the lessee vacating or discontinuing use of the leased property
   e. Adverse tax consequences
   f. The ability or willingness of the lessee to bear the cost associated with relocation or replacement of the leased property at market rental rates or to tolerate other parties using the leased property.

Performance Standby Letter of Credit. An irrevocable undertaking by a guarantor to make payments in the event a specified third party fails to perform under a nonfinancial contractual obligation.

Probable. The future event or events are likely to occur.

Related Parties. Related parties include:

1. Affiliates of the entity
2. Entities for which investments in their equity securities would be required, absent the election of the fair value option under the Fair Value Option Subsection of Section 825-10-15, to be accounted for by the equity method by the investing entity
3. Trusts for the benefit of employees, such as pension and profit-sharing trusts that are managed by or under the trusteeship of management
4. Principal owners of the entity and members of their immediate families
5. Management of the entity and members of their immediate families
6. Other parties with which the entity may deal if one party controls or can significantly influence the management or operating policies of the other to an extent that one of the transacting parties might be prevented from fully pursuing its own separate interests
7. Other parties that can significantly influence the management or operating policies of the transacting parties or that have an ownership interest in one of the transacting parties and can significantly influence the other to an extent that one or more of the transacting parties might be prevented from fully pursuing its own separate interests.

Underlying. A specified interest rate, security price, commodity price, foreign exchange rate, index of prices or rates, or other variable (including the occurrence or nonoccurrence of a specified event such as a scheduled payment under a contract). An underlying may be a price or rate of an asset or liability but is not the asset or liability itself. An underlying is a variable that, along with either a notional amount or a payment provision, determines the settlement of a derivative instrument.

Variable Interest Entity. A legal entity subject to consolidation according to the provisions of the Variable Interest Entities Subsections of Subtopic 810-10.

Warranty. A guarantee for which the underlying is related to the performance (regarding function, not price) of nonfinancial assets that are owned by the guaranteed party. The obligation may be incurred in connection with the sale of goods or services; if so, it may require further performance by the seller after the sale has taken place.

Weather Derivative. A forward-based or option-based contract for which settlement is based on a climatic or geological variable. One example of such a variable is the occurrence or nonoccurrence of a specified amount of snow at a specified location within a specified period of time.

CONCEPTS, RULES, AND EXAMPLES

Guarantees

While disclosures of at least some guarantees had been common under GAAP, the economic significance of such arrangements had rarely been measured or disclosed in the past. ASC 460, *Guarantees*, significantly altered past practice by requiring that the fair value of guarantees be recognized as a liability.

ASC 460 establishes the notion that a guarantee actually consists of two distinct components. These two obligations have quite different accounting implications.

Noncontingent obligation. The first of these components is a noncontingent obligation, namely, the obligation to stand ready to perform over the term of the guarantee in the event that the specified triggering events or conditions occur. This stand-ready obligation is unconditional and thus is not considered a contingent obligation.

Contingent obligation. The second component, which is a contingent obligation, is the obligation to make future payments if those triggering events or conditions occur.

Initial recognition. At the inception of a guarantee, the guarantor would recognize a liability for both the noncontingent and contingent obligations at their fair values. However, in the unusual circumstance that a liability is recognized under ASC 450-20 for the contingent obligation (i.e., because it is deemed probable of occurrence and reasonable of estimation that the guarantor will pay), the liability to be initially recognized for the noncontingent obligation would only be the portion, if any, of the guarantee's fair value not already recognized to comply with ASC 450-20.

It is important to stress that this does not mean that the guarantor records the entire face amount of the guarantee; rather, it is the fair value of the stand-ready obligation that would be recognized. When a guarantee is issued in a stand-alone, arm's-length transaction with an unrelated party, the fair value of the guarantee (and thus the amount to be recognized as a liability) is the premium received by the guarantor. When a guarantee is issued as part of another transaction (such as the sale or lease of an asset) or as a contribution to an unrelated party, the fair value of the liability is measured by the premium that would be required by the guarantor to issue the same guarantee in a stand-alone, arm's-length transaction with an unrelated party.

In practice, if the likelihood that the guarantor will have to perform is judged to be only "reasonably possible" or "remote," the only amount to be recorded will be the fair value of the noncontingent obligation to stand ready to perform. If, however, the contingency is probable of occurrence and can be reasonably estimated under ASC 450-20, that amount must be recognized and the liability under the guarantee arrangement will be the greater of (1) the fair value computed as explained above, or (2) the amount computed in accordance with ASC 450-20's provisions.

When initially issued, the guidance on computing guarantees where no market information is available made reference to CON 7. In so doing, FASB endorsed the use of the discounted, probability-weighted cash flow method for estimating the stand-ready obligation.

Since, in the author's opinion, in the absence of other, better input data, such as the pricing of insurance to assume the risk of performing on the guarantee, the probability-weighted present value of possible future cash flows could serve as useful input to determining the fair value of guarantees made, the following example is presented.

Example of estimating the fair value of a guarantee using CON 7 when recognition of a loss contingency under ASC 450 would not be otherwise required

Big Red Company guarantees a $1,000,000 debt of Little Blue Company for the next three years in conjunction with selling equipment to Little Blue. Big Red evaluates its risk of payment as follows:

(1) There is no possibility that Big Red will pay during year 1.
(2) There is a 15% chance that Big Red will pay during year 2. If it has to pay, there is a 30% chance that it will have to pay $500,000 and a 70% chance that it will have to pay $250,000.
(3) There is a 20% chance that Big Red will pay during year 3. If it has to pay, there is a 25% chance that it will have to pay $600,000 and a 75% chance that it will have to pay $300,000.

The expected cash flows are computed as follows:

Year 1	100% chance of paying \$0 = \$0
Year 2	85% chance of paying \$0 and a 15% chance of paying (.30 × \$500,000 + .70 × \$250,000 =) \$325,000 = \$48,750
Year 3	80% chance of paying \$0 and a 20% chance of paying (.25 × \$600,000 + .75 × \$300,000 =) \$375,000 = \$75,000

The present value of the expected cash flows is computed as the sum of the years' probability-weighted cash flows, here assuming an appropriate discount rate of 8%.

Year 1	\$0 × 1/1.08	=	\$ 0
Year 2	\$48,750 × $1/(1.08)^2$	=	41,795
Year 3	\$75,000 × $1/(1.08)^3$	=	59,537
Fair value of the guarantee			\$101,332

Based on the foregoing, a liability of \$101,332 would be recognized at inception. This would reduce the net selling price of the equipment sold to Little Blue, thereby reducing the profit to be reported on the sale transaction.

Example of estimating the fair value of a guarantee using CON 7 when recognition of a loss contingency under ASC 450 is also required

Assume the same basic facts as in the foregoing example, but now also assume that it has been determined that there is a 60% likelihood that the buyer will eventually default and, after legal process, Big Red will have to repay debt amounting to \$400,000 at the end of the fifth year. Assume also that a likelihood of 60% is deemed to make this contingent obligation "probable" under ASC 450. The present value of that payment is \$272,233, but ASC 450 does not address or seemingly anticipate the application of present value methods. Thus, it would appear that accrual of the full \$400,000 expected loss is required, unaffected by expected timing or by the probability (60%, in this example) that it will occur. Since this amount exceeds the amount computed under ASC 460, no additional amount would be recognized in connection with the noncontingent obligation to stand ready to perform.

If, instead of the immediate foregoing facts, the probable repayments were estimated to be \$75,000, then the liabilities to be recognized would total \$101,322, of which \$75,000 would be required to satisfy the provisions of ASC 450, and the incremental amount, \$26,332, would be attributed to the noncontingent obligation.

The entry to record the liability depends upon the circumstances under which the guarantee arose. If the guarantee was issued in a stand-alone transaction for a premium, the offset would be to the asset accepted for the premium's payment (most likely, cash or a receivable). If the guarantee was issued in conjunction with the sale of assets, the proceeds would be allocated between the sale of the asset and the guarantee obligation, so that the profit (loss) on the sale of the asset would be reduced (increased). If the guarantee was issued in conjunction with the formation of a business accounted for under the equity method, the offset would be an increase in the carrying amount of the investment. If the guarantee was issued to an unrelated party for no consideration, an immediate expense would be recognized. If a residual value guarantee was provided by a lessee-guarantor, the offset would be reported as prepaid rent and then amortized over the term of the lease to rent expense. The residual value of equipment by the manufacturer is recognized by the manufacturer as an asset (included in the seller/lessor's net investment in lease).

Subsequent measurement. After initial recognition, the liability is adjusted as the guarantor either is released from risk or is subject to increased risk. ASC 460 does not prescribe the accounting for guarantees subsequent to initial recognition, and there is no requirement to reassess the fair value of the guarantee after inception. In fact, ASC 460 only addresses measurement of a guarantor's liability at the inception of the guarantee and fair value is only to be used in subsequent accounting for the guarantee if the use of that method can be justified under other authoritative guidance. ASC 460 cannot be cited to support adjustments to fair value subsequent to initial recognition.

However, if the guarantor is subsequently released from risk, logically that could be recognized in one of three ways, in the authors' opinion, although no guidance is provided by ASC 460. First, the liability could simply be written off at its expiration or settlement. Second, the liability could be amortized systematically over the guarantee period. Third, the liability might be adjusted to reflect changing fair value, which presumably declines over time as the risk of having to perform decreases. Furthermore, changes dictated by the provisions of ASC 450 (e.g., as a previously "remote" contingency becomes a "probable" one) must be accounted for under that requirement, apart from the requirements of ASC 460.

Fees for guaranteeing a loan. According to ASC 605-20-25-9, fees received for guaranteeing another entity's obligation are to be recognized as income over the guarantee period, rather than at the time of receipt, consistent with other standards governing service fee income recognition. The guarantor is to perform ongoing assessments of the probability of loss related to the guarantee and recognize a liability if the conditions in ASC 450 are met. Upon entering into a guarantee arrangement, the guarantor is required to recognize the stand-ready obligation under the guarantee. The contingent aspect of the guarantee would only be recognized if the conditions defined by ASC 450 are met.

Impact of ASC 460 on revenue recognition on sales with a guaranteed minimum resale value. The authoritative GAAP governing lease accounting holds that manufacturers are precluded from recognizing sales of equipment when they provide purchasers with guarantees of resale value, unless the criteria for sales-type lease accounting are met (ASC 840-10-55-12 et seq.). It states that minimum lease payments, used to ascertain whether a given lease would be an operating or sales-type (capital) lease, are to include the difference between the initial proceeds and the guaranteed amount. Under these circumstances, the fair value of the resale value guarantee is not recognized by the manufacturer, because ASC 460 does not apply to an asset of the guarantor. Given that the manufacturer would report the residual value as an asset, the guarantee does not fall within the domain of ASC 460.

Disclosure requirements. Disclosures can be found in the checklist in the Appendix.

Product Warranties

Product warranties providing for repair or replacement of defective products may be sold separately or may be included in the sale price of the product. ASC 460-10-25-5 points out that "because of the uncertainty surrounding claims that may be made under warranties, warranty obligation fall within the definition of a contingency" and losses are accrued under the conditions in ASC 450-20-25 are met:

1. If it is *probable* that an obligation has been incurred because of a transaction or event that occurred on or before the date of the financial statements and
2. If the amount of the obligation can be *reasonably estimated*.

These conditions may be made for individual elements or groups of items and the particular parties making claims my not be identified at the time of the accrual.

If the warranty extends into the next accounting period, a current liability for the estimated amount of warranty expense expected in the next period must be recorded. If the warranty spans more than the next period, the estimated liability must be partitioned into a current and long-term portion. ASC 460 requires disclosure of product warranties in the notes to financial statements. Disclosure requirements can be found in the Appendix.

Example of product warranty expense

The Churnaway Corporation manufactures clothes washers. It sells $900,000 of washing machines during its most recent month of operations. Based on its historical warranty claims experience, it records an estimated warranty expense of 2% of revenues with the following entry:

Warranty expense	18,000	
Accrued warranty claims		18,000

During the following month, Churnaway incurs $10,000 of actual labor and $4,500 of actual materials expenses to perform repairs required under warranty claims, which it charges to the warranty claims accrual with the following entry:

Accrued warranty claims	14,500	
Labor expense		10,000
Materials expense		4,500

Churnaway also sells three-year extended warranties on its washing machines that begin once the initial one-year manufacturer's warranty expires. During one month, it sells $54,000 of extended warranties, which it records with the following entry:

Cash	54,000	
Unearned warranty revenue		54,000

This liability is unaltered for one year from the purchase date, after which the extended warranty servicing period begins. Churnaway recognizes the warranty revenue on a straight-line basis over the 36 months of the warranty period, using the following entry each month:

Unearned warranty revenue	1,500	
Warranty revenue		1,500

Software vendors/licensors often include, as part of their customary contractual terms, an indemnification clause that indemnifies the licensee against liability and damages (including costs of legal defense) that could arise in the event that a third party claims patent, copyright, trademark, or trade secret infringement with respect to the licensor's software. The indemnification requires the licensor/guarantor to make a payment to the licensee/guaranteed party based on the occurrence of an infringement claim against the licensor that results in liabilities or damages related to the licensed software being used by the licensee. Under such a scenario, an infringement claim covered by the indemnification could impair the ability of the licensee to use the licensed software if, for example, a court orders an injunction or assesses damages.

The indemnification qualifies for the scope exception in ASC 460-10-25-1(b) (discussed in the Scope and Scope Exceptions at the beginning of this chapter) as a product warranty or other guarantee for which the underlying is related to the performance of a nonfinancial asset (the software) owned (leased) by the guaranteed party since the licensed software cannot function as intended until the seller-licensor cures the alleged infringement defect.

These arrangements are subject to the same disclosure requirements imposed on other warranty obligations.

Other Sources

See ASC Location – Wiley *GAAP* Chapter …	*For information on…*
ASC 323-10-35-20	Guaranteed obligations of an investee that is accounted for using the equity method
ASC 340-10-25-3	Contractual guarantees for reimbursement of design and development costs related to long-term supply arrangements
ASC 360-20-40-41	A seller's guarantee of a return of the buyer's investment in real estate or a seller's guarantee of a return on that investment for an extended period
ASC 405-20-40-2	The guarantee obligation that results if a primary debtor becomes secondarily liable upon a release by a creditor
ASC 480-10-55-23	An entity's guarantee of the value of an asset, liability, or equity security of another entity that may require or permit settlement in the entity's equity shares
ASC 480-10-55-53 through 55-58	A freestanding put option indexed to a subsidiary's equity shares
ASC 480-10-55-59 through 55-62	Embedded put options indexed to the stock of a consolidated subsidiary
ASC 605-20-25-8 through 25-12	Recognition of guarantee fees
ASC 605-15-25-1 through 25-4	Guaranteed sales (arrangements in which customers buy products for resale with the right to return products)
ASC 605-35	For guaranteed maximum reimbursable costs of construction contracts or production contracts
ASC 718-40-25-9	An employer's guarantee of the debt of an employee stock option plan
ASC 805-30	Guarantees that represent contingent consideration in a business combination
ASC 810-10-55-25 through 55-26	Guarantees of the value of the assets or liabilities of a variable interest entity (VIE), written put options on the assets of the VIE, or similar obligations
ASC 815-10-15-77 and 810-10-45-16A	Freestanding derivative instruments indexed to, and potentially settled in, the stock of a consolidated subsidiary
ASC 815-45	Weather derivatives

See ASC Location – Wiley *GAAP* Chapter …	***For information on…***
Definition of lease term	The effect on the lease term of a provision or condition that in substance is a guarantee of a lessor's debt or a loan to a lessor by the lessee that is related to the leased property but is structured in such a manner that it does not represent a direct guarantee or loan
ASC 840-10-25-5	The effects on minimum lease payments of a guarantee by the lessee of the lessor's debt
ASC 840-10-25-6 and 840-10-55-8 through 55-10	The effects on minimum lease payments of a guarantee by the lessee of the residual value of the leased property at the expiration of the lease term
ASC 840-10-15-20	A determination of whether a residual value guarantee is subject to the requirements of Topic 815
ASC 840-10-25-21 through 25-22	Allocation of a residual value or first-loss guarantee to minimum lease payments in leases involving land and building(s)
ASC 840-10-25-42 through 25-43	The classification of a lease that includes a commitment by a lessor to guarantee performance of the leased property in a manner more extensive than a typical product warranty or to effectively protect the lessee from obsolescence of the leased property
ASC 840-10-55-12 through 55-25	A manufacturer's guarantee of the resale value of equipment to the purchaser
ASC 840-10-25-13	A lessee's indemnification for environmental contamination
ASC 840-20-30-1	A guarantee by a lessee of the leased property's residual value in an operating lease transaction
ASC 840-30-35	A guarantee by a lessee of the leased property's residual value in a capital lease transaction
ASC 840-40-25-14	The effect of providing an independent third-party guarantee of the lease payments in a sale-leaseback transaction
ASC 840-40-25-15	Classification of a lease that contains an entity's unsecured guarantee of its own lease payments
ASC 840-40-25-16	Classification of a lease that contains an unsecured guarantee of the lease payments of one member of a consolidated group by another member of the consolidated group

See ASC Location – Wiley *GAAP* Chapter ...	***For information on...***
ASC 840-40-55-9	An indemnification or guarantee of an owner-lessor against third-party claims relating to construction completion in a sale-leaseback transaction
ASC 840-40-55-15	An indemnification or guarantee of an owner-lessor against third-party damage claims other than claims caused by or resulting from the lessee's own actions or failures to act while in possession or control of the construction project in a sale-leaseback transaction
ASC 840-40-55-15	An indemnification or guarantee by the seller-lessee to a party other than the owner-lessor in a sale-leaseback transaction
ASC 840-40-55-26	A guarantee by the seller-lessee of the leased property's residual value in a sale-leaseback transaction
ASC 860-10-35-6	Subordination agreements, which are commonly thought of as guarantees issued by subordinated investors
ASC 860-20-55-20	Transactions that involve the sale of a marketable security to a third-party buyer, with the buyer's having an option to put the security back to the seller at a specified future date or dates for a fixed price
ASC 860-50-40-7 through 40-9	A sale of mortgage servicing rights with a subservicing agreement in which the seller-subservicer directly or indirectly guarantees a yield to the buyer
ASC 926-605-25-19 through 25-21	Nonrefundable minimum guarantees contained in certain film licensing arrangements
ASC 960-325-35-3	Guaranteed investment contracts held by defined benefit pension plans
ASC 970-470-25-3	An entity's agreement to either make up shortfalls in the annual debt service requirements or guarantee a tax increment financing entity's debt

33 ASC 470 DEBT

PERSPECTIVE AND ISSUES

Subtopics

ASC 470, *Debt,* consists of six subtopics:

- ASC 470-10, *Overall,* which provides guidance on classification on obligations, such as short-term debt expected to be refinanced on a long-term basis, due-on-demand loans, callable debt, sales of future revenue, increasing rate debt, debt with covenants, revolving credit agreements subject to lock-box arrangements and subjective acceleration clauses, and indexed debt.
- ASC 470-20, *Debt with Conversion and Other Options*, which provides guidance on debt and certain preferred stock with specific conversion features: debt instruments with detachable warrants, convertible securities in general, beneficial conversion features, interest forfeiture, induced conversions, conversion upon issuer's exercise of call option, convertible instruments issued to nonemployees for goods and services, and own-share lending arrangements issued in contemplation of convertible debt issuance.
- ASC 470-30, *Participating Mortgage Loans,* provides guidance on the borrower's accounting for a participating mortgage loan if the lender is entitled to participate in appreciation in the fair value of the mortgaged real estate project or the results of operations of the mortgaged real estate project.
- ASC 470-40, *Product Financing Arrangements,* which provides guidance for determining whether an arrangement involving the sale of inventory is in substance a financing arrangement.
- ASC 470-50, *Modifications and Extinguishments,* provides guidance on all debt instruments extinguishment, except for debt extinguished in a troubled debt restructuring.
- ASC 470-60, *Troubled Debt Restructurings by Debtors,* which addresses measuring and recognition from the debtor's perspective.

Scope and Scope Exceptions

ASC 470-20. ASC 470-20 is divided into two subsections:

- General
- Cash Conversion.

General Subsection. The guidance in the General Subsections does not apply to those instruments within the scope of the Cash Conversion Subsections. The guidance on own-share lending arrangements applies to an equity-classified share-lending arrangement on an entity's own shares when executed in contemplation of a convertible debt offering or other financing.

The guidance in this Section should be considered after consideration of the guidance in Subtopic 815-15 on bifurcation of embedded derivatives, as applicable (see paragraph 815-15-55-76A).

Cash Conversion Subsections. The guidance in the Cash Conversion Subsections applies only to convertible debt instruments that may be settled in cash (or other assets) upon conversion, unless the embedded conversion option is required to be separately accounted for as a derivative instrument under Subtopic 815-15.

The Cash Conversion Subsections do *not* apply to any of the following instruments:

1. A convertible preferred share that is classified in equity or temporary equity.
2. A convertible debt instrument that requires or permits settlement in cash (or other assets) upon conversion only in specific circumstances in which the holders of the underlying shares also would receive the same form of consideration in exchange for their shares.
3. A convertible debt instrument that requires an issuer's obligation to provide consideration for a fractional share upon conversion to be settled in cash but that does not otherwise require or permit settlement in cash (or other assets) upon conversion.

For purposes of determining whether an instrument is within the scope of the Cash Conversion Subsections, a convertible preferred share shall be considered a convertible debt instrument if it has both of the following characteristics:

a. It is a mandatorily redeemable financial instrument.
b. It is classified as a liability under Subtopic 480-10.

ASC 470-30. ASC 470-30 does *not* apply to creditors in participating mortgage loan arrangements and to the following transactions:

a. Participating leases
b. Debt convertible at the option of the lender into equity ownership of the property
c. Participating loans resulting from troubled debt restructurings.

ASC 470-40. The guidance in ASC 470-40 applies to product financing arrangements for "products that have been produced by or were originally purchased by the sponsor or purchased by another entity on behalf of the sponsor." The arrangement must have the following characteristics:

1. The financing arrangement requires the sponsor to purchase the product, a substantially identical product, or processed goods of which the product is a component at specified prices. The specified prices are not subject to change except for fluctuations due to finance and holding costs. This characteristic of predetermined prices also is present if any of the following circumstances exist:

   a. The specified prices in the financing arrangement are in the form of resale price guarantees under which the sponsor agrees to make up any difference between the specified price and the resale price for products sold to third parties.
   b. The sponsor is not required to purchase the product but has an option to purchase the product, the economic effect of which compels the sponsor to purchase the product; for example, an option arrangement that provides for a significant penalty if the sponsor does not exercise the option to purchase.
   c. The sponsor is not required by the agreement to purchase the product but the other entity has an option whereby it can require the sponsor to purchase the product.

2. The payments that the other entity will receive on the transaction are established by the financing arrangement, and the amounts to be paid by the sponsor will be

adjusted, as necessary, to cover substantially all fluctuations in costs incurred by the other entity in purchasing and holding the product (including interest). This characteristic ordinarily is not present in purchase commitments or contractor-subcontractor relationships.

(ASC 470-40-15-2)

ASC 470-40 does *not* apply to the following transactions and activities:

1. Ordinary purchase commitments in which the risks and rewards of ownership are retained by the seller (for example, a manufacturer or other supplier) until the product is transferred to a purchaser.
2. Typical contractor-subcontractor relationships in which the contractor is not in substance the owner of product held by the subcontractor and the obligation of the contractor is contingent on substantial performance on the part of the subcontractor.
3. Long-term unconditional purchase obligations (for example, take-or-pay contracts) specified by Subtopic 440-10. At the time a take-or-pay contract is entered into, which is an unconditional purchase obligation, either the product does not yet exist (for example, electricity) or the product exists in a form unsuitable to the purchaser (for example, unmined coal); the purchaser has a right to receive future product but is not the substantive owner of existing product.
4. Unmined or unharvested natural resources and financial instruments.
5. Transactions for which sales revenue is recognized currently in accordance with the provisions of Topic 605.
6. Typical purchases by a subcontractor on behalf of a contractor. In a typical contractor-subcontractor relationship, the purchase of product by a subcontractor on behalf of a contractor ordinarily leaves a significant portion of the subcontractor's obligation unfulfilled. The subcontractor has the risks of ownership of the product until it has met all the terms of a contract. Accordingly, the typical contractor-subcontractor relationship shall not be considered a product financing arrangement. (ASC 470-40-15-3)

ASC 470-50. ASC 470-50 does *not* apply to the following transactions and activities:

1. Conversions of debt into equity securities of the debtor pursuant to conversion privileges provided in the terms of the debt at issuance. Additionally, the guidance in this Subtopic does not apply to conversions of convertible debt instruments pursuant to terms that reflect changes made by the debtor to the conversion privileges provided in the debt at issuance (including changes that involve the payment of consideration) for the purpose of inducing conversion. Guidance on conversions of debt instruments (including induced conversions) is contained in paragraphs 470-20-40-13 and 470-20-40-15.
2. Extinguishments of debt through a troubled debt restructuring. (See Section 470-60-15 for guidance on determining whether a modification or exchange of debt instruments is a troubled debt restructuring. If it is determined that the modification or exchange does not result in a troubled debt restructuring, the guidance in this Subtopic shall be applied.)
3. Transactions entered into between a debtor or a debtor's agent and a third party that is not the creditor.

(ASC 470-50-15-3)

Overview

Long-term (or noncurrent) liabilities are liabilities that will be paid or otherwise settled over a period of more than one year, or if longer, greater than one operating cycle.

Debt remains on the books of the debtor until it is extinguished. In most cases, a debt is extinguished at maturity, when the required principal and interest payments have been made and the debtor has no further obligation to the creditor. In other cases, the debtor may extinguish the debt before its maturity. For example, if market interest rates are falling, a debtor may choose to issue debt at the new lower rate and use the proceeds to retire older higher-interest-rate debt. ASC 405-20-40-1 states that a debt is extinguished if either of two conditions is met.

1. The debtor pays the creditor and is relieved of its obligation for the liability.
2. The debtor is legally released from being the primary obligor under the liability, either judicially or by the creditor.

If a debtor experiences financial difficulties before the debt is repaid, a creditor may need to recognize an impairment of the debt. Under ASC 310-10-35-16, an impairment of the debt is recognized when the present value of the expected future cash flows discounted at the debt's original effective interest rate is less than the recorded investment in the debt. If for economic or legal reasons related to the debtor's financial difficulties, the creditor grants the debtor concessions that would not otherwise have been granted, the debtor must determine how to recognize the effects of the troubled debt restructuring (ASC 470-60).

Some debt is issued with terms that allow it to be converted to an equity instrument (common or, less often, preferred stock) at a future date. When issued, under current GAAP, no value is attributed to the conversion feature. When the debt is converted, the stock issued is generally valued at the carrying value of the debt (ASC 470). In certain situations, a debtor will modify the conversion privileges after issuance of the debt in order to induce prompt conversion of the debt into equity, in which case the debtor must recognize an expense for this consideration (ASC 470-20-40-16).

Debt can also be issued with stock warrants, which allow the holder to purchase a stated number of common shares at a certain price within a defined time period. If debt is issued with detachable warrants, the proceeds of issuance are allocated between the two financial instruments (ASC 470-20-05).

DEFINITIONS OF TERMS

Source: ASC 470

Beneficial Conversion Feature. A nondetachable conversion feature that is in the money at the commitment date.

Callable Obligation. An obligation is callable at a given date if the creditor has the right at that date to demand, or to give notice of its intention to demand, repayment of the obligation owed to it by the debtor.

Carrying Amount. For a receivable, the face amount increased or decreased by applicable accrued interest and applicable unamortized premium, discount, finance charges, or issue costs and also an allowance for uncollectible amounts and other valuation accounts. For a payable, the face amount increased or decreased by applicable accrued interest and applicable unamortized premium, discount, finance charges, or issue costs.

Convertible Security. A security that is convertible into another security based on a conversion rate. For example, convertible preferred stock that is convertible into common stock on a two-for-one basis (two shares of common for each share of preferred).

Debt. A receivable or payable (collectively referred to as debt) represents a contractual right to receive money or a contractual obligation to pay money on demand or on fixed or determinable dates that is already included as an asset or liability in the creditor's or debtor's balance sheet at the time of the restructuring.

Fair Value. The price that would be received to sell an asset or paid to transfer a liability in an orderly transaction between market participants at the measurement date.

Firm Commitment. An agreement with an unrelated party, binding on both parties and usually legally enforceable, with the following characteristics:

a. The agreement specifies all significant terms, including the quantity to be exchanged, the fixed price, and the timing of the transaction. The fixed price may be expressed as a specified amount of an entity's functional currency or of a foreign currency. It may also be expressed as a specified interest rate or specified effective yield. The binding provisions of an agreement are regarded to include those legal rights and obligations codified in the laws to which such an agreement is subject. A price that varies with the fair value of the item that is the subject of the firm commitment cannot qualify as a fixed price. For example, a price that is specified in terms of ounces of gold would not be a fixed price if the fair value of the item to be purchased or sold under the firm commitment varied with the price of gold.
b. The agreement includes a disincentive for nonperformance that is sufficiently large to make performance probable. In the legal jurisdiction that governs the agreement, the existence of statutory rights to pursue remedies for default equivalent to the damages suffered by the nondefaulting party, in and of itself, represents a sufficiently large disincentive for nonperformance to make performance probable for purposes of applying the definition of a firm commitment.

Lock-Box Arrangement. An arrangement with a lender whereby the borrower's customers are required to remit payments directly to the lender and amounts received are applied to reduce the debt outstanding. A lock-box arrangement refers to any situation in which the borrower does not have the ability to avoid using working capital to repay the amounts outstanding. That is, the contractual provisions of a loan arrangement require that, in the ordinary course of business and without another event occurring, the cash receipts of a debtor are used to repay the existing obligation.

Long-Term Obligations. Long-term obligations are those scheduled to mature beyond one year (or the operating cycle, if applicable) from the date of an entity's balance sheet.

Operating Cycle. The average time intervening between the acquisition of materials or services and the final cash realization constitutes an operating cycle.

Probable. The future event or events are likely to occur.

Product Financing Arrangement. A product financing arrangement is a transaction in which an entity sells and agrees to repurchase inventory with the repurchase price equal to the original sale price plus carrying and financing costs, or other similar transactions.

Public Entity. An entity that meets any of the following criteria:

a. Has equity securities that trade in a public market, either on a stock exchange (domestic or foreign) or in an over-the-counter market, including securities quoted only locally or regionally

b. Makes a filing with a regulatory agency in preparation for the sale of any class of equity securities in a public market
c. Is controlled by an entity covered by the preceding criteria. That is, a subsidiary of a public entity is itself a public entity.

An entity that has only debt securities trading in a public market (or that has made a filing with a regulatory agency in preparation to trade only debt securities) is not a public entity.

Reasonably Possible. The chance of the future event or events occurring is more than remote but less than likely.

Recorded Investment in the Receivable. The recorded investment in the receivable is the face amount increased or decreased by applicable accrued interest and unamortized premium, discount, finance charges, or acquisition costs and may also reflect a previous direct write-down of the investment.

Springing Lock-Box Arrangement. Some borrowings outstanding under a revolving credit agreement include both a subjective acceleration clause and a requirement to maintain a springing lock-box arrangement, whereby remittances from the borrower's customers are forwarded to the debtor's general bank account and do not reduce the debt outstanding until and unless the lender exercises the subjective acceleration clause.

Subjective Acceleration Clause. A subjective acceleration clause is a provision in a debt agreement that states that the creditor may accelerate the scheduled maturities of the obligation under conditions that are not objectively determinable (for example, if the debtor fails to maintain satisfactory operations or if a material adverse change occurs).

Substantive Conversion Feature. A conversion feature that is at least reasonably possible of being exercisable in the future absent the issuer's exercise of a call option.

Time of Issuance. The date when agreement as to terms has been reached and announced, even though the agreement is subject to certain further actions, such as directors' or stockholders' approval.

Time of Restructuring. Troubled debt restructurings may occur before, at, or after the stated maturity of debt, and time may elapse between the agreement, court order, and so forth, and the transfer of assets or equity interest, the effective date of new terms, or the occurrence of another event that constitutes consummation of the restructuring. The date of consummation is the time of the restructuring.

Troubled Debt Restructuring. A restructuring of a debt constitutes a troubled debt restructuring if the creditor for economic or legal reasons related to the debtor's financial difficulties grants a concession to the debtor that it would not otherwise consider.

Units-of-Revenue Method. A method of amortizing deferred revenue that arises under certain sales of future revenues. Under this method, amortization for a period is calculated by computing a ratio of the proceeds received from the investor to the total payments expected to be made to the investor over the term of the agreement, and then applying that ratio to the period's cash payment.

Violation of a Provision. The failure to meet a condition in a debt agreement or a breach of a provision in the agreement for which compliance is objectively determinable, whether or not a grace period is allowed or the creditor is required to give notice of its intention to demand repayment.

Working Capital. Working capital (also called net working capital) is represented by the excess of current assets over current liabilities and identifies the relatively liquid portion of total entity capital that constitutes a margin or buffer for meeting obligations within the ordinary operating cycle of the entity.

CONCEPTS, RULES, AND EXAMPLES

ASC 470-10, *Overall*

Classification. The currently maturing portion of long-term debt or of capital lease obligations are classified as current liabilities if the obligations are to be liquidated by using assets classified as current. However, if the currently maturing debt is to be liquidated by using noncurrent assets (i.e., by using a sinking fund that is properly classified as a noncurrent investment) then these obligations are to be classified as long-term liabilities.

Due on Demand Loans. Obligations that, by their terms, are due on demand (ASC 470-10-45-10) or will be due on demand within one year (or the reporting entity's operating cycle, if longer) from the statement of financial position date, even if liquidation is not expected to occur within that period, are required to be classified as current liabilities.

Even noncurrent debt may be due on demand under certain circumstances. Long-term obligations that contain creditor call provisions are to be classified as current liabilities, if as of the statement of financial position date the debtor is in violation of the agreement and either:

1. That violation makes the obligation callable, *or*
2. Unless cured within a grace period specified in the agreement, that violation will make the obligation callable.

If either of these two conditions exist, the long-term obligation is required to be classified as a current liability unless either:

1. The creditor has waived the right to call the obligation caused by the debtor's violation or the creditor has subsequently lost the right to demand repayment for more than one year (or operating cycle, if longer) from the statement of financial position date, *or*
2. The obligation contains a grace period for remedying the violation, and it is probable that the violation will be cured within the grace period.

If either of these situations applies, management is required to disclose the circumstances in the financial statements.

Demand notes with scheduled repayment terms. In some instances, a demand loan will include a repayment schedule calling for scheduled principal reductions. The loan agreement may contain language such as the following examples:

> *This term note shall mature in monthly installments as set forth herein, or on demand, whichever is earlier.*
>
> *Principal and interest are due on demand, or if demand is not made, in quarterly installments commencing on . . .*

Under ASC 470-10-45-10, an obligation containing such terms is considered due on demand even though the debt agreement specifies repayment terms. In either instance, the creditor, at its sole discretion, can demand full repayment at any time. This situation is distinguished from a subjective acceleration clause, which is addressed separately below.

Increasing-rate debt. Arrangements commonly referred to as "increasing-rate notes" are debt instruments that mature at a defined, near-term date, but which can be continually extended (renewed) by the borrower for a defined longer period of time with predefined increases in the interest rate as extensions are elected.

Management of the borrower estimates the effective outstanding term of the debt after considering its plans, ability and intent to service the debt. Based upon this estimated term, the borrower's periodic interest rate is determined using the interest method. Thus, a constant yield is computed over the estimated term resulting in the accrual of additional interest during the earlier portions of the term.

Debt interest costs are amortized over the estimated outstanding term of the debt using the interest method. Any excess accrued interest resulting from repaying the debt prior to the estimated maturity date is an adjustment of interest expense in the period of repayment. The adjustment is not permitted to be treated as an extraordinary item.

The classification of the debt as current or noncurrent is based on the expected source of repayment. Thus, this classification need not be consistent with the period used to determine the periodic interest cost. For example, the time frame used for the estimated outstanding term of the debt could be a year or less, but because of a planned long-term refinancing agreement the noncurrent classification could be used.

Furthermore, the term-extending provisions of the debt instrument are evaluated to ascertain whether they constitute a derivative financial instrument under ASC 815. If so, the derivative element of the instrument is, in all likelihood, not considered "clearly and closely related" to the host instrument (the debt), and thus would have to be reported separately at fair value with changes in fair value reported in net income each period.

Subjective acceleration clauses. Long-term obligations that contain subjective acceleration clauses are classified as current liabilities if circumstances (such as recurring losses or liquidity problems) indicate that it is probable that the lender will exercise its rights under the clause and demand repayment within one year (or one operating cycle, if longer). If, on the other hand, the likelihood of the acceleration of the due date is remote, the obligation continues to be classified as long-term debt on the statement of financial position. Situations between the probable and remote thresholds (i.e., it is deemed reasonably possible that the lender would demand repayment) require disclosure of the existence of the provision of the agreement (ASC 470-10-45).

Debt with covenants. Most commercial debt agreements contain a range of financial covenants. These covenants legally bind the borrower to comply with their requirements as a condition of the lender extending credit. The failure by the borrower to comply with these conditions often provides the lender with the contractual right to accelerate the due date, commonly to declare the full amount of the debt due and payable on demand. Unless a properly worded waiver is obtained by the borrower in such a situation, its statement of financial position would have to reflect the debt, that which would otherwise be classified as long-term, as a current liability. This in turn might create or complicate issues for management with respect to the assessment of whether there is substantial doubt about the ability of the reporting entity to continue as a going concern.

While a complete waiver, effectively a promise by the lender that it will not exercise its rights under the financial covenants for at least one year from the statement of financial position date, makes it possible to continue presenting the debt as noncurrent, great care must be exercised in interpreting the substance of such an agreement.

In practice, many waivers are not effective and cannot form the basis for continued accounting for the debt as noncurrent. For example, a waiver "as of" the current statement of financial position date provides no real comfort, since the lender is entitled to assert its rights as soon as the very next day. Likewise, a waiver pending (i.e., conditioned on) compliance with the covenants at the next scheduled submission of a borrower's covenant compliance letter (generally quarterly, possibly monthly) offers no assurance that the borrower will successfully meet its obligations, and hence also affords no basis for presentation of the debt as noncurrent.

A loan covenant may require that compliance determinations be made at quarterly or semiannual intervals. A borrower may be in violation of the covenant at the end of its fiscal year and obtain a waiver from the lender, for a period greater than one year, of the lender's right to demand repayment arising from that specific year-end violation. Often, however, the lender will include language in the waiver document that reserves its right to demand repayment should another violation occur at a subsequent measurement date, including those dates that occur during the ensuing year.

Under these circumstances, management of the borrower/reporting entity considers whether both of the following conditions exist under the specific circumstances:

1. A violation of one or more covenants that gives the lender the right to call the debt (declare it payable on demand) has occurred at the statement of financial position date, or would have occurred absent a modification of the loan, and
2. It is probable that, at measurement dates occurring during the next 12 months, the borrower will be unable to cure the default (i.e., comply with the covenant).

If both of these conditions are present, the borrower is required to classify the debt as a current liability; otherwise, it can continue to classify the debt as noncurrent.

Revolving credit agreements. Borrowings outstanding under a revolving credit agreement sometimes include both a subjective acceleration clause (as discussed above) and a requirement to maintain a lockbox into which the borrower's customers send remittances that are then used to reduce the debt outstanding. These borrowings are short-term obligations and are classified as current liabilities unless the entity has the intent and ability to refinance the revolving credit agreement on a long-term basis (i.e., the conditions in ASC 470-10-45, as discussed below, are met). However, if the lockbox is a springing lockbox, which is a lockbox agreement in which remittances from the borrower's customers are forwarded to its general bank account and do not reduce the debt outstanding unless the lender exercises the subjective acceleration clause, the obligations are still considered to be long-term since the remittances do not automatically reduce the debt outstanding if the acceleration clause has not been exercised.

Indexed debt. Occasionally, debt instruments are issued with guaranteed and contingent payments. The contingent payments may be linked to a specific index, like the S&P 500 or the price for a specific commodity. If the right to receive the indexing feature is separable from the debt instrument, the proceeds are allocated between the debt instrument and investor's stated right to receive the contingent payment. (ASC 410-10-25-3 and 25-4)

Short-term obligations expected to be refinanced. Short-term obligations that arise in the normal course of business and are due under customary trade terms are classified as current liabilities. Under certain circumstances, however, the reporting entity is permitted to exclude all or a portion of these obligations from current liabilities. To qualify for this treatment, management must have both the intent and ability to refinance the obligation on a long-term basis. Management's intent is to be supported by either of the following (ASC 470-10-45-14):

1. *Post-statement of financial position date issuance of a long-term obligation or equity securities.* After the date of the entity's statement of financial position, but before that statement of financial position is issued, a long-term obligation is incurred or equity securities are issued for the purpose of refinancing the short-term obligations on a long-term basis.
2. *Financing agreement.* Before the statement of financial position is issued, the entity has entered into a financing agreement that clearly enables the entity to refinance its

short-term obligation on a long-term basis on readily determinable terms that meet all of the following requirements:

a. The agreement is noncancelable by the lender (or prospective lender) or investor and will not expire within one year (or one operating cycle, if longer) of the statement of financial position date.
b. The replacement debt will not be callable during that period except for violation of a provision of the financing agreement with which compliance is objectively determinable or measurable.
c. At the date of the statement of financial position, the reporting entity is not in violation of the terms of the financing agreement and there is no information that a violation occurred subsequent to the statement of financial position and before issuance of the financial statements, unless such a violation was waived by the lender.
d. The lender (prospective lender) or investor is expected to be financially capable of honoring the financing agreement.

For the purposes of condition 2b above, violation of a provision is defined as a failure of the reporting entity to meet a condition included in the agreement; or the violation of a provision such as a restrictive covenant, representation, or warranty. A violation is not to be disregarded for this purpose, even if the agreement contains a grace period to cure it and/or if the lender is required to give the borrower notice. The requirement that compliance be objectively determinable or measurable precludes commitments that include subjective acceleration clauses (discussed previously) from being considered qualified financing agreements.

The above scenario is based on an assumption that the refinancing will take place subsequent to the date of the statement of financial position. If, instead, prior to the date of the statement of financial position, the reporting entity receives cash proceeds from long-term financing intended to be used to repay a short-term obligation after the date of the statement of financial position, the cash received is to be classified on the statement of financial position in noncurrent assets if the short-term obligation to be settled with that cash is classified in noncurrent liabilities.

The amount of short-term debt to be reclassified is not permitted to exceed the amount raised by the replacement debt or equity issuance, nor can it exceed the amount specified in the financing agreement. If the amount specified in the financing agreement can fluctuate, then the maximum amount of short-term debt that can be reclassified is equal to a reasonable estimate of the minimum amount expected to be available on any date from the due date of the maturing short-term obligation to the end of the succeeding fiscal year. If no estimate can be made of the minimum amount available under the financing agreement, none of the short-term debt can be reclassified as long-term.

If the short-term debt is refinanced by issuing equity instruments, the portion excluded from current liabilities is to be classified under noncurrent liabilities. Under no circumstances would the reclassified debt be shown in the equity section of the statement of financial position.

If debt or other agreements limit the ability of the reporting entity to fully utilize the proceeds of the refinancing agreement (for example, a clause in another debt agreement sets a maximum debt-to-equity ratio), then only the amount that can be borrowed without violating the limitations expressed in those other agreements can be reclassified as long-term.

ASC 470-10-45-15 states that if an entity uses current assets after the statement of financial position date to repay a current obligation, and then replaces those current assets by issuing either equity securities or long-term debt before the issuance of the statement of financial position, the currently maturing debt must continue to be classified as a current liability at the date of the statement of financial position.

Example of short-term obligations to be refinanced

Duboe Distribution Co. has obtained $3,500,000 of bridge financing in the form of a construction loan to assist it in completing construction of a new public warehouse. All construction is completed by the date of the statement of financial position, after which Duboe has the following three choices for refinancing the bridge loan:

- Enter into a 30-year fixed-rate mortgage for $3,400,000 at 7% interest, leaving Duboe with a $100,000 shortfall it would have to repay with available cash. Under this scenario, Duboe reports as current debt the $100,000, as well as $31,566, the portion of the mortgage principal due within one year, with the remainder of the mortgage itemized as long-term debt. The presentation follows:

Current liabilities:	
Current portion of construction loan payable	100,000
Current maturities of long-term debt	31,566
Noncurrent liabilities:	
Construction loan payable, to be refinanced on a long-term basis at 7% due in 2X40, net of current portion	3,368,434

- Pay off the bridge loan with Duboe's existing variable-rate line of credit (LOC), which expires in two years. The maximum allowable amount that can be borrowed under the LOC is 80% of Duboe's eligible accounts receivable, defined as those accounts receivable not more than 90 days old. Over the two-year remaining term of the LOC, the lowest level of qualifying accounts receivable is expected to be $2,700,000. Thus, only $2,160,000 ($2,700,000 × 80%) of the debt would be classified as long-term, while $1,340,000 is classified as a short-term obligation. The presentation follows:

Current liabilities:	
Current portion of construction loan payable	1,340,000
Noncurrent liabilities:	
Construction loan payable, to be refinanced on a long-term basis under a variable rate line of credit due in 20XX	2,160,000

- Obtain a 10% loan from Duboe's majority stockholders, with a balloon payment due in five years. Under the terms of this arrangement, the owner is entitled to withdraw up to $1,500,000 of funding at any time, even though $3,500,000 is currently available to Duboe. Under this approach, $1,500,000 is callable, and therefore must be classified as a short-term obligation. The remainder is classified as long-term debt. The presentation follows:

Current liabilities:	
Current portion of construction loan payable	1,500,000
Noncurrent liabilities:	
Construction loan payable, to be refinanced on a long-term basis under a five-year, 10% balloon note payable to the majority stockholder, due in 20XX	2,000,000

The presentations illustrated above would be accompanied by note disclosures under ASC 470-10-50-4 of the general terms of the financing agreement, as well as the terms of the new obligation incurred, or expected to be incurred, as a result of the refinancing. If part or all of the refinancing will be achieved through the issuance of equity, the notes should disclose a description of the securities issued or expected to be issued as a result of the refinancing. In addition, should the debtor decide on the third course of action, the notes would be supplemented with the required related-party disclosures.

ASC 470-20, *Debt with Conversion and Other Options*

Convertible Debt Without Beneficial Conversion

Purpose. Bonds are frequently issued with the right to convert into common stock of the company at the holder's option. Convertible debt is typically used for two reasons. First, when a specific amount of funds is needed, convertible debt often allows a lesser number of shares to be issued (assuming conversion) than if the funds were raised by directly issuing the shares. Thus, less dilution occurs. Second, the conversion feature allows debt to be issued at a lower interest rate and with fewer restrictive covenants than if the debt was issued without it.

Features. Features of convertible debt typically include (1) a conversion price 15–20% greater than the fair value of the stock when the debt is issued; (2) conversion features (price and number of shares) which protect against dilution from stock dividends, splits, etc.; and (3) a callable feature at the issuer's option, which is usually exercised once the conversion price is reached (thus forcing conversion or redemption).

Disadvantages. Convertible debt also has its disadvantages. If the stock price increases significantly after the debt is issued, the issuer would have been better off by simply issuing the stock. Additionally, if the price of the stock does not reach the conversion price, the debt will never be converted (a condition known as overhanging debt).

Recognition. When convertible debt is issued and the conversion price is greater than the fair value of the stock on the issuance date, no value is apportioned to the conversion feature when recording the issue (ASC 470-20-05). The debt and its interest are reported as if it were a nonconvertible debt. Upon conversion, the stock may be valued at either the book value or the fair value of the bonds.

Book value approach. If the book value approach is used, the new stock is valued at the carrying value of the converted bonds. This method is widely used since no gain or loss is recognized upon conversion, and the conversion represents the transformation of contingent shareholders into shareholders. It does not represent the culmination of an earnings cycle. The primary weakness of this method is that the total value attributed to the equity security by the investors is not given accounting recognition.

Example of book value method

Assume that a $1,000 bond with an unamortized discount of $50 and a fair value of $970 is converted into 10 shares of $10 par common stock whose fair value is $97 per share. Conversion using the book value method is recorded as follows:

Bonds payable	1,000	
Discount on bonds payable		50
Common stock		100
Additional paid-in capital		850

Market value approach. The alternative market value approach assumes the new stock issued is valued at market (i.e., the fair value of the stock issued or the fair value of the bonds converted, whichever is more easily determinable). A gain (loss) occurs when the fair value of the stocks or bonds is less (greater) than the carrying value of the bond.

Example of the market value method

Assume the same facts as the example above. The entry to record the conversion is

Bonds payable	1,000	
Loss on redemption (ordinary)	20	
Discount on bonds payable		50
Common stock		100
Additional paid-in capital		870

The weakness of this method is that a gain or loss can be reported as a result of an equity transaction. Only the existing shareholders are affected, as their equity will increase or decrease, but the firm as a whole is unaffected. For this reason, the market value approach is not widely used.

Derecognition. When convertible debt is retired, the transaction is handled in the same manner as nonconvertible debt: the difference between the acquisition price and the carrying value of the bond is reported currently as a gain or loss.

Accrued interest upon conversion of convertible debt. Per ASC 470-20-40-11, if terms of the convertible debt instrument provide that any accrued interest at the date of conversion is forfeited by the former debt holder, the accrued interest (net of income tax) from the last payment date to the conversion date should be charged to interest expense and credited to capital as a part of the cost basis of the securities issued.

Convertible bonds with a "premium put." Some convertible bonds contain mutually exclusive features, with one obviously being the right to convert to the issuer's common or preferred stock. In some instances, the other feature is the right, usually on specified dates before or at the stated maturity of the debt, to cause the issuer to repurchase the debt at a price higher than par or the issuance price. This is known as a "premium put" feature. An early view of premium puts held that the issuer should accrue a liability for the put premium over the period from the date of issuance to the initial put date, and that this accrual should continue regardless of fair value changes. It further held if the put expires unexercised and if—as would be highly likely if the holders chose to ignore the right to put the debt back to the issuer—the fair value of the common stock exceeds the put price at expiration date, the put premium should be credited to additional paid-in capital. Additionally, it held that if the put were to expire unexercised (in the situation where the debt maturity is later than the last put exercise date) and if the put price exceeds the fair value of the common stock at that date, the put premium should be amortized as a yield adjustment over the remaining term of the debt, reducing interest cost.

Under ASC 815, an embedded put is a derivative instrument subject to that standard. This "grandfathered" permission for entities not to account separately for embedded premium puts in pre-1998 or pre-1999 hybrid instruments issued at par; the earlier view was to continue to apply to an entity which elected not to separately account for the embedded derivative. However, separate accounting was required for convertible debt not "grandfathered" under this provision, and thus, ASC 815 does apply to more recently issued convertible debt having premium put features.

ASC 460-10 requires explicit recognition of guarantees at their inceptions (see the chapter on ASC 460 for complete discussion of this topic). A premium put is a form of guarantee arrangement, and thus the fair value of the put must now be recognized at the date of issuance of the convertible debt bearing this feature, unless the put is accounted for as a derivative (and thus also recorded at fair value) under ASC 815. As a practical matter, in either case a liability will be recognized for the fair value of the put option embedded in the convertible debt.

Under ASC 815 this derivative financial instrument will be marked to fair value at each financial reporting date. Whether the adjustment increases or decreases the recorded amount from one period to the next depends largely on the price performance of the issuer's stock, since increasing value of the stock raises the likelihood of conversion and thus decreases the perceived value of the put option. In the author's opinion, any adjustment to the carrying value of the put option should result in adjustments to the entity's interest expense for the period.

Debt convertible into the stock of a consolidated subsidiary. According to ASC 470-20-25, in the consolidated financial statements, (1) debt issued by a consolidated subsidiary that is convertible into that subsidiary's stock and (2) debt issued by a parent company that is convertible into the stock of a consolidated subsidiary should be accounted for in accordance with ASC 470-20-05. That is, no portion of the proceeds from the issuance of the debt should be accounted for as attributable to the conversion feature. ASC 470-20-25 did not apply to convertible debt instruments that require a cash settlement by the issuer of an in-the-money conversion feature, that provide the holder an option to receive cash for an in-the-money conversion feature, or that have a beneficial conversion feature.

Convertible instrument granted or issued to a nonemployee. ASC 470-20-30 describes the accounting for a convertible instrument that is used to pay a nonemployee for goods or services if that instrument contains a nondetachable conversion option. The measurement date under ASC 505-50 should be used to measure the intrinsic value of the conversion option rather than the commitment date. The proceeds from issuing the instrument for purposes of determining whether a beneficial conversion option exists is the fair value of the instrument or the fair value of the goods and services received, whichever is more reliably measured. The fair value of the convertible instrument can be measured by applying ASC 505-50. (For details, see the chapter on ASC 505.) Once the convertible instrument is issued, distributions paid or payable are financing costs rather than adjustments of the cost of the goods or services received.

If a purchaser of a convertible instrument that contains an embedded beneficial conversion option provides goods or services to the issuer under a separate contract, the contracts should be considered separately unless the separately stated pricing is not equal to fair value. If not equal to fair value, the terms of the respective transactions should be adjusted. The convertible instrument should be recognized at its fair value with a corresponding increase or decrease to the purchase price of the goods or services.

Convertible bonds with issuer option to settle for cash upon conversion. ASC 815-15-55 addressed a variant of convertible bonds that give the issuer (the reporting entity) the option of settling for cash, rather than stock, at the time conversion is elected by holders. In some versions of this arrangement, the debtor would be obligated to settle in cash, based on the stock price at the conversion date. In others, the issuer would have the option to deliver shares or cash based on the contractual conversion rate, or more complex formulae might cause partial settlement in cash.

ASC 815 requires that in the situation of a mandatory cash settlement upon conversion, the embedded derivative (which is a cash-settled written call option) must be accounted for separately from the debt, and changes in the derivative's fair value will be reported currently in earnings. When the conversion option can be settled in stock, however, the embedded derivative is indexed only to the issuer's stock and thus, under ASC 815-40 would not be separately accounted for.

If a convertible bond is issued with terms that require the issuer to satisfy the obligation (the amount accrued to the benefit of the holder exclusive of the conversion spread) in cash and to satisfy the conversion spread (the excess conversion value over the accreted value) in either cash or stock, the debt should be accounted for like convertible debt (that is, as a combined instrument under current GAAP) if the conversion spread meets the requirements of ASC 815-40. If the conversion spread feature does not meet those provisions, ASC 815 requires that the embedded derivative be separated from the debt host contract and accounted for by the issuer separately as a derivative instrument.

If a convertible bond is issued with terms that permit the issuer to satisfy the entire obligation in either stock or cash, the bond should be accounted for as conventional convertible debt. If the holder exercises the conversion and the issuer pays cash, the debt is extinguished and the issuer should account for the transaction in accordance with ASC 470-50. ASC 470-50-45-1 removed the mandatory extraordinary item treatment for any gain or loss on debt extinguishment, but if the criteria in ASC 225-20-45 are met (which is thought to be unlikely) extraordinary classification is still possible.

ASC 470-20-40-12 provides accounting guidance with respect to a financial instrument that contains the following provisions:

- Instrument is convertible at the option of its holder into a fixed number of shares of the issuer's common stock.
- At conversion, the issuer must settle the obligation to the holder as follows:
  - Payment in cash for the accreted value of the obligation (for a zero-coupon obligation, the accreted value is the amount received from the holder at issuance plus interest accreted from date of issuance to date of settlement)
  - Payment in either cash or stock to satisfy the conversion spread (the difference between the conversion value over the accreted value)
- If the holder does not exercise the conversion option, the issuer is obligated to settle the accreted value of the debt in cash at maturity.

Questions have arisen regarding the accounting for the *settlement* of this instrument partially in cash (the recognized liability) and partially in stock (the unrecognized equity instrument). ASC 470-20-40-12 states that only the cash payment is to be considered in computing gain or loss on settlement of the recognized liability. Shares transferred to the holder to settle the excess conversion spread represented by the embedded equity instrument are not considered part of the settlement of the debt component of the instrument.

ASC 470-20 specifies that issuers of convertible debt instruments that may be settled in cash upon conversion should separately account for the liability and equity components in a manner that will reflect the entity's nonconvertible debt borrowing rate when interest cost is recognized in subsequent periods. An exception to this rule, however, is when an embedded conversion option must be accounted for as a derivative instrument. Convertible preferred shares categorized as equity in the statement of financial position are also excluded from the effects of ASC 470.

For instruments addressed by ASC 470, initial measurement of the carrying amount of the liability component is to be determined by measuring the fair value of a similar liability (including any embedded features other than the conversion option) that does not have an associated equity component. The carrying amount of the equity component represented by the embedded conversion option is then computed by deducting the fair value of the liability component from the initial proceeds ascribed to the convertible debt instrument as a whole. Embedded features that are determined to be nonsubstantive at the issuance date are not to affect the initial measurement of the liability component. In this context, an embedded feature other than the conversion option (including an embedded prepayment option) is to be considered nonsubstantive if, at issuance, the issuer concludes that it is probable that the embedded feature will not be exercised. If the allocation to the liability component using this methodology results in a difference in basis versus that reported for tax purposes, then interperiod tax allocation (deferred tax accounting) must also be applied.

Convertible debt instruments affected by the foregoing requirements are not available to be accounted for under the fair value option. Rather, the debt must be reported in subsequent periods at amortized cost. The variance between the convertible debt's face value and the amount of proceeds that are allocated to the debt instrument, net of the amount allocated to the conversion feature, must be treated as a discount to be accreted using the effective yield method as additional interest expense. The accretion period is to be based on the expected term of a similar instrument lacking the conversion feature. The expected life is not subject to reassessment in later periods, unless there is a modification to the terms of the instrument. The equity component would not be reassessed either, unless it ceases to meet the criteria set forth in ASC 470, in which case the difference between the amount previously recognized in equity and the fair value of the conversion option at the date of the reclassification as a liability at fair value is to be accounted for as an adjustment to stockholders' equity.

ASC 470-50 provides guidance on derecognition of convertible obligations that can be settled in whole or in part for cash. It stipulates that the proceeds transferred to effect the extinguishment of the liability and the reacquisition of the associated conversion feature are to be allocated first to the extinguishment of the liability component equal to the fair value of that component immediately prior to extinguishment. Any difference between the consideration attributed to the liability component and the sum of (1) the net carrying amount of the liability component and (2) any unamortized debt issuance costs is to be recognized in the statement of financial performance as a gain or loss on debt extinguishment. Following this, any remaining settlement consideration is to be assigned to the reacquisition of the equity component, with recognition of that amount as a reduction of stockholders' equity. Any costs incurred (e.g., banker fees) are to be allocated pro rata to the debt and equity in proportion to the allocation of consideration transferred at settlement, and accounted for as debt extinguishment costs and equity reacquisition costs, respectively.

If an instrument within the scope of the above is modified such that the conversion option no longer requires or permits cash settlement upon conversion, it is necessary to account for the components of the instrument separately, unless the original instrument is required to be derecognized under ASC 470-50. If an instrument is modified or exchanged in a manner that requires derecognition of the original instrument under ASC 470-50 and the new instrument is a convertible debt instrument that may not be settled in cash upon conversion, the new instrument would be subject to ASC 470-50.

On the other hand, if a convertible debt instrument is not at first subject to this guidance, but is later modified so as to become subject to it, then ASC 470-50 is to be applied to ascertain whether the original instrument is to be derecognized. If not, the issuer is to apply the guidance prospectively from the date of the modification. In such a circumstance, the liability component is to be measured at its fair value as of the modification date, with the carrying amount of the equity component represented by the embedded conversion option to be determined by deducting the fair value of the liability component from the overall carrying amount of the convertible debt instrument as a whole. At the modification date, a portion of any unamortized debt issuance costs incurred previously is to be reclassified and accounted for as equity issuance costs based on the proportion of the overall carrying amount of the convertible debt instrument that is allocated to the equity component.

Finally, there is the matter of an induced conversion. If the terms of an instrument addressed are revised to induce early conversion (e.g., by offering a more favorable conversion ratio or paying other additional consideration in the event of conversion before a specified date), then the entity is to recognize a loss equal to the fair value of all securities and other consideration transferred in the transaction in excess of the fair value of consideration issuable in accordance with the *original* conversion terms. The settlement accounting (derecognition) treatment described above is then to be applied using the fair value of the consideration that was issuable in accordance with the original conversion terms. Derecognition transactions in which the holder does not exercise the embedded conversion option are not affected, however.

Disclosures. As of each date for which a statement of financial position is presented, the reporting entity is to disclose the following:

1. The carrying amount of the equity component
2. The principal amount of the liability component, its unamortized discount, and its net carrying amount.

As of the date of the most recent statement of financial position that is presented, the reporting entity must disclose the following:

1. The remaining period over which any discount on the liability component will be amortized.
2. The conversion price and the number of shares on which the aggregate consideration to be delivered upon conversion is determined.
3. The amount by which the instrument's if-converted value exceeds its principal amount, regardless of whether the instrument is currently convertible. (This disclosure is required only for public entities.)
4. Information about derivative transactions entered into in connection with the issuance of instruments within scope, including the terms of those derivative transactions, how those derivative transactions relate to the instruments within the scope, the number of shares underlying the derivative transactions, and the reasons for entering into those derivative transactions. (An example of a derivative transaction entered into in connection with the issuance of an instrument within the scope is the purchase of call options that are expected to substantially offset changes in the fair value of the conversion option.) This disclosure is required regardless of whether the related derivative transactions are accounted for as assets, liabilities, or equity instruments.

For each period for which a statement of financial performance is presented, the entity is to also disclose the following:

1. The effective interest rate on the liability component for the period
2. The amount of interest cost recognized for the period relating to both the contractual interest coupon and amortization of the discount on the liability component.

Own-share lending arrangements related to a convertible debt issuance. An entity may enter into a share-lending arrangement with an investment bank, whereby it lends shares to the bank to facilitate investors' ability to hedge the conversion option in the entity's convertible debt issuance. The entity issues the share in exchange for a nominal loan processing fee; the investment bank returns the shares upon the maturity or conversion of the convertible debt.

In a share-lending arrangement, the entity issuing shares measures them at their fair value and recognizes them as a debt issuance cost, which offsets the additional paid-in capital account. If it subsequently becomes probable that the counterparty will default, then the entity recognizes an expense equaling the fair value of any unreturned shares on that date, minus the fair value of probable share recoveries, which offsets the additional paid-in capital account. The entity continues to remeasure the fair value of unreturned shares until the consideration payable by the counterparty becomes fixed.

An entity having an outstanding own-share lending program should disclose the following:

1. Description of the arrangement.
2. All significant terms of the arrangement, including the number of shares involved, the agreement term, any cash settlement terms, and any counterparty collateral requirements.
3. The reason for entering into the arrangement.
4. The fair value of loaned shares at the balance sheet date.
5. The treatment of loaned shares in calculating earnings per share.
6. Classification of any issuance costs.
7. The unamortized amount of issuance costs, and the related interest cost for the reporting period.
8. Any dividends paid on the loaned shares that will not be reimbursed.
9. If the counterparty will probably default on the arrangement, the amount of expense related to the default that is reported in the statement of earnings. In subsequent periods, note any material changes in the amount of this expense.

Convertible Securities with Beneficial or Contingent Conversion Features

Beneficial conversion. Reporting entities sometimes issue convertible securities (debt or preferred stock) that are "in the money" at the issuance date (i.e., where it would be economically advantageous to the holders if the securities were converted immediately). That type of conversion feature is called an "embedded beneficial conversion feature." Variations of such securities may be converted at a fixed price, a fixed discount to the fair value at date of conversion, a variable discount to the fair value at conversion, or the conversion price may be dependent upon future events. In addition, the conversion feature can be exercisable at issuance, at a stated date in the future, or upon the happening of a future event (such as an IPO). ASC 470-20 addressed the assorted accounting issues arising for issuers of such securities (the reporting entity or debtor).

In contrast with GAAP governing convertible securities lacking this feature, embedded beneficial conversion features are valued separately at issuance. The feature is recognized as additional paid-in capital by allocating a portion of the proceeds equal to the intrinsic value of the feature. The intrinsic value is computed at the commitment date as (1) the difference between the conversion price and the fair value of the common stock (or other securities) into which the security is convertible, multiplied by (2) the number of shares into which the security is convertible.

For convertible debt securities, a discount on the debt may result from the allocation of a portion of the proceeds to the conversion feature. For convertible instruments that have a stated redemption date, a discount resulting from recording a beneficial conversion option shall be required to be amortized from the date of issuance to the stated redemption date of the convertible instrument, regardless of when the earliest conversion date occurs. For convertible instruments that do *not* have a stated redemption date, such as perpetual preferred stock, a discount resulting from the accounting for a beneficial conversion option is to be amortized from the date of issuance to the earliest conversion date. (ASC 470-20-35-7.1)

If the conversion feature has multiple steps, the computation of the intrinsic value is made using the conversion terms most beneficial to the investor. For example, if the security was convertible at a 10% discount to fair value after three months and then at a 25% discount to fair value after one year, the 25% discount terms would be used to measure the intrinsic value of the feature. Any resulting discount on the convertible debt would be amortized to the earliest date at which the particular discount (25% in this case) could be achieved (one year). However, at any financial statement date, the cumulative amortization recorded must be the greater of (1) the amount computed using the effective interest method of amortization or (2) the amount of the benefit the investor would receive if the securities were converted at that date. If the securities are converted prior to the full amortization of the discount, the unamortized discount is to be included in the amount transferred to equity upon conversion. (ASC 470-20-35-7.2)

If a convertible debt security having a beneficial feature is extinguished prior to conversion, a portion of the reacquisition price of the debt security is allocated to the beneficial conversion feature. That portion is measured as the intrinsic value of the conversion feature at the extinguishment date. Since the beneficial conversion feature was originally recognized as equity, the redemption or cancellation of this feature would give rise not to gain or loss, but rather to an adjustment within stockholders' equity. For example, if $2,000 of the redemption payment was identified with the beneficial feature to which $1,200 had originally been allocated, the net result would be that the original allocation would be eliminated and an $800 charge would be made against retained earnings (analogous to a loss on a treasury stock transaction). Any residual beyond the allocated cost of redeeming the beneficial conversion feature would be allocated to the retirement of the debt security, and a gain or loss on extinguishment would be reported in current earnings.

Contingent conversion. If the security becomes convertible only upon occurrence (or failure to occur) of a future event outside the control of the investor, or if the conversion terms change based on the occurrence (or failure to occur) of a future event, the value of the contingent beneficial conversion feature should be measured as of the commitment date; but it is not recognized in the financial statements until the contingency is resolved. This may be combined with a beneficial conversion feature. For example, a debt instrument issued with a conversion feature at 20% below then-fair value, to become effective conditioned on the consummation of a planned refinancing, would be contingently convertible with a beneficial feature. According to ASC 470-20, any contingent beneficial conversion feature should be measured at the commitment date, but not reflected in earnings until the contingent condition has been met.

The definition of "conventional contingently convertible debt instrument" is later addressed by ASC 815-40-25. The issue arises because of one of the requirements under ASC 815—namely, that embedded derivatives be bifurcated and accounted for separately under certain conditions, but with an exception for accounting for conversion privileges by issuers of certain convertible securities. Thus, instruments that provide holders the right to convert at a fixed ratio (or equivalent cash value, at the issuer's discretion), for which option exercise is based on either the passage of time or a contingent event, are deemed "conventional."

ASC 815-15 also states that, when a previously bifurcated conversion option in a convertible debt instrument no longer meets the bifurcation criteria in ASC 815, one should reclassify the fair value of the liability for the conversion option to shareholders' equity. If a debt discount was recognized when the conversion option was bifurcated, then it should continue to be amortized. Disclosure requirements include a description of the changes causing the termination of bifurcation, as well as the amount of the liability reclassified to stockholders' equity.

Convertible Securities with Beneficial Conversion Features. ASC 470-20 covers convertible securities with beneficial conversion features. The following summarizes this topic:

1. If an instrument includes both detachable instruments (e.g., stock purchase warrants) and an embedded beneficial conversion option, the proceeds of issuance should first be allocated among the convertible instrument and the other detachable instruments based on their relative fair values. Then ASC 470-20-35 should be applied to determine the amount allocated to the convertible instrument if the embedded conversion option has an intrinsic value.
2. If the conversion price could change upon the occurrence of a future event, assume that there are no changes to the current circumstances except the passage of time. Use the most favorable price that would be in effect if nothing were changed at the conversion date in order to measure the intrinsic value of an embedded conversion option. Changes to the conversion terms that are caused by future events not controlled by the issuer are recognized if and when the trigger event occurs. (ASC 470-20-25-20)
3. If there is no intrinsic value to a conversion right at issuance, but the conversion price resets after the commitment date and, upon reset, the conversion price is greater than the fair value of the underlying stock, the beneficial conversion amount is recognized when the reset occurs. The beneficial conversion amount is measured by the number of shares that will be issued upon conversion, multiplied by the decrease in price between the original conversion price and the reset price.
4. The definition of commitment date for purposes of applying ASC 470-20 should be the same as the definition of a firm commitment in ASC 815. If an instrument includes both detachable instruments and an embedded beneficial conversion option, the commitment date should also be used when determining the relative fair values of all the instruments issued.
5. If a convertible instrument has a stated redemption date, a discount resulting from recording a beneficial conversion option should be amortized from the date of issuance to the stated redemption date, regardless of when the earliest conversion occurs. If the instrument has beneficial conversion features, the unamortized discount remaining at the date of conversion should be immediately recognized as interest expense or as a dividend, as appropriate. (ASC 470-20-35-7)
6. If the terms of a contingent conversion option do not permit an issuer to compute the number of shares that the holder would receive upon conversion, the issuer should wait until the contingent event occurs and then compute the number of shares that would be received. The number of shares that would be received is compared to the number of shares that would have been received if the contingent event had not occurred to determine the excess number of shares. The number of excess shares multiplied by the stock price as of the commitment date equals the incremental intrinsic value that should be recognized. (ASC 470-20-35-1)
7. If an instrument includes a beneficial conversion option that expires at the end of a stated period and the instrument then becomes mandatorily redeemable at a premium, ASC 470-20 states that the proceeds of issuance were to be allocated between the debt and the embedded beneficial conversion features. The debt amount was then to be accreted to the redemption amount over the period to the required redemption date. ASC 480, however, requires that mandatorily redeemable stock be classified as a liability, measured initially at fair value, with a corresponding decrease to equity

and no gain or loss recognized. Thus, this situation is no longer governed by ASC 470-20.

8. If interest or dividends are paid in kind, the commitment date for the paid-in-kind securities is the commitment date for the original instrument if the payment in kind is not discretionary. (ASC 470-20-30-16) The payment is not discretionary

    (1) if neither the issuer nor the holder can elect other forms of payment for the interest or dividends and
    (2) if the original instrument is converted before dividends are declared or interest is accrued, the holder will always receive the number of shares as if all dividends or interest have been paid in kind (ASC 470-20-30-17).

    If the payment in kind is discretionary, the commitment date for the paid-in-kind securities is the date that the interest is accrued or the dividends are declared.
9. If an issuer issues a convertible instrument as repayment of a nonconvertible instrument, the fair value of the newly issued convertible instrument equals the redemption amount owed at the maturity date of the old debt. That is, the carrying amount of the old debt is the proceeds received for applying ASC 470-20 to the new debt. (ASC 470-20-30-19)

Other Issues. Several tentative conclusions have been expressed by the EITF, but have not been resolved:

1. If a convertible instrument is extinguished prior to its maturity date, no portion of the reacquisition price should be allocated to the conversion option if that option had no intrinsic value at the issuance date.
2. The intrinsic value of a conversion feature at an early extinguishment date of convertible debt is recorded as a decrease in additional paid-in capital, which may result in a reduction in additional paid-in capital that is larger than the amount originally recorded in paid-in capital at issuance.
3. If an entity redeems convertible preferred stock with a beneficial conversion feature, the intrinsic value of the conversion feature that was recorded at issuance is reversed, and the remaining reacquisition price is allocated to the reacquisition of the stock. Any excess of that portion over the carrying amount of the stock is an adjustment to earnings available to common shareholders.
4. If a company issues a warrant that allows the holder to acquire a convertible instrument for a stated price and that warrant is classified as equity, the date used to measure the intrinsic value of the conversion option is the commitment date for the warrant, not its exercise date, provided that the issuer received fair value for the warrant when issued. The deemed proceeds for determining whether a beneficial conversion option exists are equal to the sum of the proceeds received for the warrant and the exercise price of the warrant. If that sum is less than the fair value of the common stock that would be received upon exercise of the convertible instrument that would be obtained upon exercise of the warrant, the excess represents a deemed distribution to the holder of the warrant, which is to be recognized over the life of the warrant. The deemed distribution is limited to the proceeds received for the warrant; that is, if the deemed distribution is larger than the proceeds received, the difference is not recognized until the warrant is exercised. If the issuer received less than fair value for the warrant upon issuance, the exercise date of the warrant should be used to measure the intrinsic value of the conversion option.

5. If a company issues a warrant that allows the holder to acquire a convertible instrument for a stated price and that warrant is classified as a liability, the date used to measure the intrinsic value of the conversion option is the exercise date for the warrant, not its commitment date. The deemed proceeds for determining whether a beneficial conversion option exists are equal to the sum of the fair value of the warrant on the exercise date and the exercise price of the warrant.
6. If a conversion feature permits the holder to receive both common stock and warrants to acquire common stock, the intrinsic value of the conversion option is measured as the difference between (1) the proceeds allocated to the common stock portion of the conversion feature and (2) the fair value at the commitment date of the common stock to be received by the holder upon conversion.

The guidance in ASC 470-20 should be used to evaluate whether the issuer controls settlement of the conversion feature of convertible preferred stock. If the issuer does not control settlement, the convertible preferred stock is considered temporary equity.

Example 1: Intrinsic value of a conversion feature—fixed dollar terms

Software Solutions issues $1,000,000 of convertible debt, which is convertible into $10 par common stock at a price of $50 per share. The fair value of the common stock on the commitment date of the issue is $60. The intrinsic value of the conversion feature is computed as follows:

$1,000,000/$50 per share = 20,000 shares to be issued upon conversion
($60 fair value – $50 conversion price) × 20,000 shares = $200,000 intrinsic value

Software Solutions would make the following entry to recognize the issuance of the bonds at 100:

Cash	1,000,000	
Discount on bonds payable	200,000	
Bonds payable		1,000,000
Additional paid-in capital		200,000

If the price at which the bond is convertible to stock changes over the life of the bond, the intrinsic value should be computed using the terms that are most beneficial to the holder. The most favorable conversion price that would be in effect, assuming that there are no changes to the current circumstances except for the passing of time, should be used to measure the intrinsic value.

Example 2: Intrinsic value of a conversion feature—variable terms

American National Biotech issues $1,000,000 of convertible debt, convertible into $10 par common stock at a price 15% below the commitment date fair value for years 1 and 2, 20% below the commitment date fair value for years 3 to 5, and 25% below the commitment date fair value for years 6 to maturity. The fair value of the common stock on the commitment date of the issue is $50. The intrinsic value of the conversion feature is computed as follows:

The most beneficial price is the 25% discount available in years 6 to maturity
That price would be $37.50 ($50 × .75)
$1,000,000/$37.50 per share = 26,667 shares to be issued upon conversion
($50 fair value – $37.50 conversion price) × 26,667 shares = $333,337 intrinsic value

American National Biotech would make the following entry to recognize the issuance of the bonds at 100:

Cash	1,000,000	
Discount on bonds payable	333,337	
Bonds payable		1,000,000
Additional paid-in capital		333,337

In some cases the conversion price will be dependent on a future event, or the bond becomes convertible only upon the occurrence of a future event. In those cases, the contingent beneficial conversion feature should be measured at the commitment date but not recognized in earnings until the contingency is resolved.

Example 3: Intrinsic value of a conversion feature—contingent price terms

Major Manufacturing Co. issues $1,000,000 of convertible debt, which is convertible into $10 par common stock at a discount of 20% off of the conversion date fair value. The fair value of the common stock on the commitment date of the issue is $50. The intrinsic value of the conversion feature is computed as follows:

Because the conversion percentage is fixed, the intrinsic value is always $250,000.

Market price at conversion	$ 40	$ 50	$ 60	$ 70
Conversion price	$ 32	$ 40	$ 48	$ 56
Number of shares issued	31,250	25,000	20,833	17,857
Discount	$ 8	$ 10	$ 12	$ 14
Intrinsic value	$250,000	$250,000	$250,000	$250,000

Major Manufacturing Co. would make the following entry to recognize the issuance of bonds at 100:

Cash	1,000,000	
Discount on bonds payable	250,000	
Bonds payable		1,000,000
Additional paid-in capital		250,000

Example 4: Intrinsic value of a conversion feature—contingent conversion

Shoemaker Co. issues $1,000,000 of convertible debt, which is convertible into $10 par common stock at a discount of 25% below the commitment date fair value. The fair value of the common stock on the commitment date of the issue is $60, so the conversion price is $45. The debt is convertible only upon an initial public offering. The intrinsic value of the conversion feature is computed as follows:

$1,000,000/$45 per share = 22,222 shares to be issued upon conversion
($60 fair value – $45 conversion price) × 22,222 shares = $333,330 intrinsic value

Shoemaker Co. would not allocate any portion of the proceeds to the conversion feature at issuance. It would make the following entry to recognize the issuance of the bonds at 100:

Cash	1,000,000	
Bonds payable		1,000,000

Upon the occurrence of an initial public offering, Shoemaker would make the following entry:

Discount on bonds payable	333,330	
Additional paid-in capital		333,330

Example 5: Intrinsic value of a conversion feature—contingent conversion with variable terms

Food Franchisers issues $1,000,000 of convertible debt, which is convertible into $10 par common stock at a price of $50. The fair value of the common stock on the commitment date of the issue is $60. The debt is convertible only upon an initial public offering. If the stock's fair value is at least 20% higher than the IPO price one year after the IPO, the conversion price will be

70% of the then fair value. The intrinsic value of the contingent conversion feature at issuance is computed as follows:

$1,000,000/$50 per share = 20,000 shares to be issued upon conversion
($60 fair value – $50 conversion price) × 20,000 shares = $200,000 intrinsic value

The intrinsic value of the contingent conversion price change is also computed at the commitment date using the assumptions that the IPO price will be the same as the current market price and that the stock price one year after the IPO is 20% higher, as follows:

Contingent conversion price = $60 × 120% × 70% = $50.40
$1,000,000/$50.40 per share = 19,841 shares to be issued upon conversion
($72 fair value – $50.40 conversion price) × 19,841 shares = $428,565 intrinsic value

Food Franchisers would not allocate any portion of the proceeds to the conversion feature at issuance. It would make the following entry to recognize the issuance of the bonds at 100:

Cash	1,000,000	
Bonds payable		1,000,000

Upon the occurrence of an initial public offering at $55, Food Franchisers would make the following entry:

Discount on bonds payable	250,000	
Additional paid-in capital		250,000

If the stock price increased to $66 ($55 × 120%), Food Franchisers would make the following entry for the difference between the two intrinsic values:

Discount on bonds payable	178,565	
Additional paid-in capital		178,565

If a bond with an embedded beneficial conversion feature is extinguished prior to conversion, a portion of the reacquisition price is allocated to the repurchase of the conversion feature. That portion is the intrinsic value of the conversion feature at the extinguishment date, which would be recorded as a decrease in additional paid-in capital. That accounting may result in a reduction in additional paid-in capital that is larger than the amount originally recorded in paid-in capital at issuance. However, no portion of the reacquisition price should be allocated to the conversion feature if that feature had no intrinsic value at the issuance date.

Example of extinguishment of debt with an embedded conversion feature

Software Solutions (Example 1, above) repurchases $500,000 face of its debt at 140. At the date of issuance, the following entry had been made relating to the debt that is later extinguished.

Cash	500,000	
Discount on bonds payable	100,000	
Bonds payable		500,000
Additional paid-in capital		100,000

At the date of the repurchase, the fair value of the stock is $85, and the unamortized discount on the debt was $20,000. The intrinsic value of the conversion feature at the date of the repurchase is computed as follows:

$500,000/$50 per share = 10,000 shares to be issued upon conversion
($85 fair value – $50 conversion price) × 10,000 shares = $350,000 intrinsic value

Software Solutions would make the following entry to recognize the retirement of the bonds:

Bonds payable	500,000	
Additional paid-in capital	350,000	
Discount on bonds payable		20,000
Gain on extinguishment of debt		130,000
Cash		700,000

Questions have arisen regarding the accounting for the settlement of this instrument partially in cash (the recognized liability) and partially in stock (the unrecognized equity instrument). ASC 470-20-40-12 states that only the cash payment is to be considered in computing gain or loss on settlement of the recognized liability. Shares transferred to the holder to settle the excess conversion spread represented by the embedded equity instrument are not considered part of the settlement of the debt component of the instrument.

Contingent conversion rights triggered by issuer call. In some instances a debt instrument may include a contingent conversion privilege that becomes exercisable if the issuer attempts to call the debt before maturity, even if the stated contingency (e.g., the underlying stock price hitting some predefined threshold value) has not occurred, at which time the holders may elect to surrender the debt for cash (perhaps with a call premium, if the indenture contains such a provision) or to convert at a defined ratio for stock. If the debt remains outstanding until scheduled redemption, there will be no opportunity to convert. (Another variant exists where the debt has a contingent conversion feature at inception, e.g., where the debt becomes convertible if some other event, such as a refinancing, occurs, as well as if the issuer attempts to call the debt.)

ASC 470-20-40 states that no gain or loss should result from the creation of a conversion opportunity caused by the issuer's exercise of its call option, if the debt as originally issued contained a substantive conversion feature. In such circumstances, conversion of the debt to equity—assuming the existence of substantive rights in the original debt issuance—would be accounted for as a book value swap. On the other hand, if the conversion feature had not been substantive, the conversion triggered by the exercise by the issuer of its call option would be accounted for as a debt extinguishment, with the fair value of the equity being issued used to define the cost of the extinguishment. This would create a gain or loss to be recognized in virtually all situations. Such a gain or loss may no longer be permitted to be reported as extraordinary, however.

ASC 470-20-40 defines a *substantive* conversion feature as a conversion feature that was, when the debt instrument was first issued, at least *reasonably possible* of being exercisable in the future, absent the issuer's exercise of a call option—where *reasonably possible* has the same meaning as under ASC 450. In practical terms, evaluation of whether the original conversion feature had been substantive, in the context of the facts and circumstances at the date of issuance, might include consideration of the interest yield of the contingently convertible debt compared to equivalent rates then required for debt lacking that feature, the likelihood of the occurrence of the defined contingent event, and the relative value of the conversion feature versus the related debt instrument.

Disclosure of contingently convertible securities. Allegations had been raised that disclosures regarding contingently convertible securities have often been inconsistent across companies, and have often been inadequate. To address this problem, ASC 505-10-50 states how to disclose contingently convertible securities. See the chapter on ASC 505 for details.

Induced Conversion of Debt

A special situation exists in which the conversion privileges of convertible debt are modified after issuance. These modifications may take the form of reduced conversion prices or additional consideration paid to the convertible debt holder. The debtor offers these modifications or "sweeteners" to induce prompt conversion of the outstanding debt.

ASC 470-20 specifies the accounting method used in these situations and only applies when the convertible debt is converted into equity securities. Upon conversion, the debtor must recognize an expense for the excess of the fair value of all the securities and other consideration given over the fair value of the securities specified in the original conversion terms. The reported expense should not be classified as an extraordinary item.

Determining applicability of ASC 470-20. ASC 470-20 specifies the accounting for "sweeteners" used to induce the conversion of convertible debt. Traditionally, this involves enhancements offered by the debtor to encourage conversions, often motivated by the desire to bring an end to interest payments on the convertible debt. ASC 470-20-40-13 addresses the related circumstance of conversions when the enhanced terms are proposed or requested by the creditors/debtholders. In some instances, only the requesting parties are granted the sweetened terms. Thus, ASC 470-20 applies to all conversion of convertible debts that (1) occur pursuant to changed conversion privileges, (2) are exercisable only for a limited period of time, and (3) include the issuance of all of the equity securities issuable pursuant to conversion privileges included in the terms of the debt at issuance for each debt instrument that is converted, regardless of the party that initiates the offer or whether the offer relates to all debtholders.

Example of induced conversion expense

1. January 1, 20X1, XYZ Company issued ten 8% convertible bonds at $1,000 par value without a discount or premium, maturing December 31, 20Y1.
2. The bonds are initially convertible into no par common stock of XYZ at a conversion price of $25.
3. On July 1, 20X5, the convertible bonds have a fair value of $600 each.
4. To induce the convertible bondholders to quickly convert their bonds, XYZ reduces the conversion price to $20 for bondholders who convert before July 21, 20X5 (within twenty days).
5. The fair value of XYZ Company's common stock on the date of conversion is $15 per share.

The fair value of the incremental consideration paid by XYZ upon conversion is calculated for each bond converted before July 21, 20X5.

Value of securities issued to debt holders:

Face amount	$1,000	per bond
÷ New conversion price	÷ $20	per share
Number of common shares issued upon conversion	50	shares
× Price per common share	× $15	per share
Value of securities issued	$ 750	(a)
Face amount	$1,000	per bond
÷ Original conversion price	÷ $25	per share
Number of common shares issuable pursuant to original conversion privilege	40	shares
× Price per share	× $15	per share
Value of securities issuable pursuant to original conversion privileges	$ 600	(b)
Value of securities issued	$ 750	(a)
Value of securities issuable pursuant to the original conversion privileges	600	(b)
Fair value of incremental consideration	$ 150	

The entry to record the debt conversion for each bond is

Convertible debt	1,000	
Debt conversion expense	150	
Common stock—no par		1,150

Debt Issued with Stock Warrants

Warrants are certificates enabling the holder to purchase a stated number of shares of stock at a certain price within a certain time period. They are often issued with bonds to enhance the marketability of the bonds and to lower the bond's interest rate.

When bonds with detachable warrants are issued, the purchase price must be allocated between the debt and the stock warrants based on relative fair values (ASC 470-20). Since two separate instruments are involved, a fair value must be determined for each. However, if one value cannot be determined, the fair value of the other should be deducted from the total value to determine the unknown value.

Example of accounting for a bond with a detachable warrant

1. A $1,000 bond with a detachable warrant to buy 10 shares of $10 par common stock at $50 per share is issued for $1,025.
2. Immediately after the issuance the bonds trade at $995 and the warrants at $35.
3. The fair value of the stock is $48.

The relative fair value of the bonds is 96.6% [995/(995 + 35)] and the warrant is 3.4% [35/(995 + 35)]. Thus, $34.85(3.4% × $1,025) of the issuance price is assigned to the warrants. The journal entry to record the issuance is:

Cash	1,025.00	
Discount on bonds payable	9.85	
Bonds payable		1,000.00
Paid-in capital—warrants (or "Stock options outstanding")		34.85

The discount is the difference between the purchase price assigned to the bond, $990.15 (96.6% × $1,025), and its face value, $1,000. The debt itself is accounted for in the normal fashion.

The entry to record the subsequent future exercise of the warrant would be:

Cash	500.00	
Paid-in capital—warrants	34.85	
Common stock		100.00
Paid-in capital		434.85 (difference)

Assuming the warrants are not exercised, the journal entry is:

Paid-in capital—warrants	34.85	
Paid-in capital—expired warrants		34.85

Debt Issued with Conversion Features and Stock Warrants

ASC 470-20 states that when a debt instrument includes both detachable instruments such as warrants, and an embedded beneficial conversion option, the proceeds of issuance should first be allocated among the convertible instrument and the other detachable instruments based on their relative fair values. Following this, the ASC 470-20 model should be applied to the amount allocated to the convertible instrument to determine if the embedded conversion option has an intrinsic value.

Example of convertible debt issued with stock warrants

Cellular Communicators issues $1,000,000 of convertible debt with 100,000 detachable warrants. The debt is convertible into $10 par common stock at a price of $50 per share. At the commitment date of this issuance, the common stock is trading at $46 per share. Immediately after the issuance, the bonds trade at 85 and the warrants trade at $2. The issuance proceeds of $1,000,000 are allocated to the two instruments as follows:

$850,000 /($850,000 + $200,000) × $1,000,000 = $809,524 to the debt
$200,000/($850,000 + $200,000) × $1,000,000 = $190,476 to the warrants

The intrinsic value of the conversion feature is next computed as follows:

$1,000,000/$50 per share = 20,000 shares to be issued upon conversion

The effective conversion price is the bond's allocated proceeds of $809,524 divided by 20,000 shares or $40.48

($46 current fair value of the stock – $40.48 effective conversion price) × 20,000 shares = $110,476, which is the implied discount granted on the bonds in connection with the conversion feature

Cellular Communicators would make the following entry to recognize the issuance of the bonds with warrants at 100:

Cash	1,000,000	
Discount on bonds payable	110,476	
Bonds payable		809,524
Additional paid-in capital		110,476
Paid-in capital—warrants		190,476

A wide range of features may be incorporated into stock purchase warrants and it will often be a challenge to identify the substance of these features, and to then prescribe the proper accounting for each feature. One such example involves warrants that are issued with put options, sometimes called "puttable warrants." Such warrants allow the holder to purchase a fixed number of the issuer's shares at a fixed price (common to all warrants), but also are puttable by the holder at a specified date for a fixed monetary amount that the holder could require the issuer to pay in cash. For example, assume the warrants are issued when the entity's shares are trading at $12, and each warrant permits the purchase of 100 shares at $15 through April 30, 2013. If not previously exercised, the warrant holders can put each warrant back to the issuer for the equivalent of $14 per share, that is, for 100 × ($14 – $12) = $200 per warrant. The warrant holder is thus assured (given the underlying stock price at inception) of at least $2 per share income, and of course may reap a much larger reward if the share price has risen beyond $15 by the expiration date.

ASC 470-30, *Participating Mortgage Loans*

Accounting by participating mortgage loan borrowers. Certain mortgage loan agreements provide, generally in exchange for a lower interest rate, that the lender shares in price appreciation of the property securing the loan. Other arrangements provide that the lender receives a share of the earnings or cash flows from the commercial real estate for which the loan was made. ASC 470-30 establishes the borrower's accounting for a participating mortgage loan if the lender participates in increases in the fair value of the mortgaged real estate project, the results of operations of that mortgaged real estate project, or both.

It requires that certain disclosures be made in the financial statements. In addition, the codification requires the following:

1. At origination, if the lender is entitled to participate in appreciation in the fair value of the mortgaged real estate project, the borrower should determine the fair value of the participation feature and should recognize a participation liability for that amount. A corresponding debit should then be recorded to a debt-discount account. The debt discount should be amortized by the interest method, using the effective interest rate. The net result is to include the expected cost of the participating feature in the periodic interest cost associated with the loan.
2. At the end of each reporting period, the balance of the participation liability should be adjusted if necessary, so that the liability equals the fair value of the participation feature at that point in time. The corresponding debit or credit should be adjusted to the related debt-discount account. The revised discount should then be amortized prospectively.

ASC 470-40, *Product Financing Arrangements*

ASC 470-40 addresses the issues involved with product financing arrangements. A product financing arrangement is a transaction in which an entity (referred to as the "sponsor") simultaneously sells and agrees to repurchase inventory to and from a financing entity. The repurchase price is contractually fixed at an amount equal to the original sales price plus the financing entity's carrying and financing costs. The purpose of the transaction is to enable the sponsor enterprise to arrange financing of its original purchase of the inventory. The various steps involved in the transaction are illustrated by the diagram.

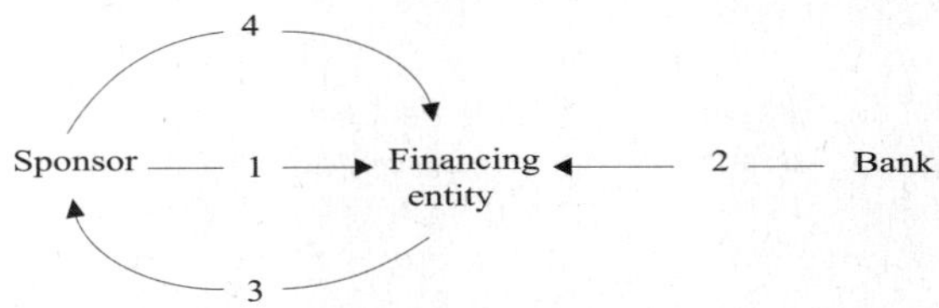

1. In the initial transaction, the sponsor "sells" inventoriable items to the financing entity in return for the remittance of the sales price and at the same time agrees to repurchase the inventory at a specified price (usually the sales price plus carrying and financing costs) over a specified period of time.
2. The financing entity borrows from a bank (or other financial institution) using the newly purchased inventory as collateral.
3. The financing entity remits the proceeds of its borrowing to the sponsor and the sponsor presumably uses these funds to pay off the debt (accounts payable) incurred for the original purchase.
4. The sponsor then, over a period of time as funds become available, repurchases the inventory from the financing entity for the specified price plus carrying and financing costs.

FASB ruled that the substance of this transaction is that of a borrowing transaction, not a sale. That is, the transaction is, in substance, no different from the sponsor directly obtaining third-party financing to purchase inventory. ASC 470-40 specifies that the proper accounting by the sponsor is to record a liability in the amount of the selling price when the funds are received from the financing entity in exchange for the initial transfer of the inventory. The sponsor proceeds to accrue carrying and financing costs in accordance with its normal accounting policies. These accruals are eliminated and the liability satisfied when the sponsor repurchases the inventory. The inventory is not removed from the statement of financial position of the sponsor and a sale is not recorded. Thus, although legal title has passed to the financing entity, for purposes of measuring and valuing inventory, the inventory is considered to be owned by the sponsor.

Example of a product financing arrangement

The Medieval Illumination Company (MIC) has borrowed the maximum amount it has available under its short-term line of credit. MIC obtains additional financing by selling $280,000 of its candle inventory to a third-party financing entity. The third party obtains a bank loan at 6% interest to pay for its purchase of the candle inventory, while charging MIC 8% interest and $1,500 per month to store the candle inventory at a public storage facility. As MIC obtains candle orders, it purchases inventory back from the third party, which in turn authorizes the public warehouse to drop ship the orders directly to MIC's customers at a cost of $35 per order. Since this is a product financing arrangement, MIC cannot remove the candle inventory from its accounting records or record revenue from sale of its inventory to the third party. Instead, the following entry records the initial financing arrangement:

Cash	280,000	
Short-term debt		280,000

After one month, MIC records accrued interest of $1,867 ($280,000 × 8% interest × 1/12 year) on the loan, as well as the monthly storage fee of $1,500, as shown in the following entry:

Interest expense	1,867	
Storage expense	1,500	
Accrued interest		1,867
Accounts payable		1,500

On the first day of the succeeding month, MIC receives a prepaid customer order for $3,800. The margin on the order is 40% and, therefore, the related inventory cost is $2,280. MIC pays the third party $2,280 to buy back the required inventory as well as $35 to the public storage facility to ship the order to the customer, and records the following entries:

Short-term debt	2,280	
Cash		2,280
To repurchase inventory from the third-party financing entity		
Cash	3,800	
Sales		3,800
To record the sale to the customer		
Cost of goods sold	2,280	
Inventory		2,280
To record the cost of the sale to the customer		
Freight out	35	
Accounts payable		35
To record the cost of fulfilling the order		

ASC 470-40 identifies variations of the terms of the above arrangement that also meet the criteria for being accounted for as product financing arrangements.

1. The third-party financing entity purchases the inventory directly from the sponsor's supplier (instead of from the sponsor) with a simultaneous agreement to sell the inventory to the sponsor.

2. The sponsor enters into an agreement with a third-party financing entity to control the disposition of product that has been purchased by the third party either from the sponsor or from the sponsor's supplier.

ASC 470-50, *Modifications and Extinguishments*

Modifications to conversion privileges. Under provisions of ASC 470-50, the debtor's (issuer's) accounting for a modification of a debt issue or an exchange for another issue is based on whether the modifications are substantial. Based on the results of the analysis, extinguishment of the original debt could be found to have occurred, with financial reporting ramifications. The SEC takes a position on this matter that adds further complexity.

ASC 470-50-40 holds that debt extinguishment accounting be used if (1) the change in the fair value of the embedded conversion option is at least 10% of the carrying value of the original debt instrument just prior to the debt being modified or exchanged, or (2) the debt instrument modification or exchange adds or eliminates a substantive conversion option. If this analysis does not result in extinguishment accounting, then an increase in the fair value of the conversion option would reduce the debt and increase additional paid-in capital, while a decrease in the fair value of the conversion option would not be recognized.

ASC 470-50-40 also holds that the modification of a convertible debt instrument will affect subsequent recognition of interest expense for the associated debt instrument for changes in the fair value of the embedded conversion option. The change in the fair value of an embedded conversion option will be calculated as the difference between the fair value of the embedded conversion option immediately before and after the modification. The value exchanged by the holder for the modification of the conversion option is to be recognized as a discount (or premium) with a corresponding increase (or decrease) in additional paid-in capital.

Finally, ASC 470-50-40 concludes that issuers should not recognize a beneficial conversion feature or reassess an existing beneficial conversion feature at the date of the modification of a convertible debt instrument.

Extinguishment of Debt. Management may reacquire or retire outstanding debt before its scheduled maturity. This decision is usually caused by changes in present or expected interest rates or in cash flows.

In-substance defeasance (irrevocably placing assets in a trust that is to be used solely to service the remaining debt payments) does not result in the extinguishment of a liability. Except for items excluded by ASC 405-20, a liability is removed from the statement of financial position only if:

1. The creditor is paid and the debtor is relieved of the obligation.
2. The debtor is released legally either by the creditor or judicially from being the primary obligor.

If a debtor becomes secondarily liable, through a third-party assumption and a release by the creditor, the original debtor becomes a guarantor. A guarantee obligation, based on the probability that the third party will pay, is to be recognized and initially measured at fair value. The amount of guarantee obligation increases the loss or reduces the gain recognized on extinguishments.

Some financial instruments can have characteristics of either assets or liabilities depending on market conditions (forward contracts, swap contracts, and written commodity options). To be derecognized, those instruments must not only meet the two criteria above, but must also meet the surrender of control criteria of ASC 405-20.

Debtor's accounting for a modification or exchange of debt instruments other than in a troubled debt restructuring. An exchange of debt instruments with substantially different terms is a debt extinguishment and should be accounted for in accordance with ASC 405-20. Any substantial modification in the terms of an existing debt, other than for a troubled debt restructuring, should similarly be reported as a debt extinguishment.

An exchange or modification is considered substantial when the present value of cash flows under the new debt instrument is at least 10% different from the present value of the remaining cash flows under the terms of the original instrument (ASC 470-50-40-10). For the purpose of the 10% test, the effective interest rate of the original debt instrument is used as the discount rate.

Cash flows can be affected by changes in principal amounts, interest rates, maturity, or by fees exchanged between the parties. Substantial change can also result from changes in the following provisions:

1. Recourse or nonrecourse features
2. Priority of the obligation
3. Collateralized or noncollateralized features
4. Debt covenants and/or waivers
5. The guarantor
6. Option features.

Assuming the 10% test is met and the debt instruments are deemed to be substantially different, the new investment should be initially recorded at fair value and that amount should be compared to the book value of the old debt to determine debt extinguishment gain or loss to be recognized, as well as the effective rate of the new instrument. (ASC 470-50-40-13) Fees paid by the debtor to the creditor or received by the debtor from the creditor should be included in determining debt extinguishment gain or loss. (ASC 470-50-40-17a) Additionally, any costs incurred with third parties should be amortized using the interest method in a manner similar to that used for debt issue costs (ASC 470-50-40-18).

Assuming the 10% test is not met and the debt instruments are not deemed to be substantially different, then the new effective interest is to be determined based on the carrying amount of the original instrument and the revised cash flows (ASC 470-50-40-14). Fees paid by the debtor to the creditor or received by the debtor from the creditor should be amortized as an adjustment to interest expense over the remaining term of the modified debt instrument using the interest method (ASC 470-50-40-17b). Additionally, any costs incurred with third parties should be expensed as incurred (ASC 470-50-40-18b).

Gain or loss on debt extinguishment. According to ASC 470-50-40-2, the difference between the net carrying value and the price paid to acquire the debt instruments is to be recorded as a gain or loss. If the acquisition price is greater than the carrying value, a loss exists. A gain is generated if the acquisition price is less than the carrying value. These gains or losses are to be recognized in the period in which the retirement took place. Debt extinguishment gains and losses are reported as extraordinary only if the event creating the gain or loss is both unusual and infrequently occurring. It is expected that extinguishments of debt will rarely, if ever, meet these dual criteria. Hence, gains and losses on debt extinguishments will be reported in earnings before extraordinary items.

The unamortized premium or discount and issue costs should be amortized to the acquisition date and recorded prior to the determination of the gain or loss. If the extinguishment of debt does not occur on the interest date, the interest payable accruing between the last interest date and the acquisition date must also be recorded.

Example of accounting for the extinguishment of debt

1. A 10%, 10-year, $200,000 bond is dated and issued on 1/2/12 at 98, with the interest payable semiannually.
2. Associated bond issue costs of $14,000 are incurred.
3. Four years later, on 1/2/16, the entire bond issue is repurchased at 102 (i.e., 102% of face value) and is retired.
4. At 1/2/16 the unamortized discount using the effective interest rate of 10.325% is $2,858.

Reacquisition price [(102%) × $200,000]		$204,000
Net carrying amount:		
Face value	$200,000	
Unamortized discount	(2,858)	
Unamortized issue costs [14,000 × (6/10)]	(8,400)	188,742
Loss on bond repurchase		$ 15,258

ASC 470-60, *Troubled Debt Restructurings by Debtors*

Troubled debt restructurings are defined by ASC 470-60 as situations in which the creditor, for economic or legal reasons related to the debtor's financial difficulties, grants the debtor a concession that would not otherwise be granted. As explained in ASC 470-60-55-5, no single characteristic or factor, taken alone, is determinative of whether a modification of terms or an exchange of a debt instrument is a troubled debt restructuring under ASC 470-60. Thus, making this determination requires the exercise of judgment. ASC 470-60-55 poses two questions to assist in making a determination of whether ASC 470-60 applies in a particular instance.

- Is the debtor experiencing financial difficulty?
- Has the creditor granted a concession?

Both of these questions must be answered in the affirmative for ASC 470-60 to be applicable.

Is the debtor experiencing financial difficulty? If the debtor's creditworthiness has deteriorated since the debt was originally issued, the debtor should evaluate whether it is experiencing financial difficulties. The following factors are indicators that this may be the case:

- The debtor is in default on some of its debt, or it is probable that the debtor will be in payment default on any of its debt in the foreseeable future without the restructuring modification
- The debtor has declared, or is in the process of declaring, bankruptcy
- There is doubt as to whether the debtor is a going concern
- The debtor's securities have been or are likely to be delisted
- The debtor forecasts that its entity-specific cash flows are insufficient to service the debt through its maturity in accordance with its terms
- The debtor cannot obtain resources at the current market rates for nontroubled debtors except through existing creditors.

(ASC 470-60-55-8)

If both of the following factors are present, it would be concluded that the debtor is not experiencing financial difficulty:

- The creditors agree to restructure the old debt solely to reflect either (1) a decrease in the current interest rates for the debtor, or (2) an increase in the debtor's creditworthiness
- The debtor is currently servicing the old debt and can obtain funds to repay the old debt at the current market rate for a nontroubled debtor.

(ASC 470-60-55-9)

Has the creditor granted a concession? The creditor has granted a concession when a restructuring results in its expectation that it will not collect all amounts due. If so, and if the payment of principal is mostly dependent on the value of collateral, the creditor should consider the current value of the collateral in deciding whether the principal will be paid.

If the creditor restructures a debt in exchange for additional collateral or guarantees, the creditor has granted a concession when the amount of these additional items is not adequate compensation for other terms of the restructuring.

If the debtor does not have access to funds at a market rate, then the creditor should consider the restructuring to be at a below-market rate; this is an indicator that the creditor has granted a concession. It may also be a concession when the interest rate in the restructuring agreement has increased, if the new rate is below the market interest rate for new debt having similar risk characteristics. If so, the creditor should consider all aspects of the restructuring agreement to determine whether it has granted a concession.

It is not a concession when a restructuring only results in a delay in payment that is insignificant. However, if the debt has been previously restructured, the creditor should consider the cumulative effect of the past restructurings when determining whether a delay in payment resulting from the most recent restructuring is insignificant.

However, in any of the following four situations, a concession granted by the creditor does not automatically qualify as a restructuring:

1. The fair value of the assets or equity interest accepted by a creditor from a debtor in full satisfaction of its receivable is at least equal to the creditor's recorded investment in the receivable.
2. The fair value of the assets or equity interest transferred by a debtor to a creditor in full settlement of its payable is at least equal to the carrying value of the payable.
3. The creditor reduces the effective interest rate to reflect a decrease in current interest rates or a decrease in the risk, in order to maintain the relationship.
4. The debtor, in exchange for old debt, issues new debt with an interest rate that reflects current market rates.

(ASC 470-60-55-12)

ASC 470-60-55-1 notes that ASC 470-60 does not apply to debtors in bankruptcy unless the restructuring does not result from a general restatement of the debtor's liabilities in bankruptcy proceedings. That is, ASC 470-60 applies only if the debt restructuring is isolated to the creditor.

A troubled debt restructuring can occur one of two ways. The first is a settlement of the debt at less than the carrying amount. The second is a continuation of the debt with a modification of terms (i.e., a reduction in the interest rate, face amount, accrued interest owed, or an extension of the payment date for interest or face amount). Accounting for such restructurings is prescribed for both debtors and creditors. ASC 470-60-15-3 points out that the debtor and creditor must separately apply ASC 470-60 to the specific fact situation, since the tests are not necessarily symmetrical and it is possible for one or the other, but not both, to have a troubled debt restructuring when the debtor's carrying amount and the creditor's recorded investment differ. ASC 310-10-35-16 specifies the accounting by creditors for troubled debt restructurings involving a modification of terms.

Recognition. If the debt is settled by the exchange of assets, a gain is recognized in the period of transfer for the difference between the carrying amount of the debt (defined as the face amount of the debt increased or decreased by applicable accrued interest and applicable unamortized premium, discount, or issue costs) and the consideration given to extinguish the debt (ASC 470-60-35-3). A two-step process is used: (1) any noncash assets used to settle the debt are revalued at fair value and the associated ordinary gain or loss is recognized and (2) the debt restructuring gain is determined and recognized. The gain or loss is evaluated under the "unusual and infrequent" criteria of ASC 225-20. If stock is issued to settle the liability, the stock is recorded at its fair value (ASC 470-60-35-4).

Example 1: Settlement of debt by exchange of assets

Assume the debtor company transfers land having a book value of $70,000 and a fair value of $80,000 in full settlement of its note payable. The note has a remaining life of five years, a principal balance of $90,000, and related accrued interest of $10,000 is recorded. The following entries are required to record the settlement:

Debtor		
Land	10,000	
Gain on transfer of assets		10,000
Note payable	90,000	
Interest payable	10,000	
Land		80,000
Gain on settlement of debt		20,000

If the debt is continued with a modification of terms, it is necessary to compare the total future cash flows of the restructured debt (both principal and stated interest) with the carrying value of the original debt. If the total amount of future cash payments is greater than the carrying value, no adjustment is made to the carrying value of the debt. However, a new lower effective interest rate must be computed. This rate makes the present value of the total future cash payments equal to the present carrying value of debt and is used to determine interest expense in future periods. The effective interest method must be used to compute the expense. If the total future cash payments of the restructured debt are less than the present carrying value, the current debt should be reduced to the amount of the future cash flows and a gain should be recognized. No interest expense would be recognized in subsequent periods, since only the principal is being repaid.

According to ASC 470-60, a troubled debt restructuring that involves only a modification of terms is accounted for *prospectively*. Thus, there is no change in the carrying value of the liability unless the carrying amount of the original debt exceeds the total future cash payments specified by the new agreement.

If the restructuring consists of part settlement and part modification of payments, the part settlement is accounted for first and then the modification of payments.

Example 2: Restructuring with gain/loss recognized (payments are less than carrying value)

Assume that the note has a principal balance of $90,000, accrued interest of $10,000, an interest rate of 5%, and a remaining life of five years. The interest rate is reduced to 4%, the principal is reduced to $72,500, and the accrued interest at date of restructure is forgiven.

Future cash flows (after restructuring):

Principal	$ 72,500
Interest (5 years × $72,500 × 4%)	14,500
Total cash to be paid	$ 87,000
Amount prior to restructure	
($90,000 principal + $10,000 accrued interest)	(100,000)
Debtor's gain	$ 13,000

The following entries need to be recorded by the debtor to reflect the terms of the agreement:

Beginning of Year 1		
Interest payable	10,000	
Note payable	3,000	
Gain on restructure of debt		13,000
End of Years 1–5		
Note payable	2,900	
Cash		2,900

NOTE: $14,500 ÷ 5 yrs. = $2,900; No interest expense is recorded in this case.

End of Year 5		
Note payable	72,500	
Cash		72,500

Example 3: Restructuring with no gain/loss recognized (payments exceed carrying value)

Modify Example 2 as follows:

Assume the $100,000 owed is reduced to a principal balance of $95,000. The interest rate of 5% is reduced to 4%.

Future cash flows (after restructuring):	
Principal	$ 95,000
Interest (5 years × $95,000 × 4%)	19,000
Total cash to be received	$ 114,000
Amount prior to restructure	
($90,000 principal + $10,000 accrued interest)	(100,000)
Interest expense/revenue over 5 years	$ 14,000

In this example, a new effective interest rate must be computed such that the present value of the future payments equals $100,000. A trial and error approach is used to calculate the effective interest rate that discounts the $95,000 principal and the $3,800 annual interest payments to $100,000, the amount owed prior to restructuring.

Trial and Error Calculation

	(n = 5, i = 2.5%)	(n = 5, i = 3%)
PV of ordinary annuity	4.64583	4.57971
PV of 1	.88385	.86261

2.5%: (.88385 × $95,000) + (4.64583 × $3,800) = $101,620

3%: (.86261 × $95,000) + (4.57971 × $3,800) = $ 99,351

Interpolation:

$$\left[\frac{101{,}620 - 100{,}000}{101{,}620 - 99{,}351}\right] \times (3\% - 2.5\%) = .357\%$$

New effective rate = 2.5% + .357% = 2.857%

Interest amortization schedule:

Year	Cash	Interest at effective rate	Reduction in carrying value	Carrying amount
				$100,000
1	$ 3,800(a)	$2,857(b)	$ 943(c)	99,057
2	3,800	2,830	970	98,087
3	3,800	2,802	998	97,089
4	3,800	2,774	1,026	96,063
5	3,800	2,745	1,055	95,000*
	$19,000			

* *Rounded*
(a) *$3,800 = $95,000 × .04*
(b) *$2,857 = $100,000 × 2.857%*
(c) *$943 = $3,800 – $2,857*

The following entries are made by the debtor to recognize the cash payments in the subsequent periods:

End of Year 1

Note payable ($3,800 – $2,857)	943	
Interest expense ($100,000 × .02857)	2,857	
Cash		3,800

End of Year 5

Note payable	95,000	
Cash		95,000

When the total future cash payments may exceed the carrying amount of the liability, no gain or loss is recognized on the books of the debtor unless the maximum future cash payments are less than the carrying amount of the debt. For example, if the debtor is required to make interest payments at a higher rate if its financial condition improves before the maturity of the debt, the debtor should assume that the larger payments would have to be made. The contingent payments would be included in the total future cash payments for comparison with the carrying amount of the debt. If the future cash payments exceed the carrying amount, a new effective interest rate should be determined. The new rate should be the rate that equates the present value of the future cash payments with the carrying amount of the liability. Interest expense and principal reduction are then recognized as the future cash payments are made.

Example 4: Contingent payments

Modify Example 2 as follows: The new agreement states that if financial condition at maturity improves as specified, an additional principal payment of $15,000 is required and additional 1% of interest must be paid in arrears for years 4 and 5.

Future cash payments:	
Required principal per agreement	$ 72,500
Required interest per agreement (5 years × $72,500 × 4%)	14,500
Contingent principal payment	15,000
Contingent interest payments (2 years × 72,500 × 1%)	1,450
	$ 103,450
Amount prior to restructure ($90,000 + $10,000)	(100,000)
	$ 3,450

When computing the new effective interest rate, only as many contingent payments as are needed to make the future cash payments exceed the carrying value are included in the calculation. Thus, the contingent principal payment would be included, but the contingent interest would not. The contingent interest payments would be recognized using the same criteria as are used in ASC 450; that is, the payments are recognized when they are both probable and reasonably estimable.

34 ASC 480 DISTINGUISHING LIABILITIES FROM EQUITY

PERSPECTIVE AND ISSUES

Subtopic

ASC 480, Distinguishing Liabilities from Equity Topic, contains one Subtopic:

- ASC 480-10, *Overall*, which provides guidance on how an issuer classifies and measures financial instruments with characteristics of both liabilities and equity.

Scope and Scope Exceptions

ASC 480 applies to all entities and to any freestanding financial instrument. This includes one that:

- Comprises more than one option or forward contract
- Has characteristics of both a liability and equity and, in some circumstances, also has characteristics of an asset.

ASC 480 does *not* address an instrument that has only characteristics of an asset. ASC 480 does not apply to:

- A feature embedded in a financial instrument that is not a derivative instrument in its entirety.
- An obligation under share-based compensation arrangements if that obligation is accounted for under Topic 718.

(Also see the Applicability of ASC 480 section in this chapter or an expanded discussion of which instruments fall under the scope of ASC 480.)

Overview

Standard setters had been struggling with the proper reporting for hybrid instruments—instruments having characteristics of both liabilities and equity. Two needs had been perceived:

- first, to establish criteria for classification for certain instruments (e.g., mandatorily redeemable stock) that nominally are equity but have key characteristics of debt, but which will significantly impact corporate statements of financial position if a "substance over form" approach is strictly enforced; and
- second, to develop the methodology for disaggregating the constituent parts of compound instruments so that they may be accounted for as debt and as equity, respectively.

ASC 480 addresses those needs.

DEFINITIONS OF TERMS

Source: ASC 480-20

Employee Stock Ownership Plan. An employee stock ownership plan is an employee benefit plan that is described by the Employee Retirement Income Security Act of 1974 and the Internal Revenue Code of 1986 as a stock bonus plan, or combination stock bonus and money purchase pension plan, designed to invest primarily in employer stock. Also called an employee share ownership plan.

Equity Shares. Equity shares refers only to shares that are accounted for as equity.

Fair Value. The price that would be received to sell an asset or paid to transfer a liability in an orderly transaction between market participants at the measurement date.

Financial Instrument. Cash, evidence of an ownership interest in an entity, or a contract that both:

a. Imposes on one entity a contractual obligation either:
   1. To deliver cash or another financial instrument to a second entity
   2. To exchange other financial instruments on potentially unfavorable terms with the second entity.
b. Conveys to that second entity a contractual right either:
   1. To receive cash or another financial instrument from the first entity
   2. To exchange other financial instruments on potentially favorable terms with the first entity.

The use of the term financial instrument in this definition is recursive (because the term financial instrument is included in it), though it is not circular. The definition requires a chain of contractual obligations that ends with the delivery of cash or an ownership interest in an entity.

Any number of obligations to deliver financial instruments can be links in a chain that qualifies a particular contract as a financial instrument.

Contractual rights and contractual obligations encompass both those that are conditioned on the occurrence of a specified event and those that are not. All contractual rights (contractual obligations) that are financial instruments meet the definition of asset (liability) set forth in FASB Concepts Statement No. 6, Elements of Financial Statements, although some may not be recognized as assets (liabilities) in financial statements—that is, they may be off-balance-sheet—because they fail to meet some other criterion for recognition.

For some financial instruments, the right is held by or the obligation is due from (or the obligation is owed to or by) a group of entities rather than a single entity.

Freestanding Financial Instrument. A financial instrument that meets either of the following conditions:

1. It is entered into separately and apart from any of the entity's other financial instruments or equity transactions.
2. It is entered into in conjunction with some other transaction and is legally detachable and separately exercisable.

Issuer. The entity that issued a financial instrument or may be required under the terms of a financial instrument to issue its equity shares.

Issuer's Equity Shares. The equity shares of any entity whose financial statements are included in the consolidated financial statements.

Mandatorily Redeemable Financial Instrument. Any of various financial instruments issued in the form of shares that embody an unconditional obligation requiring the issuer to redeem the instrument by transferring its assets at a specified or determinable date (or dates) or upon an event that is certain to occur.

Monetary Value. What the fair value of the cash, shares, or other instruments that a financial instrument obligates the issuer to convey to the holder would be at the settlement date under specified market conditions.

Net Cash Settlement. A form of settling a financial instrument under which the entity with a loss delivers to the entity with a gain cash equal to the gain.

Net Share Settlement. A form of settling a financial instrument under which the entity with a loss delivers to the entity with a gain shares of stock with a current fair value equal to the gain.

Noncontrolling Interest. The portion of equity (net assets) in a subsidiary not attributable, directly or indirectly, to a parent. A noncontrolling interest is sometimes called a minority interest.

Obligation. A conditional or unconditional duty or responsibility to transfer assets or to issue equity shares. Because Topic 480 relates only to financial instruments and not to contracts to provide services and other types of contracts, but includes duties or responsibilities to issue equity shares, this definition of obligation differs from the definition found in FASB Concepts Statement No. 6, Elements of Financial Statements, and is applicable only for items in the scope of that Topic.

Parent. An entity that has a controlling financial interest in one or more subsidiaries. (Also, an entity that is the primary beneficiary of a variable interest entity.)

Physical Settlement. A form of settling a financial instrument under which both of the following conditions are met:

a. The party designated in the contract as the buyer delivers the full stated amount of cash or other financial instruments to the seller.

b. The seller delivers the full stated number of shares of stock or other financial instruments or nonfinancial instruments to the buyer.

Securities and Exchange Commission Registrant. An entity (or an entity that is controlled by an entity) that meets any of the following criteria:

a. It has issued or will issue debt or equity securities that are traded in a public market (a domestic or foreign stock exchange or an over-the-counter market, including local or regional markets).
b. It is required to file financial statements with the Securities and Exchange Commission (SEC).
c. It provides financial statements for the purpose of issuing any class of securities in a public market.

Shares. Shares includes various forms of ownership that may not take the legal form of securities (for example, partnership interests), as well as other interests, including those that are liabilities in substance but not in form. (Business entities have interest holders that are commonly known by specialized names, such as stockholders, partners, and proprietors, and by more general names, such as investors, but all are encompassed by the descriptive term owners. Equity of business entities is, thus, commonly known by several names, such as owners' equity, stockholders' equity, ownership, equity capital, partners' capital, and proprietorship. Some entities [for example, mutual organizations] do not have stockholders, partners, or proprietors in the usual sense of those terms but do have participants whose interests are essentially ownership interests, residual interests, or both.)

Subsidiary. An entity, including an unincorporated entity such as a partnership or trust, in which another entity, known as its parent, holds a controlling financial interest. (Also, a variable interest entity that is consolidated by a primary beneficiary.)

Transfer. The term transfer is used in a broad sense consistent with its use in FASB Concepts Statement No. 6, Elements of Financial Statements (such as in paragraph 137), rather than in the narrow sense in which it is used in Subtopic 860-10.

Variable-Rate Forward Contracts. Variable-rate forward contracts are commonly used to effect equity forward transactions. The contract price on those forward contracts is not fixed at inception but varies based on changes in a specified index (for example, three-month U.S. London Interbank Offered Rate [LIBOR]) during the life of the contract.

Additional terms from the ASC Master Glossary that may be useful:

Call option. A contract that allows the holder to buy a specified quantity of stock from the writer of the contract at a fixed price for a given period.

Put option. A contract that allows the holder to sell a specific quantity of stock to the writer of the contract at a fixed price during a given period.

Warrant. A security that gives the holder the right to purchase shares of common stock in accordance with the terms of the instrument, usually upon payment of a specified amount.

CONCEPTS, RULES, AND EXAMPLES

Applicability of ASC 480

ASC 480 applies to all freestanding instruments, including those composed of more than one option or forward contract embodying obligations that require or that may require settlement by transfer of assets. It applies to three types of freestanding financial instruments:

- Mandatorily redeemable financial instruments
- Obligations to repurchase the issuer's shares by transferring assets
- Certain obligations to issue a variable number of shares.

Obligations to repurchase the issuer's equity shares by transferring assets include financial instruments, other than outstanding shares, that, at inception,

a. Embody obligations to repurchase the issuers' equity shares, or are indexed to such obligations, and
b. Require or may require the issuers to settle the obligations by transferring assets.

These must be classified as liabilities (or, rarely, as assets). Such obligations could include forward purchase contracts or written put options on an issuer's equity shares that are to be physically settled or net cash settled.

Certain obligations to issue a variable number of shares are financial instruments that embody unconditional obligations, or financial instruments other than outstanding shares that embody conditional obligations, that the issuers must or may settle by issuing variable numbers of equity shares. These obligations also must be classified as liabilities (or, rarely, as assets) if, at inception, the monetary values of the obligations are based solely or predominantly on any one of the following:

1. A fixed monetary amount known at inception (e.g., a payable settleable with a variable number of the issuer's equity shares);
2. Variations in something other than the fair value of the issuer's equity shares (e.g., a financial instrument indexed to the S&P 500 and settleable with a variable number of the issuer's equity shares); or
3. Variations inversely related to changes in the fair value of the issuer's equity shares (e.g., a written put option that could be net share settled).

If a freestanding instrument is composed of more than one option or forward contract and one of those contracts embodies an obligation to repurchase the issuer's shares that require or may require settlement by a transfer of assets, the financial instrument is a liability. In addition, if a freestanding instrument composed of more than one option or forward contract includes an obligation to issue shares, the various component obligations must be analyzed to determine if any of them would be obligations under ASC 480. If one or more would be obligations under this standard, then judgment must be used to determine if the monetary value of the obligations that would be liabilities is collectively predominant over the other component liabilities. If so, the instrument is a liability. If not, the instrument is outside the scope of ASC 480. Following is a list of examples of these types of financial instruments:

- Puttable warrants
- Warrant for shares that can be put by the holder immediately after exercise
- Warrant that allows the holder to exercise the warrant or put the warrant back to the issuer on the exercise date for a variable number of shares with a fixed monetary value
- Forward contract in which the number of shares to be issued depends on the issuer's share price on the settlement date
- Warrant with a "liquidity make-whole" put to issue additional shares to the holder if the sales price of the shares when later sold is less than the share price when the warrant is exercised

- Warrant that allows the holder to exercise the warrant or, if contingent event does not occur, put the warrant back to the issuer on the exercise date for a variable number of shares with a fixed monetary value.

Put options. ASC 480-10-55 provides examples of put options that are subject to only cash payment and also of those that could be settled by an issuance of stock. The former case is straightforward: the instrument must be classified as a liability if the share price at the reporting date is such that a cash payment would be demanded by the holders of the puttable warrants. If the share price at that date is such that exercise of the warrant would be elected over exercise of the put option, then the warrant would be included in equity, not in liabilities. In other words, classification would depend on current stock price and could change from period to period, although ASC 480-10-55 is not explicit on this point.

Other put arrangements call for settlement in shares. That is, if advantageous to do so, the warrant holders exercise the warrants and acquire shares, but if the strike price has not been attained at expiration date, the put is exercised and the reporting entity would have to settle, but instead of paying cash it would issue shares having an aggregate value equal to the put amount. Thus, at inception, the number of shares that the puttable warrant obligates the reporting entity to issue can vary, and the instrument must be examined under the provisions of ASC 480 that deal with obligations to issue a variable number of shares. The facts and circumstances must be considered in judging whether the *monetary value* of the obligation to issue a number of shares that varies is predominantly based on a fixed monetary amount known at inception; if so, it is a liability under ASC 480.

Warrant. Yet another variation illustrated by ASC 480-10-55 is the warrant for the purchase of shares, where the shares are puttable. The holder can exercise the warrant and then immediately force the issuer to repurchase the shares issued. The price at which the shares could be put would be defined in the warrant, and the likelihood that the put option would be exercised would vary with the market value of the shares. Obviously, if the shares acquired by exercise of the warrant had a greater market value than the put price, the put would not be invoked. Accordingly, whether these warrants would be classified as equity or liability would depend on the market value of the underlying shares, and this could change from the date of one statement of financial position to that of the next. However, if the shares to be issued upon warrant exercise were to have a mandatory redemption feature, then the warrants would be reportable as liabilities in any case.

ASC 480-10-55 offers several other examples, illustrating more complex features that may be found in stock purchase warrants which, depending on circumstances, might necessitate classification as liabilities in the statement of financial position.

The standard does not apply to or affect the timing of recognition of financial instruments issued as contingent consideration in a business combination, nor the measurement guidance for contingent consideration, as set forth in ASC 805. It also does not affect accounting for stock-based compensation or ESOP plans (ASC 718).

Initial and Subsequent Measurements

Mandatorily redeemable financial instruments are reported as liabilities and are initially recognized at fair value. Mandatorily redeemable financial instruments are subsequently remeasured using fair value, with any adjustments included in the periodic determination of income. In general, the value of mandatorily redeemable financial instruments will be accreted over time and the accretion will be treated as interest expense. The method of determining subsequent fair values corresponds to that set forth in the following paragraph.

Forward contracts that require physical settlement by repurchase of a fixed number of the issuer's equity shares in exchange for cash are measured initially at the fair value of the shares, as adjusted for any consideration or unstated rights or privileges. Equity is reduced by this same amount. Fair value in this context may be determined by reference to the amount of cash that would be paid under the conditions specified in the contract if the shares were repurchased immediately. Alternatively, the settlement amount can be discounted at the rate implicit at inception after taking into account any consideration or unstated rights or privileges that may have affected the terms of the transaction.

Subsequent measurement can be effected by either

- accretion (which is feasible only if the amount to be paid and the settlement date are both fixed), or
- by determining the amount of cash that would be paid under the conditions specified in the contract if settlement occurred at the reporting date (useful when either the amount to be paid or the settlement date vary based on defined conditions and terms).

In either case, the change from the amount reported in the prior period is interest expense. If accretion is appropriate, the instruments are to be measured subsequently at the present value of the amount to be paid at settlement, accruing interest cost using the rate implicit at inception.

Conditionally redeemable instruments, first classified as equity and transferred to liabilities when the condition is satisfied, are measured at fair value at that date, with no gain or loss being recognized from the reclassification. For earnings per share computation purposes, the amount of common shares that are to be redeemed or repurchased are excluded for both basic and diluted calculations.

Gain or loss on retirement of redeemable instruments. If mandatorily redeemable preferred or common stock is acquired prior to the mandatory redemption date, the financial statement implications are the same as when debt is retired. Since the mandatorily redeemable shares are categorized, for financial reporting purposes, as liabilities, not equity, the usual prohibition against reporting gain or loss on capital transactions (such as retirement of treasury stock) would not be applicable. Rather, the guidance under ASC 470-50 governing debt retirement would be pertinent. Specifically, if the price paid to redeem the shares differs from the carrying value of the shares, the difference would be a gain or loss to be reported in the current period's earnings.

FASB decided against imposing new requirements to bifurcate embedded derivatives. Furthermore, to prevent the provisions of the new standard from being circumvented by the insertion for nonsubstantive or minimal features into financial instruments, any such features are to be disregarded in applying ASC 480's classification provisions.

Mandatorily Redeemable Shares and Similar Instruments

Although mandatorily redeemable instruments may be equity in legal form, ASC 480 requires that they be reported as liabilities rather than equity instruments to the extent they represent the issuers obligation to transfer assets. Payments or accruals of "dividends" and other amounts to be paid to holders of such shares are to be reported as interest expense. The only exception to those rules is for shares that are required to be redeemed only upon the liquidation or termination of the issuer, since the fundamental "going concern assumption" underlying GAAP financial statements means that such an eventuality is not given recognition.

For all other financial instruments that are mandatorily redeemable, the classification, measurement, and disclosure provisions of ASC 480 were deferred *indefinitely* for nonpublic entities, pending further FASB action.[1]

Financial statement preparers should not presume that this application of ASC 480 will be rescinded, although that remains a possibility. There would not appear to be a conceptually sound argument for why public entities having such mandatorily redeemable instruments would be required to report these as liabilities, while granting nonpublic ones an exemption.

Note: as set forth in ASC 480-10-65, that deferral of the disclosure requirements under ASC 480, as described above, does not remove the requirements under ASC 505-10-50, which requires the disclosure of information about the pertinent rights and privileges of the various securities outstanding, including mandatory redemption requirements.

ASC 480-10-65 has also deferred indefinitely the *measurement* provisions of ASC 480, both as to the parent in consolidated financial statements and as to the subsidiary that issued the instruments that resulted in mandatorily redeemable noncontrolling interests before November 5, 2003. For those instruments, the measurement guidance for redeemable shares and noncontrolling interests under GAAP (e.g., ASC 480-10-S99) continues to apply during the deferral period. However, the *classification* provisions were not deferred.

The SEC subsequently further clarified the interaction between ASC 480 and D-98 for conditionally redeemable shares. Accounting for these shares, prior to the date on which the condition is first met, is not governed by ASC 480, but for a publicly held company the shares would not be permitted to be included in equity. A "mezzanine" classification would be acceptable until the condition is met, at which point reclassification as liabilities is necessary. Reclassification is akin to redemption, to be recognized at fair value via a charge or credit to equity, with concomitant impact on earnings per share computations in the period when the reclassification takes place.

If on the date of adoption the redemption price is greater than the book value of the shares, the company would *recognize a liability* for the redemption price of the shares that are subject to mandatory redemption, reclassifying amounts previously recognized in equity accounts. The difference between the redemption price and amounts previously recorded in equity is reported on the income statement as a cumulative effect transition adjustment loss. If the redemption price exceeds the company's equity balance, the cumulative transition loss should be reported as an excess of liabilities over assets (a deficit in the stockholders' equity section). In the opposite case, it is reported as an excess of assets over liabilities (i.e., as positive equity).

Shares are mandatorily redeemable if the issuer has an unconditional obligation to redeem the shares by transferring its assets at a specified or determinable date (or dates) or upon an event certain to occur (for example, the death of the holder). The obligation to transfer assets must be unconditional—that is, there is no specified event that is outside the control of the issuer that will release the issuer from its obligation. Thus, callable preferred shares, which are redeemable at the issuer's option, and convertible preferred shares, which are redeemable at the holder's option, are not mandatorily redeemable shares.

ASC 480 requires this reporting for all mandatorily redeemable financial instruments, unless the redemption is required to occur only upon the liquidation or termination of the reporting entity. The exception exists because the fundamental *going concern* assumption

---

[1] The main source of ASC 480 is FAS 150. Soon after the release of FAS 150, constituents raised questions about certain types of mandatorily redeemable instruments. In response, the FASB issued FSP FAS 150-3, which deferred the effective date of applying the provision of FAS 150 for mandatorily redeemable financial instruments of certain nonpublic entities and certain mandatorily redeemable noncontrolling interests. Per ASC 480-10-65, that deferral is currently in effect.

underlying GAAP financial reporting would be violated if a classification was imposed in GAAP financial statements that presumed or was conditioned on the reporting entity's cessation as a going concern. However, the exception under ASC 480 does not extend to mandatorily redeemable financial instruments of a consolidated subsidiary, in the consolidated financial statements of its parent entity. Since it is the *going concern* status of the reporting entity (i.e., the parent) that is of significance, the mandatory redemption feature of the subsidiary's instruments, albeit conditional, is to be reported consistent with ASC 480's provisions.

If the redemption price of mandatorily redeemable shares is greater than the book value of those shares, the company should report the excess as a deficit (equity), even though the mandatorily redeemable shares are reported as a liability.

After issuance, the amount of the liability for the mandatorily redeemable shares should be adjusted using the effective interest method if both the amount to be paid and the settlement date are fixed. If either the amount to be paid or the settlement date varies based on specified conditions, the liability is measured subsequently at the amount of cash that would be paid under the conditions specified in the contract if settlement occurred at the reporting date, recognizing the resulting change in that amount from the previous reporting date as interest cost.

If shares have a conditional redemption feature, which requires the issuer to redeem the shares by transferring its assets upon an event not certain to occur, the shares become mandatorily redeemable—and, therefore, become a liability—if that event occurs, the event becomes certain to occur, or the condition is otherwise resolved. The fair value of the shares is reclassified as a liability, and equity is reduced by that amount, recognizing no gain or loss.

Note that when redemption value is based on a notion of fair value, defined in the underlying agreement, the initial recognition of the difference between this computed amount and the corresponding book value will almost inevitably result in a surplus or deficit. In other words, the promised redemption amounts, measured at transition and again at the date of each statement of financial position, will not equal the book value of the equity which is subject to redemption. This discrepancy must be reflected in stockholders' equity, even though the redeemable equity is reclassified to a liability. In effect, the redemption arrangement will result in either a residual in equity (assuming that a redemption was to fully occur at the date of the statement of financial position) or a deficit, because the agreement provides that redeeming shareholders are entitled to more or less than their respective pro rata shares of the book value of their equity claims. If the redemption price of mandatorily redeemable shares is greater than the book value of those shares, the company should report the excess as a deficit (equity), even though the mandatorily redeemable shares are reported as a liability.

Common shares that are mandatorily redeemable are not included in the denominator when computing basic or diluted earnings per share. If any amounts, including contractual (accumulated) dividends, attributable to shares that are to be redeemed or repurchased have not been recognized as interest expense, those amounts are deducted in computing income available to common shareholders (the numerator of the calculation), consistently with the "two-class" method set forth in ASC 260. The redemption requirements for mandatorily redeemable shares for each of the next five years are required to be disclosed in the notes to the financial statements.

ASC 480-10-S99 addresses concerns raised by the SEC regarding the financial statement classification and measurement of securities subject to mandatory redemption requirements or whose redemption is outside the control of the issuer. Questions also arose regarding disclosures needed to comply with SEC requirements.

These rules require securities with redemption features that are not solely within the control of the issuer to be classified outside of permanent equity. The SEC staff believes that all of the events that could trigger redemption should be evaluated separately and that the possibility that *any* triggering event that is not *solely* within the control of the issuer could occur—without regard to probability—would require the security to be classified outside of permanent equity. Determining whether an equity security is redeemable at the option of the holder or upon the occurrence of an event that is solely within the control of the issuer can be complex. Accordingly, all of the individual facts and circumstances should be considered in determining how an equity security should be classified.

ASC 480-10-S99 offers several examples of complex fact patterns to help registrants in determining whether classification as a liability or as equity would be appropriate.

For example, if a preferred security has a redemption provision stating that it may be called by the issuer upon an affirmative vote by the majority of its board of directors, but the preferred security holders control a majority of the votes of the board of directors through direct representation on the board of directors or through other rights, the preferred security is effectively redeemable at the option of the holder and its classification outside of permanent equity is required. Thus, in assessing such situations, any provision that requires approval by the board of directors cannot be assumed to be within the control of the reporting entity itself. All of the relevant facts and circumstances would have to be considered.

As another example, if a security with a deemed liquidation clause that provides that the security becomes redeemable if the stockholders of the reporting entity (those immediately prior to a merger or consolidation) hold, immediately after such merger or consolidation, stock representing less than a majority of the voting power of the outstanding stock of the surviving corporation, this would not be permanent equity. A purchaser could acquire a majority of the voting power of the outstanding stock, without company approval, thereby triggering redemption.

Securities with provisions that allow the holders to be paid upon occurrence of events that are solely within the issuer's control should thus always be classified outside of permanent equity. Such events include:

1. The failure to have a registration statement declared effective by the SEC by a designated date
2. The failure to maintain compliance with debt covenants
3. The failure to achieve specified earnings targets
4. A reduction in the issuer's credit rating.

ASC 480-10-S99 notes that if a reporting entity issues preferred shares that are conditionally redeemable (e.g., at the holder's option or upon the occurrence of an uncertain event not solely within the company's control), the shares are not within the scope of ASC 480 because there is no unconditional obligation to redeem the shares by transferring assets at a specified or determinable date or upon an event certain to occur. If the uncertain event occurs, the condition is resolved, or the event becomes certain to occur, then the shares become mandatorily redeemable under FAS 150 and would require reclassification to a liability. Under SEC rules, however, these shares cannot be included in permanent equity, and thus would be displayed as a "mezzanine" equity category. Mezzanine capital is an SEC reporting concept that has no analog under GAAP rules.

ASC 480 requires that the issuer measure that liability initially at fair value and reduce equity by the amount of that initial measure, recognizing no gain or loss. ASC 480-10-S99 observes that this reclassification of shares to a liability is akin to the redemption of such shares by issuance of debt. Similar to the accounting for the redemption of preferred shares, to the extent that the fair value of the liability differs from the carrying amount of the preferred shares, upon reclassification that difference should be deducted from or added to net earnings available to common shareholders in the calculation of earnings per share.

Obligations to Issue Shares

If an entity enters into a contract that requires it or permits it at its discretion to issue a variable number of shares upon settlement, that contract is recognized as a liability if at inception the monetary value of the obligation is based solely or predominantly on one of the following criteria:

1. A fixed monetary amount known at inception (e.g., a $100,000 payable can be settled by issuing shares worth $100,000 at the then-current market value).
2. An amount that varies based on something other than the fair value of the issuer's equity shares (for example, a financial instrument indexed to the Dow that can be settled by issuing shares worth the index-adjusted amount at the then-current market value).
3. Variations inversely related to changes in the fair value of the entity's equity shares (i.e., a written put option that could be net share settled).

Contracts that meet one of the above criteria are recognized at fair value at the date of issuance and at every measurement date afterwards. The changes in the fair value are recognized in earnings unless the contract falls within the scope of ASC 718 and that statement requires the changes to be recognized elsewhere.

Obligations to Repurchase Shares

If an entity (the issuer) enters into a contract that obligates it to transfer assets to either repurchase its own equity shares or to pay an amount that is indexed to the price of its own shares, the contract is to be reported as a liability (or in certain cases, as an asset, if the fair value of the contract is favorable to the issuer). Examples of that type of financial instrument are written put options on the option writer's (issuer's) equity shares, and forward contracts to repurchase an issuer's own equity shares if those instruments require physical or net cash settlement. (If the repurchase obligation is a redemption feature of common or preferred shares issued, see "Mandatorily Redeemable Shares and Similar Instruments".)

ASC 480 requires that an issuer classify a financial instrument that is within its scope as a liability (or as an asset in some circumstances) because that financial instrument embodies an obligation of the issuer. ASC 480 addresses three types of freestanding financial instruments that embody obligations of the issuer: mandatorily redeemable financial instruments, obligations to repurchase the issuer's equity shares by transferring assets, and certain obligations to issue a variable number of shares. Instruments within the scope of ASC 480 should be classified and measured in accordance with ASC 480 per ASC 480-10-S99.

Written put options are measured initially and subsequently at fair value. Forward contracts are initially measured at the fair value of the shares to be repurchased (adjusted by any consideration or unstated rights or privileges) if the contract requires physical settlement for cash. The offset to the liability entry is a debit to equity. Subsequent to issuance, forward contracts are remeasured in one of two ways.

1. If both the amount to be paid and the settlement date are fixed, the contract is measured at the present value of the amount to be paid, computed using the rate implicit in the contract at inception.
2. If either the amount to be paid or the settlement date varies based on specified conditions, the contract is measured at the amount of cash that would be paid under the conditions specified in the contract if settlement occurred at the reporting date.

Under either measure, the amount of the change from the previous reporting date is recognized as interest cost.

An entity that has entered into a forward contract that requires physical settlement by repurchase of a fixed number of its equity shares of common stock in exchange for cash does not include those shares in the denominator when computing basic or diluted earnings per share. If any amounts, including contractual (accumulated) dividends, attributable to shares that are to be redeemed or repurchased have not been recognized as interest expense, those amounts are deducted in computing income available to common shareholders (the numerator of the calculation), consistently with the "two-class" method set forth in ASC 260.

Some corporations and partnerships, primarily closely held ones, issue shares or units that are redeemed at the death of the holder. If those shares or units represent the only shares or units in the entity, the entity reports those instruments as liabilities and describes them in its statement of financial position as shares (or units) subject to mandatory redemption, to distinguish them from other liabilities. The classification is unaffected by any insurance policies that the entity may have on the holders' lives. The entity presents interest expense and payments to holders of those instruments separately, apart from interest and payments to other creditors in its statements of income and cash flows. The entity also discloses that the instruments are mandatorily redeemable upon the death of the holders.

Application of ASC 480

Example—Obligations that require net share settlement—monetary value changes in the same direction as the fair value of the issuer's equity shares

Tyler Corp. grants 10,000 stock appreciation rights that entitle the holder to receive a number of equity shares to be determined based on the change in the fair value of Tyler's equity shares. At the date of the grant, the fair value of Tyler's equity shares is $25 per share. Subsequently, the fair value of Tyler's equity shares increases to $28 per share. Tyler is thus required to issue shares worth $30,000 [($28 – $25) × 10,000], or 1,072 shares.

This financial instrument contains an obligation to issue a number of equity shares with a value equal to the appreciation of 10,000 equity shares. The number of shares to be issued, therefore, is not fixed. Classification will depend on whether the monetary value changes in the same direction as changes in the fair value of the equity shares. In this example, the monetary value changes in the same direction as changes in the fair value of the equity shares.

The increase in fair value of the equity shares from $25 to $28 resulted in an increase in the monetary value of the obligation from $0 to $30,000. If the fair value of the equity shares increases further, for example to $30 per share, the monetary value of the obligation increases as well to $50,000 [($30 – $25) × 10,000]. If the fair value of the equity shares then decreases, for example from $30 to $27, the monetary value of the obligation decreases to $20,000 [($27 –$25) × 10,000]. Because the monetary value of the obligation changes in the same direction as the change in fair value of the issuer's equity shares, this obligation does not qualify as a liability and the equity classification is prescribed.

Example—Obligations that require net share settlement—monetary value changes in opposite direction as the fair value of the issuer's equity shares

Harrison Corp. issues equity shares to Middleboro Co. for $5 million (1 million shares at $5 each). Simultaneously, Harrison enters into a financial instrument with Middleboro, under the terms of which, if the per share value of Harrison' shares is greater than $5 on a specified date, Middleboro will transfer shares of Harrison with a value of [(share price – $5) × 1,000,000] to Harrison. If the per share is less than $5 on a specified date, Harrison transfers shares of its own equity with a value of [($5 – share price) × 1,000,000] to Middleboro.

The 1,000,000 shares issued to Middleboro do not embody an obligation. They also do not convey to the issuer the right to receive cash or another financial instrument from the holder, or to exchange other financial instruments on potentially favorable terms with the holder. Therefore, the equity classification criteria are met and the component is classified as equity.

The financial instrument issued to Middleboro contains an obligation to issue a variable number of equity shares if the fair value of Harrison' equity shares is less than $5 on a certain date. As a result, the classification will depend upon whether the monetary value is equal to the change in fair value of a fixed number of equity shares, and whether the changes are in the same direction as the fair value of the equity shares.

The first criterion is met because the monetary value of the obligation is equal to the appreciation of a fixed number (1,000,000) of the issuer's equity shares. However, the monetary value of the obligation changes in a direction opposite to the changes in the fair value of the issuer's equity shares. If the fair value of the equity shares increases, the monetary value of the obligation decreases (and may in fact be reduced to zero or result in a receivable from the counterparty). If the fair value of the equity shares decreases, the monetary value of the obligation increases. Because the monetary value of the obligation does not change in the same direction as the fair value of the equity shares, criterion (b) is not met; therefore, the obligation is not classified as equity.

Example—Written put options that require physical settlement

Carlyle Corp. writes a put option that allows a holder, Yetta Co., to put 200 shares of Carlyle stock to Carlyle for $33 per share on a specified date. The put option requires physical settlement (delivery of the shares and payment therefore). Because the put option requires Carlyle to transfer assets (cash) to settle the obligation, the component is classified as a liability.

Example—Forward purchase contract that requires physical or net cash settlement

In a fact pattern slightly at variance with the preceding example, Carlyle Corp. enters into a freestanding forward purchase arrangement with Yetta Co., under which Yetta is to transfer 200 shares of Carlyle stock to Carlyle for $33 per share on a specified date. The forward purchase agreement requires physical settlement (delivery of the shares and payment therefore). Because the forward purchase arrangement requires Carlyle to transfer assets (cash) to settle the obligation, the component is classified as a liability. The same result would hold if the contract called for a net cash settlement. While a put option (the preceding example) requires that the liability be initially recorded, and subsequently remeasured, at fair value, the forward purchase arrangement is to be recorded at fair value, and then accreted to the present value of the forward purchase price at the date of each statement of financial position, using the implicit interest rate given by the initial fair value.

Example—Written put option that require net share settlement

Dragoon Corp. writes a put option that allows the holder, Zitti Corp., to put 200 shares of Dragoon stock to Dragoon for $44 a share on a specified date. The put requires net share settlement (i.e., shares having a value equal to the spread between the option price and fair value must be delivered in settlement). Assume the fair value of the shares at the date the put is issued is $44. The monetary value of the obligation at that time is therefore zero.

Subsequently, the fair value of Dragoon's equity shares decreases to $36 and the put option is exercised. At this point, the monetary value of the obligation is $1,600 [200 shares × ($44 – $36)]. Dragoon would be required to issue about 45 shares ($1,600 divided by $36). The monetary value of the obligation increased because of a decrease in the fair value of Dragoon's equity shares. Because changes in the monetary value of the obligation are not in the same direction as changes in the fair value of Dragoon's equity shares, the component is not classified as equity, but rather as a liability. The contract is measured initially and subsequently at fair value, with changes in fair value recognized in current earnings.

Example—Unconditional obligation that must be either redeemed for cash or settled by issuing shares

If the reporting entity issues financial instruments that do not require the transfer of assets to settle the obligation but, instead, unconditionally require the issuer to settle the obligation either by transferring assets or by issuing a variable number of its equity shares, this may or may not create a liability. Because such instruments do not require the issuer to settle by transfer of assets, they are not automatically classified as liabilities under ASC 480. However, those instruments may still be classified as liabilities, if other stipulated conditions are met.

Assume that Zylog Corp. issues one million shares of cumulative preferred stock for cash equal to the stock's liquidation preference of $25 per share. Under the terms, Zylog is required either to redeem the shares on the third anniversary of the issuance, for the issuance price plus any accrued but unpaid dividends, either in cash or by issuing sufficient shares of its common stock to be worth $25 per share. This does not represent an unconditional obligation to transfer assets, and therefore the preferred stock is not a mandatorily redeemable financial instrument as that term is defined in ASC 480. However, the stock is still a liability, because the preferred shares represent an unconditional obligation that the issuer may settle by issuing a variable number of its equity shares with monetary value that is fixed and known at inception. Because the preferred shares are liabilities, payments to holders are reported as interest cost, and accrued but not-yet-paid payments are part of the liability for the shares.

Example of mandatorily redeemable preferred shares

On June 1, 20X1, Verde Corporation issues 1,000 shares of mandatorily redeemable 5% preferred stock with a par value $100 for $110,330. The shares are redeemable at $150 on May 31, 20X8. At issuance, Verde Corporation recognizes a liability of $110,330.

Example of shares that are mandatorily redeemable at the death of the holder

Mike and Ike are equal shareholders in M&I's Auto Repair, Inc. Upon the death of either shareholder, the corporation will redeem shares of the deceased for half of the book value of the corporation. The following information would be disclosed in the notes to the financial statements:

All of the corporation's shares are subject to mandatory redemption upon death of the shareholders, and are thus reported as a liability. The liability amount consists of:

Common stock—$100 par value, 1,000 shares authorized, issued and outstanding	$100,000
Undistributed earnings attributable to those shares	50,000
Accumulated other comprehensive income	(2,000)
Total liability	$148,000

Example of mandatorily redeemable preferred shares (continued)

The effective interest rate is 8.5%. Continuing the previous example, of Verde Corporation, it would recognize the following annual interest expense and liability amounts:

	Cash paid	Interest at 8.5% annually	Change in liability	Ending liability
06/01/13				110,330
05/31/14	5,000	9,378	4,378	114,708
05/31/15	5,000	9,750	4,750	119,458
05/31/16	5,000	10,154	5,154	124,612
05/31/17	5,000	10,592	5,592	130,204
05/31/18	5,000	11,067	6,068	136,271
05/31/19	5,000	11,583	6,583	142,854
05/31/20	155,000	12,146	(142,854)	0

The entry to record the first "dividend" payment would be

Interest expense	9,378	
Liability		4,378
Cash		5,000

Example of a contract with a fixed monetary amount known at inception

Numero Uno Corp. purchases equipment worth $100,000 and agrees to pay $110,000 at the end of one year or, at its option, to issue shares worth $112,000. The contract is recognized as a liability at issuance of $100,000. Subsequent to issuance the liability is remeasured at the fair value of the contract, which would be the accreted value of the cash payment amount ($110,000).

Example of a written put option on a fixed number of shares

Numero Dos Corp. writes a put allowing the purchaser to sell 100 shares of Numero Dos common stock at $20 per share in six months. The purchaser pays Numero Dos $300 for the right to put the 100 shares. Numero Dos's common stock is currently trading at $23. Numero Dos reports a liability of $300. The liability is subsequently remeasured at the fair value of the put option.

Example of a forward contract with a variable settlement date

Numero Tres Corp. enters into a contract to purchase 200 shares of its subsidiary at $25 in two years. However, if the holder of the shares dies before the settlement date, Numero Tres agrees to purchase the shares at the present value of $25 at the settlement date computed using the then-current prime rate. The shares are currently trading at $22. The liability to repurchase shares is initially reported at $4,400. At each subsequent measurement date, Numero Tres would adjust the liability to the present value of $25 at settlement date using the discount rate implicit in the contract, unless the holder of the shares had died. If the holder of the shares had died, Numero Tres would adjust the liability to the present value of $25 at settlement date using the then-current prime rate. For example, if one year from issuance date the holder is still alive, the liability would be adjusted to $4,690 using the 6.6% rate implicit in the agreement. The adjustment amount of $290 would be charged to interest expense. If instead the holder had died and the prime rate was 5%, the liability would be adjusted to $4,762 ($5,000/1.05) and the adjustment of $362 would be charged to interest expense.

35 ASC 505 EQUITY

PERSPECTIVE AND ISSUES

Subtopics

ASC 505 consists of five subtopics:

- ASC 505-10, *Overall*, provides guidance on issues not addressed in the other ASC 505 subtopics

- ASC 505-20, *Stock Dividends and Stock Splits,* provides guidance for the recipient and the issuer
- ASC 505-30, *Treasury Stock,* provides guidance on an entity's repurchase of its own shares of outstanding common stock and the subsequent retirement of those shares
- ASC 505-50, *Equity-based Payments to Nonemployees,* provides guidance for the issuer and the recipient
- ASC 505-60, *Spinoffs and Reverse Spinoffs,* provides guidance on the distribution of nonmonetary assets in spinoff transactions.

Scope and Scope Exceptions

Guidance in ASC 505 generally applies to all entities. Specific exceptions follow.

ASC 505-20 does not apply to distribution or issuance of shares of another corporation, shares of a different class, rights to subscribe for additional shares, and shares of the same class where each shareholder is given an election to receive cash or shares.

ASC 505-50 does not apply to share-based payment transactions in exchange for goods or services and modifications of existing arrangements. The guidance does not apply to transaction with employees, ESOPs, and equity instruments issued to a lender or investor that provides financing to the issuer or issued in a business combination.

ASC 505-60 does not apply to nonmonetary assets that do not constitute a business.

Overview

CON 6 defines stockholders' equity as the residual interest in the assets of an entity after deducting its liabilities. Stockholders' equity is comprised of all capital contributed to the entity plus its accumulated earnings less any distributions that have been made. There are three major categories within the equity section: paid-in capital, retained earnings, and other comprehensive income. Paid-in capital represents equity contributed by owners. Retained earnings represents the sum of all earnings less those not retained in the business (i.e., what has been paid out as dividends). Other comprehensive income represents changes in net assets, other than by means of transactions with owners, which have not been reported in earnings under applicable GAAP rules (e.g., accumulated translation gains or losses).

Earnings are not generated by transactions in an entity's own equity (e.g., by the issuance, reacquisition, or reissuance of its common or preferred shares). Depending on the laws of the jurisdiction of incorporation, distributions to shareholders may be subject to various limitations, such as to the amount of retained (accounting basis) earnings.

A major objective of the accounting for stockholders' equity is the adequate disclosure of the sources from which the capital was derived. For this reason, a number of different paid-in capital accounts may be presented in the statement of financial position. The rights of each class of shareholder must also be disclosed. Where shares are reserved for future issuance, such as under the terms of stock option plans, this fact must also be made known.

DEFINITIONS OF TERMS

Source: ASC 505 Glossary Sections

Bankruptcy Code. A federal statute, enacted October 1, 1979, as title 11 of the United States Code by the Bankruptcy Reform Act of 1978, that applies to all cases filed on or after its enactment and that provides the basis for the current federal bankruptcy system.

Business. An integrated set of activities and assets that is capable of being conducted and managed for the purpose of providing a return in the form of dividends, lower costs, or other economic benefits directly to investors or other owners, members, or participants.

Claim. As defined by Section 101(4) of the Bankruptcy Code, a right to payment, regardless of whether the right is reduced to judgment, liquidated, unliquidated, fixed, contingent, matured, unmatured, disputed, undisputed, legal, secured, or unsecured, or a right to an equitable remedy for breach of performance if such breach results in a right to payment, regardless of whether the right is reduced to a fixed, contingent, matured, unmatured, disputed, undisputed, secured, or unsecured right.

Component of an Entity. A component of an entity comprises operations and cash flows that can be clearly distinguished, operationally and for financial reporting purposes, from the rest of the entity. A component of an entity may be a reportable segment or an operating segment, a reporting unit, a subsidiary, or an asset group.

Counterparty Performance Conditions. Conditions that relate to the achievement of a specified performance target, for example, attaining a specified increase in market share for a specified product. A counterparty performance condition might pertain either to the performance of the entity as a whole or to some part of the entity, such as a division.

Employee. An individual over whom the grantor of a share-based compensation award exercises or has the right to exercise sufficient control to establish an employer-employee relationship based on common law as illustrated in case law and currently under U.S. Internal Revenue Service (IRS) Revenue Ruling 87-41. A reporting entity based in a foreign jurisdiction would determine whether an employee-employer relationship exists based on the pertinent laws of that jurisdiction. Accordingly, a grantee meets the definition of an employee if the grantor consistently represents that individual to be an employee under common law. The definition of an employee for payroll tax purposes under the U.S. Internal Revenue Code includes common law employees. Accordingly, a grantor that classifies a grantee potentially subject to U.S. payroll taxes as an employee also must represent that individual as an employee for payroll tax purposes (unless the grantee is a leased employee as described below). A grantee does not meet the definition of an employee solely because the grantor represents that individual as an employee for some, but not all, purposes. For example, a requirement or decision to classify a grantee as an employee for U.S. payroll tax purposes does not, by itself, indicate that the grantee is an employee because the grantee also must be an employee of the grantor under common law.

A leased individual is deemed to be an employee of the lessee if all of the following requirements are met:

a. The leased individual qualifies as a common law employee of the lessee, and the lessor is contractually required to remit payroll taxes on the compensation paid to the leased individual for the services provided to the lessee.
b. The lessor and lessee agree in writing to all of the following conditions related to the leased individual:
    1. The lessee has the exclusive right to grant stock compensation to the individual for the employee service to the lessee.
    2. The lessee has a right to hire, fire, and control the activities of the individual. (The lessor also may have that right.)
    3. The lessee has the exclusive right to determine the economic value of the services performed by the individual (including wages and the number of units and value of stock compensation granted).

4. The individual has the ability to participate in the lessee's employee benefit plans, if any, on the same basis as other comparable employees of the lessee.
5. The lessee agrees to and remits to the lessor funds sufficient to cover the complete compensation, including all payroll taxes, of the individual on or before a contractually agreed upon date or dates.

A nonemployee director does not satisfy this definition of employee. Nevertheless, nonemployee directors acting in their role as members of a board of directors are treated as employees if those directors were elected by the employer's shareholders or appointed to a board position that will be filled by shareholder election when the existing term expires. However, that requirement applies only to awards granted to nonemployee directors for their services as directors. Awards granted to those individuals for other services shall be accounted for as awards to nonemployees.

Fair value. The price that would be received to sell an asset or pad to transfer a liability in an orderly transaction between market participants at the measurement date.

Fair value. The amount at which an asset (or liability) could be brought (or incurred) or sold (or settled) in a current transaction between willing parties, that is, other than in a forced or liquidation sale. (ASC 505-50-20)

Market Condition. A condition affecting the exercise price, exercisability, or other pertinent factors used in determining the fair value of an award under a share-based payment arrangement that relates to the achievement of either of the following:

a. A specified price of the issuer's shares or a specified amount of intrinsic value indexed solely to the issuer's shares
b. A specified price of the issuer's shares in terms of a similar (or index of similar) equity security (securities). The term similar as used in this definition refers to an equity security of another entity that has the same type of residual rights. For example, common stock of one entity generally would be similar to the common stock of another entity for this purpose.

Operating Segment. A component of a public entity. See Section 280-10-50 for additional guidance on the definition of an operating segment.

Participation Rights. Contractual rights of security holders to receive dividends or returns from the security issuer's profits, cash flows, or returns on investments.

Preferred Stock. A security that has preferential rights compared to common stock.

Reload Feature and Reload Option. A reload feature provides for automatic grants of additional options whenever an employee exercises previously granted options using the entity's shares, rather than cash, to satisfy the exercise price. At the time of exercise using shares, the employee is automatically granted a new option, called a reload option, for the shares used to exercise the previous option.

Reporting Unit. The level of reporting at which goodwill is tested for impairment. A reporting unit is an operating segment or one level below an operating segment (also known as a component).

Reverse Spinoff. A spinoff of a subsidiary to an entity's shareholders in which the legal form of the transaction does not match its substance such that the new legal spun-off entity (the spinnee) will be the continuing entity.

Security. The evidence of debt or ownership or a related right. It includes options and warrants as well as debt and stock.

Share-based payment (or compensation) transaction. A transaction under a share-based payment arrangement, including a transaction in which an entity acquires goods or services because related parties or other holders of economic interest in that entity awards a share-based payment to an employee or other supplier of goods or services for the entity's benefit. Also called share-based compensation transactions.

Spinoff. The transfer of assets that constitute a business by an entity (the spinnor) into a new legal spun-off entity (the spinnee), followed by a distribution of the shares of the spinnee to its shareholders, without the surrender by the shareholders of any stock of the spinnor.

Stock dividend. An issuance by a corporation of its own common shares to its common shareholders without consideration and under conditions indicating that such action is prompted mainly by a desire to give the recipient shareholders some ostensibly separate evidence of a part of their respective interests in accumulated corporate earnings without distribution of cash or other property that the board of directors deems necessary or desirable to retain in the business. A stock dividend takes nothing from the property of the corporation and adds nothing to the interests of the stockholders; that is, the corporation's property is not diminished and the interests of the stockholders are not increased. The proportional interest of each shareholder remains the same.

Stock split. An issuance by a corporation of its own common shares to its common shareholders without consideration and under conditions indicating that such action is prompted mainly by a desire to increase the number of outstanding shares for the purpose of effecting a reduction in their unit market price and, thereby, of obtaining wider distribution and improved marketability of the shares. Sometimes called a stock split-up.

Terms of a share-based payment award. The contractual provisions that determine the nature and scope of a share-based payment award. For example, the exercise price of share options is one of the terms of an award of share options. The written terms of a share-based payment award and its related arrangement, if any, usually provide the best evidence of its terms, but an entity's past practice or other factors may indicate that some aspects of the substantive terms differ from the written terms. The substantive terms of a share-based payment award as those terms are mutually understood by the entity and a party (either an employee or a nonemployee) who receives the award provide the basis for determining the rights conveyed to a party and the obligations imposed on the issuer, regardless of how the award and related arrangement, if any, are structured.

CONCEPTS, RULES, AND EXAMPLES

Legal Capital and Capital Stock

Legal capital typically refers to that portion of the stockholders' investment in a corporation that is permanent in nature and represents assets that will continue to be available for the satisfaction of creditor's claims. Traditionally, legal capital was comprised of the aggregate par or stated value of common and preferred shares issued. In recent years, however, many states have eliminated the requirement that corporate shares have a designated par or stated value. States that have adopted provisions of the Model Business Corporation Act[1] have eliminated the distinction between par value and the amount contributed in excess of par.

The specific requirements regarding the preservation of legal capital are a function of the business corporation laws in the state in which a particular entity is incorporated. Accordingly, any action by the corporation that could affect the amount of legal capital (e.g., the

[1] The Model Business Corporation Act is a model created by the American Bar Association's Committee on Corporate Law and first published in 1950. It has since been extensively revised and is adopted in various forms in the majority of states.

payment of dividends in excess of retained earnings) must be considered in the context of the relevant laws of the state where the company is chartered.

Ownership interest in a corporation is made up of common and, optionally, preferred shares. The common shares represent the residual risk-taking ownership of the corporation after the satisfaction of all claims of creditors and senior classes of equity.

Preferred stock. Preferred shareholders are owners who have certain rights superior to those of common shareholders. Preferences as to earnings exist when the preferred shareholders have a stipulated dividend rate (expressed either as a dollar amount or as a percentage of the preferred stock's par or stated value). Preferences as to assets exist when the preferred shares have a stipulated liquidation value. If a corporation were to liquidate, these preferred holders would be paid a specific amount before the common shareholders would have a right to participate in any of the proceeds.

In practice, preferred shares are more likely to have preferences as to earnings than as to assets. Although unusual, preferred shares may have both preferential rights. Preferred shares may also have the following optional features:

- participation in earnings beyond the stipulated dividend rate;
- the cumulative feature, ensuring that dividends in arrears, if any, will be fully satisfied before the common shareholders participate in any earnings distribution; and
- convertibility or callability by the corporation.

Preferences must be disclosed adequately in the financial statements, either on the face of the statement of financial position or in the notes thereto.

In exchange for the preferences, the preferred shareholders' other rights or privileges are often limited. For instance, the right to vote may be restricted to common shareholders. The most important right denied to the preferred shareholders, however, is the right to participate without limitation in the earnings of the corporation. Thus, if the corporation has exceedingly large earnings for a particular period, most of these earnings would accrue to the benefit of the common shareholders. This statement is true even if the preferred stock is participating (a fairly uncommon feature) because participating preferred stock usually has some upper limitation placed upon the extent of participation.

Occasionally, several classes of stock will be categorized as common (e.g., Class A common, Class B common, etc.). Since there can be only one class of shares that represents the true residual risk-taking ownership in a corporation, it is clear that the other classes, even though described as common shareholders, must in fact have some preferential status. Typically, these preferences relate to voting rights. An example of this situation arises when a formerly closely held corporation sells shares to the public but gives the publicly held shares a disproportionately small capacity to exercise influence over the entity, thereby keeping control in the hands of the former majority owners even as they are reduced to the status of minority owners. The rights and responsibilities of each class of shareholder, even if described as common, must be fully disclosed in the financial statements.

Issuance of shares. The accounting for the sale of shares by a corporation depends upon whether the stock has a par or stated value. If there is a par or stated value, the amount of the proceeds representing the aggregate par or stated value is credited to the common or preferred stock account. The aggregate par or stated value is generally defined as legal capital not subject to distribution to shareholders. Proceeds in excess of par or stated value are credited to an additional paid-in capital account. The additional paid-in capital represents the amount in excess of the legal capital that may, under certain defined conditions, be distributed to shareholders.

A corporation selling stock below par value credits the capital stock account for the par value and debits an offsetting discount account for the difference between par value and the amount actually received. If the discount is on original issue capital stock, it serves to notify the actual and potential creditors of the contingent liability of those investors. As a practical matter, corporations avoid this problem by reducing par values to an arbitrarily low amount. This reduction in par eliminates the chance that shares would be sold for amounts below par.

Where the Model Business Corporation Act has been adopted or where corporation laws have been conformed to the guidelines of that Act, there is often no distinction made between par value and amounts in excess of par. In those jurisdictions, the entire proceeds from the sale of stock may be credited to the common stock account without distinction between the stock and the additional paid-in capital accounts. The following example illustrates these concepts:

Example—Treatment of par and no-par stock in a stock sale

Facts: A corporation sells 100,000 shares of $5 par common stock for $8 per share cash.

Cash	800,000	
Common stock		500,000
Additional paid-in capital		300,000

Facts: A corporation sells 100,000 shares of no-par common stock for $8 per share cash.

Cash	800,000	
Common stock		800,000

Preferred stock will often be assigned a par value because in many cases the preferential dividend rate is defined as a percentage of par value (e.g., 10%, $25 par value preferred stock will have a required annual dividend of $2.50).

Stock issued in exchange for property or services. If the shares in a corporation are issued in exchange for services or property rather than for cash, the transaction should be reflected at the fair value of the property or services received. If this information is not readily available, then the transaction should be recorded at the fair value of the shares that were issued. Where necessary, appraisals should be obtained in order to properly reflect the transaction. As a final resort, a valuation of the stock issued can be made by the board of directors.

Stock issued to employees for services. Stock issued to employees as compensation for services rendered should be accounted for at the fair value of the services performed, if determinable, or the value of the shares issued. If shares are given by a major shareholder directly to an employee for services performed for the entity, this exchange should be accounted for as a capital contribution to the company by the major shareholder and as compensation expense incurred by the company. Only when accounted for in this manner will there be conformity with the general principle that all costs incurred by an entity, including compensation, should be reflected in its financial statements.

Lump-sum sales. In certain instances, two or more classes of securities may be issued to investors as a unit (e.g., one share of preferred and two shares of common sold as a package). There are two methods of allocating the proceeds among the classes of stock:

- The proportional method and
- The incremental method

Where each of the classes of stock are publicly traded, the entity should use the proportional method. The proceeds from a unit offering should be allocated in proportion to the relative market values of the securities. If the entity cannot determine the fair value of all the classes of securities, then the incremental method should be used. The proceeds should be allocated to the securities that are publicly traded based on known fair value. Any excess is allocated to the other. Where the market value of neither security is known, appraisal information may be used. The imputed fair value of one class of security, particularly the preferred shares, can be based upon the stipulated dividend rate. In this case, the amount of proceeds remaining after the imputing of a value of the preferred shares would be allocated to the common stock.

Issuance costs. Equity offerings generally involve the incurrence of various costs, such as legal and accounting fees and underwriting commissions. These are offset against the proceeds of the offering, generally reducing paid-in capital, which is thus reported net of costs. If a unit offering involves debt and equity, the offering costs should be allocated proportionally against equity and debt, possibly creating a discount on the debt issuance that will be amortized as additional interest expense in the usual manner. (See the chapter on ASC 470 for a full discussion of accounting for premium or discount on debt.)

Promise to register. In certain situations, equity (or debt) is issued with a promise by the reporting entity to effect registration of the instruments by a defined date after issuance, or upon the occurrence of a contingent event. Per ASC 825-20, such obligations are recognized and measured consistent with the requirements of ASC 450, which does not alter the accounting for the associated financial instrument itself.

Stock Subscriptions

Occasionally, particularly in the case of a newly organized corporation, a contract is entered into between the corporation and prospective investors, whereby the investors agree to purchase specified numbers of shares to be paid for over some installment period. These stock subscriptions are not the same as actual stock issuances and the accounting differs.

The amount of stock subscriptions receivable by a corporation is occasionally accounted for as an asset on the statement of financial position and is categorized as current or noncurrent in accordance with the terms of payment. However, in accordance with SEC requirements, entities are required to use a contra equity account approach. Since subscribed shares do not have the rights and responsibilities of actual outstanding stock, the credit is made to a stock subscribed account instead of to the capital stock accounts.

ASC 505-10-45-2 states that a contribution to a company's equity made in the form of a note receivable should generally not be reported as an asset except on the very limited circumstances when there is substantial evidence of both the ability and intent to pay in a reasonably short period of time. The ASC notes that the most widespread practice is to report these notes as a reduction of equity. However, if the cash is received prior to the issuance of the financial statements, the note may be reported as an asset.

If the common stock has par or stated value, the common stock subscribed account is credited for the aggregate par or stated value of the shares subscribed. The excess over this amount is credited to additional paid-in capital. No distinction is made between additional paid-in capital relating to shares already issued and shares subscribed for. This treatment follows from the distinction between legal capital and additional paid-in capital. Where there is no par or stated value, the entire amount of the common stock subscribed is credited to the stock subscribed account.

As the amount due from the prospective shareholders is collected, the stock subscriptions receivable account is credited and the proceeds are debited to the cash account. Actual issuance of the shares, however, must await the complete payment of the stock subscription. Accordingly, the debit to common stock subscribed is not made until the subscribed shares are fully paid for and the stock is issued.

The following examples illustrate these concepts.

Examples of stock subscription transactions

1. 10,000 shares of $50 par preferred are subscribed at a price of $65 each; a 10% down payment is received.

Cash	65,000	
Stock subscriptions receivable	585,000	
Preferred stock subscribed		500,000
Additional paid-in capital		150,000

2. 2,000 shares of no-par common shares are subscribed at a price of $85 each, with one-half received in cash.

Cash	85,000	
Stock subscriptions receivable	85,000	
Common stock subscribed		170,000

3. All preferred subscriptions are paid and subscribed preferred shares are issued, and one-half of the remaining common subscriptions are collected in full.

Cash [$585,000 + ($85,000 × .50)]	627,500	
Stock subscriptions receivable		627,500
Preferred stock subscribed	500,000	
Preferred stock		500,000

4. The remaining common subscriptions are collected in full.

Cash ($85,000 × .50)	42,500	
Stock subscriptions receivable		42,500
Common stock subscribed	170,000	
Common stock		170,000

When a subscriber defaults on an obligation under a stock subscription agreement, the accounting will follow the provisions of the state in which the corporation is chartered. In some jurisdictions, the subscriber is entitled to a proportionate number of shares based upon the amount already paid on the subscriptions, sometimes reduced by the cost incurred by the corporation in selling the remaining defaulted shares to other stockholders. In other jurisdictions, the subscriber forfeits the entire investment upon default. In this case, the amount already received is credited to an additional paid-in capital account that describes its source.

Additional Paid-in Capital

Additional paid-in capital represents all capital contributed to a corporation other than that defined as par, stated value, no-par stock, or donated capital. Additional paid-in capital can arise from proceeds received from the sale of common and preferred shares in excess of their par or stated values. It can also arise from transactions related to the following:

1. Sale of shares previously issued and subsequently reacquired by the corporation (treasury stock)
2. Retirement of previously outstanding shares
3. Payment of stock dividends in a manner that justifies the dividend being recorded at the market value of the shares distributed
4. Lapse of stock purchase warrants or the forfeiture of stock subscriptions, if these result in the retaining by the corporation of any partial proceeds received prior to forfeiture
5. Warrants which are detachable from bonds

6. Conversion of convertible bonds
7. Other "gains" on the entity's own stock, such as that which results from certain stock option plans.

When the amounts are material, the sources of additional paid-in capital should be described in the financial statements.

Examples of additional paid-in capital transactions

ABC Company issues 2,000 shares of common stock having a par value of $1, of a total price of $8,000. The following entry records the transaction:

Cash	8,000	
Common stock		2,000
Additional paid-in capital		6,000

ABC Company buys back 2,000 shares of its own common stock for $10,000 and then sells these shares to investors for $15,000. The following entries record the buyback and sale transactions, respectively, assuming the use of the cost method of accounting for treasury stock:

Treasury stock	10,000	
Cash		10,000

Cash	15,000	
Treasury stock		10,000
Additional paid-in capital		5,000

ABC Company buys back 2,000 shares of its own $1 par value common stock (which it had originally sold for $8,000) for $9,000 and retires the stock, which it records with the following entry:

Common stock	2,000	
Additional paid-in capital	6,000	
Retained earnings	1,000	
Cash		9,000

ABC Company issues a small stock dividend of 5,000 common shares at the market price of $8 per share. Each share has a par value of $1. The following entry records the transaction:

Retained earnings	40,000	
Common stock		5,000
Additional paid-in capital		35,000

ABC Company previously has recorded $1,000 of stock options outstanding as part of a compensation agreement. The options expire a year later, resulting in the following entry:

Stock options outstanding	1,000	
Additional paid-in capital		1,000

ABC Company sells 2,000 of par $1,000 bonds, as well as 2,000 attached warrants having a market value of $15 each. Pro rata apportionment of the $2,000,000 cash received between the bonds and warrants results in the following entry:

Cash	2,000,000	
Discount on bonds payable	29,557	
Bonds payable		2,000,000
Additional paid-in capital—warrants		29,557

ABC's bondholders convert a $1,000 bond with an unamortized premium of $40 and a market value of $1,016 into 127 shares of $1 par common stock whose market value is $8 per share. This results in the following entry:

Bonds payable	1,000	
Premium on bonds payable	40	
Common stock		913
Additional paid-in capital		127

When the amounts are material, the sources of additional paid-in capital should be described in the financial statements.

Donated Capital

Donated capital can result from an outright gift to the corporation (e.g., a major shareholder donates land or other assets to the company in a nonreciprocal transfer) or may result when services are provided to the corporation. Under ASC 958-605-25-2 such nonreciprocal transactions are recognized as revenue in the period the contribution is received. Donated capital should be adequately disclosed in the financial statements.

Donations should be reflected in the income statement, which means that, after the fiscal period has ended and the books have been closed, the effect of donations will be incorporated in the reporting entity's retained earnings.

In the case of donations, historical cost is not adequate to properly reflect the substance of the transaction, since the historical cost to the corporation would be zero. Accordingly, these events should be reflected at fair market value (ASC 845-10-30-1). If long-lived assets are donated to the corporation, they should be recorded at their fair value at the date of donation. The amount so recorded should then be depreciated over the normal useful economic life of those assets. If donations are conditional in nature, they should not be reflected formally in the accounts until the appropriate conditions have been satisfied. However, disclosure might still be required in the financial statements of both the assets donated and the conditions required to be met.

Example of donated capital

A board member of the for-profit Adirondack Boys' Club (ABC) donates land to the organization that has a fair market value of $1 million. ABC records the donation with the following entry:

Land	1,000,000	
Revenue—donations		1,000,000

The same board member donates one year of accounting labor to ABC. The fair value of services rendered is $75,000. ABC records the donation with the following entry:

Salaries—accounting department	75,000	
Revenue—donations		75,000

The board member also donates one year of free rent of a local building to ABC. The annual rent in similar facilities is $45,000. ABC records the donation with the following entry:

Rent expense	45,000	
Revenue—donations		45,000

Finally, the board member pays off a $100,000 debt owed by ABC. ABC records the donation with the following entry:

Notes payable	100,000	
Revenue—donations		100,000

Following the closing of the fiscal period, the effect of all the foregoing donations will be reflected in Adirondack's retained earnings account.

Retained Earnings

Legal capital, additional paid-in capital, and donated capital collectively represent the contributed capital of the corporation. The other major source of capital is retained earnings, which represents the accumulated amount of earnings of the corporation from the date of inception (or from the date of reorganization) less the cumulative amount of distributions made to shareholders and other charges to retained earnings (e.g., from treasury stock transactions). The distributions to shareholders generally take the form of dividend payments but may take other forms as well, such as the reacquisition of shares for amounts in excess of the original issuance proceeds. The key events impacting retained earnings are:

- Dividends
- Certain treasury stock resales at amounts below acquisition cost
- Certain stock retirements at amounts in excess of book value
- Prior period adjustments
- Recapitalizations and reorganizations.

Examples of retained earnings transactions

Merrimack Corporation declares a dividend of $84,000, which it records with the following entry:

Retained earnings	84,000	
Dividends payable		84,000

Merrimack acquires 3,000 shares of its own $1 par value common stock for $15,000, and then resells it for $12,000. The following entries record the buyback and sale transactions respectively, assuming the use of the cost method of accounting for treasury stock:

Treasury stock	15,000	
Cash		15,000
Cash	12,000	
Retained earnings	3,000	
Treasury stock		15,000

Merrimack buys back 12,000 shares of its own $1 par value common stock (which it had originally sold for $60,000) for $70,000 and retires the stock, which it records with the following entry:

Common stock	12,000	
Additional paid-in capital	48,000	
Retained earnings	10,000	
Cash		70,000

Merrimack's accountant makes a mathematical mistake in calculating depreciation, requiring a prior period reduction of $30,000 to the accumulated depreciation account, and corresponding increases in its income tax payable and retained earnings accounts. Merrimack's income tax rate is 35%. It records this transaction with the following entry:

Accumulated depreciation	30,000	
Income taxes payable		10,500
Retained earnings		19,500

Retained earnings are also affected by action taken by the corporation's board of directors. Appropriation serves disclosure purposes and restricts dividend payments, but does nothing to provide any resources for the satisfaction of the contingent loss or other underlying purpose for which the appropriation has been made. Any appropriation made from retained earnings must eventually be returned to the retained earnings account. It is not permissible to charge losses against the appropriation account nor is it to credit any realized gain to that account. The use of appropriated retained earnings has diminished significantly over the years.

If a series of operating losses have been incurred or distributions to shareholders in excess of accumulated earnings have been made, and if there is a debit balance in retained earnings, the account is generally referred to as accumulated deficit.

Dividends

Dividends are the pro rata distribution of earnings to the owners of the corporation. The amount and the allocation between the preferred and common shareholders is a function of

- the stipulated preferential dividend rate;
- the presence or absence of
    1. a participation feature,
    2. a cumulative feature, and
    3. arrearages on the preferred stock; and
- the wishes of the board of directors. Dividends, even preferred stock dividends, where a cumulative feature exists, do not accrue.

Dividends only become a liability of the corporation when declared by the board of directors.

Traditionally, corporations were not allowed to declare dividends in excess of the amount of retained earnings. Alternatively, a corporation could pay dividends out of retained earnings and additional paid-in capital but could not exceed the total of these categories (i.e., they could not impair legal capital by the payment of dividends). States that have adopted the Model Business Corporation Act grant more latitude to the directors. Corporations can now, in certain jurisdictions, declare and pay dividends in excess of the book amount of retained earnings if the directors conclude that, after the payment of such dividends, the fair value of the corporation's net assets will still be a positive amount. Thus, directors can declare dividends out of unrealized appreciation that, in certain industries, can be a significant source of dividends beyond the realized and recognized accumulated earnings of the corporation. This action, however, represents a major departure from traditional practice and demands both careful consideration and adequate disclosure.

Three important dividend dates are

1. The declaration date, when a legal liability is incurred by the corporation
2. The record date, the point in time when a determination is made as to which specific registered stockholders will receive dividends and in what amounts
3. The payment date, to the date when the distribution of the dividend takes place.

These concepts are illustrated in the following example:

Example of dividends

On May 1, 20X1, the directors of River Corp. declared a $.75 per share quarterly dividend on River Corp.'s 650,000 outstanding common shares. The dividend is payable May 25 to holders of record May 15.

May 1	Retained earnings (or dividends)	487,500	
	Dividends payable		487,500
May 15	No entry		
May 25	Dividends payable	487,500	
	Cash		487,500

If a dividends account is used, it is closed to retained earnings at year-end.

Occasionally, what appear to be disproportionate dividend distributions are paid to some, but not all, of the owners of closely held corporations. Such transactions need to be carefully analyzed. In some cases these may actually represent compensation paid to the recipients. In other instances, these may be a true dividend paid to all shareholders on a pro rata basis, to which certain shareholders have waived their rights. If the former, the distribution should not be accounted for as a dividend. It should be accounted for as compensation or some other expense category and included on the income statement. If the latter, the dividend should be "grossed up" to reflect payment on a proportional basis to all the shareholders, with an offsetting capital contribution to the company recognized as having been effectively made by those to whom payments were not made.

Dividends may be made in the form of cash, property, or scrip.

- *Cash dividends* are either a given dollar amount per share or a percentage of par or stated value.
- *Property dividends* consist of the distribution of any assets other than cash (e.g., inventory or equipment).
- *Scrip dividends* are promissory notes due at some time in the future, sometimes bearing interest until final payment is made.

Property dividends. If property dividends are declared, the paying corporation may incur a gain or loss. Since the dividend should be reflected at the fair value of the assets distributed, the difference between fair value and book value is recorded at the time the dividend is declared and charged or credited to a loss or gain account.

Scrip dividends. If a corporation declares a dividend payable in scrip that is interest bearing, the interest is accrued over time as a periodic expense. The interest is not a part of the dividend itself.

Liquidating dividends. Liquidating dividends are not distributions of earnings, but rather a return of capital to the investing shareholders. A liquidating dividend is normally recorded by the declarer through charging additional paid-in capital rather than retained earnings. The exact accounting for a liquidating dividend is affected by the laws of the states where the business is incorporated.

Stock dividends. Stock dividends represent neither an actual distribution of the assets of the corporation nor a promise to distribute those assets. For this reason, a stock dividend is not considered a legal liability or a taxable transaction.

Despite the recognition that a stock dividend is not a distribution of earnings, the accounting treatment of relatively insignificant stock dividends (defined as being less than 20% to 25%

of the outstanding shares prior to declaration) is consistent with it being a real dividend. Accordingly, retained earnings are debited for the fair market value of the shares to be paid as a dividend, and the capital stock and additional paid-in capital accounts are credited for the appropriate amounts based upon the par or stated value of the shares, if any. A stock dividend declared but not yet paid is classified as such in the stockholders' equity section of the statement of financial position. Because a stock dividend never reduces assets, it cannot be a liability.

The selection of 20% to 25% as the threshold for recognizing a stock dividend as an earnings distribution is arbitrary, but it is based somewhat on the empirical evidence that small stock dividends tend not to result in a reduced market price per share for outstanding shares. The aggregate value of the outstanding shares should not change, but the greater number of shares outstanding after the stock dividend should necessitate a lower per share price. As noted, however, the declaration of small stock dividends tends not to have this impact, and this phenomenon supports the accounting treatment.

On the other hand, when stock dividends are larger in magnitude, it is observed that per-share market value declines after the declaration of the dividend. In such situations, it would not be valid to treat the stock dividend as an earnings distribution. Rather, logic suggests that it should be accounted for as a split. The precise treatment depends upon the legal requirements of the state of incorporation and upon whether the existing par value or stated value is reduced concurrent with the stock split.

If the par value is not reduced for a large stock dividend and if state law requires that earnings be capitalized in an amount equal to the aggregate of the par value of the stock dividend declared, the event should be described as a stock split effected in the form of a dividend, with a charge to retained earnings and a credit to the common stock account for the aggregate par or stated value. When the par or stated value is reduced in recognition of the split and state laws do not require treatment as a dividend, there is no formal entry to record the split but merely a notation that the number of shares outstanding has increased and the per share par or stated value has decreased accordingly. It should be noted that many companies account for stock splits as if they were a large stock dividend. By doing this, par value per share remains unchanged. The concepts of small versus large stock dividends are illustrated in the following examples.

Example of small stock dividend

Assume that stockholders' equity for the Wasatch Corp. on November 1, 20X1, is as follows.

Common stock, $1 par, 100,000 shares outstanding	$ 100,000
Paid-in capital in excess of par	1,100,000
Retained earnings	750,000

Small Stock Dividend: On November 10, 20X1, the directors of Wasatch Corp. declared a 15% stock dividend, or a dividend of 1.5 shares of common stock for every 10 shares held. Before the stock dividend, the stock is selling for $23 per share. After the 15% stock dividend, each original share worth $23 will become 1.15 shares, each with a value of $20 ($23/1.15). The stock dividend is to be recorded at the market value of the new shares issued, or $300,000 (15,000 new shares at the postdividend price of $20). The entries to record the declaration of the dividend and the issuance of stock (on November 30) by Wasatch Corp. are as follows:

Nov. 10	Retained earnings	300,000	
	Stock dividends distributable		15,000
	Paid-in capital in excess of par		285,000
Nov. 30	Stock dividends distributable	15,000	
	Common stock, $1 par		15,000

Large Stock Dividend: Because the focus of the Committee on Accounting Procedure was on small stock dividends, the accounting requirements for governing large stock dividends are less specific than those for small stock dividends. In practice, ASC 505-20-30-3 results in the par or stated value of the newly issued shares being transferred to the capital stock account from either retained earnings or paid-in capital in excess of par.

Example of large stock dividend

On November 10, 20X1, Wasatch Corp. declares a 50% large stock dividend, a dividend of one share for every two held. Legal requirements call for the transfer to capital stock of an amount equal to the par value of the shares issued. Entries for the declaration on November 10 and the issuance of 50,000 new shares (100,000 × .50) on November 30 are as follows:

Nov. 10	Retained earnings	50,000	
	Stock dividends distributable		50,000
	Or		
	Paid-in capital in excess of par	50,000	
	Stock dividends distributable		50,000
Nov. 30	Stock dividends distributable	50,000	
	Common stock, $1 par		50,000

Distributions to shareholders having cash and stock components. If a corporation makes a distribution to shareholders that allows them to elect to receive their distribution in either cash or shares of an equivalent value, and there is a limitation on the total amount of cash that shareholders can receive, then the stock portion of the distribution is considered a share issuance, not a stock dividend.

ASC 505-30, *Treasury Stock*

Treasury stock consists of a corporation's own stock that has been issued, subsequently reacquired by the firm, and not yet reissued or canceled. Treasury stock does not reduce the number of shares issued but does reduce the number of shares outstanding, as well as total stockholders' equity. These shares are not eligible to receive cash dividends. Treasury stock is not an asset although, in some very limited circumstances, it may be presented as an asset if adequately disclosed (ASC 505-30-30). Reacquired stock that is awaiting delivery to satisfy a liability created by the firm's compensation plan or reacquired stock held in a profit-sharing trust is still considered outstanding and would not be considered treasury stock. In each case, the stock would be presented as an asset with the accompanying footnote disclosure. Accounting for excesses and deficiencies on treasury stock transactions is governed by ASC 505-30-30.

Three approaches exist for the treatment of treasury stock:

- cost,
- par value, and
- constructive retirement.

Cost method. Under the cost method, the gross cost of the shares reacquired is charged to a contra equity account (treasury stock). The equity accounts that were credited for the original share issuance (common stock, paid-in capital in excess of par, etc.) remain intact. When the treasury shares are reissued, proceeds in excess of cost are credited to a paid-in capital account. Any deficiency is charged to retained earnings (unless paid-in capital from previous treasury share transactions exists, in which case the deficiency is charged to that account, with any excess charged to retained earnings). If many treasury stock purchases are made, a cost flow assumption (e.g., first-in, first-out [FIFO] or specific identification) should be adopted to compute excesses and deficiencies upon subsequent share reissuances. The advantage of the cost method is that it avoids identifying and accounting for amounts related to the original issuance of the shares and is, therefore, the simpler, more frequently used method.

The cost method is most consistent with the one-transaction concept. This concept takes the view that the classification of stockholders' equity should not be affected simply because the corporation was the middle "person" in an exchange of shares from one stockholder to another. In substance, there is only a transfer of shares between two stockholders. Since the original balances in the equity accounts are left undisturbed, the cost method is most acceptable when the firm acquires its stock for reasons other than its retirement, or when its ultimate disposition has not yet been decided.

Par value method. Under the par value method, the treasury stock account is charged only for the aggregate par (or stated) value of the shares reacquired. Other paid-in capital accounts (excess over par value, etc.) are relieved in proportion to the amounts recognized upon the original issuance of the shares. The treasury share acquisition is treated almost as a retirement. However, the common (or preferred) stock account continues at the original amount, thereby preserving the distinction between an actual retirement and a treasury share transaction.

When the treasury shares accounted for by the par value method are subsequently resold, the excess of the sale price over par value is credited to paid-in capital. A reissuance for a price below par value does not create a contingent liability for the purchaser. It is only the original purchaser who risks this obligation to the entity's creditors.

Constructive retirement method. The constructive retirement method is similar to the par value method, except that the aggregate par (or stated) value of the reacquired shares is charged to the stock account rather than to the treasury stock account. This method is superior when

1. it is management's intention not to reissue the shares within a reasonable time period or
2. the state of incorporation defines reacquired shares as having been retired.

In the latter case, the constructive retirement method is probably the only method of accounting for treasury shares that is not inconsistent with the state Business Corporation Act, even if the state law does not necessarily dictate such accounting. Certain states require that treasury stock be accounted for by this method.

The two-transaction concept is most consistent with the par value and constructive retirement methods. First, the reacquisition of the firm's shares is viewed as constituting a contraction of its capital structure. Second, the reissuance of the shares is the same as issuing new shares. There is little difference between the purchase and subsequent reissuance of treasury shares and the acquisition and retirement of previously issued shares and the issuance of new shares.

Treasury shares originally accounted for by the cost method can subsequently be restated to conform to the constructive retirement method. If shares were acquired with the intention that they would be reissued and it is later determined that such reissuance is unlikely (due, for example, to the expiration of stock options without their exercise), then it is proper to restate the transaction.

Example of accounting for treasury stock

1. 100 shares ($50 par value) that were originally sold for $60 per share are later reacquired for $70 each.
2. All 100 shares are subsequently resold for a total of $7,500.

To record the acquisition, the entry is:

Cost method			*Par value method*			*Constructive retirement method*		
Treasury stock	7,000		Treasury stock	5,000		Common stock	5,000	
Cash		7,000	Additional paid-in capital—common stock	1,000		Additional paid-in capital—common stock	1,000	
			Retained earnings	1,000		Retained earnings	1,000	
			Cash		7,000	Cash		7,000

To record the resale, the entry is:

Cost method			*Par value method*			*Constructive retirement method*		
Cash	7,500		Cash	7,500		Cash	7,500	
Treasury stock		7,000	Treasury stock		5,000	Common stock		5,000
Additional paid-in capital—treasury stock		500	Additional paid-in capital—common stock		2,500	Additional paid-in capital—common stock		2,500

If the shares had been resold for $6,500, the entry is:

Cost method			*Par value method*			*Constructive retirement method*		
Cash	6,500		Cash	6,500		Cash	6,500	
Retained earnings*	500		Treasury stock		5,000	Common stock		5,000
Treasury stock		7,000	Additional paid-in capital—common stock		1,500	Additional paid-in capital—common stock		1,500

* *"Additional paid-in capital—treasury stock" or "Additional paid-in capital—retired stock" of that issue would be debited first to the extent it exists.*

Alternatively, under the par or constructive retirement methods, any portion of or the entire deficiency on the treasury stock acquisition may be debited to retained earnings without allocation to paid-in capital. Any excesses will always be credited to an "Additional paid-in capital—retired stock" account.

The laws of some states govern the circumstances under which a corporation may acquire treasury stock and may prescribe the accounting for the stock. For example, a charge to retained earnings may be required in an amount equal to the treasury stock's total cost. In such cases, the accounting per the state law prevails. Also, some states (including those that have adopted the Model Business Corporation Act) define excess purchase cost of reacquired (i.e., treasury) shares as being "distributions" to shareholders that are no different in nature than dividends. In such cases, the financial statement presentation should adequately disclose the substance of these transactions (e.g., by presenting both dividends and excess reacquisition costs together in the retained earnings statement).

When a firm decides to formally retire the treasury stock, the journal entry is dependent on the method used to account for the stock.

Example of the cost and par value methods

Using the original sale and reacquisition data from the illustration above, the following entries would be made if the cost and par value methods, respectively, were employed:

Cost method			Par value method		
Common stock	5,000		Common stock	5,000	
Additional paid-in capital—common stock	1,000		Treasury stock		5,000
Retained earnings	1,000				
Treasury stock		7,000			

* *"Additional paid-in capital—treasury stock" may be debited to the extent it exists.*

If the constructive retirement method was used to record the treasury stock purchase, no additional entry would be necessary upon the formal retirement of the shares.

After the entry is made, the pro rata portion of all paid-in capital existing for that issue (i.e., capital stock and additional paid-in capital) will have been eliminated. If stock is purchased for immediate retirement (i.e., not put into the treasury) the entry to record the retirement is the same as that made under the constructive retirement method.

In some circumstances, shares held by current stockholders may be donated back to the reporting entity, possibly to facilitate a resale to new owners who will infuse needed capital into the business. In accounting for donated treasury stock, the intentions of management regarding these reacquired shares is key; if these are to simply be retired, the common stock account should be debited for the par or stated value (if par or stated value stock) or the original proceeds received (if no-par, no-stated-value stock). The current fair value of the shares should be credited to the "donated capital" account, and the difference should be debited or credited to a suitably titled paid-in capital account, such as "additional paid-in capital from share donations."

If the donated shares are to be sold (the normal scenario), variations on the par and cost methods of treasury stock accounting can be employed, with "donated capital" being debited and credited, respectively, when shares are received and later reissued, instead of the "treasury stock" account employed in the above illustrations. Note, however, that if the cost method is used, the debit to the donated capital account should be for the fair value of the shares, not the cost (a seeming contradiction). If the constructive retirement method is utilized instead, only a memorandum entry will be recorded when the shares are received; when reissued, the entire proceeds should be credited to "donated capital."

Other Paid-in Capital Issues

Takeover defense as cost of treasury stock. In certain instances an entity may incur costs to defend against an unwelcome or hostile attempted takeover. In some cases, in fact, putative acquirers will threaten a takeover struggle in order to extract so-called *greenmail* from the target entity, often effected through a buyback of shares held by the acquirer at a premium over market value. ASC 505-30-30 states that the excess purchase price of treasury shares should not be attributed to the shares, but rather should be attributed to the other elements of the transaction and accounted for according to their substance, which could include the receipt of stated or unstated rights, privileges, or agreements. The SEC's position is that such excess is anything over the quoted market price of the treasury shares.

Accelerated share repurchase programs. ASC 505-30-25 pertains to accelerated share repurchase programs, which are combinations of transactions that permit an entity to purchase a targeted number of shares immediately, with the final purchase price determined by an average market price over fixed periods of time. Such programs are intended to combine the immediate share retirement benefits (boosting earnings per share, etc.) of tender offers with the market impacts and pricing benefits of disciplined open market stock repurchase programs.

The ASC states that an entity should account for an accelerated share repurchase program as two separate transactions:

- first, as shares of common stock acquired in a treasury stock transaction recorded on the acquisition date, and
- second, as a forward contract indexed to its own common stock.

An entity would classify the forward contract in the above example as an equity instrument because the entity will receive cash when the contract is in a gain position but pay cash or stock when the contract is in a loss position. Changes in the fair value of the forward contract would not be recorded, and the settlement of the forward contract would be recorded in equity.

The treasury stock transaction would result in an immediate reduction of the outstanding shares used to calculate the weighted-average common shares outstanding for both basic and diluted earnings per share (EPS). The effect of the forward contract on diluted EPS would be calculated in accordance with ASC 260.

Own-share lending arrangements related to convertible debt financing. An entity may enter into a share-lending arrangement with an investment bank that is related to a convertible debt offering (ASC 470-20-05). The lending arrangement is intended to provide investors in the offering with the ability to hedge the conversion option in the convertible debt. Upon maturity of the debt, the investment bank returns the loaned shares.

On the date of issuance, the entity should record the loaned shares at their fair value and recognize them as an issuance cost, with an offset to additional paid-in capital. If it becomes probable that the counterparty to this arrangement will default, then the entity recognizes an expense equal to the value of those shares not yet returned, net of any probable recoveries. The offset to this expense is additional paid-in capital. The entity should subsequently remeasure the fair value of the unreturned shares until the amount payable by the counterparty becomes fixed.

Own-share lending arrangements call for the following disclosures:

- *Description*. A description of any outstanding share-lending arrangements, the significant terms of these arrangements, and why the entity has entered into them.
- *Fair value*. The fair value of the loaned shares outstanding.
- *Earnings per share*. The treatment of the loaned shares for EPS calculation purposes.
- *Other*. The unamortized amount of the issuance costs associated with the arrangements, the classification of these issuance costs, and the amount of any unreimbursed dividends paid to the loaned shares.

Other Equity Accounts

A principle of GAAP financial reporting is that all items of income, expense, gain, or loss (other than transactions with owners) should flow through the income statement. In fact, however, a number of important exceptions have been made, including

- translation gains or losses (ASC 830),
- certain adjustments for minimum pension obligations (ASC 715), and
- unrealized gains and losses on available-for-sale portfolios of debt or equity investments (ASC 320).

Hedging gains and losses qualifying under ASC 815 are also deferred for income measurement purposes. ASC 220 established the concept of comprehensive income (the term which denotes normal earnings plus the change in other equity accounts). Comprehensive income must be reported either in a combined statement with the income statement or as a stand-alone statement.

Refer to the chapter on ASC 220 for more information.

ASC 505-50, *Equity-based Payments to Nonemployees*

ASC 505-50 deals exclusively with those situations in which the fair value of the equity instruments delivered to other than employees is more objectively ascertainable than is the value of goods or services received. ASC 505-50 is the foundation for the discussion that follows in this section.

Measurement date. For purposes of ascertaining the amounts to be assigned for these transactions, the key concern is the determination of the measurement date. Essentially, the amount of expense or the value of the asset acquired through the issuance of equity instruments is fixed as of the measurement date, although, under certain circumstances as explained below, some subsequent adjustments may need to be made.

Per ASC 505-50, the measurement date will be the earlier of the date at which a commitment for performance is made or when the performance is actually completed. Whether or not there has been a "performance commitment" by the party providing the goods or services is a question of fact and must be determined from the surrounding circumstances, but in general will be deemed to exist if there is a "sufficiently large disincentive for nonperformance" to make performance probable. This disincentive must derive from the relationship between the equity instrument issuer/recipient of the goods or services and its counterparty. Mere risk of forfeiture is not enough to qualify as a disincentive, nor is the risk of being sued for nonperformance. When a sufficiently large disincentive exists, however, the measurement date will precede the completion of performance and, accordingly, when accrual of the related expense or recognition of the asset would otherwise be required under GAAP, it will be necessary to include the value of the equity instruments in such cost.

For example, if the agreed-upon price for the construction of a new power plant includes options on the utility company's stock, subject to a completion date of no longer than three years hence, and the contract also contains substantial financial disincentives to late completion, such as a provision for liquidated damages, then it would be concluded that there was a *performance commitment* within the meaning of ASC 505-50. On the other hand, if the price agreed to were to be fully payable even in the event of late delivery, there would be no "performance commitment" as that term is used.

In many situations in which the compensation includes significant equity instrument components, there will still be no finding of a performance commitment because the payment arrangement provides for phases of work, with payment in full for work as it is completed. For example, if a contractor agrees to build a multiplicity of sales kiosks in various air terminals for a retailing chain, with payment to be made in cash and the retailer's stock upon the completion of each kiosk, the contractor could terminate the arrangement after any intermediate completion date without significant penalty. In such cases, the measurement date would be, for each subproject, the date on which the work is completed.

When to recognize the fair value of the equity instruments. In general, the normal rules of GAAP would apply in circumstances in which stock or other equity instruments were being granted as part, or all, of the consideration for the transaction. Thus, if the services provided represented an expense of the enterprise, the expense should be recognized when incurred, which could well precede the date on which the payment was ultimately to be made.

An expense or asset measurement is made with the best information available at that time, and there is no "look back" based on subsequent events; the value assigned to the option would be credited to an appropriate paid-in capital account (e.g., "capital from expired options") if this becomes necessary.

Accounting prior to measurement date. If, under GAAP, it is necessary for the entity to recognize an expense or an asset related to the transaction involving the issuance of equity for goods or services prior to the measurement date, the then-current fair values of the equity instruments must be utilized to determine these amounts. If fair values change later, these variations are attributed to those later periods. Thus, for a transaction which calls primarily for cash payment but also, to a lesser extent, for the issuance of stock, a decline in the value of the equity portion in a later interim period would reduce the cost (or asset value) to be recognized in that period; if the stock portion is a significant component, a decline could largely eliminate the cost otherwise to be accrued or even, conceivably, cause it to become negative in a later reporting period. Of course, overall, the aggregate cost would be positive upon ultimate completion (at worst it could be zero, if the transaction were predicated only on the issuance of equity instruments, and these became worthless—an obviously unlikely scenario).

Measurement of fair value of the equity instrument portion of the transaction when certain terms are not known at inception. In some circumstances where there is a performance commitment there will also be a material uncertainty regarding the valuation of the equity instruments, either because of some question regarding the number of instruments to be delivered, the value of such instruments, or some factor dependent upon the performance of the party providing the service. For example, the arrangement may include a guarantee of the value of the instrument extending for some period subsequent to completion of performance that unless the underlying shares maintain a market price of $15 or greater for one year following delivery, or else a defined number of additional shares will be granted. This type of arrangement is referred to as a "market condition." In other circumstances, there may be a condition based on the counterparty's performance—for example, when options are granted to a tax accountant structuring a tax shelter, in which the number of options ultimately deliverable depends upon successfully surviving an IRS audit. Situations such as this are denoted "counterparty performance conditions."

Where the arrangement contains a market condition measurement of the equity instrument portion of the contracted price should be based on two elements:

- the first is the fair value of the basic equity instrument;
- the second is the fair value of the contingent commitment, such as the aforementioned promise to grant a specified number of extra shares if the market price falls below $15 during the one-year period.

In practice, the valuation of these contingencies might prove to be challenging, but clearly any such promise has some positive value, and the standard requires that this be assessed. Changes in the value of the second (contingent) element subsequent to the performance commitment date would not be recognized since, per ASC 815, a derivative financial instrument to be settled in a company's own shares (as contrasted to a settlement in cash) is not to be remeasured.

Compared to a market condition, measurement when there are counterparty performance conditions is more complicated. At the measurement date, the equity instruments are valued at the lowest of the defined alternative amounts. For example, if the value of the option award to the tax accountant noted above is $20,000 (at the performance commitment date) assuming survival against IRS challenge, but only $5,000 if the IRS ultimately prevails, then the measurement of the value of the service would be based on the $5,000 amount. However, later, when the outcome of the performance condition is known, an additional cost would have to be recognized if a more favorable outcome occurred (in this example, successful defense of the tax shelter). The added cost would be based not on the values as of the performance commitment date, but rather as of the date of resolution of the condition. If the value of the options under the "success" outcome is $28,000 at that date, and the value of the "failure" outcome is $19,000, then an added cost of ($28,000 – 19,000 =) $9,000 would be recognized.

Where a given transaction involves both market and counterparty performance conditions, the accounting specified for situations involving only counterparty performance conditions is to be applied.

Example of equity instruments issued to a third party

Carney Development Enterprises has engaged the services of Alfred Brothers Construction (ABC) to design an office tower. ABC agrees to accept 5,000 shares of Carney $1 par value common stock and 1,000 options on shares in exchange for this service, but it will only receive half the number of shares if it delivers completed drawings after the due date. Thus, there exists a sufficiently large disincentive for nonperformance. Also, if the value of Carney's stock declines below $15/share at any point during the six months subsequent to the issuance of shares to ABC, Carney agrees to issue additional shares to bring ABC's total compensation back up to the $15 level, which is capped at a maximum additional stock issuance of 2,000 shares.

Carney measures the value of its stock and options as of the performance commitment date for the initial 5,000 share payment, the 1,000 option grant, and the potential additional payment of 2,000 shares. At a price on the commitment date of $18/share, the initial share payment costs $90,000, while the additional payment costs $36,000. Carney appropriately values the stock options at $9 each, or $9,000 in total, using an option pricing model. During each of the 18 months of the design process, Carney recognizes 1/18 of the $90,000 cost of the initial stock grant and of the $9,000 option grant with the following entry:

Construction-in-progress	5,500	
Stock options outstanding		500
Accrued liabilities		5,000

ABC successfully completes the drawings by the designated deadline, triggering a stock grant of 5,000 shares that Carney records with the following entry:

Accrued liabilities	90,000	
Common stock		5,000
Additional paid-in capital		85,000

Carney's stock price drops below $18 immediately after the project is completed, so ABC never exercises the 1,000 stock options. Carney accounts for the stock options with the following entry:

Stock options outstanding	9,000	
Additional paid-in capital—expired options		9,000

The value of Carney stock subsequently declines to $10/share, which represents a shortfall of $25,000 from the guaranteed minimum share price of $15. At the current market price of $10/share, Carney would have to issue an additional 2,500 shares to ABC to make up the shortfall. However, since this liability is capped at 2,000 shares, Carney only issues 2,000 shares, using the valuation of $18 set at the commitment date, and records the transaction with the following entry:

Construction-in-progress	36,000	
Common stock		2,000
Additional paid-in capital		34,000

Reporting prior to the measurement date when certain terms are not known. When market conditions (e.g., the value of the stock underlying the options two years hence) are not known, and expenses must be accrued or assets recorded prior to the measurement date, the then-current fair values of the equity instruments at such dates should be used, with subsequent adjustments as necessary. When there are counterparty performance conditions, either alone or in conjunction with market conditions, then interim measurements should be based on the lowest of the alternative values as of each date, with subsequent changes in this same measure assigned to later periods.

Reporting after the measurement date when certain terms are not known. When market conditions (e.g., the value of the stock underlying the options two years hence) are not known, after the measurement date the principles of ASC 815 are to be applied, which generally would mean that changes in value would not be recognized. On the other hand, when there are counterparty performance conditions, with or without market conditions also being present, *modification accounting* procedures are to be utilized. This results in reporting an adjustment in subsequent periods determined with reference to the difference between the then-current fair value of the revised equity instruments and that of the old instruments immediately prior to the recognition event. In all cases, the "then-current" values are to be determined with reference to the lowest aggregate fair values under the alternative outcomes specified by the contractual arrangement.

Further guidance. Where fully vested, exercisable, nonforfeitable equity instruments are issued at the date the grantor and grantee enter into an agreement, by eliminating any obligation on the part of the counterparty to earn the equity instruments, a measurement date has been reached. The grantor should recognize the equity instruments when they are issued (in most cases, when the agreement is entered into). Whether the corresponding cost is an immediate expense or a prepaid asset (or whether the debit should be characterized as contra equity) depends on the specific facts and circumstances.

If an entity grants fully vested, nonforfeitable equity instruments that are exercisable by the grantee only after a specified period of time, and the terms of the agreement provide for earlier exercisability by the grantee only after a specified period of time, and the terms of the agreement provide for earlier exercisability if the grantee achieves specified performance conditions, the grantor should measure the fair value of the equity instruments at the date of grant and should recognize that measured cost under the same guidance as the foregoing. If, subsequent to the arrangement date, the grantee performs as specified and exercisability is accelerated, the grantor should measure and account for the increase in the fair value of the equity instruments resulting from the acceleration of exercisability using *modification accounting*. Since, generally, option-pricing models are not sensitive to exercisability restrictions, it may be necessary to provide additional guidance on how to measure the discount attributable to the exercisability restriction.

For transactions that include a grantee performance commitment, the grantee should account for the arrangement as an executory contract (that is, generally no accounting before performance) in the same manner as it would if the grantor had agreed to pay cash (upon vesting) for the goods or services. Further consideration will be directed to the accounting in cases in which the fair value at the date the equity instruments are earned is greater than or less than the fair value measured at the performance commitment date (measurement date).

Consideration for future services. ASC 505-50 discusses the appropriate statement of financial position presentation of arrangements where unvested, forfeitable equity instruments are issued to an unrelated nonemployee (the counterparty) as consideration for future services. SEC staff has since addressed situations where the grantor is entitled to recover the specific consideration paid, plus a substantial mandatory penalty, as a minimum measure of damages for counterparty nonperformance. Fair value measurement under ASC 718 is required. In practice, however, some reporting entities have made no entries until performance occurs, while others have recorded the fair value of the equity instruments as equity at the measurement date and record the offset either as an asset (future services receivable) or as a reduction of stockholders' equity (contra equity).

The SEC staff believes that if the issuer receives a right to receive future services in exchange for unvested, forfeitable equity instruments, those equity instruments should be treated as unissued for accounting purposes until the future services are received (that is, the instruments are not considered issued until they vest). Consequently, there would be no recognition at the measurement date and no entry should be recorded. This does not apply to similar arrangements in which the issuer exchanges fully vested nonforfeitable equity instruments, as those types of arrangements are addressed in ASC 505-50.

Convertible Preferred Stock

The treatment of convertible preferred stock at its issuance is no different than that of nonconvertible preferred. When it is converted, the book value approach is used to account for the conversion. Use of the market value approach would entail a gain or loss for which there is no theoretical justification, since the total amount of contributed capital does not change when the stock is converted. When the preferred stock is converted, the "Preferred stock" and related "Additional paid-in capital—preferred stock" accounts are debited for their original values when purchased, and "Common stock" and "Additional paid-in capital—common stock" (if an excess over par or stated value exists) are credited. If the book value of the preferred stock is less than the total par value of the common stock being issued, retained earnings is charged for the difference. This charge is supported by the rationale that the preferred shareholders are offered an additional return to facilitate their conversion to common stock. Many states require that this excess instead reduce additional paid-in capital from other sources.

Example of convertible preferred stock

Caspian Corporation issues 10,000 shares of $1 par value convertible preferred stock, and receives $1.25 per share. It records the initial sale with the following entry:

Cash	12,500	
Convertible preferred stock		10,000
Additional paid-in capital—preferred stock		2,500

The terms of the convertible preferred stock allow Caspian's shareholders to convert one share of preferred for one share of common stock at any time. The preferred shareholders convert all of their shares to Caspian common stock, which has a par value of $2. This requires the following entry:

Convertible preferred stock	10,000	
Additional paid-in capital—preferred stock	2,500	
Retained earnings	7,500	
Common stock		20,000

Mandatorily Redeemable Common and Preferred Stock

A mandatory redemption clause requires common or preferred stock to be redeemed (retired) at a specific date(s) or upon occurrence of an event which is uncertain as to timing, although ultimately certain to occur. This feature is in contrast to callable preferred stock, which is redeemed at the issuing corporation's option. Mandatory redemption features are not uncommon in practice; closely held corporations, for example, have "buy-sell" agreements to redeem the shares of retiring or deceased owners at formula prices, often book value. Historically, the mandatory redemption feature has been ignored in determining statement of financial position classification for nonpublic companies. On the other hand, for publicly held companies, mandatorily redeemable shares (which are almost always preferred stock in these situations) had to be displayed as either debt or as a "mezzanine equity" item separate from stockholders' equity.

Under ASC 480, discussed in detail in the chapter on ASC 480, financial instruments with mandatory redemption features must be reported as liabilities. This means that "mezzanine" presentation of redeemable preferred stock is not appropriate. It also means that some entities, having "buy-sell" agreements with all of their respective shareholders, should report no equity at all and should display all of what formerly was equity within the liabilities caption of the statement of financial position.

The only exception to this requirement exists in the circumstance where the redemption is required to occur only upon the liquidation or termination of the reporting entity. Since financial statements are prepared under the assumption of a going concern, it would be inconsistent to classify this type of redeemable stock as a liability.

If the stock subject to mandatory redemption provisions represents the only shares in the reporting entity, it must, under ASC 480, report those instruments in the liabilities section of its statement of financial position, and describe them as shares subject to mandatory redemption, so as to distinguish the instruments from other financial statement liabilities. Transition to this standard may create distress, particularly in cases in which there will be a need to modify loan agreements, restrictive covenants, and so forth, since these entities' debt/equity ratios and other financial indicators will change dramatically and in many instances immediately violate existing covenants. The use of the special caption above will serve to educate financial statements users regarding the substantive meaning of this new mode of financial statement presentation.

In some cases, stock is issued that is not subject to mandatory redemption provisions currently, but that is contingently subject to such requirements once defined events occur. An assessment must be made each reporting period to ascertain whether the triggering event has yet occurred. If it has, reclassification of the conditionally mandatorily redeemable stock to liabilities must be effected.

ASC 480 offers two such examples. First, if shares are to become mandatorily redeemable upon a change in control of the issuing corporation, these remain classified within equity until that event occurs, if ever. When it does occur, the equity is reclassified to liabilities, measured at the fair value at that date, with no gain or loss recognized. Any disparity between the carrying value of the equity and the amount transferred to liabilities would therefore remain in equity as additional paid-in capital or as a reduction to paid-in capital or to retained earnings.

Another example of conditional mandatory redemption would occur when preferred stock is issued with a mandatory redemption at a date certain, say ten years hence, conditioned on the failure of the preferred stockholders to exercise the right to convert to common stock before another defined date, say five years from issuance. For the first five years, the preferred stock would be displayed as equity, since the mandatory redemption feature has yet to become activated. If the shareholders elect to exchange the preferred stock to common stock, the usual accounting for such conversions would apply. If the five-year period elapses and the preferred shares are not exchanged, the mandatory redemption provision becomes effective, and the preferred stock is to be reclassified to liabilities, measured at fair value.

Accounting for mandatorily redeemable financial instruments of a nonpublic reporting entity must be conformed to the requirements outlined above. For all other mandatorily redeemable financial instruments issued by nonpublic entities that are not SEC registrants, the classification, measurement, and disclosure provisions are deferred indefinitely. For mandatorily redeemable noncontrolling interests that would not be classified by the subsidiary as liabilities (because they are redeemable only upon liquidation) but would be classified by the parent as liabilities on the consolidated statements, the classification and measurement provisions of ASC 480 are deferred indefinitely. For other mandatorily redeemable noncontrolling interests, the measurement provisions of ASC 480 were deferred indefinitely, but the classifications provisions are not deferred. For financial instruments created before issuance date of ASC 480 and still existing at the beginning of the interim period of adoption, transition is to be achieved by reporting the cumulative effect of a change in an accounting principle by initially measuring the financial instruments at fair value or other measurement attribute required by the statement.

In addition to the requirement of ASC 480, expanded disclosure of mandatorily redeemable common or preferred stock is required by ASC 505-10-50. Specifically, the redemption requirements for each of the next five years must be set forth in the notes to the financial statements prepared in accordance with GAAP, if the amounts are either fixed or determinable on fixed or determinable dates. Thus, readers can interpret the cash requirements on the reporting entity in a manner similar to the drawing of inferences about other fixed commitments, such as maturities of long-term debt and lease obligations.

Example of mandatorily redeemable stock

A major shareholder of the Atlantic Corporation swaps the company two tracts of prime real estate (Tract A and Tract B) in exchange for 10,000 shares and 5,000 shares, respectively, of $1 par value preferred stock. Each block of stock is mandatorily redeemable within one year if Atlantic ever sells the related tract of real estate. Tract A has a fair value of $400,000 and Tract B has a fair value of $200,000 on the initial transaction date. Since the shares are only conditionally redeemable at this time, Atlantic records a credit to equity accounts with the following entry:

Land	600,000	
Preferred stock		15,000
Additional paid-in capital		585,000

Five years later, Atlantic sells Tract A for $550,000, which is the fair value of the land. Because the status of the shares has now changed to mandatorily redeemable, Atlantic reclassifies the related 10,000 shares as a liability, measured at their fair value on the reclassification date. Since the fair value has increased by $150,000, Atlantic shifts an additional $150,000 from the additional paid-in capital account to the liability account. It uses the following entry to do so:

Preferred stock	10,000	
Additional paid-in capital	540,000	
Liabilities—shares subject to mandatory redemption		550,000

Two years later, Atlantic sells Tract B for $125,000, which is the fair value of the land. The status of these shares has also now changed to mandatorily redeemable, so Atlantic reclassifies the related 5,000 shares as a liability, measured at their fair value on the reclassification date. Since the fair value has decreased by $75,000, Atlantic retains $75,000 in the additional paid-in capital account. It uses the following entry to do so:

Preferred stock	5,000	
Additional paid-in capital	120,000	
Liabilities—shares subject to mandatory redemption		125,000

Put Warrant

A detachable put warrant can either be put back to the debt issuer for cash or can be exercised to acquire common stock. These instruments should be accounted for in the same manner as a mezzanine security. The proceeds applicable to the put warrant ordinarily are to be classified as equity and should be presented between the liability and equity sections in accordance with SEC ASR 268.

In the case of a warrant with a put price substantially higher than the value assigned to the warrant at issuance, however, the proceeds should be classified as a liability since it is likely that the warrant will be put back to the company.

Example of a put warrant

Caspian Corporation issues 100 bonds with detachable put warrants, each of which allows holders, after two years have elapsed, to purchase one share of Caspian's $1 par value common stock from the company for $20 per share, and which are puttable for a cash payment of $5. Caspian apportions $5 of the bond sale price to the warrants. Caspian's share price on the issuance date is $23. At this price, warrant holders can purchase shares from Caspian for $20 and resell them for $23, yielding a net gain of $3. Since this is less than the $5 to be gained from the put feature of the warrants, this is classified as a liability, and is recorded as such with the following entry (the remaining entries for the issuance of the bond are not given here):

Cash	500	
Liabilities—puttable warrants		500

After two years, Caspian's stock price has declined to $20, so the warrant stock purchase feature clearly has no value. Instead, a warrant holder puts 30 warrants back to the company, which requires a cash payment of $5 for each warrant, and results in the following entry:

Liabilities—puttable warrants	150	
Cash		150

Caspian's stock price then increases to $30, which allows warrant holders to achieve a $10 gain if they acquire shares with their warrants for $20. Accordingly, another warrant holder acquires shares with 50 warrants, resulting in the following entry:

Cash	1,000	
Liabilities—puttable warrants	250	
Common stock		50
Additional paid-in capital		1,200

In a separate bond issuance, Caspian again issues put warrants under the same terms, but now its stock price is $35 at the time of bond issuance, making the warrant feature more likely to be exercised than the put feature. Accordingly, Caspian records the proceeds in equity with the following entry (again, the remaining entries recording the bond issuance are omitted):

Cash	500	
Additional paid-in capital—warrants		500

Investors use all 100 warrants to acquire shares at the $20 exercise price. The entry follows:

Cash	2,000	
Paid-in capital—warrants	500	
Common stock		100
Additional paid-in capital		2,400

The original classification should not be changed because of subsequent economic changes in the value of the put. The value assigned to the put warrant at issuance, however, should be adjusted to its highest redemption price, starting with the date of issuance until the earliest date of the warrants. Changes in the redemption price before the earliest put dates are changes in accounting estimates and changes after the earliest put dates should be recognized in income. If the put is classified as equity, the adjustment should be reported as a charge to retained earnings, and if the put is classified as a liability the adjustment is reported as interest expense.

Regardless of how the put is classified on the statement of financial position, the primary and fully diluted EPS should be calculated on both an equity basis (warrants will be exercised) and on a debt basis (put will be exercised) and the more dilutive of the two methods should be used.

Disclosure Requirements

Under ASC 505-10-50, certain disclosures of an entity's capital structure are required. See the appendix for detailed information on disclosures.

FINANCIAL STATEMENT PRESENTATION

This section provides an illustration of the various financial statements that may be required to be presented and that are related to the stockholders' equity section of the statement of financial position.

Stockholders' Equity Section of a Statement of Financial Position

Capital stock:		
Preferred stock, $100 par, 7% cumulative, 30,000 shares authorized, issued, and outstanding		$ 3,000,000
Common stock, no par, stated value $10 per share, 500,000 shares authorized, 415,000 shares issued		4,150,000
Total capital stock		$ 7,150,000
Additional paid-in capital:		
Issued price in excess of par value—preferred	$ 150,000	
Issued price in excess of stated value—common	845,000	995,000
Total paid-in capital		$ 8,145,000
Donated capital		100,000
Retained earnings:		
Appropriated for plant expansion	$2,100,000	
Unappropriated	2,110,000	4,210,000
Accumulated other comprehensive income		165,000
Total capital, retained earnings, and accumulated other comprehensive income		$12,620,000
Less 10,000 common shares held in treasury, at cost		(120,000)
Total stockholders' equity		$12,500,000

Retained Earnings Statement

Balance at beginning of year, as reported	$ 3,800,000
Prior period adjustment—correction of an error in method of depreciation (less tax effect of $77,000)	115,000
Balance at beginning of year, restated	$ 3,915,000
Net income for the year	583,000
Cash dividends declared during the year	
Preferred stock	(210,000)
Common stock	(78,000)
Balance at end of year	$ 4,210,000

Statement of Changes in Stockholders' Equity

	Preferred stock Shares	Preferred stock Amount	Common stock Shares	Common stock Amount	Additional paid-in capital	Donated capital	Retained earnings	Accumulated other comprehensive income*	Treasury stock (common)	Total Stockholders' equity
Balance, 12/31/X1, as reported	–	–	400,000	$4,000,000	$840,000	$100,000	$3,800,000	$ 56,000	$(120,000)	$ 8,676,000
Correction of an error in method of depreciation	–	–	–	–	–	–	115,000		–	115,000
Balance, 12/31/X1, restated	–	–	400,000	$4,000,000	$840,000	$100,000	$3,915,000		$(120,000)	$ 8,791,000
Preferred stock issued in public offering	30,000	$3,000,000	–	–	150,000	–	–		–	3,150,000
Stock options exercised	–	–	15,000	150,000	5,000	–	–		–	155,000
Net income	–	–	–	–	–	–	583,000		–	583,000
Cash dividends declared:										
Preferred, $7.00 per share	–	–	–	–	–	–	(210,000)		–	(210,000)
Common, $.20 per share	–	–	–	–	–	–	(78,000)		–	(78,000)
Other comprehensive income								109,000		
Balance, 12/31/X1	30,000	$3,000,000	415,000	$4,150,000	$995,000	$100,000	$4,210,000	$165,000	$(120,000)	$12,500,000

* *Comprehensive income for the period:*

Net income	*$748,000*
Other comprehensive income	*109,000*
	$857,000

Other Sources

See ASC Location – Wiley *GAAP* Chapter…	***For information on…***
From ASC 505-10, *Overall*	
ASC 220-10-45-1 through 45-17	The required presentation and disclosure related to other comprehensive income
ASC 470-20	The measurement and recognition as equity of beneficial conversion features of convertible debt and certain preferred stock
ASC 470-20	The need to allocate proceeds from the sale of debt with stock purchase warrants to the debt and the warrants
ASC 480	Whether a specific financial instrument shall be classified as equity or outside of the equity classification
ASC 810-10-45-5	The treatment of shares of a parent held by its subsidiary in the consolidated balance sheet
ASC 810-10-40-1 through 40-2A	The accounting for the purchase (early extinguishment) of a wholly owned subsidiary's mandatorily redeemable preferred stock
ASC 815	The potential classification of an embedded derivative as an equity instrument
ASC 825-20	The accounting for a registration payment arrangement
ASC 505-30, *Treasury Stock*	
ASC 225-20	The income statement classification requirements applicable to the costs incurred by an entity to defend itself from a takeover attempt or the cost attributed to a standstill agreement
ASC 260	The determination of the effect of a treasury stock transaction and the effect of a forward contract that may be settled in stock or cash on the computation of earnings per share
ASC 505-60, *Spinoffs and Reverse Spinoffs*	
ASC 718	Compensation-related consequences of exchanges of share options or other equity instruments or changes to their terms in conjunction with an equity restructuring

36 ASC 605 REVENUE RECOGNITION

REVENUE RECOGNITION—GENERAL PRINCIPLES

Subtopics

ASC 605, *Revenue Recognition,* contains ten Subtopics:

- ASC 605-10, *Overall,* which provides guidance on revenues and gains and the installment and cost recovery methods.
- ASC 605-15, *Products*, which provides guidance on sales with a right of return and repurchases of products sold subject to an operating lease.
- ASC 605-20, *Services,* which provides guidance on separately priced extended warranty and product maintenance contracts, commissions from certain experience-rated or retrospective insurance arrangements, certain loan guarantee fees, in-transit freight service, and advertising barter transactions.

- ASC 605-25, *Multiple-Element Arrangements*, which provides guidance on arrangements under which a vendor will provide multiple deliverables.
- ASC 605-28, *Milestone Method*, which provides guidance on the application of the milestone method of revenue recognition in arrangements that include research or development deliverables.
- ASC 605-30, *Rights to Use,* which merely provides links to other Codification Topics on rights to use.
- ASC 605-35, *Construction-Type and Production-Type Contracts*, which provides guidance on contracts for which specifications are provided by the customer for the performance of contracts for the construction of facilities or the production of goods.
- ASC 605-45, *Gains and Losses*, which provides guidance on miscellaneous gains and losses not addressed in other FASB Codification Topics.
- ASC 605-45, *Principal-Agent Considerations*, which provides guidance on reporting revenue gross or net of certain amounts paid to others.
- ASC 605-50, *Customer Payments and Incentives*, which provides guidance on accounting by vendors and customers for consideration given by a vendor to a customer.

Revenue recognition concerns. The principles guiding recognition of revenues for financial reporting purposes are central to GAAP and in most instances are unambiguous and straightforward.

However, while the currently effective basic principles are uncomplicated, it is nonetheless true that a large percentage of financial reporting frauds over the period beginning about 1995 were the result of misapplications, often deliberate, of revenue recognition practices prescribed under GAAP. Apart from outright fraud (e.g., recording nonexistent transactions), there were several factors contributing to this unfortunate state of affairs.

First, business practices have continued to grow increasingly complex, involving, among other things, a marked shift from manufacturing to a service-based economy, where the proper timing for revenue recognition is often more difficult to ascertain. Second, there has been an undeniable increase in the willingness of managers, whose compensation packages are often directly linked to the company's stock price and reported earnings, to "stretch" accounting rules to facilitate earnings management. This has particularly been the case where GAAP requirements have been vague, complex or abstruse. And third, it has been well documented that, too often, independent auditors have been willing to accommodate managements' wishes, particularly in the absence of specific rules under GAAP to support a denial of such requests. These actions have often had disastrous consequences, if not immediately, then in the longer run.

Errors or deliberate distortions involving revenue recognition fall into two categories: situations in which revenue legitimately earned is reported in the incorrect fiscal (financial reporting) period, often referred to as "cutoff" errors, and situations in which revenue is recognized although never actually earned. Given the emphasis on periodic reporting (e.g., quarterly earnings announcements in the case of publicly held entities), even simple "cutoff" errors can have enormous impact, notwithstanding the fact that these should tend to offset over several periods. As a practical matter, all instances of improper revenue recognition constitute a challenge to all accountants attempting to properly interpret and apply GAAP, including independent auditors.

Revenue recognition—general guidelines. Revenue, whether from the sale of product or provision of services, is to be recognized only when it has been earned. According to CON 5, *Recognition and Measurement in Financial Statements of Business Enterprises*,

> *. . . An entity's revenue-earning activities involve delivering or producing goods, rendering services, or other activities that constitute its ongoing major or central operations, and revenues are considered to have been earned when the entity has substantially accomplished what it must do to be entitled to the benefits represented by the revenues. (Para. 83)*

In other words, in order to be recognized revenue must be realized or realizable, and it must have been earned.

CON 5 notes that "the two conditions (being realized or realizable, and being earned) are usually met by the time product or merchandise is delivered or services are rendered to customers, and revenues from manufacturing and selling activities and gains and losses from sales of other assets are commonly recognized at time of sale (usually meaning delivery)." Moreover, "if services are rendered or rights to use assets extend continuously over time (for example, interest or rent), reliable measures based on contractual prices established in advance are commonly available, and revenues may be recognized as earned as time passes." In other words, for most traditional and familiar types of transactions, the point at which it is appropriate to recognize revenue will be quite clear. (CON5, Para. 84a)

The SEC, reflecting on the conceptual foundation for revenue recognition, observed in Staff Accounting Bulletin (SAB) 104, that

> *. . . revenue generally is realized or realizable and earned when* **all** *of the following criteria are met:*
>
> 1. *There is persuasive evidence that an arrangement exists*
> 2. *Delivery has occurred or services have been rendered*
> 3. *The seller's price to the buyer is fixed or determinable, and*
> 4. *Collectibility is reasonably assured.*

Note that, while Securities and Exchange Commission (SEC) rules and "unofficial" guidance are not necessarily to be deemed GAAP for nonpublic companies, to the extent that these provide insights into the application of the Accounting Standards Codification (ASC), they should always be viewed as relevant guidance and followed, absent other, contradictory rules established under GAAP. In the absence of any other authoritative source, SEC pronouncements may represent the best thinking on the subject and would thus be considered authoritative for all reporting entities.

With regard to the four criteria set forth above, consideration should be directed at the following discussion, which is drawn partially from SAB 101 and SAB 104.

First, regarding persuasive evidence of an arrangement, attention must be paid to the customary manner in which the reporting entity engages in revenue-producing transactions with its customers or clients. Since these transactions are negotiated between the buyer and seller and can have unique or unusual terms, there are (and can be) no absolute standards. Thus, for an enterprise that traditionally obtains appropriate documentation (purchase orders, etc.) from its customers before concluding sales to them, advance deliveries to customers, even if later ratified by receipt of the proper paperwork, would not be deemed a valid basis for revenue recognition at the time of delivery.

When evaluating purported revenue transactions, the substance of the transactions must always be considered, and not merely their form. It has become increasingly commonplace to "paper over" transactions in ways that can create the basis for inappropriate revenue recognition. For example, transactions that are actually consignment arrangements might be described as "sales" or as "conditional sales," but revenue recognition would not be appropriate until the consigned goods are later sold to a third-party purchaser.

Careful analysis of the rights and obligations of the parties and the risks borne by each at various stages of the transactions should reveal when and whether an actual sale has occurred and whether revenue recognition is warranted. In general, if the buyer has a right to return the product in question, coupled with a deferred or conditional payment obligation and/or significant remaining performance obligations by the seller, revenue will not be recognizable by the seller at the time of initial delivery. Similarly, if there is an implicit or explicit obligation by the seller to repurchase the item transferred, a real sales transaction has not occurred. The buyer must assume the risks of ownership in all cases if revenue is to be recognized.

With regard to whether delivery has occurred or services have been rendered, ownership and risk taking must have been transferred to the buyer if revenue is to be recognized by the seller. Thus, if the seller is holding goods for delivery to the buyer because the buyer's receiving dock workers are on strike and no deliveries are being accepted, revenue generally cannot be recognized in the reporting period, even if these delayed deliveries are made subsequent to period end. (There are limited exceptions to this general principle, typically involving a written request from the buyer for delayed delivery under a "bill-and-hold" arrangement, having a valid business purpose.)

The SEC frowns upon bill-and-hold transactions. It will generally not allow revenue recognition in either of the following circumstances:

- When a company completes manufacturing of a product and segregates the inventory within its facility; or
- When a company ships products to a third-party storage facility while retaining title to the product and payment by the buyer will not occur until it is delivered to the buyer.

The SEC bases its opinion on the underlying concepts that revenue recognition does not occur until the customer takes title to the goods and assumes the risks and rewards of ownership. Consequently, the SEC uses all of the following criteria when determining whether revenue should be recognized:

1. Ownership risk must pass to the buyer;
2. The customer makes a (preferably) written commitment to buy the goods;
3. The buyer must requires that the sale be on a bill-and-hold basis, and have a substantial business purpose for doing so;
4. There is a reasonable delivery schedule for the goods;
5. The seller has no remaining performance obligations;
6. The goods have been segregated, and cannot be used to fill other orders received by the seller; and
7. The product must be complete.

The SEC further states that generally delivery has not occurred unless the product has been delivered to either the customer or another site specified by the customer. If the customer specifies delivery to a staging site but a substantial portion of the sales price is not payable until delivery is ultimately made to the customer, then revenue recognition must be delayed until final delivery to the customer has been completed.

Delivery, as used here, implies more than simply the physical relocation of the goods to the buyer's place of business. Rather, it means that the goods have actually been accepted by the customer, which, depending on the terms of the relevant contract, could be conditioned on whether inspection, testing, and/or installation have been completed, and the buyer has committed to pay for the items purchased. For revenue recognition to be justified, substantial performance of the terms of delivery must have occurred, and if any terms remain uncompleted, there should be a basis grounded on historical experience to assume that these matters will be satisfactorily attended to.

In some instances there are multiple "deliverables." in such cases, revenue is not recognized for any given element if later deliverables are essential for the functionality of the already delivered element. In other situations, such as in various licensing arrangements, physical "delivery" may occur well before product usage by the buyer can take place (e.g., software for the future year's tax preparation delivered before the current year end), and revenue is not to be recognized prior to the initial date of expected use by the buyer.

The SEC holds that revenue should not be recognized until such time as any uncertainty about customer acceptance of goods or services has been eliminated. This requires an examination of customer acceptance provisions in the purchase agreement. For example, the agreement may allow the customer to test the product or require additional services subsequent to delivery, such as product installation. If these provisions exist, the SEC assumes that the customer specifically bargained for their inclusion in the agreement, which makes them substantive parts of the agreement. Consequently, revenue cannot be recognized until either the customer has accepted the goods or services, or the acceptance provisions have lapsed.

The SEC states that formal customer sign-off on a contractual customer acceptance provision is not always necessary. Instead, the seller can demonstrate that the criteria specified in the acceptance provisions are satisfied.

The SEC considers customer acceptance provisions to take one of four general forms, which are

1. *Acceptance for trial or evaluation purposes.* The customer agrees to accept the product strictly for evaluation purposes, so title remains with the seller. The customer may then actively affirm acceptance or do so simply through the passage of time; in either case, this is essentially a consignment arrangement where the seller should not recognize revenue until the customer confirms that it will purchase the product.
2. *Acceptance granting a right to return or exchange on the basis of subjective issues.* The customer has the right to return the product if dissatisfied with it. In this case, a company can recognize revenue at the initial point of sale, but only if it can reasonably estimate the amount of future returns and accrue for them. If the seller cannot make this estimate, then it must wait until the right of return has expired before recognizing revenue.
3. *Acceptance based on seller-specified objective criteria.* The customer has a right of return or replacement if the delivered product is defective or fails to meet its published specifications. If the seller has already demonstrated that the product meets its specifications and can reasonably estimate the amount of defective products, then it can create a warranty reserve and recognize revenue at the point of sale. If the seller cannot prove that the product meets its published specifications, then it should defer revenue recognition until the specifications have been achieved.
4. *Acceptance based on customer-specified objective criteria.* The customer has created a specific set of acceptance criteria that the seller must meet before the customer will accept the delivery. This is best achieved with a formal sign-off document. Alternatively, the seller can demonstrate that the delivered product meets the customer's criteria (such as through preshipment testing). However, it may not be possible to conduct such testing prior to delivery, because performance may vary based on how the product works in combination with the customer's other systems. In this case, revenue recognition should be deferred until the product is actually installed and meets the stated criteria. Also, the seller must evaluate its ability to enforce a payment claim in the absence of a formal sign-off. If payment enforcement would be difficult, then revenue recognition should be deferred until formal customer sign-off.

This is perhaps the most subjective of the four forms of customer acceptance, so the SEC states that it will not object to a determination that is well reasoned on the basis of the guidance just described.

In the case of many service transactions, large up-front fees are often charged, nominally in recognition of the selling of a membership, the signing of a contract, or for enrolling the customer in a program. (For example, initiation fees to join a health club where the terms of membership also obligate the member to pay ongoing fees.) Unless the services provided to the customer at inception are substantial, the presumption is that the revenue received has not been earned, but rather must be deferred and recognized, usually ratably, over the period that substantive services are provided. Thus, initiation fees are amortized over the membership period.

In cases where the seller is providing a service and requires an up-front fee, the SEC prefers that the fee be accounted for as revenue on a straight-line basis; this recognition shall be either over the term of the arrangement or the expected period during which services are to be performed, whichever is longer. The only situation where revenue is not recognized on a straight-line basis is when revenue is earned or obligations are fulfilled in a different pattern.

Even in cases where the seller's obligations to the buyer are inconsequential or perfunctory, the SEC believes that the substance of these transactions indicates that the buyer is paying for a service that is delivered over a period of time, which therefore calls for revenue recognition over the period of performance.

The seller's price to the buyer is fixed or determinable when a customer does not have the unilateral right to terminate or cancel the contract and receive a cash refund. Depending on customary practice, extended return privileges might imply that this condition has not been met in given circumstances. Prices that are conditional on the occurrence of future events are not fixed or determinable from the perspective of revenue recognition.

In theory, until the refund rights have expired, or the specified future events have occurred, revenue should not be recognized. As a practical matter, however, assuming that the amount of refunds can be reliably estimated (based on past experience, industry data, etc.), revenues, net of expected refunds, can be recognized on a pro rata basis. Absent this ability to reliably estimate, however, revenue recognition is deferred.

The final factor, reasonable assurance of collectibility, implies that the accrual for bad debts (uncollectible accounts receivable) can be estimated with reasonable accuracy, both to accomplish proper periodic matching of revenue and expenses, and to enable the presentation of receivables at net realizable value, as required under GAAP. An inability to accomplish this objective necessitates deferral of revenue recognition—generally until collection occurs, or at least until it becomes feasible to estimate the uncollectible portion with sufficient accuracy.

The SEC holds that revenue may be recognized in its entirety if the seller's remaining obligation is inconsequential or perfunctory. This means that the seller should have substantially completed the terms specified in the sales arrangement in order for delivery or performance to have occurred. Any remaining incomplete actions can only be considered inconsequential if the failure to complete them would not result in the customer receiving a refund or rejecting the products or services. Further, the seller should have a history of completing the remaining tasks in a timely manner, and of being able to estimate all remaining costs associated with those activities. If revenue is recognized prior to the completion of any inconsequential items, then the estimated cost of those inconsequential items should be accrued when the revenue is recognized.

An extreme situation, calling for not merely accrual of losses from estimated uncollectible receivables, is to defer revenue recognition entirely until collectibility is assured (or actually achieved). The most conservative accounting alternative, as set forth in CON 5, is to record revenue only as collected. It states "(i)f collectibility of assets received for product, services, or other assets is doubtful, revenues and gains *may* be recognized on the basis of cash received." (Emphasis added.) The permissive language, which (it must be assumed) was deliberately selected in preference to a mandatory exhortation (e.g., "must"), suggests that even in such a situation this hyperconservative departure from accrual accounting is not truly prescriptive, but is a possible solution to a fact-specific set of circumstances.

Problems in Revenue Recognition

Certain of the more attention-getting problems in applying the general principles of revenue recognition are discussed in the following paragraphs.

Financial statement presentation: gross versus net. In general, it is well established that reporting on a "gross" basis is appropriate when the entity takes ownership of the goods being sold to its customers, with the risks and rewards of ownership accruing to it. For example, if the entity runs the risk of obsolescence or spoilage during the period it holds the merchandise, gross reporting would normally be appropriate. On the other hand, if the entity merely acts as an agent for the buyer or seller from whom it earns a commission, then "net" reporting would be more appropriate.

Enterprises may inflate the revenues reported in their income statements by reporting transactions on a "gross" basis, notwithstanding that the entity's real economic role is as an agent for buyer and/or seller. This distortion became widespread in the case of Internet commerce-based "dot-com companies" and other start-up and innovative businesses typically not reporting earnings, for which market valuations were heavily influenced by absolute levels of and trends in gross revenues. Reporting revenues "gross" rather than "net" often had an enormous impact on the perceived value of those enterprises.

Factors to consider in determining whether sales are properly reported "gross" or "net" include:

1. Whether the entity acts as a principal or an agent in the transactions
2. Whether the entity takes title to the property
3. Whether the entity has the normal risks and rewards of ownership
4. Whether the entity acts as an agent or broker (including performing services, in substance, as an agent or broker) with compensation on a commission or fee basis.

Reporting taxes collected as revenue. Most businesses must collect certain taxes which must subsequently be transmitted to governmental bodies, making the entity in effect an agent of the state. The most obvious example of this situation is the imposition of sales taxes, which are almost universally applicable to retail merchandise transactions and, increasingly, to service transactions as well. Historically accounting practice has varied, with some entities reporting gross revenue inclusive of taxes—which are then later reported as expenses when remitted—while other entities report revenue net of these taxes, treating them as purely a statement of financial position event. ASC 605-45-50-3 confirms that either methodology is acceptable, and if material, should be defined in the accounting policies note to the financial statements. As an elective accounting policy, accordingly, any change in method should be justified as being warranted as a means of improving financial reporting.

Barter transactions. Barter transactions (nonmonetary exchanges, as described in ASC 845-10) are not a problem, assuming that they represent the culmination of an earnings process. However, in recent years there have been many reports of transactions that appear to have been concocted merely to create the illusion of revenue-generating activities. Examples include advertising swaps engaged in by some entities, most commonly "dot-com" enterprises, and the excess capacity swaps of fiber optic communications concerns under "indefeasible right to use" agreements. Both of these and many other situations involved immediate recognition of revenues coupled with deferred recognition of costs, and typically in aggregate were equal exchanges not providing profits to either party. Furthermore, these examples do not represent culminations of the normal earnings process (e.g., fiber optic networks were built in order to sell communications services to end users, not for the purpose of swapping capacity with other similar operations).

In hindsight, most observers can see why these and many other aggressive reporting practices deviated from established or implied GAAP; although there are still some who insist that because GAAP failed to explicitly address these precise scenarios, the accounting for the transactions was open to interpretation. Since GAAP (even the highly rules-based US GAAP) cannot possibly hope to overtly address all the various innovative transaction structures that exist and will be invented, it is necessary to apply basic principles and reason by analogy to newly emerging circumstances. Of great importance to financial statement preparers (and internal and external auditors) is obtaining a thorough understanding of the nature and normal operations of the business enterprise being reported upon, application of "substance over form" reasoning, and the goal of faithfully representing the economics of transactions.

Channel stuffing. Many difficult issues of revenue recognition involve practices that may or may not involve GAAP departures, depending on the situation-specific facts and circumstances. Channel stuffing, a prime example of this issue, occurs when sales are actually made prior to the period-end cutoff but may have been stimulated by "side agreements," such as a promise to customers of extended return privileges or more liberal credit terms. In such circumstances, there might be a greater likelihood that a substantial portion of these sales may be subsequently nullified, as unrealistically large orders inevitably lead to later large returns made for full credit.

For purposes of financial reporting under GAAP, valuation allowances should be established for expected sales returns and allowances. (In practice, however, this is rarely done because the amounts involved are immaterial, unlike the amounts of the more familiar allowances for uncollectible accounts.) The use of valuation accounts for anticipated returns and allowances is dictated by both the matching concept (recording returns and allowances in the same fiscal period in which the revenue is recognized) as well as by the requirement to present accounts receivable at net realizable value. When the potential product returns are not subject to reasonable estimation (as when a sales promotion effort of the type just described is first being attempted by the reporting entity) but could be material, it might not be permissible to recognize revenues at all, pending subsequent developments (ASC 605-15-25). Furthermore, from the SEC's perspective, factors such as the following could require deferral of revenues at the time goods are shipped to customers, pending resolution of material uncertainties:

1. Significant levels of product inventory in the distribution channel
2. Lack of "visibility" into, or the inability to determine or observe, the levels of inventory in a distribution channel and the current level of sales to end users
3. Expected introductions of new products that may result in the technological obsolescence of, and larger than expected returns of, current products
4. The significance of a particular distributor to the company's (or a reporting segment of the company's) business, sales and marketing
5. The newness of a product
6. The introduction of competitors' products with superior technology or greater expected market acceptance could affect market demand and changing trends in that demand for an entity's products.

Mischaracterization of extraordinary or unusual transactions as components of gross revenue. Not all revenue recognition errors and frauds involve questions of when or if revenue should be recognized. In some instances, classification in the income statement is of greater concern. While matters in this group often do not result in a distortion of net results of operations, they can seriously distort important indicators of performance trends. When this occurs, it most often involves reporting unusual or infrequent gains on sales of segments or specific assets as revenue from product or service transactions. A variation on this involves reporting unusual gains as offsets to one or more categories of operating expenses, similarly distorting key financial ratios and other indicators, again without necessarily invalidating the net income measure.

Mischaracterizing transactions as involving "arm's-length" third parties, thus justifying unwarranted gain recognition. Transfers of inventory or other assets to a related entity typically defers gain or income recognition until subsequent transfer to an "arm's-length" party. In some cases, sales have been disguised as being to unrelated entities with gain being recognized, when in fact the "buyer" was a nominee of the seller, or the financing was provided or guaranteed by the seller, or the "buyer" was a "variable interest entity" that failed to meet the complex and changing requirements under GAAP required for gain recognition. Depending upon the facts of the situation, this can result in gains being improperly recognized, or the gross amount of the transaction being improperly recognized in the seller/transferor's financial statements.

Selling undervalued assets to generate reportable gains. This issue again ranges from deliberate but real economic transactions that have as a goal the inflation of reportable revenues or gains, to misrepresented events having no economic substance but the same objective. Among the former is the deliberate invasion of low-cost LIFO inventory "layers," which boosts gross margins and net profits for the period, albeit at the cost of having to later replenish inventories with higher-cost goods. To the extent that this depletion of lower-cost inventory really occurs, there is no GAAP alternative to reflecting these excess profits currently, although the threat of full disclosure may prove to be somewhat of a deterrent.

Regarding the latter category, in some instances the ability to generate gains could indicate that errors occurred in recording a previous transaction. Thus, large gains flowing from the sale of assets recently acquired in a purchase business combination transaction could well mean the purchase price allocation process was flawed. If this is true, a reallocation of purchase price would be called for, and some or all of the apparent gains would be eliminated.

Related to the foregoing is the strategy of retiring outstanding debt to generate reportable gains. In periods of higher-than-historically-typical interest rates, lenders will often agree to early extinguishment of outstanding low-coupon obligations at a discount, hence creating accounting gains for the borrower, albeit replacement debt at current yields will result in higher interest costs over future years. To the extent the debt is really retired, however, this is a real economic event, and the consequent gain is reported in current earnings under GAAP.

Deliberate misstatement of percentage of completion on long-term construction contracts. Under ASC 605-35 (detailed later in this chapter), profits on certain long-term construction-type contracts are recognized ratably over the period of construction. An obvious and often easy way to distort periodic results of operations is to deliberately over- or understate the degree to which one or more discrete projects has been completed as of period end. This, coupled with the difficulty and importance of estimating remaining costs to be incurred to complete each project, makes profit recognition under this required method of accounting challenging to verify.

Technical Alert – ASU 2014-09, Revenue from Contracts with Customers (Topic 606)

On May 28, 2014, as this volume was going to production, the FASB issued its long awaited revenue recognition standard. One of its most ambitious projects and more than ten years in the making, the update was issued as a joint project with the IASB. The FASB believes the final document meets two major goals – simplification of revenue recognition guidance and consistency globally and across markets and industries. The ASU provides a robust framework that is expected to simplify preparation of financial statements by reducing the sources of guidance and replacing it with guidance users can understand. The ASU also includes new guidance for contract modifications and consistent application for service contracts.

The ASU is over 700 pages and was released in three sections:

- Section A—Summary and Amendments That Create Revenue from Contracts with Customers (Topic 606) and Other Assets and Deferred Costs—Contracts with Customers (Subtopic 340-40)
- Section B—Conforming Amendments to Other Topics and Subtopics in the Codification and Status Tables
- Section C—Background Information and Basis for Conclusions

Effective Dates. Because of the number of organizations and line items affected, the FASB decided on a longer than usual effective date. The ASU is effective in the US as follows:

- For public organizations, the guidance in the Update is effective for annual reporting periods beginning after December 15, 2016, including interim reporting periods within that reporting period. Early application is not permitted.
- For nonpublic companies and organizations, the new guidance will be required for annual reporting periods beginning after December 15, 2017, and interim and annual reporting periods after those reporting periods. A nonpublic entity may elect early application, but no earlier than the effective date for public entities.

When the ASU was announced on May 28, 2014 and again on a June 5, 2014 webcast, the FASB left the door open to extending the implementation date. The FASB is essentially taking a "wait and see" attitude regarding changing the effective date.

Entities have the option to implement the guidance through:

- Full retrospective application or
- Modified retrospective application

Using the modified retrospective approach, the entity recognizes the cumulative effect of initially adopting the standard as an adjustment to the opening balance of retained earnings in the annual period when the standard is adopted. If the entity issues comparative statements, then it reports revenue for prior years under the guidance in effect before adoption.

Core Principle and Five Steps. The ASU articulates a core principle on which the new guidance is based:

> Recognize revenue to depict the transfer of promised goods or services to customers in an amount that reflects the consideration to which the entity expects to be entitled in exchange for those goods or services.

To achieve this core principle, an entity should follow these five steps:

1. Identify the contract with customers.
2. Identify the performance obligations (promises) in the contract.

3. Determine the transaction price.
4. Allocate the transaction price to the performance obligations in the contract.
5. Recognize revenue when (or as) the reporting organization satisfies a performance obligation.

In reviewing a transaction, each of the steps may not be needed, and they may not always be applied sequentially.

Note that the ASU is not organized by these five steps, but the FASB believes the steps offer a methodology for entities to use when deciding the appropriate accounting for a transaction.

Disclosures. The ASU includes new disclosure requirements designed to provide better information to financial statement users about contracts with customers. The requirements are comprehensive and include quantitative and qualitative information to enable users to understand the nature, amount, timing, and uncertainty of revenue and cash flow form contracts with customers. The ASU includes some exceptions for disclosure by nonpublic entities.

Other Changes. In addition to the items mentioned above, the ASU includes changes on contract cots, right of returns, warranties, principal vs. agent consideration, licenses, repurchase agreements, customer acceptance terms, and other areas.

Transition Resource Group. The FASB and the IASB have established a Joint Transition Resource Group (TRG). The objective of the TRG is to inform the Boards about potential implementation issues that could arise during the implementation period. The TRG will not issue guidance, but will bring issues to the Boards who will consider whether amendments additional guidance is needed.

LONG-TERM CONSTRUCTION CONTRACTS (ASC 605-35)

PERSPECTIVE AND ISSUES

Accounting for long-term construction contracts involves questions as to when revenue is to be recognized and how to measure the revenue to be recorded. The basic GAAP governing the recognition of long-term contract revenue is contained in ASC 605-35 and ASC 910.

The accounting for long-term construction contracts is complicated by the need to rely upon estimates of revenues, costs to be incurred, and progress toward completion.

In the process of codifying GAAP, the Financial Accounting Standards Board (FASB) made certain technical corrections to eliminate inconsistencies in the previously promulgated authoritative long-term contract literature.

The corrections clarify that:

1. To be combined for accounting purposes, contracts must meet the specified criteria discussed later in this section that are set forth in ASC 605-35-25-5, et seq., and
2. Under both the completed-contract method and percentage-of-completion method, full provision is to be made for losses on contracts in the period in which the loss becomes evident (ASC 605-35-25-45, et seq.).

DEFINITIONS OF TERMS

Back charges. Billings for work performed or costs incurred by one party (the biller) that, in accordance with the agreement, should have been performed or incurred by the party billed.

Change order. A legal document executed by a contractor and customer (which can be initiated by either) that modifies selected terms of a contract (e.g., pricing, timing and scope of work) without the necessity of redrafting the entire contract.

Claims. Amounts in excess of the agreed contract price that a contractor seeks to collect from customers for customer-caused delays, errors in specifications and designs, unapproved change orders, or other causes of unanticipated costs. (ASC 605-35)

Combining contracts. Grouping two or more contracts into a single profit center for accounting purposes.

Completed-contract method. A method of accounting that recognizes revenue only after the contract is complete.

Cost-to-cost method. A percentage-of-completion method used to determine the extent of progress toward completion on a contract. The ratio of costs incurred from project inception through the end of the current period (numerator) to the total estimated costs of the project (denominator) is applied to the contract price (as adjusted for change orders) to determine total contract revenue earned to date.

Estimated cost to complete. The anticipated additional cost of materials, labor, subcontracting costs, and indirect costs (overhead) required in order to complete a project at a scheduled time.

Percentage-of-completion method. A method of accounting that recognizes revenue on a contract as work progresses.

Precontract costs. Costs incurred before a contract has been accepted (e.g., architectural designs, purchase of special equipment, engineering fees, and start-up costs).

Profit center. A unit for the accumulation of revenues and costs for the measurement of contract performance.

Progress billings on long-term contracts. Requests for partial payments sent to the customer in accordance with the terms of the contract at agreed-upon intervals as various project milestones are reached.

Segmenting contracts. Dividing a single contract or group of contracts into two or more profit centers for accounting purposes.

Subcontractor. A second-level contractor who enters into a contract with a prime (general) contractor to perform a specific part or phase of a construction project.

Substantial completion. The point at which the major work on a contract is completed and only insignificant costs and potential risks remain.

Work-in-progress (WIP). The accumulated construction costs of the project that have been incurred since project inception.

CONCEPTS, RULES, AND EXAMPLES

Long-term construction contract revenue is recognizable over time as construction progresses rather than at the completion of the contract. This "as earned" approach to revenue recognition is justified, because under most long-term construction contracts both the buyer and the seller (contractor) obtain legally enforceable rights. The buyer has the legal right to require specific performance from the contractor and, in effect, has an ownership claim to the contractor's work in progress. The contractor, under most long-term contracts, has the right to require the buyer to make progress payments during the construction period. The substance of this business activity is that revenue is earned continuously as the work progresses.

Methods of Accounting

ASC 605-35 describes the two generally accepted methods of accounting for long-term construction contracts.

The percentage-of-completion method. ASC 605-35 states that:

> *The percentage-of-completion method recognizes income as work on a contract (or group of closely related contracts) progresses. The recognition of revenues and profits is generally related to costs incurred in providing the services required under the contract.*

Under this method, *work-in-progress* (WIP) is accumulated in the accounting records. At any point in time if the cumulative billings to date under the contract exceed the amount of the WIP plus the portion of the contract's estimated gross profit attributable to that WIP, then the contractor recognizes a current liability captioned "billings in excess of costs and estimated earnings." This liability recognizes the remaining obligation of the contractor to complete additional work prior to recognizing the excess billing as revenue.

If the reverse is true, that is, the accumulated WIP and gross profit earned exceed billings to date, then the contractor recognizes a current asset captioned "costs and estimated earnings in excess of billings." This asset represents the portion of the contractor's revenues under the contract that have been earned but not yet billed under the contract provisions. Where more than one contract exists, these assets and liabilities are determined on a project-by-project basis, with the accumulated assets and liabilities being separately stated on the statement of financial position. Assets and liabilities are not offset unless a right of offset exists. Thus, the net debit balances for certain contracts are not ordinarily offset against net credit balances for other contracts. An exception may exist if the balances relate to contracts that meet the criteria for combining described in ASC 605-35 and discussed later in this section.

Under the percentage-of-completion method, income is not based on cash collections or interim billings. Cash collections and interim billings are based upon contract terms that do not necessarily measure contract performance.

The completed-contract method. ASC 605-35 states that:

> *The completed-contract method recognizes income only when the contract is complete, or substantially complete.*

Under this method, contract costs and related billings are accumulated in the accounting records and reported as deferred items on the statement of financial position until the project is complete or substantially complete. A contract is regarded as substantially complete if remaining costs of completion are immaterial. When the accumulated costs (WIP) exceed the related billings, the excess is presented as a current asset (inventory account). If billings exceed related costs, the difference is presented as a current liability. This determination is also made on a project-by-project basis with the accumulated assets and liabilities being separately stated on the statement of financial position. An excess of accumulated costs over related billings is presented as a current asset, and an excess of accumulated billings over related costs is presented in most cases as a current liability.

Preferability assessment. ASC 605-35 deems the percentage-of-completion method to be preferable when estimates are reasonably dependable and the following conditions exist:

1. Contracts executed by the parties include provisions that clearly specify the enforceable rights regarding goods or services to be provided and received by the parties, the consideration to be exchanged, and the manner and terms of settlement.

2. The buyer can be expected to satisfy his or her obligations under the contract.
3. The contractor can be expected to perform his or her contractual obligations.

ASC 605-35 presumes that contractors generally have the ability to produce estimates that are sufficiently dependable to justify the use of the percentage-of-completion method of accounting. Persuasive evidence to the contrary is necessary to overcome this presumption.

The principal advantage of the completed-contract method is that it is based on final results, whereas the percentage-of-completion method is dependent upon estimates for unperformed work. The principal disadvantage of the completed-contract method is that when the period of a contract extends into more than one accounting period, there will be an irregular recognition of income.

These two methods are not equally acceptable alternatives for the same set of circumstances. ASC 605-35 states that, in general, when estimates of costs to complete and extent of progress toward completion of long-term contracts are reasonably dependable, the percentage-of-completion method is preferable. When lack of dependable estimates or inherent hazards cause forecasts to be doubtful, the completed-contract method is preferable.

The completed-contract method may also be acceptable when a contractor has numerous relatively short-term contracts and when results of operations do not vary materially from those that would be reported under the percentage-of-completion method.

Based on the contractor's individual circumstances, a decision is made as to whether to apply completed-contract or percentage-of-completion accounting as the entity's basic accounting policy. If warranted by different facts and circumstances regarding a particular contract or group of contracts, that contract or group of contracts is to be accounted for under the other method with accompanying financial statement disclosures of this departure from the normal policy.

Costs Incurred

Precontract costs. Precontract costs are costs incurred before a contract has been entered into, with the expectation of the contract being accepted and thereby recoverable through future billings. Precontract costs include architectural designs, costs of learning a new process, and any other costs that are expected to be recovered if the contract is accepted. ASC 720-15 requires that precontract costs be expensed as incurred, as they are the equivalent of start-up costs in other types of businesses. Consequently, precontract costs are not permitted to be included in WIP. Contract costs incurred after the acceptance of the contract are costs incurred toward the completion of the project and are accumulated in work-in-progress (WIP).

If precontract costs are incurred in connection with a current contract in anticipation of obtaining additional future contracts, those costs are nevertheless accounted for as costs of the current contract. If such costs are not incurred in connection with a current contract, then they must be expensed as incurred. There is no look-back provision permitted by this rule. A contractor may not retroactively record precontract costs as WIP if a contract is subsequently executed.

Contract costs. Contract costs are costs identifiable with or allocable to specific contracts. Generally, contract costs include all direct costs, such as direct materials, direct labor, and any indirect costs (overhead) allocable to the contracts. Contract costs can be broken down into two categories: costs incurred to date and estimated costs to complete.

The company may choose to defer costs related to producing excess goods in anticipation of future orders of the same item. Costs associated with excess production can be treated as inventory if the costs are considered recoverable.

Estimated costs to complete. These are the anticipated costs required to complete a project at a scheduled time. They are comprised of the same elements as the original total estimated contract costs and are based on prices expected to be in effect when the costs will be incurred.

The latest estimates are used to determine the progress toward completion. ASC 605-35 provides the practices to be followed when estimating costs to complete.

Systematic and consistent procedures are to be used. These procedures are to be correlated with the cost accounting system in order to facilitate a comparison between actual and estimated costs. Additionally, the determination of estimated total contract costs is to identify the significant cost elements.

Estimated costs are to reflect any expected price increases. These expected price increases are not "blanket provisions" for all contract costs, but rather specific provisions for each specific type of cost. Expected increases in each of the cost elements, such as wages, materials, and overhead items, are considered separately.

Finally, estimates of costs to complete are to be reviewed periodically to reflect new information. Estimates of costs are to be examined for price fluctuations and reviewed for possible future problems, such as labor strikes or direct material delivery delays.

Accounting for contract costs is similar to accounting for inventory. Costs necessary to ready the asset for sale (transfer of possession and occupancy by the customer) are recorded in WIP as incurred. WIP includes both direct and indirect costs but not general and administrative expenses or selling expenses, since by definition they are not identifiable with a particular contract and are therefore treated as period costs. However, general and administrative expenses may be included in contract costs under the completed contract method since this could result in better matching of revenues and costs, especially in years when no contracts were completed.

Subcontractor costs. Since a contractor may not be able to perform all facets of a construction project, one or more subcontractors may be engaged. Amounts earned by the subcontractor are included in contract costs as the work is completed. These amounts are directly attributable to the project and included in WIP, similar to direct materials and direct labor.

Back charges. Contract costs may require adjustment for back charges. A back charge is a billing by the contractor to a subcontractor (or a reduction in the amount due to that subcontractor under the subcontract) for costs incurred by the contractor to complete or correct work that the contract stipulated was to have been performed by the subcontractor. These charges are often disputed by the parties involved.

Example of a back charge situation

The subcontract (the contract between the general contractor and the subcontractor) obligates the subcontractor to raze a building and prepare the land for construction of a replacement building. The general contractor had to clear away debris left by the subcontractor before construction could begin. The general contractor expects to be reimbursed for the work since it was required to be performed by the subcontractor. The contractor back charges the subcontractor for the costs of debris removal.

The contractor treats the back charge as a receivable from the subcontractor (or a reduction in the amount payable to the subcontractor) and reduces contract costs by the amount recoverable. If the subcontractor disputes the back charge, the cost becomes a claim. Claims are an amount in excess of the agreed contract price or amounts not included in the original contract price that the contractor seeks to collect. Claims are only recorded as additional contract revenue if the requirements set forth in ASC 605-35 are met.

The subcontractor records the back charge as a payable and as additional contract costs if it is probable the amount will be paid. If the amount or validity of the liability is disputed, the subcontractor considers the probable outcome in order to determine the proper accounting treatment.

Types of Contracts

Four types of contracts are distinguished based on their pricing arrangements: (1) fixed-price or lump-sum contracts, (2) time-and-materials contracts, (3) cost-type contracts, and (4) unit-price contracts.

Fixed-price contracts are contracts for which the price is not usually subject to adjustment because of costs incurred by the contractor. The contractor bears the risks of cost overruns.

Time-and-materials contracts are contracts that provide for payments to the contractor based on direct labor hours at fixed rates and the contractor's cost of materials.

Cost-type contracts provide for reimbursement of allowable or otherwise defined costs incurred plus a fee representing profits. Some variations of cost-plus contracts are (1) cost-without-fee: no provision for a fee, (2) cost-plus-fixed-fee: contractor reimbursed for costs plus provision for a fixed fee, and (3) cost-plus-award-fee: same as (2) plus provision for an award based on performance. The contract price on a cost-type contract is determined by the sum of the reimbursable expenditures and a fee. The fee is the profit margin (revenue less direct expenses) to be earned on the contract.

Unit-price contracts are contracts under which the contractor is paid a specified amount for every unit of work performed.

Contract costs (incurred and estimated to complete) are used to compute the gross profit or loss recognized. Under the percentage-of-completion method, gross profit or loss is recognized each period. The revenue recognized is matched against the contract costs incurred (similar to cost of goods sold) to determine gross profit or loss. Under the completed contract method, the gross profit or loss is determined at the substantial completion of the contract, and no revenue or contract costs are recognized until this point.

Additionally, inventoriable costs (accumulated in WIP) are never to exceed the net realizable value (NRV) of the contract. When contract costs exceed their NRV, they must be written down, requiring a contract loss to be recognized in the current period (this will be discussed in greater detail later). This is similar to accounting for inventory.

Example of contract types

Domino Construction Inc. enters into a government contract to construct an early warning radar dome. The contract amount is for $1,900,000, on which Domino expects to incur costs of $1,750,000 and earn a profit of $150,000. Costs expected to be incurred on the project are

Concrete pad	$ 175,000
Pad installation labor	100,000
Radar dome	1,150,000
Dome installation labor	325,000
Total cost	$1,750,000

This is a two-month project, where a concrete pad is installed during the first month and a prefabricated dome is assembled on the pad during the second month. To comply with bank loan agreements, complete GAAP-basis financial statements are prepared by Domino at each month-end. Domino encounters problems pouring the concrete pad, requiring its removal and reinstallation. The extra cost incurred is $175,000. During the second month, in order to meet the completion deadline, Domino spends an extra $35,000 on overtime for the dome construction crew. Domino records different billable amounts and profits under the following five contract scenarios:

1. *Fixed-price contract.* At the end of the first month of work, Domino has already lost all of its profit and expects to incur an additional loss of $25,000. It then incurs an additional loss of $35,000 in the second month. Domino issues one billing upon completion of the project. Its calculation of losses on the contract follows:

	Month 1	*Month 2*
Total billing at completion	$ 1,900,000	$ 1,900,000
– Expected total costs	(1,750,000)	(1,925,000)
– Additional costs	(175,000)	(35,000)
+ Loss already recorded	–	25,000
= Loss to record in current period	$ (25,000)	$ (35,000)

2. *Cost-plus-fixed fee.* Domino completes the same project, but bills it to the government at cost at the end of each month, as well as a $150,000 fixed fee at the end of the project that is essentially a project management fee and which comprises all of Domino's profit. The project completion entry follows:

	Month 1	*Month 2*	*Totals*
Expected material costs	$175,000	$1,150,000	$1,325,000
+ Additional material costs	175,000	–	175,000
+ Expected labor costs	100,000	325,000	425,000
+ Additional labor costs	–	35,000	35,000
+ Fixed fee	–	150,000	150,000
= Total billing	$450,000	$1,660,000	$2,110,000

3. *Cost-plus-award.* Domino completes the same cost-plus-fixed-fee contract just described, but also bills the government an additional $50,000 for achieving the stipulated construction deadline, resulting in a total profit of $200,000. The project completion entry follows:

	Month 1	*Month 2*	*Totals*
Expected material costs	$175,000	$1,150,000	$1,325,000
+ Additional material costs	175,000	–	175,000
+ Expected labor costs	100,000	325,000	425,000
+ Additional labor costs	–	35,000	35,000
+ Fixed fee	–	150,000	150,000
+ Timely completion bonus	–	50,000	50,000
= Total billing	$450,000	$1,710,000	$2,160,000

4. *Time-and materials contract with no spending cap.* Domino completes the same project, but bills all costs incurred at the end of each month to the government. The additional material cost of the concrete pad is billed at cost, while the overtime incurred is billed at a standard hourly rate with a 25% markup. Domino's profit is contained within the markup on its labor billings. Domino records a profit on the project of $115,000 on total billings of $2,075,000. Its calculation of profits on the contract follows:

	Month 1	*Month 2*	*Totals*
Expected material costs	$175,000	$1,150,000	$1,325,000
+ Additional material costs	175,000	–	175,000
+ Expected labor costs	100,000	325,000	425,000
+ Additional labor costs	–	35,000	35,000
+ 25% profit on labor costs billed	25,000	90,000	115,000
= Total billing	$475,000	$1,600,000	$2,075,000

5. *Time and material contract with spending cap.* Domino completes the same time-and-materials project just described, but the contract authorization is divided into two task orders; one authorizes a spending cap of $450,000 on the concrete pad installation, while the second task order caps spending on the radar dome at $1,500,000. Domino records a loss of $10,000 on total billings of $1,950,000. Its calculation of profits on the contract follows:

	Month 1	*Month 2*	*Totals*
Expected material costs	$175,000	$1,150,000	$1,325,000
+ Additional material costs	175,000	–	175,000
+ Expected labor costs	100,000	325,000	425,000
+ Additional labor costs	–	35,000	35,000
+ 25% profit on labor costs billed	25,000	90,000	115,000
– Spending cap limitation	(25,000)	(100,000)	(125,000)
= Total billing	$450,000	$1,500,000	$1,950,000

Revenue Measurement

In practice, various methods are used to measure the extent of progress toward completion. The most common methods are the cost-to-cost method, efforts-expended method, units-of-delivery method, and units-of-work-performed method. Each of these methods of measuring progress on a contract can be identified as either an input or output measure.

The input measures attempt to identify progress on a contract in terms of the efforts devoted to it. The cost-to-cost and efforts-expended methods are examples of input measures. Under the cost-to-cost method, the percentage of completion is estimated by comparing total costs incurred from the inception of the job to date (numerator) to total costs expected for the entire job (denominator).

Output measures are made in terms of results by attempting to identify progress toward completion by physical measures. The units-of-delivery and units-of-work-performed methods are examples of output measures. Under both of these methods, an estimate of completion is made in terms of achievements to date.

Both input and output measures have drawbacks in certain circumstances. A significant problem of input measures is that the relationship between input and productivity is only indirect; inefficiencies and other factors can cause this relationship to change. A particular drawback of the cost-to-cost method is that costs of uninstalled materials and other up-front costs may produce higher estimates of the percentage-of-completion because of their early incurrence. These costs are excluded from the cost-to-cost computation or allocated over the contract life when it appears that a better measure of contact progress will be obtained.

A significant problem of output measures is that the cost, time, and effort associated with one unit of output may not be comparable to that of another. For example, because of the cost of the foundation, the costs to complete the first story of a twenty-story office building can be expected to be greater than the costs of the remaining nineteen floors.

Because ASC 605-35 recommends that "recognized income [is to] be that percentage of estimated total income. . . that incurred costs to date bear to estimated total costs," the cost-to-cost method has become one of the most popular measures used to determine the extent of progress toward completion.

Under the cost-to-cost method, the percentage of revenue to recognize can be determined by the following formula:

$$\left(\frac{\text{Cost to date}}{\text{Cost to date} + \text{Estimated costs to complete}} \times \begin{array}{c}\text{Contract}\\ \text{price}\end{array}\right) - \begin{array}{c}\text{Revenue}\\ \text{previously recognized}\end{array} = \begin{array}{c}\text{Current}\\ \text{revenue recognized}\end{array}$$

By slightly modifying this formula, current gross profit can also be determined.

$$\left(\frac{\text{Cost to date}}{\text{Cost to date} + \text{Estimated costs to complete}} \times \begin{array}{c}\text{Expected total}\\ \text{gross profit}\end{array}\right) - \begin{array}{c}\text{Gross profit}\\ \text{previously recognized}\end{array} = \text{Current gross profit earned}$$

Example of percentage-of-completion (cost-to-cost) and completed-contract methods with profitable contract

Assume a $500,000 contract that requires three years to complete and incurs a total cost of $405,000. The following data pertain to the construction period:

	Year 1	Year 2	Year 3
Costs incurred during the period	$150,000	$210,000	$ 45,000
Cumulative costs incurred to date	150,000	360,000	405,000
Estimated costs yet to be incurred at year-end	300,000	40,000	–
Estimated total costs	450,000	400,000	–
Progress billings made during the year	100,000	370,000	30,000
Cumulative billings to date	100,000	470,000	500,000
Collections of billings	75,000	300,000	125,000

Journal Entries Common to Completed-Contract and Percentage-of-Completion Methods

	Year 1		Year 2		Year 3	
Work-in-progress	150,000		210,000		45,000	
Cash, payables, etc.		150,000		210,000		45,000
Contract receivables	100,000		370,000		30,000	
Billings on contracts		100,000		370,000		30,000
Cash	75,000		300,000		125,000	
Contract receivables		75,000		300,000		125,000

Journal Entries for Completed-Contract Method Only

Billings on contracts	500,000	
Cost of revenues earned	405,000	
Contract revenues earned		500,000
Work-in-progress		405,000

Journal Entries for Percentage-of-Completion Method Only

Cost of revenues earned	150,000		210,000		45,000	
Work-in-progress		150,000		210,000		45,000
Billings on contracts	100,000		370,000		30,000	
Contract revenues earned		166,667		283,333		50,000
Costs and estimated earnings in excess of billings on uncompleted contracts	66,667			66,667		
Billings in excess of costs and estimated earnings on uncompleted contracts				20,000	20,000	

Income Statement Presentation

	Year 1	*Year 2*	*Year 3*	*Total*
Percentage-of-completion				
Contract revenues earned	$ 166,667*	$ 283,333**	$ 50,000***	$ 500,000
Cost of revenues earned	(150,000)	(210,000)	(45,000)	(405,000)
Gross profit	$ 16,667	$ 73,333	$ 5,000	$ 95,000
Completed-contract				
Contract revenues earned	–	–	$ 500,000	$ 500,000
Cost of revenues completed	–	–	(405,000)	(405,000)
Gross profit	–	–	$ 95,000	$ 95,000

* $\frac{\$150,000}{450,000} \times 500,000 = \$166,667$

** $\left(\frac{\$360,000}{400,000} \times 500,000\right) - \$166,667 = \$283,333$

*** $\left(\frac{\$405,000}{405,000} \times 500,000\right) - \$166,667 - 283,333 = \$50,000$

Statement of Financial Position Presentation

		Year 1	*Year 2*	*Year 3*
Percentage-of-completion				
Current assets:				
Contract receivables		$25,000	$ 95,000	*
Costs and estimated earnings in excess of billings on uncompleted contracts		66,667		
Current liabilities:				
Billings in excess of costs and estimated earnings on uncompleted contracts, year 2			20,000	
Completed-contract				
Current assets:				
Contract receivables		$25,000	$ 95,000	*
Costs in excess of billings on uncompleted contracts				
Work-in-progress	150,000			
Less billings on long-term contracts	(100,000)	$50,000		
Current liabilities:				
Billings in excess of costs on uncompleted contracts, year 2 ($470,000 – 360,000)			$110,000	

* *Since the contract was completed, there are no statement of financial position amounts at the end of year 3.*

Some contractors adopt an accounting policy of not recognizing any gross profit on a contract that is less than 10% complete. This election is usually made for two reasons:

1. The contractor is qualified to make and has made the election permitted by Internal Revenue Code §460(b)(5) to defer the recognition of such gross profit for US federal income tax purposes and wishes to avoid computational differences between applying the percentage-of-completion method for financial reporting and tax purposes, and
2. The contractor believes that this policy is prudent given the uncertainties associated with a contract that is so close to inception.

The GAAP effect of such a policy is usually immaterial and the accountant normally need not be concerned about it being a departure from GAAP.

Contract Losses

When the current estimate of total contract costs exceeds the current estimate of total contract revenues, a provision for the entire loss on the entire contract is made. Losses are recognized in the period in which they become evident under either the percentage-of-completion method or the completed-contract method. The loss is computed on the basis of the total estimated costs to complete the contract, including the contract costs incurred to date plus estimated costs (use the same elements as contract costs incurred) to complete. The loss is presented as a separately captioned current liability on the statement of financial position.

In any year when a percentage-of-completion contract has an expected loss, the amount of the loss reported in that year is computed as follows:

Reported loss = Total expected loss + All profit previously recognized

Example of percentage-of-completion and completed-contract methods with loss contract

Using the previous information, if the estimated costs yet to be incurred at the end of year two were $148,000, the total expected loss is $8,000 [$500,000 – (360,000 + 148,000)], and the total loss reported in year two would be $24,667 ($8,000 + 16,667). Under the completed-contract method, the loss recognized is simply the total expected loss, $8,000.

Journal entry at end of year 2	*Percentage-of-completion*		*Completed-contract*	
Loss on uncompleted long-term contract (expense)	24,667		8,000	
Estimated loss on uncompleted contract (liability)		24,667		8,000

Profit or Loss Recognized on Contract
(Percentage-of-Completion Method)

	Year 1	*Year 2*	*Year 3*
Contract price	$500,000	$500,000	$500,000
Estimated total costs:			
Costs incurred contract-to-date	$150,000	$360,000	$506,000*
Estimated costs yet to be incurred	300,000	148,000	–
Estimated total costs for the three-year period, actual for year 3	$450,000	$508,000	$506,000
Estimated gross profit (loss), actual for year 3	50,000	(8,000)	(6,000)

	Year 1	*Year 2*	*Year 3*
Summary of Effect on Results of Operations			
Current end-of-year estimate of gross profit (loss) actual for year 3	–	$ (8,000)	$ (6,000)
Accumulated effect of gross profit (loss) recognized in prior years	–	16,667	(8,000)
Effect on gross profit (loss) recognized in current year	–	$ (24,667)	$ 2,000

* *Assumed*

Profit or Loss Recognized on Contract
(Completed-Contract Method)

	Year 1	*Year 2*	*Year 3*
Contract price	$500,000	$500,000	$500,000
Estimated total costs:			
Costs incurred to date	$150,000	$360,000	$506,000*
Estimated cost yet to be incurred	300,000	148,000	–
Estimated total costs for the three-year period, actual for year 3	$450,000	$508,000	$506,000
Estimated profit (loss), inception-to-date, actual for year 3	$ 50,000	$ (8,000)	$ (6,000)
Loss previously recognized	–	–	$ (8,000)
Amount of estimated income (loss) recognized in the current period, actual for year 3	–	$ (8,000)	$ 2,000

* *Assumed*

Upon completion of the project during year 3, it can be seen that the actual loss was only $6,000 ($500,000 – $506,000); therefore, the estimated loss provision was overstated in previous years by $2,000. However, since this is a change of an estimate, the $2,000 difference must be handled prospectively; consequently, $2,000 of income is recognized in year 3 ($8,000 loss previously recognized – $6,000 actual loss).

Combining and Segmenting Contracts

The profit center for accounting purposes is usually a single contract, but under some circumstances the profit center may be a combination of two or more contracts, a segment of a contract, or a group of combined contracts. The contracts must meet requirements in ASC 605-35 in order to combine, or segment; otherwise, each individual contract is presumed to be the profit center.

For accounting purposes, a group of contracts may be combined if they are so closely related that they are, in substance, parts of a single project with an overall profit margin. Per ASC 605-35, a group of contracts may be combined if the contracts:

1. Are negotiated as a package in the same economic environment with an overall profit margin objective.
2. Constitute an agreement to do a single project.
3. Require closely interrelated construction activities.
4. Are performed concurrently or in a continuous sequence under the same project management.
5. Constitute, in substance, an agreement with a single customer.

Segmenting a contract is a process of breaking up a larger unit into smaller units for accounting purposes. If the project is segmented, revenues are assigned to the different elements or phases to achieve different rates of profitability based on the relative value of each element or phase to the estimated total contract revenue. According to ASC 605-35, a project may be segmented if all of the following steps were taken and are documented and verifiable:

1. The contractor submitted bona fide proposals on the separate components of the project and on the entire project.
2. The customer had the right to accept the proposals on either basis.
3. The aggregate amount of the proposals on the separate components approximated the amount of the proposal on the entire project.

A project that does not meet the above criteria may still be segmented if all of the following are applicable:

1. The terms and scope of the contract or project clearly call for the separable phases or elements.
2. The separable phases or elements of the project are often bid or negotiated separately in the marketplace.
3. The market assigns different gross profit rates to the segments because of factors such as different levels of risk or differences in the relationship of the supply and demand for the services provided in different segments.
4. The contractor has a significant history of providing similar services to other customers under separate contracts for each significant segment to which a profit margin higher than the overall profit margin on the project is ascribed.
5. The significant history with customers who have contracted for services separately is one that is relatively stable in terms of pricing policy rather than one unduly weighted by erratic pricing decisions (responding, for example, to extraordinary economic circumstances or to unique customer-contractor relationships).
6. The excess of the sum of the prices of the separate elements over the price of the total project is clearly attributable to cost savings incident to combined performance of the contract obligations (for example, cost savings in supervision, overhead, or equipment mobilization). Unless this condition is met, segmenting a contract with a price substantially less than the sum of the prices of the separate phases or elements is inappropriate even if the other conditions are met. Acceptable price variations are allocated to the separate phases or elements in proportion to the prices ascribed to each. In all other situations, a substantial difference in price (whether more or less) between the separate elements and the price of the total project is evidence that the contractor has accepted different profit margins. Accordingly, segmenting is not appropriate, and the contracts are the profit centers.
7. The similarity of services and prices in the contract segments and services and the prices of such services to other customers contracted separately are documented and verifiable.

Note that the criteria for combining and segmenting are to be applied consistently to contracts with similar characteristics and in similar circumstances.

Joint Ventures and Shared Contracts

Especially large or risky contracts are sometimes shared by more than one contractor. When the owner of the contract requests competitive bids, many contractors will form syndicates or joint ventures in order to bid on and successfully obtain a contract that each contractor individually could not perform.

When this occurs, a separate set of accounting records is maintained for the joint venture. If the percentages of interest for each of the participants are identical in more than one contract, the joint venture might keep its records in the same manner as it would if it was simply another construction company. Usually, the joint venture is for a single contract and ends upon completion of that contract.

A joint venture is a type of partnership, organized for a limited purpose. An agreement of the parties and the terms of the contract successfully bid upon will determine the nature of the accounting records. Income statements are usually cumulative statements showing totals from date of contract inception until reporting date. Each participant records its share of the amount from the venture's income statement less its previously recorded portion of the venture's income as a single line item similar to the equity method for investments. Similarly, statements of financial position of each participant present a single line asset balance, "investment in and advances to joint ventures." In most cases, footnote disclosure is similar to the equity method and presents condensed financial statements of material joint ventures.

Accounting for transactions with unrelated third parties. A participant in a collaborative arrangement recognizes revenue earned and costs incurred in transactions with third parties (parties that are not participants to the collaborative arrangement) in its income statement based on whether the participant is serving as a principal or an agent in the transaction under ASC 605-45. If the transacting participant is considered a principal in the transaction, the revenues and costs are recorded gross. If the transacting participant is considered an agent in the transaction, the revenues and costs are recorded net. Under no circumstances is a participant in a collaborative arrangement permitted to use the equity method to account for its activities associated with the collaborative arrangement.

ASC 605-45 does not provide a "bright-line" test that definitively would characterize the role of a participant in a transaction. Rather, it provides a series of indicators of gross reporting and a series of indicators of net reporting, the purpose of which is to enable management to analyze the facts and circumstances associated with the transaction to make a well-reasoned determination.

Indicators of gross reporting (principals).

- *Participant is primary obligor.* Under ASC 605-45, this is considered to be a "strong indicator" of the participant's role in the transaction.
- *Participant has authority, within reasonable limits, to establish price.* Even when subject to reasonable, preestablished economic constraints, if the participant has the authority to negotiate price with the customer, this may indicate that the participant possesses risks and rewards of a principal to the transaction.
- *Participant involvement in determining specifications.* If the participant has the authority to determine the nature, type, characteristics, or specifications of the products and/or services ordered by the customer, this may be indicative of the participant having primary responsibility for fulfillment. For the purposes of analyzing the applicability of this indicator, the evaluator considers whether the participant makes physical alterations to the product or performs services that add value sufficient to increase the selling price to the customer.
- *Participant performance.* The participant changes the product or performs part of the service.
- *Participant discretion in supplier selection.*
- *Participant exposed to inventory risks.* The participant bears inventory risk in one or both of the following manners:
    - General inventory risk either before the customer places the order or upon the return of the inventory by the customer
    - Specific risk of physical inventory loss after the customer places the order or during shipping of the inventory.
- *Participant bears credit risk.*

Indicators of net reporting (agents).

- *Participant is not the primary obligor.* The supplier of the goods or services, not the participant, is the primary obligor in the transaction.

- *Participant earnings are fixed.* The amount the participant earns is fixed.
- *Participant is not exposed to credit risk.* The supplier and not the participant bears credit risk in connection with the transaction.

Accounting for transactions between participants. In evaluating the income statement characterization of transactions between participants to a collaborative arrangement, management is to consider:

- The nature of the arrangement
- The contractual terms of the arrangement
- The nature of the participant's business operations
- Whether the transactions are included in the scope of other authoritative GAAP literature on income statement classification, either directly or by analogy.

If no authoritative GAAP is identified that is relevant directly or by analogy, management elects a reasonable and rational accounting policy to be consistently applied to all such similar transactions.

Accounting for Change Orders

Change orders are modifications of specifications or provisions of an original contract. Contract revenue and costs are adjusted to reflect change orders that are approved by the contractor and customer. According to ASC 605-35, accounting for a change order depends on the scope and price of the change.

If the scope and price have both been agreed to by the customer and contractor, contract revenue and cost are both adjusted to reflect the change order.

According to ASC 605-35, accounting for unpriced change orders depends on their characteristics and the circumstances in which they occur. Under the completed-contract method, costs attributable to unpriced change orders are deferred as contract costs if it is probable that total contract costs, including costs attributable to the change orders, will be recovered from contract revenues. Recovery is deemed probable if the future event or events are likely to occur.

Per ASC 605-35, the following guidelines apply when accounting for unpriced change orders under the percentage-of-completion method:

1. If it is not probable that the costs will be recovered through a change in the contract price, costs attributable to unpriced change orders are treated as costs of contract performance in the period in which the costs are incurred.
2. If it is probable that the costs will be recovered through a change in the contract price, the costs are deferred (excluded from the costs of contract performance) until the parties have agreed on the change in contract price, or alternatively, treated as costs of contract performance in the period in which they are incurred with a corresponding increase to contract revenue in the amount of the costs incurred.
3. If it is probable that the contract price will be adjusted by an amount that exceeds the costs attributable to the change order and both (a) the amount of the excess can be reliably estimated, and (b) realization of the full contract price adjustment is probably beyond a reasonable doubt, then the original contract price is adjusted for the full amount of the adjustment as the costs are recognized.

However, since the substantiation of the amount of future revenue is difficult, satisfaction of the condition of "realization beyond a reasonable doubt" should only be considered satisfied in circumstances in which an entity's historical experience provides such assurance or in which an entity has received a bona fide pricing offer from a customer and records only the amount of the offer as revenue.

Accounting for Contract Options

Per ASC 605-35, an addition or option to an existing contract is treated as a separate contract if any of the following circumstances exist:

1. The product or service to be provided differs significantly from the product or service provided under the original contract.
2. The price of the new product or service is negotiated without regard to the original contract and involves different economic judgments.
3. The products or services to be provided under the exercised option or amendment are similar to those under the original contract, but the contract price and anticipated contract cost relationship are significantly different.

If the addition or option does not meet the above circumstances, the contracts are combined unless the addition or option does not meet the criteria for combining, in which case it is treated as a change order.

Accounting for Claims

Claims represent amounts in excess of the agreed-upon contract price that a contractor seeks to collect from customers for unanticipated additional costs. The recognition of additional contract revenue relating to claims is appropriate if it is probable that the claim will result in additional revenue and if the amount can be reliably estimated. ASC 605-35 specifies that all of the following conditions must exist in order for the probable and estimable requirements to be satisfied:

1. The contract or other evidence provides a legal basis for the claim; or a legal opinion has been obtained, stating that under the circumstances there is a reasonable basis to support the claim.
2. Additional costs are caused by circumstances that were unforeseen at the contract date and are not the result of deficiencies in the contractor's performance.
3. Costs associated with the claim are identifiable or otherwise determinable and are reasonable in view of the work performed.
4. The evidence supporting the claim is objective and verifiable, not based on management's "feel" for the situation or on unsupported representations.

When the above requirements are met, revenue from a claim is recorded only to the extent that contract costs relating to the claim have been incurred.

When the above requirements are not met, ASC 605-35 states that a contingent asset is disclosed in accordance with ASC 450.

Accounting Changes

ASC 250 requires retroactive restatement as the standard methodology to be used for accounting for changes in accounting principle, including changes in the accounting for long-term construction contracts. (See the chapter on ASC 205 for further discussion.)

Revisions in revenue, cost, and profit estimates or in measurements of the extent of progress toward completion are changes in accounting estimates. These changes are accounted for prospectively in order for the financial statements to fully reflect the effects of the latest available estimates.

SERVICE REVENUES (ASC 605-20 AND ASC 605-45)

PERSPECTIVE AND ISSUES

Services represent over half of the transactions occurring in the US economy, but there is no official codification of accounting standards that provides specific accounting rules for them. Accounting for service transactions has evolved primarily through industry practice, and as a result, different accounting methods have developed to apply the fundamental principles of revenue and cost recognition. In fact, different accounting methods are used by similar entities for practically identical transactions.

The discussion in this section should still provide relevant guidance on service industry issues. In addition, the guidance provided by the SEC in Staff Accounting Bulletin 101 and its replacement, SAB 104, discussed in the introductory materials to this chapter, is highly relevant to accounting for service transactions and should be deemed pertinent to accounting even by nonpublic reporting entities, inasmuch as it reflects the current thinking by an authoritative source of GAAP.

DEFINITIONS OF TERMS

Collection method. A method that recognizes revenue when cash is collected.

Completed performance method. A method that recognizes revenue after the last significant act has been completed.

Direct costs. Costs that are related specifically to the performance of services under a contract or other arrangement.

Indirect costs. Costs that are incurred as a result of service activities that are not directly allocable to specific contracts or customer arrangements.

Initiation fee. A onetime, up-front charge that gives the purchaser the privilege of using a service or facilities.

Installation fee. A onetime, up-front charge for making equipment operational so that it functions as intended.

Out-of-pocket costs. Costs incurred incidental to the performance of services that are often reimbursable to the service firm by the customer either at actual cost or at an agreed-upon rate (e.g., meals, lodging, airfare, taxi fares, etc.).

Precontract or preengagement costs. Costs incurred prior to execution of a service contract or engagement letter.

Product transaction. A transaction between a seller and a purchaser in which the seller supplies tangible merchandise to the purchaser.

Proportional performance method. A method that recognizes revenue on the basis of the number of acts performed in relation to the total number of acts to be performed.

Service transaction. A transaction between a seller and a purchaser in which the seller performs work, or agrees to maintain a readiness to perform work, for the purchaser.

Specific performance method. A method that recognizes revenue after one specific act has been performed.

CONCEPTS, RULES, AND EXAMPLES

Codification defines service transactions as follows:

> *. . . transactions between a seller and a purchaser in which, for a mutually agreed price, the seller performs, agrees to perform, agrees to perform at a later date, or agrees to maintain readiness to perform an act or acts, including permitting others to use enterprise resources that do not alone produce a tangible commodity or product as the principal intended result.* (ASC 605-35-15-6j)

Generally accepted accounting principles require that revenue generally be recognized when (1) it is realized or realizable and (2) it has been earned. With respect to service transactions:

> *. . . revenue from service transactions [is to] be based on performance, because performance determines the extent to which the earnings process is complete or virtually complete.*

In practice, performance may involve the execution of a defined act, a set of similar or identical acts, or a set of related but not similar or identical acts. Performance may also occur with the passage of time. Accordingly, one of the following four methods can serve as a guideline for the recognition of revenue from service transactions:

1. The specific performance method
2. The proportional performance method
3. The completed performance method
4. The collection method.

Service versus Product Transactions

Many transactions involve the sale of a tangible product and a service; therefore, for proper accounting treatment, it must be determined whether the transaction is primarily a service transaction accompanied by an incidental product, primarily a product transaction accompanied by an incidental service, or a sale in which both a service transaction and a product transaction occur. The following criteria apply:

1. **Service transactions.** If the seller offers both a service and a product in a single transaction and if the terms of the agreement for the sale of the service are worded in such a manner that the inclusion or exclusion of the product would not change the total transaction price, the product is incidental to the rendering of the service; the transaction is a service transaction that is accounted for in accordance with one of the four methods presented. For example, fixed-price equipment maintenance contracts that include parts at no additional charge are service transactions.
2. **Product transactions.** If the seller offers both a service and a product in a single transaction and if the terms of the agreement for the sale of the product are worded in such a manner that the inclusion or exclusion of the service would not change the total transaction price, the rendering of the service is incidental to the sale of the product; the transaction is a product transaction that is accounted for as such. For example, the sale of a product accompanied by a guarantee or warranty for repair is considered a product transaction.
3. **Service and product transactions.** If the seller offers both a product and a service and the agreement states the product and service are separate elements such that the inclusion or exclusion of the service would vary the total transaction price, the transaction consists of two components: a product transaction that is accounted for

separately as such, and a service transaction that is accounted for in accordance with one of the four accepted methods.

Revenue Recognition Methods

Once a transaction is determined to be a service transaction, one of the following four methods is used to recognize revenue. The method chosen is to be based on the nature and extent of the service(s) to be performed.

1. **Specific performance method.** The specific performance method is used when performance consists of the execution of a single act. Revenue is recognized at the time the act takes place. For example, a stockbroker records sales commissions as revenue upon the sale of a client's investment.
2. **Proportional performance method.** The proportional performance method is used when performance consists of a number of identical or similar acts.

   a. If the service transaction involves a specified number of identical or similar acts, an equal amount of revenue is recorded for each act performed. For example, a refuse disposal company recognizes an equal amount of revenue for each weekly removal of a customer's garbage.

   b. If the service transaction involves a specified number of defined but not identical or similar acts, the revenue recognized for each act is based on the following formula:

$$\frac{\text{Direct cost of individual act}}{\text{Total estimated direct costs of the transaction}} \times \text{Total revenues from complete transaction}$$

   For example, a correspondence school that provides lessons, examinations, and grading would use this method. If the measurements suggested in the preceding equation are impractical or not objectively determinable, revenue is recognized on a systematic and rational basis that reasonably relates revenue recognition to service performance.

   c. If the service transaction involves an unspecified number of acts over a fixed time period for performance, revenue is recognized over the period during which the acts will be performed by using the straight-line method unless a better method of relating revenue and performance is appropriate. For example, a health club might recognize revenue on a straight-line basis over the term of a member's membership. Many professional service firms record revenues on their engagements on an "as-performed basis" by valuing labor time, as expended, at a standard hourly billing rate and accumulating these amounts as an asset, work-in-progress (WIP). For periodic reporting, ending balances of WIP (and the related revenue recognized) must be adjusted by recording valuation allowances for unbillable or unrealizable WIP.

Example of proportional performance revenue recognition

The Cheyenne Snow Removal Company enters into a contract with the Western Office Tower to plow its parking lot. The contract states that Cheyenne will receive a fixed payment of $500 to clear Western's central parking lot whenever snowfall exceeds two inches. Following an unusually snowy winter, Western elects to cap its snow removal costs by tying Cheyenne into an annual $18,000 fixed price for snow removal, no matter how many snow storms occur. Snowfall is not predictable by month, and can occur over as much as a six-month period. Western pays the full amount in advance, resulting in the following entry by Cheyenne:

Cash	18,000	
Customer advances		18,000

Though Cheyenne could recognize revenue on a straight-line basis through the contract period, it chooses to tie recognition more closely to actual performance with the proportional performance method. Its total estimated direct cost through the contract period is likely to be $12,600, based on its average costs in previous years. There is one snowstorm in October, which costs Cheyenne $350 for snow removal under the Western contract. Cheyenne's revenue recognition calculation in October is

$$\frac{\$350 \text{ direct cost}}{\$12{,}600 \text{ total direct cost}} \times \$18{,}000 \text{ total revenue} = \$500 \text{ revenue recognition}$$

Thus, Cheyenne recognizes a gross margin of $150 during the month. By the end of February, Cheyenne has conducted snow removal 28 times at the same margin, resulting in revenue recognition of $14,000 and a gross margin of $4,200. Cheyenne's cumulative entry for all performance under the Western contract to date is as follows:

Customer advances	14,000	
Direct labor expense	9,800	
Revenue		14,000
Cash		9,800

In March, Cheyenne removes snow 12 more times at a cost of $4,200. Its initial revenue recognition calculation during this month is

$$\frac{\$4{,}200 \text{ direct cost}}{\$12{,}600 \text{ total direct cost}} \times \$18{,}000 \text{ total revenue} = \$6{,}000 \text{ revenue recognition}$$

However, this would result in total revenue recognition of $20,000, which exceeds the contract fixed fee by $2,000. Accordingly, Cheyenne only recognizes sufficient revenue to maximize the contract cap, resulting in a loss of $200 for the month.

Customer advances	4,000	
Direct labor expense	4,200	
Revenue		4,000
Cash		4,200

3. **Completed performance method.** The completed performance method is used when more than one act must be performed and when the final act is so significant to the entire transaction taken as a whole that performance cannot be considered to have taken place until the performance of that final act occurs. For example, a moving company packs, loads, and transports merchandise; however, the final act of delivering the merchandise is so significant that revenue is not recognized until the goods reach their intended destination. If the services are to be performed in an indeterminable number of acts over an indeterminable period of time and if an objective measure for estimating the degree to which performance has taken place cannot be found, revenue is recognized under the completed performance method.
4. **Collection method.** The collection method is used in circumstances when there is a significant degree of uncertainty surrounding the collection of service revenue. Under this method, revenue is not recognized until the cash is collected. For example, personal services may be provided to a customer whose ability to pay is uncertain.

Expense Recognition

GAAP, in general, requires that costs be recognized as expense in the period that the revenue with which they are associated is recognized (the matching principle). Costs are deferred only when they are expected to be recoverable from future revenues. When applying these principles to service transactions, special consideration must be given to the different types of costs that might arise. The major classifications of costs arising from service transactions are as follows:

1. **Precontract or preengagement costs.** These are costs that are incurred before the service contract (or engagement letter in many professional services firms) has been executed between the parties. They can include legal fees for negotiating contract terms, costs of credit investigations, and the salaries and benefits of individuals involved in negotiating contracts with prospective clients. (See the related discussion in the Long-term Construction Contracts section of this chapter.)
2. **Direct costs.** Costs that are specifically attributable to providing service under a specific contract or contracts. For example, service labor and repair parts on a fixed-price maintenance contract.
3. **Indirect costs.** Costs that are incurred as a result of all service activity but that are not directly allocable to any specific contracts or engagements.
4. **Out-of-pocket costs.** Costs incurred incidental to the performance of services that are often reimbursable to the service firm by the customer either at actual cost or at an agreed-upon rate (e.g., meals, lodging, airfare, taxi fare, etc.).
5. **Overhead.** General costs of running the business that do not fall into any of the above categories, often referred to as selling, general, and administrative expenses. These include uncollectible receivables, advertising, sales commissions, and facilities costs (depreciation, rent, maintenance, etc.).

Accounting treatment. The costs listed above are accounted for as follows:

1. **Precontract or preengagement costs.** Expense as incurred as start-up costs under all of the service revenue recognition methods.
2. **Direct costs.** Expense as incurred under all of the service revenue recognition methods because of the close correlation between the amount of direct costs incurred and the extent of performance achieved. Direct costs incurred prior to performance, referred to as initial direct costs (e.g., expendable materials purchased for use on the job/engagement that are purchased and held by the service enterprise as a form of inventory), are deferred and recorded as prepayments (or supplies inventory, depending on the nature of the item). Under the specific performance or completed performance methods, these costs are recognized as expenses at the time of service performance at the point that revenue is recognized. Under the proportional performance method, initial direct costs are charged to expense in proportion to the recognition of service revenue (i.e., by applying the ratio of revenues recognized in the period to total expected revenues over the life of the contract).
3. **Indirect costs.** Under all of the revenue recognition methods, indirect costs are expensed as incurred.
4. **Out-of-pocket costs.** Under all of the revenue recognition methods, out-of-pocket costs are expensed as incurred with the related client billings presented as revenue in the statement of income.
5. **Overhead.** Under all of the revenue recognition methods, overhead is expensed as incurred.

Losses on service transactions. These are recognized when direct costs incurred to date plus estimated remaining direct costs of performance exceed the current estimated net realizable revenue from the contract. The loss (given as the Direct costs incurred to date + Estimated remaining direct costs – Estimated realizable revenue) is first applied to reduce any recorded deferred costs to zero, with any remaining loss recognized on the income statement and credited to an estimated liability.

Initiation and Installation Fees

Many service transactions also involve the charging of a nonrefundable initiation or activation fee with subsequent periodic payments for future services and/or a nonrefundable fee for installation of equipment essential to providing future services with subsequent periodic payments for the services. These nonrefundable fees may, in substance, be partly or wholly advance charges for future services.

Initiation or activation fees. If there is an objectively determinable value for the right or privilege granted by the fee, that value is recognized as revenue on the initiation date. Any related direct costs are recognized as expense on the initiation date. If the value of the right or privilege cannot be objectively determined, the fee is recorded as a liability for future services and recognized as revenue in accordance with one of the revenue recognition methods.

Installation fees. If the equipment and its installation costs are essential for the service to be provided and if customers cannot normally purchase the equipment in a separate transaction, the installation fee is considered an advance charge for future services. The fee is recognized as revenue over the estimated service period. The costs of installation and the installed equipment are amortized over the period the equipment is expected to generate revenue. If customers can normally purchase the equipment in a separate transaction, the installation fee is part of a product transaction that is accounted for separately as such.

Example of installation fees

Vintner Corporation has invented a nitrogen injection device for resealing opened wine bottles, calling it NitroSeal. The device is especially useful for restaurants, which can seal wine bottles opened for customers who want to take home unfinished wine. Because the NitroSeal device is massive, Vintner pays a third party to install each unit for a fixed fee of $200, charging restaurants a $300 nonrefundable installation fee plus a monthly fee for a 20-month cancelable contract. The initial entries to record an installation charge from a supplier and related installation billing to a customer are as follows:

Installation asset	200	
Accounts payable		200
Accounts receivable	300	
Unearned installation fees (liability)		300

Vintner recognizes the installation revenue and associated installation expense for each installation in 1/20 increments to match the contract length, each with the following entry:

Unearned installation fees	15	
Installation revenue		15
Installation expense	10	
Installation asset		10

A customer cancels its contract with Vintner after 5 months. As a result, Vintner accelerates all remaining amortization on the installation asset and recognizes all remaining unearned installation fees at once, using the following entries:

Unearned installation fees	225	
Installation revenue		225
Installation expense	150	
Installation asset		150

If the service contract had included a clause for a refundable installation fee, then cancellation after five months would still have resulted in immediate acceleration of amortization on the installation asset. However, the unearned installation revenue could not be recognized. Instead, the following entry would have recorded the return of the installation fee:

Unearned installation fees	225	
Cash		225

Other Guidance to Accounting for Service Transactions

Some elements of the accounting codification provide guidance to the accounting for service transactions. These are discussed in the following paragraphs.

Freight services in process. ASC 605-20-25 addresses the manner in which revenue and expense pertaining to freight services in process as of the date of the statement of financial position are to be given financial statement recognition. It holds that recognition of revenue when freight is received from the shipper or when freight leaves the carrier's terminal, with expenses recognized as incurred, is not acceptable accounting.

Reporting reimbursable costs. While not limited to service providers, a common situation for many professional service providers is the incurrence of costs that are later billed to clients, with or without a mark-up over actual cost. Examples of out-of-pocket expenses include meals, lodging, airfares, taxi fares, etc. Prior practice had been varied, with many reporting entities showing reimbursements, implicitly as offsets to expenses; others reported such reimbursements as revenue. While the net effect on reported earnings was the same under either approach, certain key performance measures, such as gross revenue, could vary considerably depending on choice of accounting method. ASC 605-45-15 mandates that any billings for out-of-pocket costs are to be classified as revenue in the statement of income and not as a reduction in expenses. This guidance is equally applicable whether expenses are billed to clients (1) as a pass-through, (i.e., at actual cost to the service firm without a mark-up), (2) at a marked-up amount, or (3) are included in the billing rate or negotiated price for the services.

Separately priced extended warranties. Extended warranties provide additional protection beyond that of the manufacturer's original warranty, lengthen the period of coverage specified in the manufacturer's original warranty, or both. Similarly, a product maintenance contract is an agreement for services to maintain a product for a certain length of time. Clearly, revenue recognition at inception is not acceptable, and it is often impossible to estimate the actual pattern of service that will be provided to the customers over the terms of the contracts. ASC 605-20-25 directs that revenue from these contracts be deferred and recognized on a straight-line basis unless evidence exists that costs are incurred on some other basis. If so, revenue is allocated to each period using the ratio of the period's cost to estimated total cost.

Direct costs of obtaining extended warranty or maintenance contracts are to be capitalized and recognized as expense in the ratio that revenues recognized each period bear to total anticipated revenues from the respective contracts. Any other costs are charged to expense as incurred. Losses on these contracts are recognized immediately if the sum of the future costs and remaining unamortized direct acquisition costs exceed the related unearned revenue. When recognizing a loss, any unamortized acquisition costs are first charged to expense, and a liability for any remaining loss is then recorded.

Example of a separately priced product maintenance contract

Salomon Heating enters into a four-year product maintenance contract with Everly Manufacturing, under which Salomon will conduct preventive maintenance and repairs to Everly's heating systems. Under the contract terms, Salomon bills Everly $1,000 during each month of the contract period, and recognizes the billed amount as revenue at once. This equates to straight-line recognition of the total contract amount.

Salomon incurred a $4,000 legal expense in writing the contract with Everly, as well as a $1,600 commission, both of which it defers and amortizes over the contract period. During the first month of work, Salomon incurs direct costs of $650 in wages, as well as $200 of repair-related materials. Its charge to expense entry follows:

Cost of goods sold—materials	200	
Cost of goods sold—labor	650	
Legal expense	83	
Commission expense	33	
Inventory—spare parts		200
Cash		650
Deferred legal costs		83
Deferred commission costs		33

At the end of two years, Salomon realizes that it must rebuild Everly's boiler. The rebuild will cost $10,000, while all expected future maintenance work will cost an additional $20,000. Unamortized legal costs equal $2,000 and unamortized commissions equal $800, while unearned revenue is $24,000. Salomon must recognize a loss of $8,800, which is the difference between all expected costs of $32,800 and unearned revenue of $24,000. To do so, Salomon accelerates all remaining amortization of the capitalized legal and commission assets, and recognizes a liability for the remainder of the loss with the following entry:

Commission expense	800	
Legal expense	2,000	
Loss on contractual obligation	6,000	
Deferred commission costs		800
Deferred legal costs		2,000
Unfulfilled contractual obligations (liability)		6,000

Salomon rebuilds Everly's boiler at the expected cost of $10,000. Since this is one-third of the remaining costs to be incurred under the contract, Salomon recognizes one-third of the $6,000 unfulfilled contractual obligation that was used to offset the loss, and charges the rest of the cost to expense with the following entry:

Unfulfilled contractual obligations (liability)	2,000	
Cost of goods sold—labor	8,000	
Cash		10,000

SALES WHEN COLLECTION IS UNCERTAIN

PERSPECTIVE AND ISSUES

Under GAAP, revenue recognition customarily does not depend upon the collection of cash. Accrual accounting techniques normally record revenue at the point of a credit sale by establishing a receivable. When uncertainty arises surrounding the collectibility of this amount, the receivable is appropriately adjusted by establishing a valuation allowance. In some cases, however, the collection of the sales price may be so uncertain that an objective measure of ultimate collectibility cannot be established. When such circumstances exist, the seller either uses the installment method or the cost recovery method to recognize the transaction (ASC 605-10-25). Both of these methods allow for a deferral of gross profit until cash has been collected.

An installment transaction occurs when a seller delivers a product or performs a service and the buyer makes periodic payments over an extended period of time. Under the installment method, revenue recognition is deferred until the period(s) of cash collection. The seller recognizes both revenues and cost of sales at the time of the sale; however, the related gross profit is deferred to those periods in which cash is collected. Under the cost recovery method, both revenues and cost of sales are recognized at the time of the sale, but none of the related gross profit is recognized until the entire cost of sales has been recovered. Once the seller has recovered all cost of sales, any additional cash receipts are recognized as revenue. ASC 605-10-25 does not specify when one method is preferred over the other. However, the cost recovery method is more conservative than the installment method because gross profit is deferred until all costs have been recovered; therefore, it is appropriate for situations of extreme uncertainty.

DEFINITIONS OF TERMS

Cost recovery method. The method of accounting for an installment basis sale whereby the gross profit is deferred until all cost of sales has been recovered.

Deferred gross profit. The gross profit from an installment basis sale that will be recognized in future periods.

Gross profit rate. The percentage computed by dividing gross profit by revenue from an installment sale.

Installment method. The method of accounting for a sale whereby gross profit is recognized in each period in which cash from the sale is collected.

Installment sale. A sales transaction for which the sales price is collected through the receipt of periodic payments over an extended period of time.

Net realizable value. The portion of the recorded amount of an asset expected to be realized in cash upon its liquidation in the ordinary course of business.

Realized gross profit. The gross profit recognized in the current period.

Repossessions. Merchandise sold by a seller under an installment arrangement that the seller physically takes back after the buyer defaults on the payments.

CONCEPTS, RULES, AND EXAMPLES

The Installment Method

The installment method was developed in response to the increasing incidence of sales contracts that allowed buyers to make payments over several years. As the payment period becomes longer, the risk of loss resulting from uncollectible accounts increases; consequently, circumstances surrounding a receivable may lead to considerable uncertainty as to whether payments will actually be received. Under these circumstances, the uncertainty of cash collection dictates that revenue recognition be deferred until the actual receipt of cash.

The installment method can be used in most sales transactions for which payment is to be made through periodic installments over an extended period of time and the collectibility of the sales price cannot be reasonably estimated. This method is applicable to the sales of real estate (covered in the last section of this chapter), heavy equipment, home furnishings, and other merchandise sold on an installment basis. Installment method revenue recognition is not in accordance with accrual accounting, because revenue recognition is not normally based upon cash collection; however, its use is justified in certain circumstances on the grounds that accrual accounting may result in "front-end loading" (i.e., all of the revenue from a transaction being recognized at the point of sale with an improper matching of related costs). For example, the application of accrual accounting to transactions that provide for installment payments over periods of ten, twenty, or thirty years may underestimate losses from contract defaults and other future contract costs.

Applying the installment method. When a seller uses the installment method, both revenue and cost of sales are recognized at the point of sale, but the related gross profit is deferred to those periods during which cash will be collected. As receivables are collected, a portion of the deferred gross profit equal to the gross profit rate times the cash collected is recognized as income. When this method is used, the seller must compute each year's gross profit rate and also must maintain records of installment accounts receivable and deferred revenue that are separately identified by the year of sale. All general and administrative expenses are normally expensed in the period incurred.

The steps to use in accounting for sales under the installment method are as follows:

1. During the current year, record sales and cost of sales in the regular manner. Record installment sales transactions separately from other sales. Set up installment accounts receivable identified by the year of sale (e.g., Installment Accounts Receivable—2012).
2. Record cash collections from installment accounts receivable. Care must be taken so that the cash receipts are properly identified as to the year in which the receivable arose.
3. At the end of the current year, transfer installment sales revenue and installment cost of sales to deferred gross profit properly identified by the year of sale. Compute the current year's gross profit rate on installment sales as follows:

$$\text{Gross profit rate} = 1 - \left(\frac{\text{Cost of installment sales}}{\text{Installment sales revenue}}\right)$$

   Alternatively, the gross profit rate can be computed as follows:

$$\text{Gross profit rate} = \frac{\text{Installment sales revenue} - \text{Cost of installment sales}}{\text{Installment sales revenue}}$$

4. Apply the current year's gross profit rate to the cash collections from the current year's installment sales to compute the realized gross profit from the current year's installment sales.

$$\text{Realized gross profit} = \begin{array}{c}\text{Cash collections from the}\\ \text{current year's installment sales}\end{array} \times \begin{array}{c}\text{Current year's}\\ \text{gross profit rate}\end{array}$$

5. Separately apply each of the previous years' gross profit rates to cash collections from those years' installment sales to compute the realized gross profit from each of the previous years' installment sales.

$$\text{Realized gross profit} = \begin{array}{c}\text{Cash collections from the}\\ \text{previous years' installment sales}\end{array} \times \begin{array}{c}\text{Previous years'}\\ \text{gross profit rate}\end{array}$$

6. Defer the current year's unrealized gross profit to future years. The deferred gross profit to carry forward to future years is computed as follows:

$$\text{Deferred gross profit (2012)} = \text{Ending balance installment account receivable (2012)} \times \text{Gross profit rate (2012)}$$

Example of the installment method of accounting

	2012	*2013*	*2014*
Sales on installment	$400,000	$450,000	$600,000
Cost of installment sales	(280,000)	(337,500)	(400,000)
Gross profit on sales	$120,000	$112,500	$200,000
Cash collections:			
2012 sales	$150,000	$175,000	$ 75,000
2013 sales		$200,000	$125,000
2014 sales			$300,000

Accounting entries are made for Steps 1 and 2 above using this data; the following computations are required for Steps 3–6:

Step 3 — Compute the current year's gross profit rate.

	2012	*2013*	*2014*
Gross profit on sales	$120,000	$112,500	$200,000
Installment sales revenue	$400,000	$450,000	$600,000
Gross profit rate	30%	25%	33 1/3%

Step 4 — Apply the current year's gross profit rate to cash collections from current year's sales.

Year	*Cash collections*		*Gross profit rate*		*Realized gross profit*
2012	$150,000	×	30%	=	$ 45,000
2013	200,000	×	25%	=	50,000
2014	300,000	×	33 1/3%	=	100,000

Step 5 — Separately apply each of the previous years' gross profit rates to cash collections from that year's installment sales.

In Year 2013

From year	*Cash collections*		*Gross profit rate*		*Realized gross profit*
2012	$175,000	×	30%	=	$52,500

In Year 2014

From year	*Cash collections*		*Gross profit rate*		*Realized gross profit*
2012	$ 75,000	×	30%	=	$22,500
2013	125,000	×	25%	=	31,250
					$53,750

Step 6 — Defer the current year's unrealized gross profit to future years.

12/31/12

Deferred gross profit (2012) = ($400,000 – 150,000) × 30% = $ 75,000

12/31/13

Deferred gross profit (2013) = ($450,000 – 200,000) × 25%	=	$ 62,500
Deferred gross profit (2012) = ($400,000 – 150,000 – 175,000) × 30%	=	22,500
		$ 85,000

12/31/14		
Deferred gross profit (2014) = ($600,000 – 300,000) × 33 1/3%	=	$100,000
Deferred gross profit (2013) = ($450,000 – 200,000 – 125,000) × 25%	=	31,250
		$131,250

Financial statement presentation. If installment sales transactions represent a significant portion of the company's total sales, the following three items of gross profit would, theoretically, be reported on the company's income statement:

1. Total gross profit from current year's sales
2. Realized gross profit from current year's sales
3. Realized gross profit from prior years' sales

Examples of income statement presentation of installment sales transactions

An income statement using the previous example would be presented as follows (assume all sales are accounted for by the installment method):

Jordan Equipment Company
Partial Income Statement
For the Years Ending December 31

	2012	*2013*	*2014*
Sales	$ 400,000	$ 450,000	$ 600,000
Cost of sales	(280,000)	(337,500)	(400,000)
Gross profit on current year's sales	120,000	112,500	200,000
Less deferred gross profit on current year's sales	(75,000)	(62,500)	(100,000)
Realized gross profit on current year's sales	45,000	50,000	100,000
Plus gross profit realized on prior years' sales	–	52,500	53,750
Total gross profit on sales	$ 45,000	$ 102,500	$ 153,750

However, when a company recognizes only a small portion of its revenues using the installment method, the illustrated presentation of revenue and gross profit may be confusing. Therefore, in practice, some companies simply report the realized gross profit from installment sales by displaying it as a single line item on the income statement as follows:

Stevens Furniture Company
Partial Income Statement
For the Year Ended December 31, 2012

Sales	$ 2,250,000
Cost of sales	(1,350,000)
Gross profit on sales	900,000
Gross profit realized on installment sales	35,000
Total gross profit on sales	$ 935,000

The statement of financial position presentation of installment accounts receivable depends upon whether installment sales are a normal part of operations. If a company sells most of its products on an installment basis, installment accounts receivable are classified as a current asset because the operating cycle of the business (the length of which is to be disclosed in the notes to the financial statements) is the average period of time covered by its installment contracts. If installment sales are not a normal part of operations, installment accounts receivable that are not to be collected for more than a year (or the length of the company's operating cycle, if different than a year) are reported as noncurrent assets. In all cases, to avoid confusion, it is desirable to fully disclose the year of maturity next to each group of installment accounts receivable.

Example of installment accounts receivable captioned by year of maturity

Current assets:		
Accounts receivable		
Customers	$180,035	
Less allowance for uncollectible accounts	(4,200)	
	175,835	
Installment accounts—collectible in 2012	26,678	
Installment accounts—collectible in 2013	42,234	$244,747

Accounting for deferred gross profit is addressed in CON 6 which states that deferred gross profit is not a liability. The reason is that the seller company is not obligated to pay cash or provide services to the customer. Rather, the deferral arose because of the uncertainty surrounding the collectibility of the sales price. CON 6 goes on to say, "deferred gross profit on installment sales is conceptually an asset valuation allowance (sometimes referred to as a 'contra asset')—that is, a reduction of an asset." However, in practice, deferred gross profit is generally presented either as unearned revenue classified in the current liability section of the statement of financial position or as a deferred credit displayed between liabilities and equity.

Example of CON 6 reduction of installment receivables for deferred gross profit

Following the guideline in CON 6, the current asset section would be presented as follows (using information from the Jordan Equipment example and assuming a 12/31/2014 statement of financial position):

Installment accounts receivable		(2013)	$125,000		
Installment accounts receivable		(2014)	300,000	$ 425,000	
Less:	Deferred gross profit	(2013)	$ 31,250		
	Deferred gross profit	(2014)	100,000	(131,250)	$293,750

Interest on installment method receivables. The previous examples ignored interest, a major component of most installment sales contracts. It is customary for the seller to charge interest to the buyer on the unpaid installment receivable balance. Generally, installment contracts call for equal payments, each with an amount attributable to interest on the unpaid balance and the remainder to the installment receivable balance. As the maturity date nears, a smaller amount of each installment payment is attributable to interest and a larger amount is attributable to principal. Therefore, to determine the amount of gross profit to recognize, the interest must first be deducted from the installment payment and then the difference (representing the principal portion of the payment) is multiplied by the gross profit rate as follows:

Realized gross profit = (Installment payment – Interest portion) × Gross profit rate

The interest portion of the installment payment is recorded as interest revenue at the time of the cash receipt. Appropriate accounting entries are required to accrue interest revenue when the collection dates do not correspond with the period end.

Example of interest-bearing installment sales contracts

To illustrate the accounting for installment sales contracts involving interest, assume that Genrich Equipment Company sells a machine for $5,000 on December 31, 2011, to a customer with a dubious credit history. The machine cost Genrich $3,750. The terms of the agreement require a $1,000 down payment on the date of the sale. The remaining $4,000 is payable in equal annual installments of $1,401.06, including 15% annual interest, at the end of each of the next four years.

For each payment it receives, Genrich must compute the portion to record as interest revenue with the remaining portion of the payment (the principal) to be applied to reduce the installment account receivable balance. Gross profit is only recognized on the principal portion of each payment that is applied to reduce the installment receivable balance. The following schedule illustrates that gross profit is recognized on the entire down payment (which contains no element of interest revenue), whereas the annual installment payments are separated into their interest and principal portions with gross profit only being recognized on the latter portion.

Schedule of Cash Receipts

Date	*Cash (debit)*	*Interest revenue (credit)*	*Installment accounts receivable (credit)*	*Installment accounts receivable balance*	*Realized gross profit*
12/31/11				$5,000.00	
12/31/11	$1,000.00	$ –	$1,000.00	4,000.00	$ 250.00[a]
12/31/12	1,401.06	600.00[b]	801.06[c]	3,198.94[d]	200.27[e]
12/31/13	1,401.06	479.84	921.22	2,277.72	230.31
12/31/14	1,401.06	341.66	1,059.40	1,218.32	264.85
12/31/15	1,401.06	182.74	1,218.32	–	304.57
	$6,604.24	$1,604.24	$5,000.00		
			Total realized gross profit		$1,250.00

Gross profit rate = 1 – ($3,750/5,000) = 25%

[a] *$1,000 × 25% = $250*
[b] *$4,000 × 15% = $600*
[c] *$1,401.06 – 600 = $801.06*
[d] *$4,000 – 801.06 = $3,198.94*
[e] *$801.06 × 25% = $200.27*

Bad debts and repossessions. The standard accounting treatment for uncollectible accounts is to accrue a bad debt loss in the year of sale by estimating the amount expected to be uncollectible. This treatment is consistent with the accrual and matching concepts. However, just as revenue recognition under the accrual basis is sometimes abandoned for certain installment basis sales, the accrual basis of recognizing bad debts is also sometimes abandoned.

When the installment method is used, it is usually appropriate to recognize bad debts by the direct write-off method (i.e., bad debts are not recognized until the receivable has been determined to be uncollectible). This practice is acceptable because most installment contracts contain a provision that allows the seller to repossess the merchandise when the buyer defaults on the installment payments. The loss on the account may be eliminated or reduced because the seller has the option of reselling the repossessed merchandise. To write off an uncollectible installment receivable, the following three steps are followed:

1. The installment account receivable and the deferred gross profit are eliminated.
2. The repossessed merchandise is recorded as used inventory at its net realizable value. Net realizable value is resale value less any selling or reconditioning costs. The repossessed asset is recorded at this fair value because any asset acquired is recorded at the best approximation of its fair value.
3. Bad debt expense and a gain or loss on repossession are recognized. The bad debt expense or repossession gain or loss is the difference between the unrecovered cost (installment account receivable minus deferred gross profit) and the net realizable value of the repossessed merchandise.

Example of uncollectible installment method receivable

Marcie Company determined that a $3,000 installment receivable is uncollectible. The deferred gross profit ratio on the original sale was 30%; thus, $900 deferred gross profit exists ($3,000 × 30%). If the repossessed equipment has a $1,500 net realizable value, a $600 repossession loss (or bad debt expense) should be recorded.

Installment account receivable	$ 3,000
Less deferred gross profit	(900)
Unrecovered cost	2,100
Less net realizable value of repossessed equipment	(1,500)
Repossession loss	$ 600

Marcie Company would record this loss by making the following entry:

Deferred gross profit	900	
Inventory—repossessed merchandise	1,500	
Repossession loss	600	
Installment account receivable		3,000

The Cost Recovery Method

The cost recovery method does not recognize any income on a sale until the cost of the item sold has been fully recovered through cash receipts. Once the seller has recovered all costs, any subsequent cash receipts are included in income. The cost recovery method is used when the uncertainty of collection of the sales price is so great that even use of the installment method cannot be justified.

Under the cost recovery method, both revenues and cost of sales are recognized at the point of sale, but the related gross profit is deferred until all costs of sales have been recovered. Each installment must also be divided between principal and interest, but unlike the installment method where a portion of the principal recovers the cost of sales and the remainder is recognized as gross profit, all of the principal is first applied to recover the cost of the asset sold. After all costs of sales have been recovered, any subsequent cash receipts are realized as gross profit.

Example of the cost recovery method

Using the information from the Genrich Company example used in the section "Interest on installment method receivables." If Genrich used the cost recovery method, gross profit would be realized as follows:

Schedule of Cash Receipts

Date	*Cash (debit)*	*Deferred interest income (credit)**	*Installment accounts receivable (credit)*	*Installment accounts receivable balance*	*Unrecovered cost*	*Realized gross profit*	*Realized interest revenue*
12/31/11				$5,000.00	$3,750.00		
12/31/11	$1,000.00	$ –	$1,000.00	4,000.00	2,750.00	$ –	$ –
12/31/12	1,401.06	600.00	801.06	3,198.94	1,948.94	–	–
12/31/13	1,401.06	479.84	921.22	2,277.72	1,027.72	–	–
12/31/14	1,401.06	(31.68)	1,059.40	1,218.32	–	–	373.34**
12/31/15	1,401.06	(1,048.16)	1,218.32	–	–	1,250.00	1,230.90***
	$6,604.24		$5,000.00			$1,250.00	$1,604.24

* *Interest received in 2012 and 2013 is credited to deferred interest income since the cost of the asset was not recovered until 2014.*

** *Computed as cash received of $1,401.06 less the portion representing unrecovered cost of $1,027.72 = $373.34. Since this amount exceeds the interest paid by the customer for the year of $341.66, the remaining $31.68 reduces deferred interest income.*

*** *Computed as cash received of $1,401.06 less the portion applied to principal of $1,218.32 = $182.74 plus the remaining deferred interest income of $1,048.16.*

The accounting entries to record the foregoing are as follows (in whole dollars):

	Debit (Credit)					
	2011	2012	2013	2014	2015	Totals
Initial Sale and Down Payment:						
Cash	1,000					
Installment accounts receivable	4,000					
Inventory	(3,750)					
Deferred gross profit	(1,250)					
Annual Payments:						
Cash		1,401	1,401	1,401	1,401	5,604
Installment accounts receivable		(801)	(921)	(1,059)	(1,219)	(4,000)
Deferred interest income		(600)	(480)	32	1,048	–
Interest income				(374)	(1,230)	(1,604)
Deferred gross profit					1,250	1,250
Recognized gross profit (revenue)					(1,250)	(1,250)

REVENUE RECOGNITION WHEN RIGHT OF RETURN EXISTS (ASC 605-15)

PERSPECTIVE AND ISSUES

In some industries, it is common practice for customers to have the right to return a product to the seller for a credit or refund. However, for companies that experience a high ratio of returned merchandise to sales, the recognition of the original sale as revenue is questionable. In fact, certain industries have found it necessary to defer revenue recognition until the return privilege has substantially expired. Sometimes the return privilege expires soon after the sale, as in the newspaper and perishable food industries. In other cases, the return privilege may last over an extended period of time, as in magazine and textbook publishing and equipment manufacturing. The rate of return normally is directly related to the length of the return privilege. An accounting issue arises when the recognition of revenue occurs in one period while substantial returns occur in later periods.

ASC 605-15-25 reduced the diversity in the accounting for revenue recognition when such rights exist.

DEFINITIONS OF TERMS

Deferred gross profit. The gross profit from a sale that is recognized in future periods because of the uncertainty surrounding the collection of the sales price.

Return privilege. A right granted to a buyer by express agreement with a seller or by customary industry practice that allows the buyer to return merchandise to the seller within a stated period of time.

CONCEPTS, RULES, AND EXAMPLES

ASC 605-15-25 provides criteria for recognizing revenue on a sale in which a product may be returned (as a matter of contract or a matter of industry practice), either by the ultimate consumer or by a party who resells the product to others. Paragraph 25-1 states the following:

> *If an enterprise sells its product but gives the buyer the right to return the product, revenue from the sales transaction [is] recognized at time of sale only if all of the following conditions are met:*
>
> *a. The seller's price to the buyer is substantially fixed or determinable at the date of sale.*
> *b. The buyer has paid the seller, or the buyer is obligated to pay the seller and the obligation is not contingent on resale of the product.*
> *c. The buyer's obligation to the seller would not be changed in the event of theft or physical destruction or damage of the product.*
> *d. The buyer acquiring the product for resale has economic substance apart from that provided by the seller.*
> *e. The seller does not have significant obligations for future performance to directly bring about the resale of the product by the buyer.*
> *f. The amount of future returns can be reasonably estimated. For purposes of this statement "returns" do not include exchanges by ultimate customers of one item for another of the same kind, quality, and price.*

If all of the above conditions are met, the seller recognizes revenue from the sales transaction at the time of the sale and any costs or losses expected in connection with returns are accrued in accordance with ASC 450, *Contingencies*. ASC 450 states that estimated losses from contingencies are accrued and charged to income when it is both probable that an asset has been impaired or a liability has been incurred, and the amount of loss can be reasonably estimated.

The interplay between ASC 605-15 and ASC 450 needs further explanation. Although ASC 605-15 requires under condition f. that the amount of returns be reasonably estimated, it does not reference the ASC 450 loss accrual criteria. Accordingly, a strict interpretation of both ASC 605-15 and ASC 450 would indicate that only when the conditions for loss accrual under ASC 450 are met (i.e., the loss is both probable and reasonably estimable) would the condition f. above under ASC 605-15 also be met, and both sales and estimated returns can be recognized. However, a more literal interpretation of ASC 605-15 indicates that, by not cross-referencing ASC 450, the FASB intended that the sole criterion for return accrual under ASC 605-15 be the "reasonably estimated" condition f. Then, whether losses are probable or reasonably possible, they would be accrued under ASC 605-15 and the sales would also be recognized. If the likelihood of losses is remote, no disclosure is required under ASC 450, and condition f under ASC 605-15 would be achieved and revenue would be recognized with no need to record an allowance for estimated returns. Under this theory, only if returns cannot be reasonably estimated, would recognition of revenue be precluded under ASC 605-15, regardless of whether losses are probable or reasonably possible.

Example of sale with right of return

Assume that Lipkis, Inc. began the sale of its new textbook on computer programming in 2012 with the following results: On December 1, 2012, 2,000 textbooks with a sales price of $45 each and total manufacturing costs of $30 each are delivered to school bookstores on account. The bookstores have the right to return the textbooks within four months of delivery date. Payments when the books are sold to final customers. Payments and returns for the initial deliveries are as follows:

	Cash receipts		*Returns*	
	Units	*Amount*	*Units*	*Amount*
November 2012				
December 2012	600	$27,000	–	–
January 2013	500	22,500	40	$1,800
February 2013	400	18,000	90	4,050
March 2013	300	13,500	30	1,350
	1,800	$81,000	160	$7,200

Lipkis, Inc. has had similar agreements with the bookstores in the past and has experienced a 15% return rate on similar sales.

Requirements for revenue recognition met. If all six of the requirements were met, the following journal entries would be appropriate:

12/1/12	Accounts receivable	90,000	
	Sales (2,000 units × $45 per unit)		90,000
	To record sale of 2,000 textbooks		
12/31/12	Cash (600 units × $45 per unit)	27,000	
	Accounts receivable		27,000
	To record cash receipts for the month		
	Cost of sales	60,000	
	Inventory (2,000 units × $30 per unit)		60,000
	To record cost of goods sold for the month		
	Sales (15% × 2,000 units × $45 per unit)	13,500	
	Cost of sales (15% × 2,000 units × $30 per unit)		9,000
	Deferred gross profit on estimated returns (15% × 2,000 units × $15 per unit)		4,500
	To record estimate of returns		
1/1/13	Cash	54,000	
to	Accounts receivable		54,000
3/31/13	*To record cash receipts*		
	Inventory (160 units × $30 per unit)	4,800	
	Deferred gross profit on estimated returns	2,400	
	Accounts receivable (160 units × $45 per unit)		7,200
	To record actual returns		
3/31/13	Cost of sales (140 units × $30 per unit)	4,200	
	Deferred gross profit on estimated returns	2,100	
	Sales (140 units × $45 per unit)		6,300
	To record expiration of return privileges and adjust estimate to actual		

The revenue and cost of goods sold recognized in 2012 are based on the number of units expected to be returned, 300 (15% × 2,000 units). The net revenue recognized is $76,500 (85% × 2,000 units × $45 per unit) and the cost of goods sold recognized is $51,000 (85% × 2,000 units × $30 per unit). The deferred gross profit balance is carried forward until either the textbooks are returned or the return privilege expires.

Requirements for revenue recognition not met. If all of the six conditions are not met, revenue and cost of sales from the sales transactions must be deferred until either the return privilege has substantially expired or the point when all the conditions are subsequently met is reached, whichever comes first.

If the facts in the Lipkis case were altered so that the bookstores were not required to pay Lipkis until the later of the date the books were actually sold, or the expiration date of the return privilege, condition b. would not be met until the store remitted payment. The following entries would be required. The return privilege is, of course, assumed to lapse when the books are sold to final customers.

12/1/12	Inventory on consignment	60,000	
	Inventory		60,000
	To record shipment of 2,000 units to retail bookstores on consignment (2,000 units × $30 = $60,000)		
12/31/12	Cash (600 units × $45 per unit)	27,000	
	Sales		27,000
	To record cash receipts for December		
	Cost of sales (600 units × $30 per unit)	18,000	
	Inventory on consignment		18,000
	To record cost of goods sold for December		
1/1/13	Cash	54,000	
to	Sales (1,200* units × $45 per unit)		54,000
3/31/13	*To record cash receipts*		
	Cost of sales (1,200 units × $30 per unit)	36,000	
	Inventory on consignment		36,000
	To record cost of goods sold on cash receipts		
	Inventory (160 units × $30 per unit)	4,800	
	Inventory on consignment		4,800
	To record product returns		
3/31/13	Accounts receivable (40 units × $45 per unit)	1,800	
	Sales		1,800
	To record expiration of return privilege on remaining units		
	Cost of sales (40** units × $30 per unit)	1,200	
	Inventory on consignment		1,200
	To record cost of goods sold on products for which return privilege expired		

* *1,800 units paid for – 600 units paid for in December*
** *2,000 units sold – 160 units returned – 1,800 units paid for*

Future returns cannot be estimated. In the relatively unlikely situation where the reporting entity is unable to make a reasonable estimate of the amount of future returns, the sale cannot be recognized until the return privilege has expired or conditions permit the loss to be estimated, at which point it would become reportable. Examples of factors that might impair the ability to reasonably estimate a loss are:

1. Susceptibility of the product to technological or other obsolescence
2. A lengthy period over which returns are permitted
3. Absence of experience with returns on similar products sold to similar markets
4. Sales are few, significant, and have unique terms (rather than a large number of relatively homogeneous sales of small dollar amounts).

Example: Future product returns – returns cannot be estimated

The SnoJet Company manufactures high-powered snowmobiles, for which it issues a six-month return policy to its distributors. It recently developed the XTR Pro model, which is an incremental enhancement of earlier models, with more horsepower and a tighter suspension. Given its similarity to earlier models, SnoJet's management is comfortable in extending the historical product return rate of 10% to sales of the XTR Pro model. In February, SnoJet sold $840,000 of XTR Pro snowmobiles that have an associated cost of $504,000 (a 60% cost of goods sold). At the same time, the company records $84,000 (10% of gross sales) in an allowance for sales returns, resulting in the following income statement presentation:

Sales	$840,000
Less: sales returns	(84,000)
Net sales	$756,000

Note that, to fully comply with the requirements of ASC 605-15, a valuation allowance for the cost of the estimated product is also to be provided for, with a corresponding reduction of cost of sales, as follows:

Cost of sales	$504,000
Less: cost of sales on estimated returns	(50,400)
Net cost of sales	$453,600

In the following month, ten XTR Pro models are returned to SnoJet. The revenue originally recorded on their sale was $24,000, with associated cost of goods sold of $14,400. However, there is some damage to the models, which will require $3,000 to repair. SnoJet records the transaction with the following entry:

Allowance for sales returns	24,000	
Inventory—rework	11,400	
Loss—returned inventory damage	3,000	
Accounts receivable		24,000
Allowance for cost of sales on product returns		14,400

SnoJet develops an entirely new, jet-powered snowmobile, called the JetPro, which requires the substantial redesign of its basic snowmobile platform. Also, it is to be sold strictly to professional snowmobile racers with whom the company has minimal sales experience, with sale terms allowing returns only within the first two months. In the first month, SnoJet has $150,000 of JetPro sales, for which the related cost of goods sold is $100,000. Given the sales return uncertainty associated with this model, SnoJet records no revenue during the first month, waiting until the second month for the product return policy to expire before recording any revenue. In the first month, its entry to record JetPro sales is:

Accounts receivable	150,000	
Unearned revenue		150,000
Inventory—customer location	100,000	
Finished goods inventory		100,000

At the end of the second month, after the right of return has expired, SnoJet uses the following entry to record the sale and its related profit:

Unearned revenue	150,000	
Revenue		150,000
Cost of goods sold	100,000	
Inventory—customer location		100,000

Note that the decision not to record revenues until after the risk of product returns has lapsed is relatively unusual in practice, and will be dependent on careful consideration of all the facts and circumstances.

REVENUE ARRANGEMENTS WITH MULTIPLE DELIVERABLES (ASC 605-25)

Another longstanding difficulty has been identifying authoritative guidance germane to the accounting for revenue arrangements (product or service sales) having more than one "deliverable." Many instances of aggressive accounting—where all or most of the total revenue was recognized at the time of delivery of the first of multiple deliverables—have come to light. ASC 605-25 comprehensively addressed these complex issues.

PERSPECTIVE AND ISSUES

Vendors may offer customers many related and unrelated products and services sold together ("bundled") or separately. The prices assigned to the various elements of a particular transaction or series of transactions on the seller's invoices and the timing of issuing those invoices are not always indicative of the actual earning of revenue on the various elements of these transactions. ASC 605-25 provides guidance on how to measure consideration received from complex, multielement arrangements and how to allocate that consideration between the different deliverables contained in the arrangement.

Terms used in ASC 605-25

The guidance provided in this Codification Topic is extensive and complex, due to the complex nature of the underlying revenue transactions. A number of key terms are used, defined as follows:

- **Contingent amount.** The portion of the total consideration to be received by a vendor under a multiple deliverable arrangement that would be realized by the vendor only if specified performance conditions were met or additional deliverables were provided to the customer.
- **Noncontingent amount.** The portion of the total consideration to be received by a vendor under a multiple deliverable arrangement that is not subject to any additional performance requirements that the vendor must meet.
- **Refund rights.** The legal right of a customer to obtain a concession or recover all or a portion of the consideration paid to a vendor under a multiple deliverable arrangement.
- **Relative selling price method.** A technique for allocating any discount in an arrangement proportionally to all of the associated deliverables on the basis of their respective selling prices.
- **Stand-alone value.** The value that a specific product or service (deliverable) has to a customer without considering other products or services that might accompany it as part of a multiple deliverable arrangement. To have value to a customer on a stand-alone basis, a deliverable must be either sold separately by any vendor or be separately resalable by the customer whether or not there is an observable market for the deliverable.
- **Vendor-specific objective evidence (VSOE).** The price that a vendor charges for a specific product or service (deliverable) when it is sold separately. If the deliverable is not currently being sold separately, a price that is established by management possessing the authority may be used under the condition that it is considered probable that the established price will not change prior to the separate market introduction of the deliverable.

Summary of guidance provided by ASC 605-25

Arrangements between vendors and their customers often include the sale of multiple products and services (deliverables). A multiple deliverable arrangement (MDA) can be structured using fixed, variable, or contingent pricing or combinations thereof. Product delivery and service performance can occur at different times, and in different locations and customer acceptance can be subject to various return privileges, or performance guarantees.

ASC 605-25 provides guidance on:

1. How a vendor determines whether an MDA consists of a single unit of accounting or multiple units of accounting
2. Allocating MDA consideration to multiple units of accounting
3. Measuring MDA consideration.

In applying these rules, it is to be presumed that separate contracts executed at or near the same time with the same entity or related parties were negotiated as a package and are to be considered together in determining how many units of accounting are contained in an MDA. That presumption can be overcome by sufficient contradictory evidence.

ASC 605-25 collectively applies to all deliverables (i.e., products, services, and rights to use assets) covered by contractually binding written, oral, or implied arrangements.

Scope exceptions are provided for the following:

1. Criteria for the timing of revenue recognition for a unit of accounting. Existing authoritative literature governs these determinations.
2. Arrangements where, conditioned upon the vendor's revenue from the customer exceeding certain cumulative levels or the customer continuing its relationship with the vendor for a specified time period:
   a. The vendor offers free or discounted products or services in the future or
   b. The vendor provides specified future cash rebates or refunds.
3. Arrangements involving the sale of award credits by a "broad-based loyalty program operator." (Presumably this exception refers to airline frequent-flyer or similar customer loyalty programs.)
4. Accounting for the direct costs incurred by a vendor relative to an MDA.

Basic principles established. ASC 605-25 set forth three basic principles, the application of which is the subject of the discussion that follows:

1. MDA are divided into separate *units of accounting* if the deliverables included in the arrangement meet all three of the criteria presented in the table below.
2. Subject to certain limits regarding contingent amounts to be received under the MDA, *relative selling prices* (as determined, in declining order, using VSOE, third-party evidence, or the vendor's best estimate of the selling price) are used to allocate MDA proceeds to the separate units of accounting. The VSOE of a selling price is based on either the price charged for a deliverable when sold separately, or (if not sold separately) the price established by management. Third-party evidence of a selling price is the price of a competitor's essentially interchangeable products in stand-alone sales to similar customers.
3. The revenue recognition criteria to be applied are determined *separately* for each unit of accounting.

Units of accounting

The following table summarizes the criteria used in determining units of accounting for MDA within the scope of ASC 605-25 and is adapted from a decision diagram contained therein:

	Criteria	*Outcome*	*Result*
1.	Does the delivered item have stand-alone value to the customer?	Yes	Go to criterion 2
		No	Do not separate item
2.	If the MDA includes a general right of return with respect to the delivered item, is delivery of the undelivered items probable and substantially controlled by the vendor?	Yes or Not Applicable	Delivered item is a separate unit of accounting
		No	Do not separate item

This separability evaluation is to be applied consistently to MDA that arise under similar circumstances or that possess similar characteristics. The evaluation is to be performed at the inception of the MDA.

If consideration is allocated to a deliverable that does not qualify as a separate unit of accounting, then the reporting entity is required to:

1. Combine the amount allocated to the deliverable with the amounts allocated to all other undelivered items included in the MDA and
2. Determine revenue recognition for the combined items as a single unit of accounting.

The determination of whether total MDA consideration is fixed or determinable disregards the effects of refund rights or performance bonuses, if any.

After applying the decision criteria, the vendor may recognize an asset representing the cumulative difference, from inception of the MDA, between amounts recognized as revenue and amounts received or receivable from the customer (this is analogous to the asset "costs and estimated earnings in excess of billings" which is used in long-term construction accounting). The amount of such assets may not exceed the total amounts to which the vendor is legally entitled under the MDA, including fees that would be earned upon customer cancellation. The amount recognized as an asset would be further limited if the vendor did not intend to enforce its contractual rights to obtain such cancellation fees from the customer.

Example of a multiple deliverable arrangement

Kensington Cellular offers a free netbook as a special promotion to those customers who sign up for a two-year data plan for the netbook, for which it charges $35 per month ($840 over the two-year term of the data plan). Kensington sells the netbook separately for $300, and also normally provides an identical data plan for $35 per month, when there is not a promotion.

The total arrangement consideration is $840. The VSOE selling price of the netbook is $300, and the VSOE selling price of the data plan is $840. The revenue allocable to the two components of the arrangement is calculated as follows:

Netbook	=	$221.05	=	$840 × [$300 ÷ ($300 netbook price + $840 data plan price)]
Data plan	=	$618.95	=	$840 × [$840 ÷ ($300 netbook price + $840 data plan price)]

Disclosures. The financial statements of a vendor are to include the following disclosures, when applicable:

1. The nature of the vendor's MDA
2. Significant deliverables
3. Delivery timing for significant deliverables

4. Whether deliverables qualify as separate units of accounting, and why
5. The timing of revenue recognition for the various units of accounting
6. The effect of changes in price for a unit of accounting if it impacts the allocation of consideration.

OTHER SPECIAL ACCOUNTING AND REPORTING ISSUES

The major categories of revenue-generating transactions, for which specialized accounting standards have been developed, have been addressed in the earlier sections of this chapter. In the following paragraphs, various miscellaneous requirements are discussed.

Reporting revenue gross as a principal versus net as an agent (ASC 605-45). A longstanding issue in financial reporting has been whether certain entities more accurately convey the nature of their operations by reporting as revenue only the "net" amount they retain when acting effectively as an agent for another entity. While in some situations the answer is obvious, in other cases it has been less clear. Historically this may not have been an urgent issue to be resolved, since users of financial statements were deemed capable of deriving correct inferences regardless of the manner of presentation of the income statement. However, in recent years an unfortunate trend developed, whereby analysts and others cited only revenue growth as an indicator of the entity's success, making the question of income statement presentation of revenue somewhat more important.

ASC 605-45 provides guidance on whether an entity is an agent for a vendor-manufacturer, and thus recognizes the net retainage (commission) for serving in that capacity, or whether that entity is a seller of goods (i.e., acting as a principal), and thus should recognize revenue for the gross amount billed to a customer and an expense for the amount paid to the vendor-manufacturer.

The codification identifies the following factors to be considered when determining whether revenue is to be reported as the net retainage (hereinafter, "net") or the gross amount billed to a customer ("gross"). None of the indicators are presumptive or determinative, although the relative strength of each indicator is to be considered.

- Is the company the primary obligor in the arrangement; that is, is the company responsible for the fulfillment of the order, including the acceptability of the product or service to the customer? If the company, rather than a supplier, is responsible, that fact is a strong indicator that the company record revenue gross. Responsibility for arranging transportation for the product is not responsibility for fulfillment. If a supplier is responsible for fulfillment, including the acceptability to the customer, that fact indicates that the company recognizes only the net retainage.
- Does the company have general inventory risk? General inventory risk exists if a company takes title to a product before the product is ordered by a customer or will take title to the product if the customer returns it (provided that the customer has a right of return). In considering this indicator, arrangements with a supplier that reduce or mitigate the company's risk level are to be considered. Unmitigated general inventory risk is a strong indicator that the company recognizes revenue gross.
- Does the company have physical loss inventory risk? Physical loss inventory risk exists if the title to the product is transferred to the company at the shipping point and then transferred to the customer upon delivery. Physical loss inventory risk also exists if a company takes title to the product after the order is received but before the product is transferred to the shipper. While less persuasive than general inventory risk, this indicator provides some evidence that a company record revenue gross.

- Does the company establish the selling price? If a company establishes the selling price, that fact may indicate that the company recognizes revenue gross.
- Is the amount earned by the company fixed? If a company earns a fixed amount per transaction or if it earns a percentage of the selling price, that fact may indicate that the company report revenue net.
- Does the company change the product or perform part of the service? If a company changes the product (beyond packaging) or performs part of the service ordered by the customer such that the selling price is greater as a result of the company's efforts, that fact is indicative that a company recognizes revenue gross. Marketing skills, market coverage, distribution system, or reputation are not to be evaluated in determining whether the company changes the product or performs part of the service.
- Does the company have multiple suppliers for the product or service ordered by the customer? If a company has the discretion to select the supplier, that fact may indicate that the company record revenue gross.
- Is the company involved in determining the nature, type, characteristics, or specifications of the product or service by the customer? If so, that fact may indicate that the company records revenue gross.
- Does the company have credit risk for the amount billed to the customer? Credit risk exists if a company must pay the supplier after the supplier performs, regardless of whether the customer has paid. If the company has credit risk, this fact provides weak evidence that the company records revenue gross. If the supplier assumes the credit risk, the company is to record revenue net.

ASC 605-45 includes thirteen examples to assist in implementation.

Accounting by a grantee for an equity instrument to be received in conjunction with providing goods or services. The accounting for such equity issuances by the reporting entity is addressed by ASC 718. ASC 505-50 has resolved the proper accounting by the recipient of such payments.

In exchange for goods or services, an entity (the grantee) may receive equity instruments that have conversion or exercisability terms that vary based on future events, such as attainment of sales levels or a successful initial public offering. This issue describes the appropriate accounting if ASC 718 does not apply because the instruments received have underlyings based on either the grantee's or issuer's performance.

The grantee measures the fair value of the equity instruments received using the stock price and measurement assumptions as of the earlier of two dates. The first date is the date on which the grantee and the issuer reach a mutual understanding of both the terms of the equity-based compensation and the goods to be delivered (or services to be performed). The second date is the date at which the performance necessary to earn the equity is completed by the grantee, that is, the grantee's rights have vested.

If the terms of the equity agreement are dependent on the achievement of a market condition, the fair value of the instrument is to include the effects on fair value of the commitment to change the terms if the market condition is met. Pricing models are available to value path-dependent equity instruments.

If the terms of the equity agreement are dependent on the achievement of certain performance goals (beyond those that initially established the goods to be delivered or services to be performed), the fair value of the instrument is computed without the effects of the commitment to change the terms if the goals are met. If those goals are subsequently met, the fair value is adjusted to reflect the new terms and the adjustment is reported as additional revenue (as described in the Share-Based Payments section in Chapter 27).

Accounting for consideration given by a vendor to a customer (ASC 605-50). ASC 605-50 provides guidance regarding the recognition, measurement, and income statement display of consideration given by a vendor to purchasers of the vendor's products. This consideration can be provided to a purchaser at any point along the distribution chain, irrespective of whether the purchaser receiving the consideration is a direct or indirect customer of the vendor. Examples of arrangements include, but are not limited to, sales incentive offers labeled as discounts, coupons, rebates, and "free" products or services as well as arrangements referred to as slotting fees, cooperative advertising, and buydowns. The issue does not apply to:

1. Coupons, rebates, and other forms of rights for free or significantly discounted products or services received by a customer in a prior exchange transaction that were accounted for by the vendor as a separate deliverable in that prior exchange, or
2. An offer to a customer, in connection with a current revenue transaction, for free or discounted products or services that is redeemable by the customer at a future date without a further exchange transaction with the vendor. Covered by ASC 605-25, summarized previously.

The issue also does not discuss the accounting for offers of free or discounted products or services that are exercisable after a customer has completed a specified cumulative level of revenue transactions or remained a customer for a specified time period (for example, "point" and loyalty programs).

ASC 605-50 contains the following separately addressed issues:

1. Cash consideration given by a vendor to a customer is presumed to be a reduction of selling price and is classified as a reduction of revenue when recognized in the vendor's income statement. That presumption is overcome and the consideration is classified as a cost incurred if, and to the extent that, both of the following conditions are met:

   a. The vendor receives, or will receive, an identifiable benefit (goods or services) in exchange for the consideration. In order to meet this condition, the identified benefit must be of a type that the vendor could have acquired in an exchange transaction with a party other than a purchaser of its products or services, that is, that the benefit must be separable from the sale of the vendor's goods or services, and
   b. The vendor can reasonably estimate the fair value of that identifiable benefit. If the amount of consideration paid by the vendor exceeds the estimated fair value of the benefit received, that excess amount is classified as a reduction of revenue when recognized in the vendor's income statement.

   If the consideration is a "free" product or service or anything other than cash (including "credits" that the customer can apply against trade amounts owed to the vendor) or equity instruments, the cost of the consideration is characterized as an expense (as opposed to a reduction of revenue) when recognized in the vendor's income statement. ASC 605-50 contains fifteen examples of the application of this issue to various fact scenarios.
2. The amounts representing reduced revenue are classified as expense only if a vendor can demonstrate that classification of those amounts as a reduction of revenue results in negative revenue for a specific customer on a cumulative basis (that is, since the inception of the overall relationship between the vendor and the customer).

However, classification as an expense would not be appropriate if a supply arrangement exists that either:

a. Provides the vendor with the right to be a provider of a certain type or class of goods or services for a specified period of time and it is probable that the customer will order the vendor's goods or services, or
b. Requires the customer to order a minimum amount of goods or services from the vendor in the future, except to the extent that the consideration given exceeds future revenue from the customer under the arrangement.

3. If the consideration (in the form of products, services, or cash) offered voluntarily by a vendor and without charge to customers can be used or becomes exercisable by a customer as a result of a single exchange transaction, and that consideration will not result in a loss on the sale, the vendor recognizes the "cost" of the consideration at the later of the following:

   a. The date the related revenue is recognized by the vendor, or
   b. The date the sales incentive is offered. (For example, a vendor recognizes a liability for a mail-in rebate coupon that requires proof of purchase, based on the estimated amount of refunds or rebates that will be claimed by customers.)

4. If the consideration (in the form of products, services, or cash) offered voluntarily by a vendor and without charge to customers can be used or becomes exercisable by a customer as a result of a single exchange transaction, and that consideration results in a loss on the sale, a vendor does not recognize a liability prior to the date on which the related revenue is recognized (this would be improper matching). However, the offer of consideration in an amount that will result in a loss on the sale of a product may indicate an impairment of existing inventory.
5. If a vendor offers a customer a rebate or refund of a specified amount of cash consideration that is redeemable only if the customer completes a specified cumulative level of purchases or remains a customer for a specified time, the vendor recognizes the cost of the offer in a systematic and rational manner over the period in which the underlying revenue transactions that qualify the customer for the rebate or refund take place. Measurement of the total rebate or refund obligation is based on the estimated number of customers that will ultimately earn and claim rebates or refunds under the offer. If the amount cannot be reasonably estimated, the maximum potential amount is to be recognized.

Accounting by a customer (including a reseller) for certain consideration received from a vendor. ASC 605-50 also addresses accounting issues from the standpoint of how the vendor's customer—either the end user or a reseller of the vendor's products or services—is to account for cash consideration it receives from its vendor.

In general, there is a rebuttable presumption that cash consideration received from a vendor is a purchase-price concession that should be recognized by the customer as a reduction of cost of goods sold (and/or the inventory of unsold units). This presumption is overcome if payment of the consideration is for either:

1. *Delivery of goods and/or services.* Payment to the customer in exchange for goods or services delivered to the vendor is accounted for by the customer as revenue. In order for the customer to recognize revenue, the goods and/or services must be "sufficiently separable" from the customer's purchase of the vendor's products by meeting two criteria.

a. The customer would have obtained the goods and/or services from a party other than the vendor and
b. The customer is able to reasonably estimate the fair value of the goods and/or services provided to the vendor.

Any excess of cash consideration received by the customer over the fair value of the goods and/or services delivered to the vendor reduces the customer's cost of sales.

2. *Reimbursement of costs.* A reimbursement of the customer's specific incremental, identifiable costs incurred to sell the vendor's products or services, which is accounted for by the customer as a reduction of that cost. To the extent the cash consideration received exceeds the actual cost being reimbursed, the excess reduces cost of sales and/or inventory.

Vendors sometimes enter into binding arrangements that offer customers specified amounts of cash rebates or refunds payable in the future only if the customer remains a customer for a specified period of time, or purchases a specified cumulative dollar amount of goods or services from the vendor. In general, these arrangements are to be recorded by the customer as reductions of cost of sales by systematically allocating a portion of the benefits to be received to each transaction that results in progress toward meeting the target that results in earning the benefit. In order to use this pro rata accounting, however, the amount of the refund must be both probable and reasonably estimable (as those terms are defined in ASC 450). The codification provided indicators that, if present, may impair the customer's ability to determine that the refund is both probable and estimable.

1. The rebate or refund applies to purchases that are to occur over a "relatively long period" (which term is undefined in the ASC)
2. An absence of historical experience with similar products or changed circumstances that make historical experience irrelevant
3. A past history of significant adjustments to expected rebates or refunds
4. Susceptibility of the product to significant external factors such as technological obsolescence or changes in demand.

If the rebate or refund is not considered both probable and estimable, it is not recognized by the customer until it is fully earned by reaching the specified milestone (e.g., the dollar amount of cumulative purchases is reached or the time period for remaining a customer has expired).

Changes in a customer's estimate of the amount of future rebates or refunds, and retroactive changes by a vendor to a previous offer are recognized using a "cumulative catch-up adjustment." This is accomplished by the customer immediately charging or crediting cost of sales in an amount that will adjust the cumulative amounts recognized under the arrangement to the changed terms. Of course, if any portion of the adjustment impacts goods still in the customer's inventory, that portion would adjust the valuation of the inventory and not cost of sales.

The SEC observer cautioned registrants to consider whether certain transactions between vendors and customers (e.g., simultaneous agreements between the parties to purchase equal amounts of each other's goods) are covered by the provisions of ASC 845 regarding nonmonetary exchanges that are not the culmination of an earning process.

Applying the foregoing guidance to sales incentives offered by manufacturers to consumers. The rule described immediately above is applicable to situations in which cash consideration is received by a customer from a vendor, and is presumed to be a reduction of the prices of the vendor's products or services. Such incentives are to be characterized as a reduction of cost of sales when recognized in the customer's income statement. There are other instances, however, where consideration is a reimbursement for incentives offered to end users (e.g., retail customers) honored by the vendor's customer (retailer). The common example is coupons given to end users to be redeemed at the retailers offering the vendor's products for sale.

ASC 605-50-45-19 states that this guidance is limited to a vendor's incentive that meets all of the following criteria:

1. The incentive can be tendered by a consumer at resellers that accept manufacturer's incentives in partial (or full) payment of the price charged by the reseller for the vendor's product;
2. The reseller receives a direct reimbursement from the vendor (or a clearinghouse authorized by the vendor) based on the face amount of the incentive;
3. The terms of reimbursement to the reseller for the vendor's sales incentive offered to the consumer are not influenced by or negotiated in conjunction with any other incentive arrangements between the vendor and the reseller, but rather, may only be determined by the terms of the incentive offered to consumers; and
4. The reseller is subject to an agency relationship with the vendor, whether expressed or implied, in the sales incentive transaction between the vendor and the consumer.

Sales incentives that do not meet all of the foregoing criteria are subject to the guidance in ASC 605-50-45-2 through 45-3, and ASC 605-50-45-12 through 45-14, as applicable.

Accounting for consideration given by a service provider to a manufacturer or reseller. There are cases, such as in the cell phone service industry, where companies provide services to their customers under arrangements that require the customers to purchase equipment in order to utilize those services. To spur demand, the companies provide incentives to the equipment manufacturers or resellers to reduce the selling price of the equipment. The accounting for this situation is addressed by ASC 605-50, which states that, if the consideration given by the service provider to the manufacturer or reseller can be linked contractually to the benefit received by the service provider's customers, then the service provider can use the guidance noted above in ASC 605-50 to properly characterize the consideration paid. If the form of consideration to be paid to the service provider's customers is not cash or the service provider does not control the type of consideration paid, then the service provider should record such payments as an expense. If the form of consideration to be paid to the service provider's customers is cash (such as a mail-in rebate), then the service provider should record such payments as a reduction of revenue. The service provider should disclose the nature of the incentive program and the amounts recognized in the statement of operations for the incentive program and their classification for each period presented.

Accounting for revenues related to vaccine stockpiles. The SEC has indicated in Accounting Standards Update (ASU) 2009-07 that it will not object if a registrant with vaccine manufacturing operations recognizes revenue from the sale of vaccines to federal government stockpile programs, even if product delivery and inventory segregation requirements have not been met. This exemption only applies to childhood disease vaccines, influenza vaccines, and other vaccines and countermeasures sold to a federal government stockpile program. A registrant using this exemption should disclose the transactions and their effect on the financial statements.

Accounting for management fees based on a formula. An arrangement may contain a performance-based incentive fee that will not be finalized until the end of a predetermined period of time; for example, a real estate management company may receive a bonus for attaining building occupancy above a specified level. The SEC has indicated in ASU 2010-04 that a registrant can either recognize such revenue at the end of the measurement period or the amount that would be due under the formula as if the contract were terminated at an interim date, though it prefers the first method. However, the SEC will object to measurements as of an interim period that are based on projected future results; it will *only* accept revenue recognition in an interim period that is based on management fees earned as of that date, as though the arrangement had been terminated at that time.

Accounting for research and development revenues using the milestone method (ASC 605-28). The milestone method can be used to recognize revenue related to research and development arrangements. A milestone is an event that occurs only due to vendor performance, and where there is substantive uncertainty that the event will be achieved. Also, the event will result in additional payments to the vendor. A milestone is not contingent solely upon the passage of time.

Under the milestone method, a vendor is allowed to recognize revenue that is contingent upon the achievement of a substantive milestone. Whether a milestone is considered achievable is decided at the beginning of the arrangement. To be substantive, the consideration a vendor earns by completing a milestone must be commensurate with either the vendor's performance to complete the milestone or the enhancement of value delivered. The consideration must also be related only to past performance, and be reasonable relative to the other deliverables and payments in the contract. It is acceptable if a vendor chooses to use some other method of revenue recognition that defers some portion of the consideration arising from a milestone.

The vendor must disclose its policy for the recognition of milestone payments as revenue, as well as a description of each arrangement involving milestone payments, and the amount of milestone consideration recognized during the period.

Fees for guaranteeing a loan. According to ASC 605-20-25-9, fees received for guaranteeing another entity's obligation are to be recognized as income over the guarantee period, rather than at the time of receipt, consistent with other standards governing service fee income recognition. The guarantor is to perform ongoing assessments of the probability of loss related to the guarantee and recognize a liability if the conditions in ASC 450 are met. Upon entering into a guarantee arrangement, the guarantor is required to recognize the stand-ready obligation under the guarantee. The contingent aspect of the guarantee would only be recognized if the conditions defined by ASC 450 are met.

37 ASC 705 COST OF SALES AND SERVICES

This Topic merely provides links to guidance in other Codification topics because the asset liability model generally results in the inclusion of guidance on costs of sales and services in other Topics.

38 ASC 710 Compensation— General

PERSPECTIVE AND ISSUES

Subtopics

ASC 710, *Compensation-General,* contains one subtopic:
ASC 710-10, *Overall,* which is divided into two subsections:

- General, which provides guidance on compensated absences, deferred compensation, and lump-sum payments under union contract
- Deferred Compensation—Rabbi Trusts.

Scope and Scope Exceptions

ASC 710 applies to all entities, but as listed in 710-10-15-5, it does *not* apply to the following transactions:

- Benefits paid to active employees other than compensated absences
- Benefits paid at retirement or provided through a pension or postretirement benefit plan including special or contractual termination benefits payable upon termination from a pension or other postretirement plan are covered by Subtopics 715-30 and 715-60
- Individual deferred compensation contracts that are addressed by Subtopics 715-30 and 715-60, if those contracts, taken together, are equivalent to a defined benefit pension plan or a defined benefit other postretirement benefit plan, respectively
- Special or contractual termination benefits that are not payable from a pension or other postretirement plan are covered by Topic 712
- Stock compensation plans that are addressed by Topic 718
- Other postemployment benefits (see Topic 712) that do not meet the conditions in paragraph 710-10-25-1 and are accounted for in accordance with Topic 450.

In addition, the Deferred Compensation—Rabbi Trusts Subsection does not address the accounting for stock appreciation rights even if they are funded through a rabbi trust (ASC 710-10-15-8).

DEFINITIONS OF TERMS

Compensated Absences. Employee absences, such as vacation, illness, and holidays, for which it is expected that employees will be paid.

Full Eligibility Date. The date at which an employee has rendered all of the service necessary to have earned the right to receive all of the benefits expected to be received by that employee (including any beneficiaries and dependents expected to receive benefits). Determination of the full eligibility date is affected by plan terms that provide incremental benefits expected to be received by or on behalf of an employee for additional years of service, unless those incremental benefits are trivial. Determination of the full eligibility date is not affected by plan terms that define when benefit payments commence or by an employee's current marital or dependency status.

Rabbi Trusts. Rabbi trusts are grantor trusts generally set up to fund compensation for a select group of management or highly paid executives. To qualify as a rabbi trust for income tax purposes, the terms of the trust agreement must explicitly state that the assets of the trust are available to satisfy the claims of general creditors in the event of bankruptcy of the employer.

Sabbatical Leave. A benefit in the form of a compensated absence whereby the employee is entitled to paid time off after working for an entity for a specified period of time. During the sabbatical, the individual continues to be a compensated employee and is not required to perform any duties for the entity.

CONCEPTS, RULES, AND EXAMPLES

Compensated Absences

Compensated absences refer to paid vacation, paid holidays, paid sick leave, and other paid leaves of absence. ASC 710 requires an employer to accrue a liability for employee's compensation for future absences if all of the following conditions are met:

1. The employee's right to receive compensation for future absences is attributable to employee services already rendered.
2. The right vests or accumulates.
3. Payment of the compensation is probable.
4. The amount of the payment can be reasonably estimated.

(ASC 710-10-25-1)

Vesting. If an employer is required to compensate an employee for unused vacation, holidays, or sick days even if employment is terminated, then the employee's right to this compensation is said to vest. Accrual of a liability for nonvesting rights depends on whether the unused rights either expire at the end of the year in which they are earned (often referred to as a "use it or lose it" policy) or accumulate and are carried forward to succeeding years. If the rights expire, a liability for future absences is not accrued at year-end because the benefits to be paid in subsequent years would not be attributable to employee services rendered in prior years. If all or a portion of the unused rights accumulate and increase the benefits otherwise available in subsequent years, a liability is accrued at year-end to the extent that it is probable that employees will be paid in subsequent years for the increased benefits attributable to the accumulated rights and the amount can be reasonably estimated. (ASC 710-10-25-2)

Sick pay. ASC 710-10-25-7 allows an exception for employee paid sick days that accumulate but do not vest. No accrued liability is required for sick days that only accumulate.

However, an employer is permitted to accrue these benefits if the four conditions are met. FASB believed that these amounts are rarely material and the low reliability of estimates of future illness coupled with the high cost of developing these estimates indicates that accrual is not necessary. The required accounting is to be determined by the employer's actual administration of sick pay benefits. If the employer routinely lets employees take time off when they are not ill and allows that time to be charged as sick pay, then an accrual is required. (ASC 710-10-25-6)

Other types of paid time off. Pay for other employee leaves of absence that represent time off for past services (jury duty, personal days) are considered compensation subject to accrual. Pay for employee leaves of absence that will provide future benefits and that are not attributable to past services rendered are not subject to accrual.

ASC 710-10-25-4 and 5 govern the accounting for sabbatical leaves or other similar benefit arrangements that require the completion of a minimum service period, and for which the benefit does not increase with additional years of service. Under these arrangements, the individual continues to be a compensated employee and is not required to perform duties for the entity during their absence. Assuming the four conditions set forth above are met, the compensation cost associated with a sabbatical or other similar arrangement must be ratably accrued over the pre-sabbatical periods of service.

Bonus Payments

Bonus payments may require estimation since the amount of the bonus may be affected by the entity's net income for the year, by the income taxes currently payable, or by other factors. Additional estimation is necessary if bonus payments are accrued on a monthly basis for purposes of interim financial reporting but are determinable only annually by using a formula whose values are uncertain until shortly before payment.

Deferred Compensation Contracts

If the aggregate deferred compensation contracts with individual employees are equivalent to a pension plan, the contracts are accounted for according to ASC 715-30. All other deferred compensation contracts are accounted for according to ASC 710.

ASC 715-60 states that the terms of the individual contract will govern the accrual of the employee's obligation for deferred compensation and the cost is to be attributed over the employee service period until full eligibility is attained.

Per ASC 710, the amount to be accrued is not to be less than the present value of the estimated payments to be made. This estimated amount is accrued in a systematic and rational manner. When elements of both current and future employment are present, only the portion attributable to the current services is accrued. (ASC 710-10-25-9) All requirements of the contract, such as continued employment for a specified period, availability for consulting services, and agreements not to compete after retirement, need to be met in order for the employee to receive future payments. Finally, the total amount is amortized to expense over the period from the date the contract is signed to the point when the employee is fully eligible to receive the deferred payments.

One benefit that may be found in a deferred compensation contract is for periodic payments to employees or their beneficiaries for life, with provisions for a minimum lump-sum settlement in the event of early death of one or all of the beneficiaries. The estimated amount to be accrued is based on the life expectancy of each individual concerned or on the estimated cost of an annuity contract, not on the minimum amount payable in the event of early death. (ASC 710-10-25-11)

Example of a deferred compensation contract

The Clear Eye Corporation enters into a deferred compensation contract with its president, Dr. Smith. Under the terms of the agreement, Clear Eye will pay Dr. Smith an amount equal to twice his annual salary in a lump sum on the date of his mandatory retirement from Clear Eye, which is four years in the future. His salary is currently $120,000. In addition, Clear Eye will pay Dr. Smith an annual pension of $45,000 beginning on his mandatory retirement date, or a minimum $200,000 lump-sum payment in the event of his early death. However, these payments are contingent upon his working the remaining four years prior to his mandatory retirement. The actuarial present value of a lifetime annuity of $45,000 that begins at Dr. Smith's expected retirement date is $392,000.

Clear Eye makes the following entry each year to record its annual expense under the lump-sum payment agreement, which is based on a lump-sum payment of $240,000:

Deferred compensation expense	60,000	
Deferred compensation liability		60,000

After two years, Dr. Smith receives a pay raise to $140,000, which increases the amount of his guaranteed lump-sum payment to $280,000. Since Clear Eye has thus far recognized a deferred compensation expense of $120,000, it must now increase its annual expense recognition to $80,000 in order to recognize additional expense totaling $160,000 over the remaining two years prior to the payment date. It makes the following entry to record the actual cash payment to Dr. Smith:

Deferred compensation liability	280,000	
Cash		280,000

Clear Eye must also record the $392,000 present value of the lifetime annuity over the remaining four years of Dr, Smith's employment rather than the smaller $200,000 early death payment, which it does with the following annual entry:

Deferred compensation expense	98,000	
Deferred compensation liability		98,000

Note that all of the foregoing entries assume that Clear Eye Corporation chooses to record the full (i.e., nondiscounted) amount of the estimated future liability pro rata each year. It would also have been acceptable under ASC 710 to record the discounted present value amounts. In that case, while the charge for deferred compensation would have been lower in the earlier years, the accrued amounts would have to be further accreted to reflect interest on the obligation, so the overall charge over the four-year accrual for the lump-sum payment would have still equaled $280,000. The charge for the lifetime annuity over the four years until the payments commence would have been less than the estimated $392,000 obligation, since the amount recorded as of the inception of the annuity (i.e., retirement date) would be the present value of the future estimated payments.

Deferred Compensation – Rabbi Trusts

The chart below gives an overview of the guidance for Rabbi Trusts.

<table>
<tr><th>Trust</th><th>Description</th><th>Accounting</th></tr>
<tr><td>Plan A</td><td>Does not permit diversification.
Must be settled by delivery of a fixed number of shares of employer stock.</td><td>Classify stock held by trust in equity, similar to treasury stock.</td></tr>
<tr><td>Plan B</td><td>Does not permit diversification.
May be settled by delivery of cash or shares of employer stock.</td><td rowspan="2">Classify employee stock in equity in a manner similar to treasury stock.
Classify deferred compensation obligation as a liability.</td></tr>
<tr><td>Plan C</td><td>Permits diversification, however, the employee has not diversified.</td></tr>
<tr><td>Plan D</td><td>Permits diversification, and the employee has diversified.</td><td>Assets accounted for in accordance with GAAP for the particular assets.
The allocation is classified as a liability.</td></tr>
</table>

39 ASC 712 COMPENSATON—NONRETIREMENT POST-EMPLOYMENT BENEFITS

PERSPECTIVE AND ISSUES

Subtopic

ASC 712, *Compensation—Nonretirement Postemployment Benefits*, contains one Subtopic:

- ASC 712-10, *Overall*, which provides guidance and links to other Topics containing guidance on nonretirement postemployment benefits.

Overview

ASC 712 provides guidance for employers that provide benefits for former or inactive employees after the employees' termination. These benefits may include counseling, pay continuation, continuation of health care benefits, etc. The FASB sees these as benefits provided in exchange for service.

DEFINITIONS OF TERMS

Inactive Employees. Employees who are not currently rendering service to the employer and who have not been terminated. They include those who have been laid off and those on disability leave, regardless of whether they are expected to return to active status.

Nonretirement Postemployment Benefits. All types of benefits, other than those provided through a pension or other postretirement plan (see Subtopics 715-30 and 715-60), provided to former or inactive employees, their beneficiaries, and covered dependents.

Other Postemployment Benefits. Benefits, other than special or contractual termination benefits, that are provided by an employer to former or inactive employees after employment but before retirement including benefits provided to beneficiaries and covered dependents.

Special Termination Benefits. Benefits that are offered for a short period of time in exchange for employees' voluntary termination of service.

Termination Benefits. Benefits provided by an employer to employees in connection with their termination of employment. They may be either special termination benefits offered only for a short period of time or contractual benefits required by the terms of a plan only if a specified event, such as a plant closing, occurs.

CONCEPTS, RULES, AND EXAMPLES

ASC 712 applies the criteria set forth by ASC 710, *Compensation—General,* to accrue an obligation for postemployment benefits other than pensions if:

- Services have been performed by employees,
- Employees' rights accumulate or vest,
- Payment is probable, and
- The amount can be reasonably estimable.

If these benefits do not vest or accumulate, ASC 450, *Contingencies,* applies. If neither ASC 710 nor ASC 450 is applicable because the amount is not reasonably estimable, this fact must be disclosed.

40 ASC 715 COMPENSATION—RETIREMENT BENEFITS

PERSPECTIVE AND ISSUES

Subtopics

ASC 715, *Compensation-Retirement Benefits,* contains six subtopics:

- ASC 715-10, *Overall,* sets the objectives and the scope for ASC 715

- ASC 715-20, *Defined Benefit Plans—General,* provides guidance for single-employer defined benefit pension and other postretirement plans
- ASC 715-30, *Defined Benefit Plans—Retirement,* provides guidance related to single-employer defined benefit pension plans
- ASC 715-60, *Defined Benefit Plans—Other Postretirement,* provides guidance on defined benefit plans other than postretirement benefit plans
- ASC 715-70, *Defined Contribution Plan,* provides guidance on defined contribution plans
- ASC 715-80, *Multiemployer Plans,* provides guidance on multi-employer plans as opposed to multiple employer plans.

Scope and Scope Exceptions

ASC 715 applies to all entities and many types of compensation arrangements including any arrangement that is in substance a postretirement benefit plan (regardless of its form or means or timing of funding), written and unwritten plans, deferred compensation contracts with individuals which taken together are the equivalent of a plan, and health and other welfare benefits for employees on disability retirement.

ASC 715 does *not* apply to contracts with "selected employees under individual contracts with specific terms determined on an individual-by-individual basis." It also does not apply to postemployment benefits paid after employment, but before retirement, like layoff benefits. (ASC 715-10-15-5)

Overview

This chapter focuses on accounting for postretirement benefits, including single-employer and multiemployer plans, defined benefit pension plans, defined contribution pension plans, and postretirement benefit plans other than pensions, such as those that help fund retiree costs of health care benefits. The accounting for such arrangements has historically been difficult, in large part because the accounting standard setters, influenced by preparers and issuers, have seen fit to include a variety of "smoothing" features that—whatever merits they may have—necessitated the use of various accruals and deferrals, and the reporting of certain elements within other comprehensive income. Thus, presentation of benefit plan expense and related items has involved lengthy and complex footnotes, and generally at least some "off the financial statement" measurements.

Accounting Standards Codification (ASC) 715-30, *Compensation—Retirement Benefits—Defined Benefit Plans, Pension,* specifies the accrual basis of accounting for pension costs. It includes three primary characteristics, which are

1. Delayed recognition (changes are not recognized immediately but are subsequently recognized in a gradual and systematic way)
2. Reporting net cost (various expense and income items are aggregated and reported as one net amount)
3. Offsetting assets and liabilities (assets and liabilities are sometimes shown net).

Estimates and averages may be used as long as material differences do not result. Explicit assumptions and estimates of future events must be used for each specified variable included in pension costs and disclosed in the notes to the financial statements.

ASC 715-30 focuses directly on the terms of the plan to assist in the recognition of compensation cost over the service period of the employees. The full amount of under- and overfunding of pension plans is reported in the statement of financial position.

The principal emphasis of ASC 715-30 is the present value of the pension obligation and the fair value of plan assets. The main accounting issues revolve around the expense to recognize on the income statement and the liability to be accrued on the statement of financial position. As noted above, the periodic expense to be recognized under GAAP is a modified version of the actual economic consequence of the employer's commitment to pay future benefits, because of the substantial use of smoothing. (Over the full time horizon, which is measured in decades, all expense is recognized in results of operations.)

ASC 715-30 establishes standards to be followed by sponsors of defined benefit pension plans when obligations are settled, plans are curtailed, or benefits are terminated.

Although there are some major differences in terminology and measurement, other postretirement benefits (commonly referred to as OPEB) accounting basically follows the fundamental framework established for defined benefit pension accounting and applies to all forms of postretirement benefits other than pensions. In most cases, the main focus is on postretirement health care benefits, since that is by far the most costly commitment made by employers to retirees. ASC 715-60, *Compensation—Retirement Benefits—Defined Benefit Plans, Other Postretirement* considers OPEB to be a form of deferred compensation and requires accrual accounting. The terms of the individual contract govern the accrual of the employer's obligation for deferred compensation and the cost is attributed to employee service periods until full eligibility to receive benefits is attained. The employer's obligation for OPEB is fully accrued when the employee attains full eligibility for all expected benefits.

As stated in ASC 715, *Compensation—Retirement Benefits,* some or all of the underfunded postretirement benefit obligations must be displayed in the statement of financial position.

ASC 715-20, *Compensation—Retirement Benefits, Defined Benefits Plans, General,* eliminates less useful information, requires some additional data deemed useful by analysts, and allows some aggregation of presentation.

DEFINITIONS OF TERMS

Source: ASC 715-20-20

Cash Equivalents. Cash equivalents are short-term, highly liquid investments that have both of the following characteristics:

1. Readily convertible to known amounts of cash
2. So near their maturity that they present insignificant risk of changes in value because of changes in interest rates.

Generally, only investments with original maturities of three months or less qualify under that definition. Original maturity means original maturity to the entity holding the investment. For example, both a three-month U.S. Treasury bill and a three-year U.S. Treasury note purchased three months from maturity qualify as cash equivalents. However, a Treasury note purchased three years ago does not become a cash equivalent when its remaining maturity is three months. Examples of items commonly considered to be cash equivalents are Treasury bills, commercial paper, money market funds, and federal funds sold (for an entity with banking operations).

Net Periodic Pension Cost. The amount recognized in an employer's financial statements as the cost of a pension plan for a period. Components of net periodic pension cost are service cost, interest cost, actual return on plan assets, gain or loss, amortization of prior service cost or credit, and amortization of the transition asset or obligation existing at the date of initial application of Subtopic 715-30. The term net periodic pension cost is used instead of net pension expense because part of the cost recognized in a period may be capitalized along with other costs as part of an asset such as inventory.

Net Periodic Postretirement Benefit Cost. The amount recognized in an employer's financial statements as the cost of a postretirement benefit plan for a period. Components of net periodic postretirement benefit cost include service cost, interest cost, actual return on plan assets, gain or loss, amortization of prior service cost or credit, and amortization of the transition obligation or asset.

Nonpublic Entity. Any entity other than one with any of the following characteristics:

a. Whose debt or equity securities trade in a public market either on a stock exchange (domestic or foreign) or in the over-the-counter market, including securities quoted only locally or regionally
b. That is a conduit bond obligor for conduit debt securities that are traded in a public market (a domestic or foreign stock exchange or an over-the-counter market, including local or regional markets)
c. That makes a filing with a regulatory agency in preparation for the sale of any class of debt or equity securities in a public market
d. That is controlled by an entity covered by a., b., or c.

Conduit debt securities refers to certain limited-obligation revenue bonds, certificates of participation, or similar debt instruments issued by a state or local governmental entity for the express purpose of providing financing for a specific third party (the conduit bond obligor) that is not a part of the state or local government's financial reporting entity. Although conduit debt securities bear the name of the governmental entity that issues them, the governmental entity often has no obligation for such debt beyond the resources provided by a lease or loan agreement with the third party on whose behalf the securities are issued. Further, the conduit bond obligor is responsible for any future financial reporting requirements.

Nonpublic Entity. Any entity that does not meet any of the following conditions:

a. Its debt or equity securities trade in a public market either on a stock exchange (domestic or foreign) or in an over-the-counter market, including securities quoted only locally or regionally.
b. It is a conduit bond obligor for *conduit debt securities* that are traded in a public market (a domestic or foreign stock exchange or an over-the-counter market, including local or regional markets).
c. It files with a regulatory agency in preparation for the sale of any class of debt or equity securities in a public market.
d. It is required to file or furnish financial statements with the Securities and Exchange Commission.
e. It is controlled by an entity covered by criteria a. through d.

Publicly Traded Entity (or Public Entity). Any entity that does not meet the definition of a nonpublic entity.

Related Parties. Related parties include:

1. Affiliates of the entity
2. Entities for which investments in their equity securities would be required, absent the election of the fair value option under the Fair Value Option Subsection of Section 825-10-15, to be accounted for by the equity method by the investing entity
3. Trusts for the benefit of employees, such as pension and profit-sharing trusts that are managed by or under the trusteeship of management

4. Principal owners of the entity and members of their immediate families
5. Management of the entity and members of their immediate families
6. Other parties with which the entity may deal if one party controls or can significantly influence the management or operating policies of the other to an extent that one of the transacting parties might be prevented from fully pursuing its own separate interests
7. Other parties that can significantly influence the management or operating policies of the transacting parties or that have an ownership interest in one of the transacting parties and can significantly influence the other to an extent that one or more of the transacting parties might be prevented from fully pursuing its own separate interests.

Settlement of a Pension or Postretirement Benefit Obligation. A transaction that is an irrevocable action, relieves the employer (or the plan) of primary responsibility for a pension or postretirement benefit obligation, and eliminates significant risks related to the obligation and the assets used to effect the settlement.

Source: ASC 715-30-20

Accumulated Benefit Obligation. The actuarial present value of benefits (whether vested or nonvested) attributed, generally by the pension benefit formula, to employee service rendered before a specified date and based on employee service and compensation (if applicable) before that date. The accumulated benefit obligation differs from the projected benefit obligation in that it includes no assumption about future compensation levels. For plans with flat-benefit or non-pay-related pension benefit formulas, the accumulated benefit obligation and the projected benefit obligation are the same.

Actual Return on Plan Assets (Component of Net Periodic Pension Cost). For a funded plan, the actual return on plan assets is determined as the difference between the fair value of plan assets at the end of the period and the fair value at the beginning of the period, adjusted for contributions and payments of benefits during the period.

Actuarial Funding Method. Any of several techniques that actuaries use in determining the amounts and incidence of employer contributions to provide for pension benefits.

Actuarial Gain or Loss. See Gain or Loss.

Actuarial Present Value. The value, as of a specified date, of an amount or series of amounts payable or receivable thereafter, with each amount adjusted to reflect the time value of money (through discounts for interest) and the probability of payment (by means of decrements for events such as death, disability, withdrawal, or retirement) between the specified date and the expected date of payment.

Allocated Contract. A contract with an insurance entity under which payments to the insurance entity are currently used to purchase immediate or deferred annuities for individual participants. See Annuity Contract.

Amortization. The process of reducing a recognized liability systematically by recognizing gains or by reducing a recognized asset systematically by recognizing losses. In accounting for pension benefits or other postretirement benefits, amortization also means the systematic recognition in net periodic pension cost or other postretirement benefit cost over several periods of amounts previously recognized in other comprehensive income, that is, gains or losses, prior service cost or credits, and any transition obligation or asset.

Annuity Contract. A contract in which an insurance entity unconditionally undertakes a legal obligation to provide specified pension benefits to specific individuals in return for a fixed consideration or premium. An annuity contract is irrevocable and involves the transfer of significant risk from the employer to the insurance entity. Annuity contracts are also called allocated contracts.

Asset Group. An asset group is the unit of accounting for a long-lived asset or assets to be held and used, which represents the lowest level for which identifiable cash flows are largely independent of the cash flows of other groups of assets and liabilities.

Assumptions. Estimates of the occurrence of future events affecting pension costs and other postretirement benefit costs (as applicable), such as turnover, retirement age, mortality, withdrawal, disablement, dependency status, per capita claims costs by age, health care cost trend rates, levels of Medicare and other health care providers' reimbursements, changes in compensation and national pension benefits, and discount rates to reflect the time value of money.

Attribution. The process of assigning pension or other postretirement benefits or costs to periods of employee service.

Benefit Approach. A group of basic approaches to attributing pension benefits or costs to periods of employee service.

Approaches in this group assign a distinct unit of benefit to each year of credited service. The actuarial present value of that unit of benefit is computed separately and determines the cost assigned to that year. The accumulated benefits approach, benefit-compensation approach, and benefit-years-of-service approach are benefit approaches.

Benefit Formula. See Pension Benefit Formula.

Benefit-Years-of-Service Approach. One of three benefit approaches. Under this approach, an equal portion of the total estimated benefit is attributed to each year of service. The actuarial present value of the benefits is derived after the benefits are attributed to the periods.

Benefits. The monetary or in-kind benefits or benefit coverage to which participants may be entitled under a pension plan or other postretirement benefit plan, including health care benefits, life insurance, legal, educational, and advisory services, pension benefits, disability benefits, death benefits, and benefits due to termination of employment.

Captive Insurer. An insurance entity that does business primarily with related entities.

Career-Average-Pay Formula. A benefit formula that bases benefits on the employee's compensation over the entire period of service with the employer. A career-average-pay plan is a plan with such a formula.

Cash Balance Plan. A plan with the following characteristics:

1. A defined principal-crediting rate as a percentage of salary
2. A defined, noncontingent interest-crediting rate that entitles participants to future interest credits at a stated, fixed rate until retirement.

A cash balance plan communicates to employees a pension benefit in the form of a current account balance that is a function of current and past salary-based principal credits and future interest credits thereon at a stated rate based on those principal credits.

In a cash balance plan, individual account balances are determined by reference to a hypothetical account rather than specific assets, and the benefit is dependent on the employer's promised interest-crediting rate, not the actual return on plan assets. The employer's financial obligation to the plan is not satisfied by making prescribed principal and interest credit contributions—whether in cash or as a hypothetical contribution to participants' accounts—for the period; rather, the employer must fund, over time, amounts that can accumulate to the actuarial present value of the benefit due at the time of distribution to each participant pursuant to the plan's terms. The employer's contributions to a cash balance plan trust and the earnings on the invested plan assets may be unrelated to the principal and interest credits to participants' hypothetical accounts.

A cash balance plan is a defined benefit plan.

Component of an Entity. A component of an entity comprises operations and cash flows that can be clearly distinguished, operationally and for financial reporting purposes, from the rest of the entity. A component of an entity may be a reportable segment or an operating segment, a reporting unit, a subsidiary, or an asset group.

Conduit Debt Securities. Certain limited-obligation revenue bonds, certificates of participation, or similar debt instruments issued by a state or local governmental entity for the express purpose of providing financing for a specific third party (the conduit bond obligor) that is not a part of the state or local government's financial reporting entity. Although conduit debt securities bear the name of the governmental entity that issues them, the governmental entity often has no obligation for such debt beyond the resources provided by a lease or loan agreement with the third party on whose behalf the securities are issued. Further, the conduit bond obligor is responsible for any future financial reporting requirements.

Contributory Plan. A plan under which retirees or active employees contribute part of the cost. In some contributory plans, retirees or active employees wishing to be covered must contribute; in other contributory plans, participants' contributions result in increased benefits.

Cost-Compensation Approach. Net pension costs under this approach are attributed to periods so that they are a constant percentage of compensation for each period.

Curtailment. See Plan Curtailment.

Defined Benefit Plan. A defined benefit plan provides participants with a determinable benefit based on a formula provided for in the plan.

1. Defined benefit health and welfare plans—Defined benefit health and welfare plans specify a determinable benefit, which may be in the form of a reimbursement to the covered plan participant or a direct payment to providers or third-party insurers for the cost of specified services. Such plans may also include benefits that are payable as a lump sum, such as death benefits. The level of benefits may be defined or limited based on factors such as age, years of service, and salary. Contributions may be determined by the plan's actuary or be based on premiums, actual claims paid, hours worked, or other factors determined by the plan sponsor. Even when a plan is funded pursuant to agreements that specify a fixed rate of employer contributions (for example, a collectively bargained multiemployer plan), such a plan may nevertheless be a defined benefit health and welfare plan if its substance is to provide a defined benefit.
2. Defined benefit pension plan—A pension plan that defines an amount of pension benefit to be provided, usually as a function of one or more factors such as age, years of service, or compensation. Any pension plan that is not a defined contribution pension plan is, for purposes of Subtopic 715-30, a defined benefit pension plan.
3. Defined benefit postretirement plan—A plan that defines postretirement benefits in terms of monetary amounts (for example, $100,000 of life insurance) or benefit coverage to be provided (for example, up to $200 per day for hospitalization, or 80 percent of the cost of specified surgical procedures). Any postretirement benefit plan that is not a defined contribution postretirement plan is, for purposes of Subtopic 715-60, a defined benefit postretirement plan. (Specified monetary amounts and benefit coverage are collectively referred to as benefits.)

Defined Contribution Plan. A plan that provides an individual account for each participant and provides benefits that are based on all of the following: amounts contributed to the participant's account by the employer or employee; investment experience; and any forfeitures allocated to the account, less any administrative expenses charged to the plan.

1. Defined contribution health and welfare plans—Defined contribution health and welfare plans maintain an individual account for each plan participant. They have terms that specify the means of determining the contributions to participants' accounts, rather than the amount of benefits the participants are to receive. The benefits a plan participant will receive are limited to the amount contributed to the participant's account, investment experience, expenses, and any forfeitures allocated to the participant's account. These plans also include flexible spending arrangements.
2. Defined contribution postretirement plan—A plan that provides postretirement benefits in return for services rendered, provides an individual account for each plan participant, and specifies how contributions to the individual's account are to be determined rather than specifies the amount of benefits the individual is to receive. Under a defined contribution postretirement plan, the benefits a plan participant will receive depend solely on the amount contributed to the plan participant's account, the returns earned on investments of those contributions, and the forfeitures of other plan participants' benefits that may be allocated to that plan participant's account.

Discount Rate. A rate or rates used to reflect the time value of money. Discount rates are used in determining the present value as of the measurement date of future cash flows currently expected to be required to satisfy the pension obligation or other postretirement benefit obligation. See Actuarial Present Value.

Expected Long-Term Rate of Return on Plan Assets. An assumption about the rate of return on plan assets reflecting the average rate of earnings expected on existing plan assets and expected contributions to the plan during the period.

Expected Return on Plan Asset. An amount calculated as a basis for determining the extent of delayed recognition of the effects of changes in the fair value of plan assets. The expected return on plan assets is determined based on the expected long-term rate of return on plan assets and the market-related value of plan assets.

Explicit Approach to Assumptions. An approach under which each significant assumption used reflects the best estimate of the plan's future experience solely with respect to that assumption. See Implicit Approach to Assumptions.

Final-Pay Formula. A benefit formula that bases benefits on the employee's compensation over a specified number of years near the end of the employee's service period or on the employee's highest compensation periods. For example, a plan might provide annual pension benefits equal to 1 percent of the employee's average salary for the last 5 years (or the highest consecutive 5 years) for each year of service. A final-pay plan is a plan with such a formula.

Flat-Benefit Formula. A benefit formula that bases benefits on a fixed amount per year of service, such as $20 of monthly retirement income for each year of credited service. A flat-benefit plan is a plan with such a formula.

Fund. Used as a verb, to pay over to a funding agency (as to fund future pension benefits or to fund pension cost). Used as a noun, assets accumulated in the hands of a funding agency for the purpose of meeting pension benefits when they become due.

Funding Method. See Actuarial Funding Method.

Funding Policy. The program regarding the amounts and timing of contributions by the employers, plan participants, and any other sources (for example, state subsidies or federal grants) to provide the benefits a pension plan or other postretirement benefit plan specifies.

Gain or Loss. A change in the value of either the benefit obligation (projected benefit obligation for pension plans or accumulated postretirement benefit obligation for other postretirement benefit plans) or the plan assets resulting from experience different from that assumed or from a change in an actuarial assumption, or the consequence of a decision to temporarily deviate from the other postretirement benefit substantive plan. Gains or losses that are not recognized in net periodic pension cost or net periodic postretirement benefit cost when they arise are recognized in other comprehensive income. Those gains or losses are subsequently recognized as a component of net periodic pension cost or net periodic postretirement benefit cost based on the recognition and amortization provisions of Subtopic 715-30 or Subtopic 715-60.

Gain or Loss (Component of Net Periodic Pension Cost). The sum of the difference between the actual return on plan assets and the expected return on plan assets and the amortization of the net gain or loss recognized in accumulated other comprehensive income. The gain or loss component is the net effect of delayed recognition of gains and losses in determining net periodic pension cost (the net change in the gain or loss) in accumulated other comprehensive income except that it does not include changes in the projected benefit obligation occurring during the period and deferred for later recognition in net periodic pension cost.

Implicit Approach to Assumptions. An approach under which two or more assumptions do not individually represent the best estimate of the plan's future experience with respect to those assumptions. Instead, the aggregate effect of their combined use is presumed to be approximately the same as that produced by an explicit approach. See Explicit Approach to Assumptions.

Interest Cost (Component of Net Periodic Pension Cost). The amount recognized in a period determined as the increase in the projected benefit obligation due to the passage of time.

Loss. See Gain or Loss.

Market-Related Value of Plan Assets. A balance used to calculate the expected return on plan assets. The market-related value of plan assets is either fair value or a calculated value that recognizes changes in fair value in a systematic and rational manner over not more than five years. Different ways of calculating market-related value may be used for different classes of assets (for example, an employer might use fair value for bonds and a five-year-moving-average value for equities), but the manner of determining market-related value is required to be applied consistently from year to year for each asset class. For a method to meet the criteria of being systematic and rational, it must reflect only the changes in the fair value of plan assets between various dates.

Mortality. The relative incidence of death in a given time or place.

Mortality Rate. The proportion of the number of deaths in a specified group to the number living at the beginning of the period in which the deaths occur. Actuaries use mortality tables, which show death rates for each age, in estimating the amount of pension benefits that will become payable.

Multiple-Employer Plan. A pension plan or other postretirement benefit plan maintained by more than one employer but not treated as a multiemployer plan. Multiple-employer plans are generally not collectively bargained and are intended to allow participating employers, commonly in the same industry, to pool their plan assets for investment purposes and to reduce the cost of plan administration. A multiple-employer plan maintains separate accounts for each employer so that contributions provide benefits only for employees of the contributing employer. Multiple-employer plans may have features that allow participating employers to have different benefit formulas, with the employer's contributions to the plan based on the benefit formula selected by the employer.

Net Periodic Pension Cost. The amount recognized in an employer's financial statements as the cost of a pension plan for a period. Components of net periodic pension cost are service cost, interest cost, actual return on plan assets, gain or loss, amortization of prior service cost or credit, and amortization of the transition asset or obligation existing at the date of initial application of Subtopic 715-30. The term net periodic pension cost is used instead of net pension expense because part of the cost recognized in a period may be capitalized along with other costs as part of an asset such as inventory.

Nonparticipating Annuity Contract. An annuity contract that does not provide for the purchaser to participate in the investment performance or in other experience of the insurance entity.

Nonpublic Entity. An entity that does not meet any of the following criteria:

1. Its debt or equity securities are traded in a public market, including those traded on a stock exchange or in the over-the-counter market (including securities quoted only locally or regionally).
2. It is a conduit bond obligor for conduit debt securities that are traded in a public market (a domestic or foreign stock exchange or an over-the-counter market, including local or regional markets).
3. Its financial statements are filed with a regulatory agency in preparation for the sale of any class of securities.

Operating Segment. A component of a public entity. See Section 280-10-50 for additional guidance on the definition of an operating segment.

Participant. Any employee or former employee, or any member or former member of a trade or other employee association, or the beneficiaries of those individuals, for whom there are pension plan benefits or other accumulated plan benefits.

Participating Annuity Contract. An annuity contract that provides for the purchaser to participate in the investment performance and possibly other experience (for example, mortality experience) of the insurance entity. Under a participating annuity contract, the insurance entity ordinarily pays dividends to the purchaser.

Participation Right. A purchaser's right under a participating contract to receive future dividends or retroactive rate credits from the insurance entity. See Participating Annuity Contract.

Pension Benefit Formula. The basis for determining payments to which participants may be entitled under a pension plan. Pension benefit formulas usually refer to the employee's service or compensation or both. Sometimes referred to as a plan's benefit formula or benefit formula.

Pension Benefits. Periodic (usually monthly) payments made pursuant to the terms of the pension plan to a person who has retired from employment or to that person's beneficiary.

Pension Fund. The assets of a pension plan held by a funding agency.

Plan Amendment. A change in the existing terms of a plan or the initiation of a new plan. A plan amendment may increase benefits (a positive plan amendment), or reduce or eliminate benefits (a negative plan amendment), including those benefits attributed to years of service already rendered.

Plan Assets. Assets—usually stocks, bonds, and other investments—that have been segregated and restricted, usually in a trust, to provide for pension benefits. The amount of plan assets includes amounts contributed by the employer, and by employees for a contributory plan, and amounts earned from investing the contributions, less benefits paid. Plan assets ordinarily cannot be withdrawn by the employer except under certain circumstances when a plan has assets in excess of obligations and the employer has taken certain steps to satisfy existing obligations. Assets not segregated in a trust or otherwise effectively restricted so that they cannot be used by the employer for other purposes are not plan assets even though it may be intended that such assets be used to provide pensions. If a plan has liabilities other than for benefits, those nonbenefit obligations may be considered as reductions of plan assets. Amounts accrued by the employer but not yet paid to the plan are not plan assets. Securities of the employer held by the plan are includable in plan assets provided they are transferable.

Plan Assets Available for Benefits. See Plan Assets.

Plan Curtailment. An event that significantly reduces the expected years of future service of present employees or eliminates for a significant number of employees the accrual of defined benefits for some or all of their future services.

Plan Suspension. An event in which the pension plan is frozen and no further benefits accrue. Future service may continue to be the basis for vesting of nonvested benefits existing at the date of suspension. The plan may still hold assets, pay benefits already accrued, and receive additional employer contributions for any unfunded benefits. Employees may or may not continue working for the employer.

Plan Termination. An event in which the pension plan or postretirement benefit plan ceases to exist and all benefits are settled by the purchase of insurance contracts (for example, annuities) or by other means. The plan may or may not be replaced by another plan. A plan termination with a replacement plan may or may not be in substance a plan termination for accounting purposes.

Plan's Benefit Formula. See Pension Benefit Formula.

Prior Service Cost. The cost of retroactive benefits granted in a plan amendment. Retroactive benefits are benefits granted in a plan amendment (or initiation) that are attributed by the benefit formula to employee services rendered in periods before the amendment.

Probable. The future event or events are likely to occur.

Projected Benefit Obligation. The actuarial present value as of a date of all benefits attributed by the pension benefit formula to employee service rendered before that date. The projected benefit obligation is measured using assumptions as to future compensation levels if the pension benefit formula is based on those future compensation levels (pay-related, final-pay, final-average-pay, or career-average-pay plans).

Reporting Unit. The level of reporting at which goodwill is tested for impairment. A reporting unit is an operating segment or one level below an operating segment (also known as a component).

Service. Employment taken into consideration under a pension plan. Years of employment before the inception of a plan constitute an employee's past service; years thereafter are classified in relation to the particular actuarial valuation being made or discussed. Years of employment (including past service) before the date of a particular valuation constitute prior service; years of employment following the date of the valuation constitute future service; a year of employment adjacent to the date of valuation, or in which such date falls, constitutes current service.

Service Cost (Component of Net Periodic Pension Cost). A component of net periodic pension cost recognized in a period determined as the actuarial present value of benefits attributed by the pension benefit formula to services rendered by employees during that period.

The service cost component is a portion of the projected benefit obligation and is unaffected by the funded status of the plan.

Settlement of a Pension or Postretirement Benefit Obligation. A transaction that is an irrevocable action, relieves the employer (or the plan) of primary responsibility for a pension or postretirement benefit obligation, and eliminates significant risks related to the obligation and the assets used to effect the settlement.

Single-Employer Plan. A pension plan or other postretirement benefit plan that is maintained by one employer. The term also may be used to describe a plan that is maintained by related parties such as a parent and its subsidiaries.

Sponsor. In the case of a pension plan established or maintained by a single employer, the employer; in the case of a plan established or maintained by an employee entity, the employee entity; in the case of a plan established or maintained jointly by two or more employers or by one or more employers and one or more employee entities, the association, committee, joint board of trustees, or other group of representatives of the parties that have established or that maintain the pension plan.

Termination Benefits. Benefits provided by an employer to employees in connection with their termination of employment. They may be either special termination benefits offered only for a short period of time or contractual benefits required by the terms of a plan only if a specified event, such as a plant closing, occurs.

Termination Indemnities. Arrangements, usually or more frequently encountered outside the United States, that are also referred to as termination allowances or severance indemnities. Termination indemnities are amounts payable to eligible employees upon termination of employment. Eligibility may be determined by law, by local custom, by the employer's policy, or by contract with the employer. Plans may or may not be in writing. Termination indemnities are normally, but not exclusively, associated with preretirement severance of employment. They are usually payable as a lump sum, or occasionally in a few payments over a short period of time.

Turnover. Termination of employment for a reason other than death or retirement.

Unallocated Contract. A contract with an insurance entity under which payments to the insurance entity are accumulated in an unallocated fund (not allocated to specific plan participants) to be used either directly or through the purchase of annuities, to meet benefit payments when employees retire. Funds held by the insurance entity under an unallocated contract may be withdrawn and otherwise invested.

Unfunded Projected Benefit Obligation. The excess of the projected benefit obligation over plan assets.

Vested Benefit Obligation. The actuarial present value of vested benefits.

Vested Benefits. Benefits for which the employee's right to receive a present or future pension benefit is no longer contingent on remaining in the service of the employer. (Other conditions, such as inadequacy of the pension fund, may prevent the employee from receiving the vested benefit.) Under graded vesting, the initial vested right may be to receive in the future a stated percentage of a pension based on the number of years of accumulated credited service; thereafter, the percentage may increase with the number of years of service or of age until the right to receive the entire benefit has vested.

Source: 715-60-20

Accumulated Postretirement Benefit Obligation. The actuarial present value as of a particular date of all future benefits attributed to an employee's service rendered to that date assuming the plan continues in effect and that all assumptions about future events are fulfilled. The accumulated postretirement benefit obligation generally reflects a ratable allocation of expected future benefits to employee service already rendered in the attribution period. Before an employee's full eligibility date, the accumulated postretirement benefit obligation as of a particular date for an employee is the portion of the expected postretirement benefit obligation attributed to that employee's service rendered to that date; on and after the full eligibility date, the accumulated and expected postretirement benefit obligations for an employee are the same.

Active Plan Participant. Any active employee who has rendered service during the credited service period and is expected to receive benefits, including benefits to or for any beneficiaries and covered dependents, under the postretirement benefit plan. See Plan Participant.

Actual Return on Plan Assets (Component of Net Periodic Postretirement Benefit Cost). The change in the fair value of the plan's assets for a period including the decrease due to expenses incurred during the period (such as income tax expense incurred by the fund, if applicable), adjusted for contributions and benefit payments during the period. For a funded plan, the actual return on plan assets shall be determined based on the fair value of plan assets (see paragraph 715-60-35-107) at the beginning and end of the period, adjusted for contributions and benefit payments. If the fund holding the plan assets is a taxable entity, the actual return on plan assets shall reflect the tax expense or benefit for the period determined in accordance with generally accepted accounting principles (GAAP). Otherwise, no provision for taxes shall be included in the actual return on plan assets.

Assumed per Capita Claims Cost (by Age). The annual per capita cost, for periods after the measurement date, of providing the postretirement health care benefits covered by the plan from the earliest age at which an individual could begin to receive benefits under the plan through the remainder of the individual's life or the covered period, if shorter. To determine the assumed per capita claims cost, the per capita claims cost by age based on historical claims costs is adjusted for assumed health care cost trend rates. The resulting assumed per capita claims cost by age reflects expected future costs and is applied with the plan demographics to determine the amount and timing of future gross eligible charges. See Gross Eligible Charges and Per Capita Claims Cost (by Age).

Attribution Period. The period of an employee's service to which the expected postretirement benefit obligation for that employee is assigned. The beginning of the attribution period is the employee's date of hire unless the plan's benefit formula grants credit only for service from a later date, in which case the beginning of the attribution period is generally the beginning of that credited service period. The end of the attribution period is the full eligibility date. Within the attribution period, an equal amount of the expected postretirement benefit obligation is attributed to each year of service unless the plan's benefit formula attributes a disproportionate share of the expected postretirement benefit obligation to employees' early years of service. In that case, benefits are attributed in accordance with the plan's benefit formula. See Credited Service Period.

Benefit Formula. The basis for determining benefits to which participants may be entitled under a postretirement benefit plan. A plan's benefit formula specifies the years of service to be rendered, age to be attained while in service, or a combination of both that must be met for an employee to be eligible to receive benefits under the plan. A plan's benefit formula may also define the beginning of the credited service period and the benefits earned for specific periods of service.

Benefits. The monetary or in-kind benefits or benefit coverage to which participants may be entitled under a pension plan or other postretirement benefit plan, including health care benefits, life insurance, legal, educational, and advisory services, pension benefits, disability benefits, death benefits, and benefits due to termination of employment.

Collateral Split-Dollar Life Insurance. A split-dollar life insurance arrangement in which the employee (or the employee's estate or a trust controlled by the employee, referred to as the employee) owns and controls the insurance policy.

Cost-Sharing (Provisions of the Plan). The provisions of the postretirement benefit plan that describe how the costs of the covered benefits are to be shared between the employer and the plan participants. Cost-sharing provisions describe retired and active plan participants' contributions toward their postretirement health care benefits, deductibles, coinsurance out-of-pocket limitations on participant costs, caps on employer costs, and so forth.

Credited Service Period. Employee service period for which benefits are earned pursuant to the terms of the plan. The beginning of the credited service period may be the date of hire or a later date. For example, a plan may provide benefits only for service rendered after a specified age. Service beyond the end of the credited service period does not earn any additional benefits under the plan. See Attribution Period.

Curtailment (of a Postretirement Benefit Plan). An event that significantly reduces the expected years of future service of active plan participants or eliminates the accrual of defined benefits for some or all of the future services of a significant number of active plan participants.

Debt Security. Any security representing a creditor relationship with an entity. It also includes preferred stock that by its terms either must be redeemed by the issuing entity or is redeemable at the option of the investor and a collateralized mortgage obligation (or other instrument) that is issued in equity form but is required to be accounted for as a nonequity instrument regardless of how that instrument is classified (that is, whether equity or debt) in the issuer's statement of financial position. However, it excludes option contracts, financial futures contracts, forward contracts, and lease contracts. Thus, the term debt security includes, among other items, U.S. Treasury securities, U.S. government agency securities, municipal securities, corporate bonds, convertible debt, commercial paper, all securitized debt instruments, such as collateralized mortgage obligations and real estate mortgage investment conduits, and interest-only and principal-only strips. Trade accounts receivable arising from sales on credit by industrial or commercial entities and loans receivable arising from consumer, commercial, and real estate lending activities of financial institutions are examples of receivables that do not meet the definition of security; thus, those receivables are not debt securities (unless they have been securitized, in which case they would meet the definition).

Dependency Status. The status of a current or former employee having dependents (for example, a spouse or other relatives) who are expected to receive benefits under a postretirement benefit plan that provides dependent coverage.

Endorsement Split-Dollar Life Insurance. A split-dollar life insurance arrangement in which the entity owns and controls the insurance policy. The employer enters into a separate agreement that splits the policy benefits between the employer and the employee. The employer owns the policy, controls all rights of ownership, and may terminate the insurance policy (and, in turn, the policy benefits promised to the employee). To effect the split-dollar arrangement, the employer endorses a portion of the death benefits to the employee (the employee designates a beneficiary for this portion of the death benefits). Upon the death of the employee, the employee's beneficiary typically receives the designated portion of the death benefits directly from the insurance entity and the employer receives the remainder of the death benefits.

Equity Security. Any security representing an ownership interest in an entity (for example, common, preferred, or other capital stock) or the right to acquire (for example, warrants, rights, and call options) or dispose of (for example, put options) an ownership interest in an entity at fixed or determinable prices. However, the term does not include convertible debt or preferred stock that by its terms either must be redeemed by the issuing entity or is redeemable at the option of the investor.

Expected Postretirement Benefit Obligation. The actuarial present value as of a particular date of the postretirement benefits expected to be paid by the employer's plan to or for each employee, the employee's beneficiaries, and any covered dependents pursuant to the terms of the plan.

Expected Return on Plan Assets. An amount calculated as a basis for determining the extent of delayed recognition of the effects of changes in the fair value of plan assets. The expected return on plan assets is determined based on the expected long-term rate of return on plan assets and the market-related value of plan assets.

Full Eligibility (for Benefits). The status of an employee having reached the employee's full eligibility date. Full eligibility for benefits is achieved by meeting specified age, service, or age and service requirements of the postretirement benefit plan. See Full Eligibility Date.

Full Eligibility Date. The date at which an employee has rendered all of the service necessary to have earned the right to receive all of the benefits expected to be received by that employee (including any beneficiaries and dependents expected to receive benefits). Determination of the full eligibility date is affected by plan terms that provide incremental benefits expected to be received by or on behalf of an employee for additional years of service, unless those incremental benefits are trivial. Determination of the full eligibility date is not affected by plan terms that define when benefit payments commence or by an employee's current marital or dependency status.

Fully Eligible Plan Participants. Collectively, that group of former employees (including retirees) and active employees who have rendered service to or beyond their full eligibility date and who are expected to receive benefits under the plan, including benefits to their beneficiaries and covered dependents.

Gain or Loss (Component of Net Periodic Postretirement Benefit Cost), The sum of all of the following:

a. The difference between the actual return on plan assets and the expected return on plan assets
b. Any gain or loss immediately recognized or the amortization of the net gain or loss recognized in accumulated other comprehensive income
c. Any amount immediately recognized as a gain or loss pursuant to a decision to temporarily deviate from the substantive plan.

The gain or loss component is generally the net effect of delayed recognition in determining net periodic postretirement benefit cost of gains and losses (the net change in the net gain or loss recognized in accumulated other comprehensive income) except that it does not include changes in the accumulated postretirement benefit obligation occurring during the period and deferred for later recognition in net periodic postretirement benefit cost.

Gross Eligible Charges. The cost of providing the postretirement health care benefits covered by the plan to a plan participant, before adjusting for expected reimbursements from Medicare and other providers of health care benefits and for the effects of the cost-sharing provisions of the plan.

Health Care Cost Trend Rate. An assumption about the annual rates of change in the cost of health care benefits currently provided by the postretirement benefit plan, due to factors other than changes in the composition of the plan population by age and dependency status, for each year from the measurement date until the end of the period in which benefits are expected to be paid. The health care cost trend rates implicitly consider estimates of health care inflation, changes in health care utilization or delivery patterns, technological advances, and changes in the health status of the plan participants. Differing types of services, such as hospital care and dental care, may have different trend rates.

Incurred Claims Cost (by Age). The cost of providing the postretirement health care benefits covered by the plan to a plan participant, after adjusting for reimbursements from Medicare and other providers of health care benefits and for deductibles, coinsurance provisions, and other specific claims costs borne by the retiree. See Net Incurred Claims Cost (By Age).

Insurance Contract. A contract in which an insurance entity unconditionally undertakes a legal obligation to provide specified benefits to specific individuals in return for a fixed consideration or premium. An insurance contract is irrevocable and involves the transfer of significant risk from the employer (or the plan) to the insurance entity.

Interest Cost (Component of Net Periodic Postretirement Benefit Cost). The increase in the accumulated postretirement benefit obligation to recognize the effects of the passage of time.

Medicare Reimbursement Rates. The health care cost reimbursements expected to be received by retirees through Medicare as mandated by currently enacted legislation. Medicare reimbursement rates vary by the type of benefits provided.

Net Incurred Claims Cost (by Age). The employer's share of the cost of providing the postretirement health care benefits covered by the plan to a plan participant; incurred claims cost net of retiree contributions. See Incurred Claims Cost (by Age).

Net Periodic Postretirement Benefit Cost. The amount recognized in an employer's financial statements as the cost of a postretirement benefit plan for a period. Components of net periodic postretirement benefit cost include service cost, interest cost, actual return on plan assets, gain or loss, amortization of prior service cost or credit, and amortization of the transition obligation or asset.

Nonparticipating Insurance Contract. An insurance contract that does not provide for the purchaser to participate in the investment performance or in other experience of the insurance entity. See Insurance Contract.

Participating Insurance Contract. An insurance contract that provides for the purchaser to participate in the investment performance and possibly other experience (for example, morbidity experience) of the insurance entity. See Insurance Contract.

Participation Right. A purchaser's right under a participating insurance contract to receive future dividends or retroactive rate credits from the insurance entity.

Pay-Related Plan. A plan that has a benefit formula that bases benefits or benefit coverage on compensation, such as a final-pay or career-average-pay plan.

Per Capita Claims Cost (by Age). The current cost of providing postretirement health care benefits for one year at each age from the youngest age to the oldest age at which plan participants are expected to receive benefits under the plan. See Assumed per Capita Claims Cost (By Age).

Plan. An arrangement that is mutually understood by an employer and its employees, whereby an employer undertakes to provide its employees with benefits after they retire in exchange for their services over a specified period of time, upon attaining a specified age while in service, or a combination of both. A plan may be written or it may be implied by a well-defined, although perhaps unwritten, practice of paying postretirement benefits or from oral representations made to current or former employees. See Substantive Plan.

Plan Demographics. The characteristics of the plan population including geographical distribution, age, sex, and marital status.

Plan Participant. Any employee or former employee who has rendered service in the credited service period and is expected to receive employer-provided benefits under the postretirement benefit plan, including benefits to or for any beneficiaries and covered dependents. See Active Plan Participant.

Postretirement Benefit Plan. See Plan.

Postretirement Benefits. All forms of benefits, other than retirement income, provided by an employer to retirees. Those benefits may be defined in terms of specified benefits, such as health care, tuition assistance, or legal services, that are provided to retirees as the need for those benefits arises, such as certain health care benefits, or they may be defined in terms of monetary amounts that become payable on the occurrence of a specified event, such as life insurance benefits.

Postretirement Benefits Other than Pensions. See Postretirement Benefits.

Postretirement Health Care Benefits. A form of postretirement benefit provided by an employer to retirees for defined health care services or coverage of defined health care costs, such as hospital and medical coverage, dental benefits, and eye care.

Retirees. Collectively, that group of plan participants that includes retired employees, their beneficiaries, and covered dependents.

Service Cost (Component of Net Periodic Postretirement Benefit Cost). The actuarial present value of benefits attributed to services rendered by employees during the period (the portion of the expected postretirement benefit obligation attributed to service in the period). The service cost component is the same for an unfunded plan, a plan with minimal funding, and a well-funded plan.

Substantive Plan. The terms of the postretirement benefit plan as understood by an employer that provides postretirement benefits and the employees who render services in exchange for those benefits. The substantive plan is the basis for the accounting for that exchange transaction. In some situations an employer's cost-sharing policy, as evidenced by past practice or by communication of intended changes to a plan's cost-sharing provisions, or a past practice of regular increases in certain monetary benefits, may indicate that the substantive plan differs from the extant written plan.

Transition Asset. The amount, as of the date Subtopic 715-60 was initially applied, of the fair value of plan assets plus any recognized accrued postretirement benefit cost or less any recognized prepaid postretirement benefit cost in excess of the accumulated postretirement benefit obligation.

Transition Obligation. The amount, as of the date Subtopic 715-60 was initially applied, of the accumulated postretirement benefit obligation in excess of the fair value of plan assets plus any recognized accrued postretirement benefit cost or less any recognized prepaid postretirement benefit cost.

Unfunded Accumulated Postretirement Benefit Obligation. The accumulated postretirement benefit obligation in excess of the fair value of plan assets.

Source 715-70-20

Fair Value. The price that would be received to sell an asset or paid to transfer a liability in an orderly transaction between market participants at the measurement date.

Multiemployer Plan. A pension or postretirement benefit plan to which two or more unrelated employers contribute, usually pursuant to one or more collective-bargaining agreements. A characteristic of multiemployer plans is that assets contributed by one participating employer may be used to provide benefits to employees of other participating employers since assets contributed by an employer are not segregated in a separate account or restricted to provide benefits only to employees of that employer. A multiemployer plan is usually administered by a board of trustees composed of management and labor representatives and may also be referred to as a joint trust or union plan. Generally, many employers participate in a multiemployer plan, and an employer may participate in more than one plan. The employers participating in multiemployer plans usually have a common industry bond, but for some plans the employers are in different industries and the labor union may be their only common bond. Some multiemployer plans do not involve a union. For example, local chapters of a not-for-profit entity (NFP) may participate in a plan established by the related national organization.

CONCEPTS, RULES, AND EXAMPLES

The principal objective of ASC 715-30 is to measure the compensation cost associated with employees' benefits and to recognize that cost over the employees' service period. This Subtopic is concerned only with the accounting aspects of pension costs. The funding (assets set aside to meet future payment obligations) of the benefits is not covered and is considered to be a financial management matter.

When an entity provides benefits that can be estimated in advance to its retired employees and their beneficiaries, the arrangement is a pension plan. The accounting for most types of retirement plans is covered by ASC 715-30. These plans include unfunded, insured, trust fund, defined contribution and defined benefit plans, and deferred compensation contracts, if equivalent. Independent deferred profit sharing plans and pension payments to selected employees on a case-by-case basis are not considered pension plans. The typical plan is written and the amount of benefits can be determined by reference to the associated documents. The plan and its provisions can also be implied, however, from unwritten but established past practices.

The establishment of a pension plan represents a commitment to employees that is of a long-term nature. Although some companies manage their own plans, this commitment usually takes the form of contributions made to an independent trustee. These contributions are used by the trustee to invest in plan assets of various types (treasury bonds and bills, certificates of deposit, annuities, marketable securities, corporate bonds, etc.). The plan assets are expected to generate a return generally in the form of interest, dividends, and/or appreciation in asset value. The return on the plan assets (and occasionally the proceeds from their liquidation) provides the trustee with cash to pay the benefits to which the employees are entitled These benefits, in turn, are defined by the plan's benefit formula. The benefit formula incorporates many factors including employee compensation, employee service longevity, employee age, and the like, and is considered to provide the best indication of pension obligations and costs. It is used as the basis for determining the pension cost recognized in the financial statements each fiscal year.

Net Periodic Pension Cost

A pension plan creates long-term obligations. It is assumed that a company will continue to provide retirement benefits well into the future. The accounting for the plan's costs is reflected in the financial statements, and these amounts are not discretionary. All pension costs incurred are recognized as expenses but, under the smoothing approach taken by ASC 715-30 and ASC 715-60, recognition of some elements of pension and postretirement benefit expense may be partially deferred until later periods.

Because pension obligations are long-term liabilities, there was a consensus of opinion, when ASC 715-30 was being written, that some current period effects should not be fully recognized in earnings as they occurred. Short-term fluctuations in interest rates, market prices of plan investments, and other factors could, if recognized as incurred, cause material swings in the net periodic pension cost and net income to be reported in the financial statements of the employer/sponsor. It was thought that such fluctuations would quite likely be offset by reversals in subsequent periods—for example, market declines in one period would be followed by market upward movements in later periods.

This possibility has traditionally been cited to justify the use of smoothing techniques in order to recognize certain of these changes in a systematic and rational manner (e.g., by amortization) instead of recognizing them immediately.

The benefits earned and costs recognized over the employees' service periods are computed by reference to the pension plan's benefit formula. Net periodic pension cost consists of the sum of the following six components:

1. Service cost
2. Interest cost on projected benefit obligation
3. Actual return on plan assets
4. Gain or loss
5. Amortization of unrecognized prior service cost
6. Amortization of unrecognized net assets or net obligation existing at date of initial application of ASC 715-30.

Pension plans may or may not be sensitive to future salary progression. The obligation, in present value terms, for future pension payments including the effects of future compensation adjustments is referred to as the *projected* benefit obligation, while the obligation computed without regard to salary progression is called the *accumulated* benefit obligation. For those plans that do not depend on salary progression, the accumulated and the projected benefit obligations are the same.

To calculate the net periodic pension cost, the accumulated benefit obligation (ABO) and the projected benefit obligation (PBO) must both be computed. Both of these obligation amounts are actuarially determined using the actuarial present value of benefits earned that are attributable to services rendered by the employee to the date of the computation. Under the provisions of most pension plans, PBO provides a more relevant measure of the estimated cost of the benefits to be paid upon retirement. This is because the benefit formula set forth in the plan normally results in increases in future pension benefits based on increases in the employee's compensation.

Pay-related, final-pay, or career-average-pay plans are examples of plans where future payments are based on future compensation levels. These plans measure benefits based on service performed to date but include assumptions as to future compensation increases, staff turnover rates, etc. In non-pay-related or flat-benefit plans, both obligations (ABO and PBO) are the same.

The following discussion employs a component-by-component analysis, providing a series of examples that cumulatively build to the comprehensive summary of net periodic pension costs and the sample pension disclosures that follow. Key amounts are cross-referenced between examples using parenthesized lowercase letters [(a), (b), etc.]. In accordance with accounting convention, obligations and increases thereto are presented in parentheses.

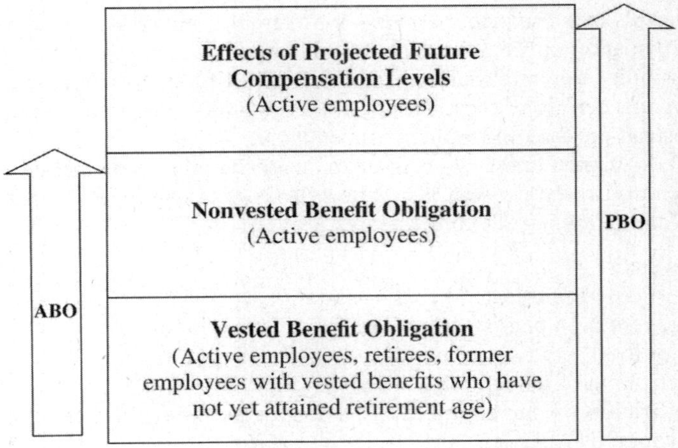

Example

	January 1, 20X3
Accumulated benefit obligation	$(1,500)
Progression of salary and wages	(400)
Projected benefit obligation	$(1,900)

The expected progression of salary and wages is added to the accumulated benefit obligation to arrive at the projected benefit obligation. These amounts are provided by the actuary in a pension plan report.

Computation of the amounts to be presented on the statement of financial position requires the determination of plan assets. Plan assets include contributions made by the employer that sponsors the pension plan (sponsor) plus the net earnings on the plan's investments (dividends, interest, and asset appreciation, less asset depreciation), less benefits paid to retired participants.

Example

Plan assets, January 1, 20X3	$1,376
Investment earnings during 20X3	158
Sponsor's contributions during 20X3	145
Benefits paid to retired participants	(160)
Plan assets, December 31, 20X3	$1,519

Service costs. This component of net periodic pension cost is the actuarial present value of benefits attributed during the current period. Under ASC 715-30, the plan's benefit formula is the key to attributing benefits to employee service periods. In most cases, this attribution is straightforward.

If the benefit formula is ambiguous, the accounting for pension service costs must be based on the substantive plan. In some cases, this means that if an employer has committed to make future amendments to provide benefits greater than those written in the plan, that commitment is the basis for the accounting. The relevant facts regarding that implicit commitment are disclosed.

Employers use pensions as a compensation tool to aid in the recruitment and long-term retention of employees. To provide incentives for employees to continue their employment with the company over time, plan participants' rights to receive present or future pension benefits are often conditioned on continued employment with the employer/plan sponsor for a specified period. As the conditions are satisfied, the employee is said to "vest" in that portion of the future benefits that become unconditional.

Vesting schedules can result in a disproportionate share of plan benefits being attributed to later years of employment. In this situation, instead of applying the benefit formula, proportions or ratios are used to attribute projected benefits to years of service in a manner that more equitably reflects the substance of timing of earning of the employee benefits. Normally, the actuary accomplishes this by attributing plan benefits to completed years of service by multiplying total benefits by the following ratio:

$$\frac{\text{Number of years of service completed by the employee}}{\text{Number of years of service required to be completed for full vesting}}$$

Certain types of benefits are not includable in vested benefits (e.g., death or disability benefit) and, thus, require a different allocation formula to attribute them to years of service. If the plan's benefit formula does not specify how to relate the benefit to years of service, the following formula is used by the actuary to attribute the benefits to years of service:

$$\frac{\text{Number of completed years of service}}{\text{Total projected years of service}}$$

ASC 715-30 actuarial assumptions must reflect plan continuation, must be consistent as to future economic expectations, and must be the best estimate in regard to each individual assumption. It is not acceptable to determine that the aggregate assumptions are reasonable if any of the individual assumptions are unreasonable.

The discount rate used in the calculation of service costs is the rate at which benefits could be settled. Examples include those rates in current annuity contracts, those published by the Pension Benefit Guaranty Corporation (PBGC), and those that reflect returns on high-quality, fixed-income investments.

Future compensation is considered in the calculation of the service cost component to the extent specified by the benefit formula. To the degree considered in the benefit formula, future compensation includes changes due to advancement, longevity, inflation, etc. Indirect effects, such as predictable bonuses based on compensation levels, and automatic increases specified by the plan also need to be considered. The effect of retroactive amendments is included in the calculation when the employer has contractually agreed to them. Service costs attributed during the period increase both the ABO and PBO, since they result in additional benefits to be payable in the future.

Example

	January 1, 20X3	*20X3 Service cost*
Accumulated benefit obligation	$(1,500)	$ (90)
Progression of salary and wages	(400)	(24)
Projected benefit obligation	$(1,900)	$(114) (a)*

* *Component of net periodic pension cost*

The current period service cost component is found in the actuarial report.

Interest on PBO. The PBO is a discounted amount. It represents the discounted actuarial present value, at the date of the valuation, of all benefits attributed under the plan's formula to employee service rendered prior to that date. Each year, when the actuary calculates the end-of-year PBO, it is one year closer to the year in which the benefits attributed in prior years will be paid to participants. Consequently, the present value of those previously attributed benefits will have increased to take into account the time value of money. This annual increase, computed by multiplying the assumed settlement discount rate times the PBO at the beginning of the year, increases net periodic pension cost and PBO.

Since this "interest" cost is accounted for as part of pension cost, it is not treated as interest for the purposes of computing capitalized interest under ASC 835-20.

Example

	January 1, 20X3	*20X3 Service cost*	*20X3 Interest cost*
Accumulated benefit obligation	$(1,500)	$ (90)	$(120)
Progression of salary and wages	(400)	(24)	(32)
Projected benefit obligation	$(1,900)	$(114) (a)*	$(152) (b)*

* *Component of net periodic pension cost*

The interest cost component is calculated by multiplying the start of the year obligation balances by an assumed 8% settlement rate. This amount is found in the actuarial report.

Benefits paid. Benefits paid to retirees are deducted from the above to arrive at the end-of-the-year statement of financial position amounts of the accumulated benefit obligation and the projected benefit obligation.

Example

	January 1, 20X3	*20X3 Service cost*	*20X3 Interest cost*	*20X3 Benefits paid*	*December 31, 20X3*
Accumulated benefit obligation	$(1,500)	$ (90)	$(120)	$160	$(1,550)
Progression of salary and wages	(400)	(24)	(32)	–	(456)
Projected benefit obligation	$(1,900)	$(114) (a)	$(152) (b)	$160	$(2,006)

Benefits of $160 were paid to retirees during the current year. This amount is found in the report of the pension plan trustee.

Actual return on plan assets. This component is the difference between the fair value of the plan assets at the end of the period and the fair value of the plan assets at the beginning of the period adjusted for contributions and payments during the period. Another way to express the result is that it is the net (realized and unrealized) appreciation and depreciation of plan assets plus earnings from the plan assets for the period.

Example

	January 1, 20X3	*20X3 Actual return on plan assets*	*20X3 Sponsor funding*	*20X3 Benefits paid*	*December 31, 20X3*
Plan assets	$1,376	$158 (c)*	$145	$(160)	$1,519

* *Component of net periodic pension cost*

The actual return on plan assets of \$158, cash deposited with the trustee of \$145, and benefits paid (\$160) are amounts found in the report of the pension plan trustee. These items increase the plan assets to \$1,519 at the end of the year. The actual return on plan assets is adjusted, however, to the expected long-term rate (9% assumed) of return on plan assets (\$1,376 × 9% = \$124). The difference (\$158 – \$124 = \$34) is a return on asset adjustment and is deferred as a gain (loss). The return on asset adjustment is a component of net periodic pension cost and is discussed in detail in the following section.

ASC 715 requires that measurements of defined benefit plan assets and obligations must (with limited exceptions) be as of the date of the statement of financial position of the respective reporting entity.

Gain or loss. Gains (losses) result from (1) changes in plan assumptions, (2) changes in the amount of plan assets, and (3) changes in the amount of the projected benefit obligation. As discussed previously, even though these gains or losses are economic events that impact the sponsor's obligations under the plan, immediately upon their occurrence, their instantaneous recognition in the sponsor's results of operations is not permitted by ASC 715-30. Instead, to provide "smoothing" of the effects of what are viewed as being short-term fluctuations, the net gain (loss) is amortized if it meets certain criteria specified below.

ASC 715 requires that actuarial gains and losses be given recognition in other comprehensive income as they occur, thus affecting statement of financial position display in full, even as the expense recognition is deferred and amortized. If actuarial gains are realized, this will give rise to a pension- or other benefit plan-related asset (or reduction in a pension- or benefit plan-related liability); if actuarial losses are incurred, these will give rise to a benefit plan liability, or reduction in an extant plan asset.

Since actuarial cost methods are based on numerous assumptions (employee compensation, mortality, turnover, earnings of the pension plan, etc.), it is not unusual for one or more of these assumptions to be invalidated by changes over time. Adjustments will invariably be necessary to bring prior estimates back into line with actual events. These adjustments are known as actuarial gains (losses). The accounting issue regarding the recognition of actuarial adjustments is their timing. All pension costs must eventually be recognized as expense. Actuarial gains (losses) are not considered prior period adjustments since they result from a refinement of estimates arising from obtaining subsequent information. These are considered changes in an estimate, and are to be recognized in current and future periods (i.e., prospectively only).

Plan asset gains (losses) result from both realized and unrealized amounts. They represent periodic differences between the actual return on assets and the expected return. The expected return is generated by multiplying the expected long-term rate of return by the market-related value of plan assets. Market-related value is a concept unique to pension accounting. It results from the previously discussed actuarial smoothing techniques under ASC 715-30.

Market-related value consists of two components. The first component is the fair value of the plan assets. The second component is an adjustment for the unrecognized portion of previous years' market gains or losses that are being amortized over a period of five years or less using a consistently applied method. Consistently applied means from year to year for each asset class (i.e., bonds, equities), since different classes of assets may have their market-related value calculated in a different manner (i.e., fair value in one case, moving average in another case). Thus, the market-related value may be fair value, but it also may be other than fair value if all or a portion of it results from calculation.

Plan asset gains (losses) include both (1) changes in the market-related value of assets (regardless of definition) from one period to another and (2) any changes that are not yet reflected in market-related value (i.e., the difference between the actual fair values of assets and the calculated market-related values). Only the former changes are recognized and amortized. The latter changes are recognized over time through the calculated market-related values. Differences between the actual amount of PBO from the assumed amount will also result in gain (loss).

Irrespective of the income smoothing techniques used, if this unrecognized net gain (loss) exceeds a "corridor" of 10% of the greater of the beginning balances of the market-related value of plan assets or the projected benefit obligation, a minimum amount of amortization is required. The excess over 10% is divided by the average remaining service period of active employees and included as a component of net pension costs. Average remaining life expectancies of inactive employees may be used if that is a better measure due to the demographics of the plan participants. ASC 715-30 sets forth a methodology for the deferred recognition of the income statement effects of actuarial changes pertaining to plan assets and obligations.

Net pension costs include only the expected return on plan assets. Any difference between actual and expected returns is deferred through the gain (loss) component of net pension cost. If actual return is greater than expected return, net pension cost is increased to adjust the actual return to the lower expected return. If expected return is greater than actual return, the adjustment results in a decrease to net pension cost to adjust the actual return to the higher expected return. If the unrecognized net gain (loss) is large enough, it is amortized. Conceptually, the expected return represents the best estimate of long-term performance of the plan's investments. In any given year, however, an unusual short-term result may occur given the volatility of financial markets.

The expected long-term rate of return used to calculate the expected return on plan assets is the average rate of return expected to be earned on invested funds to provide for pension benefits included in the PBO. Present rates of return and expected future reinvestment rates of return are considered in arriving at the rate to be used.

To summarize, net periodic pension cost includes a gain (loss) component consisting of both of the following, if applicable:

1. As a minimum, the portion of the unrecognized net gain (loss) from previous periods that exceeds the greater of 10% of the beginning balances of the market-related value of plan assets *or* the PBO, usually amortized over the average remaining service period of active employees expected to receive benefits.
2. The difference between the expected return and the actual return on plan assets.

An accelerated method of amortization of unrecognized net gain (loss) is acceptable if it is applied consistently to both gains and losses, and if the method is disclosed in the notes to the financial statements. In all cases, at least the minimum amount discussed above must be amortized.

Example

	January 1, 20X3	*20X3 Return on asset adjustment*	*20X3 Amortization*	*December 31, 20X3*
Unrecognized actuarial gain (loss)	$(210)	$34 (d)*	$2(d)*	$(174)

* *Components of net periodic pension cost*

The return on asset adjustment of $34 is the difference between the actual return of $158 and the expected return of $124 on plan assets. The actuarial loss at the start of the year ($210 assumed) is amortized if it exceeds a "corridor" of the larger of 10% of the projected benefit obligation at the beginning of the period ($1,900 × 10% = $190) or 10% of the fair value of plan assets ($1,376 × 10% = $138). In this example, $20 ($210 – $190) is amortized by dividing the years of average remaining service (twelve years assumed), with a result rounded to $2. The straight-line method is used, and it is assumed that market-related value is the same as fair value.

Amortization of unrecognized prior service cost. Prior service costs are incurred when the sponsor adopts plan amendments that increase plan benefits attributable to services rendered by plan participants in the past. These costs are accounted for as a change in estimate. Prior service costs are measured at the amendment date by the increase in the projected benefit obligation. The remaining service period of every active employee expected to receive benefits is estimated, and an equal amount of prior service cost is assigned to each future period. This is called the years-of-service amortization method.

Example of the years-of-service amortization method

The ABC Company amends its pension plan, granting $40,000 of prior service costs to its 100 employees. The employees are expected to retire in accordance with the following schedule:

Group	*Number of employees*	*Expected year of retirement*
A	10	20X4
B	15	20X5
C	20	20X6
D	20	20X7
E	35	20X8
	100	

The calculation of the service years to be recognized from this group is as follows:

	Service years					
Year	*A*	*B*	*C*	*D*	*E*	*Total*
20X4	10	15	20	20	35	100
20X5		15	20	20	35	90
20X6			20	20	35	75
20X7				20	35	55
20X8					35	35
	10	30	60	80	175	355

Consequently, there are 355 service years over which the $40,000 prior service cost can be spread, which equates to $112.68 per service year. The following table shows the annual amortization expense based on the standard charge of $112.68 per service year.

Year	*Total service years*	×	*Cost per service year*	=	*Annual amortization*
20X3	100		$112.68		$11,268
20X4	90		112.68		10,141
20X5	75		112.68		8,451
20X6	55		112.68		6,197
20X7	35		112.68		3,943
	355				$40,000

The foregoing example illustrates the years-of-service amortization method. Consistent use of an accelerated amortization method is also acceptable and must be disclosed if used.

If most of the plan's participants are inactive, remaining life expectancy is used as a basis for amortization instead of estimated remaining service period. If economic benefits will be realized by plan participants over a shorter period than remaining service period, amortization of costs is accelerated to recognize the costs in the periods that the participants benefit. If an amendment *reduces* the projected benefit obligation, unrecognized prior service costs are reduced to the extent that they exist and any excess is amortized in the manner described above for benefit increases.

Example

	January 1, 20X3	*20X3 Amortization*	*December 31, 20X3*
Unrecognized prior service cost	$320	$(27) (e)*	$293

* *Component of net periodic pension cost*

Unrecognized prior service cost ($320) is amortized over the years of average remaining service (twelve years assumed) at the amendment date with a result rounded to $27. The straight-line method was used. These amounts are found in the actuarial report.

While the vast preponderance of changes to plans increase benefits with credit for prior service, there may be plan amendments that reduce benefits, also with reference to past service. In such instances, under ASC 715, the decreases to the projected benefit obligation are given immediate recognition. The reduction in benefits is to be recognized as a credit (referred to as a prior service credit) to other comprehensive income, which is to be used to offset any remaining prior service cost included in accumulated other comprehensive income (i.e., from previous plan amendments increasing benefits). Any remaining prior service credit is to be amortized as a component of net periodic pension cost on the same basis as the cost of a benefit increase.

Thus, under requirements established by ASC 715, changes in prior service costs (and in certain other components affecting pension and other postretirement benefit costs) arising in a given reporting period, but not included in current period pension or other benefit costs (e.g., due to the above-described amortization requirements) are fully reported in other comprehensive income.

Amortization of unrecognized amount at date of initial ASC 715-30 application. ASC 715-30 has been GAAP for more than twenty years, and few plans likely still remain with unamortized transition amounts. The difference between the PBO and the fair value of plan assets minus recognized prepaid or plus accrued pension cost at the beginning of the fiscal year of the initial ASC 715-30 application was to be amortized using the straight-line method over the average remaining active employee service period. If the average remaining service period was less than fifteen years, the employer could elect to use a fifteen-year period. If all or almost all of a plan's participants were inactive, the employer used the inactive participants' average remaining life expectancy.

NOTE: Solely for purposes of illustrating amortization of an unrecognized amount at transition, implementation of ASC 715-30 is assumed to be currently taking place.

Example

	January 1, 20X3	*20X3 Amortization*	*December 31, 20X3*
Unamortized net obligation (asset) existing at ASC 715-30 application	$(6)	$3 (f)*	$(3)

* *Component of net periodic pension cost*

At initial adoption of ASC 715-30, the "transition amount" was computed as an asset of $48. This transition asset is being amortized using the straight-line method over sixteen years ($3 per year), which represents the average remaining service period of employees expected to receive benefits under the plan at transition. Thus, the unamortized balance at January 1, 20X3, was $6 and the amortization for 20X3 was $3. These amounts would be found in the actuarial report.

Summary of net periodic pension cost. The components that were identified in the above examples are summed as follows to determine the amount defined as net periodic pension cost:

		20X3
Service cost	(a)	$114
Interest cost	(b)	152
Actual return on plan assets	(c)	(158)
Gain (loss)	(d)	36
Amortization of any prior service cost or credit	(e)	27
Amortization of unrecognized net obligation (asset) existing at ASC 715-30 application	(f)	(3)
Total net periodic pension cost		$168

One possible source of confusion is the actual return on plan assets ($158) and the unrecognized gain of $36 that net to $122. The actual return on plan assets reduces pension cost because, to the extent that plan assets generate earnings, those earnings help the plan sponsor subsidize the cost of providing the benefits. Thus, the plan sponsor will not have to fund benefits as they become due, to the extent that plan earnings provide the plan with cash to pay those benefits. This reduction, however, is adjusted by increasing pension cost by the difference between actual and expected return of $34 and the amortization of the excess actuarial loss of $2, for a total of $36. The net result is to include the expected return of $124 ($158 – $34) less the amortization of the excess of $2 for a total of $122 ($158 – $36). In recognizing the components of net periodic pension costs, ASC 715-20 requires the disclosure of this expected return of $124 and the loss of $2.

Note that, while the components of periodic pension cost nominally remain the same under ASC 715 as under preamendment ASC 715-30, two of the components have changed in substance. Amortization of prior service cost previously meant the income statement recognition of what had in prior periods been an amount not given any financial statement recognition. Now, however, the prior service cost is included in accumulated other comprehensive income, and then amortized, under the formula set forth by ASC 715-30, to pension cost.

Second, the amortization of gain or loss (which pertains to actuarially driven changes to the projected benefit obligation, as well as to asset valuation adjustments not recognized in current income), which under ASC 715-30 was not given financial statement recognition before the point in time when they were to be included in pension cost, now is associated with an item incorporated in accumulated other comprehensive income.

Thus, under ASC 715 there is *display* of both prior service costs and actuarial gains or losses immediately upon the occurrence or determination of the item, but there is still *deferred recognition in expense* via the ASC 715-30-prescribed amortization process, set forth above.

If any transition amount dating from the adoption of ASC 715-30 still exists, that too must be recorded in accumulated other comprehensive income upon adoption of ASC 715, and amortization over any remaining period as originally determined when ASC 715-30 was adopted will continue as prescribed under that standard.

Under ASC 715, there will be *both* the componentized periodic pension expense *and* changes to the amounts reported in other comprehensive income, although for nonpublic entities the components of pension cost may be omitted. The suggested informative (i.e., footnote) form of disclosure consists of two tables, and is as follows for a publicly held reporting entity (these amounts, which assume partial funding of other postretirement benefits, are not related to the earlier examples):

Components of net periodic benefit cost and other amounts recognized in other comprehensive income

	Pension benefits		*Other benefits*	
	20X2	*20X3*	*20X2*	*20X3*
Net periodic benefit cost				
Service cost	$ 95	$102	$49	$57
Interest cost	80	88	58	59
Expected return on plan assets	(70)	(86)	(12)	(14)
Amortization of prior service cost	11	12	(3)	(5)
Amortization of net (gain) loss	14	9	2	2
Net periodic benefit cost	$130	$125	$94	$99

Other changes in plan assets and benefit obligations recognized in other comprehensive income

	Pension benefits		*Other benefits*	
	20X2	*20X13*	*20X2*	*20X3*
Net loss (gain)	$ 86	$102	$27	$(46)
Prior service cost (credit)	60	10	(70)	(47)
Amortization of prior service cost	(11)	(12)	3	5
Total recognized in other comprehensive income	135	100	(40)	(88)
Total recognized in net periodic benefit cost and other comprehensive income	$265	$225	$54	$11

Finally, the assumptions used in computing projected and accumulated benefits and expected return on plan assets must be disclosed. For postretirement health benefits, so-called sensitivity data must also be presented, since the amount of this often significant and most commonly unfunded future obligation is highly responsive to changes in health care cost levels. The following tables set forth these key parameters:

Assumptions

Weighted-average assumptions used to determine benefit obligations at December 31

	Pension benefits		*Other benefits*	
	20X2	*20X3*	*20X2*	*20X3*
Discount rate	6.75%	7.25%	7.00%	7.50%
Rate of compensation increase	4.25	4.50		

Weighted-average assumptions used to determine net periodic benefit cost for years ended December 31

Discount rate	7.25%	7.50%	7.50%	7.75%
Expected long-term return on plan assets	8.00	8.50	8.10	8.75
Rate of compensation increase	4.50	4.75		

Assumed health care cost trend rates at December 31

	20X2	*20X3*
Health care cost trend rate assumed for next year	12%	12.5%
Rate to which the cost trend rate is assumed to decline (the ultimate trend rate)	6%	5%
Year that the rate reaches the ultimate trend rate	20X0	20X0

Assumed health care cost trend rates have a significant effect on the amounts reported for the health care plans. A one-percentage-point change in assumed health care cost trend rates (not required for nonpublic reporting entities) would have the following effects:

	1-percentage-point increase	*1-percentage-point decrease*
Effect on total of service and interest cost	$ 42	$ (35)
Effect on postretirement benefit obligation	185	(176)

Reconciliation of Beginning and Ending ABO, PBO, and Plan Assets

The following table summarizes the 20X3 activity affecting ABO, PBO, and plan assets and reconciles the beginning and ending balances per the actuarial report:

	Accumulated benefit obligation	*Progression of salaries and wages*	*Projected benefit obligation*	*Fair value of plan assets**
Balance, January 1, 20X3	$ (1,500)	$ (400)	$ (1,900)	$ 1,376
Service cost	(90)	(24)	(114)(a)	
Interest cost	(120)	(32)	(152)(b)	
Benefits paid to retired participants	160		160	(160)
Actual return on plan assets				158 (c)
Sponsor's contributions				145
Balance, December 31, 20X3	$ (1,550)	$ (456)	$ (2,006)	$ 1,519

* *Assumed to be the same as market-related value for this illustration.*

Expanded disclosure is now required regarding the portfolio assets maintained to pay future pension and other postretirement benefits. This information should be presented in a tabular format illustrated as follows:

Plan assets. The entity's pension plan weighted-average asset allocations at December 31, 20X2 and 20X3, by asset category are as follows:

	Pension plan assets at December 31		*Other benefit plan assets at December 31*	
	20X2	*20X3*	*20X2*	*20X3*
Asset category				
Equity securities	50%	48%	60%	52%
Debt securities	30	31	30	27
Real estate	10	12	5	13
Other	10	9	5	8
Total	100%	100%	100%	100%

The foregoing allocation information should be accompanied by an entity-specific narrative description of investment policies and strategies for plan assets, including weighted-average target asset allocations, where such are used as part of those policies and strategies. If the reporting entity holds its own shares in the trusteed assets of the plan(s), this fact, and the amounts held at each reporting date, should also be set forth.

Employer's Liabilities and Assets under ASC 715-30

Accounting for defined benefit plans remains a controversial topic. In particular, the fact that plan assets and liabilities are, with certain exceptions, not considered to be the employers' assets and liabilities, continues to be a contentious issue. When ASC 715-30 was first imposed, the FASB concluded that full imposition of accrual-basis recognition rules would have caused unacceptably large adjustments to the financial statements of companies whose plans were materially underfunded. The adjustments would have been necessary to recognize previously unrecognized assets or liabilities representing the differences between PBO and the fair value of plan assets. To ease the perceived burden on these plan sponsors, FASB developed a compromise *minimum liability* approach for ASC 715-30. This minimum liability was computed by reference to the excess of the ABO (which is a smaller obligation than the PBO, since it does not recognize projected future compensation increases) over the fair value of the plan assets. Note that, for the purpose of this calculation, the fair value of the assets was used, rather than the market-related value that was used to calculate the expected return on plan assets. To the extent that there was a pension liability already recorded, the sponsor needed only to recognize the additional amount necessary to increase the recorded liability to the amount of the minimum liability.

The theory behind using the ABO was the fact that, if the pension plan were terminated at the date of the statement of financial position, the future compensation increases would never occur and the pension obligation could be settled for the smaller amount. Some might argue that this approach conflicted with the underlying going concern assumption that is fundamental to financial accounting theory. ASC 715 has eliminated the minimum liability approach of ASC 715-30, and the full amount of over- or underfunding of pension plans must now be displayed in the statement of financial position, as described later in this section.

Fair value is determined as of the financial statement date. The amount is that which would result from negotiations between a willing buyer and seller not in a liquidation sale. Fair value is measured in preferred order by market price, selling price of similar investments, or discounted cash flows at a rate indicative of the risk involved.

Regarding the additional minimum liability required under ASC 715-30 prior to being amended by ASC 715, there were several important matters impacting upon the actual computation of the amount to be displayed. First, an asset could not be recorded if the fair value of the plan assets exceeded the accumulated benefit obligation. Second, the calculation of the minimum liability required consideration of any already recorded prepaid or accrued pension cost. The net liability had to be equal to at least the unfunded accumulated benefit obligation. An already recorded prepaid pension cost would increase the amount of the recognized additional liability. An already recorded accrued pension cost would decrease it.

Third, the intangible asset was not subject to amortization. Fourth, at the time of the subsequent calculation, the amounts were to be either added to or reversed out with no effect on net income. These statement of financial position entries were entirely independent of net income and would not affect the calculation of net pension costs. Fifth, unless a significant event occurred or measures of obligations and assets as of a more current date became available, interim financial statements were to show the year-end additional minimum liability adjusted for subsequent contributions and accruals. In such a case, previous year-end assumptions regarding net pension cost would also carry over to the interim financial statements.

The advent of ASC 715 has made the minimum liability recognition, together with the associated intangible asset, extinct. Under ASC 715 the full amount (measured by projected or accumulated benefit obligations, for pensions and other postretirement benefits, respectively) of over- or underfunding will be given statement of financial position recognition, with the offsetting entry being to other comprehensive income.

A schedule showing the variables of the above example in accordance with ASC 715-20, reconciling the statement of financial position amounts with the funded status of the plan, is shown below. Assumed activity for 20X3 is provided for comparative purposes. This example is to illustrate the information required for publicly held entities; see comments below for reduced disclosure requirements applicable to nonpublicly held companies. Also, this example combines information about pension plans and other benefit plans, the latter of which are assumed data not detailed in the foregoing discussion.

	Pension benefits		*Other benefits*	
	20X2	*20X3*	*20X2*	*20X3*
Change in benefit obligation				
Benefit obligation at beginning of year	$1,800	$1,900	$612	$662
Service cost	111	114	22	30
Interest cost	144	152	35	43
Plan participant's contributions	–	–	33	13
Amendments	–	–	–	–
Actuarial loss	–	–	–	–
Acquisition	–	–	–	–
Benefits paid	(155)	(160)	(40)	(60)
Benefit obligation at end of year	1,900	2,006	662	688
Change in plan assets				
Fair value of plan assets at beginning of year	1,241	1,376	87	206
Actual return on plan assets	150	158	24	5
Acquisition	–	–	–	25
Employer contribution	140	145	152	137
Plan participants' contributions	–	–	13	20
Benefits paid	(155)	(160)	(70)	(90)
Fair value of plan assets at end of year	1,376	1,519	206	303
Funded status [plan over (under) funded]	$ (524)	$ (487)	$ (456)	$ (385)

Nonpublic reporting entities are not required to provide the information in the above tables. Instead, they are only required to disclose the employer's contributions, participants' contributions, benefit payments, and the funded status. Of course, expanded disclosures are not precluded under such circumstances.

Note that since this example disclosure addresses both pension and other postretirement plans, the captions are generically worded, but it is implicit that they refer to projected benefits for pension plans and accumulated benefits for other defined benefit plans.

ASC 715 requires the funded status of defined benefit plans to be reported in the statement of financial position, using a simple table identifying the locations in the statement of financial position where the net funded amounts are presented, as follows:

	Pension benefits		*Other benefits*	
	20X2	*20X3*	*20X2*	*20X3*
Noncurrent assets	$ 133	$ 18	$ –	$ –
Current liabilities	(225)	(125)	(150)	(99)
Noncurrent liabilities	(432)	(380)	(306)	(286)
Net amount recognized	$(524)	$(487)	$(456)	$(385)

Amounts recognized in accumulated other comprehensive income must also be identified; for this example, these consist of:

	Pension benefits		*Other benefits*	
	20X2	*20X3*	*20X12*	*20X13*
Net loss (gain)	$ 94	$ 18	$ (11)	$(48)
Prior service cost (credit)	210	160	(92)	(22)
	$304	$178	$(103)	$(70)

As set forth above, under the provisions of ASC 715 the *actual* underfunded or—for the first time—overfunded status of defined benefit pension plans will be reported without limitation in the statement of financial position of reporting sponsoring entities. Under ASC 715—for defined benefit pension arrangements—under- or overfunding will be defined by the differences between plan assets and the corresponding *projected* benefit obligations.

Thus, the measure is derived from the (almost inevitably) larger projections of future benefit payments, including the effects of anticipated salary progressions.

Additional ASC 715-30 Guidance

In situations not specifically addressed by ASC 715-30, ASC 715-30-35 states that the vested benefit obligation can be either (1) the actuarial present value of the vested benefits that the employee is entitled to if the employee separates immediately, or (2) the actuarial present value of the vested benefits to which the employee is currently entitled, but based on the employee's expected date of separation or retirement.

Pension plans sometimes are coupled with life insurance plans with the employer as beneficiary. According to ASC 325-30-35, it is not appropriate for the purchaser of life insurance to recognize income from death benefits on an actuarially expected basis.

In recent years a trend has emerged for employers to terminate classic defined benefit pension plans and replace them with "cash balance" plans, the accounting for which has not been well understood. These hybrid plans typically describe the pension benefit by reference to an account balance rather than a monthly annuity at retirement. ASC 715-30-15 considers plans that are characterized by defined principal-crediting rates as percentages of salary, and offer defined, noncontingent interest-crediting rates that entitle participants to future interest credits at stated, fixed rates until retirement. The standard states that "cash balance" plans with the foregoing attributes are to be deemed defined benefit plans, consistent with definitions set forth in ASC 715-30. This is true because an employer's contributions to a cash balance plan trust and the earnings on the invested plan assets may be unrelated to the principal and interest credits to participants' hypothetical accounts.

The standard also determined that the benefit promise in the cash balance arrangement is not pay-related and, accordingly, use of a projected unit credit method is neither required nor appropriate for purposes of measuring the benefit obligation and annual cost of benefits earned under ASC 715-30. The appropriate cost attribution approach, therefore, is the traditional unit credit method.

If an entity had been accounting for such a plan as a defined benefit plan, the effect of remeasuring the pension obligation using the guidance in this consensus was to have been calculated as of the above-mentioned measurement date. Any difference in the measurement of the obligation as a result of applying the standard was to be reported as a component of actuarial gains and losses under ASC 715-30. For an entity that has an accounting policy of immediate recognition of all gains and losses, or all gains and losses outside the 10% corridor described in ASC 715-30, the component of such gain or loss that could be attributed to the adoption of the guidance in Issue 03-4, applying a with-and-without calculation, was to have been reported as the effect of adopting the standard (in a manner similar to a cumulative-effect-type adjustment) as of the measurement date.

Reporting Funded Status: Requirements under ASC 715

ASC 715 has two major implications. First, it requires business entities having defined benefit plans (*other than* multiemployer plans) to display the funded status of those plans on the face of their statements of financial position, instead of being reported, to a greater or lesser degree, only in the informative disclosures. And second, it requires that actuarial gains and losses and prior service costs and credits arising in the reporting period, but not (under provisions of ASC 715-30 and ASC 715-60) reported in the current period's reported benefit cost, be included as items of other comprehensive income. These matters will be addressed in the following paragraphs.

Additionally, ASC 715 imposes a definitive requirement that the measurement date for plan assets and obligations be the end of the annual reporting period (that is, the date of the statement of financial position). Previously, the measurement date could be either year-end or a date not more than three months prior to that date, if used consistently.

Finally, the standard requires that additional information be presented in the notes to financial statements about certain effects on net periodic benefit cost for the upcoming fiscal year that arise as a consequence of the delayed recognition of actuarial gains or losses, prior service costs or credits, and transition asset or obligation.

ASC 715 does not change the accounting by employers participating in multiemployer defined benefit plans. For essentially practical reasons, ASC 715-30 provides that contributions made to such plans for the reporting period be recognized as net pension cost, and that any contributions due and unpaid be recognized as a liability. Thus, most of the complexities arising from smoothing were avoided in accounting for sponsors participating in multiemployer plans.

Display of funded status. The most important change wrought by ASC 715 is to move disclosure of the plan's funded status to the face of the statement of financial position proper. By requiring that the amounts of net overfunding and underfunding of benefit plans be included in assets and liabilities, respectively, there will be a very substantial improvement in financial statement users' comprehension of the implications of the defined benefit plans under which the reporting entity is obligated. Previously, this was only revealed in the benefit plan footnotes, where the funded status was reconciled to the amount presented in the statement of financial position itself.

Determination of funded status varies as between defined benefit pension plans and all other defined benefit arrangements (that is, those addressed by ASC 715-60). For the former, ASC 715 states that funded status is measured by the difference between the fair value of plan assets and the *projected* benefit obligation (explained earlier in this chapter). For the latter, it is the spread between the fair value of plan assets and the *accumulated* benefit obligation that measures funded status.

ASC 715 requires that the difference between plan assets and the *projected* benefit obligation—be used to gauge the liability to be reported. Projected benefit obligation takes into account expected salary progression, while accumulated benefit obligation does not. For all defined benefit plans, other than those that do not take salary progression into account, a larger liability will now be recognized.

The net obligations associated with underfunded plans (which will likely describe virtually all postretirement benefit plans other than pensions, as well as some pension plans) must be displayed in the statement of financial position. In contrast with the requirement for defined benefit pension plans, for these arrangements the measure is based on the *accumulated* postretirement benefit obligation, which is the actuarial present value of benefits attributed to employees as of the date of the statement of financial position, which until full eligibility is achieved, will be a lesser amount than the *projected* benefit obligation.

Reporting when there are multiple plans. When the reporting entity has multiple plans, it is not acceptable to display one single net amount of over- or underfunding. Rather, all overfunded plans must be separately aggregated, as must underfunded plans. The amount of overfunding is included in noncurrent assets, with no portion of the overfunding permitted to be displayed as a current asset. On the other hand, total underfunding is allocated between current and noncurrent liabilities, with the current portion computed (on a plan-by-plan basis) as the sum of the actuarial present value of benefits included in the benefit obligation payable over the ensuing twelve months' time, to the extent that it exceeds the fair value of plan assets.

Conceivably, an employer may have the right to use the assets of an overfunded plan to pay the obligations of another, underfunded plan. Only in such circumstances would it be acceptable to offset the overfunding asset and the underfunding liability. Such a situation would be highly unlikely to occur, however.

To illustrate, if the reporting entity has three postretirement benefit plans, one of which is overfunded and two of which are underfunded, the amount of overfunding must be included in noncurrent assets. The amount of underfunding of the two other plans must be reported in liabilities, but a portion of this total might have to be included in current liabilities. This is illustrated in the following table:

	Overfunded plan	*Underfunded plan #1*	*Underfunded plan #2*	*Statement of financial position totals*
FV of plan assets	$400,000	$700,000	$ 20,000	
PV of benefit obligation (total)	340,000	874,000	240,000	
PV of benefit obligation (due in next twelve months)	28,000	32,000	31,000	
Overfunding asset (noncurrent)	60,000			$ 60,000
Underfunding liability (noncurrent)		174,000	209,000	383,000
Underfunding liability (current)			11,000	11,000

In the table above, note that the overfunded plan results in the reporting of a noncurrent asset, and this is not mitigated by the simultaneous existence of underfunded plans. Also note that underfunded plan #1 has sufficient assets to satisfy the amounts due within one year, and therefore the sponsoring entity's statement of financial position will not report any current liability with respect to this plan. However, plan #2, which is also underfunded, has benefit payments due over the twelve months following the statement of financial position date that exceed the amount of plan assets, and thus the sponsor will have to provide additional funding in the current period. That amount must be reported as a current liability. Finally, observe that the noncurrent obligations pertaining to both underfunded plans are combined into a single statement of financial position amount.

Reporting of benefit plan transactions and events in comprehensive income. ASC 715 requires an employer to recognize all transactions and events affecting the overfunded or underfunded status of a defined benefit postretirement plan in comprehensive income (or changes in unrestricted net assets, if the entity is a not-for-profit enterprise) in the year in which they occur. Previously, many delayed-recognition elements of pension and other postretirement benefit plan expense were "off-the-books," albeit subject to disclosure in the financial statement notes.

Under ASC 715, the reporting entity must recognize as a component of other comprehensive income the gains or losses and prior service costs or credits arising during that reporting period that are not recognized as components of net periodic benefit cost of the period pursuant to ASC 715-30 and ASC 715-60. For example, if a plan amendment is adopted that credits employees with prior service, this is not reflected immediately in benefit costs, but rather is subject to amortization (i.e., it is to be recognized as part of pension or other postretirement benefit plan cost over an extended period of time). The requirements established by ASC 715 do not alter the piecemeal recognition of expense (that is, smoothing) under current GAAP, but they do make it necessary to record in other comprehensive income, in the year the amendment is effected, the full amount of the prior service cost less what is recognized in pension cost in that period.

In other words, the methodology of expense measurement has not been affected by the issuance of ASC 715, but disclosure *on the face of the statement of financial position* is now achieved. The effect of recording this debit in comprehensive income is balanced by recording an additional underfunding liability. In accordance with ASC 740, this is treated as a temporary difference, since the liability has a different basis (carrying value) for financial reporting purposes than it does for tax purposes. Hence, it must be tax effected within accumulated other comprehensive income, and a deferred tax asset (in the normal circumstances) will be recorded. The tax asset, in turn, will be subject to the "more likely than not" test for realizability, to determine whether it needs to be reduced or offset fully by an allowance.

Example

If Varga Corp., which is in the 30% tax bracket, grants its workers an amendment to a defined benefit pension plan that increases its obligation by $60,000, to be reflected in pension expense over fifteen years (i.e., amortized at $4,000 per year), under ASC 715 the following entry would be made (assuming the amendment is granted at year-end, and thus amortization will begin in the next period):

Accumulated other comprehensive income	42,000	
Deferred tax asset	18,000	
Pension liability		60,000

As noted earlier, the elements that will be reported in accumulated other comprehensive income, until taken into benefit expense as directed under ASC 715-30 or ASC 715-60, include gains and losses (i.e., those due to differences between expected and actual returns on plan assets, and those arising from actuarially determined adjustments), prior service cost or credits from plan amendments, and any remaining transition amounts deferred when ASC 715-30 was adopted. For new amounts (e.g., actuarial adjustment in the current period), there will be an entry similar to the above, whereby accumulated other comprehensive income is adjusted to reflect the full amount of the item, as well as the (offsetting) deferred tax effect thereof.

In subsequent periods, there will be opposite direction adjustments to the amount provided in other comprehensive income, as the normal, ASC 715-30-driven amortization occurs. For example, if the prior service cost recognized by Varga Corp. above is to be amortized based on average remaining service lives of current employees and the amount so determined for 20X2, the first period after the amendment, is $5,000, the following entry would be recorded:

Pension cost	5,000	
Deferred tax asset		1,500
Accumulated other comprehensive income		3,500

For each annual statement of income presented, these amounts are to be recognized in accumulated other comprehensive income, showing *separately* the amounts ascribed to net gain or loss and net prior service cost or credit. Those amounts are to be separated into amounts arising during the period and reclassification adjustments of other comprehensive income as a result of being recognized as components of net periodic benefit cost for the period.

Reporting loans to participants by defined contribution pension plans. ASC 962-310 requires that loans to the participants in an entity's defined contribution pension plan be classified as notes receivable. These loans are to be reported separately from plan investments. The proper measurement of these loans is their unpaid principal balances, plus all accrued but unpaid interest. This requirement keeps entities from recording such loans at their fair value. The reason for making this distinction is that US GAAP requires most investments by a pension plan to be recorded at their fair values, which would normally include loans to plan participants. By recording these loans as notes receivable, rather than investments, the fair value recordation requirement no longer applies.

Measurement date for year-end financial statements. ASC 715 requires that valuations be as of the date of the statement of financial position.

The only exceptions to the foregoing general statement occur in the instance of plans sponsored by consolidated subsidiaries or equity-method investees. This is a practical concession, but given that under US GAAP subsidiaries and investees are permitted to report financial results using year-ends different than the parent's or investor's, the exception is a reasonable and logical one. In those situations, the determinations of the fair values of plan assets and obligations must be as of the subsidiaries' or investees' respective dates of the statements of financial position.

Measurement date for interim financial statements. Publicly held entities must report quarterly, and private companies may choose to issue interim financial statements that are represented as being in accordance with GAAP. ASC 715 does not impose a requirement to evaluate plan assets and obligations more frequently than on an annual basis. Therefore, unless there has been an interim revaluation conducted—for example, because a plan amendment was adopted, or there had been a settlement or curtailment of a plan—it is prescribed that the funded status as of the most recent year-end be used in interim period reporting, with certain adjustments. The adjustments to be made are for subsequent accruals of service cost, interest, and return on plan assets included in current earnings (excluding, however, any amortization of amounts first recognized in other comprehensive income), subsequent contributions to the plan, and subsequent benefit payments from the plan. However, if there had been a revaluation subsequent to the prior year-end, the most recent valuation data would be used, again updated as just described, for any postvaluation accruals, contributions, and benefit payments.

Disclosure Requirements

Disclosure requirements for defined benefit pension and other postretirement plans have, of necessity, always been rather voluminous and complex. In part, this has been caused by the fact that "smoothing" (what FASB calls the "delayed recognition" of pension expense) takes place, and this results in "off the statement of financial position" plan assets and obligations. What would have otherwise been distortions of the sponsor's (reporting entity's) financial position was arguably moderated via the footnote disclosures required under ASC 715-20. Detailed disclosure requirements can be found in the Appendix.

The simplified disclosures permitted for nonpublic entities are illustrated by the following tabulation of comparative data:

	20X2	*20X3*
Funded status		
Projected benefit obligation at December 31	$1,900	$2,006
Fair value of plan assets at December 31	1,376	1,519
Funded status	$ (524)	$ (487)
Amounts recognized on the statement of financial position		
Prepaid (accrued) benefit cost	$ –	$ (23)
Amounts recognized on the income statement		
Net benefit cost for the period	$1,020	$ 890
Weighted-average assumptions		
Discount rate	7.5%	7.5%
Expected return on plan assets	9.0%	9.0%
Rate of compensation increase	4.0%	4.0%
Additional pension data		
Net periodic pension cost	$ 163	$ 168
Employer contribution	140	145
Benefits paid	155	160

ASC 715 requires that plans' under- or overfunded status and the "deferred recognition" gains and losses be formally recorded in the financial statements (the statement of financial position, specifically). ASC 715 mandates that essentially all defined benefit cost elements be included in the reporting entity's statement of financial position.

FASB has provided two prototype forms for disclosures of fair value information about plan investments, which it emphasized are not the only modes available for communicating such data to financial statement users. The following are adapted from those examples.

Example—Method One

		Fair Value Measurements at December 31, 20X3 (in millions)		
Asset Category	*Total*	*Quoted prices in active markets for identical assets (Level 1)*	*Significant observable inputs (Level 2)*	*Significant unobservable inputs (Level 3)*
Equity securities:				
US large-cap (a)	1,100	1,100		
US mid-cap growth	200	200		
International large-cap value	650	650		
Emerging markets growth	150	50	100	
Domestic real estate	200	40	160	
Fixed income securities:				
US Treasuries	400	400		
Corporate bonds (b)	400		400	
Mortgage-backed securities	100		100	
Other types of investments:				
Equity long/short hedge funds (c)	110			110
Event-driven hedge funds (d)	90			90
Global opportunities hedge funds (e)	70			70
Multistrategy hedge funds (f)	80			80
Private equity funds (g)	94			94
Real estate	150	0	0	150
Total	$4,094	$2,740	$760	$594

a. This category comprises low-cost equity index funds not actively managed that track the Standard & Poor's (S&P) 500.
b. This category represents investment grade bonds of US issuers from diverse industries.
c. This category includes hedge funds that invest both long and short in primarily US common stocks. Management of the hedge funds has the ability to shift investments from value to growth strategies, from small to large capitalization stocks, and from a net long position to a net short position.
d. This category includes investments in approximately 60% equities and 40% bonds to profit from economically, politically, and government-driven events. A majority of the investments are targeted at economic policy decisions.
e. This category includes approximately 80% investments in non-U.S. common stocks in the health care, energy, information technology, utilities, and telecommunications sectors and approximately 20% investments in diversified currencies.
f. This category invests in multiple strategies to diversify risks and reduce volatility. It includes investments in approximately 50% US common stocks, 30% global real estate projects, and 20% arbitrage investments.
g. This category includes several private equity funds that invest primarily in U.S. commercial real estate.

Example—Method Two

		Fair Value Measurements at December 31, 20X3 (in millions)		
Asset Category	*Total*	*Quoted prices in active markets for identical assets (Level 1)*	*Significant observable inputs (Level 2)*	*Significant unobservable inputs (Level 3)*
Cash	300	300		
Equity securities:				
US companies	800	800		
International companies	600	600		
Mutual funds (a)	900	640	260	
US Treasury securities	400	400		
AA corporate bonds	200		200	
A corporate bonds	200		200	
Mortgage-backed securities	100		100	
Equity long/short hedge funds (b)	110			110
Event-driven hedge funds (c)	90			90
Global opportunities hedge funds (d)	70			70
Multistrategy hedge funds (e)	160			160
Private equity funds (f)	94			94
Real estate	150	0	0	150
Total	$4,094	$2,740	$760	$594

a. 70% of mutual funds invest in common stock of large-cap US companies. 30% of the company's mutual fund investments focus on emerging markets and domestic real estate common stocks.
b. This category includes hedge funds that invest both long and short in primarily US common stocks. Management of the hedge funds has the ability to shift investments from value to growth strategies, from small to large capitalization stocks, and from a net long position to a net short position.
c. This category includes investments in approximately 60% equities and 40% bonds to profit from economically, politically, and government-driven events. A majority of the investments are targeted at economic policy decisions.
d. This category includes approximately 80% investments in non-US common stocks in the health care, energy, information technology, utilities, and telecommunications sectors and approximately 20% investments in diversified currencies.
e. This category invests in multiple strategies to diversify risks and reduce volatility. It includes investments in approximately 50% US common stocks, 30% global real estate projects, and 20% arbitrage investments.
f. This category includes several private equity funds that invest primarily in US commercial real estate.

The reporting entity is required to disclose the following information, whichever method it uses to disclose major categories of plan assets.

	Fair Value Measurements Using Significant Unobservable Inputs (Level 3)						
	Equity long/ short hedge funds	*Event-driven hedge funds*	*Global opportunities hedge funds*	*Multi-strategy hedge funds*	*Private equity funds*	*Real estate*	*Total*
Beginning balance at December 31, 20X2	$ 80	$70	$78	$70	$80	$ 20	$398
Actual return on plan assets:							
Relating to assets still held at the reporting date	(4)	10	(14)	10	4	6	12
Relating to assets sold during the period		6			4		10
Purchases, sales, and settlements	30	4			6	124	164
Transfers in and/or out of Level 3	4	-	6	0	0	0	10
Ending balance at December 31, 20X3	$110	$90	$70	$80	$94	$150	$594

Interim Financial Reporting Requirements

ASC 715-20 imposes requirements affecting both public and nonpublic company interim financial reporting. Publicly traded entities must disclose, in interim financial statements that include a statement of income, details regarding both benefit cost and contributions paid. The amount of net periodic benefit cost recognized must be set forth, showing separately the service cost component, the interest cost component, the expected return on plan assets for the period, the amortization of the unrecognized transition obligation or transition asset, the amount of recognized gains or losses, the amount of prior service cost recognized, and the amount of gain or loss recognized due to a settlement or curtailment. Additionally, the total amount of the employer's contributions paid, and expected to be paid, during the current fiscal year, must be presented, if significantly different from amounts previously disclosed pursuant to the annual reporting requirements of the standard. It is permissible to present estimated contributions in the aggregate, combining contributions required by funding regulations or laws, discretionary contributions, and noncash contributions. ASC 715 has conformed these requirements to the newly imposed regime whereby the statement of financial position fully discloses (in accumulated other comprehensive income) the deferred recognition items that formerly were "off-balance-sheet."

For nonpublic entities, disclosure is required—in interim periods when a complete set of GAAP-basis financial statements is being presented—of the total amount of the employer's contributions paid, and expected to be paid, during the current fiscal year, if significantly different from amounts previously disclosed pursuant to the annual reporting requirements of the standard. Estimated contributions may be presented in the aggregate combining contributions required by funding regulations or laws, discretionary contributions, and noncash contributions.

Remeasurement on an interim basis is neither required nor permitted under ASC 715.

Reporting and Disclosure by Not-for-Profit Entities

Not-for-profit entities sponsoring single-employer defined benefit plans are subject to ASC 715, but special rules are necessary to accommodate the fact that such entities do not report other comprehensive income as prescribed under ASC 220 for all other private sector entities. It is therefore necessary to analogize from the requirements of ASC 715. Rather than include the realized but as-yet-unrecognized net gains and losses, the unrecognized prior service cost or credit, and the unamortized transition amounts in accumulated other comprehensive income, these are to be reflected in changes in unrestricted net assets arising from a defined benefit plan. These changes will flow through the current period's statement of activities, since GAAP for not-for-profit organizations does not provide for an analogue to other comprehensive income, where nonstockholder changes in net worth are reported outside the income statement (statement of activities).

Other Pension Considerations

Annuity and insurance contracts. If annuity contracts and other insurance contracts that are equivalent in substance are valid and irrevocable, if they transfer significant risks to an unrelated insurance company (not a captive insurer), and if there is no reasonable doubt as to their payment, they are excluded from plan assets and their benefits are excluded from the accumulated benefit obligation and from the projected benefit obligation. Most other contracts are not considered annuities for ASC 715-30 purposes. If a plan's benefit formula specifies coverage by nonparticipating annuity contracts, the service component of net pension costs is the cost of those contracts. In the case of a participating annuity contract, the cost of the participation right is recognized as an asset and measured annually at its fair value. If fair value is inestimable, the cost is systematically amortized and carried at amortized cost (not to exceed net realizable value). Benefits provided by the formula beyond those provided by annuities are accounted for in the usual ASC 715-30 manner. All other insurance contracts are considered investments and are usually measured at cash surrender value, conversion value, contract value, or some equivalent.

In certain circumstances, annuity benefits are paid by employers after the insurer fails to make required payments. According to ASC 715-30-35, a loss is recognized by an employer at the time the employer assumes the benefit obligation payments to retirees for an insolvent insurance company that held these pension obligations. The loss recognized is the lesser of any gain recognized in the original contract with the insurance company or the amount of benefit obligation payments assumed by the company. Any additional loss not recognized is accounted for as a plan amendment in accordance with ASC 715-30.

Defined contribution plans. In the typical defined contribution plan, the contribution is either discretionary or derived from a formula, and that amount is the expense to be reported in the sponsor's financial statements for the year. Benefits are generally paid from the pool of accumulated contributions and are limited to the plan assets available to pay them. If, however, the defined contribution plan has defined benefits, the provision is calculated as required under ASC 715-30.

Multiemployer pension plans. A multiemployer plan is one to which two or more unrelated employers contribute, often pursuant to collectively bargained, union-sponsored agreements. It requires that the contribution for the period be recognized as net pension cost and that any contributions due and unpaid be recognized as a liability. Assets of all the employers sponsoring this type of plan are usually commingled and not segregated or restricted. A Board of Trustees usually administers these plans. If there is a withdrawal of an employer from this type of plan and if an obligation to make up any funding deficiency is either probable or reasonably possible, ASC 450 applies.

Some plans are, in substance, a pooling or aggregation of single employer plans and are ordinarily without collective-bargaining agreements. Contributions are usually based on a specified benefit formula. These plans are not considered multiemployer, and the accounting is based on each employer's respective interest in the plan.

Per ASC 715-80-55-2, the existence of an executed agreement does not require recognition by an employer of a liability beyond currently due and unpaid contributions.

Non-US pension arrangements. The terms and conditions that define the amount of benefits and the nature of the obligation determine the substance of a non-US pension arrangement. If they are, in substance, similar to pension plans, ASC 715-30 applies.

Business combinations. When an entity that sponsors a single-employer defined benefit pension plan is purchased, the purchaser must assign part of the purchase price to an asset if plan assets exceed the projected benefit obligation, or to a liability if the projected benefit obligation exceeds plan assets. The projected benefit obligation includes the effect of any expected plan curtailment or termination as a result of the change in ownership of the sponsor. This assignment eliminates any existing unrecognized components, and any future differences between contributions and net pension cost will affect the asset or liability recognized when the purchase was initially recorded.

Settlements and Curtailments of Plans

ASC 715-30 describes the accounting to be followed by obligors when all or part of defined benefit pension plans have been settled or curtailed. It establishes employer accounting procedures for benefits offered when employment is terminated.

Settlements include both the purchase of nonparticipating annuity contracts and lump-sum cash payments. The following three criteria must all be met in order to constitute a pension obligation settlement:

1. It must be irrevocable
2. It must relieve the obligor of primary responsibility for the obligation
3. It must eliminate significant risks associated with the obligation and the assets used to effect it.

Transactions that do not meet these three criteria do not qualify for treatment as a settlement under ASC 715-30. For example, an obligor could invest in a portfolio of high-quality fixed-income securities that would provide cash flows of interest and return-of-principal payments on dates that approximate the dates on which settlement payments are expected to become due. This would not meet the above criteria, however, because the employer is still primarily liable for the pension obligation and the investment is not irrevocable. Such a defeasance strategy does not constitute a settlement.

Under an annuity contract settlement, an unrelated insurance company unconditionally accepts an obligation to provide the required benefits. The following criteria must be met for this type of settlement:

1. It must be irrevocable
2. It must involve a transfer of material risk to the insurance company.

There can be no reasonable doubt as to the ability of the insurance company to meet its contractual obligation. The substance of any participating annuity contract must relieve the employer of most of the risks and rewards or it does not meet the criteria.

Curtailments include early discontinuance of employee services or cessation or suspension of a plan. Additional benefits may not be earned, although future service time may be counted towards vesting. Curtailments must meet the following criteria:

1. It must materially diminish present employees' future service or
2. It must stop or materially diminish the accumulation of benefits by a significant number of employees.

A curtailment and a settlement can occur separately or together.

Settlements. If the entire projected benefit obligation is settled, any ASC 715-30 unrecognized net gain (loss) plus any remaining unrecognized net asset existing when ASC 715-30 was initially applied are immediately recognized. A pro rata portion is recognized in the case of partial settlement. If the obligation is settled by purchasing participating annuities, the cost of the right of participation is deducted from the gain (but not from the loss) before recognition.

If the total of the interest cost and service cost components of the ASC 715-30 periodic pension cost is greater than or equal to the settlement costs during a given year, the recognition of the above gain (loss) is not required, but is permitted. However, a consistent policy must be followed in this regard. The settlement cost is generally the cash paid, or the cost of nonparticipating annuities purchased, or the cost of participating annuities reduced by the cost of the right of participation.

Example of a settlement

To use information from the previous baseline example, the company's pension plan settles the $1,150 vested benefit portion of its projected benefit obligation by using plan assets to purchase a nonparticipating annuity contract for $1,150. As a result of this settlement, nonvested benefits and the effects of projected future compensation levels remain in the plan. Also, a pro rata amount of the unrecognized net actuarial loss on assets, unrecognized prior service cost, and unamortized net asset at ASC 715-30 adoption are recognized due to settlement. Because the projected benefit obligation is reduced from $1,550 to $400, a drop of 74%, the pro rata amount used for recognition purposes is 74%. These changes are noted in the following table:

	Before settlement	Effect of settlement	After settlement
Assets and obligations:			
Vested benefit obligation	$(1,150)	$1,150	$ 0
Nonvested benefits	(400)	____	(400)
Accumulated benefit obligation	(1,550)	1,150	(400)
Effects of projected future compensation levels	(456)	____	(456)
Projected benefit obligation	(2,006)	1,150	(856)
Plan assets at fair value	1,519	(1,150)	369
Items not yet recognized in earnings:			
Funded status	(487)	0	(487)
Unrecognized net actuarial loss on assets	174	(129)	45
Unrecognized prior service cost	293	(217)	76
Unamortized net asset at ASC 715-30 adoption	(3)	2	(1)
Prepaid (accrued) benefit cost	$ (23)	$ (344)	$(367)

The entry used by the company to record this transaction does not include the purchase of the annuity contract since the pension plan acquires the contract with existing funds. The recognition of the pro rata amount of the unrecognized net actuarial loss on assets, unrecognized prior service cost, and unamortized net asset at ASC 715-30 adoption is recorded with the following entry:

Loss from settlement of pension obligation	344	
Accrued/prepaid pension cost		344

The foregoing provisions have been amended by ASC 715, necessarily, to state that the maximum gain or loss subject to recognition in earnings when an obligation is settled is the net gain or loss that is remaining in accumulated other comprehensive income, plus any transition asset remaining in accumulated other comprehensive income from the original application of ASC 715-30. The maximum gain or loss, first determined at the date of settlement, is fully reported in earnings only if the entire projected benefit obligation is settled; if it is only partially settled, only a pro rata portion of the maximum gain or loss can be recognized.

Curtailments. A curtailment results in the elimination of future years of service. The pro rata portions of any (1) unrecognized cost of retroactive plan amendments and (2) remaining unrecognized net obligation existing when ASC 715-30 was initially applied that is associated with the eliminated years of service are immediately recognized as a loss.

If curtailment results in a decrease in the projected benefit obligation, a gain is indicated. An increase in the projected benefit obligation (excluding termination benefits) indicates a loss. This indicated gain (loss) is then netted against the loss from unrecognized prior service cost recognized in accordance with the preceding paragraph. The net result is the curtailment gain or curtailment loss. This gain (loss) is accounted for as provided in ASC 450. A gain is recognized upon actual employee termination or plan suspension. A loss is recognized when both the curtailment is probable and the effects are reasonably estimable.

After the curtailment gain (loss) is calculated, any remaining unrecognized net asset existing when ASC 715-30 was initially applied is transferred from that category and combined with the gain (loss) arising after ASC 715-30 application. It is subsequently treated as a component of the new gain (loss) category.

Example of a curtailment

To use information from the previous baseline example, the company shuts down one of its factories, which terminated the employment of a number of its staff. The terminated employees have nonvested benefits of $120 and projected benefit obligation of $261. As a result of this curtailment, 19% of the projected benefit obligation has been eliminated ($381 PBO reduction resulting from the curtailment, divided by the beginning $2,006 PBO). Accordingly, 19% of the unrecognized prior service cost and unamortized net asset at ASC 715-30 adoption are recognized due to the curtailment. In addition, the total projected benefit reduction of $381 is first netted against the unrecognized net actuarial loss on assets of $174, leaving $207 to be recognized as a gain. These changes are noted in the following table:

	Before curtailment	*Effect of curtailment*	*After curtailment*
Assets and obligations:			
Vested benefit obligation	$(1,150)		$(1,150)
Nonvested benefits	(400)	$120	(280)
Accumulated benefit obligation	(1,550)	120	(1,430)
Effects of projected future compensation levels	(456)	261	(195)
Projected benefit obligation	(2,006)	381	(1,625)
Plan assets at fair value	1,519	0	1,519
Items not yet recognized in earnings:			
Funded status	(487)	381	(106)
Unrecognized net actuarial loss on assets	174	(174)	0
Unrecognized prior service cost	293	(56)	237
Unamortized net asset at ASC 715-30 adoption	(3)	1	(2)
Prepaid (accrued) benefit cost	$ (23)	$152	$ 129

The company records the recognition of the pro rata amount of the unrecognized prior service cost and unamortized net asset at ASC 715-30 adoption with the following entry, which is offset against the net gain of $207 resulting from the reduction in the planned benefit obligation:

Accrued/prepaid pension cost	152	
Gain from curtailment of pension obligation		152

ASC 715 contains guidance on accounting for curtailments of defined benefit plans. To the extent that prior service costs are included in accumulated other comprehensive income under the new mandates, and this is associated with service years no longer expected to be rendered, this must be recognized currently as a loss. This would occur if prior service cost is being amortized over a term that no longer accurately reflects expected future service by the post-curtailment workforce. Prior service cost, in this context, includes that resulting from plan amendments and also any transition obligation remaining from the initial adoption of ASC 715-30.

Curtailment gain or loss alters the projected benefit obligation. If such a gain exceeds any net loss included in accumulated other comprehensive income, or the entire gain if a net gain exists, it is reported as a curtailment gain. On the other hand, to the extent that such a loss exceeds any net *gain* included in accumulated other comprehensive income, or the entire loss if a net loss exists, this will be reported as a curtailment loss. Any transition asset remaining in accumulated other comprehensive income is to be treated as a net gain and combined with the net gain or loss arising subsequent to the ASC 715-30 transition.

Termination benefits. Termination benefits are accounted for in accordance with ASC 450. Special short time period benefits require that a loss and a liability be recognized when the offer is accepted and the amount can be reasonably estimated. Contractual termination benefits require that a loss and a liability be recognized when it is probable that employees will receive the benefits and the amount can be reasonably estimated. The cost of these benefits is the cash paid at termination and the present value of future payments. Termination benefits and curtailments can occur together.

Example of termination benefits

Again using the information from the previous baseline example, the company offers a one-time early retirement bonus payment, which is in addition to existing pension benefits. As a result of the offer, the company directly pays $200 in termination benefits. As a result of the employee retirements, the liability associated with projected future compensation levels drops by $60, while the pro rata portion of the unrecognized prior service cost associated with the retiring employees is $39. These changes are noted in the following table:

	Before termination benefit	*Effect of termination benefit*	*After termination benefit*
Assets and obligations:			
Vested benefit obligation	$(1,150)		$(1,150)
Nonvested benefits	(400)		(400)
Accumulated benefit obligation	(1,550)		(1,550)
Effects of projected future compensation levels	(456)	$ 60	(396)
Projected benefit obligation	(2,006)	$ 60	(1,946)
Plan assets at fair value	1,519	0	1,519
Items not yet recognized in earnings:			
Funded status	(487)		(427)
Unrecognized net actuarial loss on assets	174	(60)	114
Unrecognized prior service cost	293	(39)	254
Unamortized net asset at ASC 715-30 adoption	(3)		(3)
Prepaid (accrued) benefit cost	$ (23)	(39)	$ (62)
Cost of termination benefits		(200)	
Total loss on terminations		$(239)	

The company nets the $60 gain on reduction of projected future compensation levels against the existing unrecognized net actuarial loss on assets. It then records the $39 loss caused by the increased amortization of the unrecognized prior service cost and the $200 cost of the termination benefits with the following entry:

Loss on employee terminations	239	
Accrued/prepaid pension cost		39
Cash		200

Component disposal. Gains (losses), as calculated above, that result because of a disposal of a component of the entity are recognized according to the provisions of ASC 360.

Postretirement Benefits other than Pensions

ASC 715-60 established the standard for employers' accounting for other (than pension) postretirement employee benefits (commonly, if somewhat confusingly, called OPEB). This standard prescribes a single method for measuring and recognizing an employer's accumulated postretirement benefit obligation (APBO). It applies to all forms of postretirement benefits, although the most material such benefit is usually postretirement health care coverage. It uses the fundamental framework established by ASC 715-30. To the extent that the promised benefits are similar, the accounting provisions are similar. Only when there is a compelling reason is the accounting different.

ASC 715-60 requires accrual accounting and adopts the three primary characteristics of pension accounting as follows:

1. Delayed recognition (changes are not recognized immediately but are subsequently recognized in a gradual and systematic way)
2. Reporting net cost (aggregates of various items are reported as one net amount)
3. Offsetting assets and liabilities (assets and liabilities are sometimes shown net).

ASC 715-60 distinguishes between the substantive plan and the written plan. Although generally the same, the substantive plan (the one understood as evidenced by past practice or by communication of intended changes) is the basis for the accounting if it differs from the written plan.

ASC 715-60 focuses on accounting for a single-employer plan that defines the postretirement benefits to be provided. A defined benefit postretirement plan defines benefits in terms of (1) monetary amounts or (2) benefit coverage to be provided. Postretirement benefits can include tuition assistance, legal services, day care, housing subsidies, health insurance coverage (probably the most significant), and other benefits. The amount of benefits usually depends on a benefit formula. OPEB may be provided to current employees, former employees, beneficiaries, and covered dependents. This standard applies to settlement of the APBO and to curtailment of a plan as part of a special termination benefit offer. It also applies to deferred compensation contracts with individuals. Taken together, these contracts are equivalent to an OPEB plan. ASC 715-60 does not apply to benefits provided through a pension plan. If part of a larger plan with active employees, the OPEB is segregated and accounted for in accordance with this standard. If not materially different, estimates, averages, and computational shortcuts may be used.

The basic tenet of ASC 715-60 is that accrual accounting is better than cash basis accounting. Recognition and measurement of the obligation to provide OPEB is required in order to provide relevant information to financial statement users. Although funding and cash flow information is incorporated into the statement, the overall liability is the primary focus.

The standard attempts, in accordance with the terms of the substantive plan, to account for the exchange transaction that takes place between the employer, who is ultimately responsible for providing OPEB, and the employee who provides services, in part at least, to obtain the OPEB. ASC 715-60 accounting requires that the liability for OPEB be fully accrued when the employee is fully eligible for all of the expected benefits. The fact that the employee may continue to work beyond this date is not relevant, since the employee has already provided the services required to earn the OPEB.

OPEB are considered to be deferred compensation earned in an exchange transaction during the time periods that the employee provides services. The expected cost generally is attributed in equal amounts (unless the plan attributes a disproportionate share of benefits to early years) over the periods from the employee's hiring date (unless credit for the service is only granted from a later plan eligibility or entry date) to the date that the employee attains full eligibility for all benefits expected to be received. This accrual is followed even if the employee provides service beyond the date of full eligibility.

Accounting for postretirement benefits. The expected postretirement benefit obligation (EPBO) is the actuarial present value (APV) as of a specific date of the benefits expected to be paid to the employee, beneficiaries and covered dependents. Measurement of the EPBO is based on the following:

1. Expected amount and timing of future benefits
2. Expected future costs
3. Extent of cost sharing (contributions, deductibles, coinsurance provisions, etc.) between employer, employee and others (i.e., the government). The APV of employee contributions reduces the APV of the EPBO. Obligations to return employee contributions, plus interest if applicable, are recognized as a component of EPBO.

The EPBO includes an assumed salary progression for a pay-related plan. Future compensation levels represent the best estimate after considering the individual employees involved, general price levels, seniority, productivity, promotions, indirect effects, and the like.

The APBO is the APV as of a specific date of all future benefits attributable to service by an employee to that date. It represents the portion of the EPBO earned to date. After full eligibility is attained, the APBO equals the EPBO.

The APBO also includes an assumed salary progression for a pay-related plan. Thus, this term is more comparable to the projected benefit obligation (PBO) under ASC 715-30. The accumulated benefit obligation in ASC 715-30 has no counterpart in ASC 715-60.

Net periodic postretirement benefit costs include the following components:

1. Service cost—APV of benefits attributable to the current period (i.e., the portion of the EPBO earned this period)
2. Interest cost—Interest on the APBO
3. Actual return on plan assets
4. Gain or loss
5. Amortization of unrecognized prior service cost
6. Amortization of the transition asset or obligation.

Note that return on plan assets is included in the periodic expense determination, consistent with accounting for defined benefit pension plans. However, in virtually all cases, OPEB plans are unfunded, and thus there will be no asset return. If a trust has been established to fund these benefits, it does not necessarily have to be "bankruptcy proof," or insulated completely from the claims of general creditors, to qualify as plan assets in accordance with ASC 715-60-55. On the other hand, assets held in a trust that explicitly makes them available to the general creditors in bankruptcy do not qualify as plan assets under ASC 715-60. The funded status of other postretirement defined benefit plans will, under provisions of ASC 715, now be formally reported in the statement of financial position, as described above.

The transition obligation was the unrecognized and unfunded APBO for all of the participants in the plan at the date of adoption of ASC 715-60. This obligation was either (1) recognized immediately as the effect of an accounting change, subject to certain limitations, or (2) elected to be recognized on a delayed basis over future service periods with disclosure of the unrecognized amount. The delayed recognition must have resulted in at least as rapid a recognition as would have been recognized on a pay-as-you-go (cash) basis. Under ASC 715, the transition obligation that was to be given deferred recognition will be included in accumulated other comprehensive income, with a corresponding liability.

Service costs and interest costs are defined and measured in the same manner by both ASC 715-60 and ASC 715-30. However, under ASC 715-60, interest increases the APBO while under ASC 715-30, interest increases the PBO.

Under ASC 715-60, a single method is required to be followed in measuring and recognizing the net periodic cost and the liability involved. That method attributes the EPBO to employee service rendered to the full eligibility date.

Assumptions. ASC 715-60 requires the use of explicit assumptions using the best estimates available of the plan's future experience, solely with regard to the individual assumption under consideration. Plan continuity is to be presumed, unless there is evidence to the contrary. Principal actuarial assumptions include: discount rates, present value factors, retirement age, participation rates (contributory plans), salary progression (pay-related plans) and probability of payment (turnover, dependency status, mortality). Present value factors for health care OPEB include cost trend rates, Medicare reimbursement rates and per capita claims cost by age.

Current interest rates, as of the measurement date, are used for discount rates in present value calculations. Examples include high-quality, fixed-income investments with similar amounts and timing and interest rates at which the postretirement benefit obligations could be settled. The EPBO, APBO, service cost, and interest cost components use assumed discount rates.

The expected long-term rate of return on plan assets is an assumption about the average rate of return expected on contributions during the period and on existing plan assets. Current returns on plan assets and reinvestment returns are considered in arriving at the rate to be used. Related income taxes, if applicable, reduce the rate. Expected return on plan assets and the fair value of plan assets use this rate in their calculation. Since the Employee Retirement Income Security Act (ERISA) does not require OPEB plans to be funded via the separate trust vehicles used for pension plans, OPEB plans are often unfunded. Thus, there are no "plan assets." Instead, the sponsor pays benefits directly, as they become due, from general corporate assets.

Example

A sample illustration of the basic accounting for OPEB as established by ASC 715-60 follows. Kinetic Corporation established a new OPEB plan as of January 1, 20X5. Although the plan was new, it retroactively credited employees for their years of service to Kinetic prior to the establishment of the plan.

All employees had been hired at age 30 and become fully eligible for benefits at age 60. The plan is unfunded and, thus, there are no plan assets. The first calculation is the determination of the unrecognized transition obligation (UTO).

Kinetic Corporation
December 31, 20X4

Employee	*Age*	*Years of service*	*Total years when fully eligible*	*Expected retirement age*	*Remaining service to retirement*	*EPBO*	*APBO*
A	35	5	30	60	25	$ 14,000	$ 2,333
B	40	10	30	60	20	22,000	7,333
C	45	15	30	60	15	30,000	15,000
D	50	20	30	60	10	38,000	25,333
E	55	25	30	65	10	46,000	38,333
F	60	30	30	65	5	54,000	54,000
G	65	RET	–		–	46,000	46,000
H	70	RET	–		–	38,000	38,000
					85	$288,000	$226,332

Explanations

1. EPBO is usually determined by an actuary, although it can be calculated if complete data are available.
2. APBO is calculated using the EPBO. Specifically, it is EPBO × (Years of service/Total years when fully eligible)
3. The UTO is the APBO at 12/31/X1, since there are no plan assets to be deducted. The $226,332 can be amortized over the average remaining service to retirement of 14.17 (85/6) years or an optional period of 20 years, if longer. Kinetic selected the 20-year period of amortization.
4. Note that Employee F has attained full eligibility for benefits and yet plans to continue working.
5. Note that the above 20X4 table is used in the calculation of the 20X5 components of OPEB cost that follows.

After the establishment of the UTO, the next step is to determine the benefit cost for the year ended December 31, 20X5. This calculation follows the framework established by ASC 715-30. The discount rate is assumed to be 10%.

Kinetic Corporation
OPEB Cost
December 31, 20X5

1. Service cost	$ 5,500
2. Interest cost	22,633
3. Actual return on plan assets	–
4. Gain or loss	–
5. Amortization of unrecognized prior service cost	–
6. Amortization of UTO	11,317
Total OPEB Cost	$39,450

Explanations

1. Service cost calculation uses only employees not yet fully eligible for benefits.

Employee	*[a]* *12/31/X1* *EPBO*	*[b]* *Total years when fully eligible*	*[a ÷ b]* *Service cost*
A	$14,000	30	$ 467
B	22,000	30	733
C	30,000	30	1,000
D	38,000	30	1,267
E	46,000	30	1,533
			$5,000
	Interest for 20X0 ($5,000 × 10%)		500
	Total service cost		$5,500

2. Interest cost is the 12/31/X4 APBO of $226,332 × 10% = $22,633.
3. There are no plan assets so there is no return.
4. There is no gain (loss) since there are no changes yet.
5. There is no unrecognized prior service cost initially.
6. Amortization of UTO is the 12/31/X4 UTO of $226,332/20-year optional election = $11,317.

After calculation of the 20X5 benefit cost, the next step is to project the EPBO and APBO for December 31, 20X5. Assuming no changes, it is based on the December 31, 20X4 actuarial measurement and it is calculated as shown earlier in the determination of the UTO.

Kinetic Corporation
December 31, 20X5

Employee	*Age*	*Years of service*	*Total years when fully eligible*	*EPBO*	*APBO*
A	36	6	30	$ 15,400	$ 3,080
B	41	11	30	24,200	8,873
C	46	16	30	33,000	17,600
D	51	21	30	41,800	29,260
E	56	26	30	50,600	43,853
F	61	31	–	59,400	59,400
G	66	RET	–	44,620	44,620
H	71	RET	–	36,860	36,860
				$305,880	$243,546

Changes in experience or assumptions will result in gains (losses). The gain (loss) is measured by the difference resulting in the APBO or the plan assets from that projected. However, except for the effects of a decision to temporarily deviate from the substantive plan, these gains or losses have no impact in the year of occurrence. They are deferred and amortized as in ASC 715-30. Amortization of unrecognized net gain (loss) is included as a component of net postretirement cost for a year if, as of the beginning of the year, it exceeds 10% of the greater of the APBO or the market-related value of plan assets. The minimum amortization is the excess divided by the remaining average service period of active plan participants. A systematic method of amortization that amortizes a greater amount, is applied consistently to both gains and losses and is disclosed may also be used. If gains (losses) are recognized immediately, special rules of offsetting may be required.

Effect of the prescription drug benefit on OPEB computations. The Medicare Prescription Drug, Improvement, and Modernization Act of 2003 introduced a prescription drug benefit under Medicare (Medicare Part D), as well as a federal subsidy to sponsors of retiree health care benefit plans that provide a benefit that is at least actuarially equivalent to Medicare Part D. Under ASC 715-60, the effects of the Act on current period measurements of postretirement benefit costs and the APBO must be accounted for, if defined criteria are met.

The guidance regarding accounting for the subsidiary set forth in ASC 715-60 applies only to sponsors of a single-employer defined benefit postretirement health care plan for which (1) the employers have concluded that prescription drug benefits available under the plan to some or all participants for some or all future years are "actuarially equivalent" to Medicare Part D and thus qualify for the subsidy under the Act and (2) the expected subsidiaries will offset or reduce the employers' shares of the cost of the underlying postretirement prescription drug coverage on which the subsidies are based. ASC 715-60 also provides guidance for disclosures about the effects of the subsidy for employers that sponsor postretirement health care benefit plans that provide prescription drug coverage but for which the employers have not yet been able to determine actuarial equivalency.

The central question raised has been whether a subsidy is substantively similar to other Medicare benefits that existed when ASC 715-60 was issued—and therefore to be accounted for as a reduction of the APBO and net periodic postretirement benefit cost—or whether the subsidy represents a payment to the employer that is determined by reference to its plan's benefit payments but is not, in and of itself, a direct reduction of postretirement benefit costs. A secondary issue pertains to the timing of accounting recognition of the subsidy.

FASB concluded that the former interpretation is the correct one. That is, measures of the APBO and net periodic postretirement benefit cost on or after the date of enactment are to reflect the effects of the Act. When an employer initially accounts for the subsidy, its effect on the APBO is to be accounted for as an actuarial experience gain. Additionally, the subsidy reduces service cost when it is recognized as a component of net periodic postretirement benefit cost. If the estimated expected subsidy changes, the effect is to be treated as an actuarial experience gain or loss.

Plan amendments will also affect the reporting of OPEB cost and the APBO. If prescription drug benefits currently available under an existing plan are deemed not actuarially equivalent as of the date of enactment of the Act, but the plan is later amended to provide actuarially equivalent benefits, the direct effect of the amendment on the APBO and the effect on the APBO from any resulting subsidy to which the employer is expected to be entitled as a result of the amendment are to be combined, and deemed to be an actuarial experience gain if it reduces APBO. On the other hand, if the combined effect increases the APBO, it is deemed to be prior service cost that is to be accounted for consistent with ASC 715-60.

Additionally, according to ASC 715-60, if a plan that provides prescription drug benefits that previously were deemed actuarially equivalent under the Act is subsequently amended to reduce its prescription drug coverage such that the coverage is not considered actuarially equivalent, any actuarial experience gain related to the subsidy previously recognized is unaffected. The combined net effect on the APBO of (1) the subsequent plan amendment that reduces benefits under the plan and thus disqualifies the benefits as actuarially equivalent and (2) the elimination of the subsidy is to be accounted for as prior service cost (credit) as of the date the amendment is adopted.

In the periods in which the subsidy affects the employer's accounting for the plan, this will have no effect on any plan-related temporary difference accounted for under ASC 740, because the subsidy is exempt from federal taxation.

There may be a time lag before the employer is able to determine whether the benefits provided by its plan are actuarially equivalent. During the interim period, it is required to disclose: the existence of the Act and the fact that measures of the APBO or net periodic postretirement benefit cost do not reflect any amount associated with the subsidy because the employer is unable to conclude whether the benefits provided by the plan are actuarially equivalent to Medicare Part D under the Act.

In interim and annual financial statements for the first period in which an employer includes the effects of the subsidy in measuring the APBO and the first period in which an employer includes the effects of the subsidy in measuring net periodic postretirement benefit cost, it is required to disclose the following:

a. The reduction in the APBO for the subsidy related to benefits attributed to past service.
b. The effect of the subsidy on the measurement of net periodic postretirement benefit cost for the current period. That effect includes (1) any amortization of the actuarial experience gain in (a) as a component of the net amortization called for by ASC 715-60, (2) the reduction in current period service cost due to the subsidy, and (3) the resulting reduction in interest cost on the APBO as a result of the subsidy.
c. Any other disclosures required by ASC 715-20, specifically disclosure of an explanation of any significant change in the benefit obligation or plan assets not otherwise apparent in the other disclosures required by that standard.

When ASC 715-60 is initially adopted, a remeasurement of the plan's assets and APBO, including the effects of the subsidy, if applicable, as well as the other effects of the Act, is to be made as of the earlier of (1) the plan's measurement date that normally would have followed enactment of the Act or (2) the end of the employer's interim or annual period that includes the date of the Act's enactment. Alternatively, employers are permitted, but not required, to perform that remeasurement as of the date of enactment. The measurement of the

APBO is to be based on the plan provisions in place on the measurement date (i.e., later amendments are not to be anticipated in the computation).

Deferred Compensation Contracts

If the aggregate deferred compensation contracts with individual employees are equivalent to a pension plan, the contracts are accounted for according to ASC 715-30 and ASC 715-60. All other deferred compensation contracts are accounted for according to ASC 710.

ASC 715-60 states that the terms of the individual contract will govern the accrual of the employee's obligation for deferred compensation and the cost is to be attributed over the employee service period until full eligibility is attained.

41 ASC 718 COMPENSATION— STOCK COMPENSATION

PERSPECTIVE AND ISSUES

Subtopics

ASC 718, *Compensation-Stock Compensation,* provides guidance on share-based payments to employees and contains six subtopics:

- ASC 718-10, *Overall,* contains the high-level objectives for the Topic
- ASC 718-20, *Awards Classified as Equity,* deals with share-based awards to employees classified as equity
- ASC 718-30, *Awards Classified as Liabilities,* deals with share-based awards to employees classified as liabilities
- ASC 718-40, *Employee Stock Ownership Plans,* contains the following subsections:
  - General
  - Leveraged employee stock ownership plans
  - Nonleveraged employee stock ownership plans
- ASC 718-50, *Employee Share Purchase Plans,*
- ASC 718-60, *Income Taxes,* which addresses accounting for income taxes related to share-based payment arrangements.

Scope and Scope Exceptions

ASC 718 applies to all entities and to all share-based payment transactions where the entity acquires employee services by issuing or offering to issue equity instruments or incurring liabilities to an employee that meet these conditions:

1. The amounts are based in whole or in part on the price of the entity's equity instruments
2. The awards require or may require settlement by issuing the entity's equity instruments.

If the purpose of awarding the shares is other than compensation, ASC 718 does not apply. ASC 718 does not apply to share-based payments for other than employee services.

Overview

FASB has concluded that the economic substance of stock-based compensation is to provide compensation, and that results in an expense that should logically be reported by the entity using the fair value method of accounting. ASC 718 imposes fair value accounting on almost all share-based payment plans.

ASC 718 contains the accounting for employers' contributions to employee stock ownership plans (ESOP). This includes the measurement of compensation cost and the accounting for dividends paid on unallocated shares.

ASC 718 holds that freestanding financial instruments issued to employees in exchange for past or future employee services are subject to the recognition and measurement provisions of ASC 718 throughout the life of the instruments, unless their terms are modified when the holder is no longer an employee. ASC 718 also holds that, for instruments originally issued as employee compensation and then modified, and where that modification to the terms of the instrument is made *solely* to reflect an equity restructuring that occurs when the holders are no longer employees, no change in the recognition or the measurement (due to a change in classification) of those instruments will result if *both* of the following conditions are met:

1. There is no increase in the fair value of the award (or the ratio of intrinsic value to the exercise price of the award is preserved—i.e., the holder is made whole), or the antidilution provision is not added to the terms of the award in contemplation of an equity restructuring; *and*
2. All holders of the same class of equity instruments (for example, stock options) are treated in the same manner.

Other modifications of the instrument (that is, any modification that fails to meet the dual tests above) that take place when the holder is no longer an employee, are subject to the modification accounting guidance set forth by ASC 718, as addressed above. Following modification, the accounting for such instruments, no longer held by employees, must follow GAAP, including ASC 480 if applicable.

The definition of short-term inducement in the glossary of terms included the phrase *or settlement of an award*. This reference raised a question about possible interaction between different provisions of the standard. FASB did not intend for a short-term inducement deemed to be a settlement to affect the classification of the award for the period it remains outstanding (for example, change the award from an equity instrument to a liability instrument). Therefore, an offer (for a limited time period) to repurchase an award should be excluded from the definition of a short-term inducement, and not be accounted for as a modification. However, if an entity has a history of settling its awards for cash, the entity should consider whether at the inception of the awards it has a substantive liability.

DEFINITIONS OF TERMS

(Source: ASC 718-20)

Allocated shares. Allocated shares are shares in an employee stock ownership plan trust that have been assigned to individual participant accounts based on a known formula. Internal Revenue Service (IRS) rules require allocations to be nondiscriminatory generally based on compensation, length of service, or a combination of both. For any particular participant such shares may be vested, unvested, or partially vested.

Award. The collective noun for multiple instruments with the same terms and conditions granted at the same time either to a single employee or to a group of employees. An award may specify multiple vesting dates, referred to as graded vesting, and different parts of an award may have different expected terms. References to an award also apply to a portion of an award.

Blackout period. A period of time during which exercise of an equity share option is contractually or legally prohibited.

Broker-assisted cashless exercise. The simultaneous exercise by an employee of a share option and sale of the shares through a broker (commonly referred to as a broker-assisted exercise).

Generally, under this method of exercise:

1. The employee authorizes the exercise of an option and the immediate sale of the option shares in the open market.
2. On the same day, the entity notifies the broker of the sale order.
3. The broker executes the sale and notifies the entity of the sales price.
4. The entity determines the minimum statutory tax-withholding requirements.
5. By the settlement day (generally three days later), the entity delivers the stock certificates to the broker.

6. On the settlement day, the broker makes payment to the entity for the exercise price and the minimum statutory withholding taxes and remits the balance of the net sales proceeds to the employee.

Calculated value. A measure of the value of a share option or similar instrument determined by substituting the historical volatility of an appropriate industry sector index for the expected volatility of a nonpublic entity's share price in an option-pricing model.

Call option. A contract that allows the holder to buy a specified quantity of stock from the writer of the contract at a fixed price for a given period. See **Option** and **Purchased call option.**

Closed-form model. A valuation model that uses an equation to produce an estimated fair value. The Black-Scholes-Merton formula is a closed-form model. In the context of option valuation, both closed-form models and lattice models are based on risk-neutral valuation and a contingent claims framework. The payoff of a contingent claim, and thus its value, depends on the value(s) of one or more other assets. The contingent claims framework is a valuation methodology that explicitly recognizes that dependency and values the contingent claim as a function of the value of the underlying asset(s). One application of that methodology is risk-neutral valuation in which the contingent claim can be replicated by a combination of the underlying asset and a risk-free bond. If that replication is possible, the value of the contingent claim can be determined without estimating the expected returns on the underlying asset. The Black-Scholes-Merton formula is a special case of that replication.

Combination award. An award with two or more separate components, each of which can be separately exercised. Each component of the award is actually a separate award, and compensation cost is measured and recognized for each component.

Committed-to-be-released shares. Committed-to-be-released shares are shares that, although not legally released, will be released by a future scheduled and committed debt service payment and will be allocated to employees for service rendered in the current accounting period. The period of employee service to which shares relate is generally defined in the employee stock ownership plan documents. Shares are legally released from suspense and from serving as collateral for employee stock ownership plan debt as a result of payment of debt service. Those shares are required to be allocated to participant accounts as of the end of the employee stock ownership plan's fiscal year. Formulas used to determine the number of shares released can be based on either of the following:

a. The ratio of the current principal amount to the total original principal amount (in which case unearned employee stock ownership plan shares and debt balance will move in tandem)
b. The ratio of the current principal plus interest amount to the total original principal plus interest to be paid.

Shares are released more rapidly under the second method than under the first. Tax law permits the first method only if the employee stock ownership plan debt meets certain criteria.

Cross-Volatility. A measure of the relationship between the volatilities of the prices of two assets taking into account the correlation between movements in the prices of the assets.

Derived service period. A service period for an award with a market condition that is inferred from the application of certain valuation techniques used to estimate fair value. For example, the derived service period for an award of share options that the employee can exercise only if the share price increases by 25% at any time during a five-year period can be inferred from certain valuation techniques. In a lattice model, that derived service period represents the duration of the median of the distribution of share price paths on which the market condition is satisfied. That median is the middle share price path (the midpoint of the distribution of paths) on which the market condition is satisfied. The duration is the period of time from the service inception date to the expected date of satisfaction (as inferred from the valuation technique). If the derived service period is three years, the estimated requisite service period is three years, and all compensation cost would be recognized over that period, unless the market condition was satisfied at an earlier date. Compensation cost would not be recognized beyond three years even if after the grant date the entity determines that it is not probable that the market condition will be satisfied within that period. Further, an award of fully vested, deep out-of-the-money share options has a derived service period that must be determined from the valuation techniques used to estimate fair value. (See **Explicit service period, Implicit service period** and **Requisite service period**.)

Direct loan. A direct loan is a loan made by a lender other than the employer to the employee stock ownership plan. Such loans often include some formal guarantee or commitment by the employer.

Economic interest in an entity. Any type or form of pecuniary interest or arrangement that an entity could issue or be a party to, including equity securities; financial instruments with characteristics of equity, liabilities, or both; long-term debt and other debt-financing arrangements; leases; and contractual arrangements such as management contracts, service contracts, or intellectual property licenses.

Employee. An individual over whom the grantor of a share-based compensation award exercises or has the right to exercise sufficient control to establish an employer–employee relationship based on common law as illustrated in case law and currently under US Internal Revenue Service (IRS) Revenue Ruling 87-41. A reporting entity based in a foreign jurisdiction would determine whether an employee–employer relationship exists based on the pertinent laws of the jurisdiction. Accordingly, a grantee meets the definition of an employee if the grantor consistently represents that individual to be an employee under common law. The definition of an employee for payroll tax purposes under the US Internal Revenue Code includes common law employees. Accordingly, a grantor that classifies a grantee potentially subject to US payroll taxes as an employee also must represent that individual as an employee for payroll tax purposes (unless the grantee is a leased employee as described below). A grantee does not meet the definition of an employee solely because the grantor represents that individual as an employee for some, but not all, purposes. For example, a requirement or decision to classify a grantee as an employee for US payroll tax purposes does not, by itself, indicate that the grantee is an employee, because the grantee also must be an employee of the grantor under common law.

A leased individual is deemed to be an employee of the lessee if all of the following requirements are met:

1. The leased individual qualifies as a common law employee of the lessee, and the lessor is contractually required to remit payroll taxes on the compensation paid to the leased individual for the services provided to the lessee.
2. The lessor and lessee agree in writing to all of the following conditions related to the leased individual:
    a. The lessee has the exclusive right to grant stock compensation to the individual for the employee service to the lessee.
    b. The lessee has a right to hire, fire, and control the activities of the individual. (The lessor also may have that right.)
    c. The lessee has the exclusive right to determine the economic value of the services performed by the individual (including wages and the number of units and value of stock compensation granted).

d. The individual has the ability to participate in the lessee's employee benefit plans, if any, on the same basis as other comparable employees of the lessee.
e. The lessee agrees to and remits to the lessor funds sufficient to cover the complete compensation, including all payroll taxes, of the individual on or before a contractually agreed-upon date or dates.

A nonemployee director does not satisfy this definition of employee. Nevertheless, nonemployee directors acting in their role as members of a board of directors are treated as employees if those directors were elected by the employer's shareholders or appointed to a board position that will be filled by shareholder election when the existing term expires. However, that requirement applies only to awards granted to nonemployee directors for their services as directors. Awards granted to those individuals for other services shall be accounted for as awards to nonemployees.

Employee stock ownership plan (ESOP). An ESOP is an employee benefit plan described by the Employee Retirement Income Security Act (ERISA) of 1974 and the Internal Revenue Code of 1986 as a stock bonus plan, or combination stock bonus and money purchase pension plan, designed to invest primarily in employer stock. Also called an *employee share ownership plan*.

Employer loan. An employer loan is a loan made by the employer to the employee stock ownership plan, with no related outside loan.

Equity restructuring. A nonreciprocal transaction between an entity and its shareholders that causes the per-share fair value of the shares underlying an option or similar award to change, such as a stock dividend, stock split, spinoff, rights offering, or recapitalization through a large, nonrecurring cash dividend.

Excess tax benefit. The realized tax benefit related to the amount (caused by changes in the fair value of the entity's shares after the measurement date for financial reporting) of deductible compensation cost reported on an employer's tax return for equity instruments in excess of the compensation cost for those instruments recognized for financial reporting purposes.

Explicit service period. A service period that is explicitly stated in the terms of a share-based payment award. For example, an award that vests after three years of continuous employee service from a given date (usually the grant date) has an explicit service period of three years See **Derived service period**, **Implicit service period**, and **Requisite service period**.

Fair value. The amount at which an asset (or liability) could be bought (or incurred) or sold (or settled) in a current transaction between willing parties, that is, other than in a forced or liquidation sale.

Freestanding financial instrument. A financial instrument that meets either of the following conditions:

1. It is entered into separately and apart from any of the entity's other financial instruments or equity transactions.
2. It is entered into in conjunction with some other transaction and is legally detachable and separately exercisable.

Grant date. The date at which employer and employee reach a mutual understanding of the key terms and conditions of a share-based payment award. The employer becomes contingently obligated on the grant date to issue equity instruments or transfer assets to an employee who renders the requisite service. Awards made under an arrangement that is subject to shareholder approval are not deemed to be granted until that approval is obtained, unless approval is essentially a formality (or perfunctory)—for example, if management and the members of the board of directors control enough votes to approve the arrangement. Similarly, individual awards that are subject to approval by the board of directors, management, or both are not deemed to be granted until all such approvals are obtained. The grant date for an award of equity instruments is the date that an employee begins to benefit from, or be adversely affected by, subsequent changes in the price of the employer's equity shares. ASC 718-10-25-5 provides guidance on determining the grant date. See **Service inception date**.

Implicit service period. A service period that is not explicitly stated in the terms of a share-based payment award but that may be inferred from an analysis of those terms and other facts and circumstances. For instance, if an award of share options vests upon the completion of a new product design, which is deemed probable in 18 months, the implicit service period is 18 months. See **Derived service period**, **Explicit service period**, and **Requisite service period**.

Indirect loan. An indirect loan is a loan made by the employer to the employee stock ownership plan, with a related outside loan to the employer.

Intrinsic value. The amount by which the fair value of the underlying stock exceeds the exercise price of an option. For example, an option with an exercise price of $20 on a stock whose current market price is $25 has an intrinsic value of $5. (A nonvested share may be described as an option on that share with an exercise price of zero. Thus, the fair value of a share is the same as the intrinsic value of such an option on that share.)

Lattice model. A model that produces an estimated fair value based on the assumed changes in prices of a financial instrument over successive periods of time. The binomial model is an example of a lattice model. In each time period, the model assumes that at least two price movements are possible. The lattice represents the evolution of the value of either a financial instrument or a market variable for the purpose of valuing a financial instrument. In this context, a lattice model is based on a risk-neutral valuation and a contingent claims framework. See **Closed-form model** for an explanation of the terms *risk-neutral valuation* and *contingent claims framework.*

Market condition. A condition affecting the exercise price, exercisability, or other pertinent factors used in determining the fair value of an award under a share-based payment arrangement that relates to the achievement of either of the following:

1. A specified price of the issuer's shares or a specified amount of intrinsic value indexed solely to the issuer's shares
2. A specified price of the issuer's shares in terms of a similar (or index of similar) equity security (securities). The term "similar," as used in this definition, refers to an equity security of another entity that has the same type of residual rights. For example, common stock of one entity generally would be similar to the common stock of another entity for this purpose.

Measurement date. The date at which the equity share price and other pertinent factors, such as expected volatility, that enter into measurement of the total recognized amount of compensation cost for an award of share-based payment fixed.

Modification. A change in any of the terms or conditions of a share-based payment award.

Nonpublic entity. Any entity other than one that meets any of the following criteria:

1. Has equity securities that trade in a public market, either on a stock exchange (domestic or foreign) or in an over-the-counter market, including securities quoted only locally or regionally

2. Makes a filing with a regulatory agency in preparation for the sale of any class of equity securities in a public market
3. Is controlled by an entity covered by the preceding criteria.

An entity that has only debt securities trading in a public market (or that has made a filing with a regulatory agency in preparation to trade only debt securities) is a nonpublic entity.

Nonvested shares. Shares that an entity has not yet issued because the agreed upon consideration, such as employee services, has not yet been received. Nonvested shares cannot be sold. The restriction on sale of nonvested shares is due to the forfeitability of the shares if specified events occur (or do not occur).

Option. Unless otherwise stated, a call option that gives the holder the right to purchase shares of common stock from the reporting entity in accordance with an agreement upon payment of a specified amount. Options include, but are not limited to, options granted to employees and stock purchase agreements entered into with employees. Options are considered securities. See **Call option.**

Performance condition. A condition affecting the vesting, exercisability, exercise price, or other pertinent factors used in determining the fair value of an award that relates to both of the following:

1. An employee's rendering service for a specified (either explicitly or implicitly) period of time
2. Achieving a specified performance target that is defined solely by reference to the employer's own operations (or activities).

Attaining a specified growth rate in return on assets, obtaining regulatory approval to market a specified product, selling shares in an initial public offering or other financing event, and a change in control are examples of performance conditions. A performance target also may be defined by reference to the same performance measure of another entity or group of entities. For example, attaining a growth rate in earnings per share (EPS) that exceeds the average growth rate in EPS of other entities in the same industry is a performance condition. A performance target might pertain either to the performance of the entity as a whole or to some part of the entity, such as a division or an individual employee.

Probable. The future event or events are likely to occur.

Public entity. An entity that meets any of the following criteria:

1. Has equity securities that trade in a public market, either a stock exchange (domestic or foreign) or in an over-the-counter market, including securities quoted only locally or regionally
2. Makes a filing with a regulatory agency in preparation for the sale of any class of equity securities in a public market
3. Is controlled by an entity covered by the preceding criteria—that is, a subsidiary of a public entity is itself a public entity.

An entity that has only debt securities trading in a public market (or that has made a filing with a regulatory agency in preparation to trade only debt securities) is not a public entity.

Purchased call option. A contract that allows the reporting entity to buy a specified quantity of its own stock from the writer of the contract at a fixed price for a given period. See **Call option.**

Related parties. These include:

1. Affiliates of the entity
2. Entities for which investments in their equity securities would be required, absent the election of the fair value option under the Fair Value Option Subsection of Section 825-10-15, to be accounted for by the equity method by the investing entity
3. Trusts for the benefit of employees, such as pension and profit-sharing trusts that are managed by or under the trusteeship of management
4. Principal owners of the entity and members of their immediate families
5. Management of the entity and members of their immediate families
6. Other parties with which the entity may deal if one party controls or can significantly influence the management or operating policies of the other to an extent that one of the transacting parties might be prevented from fully pursuing its own separate interests
7. Other parties that can significantly influence the management or operating policies of the transacting parties or that have an ownership interest in one of the transacting parties and can significantly influence the other to an extent that one or more of the transacting parties might be prevented from fully pursuing its own separate interests.

Reload feature and reload option. A reload feature provides for automatic grants of additional options whenever an employee exercises previously granted options using the entity's shares, rather than cash, to satisfy the exercise price. At the time of exercise using shares, the employee is automatically granted a new option, called a reload option, for the shares used to exercise the previous option.

Replacement award. An award of share-based compensation that is granted (or offered to grant) concurrently with the cancellation of another award.

Requisite service period. The period or periods during which an employee is required to provide service in exchange for an award under a share-based payment arrangement. The service that an employee is required to render during that period is referred to as the requisite service. The requisite service period for an award that has only a service condition is presumed to be the vesting period, unless there is clear evidence to the contrary. If an award requires future service for vesting, the entity cannot define a prior period as the requisite service period. Requisite service periods may be explicit, implicit, or derived, depending on the terms of the share-based payment award.

Restricted share. A share for which sale is contractually or governmentally prohibited for a specified period of time. Most grants of shares to employees are better termed "nonvested shares" because the limitation on sale stems solely from the forfeitability of the shares before employees have satisfied the necessary service or performance condition(s) to earn the rights to the shares. Restricted shares issued for consideration other than employee services, on the other hand, are fully paid immediately. For those shares, there is no period analogous to a requisite service period during which the issuer is unilaterally obligated to issue shares when the purchaser pays for those shares, but the purchaser is not obligated to buy the shares. The term restricted shares refers only to fully vested and outstanding shares whose sale is contractually or governmentally prohibited for a specified period of time. Vested equity instruments that are transferable to an employee's immediate family members or to a trust that benefits only those family members are restricted if the transferred instruments retain the same prohibition on sale to third parties. See **Nonvested shares**.

Restriction. A contractual or governmental provision that prohibits sale (or substantive sale by using derivatives or other means to effectively terminate the risk of future changes in the share price) of an equity instrument for a specified period of time.

Securities and Exchange Commission (SEC) registrant. An entity (or an entity that is controlled by an entity) that meets any of the following criteria:

1. It has issued or will issue debt or equity securities that are traded in a public market (a domestic or foreign stock exchange or an over-the counter market, including local or regional markets).
2. It is required to file financial statements with the SEC.
3. It provides financial statements for the purpose of issuing any class of securities in a public market.

Service condition. A condition affecting the vesting, exercisability, exercise price, or other pertinent factors used in determining the fair value of an award that depends solely on an employee rendering service to the employer for the requisite service period. A condition that results in the acceleration of vesting in the event of an employee's death, disability, or termination without cause is a service condition.

Service inception date. The date at which the requisite service period begins. The service inception date usually is the grant date, but the service inception date may differ from the grant date (see Example 6 [see ASC 718-10-55-107]).

Settlement of an award. An action or event that irrevocably extinguishes the issuing entity's obligation under a share-based payment award. Transactions and events that constitute settlements include the following:

1. Exercise of a share option or lapse of an option at the end of its contractual term
2. Vesting of shares
3. Forfeiture of shares or share options due to failure to satisfy a vesting condition
4. An entity's repurchase of instruments in exchange for assets or for fully vested and transferable equity instruments.

The vesting of a share option is not a settlement because the entity remains obligated to issue shares upon exercise of the option.

Share-based payment arrangement. An arrangement under which either of the following conditions is met:

1. One or more suppliers of goods or services (including employees) receive awards of equity shares, equity share options, or other equity instruments
2. The entity incurs liabilities to suppliers that meet either of the following conditions:

   a. The amounts based, at least in part, on the price of the entity's shares or other equity instruments. (The phrase at least in part is used because an award may be indexed to both the price of the entity's shares and something other than either the price of the entity's shares or a market, performance, or service condition.)
   b. The awards require or may require settlement by issuance of the entity's shares.

The term shares includes various forms of ownership interest that may not take the legal form of securities (for example, partnership interests), as well as other interests, including those that are liabilities in substance but not in form. Equity shares refers only to shares that are accounted for as equity. Also called *share-based compensation arrangements*.

Share-based payment transaction. A transaction under a share-based payment arrangement, including a transaction in which an entity acquires goods or services because related parties or other holders of economic interest in that entity awards a share-based payment to an employee or other supplier of goods or services for the entity's benefit. Also called *share-based compensation transactions*.

Share option. A contract that gives the holder the right, but not the obligation, either to purchase (to call) or to sell (to put) a certain number of shares at a predetermined price for a specified period of time. Most share options granted to employees under share-based compensation arrangements are call options, but some may be put options.

Share unit. A contract under which the holder has the right to convert each unit into a specified number of shares of the issuing entity.

Short-term inducement. An offer by the entity that would result in modification of an award to which an award holder may subscribe for a limited period of time.

Suspense shares. The shares initially held by the employee stock ownership plan in a suspense account are called suspense shares. Suspense shares are shares that have not been released, committed to be released, or allocated to participant accounts. Suspense shares generally collateralize employee stock ownership plan debt.

Tandem award. An award with two or more components in which exercise of one part cancels the other(s).

Terms of a share-based payment award. The contractual provisions that determine the nature and scope of a share-based payment award. For example, the exercise price of share options is one of the terms of an award of share options. As indicated in ASC 718-10-25-5, the written terms of a share-based payment award and its related arrangement, if any, usually provide the best evidence of its terms. However, an entity's past practice or other factors may indicate that some aspects of the substantive terms differ from the written terms. The substantive terms of a share-based payment award as those terms are mutually understood by the entity and a party (either an employee or a nonemployee) who receives the award, provide the basis for determining the rights conveyed to a party and the obligations imposed on the issuer, regardless of how the award and related arrangement, if any, are structured. See ASC 718-10-30-5.

Time value. The portion of the fair value of an option that exceeds its intrinsic value. For example, a call option with an exercise price of $20 on a stock whose current market price is $25 has intrinsic value of $5. If the fair value of that option is $7, the time value of the option is $2 ($7 – $5).

Top-up shares. Top-up shares are shares or cash that an employer contributes to an employee stock ownership plan because the fair value of the shares released is less than the employer's liability for a particular benefit, such as a savings plan match.

Vest. To earn the rights to. A share-based payment award becomes vested at the date that the employee's right to receive or retain shares, other instruments, or cash under the award is no longer contingent on satisfaction of either a service condition or a performance condition. Market conditions are not vesting conditions.

The stated vesting provisions of an award often establish the requisite service period, and an award that has reached the end of the requisite service period is vested. However, as indicated in the definition of requisite service period, the stated vesting period may differ from the requisite service period in certain circumstances. Thus, the more precise (but cumbersome) terms would be options, shares, or awards for which the requisite service has been rendered and end of the requisite service period.

Volatility. A measure of the amount by which a financial variable such as a share price has fluctuated (historical volatility) or is expected to fluctuate (expected volatility) during a period. Volatility also may be defined as a probability-weighted measure of the dispersion of returns about the mean. The volatility of a share price is the standard deviation of the continuously compounded rates of return on the share over a specified period. That is the same as the standard deviation of the differences in the natural logarithms of the stock prices plus dividends, if any, over the period. The higher the volatility, the more the returns on the shares can be expected to vary—up or down. Volatility is typically expressed in annualized terms.

CONCEPTS, RULES, AND EXAMPLES

Accounting for Share-Based Payments

Under ASC 718, entities must use fair value to measure the cost of all share-based payment plans. There is still an optional exception available for nonpublic companies, where measures of stock price volatility required to apply the normal fair value approach simply do not exist, but under such circumstances a modified fair value model is prescribed, where an industry group-based surrogate for the entity's stock price volatility is employed. Thus, all stock-based compensation arrangements, where equity instruments are issued to employees, will result in compensation cost that is measured using a variant of the fair value model.

There are several ways to calculate the fair value of stock-based compensation arrangements. Lattice models provide greater flexibility than the Black-Scholes-Merton model for including or excluding variables, or changing variable parameters, from one period to the other. ASC 718 does not require the use of lattice-type models, of which the binomial model is the most widely employed, but the advantages of such approaches are worthwhile.

In determining the fair value of share options, all the features and attributes of the options must be taken into consideration, including the expected volatility of the underlying equity instrument.

In addition, ASC 718 requires that excess tax benefits be reported as a financing cash inflow rather than as a reduction of taxes paid. This is more consistent with the view that the issuance of employee stock option shares is part of the capital raising process, and the tax advantages attendant to this are equivalently part of that same process.

The business combinations codification, ASC 805, reinforces ASC 718 by requiring that an acquiring entity use ASC 718 to measure the liability associated with the replacement of an acquiree's share-based payment awards with its own share-based payment awards.

ASC 718: Detailed Explanation

ASC 718 broadly addresses share-based payments. It covers plans for employees that convey shares of the employer's stock, derivatives (such as options) related to the employer's shares, or cash in amounts tied to the value of the employer's shares. All share-based plans are considered compensatory unless the benefit to employees is no greater than that which is available to shareholders generally. The benefit to recipients is assessed based both on the discount from market price and the number of shares they are eligible to buy. Consequently, virtually all plans will be considered compensatory for accounting purposes, including employee stock purchase plans that are noncompensatory under the federal tax laws.

Additionally, ASC 718 describes (1) the prescribed pattern of compensation cost recognition, (2) the accounting for employee stock purchase plans, and (3) accounting for the income tax effects of share-based transactions. It also requires that excess tax benefits be reported in the cash flow statement as a financing activity, rather than as an operating activity (these are currently reported as a reduction of income taxes paid).

Measurement of compensation cost from share-based payment arrangements with employees. The objective is to estimate, as of the grant date, the fair value of the award that an employee earns as a result of requisite service and satisfying vesting requirements. The estimate of fair value would reflect transferability and other restrictions if they are in effect when the award vests. Compensation cost is to be recognized only for those awards that vest (which obviously demands that estimates be made).

- *Classifying awards as liabilities or equity.* ASC 718 requires that the classification criteria of ASC 480 be applied in determining whether an instrument granted to an employee is a liability or equity. In particular, some stock-based compensation awards that call for settlement by issuing an entity's own equity instruments may be classified as liabilities if they meet the criteria of ASC 480.
- *Valuation models.* In the absence of an observable market price for an award—often the reality for employee share options—reporting entities are now required to use a valuation method that takes into account the factors set forth in the standard.

While ASC 718 does not dictate a valuation model, reportedly FASB believes and prefers that most companies will use the binomial or other so-called *lattice* models of value, rather than a *closed-form* model such as the Black-Scholes-Merton. The binomial model is favored, however, because it accommodates more potential postvesting behaviors than the closed-form models.

Binomial or other lattice models value options by constructing lattices or trees that represent different possible stock prices at different future points in time. The value of the option is determined at each node or branch of the tree. To determine these values, companies need to develop information about expected volatility, dividends, and risk-free rates that will apply at each of the possible branches or nodes of the model. In addition, information about employee postvesting behavior is needed to determine likely exercise dates. Note that under ASC 718 it is necessary to use *expected volatility* of share prices.

- *Liability-classified awards.* The provisions dealing with share-based payments that involve liabilities, rather than equity, are affected by the issuance of ASC 480. Certain share-based payments create liabilities under ASC 480, (e.g., awards that result in the issuance of mandatorily redeemable shares, or those that require cash settlements or give the holders the right to demand cash, as do some stock appreciation rights). Liability-classified awards are to be remeasured at fair value each reporting period. Prior to vesting, the cumulative compensation costs would equal the proportionate amount of the award earned to date, and thus the periodic compensation cost would reflect both the passage of time (service period) and change in the fair value of the ultimate award. Subsequent to vesting, any further change in fair value would be recorded as a charge against earnings.

The use of grant date to fix the value of equity-based awards and settlement date to fix the value of liability-based awards, may seem inconsistent and/or confusing. FASB presents a rather detailed explanation for its decisions in the standard, but essentially the logic is that to recognize changes in compensation based on post-grant-date changes to the value of the underlying equity would be equivalent to recognizing changes in the value of the entity's own equity shares in earnings, which is prohibited under GAAP. Also, grant date is when the parties (the entity and its employees) have fixed the terms of their arrangement, which provides a meaningful measure of the cost to be incurred by the entity. This differs importantly from the situation with equity-based compensation that is classified as a liability because it is to be settled for cash (e.g., cash stock appreciation rights, or SARs). In that scenario, the entity is obligated to distribute assets, and the relevant measure of compensation cost, ultimately, is the amount of assets disbursed.

- *Equity-classified awards.* Equity-classified awards that are publicly traded and have observable market prices are to be valued using the market price. Few, if any, employee stock compensation awards (i.e., employee stock options) would have this characteristic, however. If not publicly traded, equity-classified awards are valued using a model such as the binomial or the Black-Scholes-Merton.

- *Valuation for graded-vesting awards.* Companies that grant awards with graded vesting are to elect whether to measure the awards as if it were a cliff-vested award, or alternatively whether they are to be treated as several separate awards. If the former is chosen, the amount expensed each year would be the pro rata portion of compensation cost determined with reference to the entire package. If the latter approach is selected, each separately vesting portion will be valued and the associated compensation cost will be accrued over the term until that portion vests.
- *Measurement alternatives for nonpublic companies.* Nonpublic companies must now choose to use either continually updated intrinsic values or fair values to measure share-option or liability-classified awards. Note that no such choice would be available for nonvested or vested stock awards, which are to be measured using grant-date fair values.

  If a nonpublic reporting entity chooses to use the intrinsic value alternative, the intrinsic value of an equity-classified award will have to be reestimated each reporting period. However, if a company uses the fair value alternative no reestimation is required, which could reduce fluctuations in reported earnings. If nonpublic companies choose the fair value approach, they will not later be able to return to the use of intrinsic value, because fair value is deemed preferable for purposes of applying ASC 250 (accounting changes).

While fair value is to be determined as of grant date, in practice there has been some ambiguity regarding the precise definition of this term. ASC 718 does set forth criteria for determining that a share-based payment award has been granted. One of the criteria is a mutual understanding by the employer and employee of the key terms and conditions of a share-based payment award. However, the "mutual" aspect may not occur until some time after the formal grant, when actual communications between employer and employee are held, sometimes not until, for example, a regularly scheduled performance review that might not occur for weeks or months thereafter. To address these practical concerns, ASC 718-10-25-5 holds that, assuming all other criteria in the grant date definition have been met, a mutual understanding of the key terms and conditions of an award to an individual employee is presumed to exist at the date the award is approved in accordance with the relevant corporate governance requirements (that is, by the board or management with the relevant authority), if both the following conditions are met:

1. The award is a unilateral grant and, therefore, the recipient does not have the ability to negotiate the key terms and conditions of the award with the employer, and
2. It is expected that the key terms and conditions of the award will be communicated to an individual recipient within a relatively short time period from the date of approval.

Recognizing compensation. Vesting can be based on a service condition, performance condition, or a combination of both.

- Service conditions are requirements to achieve a specified duration of employment (e.g., number of years' continuous full-time service).
- Performance conditions are requirements to achieve company-specific operating or financial goals (e.g., net income over $3 million).

Compensation cost is to be recognized based on the actual number of awards that eventually vest. Estimates are used to make accruals each period, and adjustments are made based on current estimates of expected future vesting until the actual number of awards that vest are known.

Under provisions of ASC 718, compensation cost for equity-based awards is to be measured at the grant date and not subsequently revised (apart from recognizing changed likelihood of forfeitures).

Market conditions affect the exercisability of an award, but not its vesting. ASC 718 defines a market condition as an exercisability requirement based on achieving a specified share price (e.g., reaching a market price of $22 per share before exercise is allowed). Market conditions can affect the grant-date fair value, and hence the compensation expense to be recognized by the reporting entity. If an employee forfeits an award because a market condition is not satisfied, compensation previously accrued is not reversed, unlike what is done in the event of ordinary forfeitures, which necessitate reversal of previously accrued compensation cost (or, equivalently, adjustment of compensation cost prospectively until the vesting date).

Under provisions of ASC 718, compensation cost for liability-based awards will be measured at the exercise or settlement date, but compensation is estimated at each reporting date from grant date to exercise or settlement date.

Modified awards. The incremental compensation cost resulting from a modification of an award will be measured as the excess of the fair value of the modified award over the fair value of the original award measured immediately prior to the modification. Modifications can occur because of repricing, extending the life, or changing the vesting condition of the award. Cancellations of existing awards and concurrent replacement with new ones have to be accounted for as modifications. In practice, modifications will rarely result in recognized compensation costs less than the fair value of the award at the grant date, but this could conceivably result if the original service or performance vesting conditions were not expected to be satisfied at the modification date.

Accounting for Employee Stock Options under ASC 718

Under ASC 718, fair value accounting must be applied in measuring compensation expense. Ideally, fair value would be market-observed. An observable market price, if available for an option with similar features, should be used as the estimate of fair value of the employee option. However, in most cases, due to the nature of employee stock options (which lack exchangeability, etc.), observable market prices will not be available. Therefore, the reporting entity will have to estimate the fair value of the employee share option using a valuation model that meets the requirements of ASC 718. The valuation model takes into account the following factors, at a minimum:

1. Exercise price of the option
2. Expected term of the option, taking into account several things including the contractual term of the option, vesting requirements, and postvesting employee termination behaviors (The SEC states in 718-10-S99 that a registrant cannot use an expected term that is shorter than the vesting period.)
3. Current price of the underlying share
4. Expected volatility of the price of the underlying share (According to the SEC in 718-10-S99, a registrant may consider historical volatility in determining expected volatility, which in turn should take into consideration historical volatility over a period generally commensurate with the expected or contractual option term, as well as regular intervals for price observations. A registrant can also ignore a period of

historical volatility if it can support a conclusion that the period is not relevant to estimating expected volatility due to nonrecurring historical events. The SEC would also not object to the use of an industry sector index to determine the expected volatility of its share price.)

5. Expected dividends on the underlying share
6. Risk-free interest rate(s) for the expected term of the option.

In practice, there are likely to be ranges of reasonable estimates for expected volatility, dividends, and option term. The closed-form models, of which Black-Scholes (now Black-Scholes-Merton) is the most widely regarded, are predicated on a set of deterministic assumptions that remain invariate over the full term of the option. In the real world, this condition is almost always not met. For this reason, current thinking is that a lattice model, of which the binomial model is an example, would be preferred. Lattice models explicitly identify nodes, such as the anniversaries of the grant date, at each of which new parameter values can be specified (e.g., expected dividends can be independently defined each period).

If a reporting entity changes from the BSM model to a binomial model, the change will be deemed a change in accounting estimate, not a change in accounting principle. A change from a binomial model back to a less desirable BSM model is to be discouraged, but apparently not prohibited if use of BSM or a similar closed-form model is supportable. The presumption is that moving from a binomial model to the BSM model would not be well received.

Other features that may affect the value of the option include changes in the issuer's credit risk, if the value of the awards contains cash settlement features (i.e., if they are liability instruments). Also, contingent features that could cause either a loss of equity shares earned or a reduction of realized gains from sale of equity instruments earned, such as a *clawback feature* (for example, where an employee who terminates the employment relationship and begins to work for a competitor is required to transfer to the issuing enterprise shares granted and earned under a share-based payment arrangement—see the illustrations in ASC 718) would be factors affecting the valuation model.

Market, performance, or service conditions may affect vesting. An award becomes vested at the date the employee's right to receive or retain shares no longer has any of these conditions. Vesting may be conditional on satisfying two or more conditions. Regardless of the conditions that must be satisfied, the existence of a market condition requires recognition of compensation cost if service has been rendered, even if the market condition is never satisfied.

The definition of an employee used in ASC 718 is that given by IRS Ruling 87-41. In addition, ASC 718 requires that nonemployee directors, acting in their role as members of the company's board of directors, be treated as employees if they were elected by the shareholders or appointed to the board and will be subject to election at the next shareholder election. Any awards granted to these individuals for their service as directors would be considered to be employee compensation.

The grant date is defined as the date when the employer and employee have a mutual understanding of the key terms and conditions of the share-based compensation arrangement and all necessary authorizations of those conditions have occurred. The service inception date is the first day of the requisite service period. Compensation cost is attributed over the service period.

If a given option plan involves the payment of compensation to the employees, such compensation cost should be recognized in the period(s) in which the services being compensated are performed. If the grant is *unconditional*, which means it effectively is in recognition of past services rendered by the employees and does not depend on the rendering of further service, then compensation is reported in full in the period of the grant. If the stock options are granted before the service inception date, compensation cost should be recognized over the periods in which the performance is scheduled to occur. Whether compensation cost is recognized ratably over the periods or not is a function of the vesting provisions of the plan. If the plan provides for cliff vesting, compensation will be accrued on an essentially straight-line basis, while if it provides for graded vesting, the pattern of recognition is subject to election and may be more complex. The accounting for graded vesting plans under ASC 718 represents a change from current practice.

Option fair value calculations. Before presenting specific examples of accounting for stock options, simple examples of calculating the fair value of options using both the Black-Scholes-Merton and the binomial/lattice methods are provided. First, an example of the Black-Scholes-Merton closed-form model is provided.

Black-Scholes-Merton actually computes the theoretical value of a so-called *European* call option, where exercise can occur only on the expiration date. *American* options, which include most employee stock options, can be exercised at any time until expiration. The value of an American-style option on dividend paying stocks is generally greater than a European-style option, since preexercise the holder does not have a right to receive dividends that are paid on the stock. (For non-dividend-paying stocks, the value of American and European options will tend to converge.) Black-Scholes-Merton ignores dividends, but this is readily dealt with, as shown below, by deducting from the computed option value the present value of expected dividend stream over the option holding period.

Black-Scholes-Merton also is predicated on constant volatility over the option term, which available evidence suggests may not be a wholly accurate description of stock price behavior. On the other hand, the reporting entity would find it very difficult, if not impossible, to compute differing volatilities for each node in the lattice model described later in this section, lacking a factual basis for presuming that volatility would increase or decrease in specific future periods.

The Black-Scholes-Merton model:

C = $SN(d_1) - Ke^{(-rt)}N(d_2)$
C = Theoretical call premium
S = Current stock price
t = time until option expiration
K = option striking price
r = risk-free interest rate
N = Cumulative standard normal distribution
e = exponential term (2.7183)

$$d_1 = \frac{ln(S/K) + (r + s^2/2)^t}{s\sqrt{t}}$$

d_2 = $d_1 - s$
s = standard deviation of stock returns
ln = natural logarithm

The Black-Scholes-Merton valuation is illustrated with the following assumed facts; note that dividends are ignored in the initial calculation, but will be addressed once the theoretical value is computed. Also note that volatility is defined in terms of the variability of the entity's stock price, measured by the standard deviation of prices over, say, the past three years, which is used as a surrogate for expected volatility over the next twelve months.

Example—Determining the fair value of options using the Black-Scholes-Merton model

Black-Scholes-Merton is a closed-form model, meaning that it solves for an option price from an equation. It computes a theoretical call price based on five parameters—the current stock price, the option exercise price, the expected volatility of the stock price, the time until option expiration, and the short-term risk-free interest rate. Of these, expected volatility is the most difficult to ascertain. Volatility is generally computed as the standard deviation of recent historical returns on the stock. In the following example, the stock is currently selling at $40 and the standard deviation of prices (daily closing prices can be used, among other possible choices) over the past several years was $6.50, yielding an estimated volatility of $6.50/$40 = 16.25%.

Assume the following facts:

S	=	$40
t	=	2 years
K	=	$45
r	=	3% annual rate
s	=	standard deviation of percentage returns = 16.25% (based on $6.50 standard deviation of stock price compared to current $40 price)

From the foregoing data, all of which is known information (the volatility, s, is computed or assumed, as discussed above), the factors d_1 and d_2 can be computed. The cumulative standard normal variates (N) of these values must then be determined (using a table or formula), following which the Black-Scholes-Merton option value is calculated, *before the effect of dividends*. In this example, the computed amounts are:

$$N(d_1) = 0.2758$$
$$N(d_2) = 0.2048$$

With these assumptions the value of the stock options is approximately $2.35. This is derived from the Black-Scholes-Merton as follows:

$$\begin{aligned} C &= SN(d_1) - Ke^{(-rt)}N(d_2) \\ &= 40(.2758) - 45(.942)(.2048) \\ &= 11.032 - 8.679 \\ &= 2.35 \end{aligned}$$

The foregone two-year stream of dividends, which in this example are projected to be $0.50 annually, have a present value of $0.96. Therefore, the net value of this option is $1.39 ($2.35 – .96).

Example—Determining the fair value of options using the binomial/lattice model

In contrast to the Black-Scholes-Merton, the binomial/lattice model is an open form, inductive model. It allows for multiple (theoretically, unlimited) branches of possible outcomes on a "tree" of possible price movements and induces the option's price. As compared to the Black-Scholes-Merton approach, this relaxes the constraint on exercise timing. It can be assumed that exercise occurs at any point in the option period, and past experience may guide the reporting entity to make certain such assumptions (e.g., that one-half the options will be exercised when the market price of the stock reaches 150% of the strike price, etc.). It also allows for varying dividends from period to period.

It is assumed that the common (Cox, Ross, and Rubinstein) binomial model will be used in practice. To keep this preliminary example relatively simple in order to focus on the concepts involved, a single-step binomial model is provided here for illustrative purposes. Assume an option is granted on a $20 stock that will expire in one year. The option exercise price equals the stock price of $20. Also, assume there is a 50% chance that the price will jump 20% over the year and a 50% chance the stock will drop 20%, and that no other outcomes are possible. The risk-free interest rate is 4%. With these assumptions there are three basic calculations.

1. Plot the two possible future stock prices.
2. Translate these stock prices into future options values.
3. Discount these future values into a single present value.

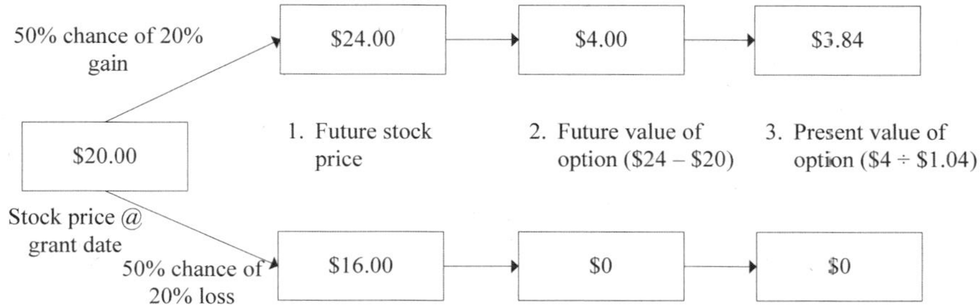

In this case, the option will only have value if the stock price increases, and otherwise the option would expire worthless and unexercised. In this simplistic example, there is only a 50% chance of the option having a value of $3.84, and therefore the option is worth $1.92 at grant date.

The foregoing was a simplistic single-period, two-outcome model. A more complicated and realistic binomial model extends this single-period model into a randomized walk of many steps or intervals. In theory, the time to expiration can be broken into a large number of ever-smaller time intervals, such as months, weeks, or days. The advantage is that the parameter values (volatility, etc.) can then be varied with greater precision from one period to the next (assuming, of course, that there is a factual basis upon which to base these estimates). Calculating the binomial model, then, involves the same three calculation steps. First, the possible future stock prices are determined for each branch, using the volatility input and time to expiration (which grows shorter with each successive node in the model). This permits computation of terminal values for each branch of the tree. Second, future stock prices are translated into option values at each node of the tree. Third, these future option values are discounted and added to produce a single present value of the option, taking into account the probabilities of each series of price moves in the model.

Example—Multiperiod option valuation using binomial model

Consider the following example of a two-period binomial model. Again, certain simplifying assumptions will be made so that a manual calculation can be illustrated (in general, computer programs will be necessary to compute option values). Eager Corp. grants 10,000 options to its employees at a time when the market price of shares is $40. The options expire in two years; expected dividends on the stock will be $0.50 per year; and the risk-free rate is currently 3%, which is not expected to change over the two-year horizon. The option exercise price is $43.

The entity's past experience suggests that, after one year (of the two-year term) elapses, if the market price of the stock exceeds the option exercise price, one-half of the options will be exercised by the holders. The other holders will wait another year to decide. If at the end of the second year—without regard to what the stock value was at the end of the first year—the market value exceeds the exercise price, all the remaining options will be exercised. The workforce has been unusually stable and it is not anticipated that option holders will cease employment before the end the option period.

The stock price moves randomly from period to period. Based on recent experience, it is anticipated that in each period the stock may increase by $5, stay the same, or decrease by $5, with equal probability, versus the price at the period year-end. Thus, since the price is $40 at grant date, one year hence it might be either $45, $40, or $35. The price at the end of the second year will follow the same pattern, based on the price when the first year ends.

Logically, holders will exercise their options rather than see them expire, as long as there is gain to be realized. Since dividends are not paid on options, holders have a motive to exercise earlier than the expiration date, which explains why historically one-half the options are exercised after one year elapses, as long as the market price exceeds the exercise price at that date, even though the exercising holders risk future market declines.

The binomial model formulation requires that each sequence of events and actions be explicated. This gives rise to the commonly seen decision tree representation. In this simple example, following the grant of the options, one of three possible events occurs: (1) the stock price rises $5 over the next year, (2) it remains constant, or (3) it falls by $5. Since these outcomes have equal *a priori* probabilities, $p = 1/3$ is assigned to each outcome of this first year event. If the price does rise, one half the option holders will exercise at the end of the first year, to reap the economic gain and capture the second year's dividend. The other holders will forego this immediate gain and wait to see what the stock price does in the second year before making an exercise decision.

If the stock price in the first year either remains flat or falls by $5, no option holders are expected to exercise. However, there remains the opportunity to exercise after the second year elapses, if the stock price recovers. Of course, holding the options for the second year means that no dividends will be received.

The cost of the options granted by Eager Corp., measured by fair value using the binomial model approach, is computed by the sum of the probability-weighted outcomes, discounted to present value using the risk-free rate. In this example, the rate is expected to remain at 3% per year throughout the option period, but it could be independently specified for each period—another advantage the binomial model has over the more rigid Black-Scholes-Merton. The sum of these present value computations measures the cost of compensation incorporated in the option grant, regardless of what pattern of exercise ultimately is revealed, since at the grant date, using the available information about stock price volatility, expected dividends, exercise behavior and the risk-free rate, this best measures the value of what was promised to the employees.

The following graphic offers a visual representation of the model, although in practice it is not necessary to prepare such a document. The actual calculations can be made by computer program, but to illustrate the application of the binomial model, the computation will be presented explicitly here. There are four possible scenarios under which, in this example, holders will exercise the options, and thus the options will have value. All other scenarios (combinations of stock price movements over the two-year horizon) will cause the holders to allow the options to expire unexercised.

First, if the stock price goes to $45 in the first year, one-half of the holders will exercise at that point, paying the exercise price of $43 per share. This results in a gain of $2 ($45 – $43) per share. However, having waited until the first year-end, they lost the opportunity to receive the $0.50 per share dividend, so the net economic gain is only $1.50 ($2.00 – $0.50) per share. As this occurs after one year, the present value is only $\$1.50 \times 1.03^{-1} = \$1.46$ per share. When this is weighted by the probability of this outcome obtaining (given that the stock price rise to $45 in the first year has only a 1/3 probability of happening, and given further that only one-half the option holders would elect to exercise under such conditions), the actual expected value of this outcome is [(1/3)(1/2)($1.46)] = $0.24. More formally,

$$[(1/3)(1/2)(\$2.00 - \$0.50)] \times 1.03^{-1} = \$0.2427$$

The second potentially favorable outcome to holders would be if the stock price rises to $45 the first year and then either rises another $5 the second year or holds steady at $45 during the second year. In either event, the option holders who did not exercise after the first year's stock price rise will all exercise at the end of the second year, before the options expire. If the price goes to $50 the second year, the holders will reap a gross gain of $7 ($50 – $43) per share; if it remains constant at $45, the gross gain is only $2 per share. In either case, dividends in both the first and second years will have been foregone. To calculate the compensation cost associated with these branches of the model, the first-year dividend lost must be discounted for one year, and the gross gain and second-year dividend must be discounted for two years. Also, the probabilities of the entire sequence of events must be used, taking into account the likelihood of the first year's stock price rise, the proclivity of holders to wait for a second year to elapse, and the likelihood of a second-year price rise or price stability. These computations are shown below.

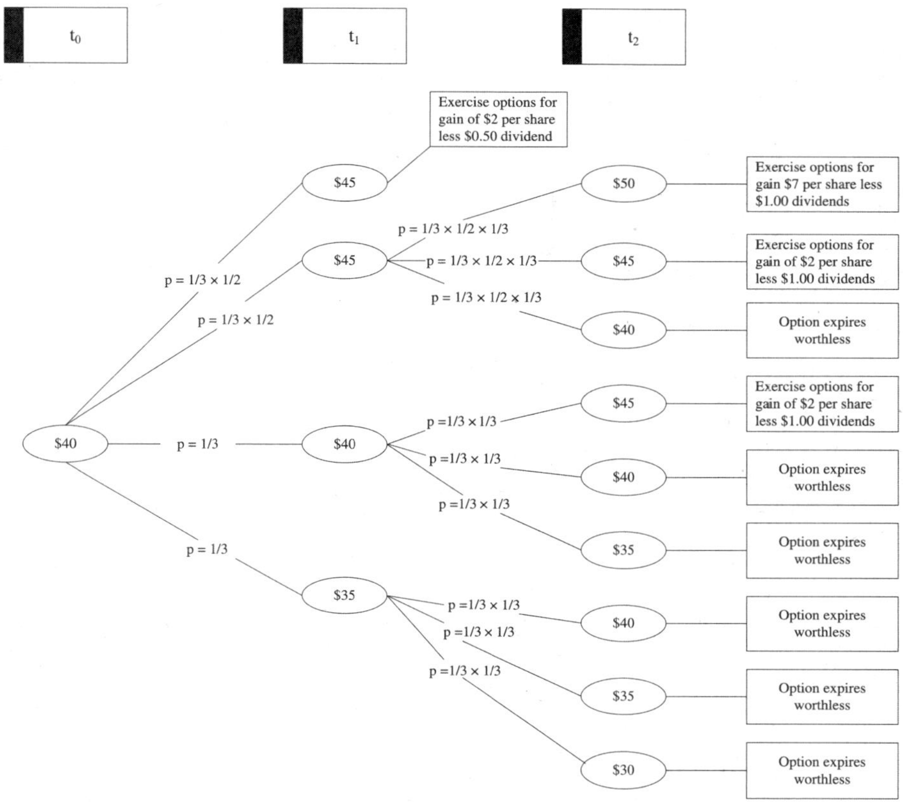

For the outcome if the stock price rises again:

$[(1/3)(1/2)(1/3)]\{[(\$7.00) \times 1.03^{-2}] - [(\$0.50) \times 1.03^{-1}] - [\$0.50 \times 1.03^{-2}]\} = [0.05544]\{\$6.59 - \$0.48 - \$0.47\} = \$0.31276$

For the outcome if the stock price remains stable:

$[(1/3)(1/2)(1/3)]\{[(\$2.00) \times 1.03^{-2}] - [(\$0.50) \times 1.03^{-1}] - [(\$0.50) \times 1.03^{-2}]\} = [0.05544]\{\$1.88 - \$0.48 - \$0.47\} = \$0.05147$

The final, favorable outcome for holders would occur if the stock price holds constant at $40 the first year but rises to $45 the second year, making exercise the right decision. Note that none of the holders would exercise after the first year given that the price, $40, was below exercise price. The calculation for this sequence of events is as follows:

$[(1/3)(1/3)]\{[(\$2.00) \times 1.03^{-2}] - [(\$0.50) \times 1.03^{-1}] - [(\$0.50) \times 1.03^{-2}]\} = [0.1111]\{\$1.88 - \$0.48 - \$0.47\} = \$0.10295$

Summing these values yields $0.709879 ($0.2427 + $0.31276 + $0.05147 + $0.10295), which is the expected value per option granted. When this per-unit value is then multiplied by the number of options granted (10,000), the total compensation cost to be recognized, $7,098.79, is derived. This would be attributed over the required service period, which is illustrated later in this section. (In the facts of this example, no vesting requirements were specified; in such cases, the employees would not have to provide future service in order to earn the right to the options, and the entire cost would be recognized upon grant.)

A big advantage of the binomial model is that it can value an option that is exercisable before the end of its term (an American-style option). This is the style that employee share-based compensation arrangements normally take. FASB prefers the binomial model, because it can incorporate the unique features of employee stock options. Two key features that FASB recommends that companies incorporate into the binomial model are vesting restrictions and early exercise. Doing so, however, requires that the reporting entity had previous experience with employee behaviors (e.g., gained with past employee option programs) that would provide it with a basis for making estimates of future behavior. In some instances, there will be no obvious bases upon which such assumptions can be developed.

The binomial model permits the specification of more assumptions than does the Black-Scholes-Merton, which has generated the perception that the binomial will more readily be manipulated so as to result in lower option values, and hence lower compensation costs, than the Black-Scholes-Merton. But this is not necessarily the case: switching from Black-Scholes-Merton to the binomial model can increase, maintain, or decrease the option's value. Having the ability to specify additional parameters, however, probably does give management greater flexibility and, accordingly, will present additional challenges for the auditors who must attest to the financial statement effects of management's specification of these variables.

To calculate option values using either the Black-Scholes-Merton or binomial models without the aid of computer software would be very difficult, but hardly impossible. Fortunately, reasonably priced software is now widely available to perform these calculations. What managers must do is determine the assumptions that should be used to create an unbiased, representative value of the options. We now turn to specific examples of accounting for share-based compensation as required under ASC 718.

NOTE: All examples ignore deferred tax effects for simplicity.

Example—Accounting for stock options for a publicly held entity

Options are granted to corporate officers to purchase 10,000 shares of $1 par stock at a price of $50 per share, which is equal to the current market price. The options may not be exercised until three years from the grant date (that is, they vest in three years). ASC 718 provides that public companies must use the fair value method to measure compensation cost associated with share-based equity programs. This means that it will be necessary to determine the expected volatility of the share price over the service period. Assume that either a lattice model or Black-Scholes-Merton has been used and that the fair value per option has been determined to be $7. Past experience suggests that forfeitures will be 4% per year, so that compensation cost under ASC 718 will be based on the net number of shares expected to vest, given as (.96 × .96 × .96 =) .885. Total share-based compensation will be ($7 × .885 × 10,000 =) $61,932. The annual entries would be:

Compensation cost	20,644	
Additional paid-in capital		20,644

If all the options are subsequently exercised, the derived proceeds of the stock issuance will be $566,000. The entry would be

Cash	500,000 (option price)	
Additional paid-in capital	61,932	
Common stock		10,000 (par)
Additional paid-in capital		551,932 (excess)

Example—Accounting for stock options for a nonpublic entity that is not an SEC registrant and elects the calculated value method

Options are granted to corporate officers to purchase 10,000 shares of $1 par stock at a price of $50 per share, which is the current market price. The options may not be exercised until three years from the grant date (that is, they vest in three years). ASC 718 provides that nonpublic companies may use a surrogate measure of fair value, called calculated fair value, when it is not possible to determine the expected volatility of the share price over the service period. Essentially, this requires that a relevant industry sector-specific index be identified for use in place of the volatility factor in the normal Black-Scholes-Merton or lattice models.

In this case, the reporting entity identifies such an index and proceeds to compute a value of $6.60 per option. The total compensation cost thereby calculated, $66,000, is accrued over the three-year period ratably. The annual entries would be:

Compensation cost	22,000	
Additional paid-in capital		22,000

If all the options are subsequently exercised, the derived proceeds of the stock issuance will be $566,000. The entry would be:

Cash	500,000 (option price)	
Additional paid-in capital	66,000	
Common stock		10,000 (par)
Additional paid-in capital		556,000 (excess)

Example—Accounting for stock options for a nonpublic entity that is not an SEC registrant and elects the intrinsic value method

As discussed above, nonpublic companies are permitted to elect the intrinsic value method of accounting for the cost of share-based compensation plans. Using this method, the intrinsic value must be measured at each reporting date, and used to accrue compensation cost for the period.

Assume again that options are granted to corporate officers to purchase 10,000 shares of $1 par stock at a price of $50 per share, which is the current market price. The options may not be exercised until three years from the grant date. These options have no intrinsic value ($50 – $50 = 0) at the grant date. The intrinsic value method and fair value method require the same measurement date (grant date) for shares and similar instruments whose fair value does not differ from their intrinsic value (and instruments with no time value). This example assumes there is no forfeiture before vesting occurs. Because of the company's decision to use the intrinsic value method, its share options are recognized at intrinsic value at each reporting date through the date of settlement, and the periodic adjustment in intrinsic value, prorated over the service period, is included in compensation cost for that period. Consequently, the compensation cost recognized each year of the three-year requisite service period will vary based on changes in the share option's intrinsic value. For example, assume that at the end of the first year, stock is valued at $55 per share, resulting in a ($55 – $50) $5 intrinsic value per share—thus, a total value of $50,000 for the award. In the first year, the compensation cost would be 1/3 of $50,000. This entry would be:

Compensation cost	16,667	
Additional paid-in capital		16,667

Assume now that at the end of the second year the stock is valued at $53 per share, and thus the intrinsic value is ($53 – $50 =) $3 per share option, for an intrinsic value of the award of $30,000 at that date. The intrinsic value of the award has declined by ($50,000 – $30,000 =) $20,000. Because services for two of the three years of service have now been rendered, the company must recognize *cumulative* compensation cost for two-thirds of the intrinsic value of the award, or ($30,000 × 2/3 =) $20,000. Because the company already recognized $16,667 in the first year, only $3,333 in further compensation cost is to be recognized in the second.

Compensation cost	3,333	
Additional paid-in capital		3,333

Note that, depending on the change in intrinsic value from the prior reporting date, the current period could be credited with *negative* compensation expense. To illustrate, assume instead that at the end of the second year, the stock is valued at $52 per share, for an intrinsic value of $20,000. Since two years of the three-year service period have elapsed, the cumulative compensation cost to be recognized is ($20,000 × 2/3 =) $13,333. Because the company already recognized $16,667 in the first year, *negative* $3,333 compensation cost is to be recognized in the second year.

Additional paid-in capital	3,333	
Compensation cost		3,333

Example of fair value accounting for stock options with cliff vesting—measurement and grant date the same

Options are granted to corporate officers to purchase 10,000 shares of $1 par stock at a price of $50 per share, which is also the market price on the grant date. The options may not be exercised until three years from the grant date, and only if the employees remain employed through that date. The company has no reason to expect that any of the options will be forfeited by the employees to whom they are granted (i.e., after the completion of the service period). The company uses the following assumptions to apply the binomial model:

Share options granted	10,000
Employees granted options	100
Expected forfeitures per year	3.0%
Share price at the grant date	$50
Exercise price	$50
Par value per share	$1
Number of years to vest	3 years
Contractual term (CT) of options	10 years
Risk-free interest rate over CT	2 to 5%
Expected volatility over CT	40 to 700%
Expected dividend yield	1.0%
Suboptimal exercise factor	2

Given these assumptions needed to construct a binomial model to value the options, a fair value estimate of approximately $6 per option is determined (details not presented). It is estimated that 3% of employees will turn over each year during the service period. The number of share options expected to vest is estimated at the grant date of (10,000 × .97 × .97 × .97 =) $9,127. The estimated fair value of the award on the grant date would be (9,127 × $6 =) $54,762. The entry to record the compensation cost [($54,762 ÷ 3) = $18,254] in each of the three years is:

Compensation cost	18,254	
Additional paid-in capital		18,254

If in the first year the actual forfeiture rate is 6% instead of the 3% expected rate, and management determines that the forfeiture rate should change to 6%, then in the second year an adjustment would be needed. The revised estimate of the number of options expected to vest is (10,000 × .94 × .94 × .94 =) 8,306. The revised cumulative compensation cost would be (8,306 × $6 =) $49,836. The cumulative adjustment to reflect adjustment of the forfeiture rate is the difference between two-thirds of the revised cost of the award and the cost already recognized in the first year The related entries and computations are:

Revised total compensation cost	$49,836
Revised cumulative cost as of the end of year 1	$16,112
Cost already recognized in year 1	$18,254
Adjustment to cost at the end of year 1	$ (2,142)

The related journal entries are:

Compensation cost	2,142	
Additional paid-in capital		2,142

Entries in years 2 and 3

Compensation cost	16,112	
Additional paid-in capital		16,112

At the end of the third year, the company would examine actual forfeitures and make any necessary adjustments to reflect compensation cost for the number of shares actually vested. Assuming vesting equals expected, the journal entry at exercise of the options would be:

Cash	500,000 (option price)	
Additional paid-in capital	49,836	
Common stock		10,000 (par)
Additional paid-in capital		539,836 (excess)

The difference between the market price of the shares and the exercise price at the date of exercise is deductible for tax purposes because the share options do not qualify as incentive stock options. The realized tax benefits result in a credit to additional paid-in capital and a reduction in the deferred tax asset.

The statement of cash flows, as amended by ASC 718, requires that the cash flow benefit that results from the tax benefit be classified as a cash inflow from financing activities and a cash outflow from operating activities.

Example of accounting for stock options with graded vesting—measurement and grant date the same

In a shift from the position espoused in the exposure draft, ASC 718 requires each reporting entity to make a policy decision about whether to recognize compensation cost for an award with only service conditions that has a graded vesting schedule either (1) on a straight-line basis over the requisite service period for each separately vesting portion of the award as if the award was, in-substance, multiple awards, or (2) on a straight-line basis over the requisite service period for the entire award (that is, over the requisite service period of the last separately vesting portion of the award). However, ASC 718 requires that the amount of compensation cost recognized at any date must at least equal the portion of the grant-date value of the award that is vested at that date.

For this example, assume the basic facts from the prior example, but now the 10,000 options vest according to a graded schedule of 25% for the first and second years of service and 50% for the third year. Using the 3% annual employee turnover forfeiture rate, 300 options are expected to never vest, leaving 9,700 options expected to vest at 25% of the award—or 2,425 options vested. In the second year, it is anticipated that another 3% will be forfeited, leaving 9,409 to vest at 25% of the award—or 2,352 options vested. In the final year another 3% are forfeited and vesting occurs at 50% of the remaining—or 4,563 vested options. (Data upon which value per option amounts are derived are not presented in this example.)

Year	*Vested option*	*Value per option*	*Compensation cost*
1	2,425	$5.00	$12,125
2	2,352	$5.50	12,936
3	4,563	$6.00	27,378
	9,340		$52,439

The value of the option is determined separately for different vesting periods after which exercise might occur. Thus, the compensation cost associated with the options is less in the earlier years, as reflected in the table above. Compensation cost is recognized over the periods of requisite service during which each group of share options is earned. In the first year, therefore, compensation cost is [$12,125 + ($12,936 ÷ 2) + ($27,378 ÷ 3) =] $27,719. The journal entry for the first year would be:

Compensation cost	27,719	
Additional paid-in capital		27,719

Accounting for Stock Appreciation Rights and Tandem Plans

Background. The accounting for variable stock plans is addressed by ASC 718. Under this standard, share-based compensation arrangements that provide for cash payments or that give to grantees the choice of receiving stock or cash in settlement are accounted for as liabilities, not equity, as compensation is accrued over the requisite service period. Publicly held entities are required to measure liabilities incurred to employees in share-based payment transactions at fair value. Nonpublic entities, on the other hand, may elect to measure their liabilities to employees incurred in share-based payment transactions at their intrinsic value.

Whether measured at fair value (using an option-pricing model such as Black-Scholes-Merton or binomial) or at intrinsic value (measured simply as the excess of market or other defined value over reference value as of the date of the statement of financial position), these amounts are updated as of each financial reporting date. Thus, when share-based compensation plans give rise to liabilities, these are continually updated as to value, whereas under the fair value measurement approach to equity instruments arising from such compensation plans, value is assessed as of the grant date in most instances, never later to be revised.

Determining whether a share-based payment should be categorized as a liability requires close attention to the guidance of ASC 718, which invokes the requirements of ASC 480. It states that, for example, a puttable share (giving the grantee the right to demand the issuer to redeem it) awarded to an employee as compensation is to be classified as a liability if either (1) the repurchase feature permits the employee to avoid bearing the risks and rewards normally associated with equity share ownership for a reasonable period of time from the date the requisite service is rendered and the share is issued, or (2) it is probable that the employer would prevent the employee from bearing those risks and rewards for a reasonable period of time from the date the share is issued. For this purpose, a period of six months or more is defined as a reasonable period of time.

Note that a share that is mandatorily or optionally redeemable upon the occurrence of a defined contingency, such as an initial public offering by the grantor entity, would not make this share-based payment a liability, unless the contingency were deemed probable of occurrence within a reasonable period of time. For example, if the entity had begun the regulatory approval and registration process, this might trigger liability classification.

ASC 718 stipulates that options or similar instruments on shares are to be categorized as liabilities if the underlying shares are classified as liabilities (which is logical) or if the reporting entity is subject to a requirement to transfer cash or other assets under any circumstances in order to settle the option. However, ASC 718-10-35-15 holds that a cash settlement feature that can be exercised only upon the occurrence of a contingent event that is outside the employee's control does not meet the condition set forth by ASC 718.

Furthermore, an option or similar instrument that is first classified as equity, but subsequently becomes a liability because the contingent cash settlement event becomes probable of occurring, is to be accounted for similar to a modification from an equity to liability award. Accordingly, on the date the contingent event becomes *probable* of occurring (thus triggering reclassification of the award as a liability) the entity recognizes a share-based liability equal to the portion of the award attributed to past service (reflecting any provision for acceleration of vesting) multiplied by the award's fair value on that date. To the extent the liability equals or is less than the amount previously recognized in equity, that is the amount transferred from equity to the liability. To the extent that the liability exceeds the amount previously recognized in equity, the excess is recognized as additional compensation cost in that period. The total recognized compensation cost for an award with a contingent cash settlement feature must at least equal the fair value of the award at the grant date.

A puttable share that does not meet either of the foregoing conditions is to be classified as equity. Options or similar instruments on shares are to be classified as liabilities if (1) the underlying shares are classified as liabilities, or (2) the reporting entity can be required under any circumstances to settle the option or similar instrument by transferring cash or other assets. If the entity grants an option to an employee that, upon exercise, would be settled by issuing a mandatorily redeemable share, the option must be classified as a liability.

According to ASC 718, a freestanding financial instrument ceases to be subject to this standard and becomes subject to the recognition and measurement requirements of ASC 480 or other applicable GAAP when the rights conveyed by the instrument to the holder are no longer dependent on the holder being an employee of the entity. Thus, once the requisite service has been provided and the grantee has, say, elected to receive stock or another instrument, guidance on the appropriate accounting would be given by ASC 480. For example, a mandatorily redeemable share becomes subject to ASC 480 or other applicable GAAP when an employee (1) has rendered the requisite service in exchange for the instrument and (2) could terminate the employment relationship and receive that share. Similarly, a share option or similar instrument that is not transferable and whose contractual term is shortened upon employment termination continues to be subject to ASC 718 until the rights conveyed by the instrument to the holder are no longer dependent on the holder being an employee of the entity (generally, when the instrument is exercised).

An award may be indexed to a factor beyond the entity's share price. ASC 718 holds that, if that additional factor is not a market, performance, or service condition, the award is to be classified as a liability. In such a case, the additional factor is to be reflected in estimating the fair value of the award. An example of such a circumstance would be an award of options whose exercise price is indexed to the market price of the commodity (e.g., wheat or gold). Another example: a share award that will vest based on the appreciation in the price of that commodity; such an award is indexed to both the value of that commodity and the issuing entity's shares. If an award is so indexed, the relevant factors (expected commodity price change) should be included in the fair value estimate of the award. ASC 718 states that the award would be classified as a liability even if the entity granting the share-based payment instrument were a producer of the commodity whose price changes are part or all of the conditions that affect an award's vesting conditions or fair value.

Stock appreciation rights and similar instruments. Stock Appreciation Rights (SARs) are a popular means of providing share-based compensation awards to employees. Essentially, the bonus arrangement is to pay employees the amount by which the share price at a defined date (say, three years hence) exceeds what it was at the measurement date. Depending on the plan, the award may be payable in the entity's shares, in cash, or in either at the option of the grantee. If the optionee has the right to demand cash or the SAR is payable in cash only, the grantor entity recognizes a liability for the accrued compensation.

If the entity is publicly held, measurement at fair value is required, with revaluation at each reporting date through final settlement. For nonpublicly held entities, an election must be made to use fair value or intrinsic value—but again, in either case, remeasurement at each reporting date until final settlement is required.

Example of accounting for SARs—Share-based liabilities

The company grants SARs with the same terms and conditions used in the examples above. Each SAR entitles the holder to receive an amount in cash equal to the increase in value of one share of company stock over $50. Using the same assumptions and option-pricing model, the fair value of the share options is computed to be $6 per SAR (details not presented). The awards cliff-vest at the end of three years. The forfeitures are expected to be 3% a year: thus, SARs expected to vest are (10,000 × .97 × .97 × .97 =) 9,127, and the fair value of the award at the beginning of the first year is (9,127 × $6 =) $54,762. It is assumed that expected and actual forfeitures are the same. The share-based compensation liability at the end of the first year is ($54,762 ÷ 3 =) $18,254. The journal entry for the first year is:

Compensation cost	18,254	
Share-based compensation SAR liability		18,254

Under ASC 718, compensation arising in connection with share-based liabilities must be valued at fair value at each reporting date. At the end of the second year, the estimated fair value is assumed to be $10 per SAR. Therefore, the award's fair value is (9,270 × $10 =) $91,270, and the corresponding liability at that date is ($91,270 × 2/3 =) $60,847 because service has now been provided for two of the three years required. Compensation cost recognized for the award in the second year is ($60,847 – $18,254 =) $42,593. The journal entry for the second year is:

Compensation cost	42,593	
Share-based compensation SAR liability		42,593

At the end of the third year, the estimated fair value is assumed to be $9 per SAR. Therefore, the award's fair value is (9,270 × $9 =) $83,430 and the corresponding liability at that date is the same because the award is fully vested. Compensation cost for the third year is ($83,430 – $42,593 – $18,254 =) $22,583. The journal entry for the third year is:

Compensation cost	22,583	
Share-based compensation SAR liability		22,583

Stock SARs. If the SARs were to be redeemed (only) in common stock of the entity, "Stock rights outstanding" (a paid-in capital account) would replace the liability account in the above entries. Fair value would be assessed at the grant date (measurement date), and then not altered over the time to final settlement, consistent with how other equity compensation awards are measured under ASC 718.

Tandem plans. Often stock option plans and SAR are joined in tandem plans, under the terms of which the exercise of one automatically cancels the other. In the absence of evidence to the contrary, however, the presumption is that the SAR, not the options, will be exercised. If the SAR portion of the tandem plan is such that classification as a liability is required, as described above, then remeasurement through the settlement date is required.

Modifications of Awards of Equity Instruments

In some instances awards previously issued but not yet settled are later modified in ways that may or may not change the classification (e.g., liability to equity). ASC 718 requires that modification of the terms or conditions of an equity award is to be treated as an exchange of the original award for a new award. In substance, the event is accounted for as if the entity repurchases the original instrument by issuing a new instrument of equal or greater value, incurring additional compensation cost for any incremental value.

Incremental compensation cost in such circumstances is to be measured as the excess, if any, of the fair value of the modified award—determined in accordance with the provisions of ASC 718—over the fair value of the original award immediately before its terms are modified.

These measures are to be based on the share price and other pertinent factors at the modification date. Any effect of the modification on the number of instruments expected to vest is also to be reflected in determining incremental compensation cost. The estimate at the modification date of the portion of the award expected to vest may also be subsequently adjusted, if necessary, as estimates or experience may dictate prior to final settlement.

The total recognized compensation cost for an equity award will at least equal the fair value of the award at the grant date, except for those instances when, at the date of the modification, the performance or service conditions of the original award are not expected to be satisfied. Accordingly, the total compensation cost measured at the date of a modification will be (1) the portion of the grant-date fair value of the original award for which the requisite service is expected to be rendered (or has already been rendered) at that date, plus (2) the incremental cost resulting from the modification.

The change in compensation cost for an equity award measured at intrinsic value (if elected for nonpublicly held companies) is to be measured by comparing the intrinsic value of the modified award, if any, with the intrinsic value of the original award, if any, immediately before the modification.

If a modification results in what had been a liability award becoming an equity award, the amount of the fair value (or implicit value, if such were elected as a measurement strategy by a nonpublic company), the amount becomes "fixed" as of the modification date, and this will differ from the amount that would have been recognized had the award been classified as equity at inception. On the other hand, if an award was originally equity and after modification becomes a liability, to the extent that the liability equals or is less than the amount recognized in equity for the original award, the offsetting debit is a charge to equity. To the extent that the liability exceeds the amount recognized in equity for the original award, the excess is recognized as compensation cost.

Example of a liability-to-equity modification

Assume that a cash payment SAR plan is created, with features similar to earlier examples (10,000 SARs granted, with three-year term, 3% forfeiture per year expectation). The share-based compensation liability is (9,127 × \$10 ÷ 3 =) \$30,423, based on reporting date fair value measurement. On January 1 of the second year, the company modifies the SAR by replacing the cash-settlement feature with a net-share settlement feature, which converts the award from a liability award to an equity award, because there is no longer an obligation to settle for cash, or an obligation classified as a liability per ASC 480. For the equity award, fair value is to be measured at grant date only. Per ASC 718, when no other terms are altered by the modification, the fair value at the modification date is used to measure the amount of the total compensation to be awarded in equity instruments.

The journal entry to reclassify the liability to equity would be:

Share-based compensation SAR liability	30,423	
Additional paid-in capital—SAR		30,423

Since no further remeasurement would be permitted, additional compensation cost of \$30,423 per year will be recorded at the end of the second and third years, with credits to the additional paid-in capital account. In this example, total compensation cost was greater because the effective measurement date was the end of the first year, but it could also have happened that compensation cost was reduced for the same reason.

Example of an equity-to-liability modification

Assume that a SAR plan, payable in shares, is created, with features similar to earlier examples (10,000 SARs granted, with three-year term, 3% forfeiture per year expectation). Using a valuation model, the amount of compensation is determined to be $40,000 in total, computed at grant date. At the end of the first year, compensation expense and additional paid-in capital of $13,333 is recorded, based on completion of one of the three years' required service. At that date the fair value of the SARs amounts to $45,000. If the plan is amended at the start of the second year to offer grantees the right to a cash payout, the equity must be reclassified to liability and the value must be remeasured at each reporting date. At the time of modification, since the fair value exceeds what had been accrued, additional compensation cost must be recognized. The entry would be:

Additional paid-in capital—SAR	13,333	
Compensation cost	1,667	
Share-based compensation—SAR liability		15,000

On the other hand, if the fair value of the liability for the SAR at the modification date had been only $30,000, the difference between the amount accrued in the first year and the modified value would have been left in the additional paid-in capital account. The entry follows:

Additional paid-in capital—SAR	10,000	
Share-based compensation—SAR liability		10,000

A share-based payment award may also be modified as a result of an acquisition. ASC 805 describes the accounting for several instances where an acquirer exchanges its share-based payment awards for rewards held by the employees of an acquiree. If the acquiring entity replaces an acquiree's share-based awards when it is not obligated to do so, then all of the fair-value replacement cost is to be recognized as postcombination compensation expense. If the acquirer's replacement award requires some additional employee service, a portion of the replacement award's fair-value cost should be attributed to postcombination compensation expense.

Accounting for Income Tax Effects of Share-Based Compensation

Under US income tax laws, the amount that is deductible in connection with a share-based compensation arrangement is limited to intrinsic value. This is generally defined by the amount by which the fair (market) value of the compensation exceeds the amount paid, if any, by the recipient, at the exercise date (not the grant date). For example, if an option grant is made when the underlying stock is trading at $34, and the option is exercisable at that price, and it is later exercised when the stock is trading at $55, the deductible amount will be $21 per share, based on the *intrinsic value* of the option as of the exercise date, which becomes observable only upon actual exercise. However, under ASC 718, compensation expense will have been recognized for the fair value of the option when granted, computed using either the Black-Scholes-Merton or lattice model as illustrated earlier in this section. Depending on other facts, that option value may have been $5, $10, or some other amount per share; it would not, however, be the same as the intrinsic amount other than by sheer coincidence.

Additionally, the timing of the compensation expense recognition will differ between tax and financial reporting. For financial reporting, expense is recognized over the expected service period, as explained above. For tax, the expense is deductible at the actual exercise date. Options not exercised (i.e., forfeited) thus never give rise to taxable deductions, whereas under GAAP the compensation cost would have been expensed.

It is thus inevitable that both the timing and the amounts of compensation expense related to share-based compensation will differ. To the extent that these are timing differences, interperiod tax allocation (deferred tax accounting) will be appropriate. The cumulative amount of compensation cost that will result in a tax deduction is to be considered a deductible temporary difference. This applies both for instruments classified as equity and for those categorized as liabilities. Any compensation cost recognized in the financial statements for instruments that will not result in a tax deduction should not be considered to result in a deductible temporary difference under ASC 740.

In general, the fair value of stock-based compensation, which is computed at grant date and recognized over the vesting period as compensation cost in the financial statements, will not be tax deductible currently, giving rise to deferred tax benefits measured with reference to the book compensation expense recognized. Ultimately, when the employee's options vest and are exercised, the company is able to deduct the intrinsic value, measured by the spread between fair value on exercise date and exercise price. To the extent this exceeds the fair value of the stock-based compensation recognized as GAAP-basis expense, the tax effect of that excess tax deduction is treated as a contribution to paid-in capital. If (less likely, but quite possible) the tax deduction is lower than the compensation already recognized for financial reporting purposes, this shortfall in tax benefits is additional compensation cost—in effect, the employer entity incurred higher compensation cost in connection with the share option program since it received less than the anticipated tax benefits related thereto.

If the exercise results in a tax deduction prior to the actual realization of the related tax benefit—because the entity, for example, has a net operating loss carryforward—then the tax benefit and the credit to additional paid-in capital for the excess deduction would not be recognized until that deduction reduces taxes payable.

However, to the extent that the excess stems from a reason *other* than changes in fair value of the entity's shares between the measurement date for accounting purposes (grant date, generally) and the later measurement date for income tax purposes (exercise date), that portion of the tax effect is to be reported in income (i.e., in the tax provision). For example, a change in the tax rate could result in such a difference.

Differences between the deductible temporary difference that arises and the tax deduction that would have resulted based on the current fair value of the entity's shares should not be considered either in measuring the gross deferred tax asset or in determining the need for a valuation allowance created by the application of ASC 718.

If there should be an excess of cumulative compensation cost recognized for financial reporting purposes over the tax deductible amount (e.g., due to options lapsing unexercised), the write-off of the deferred tax asset (net of valuation allowance, if any) is first to be offset against any remaining additional paid-in capital from previous awards accounted for under the fair value method; any remaining excess should be recognized in income (the tax provision). The additional paid-in capital available to absorb tax effects is referred to as the *APIC pool.*

Consistent with the treatment of excess tax deductions for share-based compensation as being essentially similar to capital contributions, ASC 718 requires that the realized tax benefit applicable to the excess of the deductible amount over the compensation cost recognized under GAAP be reported in the cash flow statement as both a cash inflow from financing activities and a cash outflow from operating activities. This is required whether the cash flow statement is being presented under the direct method or the indirect method.

It is possible that an entity has issued dividends to employees holding nonvested shares, nonvested share units, or outstanding options. If so, it should recognize the income tax benefit as an increase to additional paid-in-capital, but only if the deduction reduces income taxes payable.

Other ASC 718 Matters

The most common share-based compensation arrangements have been presented. Other more complicated awards have been developed. Some of these are presented below. For a further discussion with examples refer to ASC 718.

Share options with performance conditions and/or market conditions. Some option arrangements provide grants of share options with a performance condition. These types of plans permit employees to vest in differing numbers of options depending on the increase in market value of one of the company's products (or other condition) over a vesting period. These performance conditions can include factors such as market share increases, passing clinical trials, and other performance goals.

In addition to performance conditions, market conditions may also affect the option arrangements. These would include such things as indexing share prices to an industry group and the exercise price of options tied to this index. Therefore, the exercise price could go up or down depending on how the index performs. Arrangements exist for share units to have both performance and market conditions. These are accounted for in the same way as other options. The difficulty is in determining the fair values, as there are more factors contributing to uncertainty. These factors can, however, be modeled in a binomial valuation model.

Other modifications of share option awards. A company may modify the vesting conditions of an award. The accounting treatment for these modifications depends on the probability of vesting under the original conditions or the modified conditions. Other modifications are whether SAR will be settled in cash or equity or some combination, different from the original plan assumptions. A modification of vesting conditions is accounted for based on the principles set forth in ASC 718. Illustrations of different potential modifications are illustrated in ASC 718-10-55.

Other types of share-based compensation awards covered in ASC 718. Other share awards that ASC 718 addresses are outlined below.

- *Share award with a clawback feature*. These are restrictions on the employee's subsequent employment with a direct competitor, that if violated, cause the ex-employee to return the value of the share award to the company.
- *Tandem plan—share options or cash SAR*. Employees are granted awards with two separate components, in which exercise of one component cancels the other.
- *Tandem plan—phantom shares or share options*. Similar to the plan above, but the employee's choice of which component to exercise depends on the relative value of the components when the award is exercised.
- *Look-back share options*. Share options awarded under Section 423 of the Internal Revenue Code, which provides that employees will not be immediately taxed on the difference between the market price of the stock and a discounted purchase price if certain requirements are met.
- *Employee share purchase plans*. Employee share purchase plans are not compensatory if their terms are no more favorable than those available to all holders of the same class of shares and if all employees that meet limited employment qualifications may participate in the plan on an equitable basis.
- *Escrowed share arrangements*. The SEC has stated in ASC 718-10-S99 that it considers the release of shares from an escrowed share arrangement based on performance-related criteria to be compensation.
- *Book value share purchase plans (nonpublic companies only)*. Companies with two classes of stock—one of which is available to all employees and the price is based on book value.
- *Voluntary (or involuntary) change to fair-value-based method (nonpublic companies only)*. A nonpublic company elects as accounting policy the intrinsic value method and grants share awards to employees. Subsequently, the accounting for the value of these awards is changed to fair value because it is preferable under GAAP. Estimating grant

date values is very difficult in hindsight. Therefore, these companies do not have to retrospectively apply fair value methods to unvested awards at the date of change.

- *Certain instruments become subject to ASC 480.* Certain instruments will become subject to ASC 480 when an employee could terminate service and receive or retain the fair value of the instrument for the remaining contractual term of that instrument.

Reload feature and reload option. A reload feature provides for automatic grants of additional options whenever an employee exercises previously granted options using the entity's shares, rather than cash, to satisfy the exercise price. At the time of exercise using shares, the employee is automatically granted a new option, called a reload option, for the shares used to exercise the previous option.

Example of reload options

Mr. Jones has 6,000 shares of ABC Company's $1 par value common stock, as well as options to purchase an additional 8,000 shares at an exercise price of $12. It will cost Jones $96,000 to exercise the options. The current market price of ABC stock is $16, so he trades in his existing 6,000 shares, which have a market value of $96,000, to purchase 8,000 shares with his options. The option plan has a reload feature, so ABC issues 6,000 replacement options (matching the number of shares traded in), for which the exercise price is set at the current market value of $16. ABC records the stock sale with the following entry:

Treasury stock	96,000	
Common stock		8,000
Additional paid-in capital		88,000

Jones elects to exercise his options when the market value of ABC Company's stock reaches $24. At an exercise price of $16, it will again cost Jones $96,000 to purchase shares. At the current market price of $24, Jones can trade in 4,000 of his existing shares to acquire new shares. However, he chooses to trade in only 3,000 shares and pay for the remaining options with cash. ABC records the stock sale with the following entry:

Cash	24,000	
Treasury stock	72,000	
Common stock		6,000
Additional paid-in capital		90,000

The reload feature still applies, but now ABC only issues 3,000 replacement options, which matches the number of shares Jones traded in to acquire new shares. The new options are assigned at an exercise price of $24, to match the market value on the grant date.

Effect of employer payroll taxes. ASC 718-10-25-22 discusses (1) when a liability for employer payroll taxes on employee stock compensation should be recognized in the employer's financial statements and (2) how that liability should be measured. A liability for employee payroll taxes on stock compensation should be recognized and measured on the date of the event triggering the measurement and payment of the tax to the taxing authority (which would generally be the exercise date).

Payments in lieu of dividends on options. Normally dividends are not paid on shares that have not been issued; thus, unexercised options do not gain the benefit of any dividends declared on the underlying stock. However, an entity can choose to pay dividend equivalents on options.

Since the codification requires, effectively, that forfeitures be estimated and accounted for over the service period, in the author's view it would be consistent to likewise charge retained earnings only for the estimated number of options to be exercised (changing from period to period, if a lattice model is used), with the remainder of any payments in lieu of dividends charged currently to compensation expense.

Example of payments in lieu of dividends on options

Gary Ironworks declares dividends of $2 per share of common stock. Its president, Mr. Jones, has 5,000 unvested options. Gary's board of directors chooses to pay Mr. Jones dividends on the 5,000 shares represented by the unvested options, on the assumption that all the options will vest. The resulting entry follows:

Retained earnings	10,000	
Dividends payable		10,000

There are several other employees who have 20,000 unvested options. The board also declares dividends for these options, with the provision that dividends paid can be retained even if the associated options do not vest. The controller expects that only 70% of the options will vest, so she creates the following entry to charge the other 30% of the dividends to compensation expense:

Retained earnings	28,000	
Compensation expense	12,000	
Dividends payable		40,000

Disclosure requirements under ASC 718. For a company to achieve the objectives of ASC 718, the minimum information needed to achieve disclosure objectives is set forth below.

- A description of the share-based payment arrangements, including the terms of the awards. A nonpublic company should disclose its policy for measuring compensation cost.
- The most recent income statement should provide the number and weighted-average exercise prices of the share options and equity instruments.
- Each year for which an income statement is provided, a company should provide the weighted-average grant-date fair value of equity options and the intrinsic value of options exercised during the year.
- For fully vested share options and those expected to vest at date of the latest statement of financial position, the company should provide the number, weighted-average exercise price, aggregate intrinsic value, and contractual terms of options outstanding and currently exercisable.
- If more than one share-based plan is in effect, the information should be provided separately for different types of awards.
- For each year for which an income statement is provided, companies should provide the following:
  - Companies that do not use the intrinsic value method should provide a description of the method of determining fair value and a description of the assumptions used.
  - Total compensation cost for share-based payment arrangements, including tax benefits and capitalization of compensation costs, should be stated.
  - Descriptions of significant modifications and numbers of employees affected should also be provided.
- On the date of the latest statement of financial position, the total compensation cost related to nonvested awards not yet recognized and the period over which they are expected to be recognized.

- The amount of cash received from exercise of share-based compensation and the amount of cash used to settle equity instruments should be disclosed.
- Description of the company's policy for issuing shares upon share options exercise, including the source of the shares.

Accounting for Stock Issued to ESOPs

There has been a steady increase in the number of corporations that are entirely or partially employee-owned under terms of ESOPs. The accounting for ESOP is governed by ASC 718-40.

Depending on what motivated the creation of the ESOP (e.g., estate planning by the controlling shareholder, expanding the capital base of the entity, rewarding and motivating the work force), the sponsor's shares may be contributed to the plan in annual installments in a block of shares from the sponsor, or shares from an existing shareholder may be purchased by the plan.

ESOPs are defined contribution plans in which shares of the sponsoring entity are awarded to employees as additional compensation. Briefly, ESOPs are created by a sponsoring corporation which either funds the plan directly (unleveraged ESOP) or, more commonly, facilitates the borrowing of money either directly from an outside lender (directly leveraged ESOP) or from the employer, which in turn will borrow from an outside lender (indirectly leveraged ESOP).

Borrowings from outside lenders may or may not be guaranteed by the sponsor. However, since effectively the only source of funds for debt repayment is future contributions by the sponsor, GAAP requires that the ESOP's debt be considered debt of the sponsor even absent a guarantee.

When recording the direct or indirect borrowings by the ESOP as debt in the sponsor's statement of financial position, a debit to a contra equity account, not to an asset, is also reported. This is necessary since the borrowings represent a commitment (morally if not always legally) to make future contributions to the plan and this is certainly not a claim to resources. Significantly, this results in a "double hit" to the sponsor's statement of financial position (i.e., the recording of a liability and the reduction of net stockholders' equity), which is often an unanticipated and unpleasant surprise to plan sponsors. This contra equity account is referred to as "unearned ESOP shares" in accordance with provisions of ASC 718-40. If the sponsor itself lends funds to the ESOP without a "mirror loan" from an outside lender, this loan should not be reported in the employer's statement of financial position as debt, although the debit should still be reported as a contra equity account.

As the ESOP services the debt, using contributions made by the sponsor and/or dividends received on sponsor shares held by the plan, it reflects the reduction of the obligation by reducing both the debt and the contra equity account on its statement of financial position. Simultaneously, income and thus retained earnings will be impacted as the contributions to the plan are reported in the sponsor's current statement of earnings. Thus, the "double hit" is eliminated, but net worth continues to reflect the economic fact that compensation costs have been incurred.

The interest cost component of debt service must be separated from the remaining compensation expense. That is, the sponsor's income statement should reflect the true character of the expenses being incurred, rather than aggregating the entire amount into a category which might have been denoted as "ESOP contribution."

In a leveraged ESOP, shares held serve as collateral for the debt and are not allocated to employees until the debt is retired. In general, shares must be allocated by the end of the year in which the debt is repaid. However, to satisfy the tax laws, the allocation of shares may take place at a faster pace than the retirement of the principal portion of the debt.

Under ASC 718-40, the cost of ESOP shares allocated is measured based upon the fair value on the release date for purposes of reporting compensation expense in the sponsor's income statements. This is in contradistinction to the actual historical cost of the shares to the plan.

Furthermore, dividends paid on unallocated shares (i.e., shares held by the ESOP) are not treated as dividends, but rather must be reported in the sponsor's income statement as compensation cost and/or as interest expense. Of less significance to nonpublic companies is the fact that under the new rules only common shares released and committed to be released are treated as being outstanding, with the resultant need to be considered in calculating both basic and diluted EPS.

Example of accounting for ESOP transactions

Assume that Intrepid Corp. establishes an ESOP, which then borrows $500,000 from Second Interstate Bank. The ESOP then purchases 50,000 shares of Intrepid no-par shares from the company; none of these shares are allocated to individual participants. The entries would be:

Cash	500,000	
Bank loan payable		500,000
Unearned ESOP shares (contra equity)	500,000	
Common stock		500,000

The ESOP then borrows an additional $250,000 from the sponsor, Intrepid, and uses the cash to purchase a further 25,000 shares, all of which are allocated to participants.

Compensation	250,000	
Common stock		250,000

Intrepid Corp. contributes $50,000 to the plan, which the plan uses to service its bank debt, consisting of $40,000 principal reduction and $10,000 interest cost. The debt reduction causes 4,000 shares to be allocated to participants at a time when the average market value had been $12 per share.

Interest expense	10,000	
Bank loan payable	40,000	
Cash		50,000
Compensation	48,000	
Additional paid-in capital		8,000
Unearned ESOP shares		40,000

Dividends of $.10 per share are declared (only the ESOP shares are represented in the following entry, but dividends are paid equally on all outstanding shares):

Retained earnings (on 29,000 shares)	2,900	
Compensation (on 46,000 shares)	4,600	
Dividends payable		7,500

Note that in all the foregoing illustrations the effect of income taxes is ignored. Since the difference between the cost and fair values of shares committed to be released is analogous to differences in the expense recognized for tax and accounting purposes with regard to stock options, the same treatment should be applied. That is, the tax effect should be reported directly in stockholders' equity, rather than in earnings.

Other Sources

See ASC Location – Wiley *GAAP* Chapter…	***For information on…***
From ASC 718-10, *Overall*	
ASC 505-10-25-3	An investor providing stock compensation on behalf of an investee
ASC 805-20-55-50 through 51	Accounting for contractual termination benefits and curtailment losses under employee benefit plans that will be triggered by the consummation of a business combination
ASC 815-40-15-15a	Equity-linked financial instruments issued to investors for purposes of establishing a market-based measure of the grant-date fair value of employee stock options
ASC 815-10-55-46 through 55-48	Stock options in an unrelated entity given to employees
ASC 718-40, *Employee Stock Ownership Plans*	
ASC 718-740-25-6 and 718-740-45-6 and 45-7	Determining the accounting for the effect of income tax factors on employee stock ownership plans

42 ASC 720 OTHER EXPENSES

PERSPECTIVE AND ISSUES

Subtopics

ASC 720, *Other Expenses,* contains nine subtopics:

- ASC 720-10, *Overall*, which merely lists the other subtopics
- ASC 720-15, *Start-Up Costs*
- ASC 720-20, *Insurance Costs*
- ASC 720-25, *Contributions Made*
- ASC 720-30, *Real and Personal Property Taxes*
- ASC 720-35, *Advertising Costs*
- ASC 720-40, *Electronic Equipment Waste Obligations*
- ASC 720-45, *Business and Technology Reengineering*
- ASC 720-50, *Fees Paid to the Federal Government by Pharmaceutical Manufacturers and Health Insurers.*

Scope and Scope Exceptions

ASC 720-15. ASC 720-15 applies to all nongovernmental entities. Routine ongoing efforts to improve existing quality of products, services, or facilities are not start-up costs. The subtopic lists specific activities that are *not* considered start-up costs and should be accounted for in accordance with other existing authoritative literature:

1. Ongoing customer acquisition costs, such as policy acquisition costs (see Subtopic 944-30)
2. Loan origination costs (see Subtopic 310-20)
3. Activities related to routine, ongoing efforts to refine, enrich, or otherwise improve upon the qualities of an existing product, service, process, or facility
4. Activities related to mergers or acquisitions
5. Business process reengineering and information technology transformation costs addressed in Subtopic 720-45

6. Costs of acquiring or constructing long-lived assets and getting them ready for their intended uses (however, the costs of using long-lived assets that are allocated to start-up activities [for example, depreciation of computers] are within the scope of this Subtopic)
7. Costs of acquiring or producing inventory
8. Costs of acquiring intangible assets (however, the costs of using intangible assets that are allocated to start-up activities [for example, amortization of a purchased patent] are within the scope of this Subtopic)
9. Costs related to internally developed assets (for example, internal-use computer software costs) (however, the costs of using those assets that are allocated to start-up activities are within the scope of this Subtopic)
10. Research and development costs that are within the scope of Section 730-10-15
11. Regulatory costs that are within the scope of Section 980-10-15
12. Costs of fundraising incurred by NFPs
13. Costs of raising capital
14. Costs of advertising
15. Costs incurred in connection with existing contracts as stated in paragraph 605-35-25-41(d).

(ASC 720-15-15-4)

ASC 720-25. ASC 720-25 does not apply to:

- Transfers of assets that are in substance purchases of goods or services for equal value. If the donor exchanges assets or services for assets of substantially lower value, the contribution is within the scope of ASC 720-25.
- Transfers where the reporting entity acts as an agent, trustee, or intermediary, and not as a donor.
- Tax exemptions, tax incentives, or tax abatements.
- Transfers of assets from governments to business entities.

(ASC 720-25-15-2)

ASC 720-35. ASC 720-35 applies to all entities, but does not apply to the following transactions:

a. Direct-response advertising (for guidance, see Subtopic 340-20).
b. Advertising costs in interim periods (for guidance, see paragraph 270-10-45-7).
c. Costs of advertising conducted for others under contractual arrangements.
d. Indirect costs that are specifically reimbursable under the terms of a contract.
e. Fundraising by NFPs (however, this Subtopic does apply to advertising activities of NFPs).
f. Customer acquisition activities, other than advertising.
g. The costs of premiums, contest prizes, gifts, and similar promotions, as well as discounts or rebates, including those resulting from the redemption of coupons. (Other costs of coupons and similar items, such as costs of newspaper advertising space, are considered advertising costs.)

(ASC 720-35-15-3)

ASC 720-35 may or may not apply to activities, such as product endorsements and sponsorships of events, which may be performed pursuant to executory contracts. (ASC 720-35-15-4)

DEFINITIONS OF TERMS

Source: ASC 720-25

Contribution. An unconditional transfer of cash or other assets to an entity or a settlement or cancellation of its liabilities in a voluntary nonreciprocal transfer by another entity acting other than as an owner. Those characteristics distinguish contributions from exchange transactions, which are reciprocal transfers in which each party receives and sacrifices approximately equal value; from investments by owners and distributions to owners, which are nonreciprocal transfers between an entity and its owners; and from other nonreciprocal transfers, such as impositions of taxes or legal judgments, fines, and thefts, which are not voluntary transfers. In a contribution transaction, the value, if any, returned to the resource provider is incidental to potential public benefits. In an exchange transaction, the potential public benefits are secondary to the potential proprietary benefits to the resource provider. The term *contribution revenue* is used to apply to transactions that are part of the entity's ongoing major or central activities (revenues), or are peripheral or incidental to the entity (gains). See also Inherent Contribution.

(Source: ASC 720-20)

Incurred but not reported. Losses incurred by the insured entity that have not yet been reported to the insurance entity.

(Source: ASC 720-25)

Inherent contribution. A contribution that results if an entity voluntarily transfers assets (or net assets) or performs services for another entity in exchange for either no assets or for assets of substantially lower value and unstated rights or privileges of a commensurate value are not involved.

Promise to give. A written or oral agreement to contribute cash or other assets to another entity. A promise carries rights and obligations—the recipient of a promise to give has a right to expect that the promised assets will be transferred in the future, and the maker has a social and moral obligation, and generally a legal obligation, to make the promised transfer. A promise to give may be either conditional or unconditional.

(Source: ASC 720-15-20)

Start-up activities. Defined broadly as those one-time activities related to any of the following:

a. Opening a new facility
b. Introducing a new product or service
c. Conducting business in a new territory
d. Conducting business with an entirely new class of customers (for example, a manufacturer who does all of business with retailers attempts to sell merchandise directly to the public) or beneficiary
e. Initiating a new process in an existing facility
f. Commencing some new operation.

(Source: ASC 720-25)

Unconditional promise to give. A promise to give that depends only on passage of time or demand by the promisee for performance.

CONCEPTS, RULES, AND EXAMPLES

ASC 720-10, *Overall*

ASC 720-10 provides no guidance. It merely lists all the subtopics in Topic 720.

ASC 720-15, *Start-Up Costs*

ASC 720-15 provides guidance on financial reporting of start-up costs, including organization costs and requires such costs to be expensed as incurred.

ASC 720-20, *Insurance Costs*

ASC 720-20 provides guidance on:

- Retroactive contracts
- Claims-made contracts
- Multiple-year retrospectively rated contracts.

Guidance for each of the above is in a separate subsection.

The premium paid minus the amount of the premium retained by the insurer is accounted for as a deposit by the insured. This is only to "the extent that an insurance contract or reinsurance contract does not, despite its form, provide for indemnification of the insured or the ceding entity by the insurer or reinsurer against loss or liability." (ASC 720-20-25-1)

ASC 720-25, *Contributions Made*

ASC 720-25 states that contributions made are expenses in the period when the contribution is made. There should also be a decrease in assets or increase in liabilities. ASC 958 contains guidance on conditional contributions.

ASC 720-30, *Real and Personal Property Taxes*

Accrued real estate and personal property taxes represent the unpaid portion of an entity's obligation to a state, county, or other taxing authority that arises from the ownership of real or personal property, respectively. ASC 720-30 indicates that the most acceptable method of accounting for property taxes is a monthly accrual of property tax expense during the fiscal period of the taxing authority for which the taxes are levied. The fiscal period of the taxing authority is the fiscal period that includes the assessment or lien date.

A liability for property taxes payable arises when the fiscal year of the taxing authority and the fiscal year of the entity do not coincide or when the assessment or lien date and the actual payment date do not fall within the same fiscal year.

Example of accrued real estate taxes

Rohlfs Corporation is a calendar-year corporation that owns real estate in a state that operates on a June 30 fiscal year. In this state, real estate taxes are assessed and become a lien against real property on July 1. These taxes, however, are payable in arrears in two installments due on April 1 and August 1 of the next calendar year. Real estate taxes assessed were $18,000 and $22,000 for the years ended 6/30/20X2 and 6/30/X3, respectively. Rohlfs computes its accrued real estate taxes at December 31, 20X1, as follows:

Fiscal year-end of tax jurisdiction	*Assessment date/ lien date*	*Installment due dates* *April 1*	*August 1*	*Annual assessment*	*20X2 Expense*	*Portion of expense paid in 20X2*	*Accrued real estate tax at 12/31/X2*
6/30/20X2	7/1/20X1	20X2	20X2	$ 18,000	$ 9,000	$ 9,000	$ –
6/30/20X3	7/1/20X2	20X3	20X3	22,000	11,000	–	11,000
					$20,000	$ 9,000	$11,000

Proof of the accrual computation is as follows:

Annual assessment—year-end 6/30/X3 of $22,000 ÷ 12 = $1,833/month × 6 months $11,000

ASC 720-35, *Advertising Costs*

The costs of advertising are expensed either as costs are incurred or the first time the advertising takes place (e.g., when the television advertisement is aired or printed copy is published), if later (ASC 720-35-25). However, there are two exceptions:

1. Direct-response advertising
   a. Whose primary purpose is to elicit sales to customers who could be shown to have responded specifically to the advertising, and
   b. That results in probable future economic benefits; and
2. Expenditures for advertising costs that are made subsequent to recognizing revenues related to those costs.

Expenditures for direct-response advertising are deferred if both of the conditions listed above are met. The future benefits to be received are the future revenues arising as a direct result of the advertising. The company is required to provide entity-specific persuasive evidence that there is a linkage between the direct-response advertising and these future benefits. These costs are then amortized over the period in which the future benefits are expected to be received.

Advertising expenditures are sometimes made subsequent to the recognition of revenue (such as in "cooperative advertising" arrangements with customers). In order to achieve proper matching, these costs are to be estimated, accrued, and charged to expense when the related revenues are recognized.

ASC 720-40, *Electronic Equipment Waste Obligations*

ASC 720-40 contains "guidance on accounting for historical electronic equipment waste held by private households for obligations associated with Directive 2002/96/EC on Waste Electrical and Electronic Equipment adopted by the European Union." (ASC 720-40-05-01)

ASC 720-45, *Business and Technology Reengineering*

ASC 720-45 states that the cost of business process reengineering activities, should be expensed as incurred. This includes internal efforts or third-party activities.

ASC 720-50, *Fees Paid to the Federal Government by Pharmaceutical Manufacturers and Health Insurers*

ASC 720-50 provides guidance on certain provisions of the Patient Protection and Affordable Care Act, as amended by the Health Care and Education Reconciliation Act. Those acts require pharmaceutical manufacturers and health insurers to pay annual fees

The liability should be "estimated and recorded in full upon the first qualifying sale for pharmaceutical manufacturers or once the entity provides qualifying health insurance for health insurers in the applicable calendar year in which the fee is payable with a corresponding deferred cost that is amortized to expense using a straight-line method of allocation unless another method better allocates the fee over the calendar year that it is payable." (ASC 720-50-25-1)

43 ASC 730 RESEARCH AND DEVELOPMENT

PERSPECTIVE AND ISSUES

Subtopics

ASC 730, *Research and Development,* contains two subtopics:

- ASC 730-10, *Overall,* which provides guidance on the activities, elements, costs, accounting and disclosures for research and development
- ASC 730-20, *Research and Development Arrangements,* which provides guidance on arrangements used to finance research and development.

Scope and Scope Exception

ASC 730 applies to all entities and to "activities aimed at developing or significantly improving a product or service (referred to as product) or a process or technique (referred to as process) whether the product or process is intended for sale or use." (ASC 710-30-15-3)

ASC 730 does *not* apply to

- the costs of research and development activities conducted for others under a contractual arrangement,
- indirect costs,
- activities that are unique to entities in the extractive industries,
- a process for use in an entity's selling or administrative activities,
- routine alterations to existing products and processes,
- market research,
- research and development assets acquired in an acquisition by not-for-profit entity or business combination,
- internally developed computer software and costs incurred to purchase or use computer software unless it is intended for use with R&D activities.
(ASC 730-10-15-4 and 5)

Overview

ASC 730 addresses the proper accounting and reporting for research and development costs. It identifies

- those activities that are to be identified as research and development,
- the elements of costs that shall be identified with research and development activities, the accounting for these costs, and
- the financial statement disclosures related to them.
(ASC 730-10-05-1)

The central issue in regard to research and development costs is that the future benefits related to these expenditures are uncertain. Given this uncertainty, it is generally difficult to justify classifying them as an asset. Generally, entities should charge them to expense as incurred. (ASC 730-10-05- 2 and 3)

DEFINITIONS OF TERMS

Source: ASC 710-10-20 and ASC 710-20-20

Probable. A future event is likely to occur.
Related parties. Related parties include:

a. Affiliates of the entity
b. Entities for which investments in their equity securities would be required, absent the election of the fair value option under the Fair Value Option Subsection of Section 825-10-15, to be accounted for by the equity method by the investing entity
c. Trusts for the benefit of employees, such as pension and profit-sharing trusts that are managed by or under the trusteeship of management
d. Principal owners of the entity and members of their immediate families
e. Management of the entity and members of their immediate families
f. Other parties with which the entity may deal if one party controls or can significantly influence the management or operating policies of the other to an extent that one of the transacting parties might be prevented from fully pursuing its own separate interests
g. Other parties that can significantly influence the management or operating policies of the transacting parties or that have an ownership interest in one of the transacting parties and can significantly influence the other to an extent that one or more of the transacting parties might be prevented from fully pursuing its own separate interests.

Research and Development. Research is planned search or critical investigation aimed at discovery of new knowledge with the hope that such knowledge will be useful in developing a new product or service (referred to as product) or a new process or technique (referred to as process) or in bringing about a significant improvement to an existing product or process.

Development is the translation of research findings or other knowledge into a plan or design for a new product or process or for a significant improvement to an existing product or process whether intended for sale or use. It includes the conceptual formulation, design, and testing of product alternatives, construction of prototypes, and operation of pilot plants.

Sponsor. An entity that capitalizes a research and development arrangement.

CONCEPTS, RULES, AND EXAMPLES

ASC 730-10, *Research and Development – Overall*

There are three ways in which R&D costs are incurred by a business:

1. Purchase of R&D from other entities
2. Conducting R&D for others under a contractual arrangement
3. Conducting R&D activities for the benefit of the reporting entity.

The accounting treatment relative to R&D depends upon the nature of the cost. R&D costs incurred in the ordinary course of operations consist of materials, equipment, facilities, personnel, and indirect costs that can be attributed to research or development activities. These costs are expensed in the period in which they are incurred unless they have alternative future uses. Examples of such R&D costs with alternative future uses include

1. Laboratory research to discover new knowledge
2. Formulation and design of product alternatives
    a. Testing for product alternatives
    b. Modification of products or processes
3. Preproduction prototypes and models
    a. Tools, dies, etc. for new technology
    b. Pilot plants not capable of commercial production
4. Engineering activity until the product is ready for manufacture.

(ASC 730-10-55-1)

Examples of costs that are ***not*** considered R&D include:

1. Engineering during an early phase of commercial production
2. Quality control for commercial production
3. Troubleshooting during a commercial production breakdown
4. Routine, ongoing efforts to improve products
5. Adaptation of existing capacity for a specific customer or other requirements
6. Seasonal design changes to products
7. Routine design of tools, dies, etc.
8. Design, construction, startup, etc. of equipment except that used solely for R&D
9. Legal work related to patents or litigation.

(ASC 730-10-55-2)

Example of research and development

The TravelBins Corporation is developing a hard-shell plastic ski case on wheels. It assigns two staff to the design of the case, as well as a product design consultant, and also contracts with a Portuguese firm to develop suitable molds for the main case and ancillary parts. The company works its way through 17 product development and production activities before it is satisfied that the new ski case is ready for general distribution. The following matrix shows where costs are charged as various steps are completed:

Step No.	Activity	Charge to R&D expense	Charge to production overhead	Move to inventory	Capitalize
1	Cost of product design consultant	xxx			
2	Salaries related to design of the ski case	xx			
3	Purchase of design computers and rapid prototyping machines				xxx
4	Allocation of indirect development costs	xxx			
5	Cost of preliminary test molds	xxx			
6	Cost of building in which test facility is housed				xxx
7	Cost of resin pellets acquired for test runs			xxx	
8	Scrapped cases from test runs	xxx			
9	Good-quality cases from test runs			xxx	
10	Cost of independent stress test firm	xxx			
11	Patent filing cost				xxx
12	Cost to defend patent				xxx
13	Cost of final mold				xxx
14	Machine set-up time		xxx		
15	Quality control during commercial production		xxx		
16	Routine mold adjustments		xxx		
17	Production engineering to reduce scrap rate		xxx		

The cost of design computers and building are capitalized, since they can be used independently from the product development process. The cost of the final mold is capitalized and amortized over the life of the mold, while patent costs are capitalized and amortized over the life of the product (which may extend past the life of the first mold). The cost of the plastic resin and good-quality ski cases can be transferred to inventory for use in regular production and for sale to customers, respectively.

ASC 730-20, *Research and Development Arrangements*

In many cases, entities will pay other parties to perform R&D activities on their behalf. Substance over form must be used in evaluating these arrangements. A financial reporting result cannot be obtained indirectly if it would not have been permitted if accomplished directly. Thus, if costs are incurred to engage others to perform R&D activities that, in substance, could have been performed by the reporting entity itself, those costs must be expensed as incurred.

An alternative arrangement may consist of a business entering into a limited partnership where the limited partners provide funding and the business conducts the research under a contract with the partnership. Under such an arrangement, the partnership may retain legal ownership of the results of the research. The business may have an option to buy back the results of the research upon payment of a stipulated amount to the partnership.

On the other hand, if the payment is to acquire intangibles for use in R&D activities, and these assets have other uses, then the expenditure is capitalized and accounted for in accordance with ASC 350.

When R&D costs are incurred as a result of contractual arrangements, the nature of the agreement dictates the accounting treatment of the costs involved. The key determinant is the transfer of the risk associated with the R&D expenditures. Risk is not transferred to the other parties if there is a commitment by the business to repay the other parties. Examples of commitments to repay are:

- The entity guarantees repayment regardless of the outcome
- The other parties can require the entity to purchase their interests
- The other parties receive debt or equity securities issued by the entity upon completion of the project, irrespective of the outcome.

(ASC 730-20-25-4)

If the business receives funds from another party to perform R&D and is obligated to repay those funds regardless of the outcome, a liability must be recorded and the R&D costs expensed as incurred. To conclude that a liability does not exist, the transfer of the financial risk must be substantive and genuine.

Nonrefundable advance payments related to future R&D activities. Entities conducting R&D activities may make payments in advance for goods or services to be used in R&D activities. Often, these payment arrangements involve a specific R&D project and the R&D activities to be performed generally have no alternative future use at the time the arrangements are entered into. All or a portion of the advance payment may be nonrefundable to the entity conducting the R&D activities. For example, if the R&D project does not advance to a stage where the goods or services that were paid for in advance are necessary, the entity conducting the R&D activities will not recover its advance payments.

Nonrefundable advance payments are deferred and capitalized. (ASC 730-20025-13) As the related goods are delivered and services performed, the capitalized amounts are to be recognized as expense. (ASC 730-20-35-1) On a continuous basis, management should evaluate whether it expects the goods to be delivered or services rendered and to charge the capitalized advance payments to expense when there no longer is an expectation of future benefits.

This is limited to nonrefundable advance payments for goods to be used or services to be rendered in future R&D activities pursuant to an executory contractual arrangement where the goods or services have no alternative future use.

See ASC Location – Wiley *GAAP* Chapter…	*For information on…*
ASC 350-40	The costs of internal-use computer software
ASC 350-50	Website development costs
ASC 985-20-25-1	Costs incurred to establish the technological feasibility of a computer software product to be sold, leased, or otherwise marketed
ASC 985-605-25-86 through 25-87	A funded software-development arrangement
ASC 450-20	Related to loss contingencies
ASC 810-30	Whether and how a sponsor should consolidate a research and development arrangement

44 ASC 740 INCOME TAXES

PERSPECTIVE AND ISSUES

Subtopics

ASC 740, *Income Taxes,* consists of three Subtopics:

- ASC 740-10, *Overall,* which provides most of the guidance on accounting and reporting for income taxes
- ASC 740-20, *Intraperiod Tax Allocation,* which provides guidance on the process of allocating income tax benefits or expenses to different components of comprehensive income
- ASC 740-30, *Other Considerations or Special Areas,* which provides guidance for specific limited exceptions related to investments in subsidiaries and corporate joint ventures arising from undistributed earnings or other causes.
- ASC 740-270, *Interim Reporting*, which provides the guidance for interim period income taxes.

Incremental guidance may also be found in other topics, for example, Investments—Equity Method and Joint Ventures, Compensation—Stock Compensation, Business Combinations, Foreign Currency Matters, Reorganizations, Entertainment—Casinos, Extractive Activities—Oil and Gas, .Financial Services—Depository and Lending, Financial Services—Insurance, Health Care Entities, Real Estate—Common Interest Realty Associations, Regulated Operations, and U.S. Steamship Entities

Scope and Scope Exceptions

ASC 740-10 applies to income taxes accounted for in accordance with ASC 740, and thus does not apply directly or by analogy to other taxes, such as real estate, personal property, sales, excise, use taxes, or franchise taxes to the extent based on capital. The scope of ASC 740-10 includes any entity potentially subject to income taxes, including:

- Nonprofit organizations
- Flow-through entities (e.g., partnerships, limited liability companies, and S corporations)
- Entities whose income tax liabilities are subject to 100% credit for dividends paid such as real estate investment trusts (REITs) and registered investment companies.

Overview

There are two main objectives to accounting for income taxes:

1. Recognize the estimated taxes payable or refundable on tax returns for the current year as a tax liability or asset.
2. Recognize a deferred tax liability or asset for the estimated future tax effects attributable to temporary differences and carryforwards.

(ASC 740-10-05-5)

The term "tax position" is used in ASC 740-10 to refer to *each* judgment that management makes on an income tax return that has been or will be filed that affects the measurement of current or deferred income tax assets and liabilities at the date of each interim or year-end statement of financial position. Tax positions include:

1. Deductions claimed
2. Deferrals of current income tax to one or more future periods
3. Income tax credits applied
4. Characterization as capital gain versus ordinary income
5. Whether or not to report income on an income tax return
6. Whether or not to file an income tax return in a particular jurisdiction.

The effects of a tax position can result in a permanent reduction of income taxes payable or deferral of the payment of income taxes to a future year. The taking of a tax position can also affect management's estimate of the valuation allowance sufficient to reflect its estimate of the amount of deferred income tax assets that are realizable.

Reporting entities are required to file income tax returns and pay income taxes in the domestic (federal, state, and local) and foreign jurisdictions in which they do business. GAAP requires that financial statements be prepared on an accrual basis and that, consequently, the reporting entity is required to accrue a liability for income taxes owed or expected to be owed with respect to income tax returns filed or to be filed for all applicable tax years and in all applicable jurisdictions.

Uncertain income tax positions are subject to formal recognition and measurement criteria, as well as to extended disclosure requirements under GAAP.

The computation of taxable income for the purpose of filing federal, state, and local income tax returns differs from the computation of net income under GAAP for a variety of reasons. In some instances, referred to as temporary differences, the timing of income or expense recognition varies. In other instances, referred to as permanent differences, income or expense recognized for income tax purposes is never recognized under GAAP, or vice versa. An objective under GAAP is to recognize the income tax effects of transactions in the period that those transactions occur. Consequently, deferred income tax benefits and obligations frequently arise in financial statements.

The basic principle is that the deferred income tax effects of all temporary differences (which are defined in terms of differential bases in assets and liabilities under income tax and GAAP accounting) are formally recognized. To the extent that realizability of deferred income tax assets is doubtful, a valuation allowance is provided, analogous to the allowance for uncollectible receivables.

With its statement of financial position orientation, ASC 740 requires that the amounts presented be based on the amounts expected to be realized, or obligations expected to be liquidated. Use of an average effective income tax rate convention is permitted. The effects of all changes in the deferred income tax assets and liabilities flow through the income tax provision in the income statement; consequently, income tax expense is normally not directly calculable based on pretax accounting income in other than the simplest situations.

Interperiod income tax allocation, which gives rise to deferred income tax assets and liabilities, is required under GAAP.

DEFINITIONS OF TERMS

Source: ASC 740-10-20, 740-20-20, 740-30-20, 740-270-20

Alternative Minimum Tax. A tax that results from the use of an alternate determination of a corporation's federal income tax liability under provisions of the U.S. Internal Revenue Code.

Carrybacks. Deductions or credits that cannot be utilized on the tax return during a year that may be carried back to reduce taxable income or taxes payable in a prior year. An operating loss carryback is an excess of tax deductions over gross income in a year; a tax credit carryback is the amount by which tax credits available for utilization exceed statutory limitations. Different tax jurisdictions have different rules about whether excess deductions or credits may be carried back and the length of the carryback period.

Carryforwards. Deductions or credits that cannot be utilized on the tax return during a year that may be carried forward to reduce taxable income or taxes payable in a future year. An operating loss carryforward is an excess of tax deductions over gross income in a year; a tax credit carryforward is the amount by which tax credits available for utilization exceed statutory limitations. Different tax jurisdictions have different rules about whether excess deductions or credits may be carried forward and the length of the carryforward period. The terms carryforward, operating loss carryforward, and tax credit carryforward refer to the amounts of those items, if any, reported in the tax return for the current year.

Component of an Entity. A component of an entity comprises operations and cash flows that can be clearly distinguished, operationally and for financial reporting purposes, from the rest of the entity. A component of an entity may be a reportable segment or an operating segment, a reporting unit, a subsidiary, or an asset group.

Conduit debt securities. Certain limited-obligation revenue bonds, certificates of participation, or similar debt instruments issued by a state or local governmental entity (issuer) for the purpose of providing financing for a specific third party (the conduit bond obligor) that is not a part of the issuer's reporting entity. Even though these securities bear the issuer's name, the issuer often has no obligation with respect to the debt other than as provided in a lease or loan agreement with the conduit bond obligor on whose behalf the securities are issued. The conduit bond obligor is responsible for making or funding all principal and interest payments when due and is also responsible for future financial reporting requirements with respect to the securities.

Consolidated Financial Statements. The financial statements of a consolidated group of entities that include a parent and all its subsidiaries presented as those of a single economic entity.

Corporate Joint Venture. A corporation owned and operated by a small group of entities (the joint venturers) as a separate and specific business or project for the mutual benefit of the members of the group. A government may also be a member of the group. The purpose of a corporate joint venture frequently is to share risks and rewards in developing a new market, product or technology; to combine complementary technological knowledge; or to pool resources in developing production or other facilities. A corporate joint venture also usually provides an arrangement under which each joint venturer may participate, directly or indirectly, in the overall management of the joint venture. Joint venturers thus have an interest or relationship other than as passive investors. An entity that is a subsidiary of one of the joint venturers is not a corporate joint venture. The ownership of a corporate joint venture seldom changes, and its stock is usually not traded publicly. A noncontrolling interest held by public ownership, however, does not preclude a corporation from being a corporate joint venture.

Current Tax Expense (or Benefit). The amount of income taxes paid or payable (or refundable) for a year as determined by applying the provisions of the enacted tax law to the taxable income or excess of deductions over revenues for that year.

Deductible Temporary Difference. Temporary differences that result in deductible amounts in future years when the related asset or liability is recovered or settled, respectively.

Deferred Tax Asset. The deferred tax consequences attributable to deductible temporary differences and carryforwards. A deferred tax asset is measured using the applicable enacted tax rate and provisions of the enacted tax law. A deferred tax asset is reduced by a valuation allowance if, based on the weight of evidence available, it is more likely than not that some portion or all of a deferred tax asset will not be realized.

Deferred Tax Consequences. The future effects on income taxes as measured by the applicable enacted tax rate and provisions of the enacted tax law resulting from temporary differences and carryforwards at the end of the current year.

Deferred Tax Expense (or Benefit). The change during the year in an entity's deferred tax liabilities and assets. For deferred tax liabilities and assets acquired in a purchase business combination during the year, it is the change since the combination date. Income tax expense (or benefit) for the year is allocated among continuing operations, discontinued operations, extraordinary items, and items charged or credited directly to shareholders' equity.

Deferred Tax Liability. The deferred tax consequences attributable to taxable temporary differences. A deferred tax liability is measured using the applicable enacted tax rate and provisions of the enacted tax law.

Event. A happening of consequence to an entity. The term encompasses both transactions and other events affecting an entity.

Gains and Losses Included in Comprehensive Income but Excluded from Net Income. Gains and losses included in comprehensive income but excluded from net income include certain changes in fair values of investments in marketable equity securities classified as noncurrent assets, certain changes in fair values of investments in industries having specialized accounting practices for marketable securities, adjustments related to pension liabilities or assets recognized within other comprehensive income, and foreign currency translation adjustments. Future changes to generally accepted accounting principles (GAAP) may change what is included in this category.

Income taxes. Domestic and foreign federal (national), state, and local (including franchise) tax based on income.

Noncontrolling Interest. The portion of equity (net assets) in a subsidiary not attributable, directly or indirectly, to a parent. A noncontrolling interest is sometimes called a minority interest.

Nonpublic Entity. An entity that does not meet any of the following criteria:

1. Its debt or equity securities are traded in a public market, including those traded on a stock exchange or in the over-the-counter market (including securities quoted only locally or regionally).

2. It is a conduit bond obligor for conduit debt securities that are traded in a public market (a domestic or foreign stock exchange or an over-the-counter market, including local or regional markets).
3. Its financial statements are filed with a regulatory agency in preparation for the sale of any class of securities.

Not-for-Profit Entity. An entity that possesses the following characteristics, in varying degrees, that distinguish it from a business entity:

1. Contributions of significant amounts of resources from resource providers who do not expect commensurate or proportionate pecuniary return
2. Operating purposes other than to provide goods or services at a profit
3. Absence of ownership interests like those of business entities.

Entities that clearly fall outside this definition include the following:

1. All investor-owned entities
2. Entities that provide dividends, lower costs, or other economic benefits directly and proportionately to their owners, members, or participants, such as mutual insurance entities, credit unions, farm and rural electric cooperatives, and employee benefit plans.

Parent. An entity that has a controlling financial interest in one or more subsidiaries. (Also, an entity that is the primary beneficiary of a variable interest entity.)

Public entity. An entity (1) whose debt or equity securities are traded in a public market, (2) that is a conduit bond obligor for conduit debt securities traded in a public market, or (3) whose financial statements are filed with a regulatory agency in preparation for the sale of any class of securities. For the purpose of this definition, a public market can be a domestic or foreign exchange or over-the-counter market, even if the securities are only quoted locally or regionally.

Subsidiary. An entity, including an unincorporated entity such as a partnership or trust, in which another entity, known as its parent, holds a controlling financial interest. (Also, a variable interest entity that is consolidated by a primary beneficiary.)

Tax consequences. The effects on income taxes—current or deferred—of an event.

Tax Position. A position in a previously filed tax return or a position expected to be taken in a future tax return that is reflected in measuring current or deferred income tax assets and liabilities for interim or annual periods. A tax position can result in a permanent reduction of income taxes payable, a deferral of income taxes otherwise currently payable to future years, or a change in the expected realizability of deferred tax assets. The term tax position also encompasses, but is not limited to:

a. A decision not to file a tax return
b. An allocation or a shift of income between jurisdictions
c. The characterization of income or a decision to exclude reporting taxable income in a tax return
d. A decision to classify a transaction, entity, or other position in a tax return as tax exempt
e. An entity's status, including its status as a pass-through entity or a tax-exempt not-for-profit entity.

Taxable income. The excess of taxable revenue over tax deductible expenses and exemptions for the year as defined by the governmental taxing authority.

Taxable Temporary differences. Temporary differences that result in taxable amounts in future years when the related asset is recovered or the related liability is settled.

Tax-Planning Strategy. An action (including elections for tax purposes) that meets certain criteria (see paragraph 740-10-30-19) and that would be implemented to realize a tax benefit for an operating loss or tax credit carryforward before it expires. Tax-planning strategies are considered when assessing the need for and amount of a valuation allowance for deferred tax assets.

Temporary Difference. A difference between the tax basis of an asset or liability computed pursuant to the requirements in Subtopic 740-10 for tax positions, and its reported amount in the financial statements that will result in taxable or deductible amounts in future years when the reported amount of the asset or liability is recovered or settled, respectively. Paragraph 740-10-25-20 cites eight examples of temporary differences. Some temporary differences cannot be identified with a particular asset or liability for financial reporting (see paragraphs 740-10-05-10 and 740-10-25-24 through 25-25), but those temporary differences do meet both of the following conditions:

1. Result from events that have been recognized in the financial statements
2. Will result in taxable or deductible amounts in future years based on provisions of the tax law.

Some events recognized in financial statements do not have tax consequences. Certain revenues are exempt from taxation and certain expenses are not deductible. Events that do not have tax consequences do not give rise to temporary differences.

Tentative Minimum Tax. An intermediate calculation used in the determination of a corporation's federal income tax liability under the alternative minimum tax system in the United States.

Unrecognized tax benefits. The difference between a tax position taken or expected to be taken in a tax return and the benefit recognized and measured pursuant to Subtopic 740-10.

Unrelated business income. Income earned from a regularly carried-on trade or business that is not substantially related to the charitable, educational, or other purpose that is the basis of an organization's exemption from income taxes. This income subjects the otherwise tax-exempt organization to an entity-level unrelated business income tax (UBIT).

Valuation allowance. The contra asset that is to be reflected to the extent that, in management's judgment, it is "more likely than not" that the deferred income tax asset will not be realized.

CONCEPTS, RULES, AND EXAMPLES

Accounting Theory

When reporting income taxes, accounting theory has prioritized the statement of financial position. To compute deferred income taxes consistent with this balance sheet orientation requires use of the "liability method." This essentially ascertains, as of each date for which a statement of financial position is presented, the amount of future income tax benefits or obligations that are associated with the reporting entity's assets and liabilities existing at that time. Any adjustments necessary to increase or decrease deferred income taxes to the computed balance, plus or minus the amount of income taxes owed currently, determine the periodic income tax expense or benefit to be reported in the income statement. Put another way, income tax expense is the residual result of several other computations oriented to measurement in the statement of financial position.

ASC 740 requires that all deferred income tax assets are given full recognition, whether arising from deductible temporary differences or from net operating loss or tax credit carryforwards.

Under ASC 740 it is necessary to assess whether the deferred income tax asset is realizable. Testing for realization is accomplished by means of a "more-likely-than-not" criterion that indicates whether an allowance is needed to offset some or all of the recorded deferred income tax asset. While the determination of the amount of the allowance may make use of the scheduling of future expected reversals, other methods may also be employed.

In summary, interperiod income tax allocation under GAAP is based on the liability method, using comprehensive allocation. While this basic principle may be straightforward, there are a number of computational complexities to be addressed. These will be presented in the remainder of this chapter.

An example of application of the liability method of deferred income tax accounting follows.

Simplified example of interperiod income tax allocation using the liability method

Caitlyn International has no permanent differences in years 20X1 through 20X3 (these are discussed later in this chapter). The company has only two amounts on its statement of financial position with temporary differences between their income tax and financial reporting bases, property and equipment; and prepaid rent. No consideration is given to the classification of the deferred income tax amounts (i.e., current or long-term) as it is not considered necessary for purposes of this example.

Details of Caitlyn's temporary differences are as follows:

Caitlyn International Temporary Differences

Prepaid rent future deductible temporary differences

Basis at December 31	*Tax*	*GAAP*	*Future (taxable) deductible amount*
20X1	–	$(100,000)	$100,000
20X2	–	(80,000)	80,000
20X3	–	(125,000)	125,000

Property and equipment future taxable temporary difference

On January 1, 20X1, Caitlyn International purchased $400,000 of property and equipment with a 10-year estimated useful life which, under its normal accounting policy, it depreciates using the straight-line method. For income tax purposes, these assets qualify as 5-year personal property under the General Depreciation System (GDS), and consequently, income tax depreciation is computed using the Modified Accelerated Cost Recovery System (MACRS) which is equivalent to double-declining balance depreciation with a half-year assumed for the year placed in service and changing to straight-line depreciation when advantageous to the taxpayer. In addition, as permitted by IRC Section 179, Caitlyn elected to deduct $100,000 of these costs in the year placed in service. By making this election, for the purpose of computing income tax cost recovery, Caitlyn is required to reduce the depreciable basis of the eligible assets by the amount of Section 179 deduction taken during the tax year.

	20X1	*Tax*	*GAAP*	*Future (taxable) deductible amount*
A	Purchase price of assets	$400,000	$400,000	
B	Section 179 expense election	100,000	–	
C	Adjusted depreciable basis (A – B)	300,000	400,000	
D	Depreciation rate	× 20%	× 10%	
E	20X2 depreciation (C × D)	60,000	40,000	
F	Section 179 expense election (B)	100,000	–	
G	20X2 depreciation and section 179 (E + F)	160,000	40,000	
H	Basis at 12/31/X1 (A – G)	$240,000	$360,000	$(120,000)
	20X2			
I	Depreciation rate	× 32%	× 10%	
J	20X3 Depreciation (C × I)	96,000	40,000	
K	Basis at 12/31/X2 (H – J)	$144,000	$320,000	$(176,000)
	20X3			
L	Depreciation rate	× 19.2%	× 10%	
M	20X4 Depreciation (C × L)	57,600	40,000	
N	Basis at 12/31/13 (K – M)	$ 86,400	$280,000	$(193,600)

The computation of deferred income taxes is as follows:

	12/31/20X1	*12/31/20X2*	*12/31/20X3*
Future deductible temporary difference			
Prepaid rent	$ 100,000	$ 80,000	$ 125,000
Future (taxable) temporary difference			
Property and equipment	(120,000)	(176,000)	(193,600)
Net (taxable) deductible temporary difference	(20,000)	(96,000)	(68,600)
Effective tax rate	34%	34%	37%
Ending deferred income tax asset (liability)	(6,800)	(32,640)	(25,382)
Beginning deferred income tax asset (liability)	–	(6,800)	(32,640)
Deferred income tax (expense) benefit	$ (6,800)	$ (25,840)	$ 7,258

Note from the computations that, under the liability method, deferred income tax expense or benefit is the amount necessary to adjust the statement of financial position to the computed balance. No attempt is made to correlate the amount of deferred income tax expense or benefit to pretax accounting income or loss. Nor is it necessary to track the amount of each temporary difference that originates or reverses during the year.

Temporary Differences

Deferred income taxes are provided for all temporary differences, but not for permanent differences. Thus, it is important to be able to distinguish between the two. While many typical business transactions are accounted for identically for income tax and financial reporting purposes, there are many others subject to different income tax and accounting treatments, often leading to their being reported in different periods in financial statements than they are reported on income tax returns. The term "timing differences," used under prior GAAP, has been superseded by the broader term "temporary differences" under current rules. Under income statement-oriented GAAP, timing differences were said to originate in one period and to reverse in a later period. These involved such common items as alternative depreciation methods, deferred compensation plans, percentage-of-completion accounting for long-term construction contracts, and cash basis versus accrual basis accounting.

The concept of temporary differences includes all differences between the income tax basis and the financial reporting carrying value of assets and liabilities, if the reversal of those differences will result in taxable or deductible amounts in future years. Temporary differences include all the items formerly defined as timing differences, and other additional items.

Temporary differences under ASC 740 can be categorized as follows:

Revenue recognized for financial reporting purposes before being recognized for income tax purposes. Revenue accounted for by the installment method for income tax purposes, but fully reflected in current GAAP income; certain construction-related revenue recognized using the completed-contract method for income tax purposes, but recognized using the percentage-of-completion method for financial reporting purposes; earnings from investees recognized using the equity method for accounting purposes but taxed only when later distributed as dividends to the investor. These are future taxable temporary differences because future periods' taxable income will exceed GAAP income as the differences reverse; thus they give rise to deferred income tax liabilities.

Revenue recognized for income tax purposes prior to recognition in the financial statements. Certain taxable revenue received in advance, such as prepaid rental income and service contract revenue not recognized in the financial statements until later periods. These are future deductible temporary differences, because the costs of future performance will be deductible in the future years when incurred without being reduced by the amount of revenue deferred for GAAP purposes. Consequently, the income tax benefit to be realized in future years from deducting those future costs is a deferred income tax asset.

Expenses deductible for income tax purposes prior to recognition in the financial statements. Accelerated depreciation methods or shorter statutory useful lives used for income tax purposes, while straight-line depreciation or longer useful economic lives are used for financial reporting; amortization of goodwill and nonamortizable intangible assets over a 15-year life for income tax purposes while not amortizing them for financial reporting purposes unless they are impaired. Upon reversal in the future, the effect would be to increase taxable income without a corresponding increase in GAAP income. Therefore, these items are future taxable temporary differences, and give rise to deferred income tax liabilities.

Expenses recognized in the financial statements prior to becoming deductible for income tax purposes. Certain estimated expenses, such as warranty costs, as well as such contingent losses as accruals of litigation expenses, are not tax deductible until the obligation becomes fixed. In those future periods, those expenses will give rise to deductions on the reporting entity's income tax return. Thus, these are future deductible temporary differences that give rise to deferred income tax assets.

In addition to these familiar and well-understood categories, temporary differences include a number of other categories that also involve differences between the income tax and financial reporting bases of assets or liabilities. These include:

Reductions in tax-deductible asset bases arising in connection with tax credits. Under the provisions of the 1982 income tax act, taxpayers were permitted a choice of either full ACRS depreciation coupled with a reduced investment tax credit, or a full investment tax credit coupled with reduced depreciation allowances. If the taxpayer chose the latter option, the asset basis was reduced for tax depreciation, but was still fully depreciable for financial reporting purposes. Accordingly, this type of election is accounted for as a future taxable temporary difference, which gives rise to a deferred income tax liability.

Increases in the income tax bases of assets resulting from the indexing of asset costs for the effects of inflation. Occasionally proposed but never enacted, enacting such a provision to income tax law would allow taxpaying entities to finance the replacement of depreciable assets through depreciation based on current costs, as computed by the application of indices to the historical costs of the assets being remeasured. This reevaluation of asset costs would give rise to future taxable temporary differences that would be associated with deferred income tax liabilities since, upon the eventual sale of the asset, the taxable gain would exceed the gain recognized for financial reporting purposes resulting in the payment of additional tax in the year of sale.

Certain business combinations accounted for by the purchase method or the acquisition method. Under certain circumstances, the amounts assignable to assets or liabilities acquired in business combinations will differ from their income tax bases. Such differences may be either taxable or deductible in the future and, accordingly, may give rise to deferred income tax liabilities or assets. These differences are explicitly recognized by the reporting of deferred income taxes in the consolidated financial statements of the acquiring entity. Note that these differences are no longer allocable to the financial reporting bases of the underlying assets or liabilities themselves, as was the case under the old net of tax method.

A financial reporting situation in which deferred income taxes may or may not be appropriate would include life insurance (such as key person insurance) under which the reporting entity is the beneficiary. Since proceeds of life insurance are not subject to income tax under present law, the excess of cash surrender values over the sum of premiums paid is not a temporary difference, if the intention is to hold the policy until death benefits are received. On the other hand, if the entity intends to cash in (surrender) the policy at some point prior to the death of the insured (i.e., it is holding the insurance contract as an investment), which would be a taxable event, then the excess surrender value is in fact a temporary difference, and deferred income taxes are to be provided thereon.

Temporary differences from share-based compensation arrangements. ASC 718-50 contains intricate rules with respect to accounting for the income tax effects of different types of share-based compensation awards. The complexity is compounded by the complex statutes and regulations that apply under the US Internal Revenue Code (IRC).

Differences between the accounting rules and the income tax laws can result in situations where the cumulative amount of compensation cost recognized for financial reporting purposes will differ from the cumulative amount of compensation deductions recognized for income tax purposes. For more information, see the discussion in the chapter on ASC 718.

Temporary differences arising from convertible debt with a beneficial conversion feature. Issuers of debt securities sometimes structure the instruments to include a nondetachable conversion feature. If the terms of the conversion feature are "in-the-money" at the date of issuance, the feature is referred to as a "beneficial conversion feature." Beneficial conversion features are accounted for separately from the host instrument under ASC 470-20.

The separate accounting results in an allocation to additional paid-in capital of a portion of the proceeds received from issuance of the instrument that represents the intrinsic value of the conversion feature calculated at the commitment date, as defined. The intrinsic value is the difference between the conversion price and the fair value of the instruments into which the security is convertible multiplied by the number of shares into which the security is convertible. The convertible security is recorded at its par value (assuming there is no discount or premium on issuance). A discount is recognized to offset the portion of the instrument that is allocated to additional paid-in capital. The discount is accreted from the issuance date to the stated redemption date of the convertible instrument or through the earliest conversion date if the instrument does not include a stated redemption date.

For US income tax purposes, the proceeds are recorded entirely as debt and represent the income tax basis of the debt security, thus creating a temporary difference between the basis of the debt for financial reporting and income tax reporting purposes.

ASC 740-10-55 specifies that the income tax effect associated with this temporary difference is to be recorded as an adjustment to additional paid-in-capital. It would not be reported, as are most other such income tax effects, as a deferred income tax asset or liability in the statement of financial position.

Other common temporary differences. Other common temporary differences include:

Accounting for investments. Use of the equity method for financial reporting while using the cost method for income tax purposes.

Accrued contingent liabilities. These cannot be deducted for income tax purposes until the liability becomes fixed and determinable.

Cash basis versus accrual basis. Use of the cash method of accounting for income tax purposes and the accrual method for financial reporting.

Charitable contributions that exceed the statutory deductibility limitation. These can be carried over to future years for income tax purposes.

Deferred compensation. Under GAAP, the present value of deferred compensation agreements must be accrued and charged to expense over the employee's remaining employment period, but for income tax purposes these costs are not deductible until actually paid.

Depreciation. A temporary difference will occur unless the modified ACRS method is used for financial reporting over estimated useful lives that are the same as the IRS-prescribed recovery periods. This is only permissible for GAAP if the recovery periods are substantially identical to the estimated useful lives.

Estimated costs (e.g., warranty expense). Estimates or provisions of this nature are not included in the determination of taxable income until the period in which the costs are actually incurred.

Goodwill. For US federal income tax purposes, amortization over fifteen years is mandatory. Amortization of goodwill is no longer permitted under GAAP, but periodic write-downs for impairment may occur, with any remainder of goodwill being expensed when the reporting unit to which it pertains is ultimately disposed of.

Income received in advance (e.g., prepaid rent). Income of this nature is includable in taxable income in the period in which it is received, while for financial reporting purposes, it is considered a liability until the revenue is earned.

Installment sale method. Use of the installment sale method for income tax purposes generally results in a temporary difference because that method is generally not permitted to be used in accordance with GAAP.

Long-term construction contracts. A temporary difference will arise if different methods (e.g., completed-contract or percentage-of-completion) are used for GAAP and income tax purposes.

Mandatory change from the cash method to the accrual method. Generally one-fourth of this adjustment is recognized for income tax purposes each year.

Net capital loss. C corporation capital losses are recognized currently for financial reporting purposes but are carried forward to be offset against future capital gains for income tax purposes.

Organization costs. GAAP requires organization costs to be treated as expenses as incurred. For income tax purposes, organization costs are recorded as assets and amortized over a 60-month period. Also see the following section, "Permanent differences."

Uniform cost capitalization (UNICAP). Income tax accounting rules require manufacturers and certain wholesalers to capitalize as inventory costs certain costs that, under GAAP, are considered administrative costs that are not allocable to inventory.

Permanent Differences

Permanent differences are book-tax differences in asset or liability bases that will never reverse and therefore, affect income taxes currently payable but do not give rise to deferred income taxes.

Common permanent differences include:

Club dues. Dues assessed by business, social, athletic, luncheon, sporting, airline and hotel clubs are not deductible for federal income tax purposes.

Dividends-received deduction. Depending on the percentage interest of the payer owned by the recipient, a percentage of the dividends received by a corporation are nontaxable. Different rules apply to subsidiaries.

Goodwill—nondeductible. If, in a particular taxing jurisdiction, goodwill amortization is not deductible, that goodwill is considered a permanent difference and does not give rise to deferred income taxes.

Lease inclusion amounts. Lessees of automobiles whose fair value the IRS deems to qualify as a luxury automobile are required to limit their lease deduction by adding to taxable income an amount determined by reference to a table prescribed annually in a revenue procedure.

Meals and entertainment. A percentage (currently 50%) of business meals and entertainment costs is not deductible for federal income tax purposes.

Municipal interest income. A 100% exclusion is permitted for investment in qualified municipal securities. Note that the capital gains applicable to sales of these securities are taxable.

Officer's life insurance premiums and proceeds. Premiums paid for an officer's life insurance policy under which the company is the beneficiary are not deductible for income tax purposes, nor are any death proceeds taxable.

Organization and start-up costs. GAAP requires organization and start-up costs to be treated as expenses as incurred. Certain organization and start-up costs are not allowed amortization under the tax code. The most clearly defined are those expenditures relating to the cost of raising capital. Also see the prior section, "Temporary differences. . . ."

Penalties and fines. Any penalty or fine arising as a result of violation of the law is not allowed as an income tax deduction. This includes a wide range of items including parking tickets, environmental fines, and penalties assessed by the US Internal Revenue Service.

Percentage depletion. The excess of percentage depletion over cost depletion is allowable as a deduction for income tax purposes.

Wages and salaries eligible for jobs credit. The portion of wages and salaries used in computing the jobs credit is not allowed as a deduction for income tax purposes.

Treatment of Net Operating Loss Carryforwards

All temporary differences and carryforwards have been conferred identical status, and their income tax effects are given full recognition on the statement of financial position. Specifically, the income tax effects of net operating loss carryforwards are equivalent to the income tax effects of future deductible temporary differences. The deferred income tax effects of net operating losses are computed and recorded, but as is the case for all other deferred income tax assets, the need for a valuation allowance must also be assessed (as discussed below). The income tax effects of income tax credit carryforwards (e.g., general business credits, alternative minimum tax credits) are used to increase deferred income tax assets dollar-for-dollar versus being treated in the same manner as future deductible temporary differences, as illustrated in the following example.

Example—Net operating loss carryforwards and income tax credit carryforwards

Casey Corporation has the following future deductible temporary differences and available carryforwards at December 31, 20X1:

Inventory costs capitalized under Internal Revenue Code §263A	$40,000
Allowance for uncollectible accounts receivable	20,000
Net operating loss carryforward	18,000
General business credit carryforward	14,000

Casey's computation of deferred income taxes at December 31, 20X2, is as follows:

Capitalized inventory costs	$40,000
Allowance for uncollectible accounts receivable	20,000
Net operating loss carryforward	18,000
	78,000
Assumed income tax rate	× 34%
	26,520
General business credit carryforward	14,000
Deferred income tax asset	$40,520

Note the net operating loss is multiplied by the income tax rate to compute its effect on the deferred income tax asset since it is available to reduce future years' *taxable income*. In contrast, the general business credit carryforward is not multiplied by the *income tax* rate since it is available to be used to offset future years' income tax.

ASC 740 provides that the income tax benefits of net operating loss carrybacks and carryforwards, with limited exceptions (discussed below), are to be reported in the same manner as the source of either income or loss in the current year. As used in the standard, the phrase "in the same manner" refers to the classification of the income tax benefit in the income statement (i.e., as income taxes on income from continuing operations, discontinued operations, extraordinary items, etc.) or as the income tax effect of gains included in other comprehensive income but excluded from net income on the income statement. The income tax benefits are not reported in the same manner as the source of the net operating loss carryforward or income taxes paid in a prior year, or as the source of the expected future taxable income that will permit the realization of the carryforward.

For example, if the income tax benefit of a loss that arose in a prior year in connection with an extraordinary item is first given recognition in the current year, the benefit would be allocated to income taxes on income from continuing operations if the benefit offsets income taxes on income from continuing operations in the current year. The expression "first given recognition" means that the net deferred income tax asset, after deducting the valuation allowance, reflects the income tax effect of the loss carryforward for the first time.

The gross deferred income tax asset will always reflect all future deductible temporary differences and net operating loss carryforwards in the periods they arise. Thus, first given recognition means that the valuation allowance is eliminated for the first time. If it offsets income taxes on extraordinary income in the current year, then the benefits would be reported in extraordinary items. As another example, the tax benefit arising from the entity's loss from continuing operations in the current year would be allocated to continuing operations, regardless of whether it might be realized as a carryback against income taxes paid on extraordinary items in prior years. The income tax benefit would also be allocated to continuing operations in cases where it is anticipated that the benefit will be realized through the reduction of income taxes to be due on extraordinary gains in future years. (See the Intraperiod Income Tax Allocation section later in this chapter.)

Thus, the general rule is that the reporting of income tax effects of net operating losses are driven by the source of the tax benefits in the current period. There are only two exceptions to the foregoing rule. The first exception relates to existing future deductible temporary differences and net operating loss carryforwards that arise in connection with business combinations and for which income tax benefits are first recognized. This exception will be discussed below (see income tax effects of business combinations). As in the preceding paragraph, first recognized means that a valuation allowance (as discussed more fully later in this chapter) provided previously is being eliminated for the first time.

The second exception to the aforementioned general rule is that certain income tax benefits allocable to stockholders' equity are not to be reflected in the income statement. Specifically, income tax benefits arising in connection with contributed capital, employee stock options, dividends paid on unallocated ESOP shares, or temporary differences existing at the date of a quasi reorganization are reported as accumulated other comprehensive income in the stockholders' equity section of the statement of financial position and are not included in the income statement.

Certain transactions among stockholders that occur outside the company can affect the status of deferred income taxes. The most commonly encountered of these is the change in ownership of more than 50% of the company's stock, which limits or eliminates the company's ability to utilize net operating loss carryforwards, and accordingly requires the reversal of deferred income tax assets previously recognized under ASC 740. Changes in deferred income taxes caused by transactions among stockholders are to be included in current period income tax expense in the income statement, since these are analogous to changes in expectations resulting from other external events (e.g., changes in enacted income tax rates). However, the income tax effects of changes in the income tax bases of assets or liabilities caused by transactions among stockholders would be included in equity, not in the income statement, although subsequent period changes in the valuation account, if any, would be reflected in income (ASC 740-20-45).

Measurement of Deferred Income Tax Assets and Liabilities

Scheduling of the reversal years of temporary differences. There is no need to forecast (or "schedule") the future years in which temporary differences are expected to reverse except in the most exceptional circumstances. To eliminate the burden, it was necessary to endorse the use of the expected average (i.e., effective) income tax rate to measure the deferred income tax assets and liabilities and to forgo a more precise measure of marginal tax effects. Scheduling is now encountered primarily

1. when income tax rate changes are to be phased in over multiple years, and
2. in order to determine the classification (current or noncurrent) of a deferred income tax asset arising from a net operating loss carryforward or income tax credit carryforward or to determine whether such a carryforward might expire unused for the purpose of determining the amount of valuation allowance needed (as discussed in the following section of this chapter).

Determining the appropriate income tax rate. Assume C corporations with taxable income between $335,000 and $10,000,000 are taxed at an expected income tax rate equal to the 34% marginal rate and the effect of the surtax exemption has fully phased out at that level, effectively resulting in a flat tax. Thus, the computation of deferred federal income taxes for these entities is accomplished simply by applying the 34% top marginal rate to all temporary differences and net operating loss carryforwards outstanding at the date of the statement of financial position. This technique is applied to future taxable temporary differences (producing deferred income tax liabilities), and to future deductible temporary differences and net operating loss carryforwards (giving rise to deferred income tax assets). The deferred income tax assets computed must still be evaluated for realizability. Some, or all, of the projected income tax benefits may fail the "more-likely-than-not" test and consequently may need to be offset by a valuation allowance.

On the other hand, reporting entities that have historically been taxed at an effective federal income tax rate lower than the top marginal rate compute their federal deferred income tax assets and liabilities by using their expected future effective income tax rates. Consistent with the goal of simplifying the process of calculating deferred income taxes, reporting entities are permitted to apply a single, long-term expected income tax rate, without attempting to differentiate among the years when temporary difference reversals are expected to occur. In any event, the inherent imprecision of forecasting future income levels and the patterns of temporary difference reversals makes it unlikely that a more sophisticated computational effort would produce better financial statements. Therefore, absent such factors as the phasing in of new income tax rates, it is not necessary to consider whether the reporting entity's effective income tax rate will vary from year to year.

The effective income tax rate convention obviates the need to predict the impact of the alternative minimum tax (AMT) on future years. In determining an entity's deferred income taxes, the number of computations may be as few as one.

Computing deferred income taxes. To compute the gross deferred income tax provision (i.e., before addressing the possible need for a valuation allowance):

1. Identify all temporary differences existing as of the reporting date. This process is simplified if the reporting entity maintains both GAAP and income tax statements of financial position for comparison purposes.
2. Segregate the temporary differences into future taxable differences and future deductible differences. This step is necessary because a valuation allowance may be required to be provided to offset the income tax effects of the future deductible temporary differences and carryforwards, but not the income tax effects of the future taxable temporary differences.
3. Accumulate information about available net operating loss and tax credit carryforwards as well as their expiration dates or other types of limitations, if any.
4. Measure the income tax effect of aggregate future taxable temporary differences by separately applying the appropriate expected income tax rates (federal plus any state, local, and foreign rates that are applicable under the circumstances). Ensure that consideration is given in making these computations to the federal income tax deductibility of income taxes payable to other jurisdictions.
5. Similarly, measure the income tax effects of future deductible temporary differences, including net operating loss carryforwards.

Separate computations must be made for each taxing jurisdiction. In many cases, this level of complexity is not needed and a single, combined effective income tax rate can be used. However, in assessing the need for valuation allowances, it is necessary to consider the entity's ability to absorb deferred income tax benefits against income tax liabilities. Inasmuch as benefits from one tax jurisdiction will not reduce income taxes payable to another tax jurisdiction, separate calculations will be needed in these situations. Also, for purposes of presentation in the statement of financial position (discussed below), offsetting of deferred income tax assets and liabilities is only permissible within the same jurisdiction.

Separate computations are made for each taxpaying component of the primary reporting entity. If a parent company and its subsidiaries are consolidated for financial reporting purposes but file separate income tax returns, the reporting entity comprises a number of components, and the income tax benefits of any one will be unavailable to reduce the income tax obligations of the others.

The principles set forth above are illustrated by the following example.

Computation of deferred income tax liability and asset—Basic example

Assume that Humfeld Company has a total of $28,000 of future taxable temporary differences and a total of $8,000 of future deductible temporary differences. There are no available operating loss or tax credit carryforwards. Taxable income is $230,000 and the income tax rate is a flat (i.e., not graduated) 34% for the current year and not anticipated to change in the future. Also assume that there were no deferred income tax liabilities or assets in prior years.

Current income tax expense and income taxes currently payable are computed as taxable income times the current rate ($230,000 × 34% = $78,200). The deferred income tax asset is computed as $2,720, representing 34% of future deductible temporary differences of $8,000. The deferred income tax liability of $9,520 is calculated as 34% of future taxable temporary differences of $28,000. The deferred income tax expense of $6,800 is the net of the deferred income tax liability of $9,520 and the deferred income tax asset of $2,720.

The journal entry to record the required amounts is:

Current income tax expense	78,200	
Deferred income tax asset	2,720	
Income tax expense—deferred	6,800	
Deferred income tax liability		9,520
Income taxes currently payable		78,200

In 20X1, Humfeld Company has taxable income of $411,000, aggregate future taxable and future deductible temporary differences are $75,000 and $36,000 respectively, and the income tax rate remains a flat 34%.

Current income tax expense and income taxes currently payable are each $139,740 ($411,000 × 34%).

Deferred amounts are calculated as follows:

	Deferred tax liability	*Deferred tax asset*	*Income tax expense—deferred*
Required balance at 12/31/X2			
$75,000 × 34%	$25,500		–
$36,000 × 34%		$12,240	–
Balances at 12/31/X1	9,520	2,720	–
Adjustment required	$15,980	$ 9,520	$6,460

The journal entry to record the deferred amounts is:

Deferred income tax asset	9,520	
Income tax expense—deferred	6,460	
Deferred income tax liability		15,980

Because the increase in the liability in 20X2 is larger (by $6,460) than the increase in the asset for that year, the result is a deferred income tax expense for 20X2.

The Valuation Allowance for Deferred Income Tax Assets Expected to Be Unrealizable

All deferred income tax assets must be given full recognition, subject to the possible provision of an allowance when it is determined that this asset is unlikely to be realized. This approach conveys the greatest amount of useful information to the users of the financial statements.

A valuation allowance is to be provided for that fraction of the computed year-end balances of the deferred income tax assets for which it has been determined that it is more likely than not that the reported asset amount will not be realized. As used in this context, "more likely than not" represents a probability of just over 50%. Since it is widely agreed that the term probable, as used in ASC 450, denotes a much higher probability (perhaps 85% to 90%), the threshold for reflecting an impairment of deferred income tax assets is much lower than the threshold for other assets (i.e., in most cases, the likelihood of a valuation allowance being required is greater than, say, the likelihood that a long-lived asset is impaired).

Establishment of a valuation allowance

Assume that Couch Corporation has a future deductible temporary difference of $60,000 at December 31, 20X2. The tax rate is a flat 34%. Based on available evidence, management of Couch Corporation concludes that it is more likely than not that all sources will not result in future taxable income sufficient to realize an income tax benefit of more than $15,000 (25% of the future deductible temporary difference). Also assume that there were no deferred income tax assets in previous years and that prior years' taxable income was inconsequential.

At 12/31/X2 Couch Corporation records a deferred income tax asset in the amount of $20,400 ($60,000 × 34%) and a valuation allowance of $15,300 (34% of the $45,000 difference between the $60,000 of future deductible temporary differences and the $15,000 of future taxable income expected to absorb the future tax deduction arising from the reversal of the temporary difference).

The journal entry at 12/31/X2 is

Deferred income tax asset	20,400	
Valuation allowance		15,300
Income tax benefit—deferred		5,100

The deferred income tax benefit of $5,100 represents that portion of the deferred income tax asset (25%) that, more likely than not, is realizable.

Assume that at the end of 20X3, Couch Corporation's future deductible temporary difference has decreased to $50,000 and that Couch now has a net operating loss carryforward of $42,000. The total of the net operating loss carryforward ($42,000) plus the amount of the future deductible temporary difference ($50,000) is $92,000. A deferred income tax asset of $31,280 ($92,000 × 34%) is recognized at the end of 20X3. Also assume that management of Couch Corporation concludes that it is more likely than not that $25,000 of the tax asset will not be realized. Thus, a valuation allowance in that amount is required, and the balance in the allowance account of $15,300 must be increased by $9,700 ($25,000 – $15,300).

The journal entry at 12/31/X3 is

Deferred income tax asset	10,880	
Valuation allowance		9,700
Income tax benefit—deferred		1,180

The deferred income tax asset is debited $10,880 to increase it from $20,400 at the end of 20X2 to its required balance of $31,280 at the end of 20X3. The deferred income tax benefit of $1,180 represents the net of the $10,880 increase in the deferred income tax asset and the $9,700 increase in the valuation allowance.

While the meaning of the "more likely than not" criterion is clear (more than 50%), the practical difficulty of assessing whether or not this subjective threshold test is met in a given situation remains. A number of positive and negative factors need to be evaluated in reaching a conclusion as to the necessity of a valuation allowance. Positive factors (those suggesting that an allowance is not necessary) include:

1. Evidence of sufficient future taxable income, exclusive of reversing temporary differences and carryforwards, to realize the benefit of the deferred income tax asset
2. Evidence of sufficient future taxable income arising from the reversals of existing future taxable temporary differences (deferred income tax liabilities) to realize the benefit of the deferred income tax asset
3. Evidence of sufficient taxable income in prior year(s) available for realization of a net operating loss carryback under existing statutory limitations
4. Evidence of the existence of prudent, feasible tax planning strategies under management control that, if implemented, would permit the realization of the deferred income tax asset
5. An excess of appreciated asset values over their tax bases, in an amount sufficient to realize the deferred income tax asset
6. A strong earnings history exclusive of the loss creating the deferred tax asset.

While the foregoing may suggest that the reporting entity will be able to realize the benefits of the future deductible temporary differences outstanding as of the date of the statement of financial position, certain negative factors must also be considered in determining whether a valuation allowance needs to be established against deferred income tax assets. These factors include:

1. A cumulative recent history of losses
2. A history of operating losses, or of net operating loss or tax credit carryforwards that have expired unused
3. Losses that are anticipated in the near future years, despite a history of profitable operations.

Thus, the process of evaluating whether a valuation allowance is needed involves the weighing of both positive and negative factors to determine whether, based on the preponderance of available evidence, it is more likely than not that the deferred income tax assets will be realized.

Example of applying the more-likely-than-not criterion to a deferred income tax asset

Assume the following facts:

1. Foy Corporation reports on a calendar year, and it commenced operations and began applying ASC 740 in 20W6.
2. As of December 31, 20X2, it has future taxable temporary differences of $85,000 relating to income earned on equity-method investments; future deductible temporary differences of $12,000 relating to deferred compensation arrangements; a net operating loss carryforward (which arose in 20W9) of $40,000; and a capital loss carryforward of $10,000 (which arose in 20X2).
3. Foy's expected effective income tax rate for future years is 34% for both ordinary income and net long-term capital gains. Capital losses cannot be offset against ordinary income.

The first steps are to compute the deferred income tax asset and/or liability without consideration of the possible need for a valuation allowance.

Deferred income tax liability:

Future taxable temporary difference (equity-method investment)	$85,000
Effective tax rate	× 34%
Required balance	$28,900

Deferred income tax asset:	
Future deductible temporary differences and carryforwards:	
Deferred compensation	$12,000
Net operating loss carryforward	40,000
	52,000
Effective tax rate	× 34%
Required balance (a)	$17,680
Capital loss	$10,000
Effective tax rate	× 34%
Required balance (b)	$ 3,400
Total deferred income tax asset: (a) + (b)	
Ordinary	$17,680
Capital	3,400
Total required balance	$21,080

The next step is to consider the need for a valuation allowance to partially or completely offset the deferred income tax asset, based on a "more likely than not" assessment of the asset's realizability. Foy management must evaluate both positive and negative evidence to determine the need for a valuation allowance, if any. Assume that management identifies the following factors that may affect this need:

1. Before the net operating loss deduction, Foy reported taxable income of $5,000 in 20X2. Management believes that taxable income in future years, apart from net operating loss deductions, should continue at approximately the same level experienced in 20X2.
2. The future taxable temporary differences are not expected to reverse in the foreseeable future as the equity method investee is not expected to incur losses or pay dividends to Foy.
3. The capital loss arose in connection with a securities transaction of a type that is unlikely to recur. The company does not generally engage in activities that have the potential to result in capital gains or losses.
4. Management estimates that certain productive assets have a fair value exceeding their respective income tax bases by about $30,000. The entire gain, if realized for income tax purposes, would result in recapture of depreciation previously taken. Since the current plans call for a substantial upgrading of the company's plant assets, management feels it could easily accelerate those actions in order to realize taxable gains, should it be desirable to do so for income tax planning purposes.

Based on the foregoing information, Foy Corporation management concludes that a $3,400 valuation allowance is required. The reasoning is as follows:

1. There will be some taxable operating income generated in future years ($5,000 annually, based on the earnings experienced in 20X2), which will absorb a modest portion of the reversal of the deductible temporary difference ($12,000) and net operating loss carryforward ($40,000) existing at year-end 20X2.
2. More importantly, the feasible tax planning strategy of accelerating the taxable gain relating to appreciated assets ($30,000) would certainly be sufficient, in conjunction with operating income over several years, to permit Foy to fully realize the income tax benefits of the future deductible temporary difference and net operating loss carryover.
3. However, since capital losses can only be carried forward for five years, are only usable to offset future capital gains, and Foy management is unable to project future realization of capital gains, it is more likely than not that the associated tax benefit accrued ($3,400) will not be realized, and thus a valuation allowance must be recorded.

Based on this analysis, an allowance for unrealizable deferred income tax benefits in the amount of $3,400 is established by a charge against the current (20X2) income tax provision.

Among the foregoing positive and negative factors to be considered, perhaps the most difficult to fully grasp is that of available income tax planning strategies. Since ASC 740 requires that all available evidence be assessed to determine the need for a valuation allowance, the matter of the cost of implementing those strategies is irrelevant. In fact, there is no limitation regarding strategies that may involve significant costs of implementation, although in computing the amount of valuation allowance needed, any costs of implementation must be netted against the benefits to be derived.

For example, if a gross deferred income tax asset of $50,000 is recorded, and certain strategies have been identified by management that would protect realization of the future deductible item associated with the computed income tax benefit at an implementation cost of $10,000, then the net amount of income tax benefit, which is more likely than not to be realizable, would not be $50,000. Rather, it may be only $43,400, which is the gross benefit less the after-tax cost of implementation, assuming a 34% tax rate {$50,000 – [$10,000 × (1 – .34)]}. Accordingly, a valuation allowance of $6,600 is established in this example.

Impact of a qualifying tax strategy

Assume that Kruse Company has a $180,000 net operating loss carryforward as of 12/31/X2, scheduled to expire at the end of the following year. Future taxable temporary differences of $240,000 exist that are expected to reverse in approximately equal amounts of $80,000 in 20X3, 20X4, and 20X5. Kruse Company estimates that taxable income for 20X3 (exclusive of the reversal of existing temporary differences and the operating loss carryforward) will be $20,000. Kruse Company expects to implement a qualifying income tax planning strategy that will accelerate the total of $240,000 of taxable temporary differences to 20X3. Expenses to implement the strategy are estimated to approximate $30,000. The tax rate is 34%.

In the absence of the income tax planning strategy, $100,000 of the net operating loss carryforward could be realized in 20X3 based on estimated taxable income of $20,000 plus $80,000 of the reversal of future taxable temporary differences. Thus, $80,000 would expire unused at the end of 20X3 and the net amount of the deferred income tax asset at 12/31/X2 would be recognized as $34,000, computed as $61,200 ($180,000 × 34%) minus the valuation allowance of $27,200 ($80,000 × 34%).

However, by implementing the income tax planning strategy, the deferred income tax asset is calculated as follows:

Taxable income for 20X3:	
Expected amount without reversal of taxable temporary differences	$ 20,000
Reversal of taxable temporary differences due to tax-planning strategy, net of costs	210,000
	230,000
Net operating loss to be carried forward	(180,000)
Net operating loss expiring unused at 12/31/X3	$ –

The gross deferred income tax asset thus can be recorded at the full benefit amount of $61,200 ($180,000 × 34%). However, a valuation allowance is required for $19,800, representing the net-of-tax effect of the $30,000 in anticipated expenses related to implementation of the strategy. The net deferred income tax asset at 12/31/X1 is $41,400 ($61,200 – $19,800). Kruse Company will also recognize a deferred income tax liability of $81,600 at the end of 20X2 (34% of the taxable temporary differences of $240,000).

The adequacy of the valuation allowance must be assessed at the date of each statement of financial position. Adjustments to the amount of the valuation allowance are recorded by a charge against, or a credit to, current earnings, via the current period income tax expense or benefit. Thus, even if the gross amount of future deductible temporary differences has remained constant during a year, income tax expense for that year might be increased or decreased as a consequence of reassessing the adequacy of the valuation allowance at year-end. It is important that these two computational steps be separately addressed: First, the computation of the gross deferred income tax assets (the product of the expected effective income tax rate and the total amount of future deductible temporary differences) must be made; then the amount of the valuation allowance to be provided to offset the deferred income tax asset must be assessed (using the criteria set forth above). Although changes in both the deferred income tax asset and valuation allowance affect current period income tax expense, the processes of measuring these two amounts are distinct. Furthermore, ASC 740 requires disclosure of both the gross deferred income tax asset (and also the gross deferred income tax liability) and the change in the valuation allowance for the year. These disclosure requirements underline the need to separately measure these items without offsetting.

Accounting for Uncertainty in Income Taxes

Background. The process of filing income tax returns requires management, in consultation with its tax advisors, to make judgments regarding how it will apply intricate and often ambiguous laws, regulations, administrative rulings, and court precedents. If and when the income tax returns are audited by the taxing authority, sometimes years after they are filed, these judgments may be questioned or disallowed in their entirety or in part. As a result, management must make assumptions regarding the likelihood of success in defending its judgments in the event of audit in determining the accounting entries necessary to accurately reflect income taxes currently payable and/or refundable.

The primary driver behind the perceived need for guidance on uncertainty in income taxes is the notion that, in general, irrespective of the method being used to recognize and measure these assets and/or liabilities, management of reporting entities historically have not used a high degree of rigor in their determination. Consequently, especially in the case of public companies, where earnings per share are viewed as an important measure of performance, the estimation of the allowance for income taxes payable was sometimes viewed as a management tool to either improve reported earnings by reducing the allowance or to build up excess liabilities (sometimes referred to as "cookie-jar reserves") that, when needed in future periods, could be reduced in order to achieve the desired result of greater earnings.

Initial recognition and measurement. ASC 740-10 uses a two-step approach to recognition and measurement.

Initial recognition—Management is to evaluate each tax position as to whether, based on the position's technical merits, it is "more likely than not" that the position would be sustained upon examination by the taxing authority. In making this evaluation, management is required to assume that the tax position will be examined by the taxing authority and that the taxing authority will be provided with all relevant facts and will have full knowledge of all relevant information. Thus, management is prohibited from asserting that a position will be sustained because of a low likelihood that the reporting entity's income tax returns will be examined.

The term "more likely than not," consistent with its use in ASC 740-10, means that there is a probability of more than 50% that the tax position would be sustained upon examination. A judgment of more likely than not represents a positive assertion by management that the reporting entity is entitled to the economic benefits provided by the tax position it is taking. The term "upon examination" includes resolution of appeals or litigation processes, if any, necessary to settle the matter.

This is a new threshold condition for recognition. Unlike the "more likely than not" criterion in ASC 740-10-45, which governs the recognition of a valuation allowance to offset all or a portion of deferred income tax assets that have already been fully recognized, this establishes a requirement for whether to give any accounting recognition to the income tax effects of questionable tax positions being taken. Failing to meet this threshold test means that, for example, an income tax deduction being claimed would not be accompanied by recognition of a reduction of income tax expense in a GAAP-basis financial statement, and thus that an income tax liability would be required to be reported for the entire tax benefit claimed on the income tax return, notwithstanding management's assertion that a deduction claimed on its income tax return was valid.

Positions must be evaluated independently of each other without offset or aggregation. A "unit of account" approach can be taken in this evaluation if it is based on the manner in which management prepares and supports its income tax return and is consistent with the approach that the taxing authority would reasonably be expected to use in conducting an examination.

In considering the technical merits of its tax positions, management must consider the applicability of the various sources of tax authority (enacted legislation, legislative intent, regulations, rulings, and case law) to the facts and circumstances. Management may also take into account, if applicable, any administrative practices and precedents that are widely understood with respect to the manner that the taxing authority deals specifically with the reporting entity or other similar taxpayers.

Initial measurement—If a tax position meets the initial recognition threshold, it is then measured to determine the amount to recognize in the financial statements. The following considerations apply to the measurement process:

1. Consider if the position is based on clear and unambiguous tax law. If so, and management has a high level of confidence in the technical merits of the position, the position qualifies as a "highly certain tax position" and, consequently, the full benefit would be recognized in the financial statements. The measurement of the maximum amount of income tax benefit that is more than 50% likely to be realized is 100% of the benefit claimed.

NOTE: Management may deem the ***amount*** *of a tax position to be highly certain of being sustained but may not be highly certain as to the* ***timing*** *of the benefit. For example, in deciding whether to record a cost as an expense of the period in which it is incurred or to capitalize it, management may be highly certain that the cost will be deductible in some period but not be highly certain as to whether the proper period to deduct it is in the current period or ratably over multiple future periods. Under these circumstances, management would be required to measure the maximum amount that it believed was more than 50% likely to be sustained in the period that the cost is incurred.*

---

2. If it is not highly certain that the full benefit of a position would be sustained in the year claimed, then the amount to be recognized for the tax position is measured as management's *best estimate* of the *maximum* benefit that is more than 50% likely to be realized upon effective settlement with a taxing authority possessing full knowledge of all relevant information. Management is to consider the amounts and probabilities of various settlement outcomes based on the facts, circumstances, and information available at the date of the statement of financial position. As stated above, management must assume that the taxing authority will conduct an examination and may not consider the likelihood of this not occurring in this measurement process.

As explained above, measurement under ASC 740-10 can be a fairly complex process. It requires that management consider the amounts and probabilities of various effective settlement outcomes. The amount of the income tax benefit to be given financial statement recognition is the largest (i.e., most favorable) estimated outcome that is more than 50% probable, as illustrated in the following example.

Example of the two-step initial recognition and measurement process

Menkin Manufacturing planned to claim a $10,000 credit for increasing research activities (R&D credit) on its 20X2 corporate income tax return. In consultation with its tax advisor, management believes that a portion of the credit is at risk because of ambiguity regarding the technical merits of the decision to classify certain costs as qualifying to be included in the computation of the credit. Management does believe, however, that it is "more likely than not" that the reporting entity will qualify for all or a portion of the R&D credit, and thus recognition will have to be limited to only a portion of the amount it will be claiming on its income tax return.

Since the credit meets the more-likely-than-not threshold for initial recognition, management must measure the amount to be recognized. It has estimated the range of possible outcomes (i.e., of credit allowed) and related likelihoods as follows:

Estimated outcome	*Probability of occurrence*	*Cumulative probability of occurrence*
$10,000	5%	5%
8,500	35%	40%
7,500	25%	65%
7,000	20%	85%
6,500	10%	95%
6,000	5%	100%

The largest outcome above that has a more than 50% cumulative probability of being realized is $7,500, which management has estimated as having a cumulative probability of 65%. Therefore, management would recognize only $7,500 of this tax position in the reporting entity's financial statements. This would result in Menkin Manufacturing reflecting a liability for unrecognized income tax benefits in the amount of $2,500 on its statement of financial position as of December 31, 20X2.

Note, in the foregoing example, that while the income tax return will claim an R&D credit for the full $10,000, GAAP-basis financial statements will only reflect a credit of $7,500, and thus will report an accrued tax liability of $2,500 pertaining to the credit taken but not likely to be allowed upon examination. ASC 740 complies with the GAAP imperative of reporting the entity's assets and liabilities on an appropriate measurement basis. GAAP financial reporting, in other words, is not a tool to be used by management to avoid recording the accounting consequences of the tactical decisions it makes regarding the tax positions it takes.

The following diagram illustrates the application of the recognition and measurement criteria:

Probability of Position Being Sustained upon Examination

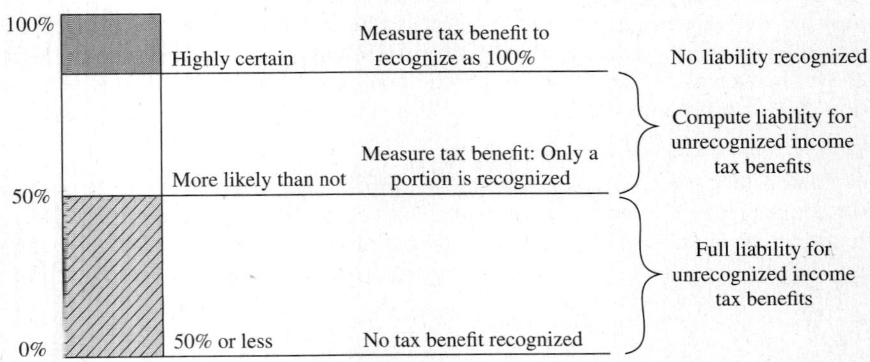

Interest. If the relevant taxing jurisdiction requires interest to be paid on income tax underpayments, the reporting entity is to recognize interest expense in the first period that interest would begin to accrue under that jurisdiction's relevant tax law. Interest is to be computed using the following formula:

Amount of tax position claimed (expected to be claimed) on income tax return
− Amount of tax position recognized in the financial statements
Portion of tax position claimed not recognized in the financial statements
× Jurisdiction's applicable statutory interest rate
× Period of time from date that interest first became accruable to reporting date
Accrued interest on tax positions taken but not recognized in the financial statements

Thus, if a tax position taken by the reporting entity fails the "more likely than not" recognition test, the presumption is that the position would not be sustained and that the entire tax benefit and associated interest (and penalties, if applicable) are to be recognized as a liability on the statement of financial position. Since interest is a period cost for the use of borrowed funds, it must be accrued until the taxing authorities reject the tax position and formally impose the demand for back taxes and interest, or the statute of limitations for the position lapses.

Penalties. If upon disallowance on examination, a position would subject the taxpayer to penalty, the reporting entity is to recognize an expense for that penalty in the period it claims or expects to claim the position in its income tax return. That is, the penalty must be accrued as the tax position becomes formalized in a tax filing. An exception is permitted if the positions taken that would be subject to penalty are under the minimum threshold that the jurisdiction uses to assess the penalty. If management later changes its assessment of whether the minimum threshold has been exceeded in a subsequent period, the penalty is to be recognized as an expense in that period.

Subsequent recognition, derecognition, and measurement. Judgments regarding initial recognition and measurement are not to be changed based on a reevaluation or reinterpretation of information that was available or should have been available in previous reporting periods. Only if new information becomes available can a new judgment be made. Management's new judgment is to consider the facts, circumstances, and information available at that time. Final certainty is not necessary for this purpose; that is, the position does not have to be subject to final settlement, court ruling, or full resolution to be remeasured.

For tax positions taken by management that do not meet the initial recognition criterion, the benefit becomes recognizable in the first interim period that the position meets any one of the following three conditions:

1. The more-likely-than-not threshold is met by the reporting date.
2. The tax position is effectively settled through examination, negotiation, or litigation.
3. The statute of limitations for the relevant taxing authority to examine and challenge the tax position has expired.

(ASC 740-10-25-8)

In determining whether the condition of "effective settlement" has occurred, ASC 740 provides that management is to evaluate whether all of the following conditions have been met:

1. The taxing authority has completed its examination procedures, including all levels of appeal and administrative reviews that are required by that authority for the specific tax position.

2. Management does not intend to appeal or litigate any aspect of the position included in the completed examination.
3. The possibility of the taxing authority examining or reexamining any aspect of the tax position is remote, considering:
    a. The authority's policy on reopening closed examinations,
    b. The specific facts and circumstances of the tax position, and
    c. The authority has full knowledge of all relevant information that might cause it to reopen an examination that had been previously closed.

(ASC 740-10-25-10)

When a taxing authority conducts an examination of a tax year, it may not choose to examine a particular tax position taken by management. Nevertheless, upon completion of the examination and all levels of appeal and review, management is permitted to consider that position effectively settled for that tax year. Management is not permitted, however, to consider that tax position or a tax position similar to it to be settled for any other open periods that were not subject to examination, nor is management permitted to use the "effectively settled" criteria for a tax position as a basis for changing its assessment of the technical merits of any tax position taken in other periods.

Tax positions recognized in previous periods that no longer meet the more-likely-than-not criterion are to be reversed ("derecognized," in FASB terminology) in the first period in which that criterion is no longer met. Importantly, it is not permitted that this objective be accomplished through the use of a valuation account or allowance to offset the recorded benefit; rather, it must be recorded as a direct reversal of the previously recorded benefit.

The accounting to record a change in judgment depends on whether the amount subject to change had been previously recognized in a prior annual period or in a prior interim period of the same fiscal year.

The effects of changes in tax positions taken in prior annual periods (including related interest and penalties, if any) are to be recognized as a "discrete item" in earnings in the period of change. Although the term "discrete item" is not defined or explained, the intent is for the change to be reported and disclosed in the same manner as the effects of a change in the enacted tax rate. This entails charging or crediting income from continuing operations for the period of change. Presumably, this would not require a separate line item on the face of the income statement (which would give disproportionate attention to the item), but would require separate disclosure in the notes to the financial statements as a significant component of income tax expense attributable to continuing operations, as specified in ASC 740.

Changes occurring in interim periods are accounted for differently. A change in judgment that applies to a tax position taken in a previous interim period of the current fiscal year is considered an integral part of the annual reporting period. Consequently, the effects of the change are recognized prospectively, through an adjustment to the estimated annual effective tax rate, in accordance with ASC 270 and ASC 740-270.

Classification. Tax liabilities resulting from applying ASC 740-10 are current tax obligations. They are *not* to be classified as deferred income tax liabilities unless they are recognized as the result of a future taxable temporary difference created by a tax position that meets the more-likely-than-not criterion.

For reporting entities that present a classified statement of financial position, the customary classification rules apply; the portion of income tax obligations recognized that are not deferred income tax liabilities under ASC 740 are classified based on management's judgment regarding whether it anticipates the payment of cash within one year or within the reporting entity's next operating cycle, if it exceeds one year. (Deferred income tax assets and liabilities are classified using the same classification as the assets or liabilities to which they relate or, if they do not relate to specific assets or liabilities, based on the year in which the temporary difference is expected to reverse.) The liability for unrecognized income tax benefits (or reduction in amounts refundable) is not permitted to be combined or netted with deferred income tax assets or liabilities.

ASC 740 provides management policy elections with respect to how it accounts for interest and penalties that are required to be accrued on the liability for unrecognized income tax positions:

Interest	Present as additional income taxes or as interest expense
Penalties	Present as additional income taxes or in another expense classification

Management is to elect which of these alternative accounting policies the reporting entity will follow, and then to disclose and consistently apply that policy.

Applicability to business combinations. ASC 805 clarifies that an acquirer is to apply its provisions to income tax positions taken by the acquiree prior to the date of the business combination. Thus, the provisions of ASC 740-10 apply to the determination of the income tax bases used to compute deferred income tax assets and liabilities as well as amounts of income taxes currently payable to or refundable from taxing authorities.

If a change occurs that affects a preexisting income tax position that was assumed as a part of the acquisition or an income tax position that arose as a result of the acquisition, the change is to be recognized as follows:

1. Changes occurring during the measurement period (as defined in ASC 805) that result from new information regarding facts and circumstances that existed on the acquisition date are recognized as an adjustment to goodwill. Should goodwill be reduced to zero, however, the remaining portion of the adjustment is to be recognized as a gain arising from a bargain purchase, in accordance with ASC 805. That standard requires recognition of such gains as part of net income and does not permit characterization as an extraordinary gain, as had been the case with the predecessor standard.
2. All other changes relating to acquired income tax positions are to be accounted for in the same manner as prescribed for other income tax positions.

The Effect of Tax Law Changes on Previously Recorded Deferred Income Tax Assets and Liabilities

General rules. The balance-sheet-oriented measurement approach of ASC 740 makes it necessary to reevaluate the deferred income tax asset and liability balances at each year-end. If changes to income tax rates or other provisions of the income tax law (e.g., deductibility of items) are enacted, the effect of these changes must be recognized so that the deferred income tax assets and liabilities are fairly presented on the statement of financial position. Any offsetting adjustments are made through the current period's income tax expense or benefit on the income statement; that is, current income tax expense or benefit reflects the income tax effect of current transactions and the revision of previously provided income tax effects for transactions which have yet to reverse.

When income tax rates are revised, this may impact not only the unreversed effects of items that were originally reported in the continuing operations section of the income statement, but also the unreversed effects of items first presented as discontinued operations, extraordinary items, or in other income statement captions. Furthermore, the impact of changes in income tax rates on the accumulated balance of deferred income tax assets or liabilities that arose through charges or credits to other comprehensive income (under ASC 220) is included in income tax expense associated with continuing operations.

For example, if an entity has unrealized gains on holding available-for-sale securities at a time when relevant income tax rates (presumably, the capital gains rates) are lowered, the reduction in the deferred income tax liability associated with these unrealized gains will reduce current period income tax expense associated with continuing operations, despite the fact that the income tax provision was originally reported in other comprehensive income (not net income) and in the equity section of the statement of financial position as accumulated other comprehensive income.

Enactment occurring during an interim period. When income tax law changes occur during an interim reporting period, the effects are reported in the interim period in which enactment occurs. The effects of the changes are included in continuing operations, whatever the source of the temporary differences being impacted. For example, if in the first fiscal quarter of a year an entity accrued a loss relating to discontinued operations, which is not tax deductible until realized, the income tax effect would be shown in the discontinued operations section of the income statement for that quarter. If income tax rates are changed in the third quarter of the same year, the deferred income tax asset recognized in connection with the loss from discontinued operations would then need to be adjusted upward or downward, based on the difference between the newly enacted income tax rates and the previously effective income tax rates. The income statement effect of this adjustment is included with income tax expense pertaining to income from continuing operations in the third quarter.

Changes in a valuation allowance for an acquired entity's deferred income tax asset. ASC 805 has specific requirements for the acquirer to recognize changes in a valuation allowance for an acquiree's deferred income tax asset. (See the chapter on ASC 805 for more detail.)

Leveraged leases. When a change in the income tax law is enacted, all components of a leveraged lease must be recalculated from the inception of the lease based upon the revised after-tax cash flows resulting from the change. For more guidance on this and other income tax aspects of leveraged leases, see the chapter on ASC 840.

Reporting the Effect of Tax Status Changes

The reporting of changes in an entity's income tax status is entirely analogous to the reporting of newly enacted income tax rate changes. Such adjustments typically arise from a change from (or to) taxable status to (or from) "flow through" or nontaxable status. When a previously taxable C corporation elects to become a flow-through entity (an S corporation), the stockholders become personally liable for income taxes on the company's earnings. This liability occurs whether the earnings are distributed to them or not, similar to the taxation of partnerships and limited liability companies.

When the income tax status change becomes effective, the effect of any consequent adjustments to deferred income tax assets and liabilities is reported in current income tax expense. This is always included in the income tax provision relating to continuing operations.

Under ASC 740, deferred income taxes are eliminated by reversal through current period income tax expense. Thus, if an entity with a net deferred income tax liability elects S corporation status, it will report an income tax benefit in the continuing operations section of its current income statement.

Similarly, if an S corporation elects to convert to a C corporation, the effect is to assume a net income tax benefit or obligation for unreversed temporary differences existing at the date the change becomes effective. Accordingly, the financial statements for the period in which the change becomes effective will include the effects of the event in current income tax expense. For example, if the entity has unreversed future taxable temporary differences at the date its income tax status change became effective, it reports income tax expense for that period. Conversely, if it had unreversed future deductible temporary differences, a deferred income tax asset (subject to the effects of any valuation allowance necessitated by applying the more-likely-than-not criterion) would be recorded, with a corresponding credit to the current period's income tax expense or benefit in the income statement.

Any entity eliminating an existing deferred income tax asset or liability, or recording an initial deferred income tax asset or liability, must fully explain the nature of the events that transpired to cause this adjustment. This is disclosed in the notes to the financial statements for the reporting period.

S corporation elections may be made prospectively at any time during the year preceding the tax year in which the election is intended to be effective and retroactively up to the 16th day of the 3rd month of the tax year in which the election is intended to be effective. The IRS normally informs the electing corporation of whether or not its election has been accepted within 60 days of filing. In practice, however, the IRS seldom denies a timely filed election, and such elections are considered essentially automatic. Consequently, if a reporting entity files an election before the end of its current fiscal year to be effective at the start of the following year, it is logical that the income tax effects would be reported in current year income. For example, an election by a C corporation to become an S corporation that is filed in December 20X1, to be effective at the beginning of the company's next fiscal year, January 1, 20X1, would give rise to the elimination of the deferred income tax assets and liabilities at the date of filing, the effect of which would be reported in the 20X2 financial statements. No deferred income tax assets or liabilities would appear on the December 31, 20X1 statement of financial position, and income tax expense or benefit for 20X2 would include the effects of the reversals of deferred income tax assets and liabilities that had been previously recognized.

There are two situations that could result in an S corporation continuing to recognize deferred income taxes. The first situation arises when the S corporation operates in one or more states that impose state income taxes on the S corporation in an amount that is material to the financial statements. In this situation, the S corporation should compute and recognize deferred state income tax assets and liabilities in the same manner that a C corporation recognizes them for federal income taxes.

The second situation is referred to as "built-in gains tax." Under current income tax law, a C corporation electing to become an S corporation may have built-in gains, which could result in a future corporate income tax liability, under defined circumstances. In such cases the reporting entity, even though it has become an S corporation, will continue to report a deferred income tax liability related to this built-in gain.

Reporting the Effect of Accounting Changes for Income Tax Purposes

Occasionally an entity will initiate or be required to adopt changes in accounting that affect income tax reporting, but which will not impact financial statement reporting. Past examples have included the change to the direct write-off method of bad debt recognition (mandated by a change in the income tax law, while the GAAP requirement to recognize an allowance for uncollectible accounts receivable continued in effect for financial reporting); and the adoption of uniform capitalization for valuing inventory for income tax purposes, while continuing to currently expense certain administrative costs not inventoriable under GAAP for financial reporting.

Generally, these mandated changes involve two distinct types of temporary differences. The first of these changes is the onetime, catch-up adjustment which either immediately or over a prescribed time period impacts the income tax basis of the asset or liability in question (net receivables or inventory, in the examples above), and which then reverses as these assets or liabilities are later realized or settled and are eliminated from the statement of financial position. The second change is the ongoing differential in the amount of newly acquired assets or incurred liabilities recognized for income tax and financial reporting purposes; these differences also eventually reverse, when the inventory is ultimately sold or the receivables are ultimately collected. This second type of change is the normal temporary difference that has already been discussed. It is the first type of change that differs from those previously discussed in this chapter, and that will now be illustrated.

Example of adjustment for prospective catch-up adjustment due to change in tax accounting

Blakey Corporation has, at December 31, 20X1, accrued interest of $80,000 on its long-term debt. Also assume that expected future taxes will be at a 34% rate and that, effective January 1, 20X2, the income tax law is revised to eliminate deductions for accrued but unpaid interest with existing accruals to be taken into income ratably over four years (referred to in tax vernacular as "a four-year spread"). A statement of financial position of Blakey Corporation prepared on January 1, 20X2, would report

1. A deferred income tax *asset* in the amount of $27,200 (i.e., $80,000 × 34%, which is the income tax effect of future deductions that Blakey will be entitled to take over the succeeding four years for the amount of interest that had been accrued and unpaid at the effective date of the tax law change, taken when specific receivables are written off and bad debts are incurred for income tax purposes);
2. A current income tax liability of $6,800 (one-fourth of the income tax obligation); and a noncurrent income tax liability of $20,400 (three-fourths of the tax income obligation).

The deferred income tax asset is *not* deemed to be identified with the liability, accrued interest (if it were, it would all be reported as a current asset), but rather with the future specific tax benefits expected to be realized from recognizing 25% of the accrual as a deduction in each of the next four years. Accordingly, the deferred income tax asset is categorized as current and noncurrent according to Blakey Corporation's best estimate of the timing of those future income tax benefits.

Income Tax Effects of Dividends Paid on Shares Held by Employee Stock Ownership Plans

ASC 740 affects the accounting for certain employee stock ownership plan (ESOP) transactions. Under ASC 718-40, dividends paid on unallocated shares are not considered to be dividends for financial reporting purposes. If used to pay down ESOP debt, these dividends are reported as reductions of debt or of accrued interest; if paid to plan participants, such dividends are reported as compensation cost. GAAP requires that the income tax benefits arising from dividends paid on unallocated shares be consistent with the reporting of those dividends. Thus, if the dividends were included in compensation cost, the tax benefit would be included in the income tax provision associated with continuing operations.

Dividends paid on allocated shares are treated as normal dividends for financial reporting purposes. However, per ASC 718-40, any income tax benefits resulting from these dividend payments are also to be credited to income tax expense reported in continuing operations. In FASB's view, income tax deductible dividends for other than unallocated ESOP-held shares represent an exemption from income tax of an equivalent amount of the payor's earnings. For that reason, it concluded that the income tax effects be reported in continuing operations.

FASB's decision regarding the presentation of the income tax effects of ESOP and other stock compensation plans are fully analogous. Given that both types of plans sometimes result in income tax deductions for amounts not recognized as compensation expense under GAAP, it was determined that the resulting income tax benefits be accounted for consistently.

Deferred Income Tax Effects of Changes in the Fair Value of Debt and Marketable Equity Securities

Unrealized gains or losses on holdings of marketable securities are not recognized for income tax purposes until realized through a sale. Thus, the gains or losses that are included in the financial statements (either in the income statement or in other comprehensive income) are temporary differences under ASC 740-10-25-18, et seq. The income tax effects of all temporary differences are recognized in the financial statements as deferred income tax assets or deferred income tax liabilities, with an additional requirement that an allowance be provided for deferred income tax assets that more likely than not will not be realized. Accordingly, adjustments to the carrying value of debt or equity investments included in either the trading or available-for-sale portfolios for changes in fair value will give rise to deferred income taxes, as will any recognition of "other-than-temporary" declines in the value of debt securities being held to maturity.

For gains or losses recognized in connection with holdings of investments classified as trading, since the fair value changes are recognized in net income currently, the deferred income tax effects of those changes will also be presented in the income statement.

Example of deferred income taxes on investments in debt and marketable equity securities

Odessa Corp. purchased Zeta Company bonds for the purpose of short-term speculation, at a cost of $100,000. At year-end, the bonds had a fair value of $75,000. Odessa has a 40% effective income tax rate. The entries to record the fair value adjustment and the related income tax effect are

Loss on holding of trading securities	25,000	
Investment in debt securities—trading portfolios		25,000
Deferred income tax benefit	10,000	
Provision for income taxes		10,000

On the other hand, if the investment in Zeta Company bonds had been classified (at the date of acquisition, or subsequently if the intentions had been revised) as available-for-sale, the adjustment to fair value would have been reported in other comprehensive income, and not included in net income. Accordingly, the income tax effect of the adjustment would also have been included in other comprehensive income. The entries would have been as follows:

Unrealized loss on securities—available-for-sale	25,000	
Investment in debt securities—available-for-sale (OCI)		25,000
Deferred income tax benefit	10,000	
Unrealized loss on securities—available-for-sale (OCI)		10,000

Finally, if the investment in Zeta Company bonds had been made with the intention and ability to hold to maturity, recognition of the decline in value would have depended upon whether it was judged to be temporary or other than temporary in nature. If the former, no recognition would be given to the decline, and hence there would be no deferred income tax effect either. If deemed to be other than temporary, the investment would need to be written down, with the loss included in net income. Accordingly, the income tax effect would also be reported in the income statement. The entries would be as follows:

Loss on decline of securities—held-to-maturity	25,000	
Investment in debt securities—held-to-maturity		25,000
Deferred income tax benefit	10,000	
Provision for income taxes		10,000

An other-than-temporary decline in value in securities available for sale would also have been recognized in net income (not merely in other comprehensive income), and accordingly the income tax effect of that loss would have been reported in net income.

As with all other transactions or events giving rise to deferred income tax assets, an evaluation must be made as to whether the entity would be MLTN to ultimately realize the income tax benefit so recorded. To the extent that it was concluded that some or all of the deferred income tax asset would not be realized, an allowance would be recorded, with the offset being either to the current income tax provision (if the income tax effect of the timing difference was reported in net income) or to OCI (if the income tax effect had been reported there).

Deferred income taxes will also be recorded in connection with unrealized gains recognized due to changes in the fair value of debt or equity investments. Deferred income tax liabilities will be reported in the statement of financial position, and the corresponding income tax provision will be reported in the income statement (for fair value gains arising from holdings of securities in the trading portfolio) or in other comprehensive income (for fair value changes relative to available-for-sale investments).

Other guidance on accounting for investments. A number of specialized issues arising in connection with short-term (or other) investments are addressed in the following paragraphs.

Tax Allocation for Business Investments

There are two basic methods for accounting for investments in the common stock of other corporations:

(1) the fair value method as set forth in ASC 320, and
(2) the equity method, as prescribed by ASC 323.

The cost method, is not appropriate, except for the exceedingly rare situation when fair value information is absolutely unavailable. If the cost method is used, however, there will be no deferred income tax consequence, since this conforms to the method prescribed for income tax reporting.

Under both the cost and fair value methods, ordinary income is recognized as dividends received by the investor, and capital gains (losses) are recognized upon the disposal of the investment. For income tax purposes, no provision is made during the holding period for the allocable undistributed earnings of the investee. There is no deferred income tax computation necessary when using the cost method, because there is no temporary difference.

Under the equity method, the investment is recorded at cost and subsequently increased by the allocable portion of the investee's net income. The investor's share of the investee's net income is then included in the investor's pretax accounting income. Dividend payments are not included in pretax accounting income but instead are considered to be a reduction in the carrying amount of the investment. For income tax purposes, however, dividends received are the only revenue realized by the investor. As a result, the investor must recognize deferred income tax expense on the undistributed net income of the investee that will be taxed in the future. The current effective GAAP in this area consists of ASC 740-30 and ASC 740-10.

Undistributed earnings of a subsidiary. These accounting requirements are set forth in ASC 740-30. While the timing of distribution of a subsidiary's net income to its parent may be uncertain, it will eventually occur, whether by means of dividends, or via the disposal of the entity and realization of capital gains. Accordingly, deferred income taxes must be provided, but the amount will be dependent upon the anticipated means of realization, which of course may change over time.

The magnitude of the income tax effects to be provided depends upon specific application of the income tax laws and management intent. If the law provides a mechanism under which the parent can recover its investment tax-free, deferred income taxes are not provided. For example, under §332 of the IRC, a parent corporation can liquidate an 80%-or-more-owned subsidiary without recognizing gain or loss for income tax purposes. Also, under IRC §368, a parent can effect a statutory merger or consolidation with its 80%-or-more-owned subsidiary, under which no taxable gain or loss would be recognized.

In other cases, the minimization or avoidance of income taxes can be achieved only if the parent company owns a stipulated share of the subsidiary's stock. A parent owning less than this threshold level of its subsidiary may express its intent to utilize a tax planning strategy to acquire the necessary additional shares to realize this benefit. In evaluating this strategy, the cost of acquiring the additional shares must be considered, and the benefits to be recognized (i.e., a reduced deferred income tax liability) must be offset by the cost of implementing the strategy as discussed earlier in this chapter.

A distinction exists in the application of ASC 740-30 between differences in income tax and financial reporting basis that are considered "inside basis differences" versus "outside basis differences," and this is clarified by ASC 830-740-25. Certain countries' income tax laws allow periodic revaluation of long-lived assets to reflect the effects of inflation with the offsetting credit recorded as equity for income tax purposes. Because this is an internal adjustment that does not result from a transaction with third parties, the additional basis is referred to as "inside basis." ASC 830-740-25 indicates that the ASC 740-30 indefinite reversal criteria only apply to "outside basis differences," and not to "inside basis differences" arising in connection with ownership of foreign subsidiaries. Therefore, a deferred income tax liability is to be provided on the amount of the increased inside basis.

Certain foreign countries tax corporate income at rates that differ depending on whether the income is distributed as dividends or retained by the corporation. Upon subsequent distribution of the accumulated earnings, the taxpayer receives a tax credit or refund for the difference between the two rates. In the consolidated financial statements of a parent company, the future income tax credit and the deferred income tax effects related to dividends that will be paid in the future are recognized based on the distributed rate if the parent provided for deferred income taxes because it did not invoke the indefinite reversal criteria of ASC 740-30. If the parent did not provide for deferred income taxes as a result of applying the ASC 740-30 criterion, the undistributed rate is to be used (ASC 740-10-25). The treatment of the tax credit in the separate financial statements of the foreign company is discussed later in this chapter in the section titled "Separate Financial Statements of Subsidiaries or Investees."

Undistributed earnings of an investee. When an entity has an equity method investee, it is presumed to be able to exercise significant influence, but lack control. Because the ability to indefinitely postpone income taxes on the investee's net income would be absent in such a case, in contrast to the parent-subsidiary situation above, GAAP requires full interperiod income tax allocation for the effects of undistributed investee net income. The facts and circumstances involved in each situation, however, will be the final determinant of whether this temporary difference is assumed to be a future dividend or a capital gain for purposes of computing the deferred income tax effect.

Example of income tax effects from investee company

To illustrate the application of these concepts, assume Investor Company owns 30% of the outstanding common stock of Investee Company and 70% of the outstanding common stock of

Subsidiary company. Additional data for Subsidiary and Investee companies for the year 20X1 are as follows:

	Investee Company	*Subsidiary Company*
Net income	$50,000	$100,000
Dividends paid	20,000	60,000

The following sections illustrate how the foregoing data are used to recognize the income tax effects of the stated events.

The pretax accounting income of Investor Company will include its equity in Investee Company net income equal to $15,000 ($50,000 × 30%). Investor's taxable income, on the other hand, will include dividend income of $6,000 ($20,000 × 30%), reduced by a deduction of 80% of the $6,000, or $4,800. This 80% dividends-received deduction is a permanent difference between pretax accounting income and taxable income and is allowed for dividends received from domestic corporations in which the taxpaying corporation's ownership is less than 80% but at least 20%. A lower dividends-received deduction of 70% is permitted when the ownership is less than 20%, and a 100% deduction is provided for dividends received from domestic corporations in which the ownership is 80% to 100%.

In this example, a temporary difference results from Investor's equity ($9,000) in Investee's undistributed income of $30,000 (= $50,000 net income less $20,000 dividends). The amount of the deferred income tax credit in 20X1 depends upon the expectations of Investor Company regarding the manner in which the $9,000 of undistributed income will be realized. If the expectation of receipt is via dividends, then the temporary difference is 20% (the net taxable portion, after the dividends-received deduction) of $9,000, or $1,800, and the deferred income tax liability associated with this temporary difference in 20X2 is the expected effective income tax rate times $1,800. However, if the expectation is that receipt will be through future sale of the investment, then the temporary difference is the full $9,000 and the deferred income tax liability is the current corporate capital gains rate times the $9,000.

The entries below illustrate these alternatives. An assumed tax rate of 34% is used for ordinary income, while a rate of 20% is used for capital gains. It is also assumed that there are no pre-20X2 temporary differences to consider. Note that the amounts in the entries below relate only to Investee Company's incremental impact upon Investor Company's income tax assets and liabilities.

	Expectations for undistributed income			
	Dividends		*Capital gains*	
Income tax expense	1,020		2,208	
Deferred income tax liability		612[b]		1,800[c]
Income taxes payable		408[a]		408[a]

[a] *Computation of income taxes payable:*

Dividend income—30% × ($20,000)	$ 6,000
Less 80% dividends-received deduction	(4,800)
Amount included in Investor's taxable income	$ 1,200
Tax liability—34% × ($1,200)	$ 408

[b] *Computation of deferred income tax liability (dividend assumption):*

Temporary difference:	
Investor's share of undistributed income—30% × ($50,000 – $20,000 = $30,000)	$ 9,000
Less 80% dividends-received deduction	(7,200)
Temporary difference	$ 1,800
Deferred income tax liability—34% × ($1,800)	$ 612

[c] *Computation of deferred income tax liability (capital gain assumption):*

Temporary difference:	
Investor's share of undistributed income—same as above	$9,000
Deferred income tax liability—20% × ($9,000)	$1,800

Example of income tax effects from subsidiary

The pretax accounting income of Investor Company will also include equity in Subsidiary income of $70,000 (70% × $100,000). This $70,000 will be included in consolidated pretax income in Investor's consolidated financial statements. For income tax purposes, Investor and Subsidiary cannot file a consolidated income tax return because the minimum level of control (i.e., 80%) is not present. Consequently, the taxable income of Investor will include dividend income of $42,000 (70% × $60,000), and there will be an 80% dividends-received deduction of $33,600. The temporary difference discussed in ASC 740-30 results from Investor's 70% equity ($28,000) in Subsidiary's undistributed earnings of $40,000. The amount of the deferred income tax liability in 20X1 depends upon the expectations of Investor Company as to the manner in which this $28,000 of undistributed income will be received. The same expectations can exist as previously discussed for Investor's equity in Investee's undistributed earnings (i.e., through future dividend distributions or capital gains).

The entries below illustrate these alternatives. A marginal tax rate of 34% is assumed for dividend income, and a rate of 20% applies to capital gains. It is also assumed that there are no pre-20X2 temporary differences to consider. The amounts in the entries below relate only to Subsidiary Company's incremental impact upon Investor Company's income tax assets and liabilities.

	Expectations for undistributed income			
	Dividends		*Capital gains*	
Income tax expense	4,760		8,456	
Deferred income tax liability		1,904[b]		5,600[c]
Income taxes payable		2,856[a]		2,856[a]

[a] *Computation of income taxes payable:*

Dividend income—70% × ($60,000)	*$ 42,000*
Less 80% dividends-received deduction	*(33,600)*
Amount included in Investor's taxable income	*$ 8,400*
Tax liability—34% × ($8,400)	*$ 2,856*

[b] *Computation of deferred income tax liability (dividend assumption):*

Temporary difference:	
Investor's share of undistributed income—70% × ($40,000)	*$ 28,000*
Less 80% dividends-received deduction	*(22,400)*
	$ 5,600
Deferred income tax liability—34% × ($5,600)	*$ 1,904*

[c] *Computation of deferred income tax liability (capital gain assumption):*

Temporary difference:	
Investor's share of undistributed income—70% × ($40,000)	*$ 28,000*
Deferred income tax liability—20% × ($28,000)	*$ 5,600*

If a company owns 80% or more of the voting stock of a subsidiary and consolidates the subsidiary for both financial reporting and income tax purposes, then no temporary differences exist between consolidated pretax income and taxable income. If, in the circumstances noted above, consolidated financial statements are prepared but a consolidated income tax return is not, IRC §243 allows the Investor to take a 100% dividends-received deduction. Accordingly, the temporary difference between consolidated pretax income and taxable income is zero if the Investor assumes the undistributed income will be realized in dividends.

Summary of Temporary Differences of Investees and Subsidiaries

Level of Ownership Interest

0%	<20%	50%	>80%	100%
Accounting				
Income recognition	Fair value method	Equity Method		
Deferred income tax on undistributed earnings	No temporary difference	Temporary difference		No temporary difference
Income tax				
Dividends recognized	30% of dividends received (70% deduction)	20% of dividends received (80% deduction)		None (100% deduction)

Separate Financial Statements of Subsidiaries or Investees

Push-down accounting. ASC 805-50 addressed a number of issues concerning whether the use of a step-up in the income tax basis of an acquired entity, as permitted by the 1982 tax law, mandated the use of push-down accounting, and the necessary allocation of the income tax provision between parent and subsidiaries if a step-up was not elected. Push-down accounting is not required for non-SEC registrants. In addition, if the acquiree continues to report its net assets on their historical basis, three alternative methods of allocating consolidated income tax expense or benefit are acceptable: (1) allocation to the acquiree on the preacquisition basis; (2) crediting the income tax benefit of basis step-up to the acquiree's stockholders' equity upon realization; and (3) crediting the income tax benefit to the income of the acquirer when realized as a permanent difference.

Tax credits related to dividend payments. Some taxing jurisdictions have differing income tax rates that are applied to taxable income based on whether that income is distributed to investors or retained in the business. For example, Germany taxes undistributed profits at a 45% rate and distributed profits at a 30% rate. When previously undistributed profits are distributed, the taxpayer earns an income tax credit for the differential between the two rates. ASC 740-10-30 specifies that the accounting for the income tax credit in the separate financial statements of the reporting entity paying the dividend is a reduction of income tax expense in the period that the credit is included in its income tax return. During the period of time that the earnings remain undistributed, the rate applied to the temporary difference in computing deferred income taxes is the rate applicable to the undistributed profits (45% in this example).

Asset Acquisitions

ASC 740-10-25 provides that in situations where an acquiring entity makes an asset acquisition:

1. When management recognizes a reduction in the reporting entity's valuation allowance that directly results from the asset acquisition, the reduction is not to enter into

the accounting for the asset acquisition. The acquiring entity is to reduce the valuation allowance and either recognize the reduction:

a. As an income tax benefit or
b. As a credit to contributed capital if related to items such as employee stock options, dividends on unallocated ESOP shares, or certain quasi reorganizations.

2. Any income tax uncertainties existing at the date of acquisition are to be accounted for in accordance ASC 740-10-45-23.

(Also see 805-740-30-3)

These specific amendments are to be applied to all asset acquisitions irrespective of when they occurred.

Intraperiod Income Tax Allocation

ASC 740 predominantly deals with the requirements of interperiod income tax allocation (i.e., deferred income tax accounting), but its scope also includes intraperiod income tax allocation. This relates to the matching of various categories of comprehensive income or expense (continuing operations, extraordinary items, corrections of errors, prior period adjustments, etc.) with the income tax effects of those items, as presented in the income (or other financial) statement. The general principle is that the income statement presentation of the effects of income taxes should be the same as items to which the income taxes relate. A "with and without" approach is prescribed as the mechanism by which the marginal, or incremental income tax effects of items other than those arising from continuing operations are to be measured. However, under ASC 740 there are some significant departures from past practice, as described in the following paragraphs.

ASC 740 prescribes an incremental calculation of income tax expense to be allocated to classifications other than continuing operations. However, rather than applying successive allocations on the "with and without" basis to determine income tax expense or benefit applicable to each succeeding income statement caption, the income tax effects of all items other than continuing operations are allocated pro rata. That is, once income tax expense or benefit allocable to continuing operations is determined, the residual income tax expense or benefit is apportioned to all the other classifications (discontinued operations, et al.) in the ratios that those other items bear, on a pretax basis, to the total of all such items. Furthermore, income tax expense or benefit on income from continuing operations includes not only income taxes on the income earned from continuing operations, as expected, but also the following items:

1. The impact of changes in income tax laws and rates, which includes the effects of such changes on items that were previously reflected directly in stockholders' equity (accumulated other comprehensive income), as described more fully below.
2. The impact of changes in the entity's taxable status.
3. Changes in estimates about whether the income tax benefits of future deductible temporary differences or net operating loss or tax credit carryforwards are more likely than not to be realizable (i.e., an adjustment to the valuation allowance for such items).
4. The income tax effects of tax-deductible dividends paid to stockholders, as discussed elsewhere in this chapter.

Under ASC 740, stockholders' equity is charged or credited directly with the initial income tax effects of items that are reported in stockholders' equity without being presented on the income statement. These items include the following:

1. Corrections of the effects of accounting errors of previous periods.
2. Gains and losses that are defined under GAAP as being part of comprehensive income but are not reported in the income statement, such as foreign currency translation adjustments under ASC 830, and the fair value adjustments applicable to available-for-sale portfolios of debt and marketable equity securities held as investments. As per ASC 220, the income tax effects of these types of items will be reported in the same financial statement where other comprehensive income items are reported. These items may be reported either in a stand-alone statement of comprehensive income, or a combined statement of income and other comprehensive income, or in an expanded version of the statement of changes in stockholders' equity.
3. Taxable or deductible increases or decreases in contributed capital, such as offering costs reported under GAAP as reductions of the proceeds of a capital stock offering, but which are either immediately deductible or amortizable for income tax purposes.
4. Increases in the income tax bases of assets acquired in a taxable business combination accounted for as a pooling of interests under GAAP, if an income tax benefit is recognized at the date of the business combination (i.e., if the income tax effects of existing future deductible temporary differences are not fully offset by a valuation allowance at that date).
5. Expenses incurred in connection with stock issued under provisions of compensatory stock option plans, which are recognized for income tax purposes but are reported for accounting purposes in stockholders' equity.
6. Dividends that are paid on unallocated shares held in an ESOP, and that are charged against retained earnings.
7. Deductible temporary differences and net operating loss and tax credit carryforwards that existed at the date of a quasi reorganization.

The effects of income tax rate or other income tax law changes on items for which the income tax effects were originally reported directly in stockholders' equity are reported in continuing operations, if they occur in any period after the original event. For example, assume the reporting entity recognized a deferred income tax asset related to an employee stock option program amounting to $34,000 in 20X2, based on the estimated future income tax deduction it would receive at the then-current and anticipated future income tax rate of 34%. If the statutory income tax rate is reduced to 25% in 20X3 before the temporary difference reverses, the adjustment to the deferred income tax asset ($34,000 – $25,000 = $9,000) is reported in income tax expense or benefit applicable to income from continuing operations in 20X3.

Comprehensive example of the intraperiod income tax allocation process

Assume $50,000 in future deductible temporary differences at 12/31/X2; these differences remain unchanged during the current year, 20X3.

	20X3
Income from continuing operations	$ 400,000
Loss from discontinued operations	(120,000)
Extraordinary gain on involuntary conversion (taxable because no replacement property purchased)	60,000
Correction of error: understatement of depreciation in 20X2	(20,000)
Income tax credits	5,000

Income tax rates are: 15% on the first $100,000 of taxable income; 20% on the next $100,000; 25% on the next $100,000; 30% thereafter.

Expected future effective income tax rates were 20% at December 31, 20X2, but are judged to be 28% at December 31, 20X3.

Retained earnings at December 31, 20X2, were $650,000.

Intraperiod tax allocation proceeds as follows:

Step 1 — Income tax on total taxable income of $320,000 ($400,000 – $120,000 + $60,000 – $20,000) is $61,000 computed as follows:

Taxable income	*Income tax rate*	*Income tax*	
$100,000	15%	$15,000	
100,000	20%	20,000	
100,000	25%	25,000	
20,000	30%	6,000	
$320,000		$66,000	Income tax before credits
		(5,000)	Tax credit
		$61,000	Income tax payable

Step 2 — Income tax on income from continuing operations of $400,000 is $85,000, net of tax credit computed as follows.

Taxable income	*Income tax rate*	*Income tax*	
$100,000	15%	$15,000	
100,000	20%	20,000	
100,000	25%	25,000	
100,000	30%	30,000	
$400,000		$90,000	Income tax before credits
		(5,000)	Tax credit
		$85,000	Income tax payable

Step 3 — The $24,000 difference is allocated pro rata to discontinued operations, extraordinary gain, and correction of the error in prior year depreciation as follows:

	Gross amount before tax	*Relative %*	*Allocation of difference*
Discontinued operations	$(120,000)	150%	$ 36,000
Extraordinary gain	60,000	(75%)	(18,000)
Error correction	(20,000)	25%	6,000
	$ (80,000)	100%	$ 24,000

Step 4 — The adjustment of the deferred income tax asset, amounting to a $4,000 increase due to an effective tax rate estimate change [$50,000 × (.28 – .20)] is allocated to continuing operations, regardless of the source of the temporary difference.

A summary combined statement of income and retained earnings for 20X3 is presented below.

Income from continuing operations, before income taxes		$400,000
Income taxes on income from continuing operations:		
Current	$90,000	
Deferred	(4,000)	
Tax credits	(5,000)	81,000
Income from continuing operations, net		319,000
Loss from discontinued operations, net of income tax benefit of $36,000		(84,000)
Extraordinary gain, net of income tax of $18,000		42,000
Net income		277,000
Retained earnings, January 1, 20X3 as originally reported		650,000
Correction of accounting error, net of income tax effects of $6,000		(14,000)
Retained earnings, January 1, 20X3, as restated		636,000
Retained earnings, December 31, 20X3		$913,000

This example does not include items that will, under provisions of ASC 220, be reported in other comprehensive income.

The income tax effect of a retroactive change in tax rates on current and deferred income tax assets and liabilities is to be determined at the enactment date, using temporary differences and currently taxable income computed as of the date of enactment. The cumulative income tax effect is included in income from continuing operations. Furthermore, the income tax effect of items not included in income from continuing operations (e.g., from discontinued operations) that arose during the current fiscal year and prior to enactment is measured based on the enacted income tax rate at the time the transaction was recognized for financial reporting purposes; the income tax effect of a retroactive change in rates on current or deferred income tax assets or liabilities related to those items is nevertheless included in income from continuing operations (ASC 740-10-45).

Classification in the Statement of Financial Position

Deferred income taxes. A reporting entity that presents a classified statement of financial position will classify its deferred income tax liabilities and assets as either current or noncurrent consistent with the classification of the related asset or liability. A deferred income tax asset or liability that is not related to an asset or liability for financial reporting purposes, such as the deferred income tax consequences related to a net operating loss carryforward or income tax credit carryforward, is classified based on the expected reversal or utilization date. These classifications must be made for each separate tax-paying component within each taxing jurisdiction.

Within each of the separate components, the current asset and liability are offset and presented as a single amount, with similar treatment for the noncurrent items. Understandably, offsetting is not permitted for different tax-paying components or for different tax jurisdictions. Thus, a statement of financial position may present current and noncurrent deferred income tax assets, along with current and noncurrent deferred income tax liabilities, under certain circumstances.

If the enterprise has recorded a valuation allowance, it must prorate the allowance between current and noncurrent according to the relative size of the gross deferred income tax asset in each classification.

Payment to retain fiscal year. S corporations and partnerships are permitted to elect tax fiscal years other than a calendar year (IRC §444). If the election is made, however, the electing entity is required to make a payment to the Internal Revenue Service in an amount that approximates the income tax that the stockholders (or partners) would have paid on the income for the period between the fiscal year-end elected and the end of the calendar year. This payment, which is not a tax, is recomputed and adjusted annually and is fully refundable to the electing entity in the future upon liquidation, conversion to a calendar tax year-end or a decline in its taxable income to zero. This "required payment" should be accounted for as an asset, analogous to a deposit (ASC 740-10-55).

Disclosures

ASC 740 is one of a handful of standards that differentiates between public and nonpublic enterprises with respect to the nature and extent of required disclosures. The Appendix, "Disclosure Checklist for Commercial Businesses," has a list of the interim and year-end disclosures related to income taxes.

Accounting for Income Taxes in Interim Periods

Basic rules. The appropriate perspective for interim period reporting is to view the interim period as an integral part of the year, rather than as a discrete period. This objective is usually achieved by projecting income for the full annual period, computing the income tax thereon, and applying the "effective rate" to the interim period income or loss, with quarterly (or monthly) revisions to the expected annual results and the income tax effects thereof, as necessary.

While the Board chose to not comprehensively address interim reporting when it deliberated ASC 740, there were certain clear contradictions between ASC 270 and the principles of ASC 740, which the Board did address. As discussed in more detail below, these issues were (1) recognizing the income tax benefits of interim losses based on expected net income of later interim or annual periods, (2) reporting the benefits of net operating loss carryforwards in interim periods, and (3) reporting the effects of income tax law changes in interim periods. Other matters requiring interpretation, which were left to the user to address without official guidance, included the classification of deferred income tax assets and liabilities on interim statements of financial position and allocation of interim period income tax provisions between current and deferred income tax expense.

The annual computation of income tax expense is based upon the current income taxes payable or refundable as indicated on the income tax return, plus or minus the adjustment necessary to adjust the deferred income tax asset and liability to the proper balances as of the date of the statement of financial position (including consideration of the need for a valuation allowance, as previously discussed). The computation of interim period income tax expense should be consistent with this asset and liability method.

ASC 740-270 introduced some unfortunate terminology that, although confusing, nevertheless must be understood in the context of interim tax computations. The term "ordinary income" as used in ASC 740-270 is not the same as that term is used in the income tax law to distinguish capital gains, for example, from operating income and deductions. The ASC 740-270 definition of "ordinary income" is, formulaically:

Pretax income or loss from continuing operations

+/– Extraordinary items
+/– Discontinued operations
+/– Cumulative effects of changes in accounting principle
+/– Significant unusual or infrequently occurring items

This "ordinary income" is used as the denominator in calculating an effective income tax rate to be used to compute income tax expense currently payable for the interim period. Note that pretax income is *not* adjusted for the effects of permanent or temporary differences.

Below is a relatively simple example that illustrates these basic principles.

Basic example of interim period accounting for income taxes

Boffa, Inc. estimates that pretax accounting income for the full fiscal year ending June 30, 20X2, will be $400,000. Boffa does not expect to have any of the items that would adjust its "ordinary income" as defined above either at year-end or during any of its interim quarters. The company expects that it will incur $60,000 of meals and entertainment expenses, of which 50% are nondeductible under the current tax law the annual premium on an officer's life insurance policy is $12,000; and dividend income (from a less than 20% ownership interest) is expected to be $100,000. The company recognized income of $75,000 in the first quarter of the year. The deferred income tax liability arises solely in connection with property and equipment temporary differences; these differences totaled $150,000 at the beginning of the year and are projected to equal

$280,000 at year-end after taking into account expected acquisitions and disposals for the remainder of the fiscal year. The graduated statutory income tax rate schedule is provided below. Boffa management used a future expected effective income tax rate of 34% to compute the beginning deferred income tax liability and does not anticipate changing that percentage at the end of the fiscal year. The change in the future taxable temporary difference during the first quarter is $30,000.

Boffa must first calculate its estimated effective income tax rate for the year. This rate is computed using all of the tax planning alternatives available to the company (e.g., tax credits, foreign rates, capital gains rates, etc.).

Estimated annual pretax accounting income (and "ordinary income" as defined in ASC 740-270)		$ 400,000
Permanent differences:		
Add: Nondeductible officers' life insurance premium	$ 12,000	
Nondeductible meals and entertainment	30,000	42,000
		442,000
Less: Dividends-received deduction ($100,000 × 70%)		(70,000)
		372,000
Less: Change in future taxable temporary difference		(130,000)
Estimated taxable income for the year		$ 242,000
Annual current tax on estimated taxable income (see below)		$ 70,530
Effective income tax rate for *current* income tax expense (computed as a percentage of "ordinary income") $70,530/400,000		17.6%

Tax rate schedule			*Taxable*	
At least	*Not more than*	*Rate*	*income*	*Tax*
$ –	$ 50,000	15%	$ 50,000	$ 7,500
50,000	75,000	25%	25,000	6,250
75,000	–	34%	167,000	56,780
				$70,530

Computation of the first quarter current income tax expense:

"Ordinary income" for first quarter	$75,000
Estimated annual effective income tax rate per above	× 17.6%
	$13,200

This amount can be "proven" as follows:

Annualized current tax computed above	$70,530
Portion of annual tax attributable to first quarter	
First quarter pretax income as a % of forecast $75,000/$400,000	× 18.75%
Result, materially the same as above	$13,224

Computation of the first quarter deferred income tax expense (same method as year-end).

	Future taxable temporary difference	*Effective tax rate estimated for reversal year(s)*	*Computed deferred tax liability*
Property and equipment			
End of first quarter	$180,000	34%	$61,200
Beginning of fiscal year	150,000	34%	51,000
First quarter deferred income tax expense			$10,200

Recap of first quarter income tax expense.

Current	$13,200
Deferred	10,200
Total	$23,400

Finally, the entry necessary to record the income tax expense at the end of the first quarter is as follows:

Income tax expense	23,400	
Income taxes payable—current		13,200
Deferred income tax liability		10,200

In the second quarter, Boffa, Inc. revises its estimate of income for the full fiscal year. It now anticipates only $210,000 of pretax accounting income ("ordinary income"), including only $75,000 of dividend income, because of dramatic changes in the national economy. Other permanent differences are still expected to total $42,000.

Estimated annual pretax accounting income (and "ordinary income" as defined in ASC 740-270)		$210,000
Permanent differences:		
Add: Nondeductible officers' life insurance premium	$12,000	
Nondeductible meals and entertainment	30,000	42,000
		252,000
Less: Dividends-received deduction ($75,000 × 70%)		(52,500)
		199,500
Less: Change in future taxable temporary difference		(130,000)
Estimated taxable income for the year		$ 69,500
Annual current tax on estimated taxable income (see below)		$ 12,375
Effective income tax rate for *current* income tax expense (computed as a percentage of "ordinary income" $12,375/$210,000)		5.2%

Tax rate schedule				
At least	*Not more than*	*Rate*	*Taxable income*	*Tax*
$ –	$ 50,000	15%	$ 50,000	$ 7,500
50,000	75,000	25%	19,500	4,875
			$69,500	$12,375

The actual "ordinary income" for the second quarter was $22,000, and the change in the temporary difference was only an additional $10,000. Income tax expense for the second quarter is computed as follows:

Computation of year-to-date and second quarter current income tax expense (benefit)

"Ordinary income" for the half year ($75,000 + $22,000)	$97,000
Estimated annual effective income tax rate per above	× 5.2%
Year-to-date current income tax expense	$ 5,044
Less: Expense recognized in first quarter	13,200
Current income tax (benefit) for second quarter	$ (8,156)

Computation of year-to-date and second quarter deferred income tax expense (benefit)

	Future taxable temporary difference	*Effective tax rate estimated for reversal year(s)*	*Computed deferred tax liability*
Property and equipment			
End of second quarter	$190,000	34%	$64,600
Beginning of fiscal year	150,000	34%	51,000
Year-to-date deferred income tax expense			13,600
Less: Expense recognized in first quarter			10,200
Deferred income tax expense for second quarter			$ 3,400

Recap of second quarter income expense (benefit)

Current	$(8,156)
Deferred	3,400
Total	$(4,756)

Under ASC 270, and also under the general principle that changes in estimate are reported prospectively (as stipulated by ASC 250), the results of prior quarters are not restated for changes in the estimated effective annual tax rate. Given the current and deferred income tax expense that was recognized in the first quarter, shown above, the following entry is required to record the income taxes as of the end of the second quarter:

Income taxes payable—current	8,156	
Income tax expense (benefit)		4,756
Deferred income tax liability		3,400

The foregoing illustrates the basic problems encountered in applying GAAP to interim reporting. In the following paragraphs, we discuss some of the items requiring modifications to the approach described in the previous example.

Net operating losses in interim periods. ASC 740-270 sets forth the appropriate accounting when losses are incurred in interim periods or when net operating loss carryforward benefits are realized during an interim reporting period.

Carryforward from prior years. The interim accounting for the utilization of a net operating loss carryforward is reflected in one of two ways.

1. If the income tax benefit of the net operating loss is expected to be realized as a result of current year "ordinary income," that income tax benefit is included as an adjustment to the effective annual tax rate computation illustrated above.
2. If the income tax benefit of the net operating loss is not expected to be realized as described in item 1, the benefit is allocated first to reduce year-to-date income tax expense from continuing operations to zero with any excess allocated to other sources of income that would provide the means to utilize the net operating loss (e.g., extraordinary items, discontinued operations, etc.).

When a valuation allowance is reduced or eliminated because of a revised judgment, the previously unrecognized income tax benefit is included in the income tax expense or benefit of the interim period in which the judgment is revised. An increase in the valuation allowance resulting from a revised judgment would cause a catch-up adjustment to be included in the current interim period's income tax expense from continuing operations. In either situation, the effect of the change in judgment is **not** prorated to future interim periods by means of the effective tax rate estimate.

Example of interim-period valuation allowance adjustments due to revised judgment

Camino Corporation has a previously unrecognized $50,000 net operating loss carryforward—that is, Camino had previously established a full valuation allowance for the deferred income tax asset arising from the net operating loss and thus had not previously recognized any deferred income tax benefit associated with the net operating loss; a flat 40% tax rate for current and future periods is assumed. Income for the full year (before net operating loss) is projected to be $80,000. Consequently, the management of Camino has revised its judgment as to the future realizability of the net operating loss. In the first quarter Camino will report a pretax loss of $10,000:

Projected annual income	$80,000
× Tax rate	40%
Projected tax liability	$32,000

Accordingly, in the income statement for the first fiscal quarter, the pretax operating loss of $10,000 will give rise to an income tax benefit of $10,000 × 40% = $4,000.

In addition, an income tax benefit of $20,000 ($50,000 net operating loss × 40%) is recognized, and is included in the current quarter's income tax benefit relating to continuing operations. Thus, the total income tax benefit for the first fiscal quarter will be $24,000 ($4,000 + $20,000).

If Camino's second quarter results in pretax operating income of $30,000, and the expectation for the full year remains unchanged (i.e., operating income of $80,000), the second quarter income tax expense is $12,000 ($30,000 × 40%).

The income tax provision for the fiscal first half-year will be a benefit of $12,000, as follows:

Cumulative pretax income through second quarter ($30,000 – $10,000)	$ 20,000
× Effective rate	40%
Income tax provision before recognition of net operating loss carryforward benefit	8,000
Benefit of net operating loss carryforward first recognized in first quarter	(20,000)
Total year-to-date tax provision (benefit)	$(12,000)
Consisting of:	
First quarter (benefit)	$(24,000)
Second quarter expense	12,000
Year-to-date benefit, per above	$(12,000)

The foregoing example assumes that during the first quarter Camino's judgment changed as to the full realizability of the previously unrecognized benefit of the $50,000 loss carryforward. Were this not the case, however, the benefit would have been recognized only as actual tax liabilities were incurred (through current period income) in amounts sufficient to offset the net operating loss benefit.

Example of recognizing net operating loss carryforward benefit as actual liabilities are incurred

To illustrate this latter situation, assume the same facts about net income for the first two quarters, and assume now that Camino's judgment about the realizability of the prior period net operating loss does not change. Tax provisions for the first quarter and first half are as follows:

	First quarter	*First half-year*
Pretax income (loss)	$(10,000)	$20,000
× Effective rate	40%	40%
Tax provision before recognition of net operating loss carryforward benefit	$ (4,000)	$ 8,000
Benefit of net operating loss carryforward recognized	–	(8,000)
Tax provision (benefit)	$ (4,000)	–

Notice that recognition of an income tax benefit of $4,000 in the first quarter is based on the expectation of at least a breakeven full year's results. That is, the benefit of the first quarter's loss was deemed more likely than not. Otherwise, no income tax benefit would have been reported in the first quarter.

Estimated loss for the year. When the full year is expected to be profitable, it is irrelevant that one or more interim periods results in a loss, and the expected effective rate for the full year is used to record interim period income tax expense and benefits, as illustrated above. However, when the full year is expected to produce a loss, the computation of the effective annual income tax benefit rate must logically take into account the extent to which a net deferred income tax asset (i.e., the asset less any related valuation allowance) will be recognized at year-end. For the first set of examples, below, assume that the realization of income tax benefits related to net operating loss carryforwards are not entirely more likely than not. That is, the full benefits will be recognized as deferred income tax assets, but those assets will be offset partially or completely by the valuation allowance.

For each of the following examples we will assume that the Gibby Corporation is anticipating a loss of $150,000 for the fiscal year. The Company's general ledger currently reflects a deferred income tax liability of $30,000; all of the liability will reverse during the fifteen-year carryforward period. Assume future income taxes will be at a 40% rate.

Example 1 – NOL carryback

Assume that the company can carry back the entire $150,000 net operating loss to the preceding three years. The income tax potentially refundable by the carryback would (remember this is only an estimate until year-end) amount to $48,000 (an assumed amount). The effective rate is then 32% ($48,000/150,000).

	Ordinary income (loss)		*Tax (benefit) expense*		
Reporting period	*Reporting period*	*Year-to date*	*Year-to date*	*Less previously provided*	*Reporting period*
1st qtr.	$ (50,000)	$ (50,000)	$(16,000)	$ –	$(16,000)
2nd qtr.	20,000	(30,000)	(9,600)	(16,000)	6,400
3rd qtr.	(70,000)	(100,000)	(32,000)	(9,600)	(22,400)
4th qtr.	(50,000)	(150,000)	(48,000)	(32,000)	(16,000)
Fiscal year	$(150,000)				$(48,000)

Note that both the income tax expense (2nd quarter) and benefit are computed using the estimated annual effective rate. This rate is applied to the year-to-date numbers just as in the previous examples, with any adjustment being made and realized in the current reporting period. This treatment is appropriate because the accrual of income tax benefits in the first, third and fourth quarters is consistent with the effective rate estimated at the beginning of the year, in contrast to those circumstances in which a change in estimate is made in a quarter relating to the realizability of income tax benefits not previously provided (or benefits for which full or partial valuation allowances were required).

Example 2 – NOL carryback

In this case assume that Gibby Corporation can carry back only $50,000 of the loss and that the remainder must be carried forward. Realization of future taxable income to fully utilize the net operating loss is not deemed to be more likely than not. The estimated carryback of $50,000 would generate an income tax refund of $12,000 (again assumed). The company is assumed to be in the 40% tax bracket (a flat rate is used to simplify the example). Although the benefit of the net operating loss carryforward is recognized, a valuation allowance must be provided to the extent that it is more likely than not that the benefit will not be realized. In this example, management has concluded that only 25% of the gross benefit will be realized in future years. Accordingly, a valuation allowance of $30,000 must be established, leaving a net of $10,000 as an estimated realizable income tax benefit related to the carryforward of the projected loss.

$150,000 loss – $50,000 carried back = $100,000 net operating loss × 40% tax rate = $40,000 benefit × 75% portion deemed unrealizable = $30,000 valuation allowance

Considered in conjunction with the carryback refund of $12,000, the company will obtain a $22,000 income tax benefit relating to the projected current year loss, for an effective income tax benefit rate of 14.7%. The calculation of the estimated annual effective rate is as follows:

Expected annual net loss			$150,000
Tax benefit from net operating loss carryback		$12,000	
Tax benefit of net operating loss carryforward ($100,000 × 40%)	$40,000		
Valuation allowance	(30,000)	10,000	
Total recognized benefit			$ 22,000
Estimated annual effective rate ($22,000 ÷ $150,000)			14.7%

	Ordinary income (loss)		*Tax (benefit) expense*			
			Year-to-date			
Reporting period	*Reporting period*	*Year-to-date*	*Computed*	*Limited to*	*Less previously provided*	*Reporting period*
1st qtr.	$ 10,000	$ 10,000	$ 1,470	$ –	$ –	$ 1,470
2nd qtr.	(80,000)	(70,000)	(10,290)	–	1,470	(11,760)
3rd qtr.	(100,000)	(170,000)	(24,990)	(22,000)	(10,290)	(11,710)
4th qtr.	20,000	(150,000)	(22,000)	–	(22,000)	–
Fiscal year	$(150,000)					$(22,000)

In the foregoing, the income tax expense (benefit) is computed by multiplying the year-to-date income or loss by the estimated annual effective rate, and then subtracting the amount of tax expense or benefit already provided in prior interim periods. It makes no difference if the current period indicates an income or a loss, assuming of course that the full-year estimated results are not being revised. However, if the cumulative loss for the interim periods to date exceeds the projected loss for the full year upon which the effective income tax benefit rate had been based, then no further tax benefits can be recorded, as is illustrated above in the benefit for the third quarter.

The foregoing examples cover most of the situations encountered in practice. The reader is referred to ASC 740-270-55 for additional examples.

Operating loss occurring during an interim period. An instance may occur in which the company expects net income for the year and incurs a net loss during one of the reporting periods. In this situation, the estimated annual effective rate, which was calculated based upon the expected net income figure, is applied to the year-to-date income or loss to arrive at year-to-date income tax expense. The amount previously provided is subtracted from the year-to-date expense to arrive at the expense for the current reporting period. If the current period operations resulted in a loss, then the period will reflect an income tax benefit.

Income tax provision applicable to interim period nonoperating items.

Unusual, infrequent, or extraordinary items. The financial statement presentation of these items and their related income tax effects are prescribed by ASC 740. Extraordinary items and discontinued operations are to be shown net of their related income tax effects. Unusual or infrequently occurring items are separately disclosed as a component of pretax income, and the income tax expense or benefit is included in the income tax expense from continuing operations. Presenting these items net of tax is strictly prohibited so the reader does not mistake them for extraordinary items.

The interim treatment accorded these items does not differ from the fiscal year-end reporting required by GAAP. However, according to ASC 270, these items are not to be included in the computation of the estimated effective annual income tax rate. The opinion also requires that these items be recognized in the interim period in which they occur rather than being prorated equally throughout the year. Examples of the treatment prescribed by the opinion follow later in this section.

Recognition of the income tax effects of a loss due to any of the aforementioned situations is permitted if the benefits are expected to be realized during the year, or if they will be recognizable as a deferred income tax asset at year-end under the provisions of ASC 740.

If a situation arises where realization is not more likely than not in the period of occurrence but becomes assured in a subsequent period in the same fiscal year, the previously unrecognized income tax benefit is reported in income from continuing operations until it reduces the income tax expense to zero, with any excess reported in those other categories of income (e.g., discontinued operations) which provided a means of realization of the tax benefit.

The following examples illustrate the treatment required for reporting unusual, infrequently occurring, and extraordinary items. Again, these items are not to be used in calculating the estimated annual tax rate. For income statement presentation, the income tax expense or benefit relating to unusual or infrequently occurring items is to be included with ordinary income from continuing operations. Extraordinary items are shown net of their applicable tax provision.

The following data apply to the next two examples:

1. Irwin Industries expects fiscal year ending June 30, 20X2 income to be $96,000 and net permanent differences to reduce taxable income by $25,500.
2. Irwin Industries also incurred a $30,000 extraordinary loss in the second quarter of the year.

Example 1 – Extraordinary, unusual, or infrequent items

In this case, assume that the loss can be carried back to prior periods and, therefore, the realization of any income tax benefit is assured. Based on the information given earlier, the estimated annual effective income tax rate can be calculated as follows:

Expected pretax accounting income	$ 96,000
Anticipated permanent differences	(25,500)
Expected taxable income	$ 70,500

Income Tax Calculation "Excluding" Extraordinary Item

$50,000	×	.15	=	$ 7,500
20,500	×	.25	=	5,125
$70,500				$12,625

Effective annual rate = 13.15% ($12,625 ÷ 96,000)

No adjustment in the estimated annual effective rate is required when the extraordinary, unusual, or infrequent item occurs. The income tax (benefit) applicable to the item is computed using the estimated fiscal year ordinary income and an analysis of the incremental impact of the extraordinary item. The method illustrated below is applicable when the company anticipates operating income for the year. When a loss is anticipated but realization of benefits of net operating loss carryforwards is not more likely than not, the company computes its estimated annual effective rate based on the amount of tax to be refunded from prior years. The income tax (benefit) applicable to the extraordinary, unusual, or infrequent item is then the decrease (increase) in the refund to be received.

Computation of the income tax applicable to the extraordinary, unusual, or infrequent item is as follows:

Estimated pretax accounting income	$ 96,000
Permanent differences	(25,500)
Extraordinary item	(30,000)
Expected taxable income	$ 40,500

Income Tax Calculation "Including" Extraordinary Item

$40,500 × .15 = $6,075

Income tax "excluding" extraordinary item	$12,625
Income tax "including" extraordinary item	6,075
Income tax benefit applicable to extraordinary, unusual, or infrequent item	$ 6,550

			Income tax (benefit) applicable to				
			Ordinary income (loss)		*Unusual, infrequent, or extraordinary item*		
Reporting period	*Ordinary income (loss)*	*Unusual, infrequent, or Extraordinary Item*	*Reporting period*	*Year-to-date*	*Year-to-date*	*Previously provided*	*Reporting period*
1st qtr.	$10,000	$ –	$ 1,315	$ 1,315	$ –	$ –	$ –
2nd qtr.	(20,000)	(30,000)	(2,630)	(1,315)	(6,550)	–	(6,550)
3rd qtr.	40,000	–	5,260	3,945	(6,550)	(6,550)	–
4th qtr.	66,000	–	8,680	12,625	(6,550)	(6,550)	–
Fiscal year	$96,000	$(30,000)	$12,625				$(6,550)

Example 2 – Extraordinary, unusual, or infrequent items

Again, assume that Irwin Industries estimates net income of $96,000 for the year with permanent differences of $25,500 which reduce taxable income. The extraordinary loss of $30,000 cannot be carried back and the ability to carry it forward is not more likely than not. Because no net deferred income tax assets exist, the only way that the loss can be deemed to be realizable is to the extent that current year ordinary income offsets the effect of the loss. As a result, realization of the loss is assured only as, and to the extent that, there is ordinary income for the year.

			Income tax (benefit) applicable to				
			Ordinary income (loss)		Unusual, infrequent, or extraordinary item		
Reporting period	*Ordinary income (loss)*	*Unusual, infrequent, or Extraordinary Item*	*Reporting period*	*Year-to-date*	*Year-to-date*	*Previously provided*	*Reporting period*
1st qtr.	$ 5,000	$ –	$ 658	$ 658	$ –	$ –	$ –
2nd qtr.	20,000	(30,000)	2,630	3,288	(3,288)[a]	–	(3,288)
3rd qtr.	(10,000)	–	(1,315)	1,973	(1,973)[a]	(3,288)	1,315
4th qtr.	81,000	–	10,652	12,625	(6,550)[a]	(1,973)	(4,577)
Fiscal year	$96,000	$(30,000)	$12,625				$(6,550)

[a] *The recognition of the income tax benefit to be realized relative to the unusual, infrequent, or extraordinary item is limited to the lesser of the total income tax benefit applicable to the item or the amount available to be realized. Because realization is based upon the amount of income tax applicable to ordinary income during the period, the year-to-date figures for the income tax benefit fluctuate as the year-to-date income tax expense relative to ordinary income fluctuates. Note that at no point does the amount of the income tax benefit exceed what was calculated above as being applicable to the unusual, infrequent, or extraordinary item.*

Discontinued operations in interim periods. Discontinued operations, according to ASC 270, are included as significant, unusual, or extraordinary items. Therefore, the computations described for unusual, infrequent, or extraordinary items will also apply to the income (loss) from the discontinued operation of the entity, including any provisions for operating gains (losses) subsequent to the measurement date.

If the decision to dispose of operations occurs in any interim period other than the first interim period, the operating income (loss) applicable to the discontinued operation has already been used in computing the estimated annual effective tax rate. Therefore, a recomputation of the total tax is not required. However, the total tax is to be divided into two components.

1. That tax applicable to ordinary income (loss)
2. That tax applicable to the income (loss) from the discontinued operation.

This division is accomplished as follows: a revised estimated annual effective rate is calculated for the income (loss) from ordinary operations. This recomputation is then applied to the ordinary income (loss) from the preceding periods. The total income tax applicable to the discontinued operation is then composed of two items.

1. The difference between the total income tax originally computed and the income tax recomputed on remaining ordinary income
2. The income tax computed on unusual, infrequent, or extraordinary items as described above.

Example – Discontinued operations

Rochelle Corporation anticipates net income of $150,000 during the fiscal year. The net permanent differences for the year will be $10,000. The company also anticipates income tax credits of $10,000 during the fiscal year. For purposes of this example, we will assume a flat statutory rate of 50%. The estimated annual effective rate is then calculated as follows:

Estimated pretax income	$150,000
Net permanent differences	(10,000)
Taxable income	140,000
Statutory rate	50%
Income tax	70,000
Anticipated credits	(10,000)
Total estimated income tax	$ 60,000
Estimated effective rate ($60,000 ÷ 150,000)	40%

The first two quarters of operations were as follows:

	Ordinary income (loss)		*Tax expense*		
Reporting period	*Reporting period*	*Year-to-date*	*Year-to-date*	*Less previously provided*	*Reporting period*
1st qtr.	$30,000	$30,000	$12,000	$ –	$12,000
2nd qtr.	25,000	55,000	22,000	12,000	10,000

In the third quarter, Rochelle made the decision to dispose of Division X. During the third quarter, the company earned a total of $60,000. Upon reclassification of Division X's property and equipment to "held-for-sale" on its statement of financial position, the company expects to incur a onetime charge to income of $75,000 and estimates that current year divisional operating losses subsequent to the disposal decision will be $20,000, all of which will be incurred in the third quarter. The company estimates revised ordinary income in the fourth quarter to be $35,000. The two components of pretax accounting income (discontinued operations and revised ordinary income) are shown below.

		Division X	
Reporting period	*Revised ordinary income*	*Loss from operations*	*Asset reclassification*
1st qtr.	$ 40,000	$(10,000)	$ –
2nd qtr.	40,000	(15,000)	–
3rd qtr.	80,000	(20,000)	(75,000)
4th qtr.	35,000	–	–
Fiscal year	$195,000	$(45,000)	$(75,000)

Rochelle must now recompute the estimated annual income tax rate. Assume that all the permanent differences are related to the revised continuing operations. However, $3,300 of the tax credits were applicable to machinery used in Division X. Because of the discontinuance of operations, the credit on this machinery would not be allowed. Any recapture of prior period credits must be used as a reduction in the income tax benefit from either operations or the loss on disposal. Assume that the company must recapture $2,000 of the $3,300 investment tax credit that is related to Division X.

The recomputed estimated annual rate for continuing operations is as follows:

Estimated (revised) ordinary income	$195,000
Less net permanent differences	(10,000)
	$185,000
Tax at statutory rate of 50%	$ 92,500
Less anticipated credits from continuing operations	(6,700)
Tax provision	$ 85,800
Estimated annual effective tax rate ($85,800 ÷ 195,000)	44%

The next step is to then apply the revised rate to the quarterly income from continuing operations as illustrated below.

	Ordinary income			*Tax provision*		
Reporting period	*Reporting period*	*Year-to-date*	*Estimated annual effective rate*	*Year-to-date*	*Less previously provided*	*Reporting period*
1st qtr.	$ 40,000	$ 40,000	44%	$17,600	$ –	$17,600
2nd qtr.	40,000	80,000	44%	35,200	17,600	17,600
3rd qtr.	80,000	160,000	44%	70,400	35,200	35,200
4th qtr.	35,000	195,000	44%	85,800	70,400	15,400
Fiscal year	$195,000					$85,800

The tax benefit applicable to the operating loss from discontinued operations and the loss from the asset reclassification and remeasurement must now be calculated. The first two quarters are calculated on a differential basis as shown below.

Reporting period	Tax applicable to ordinary income: Previously reported	Recomputed (above)	Tax (benefit) expense applicable to Division X
1st qtr.	$12,000	$17,600	$ (5,600)
2nd qtr.	10,000	17,600	(7,600)
			$(13,200)

The only calculation remaining applies to the third quarter tax benefit pertaining to the operating loss and the loss on reclassification of the assets of the discontinued operation. The calculation of this amount is made based on the revised estimate of annual ordinary income both including and excluding the effects of the Division X losses. This is shown below.

	Loss from operations of Division X	Asset reclassification
Estimated annual income from continuing operations	$195,000	$195,000
Net permanent differences	(10,000)	(10,000)
Loss from Division X operations	(45,000)	–
Provision for loss on reclassification of Division X assets	–	(75,000)
Total	$140,000	$110,000

	Loss from operations of Division X	Asset reclassification
Tax at the statutory rate of 50%	$ 70,000	$ 55,000
Anticipated credits (from continuing operations)	(6,700)	(6,700)
Recapture of previously recognized tax credits as a result of disposal	–	2,000
Taxes after effect of Division X losses	63,300	50,300
Taxes computed on estimated income before the effect of Division X losses	85,800	85,800
Tax benefit applicable to Division X	(22,500)	(35,500)
Amounts allocable to quarters one and two ($5,600 + $7,600)	(13,200)	–
Tax benefit to be recognized in the third quarter	$ (9,300)	$(35,500)

The quarterly tax provisions can be summarized as follows:

	Pretax income (loss)			Tax (benefit) applicable to		
Reporting period	Continuing operations	Operations Of Division X	Loss on asset reclassification	Continuing operations	Operations of Division X	Loss on asset reclassification
1st qtr.	$ 40,000	$(10,000)	$ –	$17,600	$ (5,600)	$ –
2nd qtr.	40,000	(15,000)	–	17,600	(7,600)	–
3rd qtr.	80,000	(20,000)	(75,000)	35,200	(9,300)	(35,500)
4th qtr.	35,000	–	–	15,400	–	–
Fiscal year	$195,000	$(45,000)	$(75,000)	$85,800	$(22,500)	$(35,500)

The following income statement shows the proper financial statement presentation of these discontinued operations. The notes to the statement indicate which items are to be included in the calculation of the annual estimated rate.

Income Statement
(ASC 740-270-55)

Net sales*		$xxxx
Other income*		xxx
		xxxx
Costs and expenses		
Cost of sales*	$xxxx	
Selling, general, and administrative expenses*	xxx	
Interest expense*	xx	
Other deductions*	xx	
Unusual items*	xxx	
Infrequently occurring items*	xxx	xxxx
Income (loss) from continuing operations before income taxes and other items listed below		xxxx
Provision for income taxes (benefit)**		xxx
Income (loss) from continuing operations before items listed below		xxxx
Discontinued operations:		
Income (loss) from operations of discontinued Division X (less applicable income taxes of $xxxx)	xxxx	
Income (loss) on reclassification of assets of Division X to held-for-sale, (less applicable taxes of $xxxx)	xxxx	xxxx
Income (loss) before extraordinary items and cumulative effect of a change in accounting principle		xxxx
Extraordinary items (less applicable income taxes of $xxxx)		xxxx
Cumulative effect on prior years of a change in accounting principle (less applicable income taxes of $xxxx)***		xxxx
Net income (loss)		$xxxx

* *Components of ordinary income (loss).*

** *Consists of total income taxes (benefit) applicable to ordinary income (loss), unusual items, and infrequently occurring items.*

*** *This amount is shown net of income taxes. Although the income taxes are generally disclosed (as illustrated), this is not required.*

45 ASC 805 BUSINESS COMBINATIONS

PERSPECTIVE AND ISSUES

Subtopics

ASC 805, *Business Combinations*, consists of six subtopics:

- ASC 805-10, *Overall,* which provides guidance on transactions accounted for under the acquisition method
- ASC 852-20, *Identifiable Assets and Liabilities, and Any Noncontrolling Interest,* deals with specific aspects of the acquisition method
- ASC 805-30, *Goodwill or Gain from Bargain Purchase, Including Consideration Transferred,* like ASC 805-20, 805-30 deals with specific aspects of the acquisition method
- ASC 805-40, *Reverse Acquisitions,* provides guidance on business combinations that are reverse acquisitions
- ASC 805-50, *Related Issue,* which offers guidance two items that are similar, but not the same, as a business combination: acquisition of assets and transactions between entities under common control
- ASC 805-740, *Income Taxes*, which provides "incremental guidance" on business combinations and on acquisitions by a not-for-profit entity.

Scope and Scope Exceptions

Transactions or other events that meet the definition of a business combination are subject to ASC 805. Excluded from the scope of ASC 805, however, are:

1. Formation of a joint venture
2. Acquisition of an asset or group of assets that does not represent a business or a nonprofit activity
3. Combinations between entities, businesses, or nonprofit activities under common control
4. An acquisition by a not-for-profit entity for which the acquisition date is before December 15, 2009, or a merger of not-for-profit entities (NFPs).
5. An event in which an NFP obtains control of a not-for-profit entity but does not consolidate that entity, as permitted or required by ASC 958-810-25.
6. If an NFP that obtained control in an event in which consolidation was permitted but not required decides in a subsequent annual reporting period to begin consolidating a controlled entity that it initially chose not to consolidate.

Overview

Historically, one of the most daunting problems facing accountants has been the determination of when it is more informative and meaningful to present the financial statements of multiple enterprises together, as if they were a single economic unit. A closely related issue was that of how to account for the acquisition of one enterprise by another, or other combination of two or more formerly unrelated entities, into one new enterprise.

Regarding this last-named concern, US GAAP had traditionally permitted two distinct methods of accounting for business combinations. The *purchase accounting method* (now known as the *acquisition method*) required that the actual cost of the acquisition be recognized, including any excess over the amounts allocable to the fair value of identifiable net assets, commonly known as goodwill. The *pooling of interest method*, available only when a set of stringent criteria were all met, resulted in combining the book values of the merging entities, without any adjustment to reflect the fair values of acquired assets and liabilities, and without any recognition of goodwill. Since pooling of interests accounting required that the mergers be achieved by means of exchanges of common stock, the use of this method was largely restricted to publicly held acquirers, which greatly preferred poolings since this averted step-ups in the carrying value of depreciable assets and goodwill recognition, the amortization of which would reduce future reported earnings.

Pooling accounting was widely seen as not being indicative of economic reality, since mergers that were true "marriages of equals" rarely, if ever, occurred, notwithstanding that this was the theoretical basis for using this method of accounting. Ultimately, the pooling method was eliminated, but gaining support for this change required a significant compromise by the FASB on the related matter of goodwill accounting: under the rules established in Accounting Standards Codification (ASC) 350, *Intangibles—Goodwill and Other,* goodwill would no longer be amortized, and the impact of business combinations on reported income would often more closely resemble that of the now-banned pooling method than the traditional purchase accounting method. Although periodic amortization is no longer reported, goodwill must be tested annually for impairment and, when impairment is found to have occurred, goodwill must be written down to fair value, with the adjustment reflected as a charge against the operating income of that period. (See the chapter on ASC 350 for a technical update on ASU 2014-02, *Intangibles—Goodwill and Other (Topic 350): Accounting for Goodwill.* The ASU introduces an alternative for private companies that allows for amortization over a period not to exceed ten years.)

DEFINITIONS OF TERMS

Source: ASC 805

Acquiree. The business or businesses that the acquirer obtains control of in a business combination. This term also includes a nonprofit activity or business that a not-for-profit acquirer obtains control of in an acquisition by a not-for-profit entity.

Acquirer. An entity that obtains control over one or more businesses in a business combination. When the acquiree is a variable interest entity (VIE), the primary beneficiary of the VIE is always the acquirer.

Acquisition by a not-for-profit entity. A transaction or other event in which a not-for-profit acquirer obtains control of one or more nonprofit activities or businesses and initially recognizes their assets and liabilities in the acquirer's financial statements. When applicable guidance in Topic 805 is applied by a not-for-profit entity, the term *business combination* has the same meaning as it has for a not-for-profit entity. Likewise, a reference to business combinations in guidance that links to Topic 805 has the same meaning as a reference to acquisitions by not-for-profit entities.

Acquisition date. The date on which control of the acquiree is obtained by the acquirer.

Business. An integrated set of assets and activities capable of being conducted and managed for the purpose of providing a return directly to investors or other owners, members, or participants. The return can be in the form of dividends, lower costs, or other economic benefits. A development stage enterprise (ASC 915) is not precluded from qualifying as a business under this definition and the guidance that accompanies it in ASC 805.

Business combination. A transaction or event that results in an acquirer obtaining control over one or more businesses. It is important to note that transactions that are sometimes referred to as "mergers of equals" or as "true mergers" are nevertheless considered to be business combinations with an acquirer and one or more acquirees.

Contingency. An existing condition, situation, or set of circumstances involving uncertainty as to possible gain (gain contingency) or loss (loss contingency) to an entity that will ultimately be resolved when one or more future events occur or fail to occur.

Contingent consideration. Usually an obligation of the acquirer to transfer additional assets or equity interests to the former owners of an acquiree as part of the exchange for control of the acquiree if specified future events occur or conditions are met. However, contingent consideration also may give the acquirer the right to the return of previously transferred consideration if specified conditions are met.

Contingent consideration might also arise when the terms of the business combination provide a requirement that the acquiree's former owners return previously transferred assets or equity interests to the acquirer under certain specified conditions.

Defensive intangible asset. An acquired intangible asset in a situation in which an entity does not intend to actively use the asset but intends to hold (lock up) the asset to prevent others from obtaining access to the asset.

Equity interests. Used broadly to mean ownership interests of investor-owned entities; owner, member, or participant interests of mutual entities; and owner or member interest in the net assets of not-for-profit entities.

Fair value. The price that would be received to sell an asset or paid to transfer a liability in an orderly transaction between market participants at the measurement date.

Goodwill. An asset representing the future economic benefits arising from other assets acquired in a business combination or an acquisition by a not-for-profit entity that are not individually identified and separately recognized. For ease of reference, this term also includes the immediate charge recognized by not-for-profit entities in accordance with ASC 958-805-25-29.

Identifiable asset. Assets (not including financial assets) that lack physical substance. (The term intangible assets is used to refer to intangible assets other than goodwill.)

Intangible asset. A nonfinancial asset that lacks physical substance. (The term intangible assets is used to refer to intangible assets other than goodwill.)

Market participants. Buyers and sellers in the principal (or most advantageous) market for the asset or liability that have all of the following characteristics:

a. They are independent of each other, that is, they are not related parties, although the price in a related-party transaction may be used as an input to a fair value measurement if the reporting entity has evidence that the transaction was entered into at market terms
b. They are knowledgeable, having a reasonable understanding about the asset or liability and the transaction using all available information, including information that might be obtained through due diligence efforts that are usual and customary
c. They are able to enter into a transaction for the asset or liability
d. They are willing to enter into a transaction for the asset or liability, that is, they are motivated but not forced or otherwise compelled to do so.

Merger of not-for-profit entities. A transaction or other event in which the governing bodies of two or more not-for-profit entities cede control of those entities to create a new not-for-profit entity.

Noncontrolling interest. The equity or net assets in a subsidiary not directly or indirectly attributable to its parent. Noncontrolling interests were formerly referred to in accounting literature as minority interests.

Nonprofit activity. An integrated set of activities and assets that is capable of being conducted and managed for the purpose of providing benefits other than goods or services at a profit or profit equivalent, as a fulfillment of an entity's purpose or mission (for example, goods or services to beneficiaries, customers, or members). As with a not-for-profit entity, a nonprofit activity possesses characteristics that distinguish it from a business or a for-profit business entity.

Not-for-profit entity. A legal entity that, in varying degrees, possesses the following characteristics that differentiate it from a business entity:

1. It receives significant amounts of resources in the form of contributions where the contributors do not expect a reciprocal monetary return,
2. It operates for purposes other than providing goods or services at a profit.
3. It does not have ownership interests similar to those of business entities.

Among the entities that are clearly not included in this definition are

1. All investor-owned entities
2. Entities that provide dividends, lower costs, or other economic benefits directly and proportionately to their owners, members, or participants, such as mutual insurance entities, credit unions, farm and rural electric cooperatives, and employee benefit plans.

See ASC 958-10-15 for a discussion of this definition and for application guidance.

Owners. Used broadly to include holders of ownership interests (equity interests) in investor-owned mutual entities, or not-for-profit entities. Owners include shareholders, partners, proprietors, or members, or participants of mutual entities. Owners also include owner and member interests in the net assets of not-for-profit entities.

Public entity. A business entity or a not-for-profit entity that meets any of the following conditions:

1. It has issued debt or equity securities or is a conduit bond obligor for conduit debt securities that are traded in a public market (a domestic or foreign stock exchange or an over-the-counter market, including local or regional markets),
2. It is required to file financial statements with the Securities and Exchange Commission (SEC),
3. It provides financial statements for the purpose of issuing any class of securities in a public market.

Reverse acquisition. An acquisition in which the entity that issues securities (the legal acquirer) is identified as the acquiree for financial accounting purposes, based on application of the guidance in ASC 805-10-55-11 through 55-15. The entity whose equity interests are acquired (the legal acquiree) must be the acquirer for accounting purposes in order for the transaction to be considered a reverse acquisition.

Reverse spin-off. A spin-off transaction in which the nominal or legal spinnor is to be accounted for as the spinnee, in order to reflect the economic reality of the spin-off transaction.

Variable interest entity. A legal entity subject to consolidation according to the provisions of the Variable Interest Entities Subsections of Subtopic 810-10.

CONCEPTS, RULES, AND EXAMPLES

Transactions and Events Accounted for as Business Combinations

A business combination results from the occurrence of a transaction or other event that results in an acquirer obtaining control of one or more businesses. This can occur in many different ways that include the following examples individually or, in some cases, in combination:

1. Transfer of cash, cash equivalents, or other assets, including the transfer of assets of another business of the acquirer
2. Incurring liabilities
3. Issuance of equity instruments
4. Obtaining variable interests in an acquiree variable interest entity (VIE) that is a business, resulting in the acquirer becoming the VIE's primary beneficiary/parent, under the provisions of ASC 810,
5. By contract alone without the transfer of consideration, such as when
   a. An acquiree business repurchases enough of its own shares to cause one of its existing investors (the acquirer) to obtain control over it
   b. There is a lapse of minority veto rights that had previously prevented the acquirer from controlling an acquiree in which it held a majority voting interest
   c. An acquirer and acquiree contractually agree to combine their businesses without a transfer of consideration between them.

Qualifying as a Business

ASC 805 provides a definition of a business. Further, it clarifies that the initial consolidation of a VIE that is a business is considered to be a business combination. This effectively provides parity between the accounting for business combinations and any related noncontrolling interests involving voting interest entities and those involving variable interest entities.

To be considered a business, an integrated group of activities and assets must be *capable* of being conducted and managed to provide a return directly to investors, or other owners, members, or participants. The return can be in the form of dividends, reduced costs, or other economic benefits. The word *capable* emphasizes the fact that the definition does not preclude a development stage entity from qualifying as a business.[1] "Other owners, members, or participants" were included to emphasize the applicability of ASC 805 to mutual entities that previously used the pooling-of-interests method of accounting for business combinations and to noncorporate entities.

The definition and related guidance elaborate further that a business consists of inputs and processes applied to those inputs that have the ability to create outputs. While outputs are usually present in a business, they are not required to qualify as a business. There simply must be the *ability* to create them.

An *input* is an economic resource that creates or has the ability to create outputs when one or more processes are applied to it. Examples of inputs include fixed assets, intangible rights to use fixed assets, intellectual property or other intangible assets, and access to markets in which to hire employees or purchase materials.

A *process* is a system, protocol, convention, or rule with the ability to create outputs when applied to one or more inputs. Processes are usually documented; however, an organized workforce with the requisite skills and experience may apply processes necessary to create outputs by following established rules and conventions. In evaluating whether an activity is a process, ASC 805 indicates that functions such as accounting, billing, payroll, and other administrative systems do not meet the definition. Thus, processes are the types of

[1] See the chapter on ASC 915 for information on a FASB project on development stage enterprises.

activities that an entity engages in to produce the products and/or services that it provides to the marketplace, rather than the internal activities it follows in operating its business.

An *output* is simply the by-product resulting from applying processes to inputs. An output provides, or has the ability to provide, the desired return to investors, members, participants, or other owners.

In analyzing a transaction or event to determine whether it is a business combination, it is not necessary that the acquirer retain, postcombination, all of the inputs or processes used by the seller in operating the business. Using the "market participant" approach to analyzing the facts, as defined in ASC 820, if market participants could, for example, acquire the business in an arm's-length transaction and continue to produce outputs by integrating the business with their own inputs and processes, then that subset of remaining inputs and processes still meets the definition of a business from the standpoint of the acquirer.

The guidance in ASC 805 provides additional flexibility by providing that it is not necessary that a business have liabilities, although that situation is expected to be rare.

If a business is not producing outputs, the acquirer must determine whether the enterprise constitutes a business by considering whether it:

1. Has started its planned principal activities,
2. Has hired employees,
3. Has obtained intellectual property,
4. Has obtained other inputs,
5. Has implemented processes that could be applied to its inputs,
6. Is pursuing a plan to produce outputs,
7. Will have the ability to obtain access to customers that will purchase the outputs.

(ASC 805-10-55-7)

It is important to note, however, that it is not required that all of these factors be present for a given set of activities and assets to qualify as a business. Again, the relevant question to ask is whether a market participant would be capable of conducting or managing the set of activities and assets as a business irrespective of whether the seller did so or the acquirer intends to do so.

Finally, ASC 805 provided what it acknowledged was circular logic in asserting that, absent evidence to the contrary, if goodwill is included in a set of assets and activities, it can be presumed to be a business. The circularity arises from the fact that, in order to apply GAAP to determine whether to initially recognize goodwill, the accountant would be required to first determine whether there had, in fact, been an acquisition of a business. Otherwise, it would not be permitted to recognize goodwill. It is not necessary, however, that goodwill be present in order to consider a set of assets and activities to be a business.

Techniques for Structuring Business Combinations

A business combination can be structured in a number of different ways that satisfy the acquirer's strategic, operational, legal, tax, and risk management objectives. Some of the more frequently used structures are:

1. One or more businesses become subsidiaries of the acquirer. As subsidiaries, they continue to operate as legal entities.
2. The net assets of one or more businesses are legally merged into the acquirer. In this case, the acquiree entity ceases to exist (in legal vernacular, this is referred to as a *statutory merger* and normally the transaction is subject to approval by a majority of the outstanding voting shares of the acquiree).

3. The owners of the acquiree transfer their equity interests to the acquirer entity or to the owners of the acquirer entity in exchange for equity interests in the acquirer.
4. All of the combining entities transfer their net assets (or their owners transfer their equity interests into a new entity formed for the purpose of the transaction). This is sometimes referred to as a *roll-up* or put-together transaction.
5. A former owner or group of former owners of one of the combining entities obtains control of the combined entities collectively.
6. An acquirer might hold a noncontrolling equity interest in an entity and subsequently purchase additional equity interests sufficient to give it control over the investee. These transactions are referred to as *step acquisitions* or business combinations achieved in stages.
7. A business owner organizes a partnership, S corporation, or LLC to hold real estate. The real estate is the principal location of the commonly owned business and that business entity leases the real estate from the separate entity.

Accounting for Business Combinations under the Acquisition Method

The acquirer accounts for a business combination using the *acquisition method.* This term represents an expansion of the now-outdated term, "purchase method." The change in terminology was made to emphasize that a business combination can occur even when a purchase transaction is not involved.

The following steps are required to apply the acquisition method:

1. Identify the acquirer.
2. Determine the acquisition date.
3. Identify the assets and liabilities, if any, requiring separate accounting because they result from transactions that are not part of the business combination, and account for them in accordance with their nature and the applicable GAAP.
4. Identify assets and liabilities that require acquisition date classification or designation decisions to facilitate application of GAAP in postcombination financial statements and make those classifications or designations based on (a) contractual terms, (b) economic conditions, (c) acquirer operating or accounting policies, and (d) other pertinent conditions existing at the acquisition date.
5. Recognize and measure the identifiable tangible and intangible assets acquired and liabilities assumed.
6. Recognize and measure any noncontrolling interest in the acquiree.
7. Measure the consideration transferred.
8. Recognize and measure goodwill or, if the business combination results in a bargain purchase, recognize a gain.

Step 1—Identify the acquirer. ASC 805 strongly emphasizes the concept that every business combination has an acquirer. In the "basis for conclusions" that accompanies FASB 141 (R), FASB asserted that

> *. . . "true mergers" or "mergers of equals" in which none of the combining entities obtain control of the others are so rare as to be virtually nonexistent . . .*

The determination of the acquirer is based on application of the provisions of ASC 810 regarding the party that possesses a controlling financial interest in another entity. In general, ASC 810 provides that direct or indirect ownership of a majority of the outstanding voting interests in another entity ". . . is a condition pointing toward consolidation." However, this is not an absolute rule to be applied in all cases. In fact, ASC 810 explicitly provides that majority owned entities are not to be consolidated if the majority-owner does not hold a controlling financial interest in the entity. Exceptions to the general majority ownership rule include, but are not limited to, the following situations:

1. An entity that is in legal reorganization or bankruptcy
2. An entity subject to uncertainties due to government-imposed restrictions, such as foreign exchange restrictions or controls, whose severity casts doubt on the majority interest owner's ability to control the entity
3. If the acquiree is a variable interest entity (VIE), the primary beneficiary of the VIE is always considered to be the acquirer.

If applying the guidance in ASC 810 does not clearly indicate the party that is the acquirer, ASC 805-10-55-10 through 15 provides factors to consider in making that determination under different facts and circumstances:

1. *Relative size*—Generally, the acquirer is the entity whose relative size is significantly larger than that of the other entity or entities. Size can be compared by using measures such as assets, revenues, or net income. (ASC 805-10-55-13)
2. *Initiator of the transaction*—When more than two entities are involved, another factor to consider (beside relative size) is which of the entities initiated the transaction. (ASC 805-10-55-14)
3. *Roll-ups or put-together transactions*—When a new entity is formed to issue equity interests to effect a business combination, one of the preexisting entities is to be identified as the acquirer. If, instead, a newly formed entity transfers cash or other assets, or incurs liabilities as consideration to effect a business combination, that new entity may be considered to be the acquirer. (ASC 805-10-55-15)
4. *Nonequity consideration*—In business combinations accomplished primarily by the transfer of cash or other assets, or by incurring liabilities, the entity that transfers the cash or other assets, or incurs the liabilities is usually the acquirer. (ASC 805-10-55-11)
5. *Exchange of equity interests*—In business combinations accomplished primarily by the exchange of equity interests, the entity that issues its equity interests is generally considered to be the acquirer. One notable exception that occurs frequently in practice is sometimes referred to as a reverse acquisition, discussed in detail later in this chapter. In a reverse acquisition, the entity issuing equity interests is legally the acquirer, but for accounting purposes is considered the acquiree. There are, however, other factors that should be considered in identifying the acquirer when equity interests are exchanged. These include:

    a. *Relative voting rights in the combined entity after the business combination*—Generally, the acquirer is the entity whose owners, as a group, retain or obtain the largest portion of the voting rights in the consolidated entity. This determination must take into consideration the existence of any unusual or special voting arrangements as well as any options, warrants, or convertible securities.
    b. *The existence of a large minority voting interest in the combined entity in the event no other owner or organized group of owners possesses a significant voting interest*—Generally, the acquirer is the entity whose owner or organized group of owners holds the largest minority voting interest in the combined entity.
    c. *The composition of the governing body of the combined entity*—Generally, the acquirer is the entity whose owners have the ability to elect, appoint, or remove a majority of members of the governing body of the combined entity.

d. *The composition of the senior management of the combined entity*—Generally the acquirer is the entity whose former management dominates the management of the combined entity.
e. *Terms of the equity exchange*—Generally, the acquirer is the entity that pays a premium over the precombination fair value of the equity interests of the other entity or entities.

(ASC 805-10-55-12)

Step 2—Determine the acquisition date. By definition, the acquisition date is that on which the acquirer obtains control of the acquiree. As discussed previously, this concept of control (or, more precisely, controlling financial interest) is not always evidenced by voting ownership. Thus, control can be obtained contractually by an acquirer absent that party holding any voting ownership interests.

The general rule is that the acquisition date is the date on which the acquirer legally transfers consideration, acquires the assets, and assumes the liabilities of the acquiree. This date, in a relatively straightforward transaction, is referred to as the *closing date*. Not all transactions are that straightforward, however. All pertinent facts and circumstances are to be considered in determining the acquisition date. The parties to a business combination might, for example, execute a contract that entitles the acquirer to the rights and obligates the acquirer with respect to the obligations of the acquiree prior to the actual date of the closing. (ASC 805-10-35-7) Thus, in evaluating economic substance over legal form, the acquirer will have contractually acquired the target on the date it executed the contract.

Step 3—Identify assets and liabilities requiring separate accounting. ASC 805 provides a basic recognition principle that, as of the acquisition date, the acquirer is to recognize, separately from goodwill, the identifiable assets acquired (whether tangible or intangible), the liabilities assumed, and, if applicable, any noncontrolling interest (previously referred to as "minority interest") in the acquiree.

In applying the recognition principle to a business combination, the acquirer may recognize assets and liabilities that had not been recognized by the acquiree in its precombination financial statements. Under ASC 805, GAAP continues to permit recognition of acquired intangibles (e.g., patents, customer lists) that would not be granted recognition if they were internally developed.

ASC 805 elaborates on the basic principle by providing that recognition is subject to the following conditions:

1. At the acquisition date, the identifiable assets acquired and liabilities assumed must meet the definitions of assets and liabilities as set forth in CON 6.[2] (ASC 805-20-25-2)
2. The assets and liabilities recognized must be part of the exchange transaction between the acquirer and the acquiree (or the acquiree's former owners) and not part of a separate transaction or transactions. (ASC 805-20-25-3)

Restructuring or exit activities. Frequently, in a business combination, the acquirer's plans include the future exit of one or more of the activities of the acquiree or the termination or relocation of employees of the acquiree. Since these exit activities are discretionary on the part of the acquirer and the acquirer is not obligated to incur the associated costs, the costs do

---

[2] *Assets are defined as "probable future economic benefits obtained or controlled by a particular entity as a result of past transactions or events" (CON 6, par. 25). Liabilities are defined as "probable future sacrifices of economic benefits arising from present obligations of a particular entity to transfer assets or provide services to other entities in the future as a result of past transactions or events" (CON 6, par. 35).*

not meet the definition of a liability and are not recognized at the acquisition date. Rather, the costs will be recognized in postcombination financial statements in accordance with ASC 420.

Boundaries of the exchange transaction. Preexisting relationships and arrangements often exist between the acquirer and acquiree prior to beginning negotiations to enter into a business combination. Furthermore, while conducting the negotiations, the parties may enter into separate business arrangements. In either case, the acquirer is responsible for identifying amounts that are not part of the exchange for the acquiree. Recognition under the acquisition method is only given to the consideration transferred for the acquiree and the assets acquired and liabilities assumed in exchange for that consideration. Other transactions outside the scope of the business combination are to be recognized by applying other relevant GAAP.

The acquirer is to analyze the business combination transaction and other transactions with the acquiree and its former owners to identify the components that comprise the transaction in which the acquirer obtained control over the acquiree. This distinction is important to ensure that each component is accounted for according to its economic substance, irrespective of its legal form.

The imposition of this condition was based on an observation that, upon becoming involved in negotiations for a business combination, the parties may exhibit characteristics of related parties. In so doing, they may be willing to execute agreements designed *primarily* for the benefit of the acquirer of the combined entity that might be designed to achieve a desired financial reporting outcome after the business combination has been consummated. Thus, the imposition of this condition is expected to curb such abuses.

In analyzing a transaction to determine inclusion or exclusion from a business combination, consideration should be given to which of the parties will reap its benefits. If a precombination transaction is entered into by the acquirer, or on behalf of the acquirer, or *primarily* to benefit the acquirer (or to benefit the to-be-combined entity as a whole) rather than for the benefit of the acquiree or its former owners, the transaction most likely would be considered to be a "separate transaction" outside the boundaries of the business combination and for which the acquisition method would not apply.

The acquirer should consider the following factors, which FASB indicates "are neither mutually exclusive nor individually conclusive," in determining whether a transaction is a part of the exchange transaction or recognized separately:

1. *Purpose of the transaction*—Typically, there are many parties involved in the management, ownership, operation, and financing of the various entities involved in a business combination transaction. Of course, there are the acquirer and acquiree entities, but there are also owners, directors, management, and various parties acting as agents representing their respective interests. Understanding the motivations of the parties in entering into a particular transaction potentially provides insight into whether or not the transaction is a part of the business combination or a separate transaction.
2. *Initiator of the transaction*—Identifying the party that initiated the transaction may provide insight into whether or not it should be recognized separately from the business combination. FASB believes that if the transaction was initiated by the acquirer, it would be less likely to be part of the business combination and, conversely, if it were initiated by the acquiree or its former owners, it would be more likely to be part of the business combination.
3. *Timing of the transaction*—Examining the timing of the transaction may provide insight into whether, for example, the transaction was executed in contemplation of the future business combination in order to provide benefits to the acquirer or the postcombination entity. FASB believes that transactions that take place during the

negotiation of the terms of a business combination may be entered into in contemplation of the eventual combination for the purpose of providing future economic benefits *primarily* to the acquirer of the to-be-combined entity and, therefore, should be accounted for separately.

(ASC 805-10-55-18)

ASC 805 provides the following presumption after analyzing the economic benefits of a precombination transaction:

***Primarily** for the benefit of*	*Transaction is likely to be*
Acquirer or combined entity	Separate transaction
Acquiree or its former owners	Part of the business combination

ASC 805 provides three examples of separate transactions that *are not* to be included in applying the acquisition method, each of which will be discussed in further detail:

1. Reimbursement to the acquiree or its former owners for paying the acquirer's acquisition-related costs,
2. A settlement of a preexisting relationship between acquirer and acquiree, and
3. Compensation to employees or former owners of the acquiree for future services

Acquisition-related costs. Acquisition-related costs are charged to expense of the period in which the costs are incurred and the related services received. Examples of these costs include

Accounting fees	Internal acquisitions department
Advisory fees	Legal fees
Consulting fees	Other professional fees
Finder's fees	Valuation fees

ASC 805 makes an exception to the general rule with respect to costs to register and issue equity or debt securities. These costs are to be recognized in accordance with other applicable GAAP. Stock issuance costs are normally charged against the gross proceeds of the issuance. Debt issuance costs are, under CON 6, to be either treated as a reduction of the amount borrowed or treated as an expense of the period in which they are incurred; however, some reporting entities have treated these costs as deferred charges and amortized them to income during the term of the debt.

Settlements of preexisting relationships between acquirer and acquiree. Prior to pursuing a business combination, business may have been transacted between the parties. The nature of the transactions may have been contractual, such as the purchase of goods and/or services, or the licensing of intellectual property. On the other hand, the parties may have had an adversarial relationship whereby they were plaintiff and defendant in pending litigation. If, in effect, a business combination settles such a preexisting relationship, the acquirer recognizes a gain or loss measured in the following manner:

1. If the relationship is noncontractual (e.g., litigation), measure at fair value
2. If the relationship is contractual, measure at the lesser of
   a. The amount by which, from the acquirer's perspective, the contract is favorable or unfavorable, or
   b. The amount of any settlement provisions stated in the contract that are available to the counterparty for which the contract is unfavorable.

If 2b is less than 2a, the difference is included as part of the accounting for the business combination.

In determining whether a contract is favorable or unfavorable to a party, the terms of the contract are compared to current market terms. It is important to note that a contract can be unfavorable to the acquirer and yet not result in a loss.

The amount of the gain or loss measured as a result of settling a preexisting relationship will, of course, depend on whether the acquirer had previously recognized related assets or liabilities with respect to that relationship.

Example of settlement of preexisting contractual supplier relationship; contract unfavorable to acquirer

Meyer Corporation (MC) and Henning, Inc. (HI) are parties to a 3-year supply contract that contains the following provisions:

1. MC is required to annually purchase 3,000 flat-panel displays from HI at a fixed price of $400 per unit for an aggregate purchase price of $1,200,000 for each of the three years.
2. MC is required to pay HI the annual $1,200,000 irrespective of whether it takes delivery of all 3,000 units and the required payment is nonrefundable.
3. The contract contains a penalty provision that would permit MC to cancel it at the end of the second year for a lump sum payment of $500,000.
4. In each of the first two years of the contract, MC took delivery of the full 3,000 units.

At December 31, 20X1, the supply contract was unfavorable to MC because MC would be able to purchase flat-panel displays with similar specifications and of similar quality from another supplier for $350 per unit. Therefore, in accordance with ARB 43, MC accrued a loss of $150,000 (3,000 units remaining under the firm purchase commitment × $50 loss per unit).

On January 1, 20X2, MC acquires HI for $30 million, which reflects the fair value of HI based on what other marketplace participants would be willing to pay. On the acquisition date, the $30 million fair value of HI includes $750,000 related to the contract with MC that consists of

Identifiable intangibles[3]	$600,000	Representing the remaining year of the contract, at prevailing market prices
Favorable pricing	150,000	Representing the portion of the contract price that is favorable to HI and unfavorable to MC
	$750,000	

HI has no other identifiable assets or liabilities related to the supply contract with MC. MC would compute its gain or loss on settlement of this preexisting relationship as follows:

1. Amount of unfavorability to acquirer (MC) at acquisition date	$150,000
2. Lump-sum settlement amount available to MC	500,000
3. Lesser of 1 or 2	150,000
4. Amount by which 1 exceeds 2	N/A

Since MC had already recognized an unrealized loss on the firm purchase commitment as of December 31, 20X1, upon its acquisition of HI, its loss of $150,000 from recognizing the lesser of items 1 and 2 in the preceding list would be offset by the elimination of the liability for the unrealized loss on the firm purchase commitment in the same amount of $150,000. Thus, under these circumstances, MC would have neither a gain nor a loss on the settlement of its preexisting relationship with HI. The entries to record these events are not considered part of the business combination accounting. It is important to note that, from the perspective of MC, when it applies the acquisition method to record the business combination, it will characterize the $600,000 "at-market" component of the contract as part of goodwill and not as identifiable intangibles. This is

[3] *In computing the valuation of HI, these amounts would represent such identifiable customer-related intangible assets as customer contract, related customer relationship, production backlog, and the like.*

the case because of the obvious fallacy of MC recognizing customer-relationship intangible assets that represent a relationship with itself.

Example of settlement of preexisting contractual supplier relationship; contract favorable to acquirer

Using the same facts as the MC/HI example above, assume that, instead of the contract being unfavorable to the acquirer MC, it was unfavorable to HI in the amount of $150,000 and that there was a cancellation provision in the contract that would permit HI to pay a penalty after year two of $100,000 to cancel the remainder of the contract.

On the acquisition date, the $30 million fair value of HI, under this scenario would include $450,000 related to the contract with MC that consists of

Identifiable intangibles	$600,000	Representing the remaining year of the contract, at prevailing market prices
Unfavorable pricing	(150,000)	Representing the portion of the contract price that is unfavorable to HI and favorable to MC
	$450,000	

Under these changed assumptions, MC would not have incurred or recorded an unrealized loss on the firm purchase commitment with HI since the contract terms were favorable to MC. The determination of MC's gain or loss would be as follows:

1. Amount of favorability to acquirer (MC) at acquisition date	$150,000
2. Lump-sum settlement amount available to HI	100,000
3. Lesser of 1 or 2	100,000
4. Amount by which 1 exceeds 2	50,000

Under this scenario, unless HI believed that the market would change in the near term, it would be economically advantageous, absent a business combination, for HI to settle the remaining contract at the acquisition date by paying the $100,000 penalty because HI would be able to sell the remaining 3,000 units covered by the contract for an aggregate price of $150,000 more than it was committed to sell those units to MC.

At the acquisition date, MC would record a gain of $100,000 to settle its preexisting relationship with HI. The entry to record the gain is not considered part of the business combination accounting.

In addition, however, since item 2 is less than item 1, the $50,000 difference is included in the accounting for the business combination, since economically, postcombination, the combined entity will not benefit from that portion of the acquisition date favorability of the contract.

As was the case in the first example, the portion of the purchase price allocated to the contract in the business combination accounting would be accounted for as goodwill for the same reason.

Contingent payments to employees or former owners of the acquiree. The acquirer assesses whether arrangements to make contingent payments to employees or selling owners of the acquiree represent contingent consideration that is part of the business combination transaction or represent separate transactions to be excluded from the application of the acquisition method to the business combination. In general, the acquirer considers:

- The reasons why the terms of the acquisition include the payment provision,
- The party that initiated the arrangement, and
- When (at what stage of the negotiations) the arrangement was entered into by the parties.

When those considerations do not provide clarity regarding whether the transaction is separate from the business combination, the acquirer considers the following indicators:

1. *Postcombination employment*—Consideration is to be given to the terms under which the selling owners will be providing services as key employees of the combined entity. The terms may be evidenced by a formal employment contract, by provisions included in the acquisition documents, or by other documents. If the arrangement provides that the contingent payments are automatically forfeited upon termination of employment, the consideration is to be characterized as compensation for postcombination services. If, instead, the contingent payments are not affected by termination of employment, this would be an indicator that the contingent payments represent additional consideration that is part of the business combination transaction and not compensation for services.
2. *Duration of postcombination employment*—If the employee is contractually bound to remain employed for a period that equals or exceeds the period during which the contingent payments are due, this may be an indicator that the contingent payments represent compensation for services.
3. *Amount of compensation*—If the amount of the employee's compensation that is not contingent is considered to be reasonable in relation to other key employees of the combined entity, this may indicate that the contingent amounts represent additional consideration and not compensation for services.
4. *Differential between amounts paid to employees and selling owners who do not become employees of the combined entity*—If, on a per-share basis, the contingent payments due to former owners of the acquiree that did not become employees are lower than the contingent payments due to the former owners that did become employees of the combined entity, this may indicate that the incremental amounts paid to the employees are compensation.
5. *Extent of ownership*—The relative ownership percentages (e.g., number of shares, units, percentage of membership interest) owned by the selling owners who remain employees of the combined entity serve as an indicator of how to characterize the substance of the contingent consideration. If, for example, the former owners of substantially all of the ownership interests in the acquiree are continuing to serve as key employees of the combined entity, this may be an indicator that the contingent payment arrangement is substantively a profit-sharing vehicle designed with the intent of providing compensation for services to be performed postcombination. Conversely, if the former owners that remained employed by the combined entity collectively owned only a nominal ownership interest in the acquiree and all of the former owners received the same amount of contingent basis on a per-share basis, this may be an indicator that the contingent payments represent additional consideration. In considering the applicability of this indicator, care must be exercised to closely examine the effects, if any, of transactions, ownership interests, and employment relationships, precombination and postcombination, with respect to parties related to the selling owners of the acquiree.
6. *Relationship of contingent arrangements to the valuation approach used*—The payment terms negotiated in many business combinations provide that the amount of the acquisition date transfer of consideration from acquirer to acquiree (or the acquiree's former owners) is computed near the lower end of a range of valuation estimates the acquirer used in valuing the acquiree. Furthermore, the formula for determining future contingent payments is derived from or related to that valuation approach. When this is the case, it may be an indicator that the contingent payments represent additional consideration. Conversely, if the formula for determining future contingent payments more closely resembles prior profit-sharing arrangements, this

may be an indicator that the substance of the contingent payment arrangement is to provide compensation for services.

7. *Formula prescribed for determining contingent consideration*—Analyzing the formula to be used to determine the contingent consideration may provide insight into the substance of the arrangement. Contingent payments that are determined on the basis of a multiple of earnings may be indicative of being, in substance, contingent consideration that is part of the business combination transaction. Alternatively, contingent consideration that is determined as a prespecified percentage of earnings would be more suggestive of a routine profit-sharing arrangement for the purposes of providing additional compensation to employees for postcombination services rendered.
8. *Other considerations*—Given the complexity of a business combination transaction and the sheer volume of legal documents necessary to affect it, the financial statement preparer is charged with the daunting, but unavoidable task of performing a comprehensive review of the terms of all of the associated agreements. These can take the form of noncompete agreements, consulting agreements, leases, guarantees, indemnifications, and, of course, the formal agreement to combine the businesses. Particular attention should be paid to the applicable income tax treatment afforded to the contingent payments. The income tax treatment of these payments may be an indicator that tax avoidance was a primary motivator in characterizing them in the manner that they are structured. An acquirer might, for example, simultaneous to a business combination, execute a property lease with one of the key owners of the acquiree. If the lease payments were below market, some or all of the contingent payments to that key owner/lessor under the provisions of the other legal agreements might, in substance, be making up the shortfall in the lease and thus, should be recharacterized as lease payments and accounted for separately from the business combination in the combined entity's postcombination financial statements. If this were not the case, and the lease payments were reflective of the market, this would be an indicator pointing to a greater likelihood that the contingent payment arrangements actually did represent contingent consideration associated with the business combination transaction.

Step 4—Classify or designate identifiable assets acquired and liabilities assumed. To facilitate the combined entity's future application of GAAP in its postcombination financial statements, management is required to make decisions on the acquisition date relative to the classification or designation of certain items. These decisions are based on contractual terms, economic and other conditions, and the acquirer's operating and accounting policies as they exist *on the acquisition date*. Examples include, but are not limited to, the following:

1. Classification of investments in certain debt and equity securities as trading, available for sale, or held to maturity under ASC 320, *Investments—Debt and Equity Securities*
2. Designation of a derivative instrument as a hedging instrument under the provisions of ASC 815, *Derivatives and Hedging*
3. Assessment of whether an embedded derivative is to be separated from the host contract under ASC 815.

In applying Step 4, specific exceptions are provided for lease contracts and insurance contracts. Generally, these contracts are classified by reference to the contractual terms and other factors that were applicable *at their inception* rather than at the acquisition date. If, however, the contracts were modified subsequent to inception and those modifications would change their classification at that date, then the accounting for the contracts is determined by the modification date facts and circumstances. Under these circumstances, the modification date could be the same as the acquisition date.

Step 5—Recognize and measure the identifiable tangible and intangible assets acquired and liabilities assumed. In general, the acquirer measures the identifiable tangible and intangible assets acquired, liabilities assumed, and, if applicable, noncontrolling interest at fair value on the acquisition date. The following guidance is followed in applying the recognition and measurement principles (subject to certain specified exceptions).

Operating leases. Irrespective of whether the acquiree is the lessee or lessor, the acquirer evaluates, as of the acquisition date, each of the acquiree's operating leases to determine whether its terms are favorable or unfavorable compared to the market terms of leases of identical or similar items. If the lease terms are favorable, the acquirer recognizes an intangible asset; if the lease terms are unfavorable, the acquirer recognizes a liability.

Even when the lease is considered to be at market terms, there nevertheless may be an identifiable intangible associated with it. This would be the case if market participants would be willing to pay to obtain it (i.e., to obtain the rights and privileges associated with it). Examples of this situation are leases for favorably positioned airport gates, and prime retail space in an economically favorable location. If, from the perspective of marketplace participants, acquiring the lease would entitle them to future economic benefits that qualify as identifiable intangible assets (discussed later in this chapter), the acquirer would recognize, separately from goodwill, the associated identifiable intangible asset.

Operating lease assets owned by an acquiree/lessor. The fair value of assets owned by the acquiree that are subject to operating leases with the acquiree being the lessor are measured separately from the underlying lease to which they are subject.

Assets with uncertain cash flows. Since fair value measurements take into account the effects of uncertainty regarding the amounts and timing of future cash flows, the acquirer does not recognize a separate valuation allowance for assets subject to such uncertainties.

Assets the acquirer plans to idle or to use in a manner that is not their highest and best use. The measurement of the identifiable assets acquired at fair value is to be made in accordance with the requirements of ASC 820. One of those requirements is that the measurement is to assume the highest and best use of the asset by market participants. In applying this requirement to assets that are acquired in a business combination, this assumption is to be used even if it differs from the manner in which the acquiree was using the assets or the manner in which the acquirer intends to use the assets. Thus, even if the acquirer intends to protect its competitive position or for other business reasons to idle an acquired asset or use it in a manner that is not its highest and best use, the acquirer is still required to initially measure the fair value of that asset using the assumption of its highest and best use and to continue to use that assumption for the purposes of subsequently testing the asset for impairment. (ASC 805-20-30-6)

Identifiable intangibles are recognized separately from goodwill. ASC 350 addresses the accounting for all intangibles and how to distinguish between separately identifiable intangibles having finite lives, those having indefinite lives, and goodwill, which is unique in being "unidentifiable" and having an indeterminate life (which makes periodic amortization impossible, in the FASB's view). CON 5, *Recognition and Measurement in Financial Statements of Business Enterprises*, states that an asset is recognized if it meets the definition of an asset (found in CON 6, *Elements of Financial Statements*), has a relevant attribute measurable with sufficient reliability, and the information about it is representationally faithful, verifiable, neutral (i.e., it is reliable), and capable of making a difference in user decisions (i.e., it is relevant). In a business acquisition, any acquired identifiable intangible asset (e.g., patents, customer lists, etc.) must be recognized separately from goodwill when it meets these CON 5 asset recognition criteria, and additionally meets either of the following two criteria:

1. *Separability criterion*—The intangible asset is capable of being separated or divided from the entity that holds it, and sold, transferred, licensed, rented, or exchanged, regardless of the acquirer's intent to do so. An intangible asset meets this criterion even if its transfer would not be alone, but instead would be accompanied or bundled with a related contract, other identifiable asset, or a liability.
2. *Legal/contractual criterion*—The intangible asset results from contractual or other legal rights. An intangible asset meets this criterion even if the rights are not transferable or separable from the acquiree or from other rights and obligations of the acquiree.

ASC 805-20-55 contains a listing of intangible assets that FASB believes have characteristics that meet one of these two criteria (legal/contractual or separability). A logical approach in practice would be for the acquirer to first consider whether the intangibles specifically included on the FASB list are applicable to the particular acquiree and then to consider whether there may be other unlisted intangibles included in the acquisition that meet one or both of the criteria for separate recognition.

ASC 805-20-55 organizes groups of identifiable intangibles into categories related to or based on

1. Marketing
2. Customers or clients
3. Artistic works
4. Contractual
5. Technological.

These categorizations are somewhat arbitrary. Consequently, some of the items listed could fall into more than one of the categories. All intangible assets acquired—whether singly, in groups, or as part of a business combination—are initially recognized and measured based on their respective fair values. Under the provisions of ASC 350, serious effort must be directed to identifying the various intangibles acquired, thus minimizing the amount of goodwill to be recognized.

Examples of identifiable intangibles included in each of the categories are as follows:

Marketing-related intangible assets.

1. *Newspaper mastheads.* The unique appearance of the title page of a newspaper or other periodical.
2. *Trademarks, service marks, trade names, collective marks, certification marks.* A *trademark* represents the right to use a name, word, logo, or symbol that differentiates a product from products of other entities. A *service mark* is the equivalent of a trademark for a service offering instead of a product. A *collective mark* is used to identify products or services offered by members affiliated with each other. A *certification mark* is used to designate a particular attribute of a product or service such as its geographic source (e.g., Colombian coffee or Florida orange juice) or the standards under which it was produced (e.g., ISO 9000 Certified).
3. *Trade dress.* The overall appearance and image (unique color, shape, or package design) of a product.

4. *Internet domain names.* The unique name that identifies an address on the Internet. Domain names must be registered with an Internet registry and are renewable.
5. *Noncompetition agreements.* Rights to assurances that companies or individuals will refrain from conducting similar businesses or selling to specific customers for an agreed-upon period of time.

Customer-related intangible assets.

1. *Customer lists.* Names, contact information, order histories, and other information about a company's customers that a third party, such as a competitor or a telemarketing firm, would want to use in its own business.
2. *Customer contracts and related customer relationships.* When a company's relationships with its customers arise primarily through contracts and are of value to buyers who can "step into the shoes" of the sellers and assume their remaining rights and duties under the contracts, and which hold the promise that the customers will place future orders with the entity or relationships between entities and their customers for which:

   a. The entities have information about the customers and have regular contacts with the customers, and
   b. The customers have the ability to make direct contact with the entity.

3. *Noncontractual customer relationships.* Customer relationships that arise through means such as regular contacts by sales or service representatives, the value of which are derived from the prospect of the customers placing future orders with the entity.
4. *Order or production backlogs.* Unfilled sales orders for goods and services in amounts that exceed the quantity of finished goods and work-in-process on hand for filling the orders.

Artistic-related intangible assets.

1. *Plays, operas, ballets.*
2. *Books, magazines, newspapers, and other literary works.*
3. *Musical works such as compositions, song lyrics, and advertising jingles.*
4. *Photographs, drawings, and clip art.*
5. *Audiovisual material including motion pictures, music videos, television programs.*

Contract-based intangible assets.

1. *License, royalty, standstill agreements.* License agreements represent the right, on the part of the licensee, to access or use property that is owned by the licensor for a specified period of time at an agreed-upon price. A royalty agreement entitles its holder to a contractually agreed-upon portion of the income earned from the sale or license of a work covered by patent or copyright. A standstill agreement conveys assurances that a company or individual will refrain from engaging in certain activities for specified periods of time.
2. *Advertising contracts.* A contract with a newspaper, broadcaster, or Internet site to provide specified advertising services to the acquiree.
3. *Lease agreements.* (Irrespective of whether the acquiree is the lessee or lessor).
4. *Construction permits.* Rights to build a specified structure at a specified location.
5. *Construction contracts.* Rights to become the contractor responsible for completing a construction project and benefit from the profits it produces, subject to the remaining obligations associated with performance (including any past-due payments to suppliers and/or subcontractors).

6. *Construction management, service, or supply contracts.* Rights to manage a construction project for a fee, procure specified services at a specified fee, or purchase specified products at contractually agreed-upon prices.
7. *Broadcast rights.* Legal permission to transmit electronic signals using specified bandwidth in the radio frequency spectrum, granted by the operation of communication laws.
8. *Franchise rights.* Legal rights to engage in a trade-named business, to sell a trademarked good, or to sell a service-marked service in a particular geographic area.
9. *Operating rights.* Permits to operate in a certain manner, such as those granted to a carrier to transport specified commodities.
10. *Use rights.* Permits to use specified land, property, or air space in a particular manner, such as the right to cut timber, expel emissions, or to land airplanes at specified gates at an airport.
11. *Servicing contracts.* The contractual right to service a loan. Servicing entails activities such as collecting principal and interest payments from the borrower, maintaining escrow accounts, paying taxes and insurance premiums when due, and pursuing collection of delinquent payments.
12. *Employment contract.* The right to succeed the acquiree as the employer under a formal contract to obtain an employee's services in exchange for fulfilling the employer's remaining duties, such as payment of salaries and benefits, as specified by the contract.

Technology-based intangible assets.

1. *Patented or copyrighted software.* Computer software source code, program specifications, procedures, and associated documentation that are legally protected by patent or copyright.
2. *Mask works.* Software permanently stored on a read-only memory chip as a series of stencils or integrated circuitry. Mask works may be provided statutory protection in some countries.
3. *Unpatented technology.* Access to knowledge about the proprietary processes and workflows followed by the acquiree to accomplish desired business results.
4. *Databases.* Databases are collections of information generally stored digitally in an organized manner. A database can be protected by copyright (e.g., the database contained on the CD-ROM version of this publication). Many databases, however, represent information accumulated as a natural by-product of a company conducting its normal operating activities. Examples of these databases are plentiful and include title plants, scientific data, and credit histories. Title plants represent historical records with respect to real estate parcels in a specified geographic location.
5. *Trade secrets.* Trade secrets are proprietary, confidential information, such as a formula, process, or recipe.

One commonly cited intangible asset deliberately omitted by the FASB from its list of identifiable intangibles is an *assembled workforce*. FASB decided that the replacement cost technique that is often used to measure the fair value of an assembled workforce is not a representationally faithful measure of the fair value of the intellectual capital acquired. It was thus decided that an exception to the recognition criteria would be made, and that the fair value of an acquired assembled workforce would remain part of goodwill.

Useful economic life. Reliably measurable identifiable intangible assets, with the exception of those meeting the criteria for nonamortization (explained below), must be amortized over their respective useful economic lives. Useful economic life is the period over which the asset is expected to contribute (whether directly or indirectly) to cash flows into the entity. Factors to be considered in estimating the useful economic life of an intangible asset to an enterprise include

1. Legal, regulatory, or contractual provisions that may limit the maximum useful life;
2. Legal, regulatory, or contractual provisions that may enable renewal or extension of the asset's legal or contractual life (provided there is evidence to support renewal or extension without substantial cost and without materially modifying the original terms);
3. The effects of obsolescence, demand, competition, and other economic factors (such as the stability of the industry, the rate of technological change, expected changes in distribution channels, and the existence of uncertainty over future legal and/or regulatory changes);
4. The expected useful life of assets or groups of assets of the enterprise that the useful life of the asset may parallel (such as mineral rights to depleting assets);
5. The expected use of the intangible asset by the enterprise; and
6. The level of maintenance expenditures required to be made in order to obtain the expected future economic benefits from the asset.

In those instances where an intangible asset is determined to have an indefinite useful economic life, it will not be amortized until its life is determined to be finite at a later date. An example of such an asset would be a broadcast license, expiring in five years, but which may be renewed indefinitely at little cost. If the acquirer intends to renew the license indefinitely, and there is evidence to support its ability to do so, and the cash flows related to that license are expected to continue indefinitely, then no amortization would be recognized until such time as these criteria are no longer met.

Residual value. Typically, the entire fair value assigned to an intangible asset will be subject to amortization, although in some instances a residual value may be determined, which reduces the asset's amortizable basis. The residual value of an amortizable intangible is assumed to be zero unless the useful life to the acquiring enterprise is shorter than the intangible asset's useful economic life, and either (1) the acquiring enterprise has a commitment from a third party to purchase the asset at the end of its useful life, or (2) the residual value can be determined by reference to an observable market for that asset and that market is expected to exist at the end of the asset's useful life. The method of amortization is to reflect the pattern in which the economic benefits of the intangible asset are to be consumed; absent the ability to ascertain this, straight-line amortization is applied. However, if impairment (determined by application of the ASC 360 criteria) is later determined to have occurred, the carrying amount will be written down to the impaired amount.

Research and development assets. ASC 805 requires the acquirer to recognize and measure all tangible and intangible assets used in research and development (R&D) activities acquired individually or in a group of assets as part of the business combination. This prescribed treatment is to be followed even if the assets are judged to have no alternative future use. These assets are measured at their acquisition-date fair values. Fair value measurements, consistent with ASC 820, must be made based on the assumptions that would be made by market participants in pricing the asset. Assets that the acquirer does not intend to use or intends to use in a manner that is not their highest and best use are, nevertheless, required to be measured at fair value.

Intangible R&D assets. Upon initial recognition, the *intangible* R&D assets are classified as indefinite-lived assets until the related R&D efforts are either completed or abandoned. In the reporting periods during which the R&D intangible assets are classified as indefinite-lived, they are not amortized. Instead, they are tested for impairment in the same manner as other indefinite-lived intangibles. Upon completion or abandonment of the related R&D efforts, management determines the remaining useful life of the intangibles and amortize them accordingly. In applying these requirements, assets that are temporarily idled are not to be considered abandoned.

Tangible R&D assets. Tangible R&D assets acquired in a business combination are accounted for according to their nature (e.g., supplies, inventory, depreciable assets).

Exceptions to the recognition and/or measurement principles. ASC 805 provides certain exceptions to its general principles for recognizing assets acquired and liabilities assumed at their acquisition date fair values. These can be summarized as follows:

Nature of exception	*Recognition*	*Measurement*
1. Assets held for sale		x
2. Contingent assets and liabilities of the acquiree	x	x
3. Indemnification assets	x	x
4. Reacquired rights		x
5. Employee benefits	x	x
6. Share-based payment awards		x
7. Income taxes	x	x

1. *Assets held for sale.* Assets classified as held for sale individually or as part of a disposal group are to be measured at acquisition date fair value less cost to sell consistent with ASC 360.

   In postacquisition periods, long-lived assets classified as held for sale are not to be depreciated *or* amortized. If the assets are part of a disposal group, interest and other expenses related to the liabilities included in the disposal group are to continue to be accrued.

   In determining fair value less cost to sell, it is important to differentiate costs to sell from expected future losses associated with the operation of the long-lived asset or disposal group to which it belongs.

   Costs to sell are defined as the incremental direct costs necessary to transact a sale. To qualify as costs to sell, the costs must result directly from the sale transaction, incurring them needs to be considered essential to the transaction, and the costs would not have been incurred by the entity absent the decision to sell the assets. Examples of costs to sell include brokerage commissions, legal fees, title transfer fees, and closing costs necessary to effect the transfer of legal title. Costs to sell are expressly not permitted to include any future losses expected to result from operating the assets (or disposal group) while it is classified as held for sale. If the expected timing of the sale exceeds one year from the date of the statement of financial position, which is permitted in limited situations by ASC 360-10-45, the costs to sell are to be discounted to their present value.

   If a loss is recognized in subsequent periods because of declines in the fair value less cost to sell, such *losses* are permitted to be restored by future periods' gains only to the extent to which the losses have been recognized cumulatively from the date the asset (or disposal group) was classified as held for sale.
2. *Contingent assets and liabilities of the acquiree.* A gain or loss contingency is defined as an existing, unresolved condition, situation, or set of circumstances that will eventually be resolved by the occurrence or nonoccurrence of one or more future events. A potential gain or loss to the reporting entity can result from the contingency's resolution.

Acquisition-date considerations. To determine whether to recognize a contingent asset or liability of the acquiree, the acquirer is to evaluate information available during the measurement period about the facts and circumstances as they existed at the measurement date. As a result of that evaluation, the acquirer is to conclude as to whether or not the *acquisition-date fair value* (ADFV) of a contingent asset acquired or contingent liability assumed can be determined during the measurement period.

a. If ADFV is considered determinable during the measurement period, the acquirer recognizes the asset or liability at its ADFV.
b. If ADFV is not considered determinable during the measurement period, an asset or liability is recognized at the acquisition date if both of the following criteria are met, following the application guidance in ASC 450 and ASC 450-20.

   - Information available prior to the end of the measurement period indicates that it is *probable* that an asset existed or that a liability had been incurred at the measurement date, *and*
   - The amount of the asset or liability can be reasonably estimated

c. If neither criterion a. nor b. is met, no asset or liability is recognized at the measurement date and the contingencies are subject to the same ASC 450 considerations as any other contingencies of the ongoing consolidated reporting entity.

   The acquirer is required, however, to initially recognize the ADFV of any preexisting contingent consideration arrangements of the acquiree that the acquirer assumes in the business combination.

   Postacquisition considerations. Management of the acquirer is to develop a "systematic and rational" basis for subsequently measuring and accounting for assets and liabilities arising from contingencies based on the nature of the contingency.

   With respect to contingent consideration arrangements of the acquiree that are assumed by the acquirer in the business combination, these are subsequently accounted for in the same manner as contingent consideration arrangements entered into between the acquirer and acquiree as a part of the business combination:

   - If additional information is obtained during the measurement period that pertains to facts and circumstances that existed at the acquisition date and affects the ADFV of the contingency, the acquirer is to reflect the effects of the new information on ADFV as a measurement period adjustment.
   - Changes in the fair value of the contingency resulting from postacquisition events, such as meeting a targeted level of earnings, reaching a specified stock price, or successfully meeting a milestone of a research and development project, are not to be reflected as measurement period adjustments. These are accounted for as follows:

     (1) If the contingent consideration was classified as equity, it is not remeasured and, when subsequently settled, it is accounted for in equity.
     (2) If the contingent consideration was classified as an asset or liability, it is remeasured at fair value in each reporting period until the contingency is resolved. Changes in fair value are charged or credited to net income unless the contingent arrangement is a hedging instrument for which ASC 15, *Derivatives and Hedging*, requires changes to be recognized initially in other comprehensive income.

3. *Indemnification assets.* Indemnification provisions are usually included in the voluminous closing documents necessary to effect a business combination. Indemnifications are contractual terms designed to fully or partially protect the acquirer from the potential adverse effects of an unfavorable future resolution of a contingency or uncertainty that exists at the acquisition date. Frequently the indemnification is structured to protect the acquirer by limiting the maximum amount of postcombination loss that the acquirer would bear in the event of an adverse outcome. A contractual indemnification provision results in the acquirer obtaining, as a part of the acquisition, an indemnification asset and simultaneously assuming a contingent liability of the acquiree.

   Acquisition-date considerations. ASC 805 requires the acquirer to recognize and measure the indemnification asset using the same measurement basis it uses to measure the indemnified obligation.

   In measuring an indemnification asset, management is to take into account any uncertainty in the amounts or timing of expected future cash flows. If the asset is measured at acquisition-date fair value, those effects are included in the measure of fair value and, therefore, a separate valuation allowance is not recognized.

   Some indemnifications relate to assets or liabilities that are exceptions to the recognition or measurement principles. Indemnifications may, for example, be related to contingencies that do not meet the previously discussed criteria for recognition in the acquisition-date financial statements. Other indemnifications may be related to uncertain income tax positions that are measured, under ASC 740, as the maximum amount that is estimated to be more likely than not of being sustained upon examination by the relevant taxing jurisdiction. In cases such as these, the indemnification asset is to be recognized and measured using assumptions consistent with those used to measure the item being indemnified. Since uncertainty with respect to the collectibility of the indemnification asset is not directly included in its measurement, collectibility is considered separately and, to the extent necessary, reflected in a valuation allowance to reduce the carrying amount of the indemnification asset.

   Postacquisition considerations. At each reporting date subsequent to the acquisition date, the acquirer is to measure an indemnification asset recognized as part of the business combination using the same basis as the indemnified item, subject to any limitations imposed contractually on the amount of the indemnification. If an indemnification asset is not subsequently measured at fair value (because to do so would be inconsistent with the basis used to measure the indemnified item), management is to assess the collectibility of the asset and, to the extent necessary, a valuation allowance should be established or adjusted. An indemnification asset is derecognized only when the asset is collected, the rights to receive the asset are sold, or the acquirer otherwise loses its right to receive it.

4. *Reacquired rights.* An acquirer and acquiree may have engaged in preacquisition business transactions such as leases, licenses, or franchises that resulted in the acquiree paying consideration to the acquirer to use tangible and/or intangible assets of the acquirer in the acquiree's business.

   Acquisition-date considerations. Upon consummation of the business combination, the acquirer may reacquire a previously granted right. Upon reacquisition, the acquirer is to account for the right as an identifiable, amortizable intangible asset separate from goodwill.

   If the terms of the contract that give rise to the reacquired right are either favorable or unfavorable to the acquirer compared to current market transactions for identical or similar rights, the acquirer is to recognize a gain or loss computed as the lesser of:

a. The amount by which, from the acquirer's perspective, the contract is favorable or unfavorable, or
b. The amount of any settlement provisions stated in the contract that are available to the counterparty for which the contract is unfavorable.

If item b is less than item a, the difference is to be included as part of the accounting for the business combination.

Postacquisition considerations. Reacquired rights recognized at the acquisition date are amortized, postcombination, on the basis of the remaining, unexpired term of the related contract. The remaining contractual term is to be used for this purpose even if market participants would consider potential future contract renewals in determining the fair value of the contract.

Should the acquirer subsequently sell the reacquired right to a third party, the carrying amount of the intangible asset is to be included in the determination of gain or loss on the sale.

5. *Employee benefits.* Liabilities (and assets, if applicable), associated with acquiree employee benefit arrangements are recognized and measured under other GAAP, as applicable.

Types of benefits	Applicable GAAP
Deferred compensation contracts including postretirement benefit aspects of split-dollar life insurance arrangements	ASC 710-10-25 ASC 715-60
Compensated absences and sabbatical leaves	ASC 710-10-15 ASC 710-10-25
Pensions, plan curtailments, and termination benefits	ASC 715-30 ASC 715-20
Postretirement benefits other than pensions, including postretirement benefit aspects of split-dollar life insurance arrangements	ASC 715-60 ASC 715-20
Postemployment benefits (benefits provided to inactive or former employees, their beneficiaries, and covered dependents after employment but before retirement) including, but not limited to: • Salary continuation • Supplemental unemployment benefits • Severance benefits • Disability-related benefits including workers' compensation • Job training and counseling (e.g., outplacement) • Continuation of benefits such as health care and life insurance	ASC 712
Onetime termination benefits	ASC 420

In researching the application of these pronouncements, it is important to consider the changes to them made by ASC 805. For example,

a. ASC 715-30 and ASC 715-60 clarify that:

(1) The acquirer is to recognize, as part of the business combination, an asset or liability that represents the funded status of a single-employer defined benefit pension plan and/or a single-employer defined benefit postretirement

plan. In determining the funded status, the acquirer is to disregard the effects of expected plan amendments, terminations, or curtailments that it has no obligation to make at the acquisition date.

(2) The projected benefit obligation assumed for a single-employer defined benefit pension plan or the accumulated postretirement benefit obligation assumed for a single-employer defined benefit postretirement plan are to reflect any other necessary changes in assumptions based on an assessment by the acquirer of relevant future events.

(3) If the acquiree participates in a multiemployer-defined benefit pension or postretirement plan, and at the acquisition date it is probable that the acquirer will withdraw from that plan, the acquirer is to recognize a withdrawal liability as of the acquisition date under ASC 450.

b. ASC 420 is amended to expand its scope to cover exit activities associated with entities that are acquired in a business combination.

6a. *Acquirer share-based payment awards exchanged for acquiree awards held by its employees.* In connection with a business combination, the acquirer often awards share-based payments to the employees of the acquiree in exchange for the employees' acquiree awards. Obviously, there are many valid business reasons for the exchange, not the least of which is ensuring smooth transition and integration as well as retention of valued employees.

The discussion that follows uses concepts and terminology from ASC 718, *Compensation—Stock Compensation*.

6b. *Acquirer not obligated to exchange.* Accounting for the replacement awards under ASC 805 is dependent on whether the acquirer is obligated to replace the acquiree awards. The acquirer is obligated to replace the acquiree awards if the acquiree or its employees can enforce replacement through rights obtained from the terms of the acquisition agreement, the acquiree awards, or applicable laws or regulations.

If the acquirer is not obligated to replace the acquiree awards, all of the fair-value-based measure (FVBM)[4] of the replacement awards is recognized as compensation cost in the postcombination financial statements.

Example of acquirer replacing acquiree awards without the obligation to do so

New Parent, Inc. (NP) acquired New Subsidiary, Inc. (NS) on January 1, 20X1. Because of the business combination, the share-based payment awards that had been previously granted by NS to its employees expired on the acquisition date.

Although NP was not obligated, legally or contractually, to replace the expired awards, its Board of Directors approved a grant of NP awards designed so that the employees of NS would not be financially disadvantaged by the acquisition transaction.

Since the replacement awards were voluntary on the part of NP, the FVBM of the replacement award is attributed wholly to the postcombination consolidated financial statements of NP and Subsidiary.

Acquirer obligated to replace acquiree awards. If the acquirer is obligated to replace the awards of the acquiree, either all or a portion of the FVBM of the replacement awards is included in measuring the consideration transferred by the acquirer in the business

[4] *Although the accompanying guidance uses the term "fair-value-based measure" to refer to the measurement of share-based awards, the guidance also applies to awards of both the acquirer and acquiree that are measured using either the calculated value method or intrinsic value method.*

combination. To the extent a portion of the replacement awards is not allocated to consideration transferred, it is accounted for as compensation for postcombination services in the acquirer's consolidated financial statements.

For the purposes of illustrating the allocation computations, the following conventions and abbreviations are used:

$FVBM_{RA}$	Acquisition date fair-value-based measure of acquirer replacement award
$FVBM_{AA}$	Acquisition date fair-value-based measure of acquiree award that is being replaced by the acquirer
RSP_{AA}	Original requisite service period[5] of acquiree awards at their grant date
RSP_{RA}	Requisite service period of the acquirer replacement awards at acquisition date
$CRSP_{AA}$	Portion of requisite service period completed at the acquisition date by employees under the acquiree awards
TSP	Total service period—the service period already satisfied by the employees at the acquisition date under the acquiree awards plus the requisite service period, if any, required by the acquirer replacement awards
PRE	Portion of $FVBM_{RA}$ attributable to precombination services performed by the employees of the acquiree
PCC	Postcombination compensation cost

$$TSP = CRSP_{AA} + RSP_{RA}$$

The following steps are followed to determine the portion of the FVBM of the replacement award to be included as part of the consideration transferred by the acquirer:

1. Compute both $FVBM_{RA}$ and $FVBM_{AA}$ by following the provisions of ASC 718.
2. Compute the portion of the replacement award that is attributable to precombination services rendered by the acquiree's employees as follows:

   a. If $RSP_{AA} > TSP$, then

   $$PRE = FVBM_{AA}\left(\frac{CRSP_{AA}}{RSP_{AA}}\right)$$

   b. If $RSP_{AA} \leq TSP$, then

   $$PRE = FVBM_{AA}\left(\frac{CRSP_{AA}}{TSP}\right)$$

3. Compute the portion of the nonvested replacement award attributable to postcombination service as follows:

   $$PCC = FVBM_{RA} - PRE$$

   This amount is to be recognized as compensation cost in the postcombination financial statements since, at the acquisition date, the requisite service conditions had not been met.

The following examples are adapted from the implementation guidance for ASC 805.

---

[5] *The term "requisite service period" includes explicit, implicit, and derived service periods during which employees are required to provide services in exchange for the award. These terms are explained in ASC 718.*

Example of acquirer replacement awards requiring no postcombination services exchanges for fully vested acquiree awards where the employees have rendered all required services by the acquisition date

New Parent, Inc. (NP) acquired New Subsidiary, Inc. (NS) on January 1, 20X1. In accordance with the acquisition agreement, NP agreed to replace share-based awards that had previously been issued by NS. Details are as follows:

	a. Acquiree Awards	*b. Acquirer Awards*
1. Acquisition date FVBM of awards	$FVBM_{AA}$ = $100	$FVBM_{RA}$ = $110
2. Original requisite service period of acquiree awards at their grant date	RSP_{AA} = 4 years	–
3. Portion of 2a completed by the acquisition date by employees of the acquiree	$CRSP_{AA}$ = 4 years	–
4. Requisite service period of acquirer replacement awards at the acquisition date	–	$RSP_{RA} = 0$
5. Total service period (3a + 4b)	–	TSP = 4 years
6. The greater of the total service period (5b) or the original requisite service period of the acquiree awards (2a)	–	4 years

Since the acquiree's employees had completed all of the services required under the prior awards applying the formula yields a result that attributes 100% of the fair value of the acquiree award that is being replaced to precombination services rendered.

$$PRE = 1a \left(\frac{3a}{6b} \right)$$

$$PRE = \$100 \left(\frac{4\ years}{4\ years} \right)$$

$$PRE = \$100$$

The $100 result, attributed to precombination services, is included by the acquirer in its computation of the consideration transferred in exchange for control of the acquiree.

The final step in the computation is to account for the difference between the acquisition date fair values of the replacement awards and the acquiree awards as follows:

Fair value of replacement awards—$FVBM_{RA}$	$110
– Allocated to consideration per above	100
Additional compensation cost recognized immediately in postcombination financial statements	$ 10

This result illustrates the basic principle in ASC 805 that any excess of FVBMRA over the $FVBM_{AA}$ is to be attributed to postcombination services and recognized as compensation cost in the postcombination financial statements.

Example of acquirer replacement awards requiring performance of postcombination services exchanged for acquiree awards for which all requisite services had been rendered by the acquiree's employees as of the acquisition date

The acquisition agreement referred to in the previous example governing the NP acquisition of NS that occurred on January 1, 20X1, contained the following provisions regarding exchange of outstanding NS awards at acquisition date for NP replacement awards:

	a. Acquiree Awards	b. Acquirer Awards
1. Acquisition date FVBM of awards	$FVBM_{AA}$ = $100	$FVBM_{RA}$ = $100
2. Original requisite service period of acquiree awards at their grant date	RSP_{AA} = 4 years	–
3. Portion of 2a completed by the acquisition date by employees of the acquiree (the acquiree employees in this example had actually completed a total of 7 years of services by the acquisition date)	$CRSP_{AA}$ = 4 years	–
4. Requisite service period of acquirer replacement awards at the acquisition date	–	RSP_{RA} = 1 year
5. Total service period (3a + 4b)	–	TSP = 5 years
6. The greater of the total service period (5b) or the original requisite service period of the acquiree awards (2a)	–	5 years

Even though the acquiree's employees had completed all of the requisite service required by the acquiree's awards three years prior to the acquisition, the imposition of an additional year of required service by the acquirer's replacement awards results in an allocation between precombination compensation cost and postcombination compensation cost as follows:

$$PRE = 1a\left(\frac{3a}{6b}\right)$$

$$PRE = \$100\left(\frac{4\ years}{5\ years}\right)$$

$$PRE = \$80$$

The $80 result, attributed to precombination services, is included by the acquirer in its computation of the consideration transferred in exchange for control of the acquirer.

The $20 difference between the $100 fair value of the replacement awards and the $80 allocated to precombination services (and included in consideration transferred) is accounted for as compensation cost in the postcombination consolidated financial statements of NP and Subsidiary under the provisions of ASC 718.

Example of acquirer replacement awards requiring performance of postcombination services exchanged for acquiree awards with remaining unsatisfied requisite service period as of the acquisition date

The acquisition agreement referred to in the previous examples governing the NP acquisition of NS that occurred on January 1, 20X1, contained the following provisions regarding exchange of outstanding NS awards at acquisition date for NP replacement awards:

	a. Acquiree Awards	b. Acquirer Awards
1. Acquisition date FVBM of awards	$FVBM_{AA}$ = $100	$FVBM_{RA}$ = $100
2. Original requisite service period of acquiree awards at their grant date	RSP_{AA} = 4 years	–
3. Portion of 2a completed by the acquisition date by employees of the acquire	$CRSP_{AA}$ = 2 years	–
4. Requisite service period of acquirer replacement awards at the acquisition date	–	RSP_{RA} = 1 year
5. Total service period (3a + 4b)	–	TSP = 3 years
6. The greater of the total service period (5b) or the original requisite service period of the acquiree awards (2a)	–	4 years

The portion of the FVBM of the replacement awards attributable to precombination services already rendered by the acquiree employees is computed as follows:

$$PRE = 1a \left(\frac{3a}{6b}\right)$$

$$PRE = \$100 \left(\frac{2\ years}{4\ years}\right)$$

$$PRE = \$50$$

Based on the computation above, at the acquisition date, NP, the acquirer, includes $50 as consideration transferred to obtain control of NS, the acquiree. The remaining $50 is attributed to postcombination services and, accordingly, recognized as compensation cost in the consolidated postcombination financial statements of NP and Subsidiary.

Example of acquirer replacement awards that do not require postcombination services exchanged for acquiree awards for which the acquiree's employees had not yet completed all of the requisite services by the acquisition date

The acquisition agreement referred to in the previous examples governing the NP acquisition of NS that occurred on January 1, 20X1 contained the following provisions regarding exchange of outstanding NS awards at acquisition date for NP replacement awards:

	a. Acquiree Awards	b. Acquirer Awards
1. Acquisition date fair-value-based measure of awards	$FVBM_{AA} = \$100$	$FVBM_{RA} = \$100$
2. Original requisite service period of acquiree awards at their grant date	$RSP_{AA} = 4$ years	–
3. Portion of 2a completed by the acquisition date by employees of the acquire	$CRSP_{AA} = 2$ years	–
4. Requisite service period of acquirer replacement awards at the acquisition date	–	$RSP_{RA} = 0$
5. Total service period (3a + 4b)	–	TSP = 2 years
6. The greater of the total service period (5b) or the original requisite service period of the acquiree awards (2a)	–	4 years

Under this scenario, the terms of the awards previously granted by NS, the acquiree, did not contain a change-in-control provision that would have fully vested them upon the acquisition by NP. If this had been the case, the outcome would be the same as the example above where neither the acquiree awards nor the replacement rewards required the completion of any service on the part of the acquiree's employees.

Since, at the acquisition date, the acquiree employees had completed only two out of the four years of required services and the replacement awards do not extend the duration of services required postcombination, the total service period (TSP) in 5b is the 2 years already completed by the acquiree's employees under their original awards in 3a ($CRSP_{AA}$).

The portion of the FVBM of the replacement awards attributable to precombination services already rendered by the acquiree employees is computed as follows:

$$PRE = 1a \left(\frac{3a}{6b}\right)$$

$$PRE = \$100 \left(\frac{2\ years}{4\ years}\right)$$

$$PRE = \$50$$

Consequently, $50 of the FVBM of the replacement awards is attributable to precombination services already performed by the acquiree employees and is, therefore, included in computing the consideration transferred in exchange for obtaining control of the acquiree.

The remaining $50 of the FVBM of the replacement awards is attributable to postcombination service. However, since the acquiree's employees are not required to provide any postcombination services under the terms of the replacement awards, the entire $50 is immediately recognized by NP, the acquirer, in its postcombination consolidated financial statements.

Although not illustrated in the preceding examples, ASC 805 requires the acquirer to estimate the number of its replacement awards for which the requisite service is expected to occur. To the extent that service is not expected to occur due to employees terminating prior to meeting the replacement award's requisite service requirements, the portion of the FVBM of the replacement awards included in consideration transferred in the business combination is reduced accordingly.

If the replacement award is subject to a graded vesting schedule, the acquirer is to recognize the related compensation cost in accordance with its policy election for other awards in accordance with ASC 718-10-35. Compensation cost is either

(1) recognized using the *graded vesting attribution method* that separates the award into tranches according to the year in which they vest and treats each tranche as if it had been a separate award, or
(2) recognized using a straight-line attribution method over the graded vesting period.

If option (2) is elected, compensation cost at any date must equal at least the amount attributable to options that actually vested on or before that date.

Finally, it is important to note that the same requirements for apportioning the replacement award between precombination and postcombination service apply to replacement awards that are classified as equity or as liabilities. All post-acquisition-date changes in the FVBM of liability awards (and their related income tax effects) are recognized in the acquirer's postcombination financial statements in the periods in which the changes occur.

7. *Income taxes.* The final exception to the general fair-value-based recognition and measurement provisions of ASC 805 is the accounting for income taxes. Since recognition and measurement of income tax assets and liabilities under US GAAP has not historically used fair value measurement or discounted present value techniques, FASB was loath to make fundamental changes to this complex area of accounting.

   The remainder of this section is devoted to describing the provisions of those standards and other related interpretive guidance related to accounting for income taxes in connection with business combinations.

   Basic principle. The basic principle that applies to income tax accounting in a business combination (carried forward without change by ASC 805) is that the acquirer is to recognize, as of the acquisition date, deferred income tax assets or liabilities for the future effects of temporary differences and carryforwards of the acquiree that either

a. Exist on the acquisition date *or*
b. Are generated by the acquisition itself

ASC 805 also clarifies ASC 740's applicability to business combinations as follows:

a. In computing the acquisition date amount of currently payable or refundable income taxes from a particular taxing jurisdiction, management is to apply the recognition and measurement provisions of ASC 740 to evaluate the amounts to record relative to prior income tax positions taken by the acquiree.
b. As a result of management's evaluation of prior tax positions and the amounts recognized in item 1, management is to adjust the income tax bases used in computing the deferred income tax assets and liabilities associated with the business combination at the acquisition date.
c. New information regarding the facts and circumstances that existed at the acquisition date that comes to the attention of management regarding those income tax positions is treated as follows:
   (1) If the information results in a change during the measurement period, the adjustment is made to goodwill. If goodwill is reduced to zero, any remaining portion of the adjustment is recorded as a bargain purchase gain.
   (2) If the information results in a post-measurement-period change, the change is accounted for in the same manner as any other ASC 740 changes.

Valuation allowances. To the extent applicable, deferred income tax assets are to be reduced by a valuation allowance for the portion of the asset not deemed MLTN to be realized.

On the acquisition date, any benefits of future deductible temporary differences or *net operating loss carryforwards* (NOLs) of an acquired entity are to be recognized if the acquirer is permitted to utilize those benefits on a consolidated income tax return under the existing income tax law. The income tax benefits will be recorded gross with an offsetting valuation allowance if it is more likely than not that the deferred income tax asset will not be realized by the reporting entity (for example, if it is estimated that there will not be sufficient future taxable income to utilize the NOL prior to its expiration).

Some jurisdictions restrict the future use of income tax benefits of the acquiree and only permit those benefits to be applied to subsequent taxable income generated by the acquiree even though the entities are permitted to file a consolidated income tax return. When this is the case, or when the acquiree is expected to file a separate income tax return, management of the consolidated reporting entity is to assess the need for a valuation allowance for those benefits based only on the acquiree's separate past and expected future taxable income.

As a result of the acquisition and the permissibility of filing a consolidated income tax return in a particular jurisdiction, the acquirer may be able to use future taxable income generated by the acquiree to obtain the tax benefits of its own NOLs for which the acquirer had previously recognized a valuation allowance. If, based on the weight of available evidence, management of the acquirer concludes that its previously recognized valuation allowance can be reduced or eliminated, the adjustment is not considered part of the accounting for the business combination. Instead, the benefit is recognized as a component of income tax expense in the period of the acquisition.

Post-acquisition-date changes in a valuation allowance with respect to an acquiree's deferred income tax asset are to be recognized as follows:

a. If the change in judgment occurs during the measurement period (as defined in ASC 805) that is not to exceed one year from the acquisition date, and results from new information bearing on facts and circumstances that existed at the acquisition date, the change is to be recognized as an adjustment to goodwill. Should the adjustment reduce goodwill to zero, the acquirer is to recognize any further reduction in the valuation allowance as a gain from a bargain purchase.
b. If the change in judgment occurs subsequent to the measurement period, it is reported as an increase or decrease in income tax expense or benefit of the period in which the judgment changed. Exceptions to this treatment are provided for changes attributable to dividends on unallocated shares of an employee stock ownership plan (ESOP), employee stock options, and certain quasi reorganizations. Accounting for these exceptions results in adjustments directly to contributed capital rather than to income tax expense.

Goodwill. Historically, amortization of goodwill was not an allowable deduction for US federal income tax purposes. To the extent that goodwill amortization is nondeductible in any applicable taxing jurisdiction, the nondeductible goodwill does not represent a temporary difference between GAAP and tax and consequently does not give rise to deferred income taxes.

The 1993 Tax Reconciliation Act amended US federal income tax law to permit the amortization of goodwill and other specified acquired intangibles over a statutory 15-year period (IRC §197). The method of determining the amount of goodwill to recognize for income tax purposes, however, differs from the method prescribed by ASC 805 for financial reporting purposes. Further complicating matters, other taxing jurisdictions to which the reporting entity is subject may not recognize goodwill amortization as deductible. This can result in onerous recordkeeping of book/tax differences in the carrying amounts of goodwill in each of the major jurisdictions in which the reporting entity is taxed.

When goodwill amortization is tax-deductible in a particular jurisdiction, it does result in a temporary difference between the income tax basis and GAAP carrying amount of the goodwill. GAAP goodwill is only written off if it becomes partially or fully impaired whereas tax goodwill is subject to periodic amortization until its income tax basis is reduced to zero.

Since goodwill represents a residual amount after considering all identifiable assets acquired and liabilities assumed in the business combination, any deferred income tax asset associated with goodwill would necessarily have to be computed in order to determine the residual. Thus, FASB prescribed the use of a simultaneous equation method to compute goodwill net of the deferred income tax asset associated with it. To operationalize this requirement, ASC 805-74-55 describes and illustrates it.

Step 6—Recognize and measure any noncontrolling interest in the acquiree. The term *noncontrolling interest* replaces the term *minority interest* to refer to the portion of the acquiree, if any, that is not controlled by the parent. The term "minority interest" had become, in some cases, an inaccurate descriptor, because under ASC 805 and ASC 810, an entity can possess a controlling financial interest in another entity without possessing a majority of the voting interests of that entity. Thus it would be inaccurate, in many cases, to refer to the party that does not possess a controlling financial interest as a "minority," since that party could, in fact, hold a majority of the voting equity of the acquiree.

ASC 805 requires the noncontrolling interest in the acquiree to be measured at fair value on the basis of a quoted price in an active market at the acquisition date. If the acquirer is not acquiring all of the shares in the acquiree and there is an active market for the remaining outstanding shares in the acquiree, the acquirer may be able to use the market price to measure the fair value of the noncontrolling interest. Otherwise, the acquirer would measure fair value using other valuation techniques.

In applying the appropriate valuation technique to determine the fair value of the noncontrolling interest, it is likely that there will be a difference in the fair value per share of that interest and the fair value per share of the controlling interest. This difference arises from what has been referred to as a "minority interest discount" applicable to the noncontrolling shares. Obviously, an investor would be unwilling to pay the same amount per share for equity shares in an entity that did not convey control of that entity than it would pay for shares that did convey control. (ASC 805-20-6 through 8)

Example of fair value of noncontrolling interest adjusted for noncontrolling interest discount

Shirley Corporation (SC) is considering acquiring an 80% interest in Jake Industries Inc. (JI), a privately held corporation. SC engages a valuation specialist to determine the fair value of JI whose shares do not trade in an active market.

The specialist's findings with respect to JI as a whole were as follows:

Aggregate fair value of JI	$ 15 million
Number of outstanding shares	375,000
Aggregate fair value per share	$ 40

In valuing the noncontrolling interest, however, the specialist made the following additional assumptions:

Aggregate fair value per share	$40
Estimated noncontrolling interest discount per share	10
Estimated fair value per share of noncontrolling interest	$30

Fair value of noncontrolling interest	
Fair value per noncontrolling share	$ 30
× # of noncontrolling shares outstanding	× 75,000
	$2,250,000

It is important to note from this analysis that, from the perspective of the acquirer, the computation of the acquisition-date fair value of the noncontrolling interest in the acquiree is not computed by simply multiplying the same fair value per share that the acquirer used to value the entity by the percentage voting interest retained collectively by the noncontrolling stockholders. Such a simplistic calculation would have yielded a different result:

$15 million aggregate fair value × 20% noncontrolling shares = $3 million

If this method had been used, the noncontrolling interest would be overvalued by $750,000 (the difference between $3 million and $2,250,000).

Step 7—Measure the consideration transferred. In general, consideration transferred by the acquiree is measured at its acquisition-date fair value. Examples of consideration that could be transferred include cash, other assets, a business, a subsidiary of the acquirer, contingent consideration, common or preferred equity instruments, options, and warrants. The aggregate consideration transferred is the sum of the following elements measured at the acquisition date:

1. The fair value of the assets transferred by the acquirer,
2. The fair value of the liabilities incurred by the acquirer to the former owners of the acquiree, and
3. The fair value of the equity interests issued by the acquirer subject to the measurement exception discussed earlier in this chapter for the portion, if applicable, of acquirer share-based awards exchanged for awards held by employees of the acquiree that is included in consideration transferred.

To the extent the acquirer transfers consideration in the form of assets or liabilities with carrying amounts that differ from their fair values at the acquisition date, the acquirer is to remeasure them at fair value and recognize a gain or loss on the acquisition date. If, however, the transferred assets or liabilities remain within the consolidated entity postcombination with the acquirer retaining control of them, no gain or loss is recognized, and the assets or liabilities are measured at their carrying amounts to the acquirer immediately prior to the acquisition date. This situation can occur, for example, when the acquirer transfers assets or liabilities to the entity being acquired rather than to its former owners.

The structure of the transaction may involve the exchange of equity interests between the acquirer and either the acquiree or the acquiree's former owners. If the acquisition-date fair value of the acquiree's equity interests is more reliably measurable than the equity interests of the acquirer, the fair value of the acquiree's equity interests is used to measure the consideration transferred.

Contingent consideration. Contingent consideration arrangements in connection with business combinations can be structured in many different ways and can result in the recognition of either assets or liabilities under ASC 805. In either case, the acquirer is to include contingent assets and liabilities as part of the consideration transferred, measured at acquisition-date fair value.

If the contingent consideration includes a future payment obligation, that obligation is to be classified as either a liability or equity under the provisions of:

- ASC 480,
- ASC 815-40, or
- Other applicable GAAP.

The acquirer is to carefully consider information obtained subsequent to the acquisition-date measurement of contingent consideration. Additional information obtained during the measurement period that relates to the facts and circumstances that existed at the acquisition date result in measurement period adjustments to the recognized amount of contingent consideration and a corresponding adjustment to goodwill or gain from bargain purchase. Changes that result from events occurring after the acquisition date, such as meeting a specified earnings target, reaching a specified share price, or reaching an agreed-upon milestone on a research and development project, do not constitute measurement period adjustments. Changes in the fair value of contingent consideration that do not result from measurement period adjustments are to be accounted for as follows:

1. If the contingent consideration is classified as equity, it is not to be remeasured and subsequent settlement of the contingency is to be reflected within equity.
2. If the contingent consideration is classified as an asset or liability, it is to be remeasured at fair value at each reporting date until resolution of the contingency. Changes in the fair value between reporting dates are to be recognized in net income unless the arrangement is a hedging instrument for which ASC 815, as amended by ASC 805, requires the changes to be initially recognized in other comprehensive income.

Step 8—Recognize and measure goodwill or gain on a bargain purchase. The last step in applying the acquisition method is the measurement of goodwill or a gain from a bargain purchase. Goodwill represents an intangible that is not specifically identifiable. It results from situations when the amount the acquirer is willing to pay to obtain its controlling interest exceeds the aggregate recognized values of the net assets acquired, measured following the principles of ASC 805. Goodwill's elusive nature as an unidentifiable, residual asset means that it cannot be measured directly but rather can only be measured by reference to the other amounts measured as a part of the business combination:

GW	=	Goodwill
NG	=	Negative goodwill
NI	=	Noncontrolling interest in the acquiree, if any, measured at fair value
CT	=	Consideration transferred, generally measured at acquisition-date fair value
PE	=	Fair value of the acquirer's previously held interest in the acquiree if the acquisition was achieved in stages
NA	=	Net assets acquired at the acquisition date—consisting of the identifiable assets acquired and liabilities assumed, measured as described in this chapter

$$(CT + NI + PE) - NA = GW \text{ or } (NG)$$

Thus, when application of the formula yields an excess of the consideration transferred, noncontrolling interest, and fair value of previously held interests over the net assets acquired, the acquirer has paid a premium for the acquisition and that premium is characterized as goodwill.

When the opposite is true, that is, when the formula yields a negative result, sometimes referred to as *negative goodwill*, the acquirer has, in fact, obtained a bargain purchase, as the value the acquirer obtained in the exchange exceeded the fair value of what it surrendered.

In a business combination in which no consideration is transferred, the acquirer is to use one or more valuation techniques to measure the acquisition-date fair value of its interest in the acquiree and substitute that measurement in the formula for CT, the consideration transferred. The techniques selected require the availability of sufficient data to properly apply them and are to be appropriate for the circumstances. If more than one technique is used, management of the acquirer is to evaluate the results of applying the techniques including the extent of data available and how relevant and reliable the inputs (assumptions) used are. Guidance on the use of valuation techniques is provided in ASC 820.

Bargain purchases. If the computation above results in negative goodwill, this constitutes a *bargain purchase*. Under ASC 805, a bargain purchase is recognized in net income as an acquisition-date gain. The gain is not characterized as an extraordinary gain. Rather, it is considered part of income from continuing operations.

Given the complexity of the computations involved, FASB prescribes a verification protocol for management to follow if the computation preliminarily results in a bargain purchase. If the computation initially yields a bargain purchase, management of the acquirer is to perform the following procedures before recognizing a gain on the bargain purchase:

1. Perform a completeness review of the identifiable tangible and intangible assets acquired and liabilities assumed to reassess whether all such items have been correctly identified. If any omissions are found, recognize the assets and liabilities that had been omitted.
2. Perform a review of the procedures used to measure all of the following items. The objective of the review is to ensure that the acquisition-date measurements appropriately considered all available information available at the acquisition date:

a. Identifiable assets acquired
b. Liabilities assumed
c. Consideration transferred
d. Noncontrolling interest in the acquiree, if applicable
e. Acquirer's previously held equity interest in the acquiree for a business combination achieved in stages.

Measurement period. More frequently than not, management of the acquirer does not obtain all of the relevant information needed to complete the acquisition-date measurements in time for the issuance of the first set of interim or annual financial statements subsequent to the business combination. If the initial accounting for the business combination has not been completed by that time, the acquirer is to report provisional amounts in the consolidated financial statements for any items for which the accounting is incomplete. ASC 805 provides for a "measurement period" during which any adjustments to the provisional amounts recognized at the acquisition date are to be retrospectively adjusted to reflect new information that management obtains regarding facts and circumstances existing as of the acquisition date. Information that has a bearing on this determination must not relate to postacquisition events or circumstances. The information is to be analyzed to determine whether, if it had been known at the acquisition date, it would have affected the measurement of the amounts recognized as of that date.

In evaluating whether new information obtained is suitable for the purpose of adjusting provisional amounts, management of the acquirer is to consider all relevant factors. Critical in this evaluation is the determination of whether the information relates to facts and circumstances as they existed at the acquisition date or instead, the information results from events occurring after the acquisition date. Relevant factors include

1. The timing of the receipt of the additional information, *and*
2. Whether management of the acquirer can identify a reason that a change is warranted to the provisional amounts.

Obviously, information received shortly after the acquisition date has a higher likelihood of relevance to acquisition-date circumstances than information received months later.

Example of consideration of new information obtained during the measurement period

Krupp Industries, Inc. (KI) acquired Miller Motor Works Corp. (MMW) on January 2, 2012. In the first quarter 2012 consolidated financial statements of Krupp Industries and Subsidiary, it assigned a provisional fair value of $40 million to an asset group consisting of a factory and related machinery that manufactures engines used in large trucks and sport utility vehicles (SUVs).

As of the acquisition date, the average cost of gasoline in the markets served by the customers of MMW was $4.30 per gallon. For the first four months subsequent to the acquisition, the per-gallon price of gasoline was relatively stable and only fluctuated slightly up or down on any given day. Upon further analysis, management was able to determine that during that four-month period, the production levels of the asset group and related order backlog did not vary substantially from the acquisition date.

In May 2012, however, due to an accident on May 3, 2012, at a large US refinery, the average cost per gallon skyrocketed to more than $6.00 a gallon. As a result of this huge spike in the price of fuel, MMW's largest customers either canceled orders or sharply curtailed the number of engines they had previously ordered.

Scenario 1: On April 15, 2012, management of KI signed a sales agreement with Joshua International (JI) to sell the asset group for $30 million. Given the fact that management was unable to identify any changes that occurred during the measurement period that would have accounted for a change in the acquisition-date fair value of the asset group, management determines that it will retrospectively reduce the provisional fair value assigned to the asset group to $30 million.

Scenario 2: On May 15, 2012, management of KI signed a sales agreement with Joshua International (JI) to sell the asset group for $30 million. Given the intervening events that affected the price of fuel and the demand for MMW's products, management determines that the $10 million decline in the fair value of the asset group from the provisional fair value it was originally assigned resulted from those intervening changes and, consequently, does not adjust the provisional fair value assigned to the asset group at the acquisition date.

In addition to adjustments to provisional amounts recognized, the acquirer may determine during the measurement period that it omitted recognition of additional assets or liabilities that existed at the acquisition date. During the measurement period, any such assets or liabilities identified are also to be recognized and measured on a retrospective basis.

In determining adjustments to the provisional amounts assigned to assets and liabilities, management should be alert for interrelationships between recognized assets and liabilities. For example, new information that management obtains that results in an adjustment to the provisional amount assigned to a liability for which the acquiree carries insurance could also result in an adjustment, in whole or in part, to a provisional amount recognized as an asset representing the claim receivable from the insurance carrier. In addition, changes in provisional amounts assigned to assets and liabilities frequently will also affect temporary differences between the items' income tax basis and GAAP carrying amount, which in turn will affect the computation of deferred income assets and liabilities.

Adjustments to the provisional amounts that are made during the measurement period are recognized retrospectively as if the accounting for the business combination had actually been completed as of the acquisition date. This will result in the revision of comparative information included in the financial statements for prior periods including any necessary adjustments to depreciation, amortization, or other effects on net income or other comprehensive income related to the adjustments.

The measurement period ends on the earlier of:

1. The date management of the acquirer receives the information it seeks regarding facts and circumstances as they existed at the acquisition date or learns that it will be unable to obtain any additional information, *or*
2. One year after the acquisition date.

After the end of the measurement period, the only revisions that are permitted to be made to the initial acquisition date accounting for the business combination are restatements for corrections of prior period errors in accordance with ASC 250, *Accounting Changes and Error Corrections*.

Application Guidance

Due to the complexity of many business combinations and the varying structures used to effect them, ASC 805 provides supplemental guidance to aid practitioners in their application.

Business combinations achieved in stages (step acquisitions). A step acquisition is a business combination in which the acquirer held an equity interest in the acquiree prior to the acquisition date on which it obtained control.

ASC 805 requires the acquirer to remeasure its previous holdings of the acquiree's equity at acquisition date fair value. Any gain or loss on remeasurement is recognized in earnings on that date.

If the acquirer had previously recognized changes in the carrying amount of the acquiree's equity in other comprehensive income (e.g., because the investment was classified as available for sale), that amount is to be reclassified and included in the computation of the acquisition date gain or loss from remeasurement.

Example of a step acquisition

On 12/31/20X1, Finestone Corporation (FC) owned 5% of the 30,000 outstanding voting common shares of Kitzes Industries (KI). On FC's 12/31/20X statement of financial position, it classified its investment in KI as available for sale. On 3/31/20X2, FC acquired additional equity shares in KI sufficient to provide FC with a controlling interest in KI and, thus, became KI's parent company.

The following table summarizes FC's initial holdings in KI, the subsequent increase in those holdings, and the computation of the gain on remeasurement at the acquisition date of 3/31/20X2:

Date	*# of Shares*	*Percent interest*	*Per share Cost*	*Per share Fair value*	*Aggregate investment Cost*	*Aggregate investment Fair value*	*Unrealized appreciation included in accumulated other comprehensive Income*
12/31/20X1	1,500	5%	$10	$16	$ 15,000	$ 24,000	$9,000
3/31/20X2	21,000	70%	20	20	420,000	420,000	
	22,500	75%					

Computation of gain (loss) on remeasurement at acquisition date:

Fair value per share on 4/1/20X2	$ 20
Number of preacquisition shares	× 1,500
Aggregate fair value of preacquisition shares on 4/1/20X2	30,000
Carrying amount of preacquisition shares on 4/1/20X2	24,000
Appreciation attributable to the 1st quarter of 20X2	6,000
Pre-2012 appreciation reclassified from accumulated OCI	9,000
Gain on remeasurement of KI stock on 3/31/20X2	$15,000

Changes in the parent's ownership interest in a subsidiary. Subsequent to a business combination, the parent may increase or decrease its ownership percentage in the acquiree/subsidiary, which may or may not affect whether the parent continues to control the subsidiary.

Changes not affecting control. The parent company may purchase or sell shares of the subsidiary after the acquisition date without affecting the determination that it controls the subsidiary. In addition, the subsidiary may issue new shares or repurchase some of its own shares as treasury stock or for retirement.

Changes in the parent's ownership interest that do not affect the determination that the parent retains a controlling financial interest in the subsidiary are accounted for as equity transactions with no gain or loss recognized in consolidated net income or in other comprehensive income. The carrying amount of the noncontrolling interest in the subsidiary is to be adjusted to reflect the change in ownership interest. Any difference between the fair value of the consideration received or paid in the transaction and the amount by which the noncontrolling interest is adjusted is to be recognized in equity attributable to the parent.

In the case of a subsidiary that has *accumulated other comprehensive income* (AOCI), if there is a change in the parent's ownership interest, the carrying amount of AOCI is to be adjusted through a corresponding charge or credit to equity attributable to the parent.

Changes resulting in loss of control. If a parent company ceases to have a controlling financial interest in a subsidiary, the parent is required to deconsolidate the subsidiary as of the date on which its control ceased. Examples of situations that can result in a parent being required to deconsolidate a subsidiary include:

1. Sale by the parent of all or a portion of its ownership interest in the subsidiary resulting in the parent no longer holding a controlling financial interest,
2. Expiration of a contract that granted control of the subsidiary to the parent,
3. Issuance by the subsidiary of stock that reduces the ownership interest of the parent to a level not representing a controlling financial interest,
4. Loss of control of the subsidiary by the parent because the subsidiary becomes subject to control by a governmental body, court, administrator, or regulator.

If a parent effects a deconsolidation of a subsidiary through a nonreciprocal transfer to owners, such as through a spin-off transaction, the transaction is accounted for under ASC 845. Otherwise, the parent is to account for the deconsolidation by recognizing, in net income, a gain or loss attributable to the parent. The gain or loss is measured as follows:

FVCR	=	Fair value of consideration received, if any
FVNIR	=	Fair value of any noncontrolling investment retained by the former parent at the deconsolidation date
CVNI	=	Carrying value of the noncontrolling interest in the former subsidiary on the deconsolidation date, including any accumulated other comprehensive income attributable to the noncontrolling interest
CVAL	=	Carrying value of the former subsidiaries assets and liabilities at the deconsolidation date.

(FVCR + FVNIR + CVNI) – CVAL = Deconsolidation Gain (Loss)

Should the parent's loss of controlling financial interest occur through two or more transactions, management of the former parent is to consider whether the transactions should be accounted for as a single transaction. In evaluating whether to combine the transactions, management of the former parent is to consider all of the terms and conditions of the transactions as well as their economic impact. The presence of one or more of the following indicators may lead to management concluding that it should account for multiple transactions as a single transaction:

1. The transactions are entered into simultaneously or in contemplation of one another,
2. The transactions, when considered in tandem, are in substance a single transaction designed to achieve an overall commercial objective,
3. The occurrence of one transaction depends on the occurrence of at least one other transaction,
4. One transaction, when considered on its own merits, does not make economic sense, but when considered together with the other transaction or transactions would be considered economically justifiable.

Obviously, this determination requires the exercise of sound judgment and attention to economic substance over legal form.

This guidance does not apply to sales of real estate or the conveyance of oil and gas mineral rights. Refer to ASC 360-20 and 976-605 for the appropriate guidance for real estate, and to ASC 932-360 for oil and gas mineral rights.

Allocation of net income and other comprehensive income to the parent and noncontrolling interest. In preparing consolidated financial statements, the parent eliminates 100% of the intercompany income or loss. This elimination is not affected by the existence of a noncontrolling interest since the consolidated financial statements purport to present the financial position and economic performance of a single economic entity. The elimination of the intercompany income or loss may be allocated between the parent and noncontrolling interests.

Revenues, expenses, gains, losses, net income or loss, and other comprehensive income are reported in the consolidated financial statements at the consolidated amounts that include amounts attributable to the owners of the parent company and the noncontrolling interest. Net income or loss, and other comprehensive income or loss, are allocated to the parent and the noncontrolling interest.

Losses allocated to the parent and to the noncontrolling interest may exceed their respective interests in the equity of the subsidiary. When this occurs, and if it continues to occur in subsequent periods, the excess as well as any further losses continue to be allocated to the parent and noncontrolling interest, even if this allocation results in a deficit balance in noncontrolling interest.

Push-Down Accounting[6]

Under new basis (or *push-down*) accounting, the amounts allocated to various assets and liabilities can be adjusted to reflect the arm's-length valuation reflected in a significant transaction, such as the sale of a majority interest in the entity. For example, the sale of 90% of the shares of a company by one shareholder to a new investor—which under the entity concept would not alter the accounting by the company itself—would, under new basis accounting, be "pushed down" to the entity. The logic is that, as under accounting for business combinations, the most objective gauge of "cost" is that arising from a recent arm's-length transaction.

Traditionally, GAAP has not permitted new basis accounting, in part because of the practical difficulty of demonstrating that the reference transaction was indeed arm's-length in nature. (Obviously, the risk is that a series of sham transactions could be used to grossly distort the "cost" and hence carrying values of the entity's assets, resulting in fraudulent financial reporting.) Also heavily debated has been where the threshold should be set (a 50% change in ownership, an 80% change, etc.) to denote when a significant event had occurred that would provide valid information on the valuation of the entity's assets and liabilities for financial reporting purposes.

Many of the more general issues of push-down accounting (those applicable to traditional business acquisitions) have yet to be dealt with. For example, proponents of push-down accounting point out that in a business combination a new basis of accounting is established, and that this new basis should be pushed down to the acquired entity and should be used when presenting that entity's own, separate financial statements. However, practical problems remain: For example, while push-down makes some sense in the case where a major block of the investee's shares is acquired in a single free-market transaction, if new basis accounting were to be used in the context of a series of step transactions, continual adjustment of the investee's carrying values for assets and liabilities would be necessary. Furthermore, the price paid for a portion of the ownership of an investee may not always be meaningfully extrapolated to a value for the investee company as a whole.

The SEC's position (ASC 805-50-S99-2) has been that push-down accounting would be required if 95% or more of the shares of the company have been acquired (unless the company has outstanding public debt or preferred stock that may impact the acquirer's ability to control the form of ownership of the company); that it would be permitted, but not mandated, if 80% to 95% has been acquired; and it would be prohibited if less than 80% of the company

---

[6] Note that the FASB has issued an exposure draft on pushdown accounting. Comments are due 7/14/2014. Updated information can be found on the FASB web site.

is acquired. The SEC also requires push-down accounting if any entity becomes substantially wholly owned by a group of investors who act together, subject to several restrictions in ASC 805-50-S99-2 relating to such matters as their independence, risk of ownership, and subsequent collaboration.

While there is no requirement under GAAP to apply this push-down concept, the SEC position is considered to be substantial authoritative support and can be referenced even for nonpublic company financial reporting. It would be defensible in any instance where there is a change in control and/or a change in ownership of a majority of the common shares, when separate financial statements of the subsidiary are to be presented. Full disclosure is to be made of the circumstances whenever push-down accounting is applied.

Example of push-down accounting

Assume that Pullup Corp. acquires, in an open market arm's-length transaction, 90% of the common stock of Pushdown Co. for $464.61 million. At that time, Pushdown Co.'s net book value was $274.78 million (for the entire company). Book and fair values of selected assets and liabilities of Pushdown Co. as of the transaction date are summarized as follows ($000,000 omitted):

	Book value		*Fair value of*	*Excess of*
	100% of entity	*90% interest*	*90% interest*	*FV over book*
Assets				
Receivables	$ 24.6	$ 22.14	$ 29.75	$ 7.61
Inventory	21.9	19.71	24.80	5.09
Property, plant, & equipment, net	434.2	390.78	488.20	97.42
All others	223.4	201.06	201.06	0.00
Additional goodwill			120.00	120.00
Total assets	$704.1	$633.69	$863.81	$230.12
Liabilities				
Bonds payable	104.9	94.41	88.65	5.76
All other liabilities	325.0	292.50	310.55	18.05
Total liabilities	429.9	386.91	399.20	12.29
Equity				
Preferred stock	40.0	36.00	36.00	0.00
Common stock	87.4	78.66	78.66	0.00
Revaluation surplus*			217.83	217.83
Retained earnings	146.8	132.12	132.12	0.00
Total equity	274.2	246.88	464.61	217.83
Liabilities + Equity	$704.1	$633.69	$863.81	$230.12

* *Net premium paid over book value by arm's-length of "almost all" common stock*

Assuming that "new basis" accounting is deemed to be acceptable and meaningful, since Pushdown Co. must continue to issue separate financial statements to its creditors and holders of its preferred stock, and also assuming that a revaluation of the share of ownership that did not change hands (i.e., the 10% noncontrolling interest in this example) should not be revalued based on the majority transaction, the entries by the subsidiary (Pushdown Co.) for purposes only of preparing stand-alone financial statements would be as follows:

Accounts receivable	7,610,000	
Inventory	5,090,000	
Plant, property and equipment (net)	97,420,000	
Goodwill	120,000,000	
Discount on bonds payable	5,760,000	
Other liabilities		18,050,000
Paid-in capital from revaluation		217,830,000

The foregoing entry would only be made for purposes of preparing separate financial statements of Pushdown Co. If consolidated financial statements of Pullup Corp. are also presented, essentially the same result will be obtained. The additional paid-in capital account would be eliminated against the parent's investment account, however, since in the context of the consolidated financial statements this would be a cash transaction rather than a mere accounting revaluation.

There is also a body of opinion holding that the separate financial statements of Pushdown Co. in this example should be "grossed up" for the imputed premium that would have been achieved on the transfer of the remaining 10% ownership interest. This is less appealing, however, given the absence of a "real" transaction involving that last 10% ownership stake, making the price at which it would have traded somewhat speculative.

The foregoing example obviously also ignored the tax effects of the transaction. Since the step-ups in carrying value would not, in all likelihood, alter the corresponding tax bases of the assets and liabilities, deferred income tax effects would also require recognition. This would be done following the procedures set forth at ASC 740. See the chapter on ASC 740 for additional information.

Accounting for Leveraged Buyouts

Another complex issue that arises in practice is the determination of the appropriate accounting treatment for a leveraged buyout (sometimes referred to as a bootstrap transaction or simply abbreviated as an LBO).

An LBO results from a highly leveraged single transaction or series of transactions in which all of the previously outstanding common stock in a target entity, "OLDCO," is acquired from the target's shareholders by "NEWCO," a financial sponsor entity often organized as a private equity limited partnership.

The source of the financing for the LBO transaction is nonrecourse debt collateralized by the underlying assets of OLDCO, the acquiree. Thus, the acquiree's own assets provide the underlying collateral to enable the acquirer to execute the transaction. The postacquisition operating cash flows expected to be generated by the acquiree are intended to provide the funding necessary to meet the debt service requirements.

When an LBO meets its initial expectations, it can provide an attractive return on the relatively minimal initial investment required by the sponsor/acquirer's investors. However, when the acquiree's postacquisition financial performance falls short of expectations, the potential for a default on the acquisition indebtedness is substantial and the previously successful business that made the target company an attractive acquisition candidate can end up in bankruptcy reorganization or in outright liquidation.

At the center of the accounting issue is the question of whether a new basis of accounting has been created by the execution of the LBO transaction notwithstanding the fact that the change in ownership occurred outside of the target entity through the purchase of shares from the target's existing owners. Generally, under GAAP, such a transaction does not affect the reporting entity since that entity was not a party to the transaction.

However, it could be argued conceptually that the change in control of the target/acquiree is economically similar to the results that would be achieved if the sponsor/acquirer were to obtain control through a business combination transaction. Proponents of this economic substance over form argument hold that the execution of the LBO transaction would warrant a step-up in the reported amounts of the target/acquiree's assets and/or liabilities. If a step-up is not recognized, the carryforward bases of the predecessor entity assets and liabilities continue to be reported in its financial statements.

The Emerging Issues Task Force (EITF) had addressed leveraged buyouts in several pre-Codification Consensuses (EITF 88-16, *Basis in Leveraged Buyout Transactions*, and EITF 90-12, *Allocating Basis to Individual Assets and Liabilities for Transactions within the Scope of Issue No. 88-16*). However, both of these Consensuses were nullified in December 2007 by the issuance of FAS 141(R), *Business Combinations*, subsequently codified as Topic ASC 805.

Since FAS 141(R) was not required to be applied to transactions that preceded its effective date, the nullified EITF consensuses represent grandfathered guidance applicable to those transactions that were within their scope.

The EITF concluded that full or partial new basis accounting is appropriate only when the transaction results in a change in control of voting interests. EITF 88-16 established a series of mechanical tests by which this change in interest was to be measured. Three groups of interests were identified: (1) shareholders in the newly created company; (2) management; and (3) shareholders in the old company (who may or may not also have an interest in the new company). Depending upon the relative interests of these groups in the old entity (OLDCO) and in the new enterprise (NEWCO), there will be either (1) a finding that the transaction was a business combination (new basis accounting applies) or (2) that it was a recapitalization or a restructuring (carryforward basis accounting applies).

Among the tests that the EITF decreed to determine proper accounting for any given LBO transaction is the *monetary test*. This test required that at least 80% of the net consideration paid to acquire OLDCO interests must have been monetary. In this context, monetary means cash, debt, and the fair value of any equity by securities given by NEWCO to selling shareholders of OLDCO. Loan proceeds provided OLDCO to assist in the acquisition of NEWCO shares by NEWCO shareholders were excluded from this definition. If the portion of the purchase effected through monetary consideration was less than 80%, but other criteria of EITF 88-16 were satisfied, there would be a step-up. This step-up was limited to the percentage of the transaction represented by monetary consideration.

EITF 88-16 presented an extensive series of examples illustrating the circumstances that would and would not meet the former purchase accounting criteria to be employed in an LBO.

Reverse Acquisitions

Introduction. A reverse acquisition is a stock transaction that occurs when one entity (the legal acquirer) issues so many of its shares to the former owners of another entity (the legal acquiree) that those former owners become the majority owners of the resultant consolidated enterprise. As a result of the transaction, the legal and accounting treatments will differ, with the legal acquiree being treated as the acquirer for financial reporting purposes. While often the legal acquirer will adopt the acquiree's name, thus alerting users of the financial statements to the nature of the organizational change, this does not necessarily occur, and, in any event, it is critical that the financial statements contain sufficient disclosure so that users are not misled. This is particularly important in the periods immediately following the transaction, and especially when comparative financial statements are presented that include periods prior to the acquisition, since comparability will be affected.

Structure of the transaction. A typical reverse acquisition (see diagram on next page) involves a public company and a nonpublic operating company. The objective is for the nonpublic entity to "go public" without the usual time-consuming and expensive registration process involved in a formal initial public offering (IPO). However, reverse acquisitions are not limited to such situations, and such transactions have occurred involving two public or two nonpublic companies.

It had become popular for private companies to use this technique by locating a *public shell* (a publicly held company that is dormant or inactive) to serve as the legal acquirer/ accounting acquiree. The staff of the SEC Division of Corporate Finance provided the following interpretive guidance in March 2001 that effectively ended the use of reverse acquisition accounting when a public shell is involved:

> *The merger of a private operating company into a nonoperating public shell corporation with nominal net assets typically results in the owners and management of the private company having actual or effective operating control of the combined company after the transaction, with shareholders of the former public shell continuing only as passive investors. These transactions are considered by the staff to be capital transactions in substance, rather than business combinations. That is, the transaction is equivalent to the issuance of stock by the private company for the net monetary assets of the shell corporation, accompanied by a recapitalization. The accounting is identical to that resulting from a reverse acquisition, except that no goodwill or other intangible should be recorded.*[7]

In addition to the foregoing SEC guidance, ASC 805-40-25-1 imposed a requirement that, in transactions occurring after its effective date, the legal acquirer meet the definition of a business. Thus, the use of a public shell entity would not give rise to goodwill and should be accounted for as described in the SEC guidance.

The reverse acquisition is effected when the shareholders of the legal acquiree obtain control of the postacquisition consolidated enterprise, and most commonly this results from a stock-for-stock exchange. The public entity issues shares of newly registered common stock (the legal acquirer) to the shareholders of the nonpublic company in exchange for their ownership interests.

Based on the application of ASC 805-10-55-11 through 55-15, and as a result of the change in control effected by the exchange of stock, the legal acquiree entity is identified as the accounting acquirer of the legal acquirer/accounting acquiree.

Continuation of the business of the legal acquiree. Following a reverse acquisition, just as in any business combination, consolidated financial statements are to be presented. Although the financial statements will be identified as being those of the legal acquirer (which will be the legal owner of the legal acquiree), in substance these will be a continuation of the financial statements of the legal subsidiary/GAAP acquirer, with the assets, liabilities, revenues, and expenses of the legal acquirer being consolidated effective with the acquisition date. Put another way, the consolidated entity will be presented as a continuation of the business of the legal subsidiary, notwithstanding the formal structure of the transaction or the name of the successor enterprise.

Comparative financial statements for earlier periods, if presented, are to be consistent, meaning that in order for them to be comparable to the postacquisition financial statements, these would also need to represent the financial statements of the legal acquiree. Since in some instances the acquiree's name is different than that shown in the heading, care must be taken to fully communicate with the readers. The fact that the prior period's financial information, identified as being that of the legal parent, is really that of the legal acquiree is obviously extremely pertinent to a reader's understanding of the financial statements.

If the legal parent/accounting subsidiary does not change its name to that of the accounting parent, it is essential that the financial statement titles be captioned in a way that clearly communicates the substance of the transaction to the readers. For example, the statements may be headed "ABC Company, Inc.—successor to XYZ Corporation."

---

[7] *"Frequently Requested Accounting and Financial Reporting Interpretations and Guidance"; Accounting staff members of the Division of Corporation Finance, US SEC; Washington, D.C.; March 31, 2001; www.sec.gov/divisions/corpfin/guidance/cfactfaq.htm.*

Structure of Typical Reverse Acquisition

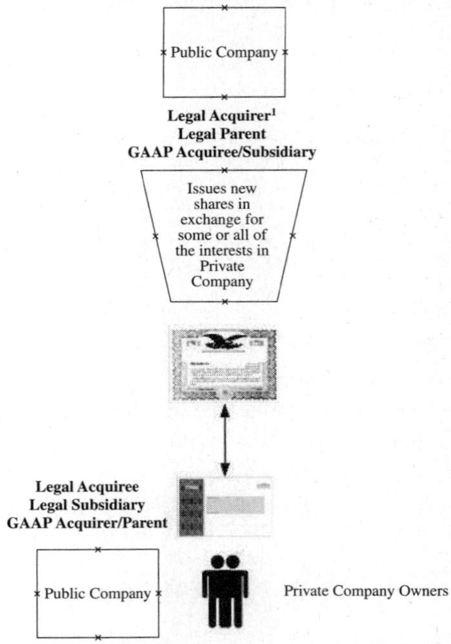

[1] The legal name of the public company/legal acquirer is used in the consolidated financial statements; however disclosure is included that the entity is a continuation of the business of the legal acquiree/subsidiary.

Equity structure adjustments. One adjustment to the financial statements is unique to a reverse acquisition. Management is to retroactively adjust the capital of the legal acquiree/GAAP acquirer to reflect the legal capital of the legal acquirer/GAAP acquiree. The adjustment is necessary in order for the consolidated statement of financial position to reflect the capital of the legal parent/GAAP subsidiary. Information presented for comparative purposes in the consolidated financial statements is also to be retroactively adjusted to reflect the legal parent's legal capital.

Consolidation procedures. The consolidated financial statements present the continuation of the financial statements of the legal subsidiary with the exception of its capital structure. Thus, those postcombination consolidated financial statements will reflect, per ASC 805-40-45-2

1. The assets and liabilities of the legal subsidiary/accounting parent recognized and measured at their precombination carrying amounts.
2. The assets and liabilities of the legal parent/accounting subsidiary recognized and measured as a business combination under ASC 805.
3. The retained earnings and other equity balances of the legal subsidiary/accounting parent *prior to* the business combination.
4. The consolidated equity structure (i.e., the number and type of equity interests issued) is to be adjusted to reflect the equity structure of the legal parent/accounting subsidiary, including the equity interests issued by the legal parent in order to effect the combination. To operationalize this adjustment, the legal subsidiary's equity structure is to be restated to reflect the number of shares of the legal parent

issued in the reverse acquisition using the exchange ratio prescribed by the acquisition agreement.

5. The noncontrolling interest's proportionate share of the legal subsidiary's precombination carrying amounts of retained earnings and other equity interests as discussed in ASC 805-40-25-2 and ASC 805-40-30-3.

Spin-offs and Reverse Spin-offs

Spin-offs. One method that is used as a means of reorganizing an entity's operations is through the use of a spin-off. This can involve the transfer of assets that constitute a business, by their holder referred to as the spinnor, into a new legal entity (spinnee), the shares of which are distributed to the spinnor's shareholders. The distribution is nonreciprocal in that the shareholders of the spinnor are not required to surrender any of their stock in the spinnor in exchange for the shares of the spinnee.

Besides facilitating a reorganization of the reporting entity, a spin-off may also qualify as a nontaxable reorganization with the distribution not being treated as a taxable gain by the spinnor or its shareholders. In addition, if the spinnee stock is subsequently sold by the shareholders, they avoid the effect of the double taxation that would occur if the company sold the company directly and distributed the net proceeds to the stockholders in a taxable cash dividend.

The accounting rules governing spin-offs and reverse spin-offs are found in ASC 505-60 and ASC 845-10-30.

In accordance with ASC 505-60-25-2, the distribution of shares of a wholly owned or consolidated subsidiary that constitutes a business to an entity's shareholders is to be recorded based on the carrying value of the subsidiary. Irrespective of whether the spun-off operations are to be sold immediately following the spin-off, management is not to account for the transaction as a sale of the spinnee followed by a distribution of the proceeds.

Further, in accordance with ASC 845-10-30-10, a pro rata distribution to owners of an entity of shares of a subsidiary or other investee entity that has been or is being consolidated or accounted for under the equity method is to be considered the equivalent of a spin-off.

Reverse spin-offs. Under certain circumstances, a spun-off subsidiary/spinnee will function as the continuing entity post-spin-off. When the spin-off of a subsidiary is structured in such a way that the legal form of the transaction does not represent its economic substance, this will be accounted for as a reverse spin-off whereby the legal spinnee is treated as if it were the spinnor for financial reporting purposes.

The determination of whether reverse spin-off accounting is appropriate is a matter of professional judgment that depends on a careful analysis of all relevant facts and circumstances. ASC 505-60-25-8 provides indicators to be considered in determining whether a spin-off should be accounted for as a reverse spin-off. No one indicator is to be considered presumptive or determinative.

1. *The sizes of the legal spinnor and the legal spinnee.* If all other factors are equal, in a reverse spin-off, the legal spinnee/accounting spinnor is larger than the legal spinnor/accounting spinnee. This comparison is to be based on assets, revenues, and earnings of the two entities with no established bright lines that should be applied.
2. *The fair value of the legal spinnor and the legal spinnee.* All other factors being equal, in a reverse spin-off, the fair value of the legal spinnee/accounting spinnor is greater than the fair value of the legal spinnor/accounting spinnee.
3. *Senior management.* All other factors being equal, in a reverse spin-off, the legal spinnee retains the senior management of the formerly consolidated entity. Senior management is generally understood to include the chairman of the board of directors,

chief executive officer, chief operating officer, chief financial officer, the divisional heads that report directly to them, or the executive committee, if applicable.

4. *Length of holding period.* All other factors being equal, in a reverse spin-off, the legal spinnee is held for a longer period than the legal spinnor. A proposed or approved plan of sale for one of the separate entities concurrent with the spin-off transaction may assist in the identification of the entity to be sold as the spinnee for accounting purposes.

The determination of the accounting spinnor and spinnee, respectively, has significant implications In a spin-off, the net book value of the spinnee is treated, in effect, as a dividend distribution to the shareholders of the spinnor. Since the net book value of these entities will differ from each other, the amount of the reduction to retained earnings of the surviving reporting entity (the accounting spinnor) will be affected by this determination. ASC 505-60 offers several examples of fact patterns which support spin-off or reverse spin-off determinations.

Finally, the accounting for a reverse spin-off is further complicated by the fact that the determination of the accounting spinnor and spinnee significantly affects the reporting of discontinued operations in accordance with ASC 360. The accounting spinnee is reported as a discontinued operation by the accounting spinnor if the spinnee is a component of an entity and meets the conditions for such reporting contained in ASC 360.

Non-Sub Subsidiaries

Another issue that has concerned accountants and the SEC is the popularity of what have been called *non-sub subsidiaries*. This situation arises when an entity plays a major role in the creation and financing of what is often a start-up or experimental operation, but does not take an equity position at the outset. For example, the sponsor might finance the entity by means of convertible debt or debt with warrants entitling it to the later purchase of common shares. The original equity in such arrangements is often provided by the creative or managerial talent engaged in the new entity's operations, who generally exchange their talents for an equity interest. If the operation prospers, the sponsor will exercise its rights and obtain a majority voting stock position; if the operation fails, the sponsor presumably avoids reflecting the losses in its financial statements.

While this strategy may seem to avoid the requirements of equity method accounting or consolidation based on majority voting ownership, the economic substance of the arrangement clearly suggests that the operating results of the sponsored entity be reflected as a subsidiary in the consolidated financial statements of the sponsor who, in substance, is fulfilling the customary role of a parent, even absent ownership of voting stock.

The entities described above are often similar in structure and purpose to what were formerly called "special-purpose entities" or "special-purpose vehicles" and which have now been identified as "variable interest entities."

46 ASC 808 COLLABORATIVE ARRANGEMENTS

PERSPECTIVE AND ISSUES

Subtopic

ASC 808-10, *Collaborative Arrangements,* contains one subtopic:

- ASC 809-10, *Overall,* which defines collaborative arrangements and gives reporting requirements.

Scope

ASC 808-10 applies to all collaborative arrangements, except for those addressed in other topics. See more on scope later in this chapter.

Overview

A collaborative arrangement (sometimes referred to in practice as "line-item" joint ventures or "virtual" joint ventures) is a contractual agreement between two or more parties (participants) to jointly conduct business activities for their mutual benefit without the formation of a separate entity in which to conduct the activities. These types of arrangements are commonly used for such purposes as

- producing motion pictures;
- designing and developing hardware and/or software; or
- developing new pharmaceutical drugs.

Determining the proper accounting treatment for the various activities included in these endeavors is the subject of Accounting Standards Codification (ASC) 808, *Collaborative Arrangements.*

DEFINITIONS OF TERMS

Source: ASC 808-10-20

Collaborative arrangement. A contractual agreement that involves a joint operating activity. These arrangements involve two (or more) parties that meet both of the following requirements:

1. They are active participants in the activity.
2. They are exposed to significant risks and rewards dependent on the commercial success of the activity.

Endeavor. The activity upon which participants in a collaborative arrangement collaborate. For example, in a biotechnology or pharmaceutical environment the endeavor may be the development and commercialization of a drug candidate. In the entertainment industry, it may be production and distribution of a motion picture.

CONCEPTS, RULES, AND EXAMPLES

Collaborative Arrangements

Joint operating activities. (ASC 808-10-15-7) As previously mentioned, collaborative arrangements are used to conduct many different types of business activities. For example,

- Two or more parties may agree to collaborate on joint operation of a facility, such as a hospital or long-term care nursing facility.
- Two professional services firms (e.g., architects, engineers, consultants) may choose to jointly submit a proposal to obtain a new engagement that neither would have the capacity and/or capability to perform on its own.
- A movie studio may collaborate with another studio because it wants to produce a film starring an actor that is under contract with another studio, or two studios may wish to spread the cost (and, of course, the risk) of producing a film.
- Frequently, in the pharmaceutical industry, two companies engage in a joint operating activity to research, develop, market, manufacture, and/or distribute a drug candidate, including the process of obtaining all necessary regulatory approvals in one or more geographic markets.

A collaborative arrangement may involve various types of activities conducted or supervised by the participants, including but not limited to research, development, branding, promotion, sales, marketing, order processing, package design, manufacturing, and distribution. In some collaborative arrangements, a legal entity may be used for certain specified activities or in certain geographic jurisdictions due, for example, to legal restrictions imposed by the jurisdiction.

The participants' roles and responsibilities vary between arrangements but can be structured where certain responsibilities are shared between the participants and other responsibilities are solely the responsibility of one of the participants.

Scope. Under ASC 808, an activity (referred to as an "endeavor") that is the subject of a joint operating arrangement is characterized as a collaborative arrangement within the scope of the pronouncement if:

1. The endeavor involves two or more parties.
2. Both (all) of the parties are:

a. Active participants in the endeavor and
b. Exposed to significant risks and rewards that depend on the endeavor's commercial success

3. The endeavor is not *primarily* conducted through a separate legal entity created for it.

Active involvement. (ASC 808-10-15-8). In evaluating whether a participant is active with respect to an endeavor, management is to consider the arrangement's specific facts and circumstances. Examples of involvement that could constitute active participation include, but are not limited to

1. Directing and executing the activities of the endeavor,
2. Participating on a steering committee or other oversight or governance body,
3. Possessing a legal or contractual right to the intellectual property that underlies the endeavor.

Solely providing financial resources to an endeavor would not constitute an active level of involvement for the purposes of ASC 808.

Significant risks and rewards. (ASC 808-10-15-10 through 13). Management of a participant is to exercise its best judgment in evaluating whether the participant is exposed to significant risks and entitled to significant rewards. Consideration is to be given to the terms and conditions of the arrangement and the facts and circumstances surrounding it, including:

- The stage of the endeavor's life cycle at which the participant is commencing its involvement
- Management's expectations regarding the duration and extent of its financial participation in relation to the total expected duration and total expected value of the endeavor.

Examples of terms and conditions of an arrangement that may indicate that a participant is not exposed to significant risks or entitled to significant rewards include:

- Market rates are paid for services provided by the participant
- Ability of a participant to exit the arrangement without cause and recover all or most of its cumulative economic participation through the exit date
- Limits on the rewards that a participant is entitled to receive
- Allocation of initial profits from the endeavor to only one participant.

Frequently, a collaborative arrangement will involve the license of intellectual property with the participants to the arrangement exchanging consideration with respect to the license at the arrangement's inception. The existence of terms of this nature are not necessarily indicative of the participants not being exposed to significant risks or entitled to significant rewards.

Timing of determination or redetermination. A participant may become involved in a collaborative arrangement at any time during the life cycle of the endeavor. From the perspective of a participant, determination of whether an endeavor is a collaborative arrangement is to be made at the inception of the arrangement or when the participant initially becomes involved in the arrangement based on the facts and circumstances existing at that time. A participant is to reevaluate whether the arrangement continues to qualify as a collaborative arrangement any time there is a change in a participant's role in the arrangement or a change in a participant's exposure to risks or entitlement to rewards from the arrangement.

Accounting for transactions with unrelated third parties. (ASC 808-10-15-1 and 15-2). A participant in a collaborative arrangement recognizes revenue earned and costs incurred in transactions with third parties (parties that are not participants to the collaborative arrangement) in its income statement based on whether the participant is serving as a principal or an agent in the transaction under ASC 605-45. (See the chapter on ASC605 for more guidance.)

Matters for which guidance is not provided. The scope of ASC 808 specifically excludes

1. Arrangements for which the accounting treatment is addressed by other authoritative literature,
2. Guidance regarding matters such as
   a. Determining the appropriate units of accounting,
   b. Determining the appropriate recognition requirements for a given unit of accounting,
   c. The timing of when recognition criteria are considered to have been met.

Example of a collaborative arrangement

Leonard Sporting Goods Company (LSG) and Maureen Metals LLC (MML) contractually agree to codevelop a new set of golf clubs using a special alloy and what they believe to be a revolutionary design. The terms of their Joint Development Agreement (JDA) are as follows:

LSG responsibilities

- Conducting all necessary research and development activities associated with the design of the club faces and shafts
- Developing the branding strategy, and designing the logo and product packaging
- Engaging a contract manufacturer and performing or supervising all manufacturing, warehousing, logistics, and order processing functions
- Carrying necessary inventories and insuring them against casualty loss
- Establishing prices, and performing all invoicing, credit checks, and collection activities.

MML responsibilities

- Conducting all necessary research and development on the development of the experimental alloy
- Handling all press relations and conducting the advertising campaign
- Filing of all patents associated with the product, its design, and materials
- Marketing the product in its home state and six surrounding states; sales orders originating in those states are to be forwarded to LSG for processing, and shipment, with LSG responsible for performing all of the activities specified above. In the specified states, MML has limited discretion regarding the pricing of the product.

Other provisions of the JDA include:

- All costs and operating profits are to be split by the participants 50%/50%.
- The participants will co-own the intellectual property arising out of the project.
- Due to legal considerations in the Grand Duchy of Leslie, all sales in that jurisdiction are required to be made by a legal entity duly established within its borders. Consequently, when orders are placed for shipment to the Duchy, LSG sells the golf clubs to Duchy Golf Sales Co. (DGS), a corporation chartered in the Duchy to enable DGS to then transact with the sporting goods retailer located in the Duchy. DGS is owned 50% each by LSG and MML, who each invested $10,000 upon its incorporation on January 2, 20X1.
- On a quarterly basis each participant is to provide the other participant a full accounting for its activities with respect to the endeavor, and whichever participant has advanced a net amount in excess of its proportionate share of the operating results is entitled to receive an "equalization payment" from the other participant.

The following summarizes the transactions associated with the endeavor for calendar year 20X1, including the final activities necessary to commence production of the product and deliver it to sporting good stores in time for the 20X1 holiday selling season.

(000s omitted)	*Total endeavor results (excluding JV)*	*50% of endeavor results*	*Joint venture DGS*
Sales	$9,200	$4,600	$500
Cost of sales	5,000	2,500	300
Gross profit	4,200	2,100	200
Operating expenses			
Advertising and promotion	500	250	
Bad debts	200	100	
Branding, package, and logo design	300	150	
Legal and patent filing fees	600	300	50
Research and development			
Alloy and metallurgy	200	100	
Club faces and shafts	300	150	
Shipping and delivery	600	300	20
Total operating expenses	2,700	1,350	70
Income from operations	$1,500		$130
× share of operating results allocable to each participant	× 50%		
	$ 750	$ 750	

The annual "equalization" payment was computed as follows, based on the transactions reported by the participants:

(000s omitted)	*Initially recorded in the accounting records of* LSG	MML
Sales	$9,200	$ –
Cost of sales	5,000	–
Gross profit	4,200	–
Operating expenses		
Advertising and promotion	–	500
Bad debts	200	–
Branding, package, and logo design	300	–
Legal and patent filing fees	–	600
Research and development		
Alloy and metallurgy	–	200
Club faces and shafts	300	–
Shipping and delivery	600	–
Total operating expenses	1,400	1,300
Income (loss) from operations prior to equalization	2,800	(1,300)
Share of operating results per agreement	750	750
Equalization payment (receivable) payable	$2,050	$(2,050)

Analysis

1. *Determine applicability of ASC 808.* The endeavor involves two parties that are both actively involved and that share equally in both risks and rewards. The existence of the separate entity (DGS) does not disqualify the arrangement, since the joint operating activities are not *primarily* conducted through the separate entity. Thus, from the perspective of the participants, the arrangement is considered a collaborative arrangement within the scope of ASC 808 for the year ended December 31, 20X1.

2. *Determine the accounting for the transactions in the separate legal entity.* DGS has no parent company that controls it via ownership as a voting interest entity or via other financial control as a variable interest entity (VIE). Thus, under ASC 323, each participant is to record its investment in DGS and apply the equity method to account for its investment in the joint venture as follows:

1/2/20X1		
Investment in DGS	10,000	
Cash		10,000
To record initial investment in Duchy Golf Sales Co. joint venture		
12/31/20X1		
Investment in DGS	65	
Equity in earnings of investee (income statement)		65
To record 50% interest in the earnings of the joint venture for the year		

3. *Apply ASC 605-45 to determine which of the participants is principal and which is agent.* Analysis under the provisions of ASC 605-45 yields the following results:

	Indicator (G=Gross; N=Net)	*LSG*	*MML*
a.	Is primary obligor	G	N
b.	Has authority, within reasonable limits, to establish price	G	N*
c.	Involved in determining specifications of product or service	G	N
d.	Changes the product or performs part of the service	G	N
e.	Has discretion in selection of suppliers	G	N

	Indicator (G=Gross; N=Net)	*LSG*	*MML*
f.	Exposed to inventory risks		
	1. General risk before order placed; upon customer return	G	N
	2. Specific risk after order placed or during shipping	G	N
g.	Exposure to credit risk	G	G
h.	Earnings fixed vs. variable	G	G

**In six states, MML has limited discretion with respect to sales price.*

Under ASC 605-45, the party that is the primary obligor is a strong indicator of the party that serves as principal to the transactions. In addition, all of the other indicators point towards LSG being the principal. This is irrespective of the fact that MML does have limited authority in certain markets to negotiate price. Even in those limited states, LSG serves as the principal to the transaction. Both participants bear credit risk equally and are not limited to a percentage commission since they share equally in the commercial success of the endeavor, thus the applicability of indicators g and h is neutral between the parties. Based on the analysis of the above factors, management of both participants concluded that LSG is the principal to the transactions associated with the collaborative arrangement and MML functions as an agent.

Note that, in this fact situation, LSG is the principal for all sales other than those made through the joint venture. In some collaborative arrangements, this will not be the case and management will be required to analyze differing sales arrangements to determine separately for each type of arrangement, the party that is the principal. As can be discerned from the analysis above, this involves the exercise of judgment in light of the specific facts and circumstances.

4. Determine the applicable GAAP for the transactions and elect an appropriate accounting policy to be disclosed and followed consistently. Management of LSG and MML summarized the various activities, revenues and expenses associated with the arrangement as follows:

		Functional classification				*Ongoing, major central operations?*	
Natural classification	*Particip. with primary responsibility under JDA*	*Directly earned or incurred as principal in transactions with third-party customers*	*Design and development of product, co-owned intellectual property*	*Development of co-owned marketing-related intangibles*	*Marketing*	*LSG*	*MML*
Sales to sporting goods stores	LSG	x				x	
R&D laboratory services; licensing	N/A						x
Advertising and promotion of product	MML				x	x	
Branding, logo, package design	LSG			x		x	
Credit, collections, bad debts	LSG	x				x	
Filing for patents	MML		x			x	x
Manufacturing, delivery, fulfillment	LSG	x				x	
R&D–Clubs	LSG		x			x	
R&D–Metals	MML		x			x	x

Based on the foregoing analysis, LSG's management determines that since it is the principal under ASC 605-45, LSG is required to present in its income statement, 100% of the sales, and cost of sales, and other related operating expenses that it incurred in connection with the endeavor. It is unable to find any authoritative GAAP that directly or by analogy would address how to account for the equalization payments it is required to make or entitled to receive. It analyzes the components of the payment and reflects them in LSG's income statement as follows:

Components of Equalization Payment to MML

Presented as additional cost of sales; in effect the sharing of its gross profit with MML results in LSG realizing a reduced margin on its sales of these codeveloped products

a.	MML share of gross profit	$2,100

Reimbursements to MML for LSG share of expenses:

These functions were performed under the JDA by MML; LSG elects to present these as operating expenses; none of the advertising expenses were capitalizable as direct response advertising or required to be deferred prior to the first time the advertising takes place under LSG's accounting policies it adopted under ASC 720-35, Advertising Costs

b.	Advertising and promotion	250
c.	Legal and patent filing fees	300

LSG records the reimbursement to MML for the metallurgical research and development as additional research and development expense analogous with outsourced contract R&D, since its laboratory did not have the experience or capability to perform such research

d.	Research and development alloy and metallurgy	100

Reimbursement from MML for MML share expenses		
	LSG elects to present these reimbursements as reductions of its recorded expenses retaining their character; it believes its arrangement with MML to share half of the endeavor's results provides it the benefit of reduced costs and that the benefits it receives from the equalization payment should be characterized in its income statement as reductions of the expenses it would otherwise have borne on its own without MML's participation.	
e.	Bad debts	(100)
f.	Branding, package, and logo design	(150)
g.	Research and development—Club faces and shafts	(150)
h.	Shipping and delivery	(300)
Net equalization payment		$2,050

Leonard Sporting Goods Company
Statement of Income
Ignoring income taxes and other transactions (000s omitted)
Year ended 12/31/20X1

	Prior to application of ASC 808		*Effects of equalization payment*	*Adjusted income statement*
Sales	$9,200			$9,200
Cost of sales				
Sales to third parties	5,000			5,000
Reimbursement to MML as agent		a	$ 2,100	2,100
Total cost of sales	5,000		2,100	7,100
Gross profit	4,200		(2,100)	2,100
Operating expenses				
Advertising and promotion	–	b	250	250
Bad debts	200	e	(100)	100
Branding, package, and logo design	300	f	(150)	150
Legal and patent filing fees	–	c	300	300
Research and development				
Alloy and metallurgy	–	d	100	100
Club faces and shafts	300	g	(150)	150
Shipping and delivery	600	h	(300)	300
Total operating expenses	1,400		(50)	1,350
Income (Loss) from operations	2,800		(2,050)	750
Equity interest in income of investee	65			65
Pretax income	$2,865		$(2,050)	$ 815

MML's management analyzed the facts and circumstances associated with the collaborative arrangement. As a research laboratory, performing research and development activities for other entities under contractual arrangements is part of MML's ongoing major and central operations.[1] MML management reached the conclusion that, since LSG is the principal in the transactions with third parties, MML, as an agent, should not recognize revenue or the related cost of that revenue at their gross amounts, nor should it present expenses in the operating expense category in its income

[1] *The phrase "ongoing, major or central operations" is used in CON 5 to differentiate activities from those that are incidental or peripheral to the reporting entity. Frequently, financial results from incidental or peripheral activities are presented in "other income and expense" if they are unusual or infrequent in nature, whereas the results from ongoing, major, or central operations are shown as components of operating income and expense.*

statement that are related to these transactions that it considers peripheral. Following this line of reasoning management classifies the activity related to the arrangement as follows:

Maureen Metals LLC
Statement of Income
Ignoring income taxes and other transactions (000s omitted)
Year ended December 31, 20X1

Revenues from collaborative arrangement			
MML share of gross profit			$2,100
Related expenses net of reimbursements			
Advertising and promotion	$500	$(250)	250
Bad debts			100
Branding, package, and logo design			150
Shipping and delivery			300
			800
Net revenues from collaborative arrangement			1,300
Intellectual property design and development			
Legal and patent filing fees	$600	$(300)	300
Research and development			
Metallurgical	200	(100)	100
Club faces and shafts			150
			550
Income from operations			750
Equity interest in income of investee			65
Pretax income			$ 815

Note MML management's position that the costs of developing the intellectual property and protecting it by filing for patents are part of its "ongoing, major, or central operations." Thus, those expenses are not considered directly related to its earnings as agent from the transactions occurring after the product was fully developed and shipments commenced. Although the details are presented for illustrative purposes, the net revenues from the collaborative arrangement could be shown as the first line in the income statement, and MML management could elect to voluntarily disclose the details in the notes to the financial statements to better inform the reader regarding the nature and results of the activities associated with the collaborative arrangement.

47 ASC 810 CONSOLIDATIONS

PERSPECTIVE AND ISSUES

Subtopics

ASC 810, *Consolidations,* consists of three subtopics:

- ASC 810-10, *Overall*, which has three subsections:
    - General
    - Variable Interest Entities
    - Consolidation of Entities Controlled by Contract
- ASC 810-20, *Control of Partnerships and Similar Entities,* which addresses the potential consolidation of those entities
- ASC 810-30, *Research and Development Arrangements,* which provides direction on whether and how those arrangements should be consolidated.

Scope and Scope Exceptions

ASC 810-10. The following are excluded from the scope of the subtopics and sections of ASC 810-10 governing variable interest entities (VIE) (ASC 810-10-15-17 et seq.):

1. Not-for-profit organizations unless the organization was organized to avoid VIE status. It is important to note, however, that a not-for-profit organization can be a related party for the purpose of determining the primary beneficiary (parent) of a VIE by applying ASC paragraphs 810-10-25-42 through 44.
2. Employers are not to consolidate an employee benefit plan subject to ASC 712, *Nonretirement Postemployment Benefits*) or to ASC 715, *Retirement Benefits*.
3. Separate accounts of life insurance entities (ASC 944-80).
4. A governmental organization.
5. A nongovernmental financing entity, unless the financing entity meets both of the following conditions:

    a. It is not a governmental organization, and
    b. It is used by a business entity in a manner similar to a VIE to attempt to circumvent VIE accounting rules.

6. Investments accounted for at fair value, as per ASC 946.
7. An entity created prior to December 31, 2003, for which, after expending "exhaustive efforts," management of the variable interest holder is unable to obtain information needed to determine whether the entity is a VIE, determine whether the holder is the primary beneficiary, or make the required consolidating/eliminating entries required by FIN 46(R).
8. An entity that qualifies to be treated as a business, as defined in ASC 810-10-30-2, need not be evaluated by a variable interest holder to determine whether it is a VIE unless one or more of the following conditions exists:

    a. The variable interest holder and/or its related parties/de facto agents[1] (de facto agents are discussed later in this chapter) participated significantly in the design or redesign of the entity. This factor is not considered when the entity is an operating joint venture jointly controlled by the variable interest holder, and either one or more independent parties, or a franchisee.
    b. The design of the entity results in substantially all of its activities either involving or being conducted on behalf of the variable interest holder and its related parties.
    c. Based on the relative fair values of interests in the entity, the variable interest holder and its related parties provide more than half of its total equity, subordinated debt, and other forms of subordinated financial support.
    d. The entity's activities relate primarily to one or both of the following:

        (1) Single-lessee leases
        (2) Securitizations or other forms of asset-backed financings.

---

[1] *For this purpose, the term "de facto agent" would exclude a party with an agreement that it cannot sell, transfer, or encumber its interests in the entity without the prior approval of the variable interest holder when that right could constrain the other party's ability to manage the economic risks or realize the economic rewards from its interests in a VIE through the sale, transfer, or encumbrance of those interests.*

ASC 810-20. An entity is in the scope of ASC 810-20 if the entity is required to apply the consolidation guidance in ASC 810-10 to its investment in a limited partnership. ASC 810-20 does not apply to:

- Limited partnerships or similar entities that are entities within the scope of the Variable Interest Entities Subsections of ASC 810-10.
- A general partner that carries its investment in the limited partnership at fair value with changes in fair value reported in a statement of operations or financial performance.
- Entities in industries in which it is appropriate for a general partner to use the pro rata method of consolidation for its investment in a limited partnership.
- Circumstances in which no single general partner in a group of general partners controls the limited partnership.
  (ASC 810-20-15-2)

ASC 810-30. ASC 810-30 is limited to those research and development arrangements in which all of the funds for the research and development activities are provided by the sponsor of the research and development arrangement. It does not apply to either:

- Transactions in which the funds are provided by third parties, which would generally be within the scope of Subtopic 730-20.
- Special-purpose entities required to be consolidated under the guidance on variable interest entities.
  (ASC 810-30-15-3)

Overview

The major accounting issues in business combinations and in the preparation and presentation of consolidated or combined financial statements are as follows:

- The proper accounting basis for the assets and liabilities of the combining entities
- The accounting for goodwill or negative goodwill (the gain from a bargain purchase), if any exists
- The elimination of intercompany balances and transactions in the preparation of consolidated or combined statements.

While the presentation of consolidated financial statements is required under GAAP, there is no parallel requirement to present combined financial statements for entities under common control (brother/sister entities). However, in certain cases, it is desirable that combined financial statements be prepared for such entities. This process is very similar to an accounting consolidation using the formerly permitted pooling accounting, except that the equity accounts for the combining entities are carried forward intact.

Consolidation of variable interest entities (VIEs) has increased substantially under the ASC 810 requirements, which were spurred on by the financial reporting scandals of the early 2000s.

The accounting for the assets and liabilities of entities acquired in a business combination is largely dependent on the fair values assigned to them at the transaction date. ASC 820, *Fair Value Measurements,* provides a framework for measuring fair value and important guidance when assigning values as part of a business combination. In essence, it favors valuations determined on the open market, but allows other methodologies if open market valuation is not practicable.

Technical Alert

In March 2014, the FASB issued ASU 2014-07, *Applying Variable Interest Entities Guidance to Common Control Leasing Arrangements,* a consensus of the Private Company Council. The ASU is effective for annual periods beginning after December 15, 2014, and interim periods within annual periods beginning after December 15, 2015. Early application is permitted for all financial statements that have not yet been made available for issuance.

Under current GAAP, a company is required to consolidate the financial reporting from an entity in which it has a controlling financial interest. Controlling financial interest is determined by:

- The voting interest model or
- The variable interest entity model.

In the VIE model, the company has a controlling financial interest when it has

a. the power to direct the activities that most significantly affect the economic performance of the entity, and
b. the obligation to absorb losses or the right to receive benefits of the entity that could be potentially significant to the entity.

A company must first determine whether it has a variable interest in the entity being evaluated for consolidation and whether that entity is a VIE.

Under the new guidance a private company may elect not to apply VIE guidance to a lessor under common control when:

a. The private company lessee and the lessor are under common control,
b. The private company lessee has a leasing arrangement with the lessor,
c. Substantially all of the activity between the private company lessee and the lessor is related to the leasing activities (including supporting leasing activities) between those two companies, and
d. If the private company lessee explicitly guarantees or provides collateral for any obligation of the lessor related to the asset leased by the private company, then the principal amount of the obligation at inception does not exceed the value of the asset leased by the private company from the lessor.

Instead of consolidating, the private company would make certain disclosures about the lessor and the leasing arrangement.

If elected, the accounting alternative should be applied to all leasing arrangements meeting the above conditions. The alternative should be applied retrospectively to all periods presented.

DEFINITIONS OF TERMS

Source: ASC 810

Acquiree. The business or businesses that the acquirer obtains control of in a business combination. This term also includes a nonprofit activity or business that a not-for-profit acquirer obtains control of in an acquisition by a not-for-profit entity.

Acquirer. The entity that obtains control of the acquiree. However, in a business combination in which a variable interest entity (VIE) is acquired, the primary beneficiary of that entity always is the acquirer.

Acquisition by a Not-for-Profit Entity. A transaction or other event in which a not-for-profit acquirer obtains control of one or more nonprofit activities or businesses and initially recognizes their assets and liabilities in the acquirer's financial statements. When applicable guidance in Topic 805 is applied by a not-for-profit entity, the term business combination has the same meaning as this term has for a for-profit entity. Likewise, a reference to business combinations in guidance that links to Topic 805 has the same meaning as a reference to acquisitions by not-for-profit entities.

Acquisition, Development, and Construction Arrangements. Acquisition, development, or construction arrangements, in which a lender, usually a financial institution, participates in expected residual profit from the sale or refinancing of property.

Business. An integrated set of activities and assets that is capable of being conducted and managed for the purpose of providing a return in the form of dividends, lower costs, or other economic benefits directly to investors or other owners, members, or participants. Additional guidance on what a business consists of is presented in paragraphs 805-10-55-4 through 55-9.

Business Combination. A transaction or other event in which an acquirer obtains control of one or more businesses. Transactions sometimes referred to as true mergers or mergers of equals also are business combinations. See also Acquisition by a Not-for-Profit Entity.

Combined Financial Statements. The financial statements of a combined group of commonly controlled entities or commonly managed entities presented as those of a single economic entity. The combined group does not include the parent.

Consolidated Financial Statements. The financial statements of a consolidated group of entities that include a parent and all its subsidiaries presented as those of a single economic entity.

Consolidated Group. A parent and all its subsidiaries.

Equity Interests. Used broadly to mean ownership interests of investor-owned entities; owner, member, or participant interests of mutual entities; and owner or member interests in the net assets of not-for-profit entities.

Expected Losses. A legal entity that has no history of net losses and expects to continue to be profitable in the foreseeable future can be a variable interest entity (VIE). A legal entity that expects to be profitable will have expected losses. A VIE's expected losses are the expected negative variability in the fair value of its net assets exclusive of variable interests and not the anticipated amount or variability of the net income or loss.

Expected Losses and Expected Residual Returns. Expected losses and expected residual returns refer to amounts derived from expected cash flows as described in FASB Concepts Statement No. 7, *Using Cash Flow Information and Present Value in Accounting Measurements*. However, expected losses and expected residual returns refer to amounts discounted and otherwise adjusted for market factors and assumptions rather than to undiscounted cash flow estimates. The definitions of expected losses and expected residual returns specify which amounts are to be considered in determining expected losses and expected residual returns of a variable interest entity (VIE).

Expected Residual Returns. A variable interest entity's (VIE's) expected residual returns are the expected positive variability in the fair value of its net assets exclusive of variable interests.

Expected Variability. Expected variability is the sum of the absolute values of the expected residual return and the expected loss. Expected variability in the fair value of net assets includes expected variability resulting from the operating results of the legal entity.

Fair Value. The price that would be received to sell an asset or paid to transfer a liability in an orderly transaction between market participants at the measurement date.

Financial Statements Are Available to Be Issued. Financial statements are considered available to be issued when they are complete in a form and format that complies with GAAP and all approvals necessary for issuance have been obtained, for example, from management, the board of directors, and/or significant shareholders. The process involved in creating and distributing the financial statements will vary depending on an entity's management and corporate governance structure as well as statutory and regulatory requirements

Foreign Entity. An operation (for example, subsidiary, division, branch, joint venture, and so forth) whose financial statements are both:

1. Prepared in a currency other than the reporting currency of the reporting entity
2. Combined or consolidated with or accounted for on the equity basis in the financial statements of the reporting entity.

Kick-Out Rights. The ability to remove the reporting entity with the power to direct the activities of a VIE that most significantly impact the VIE's economic performance.

Legal Entity. Any legal structure used to conduct activities or to hold assets. Some examples of such structures are corporations, partnerships, limited liability companies, grantor trusts, and other trusts.

Nominee Shareholder. One or more shareholders whose relationship with the physician practice management entity (which can be either the physician practice management entity itself or its controlled subsidiaries) perpetually has all of the following characteristics:

1. Time Frame:
   a. The physician practice management entity can at all times establish or effect a change in the nominee shareholder.
   b. The physician practice management entity can cause a change in the nominee shareholder an unlimited number of times, that is, changing the nominee shareholder one or more times does not affect the physician practice management entity's ability to change the nominee shareholder again and again.
2. Discretion:
   a. The physician practice management entity has sole discretion without cause to establish or change the nominee shareholder.
   b. The physician practice management entity can name anyone as a new nominee shareholder (that is, the physician practice management entity's choice of an eligible nominee is not limited).
3. Impact:
   a. The physician practice management entity and the nominally owned entity incur no more than a nominal cost to cause a change in the nominee shareholder.
   b. Neither the physician practice management entity nor the nominally owned entity is subject to any significant adverse impact upon a change in the nominee shareholder.

Noncontrolling Interest. The portion of equity (net assets) in a subsidiary not attributable, directly or indirectly, to a parent. A noncontrolling interest is sometimes called a minority interest.

Nonprofit Activity. An integrated set of activities and assets that is capable of being conducted and managed for the purpose of providing benefits, other than goods or services at a profit or profit equivalent, as a fulfillment of an entity's purpose or mission (for example, goods or services to beneficiaries, customers, or members). As with a not-for-profit entity, a nonprofit activity possesses characteristics that distinguish it from a business or a for-profit business entity.

Nonpublic Entity. Any entity other than one with any of the following characteristics:

1. Whose debt or equity securities trade in a public market either on a stock exchange (domestic or foreign) or in the over-the-counter market, including securities quoted only locally or regionally
2. That is a conduit bond obligor for conduit debt securities that are traded in a public market (a domestic or foreign stock exchange or an over-the-counter market, including local or regional markets)
3. That makes a filing with a regulatory agency in preparation for the sale of any class of debt or equity securities in a public market
4. That is controlled by an entity covered by a., b., or c.

Conduit debt securities refers to certain limited-obligation revenue bonds, certificates of participation, or similar debt instruments issued by a state or local governmental entity for the express purpose of providing financing for a specific third party (the conduit bond obligor) that is not a part of the state or local government's financial reporting entity. Although conduit debt securities bear the name of the governmental entity that issues them, the governmental entity often has no obligation for such debt beyond the resources provided by a lease or loan agreement with the third party on whose behalf the securities are issued. Further, the conduit bond obligor is responsible for any future financial reporting requirements.

Not-for-Profit Entity. An entity that possesses the following characteristics, in varying degrees, that distinguish it from a business entity:

1. Contributions of significant amounts of resources from resource providers who do not expect commensurate or proportionate pecuniary return
2. Operating purposes other than to provide goods or services at a profit
3. Absence of ownership interests like those of business entities.

Entities that clearly fall outside this definition include the following:

1. All investor-owned entities
2. Entities that provide dividends, lower costs, or other economic benefits directly and proportionately to their owners, members, or participants, such as mutual insurance entities, credit unions, farm and rural electric cooperatives, and employee benefit plans.

Ordinary Course of Business. Decisions about matters of a type consistent with those normally expected to be events or transactions that would necessitate such decisions will occur. The ordinary course of business does not include self-dealing transactions.

Owners. Used broadly to include holders of ownership interests (equity interests) of investor-owned entities, mutual entities, or not-for-profit entities. Owners include shareholders, partners, proprietors, or members or participants of mutual entities. Owners also include owner and member interests in the net assets of not-for-profit entities.

Parent. An entity that has a controlling financial interest in one or more subsidiaries. (Also, an entity that is the primary beneficiary of a variable interest entity.)

Participating Rights. The ability to block the actions through which a reporting entity exercises the power to direct the activities of a VIE that most significantly impact the VIE's economic performance. (ASC 810-10-20)

Participating Rights. Participating rights allow the limited partners to participate in certain financial and operating decisions of the limited partnership that are made in the ordinary course of business. (ASC 810-20-20)

Primary Beneficiary. An entity that consolidates a variable interest entity (VIE). See paragraphs 810-10-25-38 through 25-38G for guidance on determining the primary beneficiary.

Protective Rights. Rights designed to protect the interests of the party holding those rights without giving that party a controlling financial interest in the entity to which they relate. For example, they include any of the following:

a. Approval or veto rights granted to other parties that do not affect the activities that most significantly impact the entity's economic performance. Protective rights often apply to fundamental changes in the activities of an entity or apply only in exceptional circumstances. Examples include both of the following:
    1. A lender might have rights that protect the lender from the risk that the entity will change its activities to the detriment of the lender, such as selling important assets or undertaking activities that change the credit risk of the entity.
    2. Other interests might have the right to approve a capital expenditure greater than a particular amount or the right to approve the issuance of equity or debt instruments.
b. The ability to remove the reporting entity that has a controlling financial interest in the entity in circumstances such as bankruptcy or on breach of contract by that reporting entity.
c. Limitations on the operating activities of an entity. For example, a franchise agreement for which the entity is the franchisee might restrict certain activities of the entity but may not give the franchisor a controlling financial interest in the franchisee. Such rights may only protect the brand of the franchisor.

Public Business Entity. A public business entity is a business entity meeting any one of the criteria below. Neither a not-for-profit entity nor an employee benefit plan is a business entity.

1. It is required by the U.S. Securities and Exchange Commission (SEC) to file or furnish financial statements, or does file or furnish financial statements (including voluntary filers), with the SEC (including other entities whose financial statements or financial information are required to be or are included in a filing).
2. It is required by the Securities Exchange Act of 1934 (the Act), as amended, or rules or regulations promulgated under the Act, to file or furnish financial statements with a regulatory agency other than the SEC.
3. It is required to file or furnish financial statements with a foreign or domestic regulatory agency in preparation for the sale of or for purposes of issuing securities that are not subject to contractual restrictions on transfer.
4. It has issued, or is a conduit bond obligor for, securities that are traded, listed, or quoted on an exchange or an over-the-counter market.
5. It has one or more securities that are not subject to contractual restrictions on transfer, and it is required by law, contract, or regulation to prepare U.S. GAAP financial statements (including footnotes) and make them publicly available on a

periodic basis (for example, interim or annual periods). An entity must meet both of these conditions to meet this criterion.

An entity may meet the definition of a public business entity solely because its financial statements or financial information is included in another entity's filing with the SEC. In that case, the entity is only a public business entity for purposes of financial statements that are filed or furnished with the SEC.

Publicly Traded Entity under (or Public Entity). Any entity that does not meet the definition of a nonpublic entity.

Related Parties. Related parties include:

a. Affiliates of the entity
b. Entities for which investments in their equity securities would be required, absent the election of the fair value option under the Fair Value Option Subsection of Section 825-10-15, to be accounted for by the equity method by the investing entity
c. Trusts for the benefit of employees, such as pension and profit-sharing trusts that are managed by or under the trusteeship of management
d. Principal owners of the entity and members of their immediate families
e. Management of the entity and members of their immediate families
f. Other parties with which the entity may deal if one party controls or can significantly influence the management or operating policies of the other to an extent that one of the transacting parties might be prevented from fully pursuing its own separate interests
g. Other parties that can significantly influence the management or operating policies of the transacting parties or that have an ownership interest in one of the transacting parties and can significantly influence the other to an extent that one or more of the transacting parties might be prevented from fully pursuing its own separate interests.

Sponsor. An entity that capitalizes a research and development arrangement.

Subordinated Financial Support. Variable interests that will absorb some or all of a variable interest entity's (VIE's) expected losses.

Subsidiary. An entity, including an unincorporated entity such as a partnership or trust, in which another entity, known as its parent, holds a controlling financial interest. (Also, a variable interest entity that is consolidated by a primary beneficiary.)

Underlying. A specified interest rate, security price, commodity price, foreign exchange rate, index of prices or rates, or other variable (including the occurrence or nonoccurrence of a specified event such as a scheduled payment under a contract). An underlying may be a price or rate of an asset or liability but is not the asset or liability itself. An underlying is a variable that, along with either a notional amount or a payment provision, determines the settlement of a derivative instrument.

Variable Interest Entity. A legal entity subject to consolidation according to the provisions of the Variable Interest Entities Subsections of Subtopic 810-10.

Variable Interests. The investments or other interests that will absorb portions of a variable interest entity's (VIE's) expected losses or receive portions of the entity's expected residual returns are called variable interests. Variable interests in a VIE are contractual, ownership, or other pecuniary interests in a VIE that change with changes in the fair value of the VIE's net assets exclusive of variable interests. Equity interests with or without voting rights are considered variable interests if the legal entity is a VIE and to the extent that the investment is at risk as described in paragraph 810-10-15-14. Paragraph 810-10-25-55 explains how to determine whether a variable interest in specified assets of a legal entity is a variable interest in the entity. Paragraphs 810-10-55-16 through 55-41 describe various types of variable interests and explain in general how they may affect the determination of the primary beneficiary of a VIE.

With Cause. With cause generally restricts the limited partners' ability to dissolve (liquidate) the limited partnership or remove the general partners in situations that include, but that are not limited to, fraud, illegal acts, gross negligence, and bankruptcy of the general partners.

Without Cause. Without cause means that no reason need be given for the dissolution (liquidation) of the limited partnership or removal of the general partners.

CONCEPTS, RULES, AND EXAMPLES

Special-Purpose Entities and Variable Interest Entities

Introduction and background. ASC 810 provides the primary authority for determining when presentation of consolidated financial statements is required. The rationale underlying ASC 810 is that when one enterprise directly or indirectly holds a controlling financial interest in one or more other enterprises, consolidated financial statements are more informative to users. It further stipulates that the usual condition that best evidences which party holds a controlling financial interest is the party that holds a majority voting interest.

Managers and their advisors have devised many new and creative types of ownership structures, financing arrangements, financial instruments, and business relationships. Many, if not most, of these arrangements were originated to accomplish legitimate business objectives. Some of the arrangements, however, were financially engineered with the express intent of establishing financial control over assets or operations while the sponsoring entity avoided obtaining the voting control that served as the determinant of the need for accounting consolidation.

Examples of such arrangements abound and have been discussed in the chapter on ASC 805. Perhaps no such type of financial arrangement or structure, however, has received the level of negative publicity as the special-purpose entity (SPE). An SPE is narrowly defined as a trust or other legal vehicle to which a transferor transfers a portfolio of financial assets, such as mortgage loans, commercial loans, credit card debt, automobile loans, and other groups of homogenous borrowings.

Commonly, SPEs have been organized as trusts or partnerships (flow-through entities, to avoid double incidence of corporate income taxation), and the outside equity participant was ultimately defined as having as little as 3% of the total assets of the SPE at risk. No authoritative GAAP ever established this 3% threshold, but nevertheless it evolved somewhat by default and had been subject to varying interpretations under different sets of conditions.

In a process called a *securitization*, the SPE typically issues and sells securities that represent beneficial interests in the cash flows from the portfolio. The proceeds the SPE receives from the sale of these securities are used to purchase the portfolio from the transferor. The cash flows received by the SPE from the dividends, interest, redemptions, principal repayments, and/or realized gains on the financial assets are used to pay a return to the investors in the SPE's securities. By transferring packages of such loans to an SPE, these assets can be legally isolated and made "bankruptcy proof" (and thus made more valuable as collateral for other borrowings); various types of debt instruments can thus be used, providing the sponsor with fresh resources to fund future lending activities.

FASB's response to Enron. After the public revelations regarding Enron and its use of SPEs to conceal its true financial condition, FASB recognized the need to augment the existing consolidations model to take into account financial arrangements where parties other than the holders of a majority of the voting interests exercise financial control over another entity.

FASB decided not to refer to entities within the scope of the eventual interpretation as SPEs. This decision underscores the fact that the type of entity to which the interpretation applies is more broadly defined than entities that qualify as SPEs involved in securitization transactions or even SPEs that hold nonfinancial assets.

FASB coined the term *variable interest entity* (VIE) to designate an entity that is financially controlled by one or more parties that do not hold a majority voting interest. A party that possesses the majority of this financial control, if there is one, is referred to as the VIE's *primary beneficiary*. The definition of "parent" includes a VIE's primary beneficiary and, the definition of "subsidiary" includes a VIE that is consolidated by its primary beneficiary.

See the Scope and Scope Exceptions section at the beginning of this chapter for details on entities excluded from the ASC 810-10 guidance.

Terminology. Under ASC 810-10, VIEs that have a primary beneficiary, as defined, must be consolidated in the general-purpose financial statements of that primary beneficiary, regardless of the extent of ownership (or lack of it) by that entity. The ASC introduced a number of new terms and concepts in the attempt to explain and operationalize the accounting for VIEs.

Variable interests. (See definition in Definition of Terms section.) Variable interests are identified by thoroughly analyzing the assets, liabilities, and contractual arrangements of an entity to determine whether each item being analyzed creates variability or absorbs/receives variability. Favorable changes in the fair value of the entity's net assets and contractual arrangements that create variability comprise expected residual returns which result from estimated outcomes in which the entity outperforms the probability-weighted expected results. Unfavorable changes in the fair value of the entity's net assets and contractual arrangements that create variability comprise expected losses which result from estimated outcomes in which the entity underperforms the probability-weighted expected results.

ASC 810-10-55-16, *Identifying Variable Interests*, provides examples of potential variable interests. Each of the items below is potentially an explicit or implicit variable interest in an entity or in specified assets of an entity. Upon analysis of the specific facts, circumstances, and contractual terms, the financial statement preparer is charged with determining whether a particular item either absorbs expected losses or receives expected residual returns (collectively referred to as expected variability) or both. The absorbing/receiving of variability is the sole determinant of whether an interest is a variable interest and, in analyzing specific situations, the degree of variability can differ widely for each item:

1. At-risk equity investments in a VIE
2. Investments in subordinated debt instruments issued by a VIE
3. Investments in subordinated beneficial interests issued by a VIE
4. Guarantees of the value of VIE assets or liabilities
5. Written put options on the assets of a VIE or similar obligations that protect senior interests from suffering losses
6. Forward contracts to sell assets owned by the entity at a fixed price
7. Stand-alone or embedded derivative instruments, including total return swaps and similar arrangements
8. Contracts or agreements for fees to be paid to a decision maker (These are generally deemed to absorb variability unless the relationship between the entity and the decision maker meets specified criteria to be considered an employee/employer relationship or a "hired service provider" relationship, in which case the arrangement would not be deemed to create a variable interest. In this case, the fees would be included in computations of expected variability.)
9. Other service contracts with non-decision makers

10. Operating leases that include residual value guarantees and/or lessee option to purchase the leased property at a specified price
11. Variable interests of one VIE in another VIE
12. Interests retained by a transferor of financial assets to a VIE.

As previously stated, although all of these examples potentially qualify as variable interests, they differ widely in terms of the extent of their variability, which has a direct effect on the likelihood of their causing their holders to be considered the primary beneficiary of the VIE. Note that an interest can qualify as a variable interest but the entity in which the interest is held may not qualify as a VIE.

Variable interest entities. VIEs include any entity that, by design, possesses one of the following characteristics:

1. The total equity investment at risk is not sufficient to permit the entity to finance its activities without additional subordinated financial support from either the existing equity holders or other parties. That is, the equity investment at risk is not sufficient to absorb all of the expected losses of the entity. For this purpose, the total equity investment at risk

   a. Includes only equity investments in the entity that participate significantly in profits and losses even if those investments do not carry voting rights.
   b. Does not include equity interests that the entity issued in exchange for subordinated interests in other variable interest entities.
   c. Does not include amounts provided to the equity investor directly or indirectly by the entity or by other parties involved with the entity (for example, by fees, charitable contributions, or other payments), unless the provider is a parent, subsidiary, or affiliate of the investor that is required to be included in the same set of consolidated financial statements as the investor.
   d. Does not include amounts financed for the equity investor (for example, by loans or guarantees of loans) directly by the entity or by other parties involved with the entity, unless that party is a parent, subsidiary, or affiliate of the investor that is required to be included in the same set of consolidated financial statements as the investor.

or

2. As a group, the holders of the equity investment at risk lack any one of the following three characteristics of a controlling financial interest:

   a. The direct or indirect ability through voting or similar rights to make decisions about an entity's activities that affect the entity's success. The investors do not have that ability through voting rights or similar rights if no owners hold voting rights or similar rights (such as those of a common stockholder in a corporation or a general partner in a partnership).
   b. The obligation to absorb the expected losses of the entity. The investor or investors do not have that obligation if they are directly or indirectly protected from absorbing the expected losses or are guaranteed a return by the entity itself or by other parties with whom the entity is involved.
   c. The right to receive the expected residual returns of the entity. The investors do not have that right if their return is limited to a specified maximum amount by the entity's governing documents or arrangements with other variable interest holders or with the entity.

The equity investors as a group also are considered to lack characteristic 2a if, upon consideration of those investors' at-risk equity investments and all other interests in the entity, (1) the voting rights of some investors are not proportional to their obligations to absorb the entity's expected losses, to receive the entity's expected residual returns, or both, and (2) substantially all of the entity's activities (for example, lending activities, or asset acquisitions) either involve or are conducted on behalf of an investor that has disproportionately few voting rights.

(ASC 810-10-15-14)

In other words, VIEs are generally thinly capitalized entities that carry risks of economic losses or possibilities of economic gains beyond what the nominal owner (the *equity participant*) could absorb or will be able to benefit from, respectively. If a party provides "subordinated financial support" to the entity that exposes it to absorbing the majority of the VIE's expected losses, or entitles it to receive the majority of the VIE's expected residual returns, or both, it is generally deemed to be the primary beneficiary of that VIE and will be required to consolidate the VIE as its subsidiary, irrespective of how much, if any, equity investment it has in the VIE.

Expected variability. When estimating an entity's expected future cash flows in accordance with CON 7, *Using Cash Flow Information and Present Value in Accounting Measurements*, a range of probability-weighted expected outcomes is used. Mathematically, this is simply a weighted-average calculation. The following example illustrates the mathematical concept of expected variability:

Example of expected variability of cash flows

Mided Mining Company is computing the probability-weighted expected future cash flows from operating and disposing of a tunnel boring machine that has a remaining estimated useful life of three years. This estimate was necessitated by ASC 360, which requires an evaluation, when certain events or circumstances occur, of whether the future cash flows associated with the use and disposal of long-lived assets are sufficient to recover their carrying value over their estimated remaining depreciable lives. Because of uncertainty regarding the amounts and timing of the cash flows, Mided's management used the CON 7 probability-weighted expected cash flow model with the following results:

	20X1	*20X2*	*20X3*	*3-year outcome*	*Probability of occurrence*	*Probability-weighted expected outcome*
Expected outcome 1	$3,500	$3,200	$2,700	$9,400	20%	$1,880
Expected outcome 2	4,000	3,900	3,700	11,600	45%	5,220
Expected outcome 3	4,300	4,100	4,000	12,400	30%	3,720
Expected outcome 4	4,400	4,700	–	9,100	5%	455
					100%	
Probability-weighted expected cash flows (weighted-average)						$11,275

The $11,275 weighted-average, undiscounted, is compared to the carrying value of the tunnel boring machine to determine whether or not the carrying value is fully recoverable. The weighted-average consists of four different outcomes, each with its own estimated probability of occurrence. Since these amounts represent management's best estimates, management deems it possible that, at the end of the three-year period, any one of these outcomes could actually occur. When management considers the individual probability of occurrence for each of the four outcomes estimated above, the analysis yields the following results:

	[1] 3-year outcome	[2] Probability-weighted expected outcome	[3] [1] – [2] Variation	[4] Probability of occurrence	[5] [3] × [4] Probability-weighted variation	Positive variation	Negative variation
Expected outcome 1	$9,400	$11,275	$(1,875)	20%	$(375)	$ –	$(375)
Expected outcome 2	11,600	11,275	325	45%	146	146	–
Expected outcome 3	12,400	11,275	1,125	30%	338	338	–
Expected outcome 4	9,100	11,275	(2,175)	5%	(109)	–	(109)
				100%		$484	$(484)

Careful examination of the above analysis yields the following conclusions:

1. Variations naturally occur between expected outcomes and actual outcomes.
2. Because the expected outcome is calculated as an average, some of the amounts used to compute it will be higher than the average and some will be lower than the average.
3. When the individual variations are computed and each is multiplied by its probability of occurrence, the absolute value of the sum of the positive variations will exactly equal the absolute value of the sum of the negative variations.
4. When these two absolute values are summed ($484 + $484 = $968 in the example above), the result, the total variability in both directions is called the expected variability of the cash flows.
5. The higher the expected variability of a set of cash flow estimates, the higher the level of risk and uncertainty associated with the estimate.

The analysis of expected variability is based on the following two-step approach:

(1) Determine the nature of an entity's risks, which shall at least include the areas of credit, interest rates, foreign currency exchange, commodity prices, equity prices, and operations, and then

(2) Determine the extent of the variability the entity was designed to pass through to its interest holders by reviewing its activities, contract terms, terms of issued interests, how those interests were negotiated, and the parties participating in the entity's design.

Expected losses and expected residual returns. Expected losses represent the expected negative variability in the fair value of an enterprise's net assets exclusive of variable interests. Expected residual returns represent the expected positive variability in the fair value of an enterprise's net assets exclusive of variable interests. The expected variability in an enterprise's net income or loss is included in the determination of its expected losses and expected residual returns.

Parents and subsidiaries. As discussed previously, the definitions of parent and subsidiary have been broadened to encompass variable interest entities and their primary beneficiaries. Thus, the primary beneficiary of a VIE is now referred to as its parent, and the VIE itself is considered a subsidiary of its primary beneficiary/parent.

Noncontrolling interests. A noncontrolling interest represents the portion of equity (or net assets) in a subsidiary (VIE) that is not directly or indirectly attributable to the parent (primary beneficiary). Thus parent companies of subsidiaries that are VIEs will be required to fully record the noncontrolling interest's share of VIE losses even if recording these losses results in a deficit in noncontrolling interest. ASC 810-10-45 settles the controversial issue of how the noncontrolling interest is classified in the consolidated statement of financial position by requiring that it be reported within the equity section, separately from the equity of the parent company, and clearly identified with a caption such as "noncontrolling interest in subsidiaries." Should there be noncontrolling interests attributable to more than one consolidated subsidiary, the amounts may be aggregated in the consolidated statement of financial position.

Only equity-classified instruments issued by the subsidiary may be classified as equity in this manner. If, for example, the subsidiary had issued a financial instrument that, under applicable GAAP, was classified as a liability in the subsidiary's financial statements, that instrument would not be classified as a noncontrolling interest since it does not represent an ownership interest.

Initial determination of VIE status. Whether or not an entity qualifies as a VIE is initially determined when an entity obtains its variable interest in that entity. This determination is based on the circumstances existing at that date, taking into account future changes that are required in existing governing documents and contractual arrangements. It is not necessary, however, for an interest holder to make this determination if both of the following conditions exist:

1. It is apparent that the holder's interest would not be a significant variable interest, and
2. The holder, its related parties, and its de facto agents (as specified later in this chapter in the section entitled "Related-party considerations in determining the primary beneficiary") were not significant participants in the design or redesign of the entity.

Determination and redetermination of whether an interest holder is the primary beneficiary. A holder of a variable interest initially determines whether it is the primary beneficiary of a VIE in conjunction with the initial determination that the entity is a VIE, that is, when the holder initially obtains its interest in the entity. This initial determination of whether an interest holder is the primary beneficiary (irrespective of whether the holder is or is not considered to be the primary beneficiary) needs to be reconsidered when the changes are made to the entity's governing documents or contractual arrangements that result in a reallocation of the obligation to absorb expected losses or the right to receive expected residual returns of the VIE between the existing primary beneficiary and other unrelated parties. A variable interest holder that had previously determined that it was the VIE's primary beneficiary is required to reconsider its initial decision to consolidate that VIE if (1) it sells or otherwise disposes of all or part of its variable interest to unrelated parties, or (2) if the VIE issues new variable interests to parties other than the primary beneficiary or the primary beneficiary's related parties.

If a variable interest holder had, upon obtaining its interest, determined that it was not the primary beneficiary of a VIE, it is to reconsider this determination it if obtains additional variable interests in the VIE.

Related-party considerations in determining the primary beneficiary. Many SPE structures made use of related-party relationships, which did not, however, automatically necessitate consolidation (although disclosures were required under GAAP). For the purpose of a variable interest holder determining whether it is the primary beneficiary of a VIE, the definition of related parties is expanded from the definition set forth in ASC 850, *Related-Party Disclosures*, to include additional parties that act as "de facto agents" or "de facto principals" of the variable interest holder. The following table sets forth the related parties as prescribed by ASC 850 as well as additional related parties designated for this purpose in ASC 810-10-25-42 and 43:

Related parties

- Affiliates—Parties that directly or indirectly, through one or more intermediaries, control, are controlled by, or are under common control with the variable interest holder
- Equity-method investees of the variable interest holder
- Employee benefit trusts (e.g., pension and profit-sharing trusts) when the variable interest holder/plan sponsor or members of its management manage the plan or serve as the plan trustee
- Principal owners of the variable interest holder (owners of record or beneficial owners of > 10% of the variable interest holder's voting interests) and members of their immediate families
- Management of the variable interest holder and members of their immediate families
- Transacting parties where one party controls or significantly influences the management or operating policies of the other to the extent that it might be prevented from fully pursuing its own separate interests
- Other parties that have an ownership interest in one of the transacting parties; or control, or significantly influence the management or operating policies of the transacting parties to the extent that one or more of the transacting parties might be prevented from fully pursuing its own separate interests

De facto principals/agents

- Parties that cannot finance their operations without subordinated financial support from the variable interest holder (e.g., another VIE of which the variable interest holder is the primary beneficiary)
- Parties that received their interest in the VIE as a contribution or loan from the variable interest holder
- Officers and employees of the variable interest holder
- Members of the governing board of the variable interest holder
- Parties that have agreements not to sell, transfer, or pledge their interests in the VIE as collateral without the prior approval of the variable interest holder where that prior approval right constrains that party's ability to manage the economic risks or realize the economic rewards from its interests
- Parties with a close business relationship to the variable interest holder such as the relationship of a professional service provider to one of its significant clients.

These related-party attribution rules require consolidation of many of the currently popular SPE structures, unless the VIE is well capitalized and such subordinated support vehicles as loan guarantees are dispensed with.

If two or more related parties (including de facto principals/agents specified above) hold variable interests in the same VIE, and the aggregate variable interests held by those parties would, if held by a single party, identify that party as the primary beneficiary, then the member of the related-party group that is most closely associated with the VIE is the primary beneficiary that is required to consolidate the VIE as a subsidiary in its financial statements. In determining which party is most closely associated with the VIE, all relevant facts and circumstances are to be considered, including:

1. Whether there is a principal/agent relationship between parties within the related-party group
2. The relationship of the activities of the VIE to each of the parties in the related-party group
3. The significance of the VIE's activities to each of the parties in the related-party group
4. The extent of a party's exposure to the expected losses of the VIE
5. The structure of the VIE.

Reconsideration of VIE status. Once an initial determination is made as to whether an entity is a variable interest entity (as opposed to a voting interest entity), that initial determination need not be reconsidered unless one or more of the following circumstances occurs:

1. A change is made to the VIE's governing documents or contractual arrangements that results in changes in either the characteristics or sufficiency of the at-risk equity investment in the VIE.
2. As a result of a return of some or all of the equity investment to the equity investors, other interests become exposed to the VIE's expected losses.
3. There is an increase in the VIE's expected losses that results from the entity engaging in activities or acquiring assets that were not anticipated at either the inception of the entity or a later reconsideration date.
4. There is a decrease in the VIE's expected losses due to the entity modifying or curtailing its activities.
5. Additional at-risk equity is invested in the VIE.
6. The equity investors, as a group, lose the power to direct the activities of the VIE that most significantly impact its economic performance.

Initial measurement provisions. The initial measurement provisions of ASC 810 provide that:

1. When the primary beneficiary of the VIE and the VIE are under common control, the primary beneficiary is to initially measure the assets, liabilities, and noncontrolling interests of the VIE at their carrying amounts in the accounting records of the entity that controls the VIE, or the amounts at which they would be carried by the controlling entity if that entity issued GAAP financial statements.
2. When the primary beneficiary of the VIE and the VIE are not under common control:
   a. The initial consolidation of a VIE that is a business, discussed above, is a business combination transaction and, accordingly, is to be accounted for in accordance with the provisions of ASC 805.
   b. If an entity becomes the primary beneficiary of a VIE that is *not* a business:
      (1) The primary beneficiary is to initially measure and recognize the assets and liabilities of the VIE, except for goodwill, in accordance with ASC 805. However, any assets and liabilities transferred to the VIE by the primary beneficiary at, after, or shortly before the date the entity became the primary beneficiary are to be initially measured at the same amounts at which the assets and liabilities would have been measured if they had not been transferred. No gain or loss is to be recognized as a result of such transfers.
      (2) The primary beneficiary is to recognize a gain or loss for the difference between (a) the fair value of any consideration paid, the fair value of any noncontrolling interests, and the reported amount of any previously held interests and (b) the net amount of the VIE's identifiable assets and liabilities recognized and measured under the provisions of ASC 805. *Goodwill is not to be recognized if the VIE is not a business.*

Consolidation requirements. An entity must consolidate a VIE of which it is the primary beneficiary. The variable interest holder that is the primary beneficiary of a VIE must have *both* 1) the power to direct those activities of the VIE most significantly impacting its economic performance, and 2) the obligation to absorb VIE losses that could potentially be significant to the VIE, or the right to receive benefits from the VIE that could potentially be significant to the VIE. Only one enterprise should be identified as the primary beneficiary, with the determining factor being the power to direct those activities of the VIE most significantly impacting its economic performance. It is possible that no primary beneficiary can be identified.

If there are other (noncontrolling) interests, these are shown in the consolidated balance sheet just as minority interests are under GAAP, and likewise a share of the operating results of the VIE are allocated to the noncontrolling interests in the consolidated statements of income (operations).

ASC 810-10-25-45 et seq. provides a 10% equity threshold test, which in practice is confusing and unworkable. The interpretation indicates that an at-risk equity investment of less than 10% of the entity's total assets is presumptively not considered sufficient to permit the entity to finance its activities without obtaining additional subordinated financial support but then goes on to provide that the presumption of insufficiency can be overcome by either quantitative analysis, qualitative analysis, or both. Consequently, financial statement preparers could mistakenly rely on the 10% presumption to conclude that an entity with less than 10% at-risk equity is a VIE, when in fact, further analysis would contradict that conclusion. Conversely, the interpretation indicates that it is also possible that an entity can require at-risk equity of more than 10% in order to sufficiently finance its activities. Consequently, the financial statement preparer also cannot rely on meeting or exceeding the 10% threshold as conclusive proof that the entity is sufficiently capitalized to avoid being characterized as a VIE.

ASC 810-10-25 requires existing unconsolidated variable interest entities to be consolidated by their primary beneficiaries if the entities do not effectively disperse risks among the parties involved. Variable interest entities that effectively disperse risks will not be consolidated unless a single party holds an interest or combination of interests that effectively recombines risks that were previously dispersed.

Initial measurement with common control. If the primary beneficiary of a VIE and the VIE itself are under common control, the primary beneficiary (parent) is to initially measure the assets, liabilities, and noncontrolling interests of the newly consolidated reporting entity at their preexisting carrying amounts.

Initial measurement absent common control. The rules governing the initial measurement of the assets and liabilities of a newly consolidated VIE differ depending on the date on which the VIE is initially consolidated. These differing rules are attributable to amendments made in December 2007 to the original VIE rules to conform them more closely to the rules governing other business combinations. The following table compares the two sets of rules:

Accounting by a Primary Beneficiary (Parent)
for Initial Consolidation of a Variable Interest Entity

	Date of initial consolidation	
Recognition or measurement issue	*Before 1/1/2009*	*2009 and later*
1. Measurement date	Date that holder of variable interest(s) first becomes the primary beneficiary (PB)	Acquisition date, which is the date the acquirer/primary beneficiary obtains control of the acquiree/VIE (ASC 805-10-25-6)
2. Measurement amount for assets, liabilities, and noncontrolling interests	Fair value on measurement date	The initial consolidation of a VIE that is a business is a business combination and is to be accounted for as discussed previously in this chapter
3. Measurement exception for enterprises under common control	Carrying value (net book value or NBV) in the accounting records of the enterprise that controls the VIE with no "step-up"	

Recognition or measurement issue	*Date of initial consolidation* — *Before 1/1/2009*	*Date of initial consolidation* — *2009 and later*
4. Assets and liabilities transferred to the VIE by the PB at, after, or shortly before the date of initial consolidation where the VIE ***is not a business***	The assets and liabilities are measured at the same amounts at which the assets and liabilities would have been measured if they had not been transferred. No gain or loss is to be recognized on account of the transfer.	
5. Assets and liabilities transferred to the VIE by the PB at, after, or shortly before the date of initial consolidation where the VIE ***is a business***	Same as above, as if the VIE were not a business.	If the VIE ***is a business***, it is to follow ASC 805-10-25-20 et seq., *Determining What Is Part of the Business Combination Transaction,* to assess the substance of such transfers and whether they are to be considered part of the business combination (See previous discussion in this chapter under "Step 3, Identify assets and liabilities requiring separate accounting").
6. Recognition and measurement of goodwill	If the VIE was a business,[2] goodwill was to be recognized and measured identically with the manner that it was for business combinations under pre-Codification FAS 141/142 prior to their amendment in 12/2007. If the VIE was not a business, goodwill was not to be recognized and, instead, would have been recognized as an extraordinary loss in the period of initial consolidation.	If the VIE is a business, goodwill is recognized and measured identically with the manner described for other business combinations in this chapter under Step 8. If the VIE is not a business, goodwill is not to be recognized and, instead, is recognized as a loss in the period of initial consolidation. That loss, however, is not to be characterized as extraordinary.
7. Recognition of negative goodwill	Follows pre-Codification FAS 141/142 prior to their amendment in 12/2007; any excess of the fair values of the assets/liabilities being consolidated over the consideration exchanged would first have been recognized as a pro rata adjustment to the nonmonetary assets of the newly consolidated VIE; after reduction of those assets to zero, any remaining amount would be recognized as an extraordinary gain in the period of initial consolidation.	Irrespective of whether the VIE is a business, negative goodwill is not used to reduce the carrying values of any of the acquired assets or liabilities; rather it is recognized and measured identically with the manner described for business combinations in this chapter under Step 8 (i.e., as a gain on bargain purchase with a prohibition against characterizing the gain as extraordinary).

[2] *This determination was to be made using a different, more complex definition of what constitutes a business, which was later replaced by the definition discussed in this chapter. The major operational difference between the two definitions was that, under the current definition, a development stage enterprise could potentially qualify as a business.*

After initial measurement, the assets, liabilities, and noncontrolling interests of a consolidated variable interest entity will be accounted for as if the entity were consolidated based on majority voting interests.

Example of consolidation of a VIE

In practice, the most common situations requiring consolidation of a VIE will involve related-party leases. Consequently, this example uses a structured related-party lease to illustrate application of the consolidation provisions of ASC 810-10-30.

Arielle Aromatics Ltd. (AAL) is a manufacturer of aromatherapy products that is 100% owned by Arielle Stone. AAL's headquarters and manufacturing plant are leased pursuant to an operating lease with an S Corporation, Myles' Management, Inc. (MMI), owned by Arielle's brother, Myles.

AAL's headquarters building and the land on which it is built are the only assets owned by MMI. They have been pledged as collateral for a mortgage loan that is guaranteed by a corporate guarantee of AAL and a personal guarantee of Arielle.

MMI has been determined to be a variable interest entity (VIE) and AAL its primary beneficiary. The following is the consolidating worksheet at December 31, 20X1:

Arielle Aromatics Ltd. and Subsidiary
Consolidating Worksheet
Year Ending December 31, 20X1

(000 omitted)			*Adjustments and Eliminations*			
	AAL	*MMI*	*Debit*	*Credit*	*Noncont. interest*	*Consolidated*
Statement of income:						
Revenues						
Sales	$ 6,400					$ 6,400
Rental income		$1,200[a]	$1,200			–
Cost of sales	3,800					3,800
Gross profit	2,600	1,200	1,200			2,600
Depreciation	100	230				330
Rent expense	1,200			$1,200[a]		–
Interest expense	200	400				600
Other expenses	300	–				300
Total operating expenses and interest	1,800	630		1,200		1,230
Income before noncontrolling interest share	800	570	1,200	1,200		1,370
Noncontrolling interest share of income					$570	(570)
Net income	$ 800	$ 570	$1,200	$1,200	$570	$ 800
Statement of retained earnings:						
Retained earnings, beginning						
AAL	$ 1,200					$1,200
MMI		$ –				–
Add net income (from above)	800	570	$1,200	$1,200	$570	800
Deduct dividends paid	(100)	(500)			(500)	(100)
Retained earnings, ending	$ 1,900	$ 70	$1,200	$1,200	$ 70	$ 1,900

(000 omitted)			*Adjustments and Eliminations*			
	AAL	*MMI*	*Debit*	*Credit*	*Noncont. interest*	*Consolidated*
Statement of financial position:						
Cash	$ 2,100					$ 2,100
Accounts receivable, trade (net)	7,500					7,500
Rentals receivable		$ 100	b	$ 100		–
Inventories	1,100					1,100
Land		1,000				1,000
Depreciable property and equipment	1,200	7,000				8,200
Accumulated depreciation	(300)	(230)				(530)
Total assets	$11,600	$7,870		100		$19,370
Notes and mortgages payable	$5,000	$6,900				$11,900
Accounts payable, trade	4,400					4,400
Rent payable	100	b	$ 100			–
Total liabilities	9,500	6,900	100		–	16,300
Common stock	200	900			900	200
Retained earnings (from above)	1,900	70	1,200	1,200	$970	1,900
Noncontrolling interest					970	970
Total stockholders' equity	2,100	970	1,200	1,200		3,070
Total liabilities and stockholders' equity	$11,600	$7,870	$1,300	$1,200		$19,370

The consolidating entries posted to the December 31, 2011 worksheet are as follows:

a.	Rental income	1,200	
	Rental expense		1,200
	To eliminate intercompany rental income and rental expense at December 31, 2011		
b.	Rental payable	100	
	Rentals receivable		100
	To eliminate intercompany rent receivable and rent payable at December 31, 2011		

The consolidation process is relatively straightforward. The effects of the related-party lease, the rental income and expense and intercompany receivable and payable are eliminated so that, on a consolidated basis, the financial statements reflect the building, mortgage debt, depreciation, and interest expense.

The only difference between this consolidation of a VIE and a conventional consolidation of a voting interest entity in accordance with ASC 810-10-45 is the noncontrolling interest allocation. ASC 810-10-45-18 specifies that the elimination of intraentity profit or loss is not affected by the existence of a noncontrolling interest and that the elimination may be allocated between the parent (the controlling interest) and the noncontrolling interests.

In this example, however, the controlling interest holder, AAL, has no legal claim on the profit of MMI, since MMI's profit or loss is legally allocable to its equity owner. If this example had been a conventional consolidation of a voting interest entity, the effect of eliminating the rental income from MMI would be a remaining MMI loss of $630, computed as follows:

MMI net income	$ 570
Effect of elimination of rental income	(1,200)
MMI net loss after elimination of intercompany rental income	$ (630)

ASC 810-10-35-3 provides a special rule that the effect of eliminating fees or other sources of income or expense between the primary beneficiary and the consolidated VIE is to be attributed solely to the primary beneficiary and not to the noncontrolling interest computed as follows and illustrated above:

Net loss of VIE	$ (630)
FIN 46(R) adjustment to allocate rental expense to primary beneficiary	1,200
Adjusted VIE net income allocable to noncontrolling interest	$ 570

The net income allocation to the noncontrolling interest shown above is reduced by the dividends paid to the noncontrolling interest as follows:

Adjusted VIE net income allocable to noncontrolling interest	$ 570
Dividend paid to noncontrolling interest	(500)
Noncontrolling interest retained earnings	70
Noncontrolling interest common stock	900
Total noncontrolling interest	$ 970

The results of the consolidation can be summarized as:

Primary beneficiary rent expense	$1,200
VIE	
Depreciation	230
Interest	400
	630
Net effect, allocable to noncontrolling interest	$ 570

Consolidated net income of $800 is the same as the primary beneficiary's net income since the entire $570 of VIE net income is allocated to the noncontrolling interest. The results, however, can have a profound effect on the way that the financial statements portray the leverage of the primary beneficiary to users, which might be the difference between AAL meeting or violating its loan covenants.

Debt to equity ratio	
Primary beneficiary	4.5:1
Consolidated	5.3:1

Certain practical matters require consideration in the case of consolidating VIEs.

1. *VIE without GAAP financial statements.* Many VIEs structured as shown in this example had not previously prepared financial statements. Prior to consolidating the VIE with the primary beneficiary, the VIE's accounting records must be adjusted to eliminate any differences between GAAP and the basis on which the VIE reports for income tax purposes.
2. *Lack of prior independent CPA involvement with VIE.* VIEs that had not been subject to financial reporting in the past obviously had not needed to engage an independent CPA to perform a compilation, review, or audit engagement. Upon consolidation, the consolidated financial statements, including the VIE's (subsidiary's) financial position and results of operations, will be subject to the same level of service as the financial statements of the primary beneficiary (parent).
3. *Interaction with ASC 460-10.* ASC 460-10, *Guarantor's Accounting and Disclosure Requirements for Guarantees, Including Indirect Guarantees of Indebtedness of Others,* requires guarantors to recognize a liability at inception for the obligations embodied in the guarantee. In the example above, the guarantee of the VIE's mortgage by the primary beneficiary would be exempt from the initial recognition and measurement provision of ASC 460-10 because the guarantee is analogous to a parent guarantee of its subsidiary's debt to a third party, which is specifically exempted from the recognition and measurement provisions of ASC 460-10. However, the guarantee is not exempt from the disclosure requirements of ASC 460-10 and ASC 450-10.
4. *General-purpose financial statements.* In the example, AAL is the "parent" company. It would be precluded by ASC 810-10-45-11 from issuing separate, general-purpose financial statements that exclude MMI, since this would be a GAAP departure; however, nothing precludes MMI from issuing separate subsidiary-only financial statements.

Implicit variable interests. One of the most misunderstood aspects of this area of the literature is referred to as an implicit variable interest. The FASB staff attempts to clarify this matter in ASC 810-10-25-48 through 54 and ASC 810-10-55-88 through 89.

A party that did not explicitly issue a direct guarantee of another party's obligation can, nevertheless, be held to be an implicit guarantor of that obligation and thus, hold a variable interest in the party whose debt is implicitly guaranteed.

Example of an implicit variable interest

Consider the situation where the principal shareholder of a company personally guarantees a mortgage on the premises that the company occupies and leases from a related LLC whose sole member is the lessee's principal shareholder. Normally, the rent payments due under the related-party lease are structured to provide sufficient cash flow to the lessor to enable it to meet its debt service obligations under the mortgage. If the lessee were to become delinquent under its rent obligations to the lessor, the lessor would not have sufficient cash flow to enable it to make the payments due under its mortgage, which would cause a loan delinquency or default.

Should this occur, the following scenarios could occur:

1. The lender could repossess the property and sell it to pay off the loan,
2. The lender could enforce the guarantee and compel the shareholder to pay off the loan on behalf of the lessor or, at least to make the delinquent payments on behalf of the lessor to cure the default, or
3. The lessee could sell off assets or borrow money from its stockholder or a third party to enable it to pay its delinquent rent, thereby enabling the lessor to make its delinquent mortgage payments.

Scenario 1 would not be a desirable outcome, as the lessor would lose title to its property and the lessee, in default on its rent, could end up without the premises in which it operates its business since, upon sale of the property, the successor owner would potentially terminate the lease for nonpayment.

Under scenario 2 if the shareholder were to pay the delinquent mortgage payment on behalf of the lessor, the transactions would be recorded as follows:

Lessor Accounting Records

Rent receivable	xxx	
Rental income		xxx
To record delinquent rent due from lessee		
Mortgage payable	xxx	
Loan payable—member		xxx
To record mortgage payment made on behalf of LLC by its member as a loan payable to the member		

Lessee Accounting Records

Rent expense	xxx	
Rent payable		xxx
To record delinquent rent due to lessor		

Scenario 3 would be recorded as follows (assuming that the lessee obtains additional funds from its principal shareholder):

Lessee Accounting Records

Cash	xxx	
Loan payable—shareholder		xxx
To record loan from shareholder		

Rent payable	xxx	
Cash		xxx
To record rent payment		

Lessor Accounting Records

Cash	xxx	
Rental income		xxx
To record rent received from lessee		
Mortgage interest	xxx	
Mortgage payable	xxx	
Cash		xxx
To record mortgage payment		

The outcomes of scenarios 2 and 3 are very similar. Under scenario 2, the shareholder/member will have a loan receivable from the thinly capitalized LLC that depends solely on the delinquent corporation for its cash flow. In scenario 2, the lessee will have to raise cash in an amount sufficient to fund the LLC's repayment of its loan to the shareholder/member and keep the mortgage current. Since the LLC is dependent upon the lessee for its cash flow, the lessee has implicitly incurred an obligation to fund the LLC's loan repayment to the shareholder/member. It is, of course, in the best interest of the lessee to fund this, since it entitles the lessee to continue to benefit from the use of the leased property and, contractually, the lessee is already obligated to pay the delinquent rent.

Under scenario 3, the shareholder/member will have a loan receivable from a lessee that is experiencing difficulty in meeting its rent obligations. The lessee will have substituted a presumably interest-bearing loan payable to its shareholder for a noninterest-bearing rent payable obligation to the LLC and will, as in scenario 2, be obligated to raise cash sufficient to repay its shareholder and fund its rent obligations under the lease. In effect, the lessee will have used its available credit that it could have used for other operating purposes to help provide financial support to the LLC that would otherwise have insufficient capital to be self-sustaining. Again, implicitly, the lessee is functioning as a guarantor of the LLC's mortgage indebtedness by its willingness to provide the cash flow necessary for the LLC to meet its obligations.

Based on the foregoing analysis, in substance the lessee is the holder of an implicit variable interest in the lessor in the form of an implicit guarantee of the lessor's mortgage debt. Due to the fact that the implicit guarantee exposes the lessee/variable interest holder to the expected losses of the lessor, the lessor/LLC's sole member (and at-risk equity holder) is not the only party that potentially would absorb expected losses of the lessor.

Variable interests in "silos." A party may hold a variable interest in specific assets of a VIE (e.g., a guarantee or a subordinated residual interest). In computing expected losses and expected residual returns, a holder of a variable interest in specified assets of a VIE must determine if the interest it holds qualifies as an interest in the VIE itself. The variable interest is considered an interest in the VIE itself if either (1) the fair value of the specific assets is more than half of the total fair value of the VIE's assets or (2) the interest holder has another significant variable interest in the entity as a whole.

If the interests are deemed to be interests in the VIE itself, the expected losses and expected residual returns associated with the variable interest in the specified assets are treated as being associated with the VIE.

If the interests are not deemed to be interests in the VIE itself, the interests in the specified assets are treated as a separate VIE (referred to as a *silo*) if the expected cash flows from the specified assets (and any associated credit enhancements, if applicable) are essentially the sole source of payment for specified liabilities or specified other interests. Under this scenario, expected losses and expected residual returns associated with the silo assets are accounted for separately to the extent that the interest holder either absorbs the VIE's expected losses or is entitled to receive its expected residual returns. Any excess of expected losses or expected residual returns not borne by (received by) the variable interest holder is considered attributable to the entity as a whole.

If one interest holder is required to consolidate a silo of a VIE, other VIE interest holders are to exclude the silo from the remaining VIE.

Synthetic leases. One of the more common SPE situations under prior GAAP is that of a synthetic lease. A synthetic lease is a financing transaction whereby an independent third-party lessor (i.e., unrelated to the lessee) constructs or acquires an existing single-tenant property and leases it to a lessee. The synthetic lease transaction is generally structured with a short lease term so that the lessee accounts for it as an operating lease under GAAP, notwithstanding the fact that, for federal income tax purposes, it is treated as a "financing," which results in the lessee/taxpayer capitalizing the leased asset and deducting depreciation and interest.

When these arrangements were originally devised, prior to the establishment of consolidation rules for VIEs, they resulted in the lessee excluding the leased asset and related debt from its balance sheet. It also enabled creditworthy lessees to finance as much as 100% of the cost of the leased property, thus avoiding tying up precious working capital in a down-payment.

The lessee commits to a fixed schedule of rental payments, say for five years, so over that time there will only be a single amount of annual cash flows paid each year. The lease terms provide a purchase option to the lessee that can be exercised at any time during the lease term or upon the lease's expiration. Under the option, the lessee would pay the lessor a stipulated amount normally representing the lessor's original investment in the leased property augmented by a fixed rate of return. Thus, the lessor, to ensure it earns an acceptable return to its investors, is willing to sacrifice any appreciation of the property that exceeds the purchase price.

The lease will typically also provide, however, that if the fair value of the asset at lease expiration is less than the stipulated amount of the initial investment augmented by the agreed-upon fixed rate of return, the lessee agrees to pay the lessor for any shortfall.

In analyzing these two lease provisions, each represents a transfer of variability from one party to the other:

Lessee purchase option that enables the lessee to benefit (obtain the expected residual rewards) from excess appreciation of the leased property	This option is a variable interest that entitles its holder, the lessee, to a portion of expected residual rewards associated with the leased asset that the lessor would otherwise be entitled to. Thus it transfers from lessor to lessee a portion of the favorable variability associated with the leased asset.
Lessee residual value guarantee	This guarantee is a variable interest that obligates its holder, the lessee, to absorb a stipulated portion of any unfavorable variability associated with the leased asset that would otherwise be absorbed by the lessor upon its disposition of the leased property.

Example of application of ASC 810-10-25 to a synthetic lease

A synthetic lease is structured with a five-year term and an annual "rental" due at the end of each of those years of $50,000. The average (expected) cash flow in each of those years will be that contractual amount. The fair value of the annual cash flow in any year will be the amount defined under CON 7, which is essentially the discounted present value of the annual lease payment.

Assume 6% is the relevant discount rate, and rents are paid annually in arrears. The fair value of the first year's rent is then \$50,000 ÷ 1.06 = \$47,170; the corresponding amount for year two's rent is \$50,000 ÷ 1.06^2 = \$44,500; and so on. Since this amount is fixed, there are no expected residual rewards or expected losses from the rental stream in each of the years one through five.

It is estimated that at the lease expiration date there may be a range of fair values for the asset. Also, the lessor is entitled to a cumulative return on its investment in the leased property. It is now necessary to compute, separately, the expected (i.e., probability-weighted) discounted fair values of the shortfall amount and the excess value amount. For simplicity, assume only three discrete outcomes are estimated to be possible:

1. The asset is sold for an amount that falls short of the book value plus the promised rate of return, for a net shortfall of \$20,000;
2. The asset is sold for a net gain, after guaranteed return to the lessor, of \$10,000; or
3. The asset is sold for a net gain of \$40,000.

These outcomes are summarized as follows:

Outcome	*5th year outcome*	*Probability of occurrence*	*Probability-weighted expected outcome*
1	\$(20,000)	40%	\$ (8,000)
2	10,000	35%	3,500
3	40,000	25%	10,000
		100%	\$ 5,500

Outcome	*[1] 5th year outcome*	*[2] Probability-weighted expected outcome*	*[3] [1] – [2] Variation*	*[4] Probability of occurrence*	*[5] [3] × [4] Probability-weighted variation*	*Positive variation*	*Negative variation*
1	\$(20,000)	\$5,500	\$(25,500)	40%	\$(10,200)		\$10,200
2	10,000	5,500	4,500	35%	1,575	\$ 1,575	
3	40,000	5,500	34,500	25%	8,625	8,625	
				100%	–	\$10,200	\$10,200

Note that the expected loss equals the expected residual returns, as would always be the case, since the arithmetic average (mean) was used to compute the deviations of each projected outcome. Since the expected loss based on expected cash flow will be borne by the lessee if it occurs, and the expected residual return based on expected cash flows will benefit the lessee if one or the other occurs, the lessee is the primary beneficiary/parent of the VIE.

The actual computation would be based on the fair value of the expected cash flows. In this case, the expected fair value of the loss is given as \$–10,200 ÷ $(1.06)^5$ = \$–7,622. The expected fair value of the expected residual rewards would correspondingly be \$7,622.

The total expected variability of the lease arrangement is therefore \$15,244 (all earlier years' rental streams had zero variability), and the lessee absorbs all of this.

Note that in real-life situations there may be many other complications, such as rentals based on variables such as sales of product and the like. In addition, many of these arrangements permit the lessee to exercise its purchase option at any time during the lease term rather than limiting exercise to the end of the lease term.

In such a situation, with a wider range of the amounts and timing of possible cash flows each period, the computations will be more challenging. Also, in some situations the VIE will have a range of assets and multiple parties with whom it is in contractual arrangements, which is a complication addressed somewhat by the standard, but which requires more analysis. However, it might be possible in many cases to immediately conclude qualitatively, based on analysis of the risks, rewards, and relationships, that the VIE is indeed to be consolidated, in which case these calculations will be unnecessary. The very existence of the purchase option and residual value guarantees provide qualitative evidence that, by design, the lessor is a VIE and the lessee is its primary beneficiary.

Changing or eliminating differences in fiscal year-end. ASC 810-10-45 and ASC 810-10-50 state that the following scenarios constitute voluntary changes in accounting principle that are subject to the accounting and disclosure rules in ASC 250:

1. A consolidated entity changes its fiscal year-end to alter or eliminate a difference between its year-end and the fiscal year-end of the entity that consolidates it in its financial statements (the parent or ASC 810 primary beneficiary).
2. An investee that is accounted for by an investor using the equity method changes its fiscal year-end to alter or eliminate a difference between its year-end and the fiscal year-end of the equity method investor.

Retrospective application is not required if it is impracticable to do so. (See chapter in this volume on ASC 250.)

ASC 810-20, *Control of Partnerships and Similar Entities*

General Partnerships. Partners holding lesser interests may possess *substantive participating rights* (as that term is used in ASC 810-20-25-5) granted by a contract, lease, agreement with other partners, or court decree. When the other partners have such rights, the presumption of control by the general partner with the majority voting interest or majority financial interest is overcome. Under those circumstances, the controlling general partner would consolidate the partnership and the noncontrolling general partner would consolidate the partnership and the noncontrolling general partners would use the equity method (ASC 970-323; ASC 810-20-25-19).

Limited partnerships. The structure of many limited partnerships consists of one investor serving as general partner and having only a small equity interest and the other investors holding limited partnership (or equivalent) interests. The proper accounting for such structures is ASC 970-323, *Real Estate Investments—Equity Method and Joint Ventures,* which formally deals only with certain real estate investments but has been applied by analogy to other investments. ASC 810-10-25 provides expanded guidance to the appropriate accounting in those circumstances where the majority owner lacks control due to the existence of "substantial participating rights" by minority owners.

If the investor/holder is an entity that is required under GAAP to measure its investment in the limited partnership (LP) at fair value with changes in fair value reported in the income statement, then it follows that applicable specialized guidance with respect to accounting for its investment.

If the investee entity is a variable interest entity (VIE) under the provisions of ASC 810, the holders of interests in the entity are to use the GAAP applicable to those interests. If the investor has a controlling financial interest in the VIE, the investor is deemed to be the entity's primary beneficiary (analogous to a parent company) and is required to consolidate the investee in its financial statements.

Noncontrolling interest holders in an LP that is a VIE are to account for their interests using the equity method or the cost method. Limited partner interests that are so minor that the limited partner has virtually no influence over operating and financial policies of the partnership would be accounted for using the cost method (ASC 970-323). To be considered to be this minor, the SEC staff has indicated that an interest would not be permitted to exceed 3–5% (ASC 323-30-S99). In practice, this benchmark is also generally accepted for non-SEC registrants, since it represents the most authoritative guidance currently available with respect to making this determination.

If the LP is not a VIE and the partners are not subject to specialized industry fair value accounting rules, a determination is made as to whether a single general partner or multiple general partners control the LP. If a single general partner controls the LP, that partner is to consolidate the LP, all other general partners are to apply the equity method of accounting to their investments, and the limited partners will use either the cost method (for minor investments) or the equity method, as previously discussed.

If more than one general partner controls the partnership, ASC 810-20 provides the framework for analyzing the respective legal and contractual rights and privileges associated with each owner/investor's interests to determine control. For the purpose of applying ASC 810-20, entities under common control are considered to be a single general partner. No guidance is offered, however, in ASC 810-20 as to how to determine which of several general partners is to consolidate the partnership.

ASC 810-20 integrates certain concepts from ASC 810 into what had been only fragmentary guidance. ASC 810 introduced the concept of "kick-out rights" which, when held by limited partners, gave them the right to eject the general partner(s) of the partnership, thereby (often) preventing the general partner(s) from exercising control. ASC 810-20 holds that there is a refutable presumption that general partners in a partnership have control, regardless of their actual ownership percentage, which can be overcome if the limited partners have certain defined abilities.

If the limited partners have the *substantive ability* to dissolve (liquidate) the limited partnership or otherwise remove the general partners without cause—which is referred to as "kick-out rights"—then the general partners will be deemed to lack control over the partnership. In such cases, consolidated financial reporting would not be appropriate, but equity method accounting would almost inevitably be warranted. To qualify, the kick-out rights must be exercisable by a single limited partner or a simple majority (or fewer) of limited partners. Thus, if a super-majority of limited partner votes is required to remove the general partner(s), this would not constitute a substantive ability to dissolve the partnership and would not thwart control by the general partner(s).

There is a range of possible qualifying requirements to exercise kick-out rights that could lead to the conclusion that nominal kick-out rights are ineffective in precluding the general partner(s) from exercising control. ASC 810-20 offers a series of illustrative examples to help the preparer interpret this guidance, and should be consulted to benchmark any real-world set of circumstances. Examples of barriers to the exercise of kick-out rights include:

1. Conditions that make it unlikely the rights will be exercisable (e.g., conditions that narrowly limit the timing of the exercise)
2. Financial penalties or operational barriers associated with dissolving (liquidating) the limited partnership or replacing the general partners that would act as a significant disincentive for dissolution (liquidation) or removal
3. The absence of an adequate number of qualified replacements for the general partners or the lack of adequate compensation to attract a qualified replacement
4. The absence of an explicit, reasonable mechanism in the limited partnership agreement or in the applicable laws or regulations, by which the limited partners holding the rights can call for and conduct a vote to exercise those rights
5. The inability of the limited partners holding the rights to obtain the information necessary to exercise them.

A limited partner's unilateral right to withdraw is pointedly not equivalent to a kick-out right. However, if the partnership is contractually or statutorily bound to dissolve upon the withdrawal of one partner, that would equate to a kick-out right.

ASC 810-20 also addresses "participating rights" held by the limited partners, which it contrasts to "protective rights" as these were first defined in ASC 810. Limited partners' rights (whether granted by contract or by law) that would allow the limited partners to block selected limited partnership actions would be considered protective rights and would not overcome the presumption of control by the general partners(s). Among the actions cited by ASC 810-20 as illustrating protective (not participating) rights are:

1. Amendments to the limited partnership agreement
2. Pricing on transactions between the general partners and the limited partnership and related self-dealing transactions
3. Liquidation of the limited partnership initiated by the general partners or a decision to cause the limited partnership to enter bankruptcy or other receivership
4. Acquisitions and dispositions of assets that are not expected to be undertaken in the ordinary course of business (note that limited partners' rights relating to acquisitions and dispositions expected to be made in the ordinary course of the limited partnership's business are participating rights)
5. Issuance or repurchase of limited partnership interests.

The presence of protective rights would not serve to overcome the presumption of control by the general partner(s). Substantive participating rights, on the other hand, do overcome the presumption of general partner control. Such rights could include:

1. Selecting, terminating, and setting the compensation of management responsible for implementing the limited partnership's policies and procedures
2. Establishing operating and capital decisions of the limited partnership, including budgets, in the ordinary course of business.

ASC 810-20 states that determination of whether the presumption of general partner control is overcome is a "facts and circumstances" assessment to be made in each unique situation. For example, depending on which decisions are required to be put to a full vote of the partnership (as opposed to being reserved for the general partner), the limited partners may be found to have substantive participating rights. Another important factor weighing on this determination: the relationships among limited and general partners (using ASC 850 related-party criteria).

The assessment of the extent of limited partners' rights and the impact those have on the presumption of general partner(s) control over the partnership (for consolidated financial reporting purposes) is to be made upon initial acquisition of the general partner's interest or formation of the partnership, and again at each financial reporting (i.e., statement of financial position) date.

Limited partnerships controlled by the general partners. As previously stated, the general partners are collectively presumed to be in control of the limited partnership and, if this is substantively the case, the accounting for the general partners depends on whether control of the entity rests with a single general partner. If a single general partner controls the limited partnership, that general partner consolidates the limited partnership in its financial statements. If no single general partner controls the limited partnership, each general partner applies the equity method to account for its interest (ASC 810-20).

Noncontrolling limited partners are to account for their interests using the equity method or by the cost method. As previously discussed, limited partner interests that are so minor (not to exceed 3–5%) that the limited partner has virtually no influence over operating and financial policies of the partnership would be accounted for using the cost method (ASC 970-323).

Limited partnerships controlled by the limited partners. If the presumption of control by the general partners is overcome by applying ASC 810-20 and the limited partners control the partnership, the general partners would use the equity method to account for their interests in the partnership.

If there is a controlling limited partner, that partner would consolidate the limited partnership in its financial statements. Noncontrolling limited partners would follow the same guidance provided above that applies when the general partners control the partnership (i.e., use the equity method unless the interest is minor—in which case the cost method would be used).

Limited liability companies that maintain a specific ownership account for each investor. When an LLC maintains individual equity accounts for each member, similar to the structure of a limited partnership, the investor/member is to analogize to the guidance above that applies to accounting for investments in limited partnerships using either the cost method or equity method (ASC 272 and, by reference, ASC 970-323 and ASC 323-30-S99). In the discussion of ASC 272, it was indicated that it might be appropriate to apply this guidance by analogy to other entities that have similar specifically identifiable ownership account structures.

ASC 272 provides an exception to this general rule. Its scope does not include investments in LLCs used as securitization vehicles under ASC 860 that continue to be held by a transferor in a securitization transaction accounted for as a sale. These interests are accounted for as debt securities and categorized as either available-for-sale or trading securities under ASC 320 and are subject to specialized requirements regarding recognition of interest income and impairment (ASC 325-40).

Limited liability companies that are functionally equivalent to corporations ("analogous entities"). Some LLCs have governance structures that have characteristics that closely resemble those of corporations. These LLCs are not included in the scope of ASC 272 summarized earlier. Instead, membership interests in these LLCs are subject to different criteria to determine the proper accounting treatment to be used in the investor/member's financial statements.

The applicable GAAP relative to LLCs that are analogous entities is ASC 810-10-25. Under ASC 810-10-25, there is a similar rebuttable presumption that the majority voting interest holder(s) are in control of the investee. Management is to exercise judgment based on the relevant facts and circumstances as to whether one or more minority shareholders or members possess rights that individually or in the aggregate provide them with effective participation in the significant decisions expected to be made in the "ordinary course of business." If the minority owner or owners possess substantive participating rights, the presumption of control by the majority owners is overcome and the minority owner or owners are considered to be in control.

Again, the controlling interest holder would be required to consolidate, and the noncontrolling interest holders would apply either the equity method or cost method, depending on the extent of their respective holdings.

Display in the reporting entity's financial statements when the investee is not a corporation. Under some circumstances, investor-venturers account for undivided interests in assets by means of pro rata consolidation, including a fraction of each asset category of the investee in the investor's statement of financial position, typically commingled with the investor's own assets. This has most commonly occurred in the case of construction joint ventures, and is not a procedure formally defined under GAAP. In ASC 810-10-45, the issue addressed is whether proportional consolidation can be used to account for an investment in a partnership or a joint venture, as an alternative to full consolidation, equity method accounting, or historical cost.

The standard states that the pro rata method of consolidation is not appropriate for an investment in an unincorporated legal entity, except when the investee is in either the construction industry or an extractive industry, where there is a longstanding practice of its use. An entity is considered to be in an extractive industry only if its activities are limited to the extraction of mineral resources (such as oil and gas exploration and production) and not if its activities involve such related pursuits as refining, marketing, or transporting the extracted mineral resources.

ASC 810-30, *Research and Development Arrangements*

Sponsored research and development activities. ASC 810-30-55 discusses the accounting for a transaction in which a sponsor creates a wholly owned subsidiary with cash and rights to certain technology originally developed by the sponsor, and receives from the newly created subsidiary two classes of stock. The sponsor then distributes one of the classes of stock (e.g., Class A) to its stockholders. This class of stock has voting rights. Under a purchase option, the sponsor has the right, for a specified period of time, to repurchase all the Class A stock distributed to the stockholders for an exercise price approximating the fair value of the Class A shares. The class retained by the sponsor (e.g., Class B) conveys essentially no financial interest to the sponsor and has no voting rights other than certain blocking rights. The certificate of incorporation prohibits the subsidiary from changing its capital structure, from selling any significant portion of its assets, and from liquidating or merging during the term when the purchase option is outstanding.

The sponsor and the subsidiary enter into a development contract that requires the subsidiary to spend all the cash contributed by the sponsor for research and development activities mutually agreed upon with the sponsor. The subsidiary has no employees other than its CEO. The subsidiary contracts with the sponsor to perform, on behalf of the sponsor, all of the research and development activities under the development contract.

The sponsor accounts for the research and development contract as follows:

- The sponsor reclassifies the cash contributed to the subsidiary as restricted cash when the Class A shares are distributed to its stockholders.
- The distribution of the Class A shares by the sponsor to its stockholders is accounted for as a dividend based on the fair value of the shares distributed.
- In the financial statements of the sponsor, the Class A shares are presented similar to a minority interest.
- The sponsor recognizes research and development expense as the research and development activities are conducted.
- The research and development expense recognized by the sponsor is not allocated to the Class A shares in determining net income or in calculating earnings per share.
- If the Class A purchase option is exercised, the sponsor accounts for the purchase as the acquisition of a minority interest.
- If the Class A purchase option is not exercised by its expiration date, the sponsor reclassifies the Class A stock to additional paid-in capital as an adjustment of the original dividend.

The effect of the above guidance is quite similar to what would be achieved by consolidating the subsidiary.

Other Sources

See ASC Location – Wiley *GAAP* Chapter…	***For information on…***
ASC 480-10-55-53 through 55-58	Derivative transactions in subsidiary stock with noncontrolling interest
ASC 740-10-25-39 through 25-41	Deferred taxes on dividends of foreign operations
ASC 830-30-45-10	The elimination of intraentity profits with foreign entities
ASC 840-30-45-4	Leases sold by a manufacturer to a leasing subsidiary
ASC 860-10-55-13	Transfers of ownership interest in a subsidiary with financial assets

48 ASC 815 DERIVATIVES AND HEDGING

PERSPECTIVE AND ISSUES

Subtopics

ASC 815, Derivatives, contains eight subtopics:

- ASC 815-10, *Overall,* which contains two Subsections:
    - General
    - Certain Contracts on Debt and Equity Securities
- ASC 815-15, *Embedded Derivatives*
- ASC 815-20, *Hedging—General*
- ASC 815-25, *Fair Value Hedges*
- ASC 815-30, *Cash Flow Hedges*
- ASC 815-35, *Net Investment Hedges*
- ASC 815-40, *Contracts in Entity's Own Equity*
- ASC 815-45, *Weather Derivatives.*

ASC 815-40 and ASC 815-45 address guidance on accounting for contracts that have characteristics of derivative instruments but that are not accounted for as derivative instruments under ASC 815. The other Subtopics provide guidance on accounting for derivative instruments and hedging activities. ASC 815-10 focuses on whether a contract meets the definition of a derivative instrument.

Scope

ASC 815 applies to all entities. The following instruments are *not* included in the ASC 815 guidance, provided they meet the specific exception criterion in ASC 815-10-15-14 through 15-42:

1. Regular-way security trades
2. Normal purchases and normal sales
3. Certain insurance contracts
4. Certain financial guarantee contracts
5. Certain contracts that are not traded on an exchange
6. Derivative instruments that impede sales accounting
7. Investments in life insurance
8. Certain investment contracts
9. Certain loan commitments
10. Certain interest-only strips and principal-only strips
11. Certain contracts involving an entity's own equity
12. Leases

13. Residual value guarantees
14. Registration payment arrangements.

(ASC 815-10-15-13)

The following section expands on the information above:

1. *Regular-way security trades*—Delivery of a security readily convertible to cash within the time period generally established by marketplace regulations or conventions where the trade takes place rather than by the usual procedure of an individual enterprise. Contracts for the delivery of securities that are not readily convertible to cash are not subject to ASC 815's provisions because net settlement would not be possible.

   For example, most trades of equity securities in the United States require settlement in three business days. If an individual contract requires settlement in more than three business days (even if this is normal for a particular entity), this exception would not apply, unless (per ASC 815-10-15) the reporting entity is required, or has a continuing policy, to account for such transactions on a trade-date basis. This exception also applies to when-issued and to-be-announced securities (except for those contracts accounted for on a trade-date basis), if there is no other way to purchase or sell them and if the trade will settle within the shortest period permitted.

   Based on the foregoing, the following may be excluded: forward purchases or sales of to-be-announced securities, and when-issued, as-issued, or if-issued securities.
2. *Normal purchases and normal sales*—Contracts for future delivery of assets (other than derivative instruments or financial instruments) that are readily convertible to cash and for which there is no net settlement provision and no market mechanism to ease net settlement. Terms must be consistent with normal transactions and quantities must be reasonable in relation to needs. All relevant factors are to be considered. An example would include contracts similar to binding purchase orders. However, take or pay contracts that require little or no initial net investment, and that have products readily convertible to cash that do not qualify as normal purchases, would be a derivative instrument, and not an exception.

   The purpose of the "normal purchases and normal sales" definition was to exclude certain routine types of transactions from the required accounting as derivative instruments. This exemption includes certain contracts which do contain net settlement or market mechanisms if it is judged probable, at the inception and throughout the duration of such contracts, that they will not in fact settle net and will instead result in physical delivery. Notwithstanding, this more broadly based exemption from the accounting requirements of ASC 815, certain contracts will not qualify for exemption in any case; these include contracts the price of which are based on an underlying that is not clearly and closely related to the assets being sold or purchased, and those requiring cash settlement for any gains or losses or otherwise settled net on a periodic basis. Documentary evidence is required to support the use of the expanded exemption from the ASC 815 provisions.

   ASC 815-10-15 has further addressed the "normal purchases and sales" provisions of ASC 815. Under the amendment, power purchase or sales agreements (whether forwards, options, or some combination thereof) pertaining to delivery of electricity qualify for this exception only if a series of conditions are all met. The contracts cannot permit net settlement, but must require physical delivery, and must be capacity contracts, as differentiated from ordinary option contracts. For the seller, the quantities deliverable under the contracts must be quantities normally to be sold;

for the buyer, quantities must be those normally to be used or sold, and the buyer must be an entity which is contractually obligated to maintain sufficient capacity to meet the needs of its customers. Certain additional requirements, and further exceptions, are set forth by ASC 815-10-15.

Counterparties may reach different conclusions as to whether the contracts are a derivative instrument. Asymmetrical results are acceptable (i.e., the exception may apply to one party but not the other).

3. *Certain insurance contracts*—Contracts where the holder is only compensated when an insurable event (other than price or rate change) takes place and:

   a. The value of the holder's asset or liability is adversely changed or
   b. The holder incurs a liability.

   For example, contracts generally not considered to be derivative instruments include those within the scope of ASC 944, traditional life insurance, and traditional property and casualty insurance policies.

   Most traditional insurance contracts will not be derivative instruments. Some, however, can include embedded derivatives that must be accounted for separately. For example, embedded derivatives may be found in indexed annuity contracts, variable life and annuity contracts, and property and casualty contracts involving changes in currency rates.

4. *Certain financial guarantee contracts*—Contracts that call for payments only to reimburse for a loss from debtor failure to pay when due. However, a credit-indexed contract requiring payment for changes in credit ratings (an underlying) would not be an exception.
5. *Certain contracts that are not exchange traded*—Contracts with underlyings based on one of the following:

   a. Climatic, geological or other physical variable: for example, inches of rain or heating-degree days;
   b. Value or price involving a nonfinancial asset not readily converted to cash;
   c. Fair value of a nonfinancial liability that does not require delivery of an asset that is readily converted to cash; or
   d. Specified volumes of revenue of one of the parties: examples are royalty agreements or contingent rentals based on related sales.

   (ASC 815-10-15-59)

   In the case of a mixture of underlyings, some of which are exceptions, the predominant characteristic of the combined variable of the contract is the determinant. If there is a high correlation with the behavior of the excepted variables above, it is an exception and if there is a high correlation with the nonexcepted variables, it is a derivative instrument.

6. *Derivatives that serve as impediments to sales accounting*—A derivative instrument that affects the accounting for the transfer of an asset. For example, a call option on transferred assets under ASC 860 would prevent accounting for the transfer as a sale. This is necessary, since recognizing the call as a derivative instrument would result in double counting. For instance, a lessor guarantee of the residual value may prevent the accounting for a sales-type lease.

In addition to the foregoing, the following are not considered derivative instruments:

1. Contracts issued or held that are both:

   a. Indexed to the enterprise's own stock, and
   b. Classified in shareholders' equity.

   Derivative instruments are assets or liabilities. Items properly accounted for in shareholders' equity are thus excluded from the definition of derivatives. Contracts that can or must be settled through issuance of an equity instrument but that are indexed in part or in full to something other than the enterprise's own stock are considered derivative instruments if they qualify and they are to be classified as assets or liabilities.
2. Contracts issued in connection with stock-based compensation arrangements as addressed in ASC 718.
3. Contracts issued as contingent consideration in a business combination under ASC 805.

   Contracts in a business combination that are similar to, but are not accounted for as, contingent consideration under ASC 805, are subject to this standard as derivative instruments or embedded derivative instruments.

The exceptions for the above three issued contracts are not applicable to the counterparties.

Technical Alerts

In July 2013, the FASB issued ASU 2013-10, Derivatives and Hedging (Topic 815): *Inclusion of the Fed Funds Effective Swap Rate (or Overnight Index Swap Rate) as a Benchmark Interest Rate for Hedge Accounting Purposes.* The ASU is a consensus of the EITF. The FASB added the Overnight Index Swap rate (OIS) to the LIBOR and UST as a US benchmark for hedge accounting purposes The ASU also removes the restriction on using different benchmarks for similar hedges. The ASU is effective prospectively for qualifying new or redesignating hedging relationships entered into after July 17, 2013.

In January 2014, the FASB issued ASU 2014-03, Derivatives and Hedging (Topic 815): *Accounting for Certain Receivable–Variable, Pay-Fixed Interest Rate Swaps—Simplified Hedging Accounting Approach.* The ASU is a consensus of the Private Company Council. The ASU does not apply to public business entities, not-for-profit entities, employee benefit plans within the scope of Topics 960-965 on plan accounting, and financial institutions. It allows private companies to apply a simplified hedge accounting method to hedging relationships. Certain criteria must be met and the relationships must involve variable-rate debt and a pay-fixed, receive-floating interest rate swap. The new approach assumes no hedge ineffectiveness in the hedging relationship. This results in an income statement impact similar to what could have occurred had the company simply entered into a fixed-rate borrowing. The approach also allow private companies to measure the hedging interest rate swap at its settlement value, rather than at fair value, and gives private companies more time to put hedge documentation in place. Also included are provisions that allow certain private companies with relief from fair value measurement disclosure requirements.

ASU 2014-04 is effective for periods beginning after December 15, 2014 and interim periods beginning after December 15, 2014, with early adoption permitted.

Overview

Derivatives literature is exceedingly complex, which is largely a consequence of the rules establishing "special accounting" for hedging. Limited accounting relief (i.e., simplified accounting) for certain types of hedging activities may be provided by applying ASC 825-10-25, *Financial Instruments: Fair Value Option*.

Basic principles. ASC 815 lists four principles or cornerstones that underlie its guidance:

1. Derivative instruments represent rights or obligations that meet the definitions of assets or liabilities and should be reported in financial statements.
2. Fair value is the most relevant measure for financial instruments and the only relevant measure for derivative instruments. Derivative instruments should be measured at fair value, and adjustments to the carrying amount of hedged items should reflect changes in their fair value (that is, gains or losses) that are attributable to the risk being hedged and that arise while the hedge is in effect.
3. Only items that are assets or liabilities should be reported as such in financial statements.
4. Special accounting for items designated as being hedged should be provided only for qualifying items. One aspect of qualification should be an assessment of the expectation of effective offsetting changes in fair values or cash flows during the term of the hedge for the risk being hedged.
(ASC 815-10-10-1)

Fair value hedges. Hedges of the changes in fair value can be associated with a recognized asset or liability or of an unrecognized firm commitment. In a fair value hedge, gains and losses of both the DI and the hedged item are recognized currently in earnings. In the case of a perfectly effective hedge, these gains and losses will fully offset each period, but more typically this result will not be achieved. There will thus be a residual charge or credit to earnings each period that the hedge position is in place.

Cash flow hedges. Cash flow hedges, on the other hand, pertain to forecasted transactions. The effective portions of these hedges are initially reported in other comprehensive income and are reclassified into earnings only later, when the forecasted transactions affect earnings. Any ineffective portions of the hedges are reported currently in earnings.

Foreign currency hedges. Hedges of the foreign currency exposure of a net investment in a foreign operation also qualify for special accounting treatment. In a foreign currency net investment hedge, the gain or loss is reported in other comprehensive income as part of the cumulative translation adjustment. In the case of foreign currency hedges of unrecognized firm commitments, the gain or loss is reported the same way as a fair value hedge. A gain or loss on a foreign currency hedge that is associated with an available-for-sale security will also be reported the same way as a fair value hedge. Finally, a gain or loss arising from a hedge relating to a foreign currency-denominated forecasted transaction is reported in the same way as a cash flow hedge.

A nonderivative financial instrument generally cannot be designated as a hedge. An exception, however, occurs when that instrument is denominated in a foreign currency and is designated as a hedge of a net investment in a foreign operation or an unrecognized firm commitment.

Not-for-profit entities. Not-for-profit (NFP) entities are not permitted to use hedge accounting for forecasted transactions. This is because NFP entities do not report *other comprehensive income*—all such items are included in the statement of activity, which provides an all-inclusive measure of changes in net assets for the period. In other regards, however, ASC 815 requirements are fully applicable to NFP entities.

Hedge effectivess. Hedge effectiveness must be demonstrated if the accounting set forth in ASC 815 is to be employed. This does not require perfect effectiveness (which is almost never attainable in practice), but the guidance is not explicit regarding the degree of effectiveness that must be attained to justify the use of special hedge accounting. The method to be used for assessing the effective and ineffective portions of a hedge must be established at the inception of the hedge and must be consistent with the approach actually used by the reporting entity for managing risk. Should a hedge fail to meet a minimum threshold of effectiveness, it is to be redesignated, and hedge accounting ceases.

Summary of Accounting for Hedges

	Type of hedge—ASC 815		
Attribute	*Fair value*	*Cash flow*	*Foreign currency (FC)*
Types of hedging instruments permitted	Derivatives	Derivatives	Derivatives or nonderivatives depending on the type of hedge
Statement of financial position valuation of hedging instrument	Fair value	Fair value	Fair value
Recognition of gain or loss on changes in value of hedging instrument	Currently in earnings	Effective portion currently as a component of other comprehensive income (OCI) and reclassified to earnings in future period(s) that forecasted transaction affects earnings	**FC-denominated firm commitment** Currently in earnings **Available-for-sale (AFS) security** Currently in earnings **Forecasted FC transaction** Same as cash flow hedge
		Ineffective portion currently in earnings	**Net investment in a foreign operation** OCI as part of the cumulative translation adjustment to the extent it is effective as a hedge
Recognition of gain or loss on changes in the fair value of the hedged item	Currently in earnings	Not applicable; these hedges are not associated with recognized assets or liabilities	**FC-denominated firm** commitment Currently in earnings **Available-for-sale** security **(AFS)** Currently in earnings Forecasted **FC transaction** Not applicable; same as cash flow hedge

DEFINITIONS OF TERMS

Source: ASC 815 and FASB Codification Master Glossary

Acquiree. The business or businesses that the acquirer obtains control of in a business combination. This term also includes a nonprofit activity or business that a not-for-profit acquirer obtains control of in an acquisition by a not-for-profit entity.

Acquirer. The entity that obtains control of the acquiree. However, in a business combination in which a variable interest entity (VIE) is acquired, the primary beneficiary of that entity always is the acquirer.

Asymmetrical default provision. A nonperformance penalty provision that requires the defaulting party to compensate the nondefaulting party for any loss incurred but does not allow the defaulting party to receive the effect of favorable price changes.

Benchmark Interest Rate. A widely recognized and quoted rate in an active financial market that is broadly indicative of the overall level of interest rates attributable to high-credit-quality obligors in that market. It is a rate that is widely used in a given financial market as an underlying basis for determining the interest rates of individual financial instruments and commonly referenced in interest-rate-related transactions.

In theory, the benchmark interest rate should be a risk-free rate (that is, has no risk of default). In some markets, government borrowing rates may serve as a benchmark. In other markets, the benchmark interest rate may be an interbank offered rate.

Bid-ask spread. A bid-ask spread is the difference between the highest price a buyer will pay to acquire an instrument and the lowest price at which any investor will sell an instrument.

Business. An integrated set of activities and assets that is capable of being conducted and managed for the purpose of providing a return in the form of dividends, lower costs, or other economic benefits directly to investors or other owners, members, or participants. Additional guidance on what a business consists of is presented in ASC 805-10-55-4 through 55-9.

Business combination. A transaction or other event in which an acquirer obtains control of one or more businesses. Transactions sometimes referred to as true mergers or mergers of equals also are business combinations.

Call Option. A contract that allows the holder to buy a specified quantity of stock from the writer of the contract at a fixed price for a given period.

Capacity Contract. An agreement by an owner of capacity to sell the right to that capacity to another party so that it can satisfy its obligations. For example, in the electric industry, capacity (sometimes referred to as installed capacity) is the capability to deliver electric power to the electric transmission system of an operating control area.

Cash flow hedge. A hedge of the exposure to variability in the cash flows of a recognized asset or liability, or of a forecasted transaction, that is attributable to a particular risk.

Control Area. A control area requires entities that serve load within the control area to demonstrate ownership or contractual rights to capacity sufficient to serve that load at time of peak demand and to provide a reserve margin to protect the integrity of the system against potential generating unit outages in the control area. A control area is a portion of the electric grid that schedules, dispatches, and controls generating resources to serve area load (ultimate users of electricity) and coordinates scheduling of the flow of electric power over the transmission system to neighboring control areas.

Credit derivative. A derivative instrument that has both of the following characteristics:

1. One or more of its underlyings are related to any of the following:
   a. The credit risk of a specific entity (or group of entities)
   b. An index based on the credit risk of a group of entities.
2. It exposes the seller to potential loss from credit-risk-related events specified in the contract.

Examples of credit derivatives include, but are not limited to, credit default swaps, credit spread options, and credit index products.

Credit risk. For purposes of a hedged item in a fair value hedge, credit risk is the risk of changes in the hedge item's fair value attributable to both of the following:

1. Changes in the obligor's creditworthiness
2. Changes in the spread over the benchmark interest rate with respect to the hedge item's credit sector at inception of the hedge.

For purposes of a hedge transaction in a cash flow hedge, credit risk is the risk of changes in the hedge transaction's cash flows attributable to all of the following:

1. Default
2. Changes in the obligor's creditworthiness
3. Changes in the spread over the benchmark interest rate with respect to the related financial asset's or liability's credit sector at inception of the hedge.

Derivative instruments. In ASC 815, derivative instruments are defined by their three distinguishing characteristics, which are:

1. One or more underlyings and one or more notional amounts (or payment provisions or both);
2. No initial net investment or a smaller net investment than required for contracts expected to have a similar response to market changes; and
3. Terms that require or permit
   a. Net settlement
   b. Net settlement by means outside the contract
   c. Delivery of an asset that results in a position substantially the same as net settlement.

ASC 815 defines derivative instruments by reference to specific characteristics, rather than in terms of classes or categories of financial instruments. These distinctive features are believed to distinguish the fundamental nature of derivative instruments such as options and futures.

Embedded credit derivative. An embedded derivative that is also a credit derivative.

Embedded derivative. Implicit or explicit terms that affect some or all of the cash flows or the value of other exchanges required by a contract in a manner similar to a derivative instrument.

Exercise contingency. A provision that entitles the entity (or the counterparty) to exercise an equity-linked financial instrument (or embedded feature) based on changes in an underlying, including the occurrence (or nonoccurrence) of a specified event. Provisions that accelerate the timing of the entity's (or the counterparty's) ability to exercise an instrument and provisions that extend the length of time that an instrument is exercisable are examples of exercise contingencies.

Expected cash flow. The probability-weighted average (that is, mean of the distribution) of possible future cash flows

Face amount. See notional amount.

Fair value. Price that would be received to sell an asset or paid to transfer a liability in an orderly transaction between market participants at the measurement date.

Fair value hedge. A hedge of the exposure to changes in the fair value of a recognized asset or liability, or of an unrecognized firm commitment, that are attributable to a particular risk.

Financial instrument. Cash, evidence of an ownership interest in an entity, or a contract that both:

1. Imposes on one entity a contractual obligation either:
   a. To deliver cash or another financial instrument to a second entity
   b. To exchange other financial instruments on potentially unfavorable terms with the second entity
2. Conveys to that second entity a contractual right either:
   a. To receive cash or another financial instrument from the first entity
   b. To exchange other financial instruments on potentially favorable terms with the first entity.

The use of the term financial instrument in this definition is recursive (because the term financial instrument is included in it), though it is not circular. The definition requires a chain of contractual obligations that ends with the delivery of cash or an ownership interest in an entity. Any number of obligations to deliver financial instruments can be links in a chain that qualifies a particular contract as a financial instrument.

Contractual rights and contractual obligations encompass both those that are conditioned on the occurrence of a specified event and those that are not. All contractual rights (contractual obligations) that are financial instruments meet the definition of asset (liability) set forth in FASB Concepts Statement No. 6, *Elements of Financial Statements,* although some may not be recognized as assets (liabilities) in financial statements—that is, they may be off-balance-sheet—because they fail to meet some other criterion for recognition.

For some financial instruments, the right is held by or the obligation is due from (or the obligation is owned to or by) a group of entities rather than a single entity.

Financial statements are available to be issued. Financial statements are considered available to be issued when they are complete in a form and format that complies with GAAP and all approvals necessary for issuance have been obtained, for example, from management, the board of directors, and/or significant shareholders. The process involved in creating and distributing the financial statements will vary depending on an entity's management and corporate governance structure as well as statutory and regulatory requirements.

Firm commitment. See definition in ASC 470 chapter Definition of Terms section.

Forecasted transaction. A transaction that is expected to occur for which there is no firm commitment. Because no transaction or event has yet occurred and the transaction or event when it occurs will be at the prevailing market price, a forecasted transaction does not give an entity any present rights to future benefits or a present obligation for future sacrifices.

Foreign exchange risk. The risk of changes in a hedged item's fair value of functional-currency-equivalent cash flows attributable to changes in the related foreign currency exchange rates.

Hybrid instrument. A contract that embodies both an embedded derivative and a host contract.

Interest rate risk. The risk of changes in a hedged item's fair value or cash flows attributable to changes in the designated benchmark interest rate.

Internal derivative. A foreign currency derivative instrument that has been entered into with another member of a consolidated group (such as a treasury center).

Intrinsic value. The amount by which the fair value of the underlying stock exceeds the exercise price of an option. For example, an option with an exercise price of $20 on a stock whose current market price is $25 has an intrinsic value of $5. (A nonvested share may be described as an option on that share with an exercise price of zero. Thus, the fair value of a share is the same as the intrinsic value of such an option on that share.)

Loan commitment. Loan commitments are legally binding commitments to extend credit to a counterparty under certain prespecified terms and conditions. They have fixed expiration dates and may either be fixed-rate or variable-rate. Loan commitments can be either of the following:

1. Revolving (in which the amount of the overall line of credit is reestablished upon repayment of previously drawn amounts)
2. Nonrevolving (in which the amount of the overall line of credit is not reestablished upon repayment of previously drawn amounts).

Loan commitments can be distributed through syndication arrangements, in which one entity acts as a lead and an agent on behalf of other entities that will each extend credit to a single borrower. Loan commitments generally permit the lender to terminate the arrangement under the terms of covenants negotiated under the agreement. This is not an authoritative or all-encompassing definition.

London Interbank Offered Rate swap rate. The fixed rate on a single-currency, constant-notional interest rate swap that has its variable-rate leg referenced to the London Interbank Offered Rate (LIBOR) with no additional spread over LIBOR on that variable-rate leg. That fixed rate is the derived rate that would result in the swap having a zero fair value at inception because the present value of fixed cash flows, based on that rate, equate to the present value of the variable cash flows.

Make whole provision. A contractual option that gives a debtor (that is, an issuer) the right to pay off debt before maturity at a significant premium over the fair value of the debt at the date of settlement.

Mandatorily redeemable financial instrument. Any of various financial instruments issued in the form of shares that embody an unconditional obligation requiring the issuer to redeem the instrument by transferring its assets at a specified or determinable date (or dates) or upon an event that is certain to occur.

Net cash settlement. The party with a loss delivers to the party with a gain a cash payment equal to the gain, and no shares are exchanged.

Net share settlements. The party with a loss delivers to the party with a gain shares with a current fair value equal to the gain. The portion of equity (net assets) in a subsidiary not attributable, directly or indirectly, to a parent. A noncontrolling interest is sometimes called a minority interest.

Noncontrolling interest. The portion of equity (net assets) in a subsidiary not attributable, directly or indirectly, to a parent. A noncontrolling interest is sometimes called a minority interest.

Nonperformance risk. The risk that an entity will not fulfill an obligation. Nonperformance risk includes, but may not be limited to, the reporting entity's own credit risk.

Not-for-profit entity. An entity that possesses the following characteristics, in varying degrees, that distinguish it from a business entity:

1. Contributions of significant amounts of resources from resource providers who do not expect commensurate or proportionate pecuniary return
2. Operating purposes other than to provide goods or services at a profit
3. Absence of ownership interests like those of business entities.

Entities that clearly fall outside this definition include the following:

1. All investor-owned entities
2. Entities that provide dividends, lower costs, or other economic benefits directly and proportionately to their owners, members, or participants, such as mutual insurance entities, credit unions, farm and rural electric cooperatives, and employee benefit plans.

Not-for-profit entity. See definition in the ASC 270 chapter Definition of Terms section.

Notional amount. A number of currency units, shares, bushels, pounds, or other units specified in a derivative instrument. Sometimes other names are used. For example, the notional amount is called a face amount in some contracts.

Payment provision. A payment provision specifies a fixed or determinable settlement to be made if the underlying behaves in a specified manner.

Physical settlement. The party designated in the contract as the buyer delivers the full stated amount of cash to the seller, and the seller delivers the full stated number of shares to the buyer.

Prepayable. Able to be settled by either party before its scheduled maturity.

Private company. An entity other than a public business entity, a not-for-profit entity, or an employee benefit plan within the scope of Topics 960 through 965 on plan accounting.

Public business entity. A public business entity is a business entity meeting any one of the criteria below. Neither a not-for-profit entity nor an employee benefit plan is a business entity.

1. It is required by the U.S. Securities and Exchange Commission (SEC) to file or furnish financial statements, or does file or furnish financial statements (including voluntary filers), with the SEC (including other entities whose financial statements or financial information are required to be or are included in a filing).
2. It is required by the Securities Exchange Act of 1934 (the Act), as amended, or rules or regulations promulgated under the Act, to file or furnish financial statements with a regulatory agency other than the SEC.
3. It is required to file or furnish financial statements with a foreign or domestic regulatory agency in preparation for the sale of or for purposes of issuing securities that are not subject to contractual restrictions on transfer.
4. It has issued, or is a conduit bond obligor for, securities that are traded, listed, or quoted on an exchange or an over-the-counter market.
5. It has one or more securities that are not subject to contractual restrictions on transfer, and it is required by law, contract, or regulation to prepare U.S. GAAP financial statements (including footnotes) and make them publicly available on a periodic basis (for example, interim or annual periods). An entity must meet both of these conditions to meet this criterion.

An entity may meet the definition of a public business entity solely because its financial statements or financial information is included in another entity's filing with the SEC. In that case, the entity is only a public business entity for purposes of financial statements that are filed or furnished with the SEC.

Put Option. A contract that allows the holder to sell a specified quantity of stock to the writer of the contract at a fixed price during a given period.

Readily convertible to cash. Assets that are readily convertible to cash have both of the following:

1. Interchangeable (fungible) units
2. Quoted prices available in an active market that can rapidly absorb the quantity held by the entity without significantly affecting the price.

(Based on paragraph 83(a) of FASB Concepts Statement No. 5, *Recognition and Measurement in Financial Statements of Business Enterprises.*)

Regular-way security trades. Regular-way security trades are contracts that provide for delivery of a security within the period of time (after the trade date) generally established by regulations or conventions in the marketplace or exchange in which the transaction is being executed.

Remeasurement event. A remeasurement (new basis) event is an event identified in other authoritative accounting literature, other than the recognition of an other-than-temporary impairment, that requires a financial instrument to be remeasured to its fair value at the time of the event but does not require that financial instrument to be reported at fair value continually with the change in fair value recognized in earnings. Examples of remeasurement events are business combinations and significant modifications of debt as discussed in paragraph 470-50-40-6.

Spot rate. The exchange rate for immediate delivery of currencies exchanged.

Take-or-pay contract. Under a take-or-pay contract, an entity agrees to pay a specified price for a specified quantity of a product whether or not it takes delivery.

Trading. An activity involving securities sold in the near term and held for only a short period of time. The term trading contemplates a holding period generally measured in hours and days rather than months or years. See ASC 948-310-40-1 for clarification of the term trading for a mortgage banking entity.

Trading purposes. The determination of what constitutes trading purposes is based on the intent of the issuer or holder and shall be consistent with the definition of trading in ASC 320-10-25-1(A).

Underlying. A specified interest rate, security price, commodity price, foreign exchange rate, index of prices or rates, or other variable (including the occurrence or nonoccurrence of a specified event such as a scheduled payment under a contract). An underlying may be a price or rate of an asset or liability but is not the asset or liability itself. An underlying is a variable that, along with either a notional amount or a payment provision, determines the settlement of a derivative instrument.

Zero-coupon method. A swap valuation method that involves computing and summing the present value of each future net settlement that would be required by the contract terms if future spot interest rates match the forward rates implied by the current yield curve. The discount rates used are the spot interest rates implied by the current yield curve for hypothetical zero coupon bonds due on the date of each future net settlement on the swap.

CONCEPTS, RULES, AND EXAMPLES

Financial Instruments

Types of financial assets. The term "financial assets" encompasses a wide range of instruments including, but not limited to

Accounts receivable	General partnership interests
Beneficial interests in trusts	Limited partnership interests
Cash	LLC member interests
Certificates of deposit	Municipal bonds
Commercial paper	Mutual fund shares or units
Common and preferred stock	Notes and loans receivable
Corporate bonds	US Government securities

An unconditional contractual obligation whose economic benefit or sacrifice is to be the receipt or delivery of a financial instrument other than cash is to be considered a financial instrument. For example, a note that is payable in US Treasury bonds gives an issuer the contractual obligation to deliver and gives a holder the contractual right to receive bonds, not cash. But because the bonds represent obligations of the US Treasury to pay cash, they are considered financial instruments. Therefore, the note is also a financial instrument to both the holder of the note and the issuer of the note.

Another type of financial instrument is one that gives an entity the *contractual right* or obligation to exchange other financial instruments on *potentially* favorable or unfavorable terms. An example of this type of financial instrument would be a call option to purchase a specific US Treasury note for $100,000 in six months. The option *holder* has a contractual right, but not obligation, to exchange the financial instrument on potentially favorable terms. Six months later, if the fair value of the note exceeds $100,000, the holder will exercise the option because the terms are favorable (the option is now "in the money"). The *writer* of the call option has a contractual obligation to exchange financial instruments on potentially unfavorable terms if the holder exercises the option. The writer is normally compensated for accepting this obligation by being paid a premium, which it keeps whether or not the option is exercised.

A put option to sell a Treasury note has similar effects, although the change in fair values making it worthwhile to exercise the option will be a decline, rather than an increase. The holder of the put option, as with the call option, effectively has an unlimited profit potential and no risk of loss (the only sunk cost is the premium paid), whereas the writer of the option has unlimited risk of loss and only a fixed amount of income.

Options such as those discussed here, are derivative financial instruments because their value is derived from the value of the underlying. A bank's commitment to lend $100,000 to a customer at a fixed rate of 10% any time during the next six months at the customer's option is also a derivative financial instrument, since its value would vary as market interest rates change. It is an option, with the potential borrower being the holder and the bank being the writer (the parties are collectively referred to as the "counterparties").

An interest rate swap is a series of forward contracts to exchange, for example, fixed cash payments for variable cash receipts. The cash receipts are computed by multiplying a specified floating-rate market index by a notional amount of principal. An interest rate swap is both a contractual right and a contractual obligation of both counterparties.

Exclusions. Excluded from financial instrument classification are options and contracts that contain the right or obligation to exchange a financial instrument for a physical asset, such as bushels of wheat. For example, two entities enter a sale-purchase contract in which the purchaser agrees to take delivery of wheat or gold six months later and pay the seller $100,000 at the time of delivery. The contract is not a financial instrument because it requires the delivery of wheat or gold, which are not financial instruments.

Also excluded from financial instrument classification are contingent items that may ultimately require the payment of cash but that are not contractual. An example would be a contingent liability for tort judgments payable. However, when such an obligation becomes enforceable and is reduced to a fixed payment schedule, it then would be considered to be a financial instrument.

Derivative Financial Instruments

Derivative financial instruments are financial instruments whose fair value correlates to a specified benchmark, such as stock prices, interest rates, mortgage rates, currency rates, commodity prices, or some other agreed-upon reference (these are called "underlyings"). Option contracts and forward contracts are the two basic forms of derivatives, and they can be either publicly or privately traded. Forward contracts have symmetrical gain and loss characteristics—that is, they provide exposure to both losses and gains from market movements, although generally there is no initial premium to be paid. Forward contracts are usually settled on or near the delivery date by paying or receiving cash, rather than by physical delivery. On the other hand, option contracts have asymmetrical loss functions: They provide little or no exposure to losses (beyond the premium paid) from unfavorable market movements, but can provide large benefits from favorable market movements. Both forwards and options have legitimate roles to play in hedging programs, if properly understood and carefully managed.

Typical derivative financial instruments *include:*

1. Option contracts
2. Interest rate caps
3. Interest rate floors
4. Fixed-rate loan commitments
5. Note issuance facilities
6. Letters of credit
7. Forward contracts
8. Forward interest rate agreements
9. Interest rate collars
10. Futures
11. Swaps
12. Instruments with similar characteristics

Derivative financial instruments *exclude* all on-statement of financial position payables including:

1. Mortgage-backed securities
2. Interest-only obligations
3. Principal-only obligations
4. Indexed debt
5. Other optional characteristics incorporated within those receivables and payables (such as convertible bond conversion or call terms).

In addition, derivative financial instruments *exclude* contracts that either

1. Require exchange for a nonfinancial commodity or
2. Permit settlement by delivering a nonfinancial commodity.

Thus, most product (petroleum, grain, etc.) futures contracts would be excluded from the definition of derivative financial instrument, while swaps (if settled in cash) would be included.

As with other financial instruments, derivatives can be acquired either for investment purposes or for speculation. For enterprises which are not in the business of speculation, however, the typical purpose of derivative financial instrument is to manage risk, such as that associated with stock price movements, interest rate variations, currency fluctuations, and commodity price volatility. The parties involved tend to be brokerage firms, financial institutions, insurance companies, and large corporations, although any two or more entities of any size can hold or issue derivatives. Even small companies often engage in hedging, most commonly for risk arising from importing and exporting denominated in foreign currencies.

Derivative financial instrument are contracts which are intended to protect or hedge one or more of the parties from adverse movement in the underlying base, which can be a financial instrument position held by the entity or a commitment to acquire same at some future date, among others. These protections or hedges are rarely perfect and sometimes the hedge, once established, is later modified, even indirectly—such as by disposing of the underlying position while retaining the former hedge—so that the derivative financial instrument becomes in effect a speculative position. The derivative financial instruments themselves can become risky and, if leveraged, small adverse price or interest rate variations can produce significant losses.

The financial engineering efforts common in recent decades resulted in the creation of a wide range of derivatives, from easily understood interest rate swaps (exchanging variable- or floating-rate debt for fixed-rate debt) and interest rate caps (limiting exposure to rising interest rates) to such complicated "exotics" as structured notes, inverse floaters, and interest-only strips. At one time, most of these were not given formal statement of financial position recognition, resulting in great accounting risk (i.e., risk of loss in excess of amounts reported in the financial statements). Now, the FASB Codification includes extensive guidance on accounting for and reporting on derivatives and hedges.

ASC 815-10-55 addresses whether realized gains or losses on derivative contracts that are *not* held for trading purposes should be presented gross or net in the income statement irrespective of whether the derivative is designated as a hedging instrument.

It states that determining whether realized gains and losses on physically settled derivative contracts *not* held for trading purposes should be reported in the income statement on a gross or net basis is a matter of judgment that depends on the relevant facts and circumstances. Consideration of the facts and circumstances should be made in the context of the various activities of the entity, and not based solely on the terms of the individual contracts. For making an evaluation of the facts and circumstances in order to determine whether an arrangement should be reported on a gross or net basis, the economic substance of the transaction as well as the guidance set forth in ASC 845 relative to nonmonetary exchanges and the gross versus net reporting indicators provided in ASC 605-45 may be considered. The economic substance of the transaction should be given precedence over its legal form.

Accounting for Derivatives and Hedging Transactions per ASC 815: An Overview

ASC 815 requires standardized accounting and reporting for all derivative instruments (including derivatives which are embedded in other instruments) and for hedging activities.

Underlying principles. There are four key principles underlying ASC 815:

1. Derivative instruments are assets and liabilities and must be recognized on the financial statements.
2. Report derivatives are to be reported at fair value.
3. Gains and losses from derivative instruments are to be reported immediately in income.
4. Only designated qualifying items that are effectively offset by changes in fair value or cash flows during the term of the hedge are eligible to use the special accounting for hedging. Gains and losses on hedges are reported based on the type of hedge.

Derivative instruments represent rights and obligations, and these must be reported as assets and liabilities at fair value (which reflects the current cash equivalent). Gains and losses on derivative instruments not designated as hedges are recognized in earnings (or as a change in net assets, in the case of not-for-profit enterprises). The ability to apply hedge accounting requires that specified criteria be met, because of its elective nature and because of its reliance on management intent. Strategic risk hedges do not meet the qualifying criteria. Thus, hedge accounting is limited to relationships involving derivative instruments and certain foreign currency-denominated instruments that are designated as hedges and meet the qualifying criteria.

ASC 815-15, *Embedded Derivatives*

A reporting entity is not allowed to circumvent the requirements of ASC 815 recognition and measurement by embedding a derivative instrument in another contract. If these embedded derivative instruments would otherwise be subject to ASC 815, they are included in its scope.

Embedded derivative instruments are defined as explicit or implicit terms affecting

1. the cash flows or
2. the value of other exchanges required by contract in a way similar to a derivative instrument (one or more underlying can modify the cash flows or exchanges).

An embedded derivative instrument must be separated from the host contract and accounted for separately as a derivative instrument by both parties if, and only if, *all* three following criteria are met:

1. Risks and economic characteristics are not clearly and closely related to those of the host contract;
2. The hybrid instrument is not required to be measured at fair value under GAAP with changes reported in earnings; and
3. A separate instrument with the same terms as the embedded derivative instrument would be accounted for as a derivative instrument. For this condition, the initial net investment of the hybrid instrument is not the same as that for the embedded derivative instrument.

These three conditions for the separate accounting for embedded derivatives are explained in the following paragraphs.

Risks and economic characteristics are not clearly and closely related to those of the host contract. If the underlying is an interest rate or interest rate index that changes the net interest payments of an interest-bearing contract, it is considered clearly and closely related unless one of the following conditions exist:

1. The hybrid instrument can be settled contractually in a manner that permits any possibility whatsoever that the investor would not recover substantially all of the initial recorded investment.
2. The embedded derivative instrument could under any possibility whatsoever:
   a. At least double the investor's initial rate of return (ROR) on the host contract and
   b. Could also result in a ROR at least twice the market return for a similar contract (same host contract terms and same debtor credit quality).

The date acquired (or incurred) is the assessment date for the existence of the above conditions. Thus, the issuer and an acquirer in a secondary market could account for the instrument differently because of different points in time.

Example of embedded instruments which are separately accounted for. Assuming that the host contract is a debt instrument, the following are considered not to be clearly and closely related and would normally have to be separated out as embedded derivatives:

1. Interest rate indexes, floors, caps, and collars not meeting the criteria for exclusion (see number 2 in the next set of examples);
2. Leveraged inflation-indexed interest payments or rentals;
3. Calls and puts that do not accelerate repayment of the principal but require a cash settlement equal to the option price at date of exercise. Subsequently added options that cause one party to be exposed to performance or default risk by different parties for the embedded option than for the host contract;
4. Term extending options where there is no reset of interest rates;
5. Equity-indexed interest payments;
6. Commodity-indexed interest or principal payments;
7. A convertible debt conversion option for the investor if it qualifies as a derivative instrument (readily convertible to cash, etc.); and
8. A convertible preferred stock conversion option if the terms of the preferred stock (not the conversion option) are more similar to debt (a cumulative fixed rate with a mandatory redemption feature) than to equity (cumulative, participating, perpetual).

Example of embedded instruments which are *not* separately accounted for. Assuming that the host contract is a debt instrument, the following are considered to be clearly and closely related and would not normally have to be separated out as embedded derivative instruments:

1. Interest rate indexes (see below)
2. Interest rate floors, caps and collars, if at issuance:
   a. The cap is at or above the current market price (or rate) and/or
   b. The floor is at or below the current market price (or rate)
3. Nonleveraged inflation-indexed interest payments or rentals
4. Credit-sensitive payments (interest rate resets for debtor creditworthiness)
5. "Plain-vanilla" servicing rights not containing a separate embedded derivative instrument
6. Calls and puts that can accelerate repayment of principal unless
   a. The debt involves substantial premium or discount (zero coupon) and
   b. The call or put is only contingently exercisable (not exercisable unless default occurs) and is indexed only to credit risk or interest rates.
7. Term-extending options if the interest rate is concurrently reset to approximately the current market rate for the extended term and the host contract had no initial significant discount
8. Contingent rentals based on a variable interest rate.

Based on the foregoing, calls and puts embedded in equity instruments are normally accounted for as follows:

1. Investor—Both the call and the put are embedded derivative instruments.
2. Issuer—Only the put could be an embedded derivative instrument. The put and the call would not be embedded derivative instruments if they are both
   a. Indexed to the issuing entity's own stock and
   b. Classified in shareholders' equity.

The hybrid instrument is not required to be measured at fair value under GAAP with changes reported in earnings. For example, most unsettled foreign currency transactions are subject to ASC 830. Gains or losses are recognized in earnings and thus instruments of this nature are not considered embedded derivative instruments. Trading and available-for-sale securities that have cash flows denominated in a foreign currency also are not considered embedded derivative instruments.

A separate instrument with the same terms as the embedded derivative instrument would be accounted for as a derivative instrument. For this condition, the initial net investment of the hybrid instrument is not the same as that for the embedded derivative instrument.

To illustrate, a convertible debt conversion option for the issuer would not be an embedded derivative instrument since a separate option with the same terms would not be a derivative instrument because it is indexed to the issuer's own stock and would be classified in shareholders' equity.

To determine whether an instrument is indexed to an entity's own stock, the reporting entity is to use a two-step approach: Step 1 is to evaluate the instrument's contingent exercise provisions, if any; Step 2 is to evaluate the instrument's settlement provisions. An exercise contingency would not preclude an instrument (or embedded feature) from being considered indexed to an entity's own stock provided that it is not based on (1) an observable market, other than the market for the issuer's stock (if applicable), or (2) an observable index, other than an index calculated or measured solely by reference to the issuer's own operations (e.g., sales revenue of the issuer, EBITDA of the issuer, net income of the issuer, or total equity of the issuer). An instrument (or embedded feature) would be considered indexed to an entity's own stock if its settlement amount will equal the difference between the fair value of a fixed number of the entity's equity shares and a fixed monetary amount or a fixed amount of a debt instrument issued by the entity. An equity-linked financial instrument (or embedded feature) would not be considered indexed to the entity's own stock if the strike price is denominated in a currency other than the issuer's functional currency (including a conversion option embedded in a convertible debt instrument that is denominated in a currency other than the issuer's functional currency).

Freestanding financial instruments (and embedded features) for which the payoff to the counterparty is based, in whole or in part, on the stock of a consolidated subsidiary are not precluded from being considered indexed to the entity's own stock in the consolidated financial statements of the parent if the subsidiary is a substantive entity.

Another example of an embedded derivative determination situation would involve convertible preferred stock. A convertible preferred stock conversion option would not be an embedded derivative instrument if the terms of the preferred stock (not the conversion option) bear greater similarity to equity (e.g., cumulative, participating, perpetual) than to debt (i.e., a cumulative fixed rate with a mandatory redemption feature).

Interest-only strips and principal-only strips are specifically not subject to this standard assuming (1) the original financial instrument did not contain an embedded derivative instrument and (2) they don't incorporate any new terms from the original. In addition, foreign currency derivative instruments are specifically not separated from the host contract if (1) the currency of the primary economic environment is the functional currency of one of the parties or (2) the good or service price is routinely denominated in that currency in international commerce.

If an embedded derivative instrument is separated from the host, the accounting is as follows:

1. The embedded derivative instrument is accounted for based on ASC 815; and
2. The host contract is accounted for based on GAAP for that instrument, without the embedded derivative instrument.

If the embedded derivative instrument cannot be reliably identified and measured separately, the contract cannot be designated as a hedging instrument, and the entire contract must be measured at fair value with the gain or loss recognized in income.

The SEC's position, as articulated in ASC 815-10-S99, is that in performing an evaluation of an embedded derivative feature, the consideration of the economic characteristics and risks of the host contract should be based on all of the stated or implied substantive terms and features of the hybrid financial instrument. In evaluating the stated and implied substantive terms and features, the existence or omission of any single term or feature is not necessarily determinative of the economic characteristics and risks of the host contract (i.e., whether the nature of the host contract is more akin to a debt instrument or more akin to an equity instrument). Although the consideration of an individual term or feature may be weighted more heavily in the evaluation, judgment is required based upon an evaluation of all the relevant terms and features.

Hybrid financial instruments. By definition, financial instruments that contain embedded derivatives are known as hybrid financial instruments. ASC 815-15-25 simplifies the accounting hybrid financial instruments such as interest-only and principal-only strips by permitting fair value remeasurement for any hybrid financial instrument that contains an embedded derivative that otherwise would require bifurcation under ASC 815. ASC 815-15-25 narrows the scope exception for interest-only and principal-only strips on debt instruments to include only such strips representing rights to receive a specified portion of the contractual interest or principal cash flows.

Per ASC 815, if an embedded instrument requiring separation (because the close correlation criterion noted above is not met) from its host, but it cannot be reliably identified and measured, the entire contract must be measured at fair value. Upon recognition of a hybrid instrument that would otherwise require separation into a derivative and a host, the reporting entity may elect irrevocably to measure, on an instrument-by-instrument basis, the entire hybrid instrument at fair value. The changes in fair value are reported currently in earnings. Such an election must be supported either by concurrent documentation or by a preexisting documented policy supporting automatic election.

This fair value election is also available for remeasurement with respect to previously recognized financial instruments upon the occurrence of a business combination, a significant modification of debt, or other qualifying remeasurement event, where a new basis of accounting may be created.

Fair value measurements will often differ because they exclude transaction costs, which are included in many historical cost-based accounting entries. (For example, the fair value of stock just purchased on an exchange is lower than cost.) ASC 815 holds that any difference at inception of a recognized hybrid financial instrument for which the fair value election is applied and the transaction price is *not* to be included in current earnings (and thus is retained in the asset carrying amount) unless estimated fair value has been determined (1) from a quoted price in an active market, (2) from comparison to other observable current market transactions, or (3) using a valuation technique that incorporates observable market data.

According to ASC 815, the holder of an interest in securitized financial assets (other than holders of strips or related claims to cash flows) is to determine whether the interest is a freestanding derivative or contains an embedded derivative that would be required to be separated from the host contract and accounted for separately. That determination is to be based on an analysis of the contractual terms of the interest in securitized financial assets. This, in turn, requires understanding the nature and amount of assets, liabilities, and other financial instruments that constitute the complete securitization transaction. It is expected that the holder of an interest in securitized financial assets will obtain sufficient information about the payoff structure and the payment priority of the interest to make a determination about whether an embedded derivative exists.

Changes in cash flows that are attributable to changes in the creditworthiness of an interest resulting from securitized financial assets and liabilities (including derivative contracts) that represent the assets or liabilities that are held by the issuer are not to be considered an embedded derivative. The concentration of credit risk in the form of subordination of one financial instrument to another is also not to be considered an embedded derivative under the new standard.

ASC 815 requires statement of financial position segregation of those hybrid financial instruments that are being measured at fair value. This can be accomplished either by (1) the display of separate line items for fair value and non-fair value carrying amounts, or (2) parenthetical disclosure of fair value carrying amounts included in the aggregate of all carrying amounts. Also, disclosure must be made of the effect on earnings of changes in the fair value of recognized hybrid financial instruments.

ASC 815-20, Hedging Activities—General Requirements

Overview. While the standard requires that all derivatives be reported at fair value in the statement of financial position, the changes in fair value are reported in different ways depending on the nature and effectiveness of the hedging activities to which they are related, if held for hedging purposes. ASC 815 identifies changes in the fair values of derivatives as being the result of

1. effective hedging,
2. ineffective hedging, or
3. unrelated to hedging.

Furthermore, the hedging itself can be related to the fair value of an existing asset or liability or of a firm commitment, the cash flow associated with forecasted transactions, or foreign currency exposures.

After meeting specified conditions, a qualified derivative may be specifically designated as a total or partial (expressed as a percentage where the risk exposure profile is the same as that in the whole derivative) hedge of:

1. Changes in the fair value of:

   a. A recognized asset or liability, or
   b. An unrecognized firm commitment.

   In a fair value hedge, all gains and losses (of both the derivative instrument and the hedged item) are recognized in earnings in the period of change.

2. Variable cash flows of a forecasted transaction.

   In a cash flow hedge, the effective portion of the hedge is reported in other comprehensive income and is reclassified into earnings when the forecasted transaction affects earnings.

3. Foreign currency exposure of:

   a. A net investment in a foreign operation

      In a foreign currency net investment hedge, the gain or loss is reported in other comprehensive income as part of the cumulative translation adjustment to the extent that it is effective.

   b. An unrecognized firm commitment

      In a foreign currency unrecognized firm commitment hedge, the gain or loss is reported the same way as a fair value hedge (see category 1).

   c. An available-for-sale security

      In a foreign currency available-for-sale security hedge, the gain or loss is reported the same way as a fair value hedge (see category 1).

   d. A foreign currency-denominated forecasted transaction.

      In a foreign currency-denominated forecasted transaction hedge, the gain or loss is reported in the same way as a cash flow hedge (see category 2).

Hedge portions that are not effective are reported in earnings immediately.

A nonderivative financial instrument cannot generally be designated as a hedge. One exception, however, occurs when that instrument is denominated in a foreign currency and is designated as a hedge under 3a or 3b above. Not-for-profit enterprises cannot use hedge accounting for forecasted transactions.

Effectiveness—general observations. The method used for assessing the effective and ineffective portions of a hedge must be defined at the time of designation, must be used throughout the hedge period, and must be consistent with the approach used for managing risk. Similar hedges should usually be assessed for effectiveness in a similar manner unless a different method can be justified. If an improved method is identified and is to be applied prospectively to an existing hedge, that hedge must be discontinued. The new method can then be designated and a new hedge relationship can be established.

Factors to be included in the effectiveness assessment must be specified at inception. The effect of all excluded factors and ineffective amounts are to be included in earnings. For example, if an option contract hedge is assessed for effectiveness based on changes in the option's intrinsic value, the change due to the time value of the contract would be excluded from the effectiveness assessment, and that amount would be included in earnings. As another example, differences in key terms between the hedged item and the hedging instrument such as notional amounts, maturities, quantities, location, or delivery dates would cause ineffectiveness and that amount would be included in earnings.

ASC 815-25, Fair Value Hedges

The change in the fair value of an entire financial asset or liability for a period is computed as the fair value at the end of the period, adjusted to exclude changes in fair value (1) from payments received or made (partial recoveries or settlements) and (2) from the passage of time, minus the fair value at the beginning of the period.

Qualifications. To qualify as a fair value hedge, both the hedged items and the designated hedging instruments must meet all of the following criteria:

1. At the hedge's inception, formal documentation exists of the:

   a. Hedging relationship;
   b. Risk management objectives;
   c. Strategy for undertaking the hedge;

d. Identification of the hedged item, the hedging instrument, the nature of the risk being hedged, the method of assessing effectiveness and the components (if any) that are excluded (such as time value) from the effectiveness assessment; and the
e. Reasonable method to be used in recognizing in earnings the asset or liability representing the gain or loss in the case of a hedged firm commitment.

2. The hedging relationship is expected to be highly effective in producing offsetting fair value changes throughout the hedge period. This relationship must be assessed at least every three months and each time financial statements or earnings are reported.
3. If hedging with a written option, the combination must provide as much potential for gains from positive fair value changes as potential for losses from negative fair value changes. If a net premium is received, a combination of options is considered a written option. The combination of a written option and some other nonoption derivative is also considered a written option.

According to ASC 815, an asset or liability will be eligible for designation as a hedged item in a fair value hedge if the hedged item

1. is specifically identified as all or a specific portion of a recognized asset or liability, or an unrecognized firm commitment;
2. is exposed to fair value changes that are attributable to the hedged risk such that earnings would be affected; and
3. is not either remeasured at fair value for financial reporting purposes, or an equity-method investment, or an equity method or minority interest in a consolidated subsidiary, a firm commitment related to the foregoing, or an equity instrument issued by the entity.

Other limitations also apply, affecting held-to-maturity debt securities and nonfinancial assets.

More specifically, to be eligible for designation as a hedged item, an asset or liability must meet all of the following criteria:

1. The single item (or portfolio of similar items) must be specifically identified as hedging all or a specific portion.

   a. If similar items are aggregated and hedged, each item has to share the risk exposure that is being hedged (i.e. each individual item must respond in a generally proportionate manner to the change in fair value).
   b. A specific portion must be one of the following:

      (1) A percentage of the total asset, liability, or portfolio;
      (2) One or more selected contractual cash flows: for instance, the present value of the interest payments due in the first two years of a four-year debt instrument;
      (3) An embedded put, call, cap, or floor that does not qualify as an embedded derivative in an existing asset or liability; or
      (4) Residual value in a lessor's net investment in a sales-type or direct financing lease.

2. The item has an exposure to fair value changes that could affect earnings (this does not apply to not-for-profit enterprises).

3. The item is not
    a. Remeasured with changes reported currently in earnings; for example, a foreign currency-denominated item;
    b. An ASC 323 equity-method investment or an equity investment in a consolidated subsidiary;
    c. A minority interest;
    d. A firm commitment to enter into a business combination or to acquire or dispose of
        (1) A subsidiary;
        (2) A minority interest; or
        (3) An equity method investee; or
    e. An entity-issued equity interest classified in stockholders' equity.
4. The item is not a held-to-maturity debt security (or similar portfolio) unless the hedged risk is for something other than for fair value changes in market interest rates or foreign exchange rates; examples include hedges of fair value due to changes in the obligor's creditworthiness, and hedges of fair value due to changes in a prepayment option component.
5. If the item is a nonfinancial asset or liability (other than a recognized loan servicing right or a nonfinancial firm commitment with financial components), the designated hedged risk is the fair value change of the total hedged item (at its actual location, if applicable); ASC 815 stipulates that the price of a major ingredient cannot be used, and the price of a similar item at a different location cannot be used without adjustment.
6. If the item is a financial asset or liability, a recognized loan servicing right or a nonfinancial firm commitment with financial components, the designated hedge risk is the risk of changes in fair value from fair value changes in:
    a. The total hedged item;
    b. Market interest rates;
    c. Related foreign currency rates;
    d. The obligor's creditworthiness; or
    e. Two or more of the above, other than a.

Prepayment risk for a financial asset cannot be hedged, but an option component of a prepayable instrument can be designated as the hedged item in a fair value hedge. Embedded derivatives have to be considered also in designating hedges. For instance, in a hedge of interest rates, the effect of an embedded prepayment option must be considered in the designation of the hedge.

Reporting gains and losses from fair value hedges. The accounting for qualifying fair value hedges' gains and losses is as follows:

- On the hedging instrument, gains and losses are recognized in earnings.
- On the hedged item, gains and losses are recognized in earnings, even if they would normally be included in other comprehensive income if not hedged. For example, gains and losses on an available-for-sale security would be taken into income, if this is being hedged. The carrying amount of the hedged item is adjusted by the gains and losses resulting from the hedged risk.

Differences between the gains and losses on the hedged item and the hedging instrument are either due to amounts excluded from the assessment of hedging effectiveness, or are due to ineffectiveness. These gains and losses are to be recognized currently in earnings.

Example – Gains and losses on fair value hedges

An available-for-sale security carrying amount is adjusted by the amount resulting from the hedged risk, a fair value hedge.

Hedged item:	Available-for-sale security
Hedging instrument:	Put option
Underlying:	Price of the security
Notional amount:	100 shares of the security

On July 1, 20X1, Company XYZ purchased 100 shares of Widgetworks at a cost of $15 per share and classified it as an available-for-sale security. On October 1, 20X1, Company XYZ purchased for $350 an at-the-money put on Widgetworks with an exercise price of $25 and an expiration date of April 20X2. This put purchase locks in a profit of $650 ($1,000 spread in market price less $350 cost of the put), if the price stays at $25 or goes lower, but allows continued profitability if the price of the Widgetworks stock continues to go up. Company XYZ specifies that only the intrinsic value of the option is to be used to measure effectiveness. Thus, the time value decreases in the fair value of the put will be charged against the income of the period. Company XYZ then documents the hedge's strategy, objectives, hedging relationships, and method of measuring effectiveness. The following table shows the fair value of the hedged item and the hedging instrument.

Case 1

Hedged Item	*10/1/X1*	*12/31/X1*	*3/31/X2*	*4/17/X3*
Widgetworks share price	$ 25	$ 22	$ 20	$ 20
Number of shares	100	100	100	100
Total	$2,500	$2,200	$2,000	$2,000
Hedging Instrument				
Put option (100 shares)				
Intrinsic value	$ 0	$ 300	$ 500	$ 500
Time value	350	215	53	0
Total	$ 350	$ 515	$ 553	$ 500
Intrinsic Value Gain (Loss) on Put	$ 0	$ 300	$ 200	$ 0

Entries: Income Tax Effects and Transaction Costs Are Ignored

7/1/X1	Purchase:	Available-for-sale security	1,500	
		Cash		1,500
9/30/X1	End of Quarter:	Valuation allowance—available-for-sale security	1,000	
		Other comprehensive income		1,000
10/1/X1	Put Purchase:	Put option	350	
		Cash		350
		Case 1		
12/31/X1	End of Year:	Put option	300	
		Hedge gain (intrinsic value gain)		300
		Hedge loss	135	
		Put option (time value loss)		135
		Hedge loss	300	
		Valuation allowance—available-for-sale security (fair value loss)		300

Partial Statement of Financial Position
Effect of Hedging Relationships
December 31, 20X1
Dr (Cr)

Cash	$(1,850)
Available-for-sale securities	1,200
Plus: Valuation allowance	1,000
Put option	515
Other comprehensive income	(1,000)
Retained earnings	135

Entries

3/31/X2	End of Quarter:	Put option	200	
		Hedge gain (intrinsic value changes)		200
		Hedge loss	162	
		Put option (time value loss)		162
		Hedge loss	200	
		Available-for-sale security (fair value loss)		200
4/17/X2	Put Expires:	Put option	0	
		Hedge gain (intrinsic value changes)		0
		Hedge loss	53	
		Put option (time value changes)		53
		Hedge loss	0	
		Available-for-sale security (fair value changes)		0

Partial Statement of Financial Position
Effect of Hedging Relationships
April 17, 20X2 (Expiration of put)
Dr (Cr)

Cash	$(1,850)
Available-for-sale securities	1,500
Plus: Valuation allowance	500
Put option	500
Other comprehensive income	(1,000)
Retained earnings	350

At or before expiration, an in-the-money put must be sold or exercised. Assuming that it is sold, the entry would be

Cash	500	
Put option		500

On the other hand, if the put is exercised, the entry would be

Cash (exercise price)	2,500	
Other comprehensive income	1,000	
Available-for-sale security		1,500
Valuation allowance		500
Put option		500
Gain on sale		1,000

The net effect on retained earnings of the hedge and sale is a net gain of $650 ($1,000 – $350).

Case 2

Hedged Item	*10/1/X1*	*12/31/X1*	*3/31/X2*	*4/17/X2*
Widgetworks share price	$ 25	$ 28	$ 30	$ 31
Number of shares	100	100	100	100
Total	$2,500	$2,800	$3,000	$3,100
Hedging Instrument				
Put option (100 shares)				
Intrinsic value	$ 0	$ 0	$ 0	$ 0
Time value	350	100	25	0
Total	$ 350	$ 100	$ 25	$ 0
Intrinsic Value Gain (Loss) on Put	$ 0	$ 0	$ 0	$ 0

Entries: Income Tax Effects and Transaction Costs Are Ignored

7/1/X1	Purchase:	Available-for-sale security	1,500	
		Cash		1,500
9/30/X1	End of Quarter:	Valuation allowance—available-for-sale security	1,000	
		Other comprehensive income		1,000
10/1/X1	Put Purchase:	Put option	350	
		Cash		350
12/31/X1	End of Year:	Put option	0	
		Hedge gain (intrinsic value gain)		0
		Hedge loss	250	
		Put option (time value loss)		250
		Valuation allowance—available-for-sale security	300	
		Hedge gain (fair value gain)		300

Partial Statement of Financial Position
Effect of Hedging Relationships
December 31, 20X1
Dr (Cr)

Cash	$(1,850)
Available-for-sale securities	1,500
Plus: Valuation allowance	1,300
Put option	100
Other comprehensive income	(1,000)
Retained earnings	(50)

Entries

3/31/X2	End of Quarter:	Put option	0	
		Hedge gain (intrinsic value change)		0
		Hedge loss	75	
		Put option (time value loss)		75
		Valuation allowance—available-for-sale security	200	
		Hedge gain (fair value gain)		200
4/17/X2	Put Expires:	Put option	0	
		Hedge gain (intrinsic value change)		0
		Hedge loss	25	
		Put option (time value change)		25
		Valuation allowance—available-for-sale security	100	
		Hedge gain (fair value change)		100

Effect of Hedging Relationships
April 17, 20X2 (Expiration of put)
Dr (Cr)

Cash	$(1,850)
Available-for-sale securities	1,500
Plus: Valuation allowance	1,600
Put option	0
Other comprehensive income	(1,000)
Retained earnings	(250)

The put expired unexercised and Company XYZ must decide whether to sell the security. If it continues to hold, normal ASC 320 accounting would apply. If it continues to hold and a new put is purchased, the above example would be applicable again with the present position as a starting point. If the security is sold, the entry would be:

Cash (fair value)	3,100	
Other comprehensive income	1,000	
Available-for-sale security		1,500
Valuation allowance		1,600
Gain on sale		1,000

Measuring the effectiveness of fair value hedges. Although there are specific conditions applicable to the hedge type (fair value or cash flow), in general, the assumption of no ineffectiveness in a hedging relationship between an interest-bearing financial instrument and an interest rate swap (or a compound hedging instrument composed of an interest rate swap and a mirror-image call or put option) can be made if all of the following conditions are met:

1. The principal amount of the interest-bearing asset or liability being hedged and the notional amount of the swap match.
2. The fair value of the swap is zero at inception, if the hedging instrument is solely an interest rate swap. If the hedging instrument is a compound derivative containing the swap and a mirror-image call or put, the premium for the option must be paid or received in the same manner as the premium on the option embedded in the hedged item, and further conditions must be met depending on whether the premium on the option element of the hedged item was paid upon inception or over the life of the instrument.
3. The net settlements under the swap are computed the same way on each settlement date.
4. The financial instrument is not prepayable, but this criterion does not apply to an interest-bearing asset or liability that is prepayable only due to an embedded call option when the hedging instrument is a compound derivative composed of a swap and a mirror-image call option.
5. The terms are typical for those instruments and don't invalidate the assumption of effectiveness.
6. The maturity date of the instrument and the expiration date of the swap match.
7. No floor or ceiling on the variable interest rate of the swap exists.
8. The interval (three to six months or less) between repricings is frequent enough to assume the variable rate is a market rate.

The fixed rate on the hedged item is not required to exactly match the fixed rate on the swap. The fixed and variable rates on the swap can be changed by the same amount. As an example, a swap payment based on LIBOR and a swap receipt based on a fixed rate of 5% can be changed to a payment based on LIBOR plus 1% and a receipt based on 6%.

ASC 815 permits a "shortcut method" to compute fair value adjustments, which produces the same reporting results as when the method illustrated above has been applied. This shortcut is only appropriate for a fair value hedge of a fixed-rate asset or liability using an interest rate swap and only with the assumption of no ineffectiveness is appropriate (i.e., if the criteria above have been met). The FASB's decision to redefine interest rate risk (by permitting "benchmark rate" hedging in ASC 815-20-25) necessitated that it also address the effect on the shortcut method for fair value hedges and cash flow hedges. The steps in the shortcut method are as follows:

1. Determine the difference between the fixed rate to be received on the swap and the fixed rate to be paid on the bonds.
2. Combine that difference with the variable rate to be paid on the swap.
3. Compute and recognize interest expense using that combined rate and the fixed-rate liability's principal amount. (Amortization of any purchase premium or discount on the liability also must be considered, although that complication is not incorporated in this example.)
4. Determine the fair value of the interest rate swap.
5. Adjust the carrying amount of the swap to its fair value and adjust the carrying amount of the liability by an offsetting amount.

For fair value hedges, an assumption of no ineffectiveness is invalidated when the interest rate index embodied in the variable leg of the interest rate swap is different from the benchmark interest rate being hedged. In situations in which the interest rate index embodied in the variable leg of the swap has greater credit risk than that embodied in the benchmark interest rate, the effect of the change in the swap's credit sector spread over that in the benchmark interest rate would represent hedge ineffectiveness because it relates to an unhedged risk (credit risk) rather than to the hedged risk (interest rate risk).

In situations in which the interest rate index embodied in the variable leg of the swap has less credit risk than that embodied in the benchmark interest rate, the effect of the change in a certain portion of the hedged item's spread over the swap interest rate would also represent hedge ineffectiveness. For an entity to comply with an assumption of no ineffectiveness, the index on which the variable leg of the swap is based must match the benchmark interest rate designated as the interest rate risk being hedged for the hedging relationship.

Discontinuance of a fair value hedge. The accounting for a fair value hedge should not continue if any of the events below occur.

1. The criteria are no longer met;
2. The derivative instruments expire or are sold, terminated or exercised; or
3. The designation is removed.

If the fair value hedge is discontinued, a new hedging relationship may be designated with a different hedging instrument and/or a different hedged item, as long as the criteria established in ASC 815 are met.

Ineffectiveness of a fair value hedge. Unless the shortcut method is applicable, the reporting entity must assess the hedge's effectiveness at the inception of the hedge and at least every three months thereafter. In addition, ASC 815 requires that at the inception of the hedge the method to be used to assess hedge effectiveness must be identified. To comply, the reporting entity should decide which changes in the derivative's fair value will be considered in assessing the effectiveness of the hedge, and the method to be used to assess hedge effectiveness. Regarding the former, some derivative instruments (options) have two components: intrinsic value and time value. The intrinsic value of a call option is the excess, if any, of the market price over the strike or exercise price; the intrinsic value of an option recognizes that the price of the underlying item may move above the strike price (for a call) or below the strike price (for a put) during the exercise period. The enterprise elects to measure effectiveness either including or excluding time value; it must do so consistently once the designation is made.

Hedge effectiveness must be assessed in two different ways—in *prospective* considerations and in *retrospective* evaluations. ASC 815 provides flexibility in selecting the method the entity will use in assessing hedge effectiveness, but an entity should assess effectiveness for similar hedges in a similar manner and that the use of different methods for similar hedges should be justified.

Prospectively, the entity must, at both inception and on an ongoing basis, be able to justify an expectation that the relationship will he highly effective in achieving offsetting changes in fair value over future periods. That expectation can be based upon regression or other statistical analysis of past changes in fair values or on other relevant information. Retrospectively, the entity must, at least quarterly, determine whether the hedging relationship has been highly effective in having achieved offsetting changes in fair value through the date of periodic assessment. That assessment can also be based upon regression or other statistical analysis of past changes in fair values, as well as on other relevant information. If at inception the entity elects to use the same regression analysis approach for both prospective and retrospective effectiveness evaluations, then during the term of that hedging relationship those regression analysis calculations should generally incorporate the same number of data points. As an alternative to using regression or other statistical analysis, an entity could use the dollar-offset method to perform the retrospective evaluations of assessing hedge effectiveness.

ASC 815-20-25 addresses documentation of the method that is used to measure hedge ineffectiveness under ASC 815. ASC 815 implies that an entity must document, at inception of a hedge, the method that will be used to measure hedge ineffectiveness (in addition to the method to be used to assess effectiveness) in order to meet the documentation requirements of the standard. The FASB has stated that formal documentation is required, at the inception of a hedge, of the hedging relationship and the entity's risk management objective and strategy for undertaking the hedge, including identification of:

1. The hedging instrument,
2. The hedged item or transaction,
3. The nature of the risk being hedged,
4. The method that will be used to retrospectively and prospectively assess the hedging instrument's effectiveness, and
5. The method that will be used to measure hedge ineffectiveness.

Impairment considerations for hedging and hedged items. All assets or liabilities designated as fair value hedges are subject to the normal GAAP requirements for impairment assessment and, as needed, accounting adjustment. Those requirements are to be applied, however, only after the carrying amounts have been adjusted for the period's hedge accounting. Since the hedging instrument is a separate asset or liability, its fair value is not considered in applying the impairment criteria to the hedged item.

The hedged item is also, of course, subject to the requirement for impairment assessment. A fair value measurement represents the price at which a transaction would occur between market participants in an orderly transaction at the measurement date. The fair value is determined, as set forth by ASC 820-10, by using one of the following methods:

- Utilizing *quoted* prices in an active market (Level 1)
- Utilizing relevant *observable* inputs (Level 2)
- Utilizing significant *unobservable* inputs (Level 3).

ASC 820 stipulates that fair value represents the price at which an orderly transaction would take place between market participants. An orderly transaction is one that would not be characterized as a forced liquidation or distress sale. Thus, notwithstanding that there may be little or no market activity for an asset at the measurement date, the objective of determining fair value remains the identification of an exit price for the asset in question. Under reduced market activity conditions it would *neither* be appropriate to conclude that all market activity represents forced liquidations or distress sales, *nor* that any given transaction price is determinative of fair value.

Put another way, this admonition suggests that, in such circumstances, there may be a need to apply Level 3 measurements as described in ASC 820, if Level 1 (quoted prices) are absent or unreliable and Level 2 measures are similarly sparse or absent or no longer relevant. There would thus be a greater need to employ management's internal assumptions concerning future cash flows discounted at an appropriate risk-adjusted interest rate. When some Level 2 (observable) data is available but requires significant adjustment based on unobservable data, these should be considered to be Level 3 fair value measurements.

Example of applying fair value measurements in times of market inactivity or stress

Magna Financial holds as an investment a tranche of AA-rated mortgage-backed securities (MBS) that are collateralized by unguaranteed nonconforming residential mortgage loans. The fair value of this financial asset had heretofore been determined based on either (1) quoted prices in active markets for similar MBS (which constituted Level 2 inputs), or (2) quoted prices in inactive markets representing current transactions for the same or similar MBS not requiring significant adjustments (which were also Level 2 inputs).

As of year-end 20X1, the MBS market has grown inactive (as evidenced at first by a widening of the bid-asked spread, and subsequently by a decline in transaction volume). At the date of the statement of financial position, Magna Financial concludes that the markets for identical and similar MBS tranches are inactive. This determination was made by considering that (1) few transactions for the same MBS or similar tranches were presently observable, and (2) the few observable prices for such transactions exhibited substantial variations. Accordingly, valuation information available for Magna Financial's AA-rated MBS tranche was classified within Level 3 of the fair value hierarchy.

Magna Financial determined that use of a present value technique that would maximize the use of observable inputs (and would thus minimize the use of unobservable inputs) would be at least as representative of fair value as the market approach applied at earlier measurement dates. Specifically, Magna Financial decides to employ the "discount rate adjustment technique," under which the adjustment for risk inherent in the asset's contractual cash flows will be incorporated into the discount rate itself.

In determining the interest rate to be applied to the contractually obligated future cash flows as of year-end 20X1, Magna Financial takes into account (1) a 16% implied rate of return on the last date on which the market for an identical MBS was deemed active, and (2) the subsequent 1.5% (150 basis point) widening of credit spreads and the subsequent 4% (400 basis point) increase in liquidity risk premiums. Furthermore, Magna Financial will consider all available market information that could be obtained without due cost and effort, which in the present fact situation will include (1) previous quoted prices in markets for identical or similar MBS, (2) reports issued by analysts and rating agencies, (3) movements in relevant indexes, such as those gauging interest rates and credit risks, (4) data pertaining to the performance of the underlying mortgage loans (including delinquency and foreclosure rates, loss experience, and prepayment speeds), and

(5) two indicative (but nonbinding) broker quotes based on proprietary pricing models using Level 3 inputs, which implied rates of return of 20% and 24%, respectively.

Based on the foregoing facts, Magna Financial will be required to select an appropriate interest rate to apply in discounting the contractual cash flows of the MBS for the purpose of estimating fair value for this portfolio at year-end 20X1. Under the circumstances, Magna Financial determined that a 23% rate was to be used, as that was the result of evaluating and weighing the respective indications of the appropriate rate of the MBS tranche's return within a range of 21.5%–25.5%.The low end of the range is computed as follows:

16.0%	=	Implied rate of return as of the last date on which the market for identical MBS was active
1.5%	=	Subsequent widening of credit spreads (150 basis points)
4.0%	=	Subsequent increase in risk premiums (400 basis points)
21.5%	=	Low end of the range

The high end of the range is based on two nonbinding broker quotes that imply an average 25.5% rate of return (i.e., the average of the implied rates of 23% and 28%). Magna Financial believes that the range is reasonable and the 23% rate reflects the best estimate of the assumptions that would be made by market participants of the fair value at the measurement date and takes into account

1. nonperformance risk (consisting of both default and collateral value risks), and
2. liquidity risk (determined by the compensation a market participant would expect to receive for acquiring an asset that is difficult to sell under current market conditions).

In this instance, Magna Financial assigned slightly greater weight to its own estimate of fair value (the low end of the range, 21.5%) because

1. broker quotes were nonbinding and based on models using significant unobservable inputs, and
2. the entity was able to use market inputs relating to the performance of the underlying mortgage loans.

ASC 815-30, Cash Flow Hedges

The second major subset of hedging arrangements relate to uncertain future cash flows, as contrasted with hedged items engendering uncertain fair values. A derivative instrument may be designated as a hedge to the exposure of fluctuating expected future cash flows produced by a particular risk. The exposure may be connected with an existing asset or liability or with a forecasted transaction.

Qualifications. To qualify as a cash flow hedge, both the hedged items and the designated hedging instruments must meet all of the following criteria:

1. At the hedge's origin, formal documentation exists of the:
   a. Hedging relationship;
   b. Risk management objectives;
   c. Strategy for undertaking the hedge; and
   d. Identification of the hedged transaction, the hedging instrument, the nature of the hedged risk, the method of assessing effectiveness, and the components (if any) that are excluded (such as time value) from the effectiveness assessment.
2. Documentation must include:
   a. All relevant details;
   b. The specific nature of any asset or liability involved;
   c. When (date on or period within) a forecasted transaction is expected to occur; and

d. The expected currency amount (exact amount of foreign currency being hedged) or expected quantity (specific physical quantities such as number of items, weight, etc.) of a forecasted transaction. If a price risk is being hedged in a forecasted sale or purchase, the hedged transaction cannot

(1) Be specified solely in terms of expected currency amounts; or
(2) Be specified as a percentage of sales or purchases.

The current price of the transaction should be identified and the transaction should be described so that it is evident that a given transaction is or is not the hedged transaction. For instance, a forecasted sale of the first 2,000 units in January is proper, but the forecasted sale of the last 2,000 units is not because they cannot be identified when they occur—the month has to end before the last units sold can be identified.

3. The hedging relationship is expected to be highly effective in producing offsetting cash flows throughout the hedge period. This relationship must be assessed at least every three months and each time financial statements or earnings are reported.
4. If hedging with a written option, the combination must provide at least as much potential for positive cash flow changes as exposure to negative cash flow changes. A derivative that results from the combination of a written option and another non-option derivative is also considered a written option.
5. A link must be used to modify interest receipts or payments of a recognized financial asset or liability from one variable rate to another variable rate. It has to be between a designated asset (or group of similar assets) and a designated liability (or group of similar liabilities) and it has to be highly effective. A link occurs when the basis of one leg of an interest rate swap is the same as the basis of the interest rate receipt of a designated asset and the basis of the other leg of the swap is the same as the basis of the interest payments for a designated liability.

A nonderivative instrument cannot be designated as a hedging instrument for a cash flow hedge.

In addition to the above, to be eligible for designation as a cash flow hedge, a forecasted transaction must meet all of the following criteria:

1. The single transaction (or group of individual transactions) must be specifically identified. If individual transactions are grouped and hedged, each has to share the same risk exposure that is being hedged (i.e. each individual transaction must respond in a proportionate manner to the change in cash flow). Thus, a forecasted sale and a forecasted purchase cannot both be included in the same group of transactions.
2. The occurrence is probable.
3. It is a transaction with an external party (unless a foreign currency cash flow hedge) and it has an exposure to cash flow changes that could affect earnings.
4. The transaction is not to be remeasured under GAAP with changes reported in earnings; for example, foreign currency-denominated items would be excluded for this reason. Forecasted sales on credit and forecasted accrual of royalties on probable future sales are not considered the forecasted acquisition of a receivable. Also, if related to a recognized asset or liability, the asset or liability is not remeasured under GAAP with changes in fair value resulting from the hedged risk reported in earnings.
5. The item is not a held-to-maturity debt security (or similar portfolio) unless the hedged risk is for something other than for cash flow changes in market interest rates, as for example, in a hedge of cash flow changes due to an obligor's creditworthiness or default.

6. It does not involve:

    a. A business combination;
    b. A parent company's interest in consolidated subsidiaries;
    c. A minority interest;
    d. An equity-method investment; or
    e. An entity-issued equity interest classified in stockholders' equity.

7. If it involves a purchase or sale of a nonfinancial asset, the hedged risk is:

    a. The change in the functional-currency-equivalent cash flows resulting from changes in the related foreign currency rates; or
    b. The change in cash flows relating to the total hedged purchase or sales price (at its actual location, if applicable); for example, the price of a similar item at a different location cannot be used.

8. If it involves a purchase or sale of a financial asset or liability or the variable cash flow of an existing financial asset or liability, the hedged risk is the risk of changes in cash flow of:

    a. The total hedged item;
    b. Market interest rates;
    c. Related foreign currency rates;
    d. Obligor's creditworthiness or default; or
    e. Two or more of the above, other than a.

Prepayment risk for a financial asset cannot be hedged.

Gains and losses from cash flow hedges. The accounting for qualifying cash flow hedges' gains and losses is as follows:

1. The effective portion of the gain or loss on the derivative instrument is reported in other comprehensive income.
2. The ineffective portion of the gain or loss on the derivative instrument is reported in earnings.
3. Any component excluded from the computation of the effectiveness of the derivative instrument is reported in earnings.
4. Accumulated other comprehensive income from the hedged transaction should be adjusted to the lesser (in absolute amounts) of the following:

    a. The cumulative gain or loss on the derivative from the creation of the hedge minus any component excluded from the determination of hedge effectiveness and minus any amounts reclassified from accumulated other comprehensive income into earnings;
    b. The portion of the cumulative gain or loss on the derivative needed to offset the cumulative change in expected future cash flow on the transaction from the creation of the hedge minus any amounts reclassified from accumulated other comprehensive income into earnings.

    The adjustment of accumulated other comprehensive income should recognize in other comprehensive income either a part or all of the gain or loss on the adjustment of the derivative instrument to fair value.

5. Any remaining gain or loss is reported in earnings.

Reclassifications to earnings. In the period that the hedged forecasted transaction affects earnings, amounts in accumulated other comprehensive income should be reclassified into earnings. If the transaction results in an asset or liability, amounts in accumulated other comprehensive income should be reclassified into earnings when the asset or liability affects earnings through cost of sales, depreciation, interest expense, and the like. Any time that a net loss on the combined derivative instrument and the hedged transaction is expected, the amount that isn't expected to be recovered should immediately be reclassified into earnings.

Example of a "plain vanilla" interest rate swap

On July 1, 20X1, Abbott Corp. borrows $5 million with a fixed maturity (no prepayment option) of June 30, 20X5, carrying interest at prime + 1/2%. Interest only is due semiannually. At the same date, it enters into a "plain vanilla" type swap arrangement, calling for fixed payments at 8% and receipt of prime + 1/2%, on a notional amount of $5 million. At that date prime is 7.5%, and there is no premium due on the swap arrangement.

This swap qualifies as a cash flow hedge under ASC 815, and it is appropriate to assume no ineffectiveness, since the criteria set forth in that standard are all met.

NOTE: These criteria are that: the notional amount of the swap and the principal amount of the debt are equal; the fair value of the swap at inception is zero; the formula for computing net settlements under the swap is constant during its term; the debt may not be prepaid; all interest payments on the debt are designated as being hedged and no payments beyond the term of the swap are so designated; there is no floor or cap on the variable rate of the debt that is not likewise designated for the swap; the repricing dates of the swap match those of the variable rate debt; and the same index is designated for the hedging instrument and the underlying obligation.

Accordingly, as rates change over the term of the debt and of the swap arrangement, changes in the value of the swap are reflected in other comprehensive income, and the swap will appear on the statement of financial position as an asset or liability at fair value. As the maturity of the debt approaches, the value of the swap will converge on zero. Periodic interest expense in the income statement will be at the effective rate of 8%.

Assume that the prime rate over the four-year term of the loan, as of each interest payment date, is as follows, along with the fair value of the remaining term of the interest rate swap at those dates:

Date	*Prime rate (%)*	*Fair value of swap**
December 31, 20X1	6.5	$ – 150,051
June 30, 20X2	6.0	– 196,580
December 31, 20X2	6.5	– 111,296
June 30, 20X3	7.0	– 45,374
December 31, 20X3	7.5	0
Date	*Prime rate (%)*	*Fair value of swap**
June 30, 20X4	8.0	23,576
December 31, 20X4	8.5	24,038
June 30, 20X5	8.0	0

* *Fair values are determined as the present values of future cash flows resulting from expected interest rate differentials, based on the current prime rate, discounted at 8%.*

Regarding the fair values presented in the foregoing table, it should be assumed that the fair values are precisely equal to the present value, at each valuation date (assumed to be the interest payment dates), of the differential future cash flows resulting from utilization of the swap. Future variable interest rates (prime + 1/2%) are assumed to be the same as the existing rates at each valuation date (i.e., there is no basis for any expectation of rate changes, and therefore the best estimate is that the current rate will persist over time). The discount rate, 8%, is assumed to be constant over time.

Thus, for example, the fair value of the swap at December 31, 20X1, would be the present value of an annuity of seven payments (the number of remaining semiannual interest payments due) of $25,000 each (pay 8%, receive 7%, based on then-existing prime rate of 6.5%) to be made to the swap counterparty, discounted at an annual rate of 8% (using 4% for the semiannual discounting, which is a slight simplification). This computation yields a present value of a stream of seven $25,000 payments to the swap counterparty amounting to $150,051 at December 31, 20X1, which is a liability to be reported by the entity at that date. The offset is a debit to other comprehensive income, since the hedge is (presumably) judged to be 100% effective in this case. Semiannual accounting entries will be as follows:

December 31, 20X1

Interest expense	175,000	
Accrued interest (or cash)		175,000

To accrue or pay semiannual interest on the debt at the variable rate of prime + 1/2% (7.0%)

Interest expense	25,000	
Accrued interest (or cash)		25,000

To record net settlement on swap arrangement (8.0 – 7.0%)

Other comprehensive income	150,051	
Swap contract		150,051

To record the fair value of the swap contract as of this date (a net liability because fixed rate payable to counterparty of 8% exceeds floating rate receivable from counterparty of 7%)

June 30, 20X2

Interest expense	162,500	
Accrued interest (or cash)		162,500

To accrue or pay semiannual interest on the debt at the variable rate of prime + 1/2% (6.5%)

Interest expense	37,500	
Accrued interest (or cash)		37,500

To record net settlement on swap arrangement (8.0 – 6.5%)

Other comprehensive income	46,529	
Swap contract		46,529

To record the fair value of the swap contract as of this date (increase in obligation because of further decline in prime rate)

December 31, 20X2

Interest expense	175,000	
Accrued interest (or cash)		175,000

To accrue or pay semiannual interest on the debt at the variable rate of prime + 1/2% (7.0%)

Interest expense	25,000	
Accrued interest (or cash)		25,000

To record net settlement on swap arrangement (8.0 – 7.0%)

Other comprehensive income	150,051	
Swap contract		150,051

To record the fair value of the swap contract as of this date (decrease in obligation due to increase in prime rate)

June 30, 20X3

Interest expense	187,500	
Accrued interest (or cash)		187,500

To accrue or pay semiannual interest on the debt at the variable rate of prime + 1/2% (7.5%)

Interest expense	12,500	
Accrued interest (or cash)		12,500

To record net settlement on swap arrangement (8.0 – 7.5%)

Swap contract	65,922	
Other comprehensive income		65,922

To record the fair value of the swap contract as of this date (decrease in obligation due to further increase in prime rate)

December 31, 20X3

Interest expense	200,000	
Accrued interest (or cash)		200,000

To accrue or pay semiannual interest on the debt at the variable rate of prime + 1/2% (8.0%)

Interest expense	0	
Accrued interest (or cash)		0

To record net settlement on swap arrangement (8.0 – 8.0%)

Swap contract	45,374	
Other comprehensive income		45,374

To record the fair value of the swap contract as of this date (further increase in prime rate to the original rate of inception of the hedge eliminates fair value of the derivative)

June 30, 20X4

Interest expense	212,500	
Accrued interest (or cash)		212,500

To accrue or pay semiannual interest on the debt at the variable rate of prime + 1/2% (8.5%)

Receivable from counterparty (or cash)	12,500	
Interest expense		12,500

To record net settlement on swap arrangement (8.0 – 8.5%), counterparty remits settlement

Swap contract	23,576	
Other comprehensive income		23,576

To record the fair value of the swap contract as of this date (increase in prime rate creates net asset position for derivative)

December 31, 20X4

Interest expense	225,000	
Accrued interest (or cash)		225,000

To accrue or pay semiannual interest on the debt at the variable rate of prime + 1/2% (9.0%)

Receivable from counterparty (or cash)	25,000	
Interest expense		25,000

To record net settlement on swap arrangement (8.0 – 9.0%), counterparty remits settlement

Swap contract	462	
Other comprehensive income		462

To record the fair value of the swap contract as of this date (increase in asset value due to further rise in prime rate)

June 30, 20X5 (Maturity)

Interest expense	212,500	
Accrued interest (or cash)		212,500

To accrue or pay semiannual interest on the debt at the variable rate of prime + 1/2% (8.5%)

Receivable from counterparty (or cash)	12,500	
Interest expense		12,500
Other comprehensive income	24,038	
Swap contract		24,038

To record the fair value of the swap contract as of this date (value declines to zero as expiration date approaches)

Example of an option on an interest rate swap

The facts of this example are a variation on the previous example. Abbott Corp. anticipates as of June 30, 20X1, that as of June 30, 20X3, it will become a borrower of $5 million with a fixed maturity four years hence (June 30, 20X7). Based on its current credit rating, it expects to be able to borrow at prime + 1/2%. As of June 30, 20X1, it is able to purchase, for a single payment of $25,000, a "swaption" (an option on an interest rate swap), calling for fixed pay at 8% and variable receipt at prime + 1/2%, on a notional amount of $5 million, for a term of four years. The option will expire in two years. At June 30, 20X1, prime is 7.5%.

NOTE: The interest rate behavior in this example differs somewhat from the prior example, to better illustrate the "one-sidedness" of options, versus the obligation under a swap arrangement or other futures and forwards.

It will be assumed that the time value of the swaption expires ratably over the two years.

This swaption qualifies as a cash flow hedge under ASC 815. However, while the change in fair value of the contract is an effective hedge of the cash flow variability of the prospective debt issuance, the premium paid is a reflection of the time value of money and is thus to be expensed ratably over the period that the swaption is outstanding.

The table below gives the prime rate at semiannual intervals including the two-year period prior to the debt issuance, plus the four years during which the forecasted debt (and the swap, if the option is exercised) will be outstanding, as well as the fair value of the swaption (and later, the swap itself) at these points in time.

Date	Prime rate (%)	Fair value of swaption/swap*
December 31, 20X1	7.5	$ 0
June 30, 20X2	8.0	77,925
December 31, 20X2	6.5	0
June 30, 20X3	7.0	–84,159
December 31, 20X3	7.5	0
June 30, 20X4	8.0	65,527
December 31, 20X4	8.5	111,296
June 30, 20X5	8.0	45,374
December 31, 20X5	8.0	34,689
June 30, 20X6	7.5	0
December 31, 20X6	7.5	0
June 30, 20X7	7.0	0

* *Fair value is determined as the present value of future expected interest rate differentials, based on the current prime rate, discounted at 8%. An "out of the money" swaption is valued at zero, since the option does not have to be exercised. Since the option is exercised on June 30, 2014, the value at that date is recorded, although negative.*

The value of the swaption contract is only recorded (unless and until exercised, of course, at which point it becomes a contractually binding swap) if it is positive, since if "out of the money" the holder would forego exercise in most instances and thus there is no liability by the holder to be reported. (This example is an illustration of the opposite, however, as despite having a negative value, the option holder determines that exercise is advisable.) At June 30, 20X2, for example, the swaption is an asset, since the reference variable rate (prime + 1/2% or 8.5%) is greater than the fixed swap rate of 8%, and thus the expectation is that the option will be exercised at expiration. This would, if present rates hold steady, which is the naïve assumption, result in a series of eight semiannual payments from the swap counterparty in the amount of $12,500. Discounting this at a nominal 8%, the present value as of the debt origination date (to be June 30, 20X3) would be $84,159, which, when further discounted to June 30, 20X2, yields a fair value of $77,925.

Note that the following period (December 31, 20X2) prime drops to such an extent that the value of the swaption evaporates entirely (actually goes negative, which will not be reported since the holder is under no obligation to exercise it), and the carrying value is therefore eliminated. At expiration, the holder does (for this example) exercise, notwithstanding a negative fair value, and from that point forward the fair value of the swap will be reported, whether positive (an asset) or negative (a liability).

As noted above, assume that, at the option expiration date, despite the fact that prime + 1/2% is below the fixed pay rate on the swap, the management of Abbott Corp. is convinced that rates will climb over the four-year term of the loan, and thus exercises the swaption at that date. Accounting journal entries over the six years are as follows:

June 30, 20X1

Swaption contract	25,000	
Cash		25,000

To record purchase premium on swaption contract

December 31, 20X1

Loss on hedging transaction	6,250	
Swaption contract		6,250

To record change in time value of swaption contract—charge premium to income since this represents payment for time value of money, which expires ratably over two-year term

June 30, 20X2

Swaption contract	77,925	
Other comprehensive income		77,925

To record the fair value of the swaption contract as of this date

Loss on hedging transaction	6,250	
Swaption contract		6,250

To record change in time value of swaption contract—charge premium to income since this represents payment for time value of money, which expires ratably over two-year term

December 31, 20X2

Other comprehensive income	77,925	
Swaption contract		77,925

To record the change in fair value of the swaption contract as of this date; since contract is "out of the money," it is not written down below zero (i.e., a net liability is not reported)

Loss on hedging transaction	6,250	
Swaption contract		6,250

To record change in time value of swaption contract—charge premium to income since this represents payment for time value of money, which expires ratably over two-year term

June 30, 20X3

Other comprehensive	84,159	
Swap contract		84,159

To record the fair value of the swap contract as of this date—a net liability is reported since swap option was exercised

Loss on hedging transaction	6,250	
Swaption contract		6,250

To record change in time value of swaption contract—charge premium to income since this represents payment for time value of money, which expires ratably over two-year term

December 31, 20X3

Interest expense	200,000	
Accrued interest (or cash)		200,000

To accrue or pay interest on the debt at the variable rate of prime + 1/2% (8.0%)

Interest expense	0	
Accrued interest (or cash)		0

To record net settlement on swap arrangement (8.0 – 8.0%)

Swap contract	84,159	
Other comprehensive income		84,159

To record the change in the fair value of the swap contract as of this date

June 30, 20X4

Interest expense	212,500	
Accrued interest (or cash)		212,500

To accrue or pay interest on the debt at the variable rate of prime + 1/2% (8.5%)

Receivable from counterparty (or cash)	12,500	
Interest expense		12,500

To record net settlement on swap arrangement (8.0 – 8.5%)

Swap contract	65,527	
Other comprehensive income		65,527

To record the fair value of the swap contract as of this date

December 31, 20X4

Interest expense	225,000	
Accrued interest (or cash)		225,000

To accrue or pay interest on the debt at the variable rate of prime + 1/2% (9.0%)

Receivable from counterparty (or cash)	25,000	
Interest expense		25,000

To record net settlement on swap arrangement (8.0 – 9.0%)

Swap contract	45,769	
Other comprehensive income		45,769

To record the fair value of the swap contract as of this date

June 30, 20X5

Interest expense	212,500	
Accrued interest (or cash)		212,500

To accrue or pay interest on the debt at the variable rate of prime + 1/2% (8.5%)

Receivable from counterparty (or cash)	12,500	
Interest expense		12,500

To record net settlement on swap arrangement (8.0 – 8.5%)

Other comprehensive income	65,922	
Swap contract		65,922

To record the change in fair value of the swap contract as of this date (declining prime rate causes swap to lose value)

December 31, 20X5

Interest expense	212,500	
Accrued interest (or cash)		212,500

To accrue or pay interest on the debt at the variable rate of prime + 1/2% (8.5%)

Receivable from counterparty (or cash)	12,500	
Interest expense		12,500

To record net settlement on swap arrangement (8.0 – 8.5%)

Other comprehensive income	10,685	
Swap contract		10,685

To record the fair value of the swap contract as of this date (decline is due to passage of time, as the prime rate expectations have not changed from the earlier period)

June 30, 20X6

Interest expense	200,000	
Accrued interest (or cash)		200,000

To accrue or pay interest on the debt at the variable rate of prime + 1/2% (8.0%)

Receivable from counterparty (or cash)	0	
Interest expense		0

To record net settlement on swap arrangement (8.0 – 8.0%)

Other comprehensive income	34,689	
Swap contract		34,689

To record the decline in the fair value of the swap contract to zero as of this date

December 31, 20X6

Interest expense	200,000	
Accrued interest (or cash)		200,000

To accrue or pay interest on the debt at the variable rate of prime + 1/2% (8.0%)

Receivable from counterparty (or cash)	0	
Interest expense		0

To record net settlement on swap arrangement (8.0 – 8.0%)

Swap contract	0	
Other comprehensive income		0

No change to the zero fair value of the swap contract as of this date

June 30, 20X7 (Maturity)

Interest expense	187,500	
Accrued interest (or cash)		187,500

To accrue or pay interest on the debt at the variable rate of prime + 1/2% (7.5%)

Interest expense	12,500	
Accrued interest (or cash)		12,500

To record net settlement on swap arrangement (8.0 – 7.5%)

Other comprehensive income	0	
Swap contract		0

No change to the zero fair value of the swap contract, which expires as of this date

Effectiveness of cash flow hedges. The assumption of no ineffectiveness in a cash flow hedge between an interest-bearing financial instrument and an interest rate swap can be assumed if all of the following conditions are met:

1. The principal amount and the notional amount of the swap match;
2. The fair value of the swap is zero at origin;
3. The net settlements under the swap are computed the same way on each settlement date;
4. The financial instrument is not prepayable; and
5. The terms are typical for those instruments and don't invalidate the assumption of effectiveness.
6. All variable rate interest payments or receipts on the instrument during the swap term are designated as hedged and none beyond that term;
7. No floor or cap on the variable rate of the swap exists unless the variable rate instrument has one. If the instrument does, the swap must have a comparable (not necessarily equal) one;
8. Repricing dates match; and
9. The index base for the variable rates match.

The variable rate on the instrument is not required to exactly match the variable rate on the swap. The fixed and variable rates on the swap can be changed by the same amount.

Example of using options to hedge future purchase of inventory

Friendly Chemicals Corp. uses petroleum as a feedstock from which it produces a range of chemicals for sale to producers of synthetic fabrics and other consumer goods. It is concerned about the rising price of oil and decides to hedge a major purchase it plans to make in mid-20X1. Oil futures and options are traded on the New York Mercantile exchange and other markets; Friendly decides to use options rather than futures because it is only interested in protecting itself from a price increase; if prices decline, it wishes to reap that benefit rather than suffer the loss which would result from holding a futures contract in a declining market environment.

At December 31, 20X1, Friendly projects a need for 10 million barrels of crude oil of a defined grade to be purchased by mid-20X2; this will suffice for production through mid-20X3. The current world price for this grade of crude is $164.50 per barrel, but prices have been rising recently. Management desires to limit its crude oil costs to no higher than $165.75 per barrel, and accordingly purchases, at a cost of $2 million, an option to purchase up to 10 million barrels at a cost of $165.55 per barrel (which, when added to the option premium, would make the total cost $165.75 per barrel if the full 10 million barrels are acquired), at any time through December 20X2.

Management has studied the behavior of option prices and has concluded that changes in option prices which relate to time value are not correlated to price changes and hence are ineffective in hedging price changes. On the other hand, changes in option prices which pertain to pricing changes (intrinsic value changes) are highly effective as hedging vehicles. The table below reports the value of these options, analyzed in terms of time value and intrinsic value, over the period from December 2012 through December 20X2.

	Price of	Fair value of option relating to	
Date	oil/barrel	Time value*	Intrinsic value
December 31, 20X1	$164.50	$2,000,000	$ 0
January 31, 20X2	164.90	1,900,000	0
February 28, 20X2	165.30	1,800,000	0
March 31, 20X2	165.80	1,700,000	2,500,000
April 30, 20X2	166.00	1,600,000	4,500,000
May 31, 20X2	165.85	1,500,000	3,000,000
June 30, 20X2**	166.00	700,000	2,250,000
July 31, 20X2	165.60	650,000	250,000
August 31, 20X2	165.50	600,000	0
September 30, 20X2	165.75	550,000	1,000,000
October 31, 20X2	165.80	500,000	1,250,000
November 30, 20X2	165.85	450,000	1,500,000
December 31, 20X2***	165.90	400,000	1,750,000

* *This example does not address how the time value of options would be computed in practice.*
** *Options for 5 million barrels exercised; remainder held until end of December, then sold.*
*** *Values cited are immediately prior to sale of remaining options.*

At the end of June 20X2, Friendly Chemicals exercises options for 5 million barrels, paying $165.55 per barrel for oil selling on the world markets for $166.00 each. It holds the remaining options until December, when it sells these for an aggregate price of $2.1 million, a slight discount to the nominal fair value at that date.

The inventory acquired in mid-20X2 is processed and included in goods available for sale. Sales of these goods, in terms of the 5 million barrels of crude oil that were consumed in their production, are as follows:

Date	Equivalent barrels sold in month	Equivalent barrels on hand at month end
June 30, 20X2	300,000	4,700,000
July 31, 20X2	250,000	4,450,000
August 31, 20X2	400,000	4,050,000
September 30, 20X2	350,000	3,700,000
October 31, 20X2	550,000	3,150,000
November 30, 20X2	500,000	2,650,000
December 31, 20X2	650,000	2,000,000

Based on the foregoing facts, the journal entries prepared on a monthly basis (for illustrative purposes) for the period December 20X1 through December 20X2 are as follows:

December 31, 20X1

Option contract	2,000,000	
Cash		2,000,000

To record purchase premium on option contract for up to 10 million barrels of oil at price of $165.55 per barrel

January 31, 20X2

Loss on hedging transaction	100,000	
Option contract		100,000

To record change in time value of option contract—charge premium to income since this represents payment for time value of money, which expires ratably over two-year term and does not qualify for hedge accounting treatment

Option contract	0	
Other comprehensive income		0

To reflect change in intrinsic value of option contracts (no value at this date)

February 28, 20X2

Loss on hedging transaction	100,000	
Option contract		100,000

To record change in time value of option contract—charge premium to income since this represents payment for time value of money, which expires ratably over two-year term and does not qualify for hedge accounting treatment

Option contract	0	
Other comprehensive income		0

To reflect change in intrinsic value of option contracts (no value at this date)

March 31, 20X2

Loss on hedging transaction	100,000	
Option contract		100,000

To record change in time value of option contract—charge premium to income since this represents payment for time value of money, which expires ratably over two-year term and does not qualify for hedge accounting treatment

Option contract	2,500,000	
Other comprehensive income		2,500,000

To reflect change in intrinsic value of option contracts

April 30, 20X2

Loss on hedging transaction	100,000	
Option contract		100,000

To record change in time value of option contract—charge premium to income since this represents payment for time value of money, which expires ratably over two-year term and does not qualify for hedge accounting treatment

Option contract	2,000,000	
Other comprehensive income		2,000,000

To reflect change in intrinsic value of option contracts (further increase in value)

May 31, 20X2

Loss on hedging transaction	100,000	
Option contract		100,000

To record change in time value of option contract—charge premium to income since this represents payment for time value of money, which expires ratably over two-year term and does not qualify for hedge accounting treatment

Other comprehensive income	1,500,000	
Option contract		1,500,000

To reflect change in intrinsic value of option contracts (decline in value)

June 30, 20X2

Loss on hedging transaction	800,000	
Option contract		800,000

To record change in time value of option contract—charge premium to income since this represents payment for time value of money, which expires ratably over two-year term and does not qualify for hedge accounting treatment; since one-half the options were exercised in June, the remaining unexpensed time value of that portion is also entirely written off at this time

Option contract	1,500,000	
Other comprehensive income		1,500,000

To reflect change in intrinsic value of option contracts (further increase in value) before accounting for exercise of options on 5 million barrels

June 30 intrinsic value of options before exercise	4,500,000
Allocation to oil purchased at $165.55	2,250,000
Remaining intrinsic value of option	2,250,000

The allocation to exercised options will be maintained in other comprehensive income until transferred to cost of goods sold as a contra cost, as the 5 million barrels are sold, at the rate of 45¢ per equivalent barrel ($166.00 – $165.55).

Inventory	827,750,000	
Cash (or accounts payable)		827,750,000

To record purchase of 5 million barrels of oil at option price of $165.55/barrel

Inventory	2,250,000	
Option contract		2,250,000

To increase the recorded value of the inventory to include the fair value of options given up (exercised) in acquiring the oil (taken together, the cash purchase price and the fair value of options surrendered add to $166 per barrel, the world market price at date of purchase)

Cost of goods sold	49,800,000	
Inventory		49,800,000

To record cost of goods sold (300,000 barrels at $166) before amortizing deferred hedging gain in other comprehensive income

Other comprehensive income	135,000	
Cost of goods sold		135,000

To amortize deferred hedging gain at rate of 45¢ per barrel sold

July 31, 20X2

Loss on hedging transaction	50,000	
Option contract		50,000

To record change in time value of option contract—charge premium to income since this represents payment for time value of money, which expires ratably over two-year term, and does not qualify for hedge accounting treatment

Other comprehensive income	2,000,000	
Option contract		2,000,000

To reflect change in intrinsic value of remaining option contracts (decline in value)

Cost of goods sold	41,500,000	
Inventory		41,500,000

To record cost of goods sold (250,000 barrels at $166) before amortizing deferred hedging gain in other comprehensive income

Other comprehensive income	112,500	
Cost of goods sold		112,500

To amortize deferred hedging gain at rate of 45¢ per barrel sold

August 31, 20X2

Loss on hedging transaction	50,000	
Option contract		50,000

To record change in time value of option contract—charge premium to income since this represents payment for time value of money, which expires ratably over two-year term, and does not qualify for hedge accounting treatment

Other comprehensive income	250,000	
Option contract		250,000

To reflect change in intrinsic value of remaining option contracts (decline in value to zero)

Cost of goods sold	66,400,000	
Inventory		66,400,000

To record cost of goods sold (400,000 barrels at $166) before amortizing deferred hedging gain in other comprehensive income

Other comprehensive income	180,000	
Cost of goods sold		180,000

To amortize deferred hedging gain at rate of 45¢ per barrel sold

September 30, 20X2

Loss on hedging transaction	50,000	
Option contract		50,000

To record change in time value of option contract—charge premium to income since this represents payment for time value of money, which expires ratably over two-year term, and does not qualify for hedge accounting treatment

Option contract	1,000,000	
Other comprehensive income		1,000,000

To reflect change in intrinsic value of remaining option contracts (increase in value)

Cost of goods sold	58,100,000	
Inventory		58,100,000

To record cost of goods sold (350,000 barrels at $166) before amortizing deferred hedging gain in other comprehensive income

Other comprehensive income	157,500	
Cost of goods sold		157,500

To amortize deferred hedging gain at rate of 45¢ per barrel sold

October 31, 20X2

Loss on hedging transaction	50,000	
Option contract		50,000

To record change in time value of option contract—charge premium to income since this represents payment for time value of money, which expires ratably over two-year term, and does not qualify for hedge accounting treatment

Option contract	250,000	
Other comprehensive income		250,000

To reflect change in intrinsic value of remaining option contracts (further increase in value)

Cost of goods sold	91,300,000	
Inventory		91,300,000

To record cost of goods sold (550,000 barrels at $166) before amortizing deferred hedging gain in other comprehensive income

Other comprehensive income	247,500	
Cost of goods sold		247,500

To amortize deferred hedging gain at rate of 45¢ per barrel sold

November 30, 20X2

Loss on hedging transaction	50,000	
Option contract		50,000

To record change in time value of option contract—charge premium to income since this represents payment for time value of money, which expires ratably over two-year term, and does not qualify for hedge accounting treatment

Option contract	250,000	
Other comprehensive income		250,000

To reflect change in intrinsic value of remaining option contracts (further increase in value)

Cost of goods sold	83,000,000	
Inventory		83,000,000

To record cost of goods sold (500,000 barrels at $166) before amortizing deferred hedging gain in other comprehensive income

Other comprehensive income	225,000	
Cost of goods sold		225,000

To amortize deferred hedging gain at rate of 45¢ per barrel sold

December 31, 20X2

Loss on hedging transaction	50,000	
Option contract		50,000

To record change in time value of option contract—charge premium to income since this represents payment for time value of money, which expires ratably over two-year term, and does not qualify for hedge accounting treatment

Option contract	250,000	
Other comprehensive income		250,000

To reflect change in intrinsic value of remaining option contracts (further increase in value) before sale of options

Cost of goods sold	107,900,000	
Inventory		107,900,000

To record cost of goods sold (650,000 barrels at $166) before amortizing deferred hedging gain in other comprehensive income

Other comprehensive income	292,500	
Cost of goods sold		292,500

To amortize deferred hedging gain at rate of 45¢ per barrel sold

Cash	2,100,000	
Loss on sale of options	50,000	
Option contract		2,150,000
Other comprehensive income	1,750,000	
Gain on sale of options		1,750,000

To record sale of remaining option contracts; the cash price was $50,000 lower than carrying value of asset sold (options having unexpired time value of $400,000 plus intrinsic value of $1,750,000), but transfer of other comprehensive income to income recognizes formerly deferred gain; since no further inventory purchases are planned in connection with this hedging activity, the unrealized gain is taken into income

Note that at December 31, 20X2, other comprehensive income has a remaining credit balance of $900,000, which represents the deferred gain pertaining to the 2 million equivalent barrels of oil in inventory. As this is sold, the other comprehensive income will be transferred to cost of goods sold as a reduction of cost of sales.

Discontinuance of a cash flow hedge. The accounting for a cash flow hedge should not continue if any of the events below occur.

1. The criteria are no longer met;
2. The derivative instrument expires or is sold, terminated or exercised; or
3. The designation is removed by management.

The net gain or loss in accumulated other comprehensive income should remain there until it is properly reclassified when the hedged transaction affects earnings. If it is probable that the original forecasted transactions won't occur, the net gain or loss in accumulated other comprehensive income should immediately be reclassified into earnings.

If the cash flow hedge is discontinued, a new hedging relationship may be designated with a different hedging instrument and/or a different hedged item, as long as the criteria established in ASC 815 are met.

Ineffectiveness of a cash flow hedge. In assessing the effectiveness of a cash flow hedge, the time value of money generally will need to be considered, if significant in the circumstances. Doing so becomes especially important if the hedging instrument involves periodic cash settlements. For example, a *tailing strategy* with futures contracts is a situation in which an entity likely would reflect the time value of money. When employing such a strategy, the entity adjusts the size or contract amount of futures contracts used in a hedge so that earnings (or expense) from reinvestment (or funding) of daily settlement gains (or losses) on the futures do not distort the results of the hedge. To assess offset of expected cash flows when a tailing strategy has been used, an entity could reflect the time value of money, possibly comparing the present value of the hedged forecasted cash flow with the results of the hedging instrument.

Impairment. All assets or liabilities designated as cash flow hedges are subject to normal GAAP requirements for impairment. Those requirements are to be applied, however, after hedge accounting has been applied for the period. Since the hedging instrument is a separate asset or liability, its expected cash flow or fair value is not considered in applying the impairment criteria to the hedged item. If an impairment loss or recovery on a hedged forecasting asset or liability is recognized, any offsetting amount should be immediately reclassified from accumulated other comprehensive income into earnings.

Expanded application of interest rate hedging. ASC 815 also permits the use of hedge accounting where the interest rate being hedged is the "benchmark interest rate." As used in the standard, this rate will be either the risk-free rate (i.e., that applicable to direct Treasury borrowings – UST), the LIBOR swap rate, or the OIS. LIBOR-based swaps are the most commonly employed interest rate hedging vehicles.

The FASB has concluded that, with respect to the separation of interest rate risk and credit risk, the risk of changes in credit sector spread and any credit spread attributable to a specific borrower should be encompassed in credit risk rather than interest rate risk. Under such an approach, an entity would be permitted to designate the risk of changes in the risk-free rate as the hedged risk, and any spread above that rate would be deemed to reflect credit risk.

ASC 815 requires that all contractual cash flows be used in determining the changes in fair value of the hedged item when benchmark interest rates are being employed. In other words, cash flows pertaining to the portion of interest payments which is related to the entity's credit risk (the risk premium over the benchmark rate) cannot be excluded from the computation.

The accounting for an interest rate hedge using a benchmark rate is very similar to that illustrated previously in this chapter. However, the variable rate used, rather than reflecting the credit riskiness of the party doing the hedging (which was prime + 1/2% in that illustration), would instead be the benchmark rate (e.g., the rate on Treasury five-year notes). Since changes in the benchmark rate might not exactly track the changes in the underlying instrument (due to changes in the "credit spread" which are a reflection of changes in the underlying party's perceived credit risk), the hedge will likely be imperfect, such that a net gain or loss will be reflected in periodic earnings.

Foreign Currency Hedges

The FASB's basic objectives in hedge accounting for foreign currency exposure are:

1. To continue to permit the hedge accounting required under ASC 830; and
2. To increase the consistency of accounting guidance by broadening the scope of hedges eligible for this treatment.

Unlike ASC 830, this standard allows hedges of forecasted foreign currency transactions, including some intercompany transactions. Hedging foreign currency intercompany cash flows with foreign currency options is a common practice and was permitted under prior GAAP. ASC 815 modified that accounting rule to permit using other derivative instruments (forward contracts, etc.), on the grounds that the accounting for all derivative instruments should be the same.

Designated hedging instruments and hedged items qualify for fair value hedge accounting and cash flow hedge accounting only if all of the criteria in ASC 815 for fair value hedge accounting and cash flow hedge accounting are met. The FASB concluded that fair value hedges could be used for all recognized foreign currency-denominated asset or liability hedging situations and that cash flow hedges could be used for recognized foreign currency-denominated asset or liability hedging situations in which all of the variability in the functional currency-equivalent cash flows are eliminated by the effect of the hedge. Remeasurement of the foreign currency-denominated assets and liabilities will continue to be based on the guidance in ASC 830, which requires remeasurement based on spot exchange rates, regardless of whether a fair value hedging relationship or a cash flow hedging relationship exists.

Foreign currency net investment hedge. Either a derivative instrument or a nonderivative financial instrument (that can result in a foreign currency transaction gain or loss under ASC 830) can be designated as a hedge of a foreign currency exposure of a net investment in a foreign operation. The gain or loss from the designated instrument to the extent that it is effective is reported as a translation adjustment. The hedged net investment is accounted for under ASC 830.

Example of a foreign currency net investment hedge

Auburn Corporation has invested $15 million in a subsidiary in Germany, and for which the euro is the functional currency. The initial exchange rate is €1.2:$1, so the initial investment is worth €18,000,000. Auburn issues a debt instrument for €12 million and designates it as a hedge of the German investment. Auburn's strategy is that any change in the fair value of the loan attributable to foreign exchange risk should offset any translation gain or loss on 2/3 of Auburn's German investment.

At the end of the year, the exchange rate changes to €0.8:$1. Auburn uses the following calculation to determine the translation gain on its net investment:

€18,000,000/$0.8 = $22,500,000 less €18,000,000/$1.2 = $15,000,000 = $7,500,000

Auburn uses the following calculation to determine the translation loss on its euro-denominated debt:

€12,000,000/$0.8 = $15,000,000 less €12,000,000/$1.2 = $10,000,000 = $5,000,000

Auburn creates the following entries to record changes in the value of the translation gain on its investment and translation loss in its debt, respectively:

Investment in subsidiary	7,500,000	
Cumulative translation adjustment (equity)		7,500,000
Cumulative translation adjustment (equity)	5,000,000	
Euro-denominated debt		5,000,000

The net effect of these translation adjustments is a net increase in Auburn's investment of $2,500,000. In the following year, the exchange rates do not change, and Auburn sells its subsidiary for $17.5 million. Auburn's tax rate is 30%. Its reported annual gains and losses follow:

	Year 1	*Year 2*
Net income:		
Gain on sale of investment in ABC Company		$2,500,000
Income tax expense		(750,000)
Net gain realized in net income		1,750,000
Other comprehensive income:		
Foreign currency translation adjustment, net of tax	$1,750,000	
Reclassification adjustment, net of tax		(1,750,000)
Other comprehensive income net gain/(loss)	$1,750,000	$(1,750,000)

Foreign currency unrecognized firm commitment hedge. Either a derivative instrument or a nonderivative financial instrument (that can result in a foreign currency transaction gain or loss under ASC 830) can be designated as a fair value hedge of an unrecognized firm commitment (or a specific portion) attributable to foreign currency. If the criteria are met, this hedging relationship is accounted for as a fair value hedge.

Foreign currency available-for-sale security hedge. Only a derivative instrument can be designated as a fair value hedge of an available-for-sale debt security (or a specific portion) attributable to foreign currency. If the criteria are met, this hedging relationship is accounted for as a fair value hedge. For an available-for-sale equity security to be accounted for as a fair value hedge, it must meet all of the fair value hedge criteria and the following two requirements:

1. The security cannot be traded on an exchange (or similar marketplace) denominated in the investor's functional currency; and
2. Dividends (or other cash flows) to the holders must be denominated in the same foreign currency as that expected to be received upon the sale of the security.

If the available-for-sale equity security qualifies as a foreign currency hedge, the change in fair value from foreign exchange risk is reported in earnings and not in other comprehensive income.

Any gain or loss on a designated nonderivative hedging instrument from foreign currency risk is determined under ASC 830 (as the increase or decrease in functional currency cash flows produced by the change in spot exchange rates) and is reported in earnings along with the change in the carrying amount of the hedged firm commitment.

Foreign currency-denominated forecasted transaction. Only a derivative instrument can be designated as a cash flow hedge of a foreign currency-denominated forecasted transaction. The parties to this transaction can either be external or intercompany. To qualify for hedge accounting, all of the following criteria must be met:

1. An operating unit with foreign currency exposure is a party to the derivative instrument;
2. The transaction is denominated in a currency that is not the functional currency;
3. All of the criteria for a cash flow hedge are met (with the possible exception of allowing a qualifying intercompany transaction); and
4. If a group of individual transactions is involved, both an inflow and an outflow of foreign currency cannot be included in the same group.

If the foregoing criteria are met, this hedging relationship is accounted for as a cash flow hedge.

Using certain intercompany derivatives as hedging instruments in cash flow hedges of foreign currency risk in the consolidated financial statements. ASC 815 permits the use of intercompany derivatives as the hedging instruments in cash flow hedges of foreign currency risk in the consolidated financial statements, if those intercompany derivatives are offset by unrelated third-party contracts on a net basis. The new standard defines an "internal derivative" as a foreign currency derivative contract that has been entered into with another member of a consolidated group and that can be a hedging instrument in a foreign currency cash flow hedge of a forecasted borrowing, purchase, or sale or an unrecognized firm commitment in the consolidated financial statements only if the following two conditions are satisfied. First, from the perspective of the member of the consolidated group using the derivative as a hedging instrument, specific criteria for foreign currency cash flow hedge accounting are satisfied. Second, the members of the consolidated group who are not using the derivative as a hedging instrument must either (1) enter into a derivative contract with an unrelated third party to offset the exposure that results from that internal derivative or (2) if certain defined conditions are met, enter into derivative contracts with unrelated third parties that would offset, on a net basis for each foreign currency, the foreign exchange risk arising from multiple internal derivative contracts.

Other guidance on accounting for financial instruments. ASC 932-330-55 is directed at the accounting for derivative contracts held for trading purposes and contracts involved in energy trading and risk management activities. It concluded that energy contracts should not be marked to fair value. It determined, as well, that the common practice of carrying energy physical inventories at fair value had no basis under GAAP. Furthermore, net presentation of gains and losses derived from derivatives is required under ASC 815, even if physical settlement occurs, if the derivatives are held for trading purposes (as that term is defined in ASC 320). It was also decided that a derivative held for trading purposes may be designated as a hedging instrument, if the ASC 815 criteria are all met, on a prospective basis (i.e., from date of the consensus), notwithstanding the ASC 815 prohibition on designation of derivative instruments held for trading as "hedges."

Organizations That Do Not Report Earnings

Not-for-profits or other organizations not reporting earnings recognize gains or losses on nonhedging derivative instruments and hedging instruments as a change in net assets. Changes in the carrying amount of the hedged items are also recognized as a change in net assets.

Organizations that do not report earnings cannot use cash flow hedges. If the hedging instrument is a foreign currency net investment hedge, it is accounted for in the same manner as described above.

Derivatives Disclosures

ASC 815 imposes requirements for specific disclosures, for every annual and interim reporting period for which a statement of financial position is presented, about derivative instruments and nonderivative instruments designated and qualifying as hedging instruments.

ASC 815, in addition to the existing requirement for disclosures of information by accounting designation, requires that qualitative information be provided by *underlying risks.* The following illustrates the implementation of these qualitative requirements, including volume of activity, and also includes a nontabular presentation of the quantitative information about the hedged items in fair value hedges.

Example of disclosure of objectives and strategies for using derivative instruments by underlying risk

Utopia Company is exposed to certain risks relating to its ongoing business operations. The primary risks managed by using derivative instruments are commodity price risk and interest rate risk. Forward contracts on various commodities are entered into to manage the price risk associated with forecasted purchases of materials used in Utopia's manufacturing process. Interest rate swaps are entered into to manage interest rate risk associated with the Utopia's fixed-rate borrowings.

ASC 815 requires companies to recognize all derivative instruments as either assets or liabilities at fair value in the statement of financial position. In accordance with such requirements, Utopia designates commodity forward contracts as cash flow hedges of forecasted purchases of commodities and interest rate swaps as fair value hedges of fixed-rate borrowings.

Cash flow hedges. For derivative instruments that are designated and qualify as a cash flow hedge, the effective portion of the gain or loss on the derivative is reported as a component of other comprehensive income and reclassified into earnings in the same period or periods during which the hedged transaction affects earnings. Gains and losses on the derivative representing either hedge ineffectiveness or hedge components excluded from the assessment of effectiveness are recognized in current earnings.

As of December 31, 2012, Utopia had the following outstanding commodity forward contracts that were entered into hedge forecasted purchases:

Commodity	*Number of metric tons*
Copper	30,000
Palladium	6,000
Nickel	75,000

Fair value hedges. For derivative instruments that are designated and qualify as a fair value hedge, the gain or loss on the derivative as well as the offsetting loss or gain on the hedged item attributable to the hedged risk are recognized in current earnings.

Utopia includes the gain or loss on the hedged items (that is, fixed-rate borrowings) in the same line item—interest expense—as the offsetting loss or gain on the related interest rate swaps as follows:

Income statement classification	*Gain/loss on swaps*	*Gain/loss on borrowings*
Interest expense	$350,000	$(22,000)

As of December 31, 20X2, the total notional amount of the Utopia's receive-fixed/pay-variable interest rate swaps was $12.6 million.

Example of disclosure in tabular format of fair value amounts, and gains and losses on derivative instruments and related hedged items

Tabular Disclosures of (a) Fair Values of Derivative Instruments in a Statement of Financial Position and (b) the Effect of Derivative Instruments on the Statement of Financial Performance

Fair Values of Derivative Instruments

In millions of dollars As of December 31	*Asset Derivatives*			
	20X2		*20X1*	
	Statement of financial position location	*Fair value*	*Statement of financial position location*	*Fair value*
Derivatives designated as hedging instruments under ASC 815				
Interest rate contracts	Other assets	$xx,xxx	Other assets	$xx,xxx
Foreign exchange contracts	Other assets	xx,xxx	Other assets	xx,xxx
Equity contracts	Other assets	xx,xxx	Other assets	xx,xxx
Commodity contracts	Other assets	xx,xxx	Other assets	xx,xxx
Credit contracts	Other assets	xx,xxx	Other assets	xx,xxx
Other contracts	Other assets	xx,xxx	Other assets	xx,xxx
Total derivatives designated as hedging instruments under ASC 815		$xx,xxx		$xx,xxx
Interest rate contracts	Other assets	$xx,xxx	Other assets	$xx,xxx
Foreign exchange contracts	Other assets	xx,xxx	Other assets	xx,xxx
Equity contracts	Other assets	xx,xxx	Other assets	xx,xxx
Commodity contracts	Other assets	xx,xxx	Other assets	xx,xxx
Credit contracts	Other assets	xx,xxx	Other assets	xx,xxx
Other contracts	Other assets	xx,xxx	Other assets	xx,xxx
Total derivatives not designated as hedging instruments under ASC 815		$xx,xxx		$xx,xxx
Total derivatives		$xx,xxx		$xx,xxx
Derivatives designated as hedging instruments under ASC 815				
Interest rate contracts	Other liabilities	$xx,xxx	Other liabilities	$xx,xxx
Foreign exchange contracts	Other liabilities	xx,xxx	Other liabilities	xx,xxx
Equity contracts	Other liabilities	xx,xxx	Other liabilities	xx,xxx
Commodity contracts	Other liabilities	xx,xxx	Other liabilities	xx,xxx
Credit contracts	Other liabilities	xx,xxx	Other liabilities	xx,xxx
Other contracts	Other liabilities	xx,xxx	Other liabilities	xx,xxx
Total derivatives designated as hedging instruments under ASC 815		$xx,xxx		$xx,xxx
Derivatives not designated as hedging instruments under ASC 815 [a]				
Interest rate contracts	Other liabilities	$xx,xxx	Other liabilities	$xx,xxx
Foreign exchange contracts	Other liabilities	xx,xxx	Other liabilities	xx,xxx
Equity contracts	Other liabilities	xx,xxx	Other liabilities	xx,xxx
Commodity contracts	Other liabilities	xx,xxx	Other liabilities	xx,xxx
Credit contracts	Other liabilities	xx,xxx	Other liabilities	xx,xxx
Other contracts	Other liabilities	xx,xxx	Other liabilities	xx,xxx
Total derivatives not designated as hedging instruments under ASC 815		$xx,xxx		$xx,xxx
Total derivatives		$xx,xxx		$xx,xxx

[a] *See footnote XX for additional information on the Utopia Company's purpose for entering into derivatives not designated as hedging instruments and its overall risk management strategies.*

The Effect of Derivative Instruments on the Statement of Financial Performance for the Years Ended December 31, 20X2 and 20X1

Derivatives in ASC 815 fair value hedging relationships	*Location of gain or (loss) recognized in income on derivative* [a]	*Amount of gain or (loss) recognized in income on derivative*	
		20X2	*20X1*
Interest rate contracts	Interest income/(expense)	$xx,xxx	$xx,xxx
Foreign exchange contracts	Foreign currency gain/(loss)	xx,xxx	xx,xxx
Equity contracts	Other income/(expense)	xx,xxx	xx,xxx
Commodity contracts	Other income/(expense)	xx,xxx	xx,xxx
Credit derivatives	Other income/(expense)	xx,xxx	xx,xxx
Other contracts	Other income/(expense)	xx,xxx	xx,xxx
Total		$xx,xxx	$xx,xxx

Derivatives in ASC 815 cash flow hedging relationships	*Amount of gain on (loss) recognized in OCI on derivative (effective portion)*	
	20X2	*20X1*
Interest rate contracts	$xx,xxx	$xx,xxx
Foreign exchange contracts	xx,xxx	xx,xxx
Equity contracts	xx,xxx	xx,xxx
Commodity contracts	xx,xxx	xx,xxx
Credit derivatives	xx,xxx	xx,xxx
Other contracts	xx,xxx	xx,xxx
Total	$xx,xxx	$xx,xxx

Location of gain or (loss) reclassified from accumulated OCI into income (effective portion) [a]	*Amount of gain or (loss) reclassified from accumulated OCI into income (effective portion)*	
	20X2	*20X1*
Interest income/(expense)	$xx,xxx	$xx,xxx
Sales/revenue	xx,xxx	xx,xxx
Other income/(expense)	xx,xxx	xx,xxx
Cost of sales	xx,xxx	xx,xxx
Other income/(expense)	xx,xxx	xx,xxx
Other income/(expense)	xx,xxx	xx,xxx
	$xx,xxx	$xx,xxx

Location of gain or (loss) recognized in income on derivative (ineffective portion and amount excluded from effectiveness testing) [a]	*Amount of gain or (loss) recognized in income on derivative (ineffective portion and amount excluded from effectiveness testing)* [d]	
	20X2	*20X1*
Other income/(expense)	$xx,xxx	$xx,xxx
Other income/(expense)	xx,xxx	xx,xxx
Other income/(expense)	xx,xxx	xx,xxx
Other income/(expense)	xx,xxx	xx,xxx
Other income/(expense)	xx,xxx	xx,xxx
Other income/(expense)	xx,xxx	xx,xxx
	$xx,xxx	$xx,xxx

Derivatives in ASC 815 net investment hedging relationships	*Amount of gain or (loss) recognized in OCI on derivative (effective portion)*	
	20X2	*20X1*
Foreign exchange contracts	$xx,xxx	$xx,xxx

Location of gain or (loss) reclassified from accumulated OCI into income (effective portion)	*Amount of gain or (loss) recognized in OCI on derivative (effective portion)* 20X2	20X1
Gain or (loss) on sale of subsidiary	$xx,xxx	$xx,xxx

Location of gain or (loss) recognized in income on derivative (ineffective portion and amount excluded from effectiveness testing) [a]	*Amount of gain or (loss) recognized in income on derivative (ineffective portion and amount excluded from effectiveness testing)* [d] 20X2	20X1
Other income/(expense)	$xx,xxx	$xx,xxx

Derivatives not designated as hedging instruments under ASC 815 [b, c]	*Location of gain or (loss) recognized in income on derivative* [a]	*Amount of gain or (loss) recognized in income on derivative* 20X2	20X1
Interest rate contracts	Other income/(expense)	$xx,xxx	$xx,xxx
Foreign exchange contracts	Other income/(expense)	xx,xxx	xx,xxx
Equity contracts	Other income/(expense)	xx,xxx	xx,xxx
Commodity contracts	Other income/(expense)	xx,xxx	xx,xxx
Credit derivatives	Other income/(expense)	xx,xxx	xx,xxx
Other contracts	Other income/(expense)	xx,xxx	xx,xxx
Total		$xx,xxx	$xx,xxx

[a] *If gains and losses associated with a type of contract (for example, interest rate contracts) are displayed in multiple line items in the income statement, the entity is required to disclose the amount included in each line item.*

[b] *See footnote XX for additional information on the Utopia Company's purpose for entering into derivatives not designated as hedging instruments and its overall risk management strategies.*

[c] *For alternative disclosures about "trading derivatives," see separate table for trading activities in footnotes to the financial statements.*

[d] *The amount of gain or (loss) recognized in income represents $XXX related to the ineffective portion of the hedging relationships and $XXX related to the amount excluded from the assessment of hedge effectiveness.*

Example of tabular disclosure of nondesignated/nonqualifying derivative instruments that are included in an entity's trading activity

When the reporting entity elects the alternative disclosure for gains and losses on derivative instruments included in its trading activities, a format such as the following may be elected for use.

Note that many entities already include the required information about their trading activities in other disclosures within the financial statements, in which case it would now need to provide a cross-reference from the derivative footnote to other footnotes in which trading derivative-related information is included.

The Effect of Trading Activities on the Statement of Financial Performance for the Years Ended December 31, 20X2 and 20X1

	Trading Revenue	
Type of Instrument	*20X2*	*20X1*
Fixed income/interest rate	$xx,xxx	$xx,xxx
Foreign exchange	xx,xxx	xx,xxx
Equity	xx,xxx	xx,xxx
Commodity	xx,xxx	xx,xxx
Credit	xx,xxx	xx,xxx
Other	xx,xxx	xx,xxx
Total	$xx,xxx	$xx,xxx

Example of disclosure of contingent features in derivative instruments

This example illustrates the disclosure of credit-risk-related contingent features in derivative instruments.

Contingent Features

Certain of Utopia Company's derivative instruments contain provisions that require Utopia's debt to maintain an investment grade credit rating from each of the major credit rating agencies. If Utopia's debt were to fall below investment grade, it would be in violation of these provisions, and the counterparties to the derivative instruments could request immediate payment or demand immediate and ongoing full overnight collateralization on derivative instruments in net liability positions.

The aggregate fair value of all derivative instruments with credit-risk-related contingent features that are in a liability position on December 31, 20X2, is $XX million for which Utopia has posted collateral of $X million in the normal course of business. If the credit-risk-related contingent features underlying these agreements were triggered on December 31, 20X2, Utopia would be required to post an additional $XX million of collateral to its counterparties.

ASC 815-40, *Contracts in Entity's Own Equity*

Accounting for contracts held or issued by the reporting entity that are indexed to its own stock. ASC 815-10-15 provides that the reporting entity is not to consider contracts issued or held by that reporting entity that are both (1) indexed to its own stock and (2) classified in stockholders' equity in its statement of financial position to be derivative instruments for purposes of that topic. ASC 718-10-60-1B offers extensive examples to clarify the circumstances where the first part of this particular exemption (i.e., indexed to the entity's own stock) would apply. It applies to any freestanding financial instrument or embedded feature that has all the characteristics of a derivative in ASC 815-10-15, for purposes of determining whether that instrument or embedded feature qualifies for the first part of the scope exception in ASC 815-10-15-74. It also applies to any freestanding financial instrument that is potentially settled in an entity's own stock, regardless of whether the instrument has all the characteristics of a derivative in ASC 815-10-15, for purposes of determining whether the instrument is within the scope of ASC 815-40.

It is required that an evaluation be made of whether an equity-linked financial instrument (or embedded feature), using the following two-step approach:

- Step 1 is to evaluate the instrument's contingent exercise provisions, if any;
- Step 2 is to evaluate the instrument's settlement provisions.

An exercise contingency would not preclude an instrument (or embedded feature) from being considered indexed to an entity's own stock provided that it is not based on (1) an observable market, other than the market for the issuer's stock (if applicable), or (2) an observable index, other than an index calculated or measured solely by reference to the issuer's own operations. If the evaluation of Step 1 does not preclude an instrument from being considered indexed to the entity's own stock, the analysis would proceed to Step 2. An *exercise contingency* is a provision that entitles the entity, or counterparty, to exercise an equity-linked financial instrument (or embedded feature) based on changes in an underlying, including the occurrence (or nonoccurrence) of a specified event. Provisions that accelerate the timing of the entity's, or counterparty's, ability to exercise an instrument, and provisions that extend the length of time that an instrument is exercisable, are examples of exercise contingencies.

An instrument (or embedded feature) would be considered indexed to an entity's own stock if its settlement amount will equal the difference between the fair value of a fixed number of the entity's shares and a fixed monetary amount or a fixed amount of a debt instrument issued by the entity.

A number of examples of the application of this guidance are provided in the Topic. For example, warrants that become exercisable upon an initial public offering (IPO), at a fixed price, would meet the criteria for being deemed indexed to the entity's stock, measured by the difference between fair value and the fixed exercise price. On the other hand, if conditioned on the change in some external index (such as the Dow Industrials) over some defined period, the warrants would not be deemed linked to the entity's stock.

ASC 815-40 reached a number of conclusions. These are summarized as follows:

1. *Basis of settlement.* Initial statement of financial position classification is to be guided by the principle that contracts that require net cash settlements are assets or liabilities, and those that require settlement in shares are equity instruments. If the reporting entity has the choice of settlement modes, settlement in shares is to be assumed; if the counterparty has the option, net cash settlement is presumed. An exception occurs if the two settlement alternatives are not of equal value, in which case the economic substance should govern.
2. *Measurement.* Initial measurement should be at fair value. Contracts classed as equity are accounted for in permanent equity, with value changes being ignored, unless settlement expectations change. For publicly held companies, under defined circumstances, guidance is provided by analogy from Accounting Series Release (ASR) 268. All other contracts would be classified as assets or liabilities, to be measured continuously at fair value. If settlement in shares ultimately occurs, already recognized gains or losses are left in earnings, not reclassified or reversed.
3. *Contract reclassification.* Events may necessitate reclassification of contracts from assets/liabilities to equity. If a contract first classed as equity is later reclassified to assets/liabilities, any value change to the date of reclassification will be included in equity, not earnings. Thereafter, value changes will be reported in earnings. If partial net share settlement is permitted, the portion that can be so settled remains in equity. Appropriate disclosure under ASC 235 may be required, if more than one contract exists and different methods are applied to them.
4. *Equity classification criteria.* All the following conditions must be satisfied in order to classify a contract in equity:

    a. The contract permits settlement in unregistered shares (the assumption being that the issuer cannot effectively control the conditions for registration, making cash settlement likely unless unregistered shares can be delivered);
    b. There are sufficient authorized, unissued shares to settle the contact, after considering all other outstanding commitments;
    c. The contract contains an explicit limit on the number of shares to be issued;
    d. There are no required cash payments to the counterparty based on the issuer's failure to make timely SEC filings;
    e. There are no "make whole" provisions to compensate the holder after he sells the shares issued in the market at a price below some defined threshold value;
    f. Requirements for net cash settlement are accompanied by similar requirements for existing shareholders;
    g. There are no provisions that indicate that the counterparties have rights greater than those of the actual shareholders; and
    h. There is no requirement for any collateral posting for any reason.

5. *Hedge accounting applicability*. Contracts that are subject to this consensus cannot qualify for hedge accounting.
6. *Multiple settlement alternatives*. Contracts offering multiple settlement alternatives that require the company to receive cash when the contract is in a gain position but pay either stock or cash at the company's option when in a loss position are to be accounted for as equity. Also, such contracts requiring payment of cash when in a loss position but receipt of either cash or stock at the company's option when in a gain position must be accounted for as assets/liabilities.
7. *EPS calculations*. For EPS computation purposes, for those contracts that provide the company with a choice of settlement methods, settlement in shares is to be assumed, although this can be overcome based on past experience or stated policy. If the counterparty controls the choice, however, the more dilutive assumption must be made, irrespective of past experience or policy.

Freestanding derivatives indexed to, and potentially settled in, stock of a consolidated subsidiary. ASC 815-40 cited above, establishes a framework for accounting for freestanding derivative instruments that are indexed to, and potentially settled in, a company's own stock. The ASC does not, however, provide guidance on how to account for freestanding derivative instruments that are indexed to, and potentially settled in, a subsidiary's stock. ASC 810-10 deals with how such contracts should be classified and measured in the consolidated financial statements.

Stock of a subsidiary is not equity of the parent; therefore, derivatives indexed to and to be settled in stock of a subsidiary do not meet ASC 815-10-15's exclusion criteria. If derivatives meet the criteria (e.g., for net settlement, etc.), they must be accounted for under the provisions of ASC 815-25 through 815-35, and not of ASC 815-40. The ASC also discusses a number of exceptions based on the criteria set forth in ASC 815.

Option or forward strike prices and premiums could be indicative of impairments of the parent's investment in subsidiaries. A parent's contract to purchase a subsidiary's (minority held) common stock should not be recorded until settled; during the period of the contract, income should continue to be allocated to the minority interest. A contract to sell shares in a subsidiary, likewise, should be recorded when settled; until that time, income would not be allocated to outside interests (counterparties to the derivative).

ASC 815-40 applies to freestanding derivatives only—similar embedded derivatives are not covered Also not covered are derivatives which are issued to compensate employees or to acquire goods and services from nonemployees, when performance has yet to occur. It does apply, however, to derivatives issued to acquire goods and services from nonemployees, when performance has occurred.

FASB clarified whether a financial instrument for which the payoff to the counterparty is based, in whole or in part, on the stock of an entity's consolidated subsidiary is indexed to the reporting entity's own stock. It holds that freestanding financial instruments (and embedded features) for which the payoff to the counterparty is based, in whole or in part, on the stock of a consolidated subsidiary are not precluded from being considered indexed to the entity's own stock in the consolidated financial statements of the parent if the subsidiary is a substantive entity. If the subsidiary is not a substantive entity, however, the instrument or embedded feature would not be considered indexed to the entity's own stock. The fair value of an outstanding instrument that was previously classified as an asset or liability is to be its net carrying amount at that date (that is, the current fair value). The net carrying amount is then to be reclassified to noncontrolling interest. Gains or losses recorded during the periods that the instrument was classified as an asset or liability are not to be reversed.

ASC 815-45, *Weather Derivatives*

"Weather derivatives" are addressed by ASC 815-45. At issue was whether such contracts should be reported under accrual accounting, under settlement accounting, under insurance accounting, marked to fair value through earnings at each reporting date, or under some other method. Also at issue was whether the accounting for these derivatives should vary based on the type of contract.

ASC 815 provides that contracts that are not exchange-traded are not subject to the requirements of that statement if settlement is based on a climatic or geological variable or on some other physical variable. Any derivative based on a physical variable that eventually becomes exchange-traded automatically becomes subject to the requirements of ASC 815.

ASC 815-45 states that an entity that enters into a non-exchange-traded forward-based weather derivative in connection with nontrading activities is to account for the contract by applying an "intrinsic value method." The intrinsic value method computes an amount based on the difference between the expected results from an upfront allocation of the cumulative strike and the actual results during a period, multiplied by the contract price (for example, dollars per heating degree day). The use of external statistical sources, such as the National Weather Service, is necessary in applying this technique.

Furthermore, an entity that purchases a non-exchange-traded option-based weather derivative in connection with nontrading activities is to amortize to expense the premium paid (or due) and apply the intrinsic value method to measure the contract at the date of each interim statement of financial position. The premium asset is to be amortized in a rational and systematic manner.

Also, all entities that sell or write a non-exchange-traded option-based weather derivative are to initially recognize the premium as a liability and recognize any subsequent changes in fair value currently in earnings (the premium would not be amortized).

In addition, a purchased or written weather derivative may contain an "embedded" premium or discount when the contract terms are not consistent with current market terms. In those circumstances, the premium or discount is to be quantified, removed from the calculated benchmark strike, and accounted for as noted above.

Finally, all weather derivative contracts entered into under trading or speculative activities are to be accounted for at their fair value, with subsequent changes in fair value reported currently in earnings.

Other Guidance on Investments and Related Matters

Structured notes. Structured notes are debt obligations that are coupled with derivatives, most often related to interest rates or foreign currency exchange rates, such that a prescribed increase or decrease in the reference rate will have a large impact on some defined attribute of the debt obligation, such as its interest rate, maturity value, or maturity date. In some instances, two or more such instruments may be acquired, having essentially opposite characteristics, such that, for example, a change in a reference interest rate will cause the fair value on one holding to increase and the other to decrease, by equal amounts. In some instances, this may have been arranged in order to be able to achieve a recognizable loss on the one (losing) investment by selling it, while holding the other (winning) one as an AFS security with unrealized gains reported in other comprehensive income. ASC 320 effectively ends this practice by requiring that the related investments be accounted for as a unit while held, but if one is sold the (joint) carrying amount must be allocated based on relative fair values as of the date of sale, consistent with guidance in ASC 860. The consequence is that neither gain nor loss, recognized or included in stockholders' equity, will result from such transactions.

Accounting for freestanding derivative financial instruments indexed to, and potentially settled in, the stock of a consolidated subsidiary. ASC 815 contains a framework for accounting for freestanding derivative instruments that are indexed to, and potentially settled in, a company's own stock. It does not, however, provide guidance on the accounting for freestanding derivative instruments that are indexed to, and potentially settled in, a subsidiary's stock. ASC 810 addresses how such contracts should be classified and measured in the consolidated financial statements.

The stock of a subsidiary is not equity of the parent; therefore, derivatives indexed to and to be settled in stock of a subsidiary do not meet ASC 815's exclusion criteria. If derivatives meet the criteria of ASC 815 (e.g., for net settlement, etc.), these must be accounted for under the provisions of ASC 815. The consensus also discusses a number of exceptions based on the criteria set forth in ASC 815.

Option or forward strike prices and premiums could be indicative of impairments of the parent's investment in subsidiaries—which would need to be assessed using ASC 360. A parent's contract to purchase a subsidiary's (minority held) common stock is not recorded until settled; during the period of the contract, income continues to be allocated to the minority interest. A contract to sell shares in a subsidiary, likewise, is recorded when settled; until that time, income would not be allocated to outside interests (counterparties to the derivative).

49 ASC 820 FAIR VALUE MEASUREMENTS

PERSPECTIVE AND ISSUES

Subtopic

ASC 820 contains one subtopic:

- ASC 820-10, *Overall,* which defines fair value, describes a framework for measuring fair value and details required disclosures.

Scope and Scope Exceptions

ASC 820 does not require fair value measurement in addition to those required by other Topics in the Codification.

Scope. In pursuing an incremental approach, ASC 820 contained scope exceptions for certain, highly-complex specialized applications. It does not apply to:

1. Share-based payments transactions, except for transaction covered in ASC 718-40 which are within the scope of ASC 820
2. Measurements that are similar to fair value but that are not intended to measure fair value, including:
   a. Measurements models that are based on vendor-specific objective evidence of fair value, such as multiple-deliverable arrangements and software revenue recognition
   b. Inventory
3. Accounting principles that address fair value measurements for purposes of lease classification or measurement. The exception does *not* apply to assets acquired and liabilities assumed in a business combination or an acquisition by a not-for-profit entity that are required to be measured at fair value regardless of whether those assets and liabilities are related to leases.

In addition to the scope exceptions listed above, ASC 820 retains the practicability exceptions included in GAAP that acknowledge that it is sometimes not reasonable to estimate fair value without "undue cost or effort." When this is the case, however, management is required to inform the users of the financial statements that it has invoked this exception, as well as the reasons that it believes making fair value measurements would be impractical. (ASC 820-10-15-3)

Overview

ASC 820, *Fair Value Measurement.* Accounting Standards Codification (ASC) 820 provides

- a unified definition of fair value,
- related guidance on measurement, and
- enhanced disclosure requirements to inform financial statement users about
  - the fair value measurements included in the financial statements,
  - the methods and assumptions used to estimate them, and
  - the degree of observability of the inputs used in management's estimation process.

The standard retains the longstanding exceptions that existed in GAAP that apply when, in management's judgment, it is not practical to estimate fair value. In such instances, management is required to inform the reader in an explanatory note to the financial statements that it is unable to estimate fair value and the reasons that such an estimate cannot be made.

The practicability exception applies to certain measurements made in connection with the following matters:

GAAP measurement category	Primary GAAP
Asset retirement obligations	ASC 410-20 and 440-10-50 and 440-10-55
Business combinations, for specific items where other measures are allowed	ASC 805-20-30-10
Contributions made and received, if the value cannot be measured reliably	ASC 958 and 720-25
Financial instrument disclosures	ASC 825-10-50
Guarantees, the use of an entry price at initial recognition	ASC 460
Nonmonetary transactions	ASC 845, 605-20-25 and 605-20-50
Participation rights	ASC 715-30 and 715-60
Restructuring obligations	ASC 420

This chapter provides the reader/researcher with

1. An explanation of the fair value measurement model prescribed by ASC 820
2. Illustrations of financial statement formats and comprehensive disclosures that integrate with the disclosures required by other provisions of the ASC regarding financial instruments and fair value.

Technical Alert

ASU 2013-09. In July 2013, the FASB released *Accounting Standards Update—Fair Value Measurement (Topic 820): Deferral of the Effective Date of Certain Disclosures for Nonpublic Employee Benefit Plans in Update No. 2011-04* to defer quantitative disclosures about investments held by a nonpublic employee benefit plan in the plan sponsor's own equity securities. Stakeholders expressed concerns that certain disclosure requirements would reveal sensitive proprietary information of private companies. The ASU is effective 7/8/2013 for financial statements not yet issued.

DEFINITIONS OF TERMS

Source: ASC 820-10-20

Active market. A market in which transactions for the asset or liability occur with sufficient frequency and volume to provide pricing information on an ongoing basis.

Brokered market. A market in which brokers attempt to match buyers with sellers, but do not stand ready to trade for their own account.

Cost approach. A valuation technique that reflects the amount that currently would be required to replace the service capacity of an asset, often called current replacement cost.

Credit risk. For purposes of a hedged item in a fair value hedge, credit risk is the risk of changes in the hedged item's fair value attributable to both of the following:

1. Changes in the obligor's creditworthiness
2. Changes in the spread over the benchmark interest rate with respect to the hedged item's credit sector at inception of the hedge.

For purposes of a hedged transaction in a cash flow hedge, credit risk is the risk of changes in the hedged transaction's cash flows attributable to all of the following:

1. Default
2. Changes in the obligor's creditworthiness
3. Changes in the spread over the benchmark interest rate with respect to the related financial asset's or liability's credit sector at inception of the hedge.

Currency risk. The risk that the fair value or future cash flows of a financial instrument will fluctuate because of changes in foreign exchange rates.

Dealer market. A market in which dealers stand ready to trade (either buy or sell for their own account), thereby providing liquidity by using their capital to hold an inventory of the items for which they make a market. Typically, bid and ask prices (representing the price at which the dealer is willing to buy and the price at which the dealer is willing to sell, respectively) are more readily available than closing prices. Over-the-counter markets (for which prices are publicly reported by the National Association of Securities Dealers Automated Quotations systems or by OTC Markets Group Inc.) are dealer markets. For example, the market for U.S. Treasury securities is a dealer market. Dealer markets also exist for some other assets and liabilities, including other financial instruments, commodities, and physical assets (for example, used equipment).

Discount rate adjustment technique. A present value technique that uses a risk-adjusted discount rate and contractual, promised, or most likely cash flows.

Entry price. The price paid to acquire an asset, or received to assume a liability in an exchange transaction.

Exchange market. A market in which closing prices are both readily available and generally representative of fair value (such as the New York Stock Exchange).

Exit price. The price that would be received to sell an asset or paid to transfer a liability.

Expected cash flow. The probability-weighted average (that is, mean of the distribution) of possible future cash flows.

Fair value. The price that would be received to sell an asset or paid to transfer a liability in an orderly transaction between market participants at the measurement date.

Financial asset. Cash, evidence of an ownership interest in an entity, or a contract that conveys to one entity a right

1. to receive cash or another financial instrument from a second entity or
2. to exchange other financial instruments on potentially favorable terms with the second entity.

Financial instrument. Cash, evidence of an ownership interest in an entity, or a contract that both:

1. Imposes on one entity a contractual obligation either:
   a. To deliver cash or another financial instrument to a second entity
   b. To exchange other financial instruments on potentially unfavorable terms with the second entity.
2. Conveys to that second entity a contractual right either:
   a. To receive cash or another financial instrument from the first entity
   b. To exchange other financial instruments on potentially favorable terms with the first entity.

The use of the term financial instrument in this definition is recursive (because the term financial instrument is included in it), though it is not circular. The definition requires a chain of contractual obligations that ends with the delivery of cash or an ownership interest in an entity. Any number of obligations to deliver financial instruments can be links in a chain that qualifies a particular contract as a financial instrument.

Contractual rights and contractual obligations encompass both those that are conditioned on the occurrence of a specified event and those that are not. All contractual rights (contractual obligations) that are financial instruments meet the definitions of asset (liability) set forth in FASB Concepts Statement No. 6, Elements of Financial Statements, although some may not be recognized as assets (liabilities) in financial statements—that is, they may be off-balance-sheet—because they fail to meet some other criterion for recognition.

For some financial instruments, the rights held by or the obligation is due from (or the obligation is used to or by) a group of entities rather than a single entity.

Financial liability. A contract that imposes on one entity an obligation

1. to deliver cash or another financial instrument to a second entity or
2. to exchange other financial instruments on potentially unfavorable terms with the second entity.

Highest and best use. The use of a nonfinancial asset by market participants that would maximize the value of the asset or the group of assets and liabilities (for example, a business) within which the asset would be used.

Income approach. Valuation techniques that convert future amounts (for example, cash flows or income and expenses) to a single current (that is, discounted) amount. The fair value measurement is determined on the basis of the value indicated by current market expectations about those future amounts.

Inputs. The assumptions that market participants would use when pricing the asset or liability, including assumptions about risk, such as the following:

1. The risk inherent in a particular valuation technique used to measure fair value (such as a pricing model)
2. The risk inherent in the inputs to the valuation technique.

Inputs may be observable or unobservable.

Interest rate risk. The risk of changes in a hedged item's fair value or cash flows attributable to changes in the designated benchmark interest rate.

Legal entity. Any legal structure used to conduct activities or to hold assets. Some examples of such structures are corporations, partnerships, limited liability companies, grantor trusts, and other trusts.

Level 1 inputs. Quoted prices (unadjusted) in active markets for identical assets or liabilities that the reporting entity can access at the measurement date.

Level 2 inputs. Inputs other than quoted prices included within Level 1 that are observable for the asset or liability, either directly or indirectly.

Level 3 inputs. Unobservable inputs for the asset or liability.

Liability issued with an inseparable third-party credit enhancement. A liability that is issued with a credit enhancement obtained from a third party, such as debt that is issued with a financial guarantee from a third party that guarantees the issuer's payment obligation.

Management. Persons who are responsible for achieving the objectives of the entity and who have the authority to establish policies and make decisions by which those objectives are to be pursued. Management normally includes members of the board of directors, the chief executive officer, chief operating officer, vice presidents in charge of principal business functions (such as sales, administration, or finance), and other persons who perform similar policy-making functions. Persons without formal titles also may be members of management.

Market approach. A valuation technique that uses prices and other relevant information generated by market transactions involving identical or comparable (that is, similar) assets, liabilities, or a group of assets and liabilities, such as a business.

Market participants. Buyers and sellers in the principal (or most advantageous) market for the asset or liability that have all of the following characteristics:

1. They are independent of each other, that is, they are not related parties, although the price in the related-party transaction may be used as an input to a fair value measurement if the reporting entity has evidence that the transaction was entered into at market terms
2. They are knowledgeable, having a reasonable understanding about the asset or liability and the transaction using all available information, including information that might be obtained through due diligence efforts that are usual and customary
3. They are able to enter into a transaction for the asset or liability
4. They are willing to enter into a transaction for the asset or liability, that is, they are motivated but not forced or otherwise compelled to do so.

Market risk. The risk that the fair value or future cash flows of a financial instrument will fluctuate because of changes in market prices. Market risk comprises the following:

1. Interest rate risk
2. Currency risk
3. Other price risk.

Market-corroborated inputs. Inputs that are derived principally from or corroborated by observable market data by correlation or other means.

Most advantageous market. The market that maximizes the amount that would be received to sell the asset or minimizes the amount that would be paid to transfer the liability, after taking into account transaction costs and transportation costs.

Net asset value per share. Net asset value per share is the amount of net assets attributable to each share of capital stock (other than senior equity securities; that is, preferred stock) outstanding at the close of the period. It excludes the effects of assuming conversion of outstanding convertible securities, whether or not their conversion would have a diluting effect.

Nonperformance risk. The risk that an entity will not fulfill an obligation. Nonperformance risk includes, but may not be limited to, the reporting entity's own credit risk.

Nonpublic entity. Any entity that does not meet any of the following conditions:

1. Its debt or equity securities trade in a public market either on a stock exchange (domestic or foreign) or in an over-the counter market, including securities quoted only locally or regionally.
2. It is a conduit bond obligor for *conduit debt securities* that are traded in a public market (a domestic or foreign stock exchange or an over-the-counter market, including local or regional markets).
3. It files with a regulatory agency in preparation for the sale of any class of debt or equity securities in a public market.
4. It is required to file or furnish financial statements with the Securities and Exchange Commission.
5. It is controlled by an entity covered by criteria 1 through 4.

Not-for-profit-entity. An entity that possesses the following characteristics, in varying degrees, that distinguish it from a business entity:

1. Contributions of significant amounts of resources from resources providers who do not expect commensurate or proportionate pecuniary return
2. Operating purposes other than to provide goods or services at a profit
3. Absence of ownership interest like those of business entities.

Entities that clearly fall outside this definition include the following:

1. All investor-owned entities
2. Entities that provide dividends, lower costs, or other economic benefits directly and proportionately to their owners, members, or participants, such as mutual insurance entities, credit unions, farm and rural electric cooperatives, and employee benefit plans.

Observable inputs. Inputs that are developed using market data, such as publicly available information about actual events or transactions, and that reflect the assumptions that market participants would use when pricing the asset or liability.

Orderly transaction. A transaction that assumes exposure to the market for a period before the measurement date to allow for marketing activities that are usual and customary for transactions involving such assets or liabilities; it is not a forced transaction (for example, a forced liquidation or distress sale).

Other price risk. The risk that the fair value of future cash flows of a financial instrument will fluctuate because of changes in market prices (other than those arising from interest rate risk or currency risk), whether those changes are caused by factors specific to the individual financial instrument or its issuer or by factors affecting all similar financial instruments traded in the market.

Present value. A tool used to link future amounts (cash flows or values) to a present amount using a discount rate (an application of the income approach). Present value techniques differ in how they adjust for risk and in the type of cash flows they use.

Principal market. The market with the greatest volume and level of activity for the asset or liability.

Principal-to-principal market. A market in which transactions, both originations and resales, are negotiated independently with no intermediary. Little information about those transactions may be made available publicly.

Readily determinable fair value. An equity security has a readily determinable fair value if it meets any of the following conditions:

1. The fair value of an equity security is readily determinable if sales prices or bid-and-asked quotations are currently available on a securities exchange registered with the U.S. Securities and Exchange Commission (SEC) or in the over-the-counter market, provided that those prices or quotations for the over-the-counter market are publicly reported by the National Association of Securities Dealers Automated Quotations systems or by OTC Markets Group Inc. Restricted stock meets that definition if the restriction terminates within one year.
2. The fair value of an equity security traded only in a foreign market is readily determinable if that foreign market is of a breadth and scope comparable to one of the U.S. markets referred to above.
3. The fair value of an investment in a mutual fund is readily determinable if the fair value per share (unit) is determined and published and is the basis for current transactions.

Related parties. Related parties include:

1. Affiliates of the entity
2. Entities for which investments in their equity securities would be required, absent the election of the fair value option under the Fair Value Option Subsection of Section 825-10-15, to be accounted for by the equity method by the investing entity
3. Trusts for the benefit of employees, such as pension and profit-sharing trusts that are managed by or under that trusteeship of management
4. Principal owners of the entity and members of their immediate families
5. Management of the entity and members of their immediate families
6. Other parties with which the entity may deal if one party controls or can significantly influence the management or operating policies of the other to an extent that one of the transacting parties might be prevented from fully pursuing its own separate interests
7. Other parties that can significantly influence the management or operating policies of the transacting parties or that have an ownership interest in one of the transacting parties and can significantly influence the other to an extent that one or more of the transacting parties might be prevented from fully pursuing its own separate interests.

Risk premium. Compensation sought by risk-averse market participants for bearing the uncertainty inherent in the cash flows of an asset or a liability. Also referred to as a *risk adjustment*.

Systematic risk. The common risk shared by an asset or a liability with the other items in a diversified portfolio. Portfolio theory holds that in a market in equilibrium, market participants will be compensated only for bearing the systematic risk inherent in the cash flows. (In markets that are inefficient or out of equilibrium, other forms of return or compensation might be available.) Also referred to as *nondiversifiable risk*.

Transaction costs. The costs to sell an asset or transfer a liability in the principal (or most advantageous) market for the asset or liability that are directly attributable to the disposal of the asset or transfer of the liability and meet both of the following criteria:

1. They result directly from and are essential to that transaction.
2. They would not have been incurred by the entity had the decision to sell the asset or transfer the liability not been made (similar to costs to sell, as defined in ASC 360-10-35-38).

Transportation costs. The costs that would be incurred to transport an asset from its current location to its principal (or most advantageous) market.

Unit of account. The level at which an asset or a liability is aggregated or disaggregated in a Topic for recognition purposes.

Unobservable inputs. Inputs for which market data are not available and that are developed using the best information available about the assumptions that market participants would use when pricing the asset or liability.

Unsystematic risk. The risk specific to a particular asset or liability. Also referred to as diversifiable risk.

Variable interest entity. A legal entity subject to consolidation according to the provisions of the Variable Interest Entities Subsections of ASC 810-10.

CONCEPTS, RULES, AND EXAMPLES

The Mixed Attribute Model

Under longstanding US GAAP, assets, liabilities, and equity are measured and presented on a reporting entity's statement of financial position by applying a disjointed, inconsistent assortment of accounting methods. This current state of affairs is sometimes referred to as the "mixed attribute model." The following table summarizes the current state of the mixed attribute model and the effects of ASC 820 and ASC 825-10-25 (if any) on specified assets and liabilities of reporting entities that are not financial institutions, investment companies, or insurance companies.

Assets			**Liabilities and Equity**		
*Key**	*Caption*	*Customary measurement attribute*	*Key**	*Caption*	*Customary measurement attribute*
A	Cash and cash equivalents	Cost, or amortized cost approximating fair value	E	Notes and bonds payable	Unpaid contractual principal adjusted for accrued interest, unamortized premium or discount, unamortized debt issue costs
E	Accounts receivable (with terms not exceeding one year)	Estimated net realizable value	A, E	Accounts payable	Contractual price agreed upon by the parties; depending on the contractual terms, often will approximate fair value
E	Notes, loans and accounts receivable with terms exceeding one year	Unamortized principal due less allowance for credit losses; also subject to evaluation for impairment when holder considers it probable that it will be unable to collect all amounts due in accordance with the contractual terms	A	Payroll taxes withheld and accrued; sales taxes payable	Amounts due to taxing authorities; due to short periods during which these amounts are outstanding, they usually approximate fair value without being discounted to their present value
N	Inventory	Lower of cost or market using FIFO, LIFO, average cost, or specific identification	N	Income tax liabilities currently payable	Amounts due to taxing authorities based on positions claimed on income tax returns filed or to be filed

Assets			Liabilities and Equity		
*Key**	*Caption*	*Customary measurement attribute*	*Key**	*Caption*	*Customary measurement attribute*
N	Deposits	Cost less portion applied by the holder or for which no future benefits are expected	N	Unrecognized income tax benefits	Amounts due to taxing authorities for income tax positions claimed or to be claimed on tax returns that exceed the maximum amount that is more than 50% probable of being sustained upon audit
E	Investments in debt and marketable equity securities including those held by a not-for-profit organization	Trading and available-for-sale securities at fair value; held-to-maturity securities at amortized cost subject to evaluation for other-than-temporary impairment	N	Deferred income taxes	Future taxable temporary differences multiplied by the effective tax rate expected to apply upon their future reversal
E	Investments, cost method	Historical cost less dividends received by the investor in excess of the investee's net accumulated earnings since the date of acquisition by the investor, and subject to evaluation for other-than-temporary impairment	N	Accrued expenses	Expenses incurred or allocated to operations that have not yet been invoiced by the supplier or provider and are not yet currently payable
E	Investments, equity method	Historical cost adjusted to recognize the investor's share of investee income and losses, dividend distributions, and amortization of difference between investor cost and underlying net assets of the investee ("equity method goodwill"); subject to evaluation for other-than-temporary impairment	E	Warranty obligations	Estimated costs expected to be incurred over the warranty period
A	Derivatives	Fair value (depending on the measurement, the derivative can be an asset in one period and a liability in another period)	N	Deferred compensation arrangements, pensions, other postemployment benefits	Subject to highly complex GAAP that, in general, accrues the cost of the benefits to be provided in the future in a manner that results in compensation cost being recognized in the periods benefiting from the services provided, including factors for the time value of money, various actuarial assumptions relevant to the measurement, and when the arrangement is funded and based on assumptions regarding future investment returns

Assets			Liabilities and Equity		
*Key**	*Caption*	*Customary measurement attribute*	*Key**	*Caption*	*Customary measurement attribute*
N	Prepaid expenses	Cost less amounts consumed in operations or allocated to operations based on the passage of time	E	Guarantee liabilities	Initially recognized at fair value; reduced during the life of the guarantee as the guarantor is discharged from the obligation to stand ready to perform
N	Deferred income taxes	Future deductible temporary differences and carryforwards multiplied by the effective tax rate expected to apply upon their future reversal and less a valuation allowance for the portion, if any, that is not more than 50% probable of being realized	N	Asset retirement obligations	Initially recognized as the expected present value of the future cost associated with a legal obligation to retire an asset or group of assets; generally increased in subsequent periods for accretion of interest on the obligation
N	Property and equipment held and used	Cost less accumulated depreciation subject to evaluation for impairment upon the occurrence of certain events and circumstances	N	Contingencies	If probable that a liability has been incurred and amount is reasonably estimable, the estimated settlement amount
N	Property and equipment held for sale	Fair value less cost to sell			
N	Cash surrender value of life insurance	Amount realizable under the contract at the measurement date, net of outstanding policy loans			
N	Goodwill	Arises in business combinations: ASC 805: The excess of the purchase price over the fair values of identifiable tangible and intangible net assets acquired; subject to annual impairment tests			
N	Other intangible assets	Fair value at initial recognition; subject to considerations as to whether the intangible is amortizable and whether impaired; under ASC 805 this category includes in-process research and development assets acquired in a business combination			

**ABBREVIATION KEY:*
E—Generally eligible for fair value election under ASC 825-10-25
A—Already stated at fair value or an amount that approximates fair value
N—Not eligible for fair value election or to be measured at fair value on a recurring basis

Objectives

Definition. The term "fair value" was coined by the FASB to replace the previously used term "market value" (for which the term "fair market value" was sometimes used interchangeably) in authoritative accounting literature. This change was made to emphasize the fact that, even in the absence of active primary markets for an asset or liability, the asset or liability can be valued by reference to prices and rates from secondary markets as well. Over time, this concept has been expanded further to include the application of various fair value estimation models, such as the discounted probability-weighted expected cash flow model first introduced in CON 7.

As these broader fair value concepts were evolving in the literature and in practice, the preexisting "market-based" literature had not been revised. Further, the concepts and definitions of fair value were not consistently understood or applied in similar situations by similar reporting entities.

Measurement Principles and Methodologies

It is helpful to break down the measurement process under ASC 820 into a series of steps. Although not necessarily performed in a linear manner, the following procedures and decisions need to be applied and made, in order to value an asset or liability at fair value under ASC 820. The process will be discussed in greater detail.

1. *Identify the item to be valued and the unit of account.* Specifically identify the asset or liability, including the unit of account to be used for the measurement.
2. *Determine the principal or most advantageous market and the relevant market participants.* From the reporting entity's perspective, determine the principal market in which it would sell the asset or transfer the liability. In the absence of a principal market, consider the most advantageous market for the asset or the liability. Once the principal or most advantageous market is identified, determine the characteristics of the market participants. It is not necessary that specifically named individuals or enterprises be identified for this purpose.
3. *Select the valuation premise to be used for asset measurements.* If the item being measured is an asset, determine the valuation premise to be used by evaluating whether marketplace participants would judge the highest and best use of the nonfinancial asset on a stand-alone basis or in combination with other assets as a group or with other assets and liabilities. Note that the highest and best use and valuation premise concepts only apply to measuring of nonfinancial assets.
4. *Consider the risk assumptions applicable to liability measurements.* If the item being measured is a liability, identify the key assumptions that market participants would make regarding nonperformance risk including, but not limited to, the reporting entity's own credit risk (credit standing).
5. *Identify available inputs.* Identify the key assumptions that market participants would use in pricing the asset or liability, including assumptions about risk. In identifying these assumptions, referred to as "inputs" by ASC 820, maximize the inputs that are relevant and observable (i.e., that are based on market data available from sources independent of the reporting entity). In so doing, assess the availability of relevant, reliable market data for each input that significantly affects the valuation, and identify the level of the fair value input hierarchy in which it is to be categorized.
6. *Select the appropriate valuation technique(s).* Based on the nature of the asset or liability being valued, and the types and reliability of inputs available, determine the appropriate valuation technique or combination of techniques to use in valuing the

asset or liability. The three broad categories of techniques are the market approach, the income approach, and the cost approach.

7. *Make the measurement.* Measure the asset or liability.
8. *Determine amounts to be recognized and information to be disclosed.* Determine the amounts and information to be recorded, classified, and disclosed in interim and annual financial statements.

Item identification and unit of account. In general, the same unit of account at which the asset or liability is aggregated or disaggregated by applying other applicable GAAP pronouncements is to be used for fair value measurement purposes. ASC 820-10-35-44 prohibits adjustment to the valuation for a "blockage factor." A blockage factor is an adjustment made to a valuation that takes into account the fact that the investor holds a large quantity (block) of shares relative to the market trading volume in those shares. The prohibition applies even if the quantity held by the reporting entity exceeds the market's normal trading volume—and that, if the reporting entity were, hypothetically, to place an order to sell its entire position in a single transaction, that transaction could affect the quoted price.

There is an exception for a financial assets and financial liabilities with offsetting positions in market risks or counterparty credit risk that are managed on the basis of the entity's net exposure to the risks. If certain criteria are met, the entity can measure the fair value of net position in a manner that is consistent with how market participants would price the net position. To use the exception, ASU 820-10-35-18E indicates all the following conditions must be met. The company:

1. Manages the group of financial assets and financial liabilities on the basis of the reporting entity's net exposure to a particular market risk (or risks) or to the credit risk of a particular counterparty in accordance with the reporting entity's documented risk management or investment strategy.
2. Provides information on that basis about the group of financial assets and financial liabilities to the reporting entity's management.
3. Is required or has elected to measure those financial assets and financial liabilities at fair value in the statement of financial position at the end of each reporting period.

Principal or most advantageous market and market participants. ASC 820 requires the person performing the valuation to maximize the use of relevant assumptions (inputs) that are observable from market data obtained from sources independent of the reporting entity. In making a fair value measurement, management is to assume that the asset or liability is exchanged in an orderly transaction between market participants at the measurement date.

To characterize the exchange as orderly, it is assumed that the asset or liability will have been exposed to the market for a sufficient period of time prior to the measurement date to enable marketing activities to occur that are usual and customary with respect to transactions involving such assets or liabilities. It is also to be assumed that the transaction is not a forced transaction (e.g., a forced liquidation or distress sale).

ASC 820 also specifies that if there is a principal market for an asset or liability (determined under the SEC's Accounting Standards Release [ASR] No. 118, *Accounting for Investment Securities by Registered Investment Companies*, or otherwise), the measure of fair value is the price in that market (whether directly observable or determined indirectly using a valuation technique), even if the price in a different market is potentially more advantageous at the measurement date.

Management identifies the *principal market* for the asset or liability, if such a market exists. If the entity has access to more than one market, the principal market is the market in which the reporting entity would sell the asset or transfer the liability that has the greatest volume and activity level for the asset or liability. The greater volume of activity ensures that the measurement is based on multiple transactions potentially between multiple counterparties, and is thus more representative of fair value than if the measurement were based on less extensive data.

Note that the determination of the principal market is made from the perspective of the reporting entity. Thus, different reporting entities engaging in different specialized industries, or with access to different markets, might not have the same principal market for an identical asset or liability. Inputs from the principal market are to be used irrespective of whether the price is directly observable or determined through the use of a valuation technique.

If there is no principal market for an asset or liability from the perspective of the reporting entity, then management uses the most advantageous market for the measurement. In determining the most advantageous market, management considers transaction costs. However, once the most advantageous market had been identified, transaction costs are not used to adjust the market price used for the purposes of the fair value measurement.

ASC 820 provides a typology of markets that potentially exist for assets or liabilities. (See the Definitions of Terms section at the beginning of this chapter for descriptions of each of these markets.)

1. Active market.
2. Dealer market.
3. Brokered market.
4. Principal-to-principal market.

Market participants in the principal or most advantageous market are buyers and sellers that

1. Are unrelated third parties
2. Have the ability to enter into a transaction for the asset or liability
3. Have the motivation to voluntarily enter into a transaction for the asset or liability without being forced to do so under duress
4. Are knowledgeable about the asset or liability since they would possess a reasonable understanding of the asset or liability and the terms of the transaction based on all available information including information obtainable through the performance of usual and customary due diligence procedures.

The person determining the measurement is not required to identify specific individuals or enterprises that would potentially be market participants. Instead, it is important to identify the distinguishing characteristics of participants in the particular market by considering factors specific to the asset or liability being measured, the market identified, and the participants in that market with whom the reporting entity would enter into a transaction for the asset or liability.

Measurement considerations when markets become illiquid or less liquid. Questions have arisen regarding whether transactions occurring in less liquid markets with less frequent trades might cause those market transactions to be considered forced or distress sales, thus rendering valuations made using those prices not indicative of the actual fair value of the securities.

Under ASC 820, orderly transactions are occurring in the marketplace for an asset or liability when knowledgeable buyers and sellers independent of the reporting entity are willing and able to transact and are motivated to transact without being forced to do so. If orderly transactions are occurring in a manner that is usual and customary for the asset or liability, then the transactions are not to be characterized as forced or distress sales. Just because transaction volume in a market drops significantly from prior periods does not necessarily mean that the market is no longer active.

Determining whether there has been a significant decrease in level of activity. Management is to consider the volume and level of activity in the market compared with normal market activity for the asset or liability (or similar assets or liabilities) being measured. In making that comparison, the following indicators of declining activity may point to a decrease that is considered significant. The indicators include, but are not limited to the following (which are not to be considered of equal significance or relevance, when evaluating the weight of evidence):

1. Few recent transactions
2. Price quotations based on information that is not current
3. Price quotations vary substantially over time or among market makers (e.g., in some brokered markets)
4. Indexes that were previously highly correlated with the fair values of the asset or liability have become demonstrably uncorrelated with recent indications of fair value for that asset or liability
5. There has been a significant increase in implied liquidity risk premiums, yields, or performance indicators (such as delinquency rates or loss severities) for observed transactions or quoted prices when compared with management's estimate of expected cash flows, taking into consideration all available market data about credit and other nonperformance risk for the asset or liability being measured
6. There is a wide bid-ask spread or a significant increase in that spread
7. There is a significant decline or absence of a market for new issuances (that is, a primary market) for the asset or liability (or similar assets or liabilities)
8. Little information is publicly released (e.g., in a principal-to-principal market).

(ASC 820-10-35-54C)

Management evaluates the relevance and significance of these indicators as well as whether other indicators might be present to determine whether, based on the weight of the evidence, there has been a significant decrease in the volume and level of activity for the asset or liability.

If management concludes that a significant decrease has occurred, it must perform further analysis of the transactions or quoted prices in that market in order to determine whether it is necessary to significantly adjust the quoted prices to estimate fair value in accordance with ASC 820. It is important to note that, for the purpose of estimating fair value, management's own intention to hold an asset or liability is not relevant. Fair value is a market-based measurement, not an entity-specific measurement.

Other unrelated circumstances might also necessitate significant adjustments to quoted prices, such as when a price for a similar asset requires a significant adjustment in order to compensate for characteristics or attributes of the comparable asset that are different from those of the asset whose fair value is being measured, or when a quoted price may not be sufficiently close to the measurement date.

FASB stresses that, even if there has been a significant decrease in the market volume and level of activity for the item being measured, it is inappropriate, based solely on that judgment, to conclude that all transactions occurring in that market are not orderly transactions. Factors to consider in judging whether a transaction might not be orderly include, but are not limited to

1. Insufficient time period of exposure to the market prior to the measurement date to allow for usual or customary marketing activities for transactions involving assets or liabilities *under the current market conditions*
2. The marketing exposure period was sufficient, but the seller only marketed the item being measured to a single market participant
3. The seller is in or near bankruptcy or receivership (in other words, the seller is "distressed"), or the seller is being compelled to sell in order to meet legal or regulatory requirements (in other words, the sale is "forced")
4. The transaction price is an outlier when compared with recently occurring transactions for the same or similar item.

(ASC 820-10-35-54I)

Management considers the weight of the evidence in determining whether a particular market transaction is orderly. In making that determination, management is to consider the following guidance:

1. *Transactions considered orderly.* If the weight of the evidence indicates a transaction is *orderly,* management considers that transaction price when estimating fair value or market risk premiums. The weight to be placed on that transaction price versus other indications of fair value is dependent on the specific facts and circumstances such as
   a. The volume of shares (or units) included in the transaction,
   b. The extent of comparability between the items included in the transaction and the asset or liability being measured, and
   c. How close the transaction was to the measurement date.
2. *Transactions considered not orderly.* If the weight of the evidence indicates a transaction is *not orderly,* management is to place little, if any, weight on that transaction price as compared to other indications of fair value when estimating fair value or market risk premiums.
3. *Insufficient information to determine whether or not transactions are orderly.* If management lacks sufficient information to conclude whether or not a transaction is orderly, the transaction price is to be considered when estimating fair value or market risk premiums. However, that transaction may not be the sole or even the primary basis for estimating fair value or market risk premiums. Management is to place less weight on transactions of this nature, where sufficient information is not available to conclude whether the transaction is orderly when compared with other transactions that are known to be orderly.

(ASC 820-10-35-54J)

In making the determinations above, management is not required to make all possible efforts to obtain relevant information; however, management is not to ignore information available without undue cost and effort. Obviously, management would be prevented from asserting that it lacks sufficient information with respect to whether a transaction is orderly when the reporting entity was a party to that transaction. (ASC 820-10-35-54J)

Irrespective of what valuation technique or combination of techniques is used to measure fair value, the measurement is to include appropriate risk adjustments. According to ASC 820-10-55-8, risk-averse market participants seek compensation for bearing the uncertainties inherent in the estimated future cash flows associated with an asset or liability. This compensation is referred to as a risk premium or market risk premium and it reflects the amount that the market participant would demand in order to obtain adequate compensation for that market participant's perception of the risks associated with either the amounts or timing of the estimated future cash flows. Absent such an adjustment, a measurement would not faithfully represent fair value. While determination of the appropriate risk premium may be difficult, the degree of difficulty alone is an insufficient rationale for management excluding a risk adjustment from its fair value measurement. The risk premium adjustment, however, is to reflect an orderly transaction between market participants at the measurement date *under current market conditions*.

Quoted prices obtained from third-party pricing services or brokers may be used as inputs in the fair value measurement if management had determined that those quoted prices were determined by the third party in accordance with the principles of ASC 820 which in practical terms means that management will need to inquire of the information provider as to, among other things, the origin of the quote, the methodology followed to compute it, the types of inputs used and their sources, the level of activity in the market for market-based quotes, the age of the data used (its proximity to the measurement date), and other information relevant in the circumstances.

When there has been a significant decrease in the volume and level of activity for the asset or liability, management is to evaluate whether those quoted prices are based on current information that reflects orderly transactions (mark-to-market) or are based on application of a valuation technique reflecting market participant assumptions, including assumptions about risk premiums (mark-to-model). Management is to place less weight on quotes that are not based on the results of actual market transactions than on other indications of fair value. The type of quote is also to be considered, for example, whether the quote represents a binding offer or an indicative price, with a binding offer to be given greater weight than an indicative price.

Selection of the valuation premise for asset measurements. The measurement of the fair value of a nonfinancial asset is to assume the highest and best use of that asset from the perspective of market participants. Generally, the highest and best use is the way that market participants would be expected to deploy the asset (or a group of assets within which they would use the asset) that would maximize the value of the asset (or group). This highest and best use assumption might differ from the way that the reporting entity is currently using the asset or group of assets or its future plans for using it (them).

At the measurement date, the highest and best use must be physically possible (given the physical characteristics of the asset), legally permissible (taking into account any legal restrictions), and financially feasible (based on income or cash flows). Determination of the highest and best use of the nonfinancial asset will establish which of the two valuation premises to use in measuring the asset's fair value, the in-use valuation premise, or the in-exchange valuation premise.

Strategic buyers and financial buyers. ASC 820 differentiates between two broad categories of market participants that would potentially buy an asset or group of assets.

1. *Strategic buyers* are market participants whose acquisition objectives are to use the asset or group of assets (the "target") to enhance the performance of their existing business by achieving benefits such as additional capacity, improved technology, managerial, marketing, or technical expertise, access to new markets, improved market share, or enhanced market positioning. Thus, a strategic buyer views the purchase as a component of a broader business plan and, as a result, a strategic buyer may be willing to pay a premium to consummate the acquisition and may, in fact, be the only type of buyer available with an interest in acquiring the target. Ideally, from the standpoint of the seller, more than one strategic buyer would be interested in the acquisition which would create a bidding situation that further increases the selling price.

2. *Financial buyers* are market participants who seek to acquire the target based on its merits as a stand-alone investment. A financial buyer is interested in a return on its investment over a shorter time horizon, often three to five years, after which time their objective would typically be to sell the target. An attractive target is one that offers high growth potential in a short period of time resulting in a selling price substantially higher than the original acquisition price. Therefore, even at acquisition, a financial buyer is concerned with a viable exit strategy. A financial buyer, unlike a strategic buyer, typically does not possess a high level of industry or managerial expertise in the target's industry.

The combination valuation premise. This premise assumes that the maximum fair value to market participants is the price that would be received by the reporting entity (seller) assuming the asset would be used by the buyer with other assets as a group and further, that the other assets in the group would be available to potential buyers. The target might continue to be used as presently installed or may be configured in a different manner by the buyer. The assumptions regarding the level of aggregation (or disaggregation) of the asset and other associated assets may be different than the level used in applying other accounting pronouncements. Thus, in considering highest and best use and the resulting level of aggregation, the evaluator is not constrained by how the asset may be assigned by the reporting entity to a reportable or operating segment under ASC 820, a business, reporting unit, asset group, or disposal group (ASC 820-10-35). The assumptions regarding the highest and best use of the target should normally be consistent for all of the assets included in the group within which it would be used. Generally, the market participants whose highest and best use of an asset or group of assets would be in combination are characterized as strategic buyers, as previously described.

The stand-alone valuation premise. This premise assumes that the maximum fair value to market participants is the price that would be received by the reporting entity (seller) assuming the asset would be sold principally on a stand-alone basis.

Risk assumptions when valuing a liability. Many accountants, analysts, and others find the concept of computing fair value of liabilities and recognizing changes in fair value as they occur to be counterintuitive. Consider the case when a reporting entity's own credit standing declines (universally acknowledged as a "bad thing"). A fair value measurement that incorporates the effect of this decline in credit rating would result in a decline in the fair value of the liability and a resultant increase in stockholders' equity (a "good thing"). The justification provided in ASC 820 (and by referencing CON 7) is that

> *A change in credit standing represents a change in the relative positions of the two classes of claimants (shareholders and creditors) to an entity's assets. If the credit standing diminishes, the fair value of creditors' claims diminishes. The amount of shareholders' residual claims to the entity's assets may appear to increase but that increase is probably offset by losses that may have occasioned the decline in credit standing. Because shareholders usually cannot be called on to pay a corporation's liabilities, the amount of their residual claims approaches, and is limited by zero. Thus a change in the position of borrowers necessarily alters the position of shareholders, and vice versa. (CON 7, Paragraph 82)*

The hypothetical transaction and operational difficulties experienced in practice. Under ASC 820, fair value measurements of liabilities assume that a hypothetical transfer to a market participant occurs on the measurement date. In measuring the fair value of a liability, the evaluator assumes that the reporting entity's obligation to its creditor (i.e., the counterparty to the obligation) will continue at and after the measurement date (i.e., the obligation will not be repaid or settled prior to its contractual maturity). This being the case, this hypothetical transfer price would most likely represent the price that the current creditor (holder of the debt instrument) could obtain from a marketplace participant willing to purchase the debt instrument in a transaction involving the original creditor assigning its rights to the purchaser. In effect, the hypothetical market participant that purchased the instrument would be in the same position as the current creditor with respect to expected future cash flows (or expected future performance, if the liability is not settleable in cash) from the reporting entity.

The evaluator further assumes that the nonperformance risk related to the obligation would remain outstanding and the transferee would fulfill the obligation. Nonperformance risk is the risk that an entity will not fulfill its obligation. It is an all-encompassing concept that includes the reporting entity's own credit standing but also includes other risks associated with the nonfulfillment of the obligation. For example, a liability to deliver goods and/or perform services may bear nonperformance risk associated with the ability of the debtor to fulfill the obligation in accordance with the timing and specifications of the contract. Further, nonperformance risk increases or decreases as a result of changes in the fair value of credit enhancements associated with the liability (e.g., collateral, credit insurance, and/or guarantees).

Liabilities with inseparable third-party credit enhancements. Creditors often impose a requirement that, in connection with granting credit to a debtor, the debtor obtain a guarantee of the indebtedness from a creditworthy third party. Under such an arrangement, should the debtor default on its obligation, the third-party guarantor would become obligated to repay the obligation on behalf of the defaulting debtor and, of course, the debtor would be obligated to repay the guarantor for having satisfied the debt on its behalf.

In connection with a bond issuance, for example, the guarantee is generally purchased by the issuer (debtor) and the issuer then combines (bundles) the guarantee (also referred to as a "credit enhancement") with the bonds and issues the combined securities to investors. By packaging a bond with a related credit enhancement, the issuer improves the likelihood that the bond will be successfully marketed as well as reduces the effective interest rate paid on the bond by obtaining higher issuance proceeds than it would otherwise receive absent the bundled credit enhancement.

Scope exceptions. The following guidance *does not* apply to

1. Credit enhancements provided
   a. By a government or government agency (such as deposit insurance provided by the US Federal Deposit Insurance Corporation [FDIC])
   b. Between reporting entities within a consolidated or combined group
   c. Between entities under common control
2. The holder of the issuer's credit-enhanced liability.

Measurement. In accordance with ASC 820-10-35-18a, the issuer is not to include the effect of the credit enhancement in its fair value measurement of the liability. Thus, in determining the fair value of the liability, the issuer would consider its own credit standing and would not consider the credit standing of the third-party guarantor that provided the credit enhancement. Consequently, the unit of accounting to be used in the fair value measurement of a liability with an inseparable credit enhancement is the liability itself, absent the credit enhancement.

In the event that the guarantor is required to make payments to the creditor under the guarantee, it would result in a transfer of the issuer's obligation to repay the original creditor to the guarantor with the issuer then obligated to repay the guarantor. Should this occur, the obligation of the issuer to the guarantor would be an unguaranteed liability. Thus, the fair value of that transferred, unguaranteed obligation only considers the credit standing of the issuer.

Upon issuance of the credit-enhanced debt, the issuer is to allocate the proceeds it receives between the liability issued and the premium for the credit enhancement.

Disclosure. An issuer of debt with an inseparable credit enhancement that is covered by the scope of this guidance is required to disclose the existence of the third-party credit enhancement.

Inputs. For the purpose of fair value measurements, inputs are the assumptions that market participants would use in pricing an asset or liability, including assumptions regarding risk. An input is either observable or unobservable. Observable inputs are either directly observable or indirectly observable. ASC 820 requires the evaluator to maximize the use of relevant observable inputs and minimize the use of unobservable inputs.

An observable input is based on market data obtainable from sources independent of the reporting entity. For an input to be considered relevant, it must be considered determinative of fair value. Even if there has been a significant decrease in the volume and level of market activity for an asset or liability, it is not to be automatically assumed that the market is inactive or that individual transactions in that market are disorderly (that is, are forced or liquidation sales made under duress).

An unobservable input reflects assumptions made by management of the reporting entity with respect to assumptions it believes market participants would use to price an asset or liability based on the best information available under the circumstances.

ASC 820 provides a fair value input hierarchy (see diagram below) to serve as a framework for classifying inputs based on the extent to which they are based on observable data.

Hierarchy of Fair Value Inputs

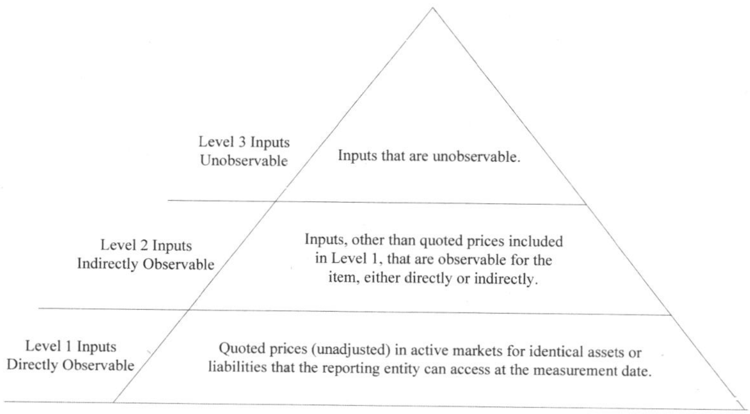

Level 1 inputs. Level 1 inputs are considered the most reliable evidence of fair value and are to be used whenever they are available. These inputs consist of quoted prices in active markets for identical assets or liabilities. The active market must be one in which the reporting entity has the ability to access the quoted price at the measurement date. To be considered an active market, transactions for the asset or liability being measured must occur frequently enough and in sufficient volume to provide pricing information on an ongoing basis.

A Level 1 input should be used without adjustment to measure fair value whenever possible. One should not adjust a Level 1 input except in these cases:

- When the entity has a large number of similar assets or liabilities, and it would be difficult to obtain pricing information for each individual item on the measurement date.
- When a quoted price in an active market does not represent the fair value of an asset or liability on the measurement date.
- When the quoted price needs to be adjusted for factors specific to the item.

The use of Level 2 or Level 3 inputs is generally prohibited when Level 1 inputs are available.

Level 2 inputs. Level 2 inputs are quoted prices for the asset or liability (other than those included in Level 1) that are either directly or indirectly observable. Level 2 inputs are to be considered when quoted prices for the identical asset or liability are not available. If the asset or liability being measured has a contractual term, a Level 2 input must be observable for substantially the entire term. These inputs include

1. Quoted prices for *similar* assets or liabilities in active markets
2. Quoted prices for identical or similar assets or liabilities in markets that are *not active*
3. Inputs other than quoted prices that are observable for the asset or liability (e.g., interest rates and yield curves observable at commonly quoted intervals; implied volatilities; credit spreads; and market-corroborated inputs).

Adjustments made to Level 2 inputs necessary to reflect fair value, if any, will vary depending on an analysis of specific factors associated with the asset or liability being measured. These factors include

1. Condition or location
2. Extent to which the inputs relate to items comparable to the asset
3. Volume or level of activity in the markets in which the inputs are observed.

Depending on the level of the fair value input hierarchy in which the inputs used to measure the adjustment are classified, an adjustment that is significant to the fair value measurement in its entirety could render the measurement a Level 3 measurement.

Level 3 inputs. Level 3 inputs are unobservable inputs. These are necessary when little, if any, market activity occurs for the asset or liability. Level 3 inputs assumptions that a market participant would use when pricing the asset or liability including assumptions about risk. The best information available in the circumstances is to be used to develop the Level 3 inputs. This information might begin with internal data of the reporting entity. Cost-benefit considerations apply in that management is not required to "undertake all possible efforts" to obtain information about the assumptions that would be made by market participants. Attention is to be paid, however, to information available to management without undue cost and effort and, consequently, management's internal assumptions used to develop unobservable inputs are to be adjusted if such information contradicts those assumptions.

Inputs based on bid and ask prices. Quoted bid prices represent the maximum price at which market participants are willing to buy an asset; quoted ask prices represent the minimum price at which market participants are willing to sell an asset. If available market prices are expressed in terms of bid and ask prices, management is to use the price within the bid-ask spread (the range of values between bid and ask prices) that is most representative of fair value irrespective of where in the fair value hierarchy the input would be classified. ASC 820 permits the use of pricing conventions such as midmarket pricing as a practical alternative for determining fair value measurements within a bid-ask spread. The use of bid prices for asset valuations and ask prices for liability valuations is permitted but not required.

Categorizing inputs. Categorization of inputs as to the level of the hierarchy in which they fall serves two purposes. First, it provides the evaluator with a means of prioritizing assumptions used as to their level of objectivity and verifiability in the marketplace. Second, as discussed later in this chapter, the hierarchy provides a framework to provide informative disclosures that enable readers to assess the reliability and market observability of the fair value estimates embedded in the financial statements.

In making a particular measurement of fair value, the inputs used may be classifiable in more than one of the levels of the hierarchy. When this is the case, the inputs used in the fair value measurement in its entirety are to be classified in the level of the hierarchy in which the lowest level input that is significant to the measurement is classified.

It is important to assess available inputs and their relative classification in the hierarchy prior to selecting the valuation technique or techniques to be applied to measure fair value for a particular asset or liability. The objective, in selecting from among alternative calculation techniques, would be to select the technique or combination of techniques that maximizes the use of observable inputs.

Valuation techniques. In measuring fair value, management employs one or more valuation techniques consistent with the market approach, the income approach, and/or the cost approach. As previously discussed, the selection of a particular technique (or techniques) to measure fair value is to be based on its appropriateness to the asset or liability being measured, maximizing the use of observable inputs and minimizing the use of unobservable inputs.

In certain situations, such as when using Level 1 inputs, use of a single valuation technique will be sufficient. In other situations, such as when valuing a reporting unit, management may need to use multiple valuation techniques. When doing so, the results yielded by applying the various techniques are evaluated considering the reasonableness of the range of values. The fair value is the point within the range that is most representative of fair value in the circumstances.

Management is required to consistently apply the valuation techniques it elects to use to measure fair value. It would be appropriate to change valuation techniques or how they are applied if the change results in fair value measurements that are equally or more representative of fair value. Situations that might give rise to such a change would be when new markets develop, new information becomes available, previously available information ceases to be available, valuation techniques improve, or market conditions change. Revisions that result from either a change in valuation technique or a change in the application of a valuation technique are to be accounted for as changes in accounting estimate under ASC 250.

Market approach. The market approach to valuation uses information generated by actual market transactions for identical or comparable assets or liabilities (including a business in its entirety). Market approach techniques often will use market multiples derived from a set of comparable transactions for the asset or liability or similar items. The evaluator needs to consider both qualitative and quantitative factors in determining the point within the range that is most representative of fair value. An example of a market approach is matrix pricing. This is a mathematical technique used primarily for the purpose of valuing debt securities without relying solely on quoted prices for the specific securities. Matrix pricing uses factors such as the stated interest rate, maturity, credit rating, and quoted prices of similar issues to develop the issue's current market yield.

Cost approach. The cost approaches are based on quantifying the amount required to replace an asset's remaining service capacity (i.e., the asset's current replacement cost). A valuation technique classified as a cost approach would measure the cost to a market participant (buyer) to acquire or construct a substitute asset of comparable utility, adjusted for obsolescence. Obsolescence adjustments include factors for physical wear and tear, improvements to technology, and economic (external) obsolescence. Thus, obsolescence is a broader concept than financial statement depreciation which simply represents a cost allocation convention and is not intended to be used as a valuation technique.

Income approach. Techniques classified as income approaches measure fair value based on current market expectations about future amounts (such as cash flows or net income) and discount them to an amount in measurement date dollars. Valuation techniques that follow an income approach include the Black-Scholes-Merton model (a closed-form model) and binomial or lattice models (open-form models), which use present value techniques, as well as the multiperiod excess earnings method that is used in fair value measurements of certain intangible assets such as in-process research and development.

Measurement considerations

Initial recognition. When the reporting entity first acquires an asset or incurs (or assumes) a liability in an exchange transaction, the transaction price is an entry price, the price paid to acquire the asset and the price received to assume the liability. Fair value measurements are based not on entry prices, but rather on exit prices—the price that would be received to sell the asset or paid to transfer the liability. While entry and exit prices differ conceptually, in many cases they may be identical and can be considered to represent fair value of the asset or liability at initial recognition. This is not always the case, however, and in assessing fair value at initial recognition, management is to consider transaction-specific factors and factors specific to the assets and/or liabilities that are being initially recognized. Examples of situations where transaction price might not represent fair value at initial recognition include

1. Related-party transactions, unless the entity has evidence that the transaction was entered into at market terms.
2. Transactions taking place under duress or the seller is forced to accept the price, such as when the seller is experiencing financial difficulties.
3. Different units of account that apply to the transaction price and the assets/liabilities being measured. This can occur, for example, where the transaction price includes other elements besides the assets/liabilities that are being measured such as unstated rights and privileges that are subject to separate measurement or when the transaction price includes transaction costs (see discussion below).
4. The exchange transaction takes place in a market different from the principal or most advantageous market in which the reporting entity would sell the asset or transfer the liability. An example of this situation is when the reporting entity is a securities dealer that enters into transactions with customers in the retail market, but the principal market for the exit transaction is with other dealers in the dealer market.

(ASC 820-10-30-3A)

If another ASC Topic requires or permits fair value measurement initially and the transaction price differs from fair value, the resulting gain or loss is recognized in earnings, unless other specified.

Transaction costs. Transaction costs are the incremental direct costs that would be incurred to sell an asset or transfer a liability. While, as previously discussed, transaction costs are considered in determining the market that is most advantageous, they are not used to adjust the fair value measurement of the asset or liability being measured. FASB excluded them from the measurement because they are not characteristic of an asset or liability being measured. (ASC 820-10-35-9B)

Transportation costs. If an attribute of the asset or liability being measured is its location, the price determined in the principal or most advantageous market is to be adjusted for the costs that would be incurred by the reporting entity to transport it to or from that market. (ASC 820-10-35-9C)

Fair Value Disclosures

Substantial disclosures regarding fair value are required by various ASC Topics. In the preparation of the financial statements, these disclosures are often placed in different informative notes including descriptions of the entity's accounting policies, financial instruments, impairment, derivatives, pensions, revenue recognition, share-based compensation, risks and uncertainties, certain significant estimates, etc. ASC 820 encourages preparers to combine disclosure requirements under ASC 820 with those of other subtopics. Plan assets of a defined benefit pension plan or other postretirement plans accounted for under ASC 715 are not subject to the ASC 820 requirements and should apply the disclosure requirements in the relevant paragraphs of ASC 715.

Objectives. ASC 820-10-50-1 requires a reporting entity to disclose information that helps financial statements users to assess:

a. For assets and liabilities that are measured at fair value on a recurring or nonrecurring basis in the statement of financial position after initial recognition, the valuation techniques and inputs used to develop those measures.
b. For recurring fair value measurements using significant unobservable inputs (Level 3), the effect of the measurements on earnings (or change to net assets) or other comprehensive income for the period. (ASC 820-10-50-1)

To meet these objectives, preparers must consider the level of detail necessary to satisfy the requirement, how much emphasis to place on each of the requirements, how much to aggregate or disaggregate, and whether additional information is needed to evaluate the information disclosed. (ASC 820-10-50-1A)

Entities must also make disclosures regarding transfers between levels, and highest and best use of a nonfinancial asset. There are no exceptions for public companies. However, nonpublic entities are not required to

- Disclose information regarding transfers between Levels 1 and 2,
- Include a narrative description regarding the sensitivity of fair value measurements to changes in unobservable inputs that result in significant changes,
- Disclose related items not reported at fair value, but for which fair value is disclosed.

Nonpublic entities are not required to disclose the level of the fair value measurement for items that are not measured at fair value in the statement of financial position but for which fair value is disclosed.

A list of the required disclosures can be found in the Appendix.

50 ASC 825 FINANCIAL INSTRUMENTS

PERSPECTIVE AND ISSUES

Subtopics

ASC 825, *Financial Instruments,* contains two Subtopics:

- ASC 825-10, *Overall,* which has two Subsections:
  - General, which provides guidance on credit losses on financial instruments with off-balance-sheet credit risk and some disclosures about financial instruments
  - Fair Value Option, which provides guidance on the circumstances under which entities may choose the fair value option and the related presentation and disclosure requirements
- ASC 825-20, *Registration Payment Arrangements.*

Scope and Scope Exceptions

The following items are eligible for the fair value option (also see the chapter on ASC 820 – the summary table in the section entitled "The Mixed Attribute Model"):

1. All recognized financial assets and financial liabilities *except*
   a. Investments in subsidiaries required to be consolidated by the reporting entity
   b. Interests in variable interest entities required to be consolidated by the reporting entity[1]
   c. Employers' and plans' obligations (unfunded or underfunded liabilities) or assets (representing net overfunded positions) for
      (1) Pension benefits

[1] *Under ASC 805, consolidated variable interest entities are referred to as subsidiaries in the same manner as consolidated voting interest entities.*

(2) Other postretirement benefits (including health care and life insurance benefits)
(3) Postemployment benefits
(4) Other deferred compensation, termination, and share-based payment arrangements such as employee stock option plans; employee stock purchase plans; compensated absences; and exit and disposal activities

d. Financial assets and financial liabilities under leases (this exception does not, however, apply to a guarantee of a third-party lease obligation or a contingent obligation associated with cancellation of a lease)
e. Deposit liabilities, withdrawable on demand, of banks; saving and loan associations; credit unions; and other similar depository institutions
f. Financial instruments that are, in whole or in part, classified by the issuer as a component of stockholders' equity (including "temporary equity," also sometimes referred to as "mezzanine") such as a convertible debt security with a noncontingent beneficial conversion feature.

(ASC 825-10-15-5)

2. Firm commitments that would otherwise not be recognized at inception and that involve only financial instruments. An example is a forward purchase contract for a loan that is not readily convertible to cash. The commitment involves only financial instruments (the loan and cash) and would not be recognized at inception since it does not qualify as a derivative.
3. A written loan commitment
4. Rights and obligations under insurance contracts or warranties that are not financial instruments[2] but whose terms permit the insurer (warrantor) to settle claims by paying a third party to provide goods and services to the counterparty (insured party or warranty claimant)
5. A host financial instrument resulting from bifurcating an embedded nonfinancial derivative instrument from a nonfinancial hybrid instrument under ASC 815-15-25. An example would be an instrument in which the value of the bifurcated embedded derivative is payable in cash, services, or merchandise but the host debt contract is only payable in cash.

(ASC 825-10-15-4)

Overview

ASC 825-10-25, *The Fair Value Option*, encourages reporting entities to elect to use fair value to measure eligible assets and liabilities in their financial statements. The objective is to improve financial reporting by mitigating the volatility in reported earnings that is caused by measuring related assets and liabilities differently. Electing entities obtain relief from the onerous and complex documentation requirements that apply to certain hedging transactions under ASC 815. ASC 825-10-25 applies to businesses and not-for-profit organizations and provides management of these entities substantial discretion in electing to measure eligible assets and liabilities at fair value.

---

[2] *Insurance contracts that require or permit the insurer to settle claims by providing goods or services instead of by paying cash are not, by definition, financial instruments. Similarly, warranties that require or permit the warrantor to settle claims by providing goods and services in lieu of cash do not constitute financial instruments.*

Management is given an extraordinary amount of discretion in selecting the assets and/or liabilities for which it chooses to make this election, the fair value option. In general, the election is made on an individual contract or item-by-item basis.

DEFINITIONS OF TERMS

Conduit Debt Securities. Certain limited-obligation revenue bonds, certificates of participation, or similar debt instruments issued by a state or local governmental entity for the express purpose of providing financing for a specific third party (the conduit bond obligor) that is not a part of the state or local government's financial reporting entity. Although conduit debt securities bear the name of the governmental entity that issues them, the governmental entity often has no obligation for such debt beyond the resources provided by a lease or loan agreement with the third party on whose behalf the securities are issued. Further, the conduit bond obligor is responsible for any future financial reporting requirements.

Fair Value. The price that would be received to sell an asset or paid to transfer a liability in an orderly transaction between market participants at the measurement date.

Financial Asset. Cash, evidence of an ownership interest in an entity, or a contract that conveys to one entity a right to do either of the following:

a. Receive cash or another financial instrument from a second entity
b. Exchange other financial instruments on potentially favorable terms with the second entity.

Financial Instrument. Cash, evidence of an ownership interest in an entity, or a contract that both:

a. Imposes on one entity a contractual obligation either:
   1. To deliver cash or another financial instrument to a second entity
   2. To exchange other financial instruments on potentially unfavorable terms with the second entity.
b. Conveys to that second entity a contractual right either:
   1. To receive cash or another financial instrument from the first entity
   2. To exchange other financial instruments on potentially favorable terms with the first entity.

The use of the term financial instrument in this definition is recursive (because the term financial instrument is included in it), though it is not circular. The definition requires a chain of contractual obligations that ends with the delivery of cash or an ownership interest in an entity. Any number of obligations to deliver financial instruments can be links in a chain that qualifies a particular contract as a financial instrument.

Contractual rights and contractual obligations encompass both those that are conditioned on the occurrence of a specified event and those that are not. All contractual rights (contractual obligations) that are financial instruments meet the definition of asset (liability) set forth in FASB Concepts Statement No. 6, *Elements of Financial Statements*, although some may not be recognized as assets (liabilities) in financial statements—that is, they may be off-balance-sheet—because they fail to meet some other criterion for recognition.

For some financial instruments, the right is held by or the obligation is due from (or the obligation is owed to or by) a group of entities rather than a single entity.

Financial Liability. A contract that imposes on one entity an obligation to do either of the following:

a. Deliver cash or another financial instrument to a second entity
b. Exchange other financial instruments on potentially unfavorable terms with the second entity.

Firm Commitment. An agreement with an unrelated party, binding on both parties and usually legally enforceable, with the following characteristics:

a. The agreement specifies all significant terms, including the quantity to be exchanged, the fixed price, and the timing of the transaction. The fixed price may be expressed as a specified amount of an entity's functional currency or of a foreign currency. It may also be expressed as a specified interest rate or specified effective yield. The binding provisions of an agreement are regarded to include those legal rights and obligations codified in the laws to which such an agreement is subject. A price that varies with the market price of the item that is the subject of the firm commitment cannot qualify as a fixed price. For example, a price that is specified in terms of ounces of gold would not be a fixed price if the market price of the item to be purchased or sold under the firm commitment varied with the price of gold.
b. The agreement includes a disincentive for nonperformance that is sufficiently large to make performance probable. In the legal jurisdiction that governs the agreement, the existence of statutory rights to pursue remedies for default equivalent to the damages suffered by the nondefaulting party, in and of itself, represents a sufficiently large disincentive for nonperformance to make performance probable for purposes of applying the definition of a firm commitment.

Liability Issued with an Inseparable Third-Party Credit Enhancement. A liability that is issued with a credit enhancement obtained from a third party, such as debt that is issued with a financial guarantee from a third party that guarantees the issuer's payment obligation.

Nonpublic Entity. Any entity that does not meet any of the following conditions:

a. Its debt or equity securities trade in a public market either on a stock exchange (domestic or foreign) or in the over-the-counter market, including securities quoted only locally or regionally.
b. It is a conduit bond obligor for conduit debt securities that are traded in a public market (a domestic or foreign stock exchange or an over-the-counter market, including local or regional markets).
c. It files with a regulatory agency in preparation for the sale of any class of debt or equity securities in a public market.
d. It is controlled by an entity covered by the preceding criteria.

Publicly Traded Company. See definition in the chapter on ASC 270.

CONCEPTS, RULES, AND EXAMPLES

ASC 825-10-25, *Financial Instruments: The Fair Value Option*

Flexibility of application. ASC 825-10-25 provides management with substantial flexibility in electing the fair value option (FVO). Once elected, however, the election is irrevocable unless, as discussed later in this section, a new election date occurs. The election can be made for a single eligible item without electing it for other identical items subject to the following limitations:

1. If the FVO is elected with respect to an investment otherwise required to be accounted for under the equity method of accounting, the FVO election is to be applied to all of the investor's financial interests in the same entity (equity and debt, including guarantees) that are eligible items.
2. If a single contract with a borrower (such as a line of credit or construction loan) involves multiple advances to that borrower and those advances lose their individual identity and are aggregated with the overall loan balance, the FVO is only permitted to be elected to apply to the larger overall loan balance and not individually with respect to each individual advance.
3. If the FVO is applied to an eligible insurance or reinsurance contract, it is also required to be applied to all claims and obligations under the contract.
4. If the FVO is elected for an eligible insurance contract (base contract) for which integrated or nonintegrated contract features or coverages (some of which are referred to as "riders") are issued either concurrently or subsequently, the FVO is required to be applied to those features and coverages. The FVO is not permitted to be elected for only the nonintegrated contract features and coverages, even though they are accounted for separately under ASC 944-30.[3]

Other than as provided in 1 and 2 above, management is not required to apply the FVO to all instruments issued or acquired in a single transaction. The lowest level of election, however, is at the single legal contract level. A financial instrument that is, in legal form, a single contract is not permitted to be separated into component parts for the purpose of electing the FVO. For example, an individual bond is the minimum denomination of that type of debt security.

An investor in an equity security of a particular issuer may elect the FVO for its entire investment in that equity security including any fractional shares issued by the investee in connection, for example, with a dividend reinvestment plan.

Management of an acquirer, parent company, or primary beneficiary[4] decides whether to elect the FVO with respect to the eligible items of an acquiree, subsidiary, or consolidated variable interest entity. That decision, however, only applies in the consolidated financial statements. FVO choices made by management of an acquiree, subsidiary, or variable interest entity continue to apply in their separate financial statements should they choose to issue them.

Timing of the election. Management may elect the FVO for an eligible item in one of two ways.

1. Based on an established policy for specified types of eligible items that it follows consistently, or
2. On the date of occurrence of one of the following events:
   a. The entity initially recognizes the item.
   b. The entity enters into an eligible firm commitment.

---

[3] *ASC 944-30-20 defines a nonintegrated contract feature in an insurance contract as a feature in which the benefits provided are not related to or dependent on the provisions of the base contract. For the purposes of applying the FVO election, neither an integrated nor a nonintegrated contract feature or coverage qualifies as a separate instrument.*

[4] *Under ASC 805 a primary beneficiary is referred to as a parent in the same manner as a company that consolidates a voting interest entity.*

c. Financial assets previously required to be reported at fair value with unrealized gains and losses included in income due to the application of specialized accounting principles cease to qualify for that accounting treatment (e.g., a subsidiary subject to ASC 946 transfers a security to another subsidiary of the same parent that is not subject to the ASC).
d. The accounting treatment for an investment in another entity changes because
   (1) The investment becomes subject to the equity method of accounting (and, for example, had previously been accounted for under ASC 320 or under the FVO)
   (2) The investor ceases to consolidate a subsidiary or variable interest entity but retains an interest in the entity
e. An event requires an eligible item to be remeasured at fair value at the time that the event occurs but does not require fair value measurements to be made at each subsequent reporting date. Specifically excluded from being considered an eligible event are
   (1) Recognition of impairment under lower-of-cost-or-market accounting, or
   (2) Other-than-temporary impairment.

(ASC 825-10-25-4)

Among the events that require initial fair value measurement or subsequent fair value remeasurements of this kind are

(1) Business combinations,
(2) Consolidation or deconsolidation of a subsidiary or variable interest entity, and
(3) Significant modifications of debt, as defined in ASC 470-50, *Debt—Modifications and Extinguishments.*

(ASC 825-10-25-5)

Financial statement presentation and disclosure

Statement of financial position. ASC 825-10-25 requires the reporting entity to report assets and liabilities for which the FVO was elected in a manner that separates those amounts from carrying amounts of similar assets and liabilities measured using another measurement method. Two alternatives are provided.

1. Present the aggregate fair value and non-fair value amounts on the same line of the statement of financial position and parenthetically provide the amount measured at fair value that is included in the aggregate amount.
2. Present two separate line items to display the fair value and non-fair value carrying amounts.

The manner in which the first alternative is illustrated in ASC 825-10-25 could potentially confuse or mislead readers.

Private equity investments ($75 at fair value)	$125

This caption could easily be misunderstood by the reader to mean that the reporting entity holds private equity investments with an aggregate carrying value of $125 whose fair value has declined to $75 thus implying a $50 unrealized loss. In fact, this caption is intended to convey the fact that the reporting entity holds private equity investments with an aggregate carrying value of $125 and that the $125 is comprised of $75 valued at fair value in accordance with an election of the FVO and $50 using another measurement attribute such as the cost method or equity method.

If using parenthetical disclosure, it would be less misleading if the amount were presented as follows:

Private equity investments	
($75 measured at fair value; $50 measured using the equity method)	$125

This can get cumbersome and is still confusing. It becomes even more unwieldy when considering the fact that reporting entities customarily present two or three years' comparative statements of financial position and that not-for-profit organizations often use tabular formats for their statements of financial position that present separate columns for unrestricted net assets, temporarily restricted net assets, and permanently restricted net assets.

Another source of confusion is the fact that existing GAAP requires certain items (such as derivatives, trading securities, and available-for-sale securities) to be stated at fair value without consideration of the FVO. Therefore, it is conceivable that a single statement of financial position will contain financial instruments that are stated at fair value due to a requirement in GAAP, financial instruments that are stated at fair value due to management's election of the FVO, and financial instruments that are stated using some other attribute such as cost method or equity method, or, as is permitted for investments in certain debt securities, using amortized cost. When this is the case, the reporting entity may wish to use a format such as the one shown in the sample "Consolidated Statement of Financial Position" for the Young Aviation Chopper and Helicopter Works, Inc.

Many variations can be derived from this method of presentation. For example, subtotals are only necessary to be presented for the total column since the notes to the financial statements provide fair value totals by major class. The financial statement preparer may wish to augment this presentation by including a column that subtotals all amounts stated at fair value irrespective of whether they are subject to the FVO election.

Separate sections of assets and liabilities could contain separate line items enumerating the eligible items within each for which the FVO was elected by management.

Young Aviation Chopper and Helicopter Works, Inc.
Consolidated Statement of Financial Position
December 31, 20X2
(Unclassified for Illustrative Purposes)

	Amounts measured under the company's customary accounting policies at other than fair value	*Amounts required to be measured at fair value or whose carrying values approximate fair value*	*Eligible amounts measured at fair value at management's election*	*Total*
Assets				
Cash and cash equivalents		$ 38		$ 38
Accounts receivable	$ 97			97
Notes receivable	400		$150	550
Inventory	134			134
Investments				
Trading securities		115		115
Securities available-for-sale		75		75
Securities held-to-maturity	32			32
Derivatives		60		60
Private equity	50		75	125
Property and equipment, net	10			10
Other assets	20	—	—	20
Total assets	$ 743	$288	$225	$1,256
Liabilities				
Borrowings under short-term line of credit	$ 128			$ 128
Long-term debt	140		$ 60	200
Accounts payable		$110		110
Accrued liabilities	130			130
Other liabilities	555	—	—	555
Total liabilities	953	110	60	1,123
Stockholders' equity				
Common stock	4			4
Additional paid-in capital	88			88
Retained earnings	42			42
Accumulated other comprehensive income	(1)	—	—	(1)
Total stockholders' equity	133	–	–	133
Total liabilities and stockholders' equity	$1,086	$110	$ 60	$1,256

Statement of cash flows. ASC 825-10-25 requires cash receipts and cash payments related to items measured at fair value to be classified in the statement of cash flows according to their nature and purpose. Inexplicably, however, ASC 825-10-25 leaves the provision of ASC 230 unchanged that requires returns on investments (interest and dividends) to be accounted for as operating activities.

Disclosure objectives. Consistent with the approach in ASC 820, ASC 825-10-25 provides financial statement preparers with the principal objectives associated with fair value option disclosures and then sets forth in detail the disclosures FASB deems necessary to meet the objective. The principal objectives are to facilitate comparisons (1) between entities that choose different measurement attributes for similar assets and liabilities, and (2) between assets and liabilities in the financial statements of an entity that elects to use different measurement attributes for similar assets and liabilities. FASB indicates that it expects the disclosures to result in

1. Information sufficient to enable financial statement users to understand
   a. The reasons why management elected or partially elected the FVO
   b. How changes in fair values affected net income for the period
   c. The differences between fair values and contractual cash flows for certain items.
2. The information that would have been required to be disclosed about certain items (e.g., equity-method investments, nonperforming loans) absent the FVO election.

Although not required by ASC 825-10-25, FASB encourages management to present the disclosures it requires in combination with related fair value disclosures required to be disclosed by parts of the codification (such as ASC 825-10-50 and ASC 820).

Example of disclosure under ASC 820 and ASC 825-10-25 combined with ASC 825-10-50 disclosures

The following example does not purport to illustrate all of the disclosure requirements specified within GAAP. Instead, it is presented to illustrate how the financial statement preparer might organize the required tabular disclosures by integrating the ASC 825-10-50 disclosures regarding the fair value of financial instruments with the ASC 820 and ASC 825-10-25 disclosures discussed in this chapter.

Young Aviation Chopper and Helicopter Works, Inc.
Notes to Financial Statements
December 31, 20X2

Note X, Fair values of financial assets and liabilities

(000 Omitted)			Fair Value Measurements at 12/31/X2				Year Ended 12/31/X2 — Changes in fair values for items elected to be measured at fair value and the caption in which they are included in the statement of income				
				Measured Using							
Description	*Total carrying amount in balance sheet 12/31/X2*	*ASC 825 estimated fair value*	*Assets/ liabilities measured at fair value 12/31/X2*	*Quoted prices in active markets for identical assets (Level 1)*	*Significant other observable inputs (Level 2)*	*Significant unobservable inputs (Level 3)*	*Trading gains and losses*	*Other gains and losses*	*Interest income on notes*	*Interest expense on long-term debt*	*Total changes in fair values included in earnings*
Asset Category											
Investments											
Trading	$115	$115	$115	$105	$10	–	$10	–	–	–	$10
Available-for-sale	75	75	75	75	–	–	–	–	–	–	–
Derivatives	60	60	60	25	15	20	–	(3)	–	–	(3)
Private equity	125	138	75	–	25	50	–	(18)	–	–	(18)
Notes receivable	550	500	150	–	100	50	–	–	30	–	30
Liability Category											
Long-term debt	(200)	(206)	(60)	(30)	(10)	(20)	–	13	–	(4)	9

Private equity investments for which the fair value option was elected represent investments that would otherwise be accounted for using the equity method of accounting. See Note 1, Summary of Significant Accounting Policies, for disclosures regarding the methods and assumptions used to value each major class of financial assets and liabilities.

51 ASC 830 FOREIGN CURRENCY MATTERS

PERSPECTIVE AND ISSUES

Subtopics

ASC 830 contains five subtopics:

- ASC 830-10, *Overall*
- ASC 830-20, *Foreign Currency Transactions*
- ASC 830-30, *Translation of Financial Statements*
- ASC 830-250, *Statement of Cash Flows*
- ASC 830-740, *Income Taxes*.

ASC 830 provides guidance about

- Foreign transaction and
- Translation of financial statements.

Scope and Scope Exceptions

ASC 830 applies to all entities. ASC 830-20 does not apply to derivative instruments. Preparers should look to ASC 815 for guidance on derivatives.

Overview

To facilitate the proper analysis of foreign operations by financial statement users, transactions and financial statements denominated in foreign currencies must be expressed in a common currency (i.e., US dollars). The GAAP governing the translation of foreign currency financial statements and the accounting for foreign currency transactions are found primarily in Accounting Standards Codification (ASC) 830, *Foreign Currency Matters.* These principles apply to the translation of:

1. Foreign currency transactions (e.g., exports, imports, and loans) that are denominated in other than a company's functional currency
2. Foreign currency financial statements of branches, divisions, subsidiaries, and other investees that are incorporated into the financial statements of a company reporting under US GAAP by combination, consolidation, or application of the equity method.

The objectives of translation are to provide

1. Information relative to the expected economic effects of rate changes on an enterprise's cash flows and equity
2. Information in consolidated statements relative to the financial results and relationships of each individual foreign consolidated entity as reflected by the functional currency of each reporting entity.

Companies sometimes use hedging strategies to attempt to manage their risk and minimize their exposure to fluctuations in the exchange rates of foreign currencies. Hedge accounting under ASC 815, *Derivatives and Hedging,* is addressed at the end of this chapter.

DEFINITIONS OF TERMS

Attribute. The quantifiable characteristic of an item that is measured for accounting purposes. For example, historical cost and current cost are attributes of an asset.

Exchange rate. The ratio between a unit of one currency and the amount of another currency for which that unit can be exchanged at a particular time.

Foreign currency. A currency other than the functional currency of the reporting entity being referred to (for example, the US dollar could be a foreign currency for a foreign entity). Composites of currencies, such as the Special Drawing Rights on the International Monetary Fund (SDR), used to set prices, denominate amounts of loans, and the like have the characteristics of foreign currency for purposes of applying ASC 830.

Foreign currency statements. Financial statements that employ as the unit of measure a functional currency that is not the reporting currency of the enterprise.

Foreign currency transactions. Transactions whose terms are denominated in a currency other than the reporting entity's functional currency. Foreign currency transactions arise when an enterprise (1) buys or sells goods or services on credit whose prices are denominated in foreign currency, (2) borrows or lends funds and the amounts payable or receivable are denominated in foreign currency, (3) is a party to an unperformed forward exchange contract, or (4) for other reasons, acquires or disposes of assets or incurs or settles liabilities denominated in foreign currency.

Foreign currency translation. The process of expressing in the enterprise's reporting currency amounts that are denominated or measured in a different currency.

Foreign entity. An operation (for example, subsidiary, division, branch, joint venture, and so forth) whose financial statements are both:

1. Prepared in a currency other than the reporting currency of the reporting entity
2. Combined or consolidated with or accounted for on the equity basis in the financial statements of the reporting entity.

Functional currency. The currency of the primary economic environment in which the entity operates; normally, the currency of the environment in which the entity primarily generates and expends cash.

Local currency. The currency of a particular country being referred to.

Noncontrolling interest. The portion of equity (net assets) in a subsidiary not attributable, directly

Reporting currency. The currency used by the entity to prepare its financial statements.

Reporting entity. An entity or group of entities whose financial statements are being referred to. Those financial statements reflect (1) the financial statements of one or more foreign operations by combination, consolidation, or equity method accounting; (2) foreign currency transactions; or (3) both.

Transaction gain or loss. Transaction gains or losses result from a change in exchange rates between the functional currency and the currency in which a foreign currency transaction is denominated. They represent an increase or decrease in (1) the actual functional currency cash flows realized upon settlement of foreign currency transactions and (2) the expected functional currency cash flows on unsettled foreign currency transactions.

Translation adjustments. Translation adjustments result from the process of translating financial statements from the entity's functional currency into the reporting currency.

CONCEPTS, RULES, AND EXAMPLES

Translation of Foreign Currency Financial Statements

Selection of the functional currency. Before the financial statements of a foreign branch, division, or subsidiary are translated into US dollars, the management of the US entity must make a decision as to which currency is the functional currency of the foreign entity. Once chosen, the functional currency cannot be changed unless economic facts and circumstances have clearly changed. Additionally, previously issued financial statements are not restated for any changes in the functional currency. The functional currency decision is crucial, because different translation methods are applied which may have a material effect on the US entity's financial statements.

FASB defines functional currency but does not list definitive criteria that, if satisfied, would with certainty result in the identification of an entity's functional currency. Rather, realizing that such criteria would be difficult to develop, FASB listed various factors that were intended to give management guidance in making the functional currency decision. These factors include:

1. Cash flows (Do the foreign entity's cash flows directly affect the parent's cash flows and are they immediately available for remittance to the parent?)
2. Sales prices (Are the foreign entity's sales prices responsive to exchange rate changes and to international competition?)
3. Sales markets (Is the foreign entity's sales market the parent's country or are sales denominated in the parent's currency?)
4. Expenses (Are the foreign entity's expenses incurred primarily in the parent's country?)
5. Financing (Is the foreign entity's financing primarily from the parent or is it denominated in the parent's currency?)

6. Intercompany transactions (Is there a high volume of intercompany transactions between the parent and the foreign entity?).

If the answers to the questions above are predominantly yes, the functional currency is the reporting currency of the parent entity (i.e., the US dollar). If the answers are predominantly no, the functional currency would most likely be the local currency of the foreign entity, although it is possible for a foreign currency other than the local currency to be the functional currency.

Translation methods. To deal with discrete circumstances, FASB chose two different methods to translate an entity's foreign financial statements into US dollars:

- The *current rate* method and
- The *remeasurement* method.

These are not alternatives, but rather are employed as circumstances dictate. The primary distinction between the methods is the classification of assets and liabilities (and their corresponding income statement amounts) that are translated at either the current or historical exchange rates.

Current rate method. The current rate method is the approach mandated by ASC 830 when the functional currency is the foreign currency (e.g., the domestic currency of the foreign subsidiary or operation). All assets and liabilities are translated at the current rates, while stockholders' equity accounts are translated at the appropriate historical rate or rates. Revenues and expenses are translated at rates in effect when the transactions occur, but those that occur evenly over the year may be translated at the weighted-average rate for the year.

Note that weighted-average, if used, must take into account the actual pace and pattern of changes in exchange rates over the course of the year, which will often not be varying at a constant rate throughout the period nor, in many instances, monotonically increasing or decreasing over the period. When these conditions do not hold, it is incumbent upon the reporting entity to develop a weighted-average exchange rate that is meaningful under the circumstances. When coupled with transactions (sales, purchases, et al.) that also have not occurred evenly throughout the year, this determination can become a fairly complex undertaking, requiring careful attention.

The theoretical basis for the current rate method is the "net investment concept," wherein the foreign entity is viewed as a separate entity in which the parent invested, rather than being considered part of the parent's operations. FASB's reasoning was that financial statement users can benefit most when the information provided about the foreign entity retains the relationships and results created in the environment (economic, legal, and political) in which the entity operates. Converting all assets and liabilities at the same current rate accomplishes this objective.

The rationale for this approach is that foreign-denominated debt is often used to purchase assets that create foreign-denominated revenues. These revenue-producing assets act as a natural hedge against changes in the settlement amount of the debt due to changes in the exchange rate. The excess (net) assets—which are the US parent entity's net equity investment in the foreign operation—will, however, be affected by this foreign exchange risk, and this effect is recognized by the parent.

Remeasurement method. The remeasurement method has also been referred to as the monetary/nonmonetary method. This approach is required by ASC 830 when the foreign entity's accounting records are *not* maintained in the functional currency (e.g., when the US dollar is designated as the functional currency for a Brazilian subsidiary). This method translates monetary assets (cash and other assets and liabilities that will be settled in cash) at the current rate. Nonmonetary assets, liabilities, and stockholders' equity are translated at the appropriate historical rates. The appropriate historical rate would be the exchange rate at the date the transaction involving the nonmonetary account originated. Also, the income statement amounts related to nonmonetary assets and liabilities, such as cost of goods sold (inventory), depreciation (property, plant, and equipment), and intangibles amortization (patents, copyrights), are translated at the same rate as used for the related statement of financial position translation. Other revenues and expenses occurring evenly over the year may be translated at the weighted-average exchange rate in effect during the period, subject to the considerations discussed above.

Recap. Thus, to summarize, if the foreign entity's local currency is the functional currency, ASC 830 requires use of the current rate method when translating the foreign entity's financial statements. If, on the other hand, the US dollar (or other nonlocal currency) is the functional currency, ASC 830 requires the remeasurement method when translating the foreign entity's financial statements. Both of these methods are illustrated below. All amounts in the following two illustrations, other than exchange rates, are in thousands.

Example of the current rate method

Assume that a US entity has a 100% owned subsidiary in Italy that commenced operations in 20X1. The subsidiary's operations consist of leasing space in an office building. This building, which cost one million euros, was financed primarily by Italian banks. All revenues and cash expenses are received and paid in euros. The subsidiary also maintains its accounting records in euros. As a result, management of the US entity has decided that the euro is the functional currency of the subsidiary.

The subsidiary's statement of financial position at December 31, 20X2, and its combined statement of income and retained earnings for the year ended December 31, 20X2, are presented below in euros.

Italian Company
Statement of Financial Position
At December 31, 20X2
(€000 omitted)

Assets		***Liabilities and Stockholders' Equity***	
Cash	€ 100	Accounts payable	€ 60
Accounts receivable	40	Unearned rent	20
Land	200	Mortgage payable	800
Building	1,000	Common stock	80
Accumulated depreciation	(20)	Additional paid-in capital	320
		Retained earnings	40
		Total liabilities and	
Total assets	€1,320	Stockholders' equity	€1,320

Italian Company
Statement of Income and Retained Earnings
For the Year Ended December 31, 20X2
(€000 omitted)

Revenues	€400
Expenses (including depreciation of €20)	340
Net income	60
Retained earnings, January 1, 20X2	–
Less dividends declared	(20)
Retained earnings, December 31, 20X2	€ 40

Various exchange rates for 20X2 are as follows:

€1 = $1.50 at the beginning of 20X2 (when the common stock was issued and the land and building were financed through the mortgage)

€1 = $1.55 weighted-average for 20X2

€1 = $1.58 at the date the dividends were declared and paid and the unearned rent was received

€1 = $1.62 at the end of 20X2

Since the euro is the functional currency, the Italian Company's financial statements must be translated into US dollars by the current rate method. This translation process is illustrated below.

Italian Company
Statement of Financial Position Translation
(The euro is the functional currency)
At December 31, 20X2
(€/$000 omitted)

	Euros	*Exchange rate*	*US dollars*
Assets			
Cash	€ 100	1.62	$ 162.00
Accounts receivable, net	40	1.62	64.80
Land	200	1.62	320.00
Building, net	980	1.62	1,587.60
Total assets	€1,320		$2,138.40
Liabilities and Stockholders' Equity			
Accounts payable	€ 60	1.62	$ 97.20
Unearned rent	20	1.62	32.40
Mortgage payable	800	1.62	1,296.00
Common stock	80	1.50	120.00
Additional paid-in capital	320	1.50	480.00
Retained earnings	40	See income statement	61.40
Translation adjustments	–	See computation below	51.40
Total liabilities and stockholders' equity	€1,320		$2,138.40

Italian Company
Statement of Income and Retained Earnings
Statement Translation
(The euro is the functional currency)
For the Year Ended December 31, 20X2
(€/$000 omitted)

	Euros	*Exchange rate*	*US dollars*
Revenues	€400	1.55	$620.00
Expenses (including depreciation of €20 [$31.00])	340	1.55	527.00
Net income	60	1.55	93.00
Retained earnings, January 1	–	–	–
Less dividends declared	(20)	1.58	(31.60)
Retained earnings, December 31	€ 40		$ 61.40

Italian Company
Statement of Cash Flows
Statement Translation
(The euro is the functional currency)
For the Year Ended December 31, 20X2
(€/$000 omitted)

	Euros	*Exchange rate*	*US dollars*
Operating activities			
Net income	€ 60	1.55	$ 93.00
Adjustments to reconcile net income to net cash provided by operating activities			
Depreciation	20	1.55	31.00
Increase in accounts receivable	(40)	1.55	(62.00)
Increase in accounts payable	60	1.55	93.00
Increase in unearned rent	20	1.58	31.60
Net cash provided by operating activities	120		186.60
Investing activities			
Purchase of land	(200)	1.50	(300.00)
Purchase of building	(1,000)	1.50	$(1,500.00)
Net cash used by investing activities	(1,200)		(1,800.00)
Financing activities			
Proceeds from issuance of common	400	1.50	600.00
Proceeds from mortgage payable	800	1.50	1,200.00
Dividends paid	(20)	1.58	(31.60)
Net cash provided by financing activities	1,180		1,768.40
Effect of exchange rate changes on cash	N/A		7.00
Increase in cash and equivalents	100		162.00
Cash at beginning of year	0		0
Cash at end of year	€ 100	1.62	$ 162.00

Note the following points concerning the current rate method:

1. All assets and liabilities are translated using the current exchange rate at the date of the statement of financial position (€1 = $1.62). All revenues and expenses are translated at the rates in effect when these items are recognized during the period. Due to practical considerations, however, weighted-average rates can be used to translate revenues and expenses (€1 = $1.55).
2. Stockholders' equity accounts are translated by using historical exchange rates. Common stock was issued at the beginning of 20X2 when the exchange rate was €1 = $1.50. The translated balance of retained earnings is the result of the weighted-average rate applied to revenues and expenses and the specific rate in effect when the dividends were declared (€1 = $1.58).
3. Translation adjustments result from translating all assets and liabilities at the current rate, while stockholders' equity is translated by using historical and weighted-average rates. The adjustments have no direct effect on cash flows. Also, the translation adjustment is due to the net investment rather than the subsidiary's operations. For these reasons, the cumulative translation adjustments balance is reported as a component of accumulated other comprehensive income (AOCI) in the stockholders' equity section of the US parent entity's consolidated statement of financial position. This balance essentially equates the total debits of the subsidiary (now expressed in US dollars) with the total credits (also in dollars). It also may be determined directly, as shown next, to verify the translation process.

4. The translation adjustments credit of $30.70 is calculated as follows for the differences between the exchange rate of $1.62 at the end of the year and the applicable exchange rates used to translate changes in net assets:

Net assets at inception (Land and buildings of $1,200,000 – Portion financed by mortgage of $800,000)	400 × ($1.62 – $1.50)	=	$48.00 credit
Net income	60 × ($1.62 – $1.55)	=	4.20 credit
Dividends declared	20 × ($1.62 – $1.58)	=	0.80 debit
Translation adjustment			$51.40 credit

5. The translation adjustments balance that appears as a component of AOCI in the stockholders' equity section is cumulative in nature. Consequently, the change in this balance during the year is disclosed as a component of other comprehensive income (OCI) for the period. In the illustration, this balance went from zero to $51.40 at the end of 20X2. In addition, assume the following occurred during the following year, 20X3:

Italian Company
Statement of Financial Position
At December 31
(€000 omitted)

	20X3	*20X2*	*Increase/(Decrease)*
Assets			
Cash	€ 200	€ 100	€100
Accounts receivable, net	–	40	(40)
Land	300	200	100
Building, net	960	980	(20)
Total assets	€1,460	€1,320	€140
Liabilities and Stockholders' Equity			
Accounts payable	€ 100	€ 60	€ 40
Unearned rent	0	20	(20)
Mortgage payable	900	800	100
Common stock	80	80	0
Additional paid-in capital	320	320	0
Retained earnings	60	40	20
Total liabilities and stockholders' equity	€1,460	€1,320	€140

Italian Company
Statement of Income and Retained Earnings
For the Year Ended December 31, 20X3
(€000 omitted)

Revenues	€440
Operating expenses (including depreciation of €20)	340
Net income	100
Retained earnings, Jan. 1, 20X3	40
Less: Dividends declared	(80)
Retained earnings, Dec. 31, 20X3	€ 60

Exchange rates were

€1 = $1.62 at the beginning of 20X3
€1 = $1.65 weighted-average for 20X3
€1 = $1.71 at the end of 20X3
€1 = $1.68 when dividends were declared in 20X3 and additional land bought by incurring mortgage

The translation process for 2013 is illustrated below.

Italian Company
Statement of Financial Position Translation
(The euro is the functional currency)
At December 31, 20X3
(€/$000 omitted)

	Euros	*Exchange rate*	*US dollars*
Assets			
Cash	€ 200	1.71	$ 342.00
Land	300	1.71	513.00
Building, net	960	1.71	1,641.60
Total assets	€1,460		$2,496.60
Liabilities and Stockholders' Equity			
Accounts payable	€ 100	1.71	$ 171.00
Mortgage payable	900	1.71	1,539.00
Common stock	80	1.50	120.00
Additional paid-in capital	320	1. 50	480.00
Retained earnings	60	See income statement	92.00
Translation adjustments	–	See computation below	94.60
Total liabilities and stockholders' equity	€1,460		$2,496.60

Italian Company
Statement of Income and Retained Earnings
Statement Translation
(The euro is the functional currency)
For the Year Ended December 31, 20X3
(€/$000 omitted)

	Euros	*Exchange rate*	*US dollars*
Revenues	€440	1.65	$726.00
Expenses (including depreciation of €10 [$12.50])	340	1.65	561.00
Net income	100	1.65	165.00
Retained earnings, January 1, 2013	40	–	61.40
Less: Dividends declared	(80)	1.68	(134.40)
Retained earnings, December 31, 2013	€ 60		$ 92.00

Italian Company
Statement of Cash Flows
Statement Translation
(The euro is the functional currency)
For the Year Ended December 31, 20X3
(€/$000 omitted)

	Euros	Exchange rate	US dollars
Operating activities			
Net income	€100	1.65	$165.00
Adjustments to reconcile net income to net cash provided by operating activities			
Depreciation	20	1.65	33.00
Decrease in accounts receivable	40	1.65	66.00
Increase in accounts payable	40	1.65	66.00
Decrease in unearned rent	(20)	1.65	(33.00)
Net cash provided by operating activities	180		297.00
Investing activities			
Purchase of land	(100)	1.68	(168.00)
Net cash used by investing activities	(100)		(168.00)
Financing activities			
Mortgage payable	100	1.68	168.00
Dividends	(80)	1.68	(134.40)
Net cash provided by financing activities	20		33.60
Effect of exchange rate changes on cash	N/A		17.40
Increase in cash and equivalents	100		180.00
Cash at beginning of year	100		162.00
Cash at end of year	€200	1.71	$342.00

Using the analysis presented before, the **change** in the translation adjustment attributable to 2013 is computed as follows:

Net assets at January 1, 20X3	€440 ($1.71 – $1.62)	=	$39.60	credit
Net income for 20X3	€100 ($1.71 – $1.65)	=	6.00	credit
Dividends for 20X3	€ 80 ($1.71 – $1.68)	=	2.40	debit
Total			$43.20	credit

The balance in the cumulative translation adjustment component of AOCI at the end of 2013 is $94.60. ($51.40 from 20X2 and $43.20 from 20X3.)

6. The use of the equity method by the US parent entity in accounting for the subsidiary would result in the following journal entries (in $000s), based upon the information presented above:

	20X2		20X3	
Original investment				
Investment in Italian subsidiary	600*		–	
Cash		600		–

* *€80 of common stock + €320 of additional paid-in capital = €400 translated at €1.50 = $600.*

	20X2		20X3	
Earnings pickup				
Investment in Italian subsidiary	93.00		165.00	
Equity in subsidiary income		93.00		165.00

Dividends received				
Cash	31.60		134.40	
Investment in Italian subsidiary		31.60		134.40
Translation adjustments				
Investment in Italian subsidiary	51.40		43.20	
OCI—Translation adjustments		51.40		43.20

Note that in applying the equity method to record this activity in the US parent entity's accounting records, the parent's stockholders' equity should be the same whether or not the Italian subsidiary is consolidated. Since the subsidiary does not report the translation adjustments on its financial statements, care should be exercised so that it is not forgotten in the application of the equity method.

7. If the US entity disposes of its investment in the Italian subsidiary, the cumulative translation adjustments balance becomes part of the gain or loss that results from the transaction and is eliminated. Guidance requires that when a parent ceases to hold a controlling interest *within* a foreign entity, the parent should apply ASC 830-30 and release any cumulative foreign translation adjustment into net income. For an equity method investment in a foreign entity, the partial sale guidance in ASC 830-40 applies.

   For example, assume that on January 2, 2014, the US entity sells its entire investment for €465 thousand. The exchange rate at this date is €1 = $1.71. The balance in the investment account at December 31, 2013, is $786,600 as a result of the entries made previously.

	Investment in Italian Subsidiary	
1/1/ X2	600.00	
	93.00	31.60
	51.40	
1/1/X3 balance	712.80	
	165.00	
	43.20	134.40
12/31/X3 balance	786.60	

The following entries would be made by the US parent entity to reflect the sale of the investment:

Cash (€465 × $1.71 conversion rate)	795.15	
Investment in Italian subsidiary		786.60
Gain from sale of subsidiary		8.55
AOCI—Translation adjustments	94.60	
Gain from sale of subsidiary		94.60

If the US entity had sold only a portion of its investment in the Italian subsidiary, only a pro rata portion of the accumulated translation adjustments balance would have become part of the gain or loss from the transaction. To illustrate, if 80% of the Italian subsidiary was sold for €372 on January 2, 20X3, the following journal entries would be made:

Cash (€372 × $1.71 exchange rate)	636.12	
Investment in Italian subsidiary (80% × $786.60)		629.28
Gain from sale of subsidiary		6.84
AOCI—Translation adjustments (80% × $94.60)	75.68	
Gain from sale of subsidiary		75.68

An exchange rate might not be available if there is a temporary suspension of foreign exchange trading. ASC 830-30-55 provides that, if exchangeability between two currencies is temporarily lacking at a transaction date or the date of the statement of financial position, the first subsequent rate at which exchanges could be made is to be used to implement ASC 830.

Example of the remeasurement method

In the previous situation, the euro was the functional currency because the Italian subsidiary's cash flows were primarily in euros. Assume, however, that the financing of the land and building was denominated in US dollars instead of euros and that the mortgage payable is denominated in US dollars (i.e., it must be repaid in US dollars). Although the rents collected and the majority of the cash flows for expenses are in euros, management has decided that, due to the manner of financing, the US dollar is the functional currency. The accounting records, however, are maintained in euros.

The remeasurement of the Italian financial statements is accomplished by use of the remeasurement method (also known as the monetary/nonmonetary method). This method is illustrated below using the same information that was presented before for the Italian subsidiary.

Italian Company
Statement of Financial Position (Remeasurement)
(The US dollar is the functional currency)
At December 31, 20X2
(€/$000 omitted)

	Euros	*Exchange rate*	*US dollars*
Assets			
Cash	€ 100	1.62	$ 162.00
Accounts receivable, net	40	1.62	64.80
Land	200	1.50	300.00
Building, net	980	1.50	1,470.00
Total assets	€1,320		$1,996.80
Liabilities and Stockholders' Equity			
Accounts payable	€ 60	1.62	$ 97.20
Unearned rent	20	1.58	31.60
Mortgage payable	800	1.62	1,296.00
Common stock	80	1.50	120.00
Additional paid-in capital	320	1.50	480.00
Retained earnings	40	(See income statement)	(28.00)
Total liabilities and stockholders' equity	€1,320		$1,996.80

Italian Company
Statement of Income and Retained Earnings (Remeasurement)
(The US dollar is the functional currency)
For the Year Ended December 31, 20X2
(€/$000 omitted)

	Euros	*Exchange rate*	*US dollars*
Revenues	€ 400	1.55	$620.00
Expenses (not including depreciation)	(320)	1.55	496.00
Depreciation expense	(20)	1.50	(30.00)
Remeasurement loss	–	See analysis below	(90.40)
Net income (loss)	60	–	(3.60)
Retained earnings, January 1	–	–	–
Less dividends declared	(20)	1.58	(31.60)
Retained earnings, December 31	€ 40		$ (28.00)

Italian Company
Remeasurement Loss
(The US dollar is the functional currency)
For the Year Ended December 31, 20X2
(€/$000 omitted)

	Euros			*US dollars*	
	Debit	*Credit*	*Exchange rate*	*Debit*	*Credit*
Cash	€ 100		1.62	$ 162.00	
Accounts receivable, net	40		1.62	64.80	
Land	200		1.50	300.00	
Building, net	980		1.50	1,470.00	
Accounts payable		€ 60	1.62		$ 97.20
Unearned rent		20	1.58		31.60
Mortgage payable		800	1.62		1,296.00
Common stock		80	1.50		120.00
Additional paid-in capital		320	1.50		480.00
Retained earnings		–	–		–
Dividends declared	20		1.58	31.60	
Revenues		400	1.55		620.00
Operating expenses	320		1.55	496.00	
Depreciation expenses	20		1.50	30.00	
Totals	€1,680	€1,680		$2,554.40	$2,644.80
Remeasurement loss				90.40	
Totals				$2,644.80	$2,644.80

Italian Company
Statement of Cash Flows (Remeasurement)
(The US dollar is the functional currency)
For the Year Ended December 31, 20X2
(€/$000 omitted)

	Euros	*Exchange rate*	*US dollars*
Operating activities			
Net income (loss)	€ 60	See income statement	$ 3.60
Adjustments to reconcile net income to net cash provided by operating activities			
Remeasurement loss	–	See income statement	90.40
Depreciation	20	1.50	30.00
Increase in accounts receivable	(40)	1.55	(62.00)
Increase in accounts payable	60	1.55	93.00
Increase in unearned rent	20	1.58	31.60
Net cash provided by operating activities	120		186.60
Investing activities			
Purchase of land	(200)	1.50	(300.00)
Purchase of building	(1,000)	1.50	(1,500.00)
Net cash used by investing activities	(1,200)		(1,800.00)
Financing activities			
Proceeds from issuance of common	400	1.50	600.00
Proceeds from mortgage payable	800	1.50	1,200.00
Dividends paid	(20)	1.58	(31.60)
Net cash provided by financing activities	1,180		1,768.40
Effect of exchange rate changes on cash	N/A		7.00
Increase in cash and equivalents	100		162.00
Cash at beginning of year	0		0
Cash at end of year	€ 100	1.62	$ 162.00

Note the following points concerning the remeasurement method:

1. Assets and liabilities that have historical cost balances (nonmonetary assets and liabilities) are remeasured by using historical exchange rates (i.e., the rates in effect when the transactions giving rise to the balance first occurred). Monetary assets and monetary liabilities, cash and those items that will be settled in cash, are remeasured by using the current exchange rate at the date of the statement of financial position. In 2012, the unearned rent from year-end 2012 of €10 would be remeasured at the rate of €1 = $1.58. The unearned rent at the end of 2012 is not considered a monetary liability. Therefore, the $1.58 historical exchange rate is used for all applicable future years. See the final Section of this chapter, titled "Accounts to Be Remeasured Using Historical Exchange Rates" for a listing of accounts that are remeasured using historical exchange rates.
2. Revenues and expenses that occur frequently during a period are remeasured, for practical purposes, by using the weighted-average exchange rate for the period. Revenues and expenses that represent allocations of historical balances (e.g., depreciation, cost of goods sold, and amortization of intangibles) are remeasured using historical exchange rates. Note that this is a different treatment as compared to the current rate method.
3. If the functional currency is the US dollar rather than the local foreign currency, the amounts of specific line items presented in the reconciliation of net income to net cash flow from operating activities will be different for nonmonetary items (e.g., depreciation).
4. The calculation of the remeasurement gain (loss), in a purely mechanical sense, is the amount needed to make the dollar debits equal the dollar credits in the Italian entity's trial balance.
5. The remeasurement loss of $90.40 is reported on the US parent entity's consolidated income statement because the US dollar is the functional currency. When the reporting currency is the functional currency, as it is in this example, it is assumed that all of the foreign entity's transactions occurred in US dollars (even if this was not the case). Accordingly, remeasurement gains and losses are taken immediately to the income statement in the year in which they occur as they can be expected to have direct cash flow effects on the parent entity. They are not deferred as a translation adjustments component of AOCI, as they were when the functional currency was the euro (applying the current rate method).
6. The use of the equity method of accounting for the subsidiary would result in the following entries by the US parent entity during 20X2:

Original investment		
Investment in Italian subsidiary	600.00	
Cash		600.00
Earnings (loss) pickup		
Investment in Italian subsidiary	3.60	
Equity in subsidiary income		3.60
Dividends received		
Cash	31.60	
Investment in Italian subsidiary		31.60

   Note that remeasurement gains and losses are included in the subsidiary's net income (net loss) as determined in US dollars before the earnings (loss) pickup is made by the US entity.
7. In economies in which—per ASC 830-10-45—cumulative inflation is greater than 100% over a three-year period, FASB requires that the functional currency be the reporting currency, that is, the US dollar. Projections of future inflation cannot be used to satisfy this threshold condition. The remeasurement method must be used in this situation even though the factors indicate the local currency is the functional currency. FASB made this decision to prevent the evaporation of the foreign entity's fixed assets, a result that would occur if the local currency was the functional currency.

Cessation of highly inflationary condition. When a foreign subsidiary's economy is no longer considered highly inflationary, the entity converts the reporting currency values into the local currency at the exchange rates on the date of change on which these values become the new functional currency accounting bases for nonmonetary assets and liabilities.

Furthermore, ASC 830-740 states that when a change in functional currency designation occurs because an economy ceases to be highly inflationary, the deferred taxes on the temporary differences that arise as a result of a change in the functional currency are treated as an adjustment to the cumulative translation adjustments portion of stockholders' equity (accumulated other comprehensive income).

Applying ASC 740 to foreign entity financials restated for general price levels. Price-level-adjusted financial statements are preferred for foreign currency financial statements of entities operating in highly inflationary economies when those financial statements are intended for readers in the United States. If this recommendation is heeded, the result is that the income tax bases of the assets and liabilities are often restated for inflation. ASC 830-740 provides guidance on applying the asset-and-liability approach of ASC 740 as it relates to such financial statements. It discusses (1) how temporary differences are to be computed under ASC 740 and (2) how deferred income tax expense or benefit for the year is to be determined.

With regard to the first issue, temporary differences are computed as the difference between the indexed income tax basis amount and the related price-level restated amount of the asset or liability. The consensus reached on the second issue is that the deferred income tax expense or benefit is the difference between the deferred income tax assets and liabilities reported at the end of the current year and those reported at the end of the prior year. The deferred income tax assets and liabilities of the prior year are recalculated in units of the current year-end purchasing power.

On a related matter, ASC 830-10-45 states that, when the functional currency changes to the reporting currency because the foreign economy has become highly inflationary, ASC 740 prohibits recognition of deferred income tax benefits associated with indexing assets and liabilities that are remeasured in the reporting currency using historical exchange rates. Any related income tax benefits would be recognized only upon their being realized for income tax purposes. Any deferred income tax benefits that had been recognized for indexing before the change in reporting currency is effected are eliminated when the related indexed amounts are realized as income tax deductions.

Summary of Current Rate and Remeasurement Methods

1. Before foreign currency financial statements can be translated into US dollars, management of the US parent entity must select the functional currency for the foreign entity whose financial statements will be incorporated into theirs by consolidation, combination, or the equity method. As the examples illustrated, this decision is important because it may have a material effect upon the financial statements of the US entity.
2. If the functional currency is the local currency of the foreign entity, the current rate method is used to translate foreign currency financial statements into US dollars. All assets and liabilities are translated by using the current exchange rate at the date of the statement of financial position. This method insures that all financial relationships remain the same in both local currency and US dollars. Owners' equity is translated using historical rates, while revenues (gains) and expenses (losses) are translated at the rates in existence during the period when the transactions occurred. A weighted-average rate can be used for items occurring frequently throughout the period. The translation adjustments (debit or credit) that result from the application

of these rules are reported in other comprehensive income and then accumulated and reported as a separate component of stockholders' equity of the US entity's consolidated statement of financial position (or parent-only statement of financial position if consolidation is deemed not to be appropriate).

3. If the functional currency is the parent entity's reporting currency (the US dollar), the foreign currency financial statements are remeasured in US dollars. All foreign currency balances are restated in US dollars using both historical and current exchange rates. Foreign currency balances that reflect prices from past transactions are remeasured using historical rates, while foreign currency balances which reflect prices from current transactions are remeasured using the current exchange rate. Remeasurement gains/losses that result from the remeasurement process applied to foreign subsidiaries that are consolidated are reported on the US parent entity's consolidated income statement.

The above summary is arranged in tabular form as shown below.

Functional currency	*Functional currency determinants*	*Translation method*	*Reporting and display*
Local currency of foreign entity	a. Operations not integrated with parent's operations b. Buying and selling activities primarily in local currency c. Cash flows not immediately available for remittance to parent d. Financing denominated in local currency	Current rate (all assets/ liabilities translated using current exchange rate; revenues/expenses use weighted-average rate; equity accounts use historical rates)	Accumulated translation adjustments are reported in the equity section of the US parent entity's consolidated statement of financial position as part of AOCI. Changes in accumulated translation adjustments reported as a component of OCI. Effect of exchange rates on cash included in reconciliation of beginning and ending cash balances on statement of cash flows.
US dollar	a. Operations integrated with parent's operations b. Buying and selling activities primarily in the United States and/or in US dollars c. Cash flows immediately available for remittance to parent d. Financing denominated in US dollars	Remeasurement (monetary assets/liabilities use current exchange rate; historical cost balances use historical rates; revenues/ expenses use weighted-average rates and historical rates, the latter for allocations like depreciation expenses).	Remeasurement gain/loss is reported on the US entity's consolidated income statement. Remeasurement gain/loss shown as a reconciliation item between net income and cash flows from operations in the statement of cash flows. Effect of exchange rates on cash included in reconciliation of beginning and ending cash balances on statement of cash flows.

Application of ASC 830 to an investment to be disposed of that is evaluated for impairment. Under ASC 830, accumulated foreign currency translation adjustments are reclassified to net income only when realized upon sale or upon complete or substantially complete liquidation of the investment in the foreign entity. ASC 830-30-45 addresses whether a reporting entity is to include the translation adjustments in the carrying amount of the investment in assessing impairment of an investment in a foreign entity that is held for disposal if the planned disposal will cause some or all of the translation adjustments to be reclassified to net income. The standard points out that an entity that has committed to a plan that will cause the translation adjustments for an equity-method investment or consolidated investment in a foreign entity to be reclassified to earnings is to include the translation adjustments as part of the carrying amount of the investment when evaluating that investment for impairment. An entity would also include the portion of the translation adjustments that represents a gain or loss from an effective hedge of the net investment in a foreign operation as part of the carrying amount of the investment when making this evaluation.

Foreign Operations in the United States

With the world economy as interconnected as it is, entities in the United States are sometimes the subsidiaries of parent companies domiciled elsewhere in the world. The financial statements of the US entity may be presented separately in the United States or may be combined as part of the financial statements in the foreign country.

In general, financial statements of US companies are prepared in accordance with US GAAP. However, adjustments may be necessary to conform these financial statements to the accounting principles of the foreign country of the parent entity where they will be consolidated.

Translation of Foreign Currency Transactions

According to ASC 830, a foreign currency transaction is a transaction ". . . denominated in a currency other than the entity's functional currency." Denominated means that the amount to be received or paid is fixed in terms of the number of units of a particular foreign currency regardless of changes in the exchange rate. From the viewpoint of a US entity, a foreign currency transaction results when it imports or exports goods or services to or from a foreign entity or makes a loan involving a foreign entity and agrees to settle the transaction in currency other than the US dollar (the functional currency of the US entity). In these situations, the US entity has "crossed currencies" and directly assumes the risk of fluctuating exchange rates of the foreign currency in which the transaction is denominated. This risk may lead to recognition of foreign exchange transaction gains or losses in the income statement of the US entity. Note that transaction gains or losses can result only when the foreign transactions are denominated in a foreign currency. When a US entity imports or exports goods or services and the transaction is to be settled in US dollars, the US entity is not exposed to a foreign exchange gain or loss because it bears no risk due to exchange rate fluctuations.

Example of foreign currency transaction translation

The following example illustrates the terminology and procedures applicable to the translation of foreign currency transactions. Assume that US Company, an exporter, sells merchandise to a customer in Italy on December 1, 20X2, for €10,000. Receipt is due on January 31, 20X3 and US Company prepares financial statements on December 31, 20X2. At the transaction date (December 1, 20X2), the spot rate for immediate exchange of foreign currencies indicates that €1 is equivalent to $1.30. To find the US dollar equivalent of this transaction, the foreign currency amount, €10,000, is multiplied by $1.30 to get $13,000. At December 1, 20X2, the foreign currency transaction is recorded by US Company in the following manner:

Accounts receivable—Italy (€ denominated)	13,000	
Sales		13,000

The accounts receivable and sales are measured in US dollars at the transaction date using the spot rate at the time of the transaction. While the accounts receivable is measured and reported in U.S. dollars, the receivable is denominated or fixed in euros. This characteristic may result in foreign exchange transaction gains or losses if the spot rate for the euro changes between the transaction date and the date the transaction is settled (January 31, 20X3).

If financial statements are prepared between the transaction date and the settlement date, all receivables and liabilities denominated in a currency other than the functional currency (the US dollar) must be restated to reflect the spot rates in effect at the statement of financial position date. Assume that on December 31, 20X2, the spot rate for euros is €1 = $1.32. This means that the €10,000 are now worth $13,200 and that the accounts receivable denominated in euros has increased by $200. The following adjustment is recorded on December 31, 2012:

Accounts receivable—Italy (€ denominated)	200	
Foreign currency transaction gain		200

Note that the $13,000 credit to sales recorded on the transaction date is not affected by subsequent changes in the spot rate. This treatment exemplifies the two-transaction viewpoint adopted by FASB. In other words, making the sale is the result of an operating decision, while bearing the risk of fluctuating spot rates is the result of a financing decision. Therefore, the amount determined as sales revenue at the transaction date is not altered because of the financing decisions to wait until January 31, 20X3, for payment of the account and to accept payment denominated in euros. The risk of a foreign exchange transaction loss can be avoided by (1) demanding immediate payment on December 1, 20X2, (2) fixing the price of the transaction in US dollars instead of in the foreign currency, or (3) by entering into a forward exchange contract to hedge the exposed asset (accounts receivable). The fact that, in the example, US Company did not take any of these actions is reflected by recognizing foreign currency transaction gains or losses in its income statement (reported as financial or nonoperating items) in the period during which the exchange rates changed. This treatment has been criticized, however, because earnings will fluctuate because of changes in exchange rates and not because of changes in the economic activities of the enterprise. The counterargument, however, is that economic reality is that earnings *are* fluctuating because the management chose to commit the reporting entity to a transaction that exposes it to economic risks and, therefore, the case can be made that the volatility in earnings faithfully represents the results of management's business decision.

On the settlement date (January 31, 20X3), assume the spot rate is €1 = $1.31. The receipt of €10,000 and their conversion into US dollars is recorded as follows:

Foreign currency (€)	13,100	
Foreign currency transaction loss	100	
Accounts receivable—Italy (€ denominated)		13,200
Cash	13,100	
Foreign currency (€)		13,100

The net effect of this foreign currency transaction was to receive $13,100 in settlement from a sale that was originally measured (and recognized) at $13,000. This realized net foreign currency transaction gain of $100 is reported on two income statements—a $200 gain in 20X2 and a $100 loss in 20X3. The reporting of the gain or loss in two income statements causes a temporary difference in the basis of the receivable for income tax and financial reporting purposes. This results because the 20X2 unrealized transaction gain of $200 is not taxable until 20X3, the year the transaction was ultimately completed or settled. Accordingly, deferred income tax accounting is required to account for the effects of this temporary difference.

It is important to note that all monetary assets and liabilities of US Company that are denominated in a currency other than US Company's functional currency (the US dollar) are required to be remeasured at the date of each statement of financial position to the extent that they are affected by increases or decreases in the exchange rate. For example, a US Company whose functional currency is the US dollar holds a bank account in France that is denominated in euros. At the date of each statement of financial position, by reference to the spot rate for the euro, US Company would remeasure the carrying amount of its French bank account and record any resulting transaction gains and losses in the same manner as above.

Intercompany Transactions and Elimination of Intercompany Profits

Gains or losses from intercompany transactions are reported on the US company's consolidated income statement unless settlement of the transaction is not planned or anticipated in the foreseeable future. In that case, which is atypical, gains and losses arising from intercompany transactions are reflected in the accumulated translations adjustments component of accumulated other comprehensive income in stockholders' equity of the US entity. In the typical situation (i.e., gains and losses reported on the US entity's income statement) gains and losses result whether the functional currency is the US dollar or the foreign entity's local currency. When the US dollar is the functional currency, foreign currency transaction gains and losses result because of one of the two situations below:

1. The intercompany foreign currency transaction is denominated in US dollars. In this case, the foreign subsidiary has a payable or receivable denominated in US dollars. This may result in a foreign currency transaction gain or loss that would appear on the foreign subsidiary's income statement. This gain or loss would be translated into US dollars and would appear on the US entity's consolidated income statement.
2. The intercompany foreign currency transaction is denominated in the foreign subsidiary's local currency. In this situation, the US entity has a payable or receivable denominated in a foreign currency. Such a situation may result in a foreign currency transaction gain or loss that is reported on the US parent entity's income statement.

The above two cases can be easily altered to reflect what happens when the foreign entity's local currency is the functional currency. The gain or loss from each of these scenarios would be reflected on the other entity's financial statements first (i.e., the subsidiary's rather than the parent's and vice versa).

The elimination of intercompany profits due to sales and other transfers between related entities is based upon exchange rates in effect when the sale or transfer occurred. Reasonable approximations and averages are allowed to be used if intercompany transactions occur frequently during the year.

Example of intercompany transactions involving foreign exchange

Cassiopeia Corporation buys an observatory-grade telescope from its Spanish subsidiary for €850,000, resulting in a profit for the subsidiary of €50,000 on the sale date at an exchange rate of $1:€0.6 (euros). The profit is eliminated at $1:€0.6. The payable to the subsidiary is due in 90 days, and is denominated in euros. On the payment date, the exchange rate has changed to $1:€0.65. Thus, rather than paying $1,416,667 to settle the payable, as would have been the case on the sale date, Cassiopeia must now pay $1,307,692 on the payable date. Cassiopeia presents the $108,975 exchange gain in its income statement in the following manner:

Sales	$ 20,000,000
Cost of sales	$(14,000,000)
Gross profit	6,000,000
Operating expenses	(5,500,000)
Other revenues/gains (expenses/losses)	
Gain on translation of foreign currencies	(108,975)
Net income	$ 608,975

In a separate series of transactions, the subsidiary sends a weekly shipment of telescope repair parts to Cassiopeia, totaling €48,000 of profits for the entire year. For these transactions, the exchange rate varies from $1:€0.6 to $1:€0.75. A reasonable estimate of the average exchange rate for all the transactions is $1:€1.67. Consequently, the €48,000 profit is eliminated at the $1:€1.67(= $71,642) average exchange rate.

Foreign Currency Hedging

ASC 815, provides complex hedging rules that permit the reporting entity to elect to obtain special accounting treatment relative to foreign currency risks with respect to the following items:

1. Recognized assets or liabilities
2. Available-for-sale debt and equity securities
3. Unrecognized firm commitments
4. Foreign-currency-denominated forecasted cash flows
5. Net investment in a foreign operation.

The chapter on ASC 815 provides a detailed discussion of derivatives and hedging. The table on the next page provides a high-level summary of the complex provisions that apply to hedges related to foreign currency exposures.

Measuring hedge effectiveness. While any entity may use hedging strategies, under the provisions of ASC 815 the transaction must meet a number of important conditions to qualify for hedge accounting. Among these conditions are the establishment, at inception, of criteria for measuring hedge effectiveness and ineffectiveness. Periodically, each hedge must be evaluated for effectiveness, using the preestablished criteria, and the gains or losses associated with hedge ineffectiveness must be reported currently in earnings and not deferred to future periods. In the instance of foreign currency hedges, ASC 815 states that reporting entities must exclude from their assessments of hedge effectiveness the portions of the fair value of forward contracts attributable to spot-forward differences (i.e., differences between the spot exchange rate and the forward exchange rate).

In practice, this means that reporting entities engaging in foreign currency hedging will recognize changes in the above-described portion of the derivative's fair value in earnings, in the same manner that changes representing hedge ineffectiveness are reported, but these are not considered to represent ineffectiveness. These entities must estimate the cash flows on forecasted transactions based on the current spot exchange rate, appropriately discounted for time value. Effectiveness is then assessed by comparing the changes in fair values of the forward contracts attributable to changes in the dollar spot price of the pertinent foreign currency to the changes in the present values of the forecasted cash flows based on the current spot exchange rate(s).

Hedging Foreign Currency Exposures

Hedges of foreign currency (FC) exposures (where FC is not the reporting entity's functional currency)

	A	***B***	***C***
Types of items that may qualify to be hedged	Fair value hedges A1. Recognized assets or liabilities A2. Available-for-sale debt securities A3. Available-for-sale equity securities A4. UFC	Cash flow hedges B1. Forecasted cash flow from recognized assets or liabilities B2. Forecasted external transactions B3. Forecasted intercompany transactions B4. UFC	C. Hedges of a net investment in a foreign operation
Risk being hedged	Changes in fair value of the hedged item that result from changes in the exchange rate (ER) of the FC in which it is denominated (which, by definition, is not the functional currency of the reporting entity)	The FC exposure to variability in the "equivalent functional currency cash flows" associated with the hedged item	Exposure of the net investment to changes in the exchange rate applicable to the functional currency of the investee
Type of instruments that qualify for use as hedging instruments	A1, A2, A3—Required to be derivatives A$ can be a derivative instrument or nonderivative financial instrument	Required to be derivatives	Can be derivative instrument or a nonderivative financial instrument; Nonderivative financial instruments, to be designated, cannot be subject to GAAP that requires that they be presented at FV since that accounting treatment would not result in foreign currency transaction gains or losses under ASC 830
Summary of accounting treatment	General Rule: When the ER changes, recognize in current earnings: (1) changes in fair value of hedged item caused by the hedged risk, (2) gain or loss on changes in fair value of the designated hedging instrument, and (3) hedge ineffectiveness, if any AFS securities: Change in fair value of the security attributable to FC risk is reported in earnings; other changes in fair value of the security, not attributable to the hedged risk continue to be reported in other comprehensive income	General Rule: The effective portion of the gain or loss on a derivative designated as a cash flow hedge is reported in OCI and the ineffective portion is reported currently in earnings. In the period or periods during which a hedged forecasted transaction affects earnings, amounts in AOCI are reclassified to earnings. Additional complex accounting provisions are provided by ASC 815-30	To the extent of hedge effectiveness, gains or losses on the hedging derivative instrument (or FC transaction gains or losses on the hedging nonderivative instrument) are accounted for in the same manner as a FC translation adjustment (i.e., reported as other comprehensive income and as a change in accumulated other comprehensive income). The hedged net investment is accounted for consistent with ASC 830 as described in this chapter; any hedge ineffectiveness is reflected as a transaction gain or loss in earnings of the period in which it arises

Applicable conditions, criteria limitations or exceptions	**Fair value hedges** a. Fair value hedges are required to meet the requirements of ASC 815-20 with respect to such matters as timely hedge designation, tests of hedge effectiveness at inception and on an ongoing basis. b. A3—(i) The AFS equity security cannot be traded on an exchange or market where transactions are denominated in the investor's functional currency, and (ii) Dividends and all other cash flows associated with holding or selling the security must be denominated in the same foreign currency. c. A2, A4—The hedged transaction must be denominated in a FC other than the hedging unit's functional currency, and if consolidated financial statements, the party to the hedging instrument must be either (i) the operating unit with the FC exposure or (ii) another member of the consolidated group (subject to certain specified restrictions and meeting certain conditions) with the same functional currency as that operating unit. d. FC derivatives entered into with another member of the consolidated group can be designated as hedging instruments in all fair value hedge transaction types (A1–A4) only if that member has entered into an offsetting contract with an unrelated third party to hedge the exposure it acquired from issuing the derivative instrument to the affiliate that initiated the hedge. **Cash flow hedges and hedges of net investments in foreign operations** e. Cash flow hedges must meet the requirements of ASC 815-20 f. Cash flow hedges of forecasted transactions must additionally meet the requirements of ASC 815-20-25 g. Cash flow hedges of forecasted transactions (B1), and hedges of net investments in foreign operations (C) must also meet the criteria in item d of this list.		
Eligibility for ASC 825-10-25 Fair Value Option (FVO)	A4—Limited eligibility when the UFC involves only financial instruments	Not eligible	Not eligible

Example of hedge effectiveness measurement

On October 1, 20X2, Braveheart Co. (a US entity) orders from its European supplier, Gemutlichkeit GmbH, a machine that is to be delivered and paid for on March 31, 20X3. The price, denominated in euros, is €4,000,000. Although Braveheart will not make the payment until the planned delivery date, it has immediately entered into a firm commitment to make this purchase and to pay €4,000,000 upon delivery. This creates a euro liability exposure to foreign exchange risk; thus, if the euro appreciates over the intervening six months, the dollar cost of the equipment will increase.

To reduce or eliminate this uncertainty, Braveheart desires to lock in the purchase cost in euros by entering into a six-month forward contract to purchase euros on the date when the purchase order is issued to and accepted by Gemutlichkeit. The spot rate on October 1, 20X2, is $1.40 per euro and the forward rate for March 31, 20X3 settlement is $1.44 per euro. Braveheart enters into a forward contract on October 1, 20X2, with the First Intergalactic Bank to pay US $5,760,000 in exchange for the receipt of €4,000,000 on March 31, 20X3, which can then be used to pay Gemutlichkeit. No premium is received nor paid at the inception of this forward contract.

The transaction is a firm commitment consistent with the requirements of ASC 815, and fair value hedge accounting is used in accounting for the forward contract.

Assume the relevant time value of money is measured at 1/2% per month (a nominal 6% annual rate). The spot rate for euros at December 31, 20X2, is $1.45, and at March 31, 20X3, it is $1.48. The forward rate as of December 31 for March 31 settlement is $1.46.

Entries to reflect the foregoing scenario are as follows:

10/1/X2	*No entries, since neither the forward contract nor the firm commitment have value on this date*		
12/31/X2	Forward currency contract	78,818	
	Gain on forward contract		78,818
	To record present value (at 1/2% monthly rate) of change in value of forward contract [= change in forward rate (1.46 – 1.44) × €4,000,000 = $80,000 to be received in three months, discounted at 6% per annum]		
	Loss on firm purchase commitment	197,044	
	Firm commitment obligation		197,044
	To record present value (at 1/2% monthly rate) of change in amount of firm commitment [= change in spot rate (1.45 – 1.40) × €4,000,000 = $200,000 to be paid in three months, discounted at 6% per annum]		
	Gain on forward contract	78,818	
	Loss on firm purchase commitment		197,044
	P&L summary (then to retained earnings)	118,226	
	To close the gain and loss accounts to net income and thus to retained earnings		
3/31/X3	Forward currency contract	81,182	
	Gain on forward contract		81,182
	To record change in value of forward contract {[= (1.48 – 1.44) × €4,000,000 = $160,000] – gain previously recognized ($78,818)}		
	Loss on firm commitment	122,956	
	Firm commitment obligation		122,956
	To record change in amount of firm commitment {[= (1.48 – 1.40) × €4,000,000] less loss previously recognized ($197,044)}		

3/31/X3	Firm commitment obligation	320,000	
	Machinery and equipment	5,600,000	
	Cash		5,920,000
	To record purchase of machinery based on spot exchange rate as of date of contractual commitment (1.40) and close out the firm commitment obligation (representing effect of change in spot rate during commitment period)		
	Cash	160,000	
	Forward contract		160,000
	To record collection of cash on net settlement of forward contract [= (1.48 – 1.44) × €4,000,000]		
	Gain on forward contract	81,182	
	P&L summary (then to retained earnings)	41,774	
	Loss on firm purchase commitment		122,956
	To close the gain and loss accounts to net income and thus to retained earnings		

Observe that in the foregoing example the gain on the forward contract did not precisely offset the loss incurred from the firm commitment. Since a hedge of an unrecognized foreign currency denominated firm commitment is accounted for as a fair value hedge, with gains and losses on hedging positions and on the hedged item both being recorded in current earnings, it may appear that the matter of hedge effectiveness is of academic interest only. However, according to ASC 815, even if both components (that is, the net gain or loss representing hedge ineffectiveness, and the amount charged to earnings that was excluded from the measurement of ineffectiveness) are reported in current period earnings, the distinction between them is still of importance.

With respect to fair value hedges of firm purchase commitments denominated in a foreign currency, ASC 815 directs that "the change in value of the contract related to the changes in the differences between the spot price and the forward or futures price would be excluded from the assessment of hedge effectiveness." As applied to the foregoing example, therefore, the net credit to income in 20X2 ($118,226) can be further analyzed into two constituent elements: the amount arising from the change in the difference between the spot price and the forward price, and the amount resulting from hedge ineffectiveness.

The former item, not attributed to ineffectiveness, arose because the spread between spot and forward price at hedge inception, (1.44 – 1.40 =) .04, fell to (1.46 – 1.45 =) .01 by December 31, for an impact amounting to (.04 – .01 =) .03 × €4,000,000 = $120,000, which, reduced to present value terms, equaled $118,227. The net credit to earnings in December 2012, ($78,818 + 118,226 =) $197,044, relates to the spread between the spot and forward rates on December 31 and is identifiable with hedge ineffectiveness.

Forward Exchange Contracts

Foreign currency transaction gains and losses on assets and liabilities that are denominated in a currency other than the functional currency can be hedged if a US entity enters into a forward exchange contract. The following example shows how a forward exchange contract can be used as a hedge, first against a firm commitment and then, following delivery date, as a hedge against a recognized liability.

A general rule for estimating the fair value of forward exchange rates under ASC 815 is to use the changes in the forward exchange rates, and discount those estimated future cash flows to a present-value basis. An entity will need to consider the time value of money if significant in the circumstances for these contracts. The following example does not apply discounting of the future cash flows from the forward contracts in order to focus on the relationships between the forward contract and the foreign currency denominated payable.

Example of a forward exchange contract

Durango, Inc. enters into a firm commitment with Dempsey Ing., Inc. of Germany, on October 1, 20X2, to purchase a computerized robotic system for €6,000,000. The system will be delivered on March 1, 2013, with payment due sixty days after delivery (April 30, 20X3). Durango, Inc. decides to hedge this foreign currency firm commitment and enters into a forward exchange contract on the firm commitment date to receive €6,000,000 on the payment date. The applicable exchange rates are shown in the table below.

Date	*Spot rates*	*Forward rates for April 30, 2013*
October 1, 2012	€1 = $1.55	€1 = $1.57
December 31, 2012	€1 = $1.58	€1 = $1.589
March 1, 2013	€1 = $1.58	€1 = $1.585
April 30, 2013	€1 = $1.60	

The example on the following pages separately presents both the forward contract receivable and the dollars payable liability in order to show all aspects of the forward contract. For financial reporting purposes, most companies present just the net fair value of the forward contract that would be the difference between the current value of the forward contract receivable and the dollars payable liability. Note that the foreign currency hedges in the illustration are not perfectly effective. However, for this example, the degree of ineffectiveness is not deemed to be sufficient to trigger income statement recognition per ASC 815.

The transactions that reflect the forward exchange contract, the firm commitment and the acquisition of the asset, and retirement of the related liability appear at the end of this section. The net fair value of the forward contract is shown below each set of entries for the forward exchange contract.

In the case of using a forward exchange contract to speculate in a specific foreign currency, the general rule to estimate the fair value of the forward contract is to use the forward exchange rate for the remainder of the term of the forward contract.

The Fair Value Option

ASC 825-10-25, encourages reporting entities to voluntarily elect to use fair value to measure eligible financial assets and financial liabilities in their financial statements. This election is referred to as the Fair Value Option (FVO). Changes in the fair values of these assets and liabilities would be reflected in earnings as they occur.

In issuing ASC 825-10-25, FASB indicated that, among the reasons it decided to permit this election was that the election would "enable entities to achieve consistent accounting and, potentially, an offsetting effect for the changes in the fair values of related assets and liabilities without having to apply complex hedge accounting provisions, thereby providing greater simplicity in the application of accounting guidance."[1]

---

[1] *ASC 825-10-25,* Financial Instruments—Fair Value Option. *Norwalk, CT: Financial Accounting Standards Board, 2007.*

Forward contract entries

(1) 10/1/11 (forward rate for 4/30/11 €1 = $1.57)

Forward contract receivable	9,420,000	
Dollars payable		9,420,000

This entry recognizes the existence of the forward exchange contract using the gross method. Under the net method, this entry would not appear at all, since the fair value of the forward contract is zero when the contract is initiated. The amount is calculated using the 10/1/10 forward rate for 4/30/12 (€6,000,000 × $1.57 = $9,420,000).

Net fair value of the forward contract = $0

Note that the net fair value of the forward exchange contact on 10/1/X0 is zero because there is an exact amount offset of the forward contract receivable of $9,420,000 with the dollars payable liability of $9,420,000. Many companies present only the net fair value of the forward contract on their balance sheets, and therefore, they would have no net amount reported for the forward contract at its inception.

(2) 12/31/X1 (forward rate for 4/30/11 €1 = $1.589)

Forward contract receivable	114,000	
Gain on hedge activity		114,000

The dollar values for this entry reflect, among other things, the change in the forward rate from 10/1/X1 to 12/31/X1. However, the actual amount recorded as gain or loss (gain in this case) is determined by all market factors.

Net increase in fair value of the forward contract = (1.589 – 1.57 = .019 × €6,000,000 = $114,000).

The increase in the net fair value of the forward exchange contract on 12/31/X0 is $114,000 for the difference between the $7,134,000 ($7,020,000 plus $114,000) in the forward contract receivable and the $7,020,000 for the dollars payable liability. Many companies present only the net fair value on their balance sheet, in this case as an asset. And, this $114,000 is the amount that would be discounted to present value, if interest is significant, to recognize the time value of the future cash flow from the forward contract.

(4) 3/1/X2 (forward rate for 4/30/10 €1 = $1.585)

Loss on hedge activity	24,000	
Forward contract receivable		24,000

Hedge against firm commitment entries

(3) 12/31/X1

Loss on hedge activity	114,000	
Firm commitment		114,000

The dollar values for this entry are identical to those in entry (2), reflecting the fact that the hedge is highly effective (100%) and also the fact that the market recognizes the same factors in this transaction as for entry (2). This entry reflects the first use of the firm commitment account, a temporary liability account pending the receipt of the asset against which the firm commitment has been hedged.

(5) 3/1/X2

Firm commitment	24,000	
Gain on hedge activity		24,000

These entries again will be driven by market factors, and they are calculated the same way as entries (2) and (3) above. Note that the decline in the forward rate from 12/31/X1 to 3/1/X2 resulted in a loss against the forward contract receivable and a gain against the firm commitment [1.585 – 1.589 = (.004) × €6,000,000 = ($24,000)].

Forward contract entries

Net fair value of the forward contract = $90,000

The net fair value of the forward exchange contract on 3/1/X1 is $90,000 for the difference between the $9,510,000 ($9,420,000 plus $114,000 minus $24,000) in the forward contract receivable and the $9,420,000 for the dollars payable liability. Another way of computing the net fair value is to determine the change in the forward contract rate from the initial date of the contract, 10/1/X1, which is $1.585 – $1.57 = $.015 × €6,000,000 = $90,000. Also note that the amount in the firm commitment temporary liability account is equal to the net fair value of the forward contract on the date the equipment is received.

(7) 4/30/12 (spot rate €1 = $1.60)

Forward contract receivable	90,000	
Gain on forward contract		90,000

The gain or loss (gain in this case) on the forward contract is calculated using the change in the forward to the spot rate from 3/1/X2 to 4/30/X2 [€6,000,000 × ($1.60 – $1.585) = $90,000]

Net fair value of the forward contract = $180,000

The net fair value of the forward exchange contract on 4/30/X2 is $180,000 for the difference between the $9,600,000 ($9,510,000 plus $90,000) in the forward contract receivable and the $9,420,000 for the dollars payable liability. The net fair value of the forward contract at its terminal date of 4/30/X2 is based on the difference between the contract forward rate of €1 = $1.57 and the spot rate on 4/30/X2 of €1 = $1.60. The forward contract receivable has reached its maturity and the contract is completed on this date at the forward rate of €1 = $1.57 as contracted on 10/1/X1. If the entity recognizes an interest factor in the forward contract over the life of the contract, then interest is recognized at this time on the forward contract, but no separate accrual of interest is required for the accounts payable in euros.

(9) 4/30/12

Dollars payable	9,420,000	
Cash		9,420,000
Foreign currency units (€)	9,600,000	
Forward contract receivable		9,600,000

This entry reflects the settlement of the forward contract at the 10/1/X1 contracted forward rate (€6,000,000 × $1.17 = $7,020,000) and the receipt of foreign currency units valued at the spot rate (€6,000,000 × $1.20 = $7,200,000).

Hedge against a recognized liability entries

(6) 3/1/X2 (spot rate €1 = $1.58)

Equipment	9,390,000	
Firm commitment	90,000	
Accounts payable (€)		9,480,000

This entry records the receipt of the equipment, the elimination of the temporary liability account (firm commitment), and the recognition of the payable, calculated using the spot rate on the date of receipt (€6,000,000 × $1.58 = $9,480,000).

(8) 4/30/X2

Transaction loss	120,000	
Accounts payable (€)		120,000

The transaction loss related to the accounts payable reflects only the change in the spot rates and ignores the accrual of interest. [€6,000,000 × ($1.60 – $1.58) = $120,000]

(10) 4/30/12

Accounts payable (€)	9,600,000	
Foreign currency units (€)		9,600,000

This entry reflects the use of the foreign currency units to retire the account payable.

As noted in the table "Hedging Foreign Currency Exposures" presented earlier in this chapter, the provisions of ASC 825-10-25 have limited applicability with respect to foreign currency risks. The election does not affect cash flow hedges or hedges of a net investment in a foreign operation. With respect to fair value hedges, the reporting entity may elect the FVO for eligible nonderivative financial assets or liabilities. An unrecognized firm commitment (UFC) may qualify as a financial instrument if it only involves financial assets and liabilities. ASC 825-10-25 provides, as an example, a forward purchase contract for a loan that is not readily convertible to cash. This instrument would qualify for the FVO. In order to achieve the desired economic offsetting that would resemble hedge accounting, the reporting entity would also have to hold assets denominated in the same foreign currency (which is not the entity's functional currency) that give rise to foreign currency transaction gains or losses that would partially or fully offset changes in the fair value of the forward purchase contract during its term and at settlement.

Elections made under the FVO are irrevocable and, if made by early adopting ASC 825-10-25, also require the reporting entity to early adopt the disclosure provisions of ASC 820 that otherwise would not be effective until the same date as ASC 825-10-25.

ACCOUNTS TO BE REMEASURED USING HISTORICAL EXCHANGE RATES

1. Marketable securities carried at cost (equity securities and debt securities not intended to be held until maturity)
2. Inventories carried at cost
3. Prepaid expenses such as insurance, advertising, and rent
4. Property, plant, and equipment
5. Accumulated depreciation on property, plant, and equipment
6. Patents, trademarks, licenses, and formulas
7. Goodwill
8. Other intangible assets
9. Deferred charges and credits, except policy acquisition costs for life insurance companies
10. Deferred income
11. Common stock
12. Preferred stock carried at issuance price
13. Revenues and expenses related to nonmonetary items
    a. Cost of goods sold
    b. Depreciation of property, plant, and equipment
    c. Amortization of intangible items such as goodwill, patents, licenses, and the like
    d. Amortization of deferred charges or credits, except policy acquisition costs for life insurance companies.

Source: ASC 830.

52 ASC 835 INTEREST

PERSPECTIVE AND ISSUES

Subtopics

ASC 835, *Interest,* contains three Subtopics:

- ASC 835-10, *Overall,* which merely points to other Topics with guidance on interest
- ASC 835-20, *Capitalization of Interest,* which provides guidance on capitalization of interest in connection with an asset investment
- ASC 835-30, *Imputation of Interest,* which provides guidance where imputation of interest is required.

Scope and Scope Exceptions

All assets that require a time period to get ready for their intended use should include a capitalized amount of interest. However, accomplishing this level of capitalization would usually violate a reasonable cost/benefit test because of the added accounting and administrative costs that would be incurred. In many such situations, the effect of interest capitalization would be immaterial. Accordingly, interest cost is only capitalized as a part of the historical cost of the following types of assets (qualifying assets) when such interest is considered to be material. (ASC 835-20-15-2) Common examples include

1. Assets constructed for an entity's own use or for which deposit or progress payments are made
2. Assets produced as discrete projects that are intended for lease or sale
3. Equity-method investments when the investee is using funds to acquire qualifying assets for principal operations that have not yet begun.

(ASC 835-20-15-5)

Many entities use threshold levels to determine whether or not interest costs related to inventory or property, plant, and equipment should be capitalized. (ASC 835-20-15-4)

The capitalization of interest costs does not apply to the following situations:

1. When the effects of capitalization would not be material, compared to the effect of expensing interest
2. When qualifying assets are already in use or ready for use
3. When qualifying assets are not being used and are not awaiting activities to get them ready for use
4. When qualifying assets are not included in a statement of financial position of the parent company and its consolidated subsidiaries
5. When principal operations of an investee accounted for under the equity method have already begun
6. When regulated investees capitalize both the cost of debt and equity capital
7. When assets are acquired with grants and gifts that are restricted by the donor (or grantor) to the acquisition of those assets, to the extent that funds are available from those grants and gifts. For this purpose, interest earned on the temporary investment of those funds that is subject to similar restriction is to be considered an addition to the gift or grant.

(ASC 835-10-15-6)

Accretion costs related to exit costs and asset retirement obligations are covered by the guidance in ASC 420 or ASC 410-20. So, too, the interest cost component of net periodic pension cost falls under the ASC 715-30 guidance.

Overview

ASC 835 provides guidance in two instances – where interest capitalization is in connection with an investment in an asset and where imputation of interest is required.

Per ASC 835-20, the recorded amount of an asset includes all of the costs necessary to get the asset set up and functioning properly for its intended use, including interest. The principal purposes accomplished by the capitalization of interest costs are:

1. To obtain a more accurate measurement of the costs associated with the investment in the asset
2. To achieve a better matching of costs related to the acquisition, construction, and development of productive assets to the future periods that will benefit from the revenues that the assets generate.

ASC 835-30 specifies when and how interest is to be imputed when the receivable is noninterest-bearing or the stated rate on the receivable is not reasonable. It applies to transactions conducted at arm's length between unrelated parties, as well as to transactions in which captive finance companies offer favorable financing to increase sales of related companies.

DEFINITIONS OF TERMS

Source: ASC 835

Activities. The term activities is to be construed broadly. It encompasses physical construction of the asset. In addition, it includes all the steps required to prepare the asset for its intended use. For example, it includes administrative and technical activities during the preconstruction stage, such as the development of plans or the process of obtaining permits from governmental authorities. It also includes activities undertaken after construction has begun in order to overcome unforeseen obstacles, such as technical problems, labor disputes, or litigation.

Capitalization Rate. Rate used to determine amount of interest to be capitalized in an accounting period.

Discount. The difference between the net proceeds, after expense, received upon issuance of debt and the amount repayable at its maturity. See Premium.

Expenditures. Expenditures to which capitalization rates are to be applied are capitalized expenditures (net of progress payment collections) for the qualifying asset that have required the payment of cash, the transfer of other assets, or the incurring of a liability on which interest is recognized (in contrast to liabilities, such as trade payables, accruals, and retainages on which interest is not recognized).

Fair Value. The price that would be received to sell an asset or paid to transfer a liability in an orderly transaction between market participants at the measurement date.

Imputed Interest Rate. The interest rate that results from a process of approximation (or imputation) required when the present value of a note must be estimated because an established exchange price is not determinable and the note has no ready market.

Intended Use. Intended use of an asset embraces both readiness for use and readiness for sale, depending on the purpose of acquisition.

Interest Cost. Interest cost includes interest recognized on obligations having explicit interest rates, interest imputed on certain types of payables in accordance with Subtopic 835-30, and interest related to a capital lease determined in accordance with Subtopic 840–30. With respect to obligations having explicit interest rates, interest cost includes amounts resulting from periodic amortization of discount or premium and issue costs on debt.

Interest Method. The method used to arrive at a periodic interest cost (including amortization) that will represent a level effective rate on the sum of the face amount of the debt and (plus or minus) the unamortized premium or discount and expense at the beginning of each period.

Premium. The excess of the net proceeds, after expense, received upon issuance of debt over the amount repayable at its maturity. See Discount.

CONCEPTS, RULES, AND EXAMPLES

ASC 835-20, *Capitalization of Interest*

Interest cost. Generally, inventories and land that are not undergoing preparation for intended use are not qualifying assets. When land is being developed, it is a qualifying asset. If land is developed for lots, the capitalized interest cost is added to the cost of the land. The capitalized interest will then be properly matched against revenues when the lots are sold. If, however, the land is developed for a building, then the capitalized interest cost is added to the cost of the building, in which case the capitalized interest will be matched against related revenues as the building is depreciated.

The amount of interest to be capitalized. Interest cost includes the following:

1. Interest on debt having explicit interest rates (fixed or floating)
2. Interest related to capital leases
3. Interest required to be imputed on payables (i.e., those due in over one year, per ASC 835-30).

Capitalization Interest Rate. The most appropriate rate to use as the capitalization rate is the rate applicable to specific new debt resulting from the need to finance the acquired assets. If there is no specific new debt, the capitalization rate is a weighted-average of the rates of the other borrowings of the entity. This reflects the fact that the previously incurred debt of the entity could be repaid if not for the acquisition of the qualifying asset. Thus, indirectly, the previous debt is financing the acquisition of the new asset and its interest is part of the cost of the new asset. The selection of borrowings to be used in the calculation of the weighted-average of rates requires judgment. The amount of interest to be capitalized is that portion which could have been avoided if the qualifying asset had not been acquired. Thus, the capitalized amount is the incremental amount of interest cost incurred by the entity to finance the acquired asset.

If the reporting entity uses derivative financial instruments as fair value hedges to affect its borrowing costs, ASC 815-25-35 specifies that the interest rate to use in capitalizing interest is the effective yield that takes into account gains and losses on the effective portion of a derivative instrument that qualifies as a fair value hedge of fixed interest rate debt. The amount of interest subject to capitalization could include amortization of the adjustments of the carrying amount of the hedged liability under ASC 815, if the entity elects to begin amortization of those adjustments during the period in which interest is eligible for capitalization. Any ineffective portion of the fair value hedge is not reflected in the capitalization rate.

Capitalizable Base. Once the appropriate rate has been established, the base to which that rate is to be applied is the average amount of accumulated net capital *expenditures* incurred for qualifying assets during the relevant time frame. Capitalized costs and expenditures are not the same terms. Theoretically, a capitalized cost financed by a trade payable for which no interest is recognized is not a capital expenditure to which the capitalization rate is applied. Reasonable approximations of net capital expenditures are acceptable, however, and capitalized costs are generally used in place of capital expenditures unless there is expected to be a material difference.

If the average capitalized expenditures exceed the specific new borrowings for the time frame involved, then the *excess* expenditures are multiplied by the weighted-average of rates and not by the rate associated with the specific debt. This requirement more accurately reflects the interest cost incurred by the entity to acquire the fixed asset.

The interest being paid on the debt may be simple or compound. Simple interest is computed on the principal alone, whereas compound interest is computed on the principal *and* on any interest that has not been paid. Most fixed assets will be acquired with debt subject to compound interest.

The total amount of interest actually incurred by the entity is the ceiling for the amount of interest cost capitalized. The amount capitalized cannot exceed the amount actually incurred during the period involved. On a consolidated basis, the ceiling is defined as the total of the parent's interest cost plus that of the consolidated subsidiaries. If financial statements are issued separately, the interest cost capitalized is limited to the amount that the separate entity has incurred, and that amount includes interest on intercompany borrowings. The interest incurred is a gross amount and is not netted against interest earned except in cases involving externally restricted tax-exempt borrowings.

Example of accounting for capitalized interest costs

1. On January 1, 2012, Daniel Corp. contracted with Rukin Company to construct a building for $2,000,000 on land that Daniel had purchased years earlier.
2. Daniel Corp. was to make five payments in 20X7, with the last payment scheduled for the date of completion, December 31, 20X7.
3. Daniel Corp. made the following payments during 20X7:

January 1, 20X7	$ 200,000
March 31, 20X7	400,000
June 30, 20X7	610,000
September 30, 20X7	440,000
December 31, 20X7	350,000
	$2,000,000

4. Daniel Corp. had the following debt outstanding at December 31, 20X7:

a. A 12%, four-year note dated 1/1 X7 with interest compounded quarterly. Both principal and interest due 12/31/Y0 (relates specifically to building project).	$850,000
b. A 10%, ten-year note dated 12/31/X1 with simple interest payable annually on December 31.	$600,000
c. A 12%, five-year note dated 12/31/X3 with simple interest payable annually on December 31.	$700,000

The amount of interest to be capitalized during 20X7 is computed as follows:

Step 1—Compute average accumulated expenditures

Average Accumulated Expenditures

Date	*Expenditure*	*Capitalization period**	*Average accumulated expenditures*
1/1/ X7	$ 200,000	12/ X7	$200,000
3/31/ X7	400,000	9/ X7	300,000
6/30/ X7	610,000	6/ X72	305,000
9/30/ X7	440,000	3/ X7	110,000
12/31/ X7	350,000	0/ X7	–
	$2,000,000		$915,000

* *The number of months between the date expenditures were made and the date interest capitalization stops (December 31, 20X7).*

Because the average accumulated expenditures of $915,000 exceed the $850,000 borrowed specifically for the project, interest will be capitalized on the excess expenditures of $65,000 by using the weighted-average interest rate on the other two notes.

Step 2—Compute the weighted-average interest rate on the Company's other borrowings

	Principal	*Interest*
10%, ten-year note	$ 600,000	$ 60,000
12%, five-year note	700,000	84,000
	$1,300,000	$144,000

$$\frac{\text{Total interest}}{\text{Total principal}} = \frac{\$144{,}000}{\$1{,}300{,}000} = 11.08\% \text{ weighted-average interest rate}$$

Step 3—Compute the potential interest cost to be capitalized

The $850,000 loan is considered first because it relates specifically to the project. Interest accretes on this loan quarterly. Since interest is not due until the loan's maturity, the interest for each quarter increases the unpaid principal amount on which further quarters' interest will be accreted.

Date	*Description*	*Interest*	*Principal*	*Balance*
1/1/20X7	Loan proceeds			$850,000
4/1/20X7	Quarterly compound interest	$ 25,500	$ (25,500)	875,500
7/1/20X7	Quarterly compound interest	26,265	(26,265)	901,765
10/1/20X7	Quarterly compound interest	27,053	(27,053)	928,818
12/31/20X7	Quarterly compound interest	27,866	(27,866)	956,684
	Totals	$106,684	$(106,684)	

The above computations can be made using specialized present value software or standard spreadsheet software. They can also be made/proved using the following formula to compute the future value of $1 for four periods at 3% per period (12% annual rate ÷ 4 periods per year quarterly compounding) where

FV = Future value of the present sum of $1
i = The interest rate at which the amount will be compounded each period, and
n = The number of periods

$$\begin{aligned} FV &= (1 + i)^n \\ &= (1 + .03)^4 \\ &= 1.03^4 \\ &= 1.12551 \\ \$850{,}000 \times 1.12551 &= \$956{,}684 \end{aligned}$$

(850,000) principal
$106,684 interest

Potential Interest Cost to Be Capitalized

Interest on the project-related loan	($850,000 × 1.12551) – $850,000	=	$106,684
Interest on remaining average accumulated expenditures	65,000 × .1108	=	7,202
	$915,000		$113,886

Step 4—Compute the actual interest cost for the period

12%, three-year note [($850,000 × 1.12551) – $850,000]	=	$106,684
10%, ten-year note ($600,000 × 10%)	=	60,000
12%, five-year note ($700,000 × 12%)	=	84,000
Total interest		$250,684

Step 5—Compute the amount of interest cost to be capitalized

The interest cost to be capitalized is the lesser of $113,886 (avoidable interest cost) or $250,684 (actual interest cost), which is $113,886. The remaining $136,798 ($250,684 – $113,886) is expensed during 20X7.

Determining the time period for interest capitalization. Three conditions must be met before capitalization commences.

1. Necessary activities are in progress to get the asset ready to function as intended
2. Qualifying asset expenditures have been made
3. Interest costs are being incurred.

As long as these conditions continue, interest costs are capitalized.

Necessary activities are interpreted in a very broad manner. They start with the planning process and continue until the qualifying asset is substantially complete and ready to function. Brief, normal interruptions do not stop the capitalization of interest costs. However, if the entity intentionally suspends or delays the activities for some reason, interest costs are not capitalized from the point of suspension or delay until substantial activities regarding the asset resume.

If the asset is completed in parts, the capitalization of interest costs stops for each part as it becomes ready. An asset that must be entirely complete before the parts can be used capitalizes interest costs until the total asset becomes ready.

Interest costs continue to be capitalized until the asset is ready to function as intended, even in cases where lower of cost or market rules are applicable and market is lower than cost. The required write-down is increased accordingly.

Capitalization of interest costs incurred on tax-exempt borrowings. If qualifying assets have been financed with the proceeds from tax-exempt, externally restricted borrowings, and if temporary investments have been purchased with those proceeds, a modification is required. The interest costs incurred from the date of borrowing must be reduced by the interest earned on the temporary investment in order to calculate the ceiling for the capitalization of interest costs. This procedure is followed until the assets financed in this manner are ready. When the specified assets are functioning as intended, the interest cost of the tax-exempt borrowing becomes available to be capitalized by other qualifying assets of the entity. Portions of the tax-exempt borrowings that are not restricted are eligible for capitalization in the normal manner.

Assets acquired with gifts or grants. Qualifying assets that are acquired with externally restricted gifts or grants are not subject to capitalization of interest. The principal reason for this treatment is the concept that there is no economic cost of financing when a gift or grant is used in the acquisition.

Summary of interest capitalization requirements. The diagram that follows summarizes the accounting for interest capitalization.

ASC 835-30, *Imputation of Interest*

Receivables. If a receivable is due on terms exceeding one year, the proper valuation is the present value of future payments to be received, determined by using an interest rate commensurate with the risks involved at the date of the receivable's creation. In many situations the interest rate commensurate with the risks involved is the rate stated in the agreement between the payee and the debtor. However, if the receivable is noninterest-bearing or if the rate stated in the agreement is not indicative of the market rate for a debtor of similar creditworthiness under similar terms, interest is imputed at the market rate. A valuation allowance is used to adjust the face amount of the receivable to the present value at the market rate. The balance in the valuation allowance is amortized as additional interest income so that interest income is recognized using a constant rate of interest over the life of

SUMMARY OF ACCOUNTING FOR INTEREST CAPITALIZATION

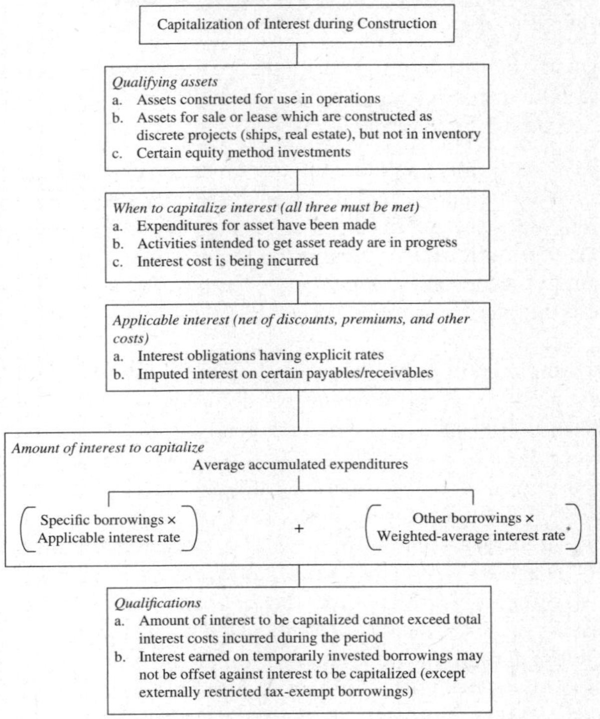

$$^{*}\textit{Weighted-average interest rate} = \frac{\textit{Total interest on other borrowings}}{\textit{Average outstanding principal during period}}$$

the agreement. Initial recording of such a valuation allowance also results in the recognition of an expense, typically (for customer receivables) reported as selling expense or as a contra revenue item (sales discounts).

ASC 835-30-25 divides receivables into three categories for discussion:

- notes issued solely for cash,
- notes issued for cash and rights or privileges, and
- notes issued in exchange for property, goods, or services.

Note issued solely for cash. When a note is issued solely for cash, its present value is necessarily assumed to be equal to the cash proceeds. The interest rate is that rate which equates the cash proceeds received by the borrower to the amounts to be paid in the future. For example, if a borrower agrees to pay $1,060 in one year in exchange for cash today of $1,000, the interest rate implicit in that agreement is 6%. A valuation allowance of $60 is applied to the face amount ($1,060) so that the receivable is included in the statement of financial position at its present value ($1,000).

Note issued for cash and rights or privileges. When a note receivable that bears an unrealistic rate of interest is issued in exchange for cash, an additional right or privilege is usually granted, unless the transaction was not conducted at arm's length. If there was an added right or privilege involved, the difference between the present value of the receivable and the cash advanced is the value assigned to the right or privilege. It will be accounted for as an addition to the cost of the products purchased for the purchaser/lender, and as additional revenue to the debtor.

Example of accounting for a note issued for both cash and a contractual right

1. Schwartz borrows $10,000 from Weiss via an unsecured five-year note. Simple interest at 2% is due at maturity.
2. Schwartz agrees to sell Weiss a car for $15,000, which is less than its market price.
3. The market rate of interest on a note with similar terms and a borrower of similar creditworthiness is 10%.

The present value factor for an amount due in five years at 10% is .62092. Therefore, the present value of the note is $6,830 [= ($10,000 principal + $1,000 interest at the stated rate) × .62092]. According to ASC 835, the $3,170 (= $10,000 – $6,830) difference between the present value of the note and the face value of the note is regarded as part of the cost/purchase price of the car. The following entry would be made by Weiss to record the transaction:

Note receivable	10,000	
Car	18,170	
Cash		25,000
Discount on note receivable		3,170

The discount on note receivable is amortized using the effective interest method, as follows:

	Effective interest (10%)	*Stated interest (2%)*	*Amortization*	*Note and interest receivable*
01/01/X1				6,830
01/01/X2	683	200	(483)	7,513
01/01/X3	751	200	(551)	8,264
01/01/X4	826	200	(626)	9,091
01/01/X5	909	200	(709)	10,000
01/01/X6	1,000	200	(800)	11,000

The entry for the first year would be

Discount on note receivable	483	
Interest receivable	200	
Interest revenue		683

Note issued in exchange for property, goods, or services. When a note is issued in exchange for property, goods, or services and the transaction is entered into at arm's length, the stated interest rate is presumed to be fair unless

1. no interest rate is stated,
2. the stated rate is unreasonable,
3. the face value of the note receivable is materially different from fair value of the property, goods, or services received, or
4. the face value of the note receivable is materially different from the current market value of the note at the date of the transaction.

According to ASC 835, when the rate on the note is not fair, the note is to be recorded at the fair market value of the property, goods, or services sold or the market value of the note, whichever is the more clearly determinable. The difference is recorded as a discount or premium and amortized to interest income.

Example of accounting for a note exchanged for goods

1. Green sells Brown inventory that has a fair market value of $8,573.
2. Green receives a two-year noninterest-bearing note having a face value of $10,000.

In this situation, the fair market value of the consideration is readily determinable and, thus, represents the amount at which the note is to be recorded. The following entry would be made by Green:

Notes receivable	10,000	
Discount on notes receivable		1,427
Sales revenue		8,573

The discount will be amortized to interest expense over the two-year period using the interest rate implied in the transaction, which is 8%. The present value factor is .8573 ($8,573/$10,000). Using a present value table for amount due in two years, .8573 is located under the 8% rate.

If neither the fair value of the property, goods, or services sold nor the fair value of the note receivable is determinable, then the present value of the note must be determined using an imputed market interest rate. This rate will then be used to establish the present value of the note by discounting all future payments on the note at that rate. General guidelines for determining the appropriate interest rate, which are provided by ASC 835, include the prevailing rates of similar instruments with debtors having similar credit ratings and the rate the debtor could obtain for similar financing from other sources. Other factors to be considered include any collateral or restrictive covenants involved, the current and expected prime rate, and other terms pertaining to the instrument. The objective is to approximate the rate of interest that would have resulted if an independent borrower and lender had negotiated a similar transaction under comparable terms and conditions. This determination is as of the issuance date, and any subsequent changes in market interest rates are irrelevant.

Notes and Bonds. The appropriate valuation of long-term debt at the date of issuance is the present value of the future payments, using an interest rate commensurate with the risks involved. In many situations this is the rate stated in the agreement between the borrower and the creditor. However, in other situations the debt may be noninterest-bearing, or the rate stated in the agreement may not be indicative of the rate applicable to a borrower having similar creditworthiness and debt having similar terms. In other words, the rate stated in the agreement is not commensurate with the risks involved. To reflect the liability at the appropriate value, interest must be imputed at the market rate, and the resulting premium or discount is amortized as interest over the life of the agreement

Notes are a common form of exchange in business transactions for cash, property, goods, and services. Notes represent debt issued to a single investor without intending for the debt to be broken up among many investors. A note's maturity, usually lasting one to seven years, tends to be shorter than that of a bond.

Bonds are primarily used to borrow funds from the general public or institutional investors when a contract for a single amount (a note) is too large for any one lender to supply. Dividing up the amount needed into $1,000 or $10,000 units makes it easier to sell the bonds. Bonds also result from a single agreement.

Notes and bonds share common characteristics. They both are promises to pay sums of money at designated maturity dates, plus periodic interest payments at stated rates. They each feature written agreements stating the amounts of principal, the interest rates, when the interest and principal are to be paid, and the restrictive covenants, if any, that must be met.

The interest rate is affected by many factors, including the cost of money, the business risk factors, and general and industry-specific inflationary expectations. The stated rate on a note or bond often differs from the market rate at the time of issuance. When this occurs, the present value of the interest and principal payments will differ from the maturity, or face value. (For a complete discussion of present value techniques see Chapter 1.) If the market rate exceeds the stated rate, the cash proceeds will be less than the face value of the debt because the present value of the total interest and principal payments discounted back to the present yields an amount that is less than the face value. Because an investor is rarely willing to pay more than the present value, the bonds must be issued at a discount. The discount is the difference between the issuance price (present value) and the face, or stated, value of the bonds. This discount is then amortized over the life of the bonds to increase the recognized interest expense so that the total amount of the expense represents the actual bond yield. When the stated rate exceeds the market rate, the bond will sell for more than its face value (at a premium) to bring the effective rate to the market rate. Amortization of the premium over the life of the bonds will decrease the total interest expense.

When the market and stated rates are equivalent at the time of issuance, no discount or premium exists and the instrument will sell at its face value. Changes in the market rate subsequent to issuance are irrelevant in determining the discount or premium or its amortization.

All commitments to pay (and receive) money at a determinable future date are subject to present value techniques and, if necessary, interest imputation with the exception of the following:

1. Normal accounts payable due within one year
2. Amounts to be applied to purchase price of goods or services or that provide security to an agreement (e.g., advances, progress payments, security deposits, and retentions)
3. Transactions between parent and subsidiary
4. Obligations payable at some indeterminable future date (e.g., warranties)
5. Lending and depositor savings activities of financial institutions whose primary business is lending money
6. Transactions where interest rates are affected by prescriptions of a governmental agency (e.g., revenue bonds, tax exempt obligations, etc.).

Summary – ASC 835-30. ASC 835-30 specifies when and how interest is to be imputed when a debt is either noninterest-bearing or the stated rate is not reasonable. ASC 835-30 divides debt into three categories for discussion. The diagram below illustrates the accounting treatment for the three types of debt.

ACCOUNTING FOR MONETARY ASSETS AND LIABILITIES

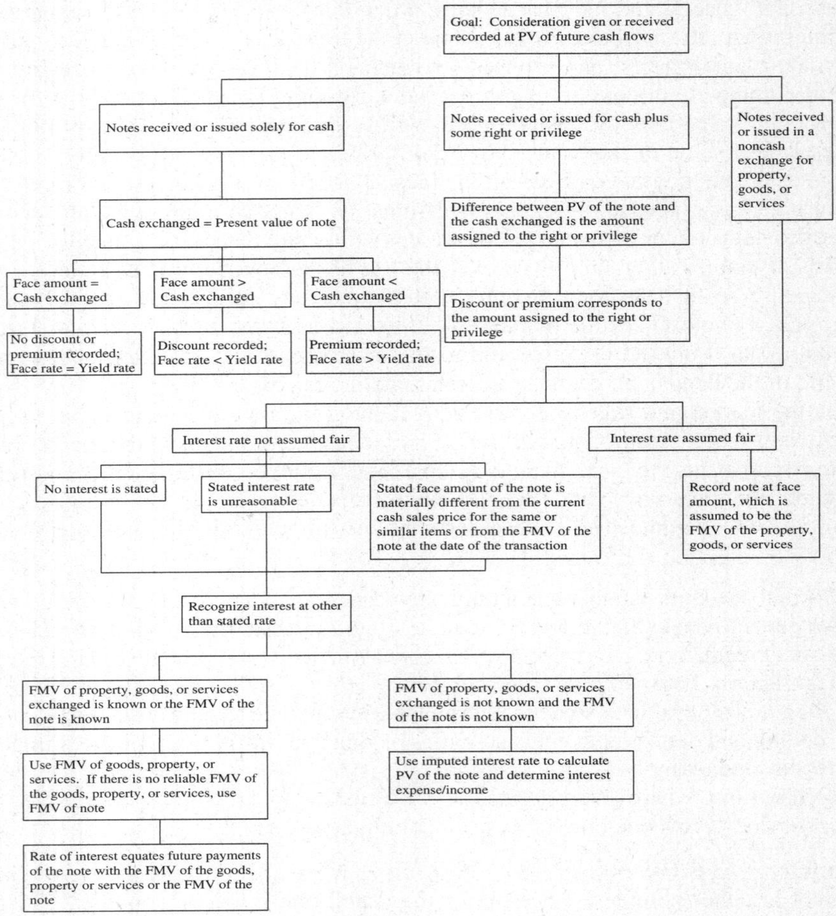

Notes issued solely for cash. When a note is issued solely for cash, its present value is assumed to be equal to the cash proceeds. The interest rate is that rate equating the cash proceeds to the amounts to be paid in the future. For example, a $1,000 note due in three years that sells for $889 has an implicit rate of 4% (= $1,000 × .889, where .889 is the present value factor at 4% for a lump sum due three years hence). This implicit rate, 4%, is to be used when amortizing the discount.

In most situations, a bond will be issued at a price other than its face value. The amount of the cash exchanged is equal to the total of the present values of all the future interest and principal payments. The difference between the cash proceeds and the face value is recorded as a premium if the cash proceeds are greater than the face value or a discount if they are less. The journal entry to record a bond issued at a premium follows:

Cash	(proceeds)	
Bonds payable		(face value)
Premium on bonds payable		(difference)

Example of bonds issued for cash

Enterprise Autos issues $100,000 of 10-year bonds bearing interest at 10%, paid semiannually, at a time when the market demands a 12% return from issuers with similar credit standings. The proceeds of the bond issuance would be $88,500, which is computed as follows:

Present value of 20 semiannual interest payments of $5,000 discounted at 12% (6% semiannually: factor = 11.4699)	$57,300
Present value of $100,000 due in 10 years, discounted at 12% compounded semiannually (factor = .31180)	31,200
Present value of bond issuance	$88,500

The journal entry would be

Cash	88,500	
Discount on bonds payable	11,500	
Bonds payable		100,000

Notes issued for cash and a right or privilege. Often when a note bearing an unrealistic rate of interest is issued in exchange for cash, an additional right or privilege is granted, such as the issuer agreeing to sell merchandise to the purchaser at a reduced rate. The difference between the present value of the receivable and the cash loaned is regarded as an addition to the cost of the products purchased for the purchaser/lender and as unearned revenue to the seller/issuer. This treatment stems from an attempt to match revenue and expense in the proper periods and to differentiate between those factors that affect income from operations and income or expense from nonoperating sources. In the situation above, the purchaser/lender will amortize the discount (difference between the cash loaned and the present value of the note) to interest income over the life of the note, and the contractual right to purchase inventory at a reduced rate will be allocated to inventory (or cost of sales) as the right expires. The seller/issuer of the note will amortize the discount to interest expense over the life of the note, and the unearned revenue will be recognized in sales as the products are sold to the purchaser/lender at the reduced price. Because the discount is amortized on a different basis than the contractual right, net income for the period is also affected.

Example of accounting for a note issued for both cash and a contractual right

1. Miller borrows $10,000 via a noninterest-bearing three-year note from Krueger.
2. Miller agrees to sell $50,000 of merchandise to Krueger at less than the ordinary retail price for the duration of the note.
3. The market rate of interest on a note with similar payment terms and a borrower of similar creditworthiness is 10%.

According to ASC 835-30, the difference between the present value of the note and the face value of the loan is to be regarded as part of the cost of the products purchased under the agreement. The present value factor for an amount due in three years at 10% is .75132. Therefore, the present value of the note is $7,513 (= $10,000 × .75132). The $2,487 (= $10,000 – $7,513) difference between the face value and the present value is to be recorded as a discount on the note payable and as unearned revenue on the future purchases by the debtor. The following entries would be made by the debtor (Miller) and the creditor (Krueger) to record the transaction:

Miller			*Krueger*		
Cash	10,000		Note receivable	10,000	
Discount on note payable	2,487		Contract right with supplier	2,487	
Note payable		10,000	Cash		10,000
Unearned revenue		2,487	Discount on note receivable		2,487

The discount on note payable (and note receivable) is to be amortized using the effective interest method, while the unearned revenue account and contract right with supplier account are amortized on a pro rata basis as the right to purchase merchandise is used up. Thus, if Krueger purchased $20,000 of merchandise from Miller in the first year, the following entries would be necessary:

Miller			*Krueger*		
Unearned revenue [$2,487 × (20,000/50,000)]	995		Inventory (or cost of sales)	995	
Sales		995	Contract right with supplier		995
Interest expense	751		Discount on note receivable	751	
Discount on note payable ($7,513 × 10%)		751	Interest revenue		751

The amortization of unearned revenue and contract right with supplier accounts will fluctuate with the amount of purchases made. If there is a balance remaining in the account at the end of the loan term, it is amortized to the appropriate account in that final year.

Noncash transactions. When a note is issued for consideration such as property, goods, or services, and the transaction is entered into at arm's length, the stated interest rate is presumed to be fair unless (1) no interest rate is stated; (2) the stated rate is unreasonable; or (3) the face value of the debt is materially different from the consideration involved or the current market value of the note at the date of the transaction. According to ASC 835-30, when the rate on the note is not considered fair, the note is to be recorded at the "fair market value of the property, goods, or services received or at an amount that reasonably approximates the market value of the note, whichever is the more clearly determinable." When this amount differs from the face value of the note, the difference is to be recorded as a discount or premium and amortized to interest expense.

Example of accounting for a note exchanged for property

1. Alexis sells Brett a machine that has a fair market value of $7,510.
2. Alexis receives a three-year noninterest-bearing note having a face value of $10,000.

In this situation, the fair market value of the consideration is readily determinable and, thus, represents the amount at which the note is to be recorded. The following entry by Brett is necessary:

Machine	7,510	
Discount on notes payable	2,490	
Notes payable		10,000

The discount will be amortized to interest expense over the three-year period using the interest rate implied in the transaction. The interest rate implied is 10%, because the factor for an amount due in three years is .75132, which when applied to the $10,000 face value results in an amount equal to the fair value of the machine.

If the fair market value of the consideration or note is not determinable, then the present value of the note must be determined using an imputed interest rate. This rate will then be used to establish the present value of the note by discounting all future payments on the note at this rate. General guidelines for imputing the interest rate, which are provided by ASC 835-30, include the prevailing rates of similar instruments from creditors with similar credit ratings and the rate the debtor could obtain for similar financing from other sources. Other determining factors include any collateral or restrictive covenants involved, the current and expected prime rate, and other terms pertaining to the instrument. The objective is to approximate the rate of interest that would have resulted if an independent borrower and lender had negotiated a similar transaction under comparable terms and conditions. This determination is as of the issuance date, and any subsequent changes in interest rates would be irrelevant.

Example of accounting for a note exchanged to property

1. Alexis sells Brett a used machine. The fair market value is not readily determinable.
2. Alexis receives a three-year noninterest-bearing note having a face value of $20,000. The market value of the note is not known.
3. Brett could have borrowed the money for the machine's purchase from a bank at a rate of 10%.

In this situation, the fair market value of the consideration is not readily determinable, so the present value of the note is determined using an imputed interest rate. The rate used is the rate at which Brett could have borrowed the money—10%. The factor for an amount due in three years at 10% is .75132, so the present value of the note is $15,026. The following entry by Brett is necessary:

Machine	15,026	
Discount on notes payable	4,974	
Notes payable		20,000

Redeemable instruments. ASC 470-10-55 addresses the classification of certain long-term debt that is subject to a demand from the holder for redemption, subject to a best efforts attempt by the issuer to remarket that date. Thus, there is a possibility that the demand for redemption would not be honored, although a bank letter of credit is also provided as additional security for the lender. Notwithstanding that possibility, this debt must be reported as a current obligation.

Sales of future revenue. ASC 470-10-25 deals with the situation in which a reporting entity receives an initial payment from another party in exchange for a promised stream of royalties or other revenue-based receipts from a defined business, which could be a segment or product line of the reporting entity. Arguably, the up-front payment could be seen as an advance against the future payments, or as a borrowing by the reporting entity. The payment is not revenue to the reporting entity.

The Codification states that the initial receipt would be accounted for as either debt or deferred revenue, depending on the facts and circumstances of the transaction. It identifies six factors that would cause the amounts to be recorded as debt, rather than as deferred income. These factors are:

1. The transaction does not purport to be a sale.
2. The reporting entity has significant continuing involvement in the generation of the cash flows due the other party (referred to as the investor in this consensus).
3. The transaction is cancelable by either party through payment of a lump sum or other transfer of assets by the entity.
4. The investor's rate of return is implicitly or explicitly limited by the terms of the transaction.
5. Variations in the reporting entity's revenue or income underlying the transaction have only a trifling impact on the investor's rate of return.
6. The investor has any recourse to the reporting entity relating to the payments due to the investor.

(ASC 470-10-25-2)

Amounts recorded as debt should be amortized under the interest method and amounts recorded as deferred income should be amortized under the units-of-revenue method. The proceeds classified as foreign-currency-denominated debt would be subject to recognition of foreign currency transaction (exchange) gains and losses under ASC 830-20.

ASC 815 established cash flow hedge accounting for hedges of the variability of the functional currency equivalent of future foreign-currency-denominated cash flows. If the proceeds are classified as deferred income, this would be a nonmonetary liability. Thus, no foreign exchange gains or losses would arise under ASC 830-20.

Effective Interest Method

The effective interest method is the preferred method of accounting for a discount or premium arising from a note or bond. Under the effective interest method, the discount or premium is amortized over the life of the debt in such a way as to result in a constant rate of interest when applied to the amount outstanding at the beginning of any given period. Therefore, interest expense is equal to the market rate of interest at the time of issuance multiplied by this beginning figure. The difference between the interest expense and the cash paid represents the amortization of the discount or premium.

Amortization tables are often created at the time of the bond's issuance to provide amounts necessary when recording the entries relating to the debt issue. They also provide a check of accuracy since the final values in the unamortized discount or premium and carrying value columns should be equal to zero and the bond's face value, respectively.

Example of applying the effective interest method

1. A 3-year, 12%, $10,000 bond is issued at 1/1/20X1, with interest payments semiannually.
2. The market rate is 10%.

The amortization table would appear as follows:

Date	*Credit cash*	*Debit int. exp.*	*Debit prem.*	*Unamort. prem. bal.*	*Carrying value*
1/1/X1				$507.61	$10,507.61(a)
7/1/X1	$ 600.00(b)	$ 525.38(c)	$ 74.62(d)	432.99(e)	10,432.99(f)
1/1/X2	600.00	521.65	78.35	354.64	10,354.64
7/1/X2	600.00	517.73	82.27	272.37	10,272.37
1/1/X3	600.00	513.62	86.38	185.99	10,185.99
7/1/X3	600.00	509.30	90.70	95.29	10,095.29
1/1/X4	600.00	504.71(g)	95.29	–	10,000.00
	$3,600.00	$3,092.39	$507.61		

(a) PV of principal and interest payments at 5% for 6 periods

$10,000(.74622)	=	*$ 7,462.20*
$ 600(5.07569)	=	*3,045.41*
		$10,507.61

(b) $10,000.00 × .12 × one-half year

(c) $10,507.61 × .10 × one-half year

(d) $600.00 – $525.38

(e) $507.61 – $74.62

(f) $10,507.61 – $74.62 (or $10,000 + $432.99)

(g) Rounding error = $.05

Although the effective interest method is the preferred method of amortizing a discount or premium, the straight-line method may be used if the results are not materially different. The amortized portion is equal to the total amount of the discount or premium divided by the life of the debt from issuance in months multiplied by the number of months the debt has been outstanding that year. Interest expense under the straight-line method is equal to the cash interest paid plus the amortized portion of the discount or minus the amortized portion of the premium.

When the interest date does not coincide with the year-end, an adjusting entry must be made to recognize the proportional share of interest payable and the amortization of the discount or premium. Within the amortization period, the discount or premium can be amortized using the straight-line method.

If bonds or notes are issued between interest payment dates, the interest and the amortization must be computed for the period between the sale date and the next interest date. The purchaser usually pays the issuer for the amount of interest that has accrued since the last payment date. That payment is recorded as a payable by the issuer. At the next interest date, the issuer pays the purchaser as though the bond had been outstanding for the entire interest period. The discount or premium is also amortized for the short period.

Example of note issued between payment dates

On June 1, 20X1, Acme Manufacturing issues a $100,000 7% bond with a three-year life at 104 (i.e., at 104% of face value). Interest is payable on July 1 and January 1. The computation of the premium would be

Proceeds	$104,000
Face value	100,000
Premium	$ 4,000

The entry to record the bond issuance and the receipt of interest from the purchaser would be

Cash	106,967	
Bonds payable		100,000
Premium on bonds		4,000
Interest payable		2,967

The bonds will be outstanding for two years and seven months. An effective interest rate must be computed that will equate the present value of the future principal and interest payments to the cash received. Using a spreadsheet facilitates the trial and error process. Many calculators with financial functions also do this calculation. Alternatively, present value tables can be used to compute the value, as shown below.

First, compute the present value of the interest and principal payments as of 7/1/X1 using a guess of 5% annually.

Present value of an annuity due of $3,500 for six periods @ 2.5% = 3,500 × 5.6458 =	19,760
Present value of a single payment of $100,000 in five periods @ 2.5% = 100,000 × .88385 =	88,385
	108,145

Then, compute the present value of that result one month earlier (at June 1, 2012) using the same interest rate.

Present value of a single payment of $108,145 in one month = 108,145/[1+(.05/12)] = 107,696

The result is more than the cash received ($106,967), so we know that the interest rate must be higher than 5%. Repeat the calculation at a 6% annual rate.

Present value of an annuity due of $3,500 for six periods @ 3% = 3,500 × 5.5797 =	19,529
Present value of a single payment of $100,000 in five periods @ 3% = 100,000 × .86261 =	86,261
	105,790
Present value of a single payment of $105,790 in one month = 105,790/[1+(.06/12)] =	105,263

The result is less than the cash received ($106,967), so we know the rate is between 5 and 6%. By interpolation, we determine that the rate is 5.3%.

$$\frac{107{,}696 - 106{,}967}{107{,}696 - 105{,}263} \times (6\% - 5\%) = .2996\%$$, which is added to 5% to get the effective rate.

The amortization of the $4,000 premium would be as follows:

	Cash paid (received)	*Interest at 5.3% annually*	*Amortization*	*Interest payable*	*Bond payable*
					104,000
06/01/X1	(2,967)			2,967	104,000
07/01/X1	3,500	459	74	(2,967)	103,926
01/01/X2	3,500	2,754	746		103,180
07/01/X2	3,500	2,734	765		102,415

	Cash paid (received)	*Interest at 5.3% annually*	*Amortization*	*Interest payable*	*Bond payable*
01/01/X3	3,500	2,714	786		101,629
07/01/X3	3,500	2,693	807		100,822
01/01/X4	103,500	2,672	822		100,000

The entry to record the first interest payment would be

Interest payable	2,967	
Interest expense	459	
Premium on bonds	74	
Cash		3,500

Costs may be incurred in connection with issuing bonds. Examples include legal, accounting, and underwriting fees; commissions; and engraving, printing, and registration costs. These costs theoretically should be treated as either an expense in the period incurred or a reduction in the related amount of debt, in much the same manner as a discount (CON 6). These costs do not provide any future economic benefit and, therefore, should not be an asset. Since these costs reduce the amount of cash proceeds, they in effect increase the effective interest rate and probably should be accounted for in the same way as an unamortized discount. However, in practice, issue costs are treated as deferred charges and amortized using the straight-line method.

53 ASC 840 LEASES

PERSPECTIVE AND ISSUES

Subtopics

ASC 840, *Leases,* and its subtopics establish standards of accounting and reporting by lessees and lessors for leases overall, and for specific classifications of leases. ASC 840 contains four subtopics:

- ASC 840-10, *Overall,*
- ASC 840-20, *Operating Leases*
- ASC 840-30, *Capital Leases*
- ASC 840-40, *Sale-Leaseback Transactions*.

Each of the subtopics contains the following Subsections:

- General
- Lessees
- Lessors.

Scope and Scope Exceptions

ASC 840 applies to all entities. However, to be considered a lease the right to use property, plant, or equipment must be transferred from one contracting party to the other. The definition of lease does not include contracts for services.

Overview

Lease transactions became enormously popular over the years as businesses sought new ways to finance long-lived assets. Leasing offered two attractive advantages: typically 100% financing, coupled very often with off-the-books obligations.

There are several economic reasons why the lease transaction is considered a viable alternative to outright purchase:

1. The lessee (borrower) is frequently able to obtain 100% financing.
2. Income tax benefits may be available to one or both of the parties.
3. The lessor receives the equivalent of interest as well as an asset with some remaining residual value at the end of the lease term.
4. In some cases, equipment or other assets are not available for outright purchase.

A lease agreement involves at least two parties, a lessor and a lessee, and an asset that is to be leased. The lessor, the party that either owns or commits to purchase the asset, agrees to grant the lessee the right to use it for a specified period of time in return for periodic rent payments.

The lease transaction derives its accounting complexity from the number of alternatives available to the parties involved. Leases can be structured to allow differing assignments of income tax benefits associated with the leased asset to meet the objectives of the transacting parties. Leases can be used to transfer ownership of the leased asset, and they can be used to transfer the risks and rewards of ownership. In any event, the substance of the transaction dictates, with certain exceptions, the accounting treatment, irrespective of its legal form. The lease transaction is probably the best example of the accounting profession's substance-over-form argument. If the transaction effectively transfers the risks and rewards of ownership to the lessee, then the substance of the transaction is that of a sale and, accordingly, it is recognized as such for accounting purposes even though the transaction is legally structured as a lease.

Variable interest entities. There later developed the practice of using nonsubstantive lessors (which often were related entities) to assist in keeping leases off the statement of financial position of lessees. These entities were frequently used to exclude liabilities from the lessee's consolidated statement of financial position in order to more favorably portray the lessee's financial condition. However, under the provisions of ASC 810, many more lessor entities are now required to be consolidated with the financial statements of the lessee, especially in situations where the lessor and lessee have common or related-party ownership.

It is necessary for the lessee to first apply ASC 810 to evaluate its relationship with the lessor and, in that respect, ASC 810 takes precedence over ASC 840, *Leases*. This is because if ASC 810 requires the lessee to consolidate the lessor, the effects of the lease transaction between the parties will be removed from the consolidated financial statements via an eliminating entry and, consequently, the consolidated reporting entity will depreciate the leased asset and reflect all of the costs of acquiring, holding, maintaining, and disposing of the asset. This makes the issue of distinguishing between operating and financial leases moot for any leases between a Variable Interest Entity (VIE) and its primary beneficiary.

The lessor will, of course, in any separately issued financial statements, account for the lease in accordance with the appropriate lease accounting requirements that would apply absent ASC 810. Certain concepts and definitions discussed in this chapter are also explained in the chapter on ASC 810 but are repeated and expanded upon here for completeness and further clarification in the context of lease transactions.

DEFINITIONS OF TERMS

Acquiree. The business or businesses that the acquirer obtains control over in a business combination. This term also includes a nonprofit activity or business that a not-for-profit acquirer obtains control of in an acquisition by a not-for-profit entity.

Acquirer. The entity that obtains control of the acquiree. However, in a business combination in which a VIE is acquired, the primary beneficiary of that entity always is the acquirer.

Bargain purchase option. A provision allowing the lessee, at his option, to renew the lease for a rental sufficiently lower than the fair rental of the property at the date the option becomes exercisable that exercise of the option appears, at lease inception, to be reasonably assured. Fair rental of a property in this context shall mean the expected rental for equivalent property under similar terms and conditions.

Bargain renewal option. A provision allowing the lessee, at his option, to renew the lease for a rental sufficiently lower than the fair rental of the property at the date the option becomes exercisable that exercise of the option appears, at lease inception, to be reasonably assured. Fair rental of a property in this context shall mean the expected rental for equivalent property under similar terms and conditions.

Capital Lease. From the perspective of a lessee, a lease that meets any of the four lease classification criteria in ASC 840-10-25-1:

1. *Transfer of ownership*. The lease transfers ownership of the property to the lessee by the end of the lease term. This criterion is met in situations in which the lease agreement provides for the transfer of title at or shortly after the end of the lease term

in exchange for the payment of a nominal fee, for example, the minimum required by statutory regulation to transfer title.

2. *Bargain purchase option.* This option is included in the lease.
3. *Lease term.* The lease term is equal to 75% or more of the estimated economic life of the leased property. However if the beginning of the lease term falls within the last 25% of the total estimated economic life of the lease property, including earlier years of use, this criterion shall not be used for purposes of classifying the lease.
4. *Minimum lease payment.* The present value at the beginning of the lease term of the minimum lease payments, excluding that portion of the payments representing executor costs such as insurance, maintenance, and taxes to be paid by the lessor, including any profit thereon, equals or exceeds 90% of the excess of the fair value of the leased property to the lessor at lease exception over any related investment tax credit retained by the lessor and expected to be realized by the lessor. If the beginning of the lease term falls within the last 25% of the total estimated economic life of the leased property, including earlier years of use, this criterion shall not be used for purposes of classifying the lease.

Contingent rentals. The increases or decreases in lease payments that result from changes occurring after lease inception in the factors (other than the passage of time) on which lease payments are based, excluding any escalation of minimum lease payments relating to increases in construction or acquisition cost of the leased property or for increases in some measure of cost or value during the construction or pre-construction period. The term *contingent rentals* contemplates an uncertainty about future changes in the factors on which lease payments are based.

Estimated economic life. The estimated remaining period during which the property is expected to be economically usable by one or more users, with normal repairs and maintenance, for the purpose for which it was intended at lease inception, without limitation by the lease term.

Estimated residual value of leased property. The estimated fair value of the leased property at the end of the lease term.

Fair value of leased property. The price that would be received to sell the property in an orderly transaction on the measurement date between market participants that are not related parties.

When the lessor is a manufacturer or dealer, the fair value of the property at the inception of the lease will ordinarily be its normal selling price net of volume or trade discounts. In some cases, due to market conditions, fair value may be less than the normal selling price or even the cost of the property.

When the lessor is not a manufacturer or dealer, the fair value of the property at the inception of the lease will ordinarily be its cost net of volume or trade discounts. However, if a significant amount of time elapses between the acquisition of the property by the lessor and the inception of the lease, fair value is determined in light of market conditions prevailing at the inception of the lease. Thus, fair value may be greater or less than the cost or carrying amount of the property.

Fair value determinations made for lease classification or measurement purposes are to be performed as defined by ASC 840, not as later set forth by ASC 820, other than as pertains to business combinations accounted for under ASC 805. For acquisition accounting applications, ASC 820 is the relevant guidance to be followed.

Incremental borrowing rate. The rate that, at lease inception, the lessee would have incurred to borrow over a similar term the funds necessary to purchase the leased asset. This definition does not proscribe the lessee's use of a secured borrowing rate as its incremental borrowing rate if that rate is determinable, reasonable, and consistent with the financing that would have been used in the particular circumstances.

Initial direct costs. Only those costs incurred by the lessor that are (1) costs to originate a lease incurred in transactions with independent third parties that (a) result directly from and are essential to acquire that lease and (b) would not have been incurred had that leasing transaction not occurred, and (2) certain costs directly related to specified activities performed by the lessor for that lease. Those activities are: evaluating the prospective lessee's financial condition; evaluating and recording guarantees, collateral, and other security arrangements; negotiating lease terms; preparing and processing lease documents; and closing the transaction. The costs directly related to those activities include only that portion of the employees' total compensation and payroll-related fringe benefits directly related to time spent performing those activities for that lease and other costs related to those activities that would not have been incurred but for that lease. Initial direct costs do not include costs related to activities performed by the lessor for advertising, soliciting potential lessees, servicing existing leases, and other ancillary activities related to establishing and monitoring credit policies, supervision, and administration. Initial direct costs do not include administrative costs, rent, depreciation, any other occupancy and equipment costs and employees' compensation and fringe benefits related to activities described in the previous sentence, unsuccessful origination efforts, and idle time.

Interest Method. The method used to arrive at a periodic interest cost (including amortization) that will represent a level effective rate on the sum of the face amount of the debt and (plus or minus) the unamortized premium or discount and expense at the beginning of each period.

Interest Rate Implicit in the Lease. The discount rate that causes the aggregate present value at the beginning of the lease term of the minimum lease payments (as described in paragraph 840-10-25-4), excluding that portion of the payments representing executory costs to be paid by the lessor, together with any profit thereon and the unguaranteed residual value, accruing to the benefit of the lessor to be equal to the fair value of the leased property to the lessor at lease inception, minus any investment tax credit retained by the lessor and expected to be realized by him. If the lessor is not entitled to any excess of the amount realized on disposition of the property over a guaranteed amount, no unguaranteed residual value would accrue to its benefit.

Lease. An agreement conveying the right to use property, plant, or equipment (land or depreciable assets or both), usually for a stated period of time.

Lease Incentive. An incentive for the lessee to sign the lease, such as an up-front cash payment to the lessee, payment of costs for the lessee (such as moving expenses), or the assumption by the lessor of the lessee's preexisting lease with a third party.

Lease Inception. The date of the lease agreement or commitment, if earlier. For purposes of this definition, a commitment shall be in writing, signed by the parties in interest to the transaction, and shall specifically set forth the principal provisions of the transaction. If any of the principal provisions are yet to be negotiated, such a preliminary agreement or commitment does not qualify for purposes of this definition.

Lease term. The fixed noncancelable term of the lease plus the following:

1. Periods covered by bargain renewal options
2. Periods for which failure to renew the lease imposes a penalty on the lessee in an amount such that renewal appears, at the inception of the lease, to be reasonably assured
3. Periods covered by ordinary renewal options during which a guarantee by the lessee of the lessor's debt directly or indirectly related to the leased property is expected to

be in effect, or a loan from the lessee to the lessor directly or indirectly related to the leased property is expected to be outstanding

4. Periods covered by ordinary renewal options preceding the date that a bargain purchase option is exercisable
5. Periods representing renewals or extensions of the lease at the lessor's option.

However, the lease term does not extend beyond the date a bargain purchase option becomes exercisable or beyond the useful life of the leased asset.

Minimum lease payments. For the lessee: The payments that the lessee is or can be required to make in connection with the leased property. Contingent rental guarantees by the lessee of the lessor's debt, and the lessee's obligation to pay executory costs, are excluded from minimum lease payments (MLPs). Additionally, if a portion of the MLPs representing executory costs is not determinable from the provisions of the lease, an estimate of executory costs is excluded from the calculation of the minimum lease payments. If the lease contains a bargain purchase option, only the minimum rental payments over the lease term and the payment called for in the bargain purchase option are included in minimum lease payments. Otherwise, MLPs include the following:

1. The minimum rental payments called for by the lease over the lease term
2. Any guarantee of residual value at the expiration of the lease term made by the lessee (or any party related to the lessee), whether or not the guarantee payment constitutes a purchase of the leased property. When the lessor has the right to require the lessee to purchase the property at termination of the lease for a certain or determinable amount, that amount is considered a lessee guarantee. When the lessee agrees to make up any deficiency below a stated amount in the lessor's realization of the residual value, the guarantee to be included in the MLP is the stated amount rather than an estimate of the deficiency to be made up. ASC 840 provides additional guidance regarding residual guarantees, as follows:
   a. Lease provisions requiring the lessee to reimburse the lessor for residual value deficiencies due to damage, extraordinary wear and tear, or excessive usage are analogous to contingent rentals, since at the inception of the lease, the amount of the deficiency is not determinable. Therefore, these payments are not included in the MLP as residual value guarantees.
   b. Some leases contain provisions limiting the lessee's obligation to reimburse the lessor for residual value deficiencies to an amount less than the stipulated residual value of the leased property at the end of the lease term. In computing the MLP associated with these leases, the amount of the lessee's guarantee is limited to the specified maximum deficiency the lessee can be required to reimburse to the lessor.
   c. A lessee may contract with an unrelated third party to guarantee the residual for the benefit of the lessor. The MLP can only be reduced by the third-party guarantee to the extent that the lessor explicitly releases the lessee from the obligation to make up the deficiency, even if the guarantor defaults. Amounts paid by the lessee to the guarantor are executory costs and are not included in the MLP.
3. Any payment that the lessee must or can be required to make upon failure to renew or extend the lease at the expiration of the lease term, whether or not the payment would constitute a purchase of the leased property.

For the lessor: The payments described above, plus any guarantee of the residual value or of the rental payments beyond the lease term by a third party unrelated to either the lessee or lessor (provided the third party is financially capable of discharging the guaranteed obligation).

Noncancelable in this context means that a lease is cancelable only if one of the following conditions is satisfied:

1. A remote contingency occurs
2. The lessor grants permission
3. The lessee enters into a new lease with the same lessor
4. The lessee pays a penalty in an amount such that continuation of the lease appears, at inception, reasonably assured.

Nonrecourse financing. Lending or borrowing activities in which, in the event of default, the collateral available to the creditor is limited to certain assets that are specifically agreed to in the loan agreement, and that collateral does not include the general assets of the debtor.

Penalty. Any requirement that is imposed or can be imposed on the lessee by the lease agreement or by factors outside the lease agreement to pay cash, incur or assume a liability, perform services, surrender or transfer an asset or rights to an asset or otherwise forego an economic benefit, or suffer an economic detriment.

Primary beneficiary. A variable interest holder that is required to consolidate a VIE. Consolidation is required when the holder of one or more variable interests would absorb a majority of the VIE's expected losses, receive a majority of the VIE's expected residual returns, or both. If one holder would absorb a majority of the VIE's expected losses and another holder would receive a majority of the VIE's expected residual returns, the holder absorbing the majority of the expected losses is the primary beneficiary and is thus required to consolidate the VIE.

Profit or Loss on Sale. The profit or loss that would be recognized on the sale if there were no leaseback. For example, on a sale of real estate subject to Topic 360, the profit on the sale to be deferred and amortized in proportion to the leaseback would be the profit that could otherwise be recognized in accordance with Topic 360.

Profit recognition. Any method to record a transaction involving real estate, other than the deposit method, or the methods to record transactions accounted for as financing, leasing, or profit-sharing arrangements. Profit recognition methods commonly used to record transactions involving real estate include, but are not limited to, the full accrual method, the installment method, the cost recovery method, and the reduced profit method.

Sale-leaseback accounting. A method of accounting for a sale-leaseback transaction in which the seller-lessee records the sale, removes all property and related liabilities from its statement of financial position, recognizes gain or loss from the sale, and classifies the leaseback in accordance with this section.

Unguaranteed residual value. The estimated residual value of the leased property, exclusive of any portion guaranteed by the lessee, by any party related to the lessee, or any party unrelated to the lessee. If the guarantor is related to the lessor, the residual value is considered unguaranteed.

Unrelated parties. All parties that are not related parties as defined above.

Variable interest. Ownership, contractual, or other monetary interests in an entity that are either entitled to received expected favorable variability ("expected residual returns") or obligated to absorb expected unfavorable variability ("expected losses").

Variable interest entity. An entity financially controlled by parties that are not its majority voting owners. Financial control is evidenced by a controlling party being exposed to the majority of the financial risks associated with the VIE performing worse than expected, *or* being entitled to the majority of the rewards associated with the VIE performing better than expected. This situation arises either because (1) the entity's at-risk equity is insufficient to absorb its expected losses *or* (2) because the entity's at-risk equity holders do not meet all three criteria necessary to be considered to possess a controlling financial interest in the entity.

CONCEPTS, RULES, AND EXAMPLES

Variable Interest Entities

From the standpoint of the lessee, it is critical for the accountant to first determine whether the relationship between the entities requires consolidation as a VIE under ASC 810. This is discussed in detail in the chapter on ASC 810. If consolidation is required, the effects of the lease recorded by the parties will be eliminated in the consolidated financial statements and the lease accounting will, in effect, be moot from the standpoint of the lessee.

In essence, a VIE is an entity that, by design, is not funded with an amount of at-risk equity sufficient to enable it to sustain itself in the face of reasonably possible losses without obtaining additional support (*"subordinated financial support"*) from existing or additional sources. In practical terms, in the context of leasing, the lessee is at risk for an amount greater than the contractual rental payments—such as for the lessor's debt arising from financing the leased property.

Determining of whether an entity is a VIE involves analysis of the individual facts, circumstances, relationships, structures, risks, and rewards associated with the entity and the parties with whom it is involved. Often, especially when related parties are involved, this analysis can be performed qualitatively without laborious numeric estimates of expected variability. That is because even a superficial review of the relationships and transaction details will reveal that the entity in question is indeed a VIE, or that it clearly is not one.

In more complex situations, however, or when qualitative analysis does not yield a conclusive answer, the holder of one or more variable interests may be required to estimate the present value of the probability-weighted expected cash flows associated with the entity in order to determine the expected variability of the entity's future cash flows as well as the portion of that expected variability that is allocable to the various holders of variable interests.

Decision diagrams. The following decision diagrams are used to discuss the illustrative examples of leasing transactions presented in this chapter.

APPLYING ASC 810

Date on which holder initially obtains interest in entity or subsequent reconsideration date.

Entity is the enterprise that is being evaluated as to whether it is a VIE.

Holder is a party that holds a variable interest in the entity and needs to determine whether the entity is a VIE and, if so, whether the holder must consolidate.

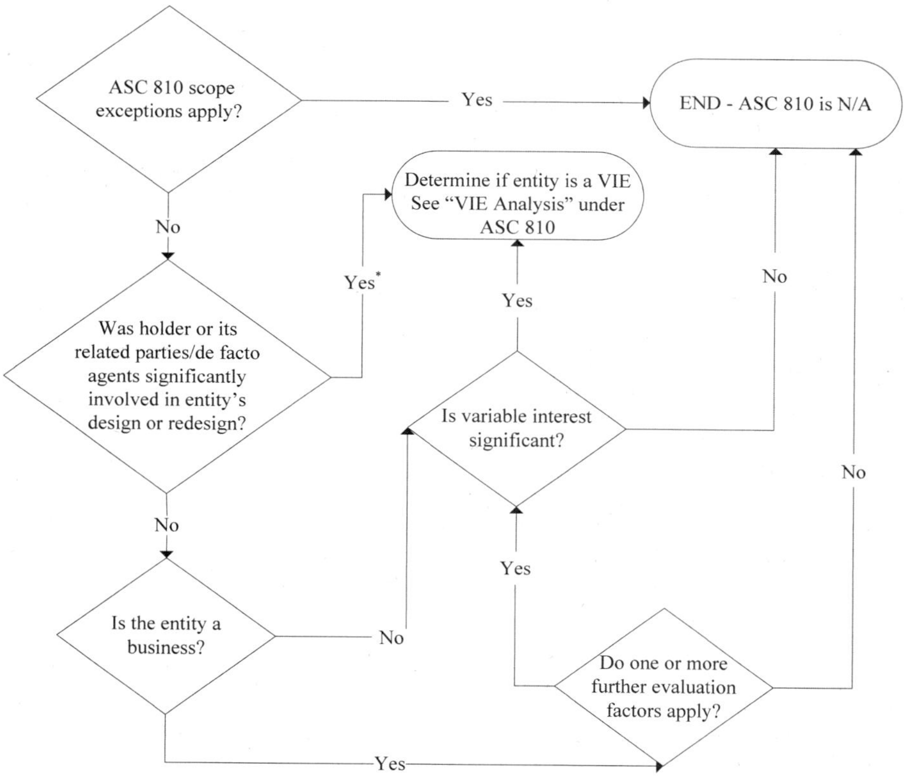

* *This factor is not considered when the entity is an operating joint venture jointly controlled by the variable interest holder, and either an independent party or a franchisee. De facto agents, for this purpose, exclude parties that require the variable interest holder's prior approval to sell, transfer, or encumber their interest in the entity.*

VIE ANALYSIS

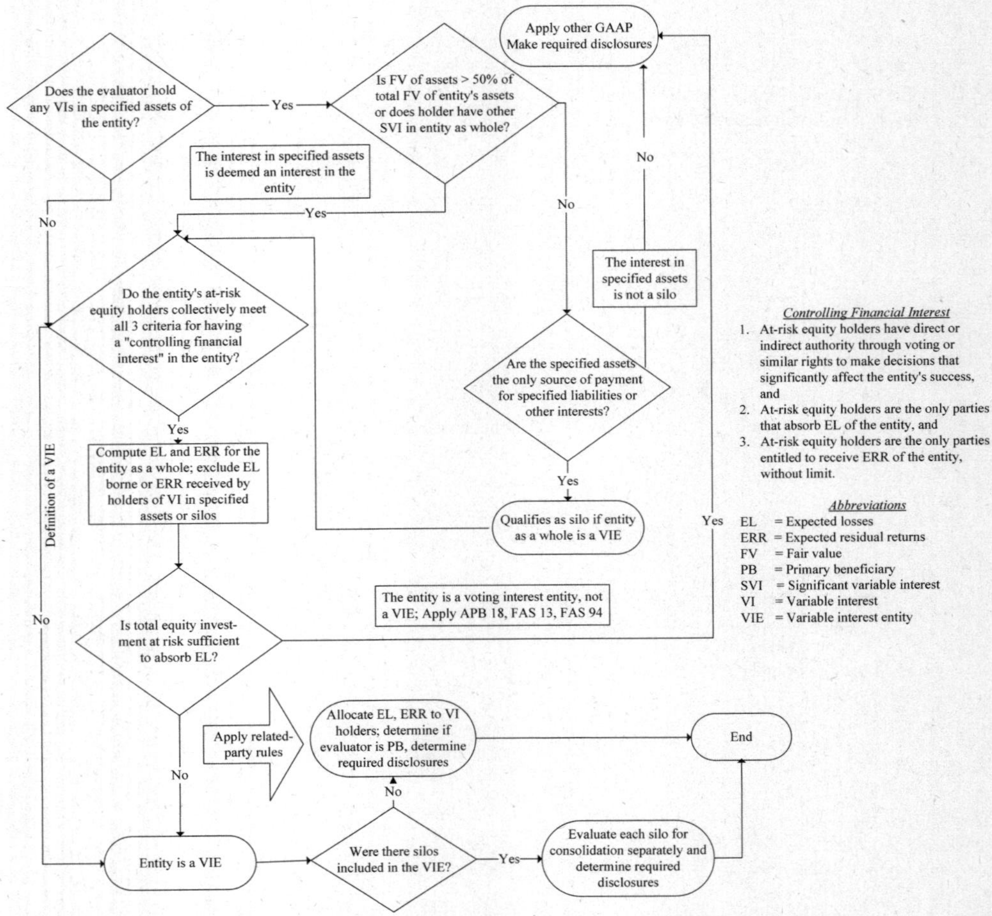

Definition of a business. A business is defined, in the context of ASC 810, as

> . . . *a self-sustaining integrated set of activities and assets conducted and managed for the purpose of providing a return to investors. A business consists of (a) inputs, (b) processes applied to those inputs, and (c) resulting outputs that are used to generate revenues. For a set of activities and assets to be a business, it must contain all of the inputs and processes necessary for it to conduct normal operations, which include the ability to sustain a revenue stream by providing its outputs to customers.*

In evaluating whether an entity is a business, consideration must be given to unique factors relating to the industry and the activities being performed including

Inputs

1. Fixed assets either owned or leased
2. Intangibles either owned or licensed
3. Access to materials or rights needed to perform its activities
4. Employees.

Processes

1. Strategic management
2. Operations
3. Resource management.

Outputs

1. Access to customers (clients).

A three-step process is provided in order to assess whether a set of activities ("set") qualifies as a business:

1. Identify elements included in the "set" (i.e., determine the existing inputs, processes, and outputs).
2. Compare the elements identified in item 1 to the elements necessary for the set of activities to be conducted as a normal business operation.
3. If any elements are missing, assess the degree of effort or investment relative to the fair value of the set of activities needed to acquire or gain access to the missing elements. If a significant effort or investment would be required, it can be concluded that the set of activities is not a business; conversely, a de minimis amount of effort or investment to supply the missing elements would lead to the conclusion that the set of activities is a business.

Variable interests in "silos." A party may hold a variable interest in specific assets of a VIE (e.g., a guarantee or a subordinated residual interest). In computing expected losses and expected residual returns, as defined above, a holder of a variable interest in specified assets of a VIE must determine if the interest it holds qualifies as an interest in the VIE itself. The variable interest is considered an interest in the VIE itself if either (1) the fair value of the specific assets is more than half of the total fair value of the VIE's assets, or (2) the interest holder has another significant variable interest in the entity as a whole.

If the interests are deemed to be interests in the VIE itself, the expected losses and expected residual returns associated with the variable interest in the specified assets are treated as being associated with the VIE.

If the interests are not deemed to be interests in the VIE itself, the interests in the specified assets are treated as a separate VIE (referred to as a "silo") if the expected cash flows from the specified assets (and any associated credit enhancements, if applicable) are essentially the sole source of payment for specified liabilities or specified other interests. Under this scenario, expected losses and expected residual returns associated with the silo assets are accounted for separately to the extent that the interest holder either bears the expected losses or is entitled to receive the expected returns. Any excess of expected losses or residual returns not borne (received) by the variable interest holder is considered attributable to the entity as a whole.

If one interest holder is required to consolidate a silo of a VIE, other VIE interest holders are to exclude the silo from the remaining VIE.

Example of application of ASC 810 to related-party leases

The most commonly encountered potential VIE situations that occur in practice involve related-party leases. Business owners often organize a partnership or LLC (for this discussion we will assume an LLC) to own property that is leased to a business with the same or similar ownership. The transaction is structured in this manner for a number of reasons that include avoidance of double taxation of the gain on the eventual sale of the property and legal protection of the building from creditors of the operating business in the event of business bankruptcy.

In attempting to avoid lessee capitalization, the lease is often structured with a short initial term (e.g., three years), with the lessee having successive options to renew the lease at similar terms. The building is pledged as collateral under a mortgage with a third-party lender. The lessor entity is thinly capitalized (i.e., it has very little owner-invested equity). Consequently, the lender, besides holding a mortgage on the building as collateral, has further protected its interests by obtaining a loan guarantee from the lessee, an assignment of rents, and a personal guarantee of the owner.

These relationships are illustrated in the following diagram:

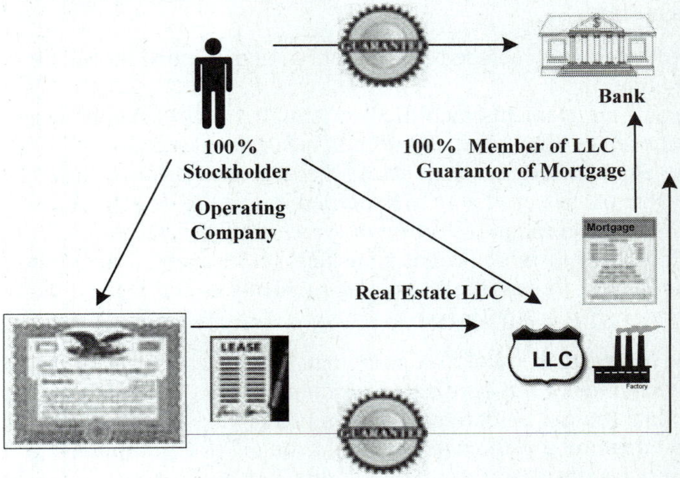

Analysis under ASC 810

Following the decision diagrams and using the related-party/de facto principal and agent rules included in ASC 810:

1. The lessee holds a variable interest in the lessor in the form of the guarantee of the lessor's mortgage debt.
2. The lessor entity is not "scoped out" of ASC 810.
3. The lessor entity is a business. It has inputs (owned fixed assets), processes for managing its investment, and outputs relative to access to the lessee.
4. The following "further evaluation factors" apply:
   a. The lessee/variable interest holder and its related parties participated significantly in the design of the lessor.
   b. The design of the lessor LLC results in all of its activities involving and being conducted on behalf of the lessee/variable interest holder.
   c. The lessee/variable interest holder and its related parties provided 100% of the subordinated financial support for the lessor entity.
   d. The lessor entity's activities relate to a single-lessee lease.
5. The lessee/evaluator and its related-party owner were involved in the design of the lessor entity.

6. The lessee's variable interest is assumed to be *significant* for the purpose of this analysis. ASC 810 does not provide guidance on making this determination.
7. The lessee's variable interest is in the leased asset.
8. The fair value of the leased asset represents 100% of the total fair value of the lessor's assets and thus is deemed to be an interest in the lessor as a whole versus an interest in just the specified assets of the lessor.
9. The at-risk equity holder of the lessor does not meet the second criterion for being considered to hold a controlling financial interest (i.e., the variable interest holder/lessee could potentially absorb expected losses of the lessor should the lessee be called upon by the lender to perform under the guarantee of the lessor's indebtedness). Note that, in this case, the other two criteria for controlling financial interest are met.
10. As a result of the analysis up to this point, it can be concluded that the lessor is a variable interest entity.
11. No silos exist, since 100% of the fair value of the assets is leased to the single lessee.
12. Application of the related-party/de facto principal and agent rules to the variable interests in the lessor indicates that 100% of the expected losses and expected residual returns from the lessor are allocable to the members of the related-party group (the lessee and the related-party owner of both). Thus, collectively, the lessee and its 100% stockholder are the primary beneficiary of the VIE/lessor. The party most closely associated with the leased property is the lessee who, consequently, is considered the primary beneficiary that is required to consolidate the lessor in its financial statements.

Other lease terms and provisions. The following discussion examines the effect that certain changes to the above facts would have on the foregoing conclusions:

Existence or absence of guarantees. Even if the stockholder/member's guarantee of the mortgage is not required by the lender and only the lessee guaranteed the debt, the analysis above would be identical. Due to the fact that the lessee/variable interest holder is exposed to the expected losses of the lessor under the terms of the guarantee, the lessor/LLC's sole member (and at-risk equity holder) is not the only party that potentially would absorb expected losses of the lessor.

Conversely, when ASC 810 was originally issued, many observers initially believed if the lessee was not required by the lender to guarantee the mortgage, and the only guarantee was that of the stockholder/member, that the absence of an explicit variable interest held by the lessee would preclude the conclusion that the lessor was a VIE.

This situation illustrates one of the most misunderstood provisions of ASC 810—referred to as an *implicit variable interest*—which the FASB staff attempts to clarify in ASC 810-10-25.

Even though the lessee did not directly guarantee the debt of the lessor, consideration must be given to the likely scenarios if the lessor/LLC should be close to a default on the mortgage payments. Realistically, what is the likelihood that the sole stockholder/sole member would perform under his or her personal guarantee obligation rather than directing the lessee to pay additional rent sufficient to enable the LLC to keep its mortgage payments current?

Clearly, it would not make economic sense for the sole stockholder/member to perform personally under the guarantee, as this would, in substance, result in the stockholder/member making a loan or capital contribution to an otherwise insolvent LLC. Instead, it would logically follow that the best course of action would be for the lessee to pay rent in amounts adequate to fund the LLC's mortgage payments so that the lessee would continue to have use of the leased premises without concern over whether the bank will foreclose on and sell the property to a third party. If the lessee were having difficulty funding the rent payments, its owner would probably authorize it to borrow money or sell assets in order to enable it to do so before its owner used personal funds to perform under the guarantee.

After analyzing this situation, with appropriate attention to the substance rather than simply its form, it can be seen that the lessee is the holder of an implicit variable interest in the lessor in the form of an implicit guarantee of the lessor's mortgage debt.

The remainder of the analysis would be identical to what was presented earlier. Due to the fact that the lessee/variable interest holder is exposed to the expected losses of the lessor under the terms of the implicit guarantee, the lessor/LLC's sole member (and at-risk equity holder) is not the only party that potentially would absorb expected losses of the lessor.

Finally, consider the situation where neither the lessee nor the owner is required to guarantee the debt. A prudent lender would probably not waive both guarantees unless the lessor was sufficiently capitalized by the owner's at-risk equity. That is, there is a presumption that the lessor in such an instance is not a VIE. Under this scenario, the lessee would perform the quantitative analysis required to estimate expected losses and estimated residual returns to determine whether the lessor is a VIE and, if it is, whether it is the primary beneficiary.

Above- or below-market rentals. Rentals due under related-party leases sometimes exceed arm's-length market rentals because the owner is using the lessor as a conduit for the lessee to indirectly provide additional salary or dividends to the owner (characterized as the excess rent).

Under ASC 810, an operating lease is generally not considered to be a variable interest unless:

1. The lease terms include a lessee residual guarantee of the fair value of the leased asset, since this results in the lessee potentially absorbing estimated negative variability that would otherwise be absorbed by the equity holder of the lessor.
2. The lease terms include an option for the lessee to purchase the property at the end of the lease term at a specified price, since this means that the lessee potentially may receive estimated positive variability that would otherwise be received by the equity holder of the lessor.
3. The lease terms are not indicative of market terms for a similar property in the same geographic location, since this would result in the lessee either receiving estimated positive variability of the lessor (if the lease terms were below market) or absorbing negative variability of the lessor (if the lease terms were above market).

Under each of the foregoing scenarios, the lease is considered a variable interest in determining the primary beneficiary, because the expected losses of the lessor that would be borne by the lessee (the excess of the rentals required over the fair value of the right to use the leased property) exceed the amounts that would have been expected had the rentals been at fair value. Thus, the stockholder/member would not be considered to have a controlling financial interest, since s/he was not the only party exposed to the lessor's expected losses.

If the situation reversed, and the rentals were below market amounts, it could be logically concluded that the lessor was absorbing negative variability of the lessee and that, therefore, the lease was a variable interest in the lessee held by the lessor that could potentially result in the lessor being considered the primary beneficiary of the lessee that would necessitate the lessor consolidating the lessee in its financial statements.

Other contractual arrangements. Leases are often accompanied by other contractual arrangements between the lessee and lessor. Such contractual arrangements can include management, marketing, brokerage, and other types of service agreements. These agreements must be carefully analyzed, as ASC 810 provides restrictive rules that often result in such agreements being characterized as variable interests.

All parties affected by these transactions should seek expert professional advice prior to either structuring a new transaction or modifying an existing transaction. For example, adverse income tax consequences could result from the transfer of property from one form of ownership to another.

Example: Arm's-length leases—computing expected losses and expected residual returns

The application of ASC 810 is, of course, not limited to related-party arrangements. The following is an example of the quantitative analysis (versus the qualitative analysis illustrated in the related-party example above) that might be necessary in an arm's-length leasing arrangement.

Lawrence Lessor, LLC (referred to herein as "the Entity" since it is the entity that the variable interest holders will be evaluating as to whether it is a VIE) is a limited liability company organized specifically for the purpose of building, owning, and operating a single-lessee retail discount warehouse club store on land that it has recently acquired. The store is the only asset owned by the Entity. The 148,000 square foot store will be occupied by Clubco, a nationally known chain that is unrelated to Lawrence Lessor.

The Entity's voting owners (the LLC members) wish only to invest a minimal amount of equity in the Entity and, consequently, the mortgage lender insisted on obtaining a third-party guarantee of the mortgage which Lawrence obtained from an unrelated third party and for which Lawrence paid a premium.

The terms of the lease with the retailer are as follows (assumed to be an operating lease):

Description of space	148,000 square foot retail discount warehouse club store
Lessee	Clubco Stores, Inc.
Initial lease term	Three years
Lease commencement date	1/1/20X1
Annual base rent	$600,000
Contingent rent	1% of annual sales over $30 million
Purchase options	$9 million—not a bargain purchase option in accordance with ASC 840
Residual guarantee	Lessee guarantees to lessor that residual value of the building at the end of the lease term will be at least equal to the $7,500,000 fair value of the store land and building at inception or it will pay the lessor the difference
Executory costs	All real estate taxes, maintenance, insurance, and common area expenses are to be borne by the lessee

The construction has been completed, the occupancy permits issued, and the construction financing settled with the proceeds of a 25-year, 6% mortgage loan on December 1, 20X1. The mortgage loan is guaranteed by an unrelated third-party guarantor. The store is opening and commencing business on January 1, 20X2.

Mortgage details are as follows:

Summary Amortization Schedule for Mortgage

25-year, 6% mortgage, original principal amount of $7,275,750

Year	*Payments*	*Interest*	*Principal*	*Balance*
Original loan				$7,275,750
20X2	$ 562,533	$ 433,022	$129,511	7,146,239
20X3	562,533	425,034	137,499	7,008,740
20X4	562,533	416,553	145,980	6,862,760
	$1,687,599	$1,274,609	$412,990	

The Entity's recorded aggregate carrying amount of $7,500,000 for the land and building represents the fair value at lease inception with the land's fair value representing 10%, or $750,000.

The rental terms for the store are considered to be at market rates. If the terms were not at market rates, additional expected variability would be assigned to the lease (in addition to the expected variability resulting from the purchase option and residual value guarantee).

Expected cash flows are discounted to their present value using an assumed 3% interest rate representing the interest rate available on risk-free investments. To simplify the example, cash flows are assumed to occur at the end of each annual period for the purpose of discounting them to present value. A copy of the statement of financial position from the Entity's annual partnership return at lease inception is as follows:

Schedule L	**Statement of Financial Position per Books**			
Assets	*Beginning of tax year*		*End of tax year*	
	(a)	(b)	(c)	(d)
1. Cash				1,000
2. a. Trade notes and accounts receivable				
b. Less allowance for bad debts				
3. Inventories				
4. US government obligations				
5. Tax-exempt securities				
6. Other current assets (*attach schedule*)				
7. Mortgage and real estate loans				
8. Other investments (*attach schedule*)				
9. a. Buildings and other depreciable assets			6,750,000	
b. Less accumulated depreciation				6,750,000
10. a. Depletable assets				
b. Less accumulated depletion				
11. Land (net of any amortization)				750,000
12. a Intangible assets (amortizable only)				
b Less accumulated amortization				
13. Other assets (*attach schedule*)				
14. Total assets				7,501,000
Liabilities and Capital				
15. Accounts payable				
16. Mortgages, notes, bonds payable in less than 1 year				
17. Other current liabilities (*attach schedule*)				
18. All nonrecourse loans				7,275,750
19. Mortgages, notes, bonds payable in 1 year or more				
20. Other liabilities (*attach schedule*)				
21. Partners' capital accounts				225,250
22. Total liabilities and capital				7,501,000

Analysis by Clubco (See the decision diagrams earlier in this chapter.)

1. Clubco holds a variable interest in Lawrence Lessor ("the Entity") in the form of the lease. Expected variability results from the purchase option and the residual value guarantee.
2. The Entity is not scoped out of ASC 810.
3. The Entity is a business.
4. Further evaluation factor d applies; that is, this is a single-lessee lease.
5. Clubco was not involved in the design of the Entity.

6. For illustrative purposes, assume that the purchase option is significant to Clubco.
7. Clubco holds a variable interest in the leased store (the specified assets) in the form of the lease containing a purchase option and residual value guarantee.
8. The fair value of the building leased by Clubco is 100% of the fair value of the Entity's assets. Therefore, Clubco is deemed to hold a variable interest in the Entity as a whole.
9. In applying the test to determine if the members of the LLC/entity have a controlling financial interest (distinguished from a controlling voting interest, which they clearly have), the following results are determined:

   a. The LLC members are the sole voting interest holders and, therefore, meet the voting test.
   b. The LLC members are *not* the only parties that absorb expected losses of the lessor due to the existence of the residual value guarantee provision in the lease that potentially could result in Clubco bearing a portion of the expected losses.
   c. The LLC members are also *not* the only parties entitled to receive the expected residual returns from the property due to the existence of the purchase option provision in the lease that potentially could result in Clubco receiving a portion of the expected residual returns.

10. As a consequence of the analysis up to this point, Clubco can conclude that its variable interest is in a lessor that is a VIE.
11. Since Clubco leases 100% of the fair value of the assets held by entity, there are no silos included therein.
12. To determine whether or not it is the primary beneficiary of the VIE/lessor, Clubco must determine whether it either will bear the majority of the expected losses, or receive the majority of the expected residual returns. One form this calculation might take is illustrated below.

Computation of expected cash flow possibilities for the lease term

	20X2					
Probability	*5%*	*15%*	*30%*	*35%*	*10%*	*5%*
Assumptions						
Annual store sales	$25,000,000	$30,000,000	$40,000,000	$50,000,000	$55,000,000	$60,000,000
Percentage rent base	$30,000,000	$30,000,000	$30,000,000	$30,000,000	$30,000,000	$30,000,000
Percentage rent rate	1%	1%	1%	1%	1%	1%
Possible cash flow outcomes						
Rent—Base	$ 600,000	$ 600,000	$ 600,000	$ 600,000	$ 600,000	$ 600,000
Rent—Percentage	–	–	100,000	200,000	250,000	300,000
Total rental income	600,000	600,000	700,000	800,000	850,000	900,000
Mortgage payments	562,533	562,533	562,533	562,533	562,533	562,533
Possible net cash flow	$ 37,467	$ 37,467	$ 137,467	$ 237,467	$ 287,467	$ 337,467
Present value, discounted at 3%	$ 36,376	$ 36,376	$ 133,463	$ 230,550	$ 279,094	$ 327,638

	20X3					
Probability	*5%*	*15%*	*30%*	*35%*	*10%*	*5%*
Assumptions						
Estimated percentage change in sales	–2.00%	0.00%	2.00%	2.50%	3.00%	4.00%
Annual store sales	$24,500,000	$30,000,000	$40,800,000	$51,250,000	$56,650,000	$62,400,000
Percentage rent base	$30,000,000	$30,000,000	$30,000,000	$30,000,000	$30,000,000	$30,000,000
Percentage rent rate	1%	1%	1%	1%	1%	1%
Possible cash flow outcomes						
Rent—Base	$ 600,000	$ 600,000	$ 600,000	$ 600,000	$ 600,000	$ 600,000
Rent—Percentage	–	–	108,000	212,500	266,500	324,000
Total rental income	600,000	600,000	708,000	812,500	866,500	924,000
Mortgage payments	562,533	562,533	562,533	562,533	562,533	562,533
Possible net cash flow	$ 37,467	$ 37,467	$ 145,467	$ 249,967	$ 303,967	$ 361,467
Present value, discounted at 3%	$ 35,316	$ 35,316	$ 137,117	$ 235,618	$ 286,518	$ 340,717

Probability	5%	15%	30%	35%	10%	5%
			20X4			
Assumptions						
Estimated percentage change in sales	–1.00%	0.00%	2.50%	3.50%	3.75%	5.00%
Annual store sales	$24,255,000	$30,000,000	$41,820,000	$53,043,750	$58,774,375	$65,520,000
Percentage rent base	$30,000,000	$30,000,000	$30,000,000	$30,000,000	$30,000,000	$30,000,000
Percentage rent rate	1%	1%	1%	1%	1%	1%

Probability	5%	15%	30%	35%	10%	5%
			20X4			
Possible cash flow outcomes						
Rent—Base	$ 600,000	$ 600,000	$ 600,000	$ 600,000	$ 600,000	$ 600,000
Rent—Percentage	–	–	118,200	230,438	287,744	355,200
Total rental income	600,000	600,000	718,200	830,438	887,744	955,200
Mortgage payments	562,533	562,533	562,533	562,533	562,533	562,533
Possible net cash flow, operations	37,467	37,467	155,667	267,905	325,211	392,667
Estimated residual amount	7,000,000	8,000,000	9,000,000	10,000,000	12,000,000	13,000,000
Mortgage repayment	6,862,760	6,862,760	6,862,760	6,862,760	6,862,760	6,862,760
Possible net sales proceeds	137,240	1,137,240	2,137,240	3,137,240	5,137,240	6,137,240
Possible net cash flow	$ 174,707	$ 1,174,707	$ 2,292,907	$ 3,405,144	$ 5,462,451	$ 6,529,907
Present value, discounted at 3%	$ 159,881	$ 1,075,023	$ 2,098,334	$ 3,116,189	$ 4,998,916	$ 5,975,790
3-year totals of present value of possible cash flows discounted at 3%	$ 231,573	$ 1,146,715	$ 2,368,914	$ 3,582,357	$ 5,564,528	$ 6,644,145

Note that, in the forecast for 20X4, the effects of the purchase option and residual value guarantee are ignored. They are considered later in the analysis of which variable interest holders participate in expected losses and expected residual returns.

13. Calculation of probability-weighted discounted expected cash flows.

Scenario	*Present value of possible cash flows*	*Estimated probability*	*Discounted probability-weighted expected cash flows*
1	$ 231,573	5%	$ 11,579
2	1,146,715	15%	172,007
3	2,368,914	30%	710,674
4	3,582,357	35%	1,253,825
5	5,564,528	10%	556,453
6	6,644,145	5%	332,207
		100%	$3,036,745

This computation uses the expected cash flow methodology prescribed by CON 7, which is also used in estimation of fair value for the purposes of impairment testing of goodwill and tangible long-lived assets, and in computing asset retirement obligations.

14. Calculations of expected losses and expected residual returns (and the related expected variability).

Scenario	*Present value of possible cash flows*	*Discounted/ probability-weighted expected cash flows*	*Variance from expected outcome*	*Estimated probability*	*Expected losses*	*Expected residual returns*
1	$ 231,573	$3,036,745	$(2,805,172)	5%	$(140,259)	
2	1,146,715	3,036,745	(1,890,030)	15%	(283,505)	
3	2,368,914	3,036,745	(667,831)	30%	(200,349)	
4	3,582,357	3,036,745	545,612	35%		$190,965
5	5,564,528	3,036,745	2,527,783	10%		252,778
6	6,644,145	3,036,745	3,607,400	5%		180,370
				100%	$(624,113)	$624,113

ASC 810 requires consideration of the "expected variability" inherent in the estimate of probability-weighted expected cash flows; in this case $3,036,745. This amount represents a weighted-average of the various expected outcomes multiplied by their respective probabilities. As is always the case when averaging numbers, the sums of the positive and negative differences between each value included in the average and the average itself are always equal. This explains why the expected losses and expected residual returns each equal $624,113. Therefore, the expected variability in both directions is the sum of the two absolute values (i.e., $624,113 + $624,113 = $1,248,226).

Another important point to note is that the terms "expected losses" and "expected residual returns" are not associated with traditional GAAP income or cash flow measures. The entity illustrated above has positive expected cash flows under all six scenarios for all three years. Notwithstanding that fact, the computation shows that it will experience expected losses and expected residual returns—variations from expectation, positive or negative, that could occur as a result of operations or of changes in the fair value of the property. This will always be the case, irrespective of how profitable an entity is or how much cash flow it generates.

15. For each scenario, the facts are analyzed to determine which of the variable interest holders will bear the expected losses. There were no silos included in the VIE; therefore, only a single primary beneficiary determination is required. The results of the analysis are aggregated as follows:

	Expected losses
Scenario 1	$(140,259)
Scenario 2	(283,505)
Scenario 3	(200,349)
	$(624,113)

Scenario	*Estimated residual value of store*	*Expected losses*	*Clubco*	*3rd-party guarantor*	*At-risk equity holders of entity*	*Mortgage lender*	*Notes*
1	7,000,000	$(140,259)	$(140,259)				$7.5MM guarantee $7 MM residual
2	8,000,000	(283,505)			$(283,505)		
3	9,000,000	(200,349)			(200,349)		
Excess of share of losses over equity				(258,604)	(258,604)		
		$(624,113)	$(140,259)	$(258,604)	$(225,250)	$ –	
		100%	22%	42%	36%	0%	

Total equity at risk is $225,250, which would not be sufficient for the entity to absorb the expected losses of $624,113 without receiving additional subordinated financial support. Consequently, the Entity (Lawrence Lessor, LLC) by definition is a VIE.

Note that, based on the analysis of the expected losses, no variable interest holder will absorb a majority (>50%) of the Entity's losses. Consequently, the expected residual returns need to be analyzed.

Scenario	*Estimated residual value of store*	*Expected residual returns*	*Clubco*	*At-risk equity holders of entity*	*Guarantor*	*Notes*
4	$10,000,000	$190,965	$190,965			Exercise of $9MM Option
5	12,000,000	252,778	252,778			Exercise of $9MM Option
6	13,000,000	180,370	180,370			Exercise of $9MM Option
		$624,113	$624,113			
		100%	100%			

16. Since 100% of the expected residual returns will be received by Clubco, it is the primary beneficiary, the party that is required to consolidate Lawrence Lessor, LLC in its financial statements.

Lease or Sale—The Interplay of Lease and Revenue Recognition Accounting

ASC 840-10-35: Determining whether an arrangement contains a lease. ASC 840 defines a lease as "an agreement conveying the right to use property, plant, or equipment (land and/or depreciable assets) usually for a stated period of time." ASC 840-10-35 provides guidance on determining when all or part of an arrangement constitutes a lease.

Scope of ASC 840-10-35. Property, plant, or equipment, as the term is used in ASC 840, includes only land and/or depreciable assets. Therefore, inventory (including equipment parts inventory) cannot be the subject of a lease because inventory is not depreciable. Although specific property, plant, or equipment may be explicitly identified in an arrangement, it is not the subject of a lease if the arrangement can be fulfilled without using the specified property, plant, or equipment. For example, if the owner/seller is obligated to deliver a specified quantity of goods or services but can provide those goods or services using property, plant, or equipment other than that specified in the arrangement, then the arrangement does not contain a lease.

In addition, ASC 840 contains specific scope exceptions with respect to agreements concerning

1. Exploration or exploitation of natural resources (e.g., oil, gas, minerals, and timber).
2. Intangible licensing rights (e.g., motion pictures, plays, manuscripts, patents, and copyrights).

Lease treatment is not precluded in situations where the owner or manufacturer of the property has extended a product warranty that includes a provision for replacement of the property if it is not operating adequately. Similarly, if the arrangement includes a provision permitting the equipment owner the right to substitute other equipment on or after a specified date, irrespective of the reason, the arrangement can still qualify as a lease.

Right to use property, plant, or equipment. The right to use the specified property, plant, or equipment is conveyed if any one of the following conditions is met:

- A *party* (for the purpose of this discussion, we will refer to this party, the potential lessee, as "the recipient" of the rights) has the ability or right to operate the property, plant, or equipment or direct others to do so as the recipient specifies, while attaining or controlling more than a minor portion of the output (or service utility),
- The recipient has the ability or right to control physical access to the specified property, plant, or equipment while attaining or controlling more than a minor portion of the output (or other service utility), or
- Analysis of the relevant facts and circumstances indicates that it is remote (as that term is used in ASC 450-20) that a party (or parties) other than the recipient will attain more than a minor amount of the output (or other service utility) that will be produced or generated by the specified property, plant, or equipment during the term of the arrangement, *and* the price that the recipient will pay for the output is neither contractually fixed per unit of output nor equal to the market price per unit of output at the time delivery of the output is received.

Timing of initial assessment and subsequent reassessments. The assessment of whether an arrangement contains a lease is to be made at the inception of the arrangement. A reassessment of whether the arrangement contains a lease is to be made only if (a) the contractual terms are modified, (b) a renewal option is exercised or the parties to the arrangement agree on an extension of its term, (c) there is a change in the determination as to whether or not fulfillment of the arrangement is dependent on the property, plant, or equipment that was originally specified, or (d) the originally specified property and equipment undergoes a substantial physical change. Remeasurement/redetermination is not permitted merely because of a change in an estimate made at inception (e.g., the number of expected units of output or the useful life of the equipment).

Aggregation of separate contracts. There is a rebuttable presumption that separate contracts between the same parties (or related parties) that are executed on or near the same date were negotiated together as a package.

This issue also provides accounting guidance for any recognized assets and liabilities existing at the time that an arrangement (or a portion of an arrangement) either ceases to qualify as a lease or commences to qualify as a lease due to a reassessment in the circumstances as described above.

Sales with a guaranteed minimum resale value. To provide sales incentives, manufacturers sometimes include in a sales contract, a guarantee that the purchaser will, upon disposition of the property, receive a minimum resale amount. Upon disposition, the manufacturer either reacquires the property at the agreed-upon minimum price or reimburses the purchaser for any shortfall between the actual sales proceeds and the guaranteed amount.

ASC 605-50-60 states that transactions containing guarantees of resale value of equipment by a manufacturer are to be accounted for as leases and not as sales. The minimum lease payments used to determine if the criteria have been met for lessor sales-type lease accounting, described later in this chapter, are computed as the difference between the proceeds received from the transferee/lessee upon initial transfer of the equipment and the amount of the residual value guarantee on its first contractual exercise date.

If the lease is accounted for as an operating lease because it does not qualify for sales-type lease accounting (as discussed and illustrated later in this chapter), the manufacturer/lessor is to record the proceeds received at inception as a liability, which is subsequently reduced by crediting revenue pro rata from the inception of the lease until the first guarantee exercise date so that, on that exercise date, the remaining liability is the guaranteed residual amount. If the lessee elects, under the terms of the arrangement, to continue to use the leased asset after the first exercise date, the manufacturer/lessor will continue to amortize the liability for the remaining residual amount to revenue to reduce it further to any remaining guarantee, if applicable.

The foregoing prescribed accounting is followed by manufacturers even when there is dealer involvement in the transaction when it is the manufacturer who is responsible for the guarantee to the purchaser.

ASC 460-10-55-17 states that ASC 460-10-55 does not apply to these transactions irrespective of whether they are accounted for as operating leases or sales-type leases because, in either case, the underlying of such a guarantee is an asset owned by the guarantor.

Equipment sold and subsequently repurchased subject to an operating lease. ASC 605-15-25-5 specifies that if four conditions are satisfied, a manufacturer can recognize a sale at the time its product is transferred to a dealer for subsequent sale to a third-party customer, even if this ultimate customer (the dealer's customer) enters into an operating lease agreement with the same manufacturer or the manufacturer's finance affiliate.

1. The dealer must be an independent entity that conducts business separately with manufacturers and customers,
2. The passage of the product from the manufacturer to the dealer fully transfers ownership,

3. The manufacturer (or finance affiliate) has no obligation to provide a lease arrangement for the dealer's customer, and
4. The dealer's customer is in control of selecting which of the many financing options available will be used.

Lessee Classification

For accounting and reporting purposes the lessee has two possible classifications for a lease.

1. Operating
2. Capital.

The proper classification of a lease is determined by the circumstances surrounding the transaction. According to ASC 840, if substantially all of the benefits and risks of ownership have been transferred to the lessee, the lessee records the lease as a capital lease at its inception. Substantially all of the risks or benefits of ownership are deemed to have been transferred if any one of the following criteria is met:

1. The lease transfers ownership to the lessee by the end of the lease term.
2. The lease contains a bargain purchase option.
3. The lease term is equal to 75% or more of the estimated economic life of the leased property, and the beginning of the lease term does not fall within the last 25% of the total economic life of the leased property.
4. The present value of the minimum lease payments at the beginning of the lease term is 90% or more of the fair value to the lessor less any investment tax credit retained by the lessor. This requirement cannot be used if the lease's inception is in the last 25% of the useful economic life of the leased asset. The interest rate, used to compute the present value, is the incremental borrowing rate of the lessee unless the implicit rate is available and lower. For the purpose of this test, lease structuring fees or lease administration fees paid by the lessee to the lessor are included as part of the minimum lease payments (ASC 840-10-25).

If a lease agreement meets none of the four criteria set forth above, it is classified as an operating lease by the lessee.

Lessor Classification

There are four possible classifications that apply to a lease from the standpoint of the lessor.

1. Operating
2. Sales-type
3. Direct financing
4. Leveraged.

The conditions surrounding the origination of the lease determine its classification by the lessor. If the lease meets any one of the four criteria specified above for lessees and both of the qualifications set forth below, the lease is classified as either a sales-type lease, direct financing lease, or leveraged lease depending upon the conditions present at the inception of the lease.

1. Collectibility of the minimum lease payments is reasonably predictable
2. No important uncertainties surround the amount of unreimbursable costs yet to be incurred by the lessor under the lease.

If a lease transaction does not meet the criteria for classification as a sales-type lease, a direct financing lease, or a leveraged lease as specified above, it is classified by the lessor as an operating lease. The classification testing is performed prior to considering the proper accounting treatment.

It is a common practice in equipment leasing transactions for the lessor to obtain, from an unrelated third party, a full or partial guarantee of the residual value of a portfolio of leased assets. These transactions are structured in such a manner that the third-party guarantor provides a guarantee of the aggregate residual value of the portfolio but does not individually guarantee the residual value of any of the individually leased assets included in that portfolio. To the extent that a specific leased asset's residual value exceeds the guaranteed minimum amount, that excess is used to offset shortfalls relating to other specific leased assets whose residual values are below the guaranteed minimum amount.

In ASC 840-30-S99, the SEC staff observer announced the SEC staff's position that the expected proceeds from these types of portfolio residual guarantees are to be *excluded* from minimum lease payments in computing the present value of the minimum lease payments for the purpose of determining the lessor's classification of the lease transaction. The SEC believes this treatment to be appropriate because, under the terms of this portfolio guarantee, the lessor is unable to determine, at lease inception, the guaranteed residual amount of any individually leased asset.

Distinctions among sales-type, direct financing, and leveraged leases. A lease is classified as a sales-type lease when the criteria set forth above have been met and the lease transaction is structured in such a way that the lessor (generally a manufacturer or dealer) recognizes a profit or loss on the transaction in addition to interest income. In order for this to occur, the fair value of the property must be different from the cost (carrying value). The essential substance of this transaction is that of a sale, and thus its name. Common examples of sales-type leases: (1) when a customer of an automobile dealership opts to lease a car in lieu of an outright purchase, and (2) the re-lease of equipment coming off an expiring lease. Note however, that a lease involving real estate must transfer title (i.e., criterion 1 in the preceding list) by the end of the lease term for the lessor to classify the lease as a sales-type lease.

A direct financing lease differs from a sales-type lease in that the lessor does not realize a profit or loss on the transaction other than interest income. In a direct financing lease, the fair value of the property at the inception of the lease is equal to the cost (carrying value). This type of lease transaction most often involves lessor entities engaged in financing operations. The lessor (a bank, or other financial institution) purchases the asset and then leases the asset to the lessee. This transaction merely replaces the conventional lending transaction in which the borrower uses the borrowed funds to purchase the asset. There are many economic reasons why the lease transaction is considered. They are as follows:

1. The lessee (borrower) is able to obtain 100% financing
2. Flexibility of use for the tax benefits
3. The lessor receives the equivalent of interest as well as an asset with some remaining value at the end of the lease term.

In summary, it may help to visualize the following chart when considering the classification of a lease from the lessor's standpoint:

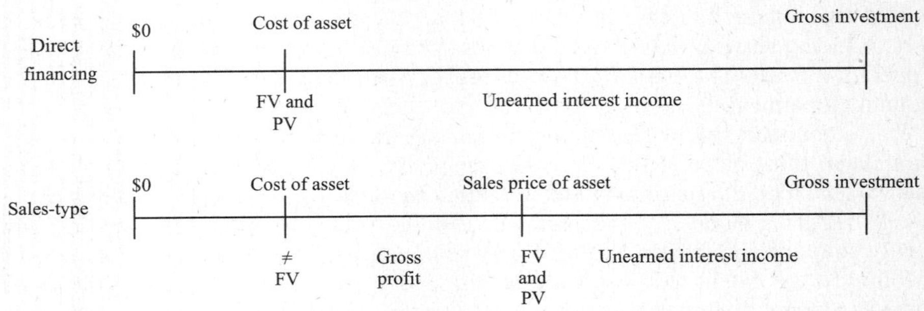

One form of a direct financing lease is a leveraged lease which is discussed later in this chapter. This type is mentioned separately because it receives a different accounting treatment by the lessor. A leveraged lease meets all the definitional criteria of a direct financing lease, but differs because it involves at least three parties: a lessee, a long-term creditor, and a lessor (commonly referred to as the equity participant). Other characteristics of a leveraged lease are as follows:

1. The financing provided by the long-term creditor must be without recourse to the general credit of the lessor, although the creditor may hold recourse with respect to the leased property. The amount of the financing must provide the lessor with substantial "leverage" in the transaction.
2. The lessor's net investment declines during the early years and rises during the later years of the lease term before its elimination.

Lessee Accounting

As discussed in the preceding section, there are two classifications that apply to a lease transaction from the standpoint of the lessee, operating or capital.

Operating leases. The accounting treatment accorded an operating lease is relatively simple; the rental payments are charged to expense as the payments are made or become payable. This assumes that the lease payments are being made on a straight-line basis (i.e., an equal payment per period over the lease term).

If the lease agreement calls for either an alternative payment schedule or a scheduled rent increase over the lease term, per ASC 840-20-25, the lease expense is recognized on a straight-line basis over the lease term unless another systematic and rational basis is a better representation of the actual physical usage of the leased property. In addition, the lessor may grant various incentives to the lessee during the lease term, such as a rent holiday, or allowances to fund leasehold improvements. Incentives paid to or incurred on behalf of the lessee by the lessor are an inseparable part of the lease agreement. These amounts are recognized as reductions to rental expense on a straight-line basis over the term of a lease, as described in the preceding paragraph.

In these instances, it is necessary to record either a prepaid asset or a liability depending upon the structure of the payment schedule. If the scheduled increase(s) is due to additional leased property, recognition is to be based on the portion of the leased property that is being utilized with the increased rents recognized over the years that the lessee has control over the use of the additional leased property.

Notice that in the case of an operating lease there is no recognition of the leased asset on the statement of financial position, because the substance of the lease is merely that of a rental. There is no reason to expect that the lessee will derive any future economic benefit from the leased asset beyond the lease term.

Capital leases. Recall that the classification of a lease is determined prior to the consideration of the accounting treatment. Therefore, it is necessary to first examine the lease transaction against the four criteria (transfer of title, bargain purchase option, 75% of useful life, or 90% of net fair value). Should the lease agreement satisfy one of these, it is accounted for as a capital (also referred to as financing) lease.

The lessee records a capital lease as an asset and an obligation (liability) at an amount equal to the present value of the minimum lease payments at the beginning of the lease term. For the purposes of the 90% test, the present value is computed using the incremental borrowing rate of the lessee unless it is practicable for the lessee to determine the implicit rate used by the lessor, and the implicit rate is less than the incremental borrowing rate. The incremental borrowing rate is defined as the rate at lease inception at which the lessee would have been able to borrow over a loan term equivalent to the lease term had it chosen to purchase the leased asset. If the lessee determines a secured borrowing rate that is reasonable and consistent with the financing that would have been used, then it is acceptable to use a secured borrowing rate.

The asset is recorded at the lower of the present value of the minimum lease payments or the fair value of the asset. When the fair value of the leased asset is less than the present value of the minimum lease payments, the interest rate used to amortize the lease obligation will differ from the interest rate used in the 90% test.

The interest rate used in the amortization will be the same as that used in the 90% test when the fair value is greater than or equal to the present value of the minimum lease payments. For purposes of this computation, the minimum lease payments are considered to be the payments that the lessee is obligated to make or can be required to make excluding executory costs such as insurance, maintenance, and taxes.

The minimum lease payments generally include the minimum rental payments, any guarantee of the residual value made by the lessee, and the penalty for failure to renew the lease, if applicable. If the lease includes a bargain purchase option (BPO), the amount required to be paid under the BPO is also included in the minimum lease payments.

The lease term used in this present value computation is the fixed, noncancelable term of the lease plus the following:

1. All periods covered by bargain renewal options
2. All periods for which failure to renew the lease imposes a penalty on the lessee
3. All periods covered by ordinary renewal options during which the lessee guarantees the lessor's debt on the leased property
4. All periods covered by ordinary renewals or extensions up to the date a BPO is exercisable
5. All periods representing renewals or extensions of the lease at the lessor's option.

Remember, if the amount computed as the present value of the minimum lease payments exceeds the fair value of the leased property at the inception of the lease, the amount recorded is limited to the fair value.

The amortization of the leased asset will depend upon how the lease qualifies as a capital lease. If the lease transaction meets the criteria of either transferring ownership, or containing a bargain purchase option, then the asset arising from the transaction is amortized over the estimated useful life of the leased property. If the transaction qualifies as a capital lease because it meets either the 75% of useful life or 90% of fair value criteria, the asset is amortized over the lease term. The conceptual rationale for this differentiated treatment arises because of the substance of the transaction. Under the first two criteria, the asset actually becomes the property of the lessee at the end of the lease term (or upon exercise of the BPO).

In the latter situations, the title to the property remains with the lessor, and thus, the lessee ceases to have the right to use the property at the conclusion of the lease term.

The leased asset is amortized (depreciated) over the lease term if title does not transfer to the lessee, while the asset is depreciated in a manner consistent with the lessee's normal depreciation policy if the title is to eventually transfer to the lessee. This latter situation can be interpreted to mean that the asset is depreciated over the useful economic life of the leased asset. The treatment and method used to amortize (depreciate) the leased asset is very similar to that used for any other long-lived asset. The amortization entry requires a debit to amortization expense and a credit to accumulated amortization. The leased asset is not amortized below the estimated residual value.

In some instances when the property is to revert back to the lessor, there may be a guaranteed residual value. This is an amount that the lessee guarantees to the lessor. If the fair value of the asset at the end of the lease term is greater than or equal to the guaranteed residual amount, the lessee incurs no additional obligation. On the other hand, if the fair value of the leased asset is less than the guaranteed residual value, then the lessee must make up the difference, usually with a cash payment. The guaranteed residual value is often used as a tool to reduce the periodic payments by substituting the lump-sum amount at the end of the term that results from the guarantee. In any event the amortization must still take place based on the estimated residual value. This results in a rational and systematic allocation of the expense to the periods of usage and avoids a large loss (or expense) in the last period as a result of the guarantee.

The annual (periodic) rent payments made during the lease term are allocated between a reduction in the obligation and interest expense in a manner such that the interest expense represents the application of a constant periodic rate of interest to the remaining balance of the lease obligation. This is commonly referred to as the effective interest method.

The following examples illustrate the treatment described in the foregoing paragraphs.

Example of accounting for a capital lease—Asset returned to lessor

1. The lease is initiated on 1/1/X1 for equipment with an expected useful life of three years. The equipment reverts back to the lessor upon expiration of the lease agreement.
2. The fair value of the equipment at lease inception is $135,000.
3. Three payments are due to the lessor in the amount of $50,000 per year beginning 12/31/X1. An additional sum of $1,000 is to be paid annually by the lessee for insurance.
4. The lessee guarantees a $10,000 residual value on 12/31/X3 to the lessor.
5. Irrespective of the $10,000 residual value guarantee, the leased asset is expected to have only a $1,000 salvage value on 12/31/X3.
6. The lessee's incremental borrowing rate is 10%. (The lessor's implicit rate is unknown.)
7. The present value of the lease obligation is as follows:

PV of guaranteed residual value	= $10,000 × 7513 *	= $ 7,513
PV of annual payments	= $50,000 × 2.4869 **	= 124,345
		$131,858

* *The present value of an amount of $1 due in three periods at 10% is .7513.*
** *The present value of an ordinary annuity of $1 for three periods at 10% is 2.4869.*

The first step in dealing with any lease transaction is to classify the lease. In this case, the lease term is for three years, which is equal to 100% of the expected useful life of the asset. Note that the 90% test is also fulfilled as the present value of the minimum lease payments ($131,858) is greater than 90% of the fair value (90% × $135,000 = $121,500). Thus, the lessee accounts for the lease as a capital lease.

In item 7, the present value of the lease obligation is computed. Note that the executory costs (insurance) are not included in the minimum lease payments and that the incremental borrowing rate of the lessee was used to determine the present value. This rate was used because the lessor's implicit rate was not determinable.

NOTE: To have used the implicit rate it would have to have been less than the incremental borrowing rate.

The entry necessary to record the lease on 1/1/X1 is

Leased equipment	131,858	
Lease obligation		131,858

Note that the lease is recorded at the present value of the minimum lease payments that, in this case, is less than the fair value. If the present value of the minimum lease payments had exceeded the fair value, the lease would have been recorded at the fair value.

The next step is to determine the proper allocation between interest and reduction of the lease obligation for each lease payment. This is done using the effective interest method as illustrated below.

Year	Cash payment	Interest expense	Reduction in lease obligation	Balance of lease obligation
Inception of lease				$131,858
20X1	$50,000	$13,186	$36,814	95,044
20X2	50,000	9,504	40,496	54,548
20X3	50,000	5,452	44,548	10,000

The interest is calculated at 10% (the incremental borrowing rate) of the balance of the lease obligation for each period, and the remainder of each $50,000 payment is allocated as a reduction in the lease obligation. The lessee is also required to pay $1,000 for insurance on an annual basis. The entries necessary to record all payments relative to the lease for each of the three years are shown below.

	12/31/X1		12/31/X2		12/31/X3	
Insurance expense	1,000		1,000		1,000	
Interest expense	13,186		9,504		5,452	
Lease obligation	36,814		40,496		44,548	
Cash		51,000		51,000		51,000

The leased equipment recorded as an asset must also be amortized (depreciated). The initial unamortized balance is $131,858; however, as with any other long-lived asset, it cannot be amortized below the estimated residual value of $1,000 (note that it is amortized down to the actual estimated residual value, not the guaranteed residual value). In this case, the straight-line amortization method is applied over a period of three years. This three-year period represents the lease term, not the life of the asset, because the asset reverts back to the lessor at the end of the lease term. Therefore, the following entry will be made at the end of each year:

Amortization expense	43,619		
Accumulated amortization		43,619	[($131,858 – 1,000) ÷ 3]

Finally, on 12/31/X3 we must recognize the fact that ownership of the property has reverted back to the owner (lessor). The lessee made a guarantee that the residual value would be $10,000 on 12/31/14; as a result, the lessee must make up the difference between the guaranteed residual value and the actual residual value with a cash payment to the lessor. The following entry illustrates the removal of the leased asset and obligation from the lessee's accounting records:

Lease obligation	10,000	
Accumulated amortization	130,858	
Cash		9,000
Leased equipment		131,858

The foregoing example illustrated a situation where the asset was to be returned to the lessor. Another situation exists (under BPO or transfer of title) where ownership of the asset is expected to transfer to the lessee at the end of the lease term. Remember that leased assets are amortized over their useful life when title transfers or a bargain purchase option exist. At the end of the lease, the balance of the lease obligation should equal the guaranteed residual value, the bargain purchase option price, or termination penalty for failure to renew the lease.

Example of accounting for a capital lease—Asset ownership transferred to lessee

1. A three-year lease is initiated on 1/1/X1 for equipment with an expected useful life of five years.
2. Three annual lease payments of $52,000 are required beginning on 1/1/X1 (note that the payment at the beginning of the year changes the present value computation from the previous example). The lessee pays $2,000 per year for insurance on the equipment and this amount is included in the annual payments.
3. The lessee can exercise a bargain purchase option on 12/31/X3 for $10,000. The expected residual value at 12/31/X3 is $18,000.
4. The lessee's incremental borrowing rate is 10% (the lessor's implicit rate is unknown).
5. The fair value of the leased property at the inception of the lease is $140,000.

Once again, the classification of the lease must be determined prior to computing the accounting entries to record it. This lease is classified as a capital lease because it contains a BPO. In this case, the 90% test is also fulfilled.

The present value of the lease obligation is computed as follows:

PV of bargain purchase option	=	$10,000	×	7513 *	= $ 7,513
PV of annual payments	=	($52,000 – $2,000)	×	2.4869 **	= 136,755
					$144,268

* .7513 is the present value of an amount due in three periods at 10%.
** 2.7355 is the present value of an annuity due for three periods at 10%.

Since the lessee pays $2,000 a year for insurance, this payment is treated as executory costs and excluded from the calculation of the present value of the annual payments. Note that the present value of the lease obligation is greater than the fair value of the asset. Because of this, the lease obligation must be recorded at the fair value of the leased asset.

1/1/X1 Leased equipment	140,000	
Obligation under capital lease		140,000

According to ASC 840, the allocation between interest and principal is determined so that interest expense is computed using a constant periodic rate of interest applied to the remaining balance of the obligation. If the fair value of the leased asset is greater than or equal to the present value of the lease obligation, the interest rate used is the same as that used to compute the present value (i.e., the incremental borrowing rate or the implicit rate). In cases such as this, when the present value exceeds the fair value of the leased asset, a new rate must be computed through a series of manual trial and error calculations. Alternatively, spreadsheet or loan amortization software can be used to solve for the unknown effective interest rate. In this situation the interest rate used was 13.267%. The amortization of the lease takes place as follows:

Date	*Cash payment*	*Interest expense*	*Reduction in lease obligation*	*Balance of lease obligation*
Inception of lease				$140,000
1/1/X1	$50,000	$ –	$50,000	90,000
1/1/X2	50,000	11,940	38,060	51,940
1/1/X3	50,000	6,891	43,109	8,831
12/31/X3	10,000	1,169	8,831	–

The following entries are required in years 20X1 through 20X3 to recognize the payment and amortization.

		20X1		20X2		20X3	
1/1	Insurance expense	2,000		2,000		2,000	
	Obligation under capital lease	50,000		38,060		43,109	
	Accrued interest payable			11,940		6,891	
	Cash		52,000		52,000		52,000
12/31	Interest expense	11,940		6,891		1,169	
	Accrued interest payable		11,940		6,891		1,169
12/31	Amortization expense	24,400		24,400		24,400	
	Accumulated amortization		24,400		24,400		24,400
	[($140,000 – $18,000) ÷ 5 years)]						
12/31	Obligation under capital lease					8,831	
	Accrued interest payable					1,169	
	Cash						10,000

Lessor Accounting

As previously noted, there are four classifications of leases with which a lessor must be concerned. They are operating, sales-type, direct financing, and leveraged.

Operating leases. As in the case of the lessee, the operating lease requires a less complex accounting treatment. The payments received by the lessor are recorded as rent revenues in the period in which the payment is received or becomes receivable. As with the lessee, if the rentals vary from a straight-line basis, the lease agreement contains a scheduled rent increase over the lease term, or the lessor grants incentives to the lessee such as a rent holiday or leasehold improvement allowance, the revenue is recorded on a straight-line basis unless an alternative basis of systematic and rational allocation is more representative of the time pattern of physical usage of the leased property. If the scheduled increase(s) is due to the lessee leasing additional property under a master lease agreement, the increase is allocated proportionally to the additional leased property and recognized on a straight-line basis over the years that the lessee has control over the additional leased property. ASC 840-20-25 prescribes that, in this case, the total revised rent be allocated between the previously leased property and the additional leased property based on their relative fair values.

The lessor presents the leased property on the statement of financial position under the caption "Investment in leased property." This caption is shown with or near the fixed assets of the lessor, and depreciated in the same manner as the lessor's other fixed assets.

Any initial direct costs are amortized over the lease term as the related lease revenue is recognized (i.e., on a straight-line basis unless another method is more representative). However, these costs may be charged to expense as incurred if the effect is not materially different from straight-line amortization.

Any incentives made by the lessor to the lessee are treated as reductions of rent and recognized on a straight-line basis over the term of the lease.

In most operating leases, the lessor recognizes rental income over the lease term and does not measure or recognize any gain or loss on any differential between the fair value of the property and its carrying value. One exception to this rule is set forth in ASC 840-40. The exception applies when an operating lease involving real estate is not classified as a sales-type lease because ownership to the property does not transfer to the lessee at the end of the lease term. In this case, if at the inception of the lease the fair value of the property is less than its carrying amount, the lessor must recognize a loss equal to that difference at the inception of the lease.

Sales-type leases. In accounting for a sales-type lease, it is necessary for the lessor to determine the following amounts:

1. Gross investment
2. Fair value of the leased asset
3. Cost.

Note that, following the promulgation of ASC 820, there was some confusion over the definition of fair value to be employed for purposes of lease determination and measurement. ASC 820 does not apply to ASC 840 determinations of lease classifications or measurements. However, ASC 820 is applicable to the determinations to be made in business combinations accounted for under ASC 805.

From these amounts, the remainder of the computations necessary to record and account for the lease transaction can be made. The first objective is to determine the numbers necessary to complete the following entry:

Lease receivable	xx	
Cost of goods sold	xx	
Sales		xx
Inventory		xx
Unearned interest		xx

The gross investment (lease receivable) of the lessor is equal to the sum of the minimum lease payments (excluding executory costs) plus the unguaranteed residual value. The difference between the gross investment and the present value of the two components of gross investment (minimum lease payments and unguaranteed residual value) is recorded as the unearned interest revenue. The present value is computed using the lease term and implicit interest rate (both of which were discussed earlier). The lease term used in this computation includes any renewal options exercisable at the discretion of the lessor. The resulting unearned interest revenue is to be amortized into income using the effective interest method. This will result in a constant periodic rate of return on the net investment (the net investment is the gross investment less the unearned income).

Recall from our earlier discussion that the fair value of the leased property is, by definition, equal to the normal selling price of the asset adjusted by any residual amount retained (this amount retained can be exemplified by an unguaranteed residual value, investment credit, etc.). The adjusted selling price used for a sales-type lease is equal to the present value of the minimum lease payments. Thus, we can say that the normal selling price less the residual amount retained is equal to the PV of the minimum lease payments.

The cost of goods sold to be charged against income in the period of the sale is computed as the historic cost or carrying value of the asset (most likely inventory) plus any initial direct costs, less the present value of the unguaranteed residual value. The difference between the adjusted selling price and the amount computed as the cost of goods sold is the gross profit recognized by the lessor at the inception of the lease (sale). Thus, a sales-type lease generates two types of revenue for the lessor.

1. The gross profit on the sale
2. The interest earned on the lease receivable.

Note that if the sales-type lease involves real estate, the lessor must account for the transaction under the provisions of ASC 360 in the same manner as a seller of the same property (see chapter on ASC 360).

The application of these points is illustrated in the example below.

Example of accounting for a sales-type lease

Price Inc. is a manufacturer of specialized equipment. Many of its customers do not have the necessary funds or financing available for outright purchase. Because of this, Price offers a leasing alternative. The data relative to a typical lease are as follows:

1. The noncancelable fixed portion of the lease term is five years. The lessor has the option to renew the lease for an additional three years at the same rental. The estimated useful life of the asset is ten years.
2. The lessor is to receive equal annual payments over the term of the lease. The leased property reverts back to the lessor upon termination of the lease.
3. The lease is initiated on 1/1/12. Payments are due annually on 12/31 for the duration of the lease term.
4. The cost of the equipment to Price Inc. is $100,000. The lessor incurs costs associated with the inception of the lease in the amount of $2,500.
5. The selling price of the equipment for an outright purchase is $150,000.
6. The equipment is expected to have a residual value of $15,000 at the end of five years and $10,000 at the end of eight years.
7. The lessor desires a return of 12% (the implicit rate).

The first step is to calculate the annual payment due to the lessor. To yield the lessor's desired return, the present value of the minimum lease payments must equal the selling price adjusted for the present value of the residual amount. The present value is computed using the implicit interest rate and the lease term. In this case, the implicit rate is given as 12% and the lease term is eight years (the fixed noncancelable portion plus the renewal period). Thus, the computation would be as follows:

Normal selling price – PV of residual value = PV of minimum lease payments

Or, in this case,

$150,000 – (.40388* × $10,000 = $4,038.80)	=	4.96764** × Annual minimum lease payment
$\frac{\$145{,}961.20}{4.96764}$	=	Annual minimum lease payment
$ 29,382.40	=	Annual minimum lease payment

* *.40388 is the present value of an amount of $1 due in eight periods at a 12% interest rate.*
** *4.96764 is the present value of an annuity of $1 for eight periods at a 12% interest rate.*

Prior to examining the accounting implications of the lease, we must first determine the lease classification. Assume that there are no uncertainties regarding the lessor's costs, and the collectibility of the lease payments is reasonably assured. In this example, the lease term is eight years (discussed above) while the estimated useful life of the asset is ten years; thus, this lease is not an operating lease because the lease term covers 80% of the asset's estimated useful life. This exceeds the previously discussed 75% criterion. (Note that it also meets the 90% of fair value criterion because the present value of the minimum lease payments of $145,961.20 is greater than 90% of the fair value [90% × $150,000 = $135,000].) Next it must be determined if this is a sales-type, direct financing, or leveraged lease. To do this, examine the fair value or selling price of the asset and compare it to the cost. Because the two are not equal, this is a sales-type lease.

Next, obtain the figures necessary for the lessor to record the entry. The gross investment is the total minimum lease payments plus the unguaranteed residual value, or:

($29,382.40 × 8 = $235,059.20) + $10,000 = $245,059.20

The cost of goods sold is the historical cost of the inventory ($100,000) plus any initial direct costs ($2,500) less the present value of the unguaranteed residual value ($10,000 × .40388 = $4,038.80). Thus, the cost of goods sold amount is $98,461.20 (= $100,000 + $2,500 – $4,038.80).

Note that the initial direct costs will require a credit entry to record their accrual (accounts payable) or payment (cash). The inventory account is credited for the carrying value of the asset, in this case $100,000.

The adjusted selling price is equal to the present value of the minimum payments, or $145,961.20. Finally, the unearned interest revenue is equal to the gross investment (i.e., lease receivable) less the present value of the components making up the gross investment (the present values of the minimum annual lease payments of $29,382.40 and the unguaranteed residual of $10,000). The computation is [$245,059.20 – ($29,382.40 × 4.96764 = $145,961.20) – ($10,000 × .40388 = 4,038.80) = $95,059.20]. Therefore, the entry necessary for the lessor to record the lease is:

Lease receivable	245,059.20	
Cost of goods sold	98,461.20	
Inventory		100,000.00
Sales		145,961.20
Unearned interest		95,059.20
Accounts payable (initial direct costs)		2,500.00

The next step in accounting for a sales-type lease is to determine the proper handling of each payment. Both principal and interest are included in each payment. Interest is recognized using the effective interest rate method so that an equal rate of return is earned each period over the term of the lease. This will require setting up an amortization schedule, as illustrated below.

Year	Cash payment	Interest	Reduction in principal	Balance of net investment
Inception of lease				$150,000.00
20X1	$ 29,382.40	$18,000.00	$ 11,382.40	138,617.00
20X2	29,382.40	16,634.11	12,748.29	125,869.31
20X3	29,382.40	15,104.32	14,278.08	111,591.23
20X4	29,382.40	13,390.95	15,991.45	95,599.78
20X5	29,382.40	11,471.97	17,910.43	77,689.35
20X6	29,382.40	9,322.72	20,059.68	57,629.67
20X7	29,382.40	6,915.56	22,466.84	35,162.83
20X8	29,382.40	4,219.57	25,162.83	10,000.00
	$235,059.20	$95,059.20	$140,000.00	

A few of the columns need to be elaborated upon. First, the net investment is the gross investment (lease receivable) less the unearned interest. Note that at the end of the lease term, the net investment is equal to the estimated residual value. Also note that the total interest earned over the lease term is equal to the unearned interest at the beginning of the lease term.

The entries below illustrate the proper accounting for the receipt of the lease payment and the amortization of the unearned interest in the first year.

Cash	29,382.40	
Lease receivable		29,382.40
Unearned interest	18,000.00	
Interest revenue		18,000.00

Note that there is no entry to recognize the principal reduction. This is done automatically when the net investment is reduced by decreasing the lease receivable (gross investment) by $29,382.40 and the unearned interest account by only $18,000. The $18,000 is 12% (implicit rate) of the net investment. These entries are to be made over the life of the lease.

At the end of the lease term the asset is returned to the lessor and the following entry is required:

Asset	10,000	
Lease receivable		10,000

Direct financing leases. The accounting for a direct financing lease holds many similarities to that for a sales-type lease. Of particular importance is that the terminology used is much the same; however, the treatment accorded these items varies greatly. Again, it is best to preface our discussion by determining our objectives in the accounting for a direct financing lease. Once the lease has been classified, it must be recorded. To do this, the following numbers must be obtained:

1. Gross investment
2. Cost
3. Residual value.

As noted, a direct financing lease generally involves a leasing company or other financial institution and results in only interest income being earned by the lessor. This is because the fair value (selling price) and the cost are equal and, therefore, no profit is recognized on the actual lease transaction. Note how this is different from a sales-type lease that involves both a profit on the transaction and interest income over the lease term. The reason for this difference is derived from the conceptual nature underlying the purpose of the lease transaction. In a sales-type lease, the manufacturer (distributor, dealer) is seeking an alternative means to finance the sale of the product, whereas a direct financing lease is a result of the consumer's need to finance an equipment purchase through a third party. Because the consumer is unable to obtain conventional financing, he or she turns to a leasing company that will purchase the desired asset and then lease it to the consumer. Here the profit on the transaction remains with the manufacturer, while the interest income is earned by the leasing company.

Like a sales-type lease, the first objective is to determine the amounts necessary to complete the following entry:

Lease receivable	xxx	
Asset		xxx
Unearned interest		xx

The gross investment is still defined as the minimum amount of lease payments exclusive of any executory costs plus the unguaranteed residual value. The difference between the gross investment as determined above and the cost (carrying value) of the asset is to be recorded as the unearned interest income because there is no manufacturer's/dealer's profit earned on the transaction. The following entry would be made to record the initial direct costs:

Initial direct costs	xx	
Cash (or accounts payable)		xx

The net investment in the lease is defined as the gross investment less the unearned interest income plus the unamortized initial direct costs related to the lease. Initial direct costs are defined in the same way that they were for purposes of the sales-type lease; however, the accounting treatment is different. For a direct financing lease, the unearned lease (interest) income and the initial direct costs are amortized to income over the lease term to yield a constant effective rate of interest on the net investment. Thus, the effect of the initial direct costs is to reduce the implicit interest rate, or yield, to the lessor over the life of the lease.

An example follows that illustrates the preceding principles.

Example of accounting for a direct financing lease

Edwards, Inc. needs new equipment to expand its manufacturing operation; however, it does not have sufficient capital to purchase the asset at this time. Because of this, Edwards has employed Samuels Leasing to purchase the asset. In turn, Edwards (the lessee) will lease the asset from Samuels (the lessor). The following information applies to the terms of the lease:

Lease information

1. A three-year lease is initiated on 1/1/X1 for equipment costing $131,858 with an expected useful life of five years. Fair value at 1/1/X2 of the equipment is $131,858.
2. Three annual payments are due to the lessor beginning 12/31/X1. The property reverts back to the lessor upon termination of the lease.
3. The unguaranteed residual value at the end of year three is estimated to be $10,000.
4. The annual payments are calculated to give the lessor a 10% return (implicit rate).
5. The lease payments and unguaranteed residual value have a present value equal to $131,858 (FMV of asset) at the stipulated discount rate.
6. The annual payment to the lessor is computed as follows:

PV of residual value	=	$10,000 × .7513* = $7,513
PV of lease payments	=	Selling price – PV of residual value
	=	$131,858 – 7,513 = $124,345

$$\text{Annual payment} = \frac{\$124{,}345}{PV_3,\ 10\%} = \frac{\$124{,}345}{2.4869^{**}} = \$50{,}000$$

* *.7513 is the present value of an amount due in three periods at 10%.*
** *2.4869 is the present value of an annuity of $1 for three periods at a 10% interest rate.*

7. Initial direct costs of $7,500 are incurred by Samuels in the lease transaction.

As with any lease transaction, the first step must be to determine the proper classification of the lease. In this case, the present value of the lease payments ($124,345) exceeds 90% of the fair value (90% × $131,858 = $118,672). Assume that the lease payments are reasonably assured and that there are no uncertainties surrounding the costs yet to be incurred by the lessor.

Next, determine the unearned interest and the net investment in the lease.

Gross investment in lease [(3 × $50,000) + $10,000]	$160,000
Cost of leased property	131,858
Unearned interest	$ 28,142

The unamortized initial direct costs are to be added to the gross investment in the lease and the unearned interest income is to be deducted to arrive at the net investment in the lease. The net investment in the lease for this example is determined as follows:

Gross investment in lease	$160,000
Add: Unamortized initial direct costs	7,500
	$167,500
Less: Unearned interest income	28,142
Net investment in lease	$139,358

The net investment in the lease (Gross investment – Unearned revenue) has been increased by the amount of initial direct costs. Therefore, the implicit rate is no longer 10%. We must recompute the implicit rate. The implicit rate is really the result of an internal rate of return calculation. We know that the lease payments are to be $50,000 per annum and that a residual value of $10,000 is expected at the end of the lease term. In return for these payments (inflows) we are giving up equipment (outflow) and incurring initial direct costs (outflows) with a net investment of $139,358 ($131,858 + $7,500). The only way to manually obtain the new implicit rate is through a trial and error calculation, as set up below.

$$\frac{50{,}000}{(1+i)^1} + \frac{50{,}000}{(1+i)^2} + \frac{50{,}000}{(1+i)^3} + \frac{10{,}000}{(1+i)^3} = \$139{,}358$$

Where i = implicit rate of interest

This computation is most efficiently performed using either spreadsheet or present value software. In doing so, the $139,358 is entered as the present value, the contractual payment stream and residual value are entered, and the software iteratively solves for the unknown implicit interest rate.

In this case, the implicit rate is equal to 7.008%. Thus, the amortization table would be set up as follows:

	(a) Lease payments	(b) Reduction in unearned interest	(c) PV × implicit rate (7.008%)	(d) Reduction in initial direct costs (b – c)	(e) Reduction in PVI net invest. (a – b + d)	(f) PVI net invest. in lease (f)(n + 1) = (f)n – (e)
						$139,358
1	$ 50,000	$13,186 (1)	$ 9,766	$3,420	$ 40,234	99,124
2	50,000	9,504 (2)	6,947	2,557	43,053	56,071
3	50,000	5,455 (3)	3,929	1,526	46,071	10,000
	$150,000	$28,145*	$20,642	$7,503	$129,358	

* *Rounded*

(b.1) $131,858 × 10% = $13,186

(b.2) [$131,858 – ($50,000 – 13,186)] × 10% = $9,504

(b.3) {$131,858 – [($50,000 – 9,504) + ($50,000 – 13,186)]} × 10% = $5,455

Here the interest is computed as 7.008% of the net investment. Note again that the net investment at the end of the lease term is equal to the estimated residual value.

The entry made to initially record the lease is as follows:

Lease receivable* [($50,000 × 3) + 10,000]	160,000	
Asset acquired for leasing		131,858
Unearned interest		28,142

* *Also the "gross investment in lease."*

When the payment of (or obligation to pay) the initial direct costs occurs, the following entry must be made:

Initial direct costs	7,500	
Cash (or accounts payable)		7,500

Using the schedule above, the following entries would be made during each of the indicated years:

	20X1		20X2		20X3	
Cash	50,000		50,000		50,000	
Lease receivable*		50,000		50,000		50,000
Unearned interest	13,186		9,504		5,455	
Initial direct costs		3,420		2,557		1,526
Interest revenue		9,766		6,947		3,929

* *Also the "gross investment in lease."*

Finally, when the asset is returned to the lessor at the end of the lease term, it must be recorded by the following entry:

Used asset	10,000	
Lease receivable*		10,000

* *Also the "gross investment in lease."*

Leveraged leases. One of the more complex accounting subjects regarding leases is the accounting for a leveraged lease. Just as is the case with sales-type and direct financing leases, the classification of the lease by the lessor has no impact on the classification of the lease by the lessee. The lessee simply considers whether the lease qualifies as an operating lease or a capital lease. The lessor's accounting issues, however, are substantially more complex.

To qualify as a leveraged lease, a lease agreement must meet the following requirements, and the lessor must account for the investment tax credit (when in effect) in the manner described below.

NOTE: Failure to do so will result in the lease being classified as a direct financing lease.

---

1. The lease must meet the definition of a direct financing lease (the 90% of fair value criterion does not apply).[1]
2. The lease must involve at least three parties.
   a. An owner-lessor (equity participant)
   b. A lessee
   c. A long-term creditor (debt participant).
3. The financing provided by the creditor is nonrecourse as to the general credit of the lessor and is sufficient to provide the lessor with substantial leverage.
4. The lessor's net investment (defined below) decreases in the early years and increases in the later years until it is eliminated.

This last characteristic poses the accounting issue.

The leveraged lease arose as a result of an effort to maximize the income tax benefits associated with a lease transaction. To accomplish this, it was necessary to involve a third party to the lease transaction (in addition to the lessor and lessee): a long-term creditor. The following diagram[2] illustrates the relationships in a leveraged lease agreement:

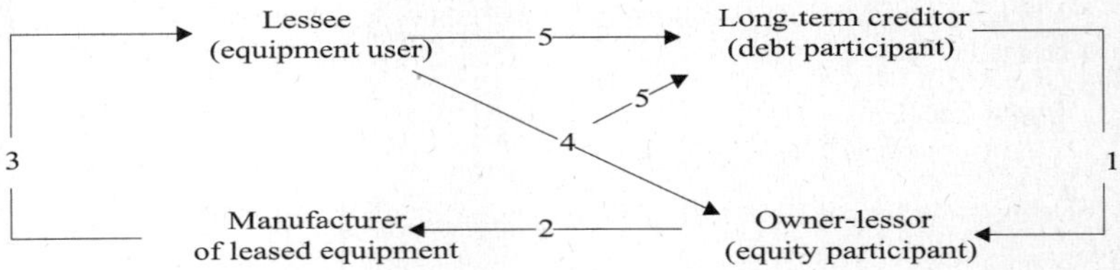

1. The owner-lessor obtains long-term financing from the creditor, generally in excess of 50% of the purchase price. ASC 840 indicates that the lessor must be provided with sufficient leverage in the transaction, therefore the 50%.
2. The owner then uses this financing along with his/her own funds to purchase the asset from the manufacturer.
3. The manufacturer delivers the asset to the lessee.
4. The lessee remits the periodic rent to the lessor.
5. The debt is guaranteed by either using the equipment as collateral, the assignment of the lease payments, or both, depending on the demands established by the creditor.

---

[1] *A direct financing lease must have its cost or carrying value equal to the fair value of the asset at the lease's inception. So even if the amounts are not significantly different, leveraged lease accounting may not be used.*

[2] *Adapted from "A Straightforward Approach to Leveraged Leasing" by Pierce R. Smith,* The Journal of Commercial Bank Lending, *July 1973, pp. 40–47.*

The FASB concluded that the entire lease agreement be accounted for as a single transaction and not a direct financing lease plus a debt transaction. The feeling was that the latter did not readily convey the lessor's net investment in the lease to the user of the financial statements. Thus, the lessor records the investment as a net amount. The gross investment is calculated as a combination of the following amounts:

1. The rentals receivable from the lessee, net of the principal and interest payments due to the long-term creditor
2. A receivable for the amount of the investment tax credit (ITC) to be realized on the transaction[3]
3. The estimated residual value of the leased asset
4. The unearned and deferred income, consisting of:
    a. The estimated pretax lease income (or loss), after deducting initial direct costs, remaining to be allocated to income
    b. The ITC remaining to be allocated to income over the remaining term of the lease.[3]

The first three amounts described above are readily obtainable; however, the last amount, the unearned and deferred income, requires additional computations. In order to compute this amount, it is necessary to create a cash flow (income) analysis by year for the entire lease term. As described in item 4 of the preceding list, the unearned and deferred income consists of the pretax lease income (Gross lease rentals – Depreciation – Loan interest) and the unamortized investment tax credit. The total of these two amounts for all of the periods in the lease term represents the unearned and deferred income at the inception of the lease.

The amount computed as the gross investment in the lease (foregoing paragraphs) less the deferred taxes relative to the difference between pretax lease income and taxable lease income is the net investment for purposes of computing the net income for the period. To compute the periodic net income, another schedule must be completed that uses the cash flows derived in the first schedule and allocates them between income and a reduction in the net investment.

The amount of income is first determined by applying a rate to the net investment. The rate to be used is the rate that will allocate the entire amount of cash flow (income) when applied in the years in which the net investment is positive. In other words, the rate is derived in much the same way as the implicit rate (trial and error), except that only the years in which there is a positive net investment are considered. Thus, income is recognized only in the years in which there is a positive net investment.

The income recognized is divided among the following three elements:

1. Pretax accounting income
2. Amortization of investment tax credit
3. The tax effect of the pretax accounting income.

The first two are allocated in proportionate amounts from the unearned and deferred income included in the calculation of the net investment. In other words, the unearned and deferred income consists of pretax lease accounting income and ITC. Each of these is recognized during the period in the proportion that the current period's allocated income is to the total

---

[3] *The ITC was repealed, effective January 1, 1986. ITC was relevant only for property placed in service prior to this date. We continue to discuss these concepts because Congress has historically reinstated this credit during economic downturns.*

income (cash flow). The last item, the income tax effect, is recognized in income tax expense for the year. The income tax effect of any difference between pretax lease accounting income and taxable lease income is charged (or credited) to deferred income taxes.

When income tax rates change, all components of a leveraged lease must be recalculated from the inception of the lease using the revised after-tax cash flows arising from the revised income tax rates.

If, in any case, the projected cash receipts (income) are less than the initial investment, the deficiency is to be recognized as a loss at the inception of the lease. Similarly, if at any time during the lease period the aforementioned method of recognizing income would result in a future period loss, the loss is to be recognized immediately.

This situation may arise as a result of the circumstances surrounding the lease changing. Therefore, any estimated residual value and other important assumptions must be reviewed on a periodic basis (at least annually). Any change is to be incorporated into the income computations; however, there is to be no upward revision of the estimated residual value.

The following example illustrates the application of these principles to a leveraged lease.

Example of simplified leveraged lease

1. A lessor acquires an asset for $100,000 with an estimated useful life of three years in exchange for a $25,000 down payment and a $75,000 three-year note with equal payments due on 12/31 each year. The interest rate is 18%.
2. The asset has no residual value.
3. The present value of an ordinary annuity of $1 for three years at 18% is 2.17427.
4. The asset is leased for three years with annual payments due to the lessor on 12/31 in the amount of $45,000.
5. The lessor uses the Accelerated Cost Recovery System (ACRS) method of depreciation (150% declining balance with a half-year convention in the year placed in service) for income tax purposes and elects to reduce the ITC rate to 4% as opposed to reducing the depreciable basis.
6. Assume a constant income tax rate throughout the life of the lease of 40%.

Chart 1 analyzes the cash flows generated by the leveraged leasing activities. Chart 2 allocates the cash flows between the investment in leveraged leased assets and income from leveraged leasing activities. The allocation requires finding that rate of return, which when applied to the investment balance at the beginning of each year that the investment amount is positive, will allocate the net cash flow fully to net income over the term of the lease. This rate can be found only by a computer program or by an iterative trial and error process. The example that follows has a positive investment value in each of the three years, and thus the allocation takes place in each time period. Leveraged leases usually have periods where the investment account turns negative and is below zero.

Allocating principal and interest on the loan payments is as follows:

($75,000 ÷ 2.17427 = $34,494)

Year	Payment	Interest 18%	Principal	Balance
Inception of lease	$ –	$ –	$ –	$75,000
1	34,494	13,500	20,994	54,006
2	34,494	9,721	24,773	29,233
3	34,494	5,261	29,233	–

Chart 1

	A	B	C	D	E	F	G	H	I
	Rent	Depr.	Interest on loan	Taxable income (loss) (A-B-C)	Income tax payable (rcvbl.) Dx40%	Loan principal payments	ITC	Cash flow (A+G-C -E-F)	Cumulative cash flow
Initial	$ –	$ –	$ –	$ –	$ –	$ –	$ –	$(25,000)	$(25,000)
Year 1	45,000	25,000	13,500	6,500	2,600	20,994	4,000	11,906	(13,094)
Year 2	45,000	38,000	9,721	(2,721)	(1,088)	24,773	–	11,594	(1,500)
Year 3	45,000	37,000	5,261	2,739	1,096	29,233	–	9,410	7,910
Total	$135,000	$100,000	$28,482	$ 6,518	$ 2,608	$75,000	$4,000	$ 7,910	

The chart below allocates the cash flows determined above between the net investment in the lease and income. Recall that the income is then allocated between pretax accounting income and the amortization of the investment credit. The income tax expense for the period is a result of applying the income tax rate to the current periodic pretax accounting income.

The amount to be allocated in total in each period is the net cash flow determined in column H above. The investment at the beginning of year one is the initial down payment of $25,000. This investment is then reduced on an annual basis by the amount of the cash flow not allocated to income.

Chart 2

	1	2	3	4	5	6	7
		Cash Flow Assumption				Income Analysis	
	Investment beginning of year	Cash flow	Allocated to investment	Allocated to income	Pretax income	Income tax expense	Investment tax credit
Year 1	$25,000	$11,906	$ 7,964	$3,942	$3,248	$1,300	$1,994
Year 2	17,036	11,594	8,908	2,686	2,213	885	1,358
Year 3	8,128	9,410	8,128	1,282	1,057	423	648
		$32,910	$25,000	$7,910	$6,518	$2,608	$4,000

Rate of return = 15.77%

1. Column 2 is the net cash flow after the initial investment, and columns 3 and 4 are the allocation based upon the 15.77% rate of return. The total of column 4 is the same as the total of column H in Chart 1.
2. Column 5 allocates column D in Chart 1 based upon the allocations in column 4. Column 6 allocates column E in Chart 1, (and, of course, is computed as 40% of column 5) and column 7 allocates column G in Chart 1 on the same basis.

The journal entries below illustrate the proper recording and accounting for the leveraged lease transaction. The initial entry represents the cash down payment, investment tax credit receivable, the unearned and deferred revenue, and the net cash to be received over the term of the lease.

The remaining journal entries recognize the annual transactions which include the net receipt of cash and the amortization of income.

	Year 1		Year 2		Year 3	
Rents receivable [Chart 1 (A – C – F)]	31,518					
Investment tax credit receivable	4,000					
Cash		25,000				
Unearned and deferred income		10,518				
Initial investment, Chart 2 (5 + 7) totals						

	Year 1		Year 2		Year 3	
Cash	10,506		10,506		10,506	
Rent receivable		10,506		10,506		10,506

Net for all cash transactions, Chart 1 (A-C-F) line by line for each year

Income tax receivable (cash)	4,000					
Investment tax credit receivable		4,000				
Unearned and deferred income	5,242		3,571		1,705	
Income from leveraged leases		5,242		3,571		1,705

Amortization of unearned income, Chart 2 (5+7) line by line for each year

The following schedules illustrate the computation of deferred income tax amount. The annual amount is a result of the temporary difference created due to the difference in the timing of the recognition of income for GAAP and income tax purposes. The income for income tax purposes can be found in column D in Chart 1, while the income for GAAP purposes is found in column 5 of Chart 2. The actual amount of deferred income tax is the difference between the income tax computed with the temporary difference and the income tax computed without the temporary difference. These amounts are represented by the income tax payable or receivable as shown in column E of Chart 1 and the income tax expense as shown in column 6 of Chart 2. A check of this figure is provided by multiplying the difference between GAAP income and tax income by the annual rate.

Year 1		
Income tax payable	$ 2,600	
Income tax expense	(1,300)	
Deferred income tax (Dr)		$1,300
Taxable income	$ 6,500	
Pretax accounting income	(3,248)	
Difference	$ 3,252	
$3,252 × 40% = $1,300		

Year 2		
Income tax receivable	$ 1,088	
Income tax expense	885	
Deferred income tax (Dr)		$1,973
Taxable loss	$ 2,721	
Pretax accounting income	2,213	
Difference	$ 4,934	
$4,934 × 40% = $1,973		

Year 3		
Income tax payable	$ 1,096	
Income tax expense	(423)	
Deferred income tax (Dr)		$ 673
Taxable income	$ 2,739	
Pretax accounting income	(1,057)	
Difference	$ 1,682	
$1,682 × 40% = $673		

Interpretive guidance.

Changes in income tax rates. ASC 840 requires that the rate of return and allocation of income to be recalculated from the date of inception of a lease and a gain or loss recognized when an important assumption is changed. Per ASC 840-30-35, the effect on a leveraged lease of a change in the income tax rate is recognized as a gain or loss in the accounting period in which the rate changes. Deferred income taxes relating to the change are recognized in accordance with ASC 740.

Change or projected changes in the timing of cash flows relative to income taxes applicable to a leveraged lease transaction. ASC 840 also provides that the projected timing of income tax cash flows attributable to a leveraged lease is to be reviewed annually during the lease term (or between annual reviews if events or changes in circumstances indicate that a change in timing either has occurred or is projected to occur in the future). Upon review, if the projected timing of the lease's income tax cash flows changes, the lessor will be required to recalculate, from the inception of the lease, the rate of return and the allocation of income to positive investment years in accordance with ASC 840-30-35. The net investment amount is adjusted to the recalculated amount with the change recognized as a gain or loss in the year that the assumptions changed. The pretax gain or loss is to be included in income from continuing operations before income taxes in the same financial statement caption in which leverage lease income is recognized with the income tax effect of the gain or loss reflected in the income tax provision or benefit.

The standard further provides that the recalculated cash flows are to exclude interest and penalties, advance payments, and deposits to the IRS (and presumably any other relevant state, local, or foreign taxing jurisdiction). The deposits or advance payments are to be included in the projected amount of the settlement with the taxing authority.

This accounting treatment is applicable only to changes or projected changes in the timing of income taxes that are directly attributable to the leveraged lease transaction. ASC 840-30-35 provides that reporting entities whose tax positions frequently vary between the alternative minimum tax (AMT) and regular tax are not required to annually recalculate the net investment in the lease unless there is an indication that the original assumptions about the leveraged lease's anticipated total after-tax net income were no longer valid.

Another factor to consider in the determination of the after-tax cash flows attributable to a leveraged lease transaction is the application of ASC 740-40-25, *Income Taxes—Recognition.* As discussed in detail in the chapter on ASC 740, the lessor is required to assess whether it is more likely than not (i.e., there is a greater than 50% chance probability) that the tax positions it takes or plans to take relative to the transaction would be sustained upon examination by the applicable taxing authorities. If the tax positions do not meet that recognition threshold, the tax benefits associated with taking those positions would be excluded from the leveraged lease calculations and, in fact, would give rise to a liability for unrecognized income tax benefits as well as an accrual for any applicable interest and penalties for all open tax years that are within the statute of limitations. This could obviously have a significant impact on the computed rate of return on the investment attributable to the years in which the net investment is positive.

If, however, the tax positions meet the recognition threshold, then they are subject to measurement to determine the maximum amount that is more than 50% probable of being sustained upon examination. The difference between the income tax position taken or planned to be taken on the income tax return (the "as-filed" benefit), and the amount of the benefit measured using the more than 50% computation, along with any associated penalties and interest, is recorded as the liability for unrecognized income tax benefits as previously described.

The only situation in which this liability, penalties, and interest would not be applicable would be if the tax positions were assessed to be highly certain tax positions, as defined in ASC 740-10-55. Under those circumstances, the entire tax benefit associated with the lease would be recognized and, of course, no interest or penalties would be recognized.

Applicability to real estate leases. The foregoing discussion involved the lease of a manufactured asset. ASC 840-40 clarifies that leases that involve land and buildings or leases in a sale-leaseback transaction potentially qualify as leveraged leases if the criteria to qualify as a leveraged lease are met.

Applicability to existing assets of the lessor. At the inception of a lease, the cost or carrying value and the fair value of an asset must be the same for the lease to be classified as a direct financing lease which is a necessary condition for leveraged lease treatment. The carrying amount of an existing asset before any write-down must equal its fair value in order for the lease to be classified as a leveraged lease (ASC 840-10-55).

Real Estate Leases

Real estate leases can be divided into the following four categories:

1. Leases involving land only
2. Leases involving land and building(s)
3. Leases involving real estate and equipment
4. Leases involving only part of a building.

Leases involving only land.

Lessee accounting. If the lease agreement transfers ownership or contains a bargain purchase option, the lessee accounts for the lease as a capital lease, and records an asset and related liability equal to the present value of the minimum lease payments. If the lease agreement does not transfer ownership or contain a bargain purchase option, the lessee accounts for the lease as an operating lease.

Lessor accounting. If the lease gives rise to dealer's profit (or loss) and transfers ownership (i.e., title), the lease is classified as a sales-type lease and accounted for under the provisions of ASC 360-20 in the same manner as a seller of the same property. If the lease transfers ownership and the criteria for both collectibility and no material uncertainties are met, but the lease does not give rise to dealer's profit (or loss), the lease is accounted for as a direct financing or leveraged lease as appropriate. If the lease does not transfer ownership, but it contains a bargain purchase option and both the collectibility and no material uncertainties criteria are met, the lease is accounted for as a direct financing, leveraged, or operating lease using the same lessor classification criteria as any other lease. If the lease does not meet the collectibility and/or no material uncertainties criteria, the lease is accounted for as an operating lease.

Leases involving land and building.

Lessee accounting. If the agreement transfers title or contains a bargain purchase option, the lessee accounts for the agreement by separating the land and building components and capitalizing each separately. The land and building elements are allocated on the basis of their relative fair values measured at the inception of the lease. The land and building components are separately accounted for because the lessee is expected to own the real estate by the end of the lease term. The building is amortized over its estimated useful life without regard to the lease term.

When the lease agreement neither transfers title nor contains a bargain purchase option, the fair value of the land must be determined in relation to the fair value of the aggregate property included in the lease agreement. If the fair value of the land is less than 25% of the aggregate fair value of the leased property, then the land is considered immaterial. Conversely, if the fair value of the land is 25% or greater of the fair value of the aggregate leased property, then the land is considered material and the land and building must be treated separately for accounting purposes.

When the land component of the lease agreement is considered immaterial (fair value land < 25% of the total fair value), the lease is accounted for as a single unit. The lessee capitalizes the lease if one of the following applies:

1. The term of the lease is 75% or more of the economic useful life of the building.
2. The present value of the minimum lease payments equals 90% or more of the fair value of the leased real estate less any lessor investment tax credit.

If neither of the above two criteria is met, the lessee accounts for the lease agreement as a single operating lease.

When the land component of the lease agreement is considered material (fair value land ≥ 25% of the total fair value), the land and building components are separated. By applying the lessee's incremental borrowing rate to the fair value of the land, the annual minimum lease payment attributed to land is computed. The remaining payments are attributed to the building. The division of minimum lease payments between land and building is essential for both the lessee and lessor. The portion of the lease involving the land is always accounted for as an operating lease. The lease involving the building(s) must meet either the 75% or 90% test to be treated as a capital lease. If neither of the two criteria is met, the building(s) are also accounted for as an operating lease.

Computing the minimum lease payments.

Construction period lease payments. Payments made by a lessee during construction of the leased asset and prior to the beginning of the lease term (sometimes called "construction period lease payments") are considered part of the minimum lease payments for the purpose of the 90% of fair value test. These advance payments are to be included in minimum lease payments at their future value, at the beginning of the lease term, with interest accreted using the same interest rate used to discount payments made during the lease term (ASC 840-10-25).

If the lease is an operating lease, these payments are accounted for as prepaid rent and amortized to expense along with other rental costs over the term of the lease, normally using the straight-line method.

Residual value guarantees. If the terms of the lease include a guarantee of the residual value of the leased property by the lessee, that guarantee is to be included in the minimum lease payments and, in accordance with ASC 840-10-25, is to be allocated entirely to the building. This treatment is consistently followed by both the lessee and the lessor.

Environmental indemnifications. An indemnification by the lessee to the lessor that any environmental contamination that the lessee causes during the lease term does not affect the lessee's classification of the lease as capital or operating.

If the lessee's indemnification covers contamination that occurred prior to the lease term, the lessee is to consider, under the ASC 450 criteria for evaluating contingencies, whether the likelihood of loss is considered remote, reasonably possible, or probable before considering any available reimbursements available from insurance companies or other third parties. If the probability of loss is considered remote, then the indemnification does not affect the lessee's classification of the lease. If, however, the probability of loss is either reasonably possible or probable, the transaction is subject to the sale-leaseback provisions of ASC 840-40 and the lessee will be considered to have purchased, sold, and then leased back the property. A lessee providing an indemnification that meets certain criteria under ASC 460 is required to record the indemnification as a guarantee and, in addition, is subject to that pronouncement's disclosure provisions.

Lessee obligation to maintain financial covenants. Leases sometimes contain financial covenants similar to those included in loan agreements that obligate the lessee to maintain certain financial ratios. Should the lessee violate these covenants, it is considered an event of default under the lease and the lessor may have a right to put the property to the lessee or require the lessee to make a payment to the lessor. In this case, for the purpose of the 90% of fair value test, the lessee includes in the minimum lease payments the maximum amount it would be required to pay in the event of default unless all of the following conditions exist:

1. The default covenant provision is customary in financing arrangements,
2. The occurrence of the event of default is objectively determinable and is not at the subjective whim of the lessor,
3. The event of default is based on predefined criteria that relate solely to the lessee and its operations, and
4. It is reasonable to assume at the inception of the lease and in considering recent lessee operating trends that the event of default will not occur.

Lessor accounting. The lessor's accounting depends on whether the lease transfers ownership, contains a bargain purchase option, or does neither of the two.

If the lease transfers ownership and gives rise to dealer's profit (or loss), the lessor classifies the lease as a sales-type lease and accounts for the lease as a single unit under the provisions of ASC 360-20 in the same manner as a seller of the same property. If the lease transfers ownership, meets both the collectibility and no important uncertainties criteria, but does not give rise to dealer's profit (or loss), the lease is accounted for as a direct financing or leveraged lease as appropriate.

If the lease contains a bargain purchase option and gives rise to dealer's profit (or loss), the lease is classified as an operating lease. If the lease contains a bargain purchase option, meets both the collectibility and no material uncertainties criteria, but does not give rise to dealer's profit (or loss), the lease is accounted for as a direct financing lease or a leveraged lease as appropriate.

If the lease agreement neither transfers ownership nor contains a bargain purchase option, the lessor should follow the same rules as the lessee in accounting for real estate leases involving land and building(s).

However, the collectibility and the no material uncertainties criteria must be met before the lessor can account for the agreement as a direct financing lease, and in no such case may the lease be classified as a sales-type lease (i.e., ownership must be transferred).

The treatment of a lease involving both land and building can be illustrated in the following examples.

Example of lessee accounting for land and building lease containing transfer of title

1. The lessee enters into a ten-year noncancelable lease for a parcel of land and a building for use in its operations. The building has an estimated remaining useful life of twelve years.
2. The fair value of the land is $75,000, while the fair value of the building is $310,000.
3. A payment of $50,000 is due to the lessor at the beginning of each of the ten years of the lease.
4. The lessee's incremental borrowing rate is 10%. (The lessor's implicit rate is unknown.)
5. Ownership will transfer to the lessee at the end of the lease.

The present value of the minimum lease payments is $337,951 ($50,000 × 6.75902).[4] The portion of the present value of the minimum lease payments to be capitalized for each of the two components of the lease is computed as follows:

FV of land			$ 75,000		
FV of building			310,000		
Total FV of leased property			$385,000		
Portion of PV allocated to land	$337,951	×	75,000 / 385,000	=	$ 65,835

[4] *6.75902 is the present value of an annuity due for ten periods at 10%.*

Portion of PV allocated to building	$337,951	×	310,000 / 385,000	=	272,116
Total PV to be capitalized					$337,951

The entry made to initially record the lease is as follows:

Leased land	65,835	
Leased building	272,116	
Lease obligation		337,951

Subsequently, the obligation will be decreased using the effective interest method. The leased building will be amortized over its expected useful life.

Example of lessee accounting for land and building lease without transfer of title or bargain purchase option

Assume the same facts as the previous example except that title does not transfer at the end of the lease.

The lease is still a capital lease because the lease term is more than 75% of the remaining useful life of the building. Since the fair value of the land is less than 25% of the aggregate fair value of the leased property, (75,000/385,000 = 19%), the land component is considered immaterial and the lease is accounted for as a single unit. The entry to record the lease is as follows:

Leased property	337,951	
Lease obligation		337,951

Assume the same facts as the previous example except that the fair value of the land is $110,000 and the fair value of the building is $275,000. Once again title does not transfer.

Because the fair value of the land exceeds 25% of the aggregate fair value of the leased property (110,000/385,000 = 29%), the land component is considered material and the lease is separated into two components. The annual minimum lease payment attributed to the land is computed as follows:

FV of land	$110,000		
PV factor	6.75902*	=	$16,275

* *6.75902 is the present value of an annuity due for ten periods at 10%.*

The remaining portion of the annual payment is attributed to the building.

Annual payment	$ 50,000
Less amount attributed to land	(16,275)
Annual payment attributed to building	$ 33,725

The present value of the minimum annual lease payments attributed to the building is then computed as follows:

Minimum annual lease payment attributed to building	$ 33,725
PV factor	× 6.75902*
PV of minimum annual lease payments attributed to building	$227,948

* *6.75902 is the present value of an annuity due for ten periods at 10%.*

The entry to record the capital portion of the lease is as follows:

Leased building	227,948	
Lease obligation		227,948

There is no computation of the present value of the minimum annual lease payment attributed to the land since the land component of the lease is treated as an operating lease. For this reason, each year $16,275 of the $50,000 lease payment will be recorded as land rental expense. The remainder of the annual payment ($33,725) will be applied against the lease obligation using the effective interest method.

Leases involving real estate and equipment. ASC 360-20-15 states that sales of integral equipment are within the scope of ASC 360-20. Consequently, the determination of whether equipment is considered to be integral equipment has increased in importance. A determination of whether equipment to be leased is integral is also necessary for proper accounting for sales-type leases by lessors.

According to ASC 360-20-15, the determination of whether equipment is integral is based on two factors.

1. The significance of the cost to remove the equipment from its existing location (which would include the costs of repairing the damage done to that location by the removal).
2. The decrease in value of the equipment that would result from its removal (which is, at minimum, the cost to ship the equipment to the new site and reinstall it). The nature of the equipment and whether others can use it are considered in determining whether there is further diminution in fair value. When the combined total of the cost to remove and any further diminution of value exceeds 10% of the fair value of the equipment (installed), the equipment is considered integral equipment.

ASC 360-20-15 clarifies that ASC 360-20 applies to all sales of real estate, including real estate with accompanying property improvements or integral equipment. Consistent with ASC 360-20-15, ASC 840-10-25 specifies that when evaluating a lease that includes integral equipment to determine the classification of the lease under ASC 840, the equipment is to be evaluated as real estate. ASC 840-10-25 also provides guidance on evaluating how to determine transfer of ownership of integral equipment when no statutory title registration system exists in the jurisdiction.

When real estate leases also involve equipment or machinery, the equipment component is separated and accounted for as a separate lease agreement by both lessees and lessors. "The portion of the minimum lease payments applicable to the equipment element of the lease shall be estimated by whatever means are appropriate in the circumstances." The lessee and lessor apply the capitalization requirements to the equipment lease independently of accounting for the real estate lease(s). The real estate leases are handled as discussed in the preceding two sections. In a sale-leaseback transaction involving real estate with equipment, the equipment and land are not separated.

Leases involving only part of a building. It is common to find lease agreements that involve only part of a building as, for example, when leasing a floor of an office building or a store in a shopping mall. A difficulty that arises in this situation is that the cost and/or fair value of the leased portion of the whole may not be objectively determinable.

Lessee accounting. If the fair value of the leased property is objectively determinable, then the lessee follows the rules and accounts for the lease as described in "Leases involving land and building." If the fair value of the leased property cannot be objectively determined, consider whether the agreement satisfies the 75% test. This calculation is made using the estimated remaining economic life of the building in which the leased premises are located. If the test is met (i.e. the term of the lease is 75% or more of the estimated remaining economic life of the building), the lease is accounted for as a capital lease. If the test is not met, the lease is accounted for as an operating lease.

Lessor accounting. From the lessor's position, both the cost and fair value of the leased property must be objectively determinable before the procedures described under "Leases involving land and building" will apply. If either the cost or the fair value cannot be determined objectively, the lessor accounts for the agreement as an operating lease.

Operating leases with guarantees. It is important to note that, for any operating lease where the terms include a guarantee of the residual value of the leased asset, two issues require consideration:

1. Since a guarantee constitutes a variable interest in the lessor or in the leased assets, does the guarantee cause the lessee to be the primary beneficiary of the lessor that would be required to consolidate the lessor? (See discussion of ASC 810 earlier in this chapter.)
2. Is the guarantee required to be recognized as a liability at inception on the statement of financial position of the lessee under ASC 460?

Lessee-incurred real estate development or construction costs. Lessees sometimes incur real estate development or construction costs prior to executing a lease with the developer/lessor. The lessee records these costs as construction in progress on its statement of financial position and any subsequent lease arrangement is accounted for as a sale-leaseback transaction under ASC 840-40, as discussed in the following section.

Sale-Leaseback Transactions

Sale-leaseback describes a transaction where the owner of property (seller-lessee) sells the property, and then immediately leases all or part of it back from the new owner (buyer-lessor). These transactions may occur when the seller-lessee is experiencing cash flow or financing problems or because of available income tax advantages. The important consideration in this type of transaction is the recognition of two separate and distinct economic events. It is important to note, however, that in a typical sale-leaseback there is not a change in the party that has the right to use the property. First, there is a sale of property, and second, there is a lease agreement for the same property in which the original seller is the lessee and the original buyer is the lessor. This is illustrated below.

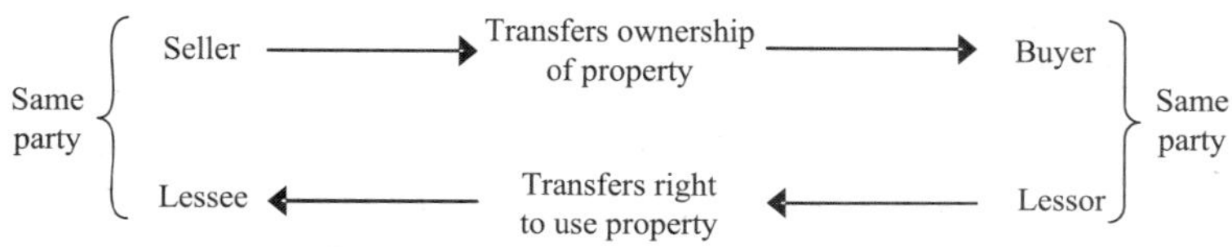

A sale-leaseback transaction is usually structured with the sales price of the asset at or above its current fair value. The result of this higher sales price is higher periodic rental payments over the lease term. The transaction is usually attractive because of the income tax benefits associated with it. The seller-lessee benefits from the higher price because of the increased gain on the sale of the property and the deductibility of the lease payments that are usually larger than the depreciation that was previously being deducted. The buyer-lessor benefits from both the higher rental payments and the larger depreciable income tax basis.

Retention of rights to use the property. The accounting treatment from the seller-lessee's point of view will depend upon the extent to which it retains the rights to use the property which can be characterized as one of the following:

1. Substantially all
2. Minor
3. More than minor but less than substantially all.

Retention of Rights to Use Property

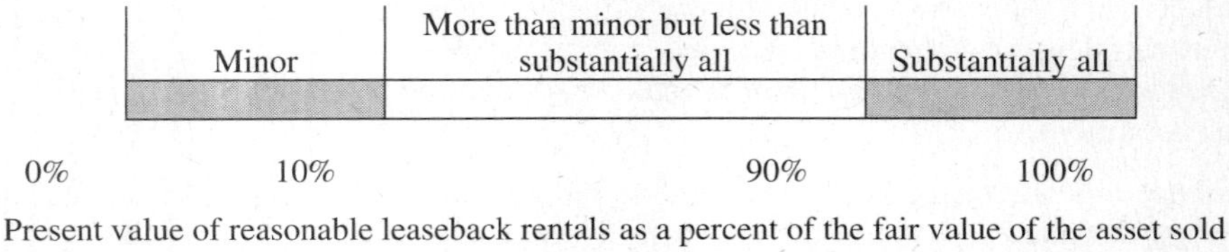

As depicted in the diagram "Retention of Rights to Use Property," the guideline for the determination of substantially all is based upon the classification criteria presented for the lease transaction. That is, if the present value of fair rental payments is equal to 90% or more of the fair value of the asset sold, the seller-lessee is presumed to have retained substantially all of the rights to use the sold property. The test for retention of minor rights would be to substitute 10% or less for 90% or more in the preceding sentence.

If substantially all the rights to use the property are retained by the seller-lessee, and the agreement meets at least one of the criteria for capital lease treatment, the seller-lessee accounts for the leaseback as a capital lease and any profit on the sale is deferred and amortized in proportion to amortization of the leased asset. If the leaseback is classified as an operating lease, it is accounted for as such, and any profit on the sale is deferred and amortized over the lease term in proportion to gross rental charges. Any loss on the sale would also be deferred unless the loss were perceived to be a real economic loss, in which case the loss would be immediately recognized and not deferred.

If only a minor portion of the rights to use are retained by the seller-lessee, the sale and the leaseback are accounted for separately. However, if the rental payments appear unreasonable based upon the existing market conditions at the inception of the lease, the profit or loss is adjusted so the rentals are at a reasonable amount. The amount created by the adjustment is deferred and amortized over the life of the property if a capital lease is involved or over the lease term if an operating lease is involved.

If the seller-lessee retains more than a minor portion but less than substantially all the rights to use the property, any excess profit on the sale is recognized on the date of the sale. For purposes of this paragraph, excess profit is derived as follows:

1. If the leaseback is classified as an operating lease, the excess profit is the portion of the profit that exceeds the present value of the minimum lease payments over the lease term including the gross amount of the guaranteed residual value. The seller-lessee uses its incremental borrowing rate to compute the present value of the minimum lease payments. If the implicit rate of interest in the lease is known and lower, it is substituted for the incremental borrowing rate in computing the present value of the minimum lease payments. The present value is amortized over the lease term while that guaranteed residual is deferred until resolution at the end of the lease term.
2. If the leaseback is classified as a capital lease, the excess profit is the portion of the profit that exceeds the recorded amount of the leased asset.

Executory costs are not to be included in the calculation of profit to be deferred in a sale-leaseback transaction (ASC 840-40-30). When the fair value of the property at the time of the leaseback is less than its undepreciated cost, the seller-lessee immediately recognizes a loss for the difference. In the example below, the sales price is less than the book value of the property. However, there is no economic loss because the fair value is greater than the book value.

Sales price	Book value	FV and PV
$85,000	$90,000	$100,000

($5,000)
Artificial loss

The artificial loss is deferred and amortized as an addition to depreciation.

The diagram below summarizes the accounting for sale-leaseback transactions.

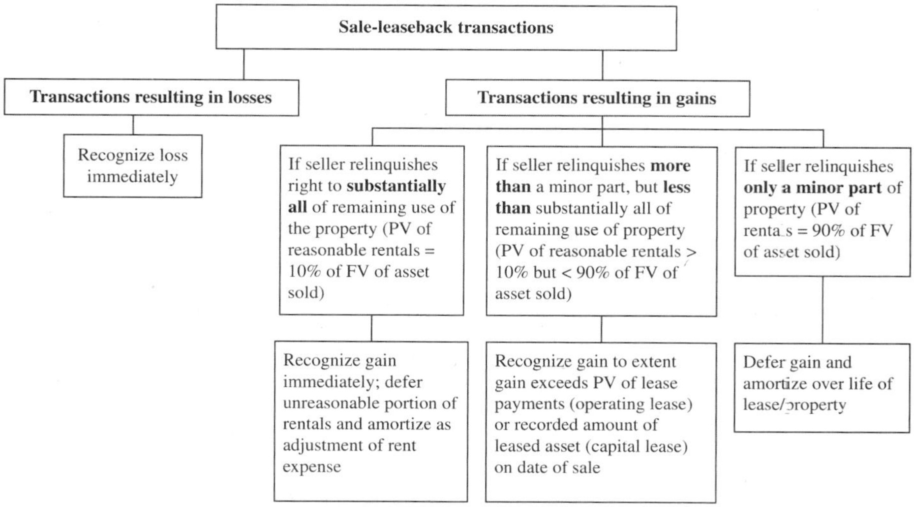

In the above circumstances, when the leased asset is land only, any amortization is recognized on a straight-line basis over the lease term, regardless of whether the lease is classified as a capital or operating lease.

The buyer-lessor accounts for the transaction as a purchase and a direct financing lease if the agreement meets the criteria of either a direct financing lease or a sales-type lease. Otherwise, the agreement is accounted for as a purchase and an operating lease.

Sale-leaseback involving real estate. Three requirements are necessary for a sale-leaseback involving real estate (including real estate with equipment) to qualify for sale-leaseback accounting treatment. Those sale-leaseback transactions not meeting the three requirements are accounted for using the deposit method or as a financing. The three requirements are:

1. The lease must be a normal leaseback (i.e., it involves active use of the leased property in the seller-lessee's trade or business during the lease term).
2. Payment terms and provisions must adequately demonstrate the buyer-lessor's initial and continuing investment in the property as prescribed by ASC 360-20.
3. Payment terms and provisions must transfer all the risks and rewards of ownership as demonstrated by a lack of continuing involvement by the seller-lessee.

Adequacy of initial and continuing investment. The buyer-lessor's initial investment is adequate if it demonstrates the buyer-lessor's commitment to pay for the property and indicates a reasonable likelihood that the seller-lessee will collect any receivable related to the leased property. The buyer-lessor's continuing investment is adequate if the buyer is contractually obligated to pay an annual amount at least equal to the amount of the annual payment sufficient to repay the principal and interest over no more than twenty years for land or the customary term of a first mortgage for other real estate.

Lack of continuing involvement by the seller-lessee. Any continuing involvement by the seller-lessee other than normal leaseback disqualifies the lease from sale-leaseback accounting treatment. Some examples of continuing involvement other than normal leaseback include

1. The seller-lessee has an obligation or option (excluding the right of first refusal) to repurchase the property
2. The seller-lessee (or party related to the seller-lessee) guarantees the buyer-lessor's investment or debt related to that investment or a specified return on that investment
3. The seller-lessee is required to reimburse the buyer-lessor for a decline in the fair value of the property below estimated residual value at the end of the lease term based on other than excess wear and tear
4. The seller-lessee remains liable for an existing debt related to the property
5. The seller-lessee's rental payments are contingent on some predetermined level of future operations of the buyer-lessor
6. The seller-lessee provides collateral on behalf of the buyer-lessor other than the property directly involved in the sale-leaseback
7. The seller-lessee provides nonrecourse financing to the buyer-lessor for any portion of the sales proceeds or provides recourse financing in which the only recourse is the leased asset
8. The seller-lessee enters into a sale-leaseback involving property improvements or integral equipment without leasing the underlying land to the buyer-lessor
9. The buyer-lessor is obligated to share any portion of the appreciation of the property with the seller-lessee
10. Any other provision or circumstance that allows the seller-lessee to participate in any future profits of the buyer-lessor or the appreciation of the leased property.

The inclusion of a put provision in the lease as a remedy for the occurrence of an event of default under the lease including for lessee noncompliance with financial covenants violates the continuing involvement criteria in ASC 840-40 when the transaction is part of a sale-leaseback. This would necessitate accounting for the transaction using the deposit method or as a financing depending on the application of ASC 360-20 to the circumstances.

When one member of a consolidated group provides an uncensored guarantee of lease payments for another member of the same consolidated group, this is not held to be continuing involvement on the part of the consolidated group. Therefore, sale-leaseback accounting is appropriate in the consolidated financial statements. In the separate financial statements of the subsidiary/seller-lessee, however, the guarantee is a form of continuing involvement that precludes sale-leaseback accounting because the guarantee provides the buyer-lessor with additional collateral that reduces the buyer-lessor's risk of loss (ASC 840-40-25).

An uncollateralized irrevocable letter of credit is not a form of continuing involvement that precludes sale-leaseback accounting unless a contract exists between the seller-lessee and third-party guarantor that would create collateral (e.g. right of offset of amounts on deposit). All written contracts between the seller-lessee and the issuer of the letter of credit must be evaluated to determine if other forms of collateral exist (ASC 840-40-25).

Example of accounting for a sale-leaseback transaction

To illustrate the accounting treatment in a sale-leaseback transaction, suppose that Seller/Lessee Corporation sells equipment that has a book value of $80,000 and a fair value of $100,000 to Buyer/Lessor Corporation for $100,000 in cash, and then immediately leases it back under the following conditions:

1. The sale date is January 1, 20X1, and the equipment has a fair value of $100,000 on that date and an estimated remaining useful life of fifteen years.
2. The lease term is fifteen years, noncancelable, and requires equal rental payments of $13,109 at the beginning of each year.
3. Seller/Lessee Corp. has the option to annually renew the lease at the same rental payments upon expiration of the original lease.
4. Seller/Lessee Corp. has the obligation to pay all executory costs.
5. The annual rental payments provide the Buyer/Lessor Corp. with a 12% return on investment.
6. The incremental borrowing rate of Seller/Lessee Corp. is 12%.
7. Seller/Lessee Corp. depreciates similar equipment on a straight-line basis.

Seller/Lessee Corp. will classify the agreement as a capital lease since the lease term exceeds 75% of the estimated remaining economic life of the equipment, and because the present value of the lease payments ($13,109 × 7.62817 = $100,000)[5] is greater than 90% of the fair value of the equipment. Assuming that collectibility of the lease payments is reasonably predictable and that no important uncertainties exist concerning the amount of unreimbursable costs yet to be incurred by Buyer/Lessor Corp., Buyer/Lessor Corp. will classify the transaction as a direct financing lease because the present value of the minimum lease payments is equal to the fair value of $100,000.

Seller/Lessee Corp. and Buyer/Lessor Corp. would make the following journal entries during the first year:

Upon Sale of Equipment on January 1, 20X1

Seller/Lessee Corp.			*Buyer/Lessor Corp.*		
Cash	100,000		Equipment	100,000	
Equipment*		80,000	Cash		100,000
Unearned profit on sale-leaseback		20,000			
Leased equipment	100,000		Lease receivable ($13,109 × 15)	196,635	
Lease obligations		100,000	Equipment		100,000
			Unearned interest		96,635

* *Assumes new equipment; for used equipment the accumulated depreciation would also be debited to remove it.*

To Record First Payment on January 1, 20X1**

Seller/Lessee Corp.			*Buyer/Lessor Corp.*		
Lease obligations	13,109		Cash	13,109	
Cash		13,109	Lease receivable		13,109

** *No interest is recorded in connection with the first payment since it is made at the inception of the lease.*

To Record Incurrence and Payment of Executory Costs

Seller/Lessee Corp.			*Buyer/Lessor Corp.*
Insurance, taxes, etc.	xxx		(No entry)
Cash (or accounts payable)		xxx	

To Record Amortization Expense on the Equipment, December 31, 20X1

Seller/Lessee Corp.			*Buyer/Lessor Corp.*
Amortization expense	6,667		(No entry)
Accum. amort.— capital leases ($100,000 ÷ 15)		6,667	

[5] *7.62817 is the present value of an annuity due for fifteen periods at a 12% interest rate.*

To Amortize Profit on Sale-Leaseback by Seller/Lessee Corp., December 31, 20X1

Seller/Lessee Corp.			Buyer/Lessor Corp.
Unearned profit on sale-leaseback	1,333		(No entry)
Amortization expense ($20,000 ÷ 15)		1,333	

To Record Interest for 20X1, December 31, 20X1

Seller/Lessee Corp.			Buyer/Lessor Corp.		
Interest expense	10,427		Unearned interest	10,427	
Accrued interest payable		10,427	Interest income		10,427

Partial Lease Amortization Schedule**

Date	*Cash payment*	*Interest expense*	*Reduction of obligation*	*Lease obligation*
Inception of lease				$100,000
1/1/X1	$13,109	$ –	$13,109	86,891
1/1/X2	13,109	10,427	2,682	84,209

** *No interest is recorded in connection with the first payment since it is made at the inception of the lease.*

Supplemental guidance. The following paragraphs provide supplemental guidance regarding the application of sale-leaseback accounting.

Property sold subject to seller's preexisting operating lease. ASC 840-40-55 considers the situation in which the reporting entity is an investor in a partnership that owns property with respect to which the reporting entity is also a lessee under an operating lease that covers all or a portion of the property. The reporting entity sells its interest in the partnership or the partnership sells the property to an independent party with the preexisting operating lease continuing in effect.

If the leased property is within the scope of ASC 840-40 (real estate or real estate with integral equipment), ASC 840-40-55 requires recognition of the transaction as a sale-leaseback if the preexisting lease is significantly modified in connection with the sale. If no changes are made to the lease, or if changes are insignificant, then profit is deferred and recognized in accordance with ASC 360-20 and ASC 840-40 for real estate, property improvements, and integral equipment.

The computation of any deferred profit is not affected by the seller-lessee's prior ownership percentage in the property. In addition, exercise of renewal options or sublease provisions contained in the preexisting lease that were included in the original minimum lease term do not affect the accounting for the transaction. ASC 840-40 would apply, however, to renewal options not contained in the original minimum lease term. These renewal options would be treated as a new lease. Finally, leases between parties under common control are not considered preexisting leases for this purpose and ASC 840-40 applies unless one of the parties is a regulated enterprise such as a public utility under the provisions of ASC 980 (ASC 840-40-55).

Sale-leaseback of an asset leased to another party. A variation of the previous issue arises when a leaseback involves an asset that is personal property falling outside coverage of ASC 840-40 and either (1) subject to an operating lease or (2) subleased or intended to be subleased to another entity under an operating lease. The standard specified that the seller-lessee-sublessor is to account for the transaction by recording the sale, removing the asset from its statement of financial position, classifying the leaseback based on the normal criteria for determining lease classification, and recognizing or deferring any gain on the transaction as previously discussed (ASC 840-40-55).

Other Lease Issues

Accounting for a sublease. A sublease is an arrangement where the original lessee re-leases the leased property to a third party (the sublessee), and the original lessee acts as a sublessor. Normally, the nature of a sublease agreement does not affect the original lease agreement, and the original lessee/sublessor retains primary liability to the lessor.

The original lease remains in effect, and the original lessor continues to account for the lease as before. The original lessee/sublessor accounts for the lease as follows:

1. If the original lease agreement transfers ownership or contains a BPO and if the new lease meets any one of the four specified criteria (i.e., transfers ownership, BPO, 75% test, or 90% test) and both the collectibility and uncertainties criteria, then the sublessor classifies the new lease as a sales-type or direct financing lease; otherwise it is classified as an operating lease. In either situation, the original lessee/sublessor continues accounting for the original lease obligation as before.
2. If the original lease agreement does not transfer ownership or contain a BPO, but it still qualifies as a capital lease, then the original lessee/sublessor (with one exception) applies the usual criteria in classifying the new agreement. If the new lease qualifies, the original lessee/sublessor accounts for it as a direct financing lease, with the unamortized balance of the asset under the original lease being treated as the cost of the leased property. However, the original lessee/sublessor should recognize a loss on the sublease if its carrying amount exceeds the total sublease rentals and the estimated residual value (ASC 840-20-25). The one exception arises when the circumstances surrounding the sublease suggest that the sublease agreement was an important part of a predetermined plan in which the original lessee played only an intermediate role between the original lessor and the sublessee. In this situation, the sublease is classified by the 75% and 90% criteria as well as collectibility and uncertainties criteria. In applying the 90% criterion, the fair value for the leased property is the fair value to the original lessor at the inception of the original lease. Under all circumstances, the original lessee continues accounting for the original lease obligation as before. If the new lease agreement (sublease) does not meet the capitalization requirements imposed for subleases, then the new lease is accounted for as an operating lease.
3. If the original lease is an operating lease, the original lessee/sublessor accounts for the new lease as an operating lease and accounts for the original operating lease as before.

Example of a direct-financing sublease

The Silver Pick Mine obtains a $300,000 ore carrier truck under a five-year capital lease at 8% interest. Annual lease payments are $75,137. Silver Pick reduces its lease liability in accordance with the following amortization table:

Year	*Cash payment*	*Interest*	*Reduction in principal*	*Balance of net investment*
Inception				$300,000
1	$ 75,137	$24,000	$ 51,137	248,863
2	75,137	19,909	55,228	193,635
3	75,137	15,419	59,646	133,989
4	75,137	10,719	64,418	69,571
5	75,137	5,566	69,571	0
	$375,685	$75,685	$300,000	

At the end of Year 2, silver prices drop too low for ongoing mining operations to be profitable, so Silver Pick subleases the ore carrier via a direct financing lease to the Lead Bottom Mine for the remaining three years of the lease at the same interest rate. Silver Pick should use the unamortized balance of $193,635 at the end of Year 2 as the cost basis of the sublease, but Lead Bottom negotiates a lower inception value of $160,000, resulting in the following amortization table:

Year	*Cash payment*	*Interest*	*Reduction in principal*	*Balance of net investment*
Inception				$160,000
3	$ 62,085	$12,800	$ 49,285	110,715
4	62,085	8,857	53,228	57,487
5	62,085	4,598	57,487	0
	$186,255	$26,255	$160,000	

At the inception of the sublease, Silver Pick records a loss of $39,156 to reflect the negotiated $33,635 drop in the cost basis of the sublease, from $193,635 to $160,000, as well as a reduction of sublease interest income of $5,521, also due to the reduced cost basis. The summary entry for the final three years of Silver Pick's payments under the original lease agreement and its receipts under the sublease follows:

	Years 3 – 5 of original lease transaction		*Total of sublease transactions*		*Variance*	
Lease liability	193,635			160,000		33,635
Interest expense	31,776			26,255		5,521
Cash		225,411	186,255		39,156	

Lease escalations. Virtually all commercial leases contain provisions obligating the lessee to pay the lessor various additional sums, often referred to as lease escalations, that supplement the specified fixed rentals. It is important that the parties to the lease properly classify these payments because the way they are characterized can affect whether the lease is accounted for in the correct manner.

Escalating base rents. These are periodic increases in the fixed monthly rentals scheduled to occur at one or more points during the lease term. Escalating base rents are included in minimum lease payments.

Variations of this type of escalation occur when the fixed (or base) rent is structured at inception to include a future escalation based on the expected growth of the lessee requiring it to physically use additional portions of the premises that it was not using at inception or an actual addition or based on the lessee actually adding space or capacity.

ASC 840-20-25 prescribes the following two rules:

1. If, at the inception of the lease, the lessee takes possession of or controls the physical use of the leased property, all rentals including the escalated rents are to be recognized by the lessee and lessor as rental expense and rental revenue, respectively, on a straight-line basis commencing with the beginning of the lease term.
2. If rents escalate under a master lease agreement because the lessee obtains access to or control of additional leased property at the time of the escalation, the escalated rents are considered by the lessee and lessor as rental expense and rental revenue respectively that is attributable to the newly leased property. This additional rental expense or rental revenue is to be computed based on the relative fair values of the original leased property and the additional leased property as determined at the inception of the lease and allocated to the time periods during which the lessee controls the use of the additional leased property.

Executory costs. These represent reimbursements to the lessor of costs associated with owning and maintaining the leased property. The most common executory costs are real estate taxes, insurance, and maintenance. Amounts paid by a lessee as consideration for a guarantee from an unrelated third party of the residual value are also considered executory costs. If executory costs are paid by the lessor, any lessor's profit on those costs is considered in the same manner as the actual executory costs. Executory costs are excluded from minimum lease payments.

Contingent rentals. These are additional rentals due that are computed based on changes that occur subsequent to the inception of the lease in factors, other than the passage of time, on which the lease payments were based. Examples of contingent rentals include real estate rentals based on a percentage of the lessee's retail sales over a certain dollar amount (often referred to as percentage rent or overage rent) and equipment rentals based on machine hours of use. One type of escalation that many commercial leases contain is a required rent increase based on increases in an index such as the prime interest rate or the Consumer Price Index (CPI). Depending on how the terms are structured, these payments might actually consist of two elements that must be separately considered. The portion attributable to the index or rate that was in effect at the inception of the lease (considered part of the minimum lease payments) and the portion representing subsequent increases in that index or rate (considered to be contingent rentals) as illustrated in the following examples.

Example 1

A three-year lease requires fixed rentals of $1,000 per month plus $10 for every full percentage point of the prime interest rate or fraction thereof determined as of the beginning of the month. The prime interest rate at the inception of the lease is 6% and on the first day of the fourth month of the lease term the prime interest rate increased to 7%.

At lease inception, the minimum rentals are computed as follows:

$1,000 + ($10 × 6 percentage points = $60) = $1,060 per month × 36 months = $38,160

The increase in rent due at the beginning of the fourth month would be allocated as follows:

Minimum rentals:	$10 × 6 percentage points	=	$60
Contingent rentals:	$10 × 1 percentage points	=	10
			$70

Example 2

Same facts as Example 1, except that the lease requires the lessee to pay fixed rentals of $1,000 per month plus $10 for every full percentage point or fraction thereof that the prime interest rate determined as of the beginning of the month exceeds 6%.

At lease inception, the minimum rentals are computed as follows:

$1,000 per month × 36 months = $36,000

The increase in rent due at the beginning of the fourth month would be allocated as follows:

Minimum rentals:			$ –
Contingent rentals:	$10 × 1 percentage point	=	10
			$10

As illustrated in the examples, amounts determined to be contingent rentals are excluded from minimum lease payments.

As discussed previously, leases for retail space often contain percentage rent provisions that obligate the lessee to pay the lessor a percentage of retail sales over a certain dollar amount. These dollar thresholds are often expressed in terms of annual targets such as one-half of one percent of annual sales over $10 million. This type of lease provision raises the accounting issue of how the lessor and lessee are to account for the lease during the interim periods prior to the attainment of the contractual target.

ASC 840-10-25 and ASC 840-10-40 prescribes the accounting as follows:

Lessor: No revenue recognition until the actual target is achieved and surpassed.

Lessee: Recognize contingent rental expense during interim periods if it is probable that the target will be reached by the end of the fiscal year. If, subsequently, the specified target is not met, previously recorded expense is reversed at the time it becomes probable that the target will not be met.

Lessee involvement in asset construction. A lessee often has substantial involvement in construction activities with respect to an asset to be leased under a long-term lease agreement. This involvement can take many forms that can include:

1. Providing the construction financing directly or indirectly
2. Guaranteeing the construction debt
3. Serving as primary or secondary obligor under construction contracts
4. Acting as the real estate developer or general contractor
5. Agreeing to purchase the asset if the construction is not completed by a specified date
6. Agreeing to fund construction cost overruns
7. Serving as an agent of the lessor for the construction, financing, or ultimate sale of the asset
8. Agreeing to a date-certain lease that obligates the lessee to commence rental payments on a certain date irrespective of whether the construction is complete by that date.

Construction period rent associated with land and building leases. In certain instances, the lessee will delay occupancy or usage of leased property until, for example, leasehold improvements have been completed. ASC 840-20-25 states that a lease conveys to the lessee the right to control the use of property, such as leased land and building, both during and after any construction period necessary to construct leasehold improvements to the property. Consequently, rental expense is required to be allocated to periods during which construction activities are occurring even though the lessee has not yet commenced operations on the premises. It further provides that the rentals allocated to the construction period are not to be capitalized as part of the cost of the leasehold improvements but rather are to be recorded as a period expense as a charge against income from continuing operations in the lessee's financial statements.

Transfer of construction period risks. A lessee is considered the owner of a real estate project during its construction period if the lessee bears substantially all of the construction period risks (ASC 840-40).

Under ASC 840-40, if the lessee is determined to bear substantially all of the construction risks, it is considered to be the owner of the asset during the construction period. If that is the case, then a sale-leaseback of the asset occurs upon the completion of construction and the commencement of the lease term.

The primary test to be used in determining if a lessee has substantially all of the construction period risks is virtually the same as the 90% of fair value test for determining if a lease is to be classified as a capital lease by a lessee. Beginning with the earlier of the date of the inception of the lease or the date that the construction terms are agreed to, if at any time during the construction period the documents governing the construction project could require, under any circumstance, that the lessee pay 90% or more of the total project costs, excluding land acquisition costs, then the lessee is considered to be the owner of the real estate project during its construction period.

Even if the present value of the lessee's maximum guarantee is less than 90% of total project costs, ASC 840-40 provides six examples of when the lessee would still be considered the owner of a real estate project.

For the purposes of this 90% test, the lessee's maximum guarantee includes any payments the lessee could be required to make in connection with the construction project. The lessee's maximum guarantee includes, but is not limited to:

1. Lease payments that must be made regardless of when or whether the project is complete
2. Guarantees of the construction financing
3. Equity investments made in the owner-lessor or any party related to the owner-lessor
4. Loans or advances made to the owner-lessor or any party related to the owner-lessor
5. Payments made by the lessee in the capacity of a developer, a general contractor, or a construction manager/agent that are reimbursed less frequently than is normal or customary
6. Primary or secondary obligations to pay project costs under construction contracts
7. Obligations that could arise from being the developer or general contractor
8. An obligation to purchase the real estate project under any circumstances
9. An obligation to fund construction cost overruns
10. Rent or fees of any kind, such as transaction costs, to be paid to or on behalf of the lessor by the lessee during the construction period
11. Payments that might be made with respect to providing indemnities or guarantees to the owner-lessor.

The scope of ASC 840-40 includes government-owned property under construction and subject to a future lease of the completed improvements (ASC 840-40-15).

Any direct or indirect financial interests of the lessee in the leased asset or in the lessor must be analyzed by the lessee to determine if

1. They require accounting recognition as a guarantee obligation under ASC 460.
2. They result in the lessee holding a variable interest in the lessor or in the lessor's specified assets (the project) that potentially could require the lessee to consolidate the lessor as the primary beneficiary of a VIE or consolidate the specified assets and related liabilities (referred to as "silo" or a "virtual VIE").

If the lessee consolidates the lessor or the project, intercompany transactions and balances will be eliminated in consolidation.

Change in residual value. For any of the foregoing types of leases, the lessor is to review the estimated residual value at least annually. If there is a decline in the estimated residual value, the lessor must make a determination as to whether this decline is temporary or permanent. If temporary, no adjustment is required; however, if the decline is other than temporary, then the estimated residual value must be revised to conform to the revised estimate. The loss that arises in the net investment is recognized in the period of decline. Under no circumstance is the estimated residual value to be adjusted to reflect an increase in the estimate. ASC 840-30-35 clarifies that this prohibition against reflecting an increase in the estimated residual value also extends to increases in the guaranteed portions of the residual value that result from renegotiations between the parties.

Example of a permanent decline in residual value

Hathaway Corporation enters into a sales-type leasing transaction as the lessor of a fire truck. The following table shows key information about the lease:

Lease term	10 years
Implicit interest rate	8%
Lease payments	One payment per year
Normal selling price	$300,000
Asset cost	$200,000
Residual value	$ 50,000

After one year, immediately after the first lease payment has been received, Hathaway determines that an indicated decline in residual value from $50,000 to $30,000 is other than temporary. The calculation it originally used to determine the annual minimum lease payment follows:

$$\frac{\text{Selling price} - (\text{Present value of residual value due in 10 years at 8\% interest} \times \text{residual value})}{\text{Present value of an annuity of \$1 for 10 years at 8\% interest}}$$

$$= \frac{\$300{,}000 - (0.46319 \times \$50{,}000)}{6.71008}$$

$$= \$41{,}257.33 \text{ Annual minimum lease payment}$$

Hathaway calculates the following reduction in the residual present value of the fire truck, using a multiplier of 0.5002 to obtain the present value of the residual value due in nine years at an interest rate of 8%:

Accreted original residual asset present value = ($50,000) × (Present value of 0.5002) = $25,010

Less: Revised residual asset present value = ($30,000) × (Present value of 0.5002) = $15,006

Equals net change in residual asset present value = ($10,004)

The following table shows the original and revised elements of Hathaway's lease transaction entry:

	*Initial entry**		*Revised residual value*		*Entry net of Residual value change*	
Less receivable	462,572			20,000	442,572	
Cost of goods sold	176,840				176,840	
Loss on residual reduction			10,004		10,004	
Inventory		200,000				200,000
Sales		276,840				276,840
Unearned interest		162,572	9,996			152,576

* *Lease receivable = (Total minimum lease payments) + (Residual asset value)*
Cost of goods sold = (Inventory cost) – (Present value of residual asset value)
Sales = (Present value of minimum lease payments)
Unearned interest = (Lease receivable) – (Present value of minimum lease payments) – (Present value of residual asset value)

The following amortization table tracks the net impact of these changes, resulting in a $30,000 residual value at the end of Year 10:

Year	*Cash payment*	*Interest*	*Reduction in principal*	*Balance of net investment*
Inception				$300,000
1	$ 41,257	$ 24,000	$ 17,257	282,743
Adjustment			10,004	272,739
2	41,257	21,819	19,438	253,301
3	41,257	20,264	20,993	232,308
4	41,257	18,584	22,673	209,635
5	41,257	16,770	24,487	185,148
6	41,257	14,811	26,446	158,702
7	41,257	12,696	28,561	130,141
8	41,257	10,411	30,846	99,295
9	41,257	7,943	33,314	65,981
10	41,257	5,276	35,981	30,000
	$412,570	$152,574	$270,000	

Thus, net of rounding errors, the total of all payments on the amortization table and the $30,000 revised residual value equals the revised lease receivable of $442,572. Similarly, the total of all interest payments on the amortization table matches the adjusted unearned interest entry.

Change in the provisions of a lease. Accounting issues arise when the lessee and lessor agree, subsequent to its inception, to change the provisions of the lease (other than by renewals or term extensions that are discussed later). If, from the standpoint of the lessee, the revised lease terms would have, at the inception of the original lease, resulted in a different lease classification (e.g., operating lease versus capital lease or vice versa), the revised agreement is considered to be a new agreement.

If the original lease was accounted for as a capital lease and the revised lease qualifies for treatment as an operating lease, they are to be accounted for as sale-leaseback transactions (discussed later in this chapter).

If the original lease was accounted for as an operating lease and the revised lease is a capital lease, then on the date of the revision, the lessee records an asset and an obligation based on the present value of the remaining lease payments (or the fair value of the leased property, if less).

Finally, if the original and revised leases are both capital leases, then the lessee adjusts the recorded asset and obligation by an amount equal to the difference between the present value of the future minimum lease payments under the revised agreement and the recorded balance of the obligation. For the purposes of this calculation, the rate of interest to be used is the rate that was used to record the lease initially. The adjustment is recognized as a gain or loss of the period in which the revision is made.

In the case of either a sales-type or direct financing lease where there is a change in the provisions of a lease, the lease is accounted for by the lessor as discussed below.

Changes in the provisions that affect the amount of the remaining minimum lease payments can result in one of the following three outcomes:

1. The change does not give rise to a new agreement. A new agreement is defined as a change that, if in effect at the inception of the lease, would have resulted in a different classification.
2. The change does give rise to a new agreement that would be classified as a direct financing lease.
3. The change gives rise to a new agreement that would be classified as an operating lease.

If either item 1 or item 2 occurs, the balance of the minimum lease payments receivable and the estimated residual value (if affected) are adjusted to reflect the effect of the change. The net adjustment is charged (or credited) to unearned income, and the accounting for the lease over its remaining term is adjusted to reflect the change.

If the new agreement is an operating lease, then the remaining net investment (lease receivable less unearned income) is written off and the leased asset is recorded by the lessor at the lower of its cost, present fair value, or carrying value. The net adjustment resulting from these entries is charged (or credited) to income of the period in which the revision is made. Thereafter, the new lease is accounted for as any other operating lease.

The lessee and the lessor may negotiate a shortened lease term and an increase in the lease payments over the revised lease term. ASC 840-20-55 observes that the nature of the modification is a matter of judgment that depends on the relevant facts and circumstances. If the modification is deemed only a change in future lease payments, the increase is amortized over the remaining term of the modified lease. On the other hand, a modification deemed a termination penalty is to be recognized in the period of modification. Termination penalties are calculated as the excess of the modified lease payments over the original lease payments that would have been required during the shortened lease term.

ASC 840-20-55 provides that consideration is to be given to (1) the length of the modified lease period compared to the remaining term of the original lease, and (2) the difference between the modified lease payments and comparable market rents in determining whether the modification is a termination penalty.

Early termination of a lease. Accounting for premature lease termination from the standpoints of the lessee and lessor follows.

Lessee accounting. Discontinuation of business activities in a particular location is considered an exit activity, the accounting for which is specified in ASC 420.

Operating leases. In connection with lease termination, the lessee may incur (1) costs to terminate the lease prior to the end of its noncancelable term and/or (2) continuing lease costs incurred during the remainder of the lease term for which the lessee receives no economic benefit because the premises are no longer in use. On the date the lessee terminates the lease, the lessee recognizes a liability for the fair value of the termination costs. The termination date is the date that the lessee provides written notice to the lessor in accordance with the notification requirements contained in the lease or the date the lessee and lessor agree to a negotiated early termination.

The fair value of rentals that continue to be incurred under the lease during its remaining term without benefit to the lessee is recognized as a liability on the date that the lessee ceases to use the property (referred to as the cease-use date). Fair value is computed based on the remaining rentals due under the lease, adjusted for any prepaid or deferred rent under the lease, and reduced by estimated sublease rentals that are reasonable to expect for the property. The fair value measurement requires that reasonable sublease rentals be included in the computation even if the lessee does not intend to sublease the property.

In periods subsequent to the recognition of these liabilities but prior to their settlement, changes in fair value are measured using the credit-adjusted risk-free rate of interest (in essence, the lessee's incremental borrowing rate) used to initially measure the liability.

Upon initial recognition of these liabilities, the related costs are recognized in the lessee's income statement as operating expense (or income from continuing operations if no measure of operations is presented) unless required to be presented as part of discontinued operations. The cumulative effects of any subsequent period changes in liabilities that result from changes in the estimates of either the amounts or timing of cash flows are reported in the same income statement caption used to initially recognize the costs. Changes to the liabilities as a result of the passage of time increase their carrying amount and are recorded as accretion expense, which is also considered an operating expense.

Capital leases. If the lease is a capital lease, it is subject to the provisions of ASC 360 with respect to long-lived assets to be disposed of other than by sale (see Chapter 14) either individually (in which case the gain or loss is recorded as a component of operating expense) or as part of a disposal group (in which case the gain or loss is presented as a part of discontinued operations). During the time period between the termination date and the cease-use date, the capital lease asset continues to be classified as "held and used," is subject to impairment evaluation, and its remaining carrying value is amortized over that shortened time period.

Lessor accounting. Lessor accounting for an early lease termination is as follows.

Sales-type and direct financing leases. The lessor records the leased equipment as an asset at the lower of its original cost, present fair value, or current carrying value. The difference between the remaining net investment in the lease and the amount of the adjustment to recognize the leased equipment is reflected in income of the period in which the lease is terminated.

Example of lessor accounting for the early termination of a sales-type lease

La Crosse Corporation enters into a sales-type leasing transaction as the lessor of a digital color copier. The following table shows key information about the lease:

Lease term	5 years
Implicit interest rate	8%
Lease payments	One payment per year
Normal selling price	$80,000
Asset cost	$50,000
Residual value	$10,000
Present value of ordinary annuity of 1 for 5 years at 8%	3.9927
Present value of 1 due in 5 years at 8%	0.6806

Based on the information in the table, La Crosse calculates an annual minimum lease payment of $18,332, which is reflected in the following amortization table:

Year	*Cash payment*	*Interest*	*Reduction in principal*	*Balance of net investment*
Inception				$80,000
1	$18,332	$ 6,400	$11,932	68,068
2	18,332	5,445	12,887	55,181
3	18,332	4,414	13,918	41,263
4	18,332	3,301	15,031	26,232
5	18,332	2,100	16,232	10,000
	$91,660	$21,660	$70,000	

At the end of Year 3, the lessee cancels the lease. At that time, the fair value of the color copier is $35,000, which is $6,263 less than the $41,263 current carrying value indicated at the end of Year 3 in the amortization table. This change is reflected in the following table, which notes the original and revised elements of La Crosse's lease transaction:

	Initial entry*		Total of transactions for first 3 years		Lease cancellation entry	
Cash			54,996			
Lease receivable	101,660			54,996		46,664
Cost of goods sold	43,194					
Inventory		50,000			35,000	
Sales		73,194				
Interest income				16,259		
Loss on early lease termination					6,263	

* *Lease receivable = (Total minimum lease payments) + (Residual asset value)*
Cost of goods sold = (Inventory cost) – (Present value of residual asset value)
Sales = (Present value of minimum lease payments)
Unearned interest = (Lease receivable) – (Present value of minimum lease payments) – (Present value of residual asset value)

Operating leases. Accounting for the leased asset is subject to the provisions of ASC 360. Between the termination date and the cease-use date, the leased asset continues to be presented as held-and-used and depreciated subject to an impairment evaluation that considers the likelihood and timing of replacing the tenant and market rents that would be realized. On the cease-use date, the leased asset is reclassified from held-and-used to the category of idle property and equipment with the associated temporary suspension of depreciation.

Upon receiving notice of termination, the lessor recognizes a receivable for the fair value of any termination fees to be received from the lessee as a result of early cancellation and a corresponding deferred rent liability that is recorded as an adjustment to any previously recorded deferred rent liability or prepaid rent. The remaining rental stream to be received thereafter is recognized on a straight-line basis over the remainder of the time period during which such payments were agreed to continue by adjusting any remaining prepaid rent, deferred rent, and/or unamortized initial direct costs so that they will be fully amortized by the date on which the lessee's payment obligation is fully satisfied.

Renewal or extension of an existing lease. The renewal or extension of an existing lease agreement affects the accounting of both the lessee and the lessor. There are two basic situations: (1) the renewal occurs and makes a residual guarantee or penalty provision inoperative or (2) the renewal agreement does not do the foregoing and the renewal is treated as a new agreement. The accounting treatment prescribed under the latter situation for a lessee is as follows:

1. If the renewal or extension is classified as a capital lease, then the (present) current balances of the asset and related obligation are adjusted by the difference between the present value of the future minimum lease payments under the revised agreement and the (present) current balance of the obligation. The present value of the minimum lease payments under the revised agreement is computed using the interest rate in effect at the inception of the original lease.
2. If the renewal or extension is classified as an operating lease, then the current balances of the asset and liability are written off and a gain (loss) recognized for the difference. The new lease agreement resulting from a renewal or extension is accounted for in the same manner as other operating leases.

Under the same circumstances, the following treatment is followed by the lessor:

1. If the renewal or extension is classified as a direct financing lease, then the existing balances of the lease receivable and the estimated residual value are adjusted for the changes resulting from the revised agreement.

NOTE: Remember that an upward adjustment to the estimated residual value is not allowed.

The net adjustment is charged or credited to unearned income.

2. If the renewal or extension is classified as an operating lease, then the remaining net investment under the existing sales-type lease or direct financing lease is written off and the leased asset is recorded as an asset at the lower of its original cost, present fair value, or current carrying amount. The difference between the net investment and the amount recorded for the leased asset is charged to income of the period that includes the renewal or extension date. The renewal or extension is then accounted for prospectively as any other operating lease.
3. If the renewal or extension is classified as a sales-type lease and it occurs at or near the end of the existing lease term, then the renewal or extension is accounted for as a sales-type lease.

NOTE: A renewal or extension that occurs in the last few months of an existing lease is considered to have occurred at or near the end of the existing lease term.

If the renewal or extension causes the guarantee or penalty provision to be inoperative, the lessee adjusts the current balance of the leased asset and the lease obligation to the present value of the future minimum lease payments (according to ASC 840 "by an amount equal to the difference between the present value of the future minimum lease payments under the revised agreement and the present balance of the obligation"). The present value of the future minimum lease payments is computed using the rate used in the original lease agreement.

Given the same circumstances, the lessor adjusts the existing balance of the lease receivable and estimated residual value to reflect the changes of the revised agreement (remember, no upward adjustments to the residual value). The net adjustment is charged (or credited) to unearned income.

Example of lessor accounting for extension of a sales-type lease

Entré Computers enters into a sales-type leasing transaction as the lessor of a corporate computer system. The following table shows key information about the lease:

Lease term	6 years
Implicit interest rate	10%
Lease payments	One payment per year
Normal selling price	\$240,000
Asset cost	\$180,000
Residual value	\$450,000
Present value of ordinary annuity of 1 for 6 years at 10%	4.3553
Present value of 1 due in 6 years at 10%	0.5645

Based on the information in the table, Entré calculates an annual minimum lease payment of $49,273, which is reflected in the following amortization table:

Year	*Cash payment*	*Interest*	*Reduction in principal*	*Balance of net investment*
Inception				$240,000
1	$ 49,273	$ 24,000	$ 25,273	214,727
2	49,273	21,472	27,801	186,926
3	49,273	18,692	30,581	156,345
4	49,273	15,634	33,639	122,706
5	49,273	12,270	37,003	85,703
6	49,273	8,570	40,703	45,000
	$295,638	$100,638	$195,000	

After making the Year 3 payment, the lessee requests a lease extension in order to reduce the annual payment amount. To do so, Entré extends the lease duration by two years and assumes the same residual value. Entré calculates the revised annual minimum lease payment under the assumption that the selling price is the balance of the net investment at the end of Year 3, as noted in the preceding amortization table.

$$\frac{\text{Selling price} - (\text{Present value of residual value due in 5 years at 10\% interest} \times \text{residual value})}{\text{Present value of an annuity of \$1 for 5 years at 10\% interest}}$$

$$= \frac{\$156{,}345 - (0.6209 \times \$45{,}000)}{3.7908}$$

$$= \$33{,}873 \text{ Annual minimum lease payment}$$

The revised lease payment and residual value is shown in the following amortization table, which includes both the first three years of the original lease agreement and the full five years of the lease extension agreement:

Year	*Cash payment*	*Interest*	*Reduction in principal*	*Balance of net investment*
Inception				$240,000
1	$ 49,273	$ 24,000	$ 25,273	214,727
2	49,273	21,472	27,801	186,926
3	49,273	18,692	30,581	156,345
4	33,873	15,635	18,238	138,107
5	33,873	13,811	20,062	118,045
6	33,873	11,805	22,068	95,977
7	33,873	9,598	24,275	71,702
8	33,873	7,171	26,702	45,000
	$317,184	$122,184	$195,000	

This change is reflected in the following table, which notes the original and revised elements of Entré's lease transaction:

	*Initial entry**		*Revised entry*		*Net entry required*	
Lease receivable	340,638		362,184		21,546	
Cost of goods sold	154,597		154,597			
Inventory		180,000		180,000		
Sales		214,597		214,597		
Unearned interest		100,638		122,184		21,546

* *Lease receivable = (Total minimum lease payments) + (Residual asset value)*
Cost of goods sold = (Inventory cost) – (Present value of residual asset value)
Sales = (Present value of minimum lease payments)
Unearned interest = (Lease receivable) – (Present value of minimum lease payments) – (Present value of residual asset value)

Leases between related parties. Leases between related parties are classified and accounted for as though the parties are unrelated, except in cases where it is certain that the terms and conditions of the agreement have been influenced significantly by the fact that the lessor and lessee are related. When this is the case, the classification and/or accounting is modified to reflect the true economic substance of the transaction rather than the legal form. Under ASC 810, discussed earlier in this chapter, many related-party lessors will qualify as VIEs. When this is the case, the lessee will present consolidated financial statements that include the lessor's assets, liabilities, and results of operations. The elimination of intercompany transactions and balances will result in the rental expense and rental income being removed from the consolidated financial statements, which will instead reflect the depreciation of the leased asset and the interest expense on any related debt.

ASC 850 requires that the nature and extent of leasing activities between related parties be disclosed. ASC 810 requires the following disclosures by the primary beneficiary of a VIE:

1. The nature, purpose, size, and activities of the VIE
2. The carrying amount and classification of consolidated assets that collateralize the VIE's obligations
3. Any lack of recourse that VIE creditors or holders of VIE beneficial interests have to the general credit of the primary beneficiary.

Indemnification provisions in lease agreements. Some lease agreements contain a provision whereby the lessee indemnifies the lessor on an after-tax basis for certain income tax benefits that the lessor might lose if a change in the income tax law should occur.

An indemnification agreement of this kind is considered a guarantee that is subject to the recognition and disclosure requirements of ASC 460. Any payments that might be required under the indemnification clause are, therefore, not considered contingent rentals.

Accounting for leases in a business combination. A business combination, in and of itself, has no effect upon the classification of a lease. However, if, in connection with a business combination, a lease agreement is modified to change the original classification of the lease, it is considered a new agreement and accounted for as previously discussed.

In most cases, a business combination will not affect the previous classification of a lease unless the provisions have been modified as indicated in the preceding paragraph.

The acquiring company applies the following procedures to account for a leveraged lease in a business combination:

1. The classification as a leveraged lease is retained.
2. The net investment in the leveraged lease is assigned a fair value (present value, net of income taxes) based upon the remaining future cash flows. Also, the estimated income tax effects of the cash flows are recognized.
3. The net investment is broken down into three components: net rentals receivable, estimated residual value, and unearned income.
4. Thereafter, the leveraged lease is accounted for as described in the discussion earlier in this chapter.

ASC 805 significantly alters the accounting for business combinations. It requires the use of the acquisition method, which requires that assets acquired and liabilities assumed in such a transaction be accounted for at fair values. This means, among other things, that capital leases under which the acquiree entity was obligated at the acquisition date are to be revalued at fair value at the date of the acquisition. The amounts of depreciation and interest to be recognized in subsequent periods by the acquirer will accordingly, in most instances, vary from the amounts that would have been recognized by the acquiree absent the business combination.

For example, if the fair value of the leased property under a capital lease is greater than its carrying value (the depreciated capitalized value as of that date), future amortization will be greater than would otherwise have been the case. Given that rental payments will not be altered by the acquisition transaction, this means that the effective interest cost will be reduced. A new effective interest rate will need to be computed in order to properly record the accounting implications of future rental payments, in such a circumstance. Contrariwise, if the fair value of the leased property is lower than its precombination carrying (book) value, the effective interest rate will be greater than had previously been determined.

ASC 805 states that the determination of the classification of an existing lease is generally not reassessed at the date of a business combination, and that the determination made at the lease inception is not to be reconsidered. However, if the terms of an operating lease are favorable or unfavorable compared with the market terms of leases of the same or similar items at the acquisition date, accounting ramifications must be addressed. The acquirer in such a circumstance is to recognize an intangible asset if the terms of an operating lease are favorable relative market terms, and is to recognize a liability if the terms are unfavorable relative to market terms.

An identifiable intangible asset may be associated with an operating lease, which may be objectively revealed by market participants' willingness to pay a price for the lease even if its terms are already at market. For example, a lease of gates at an airport or of retail space in a prime shopping area might provide entry into a market or other future economic benefits that qualify as identifiable intangible assets—for example, as a customer relationship. In that situation, the acquirer is to recognize the associated identifiable intangible asset(s). Under ASC 805, the identifiable intangible assets acquired in a business combination are to be recognized distinct from goodwill. An intangible asset is *identifiable* if it meets either the separability criterion or the contractual-legal criterion described by ASC 805.

If the acquiree in a business combination has assets (e.g., building or equipment) that are subject to operating leases (that is, the acquiree is a lessor), ASC 805 directs that such assets are to be recorded at fair value determined without regard to the terms of the associated leases. The extent to which the lease terms are favorable or unfavorable relative to the market at the acquisition date, however, will be reflected in the additional intangible asset or liability to be recognized by the acquirer.

Accounting for changes in lease agreements resulting from refunding of tax-exempt debt. Tax-exempt debt is often "refunded" by the issuer of the debt instruments. Refunding is a refinancing that enables the issuer (i.e., a municipality that issued bonds) to take advantage of favorable interest rates. A current refunding is effected when the debt becomes callable and the issuer issues new debt in order to use the proceeds to retire the original debt. An advance refunding is a more complex variation that occurs prior to the call date of the original instruments. It entails issuance of new tax-exempt debt at the lower interest rate with a similar maturity to the original issuance. The proceeds of the new debt are invested in a portfolio of market-traded US Treasury securities and other obligations that effectively "defease" the original bonds. If, during the lease term, a change in the lease results from a refunding by the lessor of tax-exempt debt (including an advance refunding) and (1) the lessee receives the economic advantages of the refunding and (2) the revised agreement can be classified as a capital lease by the lessee and a direct financing lease by the lessor, the change is accounted for as follows:

1. If the change is accounted for as an extinguishment of debt:
    a. Lessee accounting. The lessee adjusts the lease obligation to the present value of the future minimum lease payments under the revised agreement. The present

value of the minimum lease payments is computed using the interest rate applicable to the revised agreement. Any gain or loss is recognized currently as a gain or loss on the extinguishment of debt in accordance with the provisions of ASC 470-50-45 (discussed in detail in the chapter on ASC 470).

b. Lessor accounting. The lessor adjusts the balance of the lease receivable and the estimated residual value, if affected, for the difference in present values between the old and revised agreements. Any resulting gain or loss is recognized currently.

2. If the change is not accounted for as an extinguishment of debt:

   a. Lessee accounting. The lessee accrues any costs in connection with the debt refunding that are obligated to be reimbursed to the lessor. These costs are amortized by the interest method over the period from the date of refunding to the call date of the debt to be refunded.
   b. Lessor accounting. The lessor recognizes as revenue any reimbursements to be received from the lessee, for costs paid in relation to the debt refunding. This revenue is recognized in a systematic manner over the period from the date of refunding to the call date of the debt to be refunded.

Sale or assignment to third parties; nonrecourse financing. The sale or assignment of a lease or of property subject to a lease that was originally accounted for as a sales-type lease or a direct financing lease will not affect the original accounting treatment of the lease. Any profit or loss on the sale or assignment is recognized at the time of the transaction, except under the following two circumstances:

1. When the sale or assignment is between related parties, apply substance versus form provisions presented above under "leases between related parties."
2. When the sale or assignment is with recourse, it is accounted for using the provisions of ASC 860.

The sale of property subject to an operating lease is not treated as a sale if the seller (or any related party to the seller) retains "substantial risks of ownership" in the leased property. A seller may retain "substantial risks of ownership" by various arrangements. For example, if the lessee defaults upon the lease agreement or if the lease terminates, the seller may arrange to do one of the following:

1. Acquire the property or the lease
2. Substitute an existing lease
3. Secure a replacement lessee or a buyer for the property under a remarketing agreement.

A seller does not retain substantial risks of ownership by arrangements where one of the following occurs:

1. A remarketing agreement includes a reasonable fee to be paid to the seller.
2. The seller is not required to give priority to the releasing or disposition of the property owned by the third party over similar property owned by the seller.

When the sale of property subject to an operating lease is not accounted for as a sale because the substantial risk factor is present, it is accounted for as a borrowing. The proceeds are recorded by the seller as an obligation. Rental payments made by the lessee under the operating lease are recorded as revenue by the seller even if the payments are paid to the third-party purchaser. The seller accounts for each rental payment by allocating a portion to interest expense (to be imputed in accordance with the provisions of ASC 835-30), and the remainder to reduce the existing obligation. Other normal accounting procedures for operating leases are applied except that the depreciation term for the leased asset is limited to the amortization period of the obligation.

The sale or assignment of lease payments under an operating lease by the lessor are accounted for as a borrowing as described above.

Nonrecourse financing is a common occurrence in the leasing industry, whereby the stream of lease payments on a lease is discounted on a nonrecourse basis at a financial institution with the lease payments collateralizing the debt. The proceeds are then used to finance future leasing transactions. Even though the discounting is on a nonrecourse basis, the offsetting of the debt against the related lease receivable is prohibited unless a legal right of offset exists or the lease qualified as a leveraged lease at its inception.

Money-over-money lease transactions. A money-over-money lease transaction occurs when an enterprise manufactures or purchases an asset, leases the asset to a lessee and obtains nonrecourse financing in excess of the asset's cost using the leased asset and the future lease rentals as collateral. ASC 840-30-55 prescribes that this series of transactions should be accounted for as follows:

1. Record the purchase or manufacture of the asset,
2. Record the lease as an operating, direct financing, or sales-type lease as appropriate,
3. Record nonrecourse debt.

The only income that is recognizable by the reporting entity in this transaction would be any manufacturer's or dealer's profit that arises if the lease is classified as a sales-type lease. With respect to the presentation in the statement of financial position, offsetting of any assets recorded as a result of the transaction with the nonrecourse debt is not permitted unless a right of setoff exists.

Wrap-lease transactions. A wrap-lease transaction (see diagram) occurs when a reporting enterprise

1. Purchases an asset,
2. Leases the asset to a lessee,
3. Obtains nonrecourse financing using the lease rentals and/or the asset as collateral,
4. Sells the asset to an investor, subject to the lease and the nonrecourse debt, and
5. Leases the asset back while remaining the substantive principal lessor under the original lease.

If the asset is real estate, the specialized rules with respect to sale-leaseback of real estate set forth in ASC 840-40 apply (see example of accounting for a sale-leaseback transaction in this chapter).

If the asset is personal property, the accounting would be as follows:

1. The asset is removed from the accounting records of the original reporting entity
2. The leaseback is classified in accordance with the normal criteria for the classification of leases
3. Gain on the transaction is recognized or deferred/amortized following the criteria in ASC 840-40-25
4. The reporting entity reflects the following items on its statement of financial position:

    a. Any retained interest in the residual value of the leased asset
    b. Gross sublease receivable
    c. Note receivable from the investor

d. Nonrecourse third-party debt
e. Leaseback obligation
f. Deferred revenue related to any future remarketing rights for which the remarketing services had not yet been performed.

The sublease asset and related nonrecourse debt are not permitted to be offset on the statement of financial position unless a right of setoff exists.

Wrap-Lease Transaction

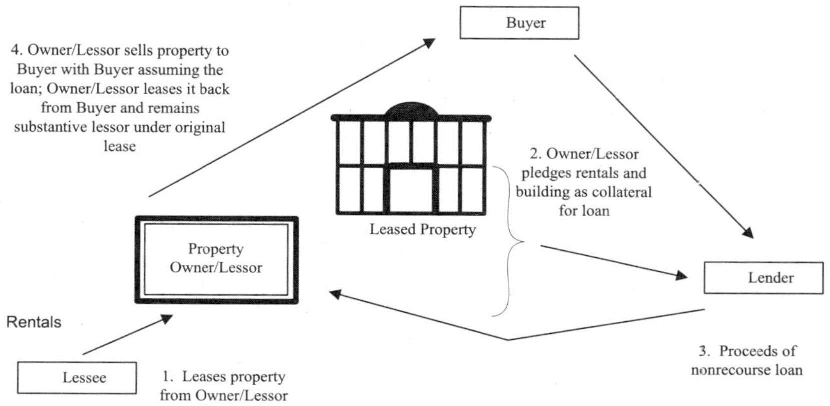

Cash Flows

Lessee pays rentals to Lessor.
Lessor pays rentals to Buyer.
Buyer pays loan principal and interest to Lender.

Transfers of residual value (ASC 860). Acquisitions of interests in residual values of leased assets may be effected by companies whose primary business is other than leasing or financing. This generally occurs through the outright purchase of the right to own the leased asset or the right to receive the proceeds from the sale of a leased asset at the end of its lease term.

In instances such as these, the rights are recorded by the purchaser at the fair value of the assets surrendered net of the present value of any liabilities assumed, unless the fair value of the residual is more objectively determinable. Increases in the estimated value of the interest in the residual (i.e., residual value accretion) to the end of the lease term are permitted to be recognized only for *guaranteed* residual values because they are financial assets. However, recognition of such increases is prohibited for *unguaranteed* residual values. A nontemporary write-down of a residual value interest (guaranteed/unguaranteed) is recognized as a loss and is not permitted to be subsequently restored. This guidance also applies to lessors who sell the related minimum lease payments but retain the interest in the residual value irrespective of whether the residual is guaranteed.

Example of the transfer of residual value

Longbottom Lease Brokers obtains an interest in the residual value of a cable placer truck as a fee for its assistance in leasing the truck to a third party. The fair value of Longbottom's interest in the residual value of the truck is estimated by an appraiser to be $47,000. Since the fair value of

Longbottom's interest in the residual value is the most clearly evident valuation, Longbottom uses it as the basis for the following entry:

Interest in asset residual value	47,000	
Revenue—leasing services rendered		47,000

In another transaction, Longbottom pays $32,000 for the residual value of an aerial truck. Longbottom records the transaction as follows:

Interest in asset residual value	32,000	
Cash		32,000

After six months, Longbottom appraises its interest in the residual value of both trucks, and finds that the value of the cable placer has declined from $47,000 to $41,000, while the residual value of the aerial truck has increased from $32,000 to $35,000. Longbottom uses the following entry to record the reduction of value in its cable placer truck:

Loss on interest in asset residual value	6,000	
Interest in asset residual value		6,000

Longbottom records no entry for the $3,000 increase in value of its aerial truck.

Leases involving government units. Leases that involve government units (i.e., airport facilities, bus terminal space, etc.) usually contain special provisions that prevent the agreements from being classified as anything but operating leases. These special provisions, referred to as fiscal funding clauses, include the governmental body's authority to abandon a facility at any time during the lease term, thus making its economic life indeterminable. These leases also do not contain a BPO or transfer ownership. The fair value is generally indeterminable because neither the leased property nor similar property is available for sale.

However, leases involving government units are subject to the same classification criteria as nongovernment units, except when all of the following six criteria are met:

NOTE: If all six conditions are met, the agreement is classified as an operating lease by both lessee and lessor.

---

1. A government unit or authority owns the leased property.
2. The leased property is part of a larger facility operated by or on behalf of the lessor.
3. The leased property is a permanent structure or part of a permanent structure that normally cannot be moved to another location.
4. The lessor, or a higher governmental authority, has the right to terminate the lease at any time under the lease agreement or existing statutes or regulations.
5. The lease neither transfers ownership nor allows the lessee to purchase or acquire the leased property.
6. The leased property or similar property in the same area cannot be purchased or leased from anyone else.

If any one of the six conditions that qualify the lease for automatic operating lease treatment is not met, then the lease is evaluated to determine the likelihood of future cancellation. Using the loss contingency criteria from ASC 450, if it is remote (i.e., the chances are slight) that the lease will be canceled, then the lease agreement qualifies as a noncancelable lease and is classified the same as any other such lease with a nongovernmental lessee. Otherwise, the lease is considered to be cancelable and accounted for as an operating lease (ASC 840-10-25).

Maintenance deposits by lessees. In some lease arrangements, the lessee may be required to make a deposit associated with the lessee's responsibility for the maintenance of the leased asset. Under a typical arrangement of this sort, the deposit is calculated based on a performance measure, such as hours of use of the leased asset, and is contractually required under the lease to be used to reimburse the lessee for required maintenance of the leased asset upon the completion of that maintenance. The lessor is thus contractually required to reimburse the lessee for the maintenance costs paid by the lessee, to the extent of the amounts on deposit. If the cumulative maintenance costs are less than the amount deposited, the excess may or may not be required to be returned to the lessee.

ASC 840-10-25 and ASC 840-10-35 address this issue. Maintenance deposits paid by a lessee under an arrangement accounted for as a lease that are refunded only if the lessee performs specified maintenance activities are to be accounted for as a deposit asset. Lessees must continue to evaluate whether it is *probable* that an amount on deposit will be returned to reimburse the costs of the maintenance activities incurred by the lessee. When an amount on deposit is less than probable of being returned, it is to be recognized as additional expense. When the underlying maintenance is performed, the maintenance cost is to be expensed or capitalized in accordance with the lessee's existing maintenance accounting policy.

Entities are to recognize the effect of the change as a change in accounting principle as of the beginning of the fiscal year in which this requirement is initially applied for all arrangements existing at the effective date. The cumulative effect of the change in accounting principle is to be recognized as an adjustment to the opening balance of retained earnings (or other appropriate components of equity or net assets in the statement of financial position) for that fiscal year, presented separately. The cumulative effect adjustment is the difference between the amounts recognized in the statement of financial position before initial application of this requirement and the amounts recognized in the statement of financial position at its initial application.

Leasehold improvements. Leasehold improvements result when tangible physical enhancements are made to property by or on behalf of the lessee of real estate. By law, when improvements are made to real property and those improvements are permanently affixed to the property, the title to those improvements automatically transfers to the owner of the property. The rationale behind this is that the improvements, when permanently affixed, are inseparable from the rest of the real estate.

As a result of this automatic title transfer, the lessee's interest in the improvements is not a direct ownership interest but rather it is an intangible right to use and benefit from the improvements during the term of the lease. Consequently, the capitalized costs incurred by a lessee in constructing improvements to property that it leases represent an intangible asset analogous to a license to use them. Thus, when allocating the costs of leasehold improvements to the periods benefited, the expense is referred to as amortization (as used in the context of amortization of intangibles) and not depreciation.

A frequently encountered issue with respect to leasehold improvements relates to determination of the period over which they are to be amortized. Normally, the cost of long-lived assets is charged to expense over the estimated useful lives of the assets. However, the right to use a leasehold improvement expires when the related lease expires, irrespective of whether the improvement has any remaining useful life. Thus, the appropriate useful life for a leasehold improvement is the lesser of the useful life of the improvement or the term of the underlying lease. ASC 840-10-35-9 reinforces this concept by requiring that leasehold improvements acquired in a business combination or leasehold improvements completed well after commencement of a lease agreement be amortized over the lesser of the useful life of the leasehold improvement or a time period that includes required lease periods as well as reasonably assured lease renewal periods.

Some leases contain a fixed, noncancelable term and additional renewal options. When considering the term of the lease for the purposes of amortizing leasehold improvements, normally only the initial fixed noncancelable term is included. There are exceptions to this general rule that arise out of the application of GAAP to the lessee's accounting for the lease. If a renewal option is a bargain renewal option, then it is probable at the inception of the lease that it will be exercised and, therefore, the option period is included in the lease term for purposes of determining the amortizable life of the leasehold improvements. Additionally, under the definition of the lease term there are other situations where it is probable that an option to renew for an additional period would be exercised. These situations include periods for which failure to renew the lease imposes a penalty on the lessee in such amount that a renewal appears, at the inception of the lease, to be reasonably assured. Other situations of this kind arise when an otherwise excludable renewal period precedes a provision for a bargain purchase of the leased asset or when, during periods covered by ordinary renewal options, the lessee has guaranteed the lessor's debt on the leased property.

In deciding whether to include the period covered by a renewal option in the calculation of the amortizable life of the leasehold improvements, management of the lessee must be consistent with its own interpretation of renewal options that it included in the minimum lease payment calculations made to determine whether the lease is a capital or operating lease.

Example

Marcie Corporation occupies a warehouse under a five-year operating lease commencing January 1, 20X1, and expiring December 31, 20X5. The lease contains three successive options to renew the lease for additional five-year periods. The options are not bargain renewals, as they call for fixed rentals at the prevailing fair market rents that will be in effect at the time of exercise. When the initial calculation was made to determine whether the lease is an operating lease or a capital lease, only the initial noncancelable term of five years was included in the calculation. Consequently, for the purpose of determining the amortizable life of any leasehold improvements made by Marcie Corporation, only the initial five-year term is used. If Marcie Corporation decides, at the beginning of year four of the lease, to make a substantial amount of leasehold improvements to the leased property, it could be argued that it would now be probable that Marcie would exercise one or more of the renewal periods, since not doing so would impose the substantial financial penalty of abandoning expensive leasehold improvements. This would trigger accounting for the lease as if it were a new agreement and would require testing to determine whether the lease, prospectively, qualifies as a capital or operating lease.

The SEC has provided the following guidance on the proper accounting treatment by a lessee for incentives or allowances provided by a lessor to a lessee under an operating lease.[6]

1. The incentives are not permitted to be netted against the leasehold improvements they were intended to subsidize. Instead, they are to be recorded as deferred rent and amortized as reductions to lease expense over the lease term.
2. The leasehold improvements are to be recorded gross, at their cost, and amortized as discussed above.
3. The lessee's cash flow statement is to reflect the cash received from the lessor as an incentive or allowance as cash provided by operating activities and the acquisition of the leasehold improvements as cash used for investing activities.

---

[6] *Letter from SEC Chief Accountant to the chairman of the American Institute of Certified Public Accountants (AICPA) Center for Public Company Audit Firms (CPCAF) dated February 7, 2005; www.sec.gov/info/accountants/staffletters/cpcaf020705.htm.*

Note that this guidance is a reasonable interpretation of GAAP as it applies to all entities, not just those subject to the jurisdiction of the SEC.

Statement of financial position classification. The balance of the lease payments receivable (lessor) and the lease obligation (lessee) must be allocated between their current and noncurrent portions. First, the current portion is computed at the date of the financial statements as the present value of the lease payments (or receipts) to be paid (received) within twelve months of the date of the statement of financial position. The noncurrent portion is computed as the difference between the current portion and the balance of the lease obligation at the end of the period. The conceptual justification for this treatment is the fact that the total lease obligation is equal to the present value of the future minimum lease payments. Therefore, it follows that the current portion is the present value of the lease payments due within one year while the noncurrent portion is the present value of all other remaining lease payments.

Summary of Accounting for Selected Items (see following page)

TREATMENT OF SELECTED ITEMS IN ACCOUNTING FOR LEASES

	Lessor		Lessee	
	Operating	*Direct financing and sales-type*	*Operating*	*Capital*
Initial direct costs	Capitalize and amortize over lease term recognized proportion to rent revenue in (normally SL basis)	Direct financing: Record in separate account Add to net investment in lease Compute new effective rate that equates gross amt. of min. lease payments and unguar. residual value with net invest. Amortize so as to produce constant rate of return over lease term Sales-type: Expense in period incurred as part of cost of sales	N/A	N/A
Investment tax credit retained by lessor	N/A	Reduces FV of leased asset for 90% test	N/A	Reduces FV of leased asset for 90% test
Bargain purchase option	N/A	Include in: Minimum lease payments 90% test	N/A	Include in: Minimum lease payments 90% test
Guaranteed residual value	N/A	Include in: Minimum lease payments 90% test Sales-type: Include PV in sales revenues	N/A	Include in: Minimum lease payments 90% test
Unguaranteed residual value	N/A	Include in: "Gross investment in lease" Not included in: 90% test Sales-type: Exclude from sales revenue Deduct PV from cost of sales	N/A	N/A
Contingent rentals	Revenue in period earned	Not part of minimum lease payments; revenue in period earned	Expense in period incurred	Not part of minimum lease payments; expense in period incurred
Amortization period	Amortize down to estimated residual value over estimated economic life of asset	N/A	N/A	Amortize down to estimated residual value over lease term or estimated economic life[b]
Revenue (expense)[a]	Rent revenue (normally SL basis) Amortization (depreciation expense)	Direct financing: Interest revenue on net investment in lease (gross investment less unearned interest income) Sales-type: Dealer profit in period of sale (sales revenue less cost of leased asset) Interest revenue on net investment in lease	Rent expense (normally SL basis)[c]	Interest expense and amortization (depreciation) expense

a *Elements of revenue (expense) listed for the above items are not repeated here (e.g., treatment of initial direct costs).*
b *If lease has automatic passage of title or bargain purchase option, use estimated economic life; otherwise, use the lease term.*
c *If payments are not on a SL basis, recognize rent expense on a SL basis unless another systematic and rational method is more representative of use or benefit obtained from the property, in which case, the other method should be used.*

54 ASC 845 NONMONETARY TRANSACTIONS

PERSPECTIVE AND ISSUES

Subtopics

ASC 845, *Nonmonetary Transactions,* has only one subtopic:

- ASC 845-10, *Overall,* which includes five Subsections:
  - General
  - Purchases and sales of inventory with the same counterparty
  - Barter transactions
  - Exchanges involving monetary consideration
  - Exchanges of a nonfinancial asset for a noncontrolling ownership interest.

Scope and Scope Exceptions

Several variants of noncash transactions are governed by ASC 845. ASC 845-10-15-4 lists scope exceptions. The following types of transactions are *not* treated as nonmonetary transactions:

1. A business combination accounted for by an entity according to the provisions of ASC 805 or a combination accounted for by a not-for-profit entity according to the provisions of ASC 958-805

2. A transfer of nonmonetary assets solely between entities or persons under common control, such as between a parent and its subsidiaries or between two subsidiaries of the same parent, or between a corporate joint venture and its owners
3. Acquisition of nonmonetary assets or services on issuance of the capital stock of an entity under ASC 718-10 and ASC 505-50
4. Stock issued or received in stock dividends and stock
5. A transfer of assets to an entity in exchange for equity interest in that entity (except for certain exchanges of a nonfinancial asset for a noncontrolling ownership interest)
6. A pooling of assets in a joint undertaking intended to find, develop, or produce oil or gas from a particular property or group of properties
7. The exchange of a part of an operating interest owned for a part of an operating interest owned by another party that is subject to ASC 932-360-55-6
8. The transfer of a financial asset within the scope of ASC 860-10-15
9. Involuntary conversions specified in ASC 605-40-15-2.

(ASC 845-10-15-4)

Overview

ASC 845, *Nonmonetary Transactions*, addresses those transactions in which no money changes hands. These transactions are most commonly associated with exchanges of fixed assets, but can also involve other items, such as inventory, liabilities, and ownership interests. They can also involve one-way, or nonreciprocal, transfers.

This chapter sets forth the basic structure and concepts of nonmonetary transactions, including the concept of commercial substance, rules regarding similar and dissimilar exchanges, involuntary conversions, and how to handle exchanges that include a certain amount of monetary consideration.

DEFINITIONS OF TERMS

Source: ASC 845-10-20

Exchange. A reciprocal transfer between two entities, resulting in one entity acquiring assets or services or satisfying liabilities by surrendering other assets or services or incurring other obligations.

Monetary Assets and Liabilities. Monetary assets and liabilities are assets and liabilities whose amounts are fixed in terms of units of currency by contract or otherwise. Examples are cash, short- or long-term accounts and notes receivable in cash, and short- or long-term accounts and notes payable in cash.

Nonmonetary assets and liabilities. Assets and liabilities other than monetary ones. Examples are inventories: investments in common stocks: property, plant, and equipment: and liabilities for rent collected in advance.

Nonreciprocal transfer. A transfer of assets or services in one direction from an entity to its owners (whether or not in exchange for their ownership interests) or another entity, or from its owners or another entity to the entity. An entity's reacquisition of its outstanding stock is an example of a nonreciprocal transfer.

Owners. Used broadly to include holders of ownership (equity interests) of investor-owned entities, mutual entities, or not-for-profit entities. Owners include shareholders, partners, proprietors, or members or participants of mutual entities. Owners also include owner and member interests in the net assets of not-for-profit entities.

Productive Assets. Productive assets are assets held for or used in the production of goods or services by the entity. Productive assets include an investment in another entity if the investment is accounted for by the equity method but exclude an investment not accounted for by that method. Similar productive assets are productive assets that are of the same general type, that perform the same function, or that are employed in the same line of business.

CONCEPTS, RULES, AND EXAMPLES

Types of Nonmonetary Transactions

There are three types of nonmonetary transactions identified in ASC 845:

1. *Nonreciprocal transfers with owners*—Examples include dividends-in-kind, nonmonetary assets exchanged for common stock, split-ups, and spin-offs.
2. *Nonreciprocal transfers with nonowners*—Examples include charitable donations of property either made or received by the reporting entity, and contributions of land by a state or local government to a private enterprise for the purpose of construction of a specified structure.
3. *Nonmonetary exchanges*—Examples include exchanges of inventory for productive assets, exchanges of inventory for similar products, and exchanges of productive assets.

(ASC 845-10-05-3)

General Rule

The primary accounting issue in nonmonetary transactions is the determination of the amount to assign to the nonmonetary assets or services transferred to or from the reporting entity.

The general rule is to value the transaction at the fair value of the asset *given up*, unless the fair value of the asset *received* is more clearly evident, and to recognize gain or loss on the difference between the fair value and carrying value of the asset. ASC 820 provides the guidance for fair value and provides that when one of the parties to a nonmonetary transaction could have elected to receive cash in lieu of the nonmonetary asset, the amount of cash that would have been received may be the best evidence of the fair value of the nonmonetary assets exchanged. The fair value of the asset surrendered should be used to value the exchange unless the fair value of the asset received is more clearly evident of the fair value.

Modification of the Basic Principle

ASC 845-10-30-3 requires states that under certain circumstances a nonmonetary exchange should be measured based on the recorded amount (after reduction, if appropriate, for an indicated impairment of value) of the nonmonetary asset relinquished, and not on the fair values of the exchanged asset, if any of the following conditions apply:

1. The fair value of neither the asset received nor the asset relinquished is determinable within reasonable limits.
2. The transaction is an exchange of a product or property held for sale in the ordinary course of business for a product of property to be sold in the same line of business to facilitate sales to customers other than the parties to the exchange.
3. The transaction lacks commercial substance.

NOTE. ASC 845 states that a transfer of a nonmonetary asset will not qualify as an exchange if the transferor has substantial continuing involvement in the transferred assets that result in the transferee not obtaining the usual risks and rewards associated with ownership of the transferred assets.

Commercial Substance

As explained in ASC 845-10-30-4, a nonmonetary exchange is subjected to a test to determine whether or not it has "commercial substance." An exchange has commercial substance if cash flows change as a result of the exchange. If determined to have commercial substance, the exchange is recorded at the fair value of the transferred asset. If the transaction is determined not to have commercial substance, the exchange is recognized using the recorded amount of the exchanged asset or assets, reduced for any applicable impairment of value.

To determine commercial substance, management estimates whether, after the exchange, the reporting entity will experience changes in its expected cash flows:

1. Because of changes in amounts, timing, and/or risks (these factors are collectively referred to as the "configuration" of the expected future cash flows), *or*
2. Because the entity-specific value of the assets received differs from the entity-specific value of the assets transferred.

If the changes in either of these criteria are significant relative to the fair values of the assets exchanged, the transaction is considered to have commercial substance. *Entity-specific value* is a concept defined in CON 7 that substitutes assumptions that an entity makes with respect to its own future cash flows for the corresponding assumptions that marketplace participants would make with respect to cash flows. The commercial substance criterion is *not* met if a transaction is structured to achieve income tax benefits or in order to achieve a specific outcome for financial reporting purposes.

Recognition of gains or losses. Entities should recognize losses incurred on all exchanges whether or not they have commercial substance. This is so that assets are not overstated. If an exchange has commercial substance, any gain should be recognized immediately. If an exchange has no commercial substance, the entity recognizes the gain through lower depreciation expense or when it sells the asset. However, if cash or "boot" is received, the entity may recognize a portion of the gain even if there is no commercial substance.

Nonreciprocal Transfers

The valuation of most nonreciprocal transfers is based upon the fair value of the nonmonetary asset (or service) given up, unless the fair value of the nonmonetary asset received is more clearly evident. This will result in recognition of gain or loss on the difference between the fair value assigned to the transaction and the carrying value of the asset surrendered.

The valuation of nonmonetary assets distributed to owners of the reporting entity in a spin-off or other form of reorganization or liquidation is based on the recorded amounts, again after first recognizing any warranted reduction for impairment. Other nonreciprocal transfers to owners are accounted for at fair value if (1) the fair value of the assets distributed is objectively measurable, and (2) that fair value would be clearly realized by the distributing reporting entity in an outright sale at or near the time of distribution to the owners. (ASC 845-10-30-10)

Example of accounting for a nonreciprocal transfer with a nonowner

1. Jacobs Corporation donated depreciable property with a book value of $10,000 (cost of $25,000 less accumulated depreciation of $15,000) to a charity during the current year.
2. The property had a fair value of $17,000 at the date of the transfer.

The transaction is valued at the fair value of the property transferred, and any gain or loss on the transaction is recognized on the date of the transfer. Thus, Jacobs recognizes a gain of $7,000 ($17,000 – $10,000) in the determination of the current period's net income. The entry to record the transaction would be as follows:

Charitable donations	17,000	
Accumulated depreciation	15,000	
Property		25,000
Gain on donation of property		7,000

Note that the gain on disposition of the donated property is reported as operating income in accordance with ASC 420 and is not to be presented in the "other income" section of the income statement.

Example of an exchange involving no boot

Company presidents Able and Baker agree to swap copiers, since each needs certain printing features only available on the other company's copier. Able's copier has a book value of $18,000 (cost of $24,000 less depreciation of $6,000). Both copiers have a fair value of $24,000. In testing for the commercial substance of the transaction, there is no difference in the fair values of the assets exchanged, nor are Able's future cash flows expected to significantly change as a result of the transfer. Under ASC 845, exchanges of assets that do not alter expected future cash flows are deemed to lack commercial substance, and are accounted for at book value. As a result of the trade, Able has the following *unrecognized* gain:

Fair value of Able copier given to Baker	$24,000
Book value of Able copier given to Baker	18,000
Total gain (unrecognized)	$ 6,000

The entry by Able to record this transaction is as follows:

Fixed assets—Office equipment; Copier received from Baker	18,000	
Accumulated depreciation—Office equipment; Copier given	6,000	
Fixed assets—Office equipment; Copier given		24,000

Able elects to depreciate its newly acquired copier over four years with an assumed salvage value of zero, which computes to monthly depreciation of $375. If Able had recorded the fair value of the incoming copier at $24,000, this would have required a higher monthly depreciation rate of $500. Thus, the unrecognized gain on the transaction is actually being recognized each month through reduced depreciation charges.

Able immediately exchanges its newly acquired copier for one owned by Charlie. However, the fair value of the copier owned by Charlie is $30,000, as compared to the $24,000 fair value of Able's copier (which is being carried at $18,000, the carryforward basis of its predecessor). In testing for the commercial substance of the transaction, there is determined to be a significant difference in the entity-specific values of the assets exchanged, so in accordance with the provisions of ASC 845 Able must record a gain on the transaction based on the difference in the fair values of the exchanged assets. This is done with the following entry:

Fixed assets—Office equipment; Copier received from Charlie	30,000	
Fixed assets—Office equipment; Copier received from Baker		18,000
Gain on disposal of office equipment		12,000

Note that the full gain from both exchanges is now being recognized, since the carryforward book value of the original copier was used as the book value of the first-acquired trade, and that carryforward amount is now being compared to the fair value of the latest trade.

Able elects to depreciate the newly acquired copier over four years with no salvage value, resulting in monthly depreciation of $625.

After ten months, Able trades his newly acquired copier to Echo. The book value has now dropped to $23,750 (cost of $30,000 less depreciation of $6,250); however, due to technology advances, its fair value has declined to $20,000. This final trade has no commercial substance, in the ASC 845-defined sense, since cash flows will not materially vary between the use of these two machines. Thus, in general, under ASC 845, fair value accounting would not be employed in an exchange of similar assets lacking commercial substance; Able is required to recognize an impairment loss under ASC 360-10-40-4 if the fair value of the asset being disposed of is less than its carrying amount. Were this not done, the new asset would be recognized at an amount in excess of its realizable amount (fair value). Able has incurred the following impairment loss resulting from the transaction, which must be fully recognized in the current period:

Fair value of Able copier given to Echo	$ 20,000
Book value of Able copier given to Echo	(23,750)
Total impairment loss (recognized)	$ (3,750)

The entry by Able to record this transaction is as follows:

Fixed assets—Office equipment; Copier received from Echo	20,000	
Accumulated depreciation—Office equipment; Copier received from Charlie	6,250	
Impairment loss on asset disposed of	3,750	
Fixed assets—Office equipment; Copier received from Charlie		30,000

Nonmonetary Exchanges That Include Monetary Consideration (Boot)

A single exception to the nonrecognition rule for an exchange without commercial substance occurs when the exchange involves both a monetary and nonmonetary asset being exchanged for a nonmonetary asset. The monetary portion of the exchange is termed *boot.* When boot is at least 25% of the fair value of the exchange, the exchange is considered a monetary transaction and both parties record the exchange at fair value. When boot less than 25% is received in an exchange, only the boot portion of the earnings process is considered to have culminated. The portion of the gain applicable to the boot is considered realized and is recognized in the determination of net income in the period of the exchange.

The formula for the recognition of the gain in an exchange involving boot of less than 25% of fair value is expressed as follows:

$$\frac{\text{Boot}}{\text{Boot + Fair value of nonmonetary asset received}} \times \text{Total gain indicated} = \text{Gain recognized}$$

Example of an exchange involving no commercial substance and boot

Amanda Excavating exchanges one of its underutilized front loaders with Dorothy Diggers, another excavator, for a bulldozer.

These assets are carried on the respective companies' statements of financial position as follows:

	Amanda (front loader)	*Dorothy (bulldozer)*
Cost	$75,000	$90,000
Accumulated depreciation	7,500	15,000
Net book value	$67,500	$75,000
Fair (appraised) value	$60,000	$78,000

The terms of the exchange require Amanda to pay Dorothy $18,000 cash (boot). Boot represents approximately 23% of the fair value of the exchange computed as follows:

	Amount	*Percent of total*
Fair value of front loader	$60,000	77%
Cash consideration (boot)	18,000	23%
Total consideration	$78,000	100%

Note that as the payer of boot, Amanda does not recognize a gain. As a receiver of boot that is less than 25% of the fair value of the consideration received, Dorothy recognizes a pro rata gain that is computed as follows:

Total gain = $78,000 consideration – $75,000 net book value of bulldozer = $3,000

Portion of gain to be recognized by Dorothy

$$\frac{\$18{,}000\text{ boot}}{\$18{,}000\text{ boot} + \$60{,}000\text{ fair value of nonmonetary asset received} = \$78{,}000} = 23\% \times \$3{,}000\text{ gain} = \$690\text{ gain recognized}$$

The accounting entries to record this transaction by Amanda and Dorothy are as follows:

	Amanda		*Dorothy*	
	Debit	*Credit*	*Debit*	*Credit*
Excavating equipment	10,500			32,310
Accum. depreciation—excavating equipment	7,500		15,000	
Cash		$18,000	18,000	
Recognized gain	--	--	--	690
	18,000	$18,000	33,000	33,000

Amanda records the increase in the carrying value of its excavating equipment to account for the difference between the $78,000 fair value of the bulldozer received and the $67,500 carrying value of the front loader exchanged. The accumulated depreciation on the front loader is reversed since, from the standpoint of Amanda, it has no accumulated depreciation on the bulldozer at the date of the exchange.

Dorothy records the cash received, removes the previously recorded accumulated depreciation on the bulldozer, records the $690 gain attributable to the boot as computed above and records the difference as an adjustment to the carrying value of its excavating equipment.

After recording the entries above, the carrying values of the exchanged equipment would be as follows:

	Amanda (bulldozer)	*Dorothy (front loader)*
Net book value exchanged	$67,500	$ 75,000
Cash paid (received)	18,000	(18,000)
Gain recognized		$ 690
Carrying value of asset received	$85,500	$ 57,690

To summarize, if boot is 25% or more of the fair value of an exchange, the transaction is considered a monetary transaction. In that case, both parties record the transaction at fair value. If the boot is less than 25%, the payer of the boot does not recognize a gain and the receiver of the boot must follow the pro rata recognition guidance in ASC 845-10-30-6. See the following section for rules regarding exchanges with boot involving real estate.

Gain on a *monetary* exchange that involves transfer by one entity of its ownership of a controlled asset, group of assets, or business to another entity in exchange for a noncontrolling ownership interest in the other entity is accounted for consistent with the guidance above for similar *nonmonetary* exchanges.

Exchanges of Real Estate Involving Monetary Consideration (Boot)

A transaction that involves the exchange of similar real estate and boot of 25% or more of the fair value of the exchange is recorded with two separate components, a monetary component and a nonmonetary component. The allocation is made based on the relative fair values of the monetary and nonmonetary portions at the time of the transaction. The party that receives the boot accounts for the monetary component of the transaction under ASC 360-20 as the equivalent of a sale of an interest in the underlying real estate and the nonmonetary component of the transaction based on the recorded amount (reduced, if applicable, for any impairment in value) of the nonmonetary asset relinquished. For the party that pays the boot, the monetary component is accounted for as an acquisition of real estate, and the nonmonetary component is accounted for based on the recorded amount (reduced, if applicable, for any impairment in value).

Inventory Purchases and Sales with the Same Counterparty

Some enterprises sell inventory to another party from whom they also acquire inventory in the same line of business. These transactions may be part of a single or separate arrangements and the inventory purchased or sold may be raw materials, work-in-process, or finished goods. These arrangements require careful analysis to determine if they are to be accounted for as a single exchange transaction under ASC 845, *Nonmonetary Transactions,* and whether they are to be recognized at fair value or at the carrying value of the inventory transferred.[1]

Determining whether transactions constitute a single exchange. ASC 845-10-15-6 states that inventory purchases and sales with the same counterparty are to be treated as a single transaction when

1. An inventory transaction is legally contingent upon the occurrence of another inventory transaction with the same counterparty, *or*
2. Two or more inventory purchase and sale transactions involving the same counterparties are entered into in contemplation of one another and are combined.

In determining whether transactions were entered into in contemplation of one another, FASB provides the following indicators, which are neither all-inclusive nor determinative (ASC 845-10-25-4):

1. The counterparties have a specific legal right of offset of their respective obligations.
2. The transactions are entered into simultaneously.
3. The terms of the transactions were "off-market" when the arrangement was agreed to by the parties.
4. The relative certainty that reciprocal inventory transactions will occur between the counterparties.

Measurement of the exchange. When management has determined that multiple transactions between the same counterparties within the same line of business are to be treated as a single exchange transaction, the measurement of the transaction depends on the type of inventory items exchanged. The rules are summarized in the following table.

---

[1] *This guidance does not apply to arrangements accounted for as derivatives under ASC 815, or to exchanges of software or real estate.*

Type of inventory transferred to counterparty	*Type of inventory received from counterparty*	*Accounting treatment*
Finished goods	Raw materials or work-in-process	Recognize the transaction at fair value if fair value is determinable within reasonable limits, and transaction has commercial substance per (ASC 845-10-30-4); otherwise, recognize at the carrying value of the inventory transferred
	Finished goods*	Recognize the transaction at the carrying value of the inventory transferred
Raw materials	Raw materials, work-in-process or finished goods	
Work-in-process		

* *NOTE: A transfer of finished goods in exchange for other finished goods is subject to ASC 845-10-30-3(b), which prescribes that when an exchange transaction involving products or property to be sold in the same line of business is made to facilitate sales to customers that are not parties to the exchange, the transaction is measured at the recorded amount of the assets relinquished, reduced for any indicated impairment of value.*

Example of counterparty inventory transfers

Shapiro Optics Corporation (SOC) manufactures lenses for cameras, binoculars, and telescopes.

Farber Products, Inc. (FPI) is a manufacturer of digital cameras. FPI internally manufactures many of the individual parts used in its cameras including all of the electronic circuitry, and the viewfinders. FPI does not have the expertise or capacity to design and manufacture lenses or camera housings, which it accordingly purchases from external suppliers.

SOC has been a long-time supplier of lenses to FPI and due to their strong business relationship, SOC wishes to purchase electronic components from FPI similar to those that FPI uses in its camera circuit boards. SOC plans to use those components as raw materials in a popular line of telescopes it manufactures. The parties negotiate and execute an agreement with the following terms:

1. FPI agrees to purchase a specified number of lenses from SOC over a two-year period.
2. At least weekly, at its discretion, FPI can settle its payable to SOC by either paying the obligation in cash, or by shipping electronic components to SOC of equivalent value.
3. SOC is obligated to accept the components in lieu of cash, should FPI choose to settle the outstanding balance in that manner.

Historically, based on its manufacturing capacity and its cash management policies, FPI has settled these transactions by shipping components and SOC has accepted those components and used them in manufacturing its telescopes. Upon delivery of its lenses to FPI, SOC reasonably expects that it will receive electronic components from FPI in return.

These transfers are to be treated as a single, nonmonetary transaction, since:

1. The agreement that governs both the purchase transactions and their settlement is evidence that they were entered into simultaneously.
2. There is a strong likelihood that each time FPI purchases lenses it will also ship components in a reciprocal inventory transaction.
3. By accepting settlement of its receivable from FPI in components rather than in cash, SOC is, in effect, allowing the offset of its receivable from FPI with its payable to FPI for its purchase of components.

From the perspective of SOC, it is relinquishing its lenses, which are accounted for in its financial statements as finished goods inventory, and exchanging the lenses for electronic components, which are accounted for as raw materials used in the production of its telescopes. Assuming the transaction passes the commercial substance test (ASC 840-10-30-4), SOC will account for the nonmonetary exchange at fair value.

Exchange of Product or Property Held for Sale for Productive Assets

An exchange of goods held for sale in the ordinary course of business for property and equipment to be used in the production process, even if they pertain to the same line of business, is recorded at fair value.

Exchanges Involving Assets That Constitute a Business

The GAAP rules for recognizing exchanges or purchases of productive assets differ materially from those that apply to acquisitions of businesses (e.g., goodwill would only be recognized in connection with the latter class of transaction, and under ASC 845 certain nonmonetary exchanges are recorded at book value).

The ASC Master Glossary defines a business as a self-sustaining integrated set of activities and assets conducted and managed for the purpose of providing a return to investors. A business consists of

(1) inputs,
(2) processes applied to those inputs, and
(3) resulting outputs that are used to generate revenues.

For a transferred set of activities and assets to be deemed a business, it must contain essentially all of the inputs and processes necessary for it to continue to conduct normal operations after the transferred assets are separated from the transferor, which includes the ability to sustain a revenue stream by providing its outputs to customers. If these criteria are not satisfied, the assets do not comprise a business and ASC 805, *Business Combinations,* does not apply to accounting for the acquisition.

Barter Transactions

Through third-party barter exchanges, many commercial enterprises exchange their goods and services to obtain barter credits that can be used in lieu of cash to obtain goods and services provided by other members of the barter exchange.

ASC 845-10-30-17 specifies two rebuttable presumptions that apply to accounting for exchanges of nonmonetary assets for barter credits.

1. The fair value of the nonmonetary asset is presumed to be more clearly evident than the fair value of the barter credits received; and
2. The fair value of the nonmonetary asset is presumed not to exceed its carrying amount.

The general rule is that when a nonmonetary asset is exchanged for barter credits, the transaction is valued at the fair value of the nonmonetary asset surrendered, since it is presumed to be the more readily determinable of the two fair values.

The first presumption can be overcome if (1) the entity is able to convert the barter credits into cash within the near term, as evidenced by past practice of doing so shortly after receipt; or (2) independent quoted market prices are available for items to be received in exchange for the barter credits. The second presumption can be overcome if persuasive evidence exists that supports a higher value.

If it subsequently becomes apparent that either of the following conditions exist, the reporting entity is to recognize an impairment loss on the barter credits:

1. The carrying value of any remaining barter credits exceeds their fair value, or
2. It is probable that the entity will not use all of the remaining barter credits.

If an exchange involves transfer or assumption of an operating lease for barter credits, impairment of the lease is to be measured as the amount of remaining lease costs (the discounted future rental payments plus the carrying amount of unamortized leasehold improvements) in excess of the fair value of the discounted amount of the probable future sublease rentals for the remaining lease term.

Involuntary Conversions

An involuntary conversion results from the forced disposition of property due to casualty, theft, condemnation, or threat of condemnation. Upon involuntary conversion, the owner of the asset forfeits it and potentially receives proceeds from filing a property/casualty insurance claim or from condemnation awards.

Certain conditions may occur that necessitate the involuntary conversion of a nonmonetary asset into a monetary asset. ASC 605-40, *Revenue Recognition—Gains and Losses,* specifies that involuntary conversions of nonmonetary assets to monetary assets are monetary transactions, and the resulting gain or loss is recognized in the period of conversion. It makes no difference that the monetary assets received are immediately reinvested in nonmonetary assets.

This rule does not apply to an interim period involuntary conversion of LIFO inventories that are intended to be replaced but have not yet been replaced by year end.

Deferred Income Taxes

A difference between the amount of gain or loss recognized for financial reporting purposes and that recognized for income tax purposes constitutes a temporary difference. The difference in the gain or loss recognized results in a difference between the income tax basis and the financial reporting basis of the asset received. The difference in the gain or loss reverses as a result of the annual charge to depreciation. The proper treatment of temporary differences is discussed in the chapter on ASC 740.

Summary

The situations involving the exchange of nonmonetary assets are summarized in the diagram on the following page.

Nonmonetary Transactions

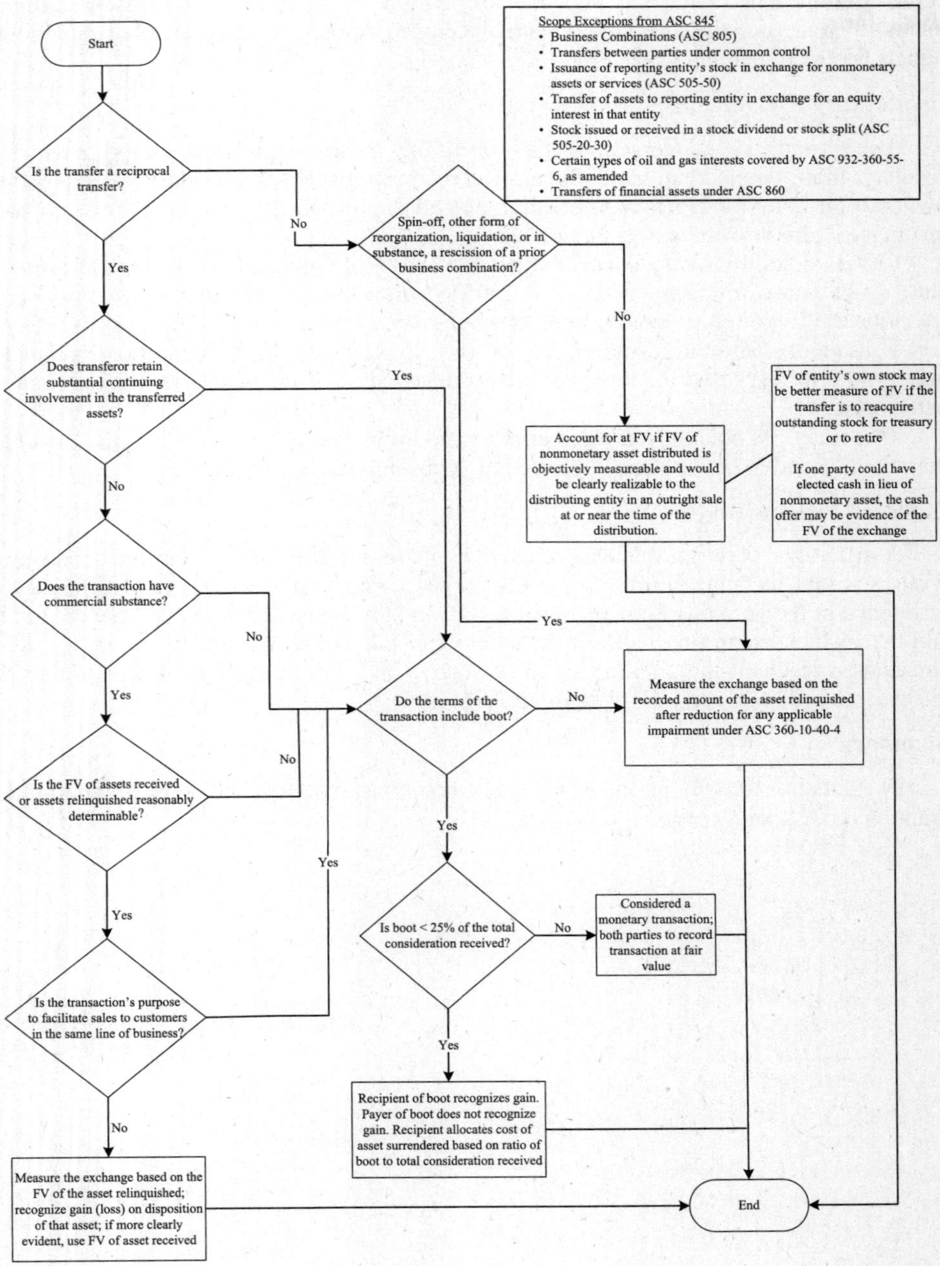

55 ASC 850 RELATED-PARTY DISCLOSURES

PERSPECTIVE AND ISSUES

Subtopic

ASC 850 contains one subtopic:

- ASC 850-10, *Overall,* which sets forth the disclosure requirements, certain significant related party transactions, and control relationships.

Scope

ASC 850 applies to all entities.

DEFINITIONS OF TERMS

Source: ASC 850-20

Affiliate. A party that, directly or indirectly through one or more intermediaries, controls, is controlled by, or is under common control with an entity.

Control. The possession, direct or indirect, of the power to direct or cause the direction of the management and policies of an entity through ownership, by contract, or otherwise.

Immediate Family. Family members who might control or influence a principal owner or a member of management, or who might be controlled or influenced by a principal owner or a member of management, because of the family relationship.

Management. Persons who are responsible for achieving the objectives of the entity and who have the authority to establish policies and make decisions by which those objectives are to be pursued. Management normally includes members of the board of directors, the chief executive officer, chief operating officer, vice presidents in charge of principal business functions (such as sales, administration, or finance), and other persons who perform similar policy-making functions. Persons without formal titles also may be members of management.

Principal Owners. Owners of record or known beneficial owners of more than 10 percent of the voting interests of the entity.

Related Parties. Related parties include:

a. Affiliates of the entity
b. Entities for which investments in their equity securities would be required, absent the election of the fair value option under the Fair Value Option Subsection of Section 825-10-15, to be accounted for by the equity method by the investing entity

c. Trusts for the benefit of employees, such as pension and profit-sharing trusts that are managed by or under the trusteeship of management
d. Principal owners of the entity and members of their immediate families
e. Management of the entity and members of their immediate families
f. Other parties with which the entity may deal if one party controls or can significantly influence the management or operating policies of the other to an extent that one of the transacting parties might be prevented from fully pursuing its own separate interests
g. Other parties that can significantly influence the management or operating policies of the transacting parties or that have an ownership interest in one of the transacting parties and can significantly influence the other to an extent that one or more of the transacting parties might be prevented from fully pursuing its own separate interests.

CONCEPTS, RULES, AND EXAMPLES

Disclosures

According to ASC 850, *Related-Party Disclosures*, financial statements are required to disclose material related-party transactions other than compensation arrangements, expense allowances, or other similar items that occur in the ordinary course of business.

A related party is essentially any party that controls or can significantly influence the management or operating policies of the company to the extent that the company may be prevented from fully pursuing its own interests. Related parties include affiliates, investees accounted for by the equity method, trusts for the benefit of employees, principal owners, management, and immediate family members of owners or management.

Transactions with related parties must be disclosed even if there is no accounting recognition made for such transactions (e.g., a service is performed without payment). Disclosures are not permitted to assert that the terms of related-party transactions were essentially equivalent to arm's-length dealings unless those claims can be substantiated. If the financial position or results of operations of the reporting entity could change significantly because of common control or common management, disclosure of the nature of the ownership or management control is required, even if there were no transactions between the entities.

The disclosures include:

1. The nature of the relationship
2. A description of transactions and the effects of those transactions reflected in the financial statements for each period for which an income statement is presented
3. The dollar amount of transactions for each period for which an income statement is presented and the effects of any change in the terms of such transactions as compared to the terms used in prior periods
4. Amounts due to and from related parties as of the date of each statement of financial position presented, together with the terms and manner of settlement.

56 ASC 852 REORGANIZATIONS

PERSPECTIVE AND ISSUES

Subtopics

ASC 852, *Reorganizations,* contains three subtopics:

- ASC 852-10, *Overall,* which provides guidance for entities that have filed petitions in the Bankruptcy Court and expect to reorganize under Chapter 11
- ASC 852-20, *Quasi-Reorganizations*
- ASC 852-740, *Income Taxes.*

Scope and Scope Exceptions

ASC 852-10 applies to all entities except governmental organizations and does not apply to debt restructurings outside of Chapter 11 and reorganizations consisting of liquidation or adoption of plans of liquidation under the Bankruptcy Code.

ASC 852-20 applies only to "readjustments in which the current income, or retained earnings or accumulated deficit account, or the income account of future years is relieved of charges that would otherwise be made against it...." Further, it does not apply to:

a. "Quasi-reorganizations involving only deficit reclassifications
b. Charges against additional paid-in capital in other types of readjustments such as readjustments for the purpose of correcting erroneous credits made to additional paid-in capital in the past
c. Financial reporting for entities that enter and intend to emerge from Chapter 11 reorganization, at the time of such reorganization."

(ASC 852-20-15-3)

Overview

Entities expected to reorganize as going concerns under Chapter 11 of the Bankruptcy Code employ so-called "fresh start" accounting if:

1. The "reorganization value of the assets of the emerging entity immediately before the date of confirmation is less than the total of all postpetition liabilities and allowed claims, and

2. Holders of existing voting shares immediately before confirmation receive less than 50 percent of the voting shares of the emerging entity."

(ASC 852-10-45-19)

DEFINITIONS OF TERMS

Source: 851-10-20

Absolute Priority Doctrine. A doctrine that provides that if an impaired class does not vote in favor of a plan, the court may nevertheless confirm the plan under the cram-down provisions of the Bankruptcy Code. The absolute priority doctrine is triggered when the cram-down provisions apply. The doctrine states that all members of the senior class of creditors and equity interests must be satisfied in full before the members of the second senior class of creditors can receive anything, and the full satisfaction of that class must occur before the third senior class of creditors may be satisfied, and so on.

Administrative Expenses. Claims that receive priority over all other unsecured claims in a bankruptcy case. Administrative expenses (sometimes referred to as administrative claims) include the actual, necessary costs and expenses of preserving the estate, including wages, salaries, or commissions for services rendered after the commencement of the case. Fees paid to professionals for services rendered after the petition is filed are considered administrative expenses.

Allowed Claim. The amount allowed by the Bankruptcy Court as a claim against the estate. This amount may differ from the actual settlement amount.

Automatic Stay Provisions. Provisions causing the filing of a petition under the Bankruptcy Code to automatically stay virtually all actions of creditors to collect prepetition debts. As a result of the stay, no party, with minor exceptions, having a security or adverse interest in the debtor's property can take any action that will interfere with the debtor or the debtor's property, regardless of where the property is located or who has possession, until the stay is modified or removed.

Bankruptcy Code. A federal statute, enacted October 1, 1979, as title 11 of the United States Code by the Bankruptcy Reform Act of 1978, that applies to all cases filed on or after its enactment and that provides the basis for the current federal bankruptcy system.

Bankruptcy Court. The United States Bankruptcy Court is an adjunct of the United States District Courts. Under the jurisdiction of the District Court, the Bankruptcy Court is generally responsible for cases filed under Chapters 7, 11, 12, and 13 of the Bankruptcy Code.

Chapter 11. A reorganization action, either voluntarily or involuntarily initiated under the provisions of the Bankruptcy Code, that provides for a reorganization of the debt and equity structure of the business and allows the business to continue operations. A debtor may also file a plan of liquidation under Chapter 11.

Chapter 7. A liquidation, voluntarily or involuntarily initiated under the provisions of the Bankruptcy Code, that provides for liquidation of the business or the debtor's estate.

Claim. As defined by Section 101(4) of the Bankruptcy Code, a right to payment, regardless of whether the right is reduced to judgment, liquidated, unliquidated, fixed, contingent, matured, unmatured, disputed, undisputed, legal, secured, or unsecured, or a right to an equitable remedy for breach of performance if such breach results in a right to payment, regardless of whether the right is reduced to a fixed, contingent, matured, unmatured, disputed, undisputed, secured, or unsecured right.

Confirmed Plan. An official approval by the court of a plan of reorganization under a Chapter 11 proceeding that makes the plan binding on the debtors and creditors. Before a plan is confirmed, it must satisfy 11 requirements in section 1129(a) of the Bankruptcy Code.

Consenting Classes. Classes of creditors or stockholders that approve the proposed plan.

Cram-Down Provisions. Provisions requiring that for a plan to be confirmed, a class of claims or interests must either accept the plan or not be impaired. However, the Bankruptcy Code allows the Bankruptcy Court under certain conditions to confirm a plan even though an impaired class has not accepted the plan. To do so, the plan must not discriminate unfairly and must be fair and equitable to each class of claims or interests impaired under the plan that has not accepted it. The Bankruptcy Code states examples of conditions for secured claims, unsecured claims, and stockholder interests in the fair and equitable requirement.

Debtor-in-Possession. Existing management continuing to operate an entity that has filed a petition under Chapter 11. The debtor-in-possession is allowed to operate the business in all Chapter 11 cases unless the court, for cause, authorizes the appointment of a trustee.

Disclosure Statement. A written statement containing information approved as adequate by the court. It is required to be presented by a party before soliciting the acceptance or rejection of a plan of reorganization from creditors and stockholders affected by the plan. Adequate information means information of a kind, and in sufficient detail, as far as is reasonably practicable in light of the nature and history of the debtor and the condition of the debtor's records, that would enable a hypothetical reasonable investor typical of holders of claims or interests of the relevant class to make an informed judgment about the plan.

Emerging Entity. An entity (sometimes referred to as the reorganized entity), that has had its plan confirmed and begins to operate as a new entity.

Impaired Claims. In determining which class of creditors' claims or stockholders' interests must approve the plan, it is first necessary to determine if the class is impaired. A class of creditors' claims or stockholders' interests under a plan is not impaired if the plan leaves unaltered the legal, equitable, and contractual right of a class, cures defaults that lead to acceleration of debt or equity interest, or pays in cash the full amount of the claim, or for equity interests, the greater of the fixed liquidation preference or redemption price.

Liquidating Bank. A bank with a substantial amount of nonperforming assets may transfer some or all of those assets to a newly created bank whose stock will be distributed to existing shareholders or to new investors. The newly created bank will be a liquidating bank; that is, it will manage the assets it receives and collect cash from loan repayments or dispositions of assets. All cash remaining after paying expenses and debt service, if any, will be distributed to the shareholders of the liquidating bank. The liquidating bank will likely be in the process of liquidation for several years.

Nonconsenting Class. A class of creditors or stockholders that does not approve the proposed plan.

Obligations Subject to Compromise. Includes all prepetition liabilities (claims) except those that will not be impaired under the plan, such as claims in which the value of the security interest is greater than the claim.

Petition. A document filed in a court of bankruptcy, initiating proceedings under the Bankruptcy Code.

Plan of Reorganization An agreement formulated in Chapter 11 proceedings under the supervision of the Bankruptcy Court that enables the debtor to continue in business. The plan, once confirmed, may affect the rights of undersecured creditors, secured creditors, and stockholders as well as those of unsecured creditors. Before a plan is confirmed by the

Bankruptcy Court, it must comply with general provisions of the Bankruptcy Code. Those provisions mandate, for example, that the plan is feasible, the plan is in the best interest of the creditors, and, if an impaired class does not accept the plan, the plan must be determined to be fair and equitable before it can be confirmed.

Postpetition Liabilities. Liabilities incurred after the filing of a petition that are not associated with prebankruptcy events. Thus, these liabilities are not considered prepetition liabilities.

Prepetition Liabilities. Liabilities that were incurred by an entity before its filing of a petition for protection under the Bankruptcy Code including those considered by the Bankruptcy Court to be prepetition claims, such as a rejection of a lease for real property.

Reorganization Items. Items of income, expense, gain, or loss that are realized or incurred by an entity because it is in reorganization.

Reorganization Proceeding. A Chapter 11 case from the time at which the petition is filed until the plan is confirmed.

Reorganization Value. The value attributed to the reconstituted entity, as well as the expected net realizable value of those assets that will be disposed of before reconstitution occurs. Therefore, this value is viewed as the value of the entity before considering liabilities and approximates the amount a willing buyer would pay for the assets of the entity immediately after the restructuring.

Secured Claim. A liability that is secured by collateral. A fully secured claim is one in which the value of the collateral is greater than the amount of the claim.

Terminal Value. A component of reorganization value. Reorganization value calculated based on the discounting of cash flows normally consists of three parts; the discounted cash flows determined for the forecast period, the residual value or terminal value, and the current value of any excess working capital or other assets that are not needed in reorganization. Terminal or residual value represents the present value of the business attributable to the period beyond the forecast period.

Trustee. A person appointed by the Bankruptcy Court in certain situations based on the facts of the case, not related to the size of the entity or the amount of unsecured debt outstanding, at the request of a party in interest after a notice and hearing.

Undersecured Claim. A secured claim whose collateral is worth less than the amount of the claim. Sometimes referred to as an undersecured claim liability.

Unsecured Claim. A liability that is not secured by collateral. In the case of an undersecured creditor, the excess of the secured claim over the value of the collateral is an unsecured claim, unless the debtor elects in a Chapter 11 proceeding to have the entire claim considered secured. The term is generally used in bankruptcy to refer to unsecured claims that do not receive priority under the Bankruptcy Code. Sometimes referred to as an unsecured claim liability.

CONCEPTS, RULES, AND EXAMPLES

Corporate Bankruptcy and Reorganizations

Entities operating under and emerging from protection of the bankruptcy laws. The going concern assumption is one of the basic postulates underlying generally accepted accounting principles and is responsible for, among other things, the historical cost convention in financial reporting. For entities that have entered bankruptcy proceedings, however, the going concern assumption will no longer be of central importance.

ASC 852 sets forth certain financial reporting standards for entities undergoing and emerging from reorganization under the bankruptcy laws. Under its provisions, assets are presented at estimated realizable values. Liabilities are set forth at the estimated amounts to be allowed in the statement of financial position, and liabilities subject to compromise are to be distinguished from those that are not. Furthermore, the codification requires that in both the statements of income and cash flows, normal transactions be differentiated from those that have occurred as a consequence of the entity's being in reorganization. While certain allocations to the latter category are rather obvious, such as legal and accounting fees incurred, others are less clear. For example, the codification suggests that if the entity in reorganization earns interest income on funds that would normally have been used to settle obligations owed to creditors, such income will be deemed to be income arising as a consequence of the bankruptcy action.

Another interesting aspect of ASC 852 is the accounting to be made for the emergence from reorganization (known as confirmation of the plan of reorganization). The ASC provides for "fresh start" financial reporting in such instances. This accounting is similar to that applied to acquistion business combinations, with the total confirmed value of the entity upon its emergence from reorganization being analogous to the purchase price in an acquisition. In both cases, this total value is to be allocated to the identifiable assets and liabilities of the entity, with any excess being allocated to goodwill. In the case of entities emerging from bankruptcy, goodwill (called reorganization value in excess of amounts allocable to identifiable assets) is measured as the excess of liabilities existing at the plan confirmation date, computed at present value of future amounts to be paid, over the reorganization value of assets. Reorganization value is calculated with reference to a number of factors, including forecasted operating results and cash flows of the new entity.

ASC 852 applies only to entities undergoing formal reorganization under the Bankruptcy Code. Less formal procedures may still be accounted for under quasi-reorganization accounting procedures.

Quasi-reorganizations

Generally, this procedure is applicable during a period of declining price levels. It is termed "quasi" since the accumulated deficit is eliminated at a lower cost and with less difficulty than a legal reorganization.

Per ASC 852-20, the procedures in a quasi-reorganization involve the:

1. Proper authorization from stockholders and creditors where required
2. Revaluation of assets to their current values: all losses are charged to retained earnings, thus increasing any deficit
3. Elimination of any deficit by charging paid-in capital:
    a. First, additional paid-in capital to the extent it exists
    b. Second, capital stock when additional paid-in capital is insufficient: the par value of the stock is reduced, creating the extra additional paid-in capital to which the remaining deficit is charged.

No retained earnings may be created by a reorganization. Any excess created by the reduction of par value is credited to "Paid-in capital from quasi-reorganization."

ASC 852-20 requires that retained earnings be dated for ten years (less than ten years may be justified under exceptional circumstances) after a quasi-reorganization takes place. Disclosure similar to "since quasi-reorganization of June 30, 20XX" is appropriate.

57 ASC 853 SERVICE CONCESSION ARRANGEMENTS

PERSPECTIVE AND ISSUES

Subtopic

ASC 853, *Service Concession Arrangements*, contains one Subtopic:

- ASC 853-10, *Overall*, which addresses the accounting for service concession arrangements between a public sector entity grantor and an operating entity where the operating entity operates the grantor's infrastructure.

Scope

ASC 853 applies to:

- The accounting *by operating entities*
- of a *service concession arrangement*
- under which a *public-sector entity grantor* enters into a contract with an operating entity
- to operate the *grantor's infrastructure.*
  [Emphasis added.]

The operating entity also may provide the construction, upgrading, or maintenance services of the grantor's infrastructure.
(ASC 853-10-15-2)

It is important to note that a service concession arrangement within the scope of ASC 853 must meet *both* of the following conditions:

a. The grantor controls or has the ability to modify or approve the services that the operating entity must provide with the infrastructure, to whom it must provide them, and at what price.
b. The grantor controls, through ownership, beneficial entitlement, or otherwise, any residual interest in the infrastructure at the end of the term of the arrangement.

(ASC 853-10-15-3)

Scope exception. A service concession arrangement meeting the scope criteria in Topic 980 on regulated operations should apply the guidance in Topic 980.

Technical Alert

ASC 853 was established through ASU 2014-05, *Service Concession Arrangement,* issued in January 2014.

Effective dates. The guidance is effective for a public business entity for annual periods and interim periods within those annual periods beginning after December 16, 2014. For all other entities, the guidance is effective for annual periods beginning after December 15, 2014, and interim periods within those annual periods beginning after December 15, 2015. However, early adoption is permitted. The provisions should be applied on a modified retrospective basis to service concessions that exist at the beginning of the fiscal year of adoption. This approach means that the cumulative effect of applying the guidance to arrangements that exist at the beginning of the period should be recognized as an adjustment to opening retained earnings.

Summary. The ASU is a consensus of the Emerging Issues Task Force (EITF) and addresses a narrow issue. However, the existing guidance was confusing, and practice was diverse. Depending on the terms, some preparers may have concluded that a service arrangement is a lease. To bring consistency in practice, the EITF decided that the arrangements described in the ASU should not be accounted for as leases. The EITF limited the scope of the guidance to arrangements in which the grantor is a public-sector entity.

DEFINITIONS OF TERMS

Source: ASC 853-10-20

Not-for-Profit Entity. An entity that possesses the following characteristics, in varying degrees, that distinguish it from a business entity:

a. Contributions of significant amounts of resources from resource providers who do not expect commensurate or proportionate pecuniary return
b. Operating purposes other than to provide goods or services at a profit
c. Absence of ownership interests like those of business entities.

Entities that clearly fall outside this definition include the following:

a. All investor-owned entities
b. Entities that provide dividends, lower costs, or other economic benefits directly and proportionately to their owners, members, or participants, such as mutual insurance entities, credit unions, farm and rural electric cooperatives, and employee benefit plans.

Public Business Entity. A public business entity is a business entity meeting any one of the criteria below. Neither a not-for-profit entity nor an employee benefit plan is a business entity.

a. It is required by the U.S. Securities and Exchange Commission (SEC) to file or furnish financial statements, or does file or furnish financial statements (including voluntary filers), with the SEC (including other entities whose financial statements or financial information are required to be or are included in a filing).
b. It is required by the Securities Exchange Act of 1934 (the Act), as amended, or rules or regulations promulgated under the Act, to file or furnish financial statements with a regulatory agency other than the SEC.

c. It is required to file or furnish financial statements with a foreign or domestic regulatory agency in preparation for the sale of or for purposes of issuing securities that are not subject to contractual restrictions on transfer.
d. It has issued, or is a conduit bond obligor for, securities that are traded, listed, or quoted on an exchange or an over-the-counter market.
e. It has one or more securities that are not subject to contractual restrictions on transfer, and it is required by law, contract, or regulation to prepare U.S. GAAP financial statements (including footnotes) and make them publicly available on a periodic basis (for example, interim or annual periods). An entity must meet both of these conditions to meet this criterion.

An entity may meet the definition of a public business entity solely because its financial statements or financial information is included in another entity's filing with the SEC. In that case, the entity is only a public business entity for purposes of financial statements that are filed or furnished with the SEC.

CONCEPTS, RULES, AND EXAMPLES

Accounting for Service Concession Arrangements

The Topic has two main provisions:

- Service concession arrangements that meet the guidelines are not to be accounted for as leases. For guidance, preparers should look to other Topics, for example, ASC 605 to recognize revenue on construction, upgrade, or operation services.
- The infrastructure involved in the arrangements should not be recognized as the operating entity's property, plant, and equipment.

Service concession arrangements. The infrastructure that the entity operates may be airports, roads, bridges, hospitals, prisons, etc. The operating entity may also provide construction or maintenance services to the grantor's infrastructure. A key feature of a service concession arrangement is that it is generally for the public good. The operator usually receives payment for the services performed over a specified time. The operator may have the right to charge users of the infrastructure. The arrangement may include unconditional guarantees for guaranteed minimum payments.

Economic substance. The grantor controls or has the ability to modify or approve the services provided and the price charged for the service. The grantor controls any residual interest in the infrastructure at the end of the term. This control is important in deciding the economic substance of the transaction and the reason why it is not appropriate for the operating entity to recognize a lease or property, plant, and equipment. (ASC 853-10-05-01 and 05-02)

58 ASC 855 SUBSEQUENT EVENTS

PERSPECTIVE AND ISSUES

Subtopic

ASC 855, *Subsequent Events,* consists of one Subtopic:

- ASC 855-10, *Overall,* which provides guidance for events or transactions occurring after the balance sheet date.

Scope and Scope Exceptions

ASC 855 applies to all entities and all transactions except for those covered in other Codification Topics.

Overview

ASC 855 describes the circumstances under which an entity should recognize events or transactions in its financial statements that occur subsequent to the balance sheet date, but before the financial statements are available to be issued. This can have a potentially significant impact on loss contingencies.

DEFINITIONS OF TERMS

Source: ASC 855-20

Financial Statements Are Available to Be Issued. Financial statements are considered available to be issued when they are complete in a form and format that complies with GAAP and all approvals necessary for issuance have been obtained, for example, from management, the board of directors, and/or significant shareholders. The process involved in creating and distributing the financial statements will vary depending on an entity's management and corporate governance structure as well as statutory and regulatory requirements.

Financial Statements Are Issued. Financial statements are considered issued when they are widely distributed to shareholders and other financial statement users for general use and reliance in a form and format that complies with GAAP. (U.S. Securities and Exchange Commission [SEC] registrants also are required to consider the guidance in paragraph 855-10-S99-2)

Revised Financial Statements. Financial statements revised only for either of the following conditions:

a. Correction of an error
b. Retrospective application of U.S. GAAP.

Securities and Exchange Commission (SEC) Filer. An entity that is required to file or furnish its financial statements with either of the following:

a. The Securities and Exchange Commission (SEC)
b. With respect to an entity subject to Section 12(i) of the Securities Exchange Act of 1934, as amended, the appropriate agency under that Section.

Financial statements for other entities that are not otherwise SEC filers whose financial statements are included in a submission by another SEC filer are not included within this definition.

Subsequent Events. Events or transactions that occur after the balance sheet date but before financial statements are issued or are available to be issued. There are two types of subsequent events:

a. The first type consists of events or transactions that provide additional evidence about conditions that existed at the date of the balance sheet, including the estimates inherent in the process of preparing financial statements (that is, recognized subsequent events).
b. The second type consists of events that provide evidence about conditions that did not exist at the date of the balance sheet but arose subsequent to that date (that is, nonrecognized subsequent events).

CONCEPTS, RULES, AND EXAMPLES

Types of Subsequent Events

The statement of financial position is dated as of the last day of the fiscal period, but a period of time usually elapses before the financial statements are issued. During this period, significant events or transactions may have occurred that materially affect the company's financial position. These events and transactions are called subsequent events. The omission of disclosure of significant events occurring between the date of the statement of financial position and issuance date of the financial statements could mislead the reader who is otherwise unaware of those events.

SEC filers and conduit bond obligors for conduit debt securities traded in a public market are required to evaluate subsequent events through the date the financial statements are issued. All other entities must evaluate subsequent events through the date the financial statements are *available* to be issued. (ASC 855-10-25-1A)

There are two types of subsequent events, which relate to when the event or transaction occurred and determine the accounting treatment:

1. *Existing conditions.* Additional evidence may arise about a condition that existed as of the balance sheet date. If so, recognize these changes within the financial statements.
2. *Subsequent events.* Evidence may arise about conditions that did not exist as of the balance sheet date, but which occurred later. Do not recognize these changes within the financial statements.

The following table presents a variety of sample situations occurring after the balance sheet date but before the financial statements are available to be issued, and that apply to these two types of subsequent events:

Event	*Accounting Treatment*
Litigation is settled for an amount different from the recorded liability	(1)
Loss on a customer receivable caused by customer bankruptcy	(1)
Loss of assets due to a natural disaster	(2)
Loss on receivables from conditions arising after the balance sheet date	(2)
Changes in the fair value of assets or liabilities	(2)
Issuing significant guarantees	(2)

(1) Recognize within the financial statements if they are not yet available to be issued.
(2) Do not recognize until the next reporting period.

An entity should disclose the date through which it has evaluated subsequent events, and whether that date is the date when the financial statements were issued or available to be issued. For revised financial statements, disclose both the dates through which subsequent events have been evaluated through the issued or available-to-be-issued financial statements, and for the revised financial statements.

If a nonrecognized event is so significant that the financial statements would be misleading without disclosure of it, note the nature of the event and an estimate of its financial effect, or a statement that the entity cannot create such an estimate.

Examples of subsequent events

1. A loss on an uncollectible trade account receivable that results from a customer's deteriorating financial condition, which led to bankruptcy subsequent to the date of the statement of financial position, would be indicative of conditions existing at the date of the statement of financial position, thereby calling for adjustment of the financial statements before their issuance. On the other hand, a loss on an uncollectible trade account receivable resulting from a customer's major casualty, such as a fire or flood subsequent to the date of the statement of financial position, would not be indicative of conditions existing at the date of the statement of financial position, and the adjustment of the financial statements would not be appropriate. However, if the amount is material, disclosure would be required.
2. A settlement of a lawsuit would require adjustment of the financial statements if the event that gave rise to the claim occurred prior to the date of the statement of financial position. However, only disclosure is required if the event that gave rise to the claim occurred after the date of the statement of financial position, and then only if the amount involved were expected to be material.
3. The second type of events (those not existing at the date of the statement of financial position) that require disclosure but not adjustment include the following:

    a. Sale of a bond or capital stock issue
    b. Purchase of a business
    c. Loss of plant or inventories as a result of fire or flood
    d. Gains or losses on certain marketable securities.

59 ASC 860 TRANSFERS AND SERVICING

PERSPECTIVE AND ISSUES

Subtopics

ASC 860 contains five Subtopics:

- ASC 860-10, *Overall*
- ASC 860-20, *Sales of Financial Assets*
- ASC 860-30, *Secured Borrowings and Collateral*
- ASC 860-50, *Servicing Assets and Liabilities.*

Scope and Scope Exceptions

ASC 860 applies to transfers and servicing of noncash financial assets. A transfer includes

- Selling a receivable,
- Transferring a receivable to a trust, or
- Using a receivable as security for a loan.

A transfer does *not* include

- The origination of a receivable,
- The settlement of a receivable, or
- The restructuring of a receivable in a troubled debt restructuring.

Those transactions are transfers involving the issuer of the receivable.

Among the types of transfers of financial assets for which ASC 860 establishes standards are:

- Financial instruments
- Financial assets
- Collateral
- Transfers of receivables with recourse (factoring with recourse)
- Transfers of undivided partial interests in receivables (retained interests)
- Transfers of receivables with servicing retained
- Transfers of minimum lease payments under sales-type and direct financing leases and any related guaranteed residual
- Putting a receivable into a securitization trust
- Repurchase agreements
- Dollar rolls
- Securities lending transactions
- Posting a receivable as collateral
- Banker's acceptances.

ASC 860-10-15-4 *excludes* the following items from the scope of ASC 860:

1. Except for transfers of servicing assets (see ASC 860-50-40) and for the transfers noted in the following paragraph, transfers of nonfinancial assets
2. Transfers of unrecognized financial assets, for example, minimum lease payments to be received under operating leases
3. Transfers of custody of financial assets for safekeeping
4. Contributions
5. Transfers of ownership interests that are in substance sales of real estate
6. Investments by owners or distributions to owners of a business entity
7. Employee benefits subject to the provisions of ASC 712
8. Leveraged leases subject to ASC 840
9. Money-over-money and wrap-lease transactions involving nonrecourse debt subject to ASC 840.

Overview

This chapter discusses the standards in Accounting Standards Codification (ASC) 860, *Transfers and Servicing*. ASC 860 describes the proper accounting for sales of financial assets to third parties and the use of financial assets as collateral in secured borrowings. This chapter also includes ASC 860's standards for repurchase agreements and securities lending. Although those two types of transfers usually involve investments, they are covered in ASC 860 because the same underlying theory—the financial components approach—is used for those transactions as is used for transfers involving receivables.

DEFINITIONS OF TERMS

Source: ASC 860 and Master Glossary

Affiliate. A party that, directly or indirectly through one or more intermediaries, controls, is controlled by, or is under common control with an entity.

Agent. A party that acts for and on behalf of another party. For example, a third-party intermediary is an agent of the transferor if it acts on behalf of the transferor.

Bankruptcy-remote entity. An entity that is designed to make remote the possibility that it would enter bankruptcy or other receivership.

Beneficial interests. Rights to receive all or portions of specified cash inflows received by a trust or other entity, including, but not limited to, all of the following:

1. Senior and subordinated shares of interest, principal, or other cash inflows to be passed-through or paid-through
2. Premiums due to guarantors
3. Commercial paper obligations
4. Residual interests, whether in the form of debt or equity.

Cleanup call option. An option held by the servicer or its affiliate, which may be the transferor, to purchase the remaining transferred financial assets, or the remaining beneficial interest not held by the transferor, its affiliates, or its agents in an entity (or in a series of beneficial interests in transferred financial assets within an entity) if the amount of outstanding financial assets or beneficial interests falls to a level at which the cost of servicing those assets or beneficial interests becomes burdensome in relation to the benefits of servicing.

Collateral. Personal or real property in which a security interest has been given.

Consolidated affiliate. An entity whose assets and liabilities are included in the consolidated, combined, or other financial statements being presented.

Continuing involvement. Any involvement with the transferred financial asset that permits the transferor to receive cash flows or other benefits that arise from the transferred financial assets or that obligates the transferor to provide additional cash flows or other assets to any party related to the transfer.

Controlled amortization method. Liquidation method used to allocate principal payments on the receivables in a trust to the investors, under which a predetermined monthly payment schedule is established so that payout to the investors will occur over a specified liquidation period. Principal payments are allocated to the investors based on their participation interests in the receivables in the trust, using one of the liquidation methods (fixed, preset, or floating). Principal payments in excess of the predetermined monthly payment, if any, are allocated to the transferor and increase the investors' ownership interests. If the principal payments allocated to the investors are insufficient to cover the predetermined monthly payment, that payment is reduced by the amount of the deficiency. If the principal payments allocated to the investors in subsequent months exceed the predetermined monthly payment, the deficiency is recovered.

Derecognize. Remove previously recognized assets or liabilities from the statement of financial position.

Derivative financial instrument. A derivative instrument that is a financial instrument.

Dollar-roll repurchase agreement. An agreement to sell and repurchase similar but not identical securities. The securities sold and repurchased are usually of the same issuer. Dollar rolls differ from regular repurchase agreements in that the securities sold and repurchased have all of the following characteristics:

1. They are represented by different certificates.
2. They are collateralized by different but similar mortgage pools (for example, conforming single-family residential mortgages).
3. They generally have different principal amounts.

Fixed coupon and yield maintenance dollar agreements comprise the most common agreement variations. In a fixed coupon agreement, the seller and buyer agree that delivery will be made with securities having the same stated interest rate as the interest rate stated on the securities sold. In a yield maintenance agreement, the parties agree that delivery will be made with securities that will provide the seller a yield that is specified in the agreement.

Embedded call option. A call option held by the issuer of a financial instrument that is part of and trades with the underlying instrument. For example, a bond may allow the issuer to call it by posting a public notice well before its stated maturity that asks the current holder to submit it for early redemption and provides that interest ceases to accrue on the bond after the early redemption date. Rather than being an obligation of the initial purchaser of the bond, and embedded call option trades with and diminishes the value of the underlying bond.

Equitable right of redemption. The right of a property owner who has defaulted on a secured obligation to recover the securing property before its sale by paying the amounts due and any appropriate fees and charges. Other creditors of or a receiver for the property owner also may be able to exercise that right. After a transfer of a financial asset, a right of redemption may allow the transferor to buy back the transferred asset.

Financial asset. Cash, evidence of an ownership interest in an entity, or a contract that conveys to one entity a right to do either of the following:

1. Receive cash or another financial instrument from a second entity
2. Exchange other financial instruments on potentially favorable terms with the second entity.

A financial asset exists if and when two or more parties agree to payment terms and those payment terms are reduced to a contract. To be a financial asset, an asset must arise from a contractual agreement between two or more parties, not from an imposition of an obligation by one party on another.

Financial instrument. Cash, evidence of an ownership interest in an entity, or a contract that both:

1. Imposes on one entity a contractual obligation, either:
   a. To deliver cash or another financial instrument to a second entity
   b. To exchange other financial instruments on potentially unfavorable terms with the second entity.
2. Conveys to that second entity a contractual right, either:
   a. To receive cash or another financial instrument from the first entity
   b. To exchange other financial instruments on potentially favorable terms with the first entity.

The use of the term financial instrument in this instance is recursive (because the term financial instrument is included in it), though it is not circular. The definition requires a chain of contractual obligations that ends with the delivery of cash or an ownership interest in an entity. Any number of obligations to deliver financial instruments can be links in a chain that qualifies a particular contract as a financial instrument.

Contractual rights and contractual obligations encompass both those that are conditioned on the occurrence of a specified event and those that are not. All contractual rights (contractual obligations) that are financial instruments meet the definition of asset (liability) set forth in FASB Concepts Statement No. 6, *Elements of Financial Statements*, although some may not be recognized as assets (liabilities) in financial statements—that is, they may be off-balance-sheet—because they fail to meet some other criterion for recognition.

For some financial instruments, the right is held by or the obligation is due from (or the obligation is owed to or by) a group of entities rather than a single entity.

Financial liability. A contract that imposes on one entity an obligation to do either of the following:

1. Deliver cash or another financial instrument to a second entity
2. Exchange other financial instruments on potentially unfavorable terms with the second entity.

Fixed participation method. Liquidation method used to allocate principal payments on the receivables in a trust to the investors, under which all principal payments on the receivables in the trust are allocated to the investors based on their respective participation interests in the credit card receivables in the trust at the end of the reinvestment period.

Floating participation method. Liquidation method used to allocate principal payments on the receivables in a trust to the investors, under which principal payments allocated to the investors are based on the investors' actual participation interests in the receivables in the trust each month. Each month, investors' participation interests in the credit card receivables in the trust are redetermined for that month's allocation of principal payments.

Freestanding call option. A call option that is neither embedded in nor attached to an asset subject to that call option.

Government National Mortgage Association Rolls. The term Government National Mortgage Association (GNMA) rolls has been used broadly to refer to a variety of transactions involving mortgage-backed securities, frequently those issued by the GNMA. There are four basic types of transactions:

Type 1. Reverse repurchase agreements for which the exact same security is received at the end of the repurchase period (vanilla repo)

Type 2. Fixed coupon dollar reverse repurchase agreements (dollar repo)

Type 3. Fixed coupon dollar reverse repurchase agreements that are rolled at their maturities, that is, renewed in lieu of taking delivery of an underlying security (GNMA roll)

Type 4. Forward commitment dollar rolls (also referred to as to-be-announced GNMA forward contracts or to-be-announced GNMA rolls), for which the underlying security does not yet exist.

Liquidation method. The method used to allocate the principal payments on the receivables in a trust to the investors.

Loan origination fees. Origination fees consist of all of the following:

1. Fees that are being charged to the borrower as prepaid interest or to reduce the loan's nominal interest rate, such as interest buy-downs (explicit yield adjustments)
2. Fees to reimburse the lender for origination activities
3. Other fees charged to the borrower that relate directly to making the loan (for example, fees that are paid to the lender as compensation for granting a complex loan or agreeing to lend quickly)

4. Fees that are not conditional on a loan being granted by the lender that receives the fee but that are, in substance, implicit yield adjustments because a loan is granted at rates or terms that would not have otherwise been considered absent the fee (for example, certain syndication fees addressed in ASC 310-20-25-19)
5. Fees charged to the borrower in connection with the process of originating, refinancing, or restructuring a loan. This term includes, but is not limited to, points, management, arrangement, placement, application, underwriting, and other fees pursuant to a lending or leasing transaction and also includes syndication and participation fees to the extent they are associated with the portion of the loan retained by the lender.

Loan participation. A transaction in which a single lender makes a large loan to a borrower and subsequently transfers undivided interest in the loan to groups of banks or other entities.

Loan syndication. A transaction in which several lenders share in lending to a single borrower. Each lender loans a specific amount to the borrower and has the right to repayment from the borrower. It is common for groups of lenders to jointly fund those loans when the amount borrowed is greater than any one lender is willing to lend.

Money-over-money lease. A transaction in which an entity manufactures or purchases an asset, leases the asset to a lessee, and obtains nonrecourse financing in excess of the asset's cost using the leased asset and the future lease rental as collateral.

Participating interest. From the date of the transfer, it represents a proportionate (pro rata) ownership interest in an entire financial asset. The percentage of ownership interests held by the transferor in the entire financial asset may vary over time, while the entire financial asset remains outstanding as long as the resulting portions held by the transferor (including any participating interest retained by the transferor, its consolidated affiliates included in the financial statements being presented, or its agents) and the transferee(s) meet the other characteristics of a participating interest. For example, if the transferor's interest in an entire financial asset changes because it subsequently sells another interest in the entire financial asset, the interest held initially and subsequently by the transferor must meet the definition of the participating interest.

Preset participation method. Liquidation method used to allocate the principal payments on the receivables in a trust to the investors. The preset participation method is similar to the fixed participation method, except that the percentage used to determine the principal payments allocated to the investors is preset higher than the investors' expected participation interests in the receivables in the trust at the end of the reinvestment period. This method results in a faster payout to the investors than the fixed participation method, because a higher percentage of the principal payment is allocated to the investors.

Recourse. The right of the transferee of receivables to receive payment from the transferor of those receivables for any of the following:

1. Failure of debtors to pay when due
2. The effects of prepayments
3. Adjustments resulting from defects in the eligibility of the transferred receivables.

Remote. The chance of the future event or events occurring is slight.

Repurchase agreement. An agreement under which the transferor (repo party) transfers a security to a transferee (repo counterparty or reverse party) in exchange for cash and concurrently agrees to reacquire that security at a future date for an amount equal to the cash exchanged plus a stipulated interest factor. Instead of cash, other securities or letters of credit sometimes are exchanged. Some repurchase agreements call for repurchase of securities that need not be identical to the securities transferred.

Repurchase financing. A repurchase agreement that relates to a previously transferred financial asset between the same counterparties (or consolidated affiliates of either counterparty) that is entered into contemporaneously with, or in contemplation of, the initial transfer.

Revolving-period securitizations. Securitizations in which receivables are transferred at the inception and also periodically (daily or monthly) thereafter for a defined period (commonly three to eight years), referred to as the revolving period. During the revolving period, the special-purpose entity uses most of the cash collections to purchase additional receivables from the transferor on prearranged terms.

Securitization. The process by which financial assets are transformed into securities.

Seller. A transferor that relinquishes control over financial assets by transferring them to a transferee in exchange for consideration.

Setoff right. A common law right of a party that is both a debtor and a creditor to the same counterparty to reduce its obligation to that counterparty if that counterparty fails to pay its obligation.

Standard representations and warranties. Representations and warranties that assert the financial asset being transferred is what it is purported to be at the transfer date.

Transfer. The conveyance of a noncash financial asset by and to someone other than the issuer of that financial asset.

A transfer includes the following:

1. Selling a receivable
2. Putting a receivable into a securitization
3. Posting a receivable as collateral.

A transfer excludes the following:

1. The origination of a receivable
2. Settlement of a receivable
3. The restructuring of a receivable into a security in a troubled debt restructuring.

Transferee. An entity that receives a financial asset, and interest in a financial asset, or a group of financial assets from a transferor.

Transferor. An entity that transfers a financial asset, and interest in a financial asset, or a group of financial assets that it controls to another entity.

Transferred financial assets. Transfers of any of the following:

1. An entire financial asset
2. A group of entire financial assets
3. Participating interest in an entire financial asset.

Unilateral ability. A capacity for action not dependent on the actions (or failure to act) of any other party.

CONCEPTS, RULES, AND EXAMPLES

Factoring results in a transfer of title of the factored receivables. Where there is a no-recourse provision or other continuing involvement with the receivables, the removal of the receivables from the borrower's statement of financial position is clearly warranted.

Another variation is known as *factoring with recourse*. Accounting for factoring with recourse requires a determination of whether the transfer is a sale or a secured borrowing. That determination is made by applying ASC 860, *Transfers and Servicing*.

Transfers of Financial Assets under ASC 860—Introduction

If receivables or other financial assets are transferred to another entity and the transferor has no continuing involvement with the transferred assets or with the transferee, it is clear that

- A sale has taken place,
- The asset should be derecognized, and
- A gain or loss on the sale is to be measured and recognized.

However, the transferor may have some form of continuing involvement with the transferred assets. It may sell the receivables with recourse for uncollectible amounts, retain an interest in the receivables, or agree to service the receivables after the sale. The more control that the transferor retains over the receivables, the more the transfer appears to be in substance a secured borrowing rather than a sale.

ASC 860 establishes the criteria and procedures used to determine whether a transfer of financial assets is a sale or a secured borrowing. ASC 860 uses a financial components approach in which a single financial asset is viewed as a mix of component assets (controlled economic benefits) and component liabilities (obligations for probable future sacrifices of economic benefits). The focus is on who controls the components and whether that control has changed as a result of a given transfer. If the transferor has surrendered control of the transferred assets, the transfer is a sale. If the transferor retains control of the transferred assets, the transfer is a secured borrowing.

To be accounted for as a disposition of financial assets, ASC 860-10-40 requires that the transferred assets must be isolated from the transferor (put presumptively out of reach of the transferor's creditors). Additionally,

- Each transferee or holder of beneficial interest must be granted the right to pledge or exchange the transferred assets, and there is no condition that both constrains the transferor from taking advantage of the right to pledge or exchange and does provide more than a trivial benefit to the transferor, and
- The transferor cannot maintain effective control over the assets.

All these conditions must be satisfied for derecognition accounting by the transferor to be appropriate.

Derecognition of financial liabilities by a debtor can be properly reflected only if the obligation is extinguished, which requires that either the debt is retired (paid off) or the debtor is legally released from being the primary obligor by either the counterparty or by judicial action (e.g., in bankruptcy proceedings). These conditions are discussed in the following sections.

Surrender of control. A transfer of financial assets (or a component of a financial asset) is recognized as a sale if the transferor surrenders control over those assets in exchange for consideration. However, control is not surrendered to the extent that the consideration received is a beneficial interest in these very same transferred assets. For example, a transferor's exchange of one form of beneficial interests in a trust for an equivalent, but different, form in the same transferred financial assets cannot be accounted for as a sale. If the trust initially issued the beneficial interests, the exchange is not even considered to be a transfer under ASC 860.

The criteria for identifying surrender of control are described in ASC 860-10-40-5:

1. *Isolation of transferred financial assets.* The financial assets transferred are beyond the reach of the transferor and its affiliates, its creditors, potential bankruptcy trustees or other receivers. This is achieved only if the transferred financial assets would be beyond the reach of the powers of a bankruptcy trustee or other receiver for the

transferor or any of its consolidated affiliates included in the financial statements being presented. For multiple-step transfers, an entity that is designed to make remote the possibility that it would enter bankruptcy or other receivership (the "bankruptcy-remote entity") is not considered a consolidated affiliate for purposes of performing the isolation analysis. Notwithstanding the isolation analysis, each entity involved in the transfer is subject to the applicable GAAP guidance on whether it must be consolidated.

NOTE: The former distinction made between qualifying special purpose entities (QSPEs) and variable interest entities (VIEs) has been eliminated and former QSPEs are now subject to consolidation, as are all VIEs, if defined criteria are met.

---

2. *Pledge or exchange rights.* Each transferee (or—if the transferee is an entity whose sole purpose is to engage in securitization or asset-backed financing activities, and if it is constrained from pledging or exchanging the assets it receives—each third-party holder of its beneficial interests) has the right to pledge or exchange the assets (or beneficial interests) it received, and no condition both (1) constrains the transferee (or third-party holder of its beneficial interests) from taking advantage of its right to pledge or exchange and (2) provides more than a trivial benefit to the transferor.
3. *Effective control.* The transferor or its consolidated affiliates included in the financial statements being presented, or its agents, does not maintain effective control over the transferred financial assets or the third-party beneficial interests related to those transferred assets. A transferor maintains effective control if (1) an agreement both entitles and obligates the transferor to repurchase or redeem the assets before their maturity, (2) the transferor has the ability to unilaterally cause the holder to return specific financial assets and that ability conveys more than trivial benefit, or (3) an agreement permits the transferee to require the transferor to repurchase the transferred financial assets at a price that is so favorable to the transferee that it is probable that the transferee will require this to occur. If the transferor can cause the holder to return assets only through a cleanup call, that ability does not indicate effective control.

All available evidence is to be assessed to determine if transferred assets would be beyond the reach of the powers of a bankruptcy trustee (or equivalent). It is irrelevant to this determination that the possibility of bankruptcy is remote at the date of the transfer. Instead, the transferor must endeavor to isolate the assets in the event of bankruptcy, however unlikely that eventuality may be. In many cases, transferors use two transfers to isolate the transferred assets. First, it transfers the assets to a wholly owned corporation that is designed in a way that prevents the transferor or its creditors from reclaiming the assets (or makes the possibility that they can reclaim them remote). Next, the wholly owned corporation transfers the assets to a trust. The trust is prevented from undertaking any business other than management of the assets and from incurring any liabilities. (Thus, there are no creditors to force bankruptcy of the trust.)

A determination that the transferred assets are beyond the reach of a bankruptcy trustee may require a legal opinion regarding the application of the laws of the relevant jurisdiction. Such legal opinions commonly address whether a "true sale" has occurred, and in practice different attorneys may reach different conclusions regarding a given transaction.

Prior to 2010, a common practice was to transfer financial assets to a related entity (a securitization trust, typically) that would qualify as a QSPE, which under then-extant GAAP would always be excluded from consolidation by the sponsoring entity. The concept of

QSPE has been entirely eliminated; such transferee entities must be evaluated for possible consolidation by the sponsoring entity under other existing GAAP requirements.

The existence of setoff rights does not impede the finding of a "true sale." In practice, while setoff rights may exist for the transferor and transferee, if either the obligor under the transferred financial asset (e.g., debtor under transferred receivable) or the transferor entity enters bankruptcy, the transferee might have only an unsecured claim, notwithstanding the nominal right of setoff.

Assets transferred by a bank or other financial institution that is subject to possible receivership by the FDIC can be considered isolated from the transferor even if the FDIC or another creditor can require their return, provided that the return can only occur in receivership, after a default, and in exchange for a payment of, at a minimum, principal and interest earned at the contractual yield to the date the investors are paid. (That rule does not apply to situations in which the transferor can require return of the assets in exchange for payment of principal and interest earned at the contractual yield to the date the investors are paid. In those cases the assets are not isolated from the transferor.)

A transferee has control of transferred assets if there is the unconstrained right to both pledge and exchange the assets. In actual practice it may be more difficult to discern whether the transferee has control if it can pledge the transferred assets but cannot sell them. The key to a determination of control by a transferee with the right to pledge *or* exchange the assets rests on whether the transferee obtains all or most of the cash inflows that are the primary economic benefits of the pledged or exchanged assets. Generally, the right of first refusal, prohibition of a sale to competitors, and the requirement to obtain transferor permission that won't be unreasonably withheld (judgment is necessary in this case) to sell or pledge won't preclude accounting as a sale. Agreements that constrain the transferee from pledge or exchange are to be accounted for as secured borrowings.

Maintaining effective control. If the transferor maintains effective control, the transfer is accounted for as a secured borrowing and not as a sale.

FASB substantially limits sale accounting, by stipulating that sale accounting can be applied only if transfers are of entire financial assets, a group of financial assets—or of a portion of those assets only if the transferor and transferee proportionately share in all the rights, risks, and benefits of the entire asset. Thus, it is difficult to employ sale accounting (and thus to recognize gains on such sales) when transferring less than an entire financial asset (or group of assets).

The concept of a *participating interest* is used to denote a portion of a financial asset that is transferred meeting criteria for sale accounting. If a given financial asset is divided into components prior to transfer, the transfer can be accounted for as a sale only if the components meet the criteria for being participating interests (see criteria, below). It is not appropriate to apply surrender of control criteria unless the component (or entire asset or group of assets) being transferred meet the definition of participating interests. If the definition of participating interest is satisfied, *and* if control is surrendered, only then will sale accounting be validly applied.

The transferor must not be able to unilaterally take back the transferred assets. Therefore, a call option, a forward purchase contract, or a removal of accounts provision will in most cases defeat the determination that a sale has taken place. The transferor cannot take back the transferred assets even through the liquidation of the VIE or other transferee.

A transferor maintains effective control over the transferred assets, and thus cannot account for the transfer as a sale, if a repurchase or redemption agreement meets all of the following conditions:

1. The financial assets covered by the agreement are the same or substantially the same as the transferred assets. In order to meet this condition, the assets transferred and those to be repurchased or redeemed must meet all of the following conditions:
   a. The same primary obligor or, in the case of government-guaranteed instruments, the same guarantor and terms of the guarantee. (If the asset is debt guaranteed by a sovereign government, central bank, government-sponsored enterprise or agency thereof, the guarantor and the terms of the guarantee must be the same.)
   b. Identical form and type providing the same risks and rights
   c. The same maturity, or, in the case of mortgage-backed pass-through or pay-through securities, have similar remaining weighted-average maturities that provide approximately the same market yield
   d. Similar assets as collateral
   e. The same aggregate unpaid principal amount or principal amounts that are within accepted "good delivery" standards for the type of security being transferred.
2. The redemption or repurchase agreement is executed concurrently with the transfer of the assets and requires repurchase or redemption prior to maturity at a fixed or determinable price.
3. The agreement is entered into simultaneously with, or in contemplation of, the transfer.

ASC 860-20-55 addresses situations where the original transferee subsequently transfers the financial assets back to the original transferor as collateral for a borrowing arrangement under a repurchase arrangement. The issue is whether this violates the surrender of control criterion of ASC 860, obviating the ability of the original transferor to record the transfer as a sale. It establishes criteria under which the secured borrowing could be evaluated separately from the initial transfer for purposes of determining proper accounting.

Under the provisions of ASC 860, the transferor and transferee are to separately account for a transfer of a financial asset and a related repurchase financing arrangement only if the two transactions have a valid and distinct business or economic purpose for being entered into separately, *and* the repurchase financing does not result in the transferor regaining control over the financial asset. The valid business purpose criterion excludes obtaining favorable accounting treatment. To qualify for separate accounting treatment, the initial transfer of a financial asset and the repurchase financing entered into, either contemporaneously with or in contemplation of each other, must meet *all* of the following conditions at inception of the transaction:

1. The initial transfer and the repurchase financing are not contractually contingent on each other, so that the pricing and performance of either the transfer or the repurchase financing will not be dependent on the terms and execution of the other.
2. The repurchase financing provides the initial transferor with recourse to the transferee upon default, which must leave the transferor exposed to the credit risk of the transferee or its affiliates, and not only exposed to the market risk of the transferred financial asset.
3. The transferee's agreement to repurchase the previously transferred financial asset is at a fixed price (generally related to the agreed interest rate on the amount financed) and not at fair value.

4. The financial asset is readily obtainable in the marketplace, and the transfer and repurchase financing are executed at market rates, and not circumvented by embedding off-market terms in a separate transaction contemplated at the time of the initial transfer or the repurchase financing.
5. The maturity date of the repurchase financing is earlier than that of the financial asset.

If the transaction satisfies each of the above-noted conditions, the initial transfer should be evaluated to determine whether, without consideration of the repurchase financing, it meets the requirements for sale accounting under ASC 860. Also, the transferor and transferee should analyze the repurchase financing as a repurchase agreement, with both parties using the same criteria.

On the other hand, if the transactions do not meet all of these conditions, the initial transfer and repurchase financing should be evaluated as a linked transaction to determine whether it meets the requirements in ASC 860 for sale accounting. If the linked transaction does not qualify for sale accounting, the linked transactions should be accounted for based on the economic substance of the combined transactions. Typically, these will represent a forward contract, to be accounted for in accordance with ASC 815.

Components of financial assets. As securitization activity increased over recent years, it became clear that more guidance was needed, particularly since a number of such arrangements appeared to feature implicit transferor guarantees or other arrangements that raised doubts about the extent to which control had really been relinquished, even as sales (and gains) were being reported by the sponsoring entity. Transferors often kept custody of the securitized assets, further adding to the difficulty in objectively assessing the transfer of control necessary to justify applying "gain on sale" accounting.

Partially in response to this specific concern, ASC 860-10-05 establishes the definition of a *participating interest* to describe when it would be appropriate to evaluate a transferred portion of a financial asset for sale accounting treatment. FASB decided that, for sales of partial interests in financial assets, it was only appropriate to apply the sale accounting conditions if the transferor and transferee proportionately share in all of the rights, risks, and benefits of the entire financial asset.

A transfer can only be treated as a sale if the transferor has surrendered control over the financial asset. If a portion, rather than the entire asset, is transferred, the transferor retains a participating interest, the character of which will determine whether sale treatment is warranted. If an entity transfers part of a financial asset and retains another portion of that asset, gain can be recognized on the portion sold only, and then only if all components qualify as participating interests; gain can be recognized, in such situations, only on the components transferred, assuming control is relinquished. However, if the entire asset (or group) is transferred in circumstances where sale accounting is warranted, and then, after first relinquishing control, the transferor obtains a beneficial interest in the transferred asset, the gain recognized on the transfer will be based on the entire transfer.

FASB has provided specific guidance on the definition of a portion of a financial asset that would be eligible for sale accounting. According to ASC 860-10-40-60, participating interest must have *all* of the following characteristics:

1. *From the date of the transfer, the participating interest represents a proportionate (pro rata) ownership interest in an entire financial asset.* The percentage of ownership interests held by the transferor in the entire financial asset may vary over time, while the entire financial asset remains outstanding, as long as the resulting portions held by the transferor (including any participating interest retained by the transferor,

its consolidated affiliates, or its agents) and the transferee(s) meet the other characteristics of a participating interest.

For example, if the transferor's interest in an entire financial asset changes because it subsequently sells another interest in the entire financial asset (a piecemeal transfer of its interests to others), the interests held initially and subsequently by the transferor will meet the definition of a participating interest.

2. *From the date of the transfer, all cash flows received from the entire financial asset are divided proportionately among the participating interest holders according to their respective shares of ownership.* Cash flows that are allocated as compensation for services performed (e.g., for loan servicing), if any, may not be included in that determination provided those cash flows are not subordinate to the proportionate cash flows of the participating interest and are not significantly above an amount that would fairly compensate a substitute service provider, should one be required, which includes any profit that would be demanded by a market participant.

   Also, any cash flows received by the transferor as proceeds of the transfer of the participating interest are to be excluded from the determination of proportionate cash flows, provided that the transfer does not result in the transferor receiving an ownership interest in the financial asset that permits it to receive disproportionate cash flows.
3. *The rights of each participating interest holder* (including the transferor, in its role as a participating interest holder) *have the same priority of cash flow, and no participating interest holder's interest is subordinated to the interest of another participating interest holder.* Priority is not subject to change in the event of bankruptcy or other receivership of the transferor, the original debtor, or any other participating interest holder. Participating interest holders can have no recourse to the transferor (or its consolidated affiliates or its agents) or to each other, other than for the standard representations and warranties, ongoing contractual obligations to service the entire financial asset and administer the transfer contract, and contractual obligations to share in any setoff benefits received by any participating interest holder. Thus, no participating interest holder can be entitled to receive cash before any other participating interest holder under its contractual rights as a participating interest holder.

   Note however, that if a participating interest holder also is the servicer of the entire financial asset, and receives cash in its role as servicer, that arrangement would not violate the requirement that all participating interest holders share the same priority.
4. *No party has the right to pledge or exchange the entire financial asset unless all participating interest holders agree to pledge or exchange the entire financial asset.*

If all the foregoing conditions are satisfied, the transfer of a portion of the entire financial asset would be accounted for as a sale, if control is relinquished. If one or more of the foregoing conditions are not met, however, the transfer would be accounted for as a lending transaction. Specifically, regarding surrender of control, the transfer is to be accounted for as a sale to the extent that consideration *other than beneficial interests* in the transferred assets is received in exchange, and if *all of the following conditions* are met:

1. *The transferred financial assets have been isolated from the transferor*—put presumptively beyond the reach of the transferor and its creditors, even in the event of bankruptcy or other receivership. The assets are effectively isolated only if the transferred financial assets would be beyond the reach of the powers of a bankruptcy trustee or other receiver for the transferor or any of its consolidated affiliates. For multiple-step

transfer structures, if an entity is designed to make remote the possibility that it would enter bankruptcy or other receivership (thus being a "bankruptcy-remote entity"), it is not considered a consolidated affiliate for the isolation analysis. (However, each entity involved in the transfer is subject to the applicable guidance on whether it must be consolidated, which is a separate determination to be made.)

2. *Each transferee has the right to pledge or exchange the assets (or beneficial interests) it received,* and there is no condition that both (1) constrains the transferee from taking advantage of its right to pledge or exchange and (2) provides more than a trivial benefit to the transferor. If the transferee is an entity whose sole purpose is to engage in securitization or asset-backed financing activities and it is constrained from pledging or exchanging the assets it receives, each third-party holder of its beneficial interests must have the right to pledge or exchange those interests.
3. *The transferor, its consolidated affiliates, and its agents, if any, do not maintain effective control over the transferred financial assets or third-party beneficial interests related to those transferred assets.* A transferor's effective control over transferred assets is exemplified by (1) an agreement that both entitles and obligates the transferor to repurchase or redeem them before their maturity, (2) an agreement that provides the transferor with both the unilateral ability to cause the holder to return specific financial assets and a more-than-trivial benefit attributable to that ability, other than through a "cleanup call" (to eliminate a small outstanding balance that would be more administratively costly to maintain than it would be worthwhile to do), and (3) an agreement that permits the transferee to require the transferor to repurchase the transferred financial assets at a price that is so favorable to the transferee that it is probable that the transferee will require the transferor to repurchase them.

Accounting for transfers. When a transfer of a participating interest that satisfies the conditions above (i.e., surrender of control over a participating interest in a financial asset) has been completed, the transferor (*seller*) is to

1. Allocate the previous carrying amount of the entire financial asset between the participating interests sold and the participating interest that continues to be held by the transferor, on the basis of relative fair values as of the date of the transfer;
2. Derecognize the participating interest(s) sold;
3. Recognize and initially measure at *fair value* servicing assets, servicing liabilities, and any other assets obtained and liabilities incurred in the sale;
4. Recognize in earnings any gain or loss on the sale; and
5. Report any participating interest or interests that continue to be held by the transferor as the difference between the previous carrying amount of the entire financial asset and the amount derecognized (i.e., the initial amount is allocated book value).

Any participating interest(s) obtained, other assets obtained, and any liabilities incurred are to be recognized and initially measured at fair value.

If, instead of a participating interest, the entire financial asset or group of financial assets is transferred, in a manner that complies with the requirements (as set forth above) for sale accounting, then the transferor (seller) is required to

1. Derecognize all transferred financial assets;
2. Recognize and initially measure at fair value servicing assets, servicing liabilities, and any other assets obtained (including a transferor's beneficial interest in the transferred financial assets) and liabilities incurred in the sale; and
3. Recognize in earnings any gain or loss on the sale.

The transferee furthermore is to recognize all assets obtained and any liabilities incurred and initially measure them at fair value (which, in the aggregate, presumptively equals the price paid).

If the transfer is accounted for as a secured borrowing, there is no adjustment to carrying value and no gain recognition.

Measuring assets and liabilities after completion of a transfer. ASC 860 addresses initial recognition and measurement. For example:

1. Interest-only strips, other beneficial interests, loans, other receivables, or other financial assets that can contractually be prepaid or otherwise settled in such a way that the holder would not recover substantially all of its recorded investment (except for derivative instruments that are within the scope of ASC 815) are to be subsequently measured like investments in debt securities classified as available-for-sale or trading under ASC 320, and thus at fair value. They cannot be reported at amortized cost, since they cannot be classified as held-to-maturity.
2. Equity securities that have readily determinable fair values are subsequently measured in accordance with ASC 320, at fair value (either available-for-sale or trading).
3. Debt securities are subsequently measured in accordance with ASC 320, ASC 948 (mortgage-backed securities), or ASC 325-40 (purchased and retained beneficial interests in securitized financial assets).
4. Derivative financial instruments are subsequently measured in accordance with ASC 815.

ASC 860-30-35-2 provides subsequent measurement guidance for pledged assets required to be reclassified that are accounted for as secured borrowings. For those assets, the transferor should follow the same measurement principles as before the transfer.

If it was initially impracticable to measure the fair value of an asset or liability but it later becomes practicable, the transferor does not remeasure the asset or liability (or the gain or loss) under ASC 860 unless it is a servicing asset or liability. (ASC 860-50-35, *Transfers and Servicing—Servicing Assets and Liabilities*, has revised accounting for servicing assets and liabilities; this is discussed in detail later in this chapter.) However, adjustment of the carrying value may be required by other standards, such as ASC 320.

The provisions of ASC 860 apply to a wide range of transfers of financial instruments. Some of those are discussed in the following paragraphs.

Transfers of receivables with recourse. Classic factoring involves the outright sale of receivables and, notwithstanding the existence of a "holdback" intended to deal with returns and allowances, are accounted for as sales. However, some entities have such a poor history of uncollectible accounts that factors are only willing to purchase their accounts if a substantial fee is collected to compensate for the risk. If the company believes that the receivables are of a better quality than the factor has assessed them, a way to avoid excessive factoring fees is to sell these receivables with recourse. This variation of factoring is, in substance, an assignment of receivables with notification to the affected customers (whereas traditional assignment does not include notification of debtors).

Structure of transfer. In a transfer of receivables with recourse, the transferor is obligated to make payments to the transferee or to repurchase receivables sold upon the occurrence of an uncertain future event. Typically, recourse provisions compensate the transferee for uncollectible accounts (sometimes amounts over a defined threshold), but they can also be written to compensate the transferee for such uncertain future events as prepayments of receivables subject to discounts or that are interest bearing, merchandise returns, or other events that change the anticipated cash flows from the receivables.

The effect of a recourse provision on the application of ASC 860's surrender of control provisions may vary by jurisdiction and by the level of recourse provided. For example, in some jurisdictions, full recourse will not place the receivables beyond the reach of the transferor and its creditors, while a limited recourse provision may have this result. Thus, some transfers of receivables with recourse will meet the criteria of ASC 860 and be accounted for as sales; other transfers will fail the criteria and be accounted for as secured borrowings. The remaining discussion in this section relates to scenarios where the arrangement qualifies for sales treatment.

Applicability of ASC 815 or ASC 460. For the recourse provision to be exempt from derivatives accounting, it must meet *all three* of the following criteria:

1. *Restricted payment.* The contract provides for payments to be made solely to reimburse the guaranteed party (the factor) for failure of the debtor to satisfy its obligations to make required payments, when due at prespecified payment dates or at dates that are earlier due to acceleration caused by a default. For the purposes of meeting this criterion, the debtor's obligation cannot be due under a contract that is accounted for as a derivative.
2. *Past due limitation.* Payment under the recourse provision is made only if the debtor's obligation under item 1 is past due.
3. *Risk of nonpayment.* At the date of inception of the factoring arrangement and subsequently throughout the term of the arrangement, the factor will be exposed to the risk of nonpayment through direct or indirect ownership of the guaranteed receivable.

If the recourse provision fails any of the three above criteria, it is considered a derivative and is accounted for by the transferor under the provisions of ASC 815.

Another accounting issue to consider is whether the recourse provision is considered a guarantee under ASC 460. ASC 460 provides that a contract that contingently requires the guarantor to make payments to the guaranteed party (in this case the factor) based on the nonoccurrence of a scheduled payment under a contract is considered a guarantee. The determination that the recourse obligation is a guarantee does not affect the measurement of that obligation because the measurement rules of ASC 460 are identical with the measurement rules for a recourse obligation that is not considered a guarantee. However, it is important to determine the applicability of that interpretation because ASC 460 requires additional disclosures not demanded by ASC 860.

Computing gain or loss. In computing the gain or loss to be recognized at the date of a transfer of receivables that meets the criteria of ASC 860, the borrower (transferor) must take into account the anticipated chargebacks from the transferee. This action requires an estimate by the transferor, based on its past experience. Adjustments are to be made at the time of sale to record the recourse obligation for the estimated effects of any bad debts, prepayments by customers (where the receivables are interest-bearing or where cash discounts are available), and any defects in the eligibility of the transferred receivables. In computing this recourse obligation, the transferor is to consider all probable credit losses over the life of the transferred receivables. The recourse obligation is to be measured at its fair value on the date of sale.

A present value method is acceptable for estimating fair value if the timings of the future cash flows are reasonably estimable. In applying a present value method, the estimated future cash flows are to be discounted using a discount rate at which the liability could be settled in an arm's-length transaction (i.e., a risk-adjusted rate versus a risk-free rate). Subsequent accruals to adjust the discounted amount are to be discounted at the interest rate inherent in determining the initial recourse obligation. ASC 860 expresses a preference for the use of the

CON 7 probability-weighted expected cash flow model over the more traditional discounting of the single point estimate of the most probable or most likely cash flows. This model is discussed and illustrated in Chapter 1.

Example of accounting for the transfer of receivables with recourse

1. Thirsty Corp. enters into an agreement with Rich Company to sell a group of its receivables with a face value of $200,000 on which a 5% allowance for uncollectible accounts had been recorded. Rich Company (the factor) will charge 20% interest computed on the weighted-average time to maturity of the receivables of thirty-six days and a 3% fee. A 5% holdback will also be retained.
2. Generally, 40% of Thirsty's customers take advantage of a 2% cash discount.
3. The factor accepts the receivables subject to recourse for nonpayment.
4. In this jurisdiction, the transfer qualifies as a sale.

Under ASC 860, Thirsty must record the recourse liability. It has accepted the obligation for all credit losses and has, in effect, guaranteed the receivables. The recourse obligation is measured as the estimate of uncollectibles (5% of face value).

The entry required to record the sale is:

Cash	180,055	
Allowance for bad debts	10,000	
Interest expense (200,000 × .20 × 36/365)	3,945	
Factoring fee (200,000 × .03)	6,000	
Factor's holdback receivable [$10,000/($10,000 + $190,000) × $190,000]	9,500	
Loss on sale of receivables	2,100	
Due to factor for discounts (200,000 × .40 × .02)		1,600
Accounts receivable		200,000
Recourse obligation		10,000

Simplified, the entry is:

Cash	180,055	
Allowance for bad debts	10,000	
Factor's holdback receivable (9,500 – 1,600)	7,900	
Loss on sale of receivables (3,945 + 6,000 + 2,100)	12,045	
Accounts receivable		200,000
Recourse obligation		10,000

The accounts receivable net of the allowance for uncollectible accounts (a valuation allowance) is removed from the transferor's accounting records, as it has been sold. Previously accrued bad debts expense is not reversed, however, as the transferor still expects to incur that expense through the recourse provision of the factoring agreement. (Alternatively, the bad debts expense could have been reversed and the new charge to loss on sale will have to be increased by $10,000.) The loss on sale of receivables is the sum of the interest charged by the factor ($3,945), the factor's fee ($6,000), the expected chargeback for cash discounts to be taken ($1,600), and the difference between the holdback receivable at face value and at carrying value ($500). The factor's holdback receivable is a retained interest in the receivables transferred, and it is measured by allocating the original carrying amount ($190,000) between the assets sold ($190,000) and the assets retained ($10,000).

If, subsequent to the sale of the receivables, the actual experience relative to the recourse terms differs from the provision made at the time of the sale, a change in an accounting estimate results. It is accounted for prospectively, as are all changes in accounting estimates, and therefore will be reflected as an additional gain or loss in the subsequent period. These changes are not to be deemed corrections of errors or other retroactive adjustments.

If the above facts apply, but the transfer does not qualify as a sale, the borrower's entry will be:

Cash	180,055	
Interest expense (or prepaid)	3,945	
Factoring fee	6,000	
Factor borrowing payable		190,000

In a secured borrowing, the accounts receivable continue to be recognized by the borrower. Both the accounts receivable and the factor borrowings payable must be cross-referenced on the face of the statement of financial position or in the notes to the financial statements. The accounting for the collateral under ASC 860 depends upon the terms of the collateral agreement. Accounting for collateral is discussed later in this chapter.

Retained interests. Interests in transferred assets that are not a part of the proceeds of a sale are considered retained interests that are still under the control of the transferor. Retained interests include participating interests for which control has not been given up by the transferor, servicing assets and liabilities, and beneficial interests in assets transferred in a securitization in a transaction that can be accounted for as a sale. In general, the more extensive an interest that the transferor of assets retains, the less likely the transaction will be classified as a sale and the more likely the transaction will be classified as a secured borrowing. The primary reason for this result is that in a true sale, the transferor no longer bears the risks or reaps the rewards associated with the transferred assets. If a determination cannot be made between classification as proceeds of a sale or as retained interests, the asset is classified as proceeds and measured at fair value.

In practice, retained interests are usually comprised of one or both of two items: the spread between the average yield on the assets securitized and the cost of the debt issued by the securitization trust, and any overcollateralization provided. Regarding the spread in yields, it is often the case that trusts can issue debt securities at a lower cost than could the transferring entity, for reasons that may include the lower risk attaching to trust instruments, which are isolated from the transferor's overall credit risk. Indeed, this is one of the major attractions of employing a securitization structure. Typically the excess of the yields on the assets placed into securitization over the costs of servicing the debt issued by the securitization trust, less credit losses and other costs incurred, revert to the transferor at the termination of the securitization. Since this event may be many years in the future, the current value of this residual interest, to the transferor, must be measured on a present value (i.e., discounted) basis, which then accretes over the term to final maturity.

Overcollateralization is the other principal residual interest held by transferors. To enhance the creditworthiness of the securities issued by the trust, it is commonly found that placing a surfeit of collateral (i.e., the underlying mortgage or other loans) into the trust (say, $100 of loans receivable for each $90 of debt to be issued by the trust) will result in a significantly reduced net interest cost incurred by the trust, and hence a greater yield spread that will ultimately revert to the transferor. Additionally, an overcollateralization structure will garner a better rating for the trust securities, making them more readily marketable (in addition to having lower coupon rates), thus insuring the ability to fully fund the trust. Alternatives to the use of an overcollateralization structure include the purchase of credit insurance and arranging for a standby letter of credit. Only overcollateralization results in a residual interest being retained by the transferor, however.

Retained interests are measured by allocating the carrying value of the transferred assets before the transfer between the assets sold (if any) and the assets retained based on their relative fair values on the date of transfer. ASC 860-50-35 specifies that the carrying value allocated is to be exclusive of any amounts included in an allowance for loan losses. Any gain recognized upon a partial sale of a loan is not to exceed the gain that would be recognized if the entire loan were sold. If the transferor retains a servicing contract, a portion of the carrying value is allocable to either a servicing asset retained or a servicing liability undertaken since ASC 860 requires all entities servicing financial assets for others to recognize either a servicing asset or servicing liability for each servicing contract.

Relative fair value determinations are to incorporate assumptions regarding interest rates, defaults, and prepayments that marketplace participants would make, as well as the expected timing of cash flows. This allocation must be applied to all transfers that have retained interests, regardless of whether or not they qualify as sales. It should be noted that this fair value allocation may result in a relative change in financial reporting basis unless the fair values are proportionate to their carrying values. Thus, the gain or loss from any sale component could also be affected.

The retained interests continue to be the transferor's assets, since control of these assets has not been transferred. Thus, the retained interest is considered continuing control over a previously owned asset (although the form may have changed). It is not to be remeasured at fair value, nor is a gain or loss recognized on it.

Example: Sale of partial interest in receivables

Facts Given

Receivables' fair value	$16,500
Receivables' book value	15,000

Seller sells 80% of receivables and agrees to service them. The benefits of servicing are just adequate to compensate for the servicing, thus there is no servicing asset or liability to be recognized.

	FV	*80% FV*	*20% FV*	*Allocated 80% BV**	*Allocated 20% BV**
Receivables sold	$16,500	$13,200		$12,000	
Retained amount (20%)			$3,300		$3,000

* *Allocated based on the relative fair values.*

Seller's Journal Entry

Cash	13,200	
Receivables		12,000
Gain		1,200

Seller reports retained amount at $3,000, which is defined by book value, not fair value.

Examples: Sale of loans with various types of retained interests

Facts Given Applicable to All Examples Below (Each Example Is Independent)

Loans' fair value and amount of cash proceeds	$16,500
Loans' book value	15,000
Fair value of recourse obligation	(900)
Fair value of call option* on portfolio of $16,500	800
Fair value of interest rate swap on portfolio of $16,500	700

* *An option that permits the seller/transferor to repurchase the same or similar loans.*

Seller's Journal Entries

1. Sale only

Cash	16,500	
Loans		15,000
Gain		1,500

2. Sale with recourse obligation

Cash	16,500	
Loans		15,000
Recourse obligation		900
Gain		600

3. Sale with recourse obligation and call option to purchase the loans sold or similar loans

Cash	16,500	
Call option	800	
Loans		15,000
Recourse obligation		900
Gain		1,400

4. Sale with recourse obligation, call, and swap (seller provides floating interest rate return although the underlying loans are at fixed interest rate terms)

Cash	16,500	
Call option	800	
Interest rate swap	700	
Loans		15,000
Recourse obligation		900
Gain		2,100

5. Partial sale with recourse obligation, call, and swap. Seller sells 80% of loans.

	FV	*80% FV*	*20% FV*	*Allocated 80% BV**	*Allocated 20% BV**
Loans	$16,500	$13,200		$11,579	
Call	800	640		561	
Swap	700	560		491	
Recourse obligation	(900)	(720)		(631)	
Retained amount (20%)			$ 3,420		$3,000
	$17,100	$13,680	$ 3,420	$12,000	$3,000

Cash	13,200	
Call	640	
Swap	560	
Loans		12,000
Recourse obligation		720
Gain		1,680

Seller reports retained amount of receivables at $3,000, at book value.

* *Allocated based on the relative fair values.*

In some transfers of receivables, the transferor provides credit enhancement (similar to a recourse provision) by retaining a beneficial interest that absorbs the credit risk. If there is no liability beyond the transferor's retained subordinated interests, the retained interest is initially measured at allocated carrying value based on relative fair value, and no recourse liability is necessary. The retained interest would be subsequently measured like other retained interests held in the same form.

Cash reserve accounts and subordinated beneficial interests created as credit enhancements are retained interests and are accounted for as such even if the seller collects the proceeds and deposits a portion in the cash reserve account. (New asset credit enhancements such as financial guarantees and credit derivatives are measured at the fair value of the amount to benefit the transferor.) ASC 860-10-35 provides guidance on estimating fair values and should be used in the case of credit enhancements.

One possible method of estimating fair value of a credit enhancement is the *cash-out method*. Using that method, cash flows are discounted from the date the credit enhancement asset becomes available to the transferor (i.e., when the cash in the credit enhancement account is expected to be paid out to the transferor). The present value can be computed using an expected present value technique with a risk-free rate or a "best estimate" technique with an appropriate discount rate. Among other transferor assumptions, time period of restrictions, reinvestment income, and potential losses due to uncertainties must be included. ASC 860 does not provide guidance concerning subsequent measurement of credit enhancements.

ASC 860-20-55-18 states that:

> *The right to receive the accrued interest receivable, if and when collected, is transferred to the securitization trust. Generally, if a securitization transaction meets the criteria for sale treatment and the accrued interest receivable is subordinated either because the asset has been isolated from the transferor (see paragraph 860-10-50-5) or because of the operation of the cash flow distribution (or waterfall) through the securitization trust, the total accrued interest receivable should be considered to be one of the components of the sale transaction. Therefore, under the circumstances described, the accrued interest receivable asset should be accounted for as a transferor's interest. It is inappropriate to report the accrued interest receivable related to securitized and sold receivables as loans receivable or other terminology implying that it has not been subordinated to the senior interest in the securitization.*

Servicing. When loans (mortgages and other) are sold to securitization trusts, the debtors are not informed that ownership has been transferred, and they will continue to make monthly (or other) payments to the original creditor. Often the transferor retains servicing, which involves collections of loan principal and interest, payment of expenses, and forwarding of net proceeds to the trustee or other transferee, to be further distributed, depending on the terms of the so-called "waterfall" provisions, to the various classes of investors in trust-issued securities. For example, if the cash flows have been assigned to different *tranches* of securities (having claims to early period cash flows, later period cash flows, principal payments only, interest payments only, etc.), the cash flows will be first used to satisfy certain securities holders, then others, in accordance with the prescribed cash-flow sequence set forth in the trust indenture.

Transferors will most commonly retain the right and obligation to perform this servicing, and will be paid a certain fee to do so, often a small percentage (say, one-quarter of 1%) of the principal amount of loans being serviced. In some cases third parties will buy the right to service loans, or, in other situations, the transferor will retain servicing and purchase rights to service yet other loans. If the fee for providing servicing exceeds the expected cost of doing so, the right to service will be a valuable asset, which will trade for a positive price. In other circumstances, a party (generally the transferor) will have to perform servicing for a fee that will not cover expected costs, in which case a servicing liability exists.

The nature of servicing. Servicing of financial assets can include such activities as

1. Collecting payments (principal, interest, and escrows)
2. Paying taxes and insurance from escrows

3. Monitoring delinquencies
4. Foreclosing
5. Investing funds temporarily prior to their distribution
6. Remitting fees to guarantors, trustees, and service providers
7. Accounting for and remitting distributions to holders of beneficial interests.

Although inherent in holding most financial assets, servicing is a distinct asset or liability only when separated contractually from the underlying financial asset. Servicers' obligations are contractually specified. Servicing is subject to significant risks due to the effects of change in interest rates and debtors' propensity for prepayment of the related obligations. As the likelihood of prepayment (known as *prepayment speed*) increases, the value of the servicing asset decreases, and vice versa.

Adequate compensation for servicing is determined by the marketplace. The concept of adequate compensation is judged by requirements that would be imposed by a new or outside servicer. It includes profit demanded by the marketplace and does not vary with the specific servicing costs of the servicer. Thus, it would not be acceptable to use a given servicer's cost plus a profit margin to estimate the fair value of a servicing asset or liability to be recognized by that particular servicer.

Other changes in economic conditions may also impact the value of servicing arrangements. Some entities having servicing contracts will attempt to hedge these risks by holding financial assets, the value of which will move in the opposite direction of the servicing contracts.

Typically, the benefits are more than adequate compensation for the servicing and the servicing contract results in an asset. The benefits to be reaped by the servicer include:

1. Fees
2. Late charges
3. Float
4. Other income.

If the above benefits are not expected to provide adequate compensation, the contract results in a liability. With regard to the sale of assets, a servicing liability would reduce the net proceeds and would affect the gain or loss calculation.

Accounting for servicing. Servicing assets are recognized at fair value if arising out of the transfer of the entire financial asset or group of financial assets, or a participating interest in financial assets, or if associated with purchased servicing rights unrelated to the assets transferred. If financial assets are transferred to an unconsolidated affiliate in a sale transaction, and the transferor retains servicing and obtains debt securities (from the securitization process) that are properly classified as held-to-maturity, the servicing rights may be reported either as a separate asset or combined with the debt instruments held.

Once a servicing asset is recognized, the asset must be expensed over the expected period over which serving income will be realized. Similarly, if a loss on servicing is anticipated, the liability must be taken into income over the appropriate time horizon. One of two acceptable methods can be employed:

1. *Amortization method:* Amortize servicing assets or servicing liabilities in proportion to and over the period of estimated net servicing income (if servicing revenues exceed servicing costs) or net servicing loss (if servicing costs exceed servicing revenues), and assess servicing assets or servicing liabilities for impairment or increased obligation based on fair value at each reporting date; or

2. *Fair value measurement method:* Measure servicing assets or servicing liabilities at fair value at each reporting date and report changes in fair value of servicing assets and servicing liabilities in earnings in the period in which the changes occur.

The method chosen can vary by class of servicing, so a given entity may be using both amortization and fair value methods simultaneously. However, all servicing in a given class must be accounted for consistently, and cannot be changed after being elected. For purposes of this requirement, a class of servicing assets and servicing liabilities is identified based on (1) the availability of market inputs used in determining the fair value of servicing assets or servicing liabilities, (2) an entity's method for managing the risks of its servicing assets or servicing liabilities, or (3) both.

A reporting entity that elects to subsequently measure a class of separately recognized servicing assets and servicing liabilities at fair value should apply that election prospectively to all new and existing separately recognized servicing assets and servicing liabilities within those classes that a servicer elects to subsequently measure at fair value. This election cannot be applied on a contract-by-contract basis.

ASC 860-50-35 requires that servicing assets or liabilities must be given recognition whenever the entity undertakes a commitment to provide servicing of financial assets, such as loans. This may arise when the entity transfers assets in a "true sale" situation (i.e., when gain or loss on the transfer is recognized, in contrast to transfers that are only secured borrowings). Additionally, it can arise from independent acquisitions or assumptions of servicing rights or obligations unrelated to financial assets of the reporting entity or its consolidated affiliates.

ASC 860-50-35 provides reporting entities with recognized servicing rights with an *optional* onetime reclassification of available-for-sale securities to trading securities, without calling into question the treatment of other available-for-sale securities under ASC 320, provided that the available-for-sale securities are identified as offsetting the entity's exposure to changes in fair value of servicing assets or servicing liabilities that a servicer elects to subsequently measure at fair value. Note that this election is not available relative to servicing assets or liabilities that will be accounted for by the amortization method. Any gains and losses associated with the reclassified securities that are included in accumulated other comprehensive income at the time of the reclassification should be reported as a cumulative-effect adjustment to retained earnings as of the beginning of the fiscal year that an entity adopts ASC 860-50-35. The carrying amount of reclassified securities and the effect of that reclassification on the cumulative-effect adjustment should be separately disclosed.

The purpose of reclassifying financial assets to trading is to have the changes in fair values reported in current earnings, rather than in other comprehensive income. Including fair value changes in current income will tend to offset, albeit not perfectly, the income effects of changes in the servicing assets and liabilities being accounted for at fair value. There is no need to test for hedging effectiveness, in contrast to hedge accounting under ASC 815, although ASC 860-50-35 does require that these assets be identified as being useful in this regard.

Finally, ASC 860-50-35 requires that servicing assets and liabilities that are being accounted for at fair value must be segregated from those being accounted for by the amortization method. This can be accomplished by using separate financial statement captions, or by footnote disclosures.

Example: Sale of receivables with servicing asset retained by transferor

Facts

Receivables' fair value, without servicing	$16,500
Receivables' book value	15,000
Servicing asset of $16,500 portfolio	800

Partial sale of receivables with servicing asset (i.e., excess of servicing fees anticipated over cost to provide services) retained. Seller sells 80% of receivables.

	FV	*80% FV*	*20% FV*	*Receivables allocated 80% BV**	*Receivables allocated 20% BV**
Receivables sold	$16,500	$13,200		$12,000	
Servicing asset**	800	640			
Retained amount (20%)			$3,460		$3,000
	$17,300	$13,840	$3,460	$12,000	$3,000

* *Allocated based on the relative fair values.*

** *Initially measured at fair value, per ASC 860-50-35.*

Journal Entry

Cash	13,200	
Servicing asset	640	
Receivables		12,000
Gain		1,840

Seller reports retained receivables at $3,000 (book value) and the servicing asset at its fair value of $640.

Example: Sale of receivables with servicing liability retained by transferor

Facts Given

Receivables' fair value, without servicing	$16,500
Receivables' book value	15,000
Servicing (liability) for $16,500 portfolio	(500)

Partial sale of receivables with servicing liability (i.e., excess cost to provide servicing over fees anticipated) retained. Seller sells 80% of receivables.

	FV	*80% FV*	*20% FV*	*Receivables allocated 80% BV**	*Receivables allocated 20% BV**
Receivables sold	$16,500	$13,200		$12,000	
Servicing liability**	(500)	(400)			
Retained amount (20%)			$3,300		$3,000
	$16,000	$12,800	$3,300	$12,000	$3,000

* *Allocated based on the relative fair values.*

** *Initially measured at fair value, if practicable, per ASC 860-50-35.*

Journal Entry

Cash	13,200	
Servicing liability		400
Receivables		12,000
Gain		800

Seller reports retained receivables at $3,000 (book value) and the servicing obligation at its fair value of $400.

ASC 860 imposes standards for both initial measurement and subsequent measurement of servicing assets and liabilities. Specifically, servicing assets or servicing liabilities from each contract are to be accounted for separately as follows:

1. Assets are to be reported separately from liabilities. They are not to be netted, since there is no right of offset.
2. Initially measure retained servicing assets and liabilities at fair values at date of sale or securitization.
3. Initially measure at fair value all purchased servicing assets, assumed servicing liabilities, and servicing liabilities undertaken in a sale or securitization.
4. Account separately for interest-only strips (future interest income from serviced assets that exceeds servicing fees).
5. Either amortize servicing assets and liabilities in proportion to and over the period of estimated net servicing income (the excess of servicing revenues over servicing costs), or adjust to fair value at each reporting date. However, if amortization is employed, impairment of servicing assets and increased obligation of servicing obligations must be accounted for, as described in the following point.
6. Evaluate and measure impairment of servicing assets as follows:

    a. Stratify recognized servicing assets based on predominant risk (asset size, type, interest rate, term, location, date of organization, etc.).
    b. Recognize impairment through a valuation allowance for individual stratum in the amount of the excess of carrying value over fair value.
    c. Adjust the valuation allowances to reflect subsequently needed changes. Excess fair value for a stratum is not recognized.

7. If amortization of servicing liabilities is employed, it is done in proportion to and over the period of net servicing loss (excess of servicing costs over servicing revenues). In cases where subsequent changes have increased the fair value of the servicing liability above the carrying value, an increased liability and a loss are recognized.
8. If servicing assets and liabilities are reported at fair value, changes in value are to be included in periodic earnings as they occur.

The fair value of a servicing asset or liability at date of transfer is best measured by quoted market prices for similar servicing responsibilities. There is the potential for significantly different estimates of fair value when a quoted market price is not available. The transferor is to analyze all available information to obtain the best estimate of the fair value of the servicing contract. These include

1. The amount that would result in a current transaction between willing parties other than in a forced or liquidation sale
2. The legitimacy of the offer
3. The third party's specific knowledge about relevant factors
4. The experience of the broker with similar contracts
5. The price of other parties that have demonstrated an interest
6. The right to benefit from cash flows of potential future transactions (late charges, ancillary revenue, etc.)
7. The nature of the assets being serviced.

In cases where there are few servicing contracts purchased or sold, present value methods may be used for estimating the fair value of servicing. Disclosure is required of the methods and significant assumptions followed to determine the estimate of fair value (unless not practicable) of recognized servicing assets and liabilities.

Examples: Sale of receivables with servicing asset retained

Facts Given Applicable to Both Examples Below (Each Example Is Independent)

Receivables' fair value	$16,500
Receivables' book value	15,000
Servicing asset fair value on portfolio of $16,500	700
Recourse obligation on portfolio of $16,500	(900)

1. Receivables sold, with servicing asset retained, no recourse obligation on receivables.

Journal Entry

Cash	16,500	
Servicing asset	700	
Receivables		15,000
Gain on transfer		2,200

2. Partial sale of receivables with servicing asset retained and recourse obligation. Seller sells 80% of receivables.

	FV	*80% FV*	*20% FV*	*Allocated 80% BV**	*Allocated 20% BV**
Receivables sold	$16,500	$13,200		$12,000	
Servicing asset	700	560			
Recourse obligation	(900)	(720)			
Retained amount (20%)	___	___	$3,300	___	$3,000
	$16,300	$13,040	$3,300	$12,000	$3,000

* *Allocated based on the relative fair values of the receivables sold and retained.*

Journal Entry

Cash	13,200	
Servicing asset	560	
Receivables		12,000
Recourse obligation		720
Gain on transfer		1,040

Seller reports retained receivables at $3,000 (book value) and servicing asset at $560, the fair value of servicing the 80% of the portfolio that has been transferred.

The foregoing example presumes that the recourse obligation does not obviate the ability to apply sale accounting for the asset transferred. While this is possible under specific circumstances, it is less likely to be acceptable under the revised ASC 860 provisions than it would have been under preamendement GAAP.

Impairment testing. In remeasuring servicing assets for impairment, this is to be based on the fair value of the contracts and not on the gain or loss from carrying out the terms of the contracts. ASC 860-50-35 requires that entities separately evaluate and measure impairment of designated strata of servicing assets. Stratification requires that judgment be used when selecting the most important characteristic. ASC 860 does not require that either the most predominant risk characteristic or more than one predominant risk characteristic be used to stratify the servicing assets for purposes of evaluating and measuring impairment.

Different stratification criteria may be used for ASC 860 impairment testing and for ASC 815 grouping of similar assets to be designated as a hedged portfolio in a fair value hedge. The stratum selected is to be used consistently; a change is to be accounted for as a change in estimate under ASC 250. The change and reasons for the change are to be included in the disclosures made in accordance with ASC 860-50-50.

A servicing liability accounted for by the amortization method, on the other hand, is to be remeasured for increases in fair value, which would be recognized as a loss. Similar to the accounting for changes in a valuation allowance for an impaired asset, increases in the servicing obligation may be recovered, but the obligation cannot be adjusted to less than the amortized measurement of its initially recognized amounts.

Subcontracted servicing. Subcontracting the servicing to another entity is not accounted for under ASC 860 because it does not involve a transfer. It is to be accounted for under other existing guidance (noting that executory contracts generally do not receive financial statement recognition under GAAP).

In the unusual case that servicing assets are assumed without a cash payment, the facts and circumstances will determine how the transaction is recorded. For example, the servicing asset may represent consideration for goods or services provided by the transferee to the transferor of the servicing. The servicing assets also might be received in full or partial satisfaction of a receivable from the transferor of the servicing. Another possibility is that the transferor (the party providing servicing) is in substance making a capital contribution to the transferee (the party receiving the servicing) in exchange for an increased ownership interest. Additionally, the possibility that there is an overstatement of the value of the servicing by the transferee must be carefully considered.

The amount to be paid to a replacement servicer under the terms of the servicing contract is not relevant to the determination of adequate compensation. This amount could, however, be relevant for determining the contractually specified servicing fees.

Rights to serviced asset income. Rights to future income from serviced assets that exceed contractually specified servicing fees are accounted for as a servicing asset, an interest-only strip, or both, depending on whether the servicer would continue to receive the value of the right to future income if a replacement servicer started servicing the assets. Generally, the value of the right to receive future cash flows from ancillary sources such as late fees is included with the servicing asset if retention of the right depends on servicing being performed satisfactorily.

An interest-only strip does not depend on satisfactory performance of servicing, and any portion that would continue to be received if servicing were shifted to a replacement servicer would be accounted for separately as a financial asset. ASC 860-50-35 specifies that interest-only strips or other interests that continue to be held by the transferor in securitizations, loans, other receivables, or other financial assets that can be prepaid or otherwise settled in such a way that the entity might not recover its investment are to be subsequently remeasured as an investment in debt securities classified as available-for-sale or trading under ASC 320.

Example of rights to future income from serviced assets

The NorthStar Bank sells a portion of its loan portfolio, but retains the obligation to service the loans and the rights to a portion of any future interest income. Accounting for the servicing asset will be on the amortization method permitted by ASC 860-50-35. NorthStar records a servicing asset of $148,000 and an interest-only strip receivable of $68,000 (based on the fair value of its retention of a portion of interest proceeds) as part of the sale transaction. The total book value of loans sold is $3,000,000, for which it receives total payment of $2,900,000. The entry to record these assets as part of the sale is

Servicing asset	148,000	
Interest-only strip receivable	68,000	
Cash	2,900,000	
Loans		3,000,000
Gain on transfer of receivables		116,000

The $3,000,000 of loans to be serviced will be contractually terminated at different times, so the estimated net servicing income and related amortization of the servicing asset will decline in accordance with the following schedule:

	Year 1	*Year 2*	*Year 3*	*Year 4*	*Year 5*
Estimated net servicing income	$120,000	$109,000	$82,000	$53,000	$19,000
Percent of total estimated servicing income	31%	28%	21%	14%	6%
Annual amortization of servicing asset	$45,880	$41,440	$31,080	$20,720	$8,880

Thus, the entry to record amortization of the servicing asset in Year 1 follows:

Amortization—servicing asset	45,880	
Servicing asset		45,880

NorthStar retains a portion of the interest income to which it is due under the original loan sale agreement. The initial interest income retention is for $23,000, and is recorded as follows:

Cash	23,000	
Interest-only strip receivable		23,000

At the beginning of Year 4, NorthStar sells its servicing business to a third party, but retains the interest-only strip receivable, whose balance has now declined to $17,500. The entry to eliminate the remaining unamortized balance of the servicing asset, covering Years 4 and 5, follows:

Amortization—servicing asset	29,600	
Servicing asset		29,600

Since the interest-only strip receivable is no longer dependent on NorthStar's satisfactory servicing activities, it shifts the remaining balance of this receivable into an available-for-sale investment account, as shown in the following entry:

Investment in debt securities—available-for-sale	17,500	
Interest-only strip receivable		17,500

Transferred servicing rights. Some organizations transfer servicing rights on loans to third parties. ASC 942 provides criteria to be considered when evaluating whether the transfer qualifies as a sale, the first three of which are cited by reference to ASC 860-50-40.

1. Has title passed?
2. Have substantially all risks and rewards of ownership been irrevocably passed to the buyer?
3. Are any protection provisions retained by the seller considered minor and are they reasonably estimable?
4. Has the seller received written approval from the investor (if required)?
5. Is the buyer a currently approved seller/servicer and not at risk of losing approved status?
6. If the sale is seller-financed:
   a. Has the buyer made a nonrefundable deposit large enough to demonstrate a commitment to pay the remaining sales price?
   b. Does the note receivable from the buyer provide full recourse to the buyer?

7. Is the seller adequately compensated in accordance with a subservicing agreement for any short-duration, temporary servicing provided?

If the servicing rights sold are on loans that are retained, the carrying amount is allocated between servicing rights and loans retained using the relative fair value method prescribed by ASC 860.

Changes resulting in transferor regaining control of financial assets sold. If a transferor is required to re-recognize financial assets in which it holds a beneficial interest because the transferor's contingent right (for example, a removal of accounts provision, known as ROAP, or other contingent call option on the transferred financial assets) becomes exercisable, no gain or loss is recognized. The transferor continues to account for its beneficial interest in those assets apart from the re-recognized assets. That is, the beneficial interest is not combined with and accounted for with the re-recognized assets. A gain or loss may be recognized upon the exercise of a ROAP or similar contingent right with respect to the "repurchased" portion of the transferred assets that were sold if the ROAP or similar contingent right held by the transferor is not accounted for as a derivative under ASC 815 and is not at-the-money. The exercise would result in a recombination of the beneficial interest with the repurchased assets.

If a transferor is required to re-recognize financial assets because the SPE becomes nonqualifying, no gain or loss is recognized with respect to the "repurchase" by the transferor of the financial assets originally sold that remain outstanding in the SPE (or the portion thereof, if the transferor retained a partial interest in those assets). The fair value of the re-recognized assets will equal the fair value of the liability assumed by the transferor, because the transferor is contractually required to pass on all of the cash flows from the re-recognized assets to the SPE for distribution in accordance with the contractual documents governing the SPE. The transferor continues to account for its beneficial interest in those assets, if any, apart from the re-recognized assets.

Under no circumstances is a valuation allowance initially recorded for assets (loans) that are re-recognized at their fair value.

The accounting for the servicing asset related to the previously sold financial assets does not change because the transferor, as servicer, is still contractually required to collect the asset's cash flows for the benefit of the SPE and otherwise service the assets. The transferor continues to recognize the servicing asset and assess it for impairment as required by ASC 860-20-55.

Sales-type and direct financing lease receivables. Lessors' lease receivables are composed of two components: minimum lease payments and residual values. Minimum lease payments are requirements for lessees to pay cash, and thus are financial assets subject to ASC 860 if transferred. Residual values are the rights to the leased equipment at the end of the lease. If the residual value is guaranteed at the inception of the lease, the right is a financial asset subject to ASC 860 if transferred. If the residual value is not guaranteed (or if it is guaranteed after the inception of the lease), transfers of that residual value are not subject to ASC 860. When entities sell lease receivables, the gross investment of the lease is allocated between minimum lease payments, residual values guaranteed at inception, and residual values not guaranteed at inception. If the reporting entity retains servicing rights, it also records a servicing asset or liability if appropriate. ASC 860 does not apply to sales of operating lease payments.

Example of sale of interest in lease payments

Lucky Leasing sells a senior interest in the guaranteed cash flows of a financing lease for $12,200. It retains a subordinated interest in the guaranteed cash flows and the residual value that is not guaranteed. The lease has the following components:

	Face value	*Present value*
Minimum lease payments	$ 8,350	$ 7,000
Guaranteed residual value	7,000	5,875
Residual value not guaranteed	1,400	1,175
Total investment in lease	$16,750	$14,050

The present values are computed using the implicit lease rate. The fair value of the subordinated interest retained is $1,200. Lucky Leasing receives no explicit compensation for servicing the lease, but it estimates that the benefits of servicing are just adequate to compensate it for its servicing responsibilities (that is, there is no servicing asset or liability). The allocation of the carrying amount for the interest sold is as follows:

	Fair value	*Allocated cost*
Senior interest sold	$12,200	$11,722
Subordinated interest retained	1,200	1,153
Totals	$13,400	$12,875

The entry to record the sale would be as follows:

Cash	12,200	
Subordinated interest	1,153	
Residual value	1,175	
Net investment in lease		14,050
Gain on sale		478

Securitizations. Entities that generate a large number of similar receivables, such as mortgages, credit card receivables, or car loans, sometimes securitize those receivables. Securitization is the transformation of the receivables into securities that are sold to other investors. For example, mortgages can be converted into mortgage-backed securities, which entitle the investors to receive specific cash flows generated by the mortgages. With an established market, issuance of the securities can cost less than using the receivables as collateral for a borrowing. Transfers in securitization transactions must be evaluated for sale accounting treatment by the criteria in ASC 860, and must be evaluated for consolidation by the usual GAAP criteria applicable to variable interest entities, set forth at ASC 810. If consolidation of the securitization entity is necessitated by the circumstances, gain cannot be recognized on the transfer.

Note that securitizations may still be treated as transfers warranting sale treatment, and thus gain recognition if justified by the facts, but the new, stricter, criteria will make this more difficult to achieve.

Securitizations may involve a single transfer to a special-purpose entity, or multiple transfers, which are designed to provide greater assurance that the transferred assets have been isolated, thus providing not only greater bankruptcy protection, but also stronger support for sale accounting treatment of the transfer. ASC 860 provides a detailed description of the conditions that would warrant this treatment.

In a typical securitization, the transferor (also called issuer or sponsor) forms a securitization mechanism (a separate corporation or a trust) to buy the assets and to issue the securities. The securitization mechanism then generates beneficial interests in the assets or resulting cash flows that are sold to investors with the sales proceeds used to pay the transferor/sponsor for the transferred assets. The form of the securities chosen depends on such things as the nature of the assets, income tax considerations, and returns to be received. The securities issued by the securitization entity may consist of a single class of interests with the characteristics of equity or multiple classes of interests, some having debt characteristics and others equity characteristics.

For example, a transferor originates long-term loans and accumulates them on its statement of financial position (referred to as warehousing). When the group of loans reaches a sufficient size, the loans are sold to a securitization entity. During the accumulation phase, the transferor finances the cost of holding the loans with prearranged lines of credit, known as warehouse lines. Often the transferor hedges the price risk of the loans as they await sale. This is referred to as an *on-statement-of-financial-position warehousing*.

Alternatively, a transferor may use a properly structured *off-statement-of-financial-position warehousing* to securitize assets. In an off-statement-of-financial-position warehouse, the transferor creates a temporary securitization vehicle. A bank typically extends credit to the securitization vehicle in the form of a variable-funding note. Using the proceeds of the note, the vehicle acquires loans from the transferor as they are originated. The principal of the note increases, up to a ceiling, as the transferor transfers additional loans to the securitization vehicle. When the loans have reached the ceiling amount of the note, the bank puts the note back to the securitization vehicle, forcing the vehicle to sell the loans to a permanent securitization entity to raise the cash to pay the note.

Payments by the securitization mechanism are usually classified as pay-through, pass-through, or revolving-period. In a *pay-through*, cash flows from the assets pay off the debt securities. The assets are essentially collateral. In a *pass-through*, undivided interests are issued and the investors share in the net cash flows. In a *revolving-period*, undivided interests are issued, but until liquidation, the net cash flows are split between buying additional assets and paying off investors. During the reinvestment period, principal repayments are reinvested in additional receivables generated by the debtors whose receivables were securitized. Under ASC 860-10-05, any gain recognized by the transferor/sponsor on the sale of credit card or other receivables to a securitization entity is limited to amounts relating to receivables existing at the date of sale. This prevents the transferor/sponsor from recognizing additional gains on transfers that are anticipated to occur during the specified reinvestment period.

In computing gain or loss on the initial transfer, the transferor/sponsor recognizes costs estimated to be incurred for all future servicing activities, including the costs of servicing the receivables that the sponsor expects to sell to the vehicle during the reinvestment period. If the initial sale results in a gain, the costs associated with the receivables to be sold during the reinvestment period may be recorded as an asset and allocated to expense using a systematic and rational method over the initial and reinvestment periods.

Various financial components arise from securitizations. Examples include servicing contracts, interest-only strips, retained interests, recourse obligations, options, swaps, and forward contracts. All controlled assets and liabilities must be recognized under ASC 860. The following examples presume that sale criteria under amended ASC 860 are met, but it is important to bear in mind that this is a facts and circumstances determination that must be made in each situation.

Example of a securitization deal involving four classes of securities

Principal of loans held by the securitizer/transferor	$10,000,000
Accrued interest on loans held by the securitizer/transferor	230,000
Deferred origination costs of loans held by the securitizer/transferor	100,000
Deferred origination fees of loans held by the securitizer/transferor	(200,000)
Loss allowance on loans held by the securitizer/transferor	(250,000)
Net carrying amount of loans	$ 9,880,000

Classes of securities issued and prices:

	Principal	*Price*	*Fair value*
Class A	$9,000,000	100	$ 9,000,000
Class B	1,000,000	90	900,000
Interest-only strip (retained)			150,000
Residual class (retained)			100,000
Total fair value			$10,150,000

Servicing is retained by the transferor and has a fair value of $75,000
Transaction costs are $100,000
Proceeds are $9,800,000 ($9,000,000 Class A + $900,000 Class B – $100,000 costs)

Allocation of carrying value:

	Fair value	*Percent*	*Allocation*	*Sold*	*Retained*
Class A	$ 9,000,000	88.0	$8,696,332	$8,696,332	
Class B	900,000	8.8	869,633	869,633	
Interest-only strip	150,000	1.5	144,939		$144,939
Residual class	100,000	1.0	96,626		96,626
Servicing	75,000	.7	72,470		72,470
Total	$10,225,000	100.0	$9,880,000	$9,565,965	$314,035

The entry to record the sale would be as follows:

Cash	9,800,000	
Interest-only strip	144,939	
Residual class	96,626	
Servicing asset	72,470	
Loan loss allowance	250,000	
Deferred origination fees	200,000	
Loans receivable		$10,000,000
Interest receivable		230,000
Deferred origination costs		100,000
Gain on sale of loans		234,035

The entry to mark the securities retained to fair value under ASC 320 would be

Interest-only strip	5,061	
Residual class	3,374	
Comprehensive income (unless trading)		8,435

Just as it is necessary to distinguish new assets, which are recorded at fair value, from retained interests, which are recorded at allocated carrying value, when accounting for a transfer to another enterprise, it is necessary to do so when accounting for a transfer to a securitization entity. In certain securitization transactions, more than one transferor contributes assets to a single securitization entity. A transferor treats the beneficial interests it receives in a securitization that commingles assets from more than one transferor as:

1. New assets, to the extent that the sources of the cash flows to be received by the transferor are assets transferred by another entity
2. Retained interests, to the extent that the sources of the cash flows are assets transferred by the transferor
3. New assets, to the extent that any derivatives, guarantees, or other contracts were entered into by the securitization entity to "transform" the transferred assets.

After a securitization, the beneficial interests held by the transferor either are in the form of securities that are accounted for under ASC 320 or are required to be accounted for as available-for-sale securities in accordance with ASC 860. Thus, the transferor must classify the beneficial interests into one of the ASC 320 categories. If beneficial interests held by the transferor after the transfer convey rights to the same cash flows as the transferor was entitled to receive from securities that it transferred to the securitization entity, the ASC 320 classification of the beneficial interests is the same as the securities held before the transfer. For example, if prior to the transfer the debt securities were accounted for as available-for-sale securities in accordance with ASC 320, the beneficial interests are to be classified as available-for-sale securities if the transferor receives the cash flows from those securities via its beneficial interest. In contrast, if the transferred assets were not ASC 320 securities prior to the transfer but the beneficial interests were issued in the form of debt securities or in the form of equity securities that have readily determinable fair values, then the transferor has the opportunity to decide the appropriate ASC 320 classification at the date of the transfer.

Revolving-period securitizations present some unique issues because they contain an implicit forward contract to sell new receivables during the revolving period. The forward contract may become valuable to the transferor or burdensome depending upon how interest rates and market conditions change. The value of the implicit forward contract arises from the difference between the rate promised to the holders of the beneficial interests and the market rate of return on similar investments. For example, if the agreed-upon rate to holders is 5% and the market rate is 7%, the forward contract's value to the transferor is 2% of the amount of the investment for each year remaining in the revolving period, after the initially transferred receivables are collected. When receivables are sold to a revolving-period securitization trust, gain or loss recognition is limited to receivables that exist and have been sold. Similarly, servicing assets or liabilities are limited to servicing receivables that exist and have already been transferred. As proceeds from collection of the receivables are used to purchase new receivables for the trusts, each additional transfer is treated as a separate sale, with its own gain or loss calculation. Those additional transfers also can result in recognition of additional servicing assets and liabilities.

ASC 860 does not address the accounting for desecuritization of securities into loans or other financial assets. ASC 320-10-25 addresses that issue. It states that the guidance in ASC 860 is to be extended by analogy to desecuritizations. Thus, the transfer of securities or beneficial interests in a securitized pool of financial assets in which the transferor receives in exchange only the financial assets underlying those securities or beneficial interests would not be accounted for as a sale.

Example of revolving period securitizations

The Mason-Dixon Auto Sales Company enters into a revolving-period securitization agreement to sell $100,000 of its car loan receivables each month to the Meridian Securitization Trust for a four-year period. Meridian guarantees a 5% rate of return to its investors for the entire four-year period. Mason-Dixon will continue to service all receivables sold to Meridian. If Mason-Dixon can create new car loans at interest rates greater than 5%, then it can recognize the difference between the actual interest rate and the rate issued to Meridian's investors as an interest-only strip.

At the end of the first month, Mason-Dixon sells $100,000 of principal on car loan receivables to Meridian, as well as $600 of accrued interest on the loans. Thus, the net carrying amount of the loans sold is $100,600. Mason-Dixon retains receivables servicing, which has a fair value of $6,000, as well as an interest-only strip receivable that recognizes the difference between the 5% guaranteed interest rate paid to Meridian's investors and the average 7% actual interest rate on the loan receivables, which has a fair value of $8,000 at the sale date.

The initial sale includes transaction costs of $5,000, which are deducted from the cash paid by Meridian to Mason-Dixon. The following entry by Mason-Dixon records the sale transaction:

Cash	95,600	
Interest-only strip receivable	8,000	
Servicing asset	6,000	
Loans receivable		100,000
Interest receivable		600
Gain on sale of loans		9,000

At the end of the next month, Mason-Dixon sells another $100,000 of receivables to Meridian, as well as $350 of accrued interest on the loans. Thus, the net carrying amount of the second group of loans is $100,350. The lower accrued interest is due to a drop in the actual interest rate on this second block of loans, which averages 4% and is below the 5% guaranteed Meridian's investors. The fair value of the servicing asset associated with these loans is $6,000. The following calculation allocates the fair value of the various elements of the transaction to the net carrying amount of the loans:

	Fair value	*Percent*	*Allocation*
Loans	$100,000	98.0	$98,343
Interest-only strip	(4,000)	(3.9)	(3,914)
Servicing asset	6,000	5.9	5,921
Totals	$102,000	100.0	$100,350

This second sale also includes transaction costs of $5,000, which are deducted from the cash paid to Mason-Dixon. The following entry records the sale transaction:

Cash	95,350	
Servicing asset	6,000	
Loss on sale of loans	3,000	
Interest-only strip receivable		4,000
Loans receivable		100,000
Interest receivable		350

Repurchase agreements. Repurchase agreements are used to obtain short-term use of funds. Under the terms of a repurchase agreement the transferor transfers financial assets to a transferee in exchange for cash. Concurrently, the transferor agrees to reacquire the financial assets at a future date for an amount equal to the cash exchanged and an interest factor. Many repurchase agreements are for short terms, often overnight.

It is necessary to determine whether the repurchase agreement meets the requirements described in the section earlier in this chapter, "Surrender of control." Usually the critical determination is whether the repurchase agreement gives the transferor effective control over the transferred assets. That determination is made by applying the criteria described in the section entitled, "Maintaining effective control." In most cases, if the repurchase is required prior to the maturity of the security transferred and the cash transferred is sufficient to repurchase the assets if the transferee defaults, the transferor retains effective control and the agreement is accounted for as a secured borrowing. For example, fixed-coupon and dollar-roll repurchase agreements, and other contracts under which the securities to be repurchased need not be the same as the securities sold, qualify as borrowings if the return of substantially the same securities as those transferred is assured. However, if a transferor does not maintain control over the transferred assets and other criteria in ASC 860 are met, the transfer is accounted for as a sale and a forward commitment. ASC 860-20-55, discussed earlier in this chapter, addresses situations where a transferee transfers the assets back to the transferor in a repurchase financing arrangement, which (depending on meeting criteria specified) may or may not interfere with derecognition of the assets by the original transferor.

Example of a repurchase agreement

Mighty Manufacturing has $1,995,000 excess cash that it desires to invest for a 7-day period. It transfers the cash to Lion Bank in exchange for $2,000,000 of commercial paper. At the end of the 7-day period, Lion Bank agrees to repurchase the commercial paper for $1,996,500. Mighty Manufacturing does not have the right to sell or pledge the commercial paper during the 7-day period.

The entries to record the origination of the agreement are as follows:

Mighty Manufacturing			*Lion Bank*		
Investment	1,995,000		Cash	1,995,000	
Cash		1,995,000	Short-term payable		1,995,000

The entries to record the termination of the agreement seven days later are as follows:

Mighty Manufacturing			*Lion Bank*		
Cash	1,996,500		Short-term payable	1,995,000	
Investment		1,995,000	Interest expense	1,500	
Interest income		1,500	Cash		1,996,500

Securities lending transactions. Broker-dealers and other financial services companies initiate securities lending transactions when they need to obtain specific securities to cover a short sale or a customer's failure to deliver securities sold. The transferor/lender provides the securities to the transferee/borrower in exchange for "collateral," usually in an amount greater than the fair value of the borrowed securities. This collateral is commonly cash but could alternatively be other securities or standby letters of credit.

When the collateral is cash, the transferor/lender invests the cash during the period that the security is loaned. The investment return on the cash collateral is larger than the fees paid by the lender under the agreement (the rebate). Because the cash collateral is usually valued daily and adjusted frequently for changes in the market value of the underlying securities, the transaction has very low credit risk.

In determining whether to account for a securities lending transaction as a sale or a secured borrowing, the same criteria used for other asset transfers are applied. Many securities lending transactions are accompanied by an agreement that entitles and obligates the transferor/lender to repurchase or redeem the transferred assets before their maturity. Thus, the transferor maintains effective control over the securities lent. If that is the case, the transaction is accounted for as a secured borrowing. The following is an example of a securities lending transaction accounted for as a secured borrowing:

Example: Securities lending transaction (30 days)

Fair value of loaned security	$16,500
Book value of loaned security	16,500
Collateral (cash)	16,995
Transferor/lender's return from investing cash	5%
Transferor/lender's rebate to transferee/borrower	4%

Transferor/lender's journal entries

At date of loan:		
Securities pledged	16,500	
Securities		16,500
To record transfer of securities as a loan		
Cash	16,995	
Loan agreement payable		16,995
To record receipt of cash collateral		
Money market instrument	16,995	
Cash		16,995
To invest cash collateral		
At end of 30 days:		
Cash	17,065	
Interest income		70
Money market instrument		16,995
To transfer cash from money market and record interest earned		
Securities	16,500	
Securities pledged		16,500
To record securities returned by transferee/borrower		
Loan agreement payable	16,995	
Interest rebate	56	
Cash		17,051
To return cash collateral and pay rebate		

Accounting for collateral. Accounting for collateral depends both on whether the secured party has the right to sell or repledge the collateral and on whether the debtor has defaulted. Ordinarily, the transferor should carry the collateral as an asset and the transferee does not record the pledged asset.

The collateral provisions of ASC 860 apply to all transfers (repurchase agreements, dollar-roll, securities lending, etc.) of financial assets pledged as collateral and accounted for as a secured borrowing. The provisions do not apply to the accounting for cash in secured borrowing transactions.

If the secured party (transferee) has the right to sell or repledge the collateral, then the debtor (transferor) reclassifies the asset used as collateral and reports it in the statement of financial position separately from other assets not similarly encumbered. That is, the debtor (transferor) continues to hold the collateral assets as its own, and the secured party (transferee) does not recognize the collateral asset. If the secured party (transferee) sells the collateral, it recognizes the proceeds from the sale and the obligation to return the collateral to the debtor (transferor).

Although collateral is required to be reclassified and reported separately by the transferor if the transferee has the right to sell or repledge the collateral, that requirement does not change the transferor's measurement of the collateral. The same measurement principles are to be used as before the transfer and the collateral is not derecognized. The subsequent measurement of the transferee's obligation to return the collateral in securities borrowing and resale agreement transactions is not addressed by ASC 860.

If the transferor defaults and is not entitled to the return of the collateral, it is to be derecognized by the transferor. If not already recognized, the transferee records its asset at fair value.

Example of accounting for collateral

Deep Water Marine enters into a loan arrangement with Key West Bank for $4,700,000, using one of its submersibles as collateral. The loan terms are monthly interest payments at an annual rate of 9%, followed by a balloon payment in five years for the entire amount of the principal. The submersible has a book value of $4,250,000, net of accumulated depreciation of $500,000, and a fair value of $4,650,000. Deep Water misses its first loan payment, so the parties renegotiate the loan agreement, allowing Key West the right to resell the submersible. Deep Water records this change by separately listing the submersible in the property, plant, and equipment section of its statement of financial position in the following manner:

Equipment used as collateral with right of sale (net of accumulated depreciation of $500,000)	$4,250,000

Two months after the loan initiation date, Deep Water defaults on the note and enters bankruptcy proceedings, so Key West takes possession of the submersible. Deep Water records the default with the following entry:

Loan payable	4,700,000	
Accrued interest payable	70,500	
Accumulated depreciation	500,000	
Fixed assets—equipment		4,750,000
Gain on loan defaults		520,500

Foreclosure of the Deep Water loan is certain. The estimated cost to sell the submersible is a 2% commission, or $93,000, which Key West includes in the following entry to record its ownership of the submersible ($4,650,000 fair value net of $93,000 commission):

Repossessed assets	4,557,000	
Bad debt expense	213,500	
Interest receivable		70,500
Loans receivable		4,700,000

Key West sells the submersible for $4,500,000, net of all sales costs. It records the transaction with the following entry:

Cash	4,500,000	
Loss on asset sale	57,000	
Repossessed assets		4,557,000

Financial assets subject to prepayment. ASC 860 requires interest-only strips, loans, other receivables, or retained interests in securitizations to be measured like investments in debt securities. If they can be contractually prepaid or settled in a way that potentially precludes recovery of substantially all of the recorded investment, they are classified as available-for-sale or trading under ASC 320 (i.e., they generally cannot be treated as held-to-maturity debt instruments). Only assets meeting all of the ASC 320 requirements and acquired late enough in life that, even if prepaid, the holder would recover substantially all of its recorded investment may be initially classified as held-to-maturity. The probability of prepayment or settlement is not relevant to the classification under ASC 320.

Although financial assets that do not meet the securities definition of ASC 320 must be measured in the same manner as investments under ASC 320, other provisions of that Statement (disclosures, etc.) are not required to be applied.

60 ASC 900s SPECIALIZED INDUSTRY GAAP

CONTRACTORS—FEDERAL GOVERNMENT (ASC 912)

PERSPECTIVE AND ISSUES

ASC 912 governs the accounting and income recognition issues concerning cost-plus-fixed-fee and fixed-price supply contracts. The fees under government cost-plus-fixed-fee contracts are recognized as income on the basis of partial performance if there is reasonable assurance of realization. Fees are also accrued as they become billable unless this accrual is not reasonably related to the proportionate performance of total work to be performed.

This pronouncement also covers renegotiation (refunds of excessive profits) and contracts terminated for the convenience of the government.

DEFINITIONS OF TERMS

Terms are from ASC 912 Glossary.

Contract. A legal agreement obligating a contractor (referred to as the "general contractor" or "prime contractor") to provide products or services to the US government. The term also refers to subcontracts obligating subcontractors to indirectly perform in a similar manner under the supervision and control of the prime contractor.

Contractors. In the context of this discussion, contractors are enterprises that sell products or services to the US government pursuant to a formal contract. The relationship to the government can be direct (a prime contract between the enterprise and the government) or indirect (a subcontract between the enterprise and a prime contractor).

Cost-plus-fixed-fee contracts. A contract under which the contractor is reimbursed for costs plus the provision for a fixed fee. (ASC 912-10-20)

Disposal credits. Amounts deducted from the contractor's termination claim receivable by reason of the contractor's retention, or sale to outsiders, of some or all of the termination inventory for which claim was made. In the circumstance of items retained, either as scrap or for use by the contractor, the amount of the credit is determined by agreement between the contractor and a representative of the government. (ASC 912-310-25-4)

No-cost settlements. A contractor whose contract is terminated may prefer to retain the termination inventory for use in other production or for disposal at the contractor's risk. For these or other reasons the contractor may prefer to make no claim against the government or a higher-tier contractor. In such no-cost settlements there is no sale of inventory or other items to the government and no occasion to accrue any profit arising from the termination. The costs otherwise applicable to the contract shall be given their usual treatment in the accounts. Items of inventory or other property retained, having been previously recorded, require no charge to purchases but shall be treated in accordance with the usual procedures applicable to such assets. (ASC 912-310-25-5)

Service contracts. Contracts in which the contractor acts only as an agent.

Subcontractor's claims. Those obligations of a contractor to a subcontractor that arise from the subcontractor's costs incurred through transactions that were related to a contract terminated but did not result in the transfer of billable materials or services to the contractor before termination (FASB ASC Master Glossary).

Supply contracts. Contract in which the contractor's services extend beyond that of an agent. Contracts include services such as the use of the contractor's own facilities and the contractor assumes responsibility to creditors for material and services, and to employees for salaries.

CONCEPTS, RULES, AND EXAMPLES

Cost-plus-fixed-fee contracts (CPFFC) are used for the manufacture and delivery of products, the construction of plants and other facilities, and for management and other services. The amount of the flat-fee payment is usually determined by the ratio of the actual expenditures to the total estimated expenditures. CPFFC may be cancelled and terminated by the government. If this occurs, the contractor is entitled to reimbursement for expenditures and an appropriate portion of the fixed fee.

Normally, profits are recognized when the right to full payment is unconditional. However, revenues can be accrued and profits recognized for partial performance when total profit can be reasonably estimated and realization is reasonably assured. The fees are usually accrued as they become billable. Because risk is minimal and there is no credit problem, billable amounts are indicative of realization. The contractor's fee is considered earned when it is billable and when the related costs are incurred or paid. Accrual based on billable amounts is an application of the percentage-of-completion method, rather than a deviation from the accrual method. The fee is considered billable when approved by the government. An alternative date is used when a determination is made that estimated and final costs are significantly different. Accrual of the fee upon delivery or based on percentage of completion is more appropriate when excess costs are substantial.

For supply contracts, reimbursable costs and fees are included in sales. For service contracts, only fees are included in sales. Unbilled amounts are included in the statement of financial position as a receivable but are to be captioned and presented separately from billed receivables. Advances in CPFFC are generally intended to assist the contractor in financing its costs. Thus, in general, advances are treated as liabilities and are not offset against contract receivables. Advances are permitted to be offset against contract receivables only when there is an expectation that the advances will be applied against those specific charges. Any such offsets require disclosure in the financial statements.

Renegotiation

Renegotiation typically addresses a refund to the government of "excessive" profits. In reality, it is more of an adjustment of the selling price. The financial statements are to disclose situations when a substantial portion of a contractor's business consists of contracts that are subject to renegotiation. When a reasonable estimate of renegotiation refunds can be made, a provision is shown as a deduction from revenue in the income statement and as a current liability on the statement of financial position. Deferred income taxes are adjusted accordingly. When a reasonable estimate cannot be made, disclosure is required along with the reasons for the inability to make an estimate. Footnote disclosure is also required regarding material uncertainties and their significance, and regarding the basis for determining the renegotiation provision.

Terminated Defense Contracts

These contracts are contracts terminated for the convenience of the government. Profits accrue as of the effective date of termination and are included in financial statements after the termination. Disclosure is made of all material facts and circumstances. Termination claims are recorded as a single amount even if they consist of several different types of cost reimbursements. Material termination claims are to be captioned separately from other receivables and such claims receivable directly from the government are to be presented separately from related claims against other contractors. Claims receivable are classified as current assets unless there is an indication of extended delay, such as a serious disagreement indicative of probable litigation. Pretermination contract advances are shown as a deduction from claims receivable and adequately explained. Termination loans are classified as current liabilities and cross-referenced to the related claims receivable.

Material termination claims are separately captioned in the revenues section of the contractor's statement of income. When inventory is reacquired by the contractor after including it in a termination claim, it is recorded as a purchase. The credit is applied against the termination claim receivable.

DEVELOPMENT STAGE ENTERPRISES (ASC 915)

PERSPECTIVE AND ISSUES

Overview

ASC 915 indicates that development stage enterprises should prepare their financial statements in accordance with the same GAAP applicable to established operating entities.

DEFINITIONS OF TERMS

Source: ASC 915-10-20

Development Stage Entity. An entity devoting substantially all of its efforts to establishing a new business and for which either of the following conditions exists:

a. Planned principal operations have not commenced.
b. Planned principal operations have commenced, but there has been no significant revenue therefrom.

CONCEPTS, RULES, AND EXAMPLES

Disclosures

ASC 915 also provides that a development stage enterprise should disclose certain additional information that would alert readers to the fact that the company is in the development stage. Disclosure requirements include

1. All disclosures applicable to operating entities (ASC 915-205-45-1)
2. Identification of the statements as those of a development stage enterprise (ASC 915-205-45-2)
3. Disclosure of the nature of development stage activities
4. A statement of financial position that, in the equity section, includes the cumulative net losses since inception (ASC 915-210-45-1)
5. An income statement showing current period revenue and expense as well as the cumulative amount from the inception of the entity (ASC 915-225-45-1)
6. A statement of cash flows showing cash flows for the period as well as those from inception (ASC 915-230-45-1)
7. A statement of stockholders' equity showing the following from the enterprise's inception:

    a. For each issuance, the date and number of equity securities issued for cash or other consideration
    b. For each issuance, the dollar amounts (per share and in total) assigned to the consideration received for equity securities
    c. For each issuance involving noncash consideration, the nature of the consideration and the basis used in assigning the valuation

    (ASC 915-215-45-1)

8. For the first period in which an enterprise is no longer a development stage enterprise, it shall disclose that in prior periods the entity was a development stage enterprise. If comparative statements are presented, the foregoing disclosure presentations (2–7) need not be shown. (ASC 915-235-45-1)

ASC 915-810 allows parent or equity method investor companies to capitalize or defer some development stage company costs that would have to be expensed by the development stage company. Costs may be deferred if recoverable within the entire entity. (ASC 915-810-45-1 and 45-2)

ENTERTAINTMENT—BROADCASTERS (ASC 920)

PERSPECTIVE AND ISSUES

ASC 920 sets forth accounting and reporting standards for the broadcasting industry. A broadcaster is an enterprise or an affiliated group of enterprises that transmits radio or television program material. Broadcasters acquire program exhibition rights through license agreements. A typical license agreement for program material (e.g., features, specials, series, or cartoons) covers several programs (a package) and grants a television station, group of stations, network, pay television, or cable television system (licensee) the right to broadcast either a specified number or an unlimited number of showings over a maximum period of time (license period) for a specified fee. Ordinarily, the fee is paid in installments over a period generally shorter than the license period. The agreement usually contains a separate license for each program in the package. The license expires at the earlier of the last telecast allowed or the end of the license period. The licensee pays the required fee whether or not the rights are exercised. If the licensee does not exercise the contractual rights, the rights revert to the licensor with no refund to the licensee.

DEFINITIONS OF TERMS

Source ASC 920 Glossary

Barter. The exchange of unsold advertising time for products or services.

Broadcaster. An enterprise or an affiliated group of enterprises that transmits radio or television program material.

Daypart. An aggregation of programs broadcast during a particular time of day (e.g., daytime, evening, late night) or programs of a similar type (e.g., sports, news, children's shows).

License agreement for program material. A typical license agreement for program material (e.g., features, specials, series, or cartoons) covers several programs (a package) and grants a television station, group of stations, network, pay television, or cable television system (licensee) the right to broadcast either a specified number or an unlimited number of showings over a maximum period of time (license period) for a specified fee.

Network affiliation agreement. A broadcaster may be affiliated with a network under a network affiliation agreement. Under the agreement the station receives compensation for the network programming that it carries based on a formula designed to compensate the station for advertising sold on a network basis and included in the network programming.

CONCEPTS, RULES, AND EXAMPLES

Accounting for License Agreements

A broadcaster accounts for a license agreement for program material as a purchase of rights. Thus, an asset and a liability are recorded for the program rights purchased and the liability incurred when the license period begins and the broadcaster has met the following requirements:

1. Knows or can reasonably determine the cost of each program
2. Has accepted the program material according to the license agreement
3. Has access to the program for the first telecast (unless an agreement with another licensee prevents the telecast).

The asset is capitalized and the liability reported at either the gross amount of the liability for program rights or, alternatively, at the fair value of the liability. If a present value technique is used to measure fair value, the difference between the gross and net liability must be accounted for as interest. Under either method, the capitalized costs are allocated to each program within a package based on the relative value of each program to the broadcaster.

The asset is separated into current and noncurrent portions based on expected time of program usage. The liability is likewise segregated according to the payment maturities.

Amortizing Capitalized Costs

The capitalized costs are amortized to expense as the program rights are used; generally based on the estimated number of program telecasts. However, licenses granting the right to unlimited broadcasts of programs such as cartoons are amortized over the license period, since the number of telecasts may be indeterminable.

Feature programs and program series require specific treatment. Feature programs are amortized program-by-program, unless amortization as a package produces approximately the same result. Syndicated programs are amortized as a series. If the broadcaster considers the first showing to be more valuable than reruns, the series is amortized using an accelerated method. If each showing is equally valuable, straight-line amortization is used.

Example of accounting for program license agreements

On July 31, 20X1, Lakie Media Company executed a license agreement for three movies, which it plans to televise on its local television station. The agreement allows the broadcast of each movie twice during the license period. Lakie is a calendar year-end company. The appropriate rate for imputing interest is 12%. Additional facts and assumptions are as follows:

	License Period			*First telecast*		*Second telecast*	
Film	*From*	*To*	*Film availability date*	*Date*	*% of Total revenue*	*Date*	*% of Total revenue*
A	10/1/X1	9/30/X3	9/1/X1	3/1/X2	60%	6/1/X3	40%
B	10/1/X1	9/30/X3	9/1/X1	5/1/X2	70%	7/1/X3	30%
C	11/1/X1	8/31/X3	10/1/X1	6/1/X2	75%	8/1/X3	25%

Payment terms and discounted present value data are as follows (Films A and B were acquired as a package):

	Payment		*Discount period**	
Film(s)	*Date*	*Amount*	*From*	*To*
A & B	7/31/X1	$1,000		
	12/31/X1	6,000	10/1/X1	12/31/X1
	12/31/X2	6,000	10/1/X1	12/31/X2
		13,000		
C	12/31/X2	3,750	11/1/X1	12/31/X2
		$16,750		

* *Discounted from the first day of the license period to the date of payment.*

Based on management's estimates of expected advertising revenues, Film A represents 70% and Film B 30% of the total package A and B.

Present value approach. When each film's license period begins, an asset and a liability are recorded at the present value of the liability. Since the first three payments apply to the package of films A and B, the $12,027 combined present value (see the amortization schedule below) must be allocated to these films according to the 70%/30% assumption stated above.

Film	Asset and liability recognized	
A	$ 8,419	($12,027 × 70%)
B	3,608	($12,027 × 30%)
	12,027	
C	3,283	
	$15,310	

In this case, all costs are capitalized in 20X1 because all of the films' licensing periods begin in that year (assuming the three conditions are met).

The amount capitalized as an asset is amortized according to the percentage of revenues to be earned each year from each film. Interest is accrued on the unpaid balance of the liability for each film. Note that for films A and B, the unpaid balance at December 31, 20X1 is $11,027 ($12,027 – the $1,000 down payment).

Amortization Schedules—Annual Compounding

Description	Date	Payment	Interest at 12%	Principal	Balance
Films A and B					
Down payment	7/31/X1	$ 1,000.00	--	$ 1,000.00	--
Discounted obligation	10/1/X1				$11,027.23
Payment	12/31/X1	6,000.00	$ 329.91	5,670.09	5,357.14
Payment	12/31/X2	6,000.00	642.86	5,357.14	--
		13,000.00	972.77	12,027.23	
Film C					
Original obligation	11/1/X1				3,283.44
Accrued interest	12/31/X2	--	64.77	(64.77)	3,348.21
Payment	12/31/X2	3,750.00	401.79	3,348.21	--
		3,750.00	466.56	3,283.44	
		$16,750.00	$1,439.33	$15,310.67	

	20X1	20X2	20X3	Total
Amortization of film rights				
Film A				
($12,027 × 70% =) $8,419 × 60%		$ 5,051		
($12,027 × 70% =) $8,419 × 40%			$3,368	$ 8,419
Film B				
($12,027 × 30% =) $3,608 × 70%		2,526		
($12,027 × 30% =) $3,608 × 30%			1,082	3,608
				12,027
Film C				
$3,283 × 75%		2,462		
$3,283 × 25%			821	3,283
Total amortization of film rights		$10,039	$5,271	15,310
Interest expense per amortization schedule				
Films A and B	$330	$ 643		973
Film C	65	402		467
	$395	$ 1,045		1,440
				$16,750

Gross method. Costs are capitalized at the gross amount of the liability.

Film	*Asset and liability recognized*	
A	$ 9,100	($13,000 × 70%)
B	3,900	($13,000 × 30%)
C	3,750	
	$16,750	

Again, since the license period for all the films begins in 2012, the assets and liabilities are recognized in that year.

Under the gross approach, no interest is accrued on the unpaid liability. Thus the only expense recognized is the amortization of the program cost.

	Year of expense recognition				*Total*
Film	*20X2*		*20X3*		
A	$5,460	(1)	$3,640	(4)	$ 9,100
B	2,730	(2)	1,170	(5)	3,900
C	2,813	(3)	937	(6)	3,750
	$11,003		$5,747		$16,750

(1) $9,100 × 60% *(4) $9,100 × 40%*
(2) $3,900 × 70% *(5) $3,900 × 30%*
(3) $3,750 × 75% *(6) $3,750 × 25%*

Accounting for Network Affiliation Agreements

A broadcaster may be affiliated with a network under a network affiliation agreement. Under the agreement, the station receives compensation for the network programming that it carries based on a formula designed to compensate the station for advertising sold on a network-wide basis and included in the network programming. Program costs, a major expense of television stations, are generally lower for a network affiliate than for an independent station because an affiliate does not incur program costs for network programs.

Upon termination of a network affiliation agreement, immediate replacement, or an agreement to replace the affiliation, the broadcaster will recognize a loss measured by the unamortized cost of the previous affiliation less the fair value of the new affiliation. No gain is recognized if the fair value exceeds the unamortized cost. If the terminated affiliation is not replaced, its unamortized cost is charged to expense.

Accounting for Barter Transactions

Broadcasters may exchange unsold advertising time for products or services. The broadcaster benefits (providing the exchange does not interfere with its cash sales) by exchanging otherwise unsold time for such things as programs, fixed assets, merchandise, other media advertising privileges, travel and hotel arrangements, entertainment, and other services or products. Such transactions are reported at the fair value of the services or products (except when advertising time is exchanged for programs).

Barter revenue is recognized when all of the following conditions are met:

1. Persuasive evidence exists of the advertising arrangement in the form of a noncancelable contract signed by both the broadcaster and the advertiser.
2. The production of the advertising is complete and has been delivered or is available for immediate and unconditional delivery in accordance with the terms of the arrangement.
3. The period of the arrangement has begun and the advertiser is entitled to use the advertising time.
4. The terms of the agreement and any fees involved are fixed and determinable.
5. Collectibility of any cash portion of the arrangement is reasonably assured.

If all of these conditions are satisfied except for the existence of a noncancelable contract, then the advertising revenue is not recognized until the advertising is aired.

The products or services received in exchange for the advertising time are reported when received or used. A liability results if products or services are received in advance of advertising revenue recognition and a receivable results if the advertising revenue is recognized prior to receipt of the products and services.

Reporting and Disclosure

The capitalized cost of program rights is reported in the statement of financial position at the lower of unamortized cost or net realizable value. Net realizable value is estimated on a package, series, program-by-program, or daypart basis. Daypart is an aggregation of programs broadcast during a particular time of day (e.g., daytime, evening, late night) or programs of a similar type (e.g., sports, news, children's shows). Broadcasters generally sell access to viewing audiences to advertisers on a daypart basis. If the broadcaster expects the usefulness of a program to diminish, the program may have to be written down from unamortized cost to estimated net realizable value. This establishes a new cost basis for the program. The write-down is not permitted to be restored in future periods.

Network affiliation agreements are reported in the statement of financial position as intangible assets.

ENTERTAINMENT—CABLE TELEVISION (ASC 922)

PERSPECTIVE AND ISSUES

ASC 922 sets forth accounting and reporting standards for the cable television industry. These standards apply to cable television systems in the prematurity period. During the prematurity period, the cable television system is partially under construction and partially in service. The prematurity period begins with the first earned subscriber revenue. Its end will vary with the system's circumstances but will be determined based on plans for completion of the first major construction period or achievement of a specified predetermined subscriber level at which no additional investment will be required for other than cable television plant. The length of the prematurity period varies with the franchise development and construction plans. Except in the smallest systems, programming is usually delivered to portions of the system, and some revenues are obtained before construction of the entire system is complete. Thus, virtually every cable television system experiences a prematurity period during which it is receiving some revenue while continuing to incur substantial costs related to the establishment of the total system.

DEFINITIONS OF TERMS

Terms are from ASC 922 Glossary.

Cable television plant. The cable television plant refers to the equipment required to render service to subscribers including:

Head-end. This includes the equipment used to receive signals of distant television or radio stations, whether directly from the transmitter or from a microwave relay system. It also includes the studio facilities required for operator-originated programming, if any.

Cable. This consists of cable and amplifiers (which maintain the quality of the signal) covering the subscriber area, either on utility poles or underground.

Drops. These consist of the hardware that provides access to the main cable, the short length of cable that brings the signal from the main cable to the subscriber's television set, and other associated hardware, which may include a trap to block particular channels.

Converters and descramblers. These devices are attached to the subscriber's television sets when more than twelve channels are provided or when special services are provided, such as "pay cable" or two-way communication.

Direct selling costs. Direct selling costs include commissions, the portion of a salesperson's compensation other than commissions for obtaining new subscribers, local advertising targeted for acquisition of new subscribers, and costs of processing documents related to new subscribers acquired. Direct selling costs do not include supervisory and administrative expenses or indirect expenses, such as rent and other facilities costs.

Subscriber-related costs. Costs incurred to obtain and retain subscribers including costs of billing and collection, bad debts, and mailings; repairs and maintenance of taps and connections; franchise fees related to revenues or number of subscribers; general and administrative system costs, such as salary of the system manager and office rent; programming costs for additional channels used in the marketing effort or costs related to revenues from, or number of subscribers to, per channel or per program service; and direct selling costs.

CONCEPTS, RULES, AND EXAMPLES

Accounting during the Prematurity Period

Before the first subscriber revenue is earned by the cable company, the beginning and end of the prematurity period must be established by management. This period generally will not exceed two years. Once the prematurity period has been established, it may not be changed except in extraordinary circumstances.

Separate accounting is required for any portion[1] of a cable television system that is in the prematurity period and that is distinct from the rest of the system. This distinction is made if the portion is characterized by a majority of the following differences:

- Accountability (e.g., separate forecasts, budgets, etc.)
- Investment decisions (e.g., separate ROI, breakeven, etc.)
- Geographical (e.g., separate franchise area)
- Mechanical (e.g., separate equipment)
- Timing (e.g., separate inception of construction or marketing).

If the portion meets these requirements, it will be charged costs of the entire system only if these costs are directly traceable to that portion. Separate projections are also developed for that portion.

During the prematurity period, costs incurred for the plant are capitalized as usual. General and administrative expenses and subscriber-related costs are considered period costs. Subscriber-related costs are costs incurred to obtain and retain subscribers to the cable television system.

System costs that will benefit the cable system upon completion (e.g., programming costs), and that will remain fairly constant despite changes in the number of subscribers, are separated into amounts benefiting current operations (which are expensed currently) and

[1] *The word "segment" has been used by some television enterprises. However, since ASC 280 uses segment in a different context, the FASB uses the word "portion" instead of "segment" to refer to the part of a cable television system that is still in the prematurity period.*

amounts allocable to future operations (which are capitalized). The amount to be currently expensed is determined by multiplying the total monthly system costs by a fraction calculated each month during the prematurity period as follows:

$$\text{Current portion of system costs benefiting future periods} = \frac{\begin{array}{l}\text{Greatest of} \\ \text{a) Average \# of subscribers expected that month as estimated at beginning of prematurity period,} \\ \text{b) Average \# of subscribers assuming straight-line progress towards estimated \# of subscribers at end of prematurity period, or} \\ \text{c) Average \# of actual subscribers}\end{array}}{\text{Total \# of subscribers expected at end of prematurity period}}$$

During the prematurity period, interest cost is capitalized using an interest capitalization rate as described in ASC 835-20. The amount of interest cost to be capitalized is determined as follows:

$$\text{Interest cost capitalized} = \text{Interest capitalization rate} \times \text{Average amount of qualifying assets during the period}$$

FAS 34 defines qualifying assets. The amount of capitalized interest cost may not exceed actual interest cost for the period.

Depreciation and amortization during the prematurity period are determined as follows:

$$\text{Depreciation and amortization expense} = \text{Monthly depreciation and amortization, of total capitalized costs expected on completion of the prematurity period (using depreciation method to be used at completion of prematurity period)} \times \text{Fraction used to determine monthly system costs to be expensed currently}$$

Amortization

Amortizable life for portions built at different times. Costs that have been capitalized for a portion of a cable television system that is in the prematurity period and that are clearly distinguishable on the basis of differences in timing between construction of that portion and the rest of the system are amortized over the same depreciation period used by the main cable plant.

Installation revenues and costs. A cable television system recognizes initial hookup revenue to the extent of the direct selling costs associated with that revenue. Any excess over the direct selling costs is deferred and amortized to income over the average period that subscribers are expected to be connected to the system.

Initial installation costs are capitalized and depreciated over a period that does not exceed the period used to depreciate the cable plant. After the initial installation, any costs incurred to disconnect or reconnect subscribers are charged to expense as incurred.

Franchise application costs. A cable television franchise is a right granted by a municipality to provide service to its residents. The treatment of franchise application costs depends upon whether or not the application is successful. If successful, the application costs are capitalized and amortized as intangible assets over the life of the franchise agreement. If unsuccessful or abandoned, all application costs are charged to expense.

Impairment. Capitalized plant and amortizable intangible assets are subject to the impairment provisions outlined in ASC 360 (discussed in detail in the chapter on ASC 360). Any of the system's intangible assets deemed to have an indefinite life are tested for impairment at least annually under the provisions of ASC 350. A separate evaluation is made for portions of the cable television system that are in their prematurity period. If total capitalized costs reach the maximum recoverable amount, capitalization continues. However, the provision to record an impairment loss to reduce capitalized costs to recoverable value is increased.

ENTERTAINMENT—CASINOS (ASC 924)

PERSPECTIVE AND ISSUES

There is some form of legalized gambling in most states, as well as on Native American land and on riverboats. Legalized gambling includes betting for horse racing, dog racing, lotteries, and jai alai. Gambling has become a considerable revenue stream for resort operators who also provide other services to attract gamblers.

There is a limited amount of guidance available for gambling entities, which is centered on ASC 924, *Entertainment—Casinos*.

DEFINITIONS OF TERMS

Source: ASC 924 Glossary

Base jackpot. The fixed, minimum amount of the payout from a slot machine for a specific combination.

Chips. Money substitutes issued by a gaming entity and used by its patrons for wagering.

Slot machine. A type of mechanical or electrical apparatus used to connection with gaming.

CONCEPTS, RULES, AND EXAMPLES

A casino typically exchanges cash from patrons for its gaming chips. When a casino exchanges gaming chips for cash, it records a liability. The casino calculates the amount of this liability by determining the difference between the total chips placed in service and the actual amount of chips in custody.

A casino should recognize revenue as the difference between gaming wins and losses, not the total amount wagered.

If a casino has immaterial base jackpots, it can charge them to revenue when established. If base jackpots are material, then it should charge them to revenue ratably over the period of time before payout is expected. If a base jackpot has not yet been charged to revenue when a jackpot is actually paid, the casino should charge it to revenue in the period when it pays the jackpot. A casino should not accrue a base jackpot before it is won if the casino can avoid paying it (such as by removing the machine from play). If the casino has an obligation to pay the jackpot, then it should accrue the jackpot in advance.

If a casino leases slot machines, a leasing condition may be to pay a percentage of wins to the machine lessor. If so, the casino records the win as revenue, and the participating fee as an expense.

ENTERTAINMENT—FILM (ASC 926)

PERSPECTIVE AND ISSUES

Overview

The production, sale, licensing, and distribution of motion pictures (and television series) are fraught with uncertainties. The industry is speculative in nature with studios routinely investing multimillion dollar sums in the hope that the production will achieve critical acclaim and that moviegoers will flock to the box office, purchase licensed merchandise tied to the film and its characters, and purchase or rent copies of the film. Due to the uncertainties involved in estimating the revenues that will be earned and costs that will be incurred over a film's life, an acceptable estimation methodology is required to achieve proper matching of costs and revenues and accurately reflect the results of the film's financial performance. This methodology is provided in ASC 926, *Entertainment—Films*.

DEFINITIONS OF TERMS

Source: ASC 926 Glossary

Cross-collateralized. A contractual arrangement granting distribution rights to multiple films, territories and/or markets to a licensee. In this type of arrangement, the exploitation results of the entire package are aggregated by the licensee in determining amounts payable to the licensor.

Distributor. The owner or holder of the rights to distribute films. Excluded from this definition, for the purposes of applying ASC 926, are entities that function solely as broadcasters, retailers (such as video stores), or movie theaters.

Exploitation costs. All direct costs incurred in connection with the film's distribution. Examples include marketing, advertising, publicity, promotion, and other distribution expenses.

Film costs. Film costs include all direct negative costs incurred in the physical production of a film, including allocations of production overhead and interest capitalized in accordance with ASC 835-20. Examples of direct negative costs include costs of story and scenario; compensation of cast members, extras, directors, producers, and miscellaneous staff; costs of set construction and operations, wardrobe and accessories; costs of sound synchronization; rental facilities on location; and postproduction costs such as music, special effects, and editing.

Film prints. The materials containing the completed audio and video elements of a film which are distributed to a theater to exhibit the film to its customers.

Firm commitment. An agreement with a third party that is binding on both parties. The agreement specifies all significant terms, including items to be exchanged, consideration, and timing of the transaction. The agreement includes a disincentive for nonperformance that is sufficiently large to ensure the expected performance. With respect to an episodic television series, a firm commitment for future production includes only episodes to be delivered within one year from the date of the estimate of ultimate revenue.

Market. A distribution channel located within a certain geographic territory for a certain type of media, exhibition, or related product. Examples include theatrical exhibition, home video (laser disc, videotape, DVD), pay television, free television, and the licensing of film-related merchandise.

Nonrefundable minimum guarantee. Amount to be paid by a customer in a variable fee arrangement that guarantees an entity a minimum fee on that arrangement. This amount applies to payments paid at inception, as well as to legally binding commitments to pay amounts over the license period.

Overall deal. An arrangement whereby an entity compensates a creative individual (e.g., producer, actor, or director) for the exclusive or preferential use of that party's creative services.

Participation costs. Frequently, persons involved in the production of a film are compensated, in part or in full, with an interest (referred to as a *participation*) in the financial results of the film. Determination of the amount of compensation payable to the participant is usually based on formulas (participations) and by contingent amounts due under provisions of collective bargaining agreements (residuals). The recipients of this compensation are referred to as participants and the costs are referred to as participation costs. Participations may be paid to creative talent (e.g. actors or writers), or to entities from whom distribution rights are licensed.

Producer. An individual or enterprise that is responsible for all aspects of a film. Although the producer's role may vary, his or her responsibilities include administration of such aspects of the project as initial concept, script, budgeting, shooting, postproduction, and release.

Revenue. Amounts earned by an entity from its direct distribution, exploitation, or licensing of a film, before deduction for any of the entity's direct costs of distribution. In markets and territories where the entity's fully or jointly owned films are distributed by third-party distributors, revenue is the net amount payable to the entity by the distributor. Revenue is reduced by appropriate allowances, estimated returns, price concessions, or similar adjustments, as applicable.

Sale. The transfer of control of the master copy of a film and all of the associated rights that accompany it.

Set for production. A film qualifies as being set for production when all of the following conditions have been met: (1) management with relevant authority authorizes (implicitly or explicitly) and commits to funding the film's production; (2) active preproduction has begun; and (3) the start of principal photography is expected to begin within six months.

Spot rate. The exchange rate for immediate delivery of currencies exchanged.

Territory. A geographic area in which a film is exploited, usually a country. In some cases, however, a territory may be contractually defined as countries with a common language.

CONCEPTS, RULES, AND EXAMPLES

ASC 926, *Entertainment—Films,* provides the authoritative guidance with respect to accounting for arrangements to sell, license, or exhibit films. The term "film" is generic and includes intellectual property produced on traditional celluloid film as well as videotape, digital, or other video-recording formats. The content or format of films includes (1) feature films, (2) television series, (3) television specials, and (4) similar products (including animated films and television programming). The guidance in the standard applies to producers and distributors who own or hold rights to distribute or exploit films. The standard does not apply to the following specialized industries or applications that have their own specialized GAAP:

1. The recording industry (ASC 928)
2. Cable television (ASC 922)
3. Broadcasters (ASC 920)

4. Computer software to be sold, leased, or otherwise marketed (ASC 985-20)
5. Software revenue recognition (ASC 985-605)
6. Entertainment and educational software products (ASC 985-705).

There are many varieties of contractual sales or licensing arrangements governing the rights or group of rights to a single or multiple films. The film's producer (referred to in the standard and in this discussion as *the entity*) may license it to distributors, theaters, exhibitors, or other licensees (referred to in the standard and in this discussion as *customers*) on an exclusive or nonexclusive basis in a particular market or territory. The terms of the license may be for a fixed (or flat) fee or the fee may be variable based on a percentage of the customer's revenue. If the arrangement is variable, it may include a nonrefundable minimum guarantee payable either in advance or over the licensing period.

Revenue Recognition

An entity recognizes revenue from a sale or licensing arrangement only when all of the following conditions are met:

1. Persuasive evidence exists of a sale or licensing arrangement with a customer.
2. The film is complete and, in accordance with the terms of the arrangement, has been delivered or is available for immediate and unconditional delivery.
3. The license period for the arrangement has started and the customer can begin exploitation, exhibition, or sale.
4. The arrangement fee is fixed or determinable.
5. Collection of the arrangement fee is reasonably assured.

If any of the above conditions has not been met, the entity defers recognizing revenue until all of the conditions are met. If the entity recognizes a receivable on its statement of financial position for advances under an arrangement for which all of the above conditions have not been met, a liability for deferred revenue of the same amount is to be recognized until such time as all of the conditions have been met.

Persuasive evidence of an arrangement. This condition is met solely by documentary evidence that sets forth, at a minimum, the following terms: (1) the license period, (2) the film or films covered by the agreement, (3) a description of the rights transferred, and (4) the consideration to be exchanged. If the agreement is ambiguous regarding the parties' rights and obligations, or if there is significant doubt as to the ability of either party to perform under the agreement, revenue is not recognized. Acceptable documentary evidence must be verifiable (e.g., a contract, a purchase order, or an online authorization).

Delivery. The delivery condition may be satisfied by an arrangement providing the customer with immediate and unconditional access to a film print held by the entity. The customer may also receive a lab access letter that authorizes it to order a film laboratory to make the film immediately and unconditionally available for its use. Under these conditions, the delivery condition is satisfied if the film is complete and available for immediate delivery.

Some licensing arrangements require the entity to make significant changes to the film after it becomes initially available. Significant changes are changes that are additive to the film and that result from the entity creating additional content after the film becomes initially available. The changes can consist of the reshooting of selected scenes or adding additional special effects. When such changes are required to be made to the film, the arrangement does not meet the delivery condition. The costs incurred for these significant changes are added to film costs and subsequently recorded as expense when the related revenue is recognized.

Changes that are not considered to be significant changes include insertion or addition of preexisting film footage, addition of dubbing or subtitles to existing footage, removal of offensive language, reformatting to fit a broadcaster's screen dimensions, or adjustments to allow for the insertion of television commercials. Such insignificant changes do not alter the film's qualification to meet the delivery condition. The expected costs of these insignificant changes are accrued and charged directly to expense by the entity at the time that revenue recognition commences even if they have not yet been incurred.

Commencement of exploitation. Some arrangements impose on the customer a release date or *street date* before which the film may not be exhibited or sold. Such a date defines the commencement date of the exploitation rights. The entity does not begin to recognize revenue on the arrangement until this restriction has expired.

Fixed or determinable arrangement fee. When there is a flat fee that covers a single film, the amount of the fee is, of course, considered fixed and determinable and the entity recognizes the entire license fee as revenue when all of the conditions set forth above have been satisfied.

If the flat fee applies to multiple films, some of which have not been produced or completed, the entity allocates the fee to each individual film by market or territory based on relative fair values of the rights to exploit each film under the licensing arrangement. The entity bases the allocations to a film or films not yet produced or completed on the amounts that would be refundable if the entity did not ultimately complete and deliver the films to the customer. The entity allocates the remaining flat fee to completed films based on the relative fair values of the exploitation rights to those films under the arrangement. These allocations may not be adjusted subsequently even if better information becomes available. After making the allocations described above, the entity recognizes revenue for each film when all of the above conditions are met with respect to that film by market and territory. If the entity is not able to determine relative fair values for the exploitation rights, then the fee is not fixed or determinable and the entity may not recognize revenue until such a determination can be made and it meets all five of the conditions.

An entity's arrangement fees may be variable based on a percentage of the customer's revenue from exploitation of the film. When all five conditions have been met, the entity commences revenue recognition as the customer exploits or exhibits the film.

Certain variable fee arrangements include a nonrefundable minimum guarantee whereby the customer guarantees to pay the entity a nonrefundable minimum amount that is applied against the variable fees on a film or group of films that are not cross-collateralized. In applying the revenue recognition conditions, the amount of the nonrefundable minimum guarantee is considered to be fixed and determinable and is recognized as revenue when all of the other conditions have been met. If the nonrefundable minimum guarantee is applied against variable fees from a group of films on a cross-collateralized basis, the amount of the minimum guarantee attributable to each individual film cannot be objectively determined. In this situation, the entity recognizes revenue as described in the preceding paragraph (i.e., when all five of the conditions have been met as the customer exhibits or exploits each film). Under this scenario, if there is a remaining portion of the nonrefundable minimum guarantee that is unearned at the end of the license period, the entity recognizes the remaining guarantee as revenue by allocating it to the individual films based on their relative performance under the arrangement.

Returns and price concessions can affect whether the arrangement fee meets the condition of being fixed and determinable. The factors to consider include the provisions of the arrangement between the entity and its customer and the entity's policies and past actions related to granting concessions or accepting product returns. If the arrangement includes a right-of-return provision or if its past practices allow for such rights, the entity must meet all of the conditions in ASC 605 in order for it to recognize revenue. Among those conditions is a requirement that the entity be able to reasonably estimate the amount of future returns. ASC 605 is discussed in detail in the chapter on ASC 605.

Barter revenue. If an entity licenses programming to television stations in exchange for a specified amount of advertising time on those stations, the exchange is accounted for as a nonmonetary exchange in accordance with ASC 845. See the discussion of nonmonetary transactions in the chapter on ASC 845.

Modifications of arrangements. If, during the term of a licensing arrangement, the entity and its customer agree to extend an existing arrangement for which all of the revenue recognition conditions have been met, the accounting follows the same rules cited above for flat-fee arrangements, variable fee arrangements, and variable fee arrangements with minimum guarantees.

For modifications that are not extensions of an existing arrangement, the modification is accounted for as a new arrangement and a termination of the former arrangement. At the time the former arrangement is terminated, the entity accrues and expenses all costs associated with the arrangement or reverses previously reported revenue to reflect refunds and concessions that result from the new arrangement. In addition, the entity adjusts accumulated film cost amortization and accrued participation costs attributable to the excess revenue. The new arrangement fee is accounted for by applying the provisions of the standard.

Example

Eva Enterprises produced a film that did not meet revenue expectations. The film was originally projected to gross $9,500,000 and to date has only earned $2,300,000.

The original arrangement called for a fixed fee of $150,000. Eva had previously met all five criteria for recognizing the $150,000 fixed fee as revenue. To placate its customers, Eva negotiated a new arrangement that reduced the original fixed fee from $150,000 to $80,000 and substituted a variable component based on 1% of the customers' revenues from exploiting the film. The effects of the new arrangement on Eva's revenue are computed as follows:

Revenue recognizable under new arrangement	
Fixed fee	$ 80,000
Variable fee earned to date (1% of $2,300,000)	23,000
	103,000
Original fixed fee recognized as revenue	150,000
Reduction in revenue due to new arrangement	$(47,000)

In addition to the adjustment above, Eva also must adjust its previously recorded accumulated amortization of film costs and accrued participation costs attributable to the excess revenue previously recorded. Prospectively, the new arrangement is accounted for in accordance with the provisions of the standard.

Product licensing. Any revenue from licensing arrangements to market film-related products is deferred until the release date of the film.

Present value. Revenue that an entity recognizes in connection with licensing arrangements is recorded at the present value of the license fee computed in accordance with ASC 835 as of the date that the entity first recognizes the revenue. A discounted cash flows model is often used to estimate fair value. FASB Concepts Statement No. 7, *Using Cash Flow Information and Present Value in Accounting Measurements,* provides guidance on the traditional and expected cash flow approaches to present value measurements.

Costs and Expenses—Components

Costs associated with the production and bringing to market of a film can be categorized as one of the following:

1. Film costs
2. Participation costs
3. Exploitation costs
4. Manufacturing costs.

Film costs. Film costs are presented separately on the entity's statement of financial position. They consist of direct negative costs, production overhead, and production period interest capitalized in accordance with ASC 835-20. Direct negative costs include costs to acquire the rights to intellectual property (e.g., film rights to books or stage plays, or original screenplays); the cost of adaptation or development of the property; compensation of the cast, directors, producers, extras, and other staff members; costs of set construction and operations, wardrobe and accessories; costs of sound synchronization; on-location rental facilities; and postproduction costs such as music, special effects, and editing. Production overhead includes allocation of costs of individuals or departments with exclusive or significant responsibility for the production of films. However, production overhead does not include general and administrative expenses, the costs of certain overall deals, or charges for losses on properties sold or abandoned. If the entity presents a classified statement of financial position, unamortized film costs are presented as a noncurrent asset. The amortization of film costs is explained later in this section.

Participation costs. Participation costs are contingent compensation paid to creative talent such as actors or writers, or to entities from whom the distribution rights are licensed, such as the publisher of a novel on which a screenplay is based (these recipients are referred to as participants). The costs are computed (accrued) based on contractual formulas (participations) and by contingent amounts due under provisions of collectively bargained union agreements (residuals). The accrual of these costs is discussed later in this section.

Exploitation costs. Exploitation costs are the direct costs associated with the film's distribution. The advertising cost component of exploitation costs is accounted for in accordance with ASC 340-20. All other exploitation costs, including marketing costs, publicity, promotion, and other distribution expenses, are expensed as incurred.

Manufacturing costs. The cost of making theatrical film prints is charged to expense over the period benefited. The cost of manufacturing and/or duplication of products to be held for sale such as videocassettes and digital video discs is charged to expense on a unit-specific basis when the related product revenue is recognized. Unsold inventories are to be evaluated at the date of each statement of financial position, for net realizable value and obsolescence.

Costs and Expenses—Amortization of Film Costs and Accrual of Participation Costs

Amortization of capitalized film costs and accrual (expensing) of participation costs commences when the film is released and the entity begins to recognize revenue from the film. The method used to compute the amortization of film costs and the accrual of participation costs is called the individual-film-forecast-computation method. This method amortizes film costs using the following formula:

$$\frac{\text{Current period actual revenue}}{\text{Estimated remaining unrecognized ultimate revenue as of the beginning of the fiscal year}} \times \text{Unamortized film costs at the beginning of the fiscal year} = \text{Film cost amortization for the fiscal year}$$

Similarly, participation costs are accrued and expensed using the following formula:

$$\frac{\text{Current period actual revenue}}{\text{Estimated remaining unrecognized ultimate revenue as of the beginning of the fiscal year}} \times \text{Unaccrued ultimate participation costs at the beginning of the fiscal year} = \text{Amount of participation costs to be accrued (expensed) for the fiscal year}$$

Irrespective of the above calculation, participation costs are subject to special rules. The liability is only accrued if it is probable that there will be a sacrifice of assets to settle the entity's obligation under the participation agreement. In addition, at the date of each statement of financial position, accrued participation costs must at least equal the amounts that the entity is obligated to pay at that date.

Using this formulaic approach, if the actual results from the exploitation of the film are realized as originally estimated, the entity would earn a constant rate of profit over the ultimate period for each film before considering exploitation costs, manufacturing costs and other period costs.

It is, of course, likely that the actual results will vary from the estimates and that the estimates will require review and refinement. At each reporting date, the entity reviews and revises estimates of ultimate revenue and ultimate participation costs to reflect the most current information available to it. As a result of this review, the denominator is revised to include only the remaining ultimate revenue at the beginning of the fiscal year of change. In this way, these changes in estimate are accounted for prospectively as of the beginning of the fiscal year of the change. The numerator is unaffected by the change since it is based on actual results. The entity uses this revised denominator in the fraction applied to the net unamortized film costs and to the film's unaccrued ultimate participation costs. The difference between expenses determined using the new estimates and any amounts previously recorded as expense during that fiscal year are charged (or credited) to the income statement in the period (e.g., quarter) during which the estimates are revised.

Ultimate revenue. In general, ultimate revenue to be included in the denominator of the fraction includes estimates of revenue to be recognized by the entity from the exploitation, exhibition, and sale of a film in all markets and territories. There are, however, certain limitations that apply to the determination of ultimate revenue.

1. The period over which ultimate revenue for a film may be estimated is limited to ten years following the date of the film's initial release.
2. For previously released films acquired as part of a film library, the period over which ultimate revenue may be estimated is limited to twenty years from the date of acquisition of the library. A film must have been initially released at least three years prior to the acquisition date of the film library in order to be categorized as part of the library for the purposes of applying this limitation.
3. Ultimate revenue includes estimates of revenue for a market or territory only if persuasive evidence exists that the revenue will be earned, or if an entity can demonstrate a history of earning revenue in that market or territory. Ultimate revenue includes estimates of revenue from newly developing territories only if an existing arrangement provides persuasive evidence that the entity will realize the revenue.
4. Ultimate revenue includes estimates of revenue from licensing arrangements with third parties to market film-related products only if there is persuasive evidence that the revenue from that arrangement will be earned for that particular film (e.g., a signed contract to receive a nonrefundable minimum guarantee or nonrefundable advance) or if the entity can demonstrate a history of earning revenue from that form of arrangement.

5. Ultimate revenue includes estimates of the portion of the wholesale or retail revenue from an entity's sale of peripheral items (such as toys and apparel) attributable to the exploitation of themes, characters, or other contents related to a particular film only if the entity can demonstrate a history of earning revenues from that form of exploitation in similar kinds of films. Under this limitation, the amount of revenue to be included in ultimate revenue is an estimate of the amount that would be earned by the entity if rights for such a form of exploitation had been granted under licensing arrangements with third parties. Thus, the entity's estimate of ultimate revenue does not include the entire gross wholesale or retail revenue from the sale of peripheral items, but rather, the amount that it would realize in net license fees from the sales.
6. Ultimate revenue excludes estimates of revenue from unproven or undeveloped technologies.
7. Ultimate revenue excludes estimates of wholesale promotion or advertising reimbursements to be received from third parties. These reimbursements are accounted for as an offset against exploitation costs.
8. Ultimate revenue excludes estimates of amounts related to the sale of film rights for periods after those identified in 1 and 2 above.

With respect to episodic television series, the following rules apply:

1. The period over which ultimate revenue for an episodic television series may be estimated is limited to ten years from the date of delivery of the first episode or, if the series is still in production, five years from the date of delivery of the most recent episode, if later.
2. Ultimate revenue includes estimates of secondary market revenue (revenue from syndication of the series to markets other than the initial market) for produced episodes only if the entity can demonstrate through its experience or industry norms that the number of episodes already produced, plus those for which a firm commitment exists and the entity expects to deliver, can be licensed successfully in the secondary market.
3. Ultimate revenue excludes estimates of amounts related to the sale of rights for periods after those identified in 1 above.

Ultimate revenue is a gross undiscounted amount and does not include amounts representing projections of future inflation. The portion of ultimate revenue that is expected to be received in a foreign currency is valued at current spot rates.

Ultimate participation costs. The estimate of unaccrued ultimate participation costs to be used in the individual-film-forecast-computation method is made using assumptions consistent with the entity's estimates of film costs, exploitation costs, and ultimate revenue subject to the limitations set forth above. If, at the date of any statement of financial position, the recognized participation costs liability exceeds the estimated unpaid ultimate participation costs for an individual film, the excess liability is first applied to reduce unamortized film costs with any remaining excess credited to income. If the entity continues to incur participation costs after the film costs have been fully amortized, the participation costs are accrued and expensed as the related revenues are recognized.

Example of individual film forecast computation method

Paula Pictures incurred film costs and earned revenues from its motion picture, Arachno-Man, as follows:

	Year 1	Year 2
1. Film cost, including capitalized interest (FC)	$15,000	
2. End-of-year estimate of ultimate revenue (UR)	36,000	$30,000
3. Remaining ultimate revenue at beginning of year* (RUR)	--	11,000
4. Actual earned revenues for the year (ER)	19,000	5,000
5. End-of-year estimate of ultimate participation costs (UPC)	3,600	3,000
6. Actual participation costs for the year (APC)	1,600	500

* *Revised estimate of ultimate revenue less actual revenue earned from date of release through the beginning of the year.*

The individual film forecast computation method is applied as follows:

Year 1

Film cost amortization:

$$\frac{\$19{,}000\text{ ER}}{\$36{,}000\text{ UR}} \times \$15{,}000\text{ FC} = \$7{,}917\text{ Film cost amortization}$$

Accrual of participation costs:

$$\frac{\$19{,}000\text{ ER}}{\$36{,}000\text{ UR}} \times \$3{,}600\text{ UPC} = \$1{,}900\text{ Accrued participation costs}$$

Year 2

Film cost amortization:

$$\frac{\$5{,}000\text{ ER}}{\$11{,}000\text{ RUR}^{*}} \times \$7{,}083^{**}\text{ Unamortized film costs} = \$3{,}220\text{ Film cost amortization}$$

* *Computed as Year 2 revised estimate of ultimate revenue of $30,000 less actual revenue recognized in prior year of $19,000.*

** *Computed as film cost of $15,000 less prior amortization expense recognized of $7,917.*

Accrual of participation costs:

$$\frac{\$5{,}000\text{ ER}}{\$11{,}000\text{ RUR}} \times \$1{,}100\text{ Remaining ultimate participation costs}^{***} = \$500$$

*** *Computed as Year 2 revised estimate for ultimate participation costs of $3,000 less the prior year accrued amount of $1,900.*

Valuation of Unamortized Film Costs

Unamoritzed film costs must be tested for impairment when there is an indication that the fair value of the film may be less than unamortized costs. Consistent with the rules for recognizing impairment of long-lived assets in ASC 360, the standard sets forth examples of events or changes in circumstances that indicate that the entity must assess whether the fair value of the film (whether it has been completed or is still in production) is less than the carrying amount of its unamortized film costs.

1. An adverse change in the expected performance of the film prior to its release
2. Actual costs substantially in excess of budgeted costs
3. Substantial delays in completion or release schedules

4. Changes in release plans, such as a reduction in the initial release pattern
5. Insufficient funding or resources to complete the film and to market it effectively
6. Actual performance subsequent to release fails to meet prerelease expectations. (ASC 926-20-35-12)

Upon making the comparison between the film's fair value and its unamortized costs, any excess of the unamortized costs over the fair value is to be written off as an operating expense on the income statement. Amounts written off may not be subsequently restored.

The fair value of a film is often estimated using a traditional discounted cash flow model. The limits regarding the number of years of revenue to include in the determination of ultimate revenue do not apply to the estimation of future cash flows associated with the film for the purpose of determining the film's fair value. Factors to be considered by management in estimating future cash inflows for a film include

1. The film's performance in prior markets, if previously released
2. The public's perception (the popularity and market appeal) of the film's story, cast, director, or producer
3. Historical results of similar films
4. Historical results of the cast, director, or producer on prior films
5. The running time of the film.

In addition to estimating the film's cash inflows, management must estimate future costs to complete the film (if any), future exploitation and participation costs, and other necessary cash outflows necessary to achieve the estimated cash inflows.

When using the traditional discounted cash flow method to estimate fair value, the estimates of future cash inflows and outflows represent management's best estimates of the most likely cash flows. The discount rate used is adjusted to consider the level of risk inherent in investing in a project of this nature.

When using the expected cash flow approach to estimate fair value (which is preferred and encouraged by ASC 360), all possible relevant future cash inflows and outflows are probability-weighted by period and the estimated average for each period used. In employing this method, the discount rate is risk-adjusted as described above only if the probable expected cash flows have not already been risk-adjusted. Guidance for applying these two estimation techniques is contained in CON 7, discussed in detail in Chapter 1.

Subsequent events. When evidence of the possible need for a write-down of unamortized film costs arises after the date of the statement of financial position but before the entity issues its financial statements, a rebuttable presumption had existed that the conditions leading to the write-off existed at the statement of financial position date. When this situation arose, whether the film was released before or after the date of the statement of financial position, the entity used this subsequent evidence to compute the adjustment necessary to record a change in estimate in its financial statements. ASU 2012-07 removed this rebuttable presumption. The relevant guidance is now ASC 820, *Fair Value,* and ASC 855, *Subsequent Events*. This aligns the guidance for film with the guidance on fair value measurements in other instances, including the impairment testing of other assets.

ENTERTAINMENT—MUSIC (ASC 928)

PERSPECTIVE AND ISSUES

ASC 928 sets forth accounting and reporting standards for the recording and music industry. In this industry, business is transacted through license agreements, contractual arrangements entered into by an owner (licensor) of a music master or copyright. License agreements are modifications of the compulsory provisions of the copyright law. The licensor grants the licensee the right to sell or distribute recordings or sheet music for a fixed fee paid to the licensor or for a fee based on sales. This section presents the proper accounting by both the licensor and the licensee for license agreements in the recording and music industry.

DEFINITIONS OF TERMS

Source: ASC 928 Glossary

Advance royalty. An amount paid to music publishers, producers, songwriters, or other artists in advance of their earning royalties from recording or sheet music sales. These amounts are based on contractual terms and are generally nonrefundable.

License agreements. Contractual arrangements entered into by an owner (licensor) of a master or music copyright and a licensee that grant the licensee the right to sell or distribute recordings or sheet music for a fixed fee paid to the licensor or for a fee based on sales.

Minimum guarantee. An amount paid in advance by a licensee to a licensor for the right to sell or distribute recordings or sheet music.

Recording (or record) master. The master tape resulting from the performance of the artist. It is used to produce tapes for use in making cartridges, cassettes, and compact discs.

Royalties. Amounts paid to producers, songwriters, or other artists for their participation in making recordings and to sheet music publishers for their copyright interest in music.

CONCEPTS, RULES, AND EXAMPLES

Accounting by Licensors

Revenues. A license agreement is considered an outright sale when the licensor has

1. Signed a noncancelable contract
2. Agreed to accept a specified fee
3. Transferred the music rights to the licensee, who is able to use them
4. Fulfilled all significant duties owed the licensee.

When all of these conditions are met, the earnings process is complete and revenue is recognized if there is reasonable assurance that the license fee is fully collectible.

In some cases the licensee pays a minimum guarantee, which is an amount paid in advance to a licensor for the right to sell or distribute recordings or sheet music. A minimum guarantee is first recorded by the licensor as a liability and then amortized to income as the license fee is earned. If the amount of the fee that is earned is indeterminable, then straight-line recognition of revenue from the guarantee is required over the license period.

Example

A licensor receives a $10,000 minimum guarantee under a five-year license agreement. The entry to record the receipt of cash is

Cash	10,000	
Liability under license agreement		10,000

The licensor recognizes revenue from the guarantee on a straight-line basis. At the end of each year of the license period, the licensor records the following entry:

Liability under license agreement	2,000	
License fees earned (revenue)		2,000

A licensor may charge fees for such items as free recordings beyond a certain number given away by a recording club. The amount of such fees is not determinable when the license agreement is made. Therefore, the licensor can recognize revenue only when the amount can be reasonably estimated or when the license agreement expires.

Cost of artist compensation. Royalties are paid to producers, songwriters, or other artists for their participation in making recordings and to music publishers for their copyright interest in music. Amounts for artists are determined by the terms of personal service contracts negotiated between the artists and media companies and usually are determined based upon a percentage of sales activity and license fee income, adjusted for estimated sales returns. Publishing royalties are generally based on copyright or other applicable laws. Royalties are recorded as a period expense of the licensor.

Advance royalties are amounts paid to music publishers, producers, songwriters, or other artists in advance of their earning royalties. Such royalties are based on contractual terms and are generally nonrefundable. Advance royalties are recorded as assets if the licensor expects that the artist's recording will be successful enough to provide for full recovery of the advance from future royalties due the artist. As royalties are subsequently earned by the artist, the capitalized advance is charged to expense. The advance must be apportioned between current and noncurrent assets according to how soon each portion is expected to be charged to expense. If it later appears that the advance will not be fully recovered from subsequent royalties earned by the artist, then the unrecoverable portion is charged to expense in the period in which the loss becomes apparent.

Cost to produce masters. A master is the media that contains the recording of the artist's performance. The costs of producing a master include (1) the cost of the musical talent (musicians, vocal background, and arrangements); (2) the cost of the technical talent for engineering, directing, and mixing; (3) costs for the use of the equipment to record and produce the master; and (4) studio facility charges. Under the standard type of artist contract, the media company bears a portion of the costs and recovers a portion of the cost from the artist out of designated royalties earned. However, either party may contractually agree to bear all or most of the cost.

The portion of the cost that is paid by the media company is recorded as an asset if the company expects that sales of the artist's recording will be successful enough to provide for full recovery of the accumulated costs. If this is not the case, then these costs are expensed. Any amount capitalized is amortized over the useful life of the recording in a manner that relates the costs to estimated net revenue to be realized. Costs to produce masters that are recoverable from the artist's royalties are treated as advanced royalties by the media company.

Accounting by Licensees

When a licensee pays a minimum guarantee in advance, the guarantee is recorded as an asset and then amortized to expense according to the terms specified in the license agreement. If it later appears that the minimum guarantee is not fully recoverable through use of the rights received under the agreement, then the unrecoverable portion is charged to expense.

Fees for which the amount is indeterminable before the agreement expires are sometimes stipulated in the license agreement. An example is a fee charged to a recording club for free recordings beyond a certain number given away. The licensee must estimate the amount of such fees and accrue them on a license-by-license basis.

EXTRACTIVE ACTIVITIES—OIL AND GAS (ASC 932)

PERSPECTIVE AND ISSUES

Oil and gas producing activities are those activities that involve the acquisition of mineral interests in properties, exploration, development, and production of crude oil, including condensate and natural gas liquids, and natural gas. Specialized GAAP does not address refining, marketing, or transportation issues. The successful efforts method of accounting adheres to a traditional historical cost basis. Property acquisition costs, whether the property is proved or unproved, are capitalized as incurred. For other costs incurred under this method, a direct relationship between the costs incurred and specific reserves discovered is required before costs are permitted to be capitalized. Under the successful efforts method, costs that cannot be directly related to the discovery of specific oil and gas reserves are expensed immediately as incurred, analogous to research and development. Oil and gas producing companies are also subject to the requirements of ASC 410 regarding the recognition of asset retirement obligations.

The use of the successful efforts method is preferred, but not required by GAAP. An oil and gas producing company is permitted to use, as an alternative to the successful efforts method, a prescribed form of the full cost method permitted by the SEC. All enterprises are required to disclose the method used for accounting for costs incurred and the method of disposition used for capitalized costs. The SEC requires additional disclosures for publicly traded companies and also provides guidance (SAB 106) on ensuring that the expected cash flows associated with asset retirement obligations are not double-counted in making computations under the full cost method.

For an enterprise that uses the full cost method of accounting, assets being depreciated, depleted, or amortized are considered to be in use in the earning activities of the enterprise and, consequently, do not qualify for interest capitalization. However, assets employed in ongoing exploration or development activities but that are not yet engaged in earning activities and not presently being depreciated, depleted or amortized, are subject to interest capitalization.

Exploratory wells or tests that are in progress at the end of the period present unique accounting issues. If, subsequent to the end of the period, but before the financial statements are issued, a well or test is found to be unsuccessful, the incurred costs, less salvage value, are expensed. Retroactively restated financial statements are not permitted.

CONCEPTS, RULES, AND EXAMPLES

The following is a discussion of the recommended treatment of oil and gas activities as per ASC 932. (Note that this treatment is recommended, but not required.)

The costs of the special types of assets used in oil and gas producing activities are capitalized when incurred. Some examples include

1. Mineral interests in properties
   a. Unproved—Properties with no proved reserves
   b. Proved—Properties with proved reserves
2. Wells and related equipment and facilities
3. Support equipment and facilities
4. Uncompleted wells, equipment, and facilities.

Costs associated with drilling exploratory wells or exploratory-type stratigraphic wells are capitalized until it is determined that the well has proved reserves at which time the capitalized costs are reclassified to wells and related equipment and facilities. If, however, proved reserves are not found, the capitalized drilling costs of the well are charged to expense. When drilling is completed if it is determined that the well has reserves but those reserves cannot be classified as proved, the reporting enterprise will continue to capitalize drilling costs if (1) the reserves found are sufficient to justify completion of the well as a producing well and, (2) the reporting enterprise is making sufficient progress assessing the reserves and the economic and operating viability of the project.

These costs are amortized as reserves are produced and, along with lifting (production) costs, are classified as costs of production. Periodically, unproved properties are evaluated for impairment. The impairment model used for drilling and mineral rights is not the same model set forth in ASC 350 for intangible assets, but rather, is based on the level of established reserves (ASC 932-350-50). If impaired, a loss is recognized.

Acquisition costs incurred to obtain oil and gas properties through purchase, lease, etc., are capitalized.

Geological and geophysical costs, unproved properties' carrying costs, and the costs of dry hole and bottom hole contributions are expensed. Drilling costs are capitalized until a determination has been made as to the success of the well. If successful, these costs are transferred to uncompleted wells, related equipment, and facilities. The cost of drilling, less residual value, is charged to expense if proved reserves are not found.

Development costs are incurred in order to

1. Get access to and prepare well locations
2. Drill and equip development wells
3. Set up production facilities
4. Provide better recovery systems.

These costs are capitalized as uncompleted equipment and facilities until drilling or construction is completed.

The cost of support equipment is capitalized and depreciated. This depreciation, along with other operating costs, is allocated to exploration, development, or production costs, as appropriate.

Production involves different costs ranging from lifting to field storage. These costs, together with depreciation, depletion, and amortization of capitalized acquisition, exploration, and development costs, are part of the cost of the oil and gas produced.

Unproved properties are reclassified to proved properties upon discovery of proved reserves. When proved reserves are found, the costs capitalized as uncompleted wells, equipment, and facilities are reclassified as completed wells, equipment, and facilities. Capitalized costs are amortized or depleted by the unit of production method. Estimated residual values must be considered when determining amortization and depreciation rates.

Any information that becomes available between the end of the period and the date when the financial statements are issued is to be considered in the evaluation of conditions existing at the date of the statement of financial position. With respect to the costs of a company's wells, related equipment, facilities, and the costs of related proved properties, the provisions for impairment as outlined in ASC 360 are applicable.

FINANCIAL SERVICES—DEPOSITORY AND LENDING (ASC 942)

PERSPECTIVE AND ISSUES

ASC 942, *Financial Services—Depository and Lending*, addresses industry-specific guidance for depository and lending institutions.

In general, certain characteristics unique to financial services entities do demand that certain accounting and financial reporting matters be given more elaboration and interpretation than do these same principles when applied to less specialized entities. These more complex areas are summarized in this section.

The thrift and (to a lesser degree) banking industries endured difficult times in the 1980s and early 1990s, largely due to very difficult interest rate environments, and a record number of banks and thrifts failed. Extraordinary steps were taken by government regulators to avert such events. Mergers were encouraged, and in some cases effectively insolvent institutions (i.e., those having liabilities in excess of assets, when both were adjusted to fair values) were acquired by healthier banks or thrifts. In some instances, acquisitions were encouraged by an unorthodox accounting treatment, whereby the net deficit was accounted for as *supervisory goodwill*, to be amortized over an agreed-upon period (typically, fifteen to twenty-five years), with the net unamortized goodwill being considered a "valid asset" for purposes of computing regulatory capital (rather than being deducted from net assets, as would otherwise have been the case).

The accounting profession objected to this treatment, since this supervisory goodwill failed to meet the usual definition of goodwill as being related to excess future earnings potential. However, the profession was ultimately forced to acquiesce. Supervisory goodwill was eliminated as an acceptable asset for banks and thrifts by controversial government legislation, spawning a wave of litigation against the federal government which continues to the present time.

Under current GAAP (ASC 350), any goodwill remaining is no longer subject to amortization, but is to be tested for impairment at least annually, more often under defined circumstances.

Banks and savings institutions are exempted from the need to present certain cash flow information. Specifically, gross amounts for such high-volume transaction categories as deposits and withdrawals need not be disclosed. Banks and thrifts are not exempt from presenting cash flow statements, however.

Lenders often incur significant costs directly related to the origination or purchase of loans and normally receive different nonrefundable fees at the inception of the loans. Historically, disparate accounting procedures had been applied in the reporting of these costs and fees. ASC 320 enumerated various categories of costs and fees and set forth the required accounting for each of them. Most fees are deferred and amortized, via the effective yield method, over the term of the arrangement.

ASC 310 requires loss recognition whenever loans are restructured, unless these involve only an extended payment schedule with full contractual rates of interest being applied to the new due dates. The banking regulators and the SEC have indicated that heightened scrutiny is to be applied to loan loss provisions, and interpretative guidance has been offered.

ASC 942 addresses the accounting and financial reporting requirements applicable to banks and saving institutions, credit unions, and finance companies. It provides revised accounting guidance for sales of loan servicing rights and makes other recommendations. It addresses GAAP for finance companies and conforms the accounting by various institutions such as banks, thrifts, credit unions, finance companies, corporate credit unions, and mortgage companies. It also is applicable to the financing activities of manufacturers, retailers, wholesalers, and other business enterprises. It eliminates differences in accounting and disclosure established by the respective financial institution AAGs, but carries forward accounting guidance for transactions determined to be unique to certain financial institutions.

The codification has the following features:

- Mortgage companies and corporate credit unions are explicitly included in its scope.
- Regulatory capital disclosures are required for mortgage companies, credit unions, banks, and thrifts.
- Credit unions report amounts placed in their deposit insurance fund as an asset if such amounts are fully refundable, due to unique legal and operational aspects of the credit union share insurance fund. Banks and thrifts expense payments to their deposit insurance fund as incurred. Both practices have been preserved because of differences in how the funds operate.
- Finance companies record purchases and sales of securities on the settlement date, whereas banks, thrifts, and credit unions follow trade date accounting. Finance companies follow trade date accounting.

ASC 310-30, *Loans and Debt Securities Acquired with Deteriorated Credit Quality,* addresses the accounting for the differences between contractual and expected future cash flows of acquired loans when these differences are attributable, at least in part, to credit quality. Under this standard, when loans are acquired with evidence of deterioration in credit quality since origination, the acquirer must estimate the cash flows expected to be collected on each loan; this is to be done both at the purchase date and periodically over the lives of the loans. Cash flows expected to be collected in excess of the purchase price will be recognized as yield, while contractual cash flows in excess of expected cash flows will not be so recognized, since to do so would probably cause later recognition of bad debts.

DEFINITIONS OF TERMS

Source: ASC 942 Glossary

Accretable yield. In the context of loans acquired in transfers, the cash flows expected to be collected in excess of the initial investment.

Carrying amount. The face amount of the interest-bearing asset plus (or minus) the unamortized premium (or discount).

Cash. Consistent with common usage, cash includes not only currency on hand but demand deposits with banks or other financial institutions. Cash also includes other kinds of accounts that have the general characteristics of demand deposits in that the customer may deposit additional funds at any time and also effectively may withdraw funds at any time without prior notice or penalty. All charges and credits to those accounts are cash receipts or payments to both the entity owning the account and the bank holding it. For example, a bank's granting of a loan by crediting the proceeds to a customer's demand deposit account is a cash payment by the bank and a cash receipt of the customer when the entry is made. (ASC 942-230-20)

Commitment fees. Fees charged for entering into an agreement that obligates the enterprise to make or acquire a loan or to satisfy an obligation of the other party under a specified condition. For purposes of this Statement, the term commitment fees includes fees for letters of credit and obligations to purchase a loan or group of loans and pass-through certificates.

General reserve. Used in the context of the special meaning this term has in regulatory pronouncements and in the US Internal Revenue Code.

Incremental direct costs. Costs to originate a loan that (1) result directly from and are essential to the lending transaction and (2) would not have been incurred by the lender had that lending transaction not occurred.

Liquidating bank. A bank with a substantial amount of nonperforming assets may transfer some or all of those assets to a newly created bank whose stock will be distributed to existing shareholders or to new investors. The newly created bank will be a liquidating bank; that is, it will manage the assets it receives and collect cash from loan repayments or dispositions of assets. All cash remaining after paying expenses and debt service, if any, will be distributed to the shareholders of the liquidating bank. The liquidating bank will likely be in the process of liquidation for several years. (ASC 942-810-20)

Long-term interest-bearing assets. For purposes of this section, these are interest-bearing assets with a remaining term to maturity of more than one year.

Net-spread method. Under this method, the acquisition of a savings and loan association is viewed as the acquisition of a leveraged whole rather than the acquisition of the separate assets and liabilities of the association.

Nonaccretable difference. In the context of loans acquired in a transfer, the excess of contractual cash flows over the amount of expected cash flows.

Origination fees. Fees charged to the borrower in connection with the process of originating, refinancing, or restructuring a loan. This term includes, but is not limited to, points, management, arrangement, placement, application, underwriting, and other fees pursuant to a lending or leasing transaction and also includes syndication and participation fees to the extent they are associated with the portion of the loan retained by the lender.

Pretax accounting income. Represents income or loss for a period, exclusive of related income tax expense, determined in conformity with generally accepted accounting principles.

Reserve for bad debts. Term is used in the context of the special meaning this term has in regulatory pronouncements and in the US Internal Revenue Code.

Separate-valuation method. Under this method, each of the identifiable assets and liabilities (assumed) of the acquired savings and loan association is accounted for in the consolidated financial statements at an amount based on fair value at the date of acquisition, either individually or by types of assets and types of liabilities.

Servicing asset or liability. A contract to service financial assets under which the estimated future revenues from contractually specified servicing fees, late charges, and other ancillary revenues are expected (asset) or not expected (liability) to adequately compensate the entity for providing the servicing.

Taxable income. Represents pretax accounting income (1) adjusted for reversal of provisions of estimated losses on loans and property acquired in settlement of loans, gains or losses on the sales of such property, and adjusted for permanent differences and (2) after giving effect to the bad debt deduction allowable by the US Internal Revenue Code assuming the applicable tax return were to be prepared based on such adjusted pretax accounting income.

CONCEPTS, RULES, AND EXAMPLES

Justifying a Change in Accounting Principle

The following sources are preferred for depository and lending institutions that must justify a change in accounting principle:

1. ASC 942, *Financial Services—Depository and Lending*
2. ASC 310-30, *Loans and Debt Securities Acquired with Deteriorated Credit Quality.*

Acquisition of a Depository or Lending Institution

The following discussion applies not only to the acquisition of a savings and loan association, but also to acquisition of savings and loan holding companies, commercial banks, mutual savings banks, credit unions, and other depository institutions with assets and liabilities of the same type.

Acquisition method. In accounting for the acquisition of a depository or lending institution, the fair value of the assets and liabilities acquired must be determined using the separate-valuation method. Under this method, each of the identifiable assets and liabilities acquired are accounted for individually, or by type, at its fair value at the date of acquisition. The total amount is reported in the consolidated financial statements.

Note that use of the net-spread method is not considered appropriate for this type of business combination. The net-spread method, which views acquisition of the institution as a leveraged whole, does not appropriately recognize the fair value of individual, or types of, assets and liabilities.

Liabilities acquired are accounted for at their present value at the date of acquisition. The present value of savings deposits due on demand equals the face amount plus interest accrued or accruable at the acquisition date. The present value of other liabilities assumed is calculated by using interest rates for similar liabilities in effect at the date of acquisition.

Identified intangible assets. The purchase price of a depository or lending institution may include intangible benefits from the purchase, such as the capacity of acquired assets to generate new business. Intangible assets that can be separately identified at a determinable fair value are to be assigned a portion of the total purchase price and are to be amortized over their estimated lives. Any portion of the purchase price that cannot be identified with specific tangible and intangible assets (less liabilities assumed) is assigned to goodwill.

Unidentifiable intangible asset. An unidentifiable intangible asset arises when the fair value of liabilities assumed exceeds the fair value of tangible and identified intangible assets acquired. This asset is amortized over a period no greater than the estimated remaining life of any long-term interest-bearing assets acquired. Amortization is applied to the carrying amount of the interest-bearing assets expected to be outstanding at the beginning of each subsequent period. If, however, the assets acquired do not include a significant portion of long-term interest-bearing assets, the unidentifiable intangible asset is amortized over a period not exceeding the estimated average remaining life of the existing customer base acquired. The amortization period may not exceed forty years.

In the sale or liquidation of a large segment, or separable group, of the operating assets of an acquired depository or lending institution, the portion of the unidentifiable intangible asset identified with that segment, or separable group, shall be included in the cost of the assets sold. If the sale or liquidation of a large portion of the interest-bearing assets significantly reduces the benefits of the unidentifiable intangible asset, any reduction shall be recognized as a charge to income.

Regulatory-assisted combinations. Bank regulatory authorities may grant financial assistance to encourage a bank acquisition. Generally, this is done when a failing bank is sold to a solvent one and the amount of any such direct assistance is less than the cost that would have been incurred honoring the deposit insurance commitment, net of recoveries on assets held by the failing bank. Under GAAP, the assistance should be accounted for as part of the combination if receipt of the assistance is probable and the amount to be received is reasonably estimable. Otherwise, assistance should be reported as a reduction of the unidentifiable asset (goodwill), with any excess over that amount being reported in income. If the grantee is required to repay all or a portion of the assistance, a liability would be recognized, together with a charge against income. Assistance received must be disclosed in the financial statements.

Elimination of special accounting for goodwill associated with bank and thrift mergers. The thrift, and later, banking crises of the 1980s gave rise to a number of unusual and often unwise practices. One of these was the invention of *supervisory goodwill*, which sometimes was used as an inducement to relatively stronger institutions to acquire those that were, on a mark-to-market (i.e., fair value) basis, already insolvent. The net liabilities assumed, in such instances, were recognized as the intangible asset goodwill, although this would not have generally qualified as such under existing GAAP, since it often did not imply excess future earnings potential, the usual working definition for goodwill. However, thrift and banking regulators permitted the combined institutions to present this asset on their statements of financial position, subject to amortization over agreed-upon periods, and to treat the unamortized balance as a qualified asset for capital computation purposes (whereas goodwill was otherwise to be deducted from equity for the purpose of making this calculation).

The accounting profession objected to the recognition of supervisory goodwill for GAAP-basis reporting purposes, but ultimately had to acquiesce. Certain parameters were established for the amortization periods to be applied to such supervisory goodwill (referred to as an "unidentifiable intangible asset" in that standard). Thus, the intangible was to be amortized over a period no longer than the estimated remaining life of interest-bearing assets (loans and investments) acquired, which would typically be shorter than the agreed-to terms under the various acquisition agreements then being encouraged by the regulators.

Beginning in 1989, supervisory goodwill was eliminated from regulatory filings, and although this did not require that such goodwill be deleted from GAAP-basis financial statements, this was largely the consequential effect. More recently, accounting for purchase business combinations has been revised in ASC 805, and the accounting for goodwill has been materially altered by ASC 350.

The requirements of ASC 850 deal with the assignment of purchase price to the various acquired assets and assumed obligations. ASC 805 also specifies that acquisitions of branches are to be accounted for as business combinations, if a branch meets the definition of a business, with the possibility of recognizing goodwill in such a transaction. If the branch does not meet the definition of a business, the transaction is to be accounted for as merely the acquisition of assets, and goodwill cannot be recognized. (The definition of a business is set forth in the Master Glossary.)

ASC 942-805 applies to combinations of mutual associations. It gives guidance on the application of long-term customer relationship intangibles often recognized in acquisitions of financial institutions—including depositor-relationship intangibles, borrower-relationship intangibles, and credit cardholder intangibles. The impairment testing of servicing assets, another commonly encountered bank or thrift intangible, is set forth by ASC 860-50.

For those intangibles that arose in business combinations, the remaining unamortized balances are to be transferred to goodwill unless they can be identified as other specific intangibles (e.g., customer relationships). Amounts reclassified to goodwill are no longer subject to amortization, but tested at least annually for impairment.

Bad-Debt Reserves

Both stock and mutual savings and loan associations are required by regulatory authorities to place a portion of their earnings into a general reserve as protection for depositors. Savings and loan associations are allowed by the IRS to maintain a bad-debt reserve and to deduct any additions to their reserve in determining taxable income. Since this method differs from the method for determining bad debt expense, pretax accounting income and taxable income will differ.

Accounting by Creditors for Impairment of a Loan

A persistent practice problem has been in the proper determination of loan loss provisions. Since such reserves are necessarily matters of judgment, the possibility of manipulation (by either understatement or overstatement) in order to manage reported earnings or otherwise bias perceptions about the thrift's or bank's performance has always existed. In more recent years, this has received greater attention, first by the issuance of a detailed standard on accounting for impaired loans (ASC 310-10-35), and later by several FASB, SEC and banking regulatory authority policy announcements.

Under ASC 310-10-35, loans are deemed impaired when it is probable that a creditor will be unable to collect all amounts contractually due, including both principal and interest. This determination is made by applying normal loan review procedures. Once impairment has been identified, the creditor institution must compute the present value of all the estimated future cash flows, using the loan's effective interest rate as the discount factor. The effective rate is defined as the loan's contractual rate as adjusted for any deferred loan fees, premiums, or discounts. It is this effective rate, and not the market rate at the time of determination of impairment, which must be used to compute the loss provision.

If the computed present value of the expected future cash flows is less than the carrying amount of the loan, an impairment will be recognized and recorded in a valuation allowance. Significant changes in the amount and/or timing of future estimated cash flows require that the creditor recalculate the amount of the loan's impairment. Adjustments, subject to the lower of cost or market (LCM) criteria, will be reflected through changes in the valuation allowance.

In the event of a formal loan restructuring through a troubled debt restructuring, the loan is remeasured at the fair market value at the date of the restructuring. This treatment differs from an impairment because it is assumed that a new, formally restructured loan reflects current market conditions; therefore, no impairment is deemed to exist.

The standard, as amended, provides that impairment losses be recognized as bad debts when measured; however, no guidance is provided on the recognition and measurement of amounts later recovered.

The FASB has indicated that loss provisions must be based only on probable losses that have occurred as of the date of the statement of financial position, even if the individual loan which may have been impaired cannot be identified. Predictions of likely future losses to be incurred, even if such predictions have been historically highly accurate, cannot be used to anticipate losses that have not yet occurred.

Losses are to be provided when it is probable that the asset has been impaired and the amount is subject to reasonable estimation. ASC 310-10-35 requires certain methods of measurement for loans that are individually considered impaired, but it does not fundamentally change the recognition criteria for loan losses. It also provides guidance on measurement and disclosure for loans that are identified for evaluation and that are individually deemed to be impaired (because it is probable that the creditor will be unable to collect all the contractual interest and principal payments as scheduled in the loan agreement). It also includes all loans that are restructured in a troubled debt restructuring involving a modification of terms, except for those loans that are excluded from the scope of the standard.

In determining the existence and extent of impairment, *environmental* factors such as existing industry, geographical, economic, and political factors, should be given consideration. Obviously, the distinction between existing environmental factors and forecasts of changes in these factors over the near-term horizon is a subtle one, but it is one which must be maintained, since the latter cannot be used to justify current period loan loss provisions. For example, even if the consensus economic forecast is for a recession (which normally results in greater loan losses being experienced as current debtors face financial difficulties) if that downturn is not being experienced at the date of the statement of financial position, loss reserves cannot be boosted to anticipate loan quality deterioration that has not yet occurred.

FASB has noted that some loans specifically identified for evaluation may be individually impaired, while other loans that are not impaired individually pursuant to ASC 310-10-35 may have specific characteristics indicating that there would be probable loss in a group of loans with those characteristics. Loans in the first category must be accounted for under ASC 310-10-35, and loans in the second category should be accounted for as a loss accrual if characteristics of a loan indicate that it is probable that a group of similar loans includes some losses even though the loss could not be identified with a specific loan. Characteristics or risk factors must be specifically identified to support an accrual for losses that have been incurred but that have not yet reached the point where it is probable that amounts will not be collected on a specific individual loan. A creditor should not ignore factors and information obtained in the evaluation of the loan's collectibility.

For example, if an individual loan specifically identified for evaluation is fully collateralized with risk-free assets, then consideration of that loan as sharing characteristics with a group of uncollateralized loans is inappropriate. A loss is recognized if characteristics of a loan indicate that it is probable that a group of similar loans includes some losses even though the loss could not be identified to a specific loan. However, a loss would be recognized only if it is probable that the loss has been incurred at the date of the financial statements and the amount of loss can be reasonably estimated.

If a creditor concludes that an individual loan specifically identified for evaluation is impaired, an allowance in addition to one measured ASC 310-10-35 may not be established. That is, the ASC 310-10-35 allowance should be the sole measure of impairment for that loan. This is equally true if the measurement of impairment results in no allowance. For example, a creditor might conclude that a given collateral-dependent loan is impaired, because it is probable that the creditor will be unable to collect all the contractual interest and principal payments as scheduled in the loan agreement. The creditor might, however, measure the impairment using the fair value of the collateral, which could result in no allowance if the fair value of the collateral is greater than the recorded investment in the loan.

Particularly objectionable is the practice of increasing (or not decreasing) the allowance for loan losses in "good" economic times to provide for losses expected to occur in the future. This income smoothing technique is invalid under all circumstances, and cannot be rationalized by citing the historical cyclicality of the economy and the reasonable likelihood that higher losses will follow periods having lower loss experience.

The SEC has noted in 310-10-S99-4 that a registrant engaged in lending activities should create a formal loan loss allowance methodology that incorporates the use of internal and external factors impacting loan collectability, lending risks, and current collateral values. An entity's management should also periodically review and update this methodology in order to yield the best possible estimate of the allowance for loan losses. An entity should also maintain supporting documentation of related internal controls, policies and procedures, loan grading systems, and changes to the loan loss allowance process.

Nonrefundable Loan Fees and Costs

Loan origination fees. These fees should be deferred and recognized over the life of the loan as an adjustment of interest income. If there are any related direct loan origination costs, the origination fees and origination costs should be netted, and only the net amount should be deferred and amortized via the interest method. Origination costs include those incremental costs such as credit checks and security arrangements, among others, pertaining to a specific loan.

The only exception to the foregoing rule would be in the instance of certain loans that also qualify as debt instruments under ASC 320. For those carried in the "trading securities" portfolio, related loan origination fees should be charged to expense when incurred; the requirement that these be carried at fair value would make adding these costs to the asset carrying amounts a useless exercise.

Example 1

Debtor Corp. wishes to take out a loan with Klein Bank for the purchase of new machinery. The fair value of the machinery is $614,457. The loan is for ten years, designed to give Klein an implicit return of 10% on the loan. The annual payment is calculated as follows:

$$\text{Annual payment} = \frac{\$614{,}457}{PV_{10},\ 10\%} = \frac{614{,}457}{6.14457} = \$100{,}000$$

Unearned interest on the loan would be $385,543 [(10 × $100,000) – $614,457].

Klein also is to receive a "nonrefundable origination fee" of $50,000. Klein incurred $20,000 of direct origination costs (for credit checks, etc.). Thus, Klein has *net* nonrefundable origination fees of $30,000. The new net investment in the loan is calculated below.

Gross investment in loan (10 × $100,000)	$1,000,000
Less: Unamortized net nonrefundable origination fees	(30,000)
	970,000
Less: Unearned interest income (from above)	385,543
Net investment in loan	$ 584,457

The new net investment in the loan can be used to find the new implicit interest rate.

$$\frac{100{,}000}{(1+i)^1} + \frac{100{,}000}{(1+i)^2} + \ldots + \frac{100{,}000}{(1+i)^{10}} = \$584{,}457$$

where i = implicit rate

Thus, the implicit interest rate is 11.002%. The amortization table for the first three years is set up as follows:

(a) Loan payments	*(b)* Reduction in unearned interest	*(c)* Interest revenue (PV × implicit rate of 11.002%)	*(d)* Reduction in net orig. fees (c-b)	*(e)* Reduction in PV of net invest (a-c)	*(f)* PV of net loan investment
					$584,457
$100,000	$61,446*	$64,302	$2,856	$35,689	548,759
100,000	57,590**	60,374	2,784	39,626	509,133
100,000	53,349***	56,015	2,666	43,985	465,148

* ($614,457 × 10%) = $61,446

** [$614,457 – ($100,000 – $61,446)] × 10% = $57,590

*** [$575,900 – ($100,000 – $57,590)] × 10% = $53,349

Commitment fees and costs. Often fees are received in advance in exchange for a commitment to originate or purchase a loan. These fees should be deferred and recognized upon exercise of the commitment as an adjustment of interest income over the life of the loan, as in Example 1 for origination costs and fees. If a commitment expires unexercised, the fees should be recognized as income upon expiration.

As with loan origination fees and costs, if both commitment fees are received and commitment costs are incurred relating to a commitment to originate or purchase a loan, the net amount of fees or costs should be deferred and recognized over the life of the loan.

If there is a remote possibility of exercise, the commitment fees may be recognized on a straight-line basis over the commitment period as "service fee income." If there is a subsequent exercise, the unamortized fees at the date of exercise shall be recognized over the life of the loan as an adjustment of interest income, as in Example 1.

In certain cases, commitment fees are determined retroactively as a percentage of available lines of credit. If the commitment fee percentage is nominal in relation to the stated rate on the related borrowing, with the borrowing earning the market rate of interest, the fees shall be recognized in income as of the determination date.

Example 2

Glass Corp. has a $2 million, 10% line of credit outstanding with Ritter Bank. Ritter charges its annual commitment fee as 0.1% of any available balance as of the end of the prior period. Ritter will report $2,000 ($2 million × 0.1%) as service fee income in its current income statement.

Fees and costs in refinancing or restructurings. (Assume this is not a troubled-debt restructuring.) When the terms of a refinanced/restructured loan are as favorable to the lender as the terms for loans to customers with similar risks who are not in a restructuring, the refinanced loan is treated as a new loan, and all prior fees of the old loan are recognized in interest income when the new loan is made.

When the above situation is not satisfied, the fees or costs from the old loan become part of the net investment in the new loan.

Example 3

Jeffrey Bank refinanced a loan receivable to $1,000,000, at 10% interest, with annual interest receipts for ten years. Jeffrey's "normal" loan in its portfolio to debtors with similar risks is for $500,000 at 9% interest for five years. Jeffrey had loan origination fees from the original loan of $20,000. These fees are recognized in income *immediately* because the terms of the restructuring are as favorable to Jeffrey as a loan to another debtor with similar risks.

Example 4

Assume the same facts as in Example 3 except that the refinanced terms are $500,000 principal, 7% interest for three years. Since the terms of the restructuring are not as favorable to Jeffrey as a loan to another debtor with similar risks, the $20,000 origination fees become part of the new investment in the loan and recognized in interest income over the life of the new loan, as in Example 1.

Purchase of a loan or group of loans. Fees paid or fees received when purchasing a loan or group of loans should normally be considered part of the initial investment; to be recognized in income over the lives of the loans. However, if the loans qualify as debt securities under ASC 320 and are held in the lender's "trading securities" portfolio, these fees should be reported in income when paid or received, and not added to the cost of the loans.

Special arrangements. Often lenders provide demand loans (loans with no scheduled payment terms). In this case, any net fees or costs should be recognized on a straight-line basis over a period determined by mutual agreement of the parties, usually over the estimated length of the loan.

Under a revolving line of credit, any net fees or costs are recognized in income on a straight-line basis over the period that the line of credit is active. If the line of credit is terminated due to the borrower's full payment, any unamortized net fees or costs are recognized in income.

Example 5

Green Bank received $50,000 as a nonrefundable origination fee on a $2 million demand loan. Green's loan dictates that any fees are to be amortized over a period of ten years. Therefore, $5,000 (= $50,000 × 1/10) of origination fees will be recognized as an addition to interest income each year for the next ten years.

Financial statement presentation. The unamortized balance of origination, commitment, and other fees/costs that are recognized as an adjustment of interest income shall be reported on the statement of financial position as part of the loan balance to which they relate. Except for any special cases as noted in the above paragraphs, the amount of net fees/costs recognized each period as an adjustment will be reported in the income statement as part of interest income.

Accounting for Loans Acquired by Transfer

Banks commonly acquire loans originated by other financial intermediaries. In some cases, these are impaired when first acquired. That is, due to changes in the borrowers' credit risks since loan inception, the expected cash flows from the purchased loans may not equal the contractual cash flows. (Note that the differences in expected cash flows versus contractual cash flows arising from changes in interest rates during the interval from loan inception to loan acquisition is a separate issue; the resulting discount or premium would be amortized by the effective yield method over the expected term of the loan.)

ASC 310-30 addresses the accounting for the differences between contractual and expected future cash flows of acquired loans when these differences are attributable, at least in part, to credit quality.

Under the provisions of ASC 310-30, purchased loans are to be displayed at the initial investment amount on the statement of financial position. The amount of any discount is not to be displayed in the statement of financial position nor should the acquirer carry over an allowance for loan losses established by the seller. This prohibition applies equally to stand-alone purchases of loans and to those which occur as part of purchase business combinations. Expanded disclosure requirements have also been established.

When loans are acquired with evidence of deterioration in credit quality since origination, the acquirer is required to estimate the cash flows expected to be collected on the loan. This exercise is to be done both at the purchase date and again periodically over the lives of the loans. Cash flows in excess of the initial investment (purchase price) expected to be collected should be recognized as yield; this is referred to as *accretable yield*. On the other hand, contractual cash flows in excess of expected cash flows (the nonaccretable difference) should not be recognized as yield. (Accretion of this amount would necessitate, in most instances, later recognition of bad debt expense, and thus would distort multiple periods' results of operations.)

Changing expectations of future cash flows are to be handled differently, depending on whether these are decreases or increases. If, subsequent to acquisition, there are decreases in the probable cash flows, impairments are to be recognized. In other words, such a development cannot be handled prospectively as a yield adjustment over the remaining lives of the loans.

By contrast, probable increases in subsequent cash flows expected to be collected should be recognized prospectively as a yield adjustment. In cases where a new, higher yield on a loan is established (due to a probable increase in cash flows to be collected), that yield should be used as the effective interest rate in any later test for impairment.

If loans are refinanced or restructured after acquisition, these cannot be accounted for as new loans, unless these are troubled debt restructurings.

Under the provisions of ASC 310-30, acquired loans are not to be aggregated for purposes of determining evidence of postorigination credit deterioration. Rather, each loan, even if purchased in a pool, must be individually evaluated. However, subsequent pooling or aggregation of smaller-balance homogeneous loans is allowed for purposes of recognition, measurement, and disclosure. To be accounted for in the aggregate, loans must have a common credit risk (such as past due status or credit score) and have a common predominant risk characteristic (such as type of loan or date of origination). Furthermore, aggregation is limited to loans purchased in the same fiscal quarter.

The codification does not provide general guidance as to the recognition of income, because that guidance does not exist for originated loans. However, income recognition will still be prohibited on loans for which an investor expects to substantially improve the collateral for resale or expects to use the collateral in operations.

Variable loans with index rate decreases, contractual cash flow decreases, and expected cash flow decreases should be evaluated based on the change in expected cash flows attributable to the decrease in index rates. Those changes should be recognized prospectively, rather than as impairments. The decrease in expected cash flows due to index rate decreases must be ascertained, and those changes are to be evaluated against the loan's contractual payments receivable, which must be calculated based on the index rate as it changes over the life of the loan.

Conforming Practice by All Financial Institutions

ASC 942, *Financial Services—Depository and Lending*, reconciled and conformed the accounting and financial reporting provisions of the former AICPA AAG applicable to banks and saving institutions, credit unions, and finance companies. It furthermore added mortgage companies and corporate credit unions to the scope of coverage. The standard applies, additionally, to all entities which finance other entities, even via normal trade credit arrangements, and thus directs the accounting to be employed by manufacturers, retailers, wholesalers, and other business enterprises.

ASC 942 provides revised accounting guidance for sales of loan servicing rights, in order to comply with the revenue recognition model set forth in ASC 860-50-40. It also adopts the basis allocation approach set forth in ASC 860.

ASC 942 requires that, to the extent management has the intent and the ability to hold them for the foreseeable future or until maturity or payoff, loans should be reported on the statement of financial position at the amount of outstanding principal adjusted for any charge-offs, the allowance for loan losses, any deferred fees or costs on originated loans, and any unamortized premiums or discounts on purchased loans. Nonmortgage loans held for sale should be reported at the lower of cost or fair value. When a decision is made to sell loans not previously held for sale, those loans should be reclassified as held-for-sale and carried at the lower of cost or fair value.

With regard to credit losses, these are to be deducted from the allowance. Loan balances should be charged off in the periods in which the loans are deemed uncollectible. Recoveries of amounts previously charged off should be recorded when received. Credit losses on off-balance-sheet instruments should be reported separately from valuation accounts for recognized instruments.

Under ASC 942, standby commitments to purchase loans are reported in one of two ways, depending on whether the settlement date is within a reasonable time and whether the entity has the intent and ability to accept delivery without selling assets. If both conditions are met, the entity should record the loans purchased at cost, net of the standby commitment fee received, on the settlement date. If one or both conditions are not met, or if the entity does not have the intent and ability to take delivery without selling assets, the standby commitment fee (which is essentially a written put option premium) should be reported as a liability. Thereafter, the liability should be reported at the greater of the initial standby commitment fee or the fair value of the written put option, with the unrealized gains or losses included in current operations.

A transfer of servicing rights should only be accounted for as a sale if the transfer qualifies as a sale under ASC 860-50-40, and if (1) the seller has written approval from the investor (if required), (2) the buyer is a currently approved seller/servicer, (3) if a seller-financed sale, the nonrefundable down payment is large enough to demonstrate the buyer's commitment to complete the transaction, and (4) the transferor receives adequate compensation for any temporary servicing it performs. Sales of servicing rights previously sold should be recognized in income consistent with this provision and the requirements under ASC 860.

ASC 942 also addresses a number of other issues. Thus, Federal Home Loan Bank and Federal Reserve Bank stock is to be classified as a restricted investment security, carried at cost, and evaluated for impairment. Also, any delinquency fees are to be recognized in income when chargeable, assuming collectibility is reasonably assured. Prepayment fees are not recognized in income until the loans or trade receivables are prepaid, except as set forth by ASC 310-20. Finally, accrual of interest income should not be affected by the possibility that rebates may be calculated using a method different than the interest method, except as set forth in ASC 310-20.

With regard to financial statement disclosures, ASC 942 requires that the summary of significant accounting policies state the basis of accounting for loans, trade receivables, and lease financings; the method used to determine the lower of cost or market of nonmortgage loans held for sale, the classification and method of accounting for interest-only strips, loans, and other receivables or retained interests in securitizations; and the method for recognizing interest income on loan and trade receivables, including the method of amortizing net deferred fees or costs. The accounting policies note should also describe the criteria for placing loans on nonaccrual status, for charging off uncollectible loans and trade receivables, and for determining past due or delinquency status.

The financial statement notes should include a description of the accounting policies and methodology used to estimate the allowance for loan losses, and any liability for off-balance-sheet credit losses, as well as the related charges for loan, trade receivable, or other credit losses. Aggregate gains or losses on sales of loans or trade receivables should be presented separately in the financial statements or disclosed in the notes thereto. Major categories of loans or trade receivables should be presented separately either in the statement of financial position or in the notes, as should the allowance for credit losses, the allowance for doubtful accounts, and any unearned income. Receivables held for sale should be separately reported.

ASC 942 also requires that foreclosed and repossessed assets be reported separately on the statement of financial position or disclosed in the notes. The recorded investment in loans and trade receivables on nonaccrual status should be disclosed, as should the amount of loans and trade receivables past due ninety days or more and still accruing.

The amount of securities deposited with state regulatory authorities (if required) should be disclosed. The carrying amount of loans, trade receivables, securities, and financial instruments that serve as collateral for borrowings should also be disclosed.

ASC 815 requires disclosure of the extent, nature, terms, and credit risk of financial instruments, not limited to derivatives with off-balance-sheet credit risk.

Previously, GAAP for banks and savings institutions did not require disclosure of capital requirements for branches of foreign banks, because those branches do not have capital. However, branches are subject to requirements to maintain certain levels of capital-equivalent deposits and may be required to maintain other specified reserves. Since failure to comply with those requirements potentially has an adverse impact on the reporting entity, disclosures about the balance requirements and a branch's compliance are required under ASC 942. Similarly, capital requirements for trust operations are unpublished, are subject to variations of interpretation as between regulatory agencies, and may not be uniformly applied to the trust operations of all institutions. Nonetheless, to the extent that an institution has been advised of an expectation that certain trust-related capital levels be maintained, its compliance with those expectations should be disclosed.

Servicing Assets and Liabilities

Financial institutions often acquire, or retain, servicing rights to financial assets, such as for loans originated and subsequently sold to other institutions or to qualified special-purpose entities. ASC 860-50-35 contains guidance on the accounting for retained or acquired servicing rights, which are to be recorded, at acquisition, at fair value. If the contractually expected fees and other revenues are expected to exceed the cost of providing the servicing, a servicing asset is recorded; if a shortfall of revenue is expected, a liability is recognized. Subsequent accounting for servicing assets and liabilities can be either by the amortization or the fair value method, with the option to elect one or the other for a given class of financial asset being serviced.

Cash Flow Statement

Banks, savings institutions, and credit unions are not required to report gross cash receipts and payments for the following:

1. Deposits placed with other financial institutions
2. Withdrawals of deposits
3. Time deposits accepted
4. Repayments of deposits
5. Loans made to customers
6. Principal collections of loans.

If an enterprise is part of a consolidated enterprise, net cash receipts and payments of the enterprise should be reported separate from the gross cash receipts and payments of the consolidated enterprise.

Other Accounting Guidance

ASC 310-20-35-13 concluded that, for situations where a lender allows a borrower to make larger payments for some number of periods (at least twelve payments), after which the borrower is then relieved of any remaining obligation, the loss related to the forgiven portion should be accrued over the period of the larger payments.

ASC 860-10-55-60 stated that forward commitment GNMA *dollar rolls* should be marked to market.

In some instances, a reporting entity may sell a loan but retain a share in the interest income, as well as the servicing rights for that loan. ASC 860-50-40-10 mandated that a gain should be recognized upon the sale of mortgage service rights that include participation in the future interest stream of the loans. On another related topic, ASC 860-50-35-18 states that servicing fee rates set by secondary market makers (GNMA, FHLMC, FNMA) should be considered normal for transactions with those agencies.

ASC 860-50-40-7 addresses events in which a mortgage loan servicer (transferor) transfers the servicing rights and related risks to an unaffiliated enterprise (transferee), which then makes a subservicing agreement whereby the transferor services the loans for a fixed fee. Income recognition should be deferred, and treatment as a sale or a financing depends on the circumstances surrounding the transaction. However, this consensus does not apply to temporary subservicing agreements. In addition, a loss should be recognized currently if loan prepayments may result in future servicing losses. When there is such a sale of mortgage servicing rights with a subservicing agreement, ASC 860-50-40 through 860-50-40-10 states that this should be accounted for as a sale if substantially all the risks and rewards of ownership have been transferred to the buyer. If substantially all the risks and rewards have not been transferred, then the transaction must be accounted for as a financing.

Normal servicing fee rates for mortgage loans are those set by federally sponsored secondary market makers (GNMA, FHLMC, FNMA). For transactions with those agencies or for mortgage loans sold to private sector investors where the seller retains servicing rights, normal servicing rates should be considered. In the latter case, a stated servicing fee rate that differs from the normal rate requires adjustment to the sales price to yield the normal rate. In either case, according to ASC 860-50-35-17 through 860-50-35-18, a loss should be accrued if expected servicing costs exceed anticipated fees based on the stated servicing fee rate. If the servicer refinances a mortgage loan and actual prepayments differ from any anticipated payments, then the servicing asset must be adjusted.

ASC 805 states that when a mutual savings and loan association converts to stock ownership and pools with another S&L, its EPS should be excluded from the restated combined EPS for years before the date of conversion. The method of presentation must be disclosed.

ASC 815 addressed equity certificates of deposit, stating that contingent interest expense resulting from equity certificates of deposit be recognized concurrently with gains relating to the assets upon which the equity is given.

Any goodwill resulting from the acquisition of a bank or thrift institution is to be amortized according to ASC 350, prohibiting amortization of goodwill but requiring annual impairment testing.

ASC 260 mandates that neither equity commitment notes nor equity contract notes should be included in earnings per share computations.

ASC 605-20-25-9 holds that a guarantor should recognize loan guarantee fees as revenue over the term of the guarantee. Any direct costs related to the guarantee must be recognized in the same manner. If material, footnote disclosure is required, and the probability of loss should be continually assessed. ASC 460 requires that a liability be recognized, at the inception of a guarantee, for the fair value of the obligation undertaken by the guarantor.

Regarding distribution fees paid by mutual funds not having front-end charges (loads), the cost deferral method should be employed. Under this method, fees expected to be received over some future period should be recognized upon receipt. Deferred incremental direct costs are amortized while indirect costs are expensed as incurred.

RAP basis accounting is no longer used in general-purpose financial statements. ASC 942-740-45-1 states that the Comptroller's Banking Circular 202, which limits the net deferred tax debits allowable on a bank's statement of condition, applies only for regulatory purposes and does not affect GAAP financial statements.

ASC 310-10-25-7 addressed purchased credit card portfolios involving premiums paid to the seller. It held that the excess of the purchase price of a credit card portfolio including cardholder relationships over the amounts due should be allocated between the credit card loans acquired and the cardholder relationships acquired. The premium related to cardholder relationships is an identifiable intangible asset and is amortized over the period of benefit. The premium related to the loans is amortized over the life of the loans.

ASC 942-405-55-1 holds that the savings accounts deposited in a credit union must be unequivocally listed as a liability if the financial statements of the credit union are to comply with the (now superseded) AICPA Credit Union Guide. The statement of financial condition must present savings accounts either as the first item in the liabilities and equity section or as a separate subtotal before total liabilities.

Lending institutions often utilize what traditionally were referred to as special-purpose entities (SPEs), and which now may or may not qualify as qualified SPEs (QSPEs) or might be simply variable interest entities (VIEs). A fairly common transaction involves securitizations of credit card receivables, which sometimes have a feature called a *removal of accounts provision* (ROAP) that allows certain accounts to be withdrawn and replaced by other receivables. ASC 860 concluded that credit card securitizations with such a provision should be recognized as sales transactions as long as the removal meets any specified terms, doesn't reduce the interests of the investor in the pool, and doesn't reduce the seller's percentage interest below a contractually specified level. The accounting implications of a ROAP depend on whether it results in the transferor maintaining effective control over the transferred assets. Unconditional ROAPs and those conditioned on a transferor's decision would preclude sale accounting when the receivables are transferred.

On a related topic, ASC 310-20-25-18 stipulated that credit card origination costs that qualify for deferral should be netted against the credit card fee charged, if any, and the net amount should be amortized on a straight-line basis over the term of the credit card or one year, depending on the significance of the fee.

Additionally, for both purchased and originated credit cards, the accounting policies, the net amount capitalized, and the amortization period should be disclosed.

Additional disclosure requirements relative to securitizations, which will impact financial reporting by banks and many other financial institutions that sponsor such arrangements, are detailed in the chapter on ASC 310.

FINANCIAL SERVICES—INSURANCE (ASC 944)

PERSPECTIVE AND ISSUES

The two major types of insurance companies are life and property and casualty. Each category is further subdivided into stock companies and mutual associations. Due to the regulated nature of the insurance industry, financial reporting may be in conformity to statutory accounting principles (SAP) or GAAP. Furthermore, publicly held companies subject to SEC accounting rules will account for certain transactions and events in other manners dictated by those requirements. While accounting principles under GAAP are broadly applicable to all types of insurance companies (including those dealing in such specialized products as mortgage insurance, title insurance, and reinsurance), the nature of the estimation process (such as for claims liabilities) differs substantially depending upon the character of the risks assumed.

The main contrasts between SAP and GAAP arise from the more conservative nature of SAP, which is a reflection of the insurance regulatory agencies' concern with protection of the policyholders' interests, and hence with the liquidity and solvency of the insurance companies. Accordingly, under SAP certain costs, such as policy acquisition expenses, are written off as incurred; certain nonliquid assets, such as property and furniture, are not recognized; and claims liabilities are very conservatively estimated. In contrast to this essentially short-term perspective, financial statements prepared on the GAAP basis are more concerned with the value of the companies' investments and net worth on a going concern basis.

The primary source of insurance industry GAAP is ASC 944, *Financial Services—Insurance*. Insurance contracts are categorized as short duration (which includes most property and liability insurance) or long duration (which includes most life, mortgage, and title insurance). Nominal insurance contracts that are effectively investment contracts, however, are not accounted for as insurance.

ASC 944 discusses those aspects of accounting and auditing unique to life and health insurance entities, and contains significant discussions of statutory accounting practices (SAP), which comprise laws, regulations, and administrative rulings adopted by various states that govern the operations and reporting requirements of life insurance entities. It does not reflect SAP under the National Association of Insurance Commissioners (NAIC) codification project.

The ASC also addresses the classification and valuation of liabilities, as well as disclosures for nontraditional annuity and life insurance contracts issued by insurance enterprises. Several of the conclusions reached on these topics are discussed later in this section.

CONCEPTS, RULES, AND EXAMPLES

Premium Income

Premium income is recognized differently for short and long duration contracts. For short-duration contracts, premium income is recognized over the contract term in proportion to the amount of insurance provided. In the case of long duration contracts, revenue is accrued as the premiums become due from policyholders, except for contracts that provide benefits over a term longer than the premium payment term (such as twenty-year life policies), in which case income is recognized over the longer period during which benefits may be provided.

Claim Cost Recognition

Costs of benefits are recognized when insured events such as property damage occur. Estimated costs are accrued for as claims incurred but not yet reported. For long-duration contracts, the present values of estimated future benefits are accrued, net of the present values of future net premiums to be collected. Accrual of these benefit obligations generally involves actuarial determinations. Accountants may be dependent on the services of specialists in such cases, as they are in computing costs related to defined benefit pension plans. Recognition of other expenses is governed by the matching concept. For example, costs that vary with acquisition activity are capitalized and amortized over the period during which premium income is earned. Catastrophic losses (as from natural disasters such as hurricanes) are accrued under the guidelines of ASC 450: when impairment of the asset or incurring of a liability is probable and the amount is reasonably estimable.

Investments

The other major concern of GAAP for insurance enterprises relates to the presentation of investments held. ASC 320 contains the accounting requirements for investments in debt and marketable equity securities. Briefly, those investments must be categorized as being either held-for-trading, available-for-sale, or held-to-maturity. Investments falling within the first two categories should be reported at fair value, with value changes affecting the trading securities portfolio being reflected in income, while changes in the available-for-sale portfolio are reported in a separate equity account. Securities to be held to maturity are accounted for at amortized historical cost, absent a permanent decline in value. Equity securities that do not meet the definition of "marketable" are also to be reported at fair value, with gains or losses reported in stockholders' equity. In addition, real estate acquired in settling mortgage guaranty and title insurance claims is to be reported at fair value. Insurance entities are subject to the disclosure requirements of ASC 942-320-50.

Deferred Income Taxes

GAAP requires that deferred income taxes be provided for temporary differences. An exception was previously provided under the *indefinite reversal criterion*, for stock life insurance companies only, for differences designated as policyholders' surplus. However, ASC 740 holds that deferred taxes must be provided, consistent with the accounting prescribed for all other temporary differences.

Other Matters

Financial guarantee insurance. Financial guarantee insurance (and reinsurance) contracts are contracts issued by insurers that provide protection to the holder of a financial obligation, such as a municipal bond or an asset-backed security, from a financial loss in the event of a default. A financial guarantee insurance contract obligates the insurer to pay a claim upon the occurrence of an event of default. Insurers are to recognize a liability for unearned premium revenue at the inception of a financial guarantee insurance contract in an amount equal to the present value of the premiums due or, if certain criteria are met and used, expected to be collected over the period of the financial guarantee insurance contract. The insurance enterprise is to determine the present value of the premiums due or expected to be collected using a discount rate that reflects the risk-free rate at the inception of the contract, based on the insurance contract period unless the insurer is permitted to consider prepayments. The discount is to be accreted on the premium receivable through earnings over that same period. The discount rate used is to be updated to a current risk-free rate only when prepayment assumptions change.

When an *expected period* is used to measure the unearned premium revenue, the insurer is to adjust the prepayment assumptions when those assumptions change. The adjustment to the unearned premium revenue will equal the adjustment to the premium receivable, and thus there will be no effect on earnings at the time of the adjustment. If the premium receivable is found to be uncollectible, it must be adjusted via a charge against earnings. Revenue is recognized over the period of insurance in proportion to the amount of coverage outstanding from period to period, which typically declines over time as the insured principal (e.g., bonds outstanding) are retired.

The insurer will recognize a claim liability on a financial guarantee insurance contract when it expects that a claim loss will exceed the unearned premium revenue for that contract based on the present value of expected net cash outflows to be paid under the insurance contract. Since the unearned premium revenue represents the stand-ready obligation under a financial guarantee insurance contract at initial recognition, if the likelihood of a default (i.e., the insured event) later increases so that the present value of the expected net cash outflows expected to be paid under the insurance contract exceeds the declining amount of unearned premium revenue, the entity must recognize a claim liability, in addition to the unearned premium revenue. The amount of recognized claim liability must be updated for new information and discounted at an updated risk-free rate for each statement of financial position presented.

Reinsurance. Another specialized topic area pertinent to insurance companies is that of reinsurance, which is addressed by ASC 944. It requires that reinsurance receivables, including amounts related to claims incurred but not reported, be reported as assets, consistent with the manner in which liabilities relating to the underlying reinsured contracts are accounted for. The standard also establishes criteria for recognition as reinsurance, and sets forth detailed accounting for long and short duration contracts, as well as disclosure requirements.

Loss reserves. ASC 944-605 concerns accounting for foreign property and liability reinsurance, and concludes that except for special circumstances, only the periodic method is acceptable in accounting for foreign reinsurance premiums. ASC 944-505-50 requires disclosures where permission was received from the National Association of Insurance Commissioners to use different accounting practices. ASC 944 also covers capitalization and amortization costs and several other matters for mutual life insurance companies, assessment enterprises, fraternal benefit societies, and stock life insurance companies.

Guaranty funds. ASC 405-30 addresses matters pertaining to guaranty funds and certain other insurance-related assessments. The key elements of this standard are discussed in the following paragraphs.

Under the standard, guaranty fund and similar assessments would be recognized when (1) it has been imposed or is deemed probable of being imposed, (2) the event obligating an entity to pay the assessment has occurred, and (3) the amount of the assessment can be reasonably estimated. All three conditions would have to be fulfilled before a liability could be accrued. Discounting to present value will be permitted. The codification offers specific guidance regarding the ability to reasonably estimate the liability for assessments.

Guaranty funds are essentially state-mandated insurance funds used to settle claims against insolvent insurers and, typically, all licensed insurers are assessed premiums based on the volume of defined lines of business they conduct in the given state. A variety of methods have been applied in determining the amounts of guaranty fund assessments (e.g., retrospectively, based on premiums written over the past two years; or prospectively, based on business written over the next several years following an insolvency of a failed insurer), with the result that entities upon which assessments are being levied have been inclined to use different methods of recognizing the cost and related obligation. In general, to warrant accrual under the codification, an insolvency of another insurer would have to have occurred, since the presumption would be that the assessments would become probable (the threshold criterion) when there has been a formal determination of another entity's insolvency. An example of an exception would be when the state uses prospective premium-based guaranty fund assessments; if the reporting entity cannot avoid the obligation by ceasing to write policies, the obligating event would be the determination of insolvency, but if it could avoid the assessment, the obligating event is the writing of premiums after the insolvency.

Surplus notes. ASC 944-470 affects accounting by certain insurance companies that issue a security known as surplus notes. It requires that these instruments be accounted for as debt and included in the liabilities caption of the statement of financial position. Furthermore, interest must be accrued over the term of the notes, whether or not payment of interest and/or principal has been approved by an insurance company. However, disclosure is required as to the status of the request for approval.

Deposit accounting. ASC 340-30 applies to entities entering into short-duration insurance and reinsurance contracts that do not transfer insurance risk, or multiple-year contracts that either do not transfer insurance risk or for which insurance risk transfer is not determinable. See the chapter on ASC 340 for more detail.

Demutualizations. ASC 944-805 addressed the increasingly common phenomenon of demutualizations (whereby formerly mutually owned insurers issue stock), as well as the formation of insurance holding companies (MIHC). A key concern is the accounting for the *closed block* of assets and liabilities, and of earnings allocable to the closed block. This pertains to mechanisms designed to protect the adjustable policy features and dividend expectations of participating life insurance policyholders from the competing interests of stockholders. Typically, the plan of demutualization describes how the closed block will operate. The closed block assets and cash returns on those assets will not inure to the stockholders of the demutualized company; instead, all cash flows from these assets will be used to benefit the closed block policyholders. The insurance enterprise remains obligated to provide for minimum guarantees under the participating policy, and it is consequently possible under certain circumstances that additional "stockholder" funds will have to be used to meet the contractual benefits of the closed block policyholders. The assets designated to the closed block are subject to the same liabilities, with the same priority in the case of insolvency or in liquidation, as assets outside the closed block. In many situations, commissions and other expenses (including management expenses) of operating and administering the closed block will not be charged to the closed block. Unless the state insurance department consents to an earlier termination, the closed block will continue in effect until the date on which none of the policies in the closed block remains in force.

Alternatives to the closed block have arisen in practice encompassing, for a number of types of contracts, various mechanisms believed by the insurance enterprise and state insurance regulators to be appropriate in the specific circumstances. Closed block alternative mechanisms have been used in lieu of closed blocks for certain participating life contracts to commit to the insurance regulator that the insurance company will continue to follow its established dividend practices. Closed block alternative mechanisms also have been used to protect nonguaranteed elements of participating and nonparticipating insurance contracts such as interest credits on deferred annuities and adjustable premiums on adjustable premium term business. In some instances, the methodology and limitations defined in the agreements with the state insurance regulators have considered only specific profit components, such as mortality experience on a block of term insurance or investment spreads on a block of annuities, and in other instances have considered virtually all components of product profitability.

Where there is a limitation on the profits that may inure to the stockholders, there generally is a formal agreement between the insurance company and the insurance regulators that defines (1) the contracts covered by the limitation, (2) the profit limitation calculation, and (3) the timing and manner (for example, as policy dividends, reduced premiums, or additional benefits) in which amounts that may not be distributed to stockholders are to be distributed to policyholders.

Some of the more important conclusions reached were as follows:

1. The classification of expenses related to a demutualization and the formation of an MIHC should be considered other than extraordinary expense.
2. Closed block assets and liabilities from the closed block should be included with the corresponding financial statement items of the insurance enterprise.
3. ASC 944 should continue to be applied after conversion to a stock company.
4. The maximum future contribution of the closed block to the earnings of the company is typically the excess of the GAAP liabilities over the GAAP assets at the date of demutualization. Under ASC 944, a dividend liability should be established for current earnings that will be paid to policyholders through future benefits. From a shareholder perspective, excess earnings of the closed block that will never inure to the shareholders should be set up as a liability. There should be a dividend liability for excess earnings due to policyholders that cannot inure to shareholders.
5. For a *distribution-form* demutualization, an insurance enterprise should reclassify all of its retained earnings as of the date of demutualization to capital stock and additional paid-in capital accounts. A *subscription-form* demutualization should not, in and of itself, result in reclassification of retained earnings. The equity accounts of the MIHC at the date of formation should be determined using the principles for transactions of companies under common control with the amount of retained earnings of the demutualized insurance enterprise, before reclassification to the capital accounts, being reported as retained earnings of the MIHC.

Nontraditional Long-Duration Contracts

ASC 944 also addresses the classification and valuation of liabilities as well as disclosures for nontraditional annuity and life insurance contracts issued by insurance enterprises. The requirements under this standard are set forth in the following paragraphs.

The portion of separate account assets representing contract holder funds are to be measured at fair value and reported in the insurance enterprise's financial statements as a summary total, with an equivalent summary total for related liabilities, if the separate account arrangement meets all the specified criteria. If the arrangement does not meet the criteria, assets representing contract holder funds should be accounted for as general account assets, and any related liability should be accounted for as a general account liability.

Assets underlying an insurance enterprise's proportionate interest in a separate account do not represent contract holder funds, and thus are not to be separately reported and valued. If a separate account arrangement meets the criteria in ASC 944 and (1) the terms of the contract allow the contract holder to invest in additional units in the separate account or (2) the insurance enterprise is marketing contracts that permit funds to be invested in the separate account, the assets underlying the insurance enterprise's proportionate interest in the separate account should be accounted for in a manner consistent with similar assets held by the general account that the insurance enterprise may be required to sell.

If the enterprise's proportionate interest in the separate account is less than 20% of the separate account, and all of the underlying investments of the separate account meet the definition of securities under the Master Glossary, or the definition of cash and cash equivalents, the enterprise may report its portion of the separate account value as an investment in equity securities classified as trading under ASC 320.

Assets transferred from the general account to a separate account should be recognized at fair value to the extent of third-party contract holders' proportionate interest in the separate account if the separate account arrangement meets the criteria set forth in the codification. Any gain related to the third-party contract holder's proportionate interest should be recognized immediately in earnings of the general account of the insurance enterprise, if the risks and rewards of ownership have been transferred to contract holders using the fair value of the asset at the date of the contract holder's assumption of risks and rewards. A guarantee of the asset's value or minimum rate of return or a commitment to repurchase the asset would indicate that the risks of ownership have not been transferred, and no gain can be recognized. If the separate account arrangement does not meet the criteria in the codification, the transfer generally should have no financial reporting effect (that is, general account classification and carrying amounts should be retained). In certain situations loss recognition may be appropriate.

The basis for determining the balance that accrues to the contract holder for a long-duration insurance or investment contract that is subject to ASC 944 is the accrued account balance. The accrued account balance equals

1. Deposit(s) net of withdrawals;
2. Plus amounts credited pursuant to the contract;
3. Less fees and charges assessed;
4. Plus additional interest (for example, persistency bonus); and
5. Other adjustments, such as appreciation or depreciation recognized under the codification, to the extent not already credited.

For contracts that have features that may result in more than one potential account balance, the accrued account balance should be the highest contractually determinable balance that will be available in cash or its equivalent at contractual maturity or the reset date, without reduction for future fees and charges. The accrued account balance should not reflect any surrender adjustments (for example, fair value annuity adjustments, surrender charges, or credits). For contracts in which amounts credited as interest to the contract holder are reset periodically, the accrued balance should be based on the highest crediting rate guaranteed or declared through the reset date.

For a contract not accounted for under ASC 815 that provides a return based on the total return of a contractually referenced pool of assets either through crediting rates or termination adjustments, the accrued account balance should be based on the fair value of the referenced pool of assets (or applicable index value) at the date of the statement of financial position, even if the related assets are not recognized at fair value.

To determine the accounting under ASC 944 for a contract that contains death or other insurance benefit features, the enterprise should first determine whether the contract is an investment or universal-life-type contract. If the mortality or morbidity risks are other than nominal and the fees assessed or insurance benefits are not fixed and guaranteed, the contract should be classified as an ASC 944 universal-life-type contract. A rebuttable presumption is that a contract has significant mortality risk where the additional insurance benefit would vary significantly in response to capital markets volatility. The determination of significance should be made at contract inception, other than at transition, and should be based on a comparison of the present value of expected excess payments (that is, insurance benefit amounts and related incremental claim adjustment expenses in excess of the account balance) to be made under insurance benefit features to the present value of all amounts expected to be assessed against the contract holder (revenue).

For contracts classified as insurance contracts that have amounts assessed against contract holders each period for the insurance benefit feature that are assessed in a manner that is expected to result in profits in earlier years and subsequent losses from that insurance benefit function, a liability should be established in addition to the account balance to recognize the portion of such assessments that compensates the insurance enterprise for benefits to be provided in future periods in accordance with the guidance in the codification.

If a reinsurer assumes the insurance benefit feature, it should assess the significance of mortality and morbidity risk within the reinsurance contract according to the guidance in ASC 944, regardless of whether there is an account balance. The reinsurer should determine the classification of the reinsurance contract as an investment contract or as an insurance contract at the inception of the reinsurance contract. For reinsurance contracts, the mortality or morbidity risk could be deemed other than nominal even if the original issuer did not determine mortality or morbidity to be other than nominal. Similarly, the issuer of a contract that provides only an insurance benefit feature that wraps a noninsurance contract, for example, a guaranteed minimum death benefit related to a mutual fund balance, should evaluate its contract in the same manner. A reinsurer or issuer of the insurance benefit features of a contract should calculate a liability for the portion of premiums collected each period that represents compensation to the insurance enterprise for benefits that are assessed in a manner that is expected to result in current profits and future losses from the insurance benefit function. That liability should be calculated using the methodology described in ASC 944.

Contracts may provide for potential benefits in addition to the account balance that are payable only upon annuitization, such as annuity purchase guarantees, guaranteed minimum income benefit (GMIB), and two-tier annuities. Insurance enterprises should determine whether such contract features should be accounted for under the provisions of ASC 815. If the contract feature is not accounted for under the provisions of ASC 815, an additional liability for the contract feature should be established if the present value of expected annuitization payments at the expected annuitization date exceeds the expected account balance at the expected annuitization date in accordance with the guidance in ASC 944.

Sales inducements provided to the contract holder, whether for investment or universal-life-type contracts, should be recognized as part of the liability for policy benefits over the period for which the contract must remain in force for the contract holder to qualify for the inducement or at the crediting date, if earlier, in accordance with the codification. No adjustments should be made to reduce the liability related to the sales inducements for anticipated surrender charges, persistency, or early withdrawal contractual features.

Sales inducements that are recognized as part of the liability under ASC 944, that are explicitly identified in the contract at inception, and that meet the criteria specified in the codification should be deferred and amortized using the same methodology and assumptions used to amortize capitalized acquisition costs.

The financial statements of an insurance enterprise should disclose information about the following:

1. Separate account assets and liabilities; the nature, extent, and timing of minimum guarantees related to variable contracts; and the amount of gains and losses recognized on assets transferred to separate accounts.
2. An insurance enterprise's accounting policy for sales inducements, including the nature of the costs capitalized and the method of amortizing those costs; the amount of costs capitalized and amortized for each of the periods presented; and the unamortized balance as of the date of each statement of financial position presented.

3. The nature of the liabilities and methods and assumptions used in estimating any contract benefits recognized in excess of the account balance pursuant to the codification.

Costs Associated with Acquiring or Renewing Insurance Contracts

ASC 944-30-25-1A specifies that only the following costs incurred in the acquisition of insurance contracts can be capitalized and subsequently amortized:

- Incremental direct costs of successfully acquiring or renewing insurance contracts; these are costs that would not have been incurred if the contract acquisition had not occurred.
- Costs directly related to underwriting, policy issuance, medical and inspection, and sales force contract selling for successfully acquired or renewed insurance contracts.

All other costs, such as market research, training, administration, and product development, should be treated as period costs. You should treat all administrative expenses as period costs.

Capitalized acquisition costs should be charged to expense in proportion to premium revenue recognized under ASC 944-605. (ASC 944-30-35-3A)

Deferred Acquisition Costs for Insurance Contract Modifications or Exchanges

ASC 944-30 addresses the accounting for deferred acquisition costs related to the internal replacement of selected insurance and investment contracts. An internal replacement is a modification of an insurance product's benefits, features, rights, or coverages (described hereafter as *benefits*) by a variety of means, including the extinguishment and replacement of a contract.

If an internal replacement occurs and the rights and obligations of the parties are essentially unchanged, then the replacement contract is considered a continuation of the replaced contract. In this case, the replaced contract's unamortized deferred acquisition costs, unearned revenue liabilities, and deferred sales inducement assets should continue to be recognized as part of the replacement contract. Also, costs incurred in connection with such a replacement are charged to expense as incurred.

A contract change must meet all of the following criteria in order to be considered a continuation of the replaced contract—if any condition is not met, the change is treated as a substantially changed contract:

1. The insured event, risk, or period of coverage has not changed.
2. The contract holder's investment return rights have not changed.
3. Either there is no change in the insurance premium, or a premium reduction is matched by a corresponding reduction in benefits.
4. Net of distributions, there is no net reduction in contract value.
5. There is no change in contractual participation or dividend features.
6. There is no change in the contract's amortization method or revenue classification.

If benefits replacement results in a substantially changed contract, then the replaced contract is considered extinguished, in which case unamortized deferred acquisition costs, unearned revenue liabilities, and deferred sales inducement assets from the replaced contract should not be deferred as part of the replacement contract.

If a contract is accounted for as a long-duration participating contract, the estimated gross profit of the replacement contract is treated as a revision of the replaced contract's gross profit when determining the amortization of deferred acquisition costs, deferred sales inducement assets, and the recognition of unearned revenues. If a contract is accounted for as nonrefundable fees, the cash flows of the replacement contract revise the cash flows of the replaced contract for purposes of calculating the interest rate amortization of unamortized deferred acquisition costs and deferred sales inducement assets.

This standard does not apply to contract modifications resulting from an election by the contract holder that was within the original contract, as long as (1) the election followed the terms of the original contract, (2) the election is not subject to any underwriting, (3) the insurance provider cannot decline the coverage or adjust contract pricing, and (4) the benefit had been accounted for since the contract inception. The standard also does not apply if a contract feature is nonintegrated (it provides coverage that is priced solely for the incremental benefits coverage, and does not alter other components of the contract), in which case it should be accounted for as a separately issued contract.

Other Accounting Guidance

ASC 944-20-S99 notes that industry practice is to amortize the present value of future profits (PVP) using an interest method with accrual of interest added to the unamortized balance. In the past, there has been some diversity in the application of this method in practice, and so the codification mandates that the interest rate used to amortize PVP should be the liability or contract rate. It also states that changes in estimates of future gross profits on contracts should be accounted for as a catch-up adjustment. And finally, PVP and any related liability should be subject to the premium deficiency test required in ASC 944-60.

ASC 944-20 includes criteria for the recognition and amounts of assets and liabilities by the assuming and ceding enterprises, respectively, and accounting for changes in coverage during the reinsurance period. A number of conditions are identified, satisfaction of which is necessary for a contract to be treated as reinsurance, and in their absence such contracts are to be accounted for by the deposit method.

ASC 944-20-25 addresses how enterprises other than insurance companies should account for contracts with insurance companies covering various types of risks such as product and environmental liability risks. ASC 944-20 also addresses *pooled risk* contracts and reinsurance contracts entered into by a captive insurer. In order for a contract to be considered insurance it must indemnify the insured party as this would result in a transfer of risk. If no transfer of risk exists, then the contract is not considered insurance, and the balance of the premium less any amount to be retained by the insurer should be accounted for as a deposit.

ASC 325-20 provided guidance on the accounting for those formerly mutual insurance companies that have undergone demutualization transactions and converted to stock enterprises. In order to effect a demutualization, a company may be required to issue consideration, often in the form of stock, to existing participating policyholders in exchange for their current membership interests. The receipt of such stock has no direct effect on the policyholders' contractual interests of their insurance policies (for example, it does not alter the cash surrender value of their life insurance policies). However, the governance of the mutual insurance company and, in particular, the participating policyholders' interest in that governance are modified. Thus, stock received from a demutualization should be accounted for at fair value with a gain recognized in income from continuing operations.

ASC 944-605 addressed the lack of uniformity of practices among foreign reinsurers, and in particular how US insurers were to account for property and liability reinsurance assumed from foreign companies.

ASC 944-505-55 illustrates disclosures for insurance enterprises that have received permission by the insurance department in their domiciliary states to use accounting practices other than those prescribed by state laws, regulations, and rules and by the National Association of Insurance Commissioners (NAIC).

ASC 944 provides guidance in accounting for mutual life insurance contracts. Capitalization and amortization of acquisition costs are discussed. Premiums are to be reported as revenue when due from policyholders. Death and surrender benefits are reported as expenses, and annual dividends are reported separately as expenses. The calculation of estimated gross margin and liability for future policy benefits is described.

ASC 405-30 addresses the diversity in practice of accounting for assessments made by government agencies against insurance activities such as workers' compensation second injury funds, this standard imposed accrual accounting requirements and set forth the conditions that must be met before a liability may be recognized.

ASC 340-30 provides guidance on how to account for insurance and reinsurance contracts that do not have the effect of transferring insurance risk. It applies to all entities and all types of insurance or reinsurance contracts, other than long duration life and health insurance contracts. The method prescribed by this standard is *deposit accounting*.

ASC 944-805 provides necessary guidance to the proper accounting for demutualization transactions and also for the formation of mutual insurance holding companies.

ASC 944-605-25 states that recognition of an unearned revenue liability representing amounts that have been assessed to compensate insurers for services to be performed over future periods is a requirement under ASC 944. Importantly, this liability is not to be used to inappropriately level or smooth out gross profit over the term of the contract or produce a level gross profit from the mortality benefit over the life of the contract.

The staff of the SEC's Division of Corporate Finance has issued guidance in its "Current Accounting and Disclosure Issues" publication regarding the proper disclosures required of publicly held property-casualty insurance companies. The disclosure about the policies and methodologies for estimating the liability for unpaid claims and claim adjustment expenses should (1) separately address each material line of business, (2) identify and describe the actuarial method used, (3) describe any policy for adjusting the liability for unpaid claims and claim adjustment expenses to an amount differing from the amount calculated by its actuaries, and (4) describe any difference in the annual and interim procedures for determining the liability for unpaid claims and claim adjustment expenses. Further, the disclosure of the reasons for incurred claims and claim adjustment expenses in the current income statement that are attributed to insured events in prior years should (1) quantify the amount by line of business and by accident year within each line, (2) describe the new events or information obtained since the last reporting period that led to any changes in estimate, and (3) explain why recognition occurred in the current period, rather than in earlier periods.

The SEC staff also requires disclosure about reserving assumptions. For each material line of business, disclosure should include (1) the key assumptions affecting the estimate of liability for unpaid claims and claim adjustment expenses, and (2) a quantification of any material assumption changes from the preceding period. Finally, registrants should disclose whether the liability for claims and claim adjustment expenses is likely to change in the future. This disclosure should include, for each material line of business, (1) the identification of key assumptions that are reasonably likely to change, (2) an explanation of why management believes each change is likely, and (3) quantification of the effect that these changes may have on future financial position, liquidity, and results of operations.

FINANCIAL SERVICES—INVESTMENT COMPANIES (ASC 946)

PERSPECTIVE AND ISSUES

An investment company pools shareholders' funds to provide shareholders with professional investment management. Investment companies' activities include selling capital shares to the public, investing the proceeds in securities, and distributing net income and net realized gains to its shareholders.

ASC 946 discusses those aspects of accounting and auditing unique to investment companies, and provides guidance on accounting for offering costs, amortization of premium or discount on bonds, liabilities for excess expense plans, reporting complex capital structures, payments by affiliates, and financial statement presentation and disclosures for investment companies and nonpublic investment partnerships.

ASC 946 provides incremental guidance to those entities that meet the assessment guidelines to be deemed investment companies. All entities regulated under the Investment Company Act of 1940 are in the scope of ASC 946. Other entities must assess the characteristics of an investment company outlined below, taking into account the entities' purpose and design. The fundamental characteristics of an investment company are that it

- Obtains funds from one or more investors,
- Provides the investors with investment management services
- Commits to its investors that its business purpose and only substantive activities are investing the funds solely for returns from capital appreciation, investment income, or both.
- Does not obtain or have the objective of obtaining returns or benefits from an investee or its affiliates that are not normally attributable to ownership interests or that are other than capital appreciation or investment income.

Typical characteristics of an investment company are:

1. It has more than one investment and investor.
2. Investors are not related parties of the parent, if any, or the investment manager.
3. Ownership interests are in the form of equity or partnership interests.
4. It manages substantially all of its investments on a fair value basis.

(ASC 946-10-15-6 and 15-7)

Entities that do not possess one or more of the characteristics may still be investment companies.

If an entity makes the assessment and judges that it is an investment company, it should account for the effect of the change from the date of the change, recognizing the effect as a cumulative effect adjustment. Entities that make the assessment and come to the conclusion that they are no longer an investment company discontinue applying the guidance and account for the effect of the change prospectively in accordance with other Topics. (ASC 946-10-15-5)

DEFINITIONS OF TERMS

Terms are from ASC 946 Glossary.

Affiliate. A party that, directly or indirectly through one or more intermediaries, controls, is controlled by, or is under common control with an entity.

Fair Value. The price that would be received to sell an asset or paid to transfer a liability in an orderly transaction between market participants at the measurement date.

Front-End Load. A sales commission or charge payable at the time of purchase of mutual fund shares.

Net Asset Value per Share. Net asset value per share is the amount of net assets attributable to each share of capital stock (other than senior equity securities, that is, preferred stock) outstanding at the close of the period. It excludes the effects of assuming conversion of outstanding convertible securities, whether or not their conversion would have a diluting effect.

Parent. An entity that has a controlling financial interest in one or more subsidiaries. (Also, an entity that is the primary beneficiary of a variable interest entity.)

Related Parties. Related parties include:

1. Affiliates of the entity
2. Entities for which investments in their equity securities would be required, absent the election of the fair value option under the Fair Value Option Subsection of Section 825-10-15, to be accounted for by the equity method by the investing entity
3. Trusts for the benefit of employees, such as pension and profit-sharing trusts that are managed by or under the trusteeship of management
4. Principal owners of the entity and members of their immediate families
5. Management of the entity and members of their immediate families
6. Other parties with which the entity may deal if one party controls or can significantly influence the management or operating policies of the other to an extent that one of the transacting parties might be prevented from fully pursuing its own separate interests
7. Other parties that can significantly influence the management or operating policies of the transacting parties or that have an ownership interest in one of the transacting parties and can significantly influence the other to an extent that one or more of the transacting parties might be prevented from fully pursuing its own separate interests.

CONCEPTS, RULES, AND EXAMPLES

Several types of investment companies exist: management investment companies, unit investment trusts, collectible trust funds, investment partnerships, certain separate accounts of life insurance companies, and offshore funds. Management investment companies include open-end funds (mutual funds), closed-end funds, special purpose funds, venture capital investment companies, small business investment companies, and business development companies.

Accounting Policies

The accounting policies for an investment company result from the company's role as a vehicle through which investors can invest as a group. These policies are largely governed by the SEC, Small Business Administration, and specific provisions of the Internal Revenue Code relating to investment companies.

Investment companies report investment securities at fair value in accordance with the guidance in ASC 825. (ASC 946-10-15-2)

Security purchases and sales are generally recorded at the trade date; therefore, the effects of all securities trades entered into by the investment company to the date of the financial statements are included in the financial report. (ASC 946-320-25-1)

Investment companies record dividend income on the ex-dividend date, not on the later record or payable date. The rationale for this treatment is that the market price of market securities may be affected by the exclusion of the declared dividend. Additionally, investment companies record a liability for dividends payable on the ex-dividend date because mutual fund shares are purchased and redeemed at prices equal to or based on net asset value. If investors purchase shares between the declaration and ex-dividend dates they are entitled to receive dividends; however, investors purchasing shares after the ex-dividend date are not entitled to receive dividends. (ASC 946-320-25-4)

Open-end investment companies often employ the practice of equalization. This theory states that the net asset value of each share of capital stock sold comprises the par value of the stock, undistributed income, and paid-in capital and other surplus. When shares are sold or repurchased, the investment company calculates the amount of undistributed income available for distribution to its shareholders. Based on the number of shares outstanding, the investment company determines the per share amount; this amount is credited to an equalization account when shares are sold. Conversely, the equalization account is charged when shares are repurchased.[2]

Accounting for High-Yield Debt Securities

The accounting by creditors for investments in *step interest* and *payment in kind (PIK)* debt securities, if these qualify as *high-yield* securities, is addressed by the ASC 946. Step interest bonds are generally unsecured debentures that pay no interest for a specified period after issuance, then pay a stipulated rate for a period, then a higher rate for another period, etc., until maturity. Thus, they combine some of the characteristics of zero-coupon bonds with some features of current interest bonds. PIK bonds pay some or all interest in the form of other debt instruments (*baby* or *bunny* bonds), which in turn may also pay interest in the form of baby bonds. All babies mature at the due date of the parent bond.

The interest method should be used for step interest bonds; to the extent that interest income is not expected to be realized, a reserve against the income should be established. For PIK bonds, the interest method is also required.

Exemptions from the Requirement to Provide a Statement of Cash Flows

The following conditions must be met for an investment company to be exempted from providing a statement of cash flows:

1. The entity's investments are carried at fair value and classified as Level 1 or Level 2 measurements per ASC 820.
2. The entity had little or no debt, based on average debt outstanding during the period, in relation to average total assets.
3. The entity provides a statement of changes in net assets.

(ASC 230-10-15-4)

Taxes

Investment companies that distribute all taxable income and taxable realized gains qualifying under Subchapter M of the Internal Revenue Code are not required to record a provision for federal income taxes. If the investment company does not distribute all taxable income and taxable realized gains, a liability should be recorded at the end of the last day of the taxable year. The rationale for recording on the last day of the year is that only shareholders of record at that date are entitled to credit for taxes paid.[3]

---

[2] See *Investment Companies–Audit and Accounting Guide*, Copyright 2014, American Institute of Certified Public Accountants.

[3] Ibid.

Commodity Pools

ASC 946-210 stipulates that investment partnerships which are commodity pools subject to regulation by the Commodity Exchange Act of 1934 are subject to its guidance. Thus, notwithstanding the rapid turnover common among such pools, the financial statements must include a schedule of investments. (ASC 946-210-50-4)

Other Accounting Guidance

ASC 946-320 concludes that for PIK and step bonds,

(1) the interest method should be used to determine interest income;
(2) a reserve against income should be established for interest income not expected to be realized;
(3) the cost plus any discount should not exceed undiscounted future cash collections.
(ASC 946-320-35-10 and 35-11)

For defaulted debt securities, any interest receivable written off that had been recognized as income constitutes a reduction of income. Write-offs of purchased interest increase the cost basis and represent an unrealized loss until the security is sold. (ASC 946-320-35-17 and 35-18) *Capital infusions* are accounted for as an addition to the cost basis, while related "workout expenditures" are recorded as unrealized losses. Any ongoing expenditures to protect the value of the investment are recorded as operating expenses. (ASC 946-320-35-14 through 16)

In ASC 946-830, it was concluded that transactions denominated in a foreign currency must originally be measured in that currency. Reporting exchange rate gains and losses separately from any gain/loss on the investment due to changes in market price is allowable but not required.

ASC 946-210-50 pertains to investment partnerships that are exempt from SEC registration under the Investment Company Act of 1940. Specifically, the statement requires that the financial statements include a condensed schedule of securities that categorizes investments by type, country or geographic region, and industry; discloses pertinent information concerning investments comprising greater than 5% of net assets; and aggregates any securities holdings less than the 5% of net assets threshold. The statement of operations for nonpublic investment companies shall be presented in conformity with requirements for public investment companies per the AAG so as to reflect their comparable operations. The financial statements shall also present management fees and disclose their computation.

ASC 946-20 requires investment companies with enhanced 12b-1 plans or board-contingent plans for which the board has committed to pay costs to recognize a liability and the related expense, for the amount of excess costs. This liability should be discounted at an appropriate current rate if the amount and timing of cash flows are reliably determinable and if distribution costs are not subject to a reasonable interest charge. Excess costs are recorded as a liability as the fund has assumed an obligation to pay the 12b-1 fee after the termination of the plan to the extent that the distributor has excess costs.

In a related matter, ASC 946-605 specifies the accounting for cash received from a third party for a distributor's right to future cash flows relating to distribution fees for previously sold shares. Revenue recognition is deemed proper when cash is received from a third party if the distributor has no continuing involvement nor recourse; any deferred costs related to the sale of shares is to be expensed concurrently. It further defines absence of continuing involvement and recourse.

ASC 946-210 affects the required display of certain contracts held by investment companies if these are fully benefit-responsive. Both the fair values of the contracts, segregated between guaranteed investment contracts and so-called wrapper contracts, and the contract (guaranteed) values, must be displayed in the investment company's statement of financial position.

A contract is deemed fully benefit-responsive if *all* five conditions set forth by the ASC are met. These conditions are defined as

1. The contract is negotiated directly between the fund and the issuer, and it prohibits the fund from assigning or selling the contract or its proceeds to another party without the consent of the issuer.
2. Either (a) the repayment of principal and interest credited to participants in the fund is guaranteed by the issuer of the investment contract, or (b) the fund provides for prospective interest crediting rate adjustments to participants in the fund on a designated pool of investments held by the fund, provided that the terms of the agreement with participants in the fund specify that the crediting interest rate cannot be less than zero. The risk of decline in the interest crediting rate below zero must be transferred to a financially responsible third party through a *wrapper* contract. If an event (e.g., decline in creditworthiness of the contract issuer or wrapper provider) has occurred that may affect the realization of full contract value for a particular investment contract, the contract no longer is to be considered fully benefit-responsive.
3. The terms of the contract require all permitted participant-initiated transactions with the fund to occur at contract value with no conditions, limits, or restrictions. Permitted participant-initiated transactions are those transactions allowed by the underlying defined-contribution plan, such as withdrawals for benefits, loans, or transfers to other funds within the plan.
4. Events that limit the ability for the fund to transact at contract value with the issuer (e.g., premature termination of the contracts by the plan, plant closings, layoffs, plan termination, bankruptcy, mergers, and early retirement incentives) must be *probable* of *not* occurring.
5. The fund itself must allow participants reasonable access to their funds.

(ASC 946-210-20)

This standard requires that statements of financial position of investment companies report separately investments, including guaranteed investment contracts, at fair value, and wrapper contracts, also at fair value. The statement of financial position must also display an additional account to bring the total assets being reported to contract amounts—that is, the amounts at which participants can transact with the fund. (ASC 946-210-45-15)

Additionally, the following information must be disclosed in footnotes to the financial statements for each investment contract, and be reconciled to corresponding line items on the statement of financial position:

1. The fair value of the wrapper contract and the fair value of each of the corresponding underlying investments;
2. Adjustment from fair value to contract value (if the investment contract is fully benefit-responsive); and
3. Major credit ratings of the issuer or wrapper provider.

(ASC 946-210-45-18)

Other expanded disclosures are mandated for investment companies having fully benefit-responsive contracts, as follows:

1. A description of the nature of the investment contracts, how they operate, and the methodology for calculating the crediting interest rate, including the key factors that

could influence future average crediting interest rates, the basis for and frequency of determining credit interest-rate resets, and any minimum crediting interest rate under the terms of the contracts. This disclosure should explain the relationship between future crediting rates and the amount reported on the statement of financial position representing the adjustment of the portion of net assets attributable to fully benefit-responsive investments from fair value to contract value.

2. A reconciliation between the beginning and ending balance of the amount presented on the statement of financial position that represents the difference between net assets at fair value and net assets for each period in which a statement of changes in net assets is presented. This reconciliation should include
   a. The change in the difference between the fair value and contract value of all fully benefit-responsive investment contracts, and
   b. The increase or decrease due to changes in the fully benefit-responsive status of the fund's investment contracts.
3. The average yield earned by the entire fund (without regard to the interest rate credited to participants in the fund) for each period for which a statement of financial position is presented.
4. The average yield earned by the entire fund with an adjustment to reflect the actual interest rate credited to participants in the fund covering each period for which a statement of financial position is presented.
5. Two different sensitivity analyses:
   a. The effect on the weighted-average crediting interest rates calculated at the latest date of a statement of financial position and the next four reset dates, under two or more scenarios where there is an immediate hypothetical increase or decrease in interest rates, with no change to the duration of the underlying investment portfolio and no contributions or withdrawals. These scenarios should include, at a minimum, immediate hypothetical changes in market yields equal to one-quarter and one-half of the current yield.
   b. The effect on the weighted-average crediting interest rates calculated at the latest date of a statement of financial position and the next four reset dates, under two or more scenarios where there are the same immediate hypothetical changes in market yields in the first analysis, combined with an immediate hypothetical 10% decrease in the net assets of the fund due to participant transfers, with no change to the duration of the portfolio.
6. A description of the events which limit the ability of the fund to transact at contract value with the issuer (for example, premature termination of the contracts by the plan, plant closings, layoffs, plan termination, bankruptcy, mergers, and early retirement incentives), including a statement that the occurrence of such events is probable or not probable.
7. A description of the events and circumstances that would allow issuers to terminate fully benefit-responsive investment contracts with the fund and settle at an amount different from contract value.

(ASC 946-210-50-14)

In order to be considered within the scope of the guidance in ASC 946-210-45-15 through 45-18, any portion of the net assets of the investment company that is not held by participants in qualified employer-sponsored defined-contribution plans as of the effective date are not permitted to increase due to gross contributions, loan repayments, or transfers into the fund. (ASC 946-210-45-18A)

FINANCIAL SERVICES—MORTGAGE BANKING (ASC 948)

PERSPECTIVE AND ISSUES

Mortgage banking comprises two activities:

1. The origination or purchase of mortgage loans and subsequent sale to permanent investors, and
2. Long-term servicing of the mortgage loan.

To the extent that mortgage banking activities discussed in this section may be undertaken by subsidiaries or divisions of commercial banks or savings institutions, the same accounting and reporting standards apply. Normal, nonmortgage lending of those enterprises, however, is accounted for in accordance with the lender's normal accounting policies for such activities.

Mortgage loans held for sale are valued at the lower of cost or market. Mortgage-backed securities are reported under ASC 320 as held-to-maturity, trading, or available-for-sale, depending on the entity's intent and ability to hold the securities.

Loan origination fees and related direct costs for loans held for sale are capitalized as part of the related loan and amortized, using the effective yield method. However, fees and costs associated with commitments to originate, sell, or purchase loans are treated as part of the commitment, which is a derivative accounted for under ASC 815.

Loan origination fees and costs for loans held for investment are deferred and recognized as an adjustment to the yield.

ASC 942, *Financial Services—Depository and Lending,* provides uniform and consistent guidance for the accounting and reporting practices for similar transactions by various types of depository and lending institutions, and has now been incorporated in a unified AAG. The standard includes in its scope, corporate credit unions and mortgage companies and, in fact, affects disclosure practices for any entity that extends credit to customers. (See the summary under the Financial Services—Banking and Lending section of this chapter for a discussion of the general disclosure requirements for all enterprises. These general requirements also apply, when applicable, to mortgage banking enterprises and are not repeated in this section.) In addition, the standard prescribes required disclosures for mortgage banking enterprises regarding their regulatory capital and net worth requirements.

DEFINITIONS OF TERMS

Source: ASC 948 Glossary

Affiliated entity. An entity that directly or indirectly controls, is controlled by, or is under common control with another entity; also, a party with which the entity may deal if one party has the ability to exercise significant influence over the other's operating and financial policies.

Current (normal) servicing fee rate. A servicing fee rate that is representative of servicing fee rates most commonly used in comparable servicing agreements covering similar types of mortgage loans.

Federal Home Loan Mortgage Corporation (FHLMC). Often referred to as *Freddie Mac*, FHLMC is a private corporation authorized by Congress to assist in the development and maintenance of a secondary market in conventional residential mortgages. FHLMC purchases and sells mortgages principally through mortgage participation certificates (PC) representing an undivided interest in a group of conventional mortgages. FHLMC guarantees the timely payment of interest and the collection of principal on the PC.

Federal National Mortgage Association (FNMA). Often referred to as *Fannie Mae*, FNMA is an investor-owned corporation established by Congress to support the secondary mortgage loan market by purchasing mortgage loans when other investor funds are limited and selling mortgage loans when other investor funds are available.

Gap commitment. A commitment to provide interim financing while the borrower is in the process of satisfying provisions of a permanent loan agreement, such as obtaining a designated occupancy level on an apartment project. The interim loan ordinarily finances the difference between the floor loan (the portion of a mortgage loan commitment that is less than the full amount of the commitment) and the maximum permanent loan.

Government National Mortgage Association (GNMA). Often referred to as *Ginnie Mae*, GNMA is a US governmental agency that guarantees certain types of securities (mortgage-backed securities) and provides funds for and administers certain types of low-income housing assistance programs.

Internal reserve method. A method for making payments to investors for collections of principal and interest on mortgage loans by issuers of GNMA securities. An issuer electing the internal reserve method is required to deposit in a custodial account an amount equal to one month's interest on the mortgage loans that collateralize the GNMA security issued.

Mortgage-backed securities. Securities issued by a governmental agency or corporation (e.g., GNMA or FHLMC) or by private issuers (e.g., FNMA, banks, and mortgage banking entitiess). Mortgage-backed securities generally are referred to as mortgage participation certificates or pass-through certificates (PC). A PC represents an undivided interest in a pool of specific mortgage loans. Periodic payments on GNMA PC are backed by the US government. Periodic payments on FHLMC and FNMA PC are guaranteed by those corporations and are not backed by the US government.

Mortgage banking entity. An entity that is engaged primarily in originating, marketing, and servicing real estate mortgage loans for other than its own account. Mortgage banking entities, as local representatives of institutional lenders, act as correspondents between lenders and borrowers.

Permanent investor. An entity that invests in mortgage loans for its own account, for example, an insurance entity, commercial or mutual savings bank, savings and loan association, pension plan, real estate investment trust, or FNMA.

Repurchase financing. A repurchase agreement that relates to a previously transferred financial asset between the same counterparties, and which is entered into contemporaneously with, or in contemplation of, the initial transfer.

CONCEPTS, RULES, AND EXAMPLES

Mortgage Banking Activities

A mortgage banking entity (MBE) acts as an intermediary between borrowers (mortgagors) and lenders (mortgagees). MBE activities include purchasing and originating mortgage loans for sale to permanent investors and performing servicing activities during the period that the loans are outstanding. The mortgage loans offered for sale to permanent investors may be originated by the MBE (in-house originations); purchased from realtors, brokers, or investors; or converted from short-term, interim credit facilities to permanent financing. The common technique used by the MBE to market and sell the loans is referred to as securitization because the mortgage loans receivable are pooled and converted to mortgage-backed securities and sold in that form.

MBEs customarily retain the rights to service the loans that they sell to permanent investors in exchange for a servicing fee. The servicing fee, normally a percentage of the mortgage's outstanding principal balance, compensates the MBE for processing of mortgagor payments of principal, interest and escrow deposits, disbursing funds from the escrow accounts to pay property taxes and insurance on behalf of the mortgagor, and remitting net proceeds to the permanent investor along with relevant accounting reports.

Mortgage loans. The MBE is required to classify mortgage loans that it holds as either (1) held-for-sale, or (2) held for long-term investment.

Loans held-for-sale. Mortgage loans held for sale are reported at the lower of cost or market as of the date of the statement of financial position. Any excess of cost over market is accounted for as a valuation allowance, changes in which are to be included in income in the period of change.

Determination of cost basis. The following matters must be considered with respect to the cost basis used for the purposes of the lower of cost or market value determination:

1. If a mortgage loan has been identified as a hedged item in a fair value hedge under ASC 815, the cost basis used reflects adjustments to the loan's carrying amount for changes in the loan's fair value attributable to the risk being hedged.
2. Purchase discounts on mortgage loans reduce the cost basis and are not amortized as interest revenue during the period that the loans are held for sale.
3. Capitalized costs attributable to the acquisition of mortgage servicing rights associated with the purchase or origination of mortgage loans are excluded from the cost basis of the mortgage loans.

Determination of market value. The market value of mortgage loans held for sale is determined by type of loan; at a minimum, separate determinations are made for residential and commercial loans. Either an aggregate or individual loan basis may be used in determining the lower of cost or market for each type of loan. Market values for loans subject to investor purchase commitments (committed loans) and loans held for speculative purposes (uncommitted loans) must be determined separately as follows:

1. For committed loans, market value is defined as fair value.
2. For uncommitted loans, market value is based on quotations from the market in which the MBE normally operates, considering
   a. Market prices and yields sought by the MBE's normal market outlets,
   b. Quoted Government National Mortgage Association (GNMA) security prices or other public market quotations of rates for long-term mortgage loans, and
   c. Federal Home Loan Mortgage Corporation (FHLMC) and Federal National Mortgage Association (FNMA) current delivery prices.

Loans held for long-term investment. Mortgage loans may be transferred from the held-for-sale classification to the held-for-long-term investment classification only if the MBE has both the intent and ability to hold the loan for the foreseeable future or until maturity. The transfer to the long-term investment classification is recorded at the lower of cost or market value on the date of transfer. Any difference between the loan's adjusted carrying amount and its outstanding principal balance (e.g., purchase discounts as discussed above) is recognized as a yield adjustment using the interest method.

If recoverability of the carrying amount of a mortgage loan held for long-term investment is doubtful and the impairment is judged to be other than temporary, the loan's carrying amount is reduced by the amount of the impairment to the amount expected to be collected with the related charge recognized as a loss. The adjusted carrying value becomes the loan's new cost basis and any eventual gain on recovery may only be recognized upon the loan's sale, maturity, or other disposition.

Mortgage-backed securities. The securitization of mortgage loans held-for-sale is accounted for as a sale of the mortgage loans and purchase of mortgage-backed securities.

Classification and valuation. After the securitization of a held-for-sale mortgage loan, any mortgage-backed securities retained by the MBE are classified as (1) trading, (2) available-for-sale, or (3) held-to-maturity under the provisions of ASC 320. As is the case with the MBE's mortgage loans held for investment, the MBE must have both the intent and ability to hold the mortgage-backed securities for the foreseeable future or until maturity in order to classify them as held-to-maturity. If the MBE had committed to sell the securities before or during the securitization process, the securities are required to be classified under the trading category. Mortgage-backed securities held by a not-for-profit entity are stated at fair value under ASC 958-320.

The fair value of uncommitted mortgage-backed securities collateralized by the MBE's own loans is ordinarily based on the market value of the securities. If the trust holding the loans may be readily terminated and the loans sold directly, fair value of the securities is based on the market value of either the loans or the securities, depending on the entity's intentions. Fair value for other uncommitted mortgage-backed securities is based on published yield data.

Repurchase agreements. Mortgage loans or mortgage-backed securities held for sale may be temporarily transferred by an MBE to another financial institution under a formal or informal agreement which serves as a means of financing these assets. Such agreements are accounted for as collateralized financing arrangements; the loans and securities transferred under the agreements are still reported by the MBE as held for sale.

A formal repurchase agreement specifies that the MBE retains control over future economic benefits and also the risk of loss relating to the loans or securities transferred. These assets are subsequently reacquired from the financial institution upon the sale of the assets by the mortgage banking entity to permanent investors.

An informal repurchase agreement exists when no formal agreement has been executed but loans or securities are transferred by an MBE that does all of the following:

1. Is the sole marketer of the assets
2. Retains any interest spread on the assets
3. Retains risk of loss in market value
4. Reacquires uncollectible loans
5. Regularly reacquires most or all of the assets and sells them to permanent investors.

When mortgage loans held for sale are transferred under a repurchase arrangement, they continue to be reported by the transferor as loans held for sale. Mortgage-backed securities sold under agreements to repurchase are reported as trading securities as defined in ASC 320.

Servicing Mortgage Loans

Rights to service mortgage loans for others are recognized as separate assets by an MBE. If the entity acquires such rights through purchase or origination of mortgage loans and retains them upon sale or securitization, the total cost of the mortgage loans must be allocated between the rights and the loans (without the rights) based on their relative fair values. If it is impossible to determine the fair value of the mortgage servicing rights apart from the mortgage, the MBE/transferor records the mortgage servicing rights at zero value (ASC 860). Otherwise, mortgage servicing rights are capitalized at their fair value and recognized as a net asset if the benefits of servicing the mortgage are expected to be more than adequate compensation to the servicer for performing the duties. If the benefits of servicing the mortgage are not expected to adequately compensate the servicer, the servicer recognizes a liability. The asset, mortgage servicing contract rights, is initially measured at its fair value. Subsequent impairment is recognized as follows:

1. The mortgage servicing assets are stratified based on predominant risk characteristics.
2. Impairment is recognized through a valuation allowance for an individual stratum. The amount of impairment equals the carrying amount for a particular stratum minus its fair value.
3. The valuation allowance is adjusted to reflect changes in the measurement of impairment after the initial measurement of impairment.

Servicing fees. Servicing fees are usually based on a percentage of the outstanding principal balance of the mortgage loan. When a mortgage loan is sold with servicing rights retained, the sales price must be adjusted if the stated rate is materially different from the current (normal) servicing fee rate so that the gain or loss on the sale can be determined. The adjustment is

Adjustment	=	Actual Sales Price	–	Estimated sales price obtainable if normal servicing fee rate had been used

This adjustment allows for recognition of normal servicing fees in subsequent years.

The adjustment and any recognized gain or loss is determined as of the sale date. If estimated normal servicing fees are less than total expected servicing costs, then this loss is accrued on the sale date as well.

Repurchase Financing

A repurchase financing involves the transfer of a previously transferred financial asset back to the lender as collateral for a financing between the borrower and the lender. The lender usually returns the financial asset to the borrower when the financing is repaid. The borrower and lender cannot separately account for an asset transfer and related repurchase financing unless the two transactions have a valid business purpose for being entered into separately, and the repurchase financing does not result in the lender retaining control over the financial asset. If a transaction meets these criteria, then evaluate the initial transfer without the repurchase financing to see if it meets the requirements for sale accounting (ASC 860). If the transaction does not meet these criteria, then the arrangement is probably a forward contract.

Sales to Affiliated Entities

When mortgage loans or mortgage-backed securities are sold to an affiliated entity, the carrying amount of the assets must be adjusted to lower of cost or market as of the date that management decides that the sale will occur. This date is evidenced by formal approval by a representative of the affiliated entity (purchaser), issuance of a purchase commitment, and acceptance of the purchase commitment by the seller. Any adjustment is charged to income.

If a group of (or all) mortgage loans are originated specifically for an affiliate, then the originator is an agent of the affiliated entity. In this case, the loans are transferred at the originator's cost of acquisition. This treatment does not apply to *right of first refusal* or similar contracts in which the originator retains all risks of ownership.

Issuance of GNMA Securities

An issuer of GNMA securities who elects the internal reserve method must pay one month's interest cost to a trustee. This cost is capitalized (at no greater than the present value of net future servicing income) and amortized.

Loan and Commitment Fees and Costs

Mortgage bankers may pay or receive loan and commitment fees as compensation for various loan administration services. These fees and costs are accounted for as described in the following paragraphs.

Loan origination fees received. Loan origination fees and related direct costs are deferred and amortized, using the effective yield method. Fees and costs associated with commitments to originate, sell, or purchase loans, however, must be considered part of the commitments, which are deemed to be derivatives under ASC 815. If the loan is held for investment, loan origination fees and costs are recognized as an adjustment of yield using the effective interest method.

Services rendered. Fees for specific services rendered by third parties as part of a loan origination (e.g., appraisal fees) are recognized when the services are performed.

Commitment fees paid to investors on loans held for sale. Residential or commercial loan commitment fees paid to permanent investors are recognized as expense when the loans are sold or when it is determined that the commitment will not be used. Since residential loan commitment fees typically cover groups of loans, the amount of fees recognized as revenue or expense relating to an individual transaction is calculated as

$$\text{Revenue or expense recognized on individual transaction} = \text{Total residential loan commitment fee} \times \frac{\text{Amount of individual loan}}{\text{Total commitment amount}}$$

Loan placement fees (fees for arranging a commitment directly between investor and borrower) are recognized as revenue once all significant services have been performed by the MBE. In some cases, an MBE secures a commitment from a permanent investor before or at the same time a commitment is made to a borrower and the latter commitment requires

1. Simultaneous assignment to the investor, and
2. Simultaneous transfer to the borrower of amounts paid by the investor.

The fees related to such transactions are also accounted for as loan placement fees.

Expired commitments or early repayment of loans. At the time that a loan commitment expires unused or is repaid before repayment is due, any related fees that had been deferred are recognized as revenue or expense.

Reporting

An MBE must, on its statement of financial position, distinguish between mortgage loans and mortgage-backed securities that are held for sale and those that are held for long-term investment. The notes to the financial statements are to disclose whether the MBE used the aggregate method or the individual-loan method to determine the lower of cost or market.

ASC 942, *Financial Services—Depository and Lending,* contains specific capital disclosure requirements including, at a minimum

1. A description of the minimum net worth requirements related to
   a. Secondary market investors, and
   b. State-imposed regulatory mandates.
2. The actual or possible material effects of noncompliance with those requirements.
3. Whether the entity is in compliance with the regulatory capital requirements including, as of the date of each statement of financial position presented, the following measures:
   a. The amount of the entity's required and actual net worth
   b. Factors that may significantly affect adequacy of net worth such as potentially volatile components of capital, qualitative factors, or regulatory mandates
4. If the entity is not in compliance with capital adequacy requirements as of the date of the most recent statement of financial position, the possible material effects of that condition on amounts and disclosures in the financial statements.
5. Loan servicers with net worth requirements imposed by more than one source are to disclose the new worth requirements of
   a. Significant servicing covenants with secondary market investors with commonly defined servicing requirements,
   b. Any other secondary market investor where violation of the net worth requirement would have an adverse effect on the business, and
   c. The most restrictive third-party agreement if not already included in the above disclosures.

The standard points out that noncompliance with minimum net worth requirements may trigger substantial doubt about the entity's ability to continue as a going concern.

FINANCIAL SERVICES—TITLE PLANT (ASC 950)

PERSPECTIVE AND ISSUES

ASC 950-350, *Financial Services—Title Plant,* presents accounting and reporting standards for costs relating to the construction and operation of title plants. A title plant comprises a record of all transactions or conditions that affect titles to land located in a specified area. The length of time spanned by a title plant depends upon regulatory requirements and the time frame required to gather sufficient information to efficiently issue title insurance. Updating occurs frequently as documentation of the current status of a title is added to the title plant.

This pronouncement applies to entitiess such as title insurance companies, title abstract companies, and title agents that use a title plant in their operations. The standard provides that costs directly incurred to construct a title plant are to be capitalized when the entity can use the title plant to do title searches and that such capitalized costs are not normally depreciated. The statement also requires that the costs of maintaining a title plant and of doing title searches be expensed as incurred.

DEFINITIONS OF TERMS

Source: ASC 950 Glossary

Backplant. A title plant that antedates the period covered by its existing title plant.

Title Plant. A historical record of all matters affecting title to parcels of land in a particular geographic area. The number of years covered by a title plant varies, depending on regulatory requirements and the minimum information period considered necessary to issue title insurance policies efficiently.

CONCEPTS, RULES, AND EXAMPLES

Acquisition Costs

The cost of constructing a title plant includes the cost of obtaining, organizing, and summarizing historical information pertaining to a particular tract of land. Costs incurred to assemble a title plant are to be capitalized until the record is usable for conducting title searches. Costs incurred to construct a backplant (a title plant that predates the time span of an existing title plant) must also be capitalized. However, an entity may capitalize only those costs that are directly related to and traceable to the activities performed in constructing the title plant or backplant.

The purchase of a title plant or backplant, or an undivided interest therein (the right to its joint use) is recorded at cost as of the date acquired. If the title plant is acquired separately, it is recorded at the fair value of consideration given.

Capitalized title plant costs are not amortized or depreciated unless an impairment in the carrying amount of the title plant occurs. The following events or changes in circumstances can indicate that the carrying amount may not be recoverable. An impairment may be indicated by the following circumstances (not intended to be an exhaustive list):

1. Changing legal or statutory requirements
2. Economic factors, such as changing demand
3. Loss of competitive advantage
4. Failure to maintain an up-to-date title plant
5. Circumstances that indicate obsolescence, such as abandonment of title plant.

The provisions of ASC 360 apply to any such impairment. See chapter on ASC 360 for a complete discussion of this topic.

Operating Costs

Costs of title plant maintenance and of conducting title searches are required to be expensed currently. A title plant is maintained through frequent, often daily, updating which involves adding reports on the current status of specific real estate titles and documentation of security or other ownership interests in such land. A title search entails a search for all information or documentation pertaining to a particular parcel of land. This information is found in the most recently issued title report.

Once a title plant is operational, costs may be incurred to convert the record from one storage and retrieval system to another or to modify the current storage and retrieval system. These costs may not be capitalized as title plant. However, they may be separately capitalized and amortized using a systematic and rational method.

Reporting Title Plant Sales

The sale of a title plant is to be reported separately. The amount to be reported is determined by the circumstances surrounding the sale as follows:

Terms of sale	*Amount reported*
Sale of title plant and waiver of all rights to future use	Amount received less adjusted cost of title plant
Sale of undivided ownership interest (rights to future joint use)	Amount received less pro rata portion of adjusted cost of title plant
Sales of copies of title plant or the right to use it	Amount received

Note that in the last instance the amount reported is simply the amount received. In this case, no cost is allocated to the item sold unless the title plant's value drops below its adjusted cost as a result of the sale.

FRANCHISORS (ASC 952)

PERSPECTIVE AND ISSUES

Overview

Franchising has become a popular growth industry with many businesses seeking to sell franchises as their primary income source and individuals seeking to buy franchises and become entrepreneurs. How to recognize revenue on the individual sale of franchise territories and on the transactions that arise in connection with the continuing relationship between the franchisor and franchisee are prime accounting issues.

Franchise fees are governed by ASC 952, *Franchisors.*

DEFINITIONS OF TERMS

Source: ASC 952 Glossary

Area franchise. An agreement that transfers franchise rights within a geographical area permitting the opening of a number of franchised outlets. Under those circumstances, decisions regarding the number of outlets, their location, and so forth are more likely made unilaterally by the franchisee than in collaboration with the franchisor. A franchisor may sell an area franchise to a franchisee who operates the franchised outlets or the franchisor may sell an area franchise to an intermediary franchisee who then sells individual franchises to other franchisees who operate the outlets.

Continuing franchise fee. Consideration for the continuing rights granted by the franchise agreement and for general or specific services during its term.

Franchise agreement. A written business agreement that meets the following principal criteria:

1. The relation between the franchisor and franchisee is contractual, and an agreement confirming the rights and responsibilities of each party is in force for a specified period.
2. The continuing relation has as its purpose the distribution of a product or service, or an entire business concept, within a particular market area.
3. Both the franchisor and the franchisee contribute resources for establishing and maintaining the franchise. The franchisor's contribution may be a trademark, a

company reputation, products, procedures, labor, equipment, or a process. The franchisee usually contributes operating capital as well as the managerial and operational resources required for opening and continuing the franchised outlet.
4. The franchise agreement outlines and describes the specific marketing practices to be followed, specifies the contribution of each party to the operation of the business, and sets forth certain operating procedures with which both parties agree to comply.
5. The establishment of the franchised outlet creates a business entity that will, in most cases, require and support the full-time business activity of the franchisee.
6. Both the franchisee and the franchisor have a common public identity. This identity is achieved most often through the use of common trade names or trademarks and is frequently reinforced through advertising programs designed to promote the recognition and acceptance of the common identity within the franchisee's market area.

The payment of an initial franchise fee or a continuing royalty fee is not a necessary criterion for an agreement to be considered a franchise agreement.

Franchisee. The party who has been granted business rights (the franchise) to operate the franchised business.

Franchisor. The party who grants business rights (the franchise) to the party (the franchisee) who will operate the franchised business.

CONCEPTS AND RULES

Franchise Sales

Franchise operations are generally subject to the same accounting principles as other commercial entitiess. Special issues arise out of franchise agreements, however, which require the application of special accounting rules.

Revenue is recognized, with an appropriate provision for bad debts, when the franchisor has substantially performed all material services or conditions. Only when revenue is collected over an extended period of time and collectibility cannot be predicted in advance would the use of the cost recovery or installment methods of revenue recognition be appropriate. Substantial performance means

1. The franchisor has no remaining obligation to either refund cash or forgive any unpaid balance due.
2. Substantially all initial services required by the agreement have been performed.
3. No material obligations or conditions remain.

Even if the contract does not require initial services, the pattern of performance by the franchisor in other franchise sales will impact the time period of revenue recognition. This can delay such recognition until services are either performed or it can reasonably be assured they will not be performed. The franchisee operations will be considered as started when such substantial performance has occurred.

If initial franchise fees are large compared to services rendered and continuing franchise fees are small compared to services to be rendered, then a portion of the initial fee is deferred in an amount sufficient to cover the costs of future services plus a reasonable profit, after considering the impact of the continuing franchise fee.

Example of initial franchise fee revenue recognition

Shanghai Asian Cuisine sells a Quack's Roast Duck franchise to Toledo Restaurants. The franchise is renewable after two years. The initial franchise fee is $50,000, plus a fixed fee of $500 per month. In exchange, Shanghai provides staff training, vendor relations support, and site selection consulting. Each month thereafter, Shanghai provides $1,000 of free local advertising. Shanghai's typical gross margin on franchise startup sales is 25%.

Because the monthly fee does not cover the cost of monthly services provided, Shanghai defers a portion of the initial franchise fee and amortizes it over the two-year life of the franchise agreement, using the following calculation:

Cost of monthly services provided $1,000 × 24 months	=	$24,000
÷ Markup to equal standard 25% gross margin	÷	.75
= Estimated revenue required to offset monthly services provided	=	$32,000
Less: Monthly billing to franchise $500 × 24 months	–	$12,000
= Amount of initial franchise fee to be deferred	=	$20,000

Shanghai's entry to record the franchise fee deferral follows:

Franchise fee revenue	20,000	
Unearned franchise fees (liability)		20,000

Shanghai recognizes 1/24 of the unearned franchise fee liability during each month of the franchise period on a straight-line basis, which amounts to $833.33 per month.

Area Franchise Sales

Sometimes franchisors sell territories rather than individual locations. In this event, the franchisor may render services to the area independent of the number of individual franchises to be established. Under this circumstance, revenue recognition for the franchisor is the same as stated above. If, however, substantial services are performed by the franchisor for each individual franchise established, then revenue is recognized in proportion to mandatory service. The general rule is that when the franchisee has no right to receive a refund, all revenue is recognized. It may be necessary for revenue recognition purposes to treat a franchise agreement as a divisible contract and allocate revenue among existing and estimated locations. Future revisions to these estimates will require that remaining unrecognized revenue be recorded in proportion to remaining services expected to be performed.

Example of revenue recognition for area franchise sales

Shanghai Asian Cuisine sells an area Quack's Roast Duck franchise to Canton Investments for $40,000. Under the terms of this area franchise, Shanghai is solely obligated to provide site selection consulting services to every franchise that Canton opens during the next twelve months, after which Canton is not entitled to a refund. Canton estimates that it will open 12 outlets sporadically throughout the year. Shanghai estimates that it will cost $2,500 for each site selection, or $30,000 in total. Based on the initial $40,000 franchise fee, Shanghai's estimated gross margin is 25%. Canton's initial payment of $40,000 is recorded by Shanghai with the following entry:

Cash	40,000	
Unearned franchise fees (liability)		40,000

After six months of preparation, Canton requests that four site selection surveys be completed. Shanghai completes the work at a cost of $10,000 and uses the following entry to record both the expenditure and related revenue:

Unearned franchise fees (liability)	13,333	
Franchise fee revenue		13,333
Site survey expense	10,000	
Accounts payable		10,000

By the end of the year, Shanghai has performed ten site selection surveys at a cost of $25,000 and recognized revenue of $33,333, leaving $6,667 of unrecognized revenue. Since Canton is no longer entitled to a refund, Shanghai uses the following entry to recognize all remaining revenue, with no related expense:

Unearned franchise fees (liability)	6,667	
Franchise fee revenue		6,667

Other Relationships

Franchisors may guarantee debt of the franchisee, continue to own a portion of the franchise, or control the franchisee's operations. Revenue is not recognized until all services, conditions, and obligations have been performed.

In addition, the franchisor may have an option to reacquire the location. Accounting for initial revenue is to consider the probability of exercise of the option. If the expectation at the time of the agreement is that the option is likely to be exercised, the entire franchise fee is deferred and not recognized as income. Upon exercise, the deferral reduces the recorded investment of the franchisor.

An initial fee may cover both franchise rights and property rights, including equipment, signs, and inventory. A portion of the fee applicable to property rights is recognized to the extent of the fair value of these assets. However, fees relating to different services rendered by franchisors are generally not allocated to these different services because segregating the amounts applicable to each service could not be performed objectively. The rule of revenue recognition when all services are substantially performed is generally upheld. If objectively determinable separate fees are charged for separate services, then recognition of revenue can be determined and recorded for each service performed.

Franchisors may act as agents for the franchisee by issuing purchase orders to suppliers for inventory and equipment. These are not recorded as sales and purchases by the franchisor; instead, consistent with the agency relationship, receivables from the franchisee and payables to the supplier are reported on the statement of financial position of the franchisor. There is, of course, no right of offset associated with these amounts, which are to be presented gross.

Continuing Franchise and Other Fees

Continuing franchise fees are recognized as revenue as the fees are earned. Related costs are expensed as incurred. Regardless of the purpose of the fees, revenue is recognized when the fee is earned and receivable. The exception is when a portion of the fee is required to be segregated and used for a specific purpose, such as advertising. The franchisor defers this amount and records it as a liability. This liability is reduced by the cost of the services received.

Sometimes, the franchisee has a period of time where bargain purchases of equipment or supplies are granted by the contract. If the bargain price is lower than other customers pay or denies a reasonable profit to the franchisor, a portion of the initial franchise fee is deferred and accounted for as an adjustment of the selling price when the franchisee makes the purchase. The deferred amount is either the difference in the selling price among customers and the bargain price, or an amount sufficient to provide a reasonable profit to the franchisor.

Costs

Direct and incremental costs related to franchise sales are deferred and recognized when revenue is recorded. However, deferred costs cannot exceed anticipated future revenue, net of additional expected costs.

Indirect costs are expensed as incurred. These usually are regular and recurring costs that bear no relationship to sales.

Repossessed Franchises

If, for any reason, the franchisor refunds the franchise fee and obtains the location, previously recognized revenue is reversed in the period of repossession. If a repossession is made without a refund, there is no adjustment of revenue previously recognized. However, any estimated uncollectible amounts are to be provided for and any remaining collected funds are recorded as revenue.

Business Combinations

Business combinations where the franchisor acquires the business of a franchisee are accounted for in accordance with the requirements of ASC 805.

No adjustment of prior revenue is made since the financial statements are not retroactively consolidated in recording a business combination. Care must be taken to ensure that the purchase is not a repossession. If the transaction is deemed to be a repossession, it is accounted for as described in the above section.

NOT-FOR-PROFIT ENTITIES (ASC 958)

PERSPECTIVE AND ISSUES

Overview

Not-for-profit entities have several characteristics that distinguish them from business entities. First, and perhaps foremost, not-for-profit entities exist to provide goods and services without the objective of generating a profit. Rather than obtaining resources by conducting exchange transactions at a profit or from capital infusions from owners, a not-for-profit organization obtains most resources from others that share its desire to serve a chosen mission—an educational, scientific, charitable, or religious goal. Although not-for-profit organizations can be "owned" or controlled by another, the ownership interest is unlike that of business entities because the "owner" cannot remove resources from the entity for personal use or gain; the resources must be used for a mission-related purpose. Examples of not-for-profit entities are: churches and religious entities, colleges and universities, health care entities, libraries, museums, performing arts entities, civic or fraternal entities, federated fund-raising entities, professional and trade associations, social clubs, research entities, cemeteries, arboretums, and zoos.

Specifically excluded from the list of not-for-profit entities are entities that exist to provide dividends, lower costs, or other economic benefits directly and proportionately to their members, participants, or owners, such as mutual insurance companies, credit unions, farm or utility cooperatives, and employee benefit plans. Further, some not-for-profit entities are governmental and are required to follow the standards of the Governmental Accounting Standards Board (GASB). Governmental entities are outside of the scope of this publication. Readers instead should refer to *Wiley GAAP for Governments 2012*.

All authoritative pronouncements in the FASB codification apply to not-for-profit entities unless the pronouncement specifically excludes not-for-profit entities from its scope. Certain standards apply specifically to not-for-profit entities. Because those standards are particularly relevant to the transactions of not-for-profit entities they are discussed in this chapter.

ASC 958, *Not-for-Profit Entities,* applies specifically to not-for-profit entities that are nongovernmental entities. (ASC 958-10-05-01) It requires not-for-profit entities to depreciate their long-lived assets and to disclose balances for the major classes of assets, depreciation for the period, accumulated depreciation, and the organization's policy for computing depreciation.

ASC 958-605 establishes standards for recognition and display of contributions received and contributions made. It requires all contributions received and made to be measured at fair value and recognized in the period the gift is made. It applies to any contribution of assets, including contributions of cash, securities, supplies, long-lived assets, use of facilities or utilities, services, intangible assets, or unconditional promises to give those items in the future.

ASC 958-205 establishes standards for the general-purpose financial statements issued by not-for-profit entities. It defines a complete set of financial statements for most entities as a statement of financial position, a statement of activities, a statement of cash flows, and accompanying notes. It requires an organization's net assets and its revenues, expenses, gains, and losses to be classified based on the existence or absence of restrictions imposed by donors.

ASC 958-320 establishes standards for investments held by not-for-profit entities. It requires equity securities with readily determinable fair values and debt securities to be reported at fair value with the resulting holding gains and losses reported in the statement of activities. It also establishes standards for reporting investment return, including losses on donor-restricted endowment funds.

ASC 958-20 establishes standards for transfers of assets to a not-for-profit organization or a charitable trust that raises or holds contributions for others. Although it primarily affects federated fund-raising entities, community foundations, and institutionally related foundations, all entities are subject to its standards because they can be the beneficiaries of the contributions raised by those entities.

Combinations in which the acquiring entity is a not-for-profit organization, unlike combinations in which the acquiring entity is a business entity, cannot be assumed to be an exchange of commensurate value. Acquired not-for-profit entities lack owners who are focused on receiving a return on and return of their investment. Moreover, the parent or governing body of an acquired organization may place its mission effectiveness ahead of achieving maximum price when negotiating a combination agreement. Thus, when two not-for-profit entities combine, it will be necessary to determine if there was an exchange of commensurate value (in which case, standards similar to ASC 850 would be applied) or if there is a contribution inherent in the transaction that would be reported in accordance with ASC 958-605.

If there is a contribution inherent in the transaction, it would be measured as the excess of the net fair values of the identifiable assets acquired and the liabilities assumed over the fair value of the consideration exchanged. If the acquired entity is a business enterprise, the contribution inherent in a combination would be measured as the excess of the fair value of the acquired business enterprise over the cost of that business enterprise. The primary difference is that no goodwill would be recognized in most contributions of not-for-profit entities, although it would be in the contributions of business entities.

In the rare cases in which the sum of the fair values of the liabilities assumed exceeds the sum of the fair values of the identifiable assets acquired, the acquiring organization would initially recognize that excess as an unidentifiable intangible asset (goodwill).

ASC 954 applies to providers of health care services, including hospitals, nursing homes, medical clinics, continuing care retirement communities, health maintenance entities, home health agencies, and rehabilitation facilities. It discusses the aspects of financial statement preparation and audit particularly relevant to the entities within its scope.

ASC 958-805, *Not-for-Profit Entity—Business Combinations*, establishes standards for determining whether a combination of not-for-profit entities is a merger or an acquisition, describes the carryover method of accounting (for a merger) and the acquisition method of accounting (for an acquisition), and notes related disclosures.

ASC 958-810 establishes standards for consolidation by not-for-profit entities of investments in for-profit entities and other not-for-profit entities. It also describes the disclosures required when related entities are not consolidated because the relationship does not meet the criteria of control and economic benefit.

ASC 958-720 establishes standards for the functional classification of expenses incurred in activities that combine program or management and general components with fund-raising. It requires that all costs of the combined activity be classified as fund-raising expenses unless three criteria—purpose, audience, and content—are met.

ASC 954-815 clarifies that the performance indicator required to be reported in the financial statements of a not-for-profit health care organization is analogous to income from continuing operations of a business (for-profit) enterprise.

This chapter contains a highly summarized discussion of accounting and reporting standards for not-for-profit entities. Readers who desire a more in-depth discussion should refer to *Wiley Not-for-Profit GAAP*.

DEFINITIONS OF TERMS

Agent. An entity that acts for and on behalf of another. For example, a not-for-profit organization acts as an agent for and on behalf of a donor if it receives resources from the donor and agrees to transfer the resources or the return generated by investing those resources to another entity named by the donor. Similarly, a not-for-profit organization acts for and on behalf of a beneficiary if it agrees to solicit contributions in the name of the beneficiary and distribute any contributions thereby received to the beneficiary.

Collections. Works of art, historical treasures, or similar assets that meet the following three criteria: (1) they are held for public exhibition, education, or research in service to the public rather than for financial gain; (2) they are protected, kept unencumbered, cared for, and preserved; and (3) they are subject to a policy requiring that the organization use the proceeds from the sale of an item to acquire another item for the collection.

Contribution. A voluntary and unconditional transfer of assets to an entity (the donee) from another entity that does not expect to receive equivalent value in exchange and does not act as an owner (the donor). A contribution can also take the form of a settlement or cancellation of the donee's liabilities.

Designated net assets. Unrestricted net assets subject to self-imposed limits by action of the governing board. Designated net assets may be earmarked for future programs, investment, contingencies, purchase or construction of fixed assets, or other uses.

Donor-imposed condition. A donor stipulation that specifies a future and uncertain event whose occurrence (or failure to occur) gives the donor the right of return of resources it has transferred or releases the donor from the obligation to transfer assets in the future.

For example, "I will contribute one dollar for each dollar raised during the month of July in excess of $10,000," includes a donor-imposed condition. If only $9,000 is raised, the donor has no obligation to transfer assets.

Donor-imposed restriction. A donor stipulation that specifies a use for contributed resources that is narrower than the limitations that result from the nature of the organization, the environment in which it operates, and the purposes specified in its articles of incorporation, bylaws, or similar documents. A restriction may be temporary or permanent. A temporary restriction is a restriction that will expire (be satisfied) either by an action of the organization (such as spending the resources for the purpose described by the donor) or by the passage of time. A permanent restriction never expires. Instead, it requires that the contrib-uted resources be maintained permanently, although it allows the organization to spend the income or to use the other economic benefits generated by those resources.

Endowment fund. A fund of cash, securities, or other assets held to provide income for the support of a not-for-profit organization. A donor-restricted endowment fund is a fund established by a donor, specifying that the gift must be invested permanently to generate support (a permanent endowment fund) or invested for a specified period of time (a term endowment fund). A quasi endowment fund is a fund established by an organization's governing board to provide income for a long, but usually unspecified, period of time. A quasi endowment fund may be created from unrestricted resources or from resources that are for a restricted purpose but not required by the donor to be invested.

Intermediary. An organization that acts as a facilitator for the transfer of resources between two or more other parties. An intermediary generally does not take possession of the assets transferred.

Natural expense classification. A method of grouping expenses according to the kinds of economic benefits received in incurring those expenses. Examples of natural expense classifications include salaries and wages, employee benefits, supplies, rent, and utilities.

Net assets. The residual interest in the assets of a not-for-profit organization that remains after deducting its liabilities. Net assets are divided into three categories—permanently restricted, temporarily restricted, and unrestricted—based on the nature and existence (or absence) of donor-imposed restrictions. Permanently restricted net assets are the portion of net assets that result from contributions and other inflows of resources that are subject to permanent donor-imposed restrictions. Permanently restricted net assets are not permitted to be expended or used up. Temporarily restricted net assets are the portion of net assets that result from contributions and other inflows of resources that are subject to temporary donor-imposed restrictions. They are permitted to be expended or used up as long as their use is consistent with the limitations imposed by the donor. Unrestricted net assets are the portion of net assets that are neither permanently nor temporarily restricted by donors. The use of unrestricted net assets is subject only to the limitations imposed by the nature of the organization, its articles of incorporation or bylaws, and the environment in which it operates.

Not-for-profit entity. An entity that possesses the following characteristics, in varying degrees, that distinguish it from a business entity:

1. Contributions of significant amounts of resources from resource providers who do not expect commensurate or proportionate pecuniary return
2. Operating purposes other than to provide goods or services at a profit
3. Absence of ownership interests like those of business entities.

Entities that clearly fall outside this definition include the following:

1. All investor-owned entities
2. Entities that provide dividends, lower costs, or other economic benefits directly and proportionately to their owners, members, or participants, such as mutual insurance entities, credit unions, farm and rural electric cooperatives, and employee benefit plans.

Promise to give. A written or oral agreement to contribute resources to another entity at a future date. A promise to give can be either conditional or unconditional. The obligation of the donor who makes a conditional promise to give is dependant on the occurrence (or failure to occur) of a donor-imposed condition. An unconditional promise to give depends only on the passage of time or demand by the donee for payment of the promised assets.

Spending rate. The portion of total return on investments used for fiscal needs of the current period, usually used as a budgetary method of reporting returns of investments. It is usually measured in terms of an amount or a specified percentage of a moving average market value. Typically, the selection of a spending rate emphasizes the use of prudence and a systematic formula to determine the portion of cumulative investment return that can be used to support fiscal needs of the current period and the protection of endowment gifts from a loss of purchasing power as a consideration in determining the formula to be used.

Trustee. An entity that holds and manages assets for the benefit of a specified beneficiary in accordance with a charitable trust agreement.

Voluntary health and welfare organization. An organization formed for the purpose of attempting to prevent or solve health and welfare problems of society, and in many cases, of particular individuals.

CONCEPTS, RULES, AND EXAMPLES

The Reporting Entity

Not-for-profit entities are exempted from the provisions of ASC 850 and ASC 350. Consequently the financial statement preparer must consider the applicability of ASC 958-810 in determining the reporting entity. It provides guidance on reporting investments in majority-owned for-profit subsidiaries, investments in common stock in which the not-for-profit organization owns a 50% or less voting interest, and certain relationships with other not-for-profit entities.

If a not-for-profit organization has a controlling financial interest in a for-profit organization (generally a majority voting interest), it follows the standards in ASC 810. Control of a related, but separate, not-for-profit entity in which the reporting entity has an economic interest may take forms other than a majority ownership interest, sole corporate membership, or majority voting interest in the board of the other entity. For example, control may be through contract or affiliation agreement. In circumstances such as these, consolidation is permitted but not required. Consolidation is, however, encouraged if *both* the following criteria are met:

1. The reporting entity controls a separate not-for-profit entity that it has an economic interest in, and that control is not control through either of the following means:
   a. A controlling financial interest in the other not-for-profit through direct or indirect ownership of a majority voting interest
   b. A majority voting interest in the board of the other not-for-profit
2. Consolidation would be meaningful.

ASC 810 does, however, include an antiabuse provision that provides that the scope exemption does not apply if the not-for-profit organization is being used by a business enterprise in a manner similar to a variable interest entity in order to circumvent ASC 810. Variable interest entities are discussed at length in the chapter on ASC 810.

If a not-for-profit organization has significant influence over the operating and financial policies of the investee (generally owns 20% or more but less than 50% of the voting stock), it either follows the standards in ASC 323 or reports the investment at fair value.

Different combinations of control and economic interest determine the appropriate accounting for relationships with other not-for-profit entities, as shown in the following table. Control is defined for this purpose as the direct or indirect ability to determine the direction of management and policies through ownership, contract, or otherwise. Economic interest is defined as an interest in another entity that exists if (1) the other entity holds or utilizes significant resources that must be used for the purposes of the reporting organization, either directly or indirectly by producing income or providing services or (2) the reporting organization is responsible for the liabilities of the other entity.

Control?	Economic interest?	Standards
Yes, via ownership of a majority voting interest	Yes	Consolidate.
Yes, via ownership of a majority voting interest	No	Consolidate.
Yes, via majority voting interest in the board of the other entity, as a majority owner	Yes	Consolidate.
Yes, via majority voting interest in the board of the other entity, as a majority owner	No	Consolidation is prohibited, and disclosure required.
Yes, via a contract or an affiliation agreement	Yes	Consolidation is permitted, but not required.
Yes, via a contract or an affiliation agreement	No	Consolidation is prohibited, and disclosure required.
No	Yes	Consolidation is prohibited, and disclosure required.
No	No	Consolidation is prohibited. No disclosure required.

Certain disclosures are necessary if consolidated statements are not presented. If consolidated statements are not presented when consolidation is permitted, but not required, the not-for-profit organization must disclose the identity of the other organization, the nature of the relationship, and summarized financial data in addition to the information required by ASC 850. If consolidation is prohibited, the not-for-profit organization must disclose the information required by ASC 850.

Complete Set of Financial Statements

Financial statements are intended to help donors, creditors, and others who provide resources to a not-for-profit organization assess the services provided by the not-for-profit organization and its ability to continue to provide those services. The statements should also help them assess whether management has properly discharged its stewardship responsibilities and whether it has performed satisfactorily in its other management duties.

ASC 958, *Not-for-Profit Entities,* requires all not-for-profit entities to present a statement of financial position, a statement of activities, a statement of cash flows, and notes to the financial statements any time it purports to present a complete set of financial statements. In addition, voluntary health and welfare entities are required to present a statement of functional expenses as an additional basic financial statement. In most ways, the content and format of those financial statements are similar to the financial statements prepared by business enterprises.

However, three major differences between not-for-profit entities and business enterprises cause differences in the content and format of financial statements of not-for-profit entities. First, there is no profit motive in the nonprofit sector, and thus no single indicator of performance comparable to a business enterprise's net income or bottom line. In fact, the best indicators of the performance of a not-for-profit organization are generally not measurable in dollar amounts but rather in the reader's qualitative judgment about the effectiveness of the organization in achieving its mission. Nevertheless, dollars are the language of financial reporting. Information to help assess performance is provided in financial statements (1) by reporting revenues and expenses gross rather than net and (2) by classifying expenses based on the mission-related programs and supporting activities they sustain, rather than by their natural classifications (salaries, utilities, depreciation, etc.).

Second, because the bottom line of a not-for-profit organization's statement of activities is not a performance measure, but simply a change in net assets for the reporting period, there is no need for not-for-profit entities to distinguish between components of comprehensive income as business enterprises do. All revenues, expenses, gains, and losses are reported in a single statement rather than being divided between an income statement and a statement of other comprehensive income.

Third, not-for-profit entities receive contributions, a type of transaction that is without counterpart in business enterprises. Those contributions often are subject to donor-imposed restrictions which can affect the types and levels of service that a not-for-profit organization can offer. Because donor-imposed restrictions are prevalent, recurring, and, in some cases, permanent, financial reporting by not-for-profit entities needs to reflect the nature and extent of donor-imposed restrictions and changes in them that occur during the reporting period.

If the reporting entity is a not-for-profit health care organization, the standard requires it to include within its statement of activities an intermediate subtotal called a performance indicator. ASC 954-815 clarifies that the performance indicator is analogous to income from continuing operations of a business (for-profit) enterprise, and thus would exclude items that are required to be reported in or reclassified from other comprehensive income, extraordinary items, the effect of discontinued operations, the cumulative effect of accounting changes, transactions with owners acting in that capacity, and equity transfers from entities that control the reporting entity, are controlled by the reporting entity, or are under common control with the reporting entity. The performance indicator also excludes restricted contributions, contributions of and reclassifications related to gifts of long-lived assets, unrealized gains and losses on investments not restricted by donors or law (except for investments classified as trading), and investment returns restricted by donors.

Net Assets and Changes in Net Assets

The nature and extent of donor-imposed restrictions are reported in the statement of financial position by distinguishing between the portions of net assets that are permanently restricted, temporarily restricted, and unrestricted. Separate line items on the face of that statement or details in the notes to the financial statements are used to meet the requirement to disclose the amounts for different types of permanent and temporary restrictions.

Changes in donor-imposed restrictions are reported in the statement of activities. The organization's revenues, expenses, gains, and losses for the period are classified into the three classes of net assets so that the statement of activities reports amounts for the change in permanently restricted net assets, the change in temporarily restricted net assets, and the change in unrestricted net assets, as well as the change in net assets in total. Transactions and events that do not change the net assets of the organization as a whole, but only their classification, are reported separately as reclassifications. Reclassifications are events that simultaneously increase one class of net assets and decrease another. For example, unrestricted net assets increase and temporarily restricted net assets decrease when the purchase of a long-lived asset fulfills a donor-imposed restriction to acquire long-lived assets with the gift (sometimes referred to as a release of restrictions).

Not-for-profit entities often use fund accounting as a tool for tracking compliance with donor-imposed restrictions and internal designations. Fund accounting is a system of recording resources whose use is limited either by donors, granting agencies, governing boards, law, or legal covenants. A separate fund (a self-balancing group of accounts composed of assets, liabilities, and net assets) is maintained for each purpose limitation. For external reporting, a fund may be classified entirely in one net asset class or it may need to be allocated among two or three classes. (For an example of the allocations necessary to restate a fund balance to net asset classes, see the discussion of endowment funds in "Investments" in this section.)

Reporting Revenues

Revenues are reported in the statement of activities as increases in unrestricted net assets unless the use of the resources received is subject to a donor-imposed restriction. Thus, contribution revenues increase unrestricted net assets, temporarily restricted net assets, or permanently restricted net assets, depending on the existence and nature of donors' restrictions. Revenues from most exchange transactions (such as sales of goods or services) are classified as unrestricted.

Revenues from exchange transactions only increase restricted net asset classes if a preexisting donor-imposed restriction limits the use of the resources received. For example, if a donor contributes a car to the local library and requires that the proceeds from the sale of the car be used to purchase children's books, the proceeds from the sale of the car (an exchange transaction) increase temporarily restricted net assets. Investment income and gains (which are also exchange transactions) increase unrestricted net assets unless a donor required that the gift be invested and the investment return used for a restricted purpose. For example, assume a donor contributes securities worth $85,000 to a zoo, requires that all dividends and gains be retained and reinvested until the accumulated value is $100,000, and states that the $100,000 must be maintained as a permanent endowment fund, the income of which is to be used for the purchase of animals. In the early years of the endowment, before the accumulated value reaches $100,000, investment income and gains increase permanently restricted net assets. Investment income and gains earned after the accumulated value of the fund reaches $100,000 increase temporarily restricted net assets with the restriction expiring upon use of those funds to purchase animals.

ASC 958-605, *Not-For-Profit Entities—Revenue Recognition*, requires contributions to be recognized as revenue at the time of the gift and measured at the fair value of the contributed assets regardless of the form of the assets contributed. Donor-imposed restrictions do not change the timing of recognition of a contribution. Donor-imposed restrictions, or the absence of them, affect only a contribution's classification as an increase in permanently restricted net assets, temporarily restricted net assets, or unrestricted net assets. Donor-imposed conditions, however, affect the timing of recognition. Because a contribution is an unconditional transfer, a transfer of assets subject to donor-imposed conditions is not a contribution yet, although it may become one at a future date. Conditional transfers are not recognized as contribution revenues until the conditions are substantially met. Thus, the distinction between donor-imposed restrictions and donor-imposed conditions is very important to the timing of recognition. If a donor's stipulations do not clearly state whether a gift depends on meeting a stated stipulation and the ambiguity cannot be resolved by communicating with the donor or by examining the circumstances surrounding the gift, a transfer is presumed to be conditional.

Unconditional promises to give cash or other assets are recognized in financial statements when the promise is made and received, provided that there is sufficient evidence in the form of verifiable documentation (written, audio, or video). If payments of the promises are due in future periods, the promise has an implied time restriction that expires on the date the payment is due. Thus, unless circumstances surrounding the receipt of the promise indicate that the donor intended the gift to support the current period's activities, unconditional promises increase temporarily restricted net assets. A present value technique is used to measure unconditional promises to give, although short-term promises (due in less than one year) may be reported at net realizable value. Conditional promises are not recognized as revenue until the conditions are substantially met; however, they are required to be disclosed in notes to the financial statements.

In a manner similar to recognizing promises to give, a beneficiary recognizes contributions held on its behalf by an agent, trustee, or intermediary. For example, if the assets held by the agent were transferred subject to a condition that is not yet met, the beneficiary does not recognize its potential rights to the assets held by the agent. If a beneficiary has an unconditional right to receive cash flows from a charitable trust or other pool of assets, the beneficiary recognizes its rights when the beneficial interest is created and measures the rights using the present value of the estimated expected cash flows. However, if the beneficiary and the agent, trustee, or intermediary are financially interrelated entities, the beneficiary reports its rights to the assets held using a method similar to the equity method of accounting for investments. (For further discussion, see Transfers Received as an Agent, Trustee, or Intermediary in this section.)

The value of volunteer services received by the organization is recognized in certain circumstances. Contributed services that create or improve a nonfinancial asset (such as building a shed or replacing a roof) are recognized as revenue as contributions either by valuing the hours of service received or by measuring the change in the fair value of the nonfinancial asset created or improved. Other contributed services are recognized only if they meet all three of the following criteria: (1) they require specialized skills, (2) they are provided by persons possessing those skills, and (3) they would typically need to be purchased if not provided by donation. If volunteer services neither meet those three criteria nor create or improve nonfinancial assets, they cannot be recognized in the organization's financial statements. However, entities are required to describe the programs or activities for which contributed services are used, the nature and extent of services received for the period (regardless of whether those services are recognized), and disclose the amount recognized as revenues.

An organization that maintains works of art, historical treasures, and similar assets in collections, as defined, does not recognize gifts of items that are added to its collections unless it also capitalizes its collections. However, gifts that are not added to collections or items given to entities that do not maintain collections in accordance with the definition are recognized as revenues and measured at the fair value of the assets received.

Reporting Expenses

Expenses are recognized in the statement of activities as decreases in unrestricted net assets. Financing an expense with donor-restricted resources does not make the expense restricted; instead, it releases the restriction on the restricted resources, causing a reclassification to be reported in the statement of activities.

Expenses must be reported by functional classifications either on the face of the statement of activities or in the notes to the financial statements. The functional classifications describe the major classes of program services and supporting activities of an organization. Program services are the mission-related activities of the organization that result in goods and services being distributed to clients, customers, or members. They are the activities that are the major purpose of and the major output of the organization. For example, a not-for-profit organization with the mission of enhancing the lives of the community's senior citizens might have senior center, home visits, transportation services, and home maintenance as its program expense classifications. Supporting activities are all activities of a not-for-profit organization other than program services. Fund raising expenses and management and general are two common supporting activity classifications.

ASC 958-205 encourages, but does not require, most not-for-profit entities to provide an analysis of expenses by natural classification. Information about expenses by natural expense classifications (salaries, benefits, rent, depreciation, and so forth) can help readers of the financial statements understand the mix of fixed and discretionary costs incurred by the organization. Only voluntary health and welfare entities are required to report information about expenses by both functional and natural classification. Those entities must provide that information in a matrix format in a statement of functional expenses. (ASC 958-205-45-6)

ASC 958-360, *Not-for-Profit Entities—Property, Plant, and Equipment,* requires the depreciation of land, buildings, and equipment used by not-for-profit entities. An exception to that requirement is provided for certain works of art, historical treasures, and similar assets. If a not-for-profit organization can demonstrate both (1) that an asset individually has cultural, historical, or aesthetic value worth maintaining in perpetuity and (2) that the organization has the ability to protect and preserve that value essentially undiminished and is doing so, depreciation need not be recognized. Depreciation expense is a natural expense classification that must be allocated to programs and supporting activities in reporting expenses by functional classification.

Many not-for-profit entities solicit contributions as part of conducting activities that also serve their program or management and general functions. For example, an organization that has a mission of reducing the incidence of cancer might conduct a direct mail campaign and include in an envelope a listing of lifestyle changes that will lessen the risks of cancer and a request for contributions. When a fund-raising activity is conducted in conjunction with an activity that serves a program or other support purpose, the activity is referred to as a joint activity. Users of the financial statements of not-for-profit entities are particularly interested in the extent to which the organization is able to minimize its fund-raising and management and general costs. Because neither of these types of costs directly benefit the beneficiaries of the organization's programs, successful entities attempt to minimize them as a percent of the organization's support and revenue. Since the effectiveness of the management of a not-for-profit organization is often judged on operating metrics of this nature, there is a natural incentive for management to maximize the portion of the costs of these joint activities that is characterized as program expenses.

ASC 958-720 established standards for reporting the costs of joint activities. It begins with the presumption that the costs of a joint activity are reportable as fund-raising expenses. To overcome that presumption, three criteria must be met: purpose, audience, and content. If all three of the criteria are met, the costs of a joint activity are to be charged as follows:

- Costs identifiable with a particular function are charged to that function.
- Joint costs are allocated between fund-raising and the appropriate program or management and general function.

Joint costs are the costs of conducting joint activities that are not directly identifiable with a particular component of the activity. Joint costs might include the costs of salaries, professional fees, paper, printing, postage, event advertising, telephones, broadcast airtime, and facility rentals.

Determining whether all three criteria are met is complicated because the purpose and audience criteria have additional tests within them. The purpose test includes a call to action test, a compensation or fees test, a similar scale and same medium test, and another evidence test. The audience criterion includes a prior donor test, an ability and likelihood to contribute test, and a need to use or reasonable potential for use test. Failure of one of the additional tests often causes the activity to fail the criterion.

If any of the three criteria is not met, all costs of the joint activity must be reported as fund-raising expense. "All costs" includes the costs that would have been considered program or management and general if they had been incurred in a different activity. There is an exception to the rule that all costs are charged to fund-raising expense if one or more of the criteria is not met. The costs of goods or services provided in an exchange transaction (sometimes referred to as a quid pro quo contribution) that is part of the joint activity are charged to cost of goods sold rather than fund-raising expense. For example, the costs of direct donor benefits, such as the value of items sold at a fund-raising auction or meals served at a fund-raising dinner, are not charged to fund-raising expenses.

ASC 958-720 requires that the method used to allocate the joint costs be rational and systematic and that it result in a reasonable allocation of costs. The method selected is to be applied consistently given similar facts and circumstances. No particular method of allocation is required by the standard, but three allocation methods are illustrated: the physical units method, the relative direct cost method, and the stand-alone joint-cost-allocation method.

Entities that allocate joint costs are required to disclose the types of activities in which joint costs have been incurred, a statement that the costs have been allocated, and the total amount of joint costs allocated, and the portion of joint costs allocated to each functional expense category. The standard also encourages disclosure of the amount of joint costs for each type of joint activity.

Transfers Received as an Agent, Trustee, or Intermediary

ASC 958-20 and ASC 958-605 establish standards for transactions in which a donor makes a contribution by using an agent, trustee, or intermediary. (Agents, trustees, and intermediaries are referred to as recipient entities.) The donor transfers assets to the recipient organization. The recipient organization accepts the assets from the donor and agrees to use the assets on behalf of or transfer the assets, their investment return, or both to another entity—the beneficiary—named by the donor. It also establishes standards for transactions that take place in a similar manner but are not contributions because the transactions are revocable, repayable, or reciprocal. It does not set standards for recipient entities that are trustees.

In general, a recipient organization reports a liability if it accepts assets from a donor and agrees to use those assets on behalf of or transfer those assets to another organization or individual specified by the donor. When it subsequently spends the assets on behalf of the beneficiary or transfers the assets, their return, or both to the beneficiary, the nonprofit organization reduces the liability it recorded earlier. If the assets received from the donor are donated materials, supplies, or other nonfinancial assets, the recipient organization may choose either to (1) report the receipt of the assets as liability to the beneficiary concurrent with recognition of the assets received or (2) not to report the transaction at all. The choice is an accounting policy that must be applied consistently from period to period and disclosed in the notes to the financial statements.

If the donor explicitly grants the recipient organization variance power, the recipient organization, rather than the beneficiary, recognizes contribution revenue. Variance power is the unilateral power to direct the transferred assets to an entity other than the specified beneficiary. Unilateral power means that the recipient organization does not have to contact the donor, the beneficiary, or any other interested party in order to substitute a different beneficiary. Variance power must be granted by the instrument transferring the assets.

If the recipient organization and the specified beneficiary are financially interrelated entities, the recipient organization reports contribution revenue and the specified beneficiary recognizes its interest in the net assets of the recipient organization using a method similar to the equity method of accounting for investments in common stock. Entities are financially interrelated if the relationship between them has both of the following characteristics: (1) one organization has the ability to influence the operating and financial decisions of the other and (2) one organization has an ongoing economic interest in the net assets of the other. The ability to influence the operating and financial decisions of the other can be demonstrated in several ways: (1) the entities are affiliates as defined in ASC 850, *Related-Party Disclosures*, (2) one organization has considerable representation on the governing board of the other, (3) the charter or bylaws of one organization limit its activities to those that are beneficial to the other, or (4) an agreement between the entities allows one organization to actively participate in the policymaking processes of the other. An ongoing economic interest in the net assets of another is a residual right to the other organization's net assets that results from an ongoing relationship. A common example of financially interrelated entities is a foundation that exists to raise, hold, and invest assets for a specific beneficiary that it supports.

In addition to establishing standards for contributions transferred to beneficiaries via agents, trustees, and intermediaries, ASC 958-20 sets standards for transfers that take place in a similar manner but are not contributions because the terms of the transfer or the relationships between the parties make the transfer revocable, repayable, or reciprocal. Transfers are recognized by the recipient organization as liabilities if one or more of the following situations are present: (1) the transfer is subject to the transferor's right to redirect the transferred assets to another beneficiary, (2) the transfer is accompanied by the transferor's conditional promise to give, (3) the transferor controls the recipient organization and specifies an unaffiliated beneficiary, or (4) the transferor specifies itself or its affiliate as the beneficiary of a transfer that is not an equity transaction. An equity transaction is a transfer that has all of the following terms: (1) the transferor specifies itself or its affiliate as beneficiary, (2) the transferor and the recipient organization are financially interrelated entities, and (3) neither the transferor nor its affiliate expects payment of the transferred assets (although payment of investment return is allowable). Equity transactions are reported by the recipient organization as a separate line item in the statement of activities.

Investments and Endowment Funds

ASC 958-320 requires investments in equity securities with readily determinable fair values and all debt securities to be reported at fair value. Although the standard applies to the same securities that ASC 320 covers for business enterprises, accounting for the resulting gains and losses is different than specified by that standard. Gains and losses (both realized and unrealized) are reported in a not-for-profit organization's statement of activities.

ASC 958 establishes standards for reporting other investments. The appropriate standards to apply depend on whether the not-for-profit organization is a college or university, a voluntary health and welfare organization, a health care organization, or another type of not-for-profit organization. Most entities have the option of reporting their other investments at either cost or at the lower of cost or market.

Not-for-profit health care entities are required to apply the provisions of ASC 815 in the same manner as business enterprises, including the provisions pertaining to cash flow hedge accounting. The gain or loss items that affect a business enterprise's income from continuing operations similarly affect the not-for-profit health care organization's performance indicator, and the gain or loss items that are excluded from a business enterprise's income from continuing operations (such as items reported in other comprehensive income) are to be excluded from the performance indicator.

Many of the investments held by not-for-profit entities are held as the investments of endowment funds. Endowment funds generally are established by gifts from donors who desire to provide support for the organization permanently (a permanently restricted endowment fund) or for a specified period of time (a term endowment fund). In addition, a governing board may determine that certain resources be invested and that only the return generated be spent by the organization. These board-designated amounts are referred to as quasiendowment funds or funds functioning as endowment. The net assets of an endowment fund are classified in accordance with the restrictions placed on the resources by donors, if any. Because a donor can place different restrictions on each source of the net assets (original gift, investment gains and losses, and investment income), each source must be examined separately to achieve the proper classification.

Each source is unrestricted unless its use is temporarily or permanently restricted by the donor or by a law that extends the donor's restriction to the source. Thus, the net assets of an endowment fund created by the governing board from a large unrestricted bequest (or from unrestricted net assets) are classified as unrestricted because no donor was involved in the transaction of creating the endowment fund and all amounts transferred to that fund are free of donor-imposed restrictions.

In contrast, assume that a donor contributes $50,000 to a museum and stipulates that the gift be invested in perpetuity and the investment income be used to purchase works of art. The donor further stipulates that any gains on the investment be added to the original gift and invested in perpetuity. The donor's original gift ($50,000) increases permanently restricted net assets because of the stipulation that the gift be invested in perpetuity. The income earned by the investment of the gift increases temporarily restricted net assets. When works of art are purchased, the restriction on net assets resulting from the income is fulfilled and the net assets are reclassified to unrestricted net assets. The realized and unrealized gains from investment of the gift increase permanently restricted net assets because the donor required that those gains also be reinvested in perpetuity.

In most cases, the classification of the original gift and the investment income is straightforward because donors explicitly state the time and purpose restrictions on them. Classification of gains and losses on the investments is not as clearly determinable unless the donor explicitly states how gains are to be used and whether losses must be restored immediately from other sources, from future gains on the investments, or not at all. However, donors are often silent in their agreements about those matters.

In the absence of explicit donor restrictions, the law in most states provides some direction about the restrictions on investment gains of donor-restricted endowment funds. The Uniform Management of Institutional Funds Act (UMIFA) extends certain donor restrictions to the net appreciation (accumulated net gains) of donor-restricted endowment funds. In states that have adopted UMIFA, net appreciation is expendable unless the donor states otherwise. UMIFA provides that the net appreciation can be spent for the uses and purposes for which the endowment fund was established. Thus, unless the donor specifies otherwise, gains increase unrestricted net assets if the endowment's income is not restricted by the donor, and gains increase temporarily restricted net assets if the endowment's income is temporarily restricted by the donor. Assume in the earlier example of the $50,000 gift to the museum that the donor was silent about the use of gains earned by investing the original gift. In a state that has adopted UMIFA, the accumulated gains on the endowment fund would be restricted to the purchase of artwork because the law requires that the donor's restriction be extended to those gains. The restrictions on those temporarily restricted net assets expire when the museum purchases works of art even if the money to purchase the work of art is not withdrawn from the fund. Thus, this single endowment fund can be composed of permanently restricted net assets (the original $50,000 gift), temporarily restricted net assets (the gains on which restrictions have not yet been met), and unrestricted net assets (the gains on which restrictions have been met).

ASC 958-205 has expanded certain disclosure requirements applicable to endowment funds. It stipulates that not-for-profit entities that are subject to an enacted version of the Uniform Prudent Management of Institutional Funds Act of 2006 (UPMIFA, a modernized version of the Uniform Management of Institutional Funds Act of 1972 [UMIFA], the model act on which 46 states and the District of Columbia had based their primary laws governing the investment and management of donor-restricted endowment funds by not-for-profit entities) are required to classify a portion of a donor-restricted endowment fund that are of a perpetual duration as being a permanently restricted net assets. The amount that is to be classified as permanently restricted should be the amount of the fund (1) that is required to be permanently retained due to an explicit stipulation by the donor, or (2) that in the absence of such donor stipulations, the organization's governing board determines must be permanently restricted to comply with applicable laws.

Losses incurred on the investments of the funds should not reduce the portion of the donor-restricted endowment fund that is to be classified as permanently restricted net assets, unless this is a requirement of the donor. Furthermore, the amount of permanently restricted net assets is not to be reduced by an organization's appropriations from the fund.

A not-for-profit organization should classify the portion of the funds that are not classified as permanently restricted net assets as temporarily restricted net assets until they are appropriated for expenditure by the organization, unless the gift instrument states otherwise. This is in accordance with the stipulation in subsection 4(a) of UPMIFA that requires, "unless stated otherwise in the gift instrument, the assets in an endowment fund are donor-restricted assets until appropriated for expenditure by the institution."

According to ASC 958-205, a not-for-profit organization, whether or not subject to UPMIFA, is to disclose information that will enable users of its financial statements to understand the net asset classification, net asset composition, changes in net asset composition, spending policies, and related investment policies of its endowment funds. Therefore, at a minimum, the following disclosures should be made:

1. A description of the governing board's interpretation of the law that supports the organization's net asset classification of donor-restricted endowment funds.
2. A description of the organization's endowment spending policies.
3. A description of the organization's endowment investment policies.
4. The make-up of the organization's endowment by net asset class at the end of the period. These amounts should be presented in total, as well as by endowment fund and should separately show donor-restricted endowment funds from board-designated endowment funds.
5. A reconciliation of the beginning and ending balance of the organization's endowment, in total and by net asset class.

6. Information about the net assets of its endowment funds such as
   a. The nature and types of any permanent restrictions or temporary restrictions.
   b. The aggregate amount of the deficiencies for all donor-restricted endowment funds where the fair value of the assets at the reporting date is less than the level required in the donor stipulations or law.

ASC 958-320 requires that losses on the investments of an endowment fund reduce temporarily restricted net assets to the extent that temporary restrictions on net appreciation have not yet been met before the loss occurs. The remainder of the loss, if any, reduces unrestricted net assets. If the losses reduce the value of the fund below the level required by the donor or by law, future gains that restore the value to the required level are classified as unrestricted net assets.

Expanding on the earlier example, assume that several years after the fund was established, the assets of the fund have increased in value to $65,000. Assume also that the classification of the net assets in the fund is: $50,000 permanently restricted (the original gift), $10,000 temporarily restricted (accumulated gains on which the restrictions have not been met), and $5,000 unrestricted (gains on which the restriction was met by purchasing a work of art with unrestricted funds in years after the inception of the fund). A market correction causes the value of the investments to fall to $58,000. The $7,000 loss decreases temporarily restricted net assets from $10,000 to $3,000. Assume that a further market correction reduces the value of the investments another $9,000 from $58,000 to $49,000. The $9,000 loss reduces temporarily restricted net assets by $3,000 (the amount remaining after the $7,000 loss decreased the original $10,000) and reduces unrestricted net assets by $6,000. After recording the loss, the classification of the $49,000 value of the endowment fund would be: $50,000 permanently restricted (the original gift) and ($1,000) deficit in unrestricted net assets. A not-for-profit organization is required to disclose the amount by which the value of the endowment fund is less than the level required by the donor.

Continuing the example, assume that the next year the value of the investments increases from $49,000 to $53,000. The $4,000 gain increases unrestricted net assets by $1,000 (the restoration of the deficit) and increases temporarily restricted net assets by $3,000. After the gain, the net assets of the endowment fund are $50,000 permanently restricted (the original gift) and $3,000 temporarily restricted for the purchase of works of art.

Collections

Not-for-profit entities are allowed an exception to the normal requirement to capitalize purchases of property, plant, and equipment. If a not-for-profit organization maintains collections of works of art, historical treasures, or similar assets in the manner defined in the Master Glossary, it can choose whether it will capitalize and report those collections in its statement of financial position. To qualify for the exception, an organization must (1) hold the items for public exhibition, education, or research in service to the public rather than for financial gain, (2) protect the items, keep them unencumbered, care for them, and preserve them, and (3) use the proceeds from the sale of any items to acquire other items for the collection. If an organization meets those criteria, it can choose one of the following policies: (1) capitalize its collections, (2) capitalize only collection items acquired after the adoption of ASC 958-605, or (3) not capitalize any collections. An organization cannot selectively choose to capitalize only certain collections.

If an organization does not capitalize its collections, transactions involving collection items must be reported separately on the face of its statement of activities. Similarly, if an organization chose to capitalize its collections prospectively when it adopted ASC 958-605, it would separately report transactions involving collection items not previously capitalized. Descriptions of the collections, including information about stewardship policies and items *deaccessed* (removed from the collection), must be included in notes to the financial statements by entities that do not capitalize their collections or that capitalize them prospectively.

Capitalization is required of works of art, historical treasures, and similar assets that are not collection items, even if those items are held by entities that regularly maintain collections. Thus, if a museum does not capitalize its collections and it is given a work of art that it does not to add to its collection (perhaps because it duplicates other collection items), the museum would recognize that contribution and report the asset in its statement of financial position as a work of art held for sale.

Split-Interest Agreements

A split-interest agreement is an arrangement in which a donor transfers assets to a not-for-profit organization or to a charitable trust and requires the benefits of ownership of those assets be split among two or more beneficiaries. Charitable gift annuities, annuity trusts, charitable remainder unitrusts, charitable lead trusts, and pooled (or life) income funds are examples of split-interest agreements. ASC 958 provides guidance for reporting the initial gifts that create these funds and the annual adjustments necessary to report them properly. Accounting for split-interest gifts is a complex area; the following discussion is highly summarized and overly simplified.

Not-for-profit entities are required to report their interests in irrevocable split-interest agreements. If another party, such as a bank, holds the assets, a not-for-profit organization recognizes its interest as an asset and contribution revenue and measures its interest at fair value, usually based on the present value of the cash flows to be received. If the not-for-profit organization holds the assets and is also a beneficiary of the agreement, it reports the fair value of the assets received from the donor as its assets and reports the actuarially computed present value of the payments to be made to other beneficiaries as its liability. The difference between the two amounts is the contribution received by the not-for-profit organization. Each year there-after, the liability to the beneficiaries is recomputed based on revaluations of the amounts to be paid, the expected lives of the beneficiaries, and other relevant actuarial assumptions.

The net assets resulting from most split-interest agreements are classified as temporarily restricted because they are subject to time restrictions and purpose restrictions. The net assets are time-restricted either because the distributions are not yet due (when amounts are held by a third party) or because the contribution amount cannot be used by the not-for-profit organization until the death of the beneficiary or some other future specified date. However, the net assets are classified as permanently restricted if the donor has permanently restricted the organization's use of the assets. (For example, the donor requires that the not-for-profit organization use the remaining assets to create a permanent endowment fund at the end of the agreement.) Similarly, if upon the establishment of the agreement the organization can immediately spend the contribution portion without restriction, as is the case for some gift annuities, the net assets would be classified as unrestricted. (ASC 958-30-45-2)

Revocable split-interest agreements are not recorded unless the not-for-profit organization holds the assets. Assets received by a not-for-profit organization that acts as trustee under a revocable agreement are recognized as refundable advances at their fair value.

Mergers and Acquisitions

ASC 958-805 establishes standards for determining whether a combination of not-for-profit entities is a merger or an acquisition, describes the carryover method of accounting (for a merger) and the acquisition method of accounting (for an acquisition), and notes related disclosures.

In many not-for-profit mergers and acquisitions, there is no transfer of consideration, so there is no fair value exchange to record. Because of this issue, different accounting methods are applied to a merger of not-for-profit entities and an acquisition by a not-for-profit entity.

In a merger, where two or more not-for-profit entities cede control to a new entity, the *carryover method* is used (ASC 958-05-25-3). Under this method, the initial financial statements of the combined entities carry forward the assets and liabilities of the combining entities, measured at their carrying amounts, less the effects of any intra-entity transactions. There is no recognition of changes in fair value. The financial history of the new entity created by the merger begins on the merger date—it does not report the prior financial results of the preceding merged entities. Key merger disclosures include the reasons for the merger, the amounts of any significant adjustments made to conform the individual accounting policies of the merged entities, and the amounts of any intra-entity balance eliminations.

An acquisition by a not-for-profit entity is accounted for using the *acquisition method*, which was described in detail earlier in this chapter. If this method is used, there are a few exceptions to the recognition principle in ASC 805. The acquirer cannot recognize an acquired donor relationship as an intangible asset. So, too, if the not-for-profit acquirer has a policy of not capitalizing collections (works of art, historical treasures, or similar assets), then the acquirer does not recognize those items as assets at acquisitions added to the collection. Instead, the acquirer recognizes the cost of the collection items purchased as a decrease in the appropriate class of net assets in the statement of activities and as a cash outflow for investing activities and does not recognize the fair value of collection items contributed. For conditional promises to give, the not-for-profit acquirer recognizes either:

- The conditional promise only if the conditions on which it depends are substantially met as of the acquisition date, or
- A transfer of assets with a conditional promise to contribute them as a refundable advance unless the conditions have been substantially met as of the acquisition date.

Key acquisition disclosures include the reasons for the acquisition, the factors that make up either goodwill recognized or the equivalent amount charged to expense, and the fair value of consideration transferred.

If an acquirer expects the operations of the acquiree to be supported primarily by contributions and returns on investments, then it should recognize as an expense on the acquisition date the amount that would otherwise be recognized as a goodwill asset. This situation arises when an acquiree's contributions and returns on investments are expected to significantly exceed all other sources of revenue.

In an acquisition, there is an *inherent contribution received*, because the acquirer receives net assets from the acquiree without any corresponding transfer of consideration.

PLAN ACCOUNTING (ASC 960, ASC 962, ASC 965)

PERSPECTIVE AND ISSUES

Employee benefit plans have become increasingly important and diverse. Using assets that are segregated from the plan sponsor, they provide benefits to employees and former employees in accordance with a plan agreement. The provisions of the plan agreement deal with such matters as eligibility, entitlement to benefits, funding, plan amendments, operation and administration, allocation of responsibilities among the fiduciaries, and fiduciaries' ability to delegate duties. A few examples of employee benefit plans are pension plans, profit-sharing plans, stock bonus plans, 401(k) plans, 403(b) plans, disability plans, health care plans, life insurance plans, unemployment benefit plans, tuition assistance plans, dependent care plans, and cafeteria/flexible benefit plans. For accounting and reporting purposes, the plans are divided into three major types: defined benefit pension plans, defined contribution pension plans, and health and welfare benefit plans.

Employee benefit plans that are sponsored by and provide benefits to the employees of state and local governmental entities are outside of the scope of this publication. Readers instead should refer to *Wiley GAAP for Governments 2012*.

All authoritative pronouncements apply to employee benefit plans unless the pronouncement specifically excludes them from its scope. Certain authoritative pronouncements apply specifically to employee benefit plans. Because those pronouncements are particularly relevant to the transactions of employee benefit plans, they are discussed in this chapter.

ASC 960, *Plan Accounting—Defined Benefit Pension Plans*, is the principal standard involving the accounting and reporting of employee benefit plans. ASC 960 applies only to ongoing plans, not to plans that are terminated or expected to be terminated. The codification describes the objectives of plan financial statements and the necessary components of a complete set of plan financial statements.

ASC 230-10-15 exempts defined benefit pension plans and certain other employee benefit plans from ASC 230's requirement to present a statement of cash flows.

ASC 960-325-35 requires defined benefit pension plans to report all investment contracts, including guaranteed investment contracts issued by insurance companies, at fair value. Only contracts that incorporate mortality or morbidity risk (insurance contracts) may be reported at contract value.

ASC 960, ASC 962, and ASC 965 set standards for defined benefit pension plans, defined contribution pension plans, and health and welfare benefit plans, respectively. In addition to providing accounting and reporting guidance for the plans, they provide summaries of statutory rules and regulations applicable to employee benefit plans and illustrative financial statements.

ASC 965, *Plan Accounting—Health and Welfare Benefit Plans,* provides the standards for health and welfare benefit plans. It divides the diverse universe of plans into two major types: defined benefit health and welfare plans and defined contribution health and welfare plans. It requires defined benefit health and welfare plans to use certain provisions of ASC 715, to measure benefit obligations. In addition, it applies many of the measurement and disclosure provisions of ASC 960 to health and welfare plans.

ASC 965-205-05 specifies the accounting for and disclosure of 401(h) features of defined benefit pension plans that offer medical benefits to retirees in addition to the normal retirement benefits.

This section presents a highly summarized discussion of accounting and reporting standards by employee benefit plans. This chapter does not describe an employer's requirements for reporting information about employee benefit plans. That information is described in the chapters on ASC 710-718.

DEFINITIONS OF TERMS

Source: ASC 960 Glossary

Accumulated plan benefits. Future benefit payments that are attributable under the provisions of a pension plan to employees' service rendered to the benefit information date. Accumulated plan benefits comprise benefits expected to be paid to any of the following:

1. Retired or terminated employees or their beneficiaries
2. Beneficiaries of deceased employees
3. Present employees or their beneficiaries.

Benefits. The monetary or in-kind benefits or benefit coverage to which participants may be entitled under a pension plan or other postretirement benefit plan, including health care benefits, life insurance, legal, educational, and advisory services, pension benefits, disability benefits, death benefits, and benefits due to termination of employment.

Defined benefit plan. A defined benefit plan provides participants with a determinable benefit based on a formula provided for in the plan.

1. Defined benefit health and welfare plans—Defined benefit health and welfare plans specify a determinable benefit, which may be in the form of a reimbursement to the covered plan participant or a direct payment to providers or third-party insurers for the cost of specified services. Such plans may also include benefits that are payable as a lump sum, such as death benefits. The level of benefits may be defined or limited based on factors such as age, years of service, and salary. Contributions may be determined by the plan's actuary or be based on premiums, actual claims paid, hours worked, or other factors determined by the plan sponsor. Even when a plan is funded pursuant to agreements that specify a fixed rate of employer contributions (for example, a collectively bargained multiemployer plan), such a plan may nevertheless be a defined benefit health and welfare plan if its substance is to provide a defined benefit.
2. Defined benefit pension plan—A pension plan that defines an amount of pension benefit to be provided, usually as a function of one or more factors such as age, years of service, or compensation. Any pension plan that is not a defined contribution pension plan is, for purposes of Subtopic 715-30, a defined benefit pension plan.
3. Defined benefit postretirement plan—A plan that defines postretirement benefits in terms of monetary amounts (for example, $100,000 of life insurance) or benefit coverage to be provided (for example, up to $200 per day for hospitalization, or 80 percent of the cost of specified surgical procedures). Any postretirement benefit plan that is not a defined contribution postretirement plan is, for purposes of Subtopic 715-60, a defined benefit postretirement plan. (Specified monetary amounts and benefit coverage are collectively referred to as benefits.)

Defined contribution plan. A plan that provides an individual account for each participant and provides benefits that are based on all of the following: amounts contributed to the participant's account by the employer or employee; investment experience; and any forfeitures allocated to the account, less any administrative expenses charged to the plan.

1. Defined contribution health and welfare plans—Defined contribution health and welfare plans maintain an individual account for each plan participant. They have terms that specify the means of determining the contributions to participants' accounts, rather than the amount of benefits the participants are to receive. The benefits a plan participant will receive are limited to the amount contributed to the participant's account, investment experience, expenses, and any forfeitures allocated to the participant's account. These plans also include flexible spending arrangements.
2. Defined contribution postretirement plan—A plan that provides postretirement benefits in return for services rendered, provides an individual account for each plan participant, and specifies how contributions to the individual's account are to be determined rather than specifying the amount of benefits the individual is to receive.

> Under a defined contribution postretirement plan, the benefits a plan participant will receive depend solely on the amount contributed to the plan participant's account, the returns earned on investments of those contributions, and the forfeitures of other plan participants' benefits that may be allocated to that plan participant's account.

Health and welfare benefit plan. Plans that provide benefits such as medical, dental, visual, or other health care, insurance, disability, vacation, education, or dependent care.

Liquidation. The process by which an entity converts its assets to cash or other assets and settles its obligations with creditors in anticipation of the entity ceasing all activities. Upon cessation of the entity's activities, any remaining cash or other assets are distributed to the entity's investors or other claimants (albeit sometimes indirectly). Liquidation may be compulsory or voluntary. Dissolution of an entity as a result of that entity being acquired by another entity or merged into another entity in its entirety and with the expectation of continuing its business does not qualify as liquidation.

Net assets. The residual interest in the assets of an employee benefit plan that remains after deducting its liabilities. The liabilities of a plan do not include its accumulated plan benefits (defined benefit pension plans) or its benefit obligation (defined benefit health and welfare plans).

Noncontributary plan. A pension or other postretirement benefit plan under which participants do not make contributions.

Participant. Any employee or former employee, or any member or former member of a trade or other employee association, or the beneficiaries of those individuals, for whom there are pension plan benefits or other accumulated plan benefits.

Pension benefits. Periodic (usually monthly) payments made pursuant to the terms of the pension plan to a person who has retired from employment or to that person's beneficiary.

Plan assets. Assets—usually stocks, bonds, and other investments—that have been segregated and restricted, usually in a trust, to provide for pension benefits. The amount of plan assets includes amounts contributed by the employer, and by employees for a contributory plan, and amounts earned from investing the contributions, less benefits paid. Plan assets ordinarily cannot be withdrawn by the employer except under certain circumstances when a plan has assets in excess of obligations and the employer has taken certain steps to satisfy existing obligations. Assets not segregated in a trust or otherwise effectively restricted so that they cannot be used by the employer for other purposes are not plan assets even though it may be intended that such assets be used to provide pensions. If a plan has liabilities other than for benefits, those nonbenefit obligations may be considered as reductions of plan assets. Amounts accrued by the employer but not yet paid to the plan are not plan assets. Securities of the employer held by the plan are includable in plan assets provided they are transferable.

Service. Employment taken into consideration under a pension plan. Years of employment before the inception of a plan constitute an employee's past service; years thereafter are classified in relation to the particular actuarial valuation being made or discussed. Years of employment (including past service) before the date of a particular valuation constitute prior service; years of employment following the date of the valuation constitute future service; a year of employment adjacent to the date of valuation, or in which such date falls, constitutes current service.

Sponsor. In the case of a pension plan established or maintained by a single employer, the employer; in the case of a plan established or maintained by an employee entity, the employee entity; in the case of a plan established or maintained jointly by two or more employers or by one or more employers and one or more employee entities, the association, committee, joint board of trustees, or other group of representatives of the parties that have established or that maintain the pension plan.

CONCEPTS, RULES, AND EXAMPLES

In addition to varying by basic type (defined benefit plan, defined contribution plan, and health and welfare benefit plan), employee benefit plans vary by operating and administrative characteristics. Plans established by one employer or a group of controlled corporations are referred to as single employer plans. Alternatively, they can include the employees of many employers who are related in some way, often by all being parties to a collective-bargaining agreement. Those plans are referred to as multiemployer plans. A plan can be either contributory or noncontributory. A contributory plan requires both the employer and the participants to fund (contribute to) the cost of the future benefits. In a noncontributory plan, the participants do not fund any part of the cost of the future benefits. Insured plans are funded through insurance contracts. Self-funded plans are funded through contributions and investment return. Split-funded plans are funded by a combination of insurance contracts, contributions, and investment return.

Complete Set of Financial Statements

The primary objective of a plan's financial statements is to provide the information necessary to assess the plan's ability to pay benefits when due. Thus, financial statements are to include information about the plan's resources, the results of transactions and events that changed the plan's resources, the stewardship of management over the plan's resources, and any other facts necessary to understand the information provided.

A complete set of financial statements includes a statement of net assets available for benefits as of the end of the plan year (statement of financial position equivalent), a statement of changes in net assets available for benefits for the plan year ended (income statement equivalent), and notes to the financial statements. In addition, defined benefit plans must include information about the actuarial present value of accumulated benefits and changes in the accumulated benefits. That information can appear either as additional financial statements or in the notes to financial statements.

ASC 230-10-15 exempts defined benefit pension plans from the requirement that a statement of cash flows be provided. Other employee benefit plans are also exempted if they report similar to defined benefit pension plans, including ASC 960's requirement to report plan investments at fair value. Although not required, presentation of a statement of cash flows is encouraged if it would provide useful information about the plan's ability to pay future liabilities, as would be the case if the plan either holds illiquid investments or purchases investments using borrowed funds.

ASC 220-10-15 requires that changes in equity other than transactions with owners be reported in financial statements in the period in which they are recognized. The statement of changes in net assets available for benefits is a comprehensive income statement because all changes in net assets available for benefits are reflected in that statement. Thus, although it did not specifically exempt employee benefit plans from its provisions, the codification did not change the reporting for employee benefit plans.

Statement of Net Assets Available for Benefits

Most investments of the plan are reported at fair value. If there is an active market, quoted market prices are used. If market quotations are not available, investments are valued "in good faith" by the plan's trustees and administrator. The selling price of similar investments or discounted cash flows can be useful in estimating fair value. The use of an independent expert may be necessary for the valuation of certain investments. Investment contracts with an insurance company, bank, or other financial institution are reported at fair value. Only insurance contracts—contracts that incorporate mortality or morbidity risk (defined benefit pension plans) or that are fully benefit-responsive (defined contribution plans and health and welfare plans)—may be reported at contract value, and then only if the plan reports at contract value in its annual report filed with government agencies. The financial statements are to identify plan investments by type of investment and indicate how fair value was determined. It is not necessary to disclose the original cost of investments in the basic financial statements. Plans are to disclose in the notes to the financial statements any investments representing 5% or more of the net assets available for benefits as of the end of the year.

Contributions receivable include those due as of the reporting date from participants, employers, withdrawing employers of a multiemployer plan, and other sources (such as a state or federal government in the case of a grant or subsidy). Receivables arise from formal commitments of an employer, legal requirements, or contractual requirements. The receivables are to be reduced by an allowance for uncollectible amounts if warranted.

Long-lived assets (such as buildings, equipment, furniture and fixtures, and leasehold improvements) that are used in the plan's operations are presented at cost less accumulated depreciation or amortization.

Statement of Changes in Net Assets Available for Benefits

The statement of changes in net assets available for benefits is a comprehensive income statement that includes all recognized transactions and events that change the net assets available for benefits. At a minimum, the statement is to include separate amounts for

1. Contributions from
    a. Employer(s)—separating cash from noncash contributions
    b. Participants, including those transmitted by the plan sponsor
    c. Other identified sources
2. Net appreciation or depreciation (realized and unrealized amounts may be combined) in fair value for each significant class of investment, presented by
    a. Investments measured by quoted market prices
    b. Investments measured by some other means
3. Investment income (not including appreciation or depreciation in fair value)
4. Payments to plan participants for benefits, excluding amounts paid by insurance contracts that are not included in plan assets
5. Payments to insurance companies to purchase contracts that are excluded from plan assets
6. Administrative expenses
7. Other changes, if necessary, with appropriate description(s).

Transactions with Related Parties (ASC 850)

Transactions between a plan sponsor and its employee benefit plans are subject to the disclosure requirements of ASC 850, *Related-Party Disclosures.*

Risks and Uncertainties

Employee benefit plans must disclose the information required by ASC 275, *Risks and Uncertainties.* Risks that are unique to employee benefit plans include

1. A significant industry downturn that could cause employees to retire early in order to avoid being laid off, especially if the plan's participants are concentrated within a particular industry or with a single employer
2. Likelihood that an employer will significantly increase pension or health and welfare benefits in order to avoid a union walkout
3. A planned downsizing that is expected to offer early retirement to employees
4. Investments in the stock of the employer.

Defined Benefit Plans

In addition to the statement of net assets available for benefits and the statement of changes in net assets available for benefits, defined benefit pension plans must provide information about the actuarial present value of accumulated plan benefits and changes in the actuarial present value of accumulated plan benefits. The information can be included as separate financial statements or as schedules in the notes to the financial statements.

Accumulated plan benefits include the present value of future benefits to retired or terminated employees or their beneficiaries, to beneficiaries of deceased employees, and to present employees or their beneficiaries. Whenever possible, plan provisions are to govern the measurement of accumulated plan benefits. If the benefits earned in each year are not determinable from the plan's provisions, a formula for measurement is provided in ASC 960. When calculating accumulated plan benefits, an ongoing plan is to be assumed, analogous to the going concern assumption used in preparing GAAP financial statements of other types of entities. Thus, interest rates used for discounting expected future payments are based on rates of return on investments for the benefit deferral period, and employee turnover and employee mortality are considered.

At a minimum, the information provided in the financial statements for accumulated plan benefits is to include

1. Vested benefits of participants currently collecting benefits
2. Other vested benefits
3. Nonvested benefits.

Either a reconciliation or a narrative description is to identify significant factors affecting the accumulated plan benefits from the beginning of the year to the end. The information is to include

1. Effects of plan amendments
2. Changes in the nature of the plan, such as a merger or a spin-off
3. Changes in actuarial assumptions
4. Benefits accumulated during the year
5. Benefits paid during the year
6. Interest component (from amortizing the discount)
7. Other changes.

The last four items can be combined into a single "other changes" category.

If the provisions of the defined benefit plan include a postretirement medical benefit component that is funded in accordance with IRC §401(h), ASC 965-205-05 specifies the accounting and disclosure rules with respect to the §401(h) component. These specialized rules are necessary due to legal requirements regarding the separate accounting for and funding of these arrangements.

Defined Contribution Plans

The three general types of defined contribution plans are profit-sharing plans, money purchase pension plans, and stock bonus plans. A profit-sharing plan is a plan that is neither a pension plan, as defined in the Internal Revenue Code, nor a stock bonus plan. Employer contributions to a profit-sharing plan are to be either discretionary or based on a fixed formula. Although the plan is called a profit-sharing plan, the contributions need not be made from the profits of the plan sponsor. A money purchase plan is a benefit plan that bases employer contributions on a fixed formula that is unrelated to profits. A stock bonus plan is a plan that makes its distributions to participants in the stock of the employer unless the participant chooses otherwise. Within these three categories of plans are more specialized plans, such as 401(k) plans, 403(b) plans, savings plans, employee stock ownership plans, target benefit plans, and Keogh plans.

The three primary attributes that distinguish a defined contribution plan from a defined benefit plan are

1. Employer contributions are determined at the discretion of the employer or according to a contractual formula, rather than being actuarially determined.
2. Individual accounts are maintained for each plan participant, rather than a single account in which all participants partake.
3. Benefits are determined based on the amount accumulated in a participant's account at the time he or she retires or withdraws from the plan, rather than being defined in the plan agreement. If vested, the account's value is either paid to the participant or used to purchase an annuity for the participant.

The liabilities of a defined contribution plan include accounts payable, amounts owed for securities purchases, and borrowings. The liabilities are not to include amounts that have not been paid to withdrawing participants. Those amounts are included in net assets available for benefits (representing the participants' equity in the plan net assets) and disclosed in the notes to the financial statements. Because those amounts are liabilities for regulatory purposes, a note to reconcile the financial statements to the Form 5500 may be necessary to comply with the Employee Retirement Income Security Act of 1974 (ERISA), as amended.

ASC 946-210-45 specifies that, if the net assets of an investment company contain fully benefit-responsive investment contracts, those assets shall be reported at their contract values, because that is the amount participants in the fund would receive if they were to initiate withdrawals under the terms of the plan. An asset is considered fully benefit-responsive if (1) the investment contract is between the fund and the issuer and prohibits the fund from assigning or selling the contract without issuer permission, (2) the issuer is obligated to repay principal and interest, or a financially responsible third party assures that the interest rate will not drop below zero, (3) all permitted participant-initiated transactions occur at contract value, and (4) an event that would limit the fund's ability to transact at contract value with the issuer is not probable. The codification also specifies disclosure requirements for this scenario.

Employee Health and Welfare Benefit Plans

Defined benefit health and welfare plans stipulate a determinable benefit amount, which may take the form of a payment directly to the participant or a payment to a third party (such as a service provider or an insurance company) on the participant's behalf. These benefits may be provided upon retirement of the participant or during the postemployment period between termination of employment and retirement. Factors such as length of employment, age, and salary level determine the level of benefits to be provided. The contributions from the employer may be determined actuarially, by actual claims paid, or by a formula established by the plan sponsor. Regardless of the manner in which the plan is funded, the plan is a defined benefit health and welfare plan if its purpose is to provide a defined benefit.

Like defined benefit pension plans, defined benefit health and welfare plans must include information in their financial statements about the actuarial present value of benefit obligations earned by having performed past service. A benefit obligation exists if all of the following conditions are met:

1. The participants' rights to receive benefits are attributable to services already rendered.
2. The participants' benefits vest or accumulate.
3. Payment of benefits is probable.
4. The amount can be reasonably estimated.

If conditions 1 and 2 are not met, the obligation exists if the event that gives rise to the liability has already occurred and the amount can be reasonably estimated. The benefit obligations are measured as of the end of the plan year and include the actuarial present value of

1. Claims payable
2. Claims incurred but not reported (IBNR)
3. Insurance premiums due
4. Accumulated eligibility credits and postemployment benefits, net of amounts currently payable
5. Postretirement benefits for retired participants and their beneficiaries, other plan participants who are eligible to receive benefits, and participants who are not yet eligible to receive benefits.

Benefit obligations of defined benefit health and welfare plans, similar to accumulated plan benefits of defined benefit pension plans, do not appear as liabilities on the statement of net assets available for benefits. Instead, they are presented either as a separate financial statement, on the face of another financial statement, such as the statement of net assets available for benefits, or in the notes to the financial statements. Regardless of the location selected, the information about benefit obligations is required to be presented in its entirety in the same location.

A reconciliation, presented as a separate statement, on the face of another financial statement, or in the notes to the financial statements, is to identify significant factors comprising the change in the benefit obligation from the beginning of the year to the end. The changes are classified into at least three categories: (1) amounts currently payable, which includes claims payable, claims IBNR, and premiums due insurance companies, (2) accumulated eligibility credits and postemployment benefits, net of amounts currently payable, and (3) postretirement benefit obligations, net of amounts currently payable and claims IBNR. The information for each category is to include, at a minimum, the effects of

1. Plan amendments
2. Changes in the nature of the plan, such as a merger or a spin-off
3. Changes in actuarial assumptions
4. Benefits accumulated during the year
5. Benefits paid during the year
6. Interest component (from amortizing the discount)
7. Other changes.

The last four items can be combined into a single "other changes" line.

ASC 965-205-50 requires the following additional disclosures:

1. The weighted-average assumed discount rate used to measure the obligation for postemployment benefits
2. Investments representing 5% or more of the net assets available for benefits as of the end of the plan year and
3. The portion of the plan's estimated cost of providing postretirement benefits that is funded by contributions from retirees.

Defined contribution health and welfare plans, like other defined contribution plans, maintain an account for each participant that determines the amount of benefits that the participant will eventually receive. The terms of a defined contribution health and welfare plan agreement determine the contribution that will be made by the employer or participant into each account. Defined contribution health and welfare plans do not report information about benefit obligations because a plan's obligation is limited to the amounts accumulated in the participants' accounts.

Government Regulations

Pursuant to the requirements of ERISA, the federal government oversees the operating and reporting practices of employee benefit plans. ERISA establishes minimum standards for participation, vesting, and funding. It defines the responsibilities of plan fiduciaries and standards for their conduct. It requires plans to annually report summarized plan information to plan participants.

The Department of Labor (DOL) and the Internal Revenue Service (IRS) are authorized to issue regulations establishing reporting and disclosure requirements for employee benefit plans that are subject to ERISA. Each year, plans are required to report certain information to the DOL, the IRS, and the Pension Benefit Guaranty Corporation (if applicable). For many plans, the information is reported using Form 5500, which includes financial statements prepared in conformity with GAAP and additional supplementary financial schedules.

Various provisions of the Internal Revenue Code apply to employee benefit plans. If an employee benefit plan qualifies under Section §401(a) of the Code, certain favorable tax treatments apply. For example, if a plan is qualified, the plan sponsor receives current deductions for contributions to the plan, and the plan participants do not pay income taxes on those contributions or the accumulated earnings on them until benefits are distributed to them. In addition, plan participants may receive favorable tax treatment on the distributions. Qualified plans are exempt from income taxes, except for taxes on unrelated business income. Nonqualified plans, which generally provide benefits selectively only to a few key employees, are not entitled to those favorable treatments.

Terminating Plans

If the liquidation of a plan is imminent before the end of the plan year, the plan is a terminating plan, even if another plan will replace the terminated plan. A terminating plan may continue to operate for as long as necessary to pay accrued benefits. Prominent disclosure of the relevant circumstances is necessary in all financial statements issued by the plan after the decision to terminate is made. Financial statements of a terminating plan are prepared on the liquidation basis of accounting for plan years ending after the determination that the termination is imminent. The liquidation basis for accumulated plan benefits (defined benefit pension plans) and benefit obligations (defined benefit health and welfare plans) may differ from the actuarial present value of benefits for an ongoing plan. For example, certain or all benefits may become vested upon plan termination.

REAL ESTATE—GENERAL (ASC 970)

PERSPECTIVE AND ISSUES

ASC 970, *Real Estate—General*, specifies the accounting for various costs in acquiring and developing real estate projects. It does not apply to

1. Real estate developed by an entity for its own use rather than for sale or rental
2. Initial direct costs of leases (discussed in the chapter on ASC 840)
3. Costs directly related to manufacturing, merchandising or service activities rather than real estate activities
4. Rental operations in which the predominant rental period is less than a month.

ASC 970 does address the accounting for costs of real estate whether rented or sold.

DEFINITIONS OF TERMS

Amenities. Features of or enhancements made to real estate projects that enhance the attractiveness of the property to potential tenants or purchasers. Amenities include golf courses, utility plants, clubhouses, swimming pools, tennis courts, indoor recreational facilities, and parking facilities.

Common costs. Costs that relate to two or more units within a real estate project.

Costs incurred to rent real estate projects. Includes costs of model units and their furnishings, rental facilities, semipermanent signs, rental brochures, advertising, "grand openings," and rental overhead including rental salaries.

Costs incurred to sell real estate projects. Includes costs of model units and their furnishings, sales facilities, sales brochures, legal fees for preparation of prospectuses, semipermanent signs, advertising, "grand openings," and sales overhead including sales salaries.

Fair value. The amount in cash or cash equivalent value of other consideration that a real estate parcel would yield in a current sale between a willing buyer and a willing seller (other than in a forced or liquidation sale). The fair value of a parcel is affected by its physical characteristics, ultimate use, and the time required to make such use of the property considering access, development plans, zoning restrictions, and market absorption factors.

Incidental operations. Revenue-producing activities engaged in during the holding or development period to reduce the cost of developing the property for its intended use, as distinguished from activities designed to generate a profit or a return from the use of the property.

Incremental costs of incidental operations. Costs that would not be incurred except in relation to the conduct of incidental operations. Interest, taxes, insurance, security, and similar costs that would be incurred during the development of a real estate project regardless of whether incidental operations were conducted are not incremental costs.

Incremental revenue from incidental operations. Revenues that would not be earned except in relation to the conduct of incidental operations.

Indirect project costs. Costs incurred after the acquisition of the property, such as construction administration, legal fees, and various office costs, that clearly relate to projects under development or construction.

Net realizable value. The estimated selling price in the ordinary course of business less estimated costs of completion, holding, and disposal.

Phase. A contractually or physically distinguishable portion of a real estate project (including time-sharing projects). That portion is distinguishable from other portions based on shared characteristics such as:

1. Units a developer has declared or legally registered to be for sale
2. Units linked to an owners association
3. Units to be constructed during a particular time period
4. How a developer plans to build the real estate project.

Preacquisition costs. Costs related to a property that are incurred for the express purpose of, but prior to, obtaining that property. Examples may be costs of surveying, zoning or traffic studies, or payments to obtain an option on the property.

Project costs. Costs clearly associated with the acquisition, development, and construction of a real estate project.

Relative fair value before construction. The fair value of each land parcel in a real estate project in relation to the fair value of the other parcels in the project, exclusive of value added by on-site development and construction activities.

CONCEPTS, RULES, AND EXAMPLES

Preacquisition Costs

Payments are generally capitalized if they relate to an option to obtain the real property or if all of the following conditions are met:

1. Costs are directly identified with the property.
2. Costs would be capitalized if the property already were acquired.
3. Acquisition of the option or property is probable. The purchaser wants the property and believes it to be available for sale and has the ability to finance its acquisition.

Once capitalized, these costs are project costs that, if not receivable in the future, or if the property is not acquired, are to be recognized as expense.

Taxes and Insurance

Real estate taxes and insurance are capitalized as property costs only when the property is undergoing activities necessary to get the property ready for its intended use. After the property is substantially complete and ready for its intended use such items are expensed.

Project Costs

Costs that are identifiable and clearly associated with acquisition, development, and construction of a real estate project are capitalized as a cost of the project.

Indirect costs that relate to several projects are capitalized and allocated to these projects. Overhead costs that do not clearly relate to any project (i.e., general and administrative expenses) are expensed as incurred.

Amenities

The costs in excess of anticipated proceeds of amenities that are to be sold or transferred in connection with the sale of individual units are treated as common costs of the project.

The costs of amenities that are to be sold separately or retained by the developer are capitalized with those costs in excess of estimated fair value treated as common costs. Fair value is determined as of the expected date of substantial physical completion and the amounts allocated to the amenity are not to be revised later. The sale of the amenity results in a gain or loss when the selling price differs from the fair value less accumulated depreciation.

Costs of amenities are allocated among land parcels benefited for which development is probable. The fair value of a parcel is affected by its physical characteristics, its highest and best use, and the time and cost required to make such use of the property. Before completion and availability for use, operating income or loss is an adjustment to common costs. After such date, operating income or loss is included in the income statement.

Incidental Operations

Revenue from incidental operations is netted with the costs of such operations and any excess of incremental revenue over incremental costs reduces capitalized project costs. If such costs exceed revenues, the excess is recognized as expense as incurred.

Allocation of Costs

Capitalized costs are allocated by specific identification. If this is not feasible, then costs prior to construction are allocated by the relative fair value of each parcel before construction and construction costs are allocated by the relative sales value of each unit.

If estimation of relative values is impractical, allocation may be based on square footage or another area method, or by using other appropriate methods.

Revisions of Estimates

Estimates made and cost allocations are to be reviewed at least annually until the project is substantially complete and available for sale. Costs are revised and reallocated as required for changes in current estimates.

Abandonment and Change in Use

Abandonment of a project requires all capitalized costs to be expensed and not reallocated to other components of the project or other projects. Real estate dedicated to governmental units is not deemed abandoned and its costs are treated as project common costs.

Changes in use require that costs incurred and expected to be incurred that exceed the estimated value of the required project (when substantially complete and ready for intended use) be charged to expense. If no formal plan for the project exists, then project costs in excess of current net realizable value are expensed.

Selling Costs

Costs incurred to sell are capitalized if they are

1. Reasonably expected to be recovered from sale of the project or from incidental operations, and
2. Incurred for tangible assets used directly throughout the selling period to assist the selling process or incurred for services required to obtain regulatory approval of sales.

Other costs may be capitalized as prepaid expenses if directly associated with sales, cost recovery is reasonably expected from sales and the full accrual method cannot be used.

All other costs are expensed in the period incurred. Capitalized costs are expensed in the period in which the related revenue is earned.

Rental Costs

Costs related to and reasonably expected to be recoverable from future rental operations are capitalized. This excludes initial direct costs as defined and described in accounting for leases. Costs that do not qualify for capitalization are expensed as incurred.

Capitalized costs are amortized over the term of the lease, if directly related to a specific operating lease, or over the period of expected benefit. Amortization begins when the project is substantially completed and available for occupancy. Estimated unrecoverable amounts are expensed when it is probable that the lease will be terminated.

A project is substantially completed and available for occupancy when tenant improvements are completed or after one year from the end of major construction activity. Then normal operations take place with all revenues and costs (including depreciation and other amortized costs) recognized in the income statement. If part of a project is occupied but other parts are not yet complete, completed portions are considered separate projects.

Impairment and Recoverability

As discussed in the chapter on ASC 360, real estate projects must be evaluated, when warranted by events and circumstances, to determine whether their carrying value is recoverable from estimated future cash flows. ASC 360 provides guidance on grouping assets that are being held and used into "asset groups" and assets being held for sale into "disposal groups" for the purpose of the evaluation of recoverability and impairment computations. ASC 360 applies to real estate held for development and sale, property to be developed in the future, and property currently undergoing development.

Generally, under ASC 360, recoverability is evaluated at the "lowest level for which identifiable cash flows are largely independent of the cash flows of other assets and liabilities." If a project has identifiable elements with separate cash flows such as residential and commercial, or houses and condominiums, then each element is evaluated separately and not combined for the whole project. Projects are not combined in order to avoid recognizing impairment of one of the components.

Once impairment losses are recognized on property, similar to inventory, a new cost basis is adopted and future recoveries in value are not recognized.

Real estate special assessments. The laws of various states permit the formation of Tax Increment Financing Entities (TIFEs). Although their structure and characteristics differ between jurisdictions, TIFEs are generally special taxing districts established to finance and operate infrastructure owned by the municipality, such as roads, water mains, electric lines, sewers, and the like. These infrastructure improvements are used to revitalize a discrete geographic area by facilitating the private development of adjoining residential and commercial real estate. The TIFE or, absent a TIFE, the municipality typically issues bonds to finance the construction of the infrastructure improvements. The bonds may offer investors favorable after-tax yields by qualifying for tax-exempt status under IRC §141. Generally, the bonds are repaid from special assessments specifically designated for this purpose by the TIFE (or the municipality) such as user fees, tolls, sales taxes, real estate taxes, hotel bed taxes, and the like.

Besides paying for the debt service, these special assessments also fund ongoing operating costs, such as routine infrastructure repairs and maintenance. The infrastructure improvements made with the bond proceeds directly benefit the adjoining property owners and, in fact, the terms of these arrangements are often jointly negotiated between residential and commercial real estate developers and the municipality as an inducement to the developers to invest in a local development project.

Depending on an analysis of the specific facts and circumstances, including the relevant statute, ordinance, bond indenture, and other legal documents, the property owner or developer may potentially be required to record a liability for:

1. A liability for a special assessment by the TIFE or municipality if that assessment is levied on each individual property owner at an amount that is fixed or determinable and that covers a determinable period of time (ASC 970-470).
2. A guarantee liability under ASC 460 if, for example, it has:
   a. Contractually agreed to cover all or a portion of any shortfalls in the required annual debt service of the bond obligations of the issuing TIFE or municipality.
   b. Pledged company assets as collateral for the bond obligations.
   c. Provided a letter of credit or other credit enhancements to support all or a portion of the bond obligations.

Other Guidance to Accounting for Real Estate Operations

ASC 970-360 holds that when a seller of real estate agrees to make up any rental shortfalls for a period of time, payments to and receipts from the seller are adjustments to the cost of the property and will affect future depreciation charges.

ASC 974-323-25 addresses the accounting by a REIT in a service corporation (SC). In determining a REIT's accounting for its investment in an SC, the SC must be evaluated as a potential VIE under ASC 810. If the SC is subject to ASC 810, this codification section does not apply to the determination of the REIT's accounting. If, however, the SC is not subject to ASC 810, this section continues to apply to the determination of the method of accounting that the REIT should use to record its investment (consolidation, equity method, or cost method). The codification includes a list of factors that indicate that the equity method of accounting is to be used. Regardless of the method of accounting used by a REIT for its investment in an SC, the SC is not considered an independent third party for the purpose of capitalizing lessor initial direct costs under ASC 310-20. Consequently, leasing costs capitalized by a REIT as initial direct costs may not exceed the amounts allowable if the REIT had incurred the costs directly.

As noted in the preceding section of this chapter, ASC 978 addresses the accounting for time-share operations. ASC 978 also establishes accounting requirements for incidental operations. In particular, rental and other operations during holding periods, including sampler programs and minivacations, are to be accounted for as incidental operations. The excess, if any, of revenue over costs of such operations is to be recorded as a reduction of inventory costs.

REAL ESTATE—RETAIL LAND (ASC 976)

PERSPECTIVE AND ISSUES

The substance of a sale of any asset is that the transaction unconditionally transfers the risks and rewards of ownership to the buyer. However, the economic substance of many real estate sales is that the risks and rewards of ownership have not been clearly transferred. The turbulent and cyclical environments in the real estate and debt markets have led to the evolution of many complex methods of financing real estate transactions. For example, in some transactions the seller, rather than an independent third party, finances the buyer, while in others, the seller may be required to guarantee a minimum return to the buyer or continue to operate the property for a specified period of time. In many of these complex transactions, the seller still has some association with the property even after the property has been sold. The question that must be answered in these transactions is: At what point does the seller become disassociated enough from the property that profit may be recognized on the transaction?

Accounting for sales of real estate is governed by ASC 976. The purpose of this section is to present the guidelines that need to be considered when analyzing nonretail real estate transactions. ASC 840-40 dealing with sales-type real estate leases and sales-leaseback real estate transactions is covered in the chapter on ASC 840.

A specialized situation involving the sale of real estate pertains to time-share projects, which are addressed by ASC 978, as discussed in this chapter.

DEFINITIONS OF TERMS

Buy-sell agreement. A contractual arrangement that gives both investors in a jointly owned entity the ability to offer to buy the other's interest.

Continuing investment. Payments that the buyer is contractually required to pay on its total debt for the purchase price of the property.

Cost recovery method. A method which defers the recognition of gross profit on a real estate sale until the seller recovers the cost of the property sold.

Deposit method. A method which records payments by the buyer as deposits rather than a sale. The seller continues to report the asset and related debt on the statement of financial position until the contract is canceled or until the sale has been achieved.

First mortgage (primary debt). The senior debt the seller has on the property at the time the buyer purchases the property. A first mortgage lender (mortgagee) has foreclosure rights superior to those of second (or junior) mortgage lenders (i.e., proceeds from sale of the foreclosed property are used first to repay the first mortgage lender in full with only the remainder available to satisfy the junior lenders' balances).

Full accrual method. A method that recognizes all profit from a real estate sale at the time of sale.

Initial investment. The sales value received by the seller at the time of sale. It includes a cash down payment, buyer's notes supported by an irrevocable letter of credit, and payments by the buyer to third parties to reduce or eliminate the seller's indebtedness on the property.

Installment method. A method that recognizes revenue on the basis of payments made by the buyer on debt owed to the seller and payments by the buyer to the holder of primary debt. Each payment is apportioned between profit and cost recovery.

Lien. A claim or charge a creditor has on property which serves as security for payment of debt by the debtor.

Minimum initial investment. The minimum amount that an initial investment must equal or exceed so that the criterion for using the full accrual method is met.

Partial sale. A sale in which the seller retains an equity interest in the property or has an equity interest in the buyer.

Property improvements. An addition made to real estate, usually consisting of buildings but that may also include any permanent structure such as streets, sidewalks, sewers, utilities, and the like.

Reduced profit method. A method which recognizes profit at the point of sale, but only a reduced amount. The remaining profit is deferred to future periods.

Release provision. An agreement that provides for the release of property to the buyer. This agreement releases the property to the buyer free of any previous liens.

Sales value. The sales price of the property increased or decreased for other consideration in the sales transaction that are, in substance, additional sales proceeds to the seller.

Subordination. The process by which a party's rights are ranked below the rights of others.

CONCEPTS, RULES, AND EXAMPLES

Real Estate Sales Other than Retail Land Sales

ASC 976 scope. ASC 976, *Real Estate—Retail Land*, contains standards applicable to all real estate sales for all types of businesses.

ASC 360-20-15 explicitly states that real estate sales transactions under ASC 976 include real estate with property enhancements or integral equipment. This defines property improvements and integral equipment as "any physical structure or equipment attached to real estate or other parts thereof, that cannot be removed and used separately without incurring significant cost." Examples include an office building or manufacturing plant.

Transactions excluded from the provisions of ASC 976 are as follows:

1. A sale of improvements or integral equipment with no sale or plans for a sale of the land.
2. A sale of stock, net assets of a business, or a segment of a business which contain real estate except in cases in which an "in-substance" real estate sale occurs.
3. Securities accounted for under ASC 320.

Profit recognition methods. Profit from real estate sales is recognized in full, provided the following:

1. The profit is determinable (i.e., the collectibility of the sales price is reasonably assured or the amount that will not be collectible can be estimated).
2. The earnings process is virtually complete, that is, the seller is not obliged to perform significant activities after the sale to earn the profit.

When both of these conditions are satisfied, the method used to recognize profits on real estate sales is referred to as the full accrual method. If both of these conditions are not satisfied, recognition of all or part of the profit is postponed.

For real estate sales, the collectibility of the sales price is reasonably assured when the buyer has demonstrated a commitment to pay. This commitment is supported by a substantial initial investment, along with continuing investments that give the buyer a sufficient stake in the property such that the risk of loss through default motivates the buyer to honor its obligations to the seller. Collectibility of the sales price is also assessed by examining the conditions surrounding the sale (e.g., credit history of the buyer; age, condition, and location of the property; and history of cash flows generated by the property).

The full accrual method is appropriate and profit is recognized in full at the point of sale for real estate transactions when all of the following criteria are met:

1. A sale is consummated.
2. The buyer's initial and continuing investments are adequate to demonstrate a commitment to pay for the property.
3. The seller's receivable is not subject to future subordination.

4. The seller has transferred to the buyer the usual risks and rewards of ownership in a transaction that is in substance a sale, and the seller does not have a substantial continuing involvement in the property.

On sales in which an independent third party provides all of the financing for the buyer, the seller is most concerned that criterion 1 is met. For such sales, the sale is usually consummated on the closing date. When the seller finances the buyer, the seller must analyze the economic substance of the agreement to ascertain that criteria 2, 3, and 4 are also met (i.e., whether the transaction clearly transfers the risks and rewards of ownership to the buyer).

ASC 360-20 provides the following guidelines for a seller of real estate to follow when considering the various forms of financing that may be applicable to the transaction:

1. The ASC 976 conditions for obtaining sufficient initial and continuing investment from the buyer before full accrual profit recognition is allowed must be applied unless the seller receives as the full sales value of the property
   a. Cash without any seller contingent liability on any debt on the property incurred or assumed by the buyer,
   b. The buyer's assumption of the seller's existing nonrecourse debt on the property,
   c. The buyer's assumption of all recourse debt on the property with the complete release of the seller from those obligations, or
   d. Any combination of such cash and debt assumption.
2. In computing the buyer's initial investment, debt incurred by the buyer that is secured by the property is not considered part of the buyer's initial investment. This is true whether the debt was incurred directly from the seller or other parties or indirectly through assumption. Payments to the seller from the proceeds of such indebtedness are not included as part of the buyer's initial investment.
3. If the transaction does not qualify for full accrual accounting and, consequently, is being accounted for using installment, cost recovery or reduced profit methods, payments made on debt described in 2 above are not considered to be buyer's cash payments. However, if the profit deferred under the applicable method exceeds the outstanding amount of seller financing and the outstanding amount of buyer's debt secured by the property for which the seller is contingently liable, the seller recognizes the excess in income.

Consummation of a sale. A sale is considered consummated when the following conditions are met:

1. The parties are bound by the terms of a contract.
2. All consideration has been exchanged.
3. Any permanent financing for which the seller is responsible has been arranged.
4. All conditions precedent to closing have been performed.

When a seller is constructing office buildings, condominiums, shopping centers, or similar structures, item 4 may be applied to individual units rather than the entire project. These four conditions are usually met on or after closing, not at the point the agreement to sell is signed or at a preclosing meeting. Closing refers to the final steps of the transaction (i.e., when consideration is paid, the mortgage is secured, and the deed is delivered or placed in escrow). If the consummation criteria have not been satisfied, the seller uses the deposit method of accounting until all of the criteria are met (i.e., the sale has been consummated).

Adequacy of the buyer's initial investment. Once the sale is consummated, the next step is to determine whether the buyer's initial investment adequately demonstrates a commitment to pay for the property and the reasonable likelihood that the seller will collect it. This determination is made by comparing the buyer's initial investment to the sales value of the property. ASC 976 specifically details items that are includable as the initial investment and the minimum percentages that the initial investment must bear to the sales value of the property. To make the determination of whether the initial investment is adequate, the sales value of the property must also be computed.

Computation of sales value. The sales value of property in a real estate transaction is computed as follows:

	Stated sales price
+	Proceeds from the issuance of an exercised purchase option
+	Other payments that are, in substance, additional sales proceeds (e.g., management fees, points, prepaid interest, or fees required to be maintained in advance of the sale that will be applied against amounts due to the seller at a later point)
–	A discount that reduces the buyer's note to its present value
–	Net present value of services seller agrees to perform without compensation
–	Excess of net present value of services seller performs over compensation that seller will receive
=	Sales value of the property

Composition of the initial investment. Sales transactions are characterized by many different types of payments and commitments made between the seller, buyer, and third parties; however, the buyer's initial investment only includes the following:

1. Cash paid to the seller as a down payment
2. Buyer's notes given to the seller that are supported by irrevocable letters of credit from independent lending institutions
3. Payments by the buyer to third parties that reduce existing indebtedness the seller has on the property
4. Other amounts paid by the buyer that are part of the sales value
5. Other consideration received by the seller that can be converted to cash without recourse to the seller; for example, other notes of the buyer.

ASC 976 specifically states that the following items are not included as initial investment:

1. Payments by the buyer to third parties for improvements to the property
2. A permanent loan commitment by an independent third party to replace a loan made by the seller
3. Funds that have been or will be loaned, refunded, or directly or indirectly provided to the buyer by the seller or loans guaranteed or collateralized by the seller for the buyer.

Size of initial investment. Once the initial investment is computed, its size must be compared to the sales value of the property. To qualify as an adequate initial investment, the initial investment must be equal to at least a major part of the difference between usual loan limits established by independent lending institutions and the sales value of the property. The minimum initial investment requirements for real estate sales (other than retail land sales) vary depending upon the type of property being sold. The following table from ASC 976 provides the limits for the various properties:

Type of property	*Minimum initial investment expressed as a percentage of sales value*
Land	
Held for commercial, industrial, or residential development to commence within two years after sale	20
Held for commercial, industrial, or residential development to commence more than two years after sale	25
Commercial and Industrial Property	
Office and industrial buildings, shopping centers, and so forth:	
Properties subject to lease on a long-term lease basis to parties with satisfactory credit rating; cash flow currently sufficient to service all indebtedness	10
Single-tenancy properties sold to a buyer with a satisfactory credit rating	15
All other	20
Other income-producing properties (hotels, motels, marinas, mobile home parks, and so forth):	
Cash flow currently sufficient to service all indebtedness	15
Start-up situations or current deficiencies in cash flow	25
Multifamily Residential Property	
Primary residence:	
Cash flow currently sufficient to service all indebtedness	10
Start-up situations or current deficiencies in cash flow	15
Secondary or recreational residence:	
Cash flow currently sufficient to service all indebtedness	15
Start-up situations or current deficiencies in cash flow	25
Single-Family Residential Property (including condominium or cooperative housing)	
Primary residence of the buyer	5[a]
Secondary or recreational residence	10[a]

[a] *If collectibility of the remaining portion of the sales price cannot be supported by reliable evidence of collection experience, the minimum initial investment [is to] be at least 60% of the difference between the sales value and the financing available from loans guaranteed by regulatory bodies such as the Federal Housing Authority (FHA) or the Veterans Administration (VA), or from independent, established lending institutions. This 60% test applies when independent first-mortgage financing is not utilized and the seller takes a receivable from the buyer for the difference between the sales value and the initial investment. If independent first mortgage financing is utilized, the adequacy of the initial investment on sales of single-family residential property [is] determined [as described in the next paragraph].*

Lenders' appraisals of specific properties often differ. Therefore, if the buyer has obtained a permanent loan or firm permanent loan commitment for maximum financing of the property from an independent lending institution, the minimum initial investment must be the greater of the following:

1. The minimum percentage of the sales value of the property specified in the above table or
2. The lesser of
   a. The amount of the sales value of the property in excess of 115% of the amount of a newly placed permanent loan or firm loan commitment from a primary lender that is an independent established lending institution
   b. 25% of the sales value.

To illustrate the determination of whether an initial investment adequately demonstrates a commitment to pay for property, consider the following example.

Example of determining adequacy of initial investment

Marcus, Inc. exercised a $2,000 option for the purchase of an apartment building from Rubin, Inc. The terms of the sales contract required Marcus to pay $3,000 of delinquent property taxes, pay a $300,000 cash down payment, assume Rubin's recently issued first mortgage of $1,200,000, and give Rubin a second mortgage of $500,000 at a prevailing interest rate.

Step 1 — Compute the sales value of the property.

Payment of back taxes to reduce Rubin's liability to local municipality	$ 3,000
Proceeds from exercised option	2,000
Cash down payment	300,000
First mortgage assumed by Marcus	1,200,000
Second mortgage given to Rubin	500,000
Sales value of the apartment complex	$2,005,000

Step 2 — Compute the initial investment.

Cash down payment	$ 300,000
Payment of back taxes to reduce Rubin's liability to local municipality	3,000
Proceeds from exercised option	2,000
	$ 305,000

Step 3 — Compute the minimum initial investment required.

a. The minimum percentage of the sales value of the property as specified in the table is 200,500 (= $2,005,000 × 10%).

b. 1. The amount of the sales value of the property in excess of 115% of the recently placed permanent mortgage is $625,000 (sales value of $2,005,000 – $1,380,000 [= 115% of $1,200,000]).

2. 25% of the sales value ($2,005,000) is $501,250.

The lesser of b.1 and b.2 is b.2, $501,250. The greater of a and b is b, $501,250. Therefore, to record this transaction under the full accrual method (assuming all other criteria are met), the minimum initial investment must be equal to or greater than $501,250. Since the actual initial investment is only $305,000, all or part of the recognition of profit from the transaction must be postponed.

If the sale has been consummated but the buyer's initial investment does not adequately demonstrate a commitment to pay, the transaction is accounted for using the installment method when the seller is reasonably assured of recovering the cost of the property if the buyer defaults. However, if the recovery of the cost of the property is not reasonably assured should the buyer default or if the cost has been recovered and the collection of additional amounts is uncertain, the cost recovery or deposit method is used.

Adequacy of the buyer's continuing investments. The collectibility of the buyer's receivable must be reasonably assured; therefore, for full profit recognition under the full accrual method, the buyer must be contractually required to pay each year on its total debt for the purchase price of the property an amount at least equal to the level annual payment that would be needed to pay that debt (both principal and interest) over a specified period. This period is no more than twenty years for land, and no more than the customary amortization term of a first mortgage loan by an independent lender for other types of real estate. For continuing investment purposes, the contractually required payments must be in a form that is acceptable for an initial investment. If the seller provides funds to the buyer, either directly or indirectly, these funds must be subtracted from the buyer's payments in determining whether the continuing investments are adequate.

The indebtedness on the property does not have to be reduced proportionately. A lump-sum (balloon) payment will not affect the amortization of the receivable as long as the level annual payments still meet the minimum annual amortization requirement. For example, a land real estate sale may require the buyer to make level annual payments at the end of each of the first five years and then a balloon payment at the end of the sixth year. The continuing investment criterion is met provided the level annual payment required in each of the first five years is greater than or equal to the level annual payment that would be made if the receivable were amortized over the maximum twenty-year (land's specified term) period.

Continuing investment not qualifying. If the sale has been consummated and the minimum initial investment criteria have been satisfied but the continuing investment by the buyer does not meet the stated criterion, the seller recognizes profit by the reduced profit method at the time of sale if payments by the buyer each year will at least cover both of the following:

1. The interest and principal amortization on the maximum first mortgage loan that could be obtained on the property
2. Interest, at an appropriate rate, on the excess of the aggregate actual debt on the property over such a maximum first mortgage loan.

If the payments by the buyer do not cover both of the above, the seller recognizes profit by either the installment or cost recovery method.

Release provisions. An agreement to sell real estate may provide that part or all of the property sold will be released from liens by payment of an amount sufficient to release the debt or by an assignment of the buyer's payments until release. To meet the criteria of an adequate initial investment, the investment must be sufficient both to pay the release on property released and to meet the initial investment requirements on property not released. If not, profit is recognized on each released portion as if it were a separate sale when a sale has been deemed to have taken place.

Seller's receivable subject to future subordination. The seller's receivable should not be subject to future subordination. Future subordination by a primary lender would permit the lender to obtain a lien on the property, giving the seller only a secondary residual claim. This subordination criterion does not apply if either of the following occur:

1. A receivable is subordinate to a first mortgage on the property existing at the time of sale.
2. A future loan, including an existing permanent loan commitment, is provided for by the terms of the sale and the proceeds of the loan will be applied first to the payment of the seller's receivable.

If the seller's receivable is subject to future subordination, profit is recognized using the cost recovery method. The cost recovery method is justified because the collectibility of the sales price is not reasonably assured in circumstances when the receivable may be subordinated to amounts due to other creditors.

Seller's continuing involvement. Sometimes sellers continue to be involved with property for periods of time even though the property has been legally sold. The seller's involvement often takes the form of profit participation, management services, financing, guarantees of return, construction, etc. The seller does not have a substantial continuing involvement with property unless the risks and rewards of ownership have been clearly transferred to the buyer.

If the seller has some continuing involvement with the property and does not clearly transfer substantially all of the risks and rewards of ownership, profit is recognized by a method other than the full accrual method. The method chosen is determined by the nature and extent of the seller's continuing involvement. As a general rule, profit is only recognized at the time of sale if the amount of the seller's loss due to the continued involvement with the property is limited by the terms of the sales contract. In this event, the profit recognized at this time is reduced by the maximum possible loss from the continued involvement.

Leases involving real estate. ASC 840-40 dealing with sales-type real estate leases and sale-leaseback real estate transactions is covered in the chapter on ASC 840

Profit-sharing, financing, and leasing arrangements. In real estate sales, it is often the case that economic substance takes precedence over legal form. Certain transactions, though possibly called sales, are in substance profit-sharing, financing, or leasing arrangements and are accounted for as such. These include situations in which:

1. The seller has an obligation to repurchase the property, or the terms of the transaction allow the buyer to compel the seller to repurchase the property or give the seller an option to do so.
2. The seller is a general partner in a limited partnership that acquires an interest in the property sold and holds a receivable from the buyer for a significant part (15% of the maximum first-lien financing) of the sales price.
3. The seller guarantees the return of the buyer's investment or a return on that investment for an extended period of time.
4. The seller is required to initiate or support operations, or continue to operate the property at its own risk for an extended period of time.

Options to purchase real estate property. Often a buyer will buy an option to purchase land from a seller with the hopeful intention of obtaining a zoning change, building permit, or some other contingency specified in the option agreement. Proceeds from the issue of an option by a property owner (seller) are accounted for by the deposit method. If the option is exercised, the seller includes the option proceeds in the computation of the sales value of the property. If the option is not exercised, the seller recognizes the option proceeds as income at the time the option expires.

Partial sales of property. Per ASC 976, "a sale is a partial sale if the seller retains an equity interest in the property or has an equity interest in the buyer." Profit on a partial sale may be recognized on the date of sale if the following occur:

1. The buyer is independent of the seller.
2. Collection of the sales price is reasonably assured.
3. The seller will not be required to support the operations of the property on its related obligations to an extent greater than its proportionate interest.

If the buyer is not independent of the seller, the seller may not be able to recognize any profit that is measured at the date of sale (see the following Buy-sell agreements section).

If the seller is not reasonably assured of collecting the sales price, the cost recovery or installment method is used to recognize profit on the partial sale.

A seller who separately sells individual units in condominium projects or time-sharing interests recognizes profit by the percentage-of-completion method on the sale of individual units or interests if all of the following criteria are met:

1. Construction is beyond a preliminary stage (i.e., engineering and design work, execution of construction contracts, site clearance and preparation, excavation, and completion of the building foundation have all been completed).

2. The buyer is unable to obtain a refund except for nondelivery of the units or interest.
3. Sufficient units have been sold to assure that the entire property will not revert to being rental property.
4. Sales prices are collectible.
5. Aggregate sales proceeds and costs can be reasonably estimated.

The deposit method is used to account for these sales up to the point all the criteria are met for recognition of a sale.

Buy-sell agreements. A buy-sell clause is not a prohibited form of continuing involvement precluding partial sales treatment, but only if (1) the buyer can act independently from the seller, or if (2) the seller is not compelled to reacquire the other investor's interest in the jointly owned entity. The decision is judgmental, requiring consideration of numerous factors.

Factors to consider in determining whether the buyer cannot act independently from the seller are (1) the presence of a predetermined buy-sell price, (2) the seller has a strategic necessity barring it from relinquishing its ownership rights to the buyer, (3) the seller has business arrangements with the jointly owned entity that economically require it to reacquire the real estate to avoid losing economic benefits or escaping negative consequences of the arrangements, or (4) tax implications compelling the seller to acquire the buyer's interest in the entity.

Factors to consider in determining if the buyer can compel the seller to repurchase the property include (1) the buyer is financially unable to acquire the seller's interest, (2) the buy-sell clause contains a specified rate of return for either party, (3) the buyer has a strategic necessity requiring it to sell its interest to the seller, (4) the buyer is legally restricted from acquiring the seller's interest, (5) the buyer cannot realize its economic interest by sale to a third party, due to the integration of the real estate into the seller's business, or (6) tax implications compelling the buyer to sell its interest to the seller.

Selection of method. If a loss is apparent (e.g., the carrying value of the property exceeds the sum of the deposit, fair value of unrecorded note receivable, and the debt assumed by the buyer), then immediate recognition of the loss is required.

The installment method is used if the full accrual method cannot be used due to an inadequate initial investment by the buyer, provided that recovery of cost is reasonably assured if the buyer defaults. The cost recovery method or the deposit methods are used if such cost recovery is not assured.

The reduced profit method is used when the buyer's initial investment is adequate but the continuing investment is not adequate, and payments by the buyer at least cover the sum of (1) the amortization (principal and interest) on the maximum first mortgage that could be obtained on the property and (2) the interest, at an appropriate rate, on the excess of aggregate debt over the maximum first mortgage.

Methods of Accounting for Real Estate Sales other than Retail Land Sales

Full accrual method. This method of accounting for nonretail sales of real estate is appropriate when all four of the recognition criteria have been satisfied. The full accrual method is simply the application of the revenue recognition principle. A real estate sale is recognized in full when the profit is determinable and the earnings process is virtually complete. The profit is determinable when the first three criteria have been met (the sale is consummated, the buyer has demonstrated a commitment to pay, and the seller's receivable is not subject to future subordination). The earnings process is virtually complete when the fourth criterion has been met (the seller has transferred the risks and rewards of ownership and does not have a substantial continuing involvement with the property). If all of the criteria have not been met, the seller records the transaction by one of the following methods as indicated by ASC 976:

1. Deposit
2. Cost recovery
3. Installment
4. Reduced profit
5. Percentage-of-completion (see the section on Long-Term Construction Contracts in this chapter).

Profit under the full accrual method is computed by subtracting the cost basis of the property surrendered from the sales value given by the buyer. Also, the computation of profit on the sale includes all costs incurred that are directly related to the sale, such as accounting and legal fees.

Installment method. Under the installment method, each cash receipt and principal payment by the buyer on debt assumed with recourse to the seller consists of part recovery of cost and part recovery of profit. The apportionment between cost recovery and profit is in the same ratio as total cost and total profit bear to the sales value of the property sold. Therefore, under the installment method, the seller recognizes profit on each payment that the buyer makes to the seller and on each payment the buyer makes to the holder of the primary debt. When a buyer assumes debt that is without recourse to the seller, the seller recognizes profit on each payment made to the seller and on the entire debt assumed by the buyer. The accounting treatment differs because the seller is subject to substantially different levels of risk under the alternative conditions. For debt that is without recourse, the seller recovers a portion, if not all, of the cost of the asset surrendered at the time the buyer assumes the debt.

Example of the installment method

Assume Tucker sells to Price a plot of undeveloped land for $2,000,000. Price will assume, with recourse, Tucker's existing first mortgage of $1,000,000 and also pay Tucker a $300,000 cash down payment. Price will pay the balance of $700,000 by giving Tucker a second mortgage payable in equal installments of principal and interest over a ten-year period. The cost of the land to Tucker was $1,200,000 and Price will commence development of the land immediately.

1. Computation of sales value:

Cash down payment	$ 300,000
First mortgage	1,000,000
Second mortgage	700,000
Sales value	$2,000,000

2. Computation of the initial investment:

Cash down payment	$ 300,000

3. Computation of the minimum required initial investment:

   a. $400,000 ($2,000,000 × 20%)
   b. 1. $850,000 [$2,000,000 – (115% × 1,000,000)]
      2. $500,000 ($2,000,000 × 25%)

The minimum initial investment is $500,000 since b.2 is less than b.1 and b.2 is greater than a.

The initial investment criterion has not been satisfied because the actual initial investment is less than the minimum initial investment. Therefore, assuming the sale has been consummated and Tucker is reasonably assured of recovering the cost of the land from Price, the installment method is to be used. The gross profit to be recognized over the installment payment period by Tucker is computed as follows:

Sales value	$ 2,000,000
Cost of land	(1,200,000)
Gross profit	$ 800,000

The gross profit percentage to apply to each payment by Price to Tucker and the primary debt holder is 40% ($800,000/$2,000,000).

If Price also pays $50,000 of principal on the first mortgage and $70,000 of principal on the second mortgage in the year of sale, Tucker would recognize the following profit in the year of sale:

Profit recognized on the down payment ($300,000 × 40%)	$120,000
Profit recognized on the principal payments:	
First mortgage ($50,000 × 40%)	20,000
Second mortgage ($70,000 × 40%)	28,000
Total profit recognized in year of sale	$168,000

Note that Tucker recognizes profit only on the payment applicable to the first mortgage. This is because Tucker may be called upon to satisfy the liability on the first mortgage if Price defaults.

If Tucker's first mortgage was assumed without recourse, Tucker would recognize the following profit in the year of sale:

Profit recognized on the down payment ($300,000 × 40%)	$120,000
Profit recognized on Price's assumption of Tucker's first mortgage without recourse ($1,000,000 × 40%)	400,000
Profit recognized on the principal payment of the second mortgage ($70,000 × 40%)	28,000
Total profit recognized in year of sale	$548,000

The income statement (or related footnotes) for the period of sale includes the sales value received, the gross profit recognized, the gross profit deferred, and the costs of sale. In future periods when further payments are made to the buyer, the seller realizes gross profit on these payments. This amount is presented as a single line item in the revenue section of the income statement.

If, in the future, the transaction meets the requirements for the full accrual method of recognizing profit, the seller may change to that method and recognize the remaining deferred profit as income at that time.

Cost recovery method. When the cost recovery method is used (e.g., when the seller's receivable is subject to subordination or the seller is not reasonably assured of recovering the cost of the property if the buyer defaults), no profit is recognized on the sales transaction until the seller has recovered the cost of the property sold. If the buyer assumes debt that is with recourse to the seller, profit is not recognized by the seller until the cash payments by the buyer, including both principal and interest on debt due the seller and on debt assumed by the buyer, exceed the seller's cost of the property sold. If the buyer assumes debt that is without recourse to the seller, profit may be recognized by the seller when the cash payments by the buyer, including both principal and interest on debt due the seller, exceed the difference between the seller's cost of the property and the nonrecourse debt assumed by the buyer.

For the cost recovery method, principal collections reduce the seller's related receivable, and interest collections on such receivable increase the deferred gross profit on the statement of financial position.

Example of the cost recovery method

Assume that on January 1, 2012, Simon, Inc. purchased undeveloped land with a sales value of $365,000 from Davis Co. The sales value is represented by a $15,000 cash down payment,

Simon assuming Davis's $200,000 first mortgage (10%, payable in equal annual installments over the next twenty years), and Simon giving Davis a second mortgage of $150,000 (12%, payable in equal annual installments over the next ten years). The sale has been consummated, but the initial investment is below the minimum required amount and Davis is not reasonably assured of recovering the cost of the property if Simon defaults. The cost of the land to Davis was $300,000. The circumstances indicate the cost recovery method is appropriate. The transaction is recorded by Davis as follows:

1/1/X1	Notes receivable	150,000	
	First mortgage payable	200,000	
	Cash	15,000	
	Revenue from sale of land		365,000
	Revenue from sale of land	365,000	
	Land		300,000
	Deferred gross profit		65,000

Case 1 — The first mortgage was assumed with recourse to Davis. Immediately after the sale, the unrecovered cost of the land is computed as follows:

Land	$300,000
Less: Cash down payment	(15,000)
Unrecovered cost	$285,000

The note (second mortgage) is reported as follows:

Note receivable	$150,000	
Less: Deferred gross profit	(65,000)	$ 85,000

At the end of the year Simon pays $26,547.64 ($8,547.64 principal and $18,000.00 interest) on the second mortgage note and $23,491.94 ($3,491.94 principal and $20,000.00 interest) on the first mortgage. At 12/31/12 the unrecovered cost of the land is computed as follows:

Previous unrecovered cost		$285,000.00
Less: Note receivable payment	$26,547.64	
First mortgage payment	23,491.94	(50,039.58)
Unrecovered cost		$234,960.42

The receivable is reported on the 12/31/X1 statement of financial position as follows:

Note receivable ($150,000 – 8,547.64)	$141,452.36	
Less: Deferred gross profit ($65,000 + 18,000)	83,000.00	$58,452.36

Case 2 — The first mortgage is assumed without recourse to Davis. The reporting of the note is the same as Case 1; however, the unrecovered cost of the property is different. Immediately after the sale, the unrecovered cost of the property is computed as follows:

Land	$ 300,000
Less: Cash down payment	(15,000)
Nonrecourse debt assumed by Simon	(200,000)
Unrecovered cost	$ 85,000

After Simon makes the payments at the end of the year, the unrecovered cost is computed as follows:

Previous unrecovered cost	$85,000.00
Less: Notes receivable payment	26,547.64
Unrecovered cost	$58,452.36

For the cost recovery method, the income statement for the year the real estate sale occurs includes the sales value received, the cost of the property given up, and the gross profit deferred. In future periods, after the cost of the property has been recovered, the income statement includes the gross profit earned as a separate revenue item.

If, after accounting for the sale by the cost recovery method, circumstances indicate that the criteria for the full accrual method are satisfied, the seller may change to the full accrual method and recognize any remaining deferred gross profit in full.

Deposit method. When the deposit method is used (e.g., when the sale is, in substance, the sale of an option and not real estate), the seller does not recognize any profit, does not record a receivable, continues to report in its financial statements the property and the related existing debt even if the debt has been assumed by the buyer, and discloses that those items are subject to a sales contract. The seller also continues to recognize depreciation expense on the property for which the deposits have been received, unless the property has been classified as held for sale (per ASC 360-10). Cash received from the buyer (initial and continuing investments) is reported as a deposit on the contract. However, some amounts of cash may be received that are not subject to refund, such as interest on the unrecorded principal. These amounts are used to offset any carrying charges on the property (e.g., property taxes and interest on the existing debt). If the interest collected on the unrecorded receivable is refundable, the seller records this interest as a deposit before the sale is consummated and then includes it as a part of the initial investment once the sale is consummated. If deposits on retail land sales are eventually recognized as sales, the interest portion of the deposit is separately recognized as interest income. For contracts that are canceled, the nonrefundable amounts are recognized as income and the refundable amounts returned to the depositor at the time of cancellation.

As stated, the seller's statement of financial position continues to present the debt assumed by the buyer (this includes nonrecourse debt) among its other liabilities. However, the seller reports any principal payments on the mortgage debt assumed as additional deposits, while correspondingly reducing the carrying amount of the mortgage debt.

Example of a deposit transaction

Elbrus Investments enters into two separate property acquisition transactions with the Buena Vista Land Company.

1. Elbrus pays a $50,000 deposit and promises to pay an additional $800,000 to buy land and a building in an area not yet properly zoned for the facility Elbrus intends to construct. Final acquisition of the property is contingent upon these zoning changes. Buena Vista does not record the receivable, and records the deposit with the following entry:

Cash	50,000	
Customer deposits		50,000

Part of the purchase agreement stipulates that Buena Vista will retain all interest earned on the deposit, and that 10% of the deposit is nonrefundable. Buena Vista earns 5% interest on Elbrus' deposit over a period of four months, resulting in $208 of interest income that is offset against the property tax expenses of the property with the following entry:

Cash	208	
Property tax expense		208

Immediately thereafter, the required zoning changes are turned down, and Elbrus cancels the sales contract. Buena Vista returns the refundable portion of the deposit to Elbrus and records the nonrefundable portion as income with the following entry:

Customer deposits	50,000	
Income from contract cancellation		10,000
Cash		40,000

2. Elbrus pays a $40,000 deposit on land owned and being improved by Buena Vista. Elbrus immediately begins paying $5,000/month under a four-year, 7% loan agreement totaling $212,000 of principal payments, and agrees to pay an additional $350,000 at closing, subject to the land being approved for residential construction. After two months, Buena Vista has earned $167 of refundable interest income on Elbrus' deposit and has been paid $7,689 of refundable principal and $2,311 of refundable interest on the debt. Buena Vista records these events with the following entry:

Cash	10,167	
Customer deposits		10,167

The land is approved for residential construction, triggering sale of the property. Buena Vista's basis in the property is $520,000. Buena Vista uses the following entry to describe completion of the sale:

Cash	350,000	
Note receivable	204,311	
Customer deposits	50,167	
Gain on asset sale		84,478
Land		520,000

Reduced profit method. The reduced profit method is appropriate when the sale has been consummated and the initial investment is adequate but the continuing investment does not clearly demonstrate the buyer's willing commitment to pay the remaining balance of the receivable. For example, a buyer may purchase land under an agreement in which the seller will finance the sale over a thirty-year period. ASC 976 specifically states twenty years as the maximum amortization period for the purchase of land; therefore, the agreement fails to meet the continuing investment criteria.

Under the reduced profit method, the seller recognizes a portion of the profit at the time of sale with the remaining portion recognized in future periods. The amount of reduced profit recognized at the time of sale is determined by discounting the receivable from the buyer to the present value of the lowest level of annual payments required by the sales contract over the maximum period of time specified for that type of real estate property (twenty years for land and the customary term of a first mortgage loan set by an independent lending institution for other types of real estate). The remaining profit is recognized in the periods that lump-sum or other payments are made.

Example of the reduced profit method

Assume Levinson, Inc. sells a parcel of land to Raemer Co. Levinson receives sales value of $2,000,000. The land cost $1,600,000. Raemer gave Levinson the following consideration:

Cash down payment	$ 500,000
First mortgage note payable to an independent lending institution (payable in equal installments of principal and 12% interest, $133,887 payable at the end of each of the next twenty years)	1,000,000
Second mortgage note payable to Levinson (payable in equal installments of principal and 10% interest, $53,039 payable at the end of each of the next thirty years)	500,000
Total sales value	$2,000,000

The amortization term of the second mortgage (seller's receivable) exceeds the twenty-year maximum permitted by ASC 976. It is assumed that the payments by the buyer will cover the interest and principal on the maximum first mortgage loan that could be obtained on the property and interest on the excess aggregate debt on the property over such a maximum first mortgage loan; consequently, the reduced profit method is appropriate. It is also assumed that the market interest rate on similar agreements is 14%.

The present value of $53,039 per year for twenty years at the market rate of 14% is $351,278 ($53,039 × 6.623).

The gross profit on the sale ($400,000) is reduced by the difference between the face amount of the seller's receivable ($500,000) and the reduced amount ($351,278) or $148,722. The profit recognized at the time of sale is the sales value less the cost of the land less the difference between the face amount of the receivable and the reduced amount. Therefore, the reduced profit recognized on the date of sale is computed as follows:

Sales value	$ 2,000,000
Less: Cost of land	(1,600,000)
Excess	(148,722)
Reduced profit	$ 251,278

Under the reduced profit method, the seller amortizes its receivable at the market rate, not the rate given on the second mortgage. The receivable's carrying balance is zero after the specified term expires (in this case, twenty years). The remaining profit of $148,722 is recognized in the years after the specified term expires as the buyer makes payments on the second mortgage (years twenty-one through thirty).

Profit Recognition on Retail Land Sales

A single method of recognizing profit is applied to all consummated sales transactions within a project.

Full accrual method. The full accrual method of accounting is applied if all of the following conditions are met and a sale can be recorded:

1. **Expiration of refund period.** The buyer has made the down payment and each required subsequent payment until the period of cancellation with refund has expired. That period is the longest period of those required by local law, established by the seller's policy, or specified in the contract.
2. **Sufficient cumulative payments.** The cumulative payments of principal and interest equal or exceed 10% of the contract sales price.
3. **Collectibility of receivables.** Collection experience for the project in which the sale is made or for the seller's prior projects indicates that at least 90% of the contracts in the project in which the sale is made that are in force six months after sale will be collected in full. The collection experience with the seller's prior projects may be applied to a new project if the prior projects have:

    a. The same characteristics (type of land, environment, clientele, contract terms, sales methods) as the new project
    b. A sufficiently long collection period to indicate the percentage of current sales of the new project that will be collected to maturity

    A down payment of at least 20% is an acceptable indication of collectibility.
4. **Nonsubordination of receivables.** The receivable from the sale is not subject to subordination to new loans on the property except that subordination by an individual lot buyer for home construction purposes is permissible if the collection experience on those contracts is the same as on contracts not subordinated.
5. **Completion of development.** The seller is not obligated to complete improvements of lots sold or to construct amenities or other facilities applicable to lots sold.

Percentage-of-completion method. The percentage-of-completion method is used if criteria 1, 2, 3, and 4 above are met, and full accrual criteria are not met (criterion 5 is not satisfied). However, additional criteria (6 and 7) must be satisfied.

6. **There has been progress on improvements.** The project's improvements progressed beyond preliminary stages and the work apparently will be completed according to plan. Some indications of progress are

   a. The expenditure of funds
   b. Initiation of work
   c. Existence of engineering plans and work commitments
   d. Completion of access roads and amenities such as golf courses, clubs, and swimming pools.

   Additionally, there should be no indication of significant delaying factors, such as the inability to obtain permits, contractors, personnel, or equipment. Finally, estimates of costs to complete and extent of progress toward completion should be reasonably dependable.
7. **Development is practical.** There is an expectation that the land can be developed for the purposes represented and the properties will be useful for those purposes; restrictions, including environmental restrictions, will not seriously hamper development; and that improvements such as access roads, water supply, and sewage treatment or removal are feasible within a reasonable time period.

Installment method. The installment method is appropriate if criteria a and b are met, full accrual criteria are not met, and the seller is financially capable, as shown by capital structure, cash flow, or borrowing capacity. If the transaction subsequently meets the requirements for the full accrual method, the seller is permitted to change to that method. This would be a change in accounting estimate. This method may be changed to the percentage-of-completion method when all of the criteria are met.

Deposit method. If a retail land sale transaction does not meet any of the above criteria, the deposit method is appropriate.

REAL ESTATE TIME-SHARING ACTIVITIES (ASC 978)

PERSPECTIVE AND ISSUES

Overview

A major segment of the real estate industry has evolved in recent decades to market and sell time-shares, whereby parties acquire the right to use property (typically, resort condominiums or other vacation-oriented property) for a fixed number of weeks per year (known as intervals). While a vast variety of property types and transaction structures exist, there are certain common features and complexities that have challenged the accounting profession. Time-sharing transactions are characterized by the following:

1. Volume-based, homogeneous sales
2. Seller financing
3. Relatively high selling and marketing costs
4. Upon default, recovery of the time-sharing interval by the seller and some forfeiture of principal by the buyer.

Time-share transactions are to be accounted for as nonretail land sales, while time-share transactions are excluded from certain provisions otherwise applicable to incidental rental operations.

DEFINITIONS OF TERMS

Source: ASC 978 Glossary

Fixed Time. A time-sharing arrangement in which ownership is passed through a deed and the buyer purchases a specific period (generally, a specific week) during the year.

Floating Time. A time-sharing arrangement in which ownership is passed through a deed but the buyer is not limited to a specific period (generally, a specific week) during the year.

Fractional interest. A partial ownership interest in real estate that typically includes larger blocks of time on an annual basis (for example, three weeks or more).

Interval. The specific period (generally, a specific week) during the year that a time-sharing unit is specified by agreement to be available for occupancy by a particular customer. Also denoted Time-Sharing Interest or Time-Share.

Phase. A contractually or physically distinguishable portion of a real estate project (including time-sharing projects). That portion is distinguishable from other portions based on shared characteristics such as:

1. Units a developer has declared or legally registered to be for sale
2. Units linked to an owners association
3. Units to be constructed during a particular time period
4. How a developer plans to build the real estate project.

Points. Purchased vacation credits that a buyer may redeem for occupancy at various sites. The number of points redeemed depends on such factors as unit type and size, site location, and season.

Project. A time-sharing development; some projects may be completed in a single phase, such as a single, one-story building containing several time-sharing units. Other projects may be completed in several phases, for example:

a. A hotel that is being converted to time-sharing units one floor at a time while the unconverted units continue to be rented
b. A number of buildings, each containing several time-sharing units, being built on a piece of property over an extended period of time.

Tenancy-for-Years. A time-sharing arrangement in which a customer has a qualified right to possession and use of a time-sharing interval for a certain number of years, after which it reverts to the seller or a third party. Also known as Estate-for-Years or Term-for-Years.

Time-Share. See Interval.

Time-Sharing. An arrangement in which a seller sells or conveys the right to occupy a dwelling unit for specified periods in the future. Forms of time-sharing arrangements include but are not limited to fixed and floating time, interval ownership, undivided interests, points programs, vacation clubs, right-to-use arrangements such as tenancy-for-years arrangements, and arrangements involving special-purpose entities. In this context, an undivided interest is a time-sharing arrangement that involves a tenant-in-common interest in a condominium unit or entire improved property, and in which the interest holder is assigned a specific period (generally, a specific week). The interest holder is also assigned a specific unit if the undivided interest is in the entire improved property.

Time-Sharing Interest. See Interval.

Time-Sharing Special-Purpose Entity. An entity, typically a corporation or a trust, to which a seller transfers time-sharing real estate in exchange for the entity's stock, membership interests, or beneficial interests.

CONCEPTS, RULES, AND EXAMPLES

Accounting for time-share transactions. ASC 978 provides guidance for a seller's accounting for real estate time-sharing transactions, including

1. Fee simple transactions in which nonreversionary title and ownership of the real estate pass to the buyer or an SPE
2. Transactions in which title and ownership of all or a portion of the real estate remain with the seller
3. Transactions in which title and ownership of all or a portion of the real estate pass to the buyer and subsequently revert to the seller or transfer to a third party
4. Transactions by a time-share reseller.

The major conclusions of this very detailed, specialized section of the ASC are as follows:

Profit recognition. A time-share seller should recognize profit on time-sharing transactions as set forth by the provisions of ASC 978 that specify the accounting for other than retail land sales. In order to justify recognizing profit, nonreversionary title must be transferred. If title transfer is reversionary, on the other hand, the seller must account for the transaction as if it were an operating lease.

For a time-sharing transaction to be accounted for as a sale, it must meet the following criteria:

1. The seller transfers nonreversionary title to the time-share;
2. The transaction is *consummated*;
3. The buyer makes cumulative payments (excluding interest) of at least 10% of the sales value of the time-share; and
4. Sufficient time-shares would have been sold to reasonably assure that the units will not become rental property.

Effect of sales incentives. The codification requires that certain sales incentives provided by a seller to a buyer to consummate a transaction are to be recorded separately, by reducing the stated sales price of the time-share by the excess of the fair value of the incentive over the amount paid by the buyer. For purposes of testing for buyer's financial commitment as set forth under ASC 978, the seller must reduce its measurement of the buyer's initial and continuing investments by the excess of the fair value of the incentive over the stated amount the buyer pays, except in certain situations in which the buyer is required to make specific payments on its note in order to receive the incentive.

Reload transactions. A reload transaction is considered to be a separate sale of a second interval, and the second interval is accounted for in accordance with the profit recognition guidance of ASC 978. For an upgrade transaction, that guidance is applied to the sales value of the new (upgrade) interval, and the buyer's initial and continuing investments from the original interval are included in the profit recognition tests related to the new interval.

Uncollectibles. The term uncollectibles is used in ASC 978 to include all situations in which, as a result of credit issues, a time-share seller collects less than 100% of the contractual cash payments of a note receivable, except for certain transfers of receivables to independent third parties by the seller. An estimate of uncollectibility that is expected to occur should be recorded as a reduction of revenue at the time that profit is recognized on a time-sharing sale recorded under the full accrual or percentage-of-completion method. Historical and statistical perspectives are used in making such a determination of anticipated uncollectible amounts. Subsequent changes in estimated uncollectibles should be recorded as an adjustment to estimated uncollectibles and thereby as an adjustment to revenue. Under the relative sales value method, the seller effectively does not record revenue, cost of sales, or inventory relief for amounts not expected to be collected. There generally is no accounting effect on inventory when, as expected, a time-share is repossessed or otherwise reacquired.

Cost of sales. The seller should account for cost of sales and time-sharing inventory in accordance with the relative sales value method.

Costs charged to current period expense. All costs incurred to sell time-shares would be charged to expense as incurred except for certain costs that are:

- Incurred for tangible assets used directly in selling the time-shares;
- Incurred for services performed to obtain regulatory approval of sales; or
- Direct and incremental costs of successful sales efforts under the percentage-of-completion, installment, reduced profit, or deposit methods of accounting.

Incidental operations. Rental and other operations during holding periods, including sampler programs and minivacations, should be accounted for as incidental operations. This requires that any excess of revenue over costs be recorded as a reduction of inventory costs.

VIEs and other complex structures. The accounting treatment for more complex time-sharing structures such as time-sharing special-purpose entities (variable interest entities [VIEs], which were formerly known as *special-purpose entities*, or SPEs), points systems, and vacation clubs should be determined using the same profit recognition guidance as for simpler structures, provided that the time-sharing interest has been sold to the end user. For statement of financial position presentation purposes, a VIE should be viewed as an entity lacking economic substance and established for the purpose of facilitating sales if the VIE structure is legally required for purposes of selling intervals to a class of nonresident customers, and the VIE has no assets other than the time-sharing intervals and has no debt. In those circumstances, the seller should present on its statement of financial position as time-sharing inventory the interests in the VIE not yet sold to end users.

Continuing involvement by seller or related entities. If the seller, seller's affiliate, or related party operates an exchange, points, affinity, or similar program, the program's operations constitute continuing involvement by the seller, and the seller should determine its accounting based on an evaluation of whether it will receive compensation at prevailing market rates for its program services.

REGULATED OPERATIONS (ASC 980)

PERSPECTIVE AND ISSUES

Although various businesses are subject to regulatory oversight to greater or lesser degrees, as used in GAAP the term regulated operations refers primarily to public utilities, whose ability to set selling prices for the goods or services they offer is constrained by government actions. Generally, the regulatory process has been designed to permit such enterprises to recover the costs they incur, plus a reasonable rate of return to stockholders. However, given the political process of rate-setting by regulatory authorities, and the fact that costs such as those for plant construction have escalated, the ability to recover all costs through rate increases has become less certain. For this and other reasons, specialized GAAP has been promulgated.

CONCEPTS, RULES, AND EXAMPLES

These accounting principles apply to regulated enterprises only if they continue to meet certain criteria, which relate to the intended ability to recover all costs through the rate-setting process. When and if these conditions are no longer met, due to deregulation or a shift to rate-setting which is not based on cost recovery, then application of the specialized GAAP is to terminate.

Asset Recognition

If certain costs are not recognized for current rate-setting purposes, but it is probable that the costs will be recovered through future revenue, then these costs can be capitalized even though a nonregulated enterprise would be required to expense these costs currently. Deferred costs can include an imputed cost of equity capital, if so accounted for rate-setting purposes, even though this would not normally be permitted under GAAP. Thus, the regulatory process can result in the accounting recognition of an asset that would not otherwise be recognized by a commercial enterprise. If at any time it becomes apparent that the incurred cost will not be recovered through generation of future revenue, that cost is to be charged to expense. If a regulator subsequently excludes specific costs from allowable costs, the carrying value of the asset recognized is to be reduced to the extent of the excluded costs. Should the regulator allow recovery of these previously excluded costs or any additional costs, a new asset is to be recognized and classified as if these costs had been initially included in allowable costs.

Imposition of Liabilities

In other situations, the regulatory process can result in the accounting recognition of a liability. This usually occurs when regulators mandate that refunds be paid to customers, which must be accrued when probable and reasonably estimable, per ASC 450, *Contingencies.* Furthermore, regulatory rates may be set at a higher level, in order to recover costs expected to be incurred in the future, subject to the caveat that such amounts will be refunded to customers if it later becomes apparent that actual costs incurred were less than expected. In such cases, the incremental rate increase related to recovery of future costs must be accounted for as a liability (unearned revenue), until the condition specified is satisfied. Finally, regulators may stipulate that a gain realized by the utility will be returned to customers over a specified future period; this will be accounted for by accrual of a liability rather than by recognition of the gain for accounting purposes.

Abandonment

Accounting for abandonments is also stipulated for regulated enterprises. If an abandonment occurs or becomes probable, any costs which are probable of not being recovered are required to be written off as a loss. Furthermore, if the return on the investment that will be recoverable will not be equal to the normal rate of return, then an additional loss accrual must be recognized currently. This loss is measured by the difference between the projected future revenues, discounted at the enterprise's incremental borrowing rate, and the remaining costs to be recovered. The amount of loss to be recognized obviously depends on the enterprise's estimate of time to elapse until rate increases are effective, and the length of time over which the increases will remain in effect. These estimates may change over time, and the effect of revisions in the estimate will be reflected in earnings in the periods the new estimates are made.

The carrying value of the costs of an abandoned plant is increased during the period from the abandonment until recovery occurs through rate increases as promised by the regulatory authorities. If full return of investment is anticipated, the cost of abandoned assets is accreted at the rate (the enterprise's overall cost of capital) permitted for rate-setting purposes. If partial or no return on investment is expected, the asset value is accreted at the same rate that was used to compute the loss accrual, which is the enterprise's incremental borrowing rate. During the recovery period, the costs of the abandoned plant are amortized. If full return on investment is expected, this amortization is to be computed on the same basis as is permitted for rate-setting purposes. If partial or no return is expected, amortization is recognized in amounts that provide a constant rate of return on the unamortized balance of the investment in the costs of the abandoned plant.

Accounting for Liabilities Related to Asset Retirement Obligations

Historically, and particularly since the advent of nuclear energy generation, public utilities have faced the problem of accounting for costs which are expected to be incurred attendant upon the retirement from service of the generating facilities. Environmental and other laws and regulations typically mean that very substantial costs have to be borne, in order to dispose of waste, restore the land (not merely the power generating facility site, but, in the case of coal-fired plants, restoration of the strip mining locations) and ameliorate other problems. These issues are addressed by ASC 410-20, *Asset Retirement Obligations*.

The chapter on ASC 410 presents a detailed examination of ASC 410-20, and that discussion is not duplicated here. In brief, this pronouncement establishes standards for measuring the future cost to retire an asset and recognizing it in the financial statements as a liability and correspondingly, as part of the depreciable cost of the asset. ASC 410-20 applies to legal obligations associated with the retirement of tangible long-lived assets that result from their acquisition, construction, development and/or normal operation. It does not apply to situations where moral suasion is to be applied to encourage cleanup efforts, even if the reporting entity has a history of making such voluntary gestures. However, the principle of "promissory estoppel" does create legal obligations even absent contractual or statutory requirements, in some cases.

If costs, such as those related to nuclear decommissioning, are legal obligations, the present value of the future expenditures is recognized as an added cost of the asset, and as a liability, at acquisition. Further cost accretion is required due to the passage of time. Depreciation charges are based on the recorded cost of the asset, including the estimated future retirement costs. Changes in estimates, which are inevitable, are handled differently if they are increases versus decreases, as described in the chapter on ASC 360.

Accounting for Asset Impairments

While not unique to regulated industries (public utilities, in particular), the issue of asset impairment will often be dealt with in these operations, due to the large investment in very long-lived fixed assets and the potential impact of changes in technology over time. ASC 360 addresses this issue. Briefly, under defined conditions, assets must be reviewed to determine whether their carrying value will be fully recovered from future cash flows from using and disposing of them. If the future estimate of cash flows over the asset's (or group of assets') remaining estimated useful life, undiscounted, is less than the carrying value, the asset is considered impaired, and the carrying value is reduced to the fair value of the asset with the impairment loss being charged to expense in the current period. Typically, a projected cash flows approach is used in estimating value, although in some instances a more direct approach, relying on market prices, might be usable.

Accounting for Deregulation and "Stranded Costs"

The utilities industries have undergone varying degrees of deregulation. This has significant effects on the financial reporting of many of the entities operating in these industries, since under GAAP many had recognized regulatory assets and regulatory liabilities which will no longer be recognizable once full deregulation occurs. Also, certain costs may no longer be recoverable in a deregulated environment, transforming certain assets into *stranded costs*.

ASC 980-20-35 addresses the matter of deregulation. When deregulation legislation has been enacted affecting all or a portion of the entity's operations, it is to cease applying ASC 980 to the affected operations. In cases in which the effects of deregulation are imposed by means of a rate order, such an order would have to be sufficiently detailed so that the entity would be able to determine how it will be affected. Regulatory assets would not, however, be immediately written off; instead, an evaluation of regulatory cash flows would be conducted to determine whether an impairment had occurred and to determine whether the portion of the business from which the regulatory cash flows are derived is still subject to ASC 980. Only if the asset is impaired (applying ASC 360 criteria) or if ASC 980 is no longer applicable would the asset be written off before being recovered. Similarly, regulatory liabilities would not be reclassified into income until the obligation is eliminated by the regulatory authority.

A related concern is whether the new regulatory assets or liabilities must be given recognition to reflect expenses and obligations that will arise from the portion of the business being deregulated. The same "source of cash flow" type of analysis noted above is to be applied to make these determinations. Thus, a cost or obligation is recognized as a regulatory asset or liability, respectively, once it is expensed or incurred after ASC 980 is applied to that portion of the operations, if it has been designated for recovery or settlement, respectively, via regulated cash flows.

Other Accounting Guidance

ASC 980-605-25 states that Nonutility Generators (NUG) are to recognize the lesser of (1) the amount billable under the contract or (2) a formula-based pricing arrangement, as revenue. The formula-based pricing arrangement is determined by the kilowatt-hours (kwhs) made available during the period multiplied by the estimated average revenue per kwh over the term of the contract for the fixed or scheduled price period of the contract. Revenue is not to be recognized utilizing the formula-based pricing arrangement if its only purpose is to establish liquidating damages. Additionally, a receivable arises when the amounts billed are less than the amount computed pursuant to the formula-based pricing arrangement and if the contract requires a payment, probable of recovery, to the NUG at the end of the contract term.

ASC 980-605-25 also addresses the treatment of additional revenues of rate-regulated utility companies that are to be billed in the future under alternative revenue programs. It identifies two types of alternative revenue programs, defined as Type A and Type B. The revenues from alternative revenue programs are to be recognized when the events permitting billing of the revenues have occurred and three specific criteria that are discussed in the abstract are met.

Also, rate-regulated utilities recognizing revenues from an alternative revenue program that do not meet the conditions of this consensus must amend the plan or change the program to meet the conditions.

ASC 980-715-25 holds that, if the regulator includes other postemployment benefits (OPEB), costs in rates on a pay-as-you-go basis, the regulatory asset relating to the cost under ASC 715 is not to be recognized. Further, the regulatory asset for a rate-regulated enterprise is to recognize the difference between ASC 715 costs and the OPEB costs if future revenue will at least offset the deferred cost and meet four specific criteria, which are discussed in the standard.

Regarding the accounting for regulatory assets, ASC 980-715-25-8 states that a rate-regulated enterprise that fails to initially meet the asset recognition criteria can recognize a regulatory asset for other postemployment benefits costs in a future period when applicable criteria are met. This consensus applies also to all regulatory assets recognized pursuant to ASC 980-10-05 criteria.

Additionally, it was noted that the carrying amount of the regulatory asset to be recognized is to be reduced by any impairment that may have occurred.

Fixed price arrangements are to be handled in accordance with ASC 980-605-25. Variable price arrangements in which the rate is at least equal to expected costs are to recognize revenue as billed, in accordance with the provisions of the contract for that variable price period. A long-term power sales contract is to be reviewed periodically to determine whether it is a loss contract, in which case the loss is to be recognized immediately. Finally, any premium related to a contractual rate in excess of the current market rate is to be amortized over the remaining portion of the contract for long-term power sales contracts acquired in a purchase business combination.

SOFTWARE (ASC 985)

PERSPECTIVE AND ISSUES

Overview

As technology has come to play a more important role in businesses, increasing levels of activity have been devoted to the development of computer software. This involves a number of undertakings.

- Software licensed, purchased, or leased from others for internal use
- Software obtained from others for resale in the normal course of business (either on a stand-alone basis or as part of a larger product)
- Software developed internally for sale to others
- Software developed internally for the developer's own use.

Software can be licensed, purchased, or leased and can reside on the user's hardware or be "hosted" by an application service provider (ASP) and leased to the user for remote use over the Internet. A growing set of accounting standards deal with some, but not all, of these issues.

The accounting for the cost of software developed internally for sale (or lease, etc.) to others is addressed by ASC 985-605; it provides that costs incurred prior to the point at which technological feasibility has been demonstrated are to be expensed as research and development costs, but specified costs incurred subsequently are capitalized, and later amortized or expensed (e.g., as cost of sales) as appropriate.

The cost of software acquired from others for resale in the normal course of business is not separately addressed by GAAP, but would be handled as are any other inventory costs. The usual inventory costing methods (LIFO, FIFO, etc.) and financial reporting concerns (lower of cost or market, etc.) are applicable to such situations.

ASC 350-40 addresses accounting for the costs of software acquired from others, or developed internally, for internal use. Internal-use software and the related rules regarding costs of developing Web sites are discussed in connection with the discussion of intangible assets in the chapter on ASC 350. This standard establishes the conditions that must be met before internal use software costs are capitalized. To qualify for capitalization, costs must have been incurred subsequent to the completion of the conceptual formulation, design and testing of possible project alternatives (including the process of vendor selection for purchased software). In addition, management at the appropriate level of authority must have authorized funding for the development project and conclude that it is probable that the project will be completed and the software will be used to perform the intended functions. This prerequisite is roughly analogous to the "technological feasibility" threshold prescribed by ASC 985 for software to be sold or leased to customers. Costs that are eventually capitalized under ASC 350-40 will be amortized over the period of expected economic benefit, as is the case with all other long-lived assets used in the business.

The increasingly central role of technology has received the attention of accounting standard setters in another arena as well. For enterprises that sell computer software and associated goods and services (program upgrades, maintenance agreements, etc.), complicated issues of revenue recognition arise.

DEFINITIONS OF TERMS

Terms are from ASC 985 Glossary.

Coding. Generating detailed instructions in a computer language to carry out the requirements described in the detail program design. The coding of a computer software product may begin prior to, concurrent with, or subsequent to the completion of the detail program design.

Customer support. Services performed by an enterprise to assist customers in their use of software products. Those services include any installation assistance, training classes, telephone question and answer services, newsletters, on-site visits, and software or data modifications.

Detail program design. The specifications of a computer software product that take product functions, features, and technical requirements to their most detailed, logical form and enables coding of the product.

Maintenance. Activities undertaken after the product is available for general release to customers to correct errors (commonly referred to as "bugs") or keep the product updated with current information. Those activities include routine changes and additions.

Product design. A logical representation of all product functions in sufficient detail to serve as product specifications.

Product enhancement. Improvements to an existing product that are intended to extend the life or improve significantly the marketability of the original product. Enhancements normally require their own product design and may require a redesign of all or part of the existing product.

Product masters. A completed version, ready for copying, of the computer software product, the documentation, and the training materials that are to be sold, leased, or otherwise marketed.

Testing. Performing the steps necessary to determine whether the coded computer software product meets function, feature, and technical performance requirements set forth in the product design.

Working model. An operative version of the computer software product that is completed in the same software language as the product to be ultimately marketed, performs all the major functions planned for the product, and is ready for initial customer testing (usually referred to as **beta testing**).

CONCEPTS, RULES, AND EXAMPLES

Costs of Software Developed Internally for Sale or Lease

A separate set of accounting issues arise in connection with the costs of computer software developed internally for lease or sale to others. The principal issue relates to the point in the development process at which development efforts are no longer characterized as research and development (R&D). The costs of R&D activities are required to be expensed currently as discussed in the chapter on ASC 730. The determination of this milestone has important accounting significance because specified costs incurred subsequent to the completion of R&D may be deferred (i.e., inventoried) and later reclassified as cost of sales as the finished products are sold or leased.

ASC 985 established the concept of technological feasibility to demarcate the point at which it is proper to begin to defer costs. According to this standard, all costs of development are considered research and development costs until technological feasibility has been established. This point is reached when all the necessary planning, designing, coding, and testing activities have been completed, to the extent these activities are necessary to establish that the product in question can meet its design specifications. Design specifications, in turn, may include such product aspects as functions, features, and technical performance requirements.

If the process of creating the software involves a detail program design, evidence of having achieved technological feasibility includes having performed these steps:

1. The product design (the logical representation of the product) and detailed program design have been completed. This step includes having demonstrated that the necessary skills, hardware, and software technologies are accessible to the entity for completion of product development.
2. The detailed program design has been documented and traced to product specifications, thus demonstrating completeness and consistency.
3. The detailed program design has been reviewed for any high-risk elements, such as unproven functions or product innovations, and any such high-risk elements have been resolved through coding and testing.

If the software development effort does not involve creation of a detailed program design, then the following steps would require completion to demonstrate technological feasibility:

1. A product design and working model of the software have been completed.
2. The completeness of the working model and its consistency with the product design have been confirmed by testing.

If all the foregoing steps in either of the above listings have been completed as applicable, then technological feasibility has been demonstrated, and qualifying costs of producing product masters incurred thereafter are capitalized as production costs. Such costs include additional coding and testing activities that occur after the establishment of technological feasibility. The costs of producing product masters include not only the master copy of the software itself but also related user documentation and training materials. Capitalized production costs may include allocated indirect costs (e.g., occupancy costs related to programmers). (ASC 985-20-25-5)

Capitalization of software costs ceases once the product is available for general release to customers of the entity. Period costs, such as maintenance and ongoing customer support efforts, are expensed as incurred.

The capitalized production costs must be amortized, beginning when the product is first available for general release to customers. Amortization is computed on a product-by-product basis, which means that costs related to development of earlier products cannot be "rolled forward" into the costs of newer products, thereby delaying expense recognition. Periodic amortization must be the greater of (1) an amount determined with reference to total estimated revenues to be generated by the product, or (2) an amount computed on a straight-line basis with reference to the product's expected life cycle.

Example of amortization of capitalized computer software development costs

Assume total costs of $30,000 have been capitalized at the point product sales begin. Management estimates that the product will eventually generate revenues of $5,100,000 over a period of four years. For the current period (1/2 of a year), revenues of $600,000 have been earned. Capitalized costs of $3,750 must be amortized, which is the greater of the pro rata amount based on estimated total revenues to be derived from product sales [($600,000 ÷ $5,100,000) × $30,000 = $3,529] or the amount determined on a straight-line basis ($30,000 ÷ 4 × 1/2 = $3,750).

Other costs, such as product duplication, training material publication, and packaging, are capitalized as inventory on a unit-specific basis and expensed as cost of sales when product sales revenues are recognized.

Capitalized production costs are subject to annual evaluation for net realizable value; if impairment adjustments are recognized, the written-down amount becomes the new cost basis for further amortization purposes, as well as for comparison to net realizable value in the following period.

Capitalized inventory costs are subject to the same lower of cost or market evaluation as is required for inventories of tangible goods.

Software Revenue Recognition

The basic principles underlying ASC 985-605 are set forth in the following paragraphs.

Licensing vs. sales. Standards setters were concerned that transfers of rights to software by licenses rather than by outright sales (a technique widely employed to provide vendors with legal recourse when others engage in unauthorized duplication of their products) were being accounted for differently. The standard setters concluded that any legal distinction between a license and a sale should not cause revenue recognition to differ.

Product may not equate with delivery of software. Arrangements to deliver software, whether alone or in conjunction with other products, often include services. Services to be provided in such contexts commonly involve significant production, modification, or customization of the software. Thus, physical delivery of the software might not constitute the delivery of the final product contracted for, absent those alterations, resulting in the requirement that such arrangements be accounted for as construction-type or production-type contracts in conformity with ASC 605-35. However, if the services do not entail significant production, modification, or customization of the software, the services are accounted for as a separate element.

Delivery is the key threshold issue for revenue recognition. This is consistent with the principles set forth in CON 5, *Recognition and Measurement in Financial Statements of Business Enterprises*, which states that

An entity's revenue-earning activities involve delivering or producing goods, rendering services, or other activities that constitute its ongoing major or central operations, and revenues are considered to have been earned when the entity has substantially accomplished what it must do to be entitled to the benefits represented by the revenues... [t]he two conditions (being realized or realizable and being earned) are usually met by the time the product or merchandise is delivered . . . to customers, and revenues . . . are commonly recognized at time of sale (usually meaning delivery).

Revenue must be allocated to all elements of the sales arrangement, with recognition dependent upon meeting the criteria on an element-by-element basis. Under prior GAAP, the accounting for vendor obligations remaining after delivery of software was dependent upon whether or not the obligation was deemed to be significant. Under ASC 985-605-25, however, all obligations are accounted for and revenue is allocated to each element of the arrangement, based on vendor-specific objective evidence (VSOE) of the fair values of the elements. Revenue associated with a particular element is not recognized until the revenue-recognition conditions established by the ASC are met, as the earnings process related to that element will not be considered complete until that time.

Fair values for revenue allocation purposes must be vendor-specific. When there are multiple elements of an arrangement, revenue is generally recognized on an element-by-element basis as individual elements are delivered. Revenue is allocated to the various elements in proportion to their relative fair values. Under ASC 985-605-25, this allocation process requires that VSOE of fair value be employed, regardless of any separate prices stated in the contract for each element, since prices stated in a contract may not represent fair value and, accordingly, might result in an unreasonable allocation of revenue. If an element is not yet being sold separately, then the price established by management is acceptable as a substitute. Separate transaction prices for the individual elements comprising the arrangement, if they are also being sold on that basis, would be the best such evidence, although under some circumstances (such as when prices in the arrangement are based on multiple users rather than the single user pricing of the element on a stand-alone basis) even that information could conceivably be invalid for revenue allocation purposes. Relative sales prices of the elements included in the arrangement are to be used whenever possible.

The earnings process is not complete if fees are subject to forfeiture. Even when elements have been delivered, if fees allocated to those elements are subject to forfeiture, refund, or other concession if the vendor does not fulfill its delivery responsibilities relative to other elements of the arrangement, those fees are not treated as having been earned. The potential concessions are an indication that the customer would not have licensed the delivered elements without also licensing the undelivered elements. For that reason, there must be persuasive evidence that fees allocated to delivered elements are not subject to forfeiture, refund, or other concessions before revenue recognition can be justified. Thus, for example, in determining the persuasiveness of the evidence, the vendor's history of making concessions that were not required by the provisions of an arrangement is more persuasive than are terms included in the arrangement that indicate that no concessions are required.

Exclusions. The ASC provides that software revenue recognition guidance does *not* apply when a tangible product contains software and non-software components that function together to deliver its essential functionality. Further, an entity should always exclude hardware components of a tangible product from software revenue guidance. The exclusion also applies to any software contained within a tangible product, and which is essential to its functionality (including essential software sold with the product). An example of a tangible product that would be excluded from software revenue recognition guidance is a computer sold with an included operating system. Conversely, an example of a tangible product that would *not* be excluded from software revenue recognition guidance is a computer sold with a bundle of software productivity software; this software is not essential to the operation of the computer, and so is not excluded from the software revenue recognition guidance.

Consider the following factors when deciding if a specific scenario is governed by these exclusions:

- Infrequent sales of the tangible product without the software elements indicate that the software elements are essential to the product's functionality.
- If an entity sells multiple similar products that primarily differ only in the presence or absence of a software component, then consider them the same for the purposes of reviewing the exclusion applicability.
- The separate sale of software that is also contained within a tangible product does not necessarily mean that the software is not essential to the tangible product.
- A software element may be considered essential to a tangible product even it is not embedded within the product.
- The non-software elements of a tangible product must substantially contribute to its functionality.
- If there is an undelivered element of a deliverable that can be subdivided into elements that are excluded from and applicable to software revenue guidance, then bifurcate them into software and non-software deliverable.

Operational Rules Established by ASC 985-605

1. If an arrangement to deliver software or a software system, either alone or together with other products or services, requires significant production, modification, or customization of software, the entire arrangement is accounted for in conformity with ASC 605-35.
2. If the arrangement does not require significant production, modification, or customization of software, revenue is recognized when all of the following criteria are met:

   a. Persuasive evidence of an arrangement exists;
   b. Delivery has occurred;
   c. The vendor's fee is fixed or determinable; and
   d. Collectibility is probable.

3. For software arrangements that provide licenses for multiple software deliverables (multiple elements), some of which may be deliverable only on a when-and-if-available basis, these deliverables are considered in determining whether an arrangement includes multiple elements. The requirements with respect to arrangements that consist of multiple elements are applied to all additional products and services specified in the arrangement, including those described as being deliverable only on a when-and-if-available basis.
4. For arrangements having multiple elements, the fee is allocated to the various elements based on VSOE of fair value, regardless of any separate prices stated for each element within the contract. VSOE of fair value is limited to the following:

   a. The price charged when the same element is sold separately; or
   b. For an element not yet being sold separately, the price established by management, if it is probable that the price, once established, will not change before the separate introduction of the element into the marketplace.

   The revenue allocated to undelivered elements cannot later be adjusted. However, if it becomes probable that the amount allocated to an undelivered element of the arrangement will result in a loss on that element, the loss must be immediately recognized. When a vendor's pricing is based on multiple factors such as the number of products and the number of users, the amount allocated to the same elements when sold separately must consider all the relevant factors of the vendor's pricing structure.

In ASC 985-605, multiple-element arrangements are not accounted for as long-term construction contracts when (1) there is VSOE of the fair values of all undelivered elements, (2) VSOE does not exist for one or more of the delivered elements, and (3) all other revenue recognition criteria have been satisfied. In such cases, "residual" method of allocation of selling price is to be utilized. This results in deferral of the aggregate fair value of the undelivered elements of the arrangement (to be recognized later as delivery occurs), with the excess of the total arrangement fee over the deferred portion being recognized in connection with the delivered components. This change was made to accommodate the situation whereby software is commonly sold with one "free" year of support, where additional years of support are also marketed at fixed prices; in this case, the fair value of the "free" support is deferred (and amortized over the year), while the software itself is assigned a revenue amount which is the difference between the package price and the known price of one year's support.

5. If a discount is offered in a multiple-element arrangement, a proportionate amount of the discount is applied to each element included in the arrangement, based on each element's fair value without regard to the discount. However, no portion of the discount is allocated to any upgrade rights.
6. If sufficient VSOE does not exist for the allocation of revenue to the various elements of the arrangement, all revenue from the arrangement is deferred until the earlier of the point at which (1) such sufficient VSOE does exist, or (2) all elements of the arrangement have been delivered. The exceptions to this guidance, provided in ASC 985-605, are as follows:

   a. If the only undelivered element is postcontract customer support (PCS), the entire fee is recognized ratably over the contractual PCS period, or when the PCS rights are implicit in the arrangement, over the period that PCS is expected to be provided to the customer.
   b. If the only undelivered element is services that do not involve significant production, modification, or customization of the software (e.g., training or installation), the entire fee is recognized over the period during which the services are expected to be performed.
   c. If the arrangement is in substance a subscription, the entire fee is recognized ratably over the term of the arrangement, if stated, otherwise over the estimated economic life of the products included in the arrangement.
   d. If the fee is based on the number of copies delivered, how the arrangement is accounted for depends on whether the total fee is fixed, and on whether the buyer can alter the composition of the copies to be received, as follows:

      (1) If the arrangement provides customers with the right to reproduce or obtain copies of two or more software products at a specified price per copy (not per product) up to the total amount of the fixed fee, an allocation of the fee to the individual products generally cannot be made, because the total revenue allocable to each software product is unknown at inception and depends on subsequent choices to be made by the customer and, sometimes, on future vendor development activity. Nevertheless, certain arrangements that include products that are not deliverable at inception impose a maximum number of copies of the undeliverable product(s) to which the customer is entitled. In such arrangements, a portion of the arrangement fee is allocated to the undeliverable

product(s). This allocation is made assuming that the customer will elect to receive the maximum number of copies of the undeliverable product(s).

(2) In arrangements in which no allocation can be made until the first copy or product master of each product covered by the arrangement has been delivered to the customer, and assuming the four conditions set forth above are met, revenue is recognized as copies of delivered products are either (a) reproduced by the customer, or (b) furnished to the customer if the vendor is duplicating the software. Once the vendor has delivered the product master or the first copy of all products covered by the arrangement, any previously unrecognized licensing fees are recognized, since only duplication of the software is required to satisfy the vendor's delivery requirement and such duplication is incidental to the arrangement. Consequently, the delivery criterion is deemed to have been met upon delivery to the customer of the product master or first copy. When the arrangement terminates, the vendor recognizes any licensing fees not previously recognized. Revenue is not recognized fully until at least one of the following conditions is met: either (a) delivery is complete for all products covered by the arrangement, or (b) the aggregate revenue attributable to all copies of the software products delivered is equal to the fixed fee, provided that the vendor is not obligated to deliver additional software products under the arrangement.

(3) The revenue allocated to the delivered products is recognized when the product master or first copy is delivered. If, during the term of the arrangement, the customer reproduces or receives enough copies of these delivered products so that revenue allocable to the delivered products exceeds the revenue previously recognized, the additional revenue is recognized as the copies are reproduced or delivered. The revenue allocated to the undeliverable product(s) is reduced by a corresponding amount.

7. The portion of the fee allocated to a contract element is recognized when the four revenue recognition criteria are met with respect to the element. In applying those criteria, the delivery of an element is considered not to have occurred if there are undelivered elements that are essential to the functionality of the delivered element, because functionality of the delivered element is considered to be impaired.
8. No portion of the fee can be deemed to be collectible if the portion of the fee allocable to delivered elements is subject to forfeiture, refund, or other concession if any of the undelivered elements are not delivered. If management represents that it will not provide refunds or concessions that are not required under the provisions of the arrangement, this assertion must be supported by reference to all available evidence. This evidence may include the following:

   a. Acknowledgment in the arrangement regarding products not currently available or not to be delivered currently;
   b. Separate prices stipulated in the arrangement for each deliverable element;
   c. Default and damage provisions as defined in the arrangement;
   d. Enforceable payment obligations and due dates for the delivered elements that are not dependent on the delivery of future deliverable elements, coupled with the intent of the vendor to enforce rights of payment;
   e. Installation and use of the delivered software; and
   f. Support services, such as telephone support, related to the delivered software being provided currently by the vendor.

Other Accounting Guidance

As a complex and still evolving area, the use of technology in general, and computer software in particular, has created many accounting concerns.

Both software developers and motion picture companies engage in development of software products that combine entertainment (e.g., including well-known cartoon characters and film storylines in the software) and education. The term *edutainment* has been coined to refer to these hybrid products. Diversity in accounting practice had arisen whereby different companies engaged in edutainment development were using different combinations of GAAP to account for the same activities.

In ASC 985-705-S99 the SEC staff announced that

1. Entertainment and educational products developed for sale or lease, or that are otherwise marketed are to be accounted for under ASC 985-20.
2. Costs subject to ASC 985-20 accounting include film costs incurred in the development of the product that would otherwise be accounted for under ASC 926 (discussed earlier in this chapter).
3. Exploitation costs (marketing, advertising, publicity, promotion, and other distribution expenses) are to be expensed as incurred unless they qualify for capitalization as direct response advertising under ASC 340-20.

The SEC announcement should be deemed the most meaningful guidance on this topic.

In ASC 720-45-25, all expenditures incurred for business process reengineering activities (either by insiders or outsiders) are to be expensed as incurred. This guidance also applies when business process reengineering activities are part of development or implementation of internal-use software. Finally, the accounting for internal-use software development and acquisition of property, plant, and equipment are not affected by this consensus.

ASC 720-45-30-1 also states that, in cases where a third party is engaged for a business process reengineering project, the entire consulting contract price is to be allocated to each activity on the basis of the relative fair values of the separate components.

Some software users do not actually receive and load applications software on their computers, but instead merely access and use it via the Internet, on the vendor's or a third party's server, on an as-needed basis. (Commonly, the applications are "hosted" by companies known as application service providers, or ASPs.) In such arrangements, the customer is paying for two elements—the right to use the software and the storage of the software (and sometimes, the customer's proprietary data) on the provider's hardware. ASC 985-605 has addressed certain concerns arising in such circumstances.

When a vendor provides hosting, several revenue recognition issues may arise. First, the relationship between the customer and the ASP may be structured in the form of a service agreement providing Internet access to the specified site, without a corresponding software license. In such instances, the application of ASC 985-605 to the arrangement was unclear. Second, when the transaction is structured as a software license with a service element, evaluation of how the arrangement meets the delivery requirement of ASC 985-605 was unclear.

ASC 985-605 only applies if the customer has the right to take possession of the software at any time during the hosting period, without significant penalty, and install the software on its own hardware or contract with another service provider to host it. Most, if not all, ASP arrangements would not provide this option to the customer and therefore ASC 985-605 would not apply.

For those few hosting arrangements meeting the foregoing criteria, and thus subject to ASC 985-605, software delivery is deemed to have occurred when the customer first has the option to take possession. The criteria of ASC 985-605 must be met in order for the ASP to recognize revenue allocable to the software element; revenue relating to the hosting element is recognized as that service is provided.

Finally, ASC 985-605 provides authoritative guidance regarding the amounts and timing of revenue recognition in transactions involving the sale or license of computer software. Such transactions are often structured to bundle other software-related "elements" with the software such as future upgrades, postcontract customer support (PCS), training, customization, or other services. Those bundled arrangements are referred to as multiple-element arrangements (MEA).

ASC 985-605-15-3 states that in an MEA that includes software that is "more than incidental" to the arrangement, ASC 985-605 applies to the software-related elements enumerated above as well as any nonsoftware element for which the software element is essential to its functionality.

NOTES:

1. *ASC 460-10-30 provides that, at the inception of the guarantee, the guarantor may be required under ASC 450 to recognize a liability for a contingent loss. In the circumstances described here, this would result in the developer or property owner recording the TIFE or municipality debt as their own obligation. In fact, ASC 970-470 specifies that if the property owner is constructing facilities for its own use or operation, the presence of any of the above factors a. through c. would create a presumption that the TIFE debt be recognized as a company obligation.*
2. *Consolidation of the TIFE by the property owner or developer will most likely be prohibited under ASC 810, since governmental organizations and financing entities established by governmental organizations are exempt from consolidation unless the property owner or developer is using the arrangement in an attempt to circumvent ASC 810.*

Real estate developers follow the guidance in ASC 970. Under ASC 970, the developer capitalizes any portion allocable to the production period as part of the cost of the property being developed. The remaining portion is charged to expense because it is attributable to the period after the project is substantially complete and ready for intended use.

Reporting entities developing the property for their own use are not included in the scope of ASC 970 and, therefore need to consider the best of the available alternatives. The author favors analogizing from ASC 970 and the literature on interest capitalization on self-constructed assets, and accordingly following the same accounting as described in the previous paragraph.

Appendix
Disclosure Checklist for Commercial Businesses

The disclosure checklist presented below provides a quick reference to those disclosures that are common to the financial statements of most commercial business enterprises. This checklist does not purport to be suitable for use as a comprehensive SEC disclosure checklist, nor is it designed to be used for reporting entities that are not-for-profit organizations, state or local governments, or that are engaged in other industries that are subject to specialized accounting and reporting rules. Readers are advised to access the FASB Codification for additional details on requirements.

Numbers preceding the topics refer to the relevant FASB ASC Topic. For each Topic, the related chapter in *Wiley GAAP 2015* offers more information about implementing the requirements and gives examples.

CONTENTS

Broad Transactions

PRESENTATION

In the far right column, indicate:

Yes – If the disclosure has been made.
No – If the disclosure is required, but has not been made
N/A – If the disclosure is not applicable to the entity.

205 Presentation of Financial Statements

1. Full set of financial statements shows:

   a. Financial position _____
   b. Earnings for the period as a separate statement or within a continuous statement of comprehensive income _____
   c. Comprehensive income in one statement or two separate but consecutive statements _____
   d. Cash flows _____
   e. Investments by and distributions to owners during this period. _____

(FASB ASC 205-10-45-1A)

2. Comparative statements of financial position, income, and changes in equity are preferable. _____

(FASB ASC 205-10-45-2)

3. Include name of entity for which statements are being presented (if d/b/a different name than legal name, indicate both). _____
4. Titles of statements should be appropriate (certain titles denote and should be reserved for GAAP financial statements; other titles denote other comprehensive basis of accounting [OCBOA] financial statements). _____
5. Dates and periods covered should be clearly stated. _____
6. If one or more consolidated subsidiaries have different fiscal periods than the parent (not to exceed 3 months), disclose any intervening events that materially affect financial position or results of operations. _____
7. If comparative statements are presented, repeat footnotes from prior years to extent they continue to be significant. _____

(FASB ASC 205-10-45-4)

8. Differences between "economic" entity and legal entity being presented should be noted (e.g., consolidated or not, subsidiaries included and excluded, combined statements, etc.). Disclose summarized financial information for previously unconsolidated subsidiaries. _____
9. Identify new accounting principles not yet adopted and expected impact of adoption. *(SEC SAB Topic 11)* _____
10. For reclassifications or other reasons, if changes have occurred in the manner or basis of presenting corresponding items in two or more periods, disclose the explanation of the change. _____

(FASB ASC 205-10-50-1)

205-20 Discontinued Operations—Extant Guidance[1]

Assets Sold or Held for Sale

1. For assets (or disposal groups) either sold or reclassified from held-and-used to held-for-sale during the period
   a. The facts and circumstances leading to the expected disposal, the expected manner and timing of the disposal, and if not separately presented on the face of the statement of financial position, the carrying amounts of the major classes of assets and liabilities included as part of the disposal group. _____
   b. Gain or loss recognized for initial or subsequent write-downs to fair value less cost to sell, and, if not separately stated, the income statement caption in which included. _____
   c. Amounts of revenue and pretax profit or loss reported as discontinued operations, if applicable. _____
   d. If applicable, the segment in which the long-lived asset (disposal group) is reported under Topic 280. _____

(FASB ASC 205-20-50-1—extant guidance)

[1] In April 2014, the FAB issued ASU 2014-08, *Reporting Discontinued Operations and Disclosures of Disposals of Components of an Entity.* At the end of this section the ASU 2014-08 guidance is included. Please see the Technical Alert in the chapter on ASC 205 for more information and effective dates.

Long-Lived Asset of Disposal Group Classified as Held for Sale

2. In the period of disposal, the major classes of assets and liabilities classified as held for disposal (either on the face of the income statement or in the notes to the financial statements). _____

(FASB ASC 205-20-50-2 – Note: this paragraph superseded by ASU 2014-08)

Change to a Plan of Sale

3. For assets (or groups) reclassified from held-for-sale to held-and-used during the period, including the removal of individual assets or liabilities from a disposal group to be sold,
   a. The facts and circumstances leading to the decision to change the plan to sell the long-lived asset (disposal group). _____
   b. The effect of the changed decision on the results of operations for the period in which the decision was made and any prior periods presented. _____

(FASB ASC 205-20-50-3 – extant guidance)

Continuing Cash Flows

4. For each discontinued operation that generates continuing cash flows:
   a. The nature of the activities that give rise to continuing cash flows. _____
   b. The period of time continuing cash flows are expected to be generated. _____
   c. The principal factors used to conclude that the expected continuing cash flows are not direct cash flows of the disposed component. _____

(FASB ASC 205-20-50-4—extant guidance)

Adjustments to Previously Reported Amounts

5. The nature and amount of adjustments to amounts previously reported in discontinued operations that are directly related to the disposal of a component of an entity in a prior period. _____

(FASB ASC 205-20-50-5 – Note: this paragraph superseded by ASU 2014.08)

Continuing Involvement by Ongoing Entity

6. In the period in which the discontinued operations are initially classified and for each discontinued operation in which the ongoing entity will engage in a continuation of activities after disposal and for which revenues and expenses that were intra-entity transactions are included in revenue, disclose those intra-entity amounts and the types of continuing involvement. _____

(FASB ASC 205-20-50-6 – Note this paragraph superseded by 2014-08)

205-20 Discontinued Operations – Guidance Based on ASU 2014-08

The following requirements for ASC 205-20-50 are based on new guidance in ASU 2014-08. See the chapter on ASC 205 for information on implementation and effective dates.

1. For periods in which a discontinued operation has been disposed of or is classified as held-for-sale
   a. The facts and circumstances leading to the disposal or expected disposal, _____
   b. The expected manner and timing of the disposal, _____
   c. If not separately presented on the face of the income statement as part of discontinued operations, gain or loss recognized on the disposal or loss recognized on classification as held for sale in accordance with the relevant guidance in other subtopics, _____

   d. If applicable, the segment in which the discontinued operation is reported under Topic 280. _____

(FASB ASC 205-20-50-1 – reflecting ASU 2014-08)

Change to a Plan of Sale

3. If an entity changes its plan of sale, in the period in which that decision is made, in the notes,
   a. The facts and circumstances leading to the decision _____
   b. The effect of the change on the results of operations for all periods presented _____

(FASB ASC 205-20-50-3 – reflecting ASU 2014-08)

Adjustments to Previously Recorded Amounts

4. The nature and amount of adjustments to amounts previously reported in discontinued operations.

(FASB ASC 205-20-50-3A – reflecting ASU 2014-08)

5. For as long as the discontinued operation is presented separately, information about the entity's significant continuing involvement with a discontinued operation after the disposal date _____

(FASB ASC 205-20-50-4A – reflecting ASU 2014.08)

6. For each discontinued operation in which the entity retains significant continuing involvement after the disposal date:
   a. Description of the nature of the activities that give rise to the continuing involvement. _____
   b. Period of time the involvement is expected to continue _____
   c. The amount of any cash flows _____
   d. Revenues or expenses in continuing operations after the disposal transaction that were eliminated in consolidate financial statements as intra-entity transactions. _____
   e. Where an entity retains an equity method investment after the disposal:
      i. The pretax income of the investee _____
      ii. The ownership interest in the discontinued operation before and after the disposal. _____
      iii. Share of the income or loss of the investee in the period after the disposal and where on the income statement that is reported. _____

(FASB ASC 205-20-50-4B – reflecting ASU 2014-08)

Disclosures Required for a Discontinued Operation Comprising a Component or Group of Components of an Entity

7. For discontinued operations, to the extent not presented on the face of the financial statements as part of discontinued operations:
   a. Pretax profit or loss. _____
   b. Major classes of line items making up the pretax profit or loss. _____
   c. For the periods in which the results of discontinued operations are presented in the income statement either the total operating and investing cash flows of the discontinued operation or the depreciation, amortization, capital expenditures, and significant operating and investing noncash items. _____
   d. The pretax profit or loss attributable to the parent if the discontinued operation includes a noncontrolling interest. _____

e. Carrying amounts of major classes of assets and liabilities included in discontinued operations for the period in which it is classified as held for sale and all prior periods presented. _____

(FASB ASC 205-20-50-5B – reflecting ASU 2014-08)

8. If the above disclosures are provided in a note,

   a. For the initial period in which a disposal group is classified as held for sale and all prior periods, reconciliation of the amounts disclosed in 205-20-50-5B(e) and total assets and liabilities classified as held for sale that are presented separately on the face of the statement of financial position. The entity may aggregate amounts that are not considered major. _____
   b. For the periods in which the results of operations of the discontinued operations are recorded in the income statement, the amounts disclosed in 205-20-50-5B(a) and (b) and the after-tax profit or loss from discontinued operations. _____

(FASB ASC 205-20-50-5C and 5D – reflecting ASU 2014-08)

Disclosures Required for a Discontinued Operation Comprising an Equity Method Investment

9. Summarized information about the assets, liabilities and results of operations of the investee if that information was disclosed in periods before the disposal _____

(FASB ASC 205-20-50-7 – reflecting ASU 2014-08)

205-30 Liquidation Basis of Accounting

1. Disclose information requited by other Topics relevant to understanding the statement of net assets in liquidation and statement of changes in net assets in liquidation, informing readers about the amount of cash or other consideration that the entity expects to collect and the amount that the entity is obligated or expects to be obligated to pay during the course of liquidation. _____

(FASB ASC 205-30-50-1)

2. Disclose all of the following when for financial statements using the liquidation basis of accounting:

   a. That the financial statements are prepared using the liquidation basis of accounting, including the facts and circumstances surrounding the adoption of the liquidation basis of accounting and the entity's determination that liquidation is imminent. _____
   b. A description of the entity's plan for liquidation, including a description of each of the following:

      1. The manner by which it expects to dispose of its assets and other items it expects to sell that it had not previously recognized as assets (for example, trademarks) _____
      2. The manner by which it expects to settle its liabilities _____
      3. The expected date by which the entity expects to complete its liquidation. _____

   c. The methods and significant assumptions used to measure assets and liabilities, including any subsequent changes to those methods and assumptions. _____
   d. The type and amount of costs and income accrued in the statement of net assets in liquidation and the period over which those costs are expected to be paid or income earned. _____

(FASB ASC 205-30-50-2)

210 Balance Sheet

The amounts at which current assets supplemented by information that reveals, for the various classifications of inventory items, the basis upon which their amounts are stated and, where practicable, indication of the method of determining the cost—for example, average cost, first-in first-out (FIFO), last-in first-out (LIFO), and so forth.

(FASB ASC 210-10-50-1)

210-20 Offsetting

1. The disclosures below apply to both of the following:
   a. Recognized derivative instruments that are offset in accordance with either Section 210-20-45 or Section 815-10-45. _____
   b. Recognized derivative instruments that are subject to an enforceable master netting arrangement or similar agreement, irrespective of whether they are offset in accordance with either Section 210-20-45 or Section 815-10-45. _____

(FASB ASC 210-20-50-1)

2. Information to enable financial statements users to evaluate the effect or potential effect of netting arrangements on its financial position. This includes the effect or potential effect of rights of setoff associated with an entity's recognized assets and recognized liabilities that are in the scope of ASC 210-20-50-1. _____

(FASB ASC 210-20-50-2)

3. At the end of the reporting period the following quantitative information separately for assets and liabilities that are within the scope of paragraph 210-20-50-1:
   a. The gross amounts of those recognized assets and those recognized liabilities. _____
   b. The amounts offset in accordance with the guidance in Sections 210-20-45 and 815-10-45 to determine the net amounts presented in the statement of financial position. _____
   c. The net amounts presented in the statement of financial position. _____
   d. The amounts subject to an enforceable master netting arrangement or similar agreement not otherwise included in (b):
      (1) The amounts related to recognized financial instruments and other derivative instruments that either:
         (a) Management makes an accounting policy election not to offset _____
         (b) Do not meet some or all of the guidance in either Section 210-20-45 or Section 815-10-45. _____
      (2) The amounts related to financial collateral (including cash collateral). _____
   e. The net amount after deducting the amounts in (d) from the amounts in (c). _____

(FASB ASC 210-20-50-3)

4. Present the information required above in a tabular format, separately for assets and liabilities, unless another format is more appropriate. The total amount disclosed in accordance with paragraph 210-20-50-3(d) for an instrument should not exceed the amount disclosed in accordance with paragraph 210-20-50-3(c) for that instrument. _____

(FASB ASC 210-20-50-4)

5. A description of the rights of setoff associated with an entity's recognized assets and recognized liabilities subject to an enforceable master netting arrangement or similar agreement disclosed in accordance with paragraph 210-20-50-3(d), including the nature of those rights.

(FASB ASC 210-20-50-5)

225 Income Statement

225-20 Extraordinary and Unusual Items

1. Present descriptive captions and the amounts for individual extraordinary events or transactions, preferably on the face of the income statement, if practicable; otherwise disclosure in related notes is acceptable. Describe the nature of an extraordinary event or transaction and the principal items entering into the determination of an extraordinary gain or loss. Disclose the income taxes applicable to extraordinary items on the face of the income statement; alternatively, disclosure in the related notes is acceptable. _____

(FASB 225-20-45-11)

2. Present earnings per share information related to extraordinary items either on the face of the income statement or in the notes. _____

(FASB ASC 225-20-45-12)

3. Each adjustment in the current period of an element of an extraordinary item that was reported in a prior period shall be separately disclosed as to year of origin, nature, and amount. _____

(FASB ASC 225-20-50-2)

Unusual or Infrequent Items

4. Disclose the nature and financial effects of each event or transaction on the face of the income statement or, alternatively, in notes to financial statements. _____

(FASB ASC 225-20-50-3)

230 Statement of Cash Flows

1. Policy for determining which items are treated as cash equivalents _____

(FASB ASC 230-10-50-1)

2. Disclose both interest and income taxes paid in a schedule following the statement or in the notes, if the indirect method of reporting net cash flows from operating activities is used. _____

(FASB ASC 230-10-50-2)

3. Information about all investing and financing activities of an entity during a period that affect recognized assets or liabilities but that do not result in cash receipts or cash payments in the period shall be disclosed. Those disclosures may be either narrative or summarized in a schedule and should clearly relate the cash and noncash aspects of transactions involving similar items. _____

(FASB ASC 230-10-50-3)

4. Examples of noncash investing and financing transactions are converting debt to equity; acquiring assets by assuming directly related liabilities, such as purchasing a building by incurring a mortgage to the seller; obtaining an asset by entering into a capital lease; obtaining a building or investment asset by receiving a gift; and exchanging noncash assets or liabilities for other noncash assets or liabilities. _____

(FASB ASC 230-10-50-4)

5. Some transactions are part cash and part noncash; only the cash portion should be reported in the statement of cash flows. _____

(FASB ASC 230-10-50-5)

6. If there are only a few such noncash transactions, it may be convenient to include them on the same page as the statement of cash flows. Otherwise, the transactions may be reported elsewhere in the financial statements, clearly referenced to the statement of cash flows. _____

(FASB ASC 230-10-50-6)

235 Notes to Financial Statements

1. Identify and describe significant accounting principles followed and methods of applying them that materially affect statements; disclosures should include principles and methods that involve
    a. Selection from acceptable alternatives _____
    b. Principles and methods peculiar to the company's industry _____
    c. Unusual or innovative applications of generally accepted accounting principles. _____

(FASB ASC 235-10-50-3)

2. Among others, common accounting policies are:
    a. Basis of consolidation _____
    b. Depreciation methods _____
    c. Amortization of intangibles _____
    d. Inventory pricing _____
    e. Accounting for recognition of profit on long-term construction-type contracts _____
    f. Recognition of revenue from franchising and leasing operation _____
    g. Use of estimates _____
    h. Cash equivalents _____
    i. Impairment _____
    j. Property _____
    k. Interperiod tax allocation. _____

(FASB ASC 235-10-50-4)

3. Accounting policies disclosures do not duplicate details presented elsewhere. It may be appropriate to refer to related details presented elsewhere in the financial statements. _____

(FASB ASC 235-10-50-5)

4. It is preferable to disclose significant accounting policies in a separate summary preceding the notes to financial statements, or as the initial note, under the same or a similar title. _____

(FASB ASC 235-10-50-6)

250 Accounting Changes and Error Corrections

Change in Accounting Principle

1. Nature and justification of change in accounting principle:

   a. The nature of and reasons for making the change, addressing preferability of the newly adopted principle. _____
   b. Descriptions of prior period items that have been restated. _____
   c. The effects of the change for both current period and prior period(s) being presented; specific quantification of the effects on income from continuing operations, net income, any other financial statement caption materially affected, and corresponding per-share amounts for each. _____
   d. The cumulative effect on retained earnings at the beginning of the earliest period's financial statements presented. _____
   e. As of the beginning of the earliest statement presented, the cumulative effect of the change in retained earnings or other components of equity or net assets in the statement of financial position. _____
   f. If ASC 250 requirement to restate prior periods is not adhered to, based on impracticability criterion, explain and provide details regarding method of accounting applied. _____
   g. When indirect effects of change in accounting principle are included, describe these effects and state the amounts recognized in the current reporting period, together with per-share amounts. If possible, also state the indirect effects of the change in each of the prior periods being presented. _____

(FASB ASC 250-10-50-1)

2. For interim reports after the date of adoption of a new accounting principle,

   a. the effect of the change on income from continuing operations, _____
   b. net income (or other appropriate captions of changes in the applicable net assets or performance indicator), and _____
   c. related per-share amounts for those post-change interim periods. _____

(FASB ASC 250-10-50-3)

Change in Accounting Estimate

3. For a change in accounting estimate, if the change affects several future periods (e.g., for change in useful lives of fixed assets), disclose the effect on income from continuing operations and net income of current period (and related per-share amounts). For a change in estimate not having material effect in the current period, but which is deemed likely to have material effects on later periods, describe the change. _____

(FASB ASC 250-10-50-4)

Change in Reporting Entity

4. For change in reporting entity, nature of change and reason for it; also, effect of change on income before extraordinary items, net income, and comprehensive income for all periods presented (also per-share amounts). For a change in entity not having material effect currently but anticipated to have such effect in later periods, the nature of the change and reason the change was made. _____

(FASB ASC 250-10-50-6)

Correction of an Error in Previously Issued Financial Statements

5. For the correction of an error, disclose that the previously issued statements have been reissued and the nature of the error in previously issued statements and the effect of its correction on each financial statement line item (only in period of discovery and correction), with per-share equivalents. Also, the cumulative effect on retained earnings or other appropriate components of equity or net assets. _____

(FASB ASC 250-10-50-7)

6. The effects (both gross and net of applicable income tax) of prior period adjustments on the net income of prior periods in the annual report for the year in which the adjustments are made and in interim reports issued during that year after the date of recording the adjustments. _____

(FASB ASC 250-10-50-8)

7. For single period only financial statements, indicate the effects of such restatement on the balance of retained earnings at the beginning of the period and on the net income of the immediately preceding period. For financial statements with more than one period presented, the effects for each of the periods included in the statements. Include the amounts of income tax applicable to the prior period adjustments. Disclosure of restatements in annual reports issued after the first such post-revision disclosure would ordinarily not be required. _____

(FASB ASC 250-10-50-9)

Error Corrections Related to Prior Interim Periods of the Current Fiscal Year

8. The effect on income from continuing operations, net income, and related per-share amounts for each prior interim period of the current fiscal year and income from continuing operations, net income, and related per-share amounts for each prior interim period restated in accordance with paragraph 250-10-45-26. _____

(FASB ASC 250-10-50-11)

260 Earnings per Share

1. Earnings per-share amounts for income from continuing operations and net income, shown on the face of income statement for all periods presented. _____

(FASB ASC 260-10-45-2)

2. If applicable, per-share amounts for discontinued operations, extraordinary items, and cumulative effect of an accounting change, presented either on face of income statement or in notes to financial statements. _____

(FASB ASC 260-10-45-3)

3. For each income statement presented
   a. Reconciliation of the numerators and the denominators of the basic and diluted per-share computations for income from continuing operations. _____
   b. Effect that has been given to preferred dividends in arriving at income available to common stockholders in computing basic EPS. _____
   c. Securities (including those issuable pursuant to contingent stock agreements) that could potentially dilute basic EPS in the future that were not included in the computation of diluted EPS because to do so would have been antidilutive for the period(s) presented. _____

(FASB ASC 260-10-50-1)

4. Amounts should be restated when stock dividends, splits, or reverses occur after close of period but before statements are issued with appropriate disclosure. _____

(FASB ASC 260-10-50-2)

270 Interim Financial Information

1. Provide, at a minimum, the captions and disclosures required when publicly traded entities report summarized interim financial information. These required disclosures are

    a. Sales or gross revenues, provision for income taxes, extraordinary items including related income tax effects, cumulative effect of a change in principle, net income, and comprehensive income. _____
    b. Basic and diluted earnings per share for each period presented. _____
    c. Seasonal revenues, costs, and expenses. _____
    d. Significant changes in income tax estimates or provisions. _____
    e. Disposal of a component of an entity and extraordinary, unusual, or infrequently occurring items. _____
    f. Contingencies. _____
    g. Changes in accounting principles or estimates. _____
    h. Significant changes in financial position. _____
    i. Information regarding reportable operating segments including provisions related to restatement of segment information in previously issued financial statements.

        (1) Revenues from external customers. _____
        (2) Intersegment revenues. _____
        (3) A measure of segment profit or loss. _____
        (4) Total assets for which there has been a material change from the amount disclosed in the last annual report. _____
        (5) A description of differences from the last annual report in the basis of segmentation or in the measurement of segment profit or loss. _____
        (6) A reconciliation of the total of the reportable segments' measures of profit or loss to the enterprise's consolidated pretax income, extraordinary items, discontinued operations. However, if, for example, an entity allocates items such as income taxes and extraordinary items to segments, the entity may choose to reconcile the total of the segments' measures of profit or loss to consolidated income after those items. Significant reconciling items shall be separately identified and described in that reconciliation. _____

    j. The following information regarding defined benefit pension plans and other defined benefit postretirement benefit plans, disclosed for interim statements that include an income statement:

        (1) The amount of the net periodic benefit cost recognized, for each period for which a statement of income is presented, separately showing the service cost component, interest cost component, expected return on plan assets for the period, gain or loss component, prior service cost or credit component, transition asset or obligation component, and gain or loss recognized due to a settlement or curtailment. _____
        (2) The total amount of the employer's contributions paid, and expected to be paid during the current fiscal year, if significantly different from amounts previously disclosed. Estimated contributions may be presented in the aggregate, combining contributions required by funding laws or regulations, discretionary contributions, and noncash contributions. _____

k. Information about the use of fair value to measure assets and liabilities recognized in the statement of financial position as required by ASC 820-10-50. ____
l. Information about derivative instruments required by ASC 815-10-50, 815-20-50, 815-30-50, and 815-35-50. ____
m. The information about fair value of financial instruments as required by Section 825-10-50. ____
n. The information about certain investments in debt and equity securities as required by Sections 320-10-50 and 942-320-50. ____
o. The information about other-than-temporary impairments as required by Sections 320-10-50, 325-20-50, and 958-320-50. ____
p. All of the following information about the credit quality of financing receivables and the allowance for credit losses determined in accordance with the provisions of Topic 310:
   (1) Nonaccrual and past-due financing receivables (see paragraphs 310-10-50-5A through 50-7B) ____
   (2) Allowance for credit losses related to financing receivables (see paragraphs 310-10-50-11A through 50-11C) ____
   (3) Impaired loans (see paragraphs 310-10-50-14A through 50-15) ____
   (4) Credit quality information related to financing receivables (see paragraphs 310-10-50-27 through 50-30) ____
   (5) Modifications of financing receivables (see paragraphs 310-10-50-31 through 50-34). ____
q. The gross information and net information required by paragraphs 210-20-50-1 through 50-6. ____
r. The information about changes in accumulated other comprehensive income required by ASC 220-10-45-14A and ASC 220-10-45-17 through 45-17B. ____
s. The carrying amount of foreclosed residential real estate (see 310-10-50-1) and the amount of loans in the process of foreclosure (see 310-10-50-35) ____

If summarized financial data are regularly reported on a quarterly basis, the foregoing information with respect to the current quarter and the current year to date or the last 12 months to date should be furnished together with comparable data for the preceding year.

(FASB ASC 270-10-50-1)

2. In the absence of a separate fourth quarter report or disclosure of the results (as outlined in the preceding paragraph) for that quarter in the annual report, disclose disposals of components of an entity and extraordinary, unusual, or infrequently occurring items recognized in the fourth quarter, as well as the aggregate effect of year-end adjustments that are material to the results of that quarter (see paragraphs 270-10-05-2 and 270-10-45-10) in the annual report in a note to the annual financial statements. If a publicly traded company that regularly reports interim information makes an accounting change during the fourth quarter of its fiscal year and does not report the data specified by the preceding paragraph in a separate fourth quarter report or in its annual report, make the disclosures about the effect of the accounting change on interim periods that are required by paragraphs 270-10-45-12 through 45-14 or by paragraph 250-10-45-15, as appropriate, in a note to the annual financial statements for the fiscal year in which the change is made. ____

(FASB ASC 270-10-50-2)

3. Disclosure of the impact of the financial results for interim periods of the matters discussed in paragraphs 270-10-45-12 through 45-16 and 270-10-50-5 through 50-6 is desirable for as many subsequent periods as necessary to keep the reader fully informed. There is a presumption that users of summarized interim financial data will have read the latest published annual report, including the financial disclosures required by generally accepted accounting principles (GAAP) and management's commentary concerning the annual financial results, and that the summarized interim data will be viewed in that context. In this connection, management is encouraged to provide commentary relating to the effects of significant events upon the interim financial results. _____

(FASB ASC 270-10-50-3)

4. Publicly traded companies are encouraged to publish balance sheet and cash flow data at interim dates since these data often assist users of the interim financial information in their understanding and interpretation of the income data reported. If condensed interim balance sheet information or cash flow data are not presented at interim reporting dates, significant changes since the last reporting period with respect to liquid assets, net working capital, long-term liabilities, or stockholders' equity shall be disclosed. _____

(FASB ASC 270-10-50-4)

5. Extraordinary items shall be disclosed separately and included in the determination of net income for the interim period in which they occur. In determining materiality, extraordinary items shall be related to the estimated income for the full fiscal year. In addition, matters such as unusual seasonal results, business combinations, and acquisitions by not-for-profit entities shall be disclosed to provide information needed for a proper understanding of interim financial reports. _____

(FASB ASC 270-10-50-5)

6. Contingencies and other uncertainties that could be expected to affect the fairness of presentation of financial data at an interim date shall be disclosed in interim reports in the same manner required for annual reports. Such disclosures shall be repeated in interim and annual reports until the contingencies have been removed, resolved, or have become immaterial. The significance of a contingency or uncertainty should be judged in relation to annual financial statements. Disclosures of such items shall include, but not be limited to, those matters that form the basis of a qualification of an independent auditor's report. _____

(FASB ASC 270-10-50-6)

7. The following may not represent all references to interim disclosure:

   a. For business combinations and combinations accounted for by not-for-profit entities, see Sections 805-10-50, 805-20-50, 805-30-50, 805-740-50, and 958-805-50. _____
   b. For compensation-related costs, see paragraphs 715-60-50-3 and 715-60-50-6 _____
   c. For disclosures required for entities with oil- and gas-producing activities, see paragraph 932-270-50-1. _____
   d. For disclosures related to prior interim periods of the current fiscal year, see paragraph 250-10-50-11. _____
   e. For fair value requirements, see Section 820-10-50. _____
   f. For guarantors, see Section 460-10-50. _____
   g. For pensions and other postretirement benefits, see paragraphs 715-20-50-6 through 50-7. _____
   h. For reportable segments, see paragraphs 280-10-50-39 and 280-10-55-16. _____
   i. For suspended well costs and interim reporting, see Section 932-235-50. _____

j. For applicability of disclosure requirements related to risks and uncertainties, see paragraph 275-10-15-3. ____

(FASB ASC 270-10-50-7)

275 Risks and Uncertainties

1. Nature of operations including description of major products, services, principal markets served locations, and relative importance of operations in various businesses and basis for determination of relative importance (e.g., sales volume, profits, etc.). Convey relative importance, but disclosures need not be quantified. ____

(FASB ASC 275-10-50-2)

2. Explanation that the preparation of financial statements requires the use of management's estimates. ____

(FASB ASC 275-10-50-4)

3. Significant estimates used in the determination of the carrying amounts of assets or liabilities or in the disclosure of gain or loss contingencies when, based on information known to management prior to issuance of the financial statements, it is at least reasonably possible that the effect on the financial statements of a condition or situation existing at the statement of financial position date for which an estimate has been made will change in the near term due to one or more future confirming events. (If the estimate involves a loss contingency covered by ASC 450, include an estimate of the possible loss or range of loss, or state such estimate cannot be made.) Indicate the nature of the uncertainty and that it is at least reasonably possible that a change in estimate may occur in the near term. ____

(FASB ASC 275-10-50-6 through 9)

4. Vulnerability because of concentrations in the volume of business with a particular customer, supplier, or lender; revenue from particular products or services; available sources of supply of materials, labor, or other inputs; and market or geographic area. (For concentrations of labor subject to collective bargaining agreements, disclose both the percentage of the labor force covered by a collective bargaining agreement and the percentage of the labor force covered by a collective bargaining agreement that will expire within one year. For concentrations of operations located outside of the entity's home country, disclose the carrying amounts of net assets and the geographic areas in which they are located.) ____

(FASB ASC 275-10-50-16 through 21)

280 Segment Reporting

1. General information on segments including
   a. Factors used to identify the enterprise's reportable segments, including the basis of organization (e.g., whether management has chosen to organize the enterprise around differences in products and services, geographic areas, regulatory environments, or a combination of factors and whether operating segments have been aggregated). ____
   b. Types of products and services from which each reportable segment derives its revenues. ____

(FASB ASC 280-10-50-21)

2. The following about each reportable segment if the specified amounts are included in the measure of segment profit or loss reviewed by the chief operating decision maker:

a. Revenues from external customers. _____
b. Revenues from transactions with other operating segments of the same enterprise. _____
c. Interest revenue. _____
d. Interest expense. _____
e. Depreciation, depletion, and amortization expense. _____
f. Unusual items. _____
g. Equity in the net income of investees accounted for by the equity method. _____
h. Income tax expense or benefit. _____
i. Extraordinary items. _____
j. Significant noncash items other than depreciation, depletion, and amortization expense. _____

(FASB ASC 280-10-50-22)

3. Interest revenue and interest expense included in reported segment profit or loss is intended to provide information about the financing activities of a segment. _____

(FASB ASC 280-10-50-23)

4. If a segment has no or only immaterial financial operations, no information about interest is required. For segments that are primarily a financial operation where interest revenue probably constitutes most of segment revenues and interest expense constitutes most of the difference between reported segment revenues and reported segment profit or loss, disclose interest revenue separately from interest expense. _____

(FASB ASC 280-10-50-24)

5. Disclose the following about each reportable segment if the specific amounts are included in the determination of segment assets reviewed by the chief operating decision maker:

a. The amount of investment in equity method investees. _____
b. Total expenditures for additions to long-lived assets other than financial instruments, long-term customer relationships of a financial institution, mortgage and other servicing rights, deferred policy acquisition costs, and deferred tax assets. _____

(FASB ASC 280-10-50-25)

6. If no asset information is provided for a reportable segment, disclose that fact and the reason. _____

(FASB ASC 280-10-50-26)

7. An explanation should be provided of the measurements of segment profit or loss and segment assets for each reportable segment; at a minimum, these shall include the following:

a. The basis of accounting for any transactions between reportable segments. _____
b. The nature of any differences between the measurements of the reportable segments' profits or losses and the company's consolidated income before income taxes, extraordinary items, discontinued operations, and the cumulative effect of changes in accounting principles (if not apparent from the reconciliations); for example, accounting policies and policies for allocation of centrally incurred costs that are necessary for an understanding of the reported segment information. _____
c. The nature of any differences between the measurements of the reportable segments' assets and the company's consolidated assets (if not apparent from the reconciliations); for example, accounting policies and policies for allocation of jointly used assets that are necessary for an understanding of the reported segment information. _____

d. The nature of any changes from prior periods in the measurement methods used to determine reported segment profit or loss and the effect, if any, of those changes on the measure of segment profit or loss. ____
e. The nature and effect of any asymmetrical allocations to segments; for example, an enterprise might allocate depreciation expense to a segment without allocating the related depreciable assets to that segment. ____

(FASB ASC 280-10-50-29)

8. Reconciliations of the totals of segment revenues, reported profit or loss, assets, and other significant items to corresponding company amounts, as follows:

   a. The total of the reportable segments' revenues to the enterprise's consolidated revenues. ____
   b. The total of the reportable segments' measures of profit or loss to the company's consolidated income before income taxes, extraordinary items, discontinued operations, and the cumulative effect of changes in accounting principles. ____
   c. The total of the reportable segments' assets to the company's consolidated assets. ____
   d. The total of the reportable segments' amounts for every other significant item of information disclosed to the corresponding consolidated amount. ____

(FASB ASC 280-10-50-30)

9. Identify and describe separately all significant reconciling items. ____

(FASB ASC 280-10-50-31)

10. For a public entity disclose all of the following about each reportable segment in condensed financial statements of interim periods:

   a. Revenues from external customers ____
   b. Intersegment revenues ____
   c. A measure of segment profit or loss ____
   d. Total assets for which there has been a material change from the amount disclosed in the last annual report ____
   e. A description of differences from the last annual report in the basis of segmentation or in the basis of measurement of segment profit or loss ____
   f. A reconciliation of the total of the reportable segments' measures of profit or loss to the public entity's consolidated income before income taxes, extraordinary items, and discontinued operations. However, if a public entity allocates items such as income taxes and extraordinary items to segments, the public entity may choose to reconcile the total of the segments' measures of profit or loss to consolidated income after those items. Significant reconciling items shall be separately identified and described in that reconciliation. ____

(FASB ASC 280-10-50-32)

11. Interim disclosures are required for the current quarter and year-to-date amounts. Paragraph 270-10-50-1 states that when summarized financial data are regularly reported on a quarterly basis, the information in the previous paragraph with respect to the current quarter and the current year to date or the last 12 months to date should be furnished together with comparable data for the preceding year. ____

(FASB ASC 280-10-50-33)

12. If revenues from transaction with a single external customer amount to ten percent or more of an enterprise's revenues, disclose that fact, the total amount of revenues from each such customer, and the identity of the segment or segments reporting the revenues. ____

(FASB ASC 280-10-50-42)

13. Depreciation and amortization expense for each reportable segment, when the chief operating decision maker evaluates the performance of its segments based on earnings before interest, taxes, depreciation, and amortization. _____

(FASB ASC 280-10-55-13)

ASSETS

310 Receivables

1. Basis of accounting for loans and trade receivables _____
2. Method used in determining the lower of cost or fair value of nonmortgage bonds held for sale _____
3. Classification and method of accounting for interest-only strips, loans, other receivables or retained interests in securitizations that can contractually be prepaid or otherwise settled in a way that the holder would not recover substantially all of its recorded investment _____
4. Methods for recognizing interest income on load and trade receivables. _____

(FASB ASC 310-10-50-2)

For loans and trade receivables:

5. Separately report each major category of loans and trade receivables either on the face of the statement of financial position or in the notes. _____

(FASB ASC 310-10-50-3)

6. State the allowance for doubtful accounts or credit losses and any unearned income, unamortized premiums or discounts, and any net unamortized deferred fees and costs. _____

(FASB ASC 310-10-50-4)

7. Except for credit card receivables, disclose the policy for charging off uncollectible trade accounts receivable that have a contractual maturity of one year or less **and** that arose from the sale of goods or services. _____

(FASB ASC 310-10-50-4A)

8. The carrying amount of financial instruments that serve as collateral for borrowings. (See also 860-30-50-1A) _____

(FASB ASC 310-10-50-5)

9. By class of financing receivable, with some exceptions (FASB ASC 310-10-50-5b) accounting policies for financing receivables, including policies related to nonaccrual status, for recording payments received on nonaccrual financing receivables, for resuming accrual of interest, and for determining past due or delinquent status. _____

(FASB ASC 310-10-50-6)

10. For nonaccrual and past due financing receivables as of each balance sheet date:
    a. State the recorded investment in loans (and trade receivables, if applicable on nonaccrual status) _____
    b. State the recorded investment in financing receivables past due 90 days or more and still accruing. _____

(FASB ASC 310-10-50-7)

11. Present an analysis of the age of the recorded investment in financing receivables. _____

(FASB ASC 310-10-50-7a)

12. Policies and methodology used to estimate liability for off-balance-sheet credit exposures and related charges for those credit exposures. _____

(FASB ASC 310-10-50-9)

13. The amount of foreclosed or repossessed assets, which can be included in the other assets category if the notes to the financial statements disclose the amount and the carrying amount of foreclosed residential real estate properties held at the reporting date as a result of obtaining physical possession as per 310-40-40-6 and 310-40-55-10A.[2] _____

(FASB ASC 310-10-50-11)

14. All of the following by portfolio segment:
    a. A description of the entity's accounting policies and methodology used to estimate the allowance for credit losses, including all of the following:
        (1) A description of the factors that influenced management's judgment, including both of the following:
            (a) Historical losses _____
            (b) Existing economic conditions. _____
        (2) A discussion of risk characteristics relevant to each portfolio segment _____
        (3) Identification of any changes to the entity's accounting policies or methodology from the prior period and the entity's rationale for the change. _____
    b. A description of the policy for charging off uncollectible financing receivables _____
    c. The activity in the allowance for credit losses for each period, including all of the following:
        (1) The balance in the allowance at the beginning and end of each period _____
        (2) Current period provision _____
        (3) Direct write-downs charged against the allowance _____
        (4) Recoveries of amounts previously charged off. _____
    d. The quantitative effect of changes identified in item (a)(3) on item (c)(2) _____
    e. The amount of any significant purchases of financing receivables during each reporting period _____
    f. The amount of any significant sales of financing receivables or reclassifications of financing receivables to held for sale during each reporting period _____
    g. The balance in the allowance for credit losses at the end of each period disaggregated on the basis of the entity's impairment method _____
    h. The recorded investment in financing receivables at the end of each period related to each balance in the allowance for credit losses, disaggregated on the basis of the entity's impairment methodology in the same manner as the disclosure in item (g). _____

(FASB ASC 310-50-11B)

15. To disaggregate the information required by items (g) and (h) above on the basis of the impairment methodology, separately disclose:
    a. Amounts collectively evaluated for impairment (determined under Subtopic 450-20) _____
    b. Amounts individually evaluated for impairment (determined under Section 310-10-35) _____

---

[2] The latter part of this requirement is based on guidance in ASU 2014-04. See the chapter on ASC 310 for effective dates and more information.

c. Amounts related to loans acquired with deteriorated credit quality (determined under Subtopic 310-30). _____

(FASB ASC 310-10-50-11C)

16. For each class of financing receivable, for loans that are impaired, disclose the accounting for and the amount of impaired loans. _____

(FASB ASC 310-10-50-14A)

17. For loans that meet the definition of an impaired loan by class of financing receivable:

    a. The recorded investment in the impaired loans and the amount for which there is a related allowance for credit losses, the amount of that allowance, and the amount of the investment for which there is no allowance for credit losses. _____
    b. The total unpaid principal balance of the impaired loans. _____
    c. The policy for recognizing interest income on impaired loans, including how cash receipts are recorded _____
    d. The average recorded investment in the impaired loans _____
    e. The related amount of interest income recognized during the time within that period that the loans were impaired _____
    f. The amount of interest income recognized using a cash-basis method of accounting during the time within that period that the loans were impaired, if practicable. _____
    g. The entity's policy for determining which loans the entity assesses for impairment _____
    h. The factors considered in determining that the loan is impaired. _____

(FASB ASC 310-10-50-15)

18. Disclose items in ASC 310-10-50-15 for impaired loans that have been charged off partially. _____

(FASB ASC 310-10-50-16)

19. Information that enables financial statement users to understand how and to what extent management monitors the credit quality of its financing receivables in an ongoing manner assess the quantitative and qualitative risks arising from the credit quality of its financing receivables. _____

(FASB ASC 310-10-50-28)

20. Provide quantitative and qualitative information by class about credit quality of financing receivables, including a description of the credit quality indicator, the recorded investment in financing receivables by credit quality indicator, and for each credit quality indicator, the date or range of dates in which the information was updated for that indicator. _____

(FASB ASC 310-10-50-29)

21. If the entity discloses internal risk ratings, qualitative information on how those internal risk ratings relate to the likelihood of loss. _____

(FASB ASC 310-10-50-30)

Modifications

22. For troubled debt restructurings of financing receivables that occurred during the period:
    a. By class of financing receivable, qualitative and quantitative information, including how the financing receivables were modified and the financial effects of the modifications ____
    b. By portfolio segment, qualitative information about how such modifications are factored into the determination of the allowance for credit losses. ____

(FASB ASC 310-10-50-33)

23. For financing receivables modified as troubled debt restructurings within the previous 12 months and for which there was a payment default during the period:
    a. By class of financing receivable, qualitative, and quantitative information about those defaulted financing receivables, including types of financing receivables that defaulted and the amount that defaulted. ____
    b. By portfolio segment, qualitative information about how such defaults are factored into the determination of the allowance for credit losses. ____

(FASB ASC 310-10-50-34)

24. The recorded investment in consumer mortgage loans secured by residential real estate properties where formal disclosure procedures are in process.[3] ____

(FASB ASC 310-10-50-35)

310-20 Nonrefundable Fees and Other Costs

1. The method for recognizing interest income on trade and loan receivables, including a statement about the entity's policy for treatment of related fees and costs, including the method of amortizing net deferred fees or costs. ____

(FASB ASC 310-20-50-1)

2. If prepayments are anticipated in applying the interest method, the significant assumptions underlying the prepayment estimates. ____

(FASB ASC 310-20-50-2)

3. The unamortized net fees and costs are reported as a part of each loan category. Additional disclosures such as unamortized net fees and costs may be included in the footnotes to the financial statements if the lender believes that such information is useful to the users of financial statements. ____

(FASB ASC 310-20-50-3)

4. For credit card fees, the accounting policy for credit card fees, net amount capitalized at the balance sheet date, and the amortization period(s). ____

(FASB ASC 310-20-50-4

310-30 Loans and Debt Securities Acquired with Deteriorated Credit Quality

1. For certain loans or debt securities acquired with deteriorated credit quality, the following disclosures are required:

---

[3] This requirement is based on guidance on ASU 2014-04. For more information and effective dates, see the chapter on ASC 310.

a. How prepayments on loans receivable are considered in the determination of contractual cash flows and cash flows expected to be collected. _____

(FASB ASC 310-30-50-1)

b. For loans acquired through purchase, including in a business combination, separately for loans accounted for as debt securities and for those not accounted for as debt securities

(1) The outstanding balance (undiscounted cash flows owed and the carrying amount at the beginning and end of the period). _____
(2) The amount of accretable yield at the beginning of the period to the amount of accretable yield at the end of the period, reconciled for additions, accretion, disposals of loans, and reclassifications to or from nonaccretable difference during the period. _____
(3) For loans acquired in the current period

(a) The contractually required payments receivable. _____
(b) The cash flows expected to be collected. _____
(c) The fair value at acquisition. _____
(d) The carrying amount of any acquired loans in nonaccrual status. _____

(4) The carrying amount of all loans in a nonaccrual status. _____
(5) For loans not accounted for as debt securities

(a) The amount of any expense recognized for impairment. _____
(b) The amount of any reduction in a valuation allowance for losses that results from an increase in cash flows previously expected to be collected. _____
(c) The amount of the allowance for uncollectible loans at the beginning and the end of the period. _____

(FASB ASC 310-30-50-2)

310-40 Troubled Debt Restructurings by Creditors

1. In the body of the financial statements or in the accompanying notes, the amount of commitments, if any, to lend additional funds to debtors owing receivables whose terms have been modified in a troubled debt restructuring. _____

(FASB ASC 310-40-50-1)

2. If both of the following conditions exist, it is not necessary to disclose information about an impaired loan that has been restructured in a troubled debt restructuring involving a modification of terms need not be included in the disclosures required by paragraphs 310-10-50-15(a) and 310-10-50-15(c) in years after the restructuring:

a. The restructuring agreement specifies an interest rate equal to or greater than the rate that the creditor was willing to accept at the time of the restructuring for a new loan with comparable risk. _____
b. The loan is not impaired based on the terms specified by the restructuring agreement. _____

(FASB ASC 310-40-50-2)

3. Apply consistently the exception in ASC 310-40-50-2 for paragraph 310-10-50-15(a) and 310-10-50-15(c) to all loans restructured in a troubled debt restructuring that meet the criteria in that paragraph. _____

(FASB ASC 310-40-50-3)

4. For a loan whose terms are modified in a troubled debt restructuring and is already written and the measure of the restructured loan is equal to or greater than the recorded investment, no impairment would be recognized under ASC 310-40. Disclose the amount of the write-down and the recorded investment in the year of the write-down, but not in later years if the two criteria of paragraph 310-40-50-2 are met. _____

(FASB ASC 310-40-50-4)

5. For a loan restructured in a troubled debt restructuring into two (or more) loan agreements, consider the restructured loans separately when assessing the applicability of the disclosures in paragraph 310-10-50-15 in years after the restructuring. _____

(FASB ASC 310-40-50-5)

320 Investments—Debt and Equity

1. The disclosures for investments in debt and equity securities are required for all interim and annual periods. In determining whether disclosure for a particular security type is necessary and whether it is necessary to further separate a particular security type into greater detail, consider (shared) activity or business sector, vintage, geographic concentration, credit quality, and economic characteristic. _____

(FASB ASC 320-10-50-1A and B)

2. For securities classified as available-for-sale, disclose by major security type as of each date for which a statement of financial position is presented.
   a. The amortized cost basis. _____
   b. Aggregate fair value. _____
   c. Total other-than-temporary impairment recognized in accumulated other comprehensive income. _____
   d. Total gains for securities with net gains in accumulated other comprehensive income. _____
   e. Total losses for securities with net losses in accumulated other comprehensive income. _____

(FASB ASC 320-10-50-2)

3. Combined maturity information in appropriate groupings. _____

(FASB ASC 320-10-50-3)

4. For securities classified as held-to-maturity, by major security type as of each date for which a statement of financial position is presented
   a. Amortized cost basis. _____
   b. Aggregate fair value. _____
   c. Gross unrecognized holding gains. _____
   d. Gross unrecognized holding losses. _____
   e. Net carrying amount. _____
   f. Total OTTI recognized in AOCI. _____
   g. Gross gains and losses in AOCI for any derivatives that hedged the forecasted acquisition of the held-to-maturity securities. _____

h. Information about the contractual maturities of those securities as of the date of the most recent statement of financial position presented. (Maturity information may be combined in appropriate groupings. In complying with this requirement, financial institutions [see paragraph 942-320-50-1] shall disclose the fair value and the net carrying amount (if different from fair value) of debt securities on the basis of at least the following four maturity groupings:

1. Within one year
2. After one year through five years
3. After 5 years through 10 years
4. After 10 years).

May separately disclose securities not due at a single maturity date, such as mortgage-backed securities. If allocated, disclose the basis for allocation. ____

(FASB ASC 320-10-50-5)

5. For SEC reporting—Substantial post–statement of financial position market decline.

Impairment of Securities

6. For all investments for which there is an unrealized loss where impairment has not been recognized because the loss is not considered "other than temporary"

   a. Quantitative disclosure in tabular form and aggregated by category of investment under ASC 320 and ASC 958-320, and cost-method investments, as of the date of each statement of financial position presented. ____

   NOTE: *The disclosures in (1) and (2) below are to be segregated by those investments that have been in a continuous unrealized loss position for less than 12 months and those that have been in a continuous unrealized loss position for 12 months or longer.*

   (1) The aggregate related fair value of investments with unrealized losses. ____
   (2) The aggregate amount of unrealized losses. ____

   b. A narrative as of the date of the most recent statement of financial position that provides sufficient information to enable the reader of the financial statements to understand the disclosures in a. above, as well as both the positive and negative information that the investor considered in reaching the conclusion that the impairment is not other than temporary. ____

   NOTE: *These disclosures may be aggregated by investment category; however, individually significant unrealized losses should not be aggregated.*

   Examples of relevant information that could be included in this narrative are

   - The nature of the investments
   - The causes(s) of the impairment(s)
   - The number of investment positions in an unrealized loss position
   - The severity and duration of the impairment(s)

   c. Other evidence considered by the investor in concluding that the impairment is not other than temporary (e.g., reports from industry analysts, sector credit ratings, volatility data regarding the fair value of the security, and/or any other relevant information that the investor considered). ____

(FASB ASC 320-10-50-6 and 7)

7. The reference point for determining how long an investment has been in a continuous unrealized loss position is the balance sheet date of the reporting period in which the impairment is identified. For entities that do not prepare interim financial information, the reference point is the annual balance sheet date of the period during which the impairment was identified. The continuous unrealized loss position ceases upon either of the following:

   a. The recognition of the total amount by which amortized cost basis exceeds fair value as an other-than-temporary impairment in earnings _____
   b. The investor becoming aware of a recovery of fair value up to (or beyond) the amortized cost basis of the investment during the period. _____

(FASB ASC 320-10-5-8)

8. For interim and annual periods in which an other-than-temporary impairment of a debt security is recognized and only the amount related to a credit loss was recognized in earnings, an entity shall disclose by major security type, the methodology and significant inputs used to measure the amount related to credit loss. Examples of significant inputs include, but are not limited to, all of the following:

   a. Performance indicators of the underlying assets in the security, including all of the following:

      (1) Default rates
      (2) Delinquency rates
      (3) Percentage of nonperforming assets _____

   b. Loan-to-collateral-value ratios _____
   c. Third-party guarantees _____
   d. Current levels of subordination _____
   e. Vintage _____
   f. Geographic concentration _____
   g. Credit ratings. _____

(FASB ASC 320-10-5-8A)

9. Disclose a tabular rollforward of the amount related to credit losses recognized in earnings in accordance with paragraph 320-10-35-34D, which include at a minimum:

   a. The beginning balance of the amount related to credit losses on debt securities held by the entity at the beginning of the period for which a portion of an other-than-temporary impairment was recognized in other comprehensive income _____
   b. Additions for the amount related to the credit loss for which an other-than-temporary impairment was not previously recognized _____
   c. Reductions for securities sold during the period (realized) _____
   d. Reductions for securities for which the amount previously recognized in other comprehensive income was recognized in earnings because the entity intends to sell the security or more likely than not will be required to sell the security before recovery of its amortized cost basis _____
   e. If the entity does not intend to sell the security and it is not more likely than not that the entity will be required to sell the security before recovery of its amortized cost basis, additional increases to the amount related to the credit loss for which an other-than-temporary impairment was previously recognized _____
   f. Reductions for increases in cash flows expected to be collected that are recognized over the remaining life of the security (see paragraph 320-10-35-35) _____

g. The ending balance of the amount related to credit losses on debt securities held by the entity at the end of the period for which a portion of an other-than-temporary impairment was recognized in other comprehensive income. _____

(FASB ASC 320-10-50-8B)

10. For sales, transfers, and related matters that occurred during the period:

    a. The proceeds from sales of available-for-sale securities and the gross realized gains and gross realized losses that have been included in earnings as a result of those sales. _____
    b. The basis on which the cost of a security sold or the amount reclassified out of AOCI into earnings was determined. _____
    c. The gross gains and gross losses included in earnings from transfers of securities from the available-for-sale category into the trading category. _____
    d. The amount of the net unrealized holding gains or losses on available-for-sale securities for the period that are included in AOCI and the amount of gains and losses reclassified out of AOCI into earnings for the period. _____
    e. The portion of trading gains and losses for the period that relates to trading securities still held at the reporting date. _____

(FASB ASC 320-10-50-9)

11. For any sales/transfers from held-to-maturity classification, disclose

    a. Net carrying amount. _____
    b. Net gain or loss in AOCI for any derivative that hedged the forecasted acquisition of the held-to-maturity security. _____
    c. Realized or unrealized gain or loss. _____
    d. Circumstances leading to decision to sell or transfer the security. (These transfers should be rare. See ASC 320-10-25-14 for the conditions under which sales of debt securities may be considered as maturities.) _____

(FASB ASC 320-10-50-10 and 11)

323 Investments—Equity Method and Joint Ventures

1. If the investor has more than one investment in common stock, disclosures wholly or partly on a combined basis may be appropriate. Consider the significance of an investment to the investor's financial position and results of operations. _____

(FASB ASC 323-10-50-2)

2. Name of each investee and the percentage of ownership of common stock. _____
3. Accounting policies with respect to each of the investments. _____
4. Difference between the carrying amount for each investment and its underlying equity in the investee's net assets and the accounting treatment of the difference between these amounts. _____
5. For those investments which have a quoted market price, the aggregate value of each investment. _____
6. If investments in corporate joint ventures or other investments accounted for under the equity method are considered to have a material effect on the investor's financial position and operating results, summarized data for the investor's assets, liabilities, and results of operations. _____
7. If potential conversion of convertible securities and exercise of options and warrants would have material effects on the investor's percentage of the investee. _____

(FASB ASC 323-10-50-3)

323-740 Investments—Equity Method and Joint Ventures—Income Taxes

1. A reporting entity with an investment in a Qualified Affordable Housing Project should disclose information that helps investors understand the nature of the investment and effect of the measurement of its investment and related tax credits on financial position and results of operations. These disclosures may include:

   a. The amount of tax benefits recognized during the year _____
   b. The balance of the investment. _____
   c. For those investments accounted for using the proportional amortization method, the amount recorded as a component of income tax expense or benefit. _____
   d. For those investments accounted for using the equity method, the investment income or loss included in pretax income. _____
   e. Any commitments or contingent commitments. _____
   f. Amount and nature of impairment losses from the forfeiture or ineligibility of tax credits. _____

(ASC 323-740-50-1 and 50-2)[4]

325 Investments—Other

Cost Method Investments

1. For investments valued using the cost method, as of the date of each statement of financial position presented in the annual financial statements

   a. The aggregate carrying amount of all investments valued using the cost method. _____
   b. The aggregate carrying amount of cost-method investments not evaluated for impairment by the investor. _____
   c. The fact that the fair value of a cost-method investment is not estimated by management if no events or changes in circumstances have been identified that potentially would have a significant adverse effect on the investment's fair value, and any of the following:

      (1) The investor determined that it is not practicable to estimate the fair value of the investment, or _____
      (2) The investor is exempt from estimating fair value. _____
      (3) The entity is exempt from estimating interim fair value because it does not meet the FASB ASC definition of a publicly traded company. _____

(FASB ASC 325-20-50-1)

Investments in Insurance Contracts

2. If a policyholder, contractual restrictions on the ability to surrender a policy. _____

(FASB ASC 325-30-50-1)

3. Accounting policy for life settlement contracts including the classification of cash receipts and cash disbursements in statement of cash flows. _____

(FASB ASC 325-30-50-2)

[4] These disclosures are required by ASU 2014-01. See the Technical Alert in the chapter on ASC 323 for effective date and other information.

4. All of the following for life settlement contracts accounted for under the investment method based on the remaining life expectancy for each of the first five succeeding years from the date of the statement of financial position and thereafter, as well as in the aggregate: the number of life settlement contracts and their carrying value and the face value of underlying life insurance policies. _____

(FASB ASC 325-30-50-4)

5. As of the date of the most recent statement of financial position, the life insurance premiums anticipated to be paid for each of the five succeeding fiscal years in order to keep the life settlement contracts in force. _____

(FASB ASC 325-30-50-5)

6. The nature of new or updated information that causes the investor to change its expectations on the timing of the realization of proceeds from the investments in life settlement contracts. Include the information and the related effect on the timing of the realization of proceeds from the life settlement contracts. _____

(FASB ASC 325-30-50-6)

7. The method and significant assumptions used to estimate the fair value of investments in life settlement contracts, including any mortality assumptions. _____

(FASB ASC 325-30-50-7)

8. For life settlement contracts accounted for under the fair value method based on remaining life expectancy for each of the first five succeeding years from the date of the statement of financial position and thereafter, as well as in the aggregate: the number and carrying value of life settlement contracts and the face value (death benefits) of the life insurance policies underlying the contracts. _____

(FASB ASC 325-30-50-8)

9. The reasons for changes in its expectation of the timing of the realization of the investments in life settlement contracts. _____

(FASB ASC 325-30-50-9)

10. For each reporting period presented in the income statement, the gains or losses recognized during the period on investments sold during the period and the unrealized gains or losses recognized during the period on investments that are still held at the date of the statement of financial position. _____

(FASB ASC 325-30-50-10)

330 Inventory

1. Change in basis of stating inventories and its effect. _____

(FASB ASC 330-10-50-1)

2. Lower of cost or market "losses," if material. _____

(FASB ASC 330-10-50-2)

3. Goods stated above cost. _____

(FASB ASC 330-10-50-3)

4. Inventories stated at sales price. _____

(FASB ASC 330-10-50-4)

5. Amount of net losses on firm purchase commitments accrued under 330-10-35-1. _____

(FASB ASC 330-10-50-5)

340 Other Assets and Deferred Costs

340-20 Capitalized Advertising Costs

1.
   a. The accounting policy selected from the two alternatives in paragraph 720-35-25-1 for reporting advertising, indicating whether such costs are expensed as incurred or the first time the advertising takes place ____
   b. A description of the direct-response advertising reported as assets (if any), the accounting policy for it, and the amortization method and period ____
   c. The total amount charged to advertising expense for each income statement presented, with separate disclosure of amounts, if any, representing a write-down to net realizable value ____
   d. The total amount of advertising reported as assets in each balance sheet presented. ____

(FASB ASC 340-20-50-1)

340-30 Insurance Contracts That Do Not Transfer Insurance Risk

1. A description of the contracts accounted for as deposits and the separate amounts of total deposit assets and total deposit liabilities reported in the statement of financial position. ____

(FASB ASC 340-30-50-1)

2. Insurance entities—the changes in the recorded amount of the deposit arising from an insurance or reinsurance contract that transfers only significant underwriting risk. ____

(FASB ASC 340-30-50-2)

350 Intangibles—Goodwill and Other

350-20 Goodwill

1. For goodwill, a reconciliation of changes in the carrying amount during the period, showing separately
   a. The gross amount and accumulated impairment losses at the beginning of the period. ____
   b. Additional goodwill recognized during the period, except goodwill that is included in a disposal group that, upon acquisition, meets the criteria in ASC 360 to be classified as held for sale. ____
   c. Adjustments resulting from the subsequent recognition of deferred tax assets during the period in accordance with ASC 805-740. ____
   d. Goodwill included in a disposal group classified as held for sale in accordance with 360-10-45-9 and goodwill derecognized during the period without having previously been reported in a disposal group classified as held for sale. ____
   e. Impairment losses recognized during the period. ____
   f. Net foreign exchange differences arising during the period. ____
   g. Any other changes in carrying amounts during the period. ____
   h. The gross amount and accumulated impairment losses at the end of the period. ____

   For entities that report segment information in accordance with Topic 280, provide the above information about goodwill in total and for each reportable segment and disclose any significant changes in the allocation of goodwill by reportable segment. If any portion of goodwill has not yet been allocated to a reporting unit at the date the financial statements are issued, disclose that unallocated amount and the reasons for not allocating that amount.

(FASB ASC 350-20-50-1)

2. Goodwill impairment losses recognized during the period

   a. The facts and circumstances causing the impairment. ____
   b. The amount of the impairment loss and the method of determining fair value of the associated reporting unit (whether based on quoted market prices; prices of comparable businesses; or present value or other valuation techniques; or a combination of these methods). ____
   c. If the amount recognized is an estimate that has not yet been finalized, that fact and the reasons why the estimate is not yet complete. ____

(FASB ASC 350-20-50-2)

3. The quantitative disclosures about significant unobservable inputs used in fair value measurements categorized within Level 3 of the fair value hierarchy required by paragraph 820-10-50-2(bbb) are not required for fair value measurements related to the financial accounting and reporting for goodwill after its initial recognition in a business combination. ____

(FASB ASC 350-20-50-3)

Accounting Alternative[5]

4. For those entities who choose the accounting alternative,

   a. For any addition to goodwill for each period for which a statement of financial position is presented:

      i. Amount assigned to goodwill and the weighted average amortization period in total and by major business combination or by reorganization event that results in fresh-start reporting. ____

(FASB ASC 350-20-50-4)

   b. For each period for which a statement of financial position is presented:

      i. The gross carrying amount of:

         a) Goodwill ____
         b) Accumulated amortization ____
         c) Accumulated impairment loss ____

      ii. Aggregate amortization expense ____
      iii. Goodwill in a disposal group classified as held for sale ____
      iv. Goodwill recognized during the period without having previously been reported in a disposal group classified as held for sale ____

(FASB ASC 350-20-50-5)

   c. For each goodwill impairment loss:

      i. Description of the facts and circumstances leading to the impairment ____
      ii. Amount of the loss and how the fair value of the entity or reporting unit was determined. ____
      iii. Where the impairment loss is included in the income statement amount, ____
      iv. Method used to allocate the loss to the individual amortizable units of goodwill ____

(FASB ASC 350-20-50-6)

---

[5] ASC 350-20-50-4 through 50-7 are included by ASU 2014-02, a consensus of the Private Company Council. See the technical alert in the chapter on ASC 350 for information on the entities eligible for the "accounting alternative" and the effective date.

d. Quantitative disclosures about significant unobservable inputs used in fair value measurements categorized in level 3 required by 820-10-50-2 (bbb) are not required for fair value measurements related to the financial accounting and reporting for goodwill after its initial recognition in a business combination. _____

(FASB ASC 350-20-50-7)

350-30 General Intangibles Other Than Goodwill

1. For each major class of intangible asset, for each period-end for which a statement of financial position is presented:
   a. For intangible assets subject to amortization, all of the following:
      (1) The total amount assigned and the amount assigned to any major intangible asset class _____
      (2) The amount of any significant residual value, in total and by major intangible asset class _____
      (3) The weighted-average amortization period, in total and by major intangible asset class. _____

(FASB ASC 350-30-50-1a)

   b. For intangible assets not subject to amortization, the total carrying amount and the carrying amount for each major intangible asset class. _____

(FASB ASC 350-30-50-1b)

   c. The amount of research and development assets acquired in a transaction other than a business combination or an acquisition by a not-for-profit entity and written off in the period and the line item in the income statement in which the amounts written off are aggregated. _____

(FASB ASC 350-30-50-1c)

   d. For intangible assets with renewal or extension terms, the weighted-average period before the next renewal or extension (both explicit and implicit), by major intangible asset class.

(FASB ASC 350-30-50-1d)

2.
   a. Gross carrying amount and accumulated amortization, in total and by major class of intangible asset. _____
   b. Amortization expense for the period. _____
   c. Estimated aggregate amortization expenses for each of the five succeeding fiscal years as of the date of the latest statement of financial position presented. _____

(FASB ASC 350-30-50-2a)

3. For intangible asset not subject to amortization, the total carrying amount and the carrying amount for each major intangible asset class. _____

(FASB ASC 350-30-50-2b)

4. The entity's accounting policy on the treatment of costs incurred to renew or extend the term of a recognized intangible asset. _____

(FASB ASC 350-30-50-2c)

5. The entity's accounting policy on the treatment of costs incurred to renew or extend the term of a recognized intangible asset. _____

(FASB ASC 350-30-50-6)

6. For intangible assets that have been renewed or extended in the period for which the statement of financial position is presented
   (1) For entities that capitalize renewal or extension costs, the total amount of costs incurred in the period to renew or extend the term of a recognized intangible asset, by major intangible asset class. _____
   (2) The weighted-average period prior to the next renewal or extension (both explicit and implicit), by major intangible asset class. _____

(FASB ASC 350-30-50-2d)

7. For each impairment loss recognized related to an intangible asset, the following disclosures are to be made in financial statements that include the period the loss is recognized:
   a. A description of the impaired intangible asset and the facts and circumstances that caused the impairment. _____
   b. The amount of the impairment loss and the method used to determine fair value. _____
   c. The caption of the income statement in which it is included. _____
   d. If applicable, the segment in which the impaired intangible asset is reported under Topic 280. _____

(FASB ASC 350-30-50-3)

8. A nonpublic entity is not required to disclose the quantitative information about significant unobservable inputs used in fair value measurements categorized within Level 3 of the fair value hierarchy required by paragraph 820-10-50-2(bbb) that relate to the financial accounting and reporting for an indefinite-lived intangible asset after its initial recognition. _____

(FASB ASC 350-30-50-3A)

9. For a recognized intangible asset, information that enables users of financial statements to assess the extent to which the expected future cash flows associated with the asset are affected by the entity's intent and/or ability to renew or extend the arrangement. _____

(FASB ASC 350-30-50-4)

360 Property, Plant, and Equipment

1. Depreciation expense for the period _____
2. Balances of major classes of depreciable assets, by nature or function, at the balance sheet date _____
3. Accumulated depreciation, either by major classes of depreciable assets or in total, at the balance sheet date _____
4. A general description of the method or methods used in computing depreciation with respect to major classes of depreciable assets. _____

(FASB ASC 360-10-50-1)

5. In the period in which an impairment loss is incurred:
   a. A description of the impaired long-lived asset (asset group) and the facts and circumstances leading to the impairment _____
   b. If not separately presented on the face of the statement, the amount of the impairment loss and the caption in the income statement or the statement of activities that includes that loss _____
   c. The method or methods for determining fair value (whether based on a quoted market price, prices for similar assets, or another valuation technique) _____

d. If applicable, the segment in which the impaired long-lived asset (asset group) is reported under Topic 280. _____

(FASB ASC 360-10-50-2)

LIABILITIES

405-40 Obligations Resulting from Joint and Several Liability Arrangements

1. About each obligation, or each group of similar obligations, resulting from joint and several liability arrangements for which the total amount under the arrangement is fixed at the reporting date, the nature of the arrangement (including how the liability arose, the relationship with other co-obligors, terms and conditions of the arrangement); the total outstanding amount under the arrangement (not reduced by the effect of any amounts that may be recoverable from other entities); the carrying amount of the liability and the carrying amount of any receivable recognized; the nature of any recourse provisions that would enable recovery from other entities of the amounts paid, including any limitations on the amounts that might be recovered; in the period the liability is initially recognized and measured or in a period the measurement changes significantly, the corresponding entry and where the entry was recorded in the financial statements. _____

(FASB ASC 405-40-50-2)

2. The disclosure requirements in this Section are incremental to related party disclosures required. _____

(FASB ASC 405-40-50-2)

410 Asset Retirement and Environmental Obligations

Asset Retirement Obligations

1. General description of asset retirement obligations and the related long-lived assets. _____
2. Fair value of assets, if any, that are legally restricted to satisfy the liability. _____
3. Reconciliation of the beginning and ending aggregate carrying amount of the liability separately, whenever there is a significant change in any of these components during the reporting period, showing the changes resulting from

   a. Additional liability incurred during the current period. _____
   b. Settlements of the liability during the current period. _____
   c. Accretion expense. _____
   d. Revisions in estimated cash flows. _____

(FASB ASC 410-20-50-1)

4. If the fair value of an asset retirement obligation cannot be reasonably estimated, that fact and the reasons therefor shall be disclosed. _____

(FASB ASC 410-20-50-2)

Environmental Obligations

5. Whether the accrual for environmental remediation liabilities is measured on a discounted basis. If an entity utilizes present-value measurement techniques, additional disclosures are appropriate. See ASC 410-30-50-7. _____

(FASB ASC 410-30-50-4)

6. With respect to recorded accruals for environmental remediation loss contingencies and assets for third-party recoveries related to environmental remediation obligations, disclose if any portion of the accrued obligation is discounted, the undiscounted amount of the obligation, and the discount rate used in the present-value determinations. _____

(FASB ASC 410-30-50-7)

7. May include a contingency conclusion that addresses the estimated total unrecognized exposure to environmental remediation and other loss contingencies. _____

(FASB ASC 410-30-50-14)

8. Optionally, a description of the general applicability and impact of environmental laws and regulations upon the business and how the laws and regulations may give rise to loss contingencies for future environmental remediation. _____

(FASB ASC 410-30-50-17)

420 Exit or Disposal Cost Obligations

1. All of the following information shall be disclosed in notes to financial statements that include the period in which an exit or disposal activity is initiated and any subsequent period until the activity is completed:

   a. A description of the exit or disposal activity, including the facts and circumstances leading to the expected activity and the expected completion date _____
   b. For each major type of cost associated with the activity (for example, onetime employee termination benefits, contract termination costs, and other associated costs), both of the following shall be disclosed:

      (1) The total amount expected to be incurred in connection with the activity, the amount incurred in the period, and the cumulative amount incurred to date _____
      (2) A reconciliation of the beginning and ending liability balances showing separately the changes during the period attributable to costs incurred and charged to expense, costs paid or otherwise settled, and any adjustments to the liability with an explanation of the reason(s) why. _____

   c. Line item(s) in the income statement or the statement of activities in which the costs in b. are aggregated. _____
   d. For each reportable segment, as defined in Subtopic 280-10, the total amount of costs expected to be incurred in connection with the activity, the amount incurred in the period, and the cumulative amount incurred to date, net of any adjustments to the liability with an explanation of the reason(s) why. _____
   e. If a liability for a cost associated with the activity is not recognized because fair value cannot be reasonably estimated, that fact and the reasons why. _____

(FASB ASC 420-10-50-1)

440 Commitments

1. All of the following:

   a. Unused letters of credit _____
   b. Long-term leases _____
   c. Assets pledged as security for loans _____
   d. Pension plans _____
   e. The existence of cumulative preferred stock dividends in arrears _____

f. Commitments, including a commitment for plant acquisition, and obligations to reduce debts, maintain working capital, and restrict dividends. _____

(FASB ASC 440-10-50-1)

2. Unconditional purchase obligations are to be disclosed in accordance with FASB ASC 440-10-50-4 (if not recorded on the statement of financial position) or FASB ASC 440-10-50-6 (if recorded on the statement of financial position), if all the following criteria are met:

   a. It is noncancelable, or cancelable only

      (1) Upon the occurrence of some remote contingency _____
      (2) With the permission of the other party _____
      (3) If a replacement agreement is signed between the same parties _____
      (4) Upon payment of a penalty in an amount such that continuation of the agreement appears reasonably assured; _____

   b. It is negotiated as part of a supplier's product financing arrangement for the facilities that will provide the contracted goods or services or for costs related to those goods or services (e.g., carrying costs for contracted goods); and _____
   c. It has a remaining term in excess of one year. _____

(FASB ASC 440-10-50-2)

3. If the obligation meets the criteria of FASB ASC 440-10-50-2 and is not recorded on the statement of financial position, then the following footnote disclosures are required:

   a. The nature and term of the obligation(s). _____
   b. The amount of the fixed and determinable portion of the obligation(s) at the statement of financial position date in the aggregate and for each of the next five years, if determinable. _____
   c. The nature of any variable components of the obligation(s). _____
   d. The amounts purchased under the obligation(s) (as in take-or-pay or through-put contracts) for each period for which an income statement is presented. _____

(FASB ASC 440-10-50-4)

4. If the obligation fulfills the criteria in FASB ASC 440-10-50-2 and is recorded on the statement of financial position, disclose the aggregate amount of payments to be made for each of the five years following the date of the balance sheet. _____

(FASB ASC 440-10-50-6)

450 Contingencies

450-20 Loss Contingencies

1. If necessary to avoid misleading statements, the nature of the loss accrual and the amount accrued. _____

(FASB ASC 450-20-50-1)

2. If prior to issuance of financial statements, management has an indication that it is at least reasonably possible that a change in an entity's estimate of its probable liability could occur in the near term, disclose that information. (See FASB ASC 275-10-50- 8 and 9). _____

(FASB ASC 450-20-50-2)

3. Disclose the contingency if there is at least a reasonable possibility that a loss or an additional loss may have been incurred and the contingency does not meet the criteria for accrual or an exposure to loss exists in excess of the amount accrued. _____

(FASB ASC 450-20-50-3)

4. When accruals are not made because probable loss could not be estimated, describe
   a. The nature of the contingency _____
   b. Provide an estimate of the possible loss or range of loss or a statement that such an estimate cannot be made. _____

(FASB ASC 450-20-50-4)

5. Disclosure is preferable to accrual when a reasonable estimate of loss cannot be made or it is reasonably possible that a loss has occurred. _____

(FASB ASC 450-20-50-5)

6. Describe the nature of the loss and an estimate of the range of loss for unasserted claims for which it is both probable that a claim will be asserted, and reasonably possible that an unfavorable outcome will result. _____

(FASB ASC 450-20-50-6)

7. Disclose events occurring after the date of the statement of financial position but before those financial statements are issued that may give rise to a loss contingency, including the nature of the loss or loss contingency and an estimate of the possible loss or range of loss, or a statement that an estimate cannot be made. _____

(FASB ASC 450-20-50-9 through 10)

450-30 Gain Contingencies

1. Gain contingencies, if described such that the likelihood of realization is not overstated. _____

(FASB ASC 450-30-50-1)

460 Guarantees

1. Disclose about guarantees, including guarantees of the indebtedness of others:
   a. The nature of the guarantee, including the approximate term, how the guarantee arose, the events or circumstances that would require the guarantor to perform under the guarantee, and the current status (that is, as of the date of the statement of financial position) of the payment/performance risk of the guarantee. For example, the current status of the payment/performance risk of a credit-risk-related guarantee could be based on either recently issued external credit rating or current internal groupings used by the guarantor to manage its risks. An entity that uses internal groupings shall disclose how those groupings are determined and used for managing risk. _____
   b. The maximum potential amount of the future payments (undiscounted) that the entity would be required to make, or if the guarantee provides no limitation on future payments, that fact. _____
   c. The reasons why the maximum future payments cannot be estimated, if the entity is unable to estimate that amount. _____
   d. The current carrying amount of the liability. _____
   e. The nature of any recourse provisions that would enable the entity to recover from third parties any amounts paid under the guarantee, and the extent to which the proceeds are expected to cover the amount in b. above. _____

f. The nature of any assets (collateral) that can be liquidated to recover amounts paid under the guarantee, and the extent to which the proceeds from liquidation are expected to cover the amount in b. above. ____

(FASB ASC 460-10-50-4)

2. For product warranties:

   a. Information required by FASB ASC 460-10-50-4 except for b. above. ____
   b. Accounting policy and method used in determining liability for product warranties. ____
   c. Tabular reconciliation of the changes in aggregate product warranty liability for the period, including the beginning and ending balances, the aggregate reductions for payments made, and aggregate changes in the liability related to product warranties issued during the reporting period. ____

(FASB ASC 460-10-50-8)

470 Debt

1. Long-Term Obligations

   a. The combined aggregate amount of maturities and sinking fund requirements for all long-term borrowings for each of the five years following the date of the latest balance sheet presented. ____

(FASB ASC 470-10-50-1)

2. Long-term debt is classified as current if the debtor is in violation of a debt covenant at the statement of financial position date which

   a. Makes the obligation callable within one year, or ____
   b. Will make the obligation callable within one year if the violation is not cured within a specified grace period. ____

(FASB ASC 470-10-50-3)

3. The debt referred to in d. above need not be reclassified if either of the following conditions are met:

   a. The creditor has waived or has subsequently lost the right to demand repayment for one year (or, if longer, the operating cycle) from the statement of financial position date, or ____
   b. It is probable (likely) that the violation will be cured by the debtor within the grace period stated in the terms of the debt agreement, thus preventing the obligation from being called. ____

(FASB ASC 470-10-45-11)

4. If a short-term obligation is expected to be refinanced under 470-10, include in the notes a general description of the financing agreement and the terms of any new obligations incurred or expected to be incurred or equity securities issued or expected to be issued as a result of a refinancing. ____

(FASB ASC 470-10-50-4)

470-20 Debt with Conversion and Other Options

Own-Share Lending Arrangements Issued in Contemplation of Convertible Debt Issuance

1. Make the following disclosures if there is a share-lending arrangement of an entity's own shares in contemplation of a convertible debt offering or other financing:

a. Describe outstanding share-lending arrangements on the entity's own stock. _____
b. All significant terms of the arrangement, including the number of shares, the term, circumstances under which cash settlement would be required, and any collateral requirements for the counterparty. _____
c. The reasons for entering into the arrangement. _____
d. The fair value of the loaned shares. _____
e. The treatment of the share-lending arrangement for calculating earnings per share. _____
f. The unamortized amount of issuance costs associated with the arrangement. _____
g. The classification of issuance costs associated with the arrangement. _____
h. The amount of interest cost associated with the share-lending arrangement. _____
i. The amount of dividends paid related to the loaned shares that will not be reimbursed. _____

(FASB ASC 470-20-50-2A)

j. If it is probable in the current period that the counterparty will default, disclose the amount of expense related to the default. In subsequent periods, disclose material changes in the fair value of the shares or probable recoveries. If default is probable but has not yet occurred, disclose the number of shares related to the arrangement that will be included in basic and diluted earnings per share when there is a default. _____

(FASB ASC 470-20-50-2C)

2. With respect to convertible debt instruments that were outstanding during any of the periods presented and that are within the scope of ASC 470-20 disclose:

   a. As of each date for which a statement of financial position is presented

      (1) The carrying amount of the equity component. _____
      (2) The principal amount, unamortized discount, and net carrying amount of the liability component. _____

(FASB ASC 470-20-50-4)

3. As of the date of the *most recent* statement of financial position presented:

   a. The remaining period over which any discount on the liability component will be amortized. _____
   b. The conversion price and the number of shares on which the aggregate consideration to be delivered on conversion is determined. _____
   c. For public entities (as defined in the Master Glossary), the amount by which the if-converted value of the instrument exceeds its principal amount, irrespective of whether the instrument is currently convertible. _____
   d. Information about derivative transactions entered into in connection with the issuance of the instruments, including the terms of those derivative transactions, how those transactions relate to the instruments, the number of shares underlying the derivative transactions, and the reasons for entering into those derivatives transactions. This disclosure is required regardless of whether the related derivative transactions are accounted for as assets, liabilities, or equity instruments. _____

(FASB ASC 470-20-50-5)

4. For each period for which a statement of financial performance is presented

   a. The effective interest rate for the period on the liability component. _____
   b. The amount of interest cost recognized in the period relating to both the contractual interest coupon and amortization of the discount on the liability component. _____

(FASB ASC 470-20-50-6)

470-30 Participating Mortgage Loans

1. The aggregate amount of participating mortgage obligations at the balance sheet date, with separate disclosure of the aggregate participation liabilities and related debt discounts _____
2. Terms of the participations by the lender in either the appreciation in the fair value of the mortgaged real estate project or the results of operations of the mortgaged real estate project, or both. _____

(FASB ASC 470-30-50-1)

470-60 Troubled Debt Restructurings by Debtors

1. Disclosures by the debtor
   a. A description of the changes in terms and/or major features of the settlement. _____
   b. The aggregate gain on restructuring and the related tax effect. _____
   c. The aggregate net gain or loss on the transfer of assets recognized during the period. _____
   d. The per share amount of the aggregate gain or loss. _____

(ASC 470-60-50-1)

2. Disclose in financial statements for periods after a troubled debt restructuring the extent to which amounts contingently payable are included in the carrying amount of restructured payables pursuant to the provisions of paragraph 470-60-35-7. If required by paragraphs 450-20-50-1 through 50-6 and 450-20-50-9 through 50-10, disclose in those financial statements total amounts that are contingently payable on restructured payables and the conditions under which those amounts would become payable or would be forgiven. _____

(FASB ASC 470-60-50-2)

480 Distinguishing Liabilities from Equity

1. Issuers of financial instruments within the scope of 480-10-25 must disclose
   a. The nature and terms of the financial instruments. _____
   b. The rights and obligations embodied therein. _____
   c. Settlement alternatives, if any, in the contract. _____
   d. The entity that controls the settlement alternatives. _____

(FASB ASC 480-10-50-1)

2. For all outstanding financial instruments and for each settlement alternative, issuers disclose
   a. The amount that would be paid, or the number and fair value of shares that would be issued, determined under the conditions specified in the contract, if the settlement were to occur at the reporting date. _____
   b. How changes in the fair value of the issuer's equity shares would affect those settlement amounts. _____
   c. The maximum amount that the issuer could be required to pay to redeem the instrument by physical settlement, if applicable. _____
   d. The maximum number of shares that could be required to be issued, if applicable _____
   e. That a contract does not limit the amount that the issuer could be required to pay or the number of shares that the issuer could be required to issue, if applicable. _____
   f. For a forward contract or an option indexed to the issuer's equity shares, the forward price or option strike price, the number of issuer's shares to which the contract is indexed, and the settlement date or dates of the contract, as applicable. _____

(FASB ASC 480-10-50-2)

3. For entities having no equity instruments outstanding but having financial instruments in the form of shares, all of which are mandatorily redeemable financial instruments required to be classified as liabilities, disclose the components of the liability that would otherwise be related to shareholders' interest and other comprehensive income (if any) subject to the redemption feature. _____

(FASB ASC 480-10-50-4)

EQUITY

505 Equity

1. If both financial position and results of operations are presented, disclose changes in the separate accounts comprising shareholders' equity (in addition to retained earnings) and the changes in the number of shares of equity securities during at least the most recent annual fiscal period and any subsequent interim period presented. Disclosure of such changes may take the form of separate statements or may be made in the basic financial statements or notes thereto. _____

(FASB ASC 505-10-50-2)

2. Explain, in summary form within its financial statements, the pertinent rights and privileges of the various securities outstanding. Examples of information that shall be disclosed are dividend and liquidation preferences, participation, call prices and dates, conversion or exercise prices or rates and pertinent dates, sinking-fund requirements, unusual voting rights, and significant terms of contracts to issue additional shares. An entity shall disclose within its financial statements the number of shares issued upon conversion, exercise, or satisfaction of required conditions during at least the most recent annual fiscal period and any subsequent interim period presented. _____

(FASB ASC 505-10-50-3)

3. An entity that issues preferred stock (or other senior stock) that has a preference in involuntary liquidation considerably in excess of the par or stated value of the shares shall disclose the liquidation preference of the stock (the relationship between the preference in liquidation and the par or stated value of the shares). That disclosure shall be made in the equity section of the statement of financial position in the aggregate, either parenthetically or in short, rather than on a per-share basis or through disclosure in the notes. _____

(FASB ASC 505-10-5-4)

4. In addition, disclose both of the following within its financial statements (either on the face of the statement of financial position or in the notes thereto):

    a. The aggregate or per-share amounts at which preferred stock may be called or is subject to redemption through sinking-fund operations or otherwise _____
    b. The aggregate and per-share amounts of arrearages in cumulative preferred dividends. _____

(FASB ASC 505-10-50-5)

5. To comply with the general disclosure requirements of paragraph 505-10-50-3, disclose the significant terms of the conversion features of the contingently convertible security to enable users of financial statements to understand the circumstances of the contingency and the potential impact of conversion. Quantitative and qualitative terms of the contingently convertible security, disclosure of which would be helpful in understanding both the nature of the contingency and the potential impact of conversion include all of the following:

a. Events or changes in circumstances that would cause the contingency to be met and any significant features necessary to understand the conversion rights and the timing of those rights (for example, the periods in which the contingency might be met and the securities may be converted if the contingency is met) _____
b. The conversion price and the number of shares into which a security is potentially convertible _____
c. Events or changes in circumstances, if any, that could adjust or change the contingency, conversion price, or number of shares, including significant terms of those changes _____
d. The manner of settlement upon conversion and any alternative settlement methods (for example, cash, shares, or a combination). _____

(FASB ASC 505-10-50-6)

6. In order to meet the disclosure requirements of the preceding paragraph, disclose the possible conversion prices and dates as well as other significant terms for each convertible instrument. _____

(FASB ASC 505-10-50-7)

7. Additionally, the issuer shall disclose in the footnotes to its financial statements the terms of the transaction, including the excess of the aggregate fair value of the instruments that the holder would receive at conversion over the proceeds received and the period over which the discount is amortized. _____

(FASB ASC 505-10-50-8)

8. Indicate whether the shares that would be issued if the contingently convertible securities were converted are included in the calculation of diluted earnings per share (EPS) and the reasons why or why not. _____

(FASB ASC 505-10-50-9)

9. Disclosures of information about derivative instruments entered into in connection with the issuance of the contingently convertible securities may be useful in terms of fully explaining the potential impact of the contingently convertible securities. That information might include the terms of those derivative instruments (including the terms of settlement), how those instruments relate to the contingently convertible securities, and the number of shares underlying the derivative instruments. One example of a transaction entered into in connection with the issuance of a contingently convertible security is the purchase of a call option such that the terms of the purchased call option would be expected to substantially offset changes in value of the written call option embedded in the convertible security. Derivative instruments are also subject to disclosure information, as required by Topic 815. _____

(FASB ASC 505-10-50-10)

10. An entity that issues redeemable stock shall disclose the amount of redemption requirements, separately by issue or combined, for all issues of capital stock that are redeemable at fixed or determinable prices on fixed or determinable dates in each of the five years following the date of the latest statement of financial position presented. _____

(FASB ASC 505-10-50-11)

505-20 Stock Dividends and Stock Splits

1. Paragraph 505-20-25-2 identifies a situation in which a stock dividend in form is a stock split in substance. In such instances make every effort to avoid the use of the word dividend in related corporate resolutions, notices, and announcements and that, in those cases in which because of legal requirements this cannot be done, the transaction be described, for example, as a stock split effected in the form of a dividend. _____

(FASB ASC 505-20-50-1)

505-30 Treasury Stock

1. State laws may affect an entity's repurchase of its own outstanding common stock. If state laws relating to an entity's repurchase of its own outstanding common stock restrict the availability of retained earnings for payment of dividends or have other effects of a significant nature, those facts shall be disclosed. _____

(FASB ASC 505-30-50-2)

2. A repurchase of shares at a price significantly in excess of the current market price creates a presumption that the repurchase price includes amounts attributable to items other than the shares repurchased. A repurchase of shares at a price significantly in excess of the current market price may require an entity to allocate amounts to other elements of the transaction under the requirements of paragraph 505-30-30-23. _____

(FASB ASC 505-30-50-4)

505-50 Equity-Based Payments to Non-Employees

1. For an entity that acquires goods or services other than employee services in share-based payment transactions, make disclosures similar to those required by paragraphs 718-10-50-1 through 50-2 to the extent that those disclosures are important to an understanding of the effects of those transactions on the financial statements. _____

(FASB ASC 505-50-50-1)

2. In accordance with paragraphs 845-10-50-1 through 50-2, disclose, in each period's financial statements, the amount of gross operating revenue recognized as a result of nonmonetary transactions addressed by the guidance in this subtopic. _____

(FASB ASC 505-50-50-2)

REVENUE

605 Revenue

605-20 Services

Advertising Barter Transactions

1. Disclose the amount of revenue and expense recognized from advertising barter transactions for each income statement period presented. In addition, if an entity engages in advertising barter transactions for which the fair value is not determinable within the limits of paragraphs 605-20-25-15 through 25-18, information regarding the volume and type of advertising surrendered and received (such as the number of equivalent pages, the number of minutes, or the overall percentage of advertising volume) shall be disclosed for each income statement period presented. _____

(FASB ASC 605-20-50-1)

605-25 Multiple Element Arrangements

1. In addition to specifically required disclosures, any other qualitative and quantitative information that will provide both qualitative and quantitative information about revenue arrangements and about the significant judgments made about the application of the requirements in the 605-25 guidance and changes in those judgments or in the application that may significantly affect the timing or amount of revenue recognition. _____

(FASB ASC 605-25-50-1)

2. If the company is a party to multiple-deliverable arrangements

   a. The nature of the entity's multiple-deliverable arrangements. ____
   b. Significant deliverables within the arrangements. ____
   c. General timing of the delivery of goods or performance of services. ____
   d. Performance, cancellation, termination, and refund provisions. ____
   e. Significant factors, inputs, assumptions, and methods used to determine selling price for significant deliverables. ____
   f. Whether significant deliverables are separable into units of accounting and the reasons they do not qualify as separate units of accounting if applicable. ____
   g. General timing of revenue recognition for significant units of accounting. ____
   h. The effect of changes in selling price or the methods used to determine the selling price for a unit of accounting if the change has a significant effect on the allocation of consideration in an arrangement. ____

(FASB ASC 605-25-50-1 and 2)

605-28 Milestone Method

1. If an entity uses the milestone method of revenue recognition, disclose the following:

   a. The accounting policy for using the milestone method. ____
   b. Describe each such arrangement. ____
   c. Describe each milestone and related contingent consideration. ____
   d. Note whether each milestone is substantive. ____
   e. The factors considered in determining whether the milestones are substantive. ____
   f. The amount of consideration recognized during the period for the milestones. ____

(FASB ASC 605-28-50-2)

605-35 Construction-Type and Production-Type Contracts

Percentage of Completion Method

1. If the percentage-of-completion method is used, the method of measuring extent of progress toward completion (e.g., cost-to-cost, efforts-expended). ____

(FASB ASC 605-35-50-2)

2. An entity that departs from use of the percentage-of-completion method as its basic accounting policy in the circumstances described in paragraph 605-35-25-61 shall disclose such a departure from the basic policy. ____

(FASB ASC 605-35-50-3)

Completed-Contract Method

3. If the completed-contract method is used, disclose the specific criterion used to determine when a contact is substantially completed. ____

(FASB ASC 605-35-50-4)

4. An entity that departs from use of the completed-contract method as its basic accounting policy in the circumstances described in paragraph 605-35-25-95 shall disclose such a departure. ____

(FASB ASC 605-35-50-5)

Contract Claims

5. As indicated in paragraph 605-35-25-31, if certain requirements are met, revenue from a claim is recorded only to the extent that contract costs relating to the claim have been incurred. The amounts recorded shall be disclosed in the notes to financial statements. _____

(FASB ASC 605-35-50-6)

6. As indicated in paragraph 605-35-25-31, a practice such as recording revenues from claims only when the amounts have been received or awarded may be used. If that practice is followed, the amounts shall be disclosed in the notes to financial statements. _____

(FASB ASC 605-35-50-7)

7. If the requirements in paragraph 605-35-25-31 are not met or if those requirements are met but the claim exceeds the recorded contract costs, a contingent asset shall be disclosed in accordance with paragraph 450-30-50-1. _____

(FASB ASC 605-35-50-8)

Revision of Estimates

8. Although estimating is a continuous and normal process for contractors, paragraph 250-10-50-4 requires disclosure of the effect of revisions if the effect is material. _____

(FASB ASC 605-35-50-9)

9. Events occurring after the date of the financial statements that are outside the normal exposure and risk aspects of the contract shall not be considered refinements of the estimating process of the prior year but should be disclosed as subsequent events. _____

(FASB ASC 605-35-50-10)

605-45 Principal Agent Considerations

1. For significant shipping or handling costs, both the amount of such costs and the line item or items on the income statement that include them. _____

(FASB ASC 605-45-50-2)

2. The presentation of taxes within the scope of this Subtopic on either a gross or a net basis (excluded from revenues) is an accounting policy decision that shall be disclosed pursuant to Topic 235. _____

(FASB ASC 605-45-50-2)

3. For any such taxes, significant in amount, that are reported on a gross basis, the amounts of those taxes in interim and annual financial statements for each period for which an income statement is presented. The disclosure of those taxes can be done on an aggregate basis. _____

(FASB ASC 605-45-50-2)

605-50 Customer Payments and Incentives

1. If significant, the nature of incentive programs and the amounts recognized in the statement of operations for those incentive programs and their related classification for each period presented. _____

(FASB ASC 605-50-50-1)

EXPENSES

710 Compensation—General

Compensated Absences

1. If the employer's obligation is from service already rendered, the obligation vests or accumulates, and payment is probable, but the amount cannot be estimated, disclose that fact. _____

(FASB ASC 710-10-50-1)

712 Compensation—Nonretirement Postemployment Benefits

1. If an obligation for other postemployment benefits is not accrued only because the amount cannot be reasonably estimated, the financial statements shall disclose that fact. _____

(FASB ASC 712-10-50-2)

715 Compensation—Retirement Benefits

1. An employer that sponsors one or more defined benefit pension plans or one or more other defined benefit postretirement plans is to provide the following information, separately for pension plans and postretirement plans. Amounts related to the employer's results of operations are to be included for each period for which an income statement is presented. Amounts related to the employer's financial position are to be disclosed as of the date of each statement of financial position presented. _____
2. Note that the term "changes in foreign currency exchange rates" as used herein is applicable to plans of a foreign operation whose functional currency is not the reporting currency, as those terms are defined in FASB ASC 830-10-45. _____

715-20 Defined Benefit Plans – General

Disclosures by Public Entities

1. Defined benefit plans and other postretirement plans
   a. Shown separately for each plan, schedule reconciling beginning and ending balances of the benefit obligation, (for defined benefit pension plans, the benefit obligation is the projected benefit obligation; for defined benefit postretirement plans, the benefit obligation is the accumulated postretirement benefit obligation) separately showing if applicable, the effects during the period attributable to each of the following (not required for nonpublic entities)
      (1) Service cost. _____
      (2) Interest cost. _____
      (3) Contributions by plan participants. _____
      (4) Actuarial gains and losses. _____
      (5) Changes in foreign currency exchange rates. _____
      (6) Benefits paid. _____
      (7) Plan amendments. _____
      (8) Business combinations. _____
      (9) Divestitures. _____
      (10) Curtailments. _____
      (11) Settlements. _____
      (12) Special and contractual termination benefits. _____

b. Schedule reconciling beginning and ending balances of the fair value of plan assets, separately showing if applicable (not required for nonpublic entities)

   (1) Actual return on plan assets. _____
   (2) Changes in foreign currency exchange rates. _____
   (3) Employer contributions. _____
   (4) Contributions by plan participants. _____
   (5) Benefits paid. _____
   (6) Business combinations. _____
   (7) Divestitures. _____
   (8) Settlements. _____

c. Information on the funded status of the plan(s), and amounts recognized in the statement of financial position, separately presenting the assets and current and noncurrent liabilities recognized (not required for nonpublic entities). _____

d. When making the disclosures that follow, consider the objectives of the disclosures about postretirement benefit plan assets are to provide users of financial statements with an understanding of:

   (1) How investment allocation decisions are made, including the factors that are pertinent to an understanding of investment policies and strategies _____
   (2) The classes of plan assets _____
   (3) The inputs and valuation techniques used to measure the fair value of plan assets _____
   (4) The effect of fair value measurements using significant unobservable inputs (Level 3) on changes in plan assets for the period _____
   (5) Significant concentrations of risk within plan assets. _____

e. The following information regarding assets of the plan:

   (1) A narrative description of investment policies and strategies, including target allocation percentages or ranges of percentages considering the major categories of plan assets disclosed pursuant to (2) below, as of the latest statement of financial position presented (on a weighted-average basis for employers with more than one plan), and other factors pertinent to an understanding of those policies and strategies such as investment goals, risk management practices, permitted and prohibited investments including the use of derivatives, diversification, and the relationship between plan assets and benefit obligations. For investment funds disclosed as major categories as described in (2) below, a description of the significant investment strategies of those funds shall be provided. _____
   (2) The fair value of each major category of plan assets as of each date for which a statement of financial position is presented. Asset categories shall be based on the nature and risks of assets in an employer's plan(s). Examples of major categories include, but are not limited to, the following: cash and cash equivalents; equity securities; debt securities issued by national, state and local governments; corporate debt securities; asset-backed securities; structured debt; derivatives on a gross basis (segregated by type of underlying risk in the contract); investment funds (segregated by type of fund); and real estate. Those examples are not meant to be all-inclusive. _____
   (3) A narrative description of the basis used to determine the overall expected long-term rate-of-return-on-assets assumption, such as the general approach used, the extent to which the overall rate-of-return-on-assets assumption was based on historical returns, the extent to which adjustments were made to those historical returns to reflect expectations of future returns, and how those adjustments were determined. The description should consider the major categories of assets described in (2) above, as appropriate. _____

(4) Information that enables users of financial statements to assess the inputs and valuation techniques used to develop fair value measurements of plan assets at the reporting date. For fair value measurements using significant unobservable inputs, an employer shall disclose the effect of the measurements on changes in plan assets for the period. To meet those objectives, the employer shall disclose the following information for each major category of plan assets disclosed pursuant to (3) above:

(a) The level of the fair value hierarchy in which the fair value measurements in their entirety fall, segregating fair value measurements using quoted prices in active markets for identical assets and liabilities (Level 1), significant other observable inputs (Level 2), and significant unobservable inputs (Level 3) _____

(b) For fair value measurements of plan assets using significant unobservable inputs (Level 3), a reconciliation of the beginning and ending balances, separately presenting changes during the period attributable to the following: actual return on plan assets, separately identifying the amount related to assets still held at the reporting date and the amount related to assets sold during the period; purchases, sales, and settlements net; and transfers in and/or out of Level 3. _____

(c) Information about the valuation technique(s) and inputs used to measure fair value and a discussion of changes in valuation techniques and inputs, if any, during the period. _____

f. Defined benefit pension plans: The accumulated benefit obligation. _____

g. The benefits, as of the date of the latest statement of financial position presented, that are expected to be paid in each of the next five fiscal years, and in the aggregate for the five fiscal years thereafter. The estimate of expected benefits is to be based on the same assumptions used to measure the entity's benefit obligation at the end of the year and is to include benefits attributable to estimated future service by employees. _____

h. The best estimate of the employer, as soon as reasonably determinable, of contributions expected to be paid to the plan during the next fiscal year that begins after the date of the latest statement of financial position presented. Estimated contributions are permitted to be presented in the aggregate combining

(1) Contributions required by funding laws and regulations _____
(2) Discretionary contributions _____
(3) Noncash contributions. _____

i. The amount of net benefit cost recognized, separately showing (not required for nonpublic entities)

(1) Service cost component _____
(2) Interest cost component _____
(3) Expected return on plan assets for the period _____
(4) The gain or loss _____
(5) The prior service cost or credit component _____
(6) The transition asset or obligation component _____
(7) The gain or loss recognized due to settlements or curtailments. _____

j. Separate disclosure of the net gain or loss and net prior service cost or credit recognized in other comprehensive income (OCI) for the period and reclassification adjustments of OCI for the period, as those amounts, including amortization of the net transition asset or obligation, are recognized as components of net periodic benefit cost. _____

k. The amounts in accumulated other comprehensive income (AOCI) not yet recognized as components of net periodic benefit cost, separately presenting the net gain or loss, net prior service cost or credit, and net transition asset or obligation. _____

l. The following assumptions used in the accounting for the plans, on a weighted-average basis specifying in a tabular format:

 (1) Assumed discount rates. _____
 (2) For pay-related plans, rates of compensation increase. _____
 (3) Expected long-term rates of return on plan assets. _____

m. Assumed health-care cost trend rate(s) for the next year used to measure the expected cost of benefits covered by the plan (gross eligible charges), and a general description of the direction and pattern of change in the assumed trend rates thereafter, along with the ultimate trend rate(s) and when that rate is expected to be achieved. _____

n. The effect of both a 1% increase and a 1% decrease in the assumed health-care cost trend rates on each of the following: (not required for nonpublic entities)

 (1) Service and interest cost components (aggregated) of the net periodic postretirement health-care benefit costs. _____
 (2) Health-care accumulated postretirement benefit obligation for health-care benefits (APBO) (based on the substantive plan and while holding all other assumptions constant). _____

o. If applicable

 (1) Amounts and types of employer and related-party securities included in plan assets. _____
 (2) Approximate amount of future annual benefits covered by insurance contracts by the employer and related parties. _____
 (3) Any significant transactions between the employer and related parties with the plan during the period. _____

p. Any alternative method used to amortize prior service amounts or net gains and losses, if applicable (not required for nonpublic entities). _____

q. Any substantive commitments, such as past practice or a history of regular benefit increases, used as the basis for accounting for the benefit obligation, if applicable (not required for nonpublic entities). _____

r. Cost of providing special or contractual termination benefits recognized during the period (not required for nonpublic entities) including a description of the

 (1) Nature of the event. _____
 (2) Cost. _____

s. An explanation (not required for nonpublic entities) of matters of significance in regard to changes in

 (1) Benefit obligation. _____
 (2) Plan assets. _____

t. The amounts in AOCI expected to be recognized as components of net periodic benefit cost during the fiscal year following the most recent annual statement of financial position presented, separately presenting

 (1) Net gain or loss. _____
 (2) Net prior service cost or credit. _____
 (3) Net transition asset or obligation. _____

u. The amount and timing of any plan assets expected to be returned to the business entity during the 12-month period, or operating cycle if longer, that follows the most recent annual statement of financial position presented. _____

(FASB ASC 715-20-50-1)

Entities (Public and Nonpublic) with Two or More Plans

2. Employers with two or more defined benefit plans (pension, postretirement, or both) are, in general, to separately aggregate all of the employer's defined benefit pension plans and all of the employer's defined benefit postretirement plans.

   a. Disaggregate into groups if otherwise required or if it would provide useful information. _____

(FASB ASC 715-20-50-2)

   b. Generally, the entity is permitted to aggregate disclosures regarding pension plans with assets in excess of the ABO with disclosures regarding pension plans with ABO in excess of assets. The same aggregation is permitted for other postretirement benefit plans. If the disclosures are aggregated, however, the employer is to disclose

      (1) For plans where the ABO is in excess of plan assets as of the measurement date of each statement of financial position presented, disclose the

         (a) Aggregate benefit obligation. _____
         (b) Aggregate fair value of plan assets. _____

      (2) For pension plans where the ABO is in excess of plan assets, disclose the

         (a) Aggregate pension accumulated benefit obligation. _____
         (b) Aggregate fair value of plan assets. _____

(FASB ASC 715-20-50-3)

   c. US pension and OPEB plans and plans outside the US may be combined unless benefit obligations outside the US are significant relative to the total benefit obligation and those plans use significantly different assumptions. A foreign reporting entity that prepares financial statements in conformity with US GAAP applies this guidance to its domestic and foreign plans. _____

(FASB ASC 715-20-50-4)

Disclosures by Nonpublic Entities

3. A nonpublic entity sponsoring one or more defined benefit pension plans or one or more other defined benefit postretirement plans is to provide the following information, separately for pension plans and other postretirement benefit plans. Amounts related to the employer's results of operations are to be disclosed for each period for which an income statement is presented. Amounts related to the employer's financial position are to be disclosed at the date of each statement of financial position presented.

   a. Benefit obligation, fair value of plan assets, funded status of plan. _____
   b. Employer contributions, participant contributions, benefits paid. _____
   c. When providing the information below, consider the objectives of the disclosures about postretirement benefit plan assets to provide users of financial statements with an understanding of:

      (1) How investment allocation decisions are made, including the factors that are pertinent to an understanding of investment policies and strategies _____

(2) The classes of plan assets _____
(3) The inputs and valuation techniques used to measure the fair value of plan assets _____
(4) The effect of fair value measurements using significant unobservable inputs (Level 3) on changes in plan assets for the period _____
(5) Significant concentrations of risk within plan assets. _____

d. Information about plan assets

(1) A narrative description of the plan's investment policies and strategies, including target allocation percentages or range of percentages considering the major categories of plan assets disclosed pursuant to (2) below, as of the latest statement of financial position presented (on a weighted-average basis for employers with more than one plan), and other factors pertinent to understanding those policies or strategies, such as investment goals, risk management practices, permitted and prohibited investments including the use of derivatives, diversification, and the relationship between plan assets and benefit obligations. For investment funds disclosed as major categories as described in (2) below, a description of the significant investment strategies of those funds shall be provided. _____
(2) The fair value of each major category of plan assets as of each date for which a statement of financial position is presented. Asset categories shall be based on the nature and risks of assets in an employer's plan(s). Examples of major categories include, but are not limited to, the following: cash and cash equivalents; equity securities (segregated by industry type, company size, or investment objective); debt securities issued by national, state, and local government; corporate debt securities; asset-backed securities; structured debt; derivatives on a gross basis (segregated by type of underlying risk in the contract); investment funds (segregated by type of fund); and real estate. Those are examples but are not meant to be all-inclusive. _____
(3) A narrative description of the basis used to determine the overall expected long-term rate-of-return-on-assets assumption, such as the general approach used, the extent to which the assumption was based on historical returns, the extent to which adjustments were made to those historical returns to reflect expectations of future returns, and how those adjustments were determined. The description should consider the major categories of assets described in (2) above, as appropriate. _____
(4) Information that enables users of financial statements to assess the inputs and valuation techniques used to develop fair value measurements of plan assets at the reporting date. For fair value measurements using significant unobservable inputs, an employer shall disclose the effect of the measurements on changes in plan assets for the period. To meet those objectives, the employer shall disclose the following information for each major category of plan assets disclosed pursuant to (3) above:

(a) The level within the fair value hierarchy in which the fair value measurements in their entirety fall, segregating fair value measurements using quoted prices in active markets for identical assets and liabilities (Level 1), significant other observable inputs (Level 2), and significant unobservable inputs (Level 3). _____

(b) For fair value measurements of plan assets using significant unobservable inputs (Level 3), a reconciliation of the beginning and ending balances, separately presenting changes during the period attributable to the following: actual return on plan assets, separately identifying the amount related to assets still held at the reporting date and the amount related to assets sold during the period; purchases, sales, and settlements net; and transfers in and/or out of Level 3. _____

(c) Information about the valuation technique(s) and inputs used to measure fair value and a discussion of changes in valuation techniques and inputs, if any, during the period. _____

e. For defined benefit plans, the accumulated benefit obligation (ABO). _____

f. As of the date of the latest statement of financial position presented, the benefits expected to be paid in each of the next five fiscal years, and in the aggregate for the five fiscal years thereafter. The expected benefits are to be estimated using the same assumptions used to measure the entity's end-of-year benefit obligation and are to include benefits attributable to estimated future service by employees. _____

g. The employer's best estimate, as soon as it can be determined reasonably, of contributions expected to be paid to the plan during the next fiscal year beginning after the date of the latest statement of financial position presented. Estimated contributions may be presented in the aggregate, combining

(1) Contributions required by funding laws or regulations. _____
(2) Discretionary contributions. _____
(3) Noncash contributions. _____

h. The amounts recognized in the statements of financial position, showing separately the postretirement benefit assets and current and noncurrent postretirement benefit liabilities. _____

i. Separate disclosure of the net gain or loss, and the net prior service cost or credit recognized in OCI for the period, and reclassification adjustments of OCI for the period as those amounts, including amortization of the net transition asset or obligation, are recognized as components of net periodic benefit cost. _____

j. The amounts in AOCI that have not yet been recognized as components of net periodic benefit cost, separately presenting the net gain/loss, net prior service cost/credit, and net transition asset/obligation. _____

k. On a weighted-average basis, all of the following assumptions used in the accounting for the plans, specifying in a tabular format, the assumptions used to determine the benefit obligation and the assumptions used to determine net benefit cost:

(1) Assumed discount rates for a discussion of representationally faithful disclosure _____
(2) Rates of compensation increase (for pay-related plans) _____
(3) Expected long-term rates of return on plan assets. _____

l. The assumed health-care cost trend rate(s) for the next year used to measure the expected cost of benefits covered by the plan (gross eligible charges), and a general description of the direction and pattern of change in the assumed trend rates thereafter, together with the ultimate trend rate(s) and when the rate is expected to be achieved. _____

m. The amounts and types of securities, if applicable, of the employer and related partied included in plan assets, the approximate amount of future annual benefits of plan participants covered by insurance contracts, including annuity contracts, issued by the employer or related parties, and any significant transactions between the employer or related parties and the plan during the period. _____

n. The nature and effect of significant nonroutine events, such as amendments, combinations, divestitures, curtailments, and settlements. _____
o. The amounts in AOCI expected to be recognized as components of net periodic benefit cost over the fiscal year following the date of the most recent annual statement of financial position presented, with separate presentation of the net gain/loss, net prior service cost/credit, and net transition asset/obligation. _____
p. The amount and timing of any plan assets expected to be returned to the employer during the 12-month period (or operating cycle, if longer) following the most recent annual statement of financial position presented. _____
q. The amount of net periodic benefit recognized. _____

(FASB ASC 715-20-50-5)

Disclosures Related to Expected Rate of Return on Plan Assets

4. If the weighted-average expected rate of return on plan assets changes because of interim measurement, disclose the beginning and most recently assumed rate or a weighted combination of the two. _____

(FASB ASC 715-20-50-8)

715-60 Defined Benefit Plans—Other Postretirement

This subsection provides guidance on disclosures regarding the effect of the Medicare subsidy. This subsection also provides guidance on the disclosures about the effects of the subsidy for an employer that sponsors a postretirement health care benefit plan that provides prescription drug coverage but for which the employer has not yet been able to determine actuarial equivalency. _____

(FASB ASC 715-60-50-2)

1. In interim and annual financial statements for the first period in which an employer includes the effects of the subsidy in measuring the accumulated postretirement benefit obligation and the first period in which an employer includes the effects of the subsidy in measuring net periodic postretirement benefit cost, it shall disclose all of the following:

   a. The reduction in the accumulated postretirement benefit obligation for the subsidy related to benefits attributed to past service. _____
   b. The effect of the subsidy on the measurement of net periodic postretirement benefit cost for the current period. That effect includes any amortization of the actuarial gain in a. of this paragraph as a component of the net amortization called for by paragraphs 715-60-35-29 through 35-30, the reduction in current period service cost due to the subsidy, and the resulting reduction in interest cost on the accumulated postretirement benefit obligation as a result of the subsidy. _____
   c. Any other disclosures required by paragraph 715-20-50-1(r). _____

(FASB ASC 715-60-50-3)

2. For purposes of the disclosures required by paragraph 715-20-50-1(a) and 715-20-50-1(f), disclose gross benefit payments (paid and expected, respectively), including prescription drug benefits, and separately the gross amount of the subsidy receipts (received and expected, respectively). _____

(FASB ASC 715-60-50-4)

3. Until an employer is able to determine whether benefits provided by its plan are actuarially equivalent disclose both of the following in financial statements for interim or annual periods:

   a. The existence of the Medicare Prescription Drug, Improvement, and Modernization Act. _____

b. That measures of the accumulated postretirement benefit obligation or net periodic postretirement benefit cost do not reflect any amount associated with the subsidy because the employer is unable to conclude whether the benefits provided by the plan are actuarially equivalent to Medicare Part D under the Act. _____

(FASB ASC 715-60-50-6)

715-70 Defined Contribution Plans

1. Separately from disclosures regarding defined benefit plans, the employer is to disclose the following information for all periods presented:

   a. Cost recognized for defined contribution pension plans. _____
   b. Cost recognized for other defined contribution postretirement benefit plans. _____
   c. Description of the nature and effect of any significant changes during the period affecting comparability, such as a change in the employer contribution rate, a business combination, or a divestiture. _____

(FASB ASC 715-70-50-1)

715-80 Multiemployer Plans

1. Apply the accounting and disclosure provisions of ASC 450, *Contingencies,* in situations where it is either reasonably possible or probable that

   (a) The employer would withdraw from the plan under circumstances resulting in an obligation to the plan for a portion of the unfunded pension plan benefit obligation, *or* _____
   (b) The employer's contributions to the fund would be increased during the remainder of the contract period to make up for a shortfall in the funds needed to maintain the negotiated level of benefit coverage (referred to as a "maintenance of benefits" clause). _____

(FASB ASC 715-80-50-2)

2. An employer shall apply the provisions of Topic 450 to its participation in a multiemployer plan if it is either probable or reasonably possible that either of the following would occur:

   a. An employer would withdraw from the plan under circumstances that would give rise to an obligation. _____
   b. An employer's contribution to the fund would be increased during the remainder of the contract period to make up a shortfall in the funds necessary to maintain the negotiated level of benefit coverage (a maintenance of benefits clause). _____

(FASB ASC 715-80-50-2)

Multiemployer Plans That Provide Pension Benefits

3. Provide the disclosures required by paragraphs 715-80-50-4 through 50-10 in annual financial statements. The disclosures of the employer's contributions made to the plan in paragraphs 715-80-50-4 through 50-10 include all items recognized as net pension costs. The disclosures based on *the most recently available* information are the most recently available through the date at which the employer has evaluated subsequent events. _____

(FASB ASC 715-80-50-3)

4. For an employer that participates in a multiemployer plan that provides pension benefits, a narrative description both of the general nature of the multiemployer plans that provide pension benefits and of the employer's participation in the plans that would indicate how the risks of participating in these plans are different from single-employer plans. _____

(FASB ASC 715-80-50-4)

5. When feasible, present the information required by this paragraph in a tabular format. Information that requires greater narrative description may be provided outside the table. For each individually significant multiemployer plan that provides pension benefits, disclose the following:

   a. Legal name of the plan. _____
   b. The plan's Employer Identification Number and, if available, its plan number. _____
   c. For each statement of financial position presented, the most recently available certified zone status provided by the plan, as currently defined by the Pension Protection Act of 2006 or a subsequent amendment of that Act. The disclosure shall specify the date of the plan's year-end to which the zone status relates and whether the plan has utilized any extended amortization provisions that affect the calculation of the zone status. If the zone status is not available, an employer shall disclose, as of the most recent date available, on the basis of the financial statements provided by the plan, the total plan assets and accumulated benefit obligations, whether the plan was:

      (1) Less than 65 percent funded _____
      (2) Between 65 percent and 80 percent funded _____
      (3) At least 80 percent funded. _____

   d. The expiration date(s) of the collective-bargaining agreement(s) requiring contributions to the plan, if any. If more than one collective-bargaining agreement applies to the plan, the employer shall provide a range of the expiration dates of those agreements, supplemented with a qualitative description that identifies the significant collective-bargaining agreements within that range as well as other information to help investors understand the significance of the collective-bargaining agreements and when they expire (for example, the portion of employees covered by each agreement or the portion of contributions required by each agreement). _____
   e. For each period that a statement of income (statement of activities for nonpublic entities) is presented:

      (1) The employer's contributions made to the plan _____
      (2) Whether the employer's contributions represent more than 5 percent of total contributions to the plan as indicated in the plan's most recently available annual report (Form 5500 for US plans). The disclosure shall specify the year-end date of the plan to which the annual report relates. _____

   f. As of the end of the most recent annual period presented:

      (1) Whether a funding improvement plan or rehabilitation plan (for example, as those terms are defined by the Employment Retirement Security Act of 1974) had been implemented or was pending _____
      (2) Whether the employer paid a surcharge to the plan _____
      (3) A description of any minimum contribution(s), required for future periods by the collective-bargaining agreement(s), statutory obligations, or other contractual obligations, if applicable. _____

Factors other than the amount of the employer's contribution to a plan, for example, the severity of the underfunded status of the plan, may need to be considered when determining whether a plan is significant.

(FASB ASC 715-80-50-5)

6. Provide a description of the nature and effect of any significant changes that affect comparability of total employer contributions from period to period, such as:

   a. A business combination or a divestiture ____
   b. A change in the contractual employer contribution rate ____
   c. A change in the number of employees covered by the plan during each year. ____

(FASB ASC 715-80-50-6)

7. The requirements in paragraph 715-80-50-5 assume that the other information about the plan is available in the public domain. For example, for US plans, the plan information in Form 5500 is publicly available. In circumstances in which plan level information is not available in the public domain, disclose, in addition to the requirements of paragraphs 715-80-50-5 through 50-6, the following information about each significant plan:

   a. A description of the nature of the plan benefits ____
   b. A qualitative description of the extent to which the employer could be responsible for the obligations of the plan, including benefits earned by employees during employment with another employer ____
   c. Other quantitative information, to the extent available, as of the most recent date available, to help users understand the financial information about the plan, such as total plan assets, actuarial present value of accumulated plan benefits, and total contributions received by the plan. ____
   d. If the quantitative information in paragraph 715-80-50-5(c), 715-80-50-5(e)(2), or 715-80-50-7(c) cannot be obtained without undue cost and effort, that quantitative information may be omitted and the employer shall describe what information has been omitted and why. In that circumstance, the employer also shall provide any qualitative information as of the most recent date available that would help users understand the financial information that otherwise is required to be disclosed about the plan. ____

(FASB ASC 715-80-50-7)

8. Disclosures about multiemployer plans that are subject to the guidance in the preceding paragraph shall be included in a separate section of the tabular disclosure required by paragraph 715-80-50-5. ____

(FASB ASC 715-80-50-8)

9. In addition to the information about the significant multiemployer plans that provide pension benefits required by paragraphs 715-80-50-5 and 715-80-50-7, disclose in a tabular format for each annual period for which a statement of income or statement of activities is presented, both of the following:

   a. Its total contributions made to all plans that are not individually significant ____
   b. Its total contributions made to all plans. ____

(FASB ASC 715-80-50-9)

Multiemployer Plans That Provide Postretirement Benefits Other Than Pensions

10. An employer shall disclose the amount of contributions to multiemployer plans that provide postretirement benefits other than pensions for each annual period for which a statement of income or statement of activities is presented. The disclosures shall include a description of the nature and effect of any changes that affect comparability of total employer contributions from period to period, such as:

    a. A business combination or a divestiture _____
    b. A change in the contractual employer contribution rate _____
    c. A change in the number of employees covered by the plan during each year. _____

    The disclosures also shall include a description of the nature of the benefits and the types of employees covered by these benefits, such as medical benefits provided to active employees and retirees.

(FASB ASC 715-80-50-11)

718 Compensation—Stock Compensation

1. For an entity with one or more share-based payment arrangements, information that enables users of the financial statements to understand all of the following:

    a. The nature and terms of such arrangements that existed during the period and the potential effects of those arrangements on shareholders _____
    b. The effect of compensation cost arising from share-based payment arrangements on the income statement _____
    c. The method of estimating the fair value of the goods or services received, or the fair value of the equity instruments granted (or offered to grant), during the period _____
    d. The cash flow effects resulting from share-based payment arrangements. _____

This disclosure is not required for interim reporting.

(FASB ASC 718-10-50-1)

***NOTE:** If the reporting entity grants equity or liability instruments under multiple share-based payment arrangements with employees, the information specified in a. through e. is to be provided separately for each different type of award to the extent that differences in the awards' characteristics make separate disclosure important to understanding the way the reporting entity uses share-based compensation.*

---

1. Plan description, including general terms of awards such as requisite service period(s) and other substantive conditions including vesting requirements, maximum contractual term of equity (or liability) share options or similar instruments, the number of shares authorized for awards of equity share options or other equity instruments, and the method used to measure compensation cost under share-based payment arrangements with employees. _____

(FASB ASC 718-10-50-2a through 2b)

2. For the most recent year for which an income statement is provided

    a. The number and weighted-average exercise prices (or conversion ratios) for each of the groups of share options or share units

        (1) Outstanding at the beginning of the year. _____
        (2) Granted during the year. _____
        (3) Exercised or converted during the year. _____
        (4) Forfeited during the year. _____

(5) Expired during the year. _____
(6) Exercisable or convertible at the end of the year. _____
(7) Outstanding at the end of the year. _____

(FASB ASC 718-10-50-2c1)

b. The number and weighted-average grant-date fair value (or calculated value or intrinsic value when permitted to be used) of equity instruments not specified in (1) above (such as shares of nonvested stock) for each of the following groups of equity instruments:

(1) Nonvested at the beginning of the year. _____
(2) Granted during the year. _____
(3) Vested during the year. _____
(4) Forfeited during the year. _____
(5) Nonvested at the end of the year. _____

(FASB ASC 718-10-50-2c2)

c. For each year for which an income statement is provided:

(1) Weighted-average grant-date fair value (calculated value or intrinsic value for those reporting entities permitted to use those methods) of equity options or other equity instruments granted during the year. _____
(2) The total intrinsic value of options exercised (or share units converted), share-based liabilities paid, and the total fair value of shares vested during the year. _____

(FASB ASC 718-10-50-2d)

d. For fully vested share options (or share units) and share options expected to vest at the date of the latest statement of financial position:

(1) The number, weighted-average exercise price (or conversion ratio), the aggregate intrinsic value (except for nonpublic entities), and the weighted-average remaining contractual term of options (or share units) outstanding. _____
(2) The number, weighted-average exercise price (or conversion ratio), the aggregate intrinsic value (except for nonpublic entities), and the weighted-average remaining contractual term of options (or share units) currently exercisable (or convertible). _____

(FASB ASC 718-10-50-2e)

e. For awards not accounted for using the intrinsic value method, for each year for which an income statement is presented

(1) A description of the method used during the year to estimate the fair value (or calculated value) of awards under share-based payment arrangements. _____
(2) A description of the significant assumptions used during the year to estimate the fair value (or calculated value) of share-based compensation awards including, where applicable:

(a) Expected term of share options and similar instruments, including a discussion of the method used to incorporate the contractual term of the instrument and the employees' expected exercise and postvesting employment termination behavior into the fair value (or calculated value) of the instrument. _____
(b) Expected volatility of the entity's shares and the method used to estimate it. _____

(c) If the entity uses a valuation method that employs different volatilities during the contractual term

1] The range of expected volatilities used. _____

2] The weighted-average expected volatility. _____

(d) If the entity is a nonpublic entity that uses the calculated value method

1] The reasons why it is not practicable for it to estimate the expected volatility of its share price. _____

2] The appropriate industry sector index it has selected and the reasons for selecting that particular index. _____

3] How it has calculated historical volatility using that index. _____

(e) Expected dividends and, if the entity uses a method employing different dividend rates during the contractual term, the range of expected dividends used and the weighted-average expected dividends. _____

(f) Risk-free rate(s) and, if the entity uses a method employing different risk-free rates, the range of risk-free rates used. _____

(g) The discount for postvesting restrictions and the method used to estimate it. _____

(FASB ASC 718-10-50-2f)

f. If an entity that grants equity or liability instruments under multiple share-based payment arrangements with employees, the information specified in paragraphs ASC 718-10-50 (a) through (f) separately for different types of awards to the extent that the differences in the characteristics of the awards make separate disclosure important to an understanding of the entity's use of share-based compensation. For example, separate disclosure of weighted-average exercise prices (or conversion ratios) at the end of the year for options (or share units) with a fixed exercise price (or conversion ratio) and those with an indexed exercise price (or conversion ratio); segregation of the number of options (or share units) not yet exercisable into those that will become exercisable (or convertible) based solely on fulfilling a service condition and those for which a performance condition must be met for the options (share units) to become exercisable (convertible), and separate disclosures for awards that are classified as equity and those classified as liabilities. In addition, an entity that has multiple share-based payment arrangements with employees must disclose information separately for different types of awards under those arrangements to the extent that differences in the characteristics of the awards make separate disclosure important to an understanding of the entity's use of share-based compensation. _____

(FASB ASC 718-10-50-2g)

g. For each year for which an income statement is presented:

(1) Total compensation cost for share-based payment arrangements recognized in income, the associated income tax benefit recognized, and the total compensation cost capitalized as part of the cost of an asset. _____

(2) A description of significant modifications, including the terms of the modifications, number of affected employees, and the total incremental compensation cost resulting from the modifications. _____

(FASB ASC 718-10-50-2h)

h. As of the latest statement of financial position date presented, the total compensation cost related to nonvested awards not yet recognized and the weighted-average period over which it is expected to be recognized. _____

(FASB ASC 718-10-50-2i)

i. The amount of cash received from exercise of share options and similar instruments granted under share-based payment arrangements and the tax benefit realized from stock options exercised during the annual period. _____

(FASB ASC 718-10-50-2j)

j. The amount of cash used to settle equity instruments granted under share-based payment arrangements. _____

(FASB ASC 718-10-50-2k)

k. A description of the reporting entity's policy (if any) for issuing shares upon share option exercise (or share unit conversion), including the source of the shares (i.e., newly issued shares or treasury shares). If, as a result of this policy, the entity expects to repurchase shares in the following annual period, an estimate of the amount (or range, if more appropriate) of shares to be repurchased during that period. _____

(FASB ASC 718-10-50-2l)

718-40 Employee Stock Ownership Plans (ESOP)

1. Description of the plan, including basis for determining contributions, groups covered, nature and effect of matters affecting comparability of information across periods. _____
2. The basis for releasing shares by leveraged and pension reversion ESOP. _____
3. Accounting policies pertinent to ESOP transactions. _____
4. Compensation cost recognized during the period. _____
5. Numbers of shares allocated, committed to be released, and held in suspense by the ESOP. _____
6. Fair value amount of unearned compensation at year-end. _____
7. Nature of any repurchase obligations and aggregate fair value thereof. _____
8. If material, the amount and treatment in the EPS computation of the tax benefit related to dividends paid to any employee stock ownership plan. _____

(FASB ASC 718-40-50-1)

720-20 Other Expenses—Insurance Costs

1. If the entity has changed from occurrence-based insurance to claims-made insurance or elects to significantly reduce or eliminate its insurance coverage, disclose if it is at least reasonably possible that a loss has been incurred and consider possible disclosures with respect to unasserted claims. (See 450-20-50-3 through 50-6 for additional details.) _____

(FASB ASC 720-20-50-1)

720-35 Other Expenses—Advertising Costs

1. The accounting policy for reporting advertising, indicating whether such costs are expensed as incurred or the first time the advertising takes place. _____

(FASB ASC 720-35-50-1a)

2. The total amount charged to advertising expense for each income statement presented. _____

(FASB ASC 720-35-50-1b)

730 Research and Development

1. Total research and development costs charged to expense, including research and development costs incurred for a computer software product to be sold, leased, or otherwise marketed. _____

(FASB ASC 730-10-50-1)

2. R&D arrangements
   a. Terms including royalties, purchase provisions, license agreements and funding. _____
   b. Amounts earned and costs incurred each period for which an income statement is presented. _____

(FASB ASC 730-20-50-1)

If a party to more than one research and development arrangement, aggregation of similar arrangements by type may be appropriate. Separately disclose each arrangement if necessary to understand the effects on the financial statements.

(FASB ASC 730-20-50-3)

740 Income Taxes

1. The components of the net deferred tax liability or asset recognized in an entity's statement of financial position shall be disclosed as follows:
   a. The total of all deferred tax liabilities. _____

(FASB ASC 740-10-50-2a)

   b. The total of all deferred tax assets. _____

(FASB ASC 740-10-50-2b)

   c. The total valuation allowance recognized for deferred tax assets. _____

(FASB ASC 740-10-50-2c)

2. The net change during the year in the total valuation allowance. _____

(FASB ASC 740-10-50-2)

3. Both of the following:
   a. The amounts and expiration dates of operating loss and tax credit carryforwards for tax purposes. _____

(FASB ASC 740-10-50-3a)

   b. Any portion of the valuation allowance for deferred tax assets for which subsequently recognized tax benefits will be credited directly to contributed capital (see paragraph 740-20-45-11). _____

(FASB ASC 740-10-50-3b)

4. If a change in an entity's tax status becomes effective after year-end in Year 2 but before the financial statements for Year 1 are issued or are available to be issued, disclose in the entity's financial statements for Year 1 the change in the entity's tax status for Year 2 and the effects of that change, if material. _____

(FASB ASC 740-10-50-4)

5. For a public entity, the approximate tax effect of each type of temporary difference and carryforward that gives rise to a significant portion of deferred tax liabilities and deferred tax assets (before allocation of valuation allowances). _____

(FASB ASC 740-10-50-6)

6. For a nonpublic entity, the types of significant temporary differences and carryforwards but may omit disclosure of the tax effects of each type. _____

(FASB ASC 740-10-50-8)

7. State amounts allocated to

   a. Current tax expense or benefit. _____
   b. Deferred tax expense or benefit (exclusive of the effects of other components listed below). _____
   c. Investment tax or other credits. _____
   d. Government grants (to the extent recognized as a reduction of income tax expense). _____
   e. The benefits of operating loss carryforwards. _____
   f. Tax expense that results from allocating certain tax benefits directly to contributed capital. _____
   g. Adjustments of a deferred tax liability or asset for enacted changes in tax laws or rates or a change in the tax status of the enterprise. _____
   h. Adjustments of the beginning-of-the-year balance of a valuation allowance because of a change in circumstances that causes a change in judgment about the realizability of the related deferred tax asset in future years. _____

(FASB ASC 740-10-50-9)

8. Amounts allocated to

   a. Continuing operations. _____
   b. Discontinued operations. _____
   c. Extraordinary items. _____
   d. Cumulative effect of accounting changes. _____
   e. Prior period adjustments. _____
   f. Other comprehensive income _____
   g. Items charged or credited directly to shareholders' equity. _____

(FASB ASC 740-10-50-10)

9. Reconcile statutory tax rates to actual rates for significant items (nonpublic enterprises need only disclose the nature of significant reconciling items). _____

(FASB ASC 740-10-50-11 through 13)

10. The nature and effect of any other significant matters affecting comparability of information for all periods presented. _____

(FASB ASC 740-10-50-14)

11. All of the following at the end of each annual reporting period presented:

   a. The total amounts of interest and penalties recognized in the statement of operations and the total amounts of interest and penalties recognized in the statement of financial position _____
   b. For positions for which it is reasonably possible that the total amounts of unrecognized tax benefits will significantly increase or decrease within 12 months of the reporting date:

      (1) The nature of the uncertainty _____

(2) The nature of the event that could occur in the next 12 months that would cause the change _____
(3) An estimate of the range of the reasonably possible change or a statement that an estimate of the range cannot be made. _____

c. A description of tax years that remain subject to examination by major tax jurisdictions. _____

(FASB ASC 740-10-50-15)

12. For public entities, both of the following at the end of each annual reporting period presented:

a. A tabular reconciliation of the total amounts of unrecognized tax benefits at the beginning and end of the period, which shall include at a minimum:

(1) The gross amounts of the increases and decreases in unrecognized tax benefits as a result of tax positions taken during a prior period _____
(2) The gross amounts of increases and decreases in unrecognized tax benefits as a result of tax positions taken during the current period _____
(3) The amounts of decreases in the unrecognized tax benefits relating to settlements with taxing authorities _____
(4) Reductions to unrecognized tax benefits as a result of a lapse of the applicable statute of limitations. _____

b. The total amount of unrecognized tax benefits that, if recognized, would affect the effective tax rate. _____

(FASB ASC 740-10-50-15A)

13. For public entities, state if entity is not subject to income taxes because income is taxed directly to owners. State the net difference between tax and book bases of assets and liabilities. _____

(FASB ASC 740-10-50-16)

14. If consolidated return filed, separately issued financial statements should state

a. Amount of current and deferred tax expense for each income statement and the tax-related balances due to or from affiliates for each statement of financial position. _____
b. The method of allocating consolidated amounts of current and deferred tax expense and effects of any change in that methodology. _____

(FASB ASC 740-10-50-17)

15. Policy on classification of interest and penalties in accordance with the alternatives permitted in paragraph 740-10-45-25 in the notes to the financial statements. _____

(FASB ASC 740-10-50-19)

16. Method of accounting for the investment credit (deferral or flow-through method) and amounts involved, when material. _____

(FASB ASC 740-10-50-20)

740-30 Income Taxes—Other Considerations or Special Areas

1. When a deferred tax liability is not recognized because of the exceptions to comprehensive recognition of deferred taxes, the following information shall be disclosed:

a. A description of the types of temporary differences for which a deferred tax liability has not been recognized and the types of events that would cause those temporary differences to become taxable. _____
b. The cumulative amount of each type of temporary difference. _____
c. The amount of the unrecognized deferred tax liability for temporary differences related to investments in foreign subsidiaries and foreign corporate joint ventures that are essentially permanent in duration if determination of that liability is practicable or a statement that determination is not practicable. _____
d. The amount of the deferred tax liability for temporary differences other than those in c. above (i.e., undistributed domestic earnings, the bad-debt reserve for tax purposes of a US savings and loan association or other qualified thrift lender, the policyholders' surplus of a life insurance enterprise, and the statutory reserve funds of a US steamship enterprise) that is not recognized. _____

(FASB ASC 740-30-50-2)

740-270 Income Taxes—Interim Reporting

1. In the interim period financial statements, the reasons for significant variations in the customary relationship between income tax expense and pretax accounting income, if they are not otherwise apparent from the financial statements or from the nature of the entity's business. _____

(FASB ASC 740-270-50-1)

BROAD TRANSACTIONS

805 Business Combinations

1. Business combinations *occurring during the reporting period* or after the reporting date but before the financial statements are issued. _____

(FASB ASC 805-10-50-1)

2. The acquirer is to disclose the following information for each business combination that occurs during the reporting period

   a. The name and a description of the acquiree. _____
   b. The acquisition date. _____
   c. The percentage of voting equity interest acquired. _____
   d. The primary reasons for the business combination and a description of how the acquirer obtained control over the acquiree. _____
   e. For transactions that are recognized separately from the acquisition of assets and assumptions of liabilities in the business combination (see paragraph 805-10-25-20), a description of each transaction, how the acquirer accounted for each transaction, the amounts recognized for each transaction and the line item in the financial statements in which each amount is recognized, and if the transaction is the effective settlement of a preexisting relationship, the method used to determine the settlement amount. _____
   f. For transactions required in e., include the amount of acquisition-related costs, the amount recognized as an expense, and the line item or items in the income statement in which those expenses are recognized, and the amount of any issuance costs not recognized as an expense and how they were recognized. _____
   g. In a business combination achieved in stages, all of the following:

      (1) The acquisition-date fair value of the equity interest in the acquiree held by the acquirer immediately before the acquisition date _____

(2) The amount of any gain or loss recognized as a result of remeasuring to fair value the equity interest in the acquiree held by the acquirer immediately before the business combination (see paragraph 805-10-25-10) and the line item in the income statement in which that gain or loss is recognized _____

(3) The valuation techniques used to measure the acquisition-date fair value of the equity interest in the acquiree held by the acquirer immediately before the business combination _____

(4) Information that enables users of the acquirer's financial statements to assess the inputs used to develop the fair value measurement of the equity interest in the acquiree held by the acquirer immediately before the business combination. _____

h. If the acquirer is a public business entity, all of the following:

(1) The amounts of revenue and earnings of the acquiree since the acquisition date included in the consolidated income statement for the reporting period. _____

(2) If comparative financial statements are not presented, the revenue and earnings of the combined entity for the current reporting period as though the acquisition date for all business combinations that occurred during the year had been as of the beginning of the annual reporting period (supplemental pro forma information). _____

(3) If comparative financial statements are presented, the revenue and earnings of the combined entity as though the business combination(s) that occurred during the current year had occurred as of the beginning of the comparable prior annual reporting period (supplemental pro forma information). _____

(4) The nature and amount of any material, nonrecurring pro forma adjustments directly attributable to the business combination(s) included in the reported pro forma revenue and earnings (supplemental pro forma information). _____

i. If disclosure of any of the information required by (h) is impracticable, the acquirer discloses that fact and explains why the disclosure is impracticable.

(FASB ASC 805-10-50-2)

3. For individually immaterial business combinations occurring during the reporting period that are material collectively, discloses the information required by (e) through (h) in the preceding paragraph in the aggregate. _____

(FASB ASC 805-10-50-3)

4. If the acquisition date is after the reporting date but before the financial statements are issued or available to be issued, disclose the information required by FASB ASC 805-20-50-2. If the accounting is incomplete at that time, describe which disclosures could not be made and why. _____

(FASB ASC 805-10-50-4)

5. Disclose financial effects of adjustments during the current period that relate to business combinations that occurred in the current or previous reporting periods. _____

(FASB ASC 805-10-50-5)

6. In a business combination, if the initial accounting for particular items is incomplete, disclose the reasons why, the items for which accounting is incomplete, and the nature and amount of any measurement period adjustments recognized during the reporting period. _____

(FASB ASC 805-10-50-6)

7. If the specific disclosures do not meet the disclosure objectives of this Topic whatever additional information is necessary to meet those objectives. _____

(FASB ASC 805-10-50-7)

805-20 Identifiable Assets and Liabilities and Any Noncontrolling Interest

1. Make the following disclosures for identifiable assets and liabilities and any noncontrolling interest.

   a. For indemnification assets:

      (1) The amount recognized as of the acquisition date _____
      (2) A description of the arrangement and the basis for determining the amount of the payment. _____

   An estimate of the range of outcomes (undiscounted) or, if a range cannot be estimated, that fact and the reasons why. Disclose if the maximum amount of the payment is unlimited

   b. For acquired receivables such as loans, direct finance leases under ASC 840, and any other class of receivables

      (1) The fair value of the receivables. _____
      (2) The gross contractual amount of the receivables. _____
      (3) The best estimate at the acquisition date of the contractual cash flows not expected to be collected. _____

   c. The amounts recognized as of the acquisition date for each major class of assets acquired and liabilities assumed. _____
   d. For contingencies, the following:

      (1) For assets and liabilities arising from contingencies recognized at the acquisition date:

         (a) The amounts recognized at the acquisition date and the measurement basis applied (that is, at fair value or at an amount recognized in accordance with Topic 450 and Section 450-20-25) _____
         (b) The nature of the contingencies. _____

      An acquirer may aggregate disclosures for assets or liabilities arising from contingencies that are similar in nature.

      (2) For contingencies that are not recognized at the acquisition date, the disclosures required by Topic 450 if the criteria for disclosures in that Topic are met. _____

      An acquirer may aggregate disclosures for assets and liabilities arising from contingencies that are similar in nature.

   e. For each business combination in which the acquirer holds less than 100 percent of the equity interest in the acquiree, the fair value of the noncontrolling interest in the acquiree and the valuation technique and significant inputs used to measure the fair value. _____

(FASB ASC 805-20-50-1)

2. If individually immaterial business combinations occurring during the reporting period are material collectively, disclose the information in FAS ASC 805-20-50-1 in the aggregate. _____

(FAS ASC 805-20-50-2)

3. If the acquisition date of a business combination is after the reporting date but before the financial statements are issued or are available to be issued (as discussed in Section 855-10-25), disclose the information required above. If the initial accounting for the business combination is incomplete at the time the financial statements are issued or are available to be issued, describe which disclosures could not be made and the reason why. _____

(FAS ASC 805-20-50-3)

805-30 Goodwill or Gain from Bargain Purchase

1. For each business combination that occurs during the reporting period:

   a. A qualitative description of the factors that make up goodwill recognized (e.g., expected synergies from combining acquiree operations with those of the acquirer, intangible assets that do not qualify for recognition separately from goodwill, or other factors). _____
   b. The acquisition-date fair value of the total consideration transferred and the acquisition-date fair value of each major classs of consideration, such as cash, other tangible or intangible assets, liabilities incurred, equity interests of the acquirer. _____
   c. For contingent consideration arrangements, the amount recognized as of the acquisition date, a description of the arrangement and the basis for determining the payment, an estimate of the range of outcomes or the reason why a range cannot be estimated, and if the maximum amount of the payment is unlimited. _____
   d. The total amount of goodwill that is expected to be deductible for tax purposes. _____
   e. If the acquirer is required to disclose segment information, the goodwill by segment. If the assignment of goodwill to reporting units has not been completed on the financial statements' issuance date, the acquirer is to disclose that fact. _____
   f. Bargain purchases

      (1) The amount of gain recognized. _____
      (2) The line item in the income statement in which the gain is recognized. _____
      (3) A description of the reasons why the transaction resulted in a gain. _____

(FASB ASC 805-30-50-1)

2. If business combinations occurring during the reporting period are individually immaterial, but material collectively, information required by the preceding paragraph in the aggregate. _____

(FASB ASC 805-30-50-2)

3. If the acquisition date of a business combination is after the reporting date but before the financial statements are issued or are available to be issued, the information required by paragraph 805-30-50-1. If the accounting for the business combination is incomplete at the time the financial statements are issued or are available to be issued, describe which disclosures could not be made and the reason why they could not be made. _____

(FASB ASC 805-30-50-3)

4. For each material business combination or in the aggregate for individually immaterial business combinations that are material collectively:

   a. For each reporting period after the acquisition date until the entity collects, sells, or otherwise loses the right to a contingent consideration asset, or until the entity settles a contingent consideration liability or the liability is cancelled or expires, all of the following:

(1) Any changes in the recognized amounts, including any differences arising upon settlement _____
(2) Any changes in the range of outcomes (undiscounted) and the reasons for those changes _____
(3) The fair value disclosures required by Section 820-10-50. _____

b. A reconciliation of the carrying amount of goodwill at the beginning and end of the reporting period as required by paragraph 350-20-50-1. _____

(FASB ASC 805-30-50-4)

805-50 Business Combinations—Related Issues

1. The nature of and effects on earnings per share (EPS) of nonrecurring intra-entity transactions involving long-term assets and liabilities. _____

(FASB ASC 805-50-50-2)

2. In the notes to financial statements of the receiving entity, the following for the period in which the transfer of assets and liabilities or exchange of equity interests occurred:

a. The name and brief description of the entity included in the reporting entity as a result of the net asset transfer or exchange of equity interests _____
b. The method of accounting for the transfer of net assets or exchange of equity interests. _____

(FASB ASC 805-50-50-3)

808 Collaborative Arrangements

1. In the initial interim or annual period and all annual periods thereafter, a participant to a collaborative arrangement discloses the following information. Disclose this information separately for each individually significant collaborative arrangement:

a. Information regarding the nature and purpose of its collaborative arrangements. _____
b. The entity's rights and obligations under the arrangements. _____
c. The accounting policy for collaborative arrangements. _____
d. The amounts attributable to transactions arising from the collaborative arrangement between participants for each period an income statement is presented and their classification in the income statement. _____

(FASB ASC 808-10-50-1)

810 Consolidations

Consolidation Policy

1. Consolidated financial statements shall disclose the consolidation policy that is being followed. In most cases this can be made apparent by the headings or other information in the financial statements, but in other cases a footnote is required. _____

(FASB ASC 810-10-50-1)

2. A parent with one or more less-than-wholly-owned subsidiaries discloses for each reporting period:

a. Separately on the face of the consolidated financial statements, the amounts of consolidated net income and consolidated comprehensive income and the related amounts of each attributable to the parent and the noncontrolling interest. _____

b. Either on the face of the consolidated income statement or in the notes, amounts attributable to the parent for the following items, if reported in the consolidated financial statements:

(1) Income from continuing operations. _____
(2) Discontinued operations. _____
(3) Extraordinary items. _____

c. Either in the consolidated statement of changes in equity if presented, or in the notes, a reconciliation of beginning of period and end of period carrying amounts of total equity, equity attributable to the parent, and equity attributable to the noncontrolling interest, separately disclosing

(1) Net income. _____
(2) Transactions with owners acting in their capacity as owners, separately showing contributions and distributions. _____
(3) Each component of other comprehensive income _____

d. A separate schedule in the notes to the consolidated financial statements showing the effects of any changes in the parent's ownership interest in a subsidiary on the equity attributable to the parent. _____

(FASB ASC 810-10-50-1A)

3. If a subsidiary is deconsolidated during the reporting period, the parent is to disclose

a. The amount of gain or loss recognized. _____
b. The portion of any gain or loss that relates to the remeasurement to fair value of any investment retained by the former parent in its former subsidiary. _____
c. The caption in the income statement in which the gain or loss is recognized unless presented separately on the face of the income statement. _____
d. Description of the valuation techniques used to measure the fair value of the former investment. _____
e. Enough information for users to assess the inputs used in the development of fair value of the former investment. _____
f. The nature of any continuing involvement with the entity acquiring the assets. _____
g. Whether the transaction was with a related party. _____
h. Whether the former subsidiary or entity acquiring the assets will be a related party after the deconsolidation. _____

(FASB ASC 810-10-50-1B)

A Change in the Difference Between Parent and Subsidiary Fiscal Year-Ends

4. For all entities that change (or eliminate) a previously existing difference between the reporting periods of a parent and a consolidated entity or an investor and an equity method investee, the disclosures required by Topic 250. This paragraph does not apply in situations in which a parent entity or an investor changes its fiscal year-end. _____

(FASB ASC 810-10-50-2)

5. Disclosures to be made by the primary beneficiary of a variable interest entity (unless that party also holds a majority voting interest). The principal objectives of these disclosures are to provide the users of the financial statements with information to enable an understanding of:

a. the significant judgments and assumptions made by management in determining whether it must consolidate a VIE and/or disclose information about its involvement in a VIE; _____

b. the nature of restrictions on a consolidated VIE's assets and on the settlement of its liabilities reported by a reporting entity in its statement of financial position, including the carrying amounts of such assets and liabilities; _____
c. the nature of, and changes in, the risks associated with the reporting entity's involvement with the VIE; and _____
d. how a reporting entity's involvement with the VIE affects its financial position, financial performance, and cash flows. _____

(FASB ASC 810-10-50-2AA)

Accounting Alternative[6]

6. For a private company that elects the accounting alternative (see 810-10-15-17A),

   a. Amount and key terms of liabilities that are recognized by the lessor and expose the lessee to providing financial support to the lessor legal entity. _____
   b. Qualitative description of circumstances not recognized by the lessor and that expose the lessee to providing financial support to the legal entity. _____

(FASB ASC 810-10-50-2AD)

7. In applying the disclosures above, the lessee should consider exposures through implicit guarantees, including

   a. The existence of an economic incentive for the lessee to act as guarantor or to make funds available. _____
   b. Those action have occurred in similar past situations _____
   c. The lessor acting as guarantor or making funds available. _____

(FASB ASC 810-10-50-2AE)

8. When disclosing lessor legal entity information, the private company lessee should combine the disclosures with disclosures requested by other guidance, such as guarantees, related party disclosures, and leases. These can be combined in a single note or through cross references. _____

(FASB ASC 810-10-50-2AF)

(Note: this ends the guidance from ASU 2014-07.)

Primary Beneficiary

9. The primary beneficiary of a VIE that is a business is to provide the disclosures required by other guidance. The primary beneficiary of a VIE that is not a business is to disclose the amount of any gain or loss recognized on the initial consolidation of the VIE. In addition to other disclosures required by this topic, the primary beneficiary (PB) of a VIE is to disclose the following:

   a. The carrying amounts and classification of the VIE's assets and liabilities in the statement of financial position that are consolidated, including qualitative information about the relationships between those assets and liabilities. _____
   b. Lack of recourse if creditors (or holders of beneficial interests) of a consolidated VIE have no recourse to the general credit of the PB. _____
   c. Terms or arrangements, giving consideration to both explicit arrangements and implicit variable interests that could require the reporting entity to provide financial support to the VIE, including events or circumstances that could expose the reporting entity to a loss. _____

(FASB ASC 810-10-50-3)

---

[6] The disclosures related to the Accounting Alternative are based on guidance in ASU 2014-07. Information about that guidance and entity eligibility can be found in the chapter on ASC 810.

10. In addition to disclosure required by other guidance, a reporting entity that holds a variable interest in a VIE but is not the VIE's primary beneficiary is to disclose

    a. The carrying amounts and classification of the assets and liabilities in the statement of financial position of the reporting entity that relate to the reporting entity's variable interest in the VIE. _____
    b. The entity's maximum exposure to loss as a result of its involvement with the VIE, including how the maximum exposure is determined and the significant sources of the reporting entity's exposure to the VIE. If management is unable to quantify the maximum exposure to loss, that fact is to be disclosed. _____
    c. A tabular comparison of the carrying amounts of the assets and liabilities, as required in a. above, and the enterprise's maximum exposure to loss as required in b. above. Management is to provide qualitative and quantitative information to enable financial statement users to understand the differences between the two amounts. The discussion is to include, but not be limited to, the terms of arrangements, giving consideration to both explicit arrangements and implicit variable interests, that could require the reporting entity to provide financial support to the VIE (such as liquidity arrangements and obligations to purchase assets), including events or circumstances that could expose the reporting entity to loss. _____
    d. Encouraged but not required, information regarding any liquidity arrangements, guarantees, and/or other commitments by third parties that may affect the fair value or risk of the reporting entity's VIE is encouraged to be provided. _____
    e. If applicable, significant factors and judgments made in determining the power to direct the activities of a VIE that most significantly impact the VIE's economic performance is shared. _____

(FASB ASC 810-10-50-4)

11. A reporting entity that is a primary beneficiary of a VIE or a reporting entity that holds a variable interest in a VIE but is not the entity's primary beneficiary is to disclose

    a. The methodology used to determine whether the reporting entity is the PB of a VIE, including, but not limited to, significant judgments and assumptions made. _____
    b. If facts and circumstances change, resulting in a change to the conclusion to consolidate a VIE in the most recent financial statements, the primary factors that caused the change and the effect on the financial statements of the reporting entity. _____
    c. Whether the reporting entity has provided financial or other support (explicitly or implicitly) during the periods presented to the VIE that it was not previously contractually required to provide or whether the reporting entity intends to provide that support, including both of the following

        (1) The type and amount of support, including situations in which the reporting entity assisted the VIE in obtaining another type of support. _____
        (2) The primary reasons for providing the support. _____

    d. Qualitative and quantitative information about the reporting entity's involvement with the VIE (considering both explicit arrangements and implicit variable interest) including, but not limited to, the nature, purpose, size, and activities of the VIE, and how the VIE is financed. _____

(FASB ASC 810-10-50-5A)

12. A VIE may issue voting equity interests, and the entity that holds a majority voting interest also may be the primary beneficiary of the VIE. If so, and if the VIE meets the definition of a business and the VIE's assets can be used for purposes other than the settlement of the VIE's obligations, the disclosures in the preceding paragraph are not required. ____

(FASB ASC 810-10-50-5B)

13. An enterprise that does not apply ASC 810 to one or more VIE or potential VIE because after exhaustive efforts it is unable to obtain the necessary information is to make the following disclosures:

    a. The number of legal entities to which ASC 810 is not being applied and the reason why the information required to apply ASC 810 is not available. ____
    b. The nature, purpose, size (if the information is available), and activities of the VIE or potential VIE and the nature of the enterprise's involvement with those entities. ____
    c. The enterprise's maximum exposure to loss as a result of its involvement with the entity or entities ____
    d. The amount of income, expense, purchases, sales, or other measure of activity between the reporting enterprise and the entity (entities) for all periods presented. (If not practicable to present the prior period information in the first set of financial statements to which this requirement applies, that prior period information may be omitted.) ____

(FASB ASC 810-10-50-6)

14. Disclosures about VIEs may be reported in the aggregate for similar entities if separate reporting would not provide more useful information to financial statement users. A reporting entity shall disclose how similar entities are aggregated and shall distinguish between:

    a. VIEs that are not consolidated because the reporting entity is not the primary beneficiary but has a variable interest ____
    b. VIEs that are consolidated. ____

    In determining whether to aggregate VIEs, the reporting entity shall consider quantitative and qualitative information about the different risk and reward characteristics of each VIE and the significance of each VIE to the entity. The disclosures shall be presented in a manner that clearly explains to financial statement users the nature and extent of an entity's involvement with VIEs.

(FASB ASC 810-10-50-9)

815 Derivatives and Hedging

1. Entities with derivative instruments are to disclose information that will enable users of the financial statements to understand

    a. How and why the entity uses derivatives. ____
    b. How derivatives and related hedged items are accounted for. ____
    c. How derivatives and related hedged items affect the entity's financial position, financial performance, and cash flows. ____

(FASB ASC 815-10-50-1)

2. Entities that hold or issue derivative instruments (or nonderivative instruments that are designated and qualify as hedging instruments) are to disclose the following information for every interim and annual reporting period for which a statement of financial position and income statement are presented:

a. The objectives for holding or issuing those instruments. _____
b. The context needed to understand those objectives. _____
c. The strategies for achieving those objectives. _____
d. Information to enable users of the financial statements to understand the volume of the entity's derivative activity. _____

(FASB ASC 815-10-50-1A)

3. The entity is to select the format and specifics of these volume-related disclosures that are most relevant and practical for their individual facts and circumstances. Information regarding these instruments is to be disclosed in the context of each instrument's underlying risk exposure (e.g., interest rate, credit, foreign exchange rate, or overall price). These instruments are also to be distinguished between those used for risk management purposes and those used for other purposes. Derivatives used for risk management purposes include those designated as hedging instruments as well as those used as economic hedges for other purposes with respect to the risk exposures of the entity. _____

(FASB ASC 815-10-50-1B)

4. The description is to distinguish between hedging instruments designated as fair value hedges, cash flow hedges, and hedges of foreign currency exposure in a net investment in a foreign operation, and derivative instruments used as economic hedges and for other purposes related to the entity's risk exposures, and for other purposes. _____

(FASB ASC 815-10-50-2)

5. If an entity opts to apply the simplified hedge approach[7] (815-20-25-131A through 131E) in accounting for a qualifying receivable-variable, pay-fixed interest rate swap, the entity may use the settlement value of the swap in place of fair value in the disclosures required by ASC 815 or in other fair value disclosures. The entity must clearly state the amounts are the settlement value. Those amounts must be disclosed separately from amounts disclosed at fair value. _____
6 For derivatives not designated as hedging instruments, the description is to indicate the purpose of the derivative activity for which the derivatives are held or issued. _____

(FASB ASC 815-10-50-4)

7. Present, in a tabular format, all of the following information regarding the location and fair value amounts of derivative instruments reported in the statement of financial position. _____
8. For an entity that holds or issues derivative instruments (and nonderivative instruments that are designated and qualify as hedging instruments pursuant to paragraphs 815-20-25-58 and 815-20-25-66), disclose all of the following for every annual and interim reporting period for which a statement of financial position and statement of financial performance are presented:

   a. The location and fair value amounts of derivative instruments (and such nonderivative instruments) reported in the statement of financial position _____
   b. The location and amount of the gains and losses on derivative instruments (and such nonderivative instruments) and related hedged items reported in any of the following:

      (1) The statement of financial performance _____

---

[7] ASC 815-10-50-3 was added by ASU 2014-03, a consensus of the Private Company Council. See the technical alert in the chapter on ASC 815 for information on the entities eligible for the "accounting alternative" and the effective date.

(2) The statement of financial position (for example, gains and losses initially recognized in other comprehensive income). _____

(FASB ASC 815-10-50-4A)

9. For the disclosures required by paragraph a above:

   a. Present the fair value of derivative instruments on a gross basis even when the instruments are subject to master netting arrangements and qualify for net presentation in the statement of financial position under ASC 815-10-45. _____
   b. Cash collateral payables and receivables associated with derivative instruments are not to be added to or netted against the fair value amounts. _____
   c. Present fair value amounts as separate asset and liability values segregated between derivatives designated and qualifying as hedging instruments and those that are not. Within each of these two broad categories, fair value amounts are to be presented separately by type of derivative contract (e.g., interest rate contracts, foreign exchange contracts, equity contracts, commodity contracts, credit contracts, etc.). _____
   d. The disclosure is to identify the line item or items in the statement of financial position in which the fair value amounts for these categories are included. _____

   Present amounts required to be reported for nonderivative instruments at the carrying value of the nonderivative hedging instrument, which includes the adjustment for the foreign currency transaction gain or loss on that instrument.

(FASB ASC 815-10-50-4B)

10. For the gains and losses disclosed pursuant to paragraph 815-10-50-4A(b) present separately for all of the following by type of contract (as discussed in the following paragraph):

    a. Derivative instruments designated and qualifying as fair value hedges and the related hedged items. _____
    b. The effective portion of gains and losses on derivative instruments designated and qualifying in cash flow hedges and net investment hedges that was recognized in OCI during the current period. _____
    c. The effective portion of gains and losses on derivative instruments designated and qualifying as cash flow hedges and net investment hedges recorded in accumulated other comprehensive income (AOCI) during the term of the hedging relationship and reclassified to earnings during the current period. _____
    d. The portion of gains and losses on derivative instruments designated and qualifying in cash flow hedges and net investment hedges representing

       (1) The amount of the hedges' ineffectiveness, and _____
       (2) The amount, if any, excluded from the assessment of hedge effectiveness. _____

    e. Derivative instruments not designated or qualifying as hedging instruments. _____

(FASB ASC 815-10-50-4C)

11. Disclosures required by FASB ASC 815-10-50-4C shall both

    a. Be presented separately by type of contract (e.g., interest rate, foreign exchange, equity, commodity, credit, and other contracts) and _____
    b. Identify the line item in the statement of financial position in which the gains and losses for these categories are included. _____

(FASB ASC 815-10-50-4D)

12. Present, in a tabular format, the disclosures required by 815-10-40-4A(a) and 50-4A(b), except for the information required for hedged items by 815-10-50-4C(a). For a derivative instrument where a portion is a hedging instrument and a portion is not a hedging instrument, allocate the related amounts to the appropriate categories with the disclosure table. _____

(FASB ASC 815-10-50-4E)

13. For derivative instruments that are not designated or qualifying as hedging instruments, if the entity's policy is to include these derivative instruments in its trading activities (such as part of a trading portfolio that includes derivative and nonderivative or cash instruments), management can elect not to separately disclose gains and losses as required by FASB ASC 815-10-50-4C(e), provided all of the following information is disclosed:

    a. The gains and losses on its trading activities (including both derivative and nonderivative instruments) recognized in the income statement, separately by major types of items (e.g., fixed income/interest rates, foreign exchange, equity, commodity, and credit). _____
    b. The line items in the income statement that include gains and losses from trading activities. _____
    c. A description of the nature of the entity's trading activities and related risks and how the entity manages those risks. _____

    If the disclosure is elected, include a footnote in the required tables referencing the use of the alternative disclosures for trading activities.

(FASB ASC 815-10-50-4F)

Credit-Risk-Related Contingent Features

14. For derivative instruments and nonderivative hedging instruments, disclose all of the following:

    a. The existence and nature of credit-risk-related contingent features _____
    b. The circumstances that could trigger the features in derivative instruments that are in a net liability position at the end of the reporting period. _____
    c. The aggregate fair value amounts of derivative instruments that contain credit-risk-related contingent features that are in a net liability position at the end of the reporting period. _____
    d. The aggregate fair value of assets that are already posted as collateral at the end of the reporting period, and _____
    e. The aggregate fair value of additional assets that would be required to be posted as collateral, and/or _____
    f. The aggregate fair value of assets needed to settle the instrument immediately, if the credit-risk-related contingent features were triggered at the end of the reporting period. _____
    g. The amounts required to be reported for nonderivative instruments designated and qualifying as hedging instruments are the carrying value of the nonderivative hedging instrument, including the adjustment for the foreign currency transaction gain or loss on that instrument. _____

(FASB ASC 815-10-50-4H)

Information in More than One Footnote

15. If information about derivative instruments (or nonderivative instruments that are designated and qualify as hedging instruments) is disclosed in more than a single note, cross-reference from the derivative note to other notes in which derivative-related information is disclosed. _____

(FASB ASC 815-10-50-4I)

Credit Derivatives

16. Credit derivatives disclosures are to be made by the seller (the party that assumes credit risk), which could be a guarantor in a guarantee-type contact, and any party that provides the credit protection in an option-type contract, a credit default swap, or any other credit derivative contract. _____

(FASB ASC 815-10-50-4J)

17. The seller of credit derivatives is to disclose information about its credit derivatives and hybrid instruments that have embedded credit derivatives to enable users of the financial statements to assess their potential effect on the seller's financial position, financial performance, and cash flows for each statement of financial position presented. The seller of a credit derivative should disclose the following information and

    a. The nature of the credit derivative, including

        (1) The approximate terms. _____
        (2) The reason(s) for entering into the credit derivative. _____
        (3) The events or circumstances that would require the seller to perform under the credit derivative. _____
        (4) The current status of the payment/performance risk of the credit derivative. _____
        (5) If the entity uses internal groupings for purposes of item (a)(4), how those groupings are determined and used for managing risk. _____

    b. All of the following information about the maximum potential amount of future payments under the credit derivative:

        (1) The maximum potential amount of future payments (undiscounted) the seller could be required to make under the credit derivative. _____
        (2) The fact that the terms of the credit derivative provide for no limitation to the maximum potential future payments under the contract, if applicable. _____
        (3) If the seller is unable to develop an estimate of the maximum potential amount of future payments under the credit derivative, the reasons why it cannot estimate the maximum potential amount _____

    c. The fair value of the credit derivative as of the date of the statement of financial position. _____
    d. The nature of any recourse provisions that would enable the seller to recover from third parties any of the amounts paid under the credit derivative. _____
    e. Any assets held either as collateral or by third parties that, upon the occurrence of any specified triggering event or condition under the credit derivative, the seller can obtain and liquidate to recover all or a portion of the amounts paid under the credit derivative. _____
    f. If estimable, the approximate extent to which the proceeds from liquidation of assets held either as collateral or by third parties would be expected to cover the maximum potential amount of future payments under the credit derivative. In its estimate of potential recoveries, the seller of credit protection shall consider the effect of any purchased credit protection with identical underlying(s). _____

g. These disclosures do not apply to an embedded derivative feature related to the transfer of credit risk that is only in the form of subordination of one financial instrument to another. _____

(FASB ASC 815-10-50-4K)

Qualitative Disclosures

18. Qualitative disclosures about an entity's objectives and strategies for using derivative instruments (and nonderivative instruments that are designated and qualify as hedging instruments pursuant to paragraphs 815-20-25-58 and 815-20-25-66) may be more meaningful if such objectives and strategies are described in the context of an entity's overall risk exposures relating to all of the following:

    a. Interest rate risk _____
    b. Foreign exchange risk _____
    c. Commodity price risk _____
    d. Credit risk _____
    e. Equity price risk. _____

    Those additional qualitative disclosures, if made, should include a discussion of those exposures even though the entity does not manage some of those exposures by using derivative instruments. An entity is encouraged, but not required, to provide such additional qualitative disclosures about those risks and how they are managed.

(FASB ASC 815-10-50-5)

Unconditional Purchase Obligations

19. If an unconditional purchase obligation is subject to the requirements of both Topic 440 and subtopic 815-10-50, comply with both sets of disclosure requirements. _____

(FASB ASC 815-10-50-6)

Balance Sheet Offsetting

20. Disclose the policy to offset or not offset in accordance with paragraph 815-10-45-6. _____

(FASB ASC 815-10-50-7)

The information required by paragraphs 210-20-50-1 through 50-6 for all recognized derivative instruments accounted for in accordance with Topic 815, including bifurcated embedded derivatives, which are either:

a. Offset in accordance with either Section 210-20-45 or Section 815-10-45
b. Subject to an enforceable master netting arrangement or similar agreement.

(FASB ASC 815-10-50-7A)

21. Disclose the amounts recognized at the end of each reporting period for the right to reclaim cash collateral or the obligation to return cash collateral as follows:

    a. A reporting entity that has made an accounting policy decision to offset fair value amounts shall separately disclose amounts recognized for the right to reclaim cash collateral or the obligation to return cash collateral that have been offset against net derivative positions in accordance with paragraph 815-10-45-5. _____
    b. A reporting entity shall separately disclose amounts recognized for the right to reclaim cash collateral or the obligation to return cash collateral under master netting arrangements that have not been offset against net derivative instrument positions. _____

c. A reporting entity that has made an accounting policy decision to not offset fair value amounts shall separately disclose the amounts recognized for the right to reclaim cash collateral or the obligation to return cash collateral under master netting arrangements. _____

(FASB ASC 815-10-50-8)

Certain Contracts on Debt and Equity Securities

22. Disclose the accounting policy for the premium paid to acquire an option that is classified as held to maturity or available for use. _____

(FASB ASC 815-10-50-9)

815-15 Embedded Derivatives

Hybrid Instruments That Are Not Separated

1. With respect to hybrid instruments that have embedded credit derivatives, the seller of the embedded credit derivative is to disclose the required information for the entire hybrid instrument, not just the embedded credit derivatives. _____

(FASB ASC 815-15-50-1)

2. Information that will allow users to understand the effect of changes in fair value of hybrid financial instruments measured at fair value under the election and under the practicability exception in paragraph 815-15-30-1 on earnings. _____

(FASB ASC 815-15-50-2)

Embedded Conversion Option That Is No Longer Bifurcated

3. Disclose both of the following for the period in which an embedded conversion option previously accounted for as a derivative instrument no longer meets the separation criteria under this subtopic:

   a. A description of the principal changes causing the embedded conversion option to no longer require bifurcation. _____
   b. The amount of the liability for the conversion option reclassified to stockholders' equity. _____

(FASB ASC 815-15-50-3)

815-25 Fair Value Hedges

1. Disclosures for every interim and annual reporting period for which a statement of financial position and income statement are presented are to include the following for derivative instruments as well as nonderivative instruments that may give rise to foreign currency transaction gains or losses under ASC 830-20, that have been designated and have qualified as fair value hedging instruments and for the related hedged items

   a. The net gain or loss recognized in net income during the reporting period representing

      (1) The amount of the hedges' ineffectiveness, and _____
      (2) The component of the derivative instrument's gain or loss, if any, excluded from the assessment of hedge effectiveness. _____

   b. The amount of net gain or loss recognized in net income when a hedged firm commitment no longer qualifies as a fair value hedge. _____

(FASB ASC 815-25-50-1)

815-30 Cash Flow Hedges

1. For cash flow hedges

    a. For derivative instruments that have been designated and have qualified as cash flow hedging instruments and for the related hedging transactions:

        (1) A description of the transactions or other events that will result in the reclassification into earnings of gains and losses that are reported in accumulated other comprehensive income, and _____

        (2) The estimated net amount of the existing gains or losses at the reporting date that is expected to be reclassified into earnings within the next 12 months. _____

        (3) The maximum length of time over which the entity is hedging its exposure to the variability in future cash flows for forecasted transactions excluding those forecasted transactions related to the payment of variable interest on existing financial instruments. _____

        (4) The amount of gains or losses reclassified into earnings as a result of the discontinuance of cash flow hedges because it is probable that the original forecasted transactions will not occur by the end of the originally specified time period or within the additional period of time as specified by ASC 815-30-40. _____

(FASB ASC 815-30-50-1)

2. As part of the disclosures of accumulated other comprehensive income, pursuant to paragraph 220-10-45-14 through 45-14A, separately disclose all of the following:

    a. The beginning and ending accumulated derivative instrument gain or loss _____

    b. The related net change associated with current period hedging transactions _____

    c. The net amount of any reclassification into earnings. _____

(FASB ASC 815-30-50-2)

815-35 Net Investment Hedges

1. Quantitative disclosures about derivative instruments may be more useful and less likely to be considered out of context or otherwise misunderstood, if similar information is disclosed about other financial instruments or nonfinancial assets and liabilities to which the derivative instruments are related by activity. In those situations, management is encouraged, but not required, to present a more complete picture of its activities by disclosing that information. _____

(FASB ASC 815-35-50-1)

815-40 Contracts in Entity's Own Entity

1. Disclose changes in the fair value of all contracts classified as assets or liabilities. _____

(FASB ASC 815-40-50-1)

2. If the contracts meet the definition for a derivative instrument, present disclosures required for derivatives. _____

(FASB ASC 815-40-50-2)

Reclassifications and Related Accounting Policy Disclosures

3. Disclose contract classifications, the reason for the reclassification, and the effect on the financial statements. _____

(FASB ASC 815-40-50-3)

4. Accounting policy decision regarding the determination of how to partially reclassify contracts subject to this Subtopic. _____

(FASB ASC 815-40-50-4)

Interaction with Disclosures About Capital Structure

5. The disclosures required by ASC Topic 505-10, *Equity—Overall* apply to all contracts within the scope of ASC Topic 815-40 as follows:
   a. For an option or forward contract indexed to the issuer's equity:
      1. The forward rate _____
      2. The option strike price _____
      3. The number of issuer's shares to which the contract is indexed _____
      4. The settlement date or dates of the contract _____
      5. The issuer's accounting for the contract (that is, as an asset, liability, or equity). _____
   b. If the terms of the contract provide settlement alternatives, those settlement alternatives, including both of the following:
      1. Who controls the settlement alternatives _____
      2. The maximum number of shares that could be required to be issued to net share settle a contract, if applicable. Paragraph 505-10-50-3 requires additional disclosures for actual issuances and settlements that occurred during the accounting period. _____
   c. For a contract does not have a fixed or determinable maximum number of shares that may be required to be issued, the fact that a potentially infinite number of shares could be required to be issued to settle the contract _____
   d. A contract's current fair value for each settlement alternative (denominated, as relevant, in monetary amounts or quantities of shares) and how changes in the price of the issuer's equity instruments affect those settlement amounts (For some issuers, a tabular format may provide the most concise and informative presentation of these data.) _____
   e. The disclosures required by paragraph 505-10-50-11 for any equity instrument in the scope of this Subtopic that is (or would be if the issuer were a public entity) classified as temporary equity. (That paragraph applies to redeemable stock issued by nonpublic entities, regardless of whether the private entity chooses to classify those securities as temporary equity.) _____

(FASB ASC 815-40-50-5)

815-45 Weather Derivatives

1. Entities that enter into weather derivatives contracts follow the disclosure requirements under ASC 825-10. _____

(FASB ASC 815-45-50-1)

820 Fair Value

Notes to the preparer

- Unless otherwise indicated, the disclosures included in this section are required to be presented in interim and annual financial statements.
- Disclosures required to be made separately for each major category of assets and liabilities measured at fair value on a recurring basis in periods subsequent to initial recognition.
- Quantitative Disclosures required by FASB ASC 820-10-50 should be presented in tabular format.

(FASB ASC 820-10-50-8)

1. Disclose information that allows users to assess:

    a. For assets and liabilities that are measured at fair value on a recurring or nonrecurring basis in the periods subsequent to initial recognition, the valuation techniques and inputs used to develop those measurements _____
    b. For recurring fair value measurements using significant unobservable inputs (Level 3), the effect of the measurements on earnings (or changes in net assets) or other comprehensive income for the period. _____

(FASB ASC 820-10-50-1)

2. To meet the reporting objectives, consider all of the following:

    a. The level of detail necessary to satisfy the disclosure requirements _____
    b. How much emphasis to place on each of the various requirements _____
    c. How much aggregation or disaggregation to undertake _____
    d. Whether users of financial statements need additional information to evaluate the quantitative information disclosed. _____

(FASB ASC 820-10-50-1A)

3. For each class of assets and liabilities measured at fair value in the statement of financial position after initial recognition:

    a. For recurring and nonrecurring fair value measurements, the fair value measurement at the end of the reporting period, and for nonrecurring fair value measurements, the reasons for the measurement. Recurring fair value measurements of assets or liabilities are those that other Topics require or permit in the statement of financial position at the end of each reporting period. Nonrecurring fair value measurements of assets or liabilities are those that other Topics require or permit in the statement of financial position in particular circumstances (for example, when a reporting entity measures a long-lived asset or disposal group classified as held for sale at fair value less costs to sell in accordance with Topic 360 because the asset's fair value less costs to sell is lower than its carrying amount). _____
    b. For recurring and nonrecurring fair value measurements, the level of the fair value hierarchy within which the fair value measurements are categorized in their entirety (Level 1, 2, or 3).

        (1) For assets and liabilities held at the end of the reporting period that are measured at fair value on a recurring basis, the amounts of any transfers between Level 1 and Level 2 of the fair value hierarchy, the reasons for those transfers, and the reporting entity's policy for determining when transfers between levels are deemed to have occurred. Transfers into each level shall be disclosed and discussed separately from transfers out of each level. _____
        (2) For recurring and nonrecurring fair value measurements categorized within Level 2 and Level 3 of the fair value hierarchy, a description of the valuation technique(s) and the inputs used in the fair value measurement. If there has been a change in valuation technique (for example, changing from a market approach to an income approach or the use of an additional valuation technique), the reporting entity shall disclose that change and the reason(s) for making it. For fair value measurements categorized within Level 3 of the fair value hierarchy, a reporting entity shall provide quantitative information about the significant unobservable inputs used in the fair value measurement. A reporting entity is not required to create quantitative information to comply with this disclosure requirement if quantitative unobservable inputs are not developed by the reporting entity when measuring

fair value (for example, when a reporting entity uses prices from prior transactions or third-party pricing information without adjustment). However, when providing this disclosure, a reporting entity cannot ignore quantitative unobservable inputs that are significant to the fair value measurement and are reasonably available to the reporting entity.[8] ____

c. For recurring fair value measurements categorized within Level 3 of the fair value hierarchy, a reconciliation from the opening balances to the closing balances, disclosing separately changes during the period attributable to the following:

   (1) Total gains or losses for the period recognized in earnings (or changes in net assets), and the line item(s) in the statement of income (or activities) in which those gains or losses are recognized

      (a) Total gains or losses for the period recognized in other comprehensive income, and the line item(s) in other comprehensive income in which those gains or losses are recognized ____

   (2) Purchases, sales, issues, and settlements (each of those types of changes disclosed separately) ____

   (3) The amounts of any transfers into or out of Level 3 of the fair value hierarchy, the reasons for those transfers, and the reporting entity's policy for determining when transfers between levels are deemed to have occurred. Transfers into Level 3 shall be disclosed and discussed separately from transfers out of Level 3. ____

d. For recurring fair value measurements categorized within Level 3 of the fair value hierarchy, the amount of the total gains or losses for the period in (c)(1) included in earnings (or changes in net assets) that is attributable to the change in unrealized gains or losses relating to those assets and liabilities held at the end of the reporting period, and the line item(s) in the statement of income (or activities) in which those unrealized gains or losses are recognized. ____

e. For recurring and nonrecurring fair value measurements categorized within Level 3 of the fair value hierarchy, a description of the valuation processes used by the reporting entity (including, for example, how an entity decides its valuation policies and procedures and analyzes changes in fair value measurements from period to period). ____

f. For recurring fair value measurements categorized within Level 3 of the fair value hierarchy, a narrative description of the sensitivity of the fair value measurement to changes in unobservable inputs if a change in those inputs to a different amount might result in a significantly higher or lower fair value measurement. If there are interrelationships between those inputs and other unobservable inputs used in the fair value measurement, a reporting entity shall also provide a description of those interrelationships and of how they might magnify or mitigate the effect of changes in the unobservable inputs on the fair value measurement. To comply with that disclosure requirement, the narrative description of the sensitivity to changes in unobservable inputs shall include, at a minimum, the unobservable inputs disclosed when complying with paragraph 820-10-50-2(bbb). ____

---

[8] ASU 2013-09 indefinitely defers the requirement for all employee benefit plans other than those subject to the SEC's filing requirements to disclose fair value measurements of investments in nonpublic entity equity securities issued by the plan sponsor and nonpublic entity equity securities of the plan sponsor's affiliated entities.

g. For recurring and nonrecurring fair value measurements, if that of a nonfinancial asset differs from its current use, a reporting entity shall disclose that fact and why the nonfinancial asset is being used in a manner that differs from its highest and best use. _____

(FASB ASC 820-10-50-2)

4. Determine the appropriate classes of assets and liabilities on the basis of the nature, characteristics, and risks of the asset or liability and the level of the fair value hierarchy within which the fair value measurement is categorized. _____

   The number of classes may need to be greater for fair value measurements categorized within Level 3 of the fair value hierarchy because those measurements have a greater degree of uncertainty and subjectivity. Determining appropriate classes of assets and liabilities for which disclosures about fair value measurements should be provided requires judgment. A class of assets and liabilities will often require greater disaggregation than the line items presented in the statement of financial position. However, a reporting entity shall provide information sufficient to permit reconciliation to the line items presented in the statement of financial position. If another Topic specifies the class for an asset or a liability, a reporting entity may use that class in providing the disclosures required in this Topic if that class meets the requirements in this paragraph.

(FASB ASC 820-10-50-2B)

5. Disclose the policy for determining when transfers between levels of the fair value hierarchy are deemed to have occurred in accordance with paragraph 820-10-50-2(bb) and (c)(3). The policy about the timing of recognizing transfers shall be the same for transfers into the levels as for transfers out of the levels. _____

(FASB ASC 820-10-50-2C)

6. Disclose an accounting policy decision to use the exception in paragraph 820-10-35-18D regarding net positions for groups of assets. The policy about the timing of recognizing transfers shall be the same for transfers into the levels as for transfers out of the levels. _____

(FASB ASC 820-10-50-2D)

7. If a class of assets and liabilities is not measured at fair value in the statement of financial position, but the fair value is disclosed, disclose the level of the fair value hierarchy used to measure the items; for Level 2 and 3 items, disclose the valuation techniques and inputs used; and if the highest and best use of a nonfinancial asset is not its current use, disclose that and explain why. _____

(FASB ASC 820-10-50-2E)

8. A nonpublic entity is not required to disclose the information required by paragraph 820-10-50-2(bb) and (g) and paragraph 820-10-50-2E unless required by another Topic. _____

(FASB ASC 820-10-50-2F)

9. For derivative assets and liabilities, the reporting entity shall present both of the following:

   a. The fair value disclosures required by paragraph 820-10-50-2(a) through (bb) on a gross basis (which is consistent with the requirement of paragraph 815-10-50-4B[a]) _____

b. The reconciliation disclosure required by paragraph 820-10-50-2(c) through (d) on either a gross or a net basis. _____

(FASB ASC 820-10-50-3)

10. For a liability measured at fair value and issued with an inseparable third-party credit enhancement, disclose the existence of that credit enhancement. _____

(FASB ASC 820-10-50-4A)

11. For investments that are within the scope of paragraphs 820-10-15-4 through 15-5 (regardless of whether the practical expedient in paragraph 820-10-35-59 has been applied) and measured at fair value on a recurring or nonrecurring basis during the period, a reporting entity shall disclose information that helps users of its financial statements to understand the nature and risks of the investments and whether the investments are probable of being sold at amounts different from net asset value per share (or its equivalent, such as member units or an ownership interest in partners' capital to which a proportionate share of net assets is attributed). To meet that objective, to the extent applicable, a reporting entity shall disclose, at a minimum, the following information for each class of investment:

    a. The fair value measurement (as determined by applying paragraphs 820-10-35-59 through 35-62) of the investments in the class at the reporting date and a description of the significant investment strategies of the investee(s) in the class. _____
    b. For each class of investment that includes investments that can never be redeemed with the investees, but the reporting entity receives distributions through the liquidation of the underlying assets of the investees, the reporting entity's estimate of the period of time over which the underlying assets are expected to be liquidated by the investees. _____
    c. The amount of the reporting entity's unfunded commitments related to investments in the class. _____
    d. A general description of the terms and conditions upon which the investor may redeem investments in the class (for example, quarterly redemption with 60 days' notice). _____
    e. The circumstances in which an otherwise redeemable investment in the class (or a portion thereof) might not be redeemable (for example, investments subject to a lockup or gate). Also, for those otherwise redeemable investments that are restricted from redemption as of the reporting entity's measurement date, the reporting entity shall disclose its estimate of when the restriction from redemption might lapse. If an estimate cannot be made, the reporting entity shall disclose that fact and how long the restriction has been in effect. _____
    f. Any other significant restriction on the ability to sell investments in the class at the measurement date. _____
    g. If a reporting entity determines that it is probable that it will sell an investment(s) for an amount different from net asset value per share (or its equivalent) as described in paragraph 820-10-35-62, the reporting entity shall disclose the total fair value of all investments that meet the criteria in paragraph 820-10-35-62 and any remaining actions required to complete the sale. _____
    h. If a group of investments would otherwise meet the criteria in paragraph 820-10-35-62 but the individual investments to be sold have not been identified (for example, if a reporting entity decides to sell 20 percent of its investments in private equity funds but the individual investments to be sold have not been identified), so the investments continue to qualify for the practical expedient in paragraph 820-10-35-59, the reporting entity shall disclose its plans to sell and any remaining actions required to complete the sale(s). _____

(FASB ASC 820-10-50-6)

12. Present the quantitative disclosures required by this Topic in a tabular format. _____

(FASB ASC 820-10-50-8)

825 Financial Instruments

Entities

1. For interim reporting periods, the disclosure guidance in this subsection applies to all entities but is optional for those entities that do not meet the definition of a publicly traded company. _____

(FASB ASC 825-10-50-2A)

2. Except as noted in (FASB ASC 825-10-50-3A the disclosure guidance related to fair value of financial instruments in paragraphs 825-10-50-10 through 50-19 applies to all entities but is optional for an entity that meets *all* of the following criteria:

   a. The entity is a nonpublic entity. _____
   b. The entity's total assets are less than $100 million on the date of the financial statements. _____
   c. The entity has no instrument that, in whole or in part, is accounted for as a derivative instrument under Topic 815 other than commitments related to the origination of mortgage loans to be held for sale during the reporting period. If the entity has chosen to apply the simplified hedge accounting approach[9] to a receivable-variable, pay-fixed interest rate swap that instrument is not accounted for as a derivative under Topic 815. _____

(FASB ASC 825-10-50-3)

3. A nonpublic entity is not required to provide the disclosure in paragraph 825-10-50-10(d) for items disclosed at fair value but not measured at fair value in the statement of financial position. Apply this criteria to the most recent year presented in comparative financial statements to determine applicability of this subsection. _____

(FASB ASC 825-10-50-3A-4)

4. If disclosures are not required in the current period, the disclosures for previous years may be omitted if financial statements for those years are presented for comparative purposes. _____

(FASB ASC 825-10-50-5)

5. If disclosures are required in the current period, disclosures that have not been reported previously need not be included in financial statements that are presented for comparative purposes. _____

(FASB ASC 825-10-50-6)

Transactions

6. The disclosures about fair value prescribed in paragraphs 825-10-50-10 through 50-16 are not required for any of the following:

   a. Employers' and plans' obligations for pension benefits, other postretirement benefits including health care and life insurance benefits, postemployment benefits, employee stock option and stock purchase plans, and other forms of deferred compensation arrangements (see Topics 710; 712; 715; 718, and 960) _____

---

[9] See footnote 7 for important information on the simplified hedge accounting approach.

b. Substantively extinguished debt subject to the disclosure requirements of Subtopic 405-20 ____
c. Insurance contracts, other than financial guarantees (including financial guarantee insurance contracts within the scope of Topic 944) and investment contracts, as discussed in Subtopic 944-20 ____
d. Lease contracts as defined in Topic 840 (A contingent obligation arising out of a cancelled lease and a guarantee of a third-party lease obligation are not lease contracts and are subject to the disclosure requirements in this subsection.) ____
e. Warranty obligations (see Topic 450 and the Product Warranties Subsections of Topic 460) ____
f. Unconditional purchase obligations as defined in paragraph 440-10-50-2 ____
g. Investments accounted for under the equity method in accordance with the requirements of Topic 323 ____
h. Noncontrolling interests and equity investments in consolidated subsidiaries (see Topic 810) ____
i. Equity instruments issued by the entity and classified in stockholders' equity in the statement of financial position (see Topic 505) ____
j. Receivable-variable, pay-fixed interest rate swaps for which the simplified hedge accounting approach is applied.[10] ____

(FASB ASC 825-10-50-8)

Fair Value of Financial Instruments

7. Disclosures required as of each interim and annual statement of financial position date:

    a. The fair value of financial instruments for which it is practicable to estimate that value, either in the body of the financial statements or in the notes. ____

(FASB ASC 825-10-50-10a)

    b. The method(s) and significant assumptions used to estimate the fair value of financial instruments consistent with the requirements of paragraph 820-10-50-2(bbb) except that a reporting entity is not required to provide the quantitative disclosures about significant unobservable inputs used in fair value measurements categorized within Level 3 of the fair value hierarchy required by that paragraph. ____

(FASB ASC 825-10-50-10b)

    c. A description of the changes in the method(s) and significant assumptions used to estimate the fair value of financial instruments, if any, during the period. ____

(FASB ASC 825-10-50-10c)

    d. The level of the fair value hierarchy within which the fair value measurements are categorized in their entirety (Level 1, 2, or 3). ____

(FASB ASC 825-10-50-10d)

    e. Present fair value with the related carrying amount in a form that clarifies whether the fair value and carrying amount represent assets or liabilities and how the carrying amounts relate to what is reported in the statement of financial position. ____

(FASB ASC 825-10-50-11)

---

[10] See footnote 7 for important information on the simplified hedge accounting approach.

8. If the fair value of financial instruments is disclosed in more than a single note, one of the notes shall include a summary table. The summary table shall contain the fair value and related carrying amounts and cross-references to the location(s) of the remaining disclosures required by this Section. _____

(FASB ASC 825-10-50-12)

9. In disclosing the fair value of a financial instrument, an entity shall not net that fair value with the fair value of other financial instruments—even if those financial instruments are of the same class or are otherwise considered to be related (for example, by a risk management strategy)—except to the extent that the offsetting of carrying amounts in the statement of financial position is permitted under either of the following:

   a. The general principle in paragraph 210-20-45-1 _____
   b. The exceptions for master netting arrangements in paragraph 815-10-45-5 and for amounts related to certain repurchase and reverse repurchase agreements in paragraphs 210-20-45-11 through 45-17. _____

(FASB ASC 825-10-50-15)

10. If it is not practicable to estimate the fair value of a financial instrument or a class of financial instruments, disclose information pertinent to estimating the fair value of that financial instrument or class of financial instruments (such as the carrying amount, effective interest rate, and maturity) and the reasons why it is not practicable to estimate fair value. _____

(FASB ASC 825-10-50-16)

Concentrations of Credit Risk of All Financial Instruments

11. Disclose all significant concentrations of credit risk arising from all financial instruments, whether from an individual counterparty or groups of counterparties. _____

(FASB ASC 825-10-50-20)

12. Except as indicated in the following paragraph, disclose all of the following about each significant concentration:

   a. Information about the (shared) activity, region, or economic characteristic that identifies the concentration _____
   b. The maximum amount of loss due to credit risk that, based on the gross fair value of the financial instrument, the entity would incur if parties to the financial instruments that make up the concentration failed completely to perform according to the terms of the contracts and the collateral or other security, if any, for the amount due proved to be of no value to the entity _____
   c. With respect to collateral, all of the following:

      (1) The entity's policy of requiring collateral or other security to support financial instruments subject to credit risk _____
      (2) Information about the entity's access to that collateral or other security _____
      (3) The nature and a brief description of the collateral or other security supporting those financial instruments. _____

   d. With respect to master netting arrangements, all of the following:

      (1) The entity's policy of entering into master netting arrangements to mitigate the credit risk of financial instruments _____
      (2) Information about the arrangements for which the entity is a party _____

(3) A brief description of the terms of those arrangements, including the extent to which they would reduce the entity's maximum amount of loss due to credit risk. _____

(FASB ASC 825-10-50-21)

13. The requirements of the preceding paragraph do not apply to the following financial instruments, whether written or held:

    a. The financial instruments described in paragraph 825-10-50-8(a); (c); (e); and (f), except for reinsurance receivables and prepaid reinsurance premiums _____
    b. Financial instruments of a pension plan, including plan assets, if subject to the accounting and reporting requirements of Topic 715. _____

    Financial instruments of a pension plan, other than the obligations for pension benefits, if subject to the accounting and reporting requirements of Topic 960, are subject to the requirements of paragraphs 825-10-50-20 through 50-21.

(FASB ASC 825-10-50-22)

14. An entity is encouraged, but not required, to disclose quantitative information about the market risks of financial instruments that is consistent with the way it manages or adjusts those risks. Appropriate ways of reporting that quantitative information will differ for different entities and will likely evolve over time as management approaches and measurement techniques evolve. Possibilities include disclosing any of the following:

    a. More details about current positions and perhaps activity during the period _____
    b. The hypothetical effects on comprehensive income (or net assets), or annual income, of several possible changes in market prices _____
    c. A gap analysis of interest rate repricing or maturity dates _____
    d. The duration of the financial instruments _____
    e. The entity's value at risk from derivatives and from other positions at the end of the reporting period and the average value at risk during the year. _____

    This list is not exhaustive, and an entity is encouraged to develop other ways of reporting quantitative information.

(FASB ASC 825-10-50-23)

15. The reasons that management elected the fair value option for each eligible item or group of similar eligible items. _____

(FASB ASC 825-10-50-28a)

16. If management elected the fair value option for some but not all of the eligible items within a group of similar items,

    a. A description of the items in the group and the reasons for the partial election _____
    b. Information sufficient to enable users to understand how the group of similar items relates to the individual line items presented on the statement of financial position. _____

(FASB ASC 825-10-50-28b)

17. For each statement of financial position line item that includes one or more items for which the fair value option was elected

    a. Information sufficient to enable users to understand how each statement of financial position line item relates to major categories of assets and liabilities presented in accordance with the fair value disclosure requirements of ASC 820 (see above) that provide the reader with information with respect to the level or levels within the fair value hierarchy in which the assumptions used to measure fair value (referred to as "inputs") are derived. _____
    b. The aggregate carrying amount of items included in each statement of financial position line item, if any, that are not eligible for the fair value option. _____

(FASB ASC 825-10-50-28c)

18. The difference between the aggregate fair value and the aggregate unpaid principal balance of

    a. Loans and long-term receivables (other than securities subject to ASC 820) with contractual principal amounts and for which the FVO has been elected. _____
    b. Long-term debt instruments that have contractual principal amounts and for which the FVO has been elected. _____

(FASB ASC 825-10-50-28d)

19. For loans held as assets for which the FVO has been elected

    a. The aggregate fair value of loans that are 90 or more days past due. _____
    b. The aggregate fair value of loans on nonaccrual status if the entity's policy is to recognize interest income separately from other changes in fair value. _____
    c. The difference between the aggregate fair value and the aggregate unpaid principal balance for loans that are 90 or more days past due, in nonaccrual status, or both. _____

(FASB ASC 825-10-50-28e)

20. For investments that, absent election of the FVO, would have been accounted for under the equity method, the following disclosures from ASC 323 are to be made. The extent of disclosures necessary to inform the reader of the financial position and results of operations of an investee is based on management's evaluation of the significance of an investment to the financial position and results of operations of the reporting entity.

    a. Parenthetical disclosure, or disclosure in the notes to the financial statements or in separate statements or schedules of

        (1) The name of each investee and the percentage of ownership of its common stock held by the reporting entity. _____
        (2) The accounting policies of the investor with respect to investments in common stock. _____

    b. When investments in common stock of corporate joint ventures or other investments accounted for under the equity method are, in the aggregate, material to the investor's financial position and results of operations, it may be necessary to present in the notes, or in separate statements, either individually or in groups, summarized information as to assets, liabilities, and results of operations of the investees. _____

(FASB ASC 825-10-50-28f)

21. Disclosures required in each interim and annual period for which an income statement is presented about items for which the FVO has been elected

    a. For each line item in the statement of financial position, the amounts of gains and losses from changes in fair value included in net income during the period and the specific line in the income statement on which those gains and losses are reported. ASC 825-10-25 permits management to meet this requirement by aggregating these disclosures with respect to items for which the FVO was elected with the amounts of gains and losses from changes in fair value with respect to other items measured at fair value as required by other authoritative literature. ____

(FASB ASC 825-10-50-30a)

    b. A description of how interest and dividends are measured and where they are reported in the statement of income. ____

(FASB ASC 825-10-50-30b)

    c. With respect to gains and losses included in net income during the period attributable to changes in instrument-specific credit risk associated with loans and other receivables held as assets:

        (1) The estimated amount of such gains or losses. ____
        (2) How the gains or losses were determined. ____

(FASB ASC 825-10-50-30c)

22. For liabilities with fair values that have been significantly affected during the reporting period by changes in instrument-specific credit risk:

    a. The estimated amount of gains and losses from changes in fair value included in net income attributable to changes in the instrument-specific credit risk. ____
    b. How the gains and losses were determined. ____
    c. Qualitative information regarding the reasons for those changes. ____

(FASB ASC 825-10-50-30d)

Other Required Disclosures

23. In annual financial statements only, the methods and significant assumptions used to estimate the fair value of items for which the FVO was elected. ____

(FASB ASC 825-10-50-31)

24. If management elects the FVO upon the occurrence of an event where (1) an investment newly becomes subject to the equity method, (2) a subsidiary or a variable interest entity that the investor previously consolidated ceases to qualify for consolidation but the investor continues to hold common stock in the entity, or (3) an eligible item is required to be measured or remeasured at fair value at the time of the event but is not required to be subsequently remeasured at each succeeding reporting date, the following disclosures are required in the financial statements covering the period of the election:

    a. Qualitative information about the nature of the event. ____
    b. Quantitative information by statement of financial position line item indicating which line items in the income statement include the effect on net income of initially electing the FVO for the item. ____

(FASB ASC 825-10-50-32)

25. The issuer of a registration payment arrangement shall disclose the following information about each registration payment arrangement or each group of similar arrangements. These disclosures are incremental to the disclosures that may be required under other applicable GAAP and are required even if the likelihood of the issuer having to make any payments under the arrangement is remote.

    a. The nature of the registration payment arrangement, including the approximate term of the arrangement, the financial instrument(s) subject to the arrangement, and the events or circumstances that would require the issuer to transfer consideration under the arrangement. _____
    b. Any settlement alternatives contained in the terms of the registration payment arrangement, including the party that controls the settlement alternatives. _____
    c. The maximum potential amount of consideration, undiscounted, that the issuer could be required to transfer under the registration payment arrangement (including the maximum number of shares that may be required to be issued). If the terms of the arrangement provide for no limitation to the maximum potential consideration (including shares) to be transferred, that fact shall be disclosed. _____
    d. The current carrying amount of the liability representing the issuer's obligations under the registration payment arrangement and the income statement classification of any gains or losses resulting from changes in the carrying amount of that liability. _____

(FASB ASC 825-20-50-1)

830 Foreign Currency

830-20 Foreign Currency Transactions

1. Aggregate transaction gain or loss that is included in the entity's net income. _____

(FASB ASC 830-20-50-1)

Subsequent Rate Changes

2. If significant, a rate change that occurs after the date of the reporting entity's financial statements and its effects on unsettled balances pertaining to foreign currency transactions. Include consideration of changes in unsettled transactions from the date of the financial statements to the date the rate changed. If it is not practicable to determine these changes, state that fact. _____

(FASB ASC 830-20-50-2)

Effects of Rate Changes on Results of Operations

3. To assist financial report users in understanding the implications of rate changes and to compare recent results with those of prior periods, entities are encouraged but not required, to supplement required disclosures an analysis and discussion of the effects of rate changes on the reported results of operations. _____

(FASB ASC 830-20-50-3)

830-30 Translation of Financial Statements

1. Analysis of changes in accumulated translation adjustments which are reported as other comprehensive income. At a minimum, the disclosures should include

    a. Beginning and ending amounts of the translation adjustments account. _____
    b. Aggregate adjustment for the period resulting from translation adjustments, and gains and losses from certain hedges and intercompany balances. _____
    c. Amount of income taxes for the period allocated to translation adjustments. _____

d. Amounts transferred from the translation adjustments account and included in determining net income as a result of the (partial) sale or liquidation of the foreign operation. ____

(FASB ASC 830-30-50-1)

2. Significant rate changes subsequent to the date of the financial statements including effects on unsettled foreign currency transactions. Rate changes subsequent to the statement of financial position date are not incorporated into the financial statements for the period just ended. ____

(FASB ASC 830-30-50-2)

835-20 Interest—Capitalization of Interest

1. An entity discloses the following information with respect to interest costs in the financial statements or related notes:
   a. For an accounting period in which no interest cost is capitalized, the amount of interest cost incurred and charged to expense during the period. ____
   b. For an accounting period in which some interest cost is capitalized, the total amount of interest cost incurred during the period and the amount thereof that has been capitalized. ____

(FASB ASC 835-20-50-1)

840 Leases

1. Disclose the nature and extent of leasing transactions with related parties. ____

(FASB ASC 840-10-50-1)

Lessees

2. The lessee shall disclose, in its financial statements or footnotes, a general description of its leasing arrangements including, but not limited to, all of the following:
   a. The basis on which contingent rentals are determined. ____
   b. The existence and terms of renewal or purchase options and escalation clauses. ____
   c. Restrictions imposed by lease agreements, such as those concerning dividends, additional debt, and further leasing. ____

(FASB ASC 840-10-50-2)

Lessors

3. If leasing, exclusive of leveraged leasing, is a significant part of the lessor's business activities in terms of revenue, net income, or assets, in the financial statements or footnotes thereto a general description of the lessor's leasing arrangements. ____

(FASB ASC 840-10-50-4)

4. Lessor's accounting policy for contingent rental income. If a lessor accrues contingent rental income before the lessee's achievement of the specified target (provided achievement of that target is considered probable), disclosure of the impact on rental income shall be made as if the lessor's accounting policy was to defer contingent rental income until the specified target is met. ____

(FASB ASC 840-10-50-5)

840-20 Operating Leases

1. For all operating leases
   a. Present rental expense disclosing separately the amount for minimum rentals, contingent rentals, and sublease rentals. _____
   b. Rental payments for leases with terms of a month or less that were not renewed may be excluded. _____

(FASB ASC 840-20-50-1)

2. For operating leases having a remaining noncancelable term in excess of one year, disclose
   a. Future minimum lease payments in the aggregate and for each of the next five fiscal years. _____
   b. Total of minimum rentals that will be received under noncancelable subleases. _____

(FASB ASC 840-20-50-2)

3. For operating leases, disclose
   a. The cost and carrying amount (if different) of property leased or held for leasing, segregated by major classes of property according to function or nature, and the total amount of accumulated depreciation. _____
   b. Minimum rentals on noncancelable leases in the aggregate and for each of the next five fiscal years. _____
   c. Total contingent rentals included in income for each period for which an income statement is presented. _____

(FASB ASC 840-20-50-4)

840-30 Capital Leases

1. For capital leases, disclose
   a. The gross amount of assets recorded under capital leases presented by major classes according to function or nature. _____
   b. Future minimum lease payments in the aggregate and for each of the next five fiscal years with separate deductions made for executory costs (including any profit thereon) included in the minimum lease payments, and the amount of imputed interest needed to reduce the net minimum lease payments to present value. _____
   c. Total of minimum sublease rentals to be received in the future under noncancelable subleases. _____
   d. Total contingent rentals actually incurred for each period for which an income statement is presented. _____

(FASB ASC 840-30-50-1)

2. For sales-type and direct financing leases, disclose
   a. Components of the net investment in leases including the following:
      (1) Future minimum lease payments to be received with separate deductions for amount representing executory costs (including any profit thereon), and the accumulated allowance for uncollectible lease payments. _____
      (2) Unguaranteed residual values accruing to benefit of lessor. _____
      (3) For direct financing leases only, initial direct costs. _____
      (4) Unearned interest income. _____

b. Future minimum lease payments to be received for each of the next five fiscal years. _____
c. Total contingent rentals included in income for each period for which an income statement is presented. _____

(FASB ASC 840-30-50-4)

3. For a significant investment in leveraged leases recorded net of the nonrecourse debt, the net of the balances of following accounts shall represent the initial and continuing investment in leveraged leases:

   a. Rentals receivable. _____
   b. Investment tax credit receivable. _____
   c. Estimated residual value of leased asset. _____
   d. Unearned and deferred income. _____

(FASB ASC 840-30-50-5)

4. If accounting for the effect on leveraged leases of the change in tax rates results in a significant variation from the customary relationship between income tax expense and pretax accounting income and the reason for that variation is not otherwise apparent, the reason for that variation. _____

(FASB ASC 840-30-50-6)

840-40 Sale-Leaseback Transactions

1. For sale-leaseback transactions, disclose

   a. In addition to requirements of ASC 840 and ASC 360, financials of seller-lessee shall describe terms of sale-leaseback transaction, including future commitments, obligations, provisions, or circumstances requiring or resulting in seller-lessee's involvement. _____

(FASB ASC 840-40-50-1)

Transactions that Do Not Qualify for Sale-Leaseback Accounting

2. The financial statements of a seller-lessee that has accounted for a sale-leaseback transaction by the deposit method or as a financing according to the guidance in this subtopic also shall disclose both of the following:

   a. The obligation for future minimum lease payments as of the date of the latest statement of financial position presented in the aggregate and for each of the five succeeding fiscal years. _____
   b. The total of minimum sublease rentals, if any, to be received in the future under noncancelable subleases in the aggregate and for each of the five succeeding fiscal years. _____

(FASB ASC 840-40-50-2)

845 Nonmonetary Transactions

1. Nature of transaction. _____
2. Basis of accounting for the assets transferred. _____
3. Gain or loss and basis of accounting for assets transferred. _____

(FASB ASC 845-10-50-1)

4. Amount of gross operating revenue recognized as a result of nonmonetary transactions. _____

(FASB ASC 845-10-50-2)

850 Related-Party Disclosures

1. Nature of relationship and amounts due to or from related parties with significant terms and manner of settlement. _____
2. A description of the transactions, including transactions to which no amounts or nominal amounts were ascribed, for each of the periods for which income statements are presented, and such other information deemed necessary to an understanding of the effects of the transactions on the financial statements. _____
3. For each income statement presented, a description of and dollar amounts of transaction, including those to which no or nominal amounts are assigned, as well as guarantees or other terms which are needed for understanding of financial statement impact, and description of any change in terms. _____
4. Amount due from or to related parties and manner of settlement as of the date of each balance sheet. _____
5. For additional requirements, see requirements for FASB ASC 740-10-50-17 previously in this checklist. _____

(FASB ASC 850-10-50-1)

6. Show separately, and not included under a general heading such as notes receivable or accounts receivable, notes or accounts receivable from officers, employees, or affiliated entities. _____

(FASB ASC 850-10-50-2)

7. In some cases, aggregation of similar transactions by type of related party may be appropriate. Sometimes, the effect of the relationship between the parties may be so pervasive that disclosure of the relationship alone will be sufficient. If necessary to the understanding of the relationship, the name of the related party shall be disclosed. _____

(FASB ASC 850-10-50-3)

8. It is not necessary to duplicate disclosures in a set of separate financial statements that is presented in the financial report of another entity (the primary reporting entity) if those separate financial statements also are consolidated or combined in a complete set of financial statements and both sets of financial statements are presented in the same financial report. _____

(FASB ASC 850-10-50-4)

9. Transactions involving related parties cannot be presumed to be carried out on an arm's-length basis. Representations about transactions with related parties must not imply that the related party transactions were consummated on terms equivalent to those that prevail in arm's-length transactions unless such representations can be substantiated. _____

(FASB ASC 850-10-50-5)

10. The nature of control relationship, even absent any transactions, of companies under common ownership or management control, if such could lead to operating results or financial position significantly different than what would have resulted if entities were autonomous. _____

(FASB ASC 850-10-50-6)

852 Reorganizations

1. Disclose both in the notes to financial statements of an entity in Chapter 11:
   a. Claims not subject to reasonable estimation based on the provisions of Subtopic 450-20 _____
   b. The principal categories of the claims subject to compromise. _____

(FASB ASC 852-10-1-50-2)

2. Disclose the extent to which reported interest expense differs from stated contractual interest. It may be appropriate to disclose this parenthetically on the face of the statement of operations. _____

(FASB ASC 852-10-50-3)

3. Disclose intra-entity receivables and payables of entities in reorganization proceedings in the condensed combined financial statements referred to in paragraph 852-10-45-14. _____

(FASB ASC 852-10-50-3)

Financial Reporting When Entities Emerge from Chapter 11 Reorganization and Adopt Fresh-Start Reporting

4. Paragraph 852-10-45-21 requires additional information to be disclosed in the notes to the initial fresh-start financial statements when fresh-start reporting is adopted. That additional information consists of all of the following:
   a. Adjustments to the historical amounts of individual assets and liabilities _____
   b. The amount of debt forgiveness _____
   c. Significant matters relating to the determination of reorganization value, including all of the following:
      (1) The method or methods used to determine reorganization value and factors such as discount rates, tax rates, the number of years for which cash flows are projected, and the method of determining terminal value _____
      (2) Sensitive assumptions—that is, assumptions about which there is a reasonable possibility of the occurrence of a variation that would have significantly affected measurement of reorganization value _____
      (3) Assumptions about anticipated conditions that are expected to be different from current conditions, unless otherwise apparent. _____

(FASB ASC 852-10-50-7)

852-20 Reorganizations—Quasi Reorganizations

1. After readjustment under Topic 852-20, retained earnings previously accumulated cannot properly be carried forward under that title. A new retained earnings account must be established, dated to show that it runs from the effective date of the readjustment. Disclose this dating until such time as the effective date is no longer deemed to possess any special significance. _____

(FASB ASC 852-20-50-2)

855 Subsequent Events

1. For non-SEC filers, disclose both of the following:
   a. The date through which subsequent events have been evaluated _____
   b. Whether that date is either of the following:

(1) The date the financial statements were issued _____
(2) The date the financial statements were available to be issued. _____

(FASB ASC 855-10-50-1)

2. For nonrecognized subsequent events that, by their nature, their disclosure is necessary in order to prevent the financial statements from being misleading, disclose the following:

   a. The nature of the event _____
   b. An estimate of the financial effect of the event, or a statement that an estimate cannot be made. _____

(FASB ASC 855-10-50-2)

3. If the nonrecognized subsequent event is so significant that disclosure is best made by presenting pro forma financial data, management is to consider supplementing the historical financial statements with that data that would give effect to the event as if it had occurred on the date of the statement of financial position. In some situations, management is also to consider presenting pro forma statements, usually a statement of financial position only, in columnar form on the face of the historical financial statements. _____

(FASB ASC 855-10-50-3)

4. Disclose the date through which management has evaluated subsequent events and specify whether that date represents the date the financial statements were issued, or the date the financial statements were available to be issued. _____

(FASB ASC 855-10-50-4)

5. If the financial statements are reissued, management is to disclose the date through which subsequent events were evaluated with respect to both the originally issued financial statements and the revised financial statements. _____

(FASB ASC 855-10-50-5)

860 Transfers and Servicing of Financial Assets

860-20 Sales of Financial Assets

1. For securitizations, asset-backed financing arrangements, and similar transfers accounted for as sales when the transferor has continuing involvement with the transferred financial assets

   a. For each income statement presented

      (1) The characteristics of the transfer (including a description of the transferor's continuing involvement with the transferred financial assets, the nature and initial fair value of the assets obtained as proceeds and the liabilities incurred in the transfer, and the gain or loss from sale of transferred financial assets. For initial fair value measurements of assets obtained and liabilities incurred in the transfer, the following information:

         (a) The level within the fair value hierarchy in which the fair value measurements fall in their entirety; segregating Level 1, Level 2, and Level 3 measurements. _____

(b) The key inputs and assumptions used in measuring the fair value of assets obtained and liabilities incurred as a result of the sale that relate to the transferor's continuing involvement (including at a minimum, but not limited to, and if applicable, quantitative information about discount rates, expected prepayments including the expected weighted-average life of prepayable financial assets, and anticipated credit losses, including expected static pool losses). _____

(c) The valuation technique(s) used to measure fair value. _____

(2) Cash flows between a transferor and transferee, including proceeds from new transfers, proceeds from collections reinvested in revolving-period transfers, purchases of previously transferred financial assets, servicing fees, and cash flows received from a transferor's beneficial interests. _____

(FASB ASC 860-20-50-3)

b. For each statement of financial position presented, irrespective of when the transfer occurred

(1) Qualitative and quantitative information about the transferor's continuing involvement with transferred financial assets sufficient to provide users of the financial statements with needed information to assess the reasons for the continuing involvement and the risks related to the transferred financial assets to which the transferor continues to be exposed after the transfer and the extent that the transferor's risk profile has changed as a result of the transfer (including, but not limited to, credit risk, interest rate risk, and other risks) including

(a) The total principal amount outstanding, the amount that has been derecognized, and the amount that continues to be recognized in the statement of financial position. _____

(b) The terms of any arrangements that could require the transferor to provide financial support to the transferee or its beneficial interest holders, including a description of any events or circumstances that could expose the transferor to loss and the amount of the maximum exposure to loss. _____

(c) Whether the transferor has provided financial or other support during the periods presented that it was not previously contractually required to provide to the transferee or its beneficial interest holders, including when the transferor assisted the transferee or its beneficial interest holders in obtaining support, including

1] The type and amount of support. _____

2] The primary reasons for providing the support. _____

(d) Information is encouraged to be provided regarding any liquidity arrangements, guarantees, and/or other commitments provided by third parties related to the transferred financial assets that may affect that transferor's exposure to loss or risk of the related transferor's interest. _____

(2) The entity's accounting policies for subsequently measuring assets or liabilities that relate to the continuing involvement with the transferred financial assets. _____

(3) The key inputs and assumptions used in measuring the fair value of assets or liabilities that relate to the transferor's continuing involvement (including, at a minimum, but not limited to, and if applicable, quantitative information about discount rates, expected prepayments including the expected weighted-average life of prepayable financial assets, and anticipated credit losses, including expected static pool losses. _____

(4) For the transferor's interests in the transferred financial assets, a sensitivity analysis or stress test showing the hypothetical effect on the fair value of those interests (including any servicing assets or servicing liabilities) or two or more unfavorable variations from the expected levels for each key assumption reported, independently from any change in another key assumption, and a description of the objectives, methodology, and limitation of the sensitivity analysis or stress test. _____

(5) Information about the asset quality of transferred financial assets and any other assets that it manages together with them. This information should be separated between assets that have been derecognized and assets that continue to be recognized in the statement of financial position. This information is intended to provide financial statement users with an understanding of the risks inherent in the transferred financial assets as well as in other assets and liabilities that it manages together with transferred financial assets. For example, information regarding receivables is to include, but not be limited to

(a) Delinquencies at the end of the period. _____

(b) Credit losses, net of recoveries, during the period. _____

(FASB ASC 860-20-50-4)

2. The aggregate amount of gains or losses on sales of loans or trade receivables (including adjustments to record loans held for sale at the lower of cost or fair value) shall be presented separately in the financial statements or disclosed in the notes to financial statements. _____

(FASB ASC 860-20-50-5)

860-30 Secured Borrowing and Collateral

1. An entity shall disclose all of the following for collateral:

a. If the entity has entered into repurchase agreements or securities lending transactions, it shall disclose its policy for requiring collateral or other security. _____

b. As of the date of the latest statement of financial position presented, both of the following:

(1) The carrying amount and classifications of both of the following:

(a) Any assets pledged as collateral that are not reclassified and separately reported in the statement of financial position in accordance with paragraph 860-30-25-5(a). _____

(b) Associated liabilities. _____

(2) Qualitative information about the relationship(s) between those assets and associated liabilities; for example, if assets are restricted solely to satisfy a specific obligation, a description of the nature of restrictions placed on those assets. _____

c. If the entity has accepted collateral that it is permitted by contract or custom to sell or repledge, it shall disclose all the following:

(1) The fair value as of the date of each statement of financial position presented of that collateral _____

(2) The fair value as of the date of each statement of financial position presented of the portion of that collateral that it has sold or repledged _____
(3) Information about the sources and uses of that collateral. _____

(FASB ASC 860-30-50-1A)

860-50 Servicing Assets and Liabilities

1. For all servicing assets and liabilities

   a. Management's basis for determining its classes of servicing assets and liabilities. _____
   b. A description of the risks inherent in servicing assets and servicing liabilities and, if applicable, the instruments used to mitigate the effect on the income statement of changes in fair value of the servicing assets and servicing liabilities. Note that it is encouraged, but not required, that management provide disclosure of quantitative information about the instruments used to manage the risks inherent in servicing assets and servicing liabilities, including the fair value of those instruments at the beginning and end of the period. _____
   c. The amount of contractually specified servicing fees, late fees, and ancillary fees earned for each period for which results of operations are presented, including a description of where each amount is reported in the income statement. _____
   d. Encouraged but not required, quantitative and qualitative information about the assumptions used to estimate the fair value (for example, discount rates, anticipated credit losses, and prepayment speeds). (An entity that voluntarily provides the encouraged quantitative information about the instruments used to manage risks inherent in the servicing assets and servicing liabilities is also encouraged to disclose quantitative and qualitative information about the assumptions used to estimate the fair value of those instruments). _____

(FASB ASC 860-50-50-2)

2. For servicing assets and servicing liabilities subsequently measured at fair value

   a. For each class of servicing assets and servicing liabilities, the activity in the balance of servicing assets and the activity in the balance of servicing liabilities (including a description of where changes in fair value are reported in the income statement for each period for which results of operations are presented), including but not limited to the following:

      1. The beginning and ending balances. _____
      2. Additions (through purchases of servicing assets, assumptions of servicing obligations, and recognition of servicing obligations resulting from transfers of financial assets). _____
      3. Disposals. _____
      4. Changes in fair value during the period resulting from changes in valuation inputs or assumptions used in the valuation model. _____
      5. Other changes in fair value and a description of those changes. _____
      6. Other changes that affect the balance and a description of those changes. _____

(FASB ASC 860-50-50-3)

3. For servicing assets and servicing liabilities subsequently amortized in proportion to and over the period of estimated net servicing income or loss and assessed for impairment or increased obligation

   a. For each class of servicing assets and servicing liabilities, the activity in the balance of servicing assets and the activity in the balance of servicing liabilities (including a description of where changes in the carrying amount are reported in the income statement for each period for which results of operations are presented), including, but not limited to, the following:

(1) The beginning and ending balances. _____
(2) Additions (through purchases of servicing assets, assumptions of servicing obligations, and recognition of servicing obligations resulting from transfers of financial assets). _____
(3) Disposals. _____
(4) Amortization. _____
(5) Application of valuation allowance to adjust carrying value of servicing assets. _____
(6) Other-than-temporary impairments. _____
(7) Other changes affecting the balance and a description of those changes. _____

b. For each class of servicing assets and servicing liabilities, the fair value of recognized servicing assets and servicing liabilities at the beginning and end of the period. _____
c. The risk characteristics of the underlying financial assets used to stratify recognized servicing assets for purposes of measuring impairment. _____
d. The activity by class in any valuation allowance for impairment of recognized servicing assets—including beginning and ending balances, aggregate additions charged and recoveries credited to operations, and aggregate write-downs charged against the allowance—for each period for which results of operations are presented. _____

(FASB ASC 860-50-50-4)

4. If an entity elects to subsequently measure a class of servicing assets and servicing liabilities at fair value at the beginning of the fiscal year, disclose separately the amount of the cumulative-effect adjustment to retained earnings. _____

(FASB ASC 860-50-50-5)

INDEX

Index compiled by Indexing Specialists (UK) Ltd